BEETLE

American Warriors

Throughout the nation's history, numerous men and women of all ranks and branches of the United States military have served their country with honor and distinction. During times of war and peace, there are individuals whose exemplary achievements embody the highest standards of the U.S. armed forces. The aim of the American Warriors series is to examine the unique historical contributions of these individuals, whose legacies serve as enduring examples for soldiers and citizens alike. The series will promote a deeper and more comprehensive understanding of the U.S. armed forces.

Series editor: Roger Cirillo

An AUSA Book

BEETLE

★ ★ ★ ★

The Life of
General Walter Bedell Smith

D. K. R. CROSSWELL

THE UNIVERSITY PRESS OF KENTUCKY

Scholarly publisher for the Commonwealth,
serving Bellarmine University, Berea College, Centre College of Kentucky, Eastern
Kentucky University, The Filson Historical Society, Georgetown College, Kentucky
Historical Society, Kentucky State University, Morehead State University, Murray
State University, Northern Kentucky University, Transylvania University, University
of Kentucky, University of Louisville, and Western Kentucky University.
All rights reserved.

Editorial and Sales Offices: The University Press of Kentucky
663 South Limestone Street, Lexington, Kentucky 40508-4008
www.kentuckypress.com

Maps from Thomas Greiss, ed., *West Point Atlas for the Second World War: Europe
and the Mediterranean,* www.military.com/Resources. Photographs courtesy of the
Dwight D. Eisenhower Library.

16 15 14 13 12   5 4 3 2 1

The Library of Congress has catalogued the hardcover edition as follows:

Crosswell, D. K. R. (Daniel K. R.)
   Beetle : the life of general Walter Bedell Smith / D.K.R. Crosswell.
      p. cm. — (American warriors)
   Includes bibliographical references and index.
   ISBN 978-0-8131-2649-4 (hardcover : alk. paper)
   1. Smith, Walter Bedell, 1895–1961. 2. Generals—United States—Biography.
3. United States. Army—Biography. 4. Statesmen—United States—Biography.
5. United States—History, Military—20th century. I. Title.
   E745.S57C75 2010
   355.0092—dc22
   [B]   2010026300
   ISBN 978-0-8131-3658-5 (paperback : alk. paper)

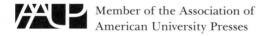

To my parents:
by birth—Earl Edward and Kathleen Crosswell;
and by choice—Willard James and Betty Marie Kaylor

Contents

Part Four: The Mediterranean Campaign

Part Five: France 1944

Part Six: The Victory Campaign

Appendixes

Illustrations

Acknowledgments

This project began in an odd way. Henry Gerard "Red" Phillips, author of *The Making of a Professional: Manton S. Eddy,* suggested to Roger Cirillo, director of the Association of the United States Army (AUSA) book program, that my first book be released in paperback. When Cirillo approached me with the idea, I asked whether we should consider a new book on Smith. The notion of the same author writing a second biography of Smith struck me as a little unconventional, but Roger ran with it. Without these two colonels, this book would never have been written; I owe them both a huge debt of gratitude.

Research for the book took place in stages. I owe the late Merle Miller a great deal. Unbeknownst to Miller, he funded the lion's share of the research for the first Smith book. Stung by the controversy emerging out of the publication of *Plain Speaking: An Oral History of Harry S. Truman,* Miller wanted his biography of Eisenhower to be fully documented and employed me as his lead researcher. Miller provided ample funding that allowed me to amass sources from the Dwight David Eisenhower Presidential Library, the Command and General Staff College, the War College, the Manuscript Division of the National Archives, the Library of Congress, and a number of British depositories. A two-year stint at James Madison University allowed me to build on this foundation, given the proximity to Washington, to Carlisle, Pennsylvania, and to the George C. Marshall Library in Lexington, Virginia. My exile to Singapore in 1990 imposed impediments, but I still managed research forays back to Washington, Carlisle, and Abilene and Leavenworth, Kansas. If I date this project back to Miller, it has been in the works for twenty-eight years and has outlived many of the people who lent invaluable assistance along the way: Forrest Pogue via letters; Russell Vitrup and Carter Burgess via interviews; Larry Bland of the Marshall Library, who was enormously helpful as I charted my way through the vertical file-card collection Pogue compiled for *Supreme Command;* and Judge Leon LeSueur of Napoleonville, Louisiana, a veteran of Normandy who read and commented on my first book. I extend my gratitude to the many archivists who aided me over the years, especially David Haight and Tom Branigar, now both retired from the Eisenhower Library, and David Keough of the U.S. Army Military History Institute. Similarly, I thank the staffs of the Indiana State Library, Indianapolis; Watson Library, University of Kansas; Hale Library, Kansas State University; Central Library, National University of Singapore; Singapore Armed Forces Military Institute library; and Willard Library, Battle Creek, Michigan.

Roger Cirillo has been the driving force behind this project from its inception. The funny thing is, twice I traveled to Washington, in part to meet and thank Roger, but both times he mysteriously went AWOL, making me wonder if he actually existed. He does, as his many emails testify. Roger ran interference, provided moral support and good cheer, and shared his amazing command of sources and the knowledge derived not only from his academic background as a historian, educator, and editor but also from his wide experience as a staff officer. Roger subtly weaned me away from my biases and added enormously to my understanding of the way things work in a headquarters or on the ground. Simply put, this project never would have happened without Roger, and I cannot begin to thank him enough; perhaps someday I might get the chance to do so in person.

Many other people have rendered invaluable assistance along the way, including Richard Grismore of Emmerich Manual High School and Sondrea Ozolins of Butler University, both in Indianapolis, who filled in the gaps in Smith's educational record; Lynsey Robertson of the Churchill Archives Centre and Lianne Smith of the Liddell Hart Centre for Military Archives, who provided amazingly prompt responses to my queries; and particularly MG David T. Zabecki AUS (Ret.), who read and critiqued the manuscript. Overdue thanks to Dominick "Toby" Graham—Military Cross recipient, Olympian, and professor at the University of New Brunswick—who made a trip to the depths of southwestern Missouri to visit and counsel a struggling young academic. I am constantly reminded of the debt owed to the members of my dissertation committee: Emeritus Professor Robin Higham and Professor Donald Mrozek of Kansas State University and Jake Kipp, deputy director of the U.S. Army School of Advanced Military Studies and director of the Foreign Military Studies Office, Fort Leavenworth, Kansas. The late George Kren's healthy skepticism of the workings of the world has always served me as a guide.

A number of people helped sustain my spirits during this long process. Stanley McCool and his wife Loretta Lauinger of Lawrence and

Eric Matta and his wife Meliz of Manhattan offered their hospitality during my sorties back to Kansas. The same applies to Jim Chalker in Philadelphia—who executed some key research for me in Washington—and Steve Sine and Emily Deterding of McGaheysville, Virginia. My family—Frank, Marilyn, Dave, and Jim in Windsor and Suzanne, Anna Marie, and Barry in Niagara Falls—tolerated my frequent impositions, especially Suzanne for letting me hole up with her during the last hectic months of preparing the final manuscript. I could never have finished it without her. My fellow castaways—Jack Fairey, Brian Farrell, Mick Kelly, and Malcolm Murfett—in Singapore, many former students (particularly Pang Yang Huei and Norman Chua, who provided key archival material), and the Saturday softball crew all provided much needed aid and comfort, as did the hundreds of folks, above all my players, involved in the baseball program over the years in Singapore. The "field of dreams" always gave me solace.

I owe a great debt to many people at the University Press of Kentucky. Steve Wrinn, director of the press, has supported this project from the beginning. He did a lot of handholding in the weeks before the final submission deadline, and I thank him for it and much more. The same applies to assistant editor Candace Chaney, who has since gone on to pursue her own writing ambitions; I wish her the best of luck. Candace handed off to Ila McEntire, who supervised the editing. Linda Lotz had the unenviable task of doing the copy edit, which she executed with great patience and skill. The same applies to David DenBoer, who performed the indexing. Their professionalism is matched only by their affability. All mistakes are wholly mine.

Grateful acknowledgment is made to the trustees of the Churchill Archives Centre, Churchill College, Cambridge University and to the Liddell Hart Centre for Military History Archives, Kings College, London, for permission to quote from various collections. I am appreciative of the generous support provided by the AUSA; the association paid for the index, saving me untold angst.

Last but not least stands my muse, my wife, Karen Kaylor, who exhibited amazing fortitude during the many ups and downs over the years spent researching, writing, and editing this work.

Abbreviations

AAF	Army Air Forces
ABDA	American-British-Dutch-Australian
ACM	Air Chief Marshal
ADM	Admiral
ADSEC	advance section
AEAF	Allied Expeditionary Air Force
AEF	American Expeditionary Force
AEFHQ	American Expeditionary Force Headquarters
AFHQ	Allied Force Headquarters
AG	Adjutant General
AGF	Army Ground Forces
AIOC	Anglo-Iranian Oil Company
AM	Air Marshal
AMGOT	Allied Military Government of Occupied Territory
ANCXF	Allied Naval Commander in Chief, Expeditionary Force
ANZUS	Australia, New Zealand, United States security treaty
ASF	Army Service Forces
ASTP	Army Specialized Training Program
AVM	Air Vice Marshal
AWOL	absent without leave
BCOS	British Chiefs of Staff
BG	Brigadier General
BOB	Bureau of the Budget
CAO	chief administrative officer
CCS	Combined Chiefs of Staff
CDR	Commander
CDRE	Commodore
CGSS	Command and General Staff School
CIA	Central Intelligence Agency
CIGS	chief of the imperial general staff
CMTC	Civilian Military Training Camp

CNL	Committee for National Liberation
CNO	chief of naval operations
COL	Colonel
ComZ	Communications Zone
COS	Chief of Staff
COSSAC	Chief of Staff, Supreme Allied Command
CPT	Captain
DCI	director of central intelligence
DRV	Democratic Republic of Vietnam
EAC	European Advisory Commission
EDC	European Defense Community
ESB	Engineer Special Brigade
ETO	European Theater of Operations
FBI	Federal Bureau of Investigation
FCNL	French Committee of National Liberation
FECZ	forward echelon
FFI	French Forces of the Interior
FM	Field Marshal; Field Manual
FSRs	Field Service Regulations
GEN	General
IAC	Intelligence Advisory Committee
IG	Inspector General
JCS	Joint Chiefs of Staff
JIC	Joint Intelligence Committee
JPC	Joint Planning Committee
L of C	line of communication
LST	landing ship/tank
LT	Lieutenant
LTC	Lieutenant Colonel
LTG	Lieutenant General
MAJ	Major
MG	Major General
MP	military police
MTCA	Military Training Camp Association
NAEB	North African Economic Board
NASB	North African Shipping Board
NATO	North Atlantic Treaty Organization; North African Theater of Operations
NATOUSA	North African Theater of Operations
NDA	National Defense Act
NNSC	Neutral Nations Supervisory Commission

NSA	National Security Agency
NSC	National Security Council
OCB	Operations Coordinating Board
OKH	*Oberkommando des Heeres* (Army High Command)
OKW	*Oberkommando der Wehrmacht* (German Armed Forces High Command)
OPC	Office of Policy Coordination
OPD	Operations Division
OSO	Office of Special Operations
OSS	Office of Strategic Services
PM	prime minister
POL	petrol, oil, and lubricants
POW	prisoner of war
PX	post exchange
RADM	Rear Admiral
RAF	Royal Air Force
ROTC	Reserve Officers' Training Corps
RSI	Italian Social Republic
SEATO	Southeast Asia Treaty Organization
SGS	secretary of the general staff
SHAEF	Supreme Headquarters, Allied Expeditionary Force
SOE	Special Operations Executive
SOLOC	southern line of communication
SOS	Services of Supply
SS	*Schutzstaffeln*
T/O	table of organization
USAAF	U.S. Army Air Force
USSTAF	U.S. Strategic Air Forces
VADM	Vice Admiral
VAM	Vice Air Marshal
WAC	Women's Army Corps
WDGS	War Department General Staff
WPA	Works Progress Administration
WPB	War Production Board
WPD	War Plans Division

Introduction

One pitfall in writing a biography is the risk of becoming too immersed in the topic. You spend so much time with the historic figure you begin to feel like you know the person and those in his or her circle. This project has consumed me—with varying degrees of intensity—since 1982. I first encountered Beetle Smith when acting as Merle Miller's researcher for his biography of Dwight Eisenhower, *Ike the Soldier: As They Knew Him*. Smith's career as Eisenhower's chief of staff became the subject of my dissertation; then I worked the dissertation into a book, published by Greenwood in 1991. As a first book, it was not without some merit—it received some solid reviews and commendation by *Choice*—but its publication left me with no sense of closure. Blame it on a callow academic too eager to publish his first book, but I fell victim to the temptation of uncritically accepting received wisdom—in this case, the "good cop" (Eisenhower)–"bad cop" (Smith) school. Basically, I took the easy way out and followed a well-worn path, merely inserting Smith into the story. During my first month as a PhD student at Kansas State, my mentor, Professor Robin Higham, invited D. Clayton James, then a scholar in residence at the Command and General Staff College, to present a talk on his experiences writing the biography of Douglas MacArthur. "Some days I wake up and think MacArthur was the greatest general who ever lived," he recounted. "Others, I concluded he was the biggest SOB who ever lived." With Smith, it proved all too easy to accept his reputation as a one-dimensional SOB, because that was precisely the persona he labored so hard to project. But his friend Hastings Ismay knew better, noting that Smith "was never the terrible Beetle in [Harry C.] Butcher's book" *My Three Years with Eisenhower*, based on the household and headquarters diaries of Eisenhower's naval aide and confidant. The truth is I did not know Smith very well in 1991, and my first book did him an injustice—albeit completely unintended. As it turned out, there were several facets to Beetle Smith. He was much more than advertised, and his boss, Eisenhower, considerably less.

This book's structure is unorthodox. Instead of following a chronological format, I begin with a section on Smith's postwar career serving two presidents: as ambassador to the Soviet Union and director of the Central Intelligence Agency under Truman, and as undersecretary of state and government adviser in the Eisenhower administration. Smith's contributions as ambassador in Moscow when American-Soviet relations entered the deep freeze, as founding father of the CIA, and as number two to John Foster Dulles, especially the parts he played in the Iranian and Guatemalan coups and the Indochina portion of the Geneva conference of 1954, are themselves worthy of serious interest. Essentially, this work is a military biography, and for that reason, I resorted to the device of front-loading Smith's postwar career. Whether this works must be left to the reader's judgment.

Aside from providing an account of Smith's remarkable career and his contributions to the Allied victory in Europe as Eisenhower's chief of staff, this volume has two other objectives. American military biographers tend to shy away from controversial topics; reflecting public tastes, they prefer to cast their subjects in bronze. Political scientists and political historians have engaged in a healthy discourse on Eisenhower and his leadership style virtually since his inaugural, but nothing similar exists in the military history literature. Biographies of Eisenhower still constitute something of a cottage industry. The title of the latest, Michael Korda's *Ike: An American Hero,* perfectly sums up the popular view: Eisenhower as American Everyman, the poor boy who grew up to be president after first liberating Europe from the scourge of fascism. Even the best of them, Carlo D'Este's *Eisenhower: A Soldier's Life,* portrays Eisenhower warts and all, but it still leaves the reader with the image of Ike as Frank Merriwell, the all-American boy. There is a good reason for this: Eisenhower personified a whole array of cherished American ideals. Another reason is that Eisenhower remains an elusive subject.

Eisenhower's detractors—both during the war and after—portray him as a mere chairman of the Allied corporate board, who, though binding the alliance together and achieving victory in Europe, never wielded decisive leadership. He was prone to maddening bouts of indecision and preferred compromise to affirmative control, and this leadership style left him prey to his fractious and willful senior subordinates. Closing his mind to more ambitious schemes for ending the war, his decisions instead lengthened it. His defenders paint an entirely different canvas. As an American supreme commander of an international coalition, Eisenhower skillfully plotted his course, balancing the need to preserve the support of his political chiefs with the need to buttress Allied public opinion, while selectively employing the formal powers conferred on him to fulfill his mission. Attacks on his reputation as a strategist and organizer—and the impression that he reigned more than he ruled—constitute only one of the personal sacrifices Eisenhower made in preserving Allied unity. The truth is Eisenhower fits both portrayals.

Any treatment of Smith as a chief of staff must center on Eisenhower—his character, his approach to problem solving and people, and his strengths and weaknesses as a supreme commander. Two aspects of Eisenhower's personality lay at the center of his leadership style: his predilection to disassociate himself from his actions, and his lifelong refusal to engage in personal conflict. Eisenhower proved decisive only when the decision was not to do something. A product of the interwar U.S. Army, Eisenhower's hierarchical and conservative bent explains not only the thinking behind his command decisions but also why he failed to confront the perpetual problems historically faced by the U.S. Army in war: manpower, supply of forces in the field, and civil affairs. Ego, ambition, envy, and suspicion were ubiquitous and occasionally decisive, and Eisenhower's penchant for personalized command produced his biggest headaches. Part of the reason for Eisenhower's successful high-wire act of managing personalities was, of course, the character of the supreme commander, but also vital was the role played by Beetle Smith.

Many years ago Toby Graham offered sage advice. He said nobody would read logistics history unless it was related to operations. Acting on this caveat, the other goal of this book is to make the connection between command decisions and the limitations imposed by logistics broadly defined. Military historians generally ignore logistics—the economics of warfare—in part because it is difficult to research and write about, but mostly because nobody cares about such arcane topics as organizational theories, manpower policies, and the functioning of incredibly complex supply organizations. There are long, densely written discourses on these admittedly not very interesting subjects, but in my view, *Materialschlacht*—the war for materiel but also for manpower—rests at the core of any explanation of why American forces eventually triumphed in North Africa and northwestern Europe, as well as why opportunities for ending the war sooner and at less cost miscarried. The first Allied invasion—Operation Torch in northwestern Africa—was nearly postponed or even canceled owing to the near breakdown of American logistics in the United Kingdom during the buildup and mounting phase. Allied efforts in Tunisia initially failed in large part because of the chaos in American supply. A succession of crises in 1944—first fuel and then ammunition and winter clothing, climaxing in the debilitating manpower crunch—

left enervated American forces stalemated and vulnerable astride the French-Belgian-German frontiers, giving rise to serious concerns about the war's outcome. Other than Roland Ruppenthal's two-volume official history, *Logistical Support of the Armies,* and the odd book or article dealing with a particular campaign, there is no major treatment of this crucial aspect of war making covering the span of American participation in Europe during World War II. Much of the blame for this operations-supply disconnect rested in Eisenhower's obstinate refusal to alter the headquarters structure. Smith fought and lost numerous battles with Eisenhower over this issue. By examining command decisions through the prism of logistics, a different picture emerges of both Eisenhower as commander and the conduct of operations in North Africa, Italy, and Europe.

Several bromides exist about the roles played by chiefs of staff. Behind every great commander stands his chief of staff. Other than commander, no position in a large, modern bureaucratic military organization is as vital as chief of staff. Chiefs of staff, the linchpins of all military staffs, toil in the shadows, performing the meticulous and anonymous work that wins campaigns. Chiefs of staff translate the will of the commander into practical plans; they harmonize and integrate the actions of headquarters, issuing succinct guidance to their principal staff subordinates while coordinating actions with higher, lateral, and lower staffs. Chiefs of staff must possess not only intelligence and a thorough grasp of detail but also tact and diplomatic skills. Despite the instrumental role played by chiefs of staff, military historians write surprisingly little about them.

Smith discharged all these functions as chief of staff and more. A study of Smith reveals the evolution of the institutional machinery for the higher direction of combined and joint war. If Smith had never served under Eisenhower, he would still command attention for his pivotal role in forging the Combined and Joint Chiefs of Staff apparatuses in Washington in 1942. Enjoying a wide grant of authority from Eisenhower, Smith fashioned and ran Allied headquarters in the Mediterranean and northwestern Europe. Through Smith we observe the inner workings of the complex and rarely smooth relationships among these headquarters and the political heads (Roosevelt, Churchill, and de Gaulle), the uniformed chiefs who stood above (the Combined Chiefs of Staff; the American Joint Chiefs of Staff, principally Marshall; and the British Chiefs of Staff, principally Brooke), and the operational commanders below them (chiefly Alexander and Montgomery for the British and Bradley, Devers, Patton, and Hodges for the Americans). Smith always backstopped Eisenhower in his military decisions and in his dealings with senior American and British politicians and officers. Except when he could not avoid it, Eisenhower delegated to Smith responsibilities for handling Allied and associated entities, most importantly the French. In the absence of direction from above, and exceeding the authority normally vested in a chief of staff, Smith frequently made key policy decisions in areas Eisenhower would not deign to touch, mostly related to military government and civil affairs programs. In effect, Smith acted as the headquarters "general manager" and as Eisenhower's foreign minister; in the latter role he conducted negotiations and signed the surrenders of Italy and Germany.

Higher command in war is a team activity. The commander–chief of staff relationship works best when the two personalities are complementary but not wholly congruent. Although little separated Eisenhower and Smith in terms of their respective professional outlooks and prewar experiences, the two possessed widely divergent personalities. Smith's primary value lay in compensating for Eisenhower's deficiencies. Smith could not play the faceless staff officer because Eisenhower's command style required a proactive chief of staff. If Eisenhower hoped to dodge unpopular decisions and the personal culpability that came with them, if he hoped to evade personal altercations, then as Allied supreme commander, he was in a very strange business. What he needed was a junior partner who was not afraid to go out on a limb, who never avoided a fight, and who at least gave the appearance of having a thick skin. Eisenhower may have stretched the truth when he described Smith as "the best chief of staff ever," but in Beetle he possessed the perfect foil.

Part One

★ ★ ★ ★

Epilogue as Prologue— Soldier, Diplomat, Spymaster

★ **1** ★

Soldier Turned Diplomat

The featured stories in the Washington newspapers on 14 August 1961 dealt with the East Germans sealing the border in Berlin and the latest exploits of Mickey Mantle in his pursuit of Babe Ruth's home run record. Other than the obligatory obituaries—unimaginative pieces mostly gleaned from *Current Biography*—the death and funeral of yet another senior U.S. Army officer from World War II received little attention. Five days before, GEN Walter Bedell Smith had died in an ambulance en route to Walter Reed Hospital. His heart, "always too big for his body" in the estimate of one of his British friends, finally gave out. For years Smith had existed on "bourbon and Dexedrine," his frail body devoured by an assortment of maladies related to a chronic ulcer condition.[1]

Whatever wartime celebrity Smith enjoyed derived largely from two events. In September 1943, fittingly enough under an olive tree, a frozen-faced Beetle Smith accepted the capitulation of Italy. Twenty months later, in a French schoolhouse, Smith, still without any exterior sign of emotion, affixed his name to the unconditional surrender of Nazi Germany. In the postwar period he continued to serve his country as diplomat and chief of intelligence. "Only President Eisenhower and the late General of the Army George C. Marshall," noted the *New York Times*, "were said to have matched the range and duration of 'Beetle' Smith's more than four decades of service in the military and civilian branches of the government."[2] The comparison to Eisenhower and Marshall proved particularly apt.

The men Smith served recognized his value, even if the public never did. Marshall spoke of his "admiration for the manner in which you have discharged your vast responsibilities" as Eisenhower's chief of staff in Europe, assuring Smith that he had carved out his "place in the his-

9

tory of a great and terrible epoch." British Prime Minister Winston Churchill pointed to Smith's "comradeship, tested in war and always found to be of the finest steel." President Harry Truman considered Smith's contribution in reforming the Central Intelligence Agency of "immeasurable value," calling him "a real patriot, and a public administrator of the highest caliber." Most telling of all, Dwight Eisenhower posited in July 1945 that "no single man in Europe contributed more to Allied victory" than Smith.[3]

Sixteen years before his death, Smith had crossed the Arlington Memorial Bridge in happier circumstances. On 18 June 1945 Eisenhower made his triumphant return to Washington. As the procession left National Airport, Eisenhower and Marshall sat in the first car, with Smith positioned in the second. After a brief ceremony at the Pentagon, Marshall excused himself. Eisenhower would give a speech at the Capitol after a parade up Independence Avenue, and true to form, Marshall did not want to steal any of the limelight. Smith assumed Marshall's place in the lead vehicle. No doubt Smith hoped this switch was a portent of the future. Although Smith's name remained forever linked with Eisenhower's—and he always maintained his fealty to Ike—in his heart, Smith was first and foremost a "Marshall man." "I wish that I could be like you," he confided to Marshall in a rare show of sentiment. "I never can, of course . . . but I have tried very hard to be, and will continue to do so as long as I live."[4] Eisenhower succeeded Marshall as army chief of staff in November 1945, and Smith harbored hope that he might eventually follow his wartime bosses into the same chair. Although he had no way of knowing it at the time, the round of victory celebrations that started in Paris with GEN Charles de Gaulle awarding him the Grand-Croix de la Légion de Mérite at the Arc de Triomphe and ended, fittingly, in Indianapolis, the city Smith had left twenty-eight years before as a young lieutenant, marked the climax of Smith's military career.

Passed Over

Smith's postwar career produced nothing but frustration. The long train of setbacks started in April 1945, when he discovered he would not become Eisenhower's deputy theater commander and proconsul in occupied Germany. He considered the appointment his due—a view shared by Marshall but not by President Franklin Roosevelt or his secretary of war, Henry Stimson. The job went to LTG Lucius Clay. In early September Eisenhower recommended that Smith succeed him as theater commander and discussed the matter with Marshall during his visit to the States. After returning to Europe, Eisenhower put his request in writing. He offered a roster of possible successors that included Carl Spaatz, George Patton, and Jacob Devers, with Smith at the top of the list. The officer selected must be a "many-sided character" because the job required an ability to work with the Allied Control Council and the Russians, British, and French in occupied Germany. Smith "would be completely acceptable to everyone," Eisenhower argued, "and because of his splendid background, would be in better position than anyone else to carry on without interruption." Eisenhower knew that his suggestion was "probably an impossible one" because it would require Smith's fast-track promotion to four stars and elevation over Patton. "This would not be particularly serious in my opinion," he concluded.[5]

Marshall did not share Eisenhower's optimism. Instead, Marshall appointed his former deputy, GEN Joseph McNarney, in the dual capacity of theater commander and military governor of Germany. A four-star general since March 1945, McNarney had assumed command of U.S. forces in the Mediterranean theater as deputy supreme commander in November 1944. Although he had been a classmate, Eisenhower did not think much of McNarney's appointment and resented Marshall's ignoring his recommendation and bringing in an outsider. As Eisenhower told Marshall, his misgivings centered on McNarney's character, "certain details [of which] I think I had better forget."[6] With McNarney's appointment "fixed," Eisenhower advanced Smith as successor to GEN Brehon Somervell, head of the Army Service Forces, who would leave his post in tandem with Marshall in November.[7] Eisenhower's proposal met with no enthusiasm in the War Department, and Marshall quietly let the matter die.

Although not the decisive consideration, the precarious state of Smith's health may have influenced Marshall's thinking. Before D-day, Smith wondered if he could tough out the strain of another campaign, and he limped across the finish line in May 1945. Despite his relative youth—he would not turn fifty until October—Smith was a physical wreck by war's end. Reassuring Marshall, he spoke of plans to spend a week fishing—he had commandeered a Bavarian estate as a lodge—and reported that he looked "forward to it like a small boy to summer vacation." He figured that after a spell on a trout stream, "I should be good for another year or so if necessary."[8] The time off no doubt did him good, but it could not cure what ailed him. Despite his reunion with wife Nory, whom he had not seen since October 1943, the victory tour in the States produced another serious recurrence of his stomach disorder. "Beetle is much improved in health," Eisenhower reported in early

August to their mutual friend, industrialist Louis Marx, "but he did give me a bad scare for a week or two." Eisenhower thought that if Smith took care of himself, he would be all right. "I don't know what I would do without him."[9] That Eisenhower relied so heavily on his chief of staff in no small measure accounted for Smith's health issues, as did his overweening sense of duty and refusal to abdicate authority. The mounting disillusionment over his future prospects added to Smith's complaints.

With Eisenhower slatted for army chief of staff, many things weighed on his mind in late summer 1945—chiefly, reorganizing the War Department and finding suitable billets for his friends—but orchestrating the American occupation of Germany was not among them. Eisenhower typically avoided anything smacking of politics—a lesson driven home by the Darlan affair in North Africa—and nothing appeared more fraught with political dangers than managing the occupation. He delegated those responsibilities, and all the complex details, to Smith and Clay.

Eisenhower was right to steer clear of any close identification with the occupation. Unlike during the war, the theater command could not blanket its activities behind a wall of censorship. It soon became evident to journalists that the Americans lacked affirmative programs for administering Germany, in sharp contrast to the Soviets, who experienced no problems integrating their military and political policies. By attitude, training, or experience, senior American officers proved inapt as military governors, and none more so than Patton.

As Robert Murphy, the political adviser for the occupation, observed, "there was no love lost between Smith and Patton." In fact, the two men shared an odd love-hate relationship. In mid-September 1945 Smith telephoned Patton and inexplicably told him, "You're my best friend, George. Probably that is the reason why you always give me my worst headaches." Smith's current headache grew out of Patton's apparent nonenforcement of the denazification program. Patton did not buy Smith's avowal of friendship; he saw Smith as the primary architect in a conspiracy to remove Patton from command of his beloved Third Army. After he put down the receiver, Patton turned to a member of his staff and pronounced Smith "a goddamn snake."[10]

Reports streamed into the Frankfurt headquarters concerning Patton's increasingly bizarre behavior. As Smith remarked, "There is no rational explanation for what General Patton is doing. I don't doubt that old George has lost his marbles." Patton lapsed into a downward spiral of depression. "Another war has ended," he lamented, "and with it my usefulness to the world."[11] He indulged in wild talk about "the horrors of peace, pacaficism [sic], and unions" and how much "real fun [it would be] killing Mongols."[12] Patton's rants against Jews, displaced persons, the Soviets, and his superiors; his flouting of the rules against fraternization; and his disavowal of denazification all indicated that Smith was probably right. Alarmed, Smith suggested that Eisenhower cut short his vacation on the Riviera and return to headquarters. If the problem spun out of control, it might bear on Eisenhower's forthcoming appointment.[13]

The *New York Times* quoted Patton as saying at a news conference on 22 September that "far too much fuss has been made regarding denazification of Germany; that this Nazi thing is just like a Democratic and Republican election fight, and that the best hope for the future lies in showing the German people what grand fellows we are."[14] Although buried on page eighteen, the story possessed explosive potential. The *Times* suggested, and Marshall concurred, that Patton's "remarks should [not] go unchallenged either by his commanding officer General Eisenhower, or by his superiors in Washington." Something did detonate: Eisenhower "erupted in the granddaddy of all tempers."[15] A curious aspect of Eisenhower's leadership style grew out of his lifetime struggle to control his anger; as a result, he avoided personal confrontations. His effectiveness remained rooted in his affability; everybody had to like Ike. This meant somebody had to wield the stick, and that somebody was Smith. To Smith fell the dirty jobs. Eisenhower returned to Frankfurt to deal with the latest Patton episode but insisted, as he always did, that Smith act as front man.

Patton claimed he had been misquoted, and Smith suggested he hold a press conference to "set the record straight." An unapologetic Patton followed Smith's advice, but his words merely fanned the flames. On 26 September Smith held his own meeting with the press in an attempt to contain the conflagration. "Growling that General Eisenhower would tolerate no insubordination," *Time* reported, "General Smith then spoke as one professional soldier practically never speaks of another: '[Patton's] mouth does not always carry out the functions of his brain. George acts on the theory that it is better to be damned than say nothing—that some publicity is better than none.'"[16] Asked "whether you think that [Eisenhower's denazification] program can be carried out by people who are temperamentally and emotionally in disagreement with it," Smith replied he did not think that categorization applied to Patton. After fielding a series of hostile questions, Smith finally admitted, "I am not prepared to state that it [denazification] has been carried out effectively in every case." He assured within a week they could expect a "marked improvement" and finished by saying, "General Patton is a soldier and will carry out his orders."[17]

Two days later Patton traveled to Canossa, in this case theater headquarters in Frankfurt. Eisenhower put on his trademark grin, but it was forced. Smith sat in on the meeting. When Patton proved impenitent, the grin disappeared. Patton stood among Eisenhower's oldest friends, a man he greatly admired and owed much, but this time "Old Blood and Guts" went too far. Eisenhower's secretary, Kay Summersby, recorded that Eisenhower "aged ten years in reaching the decision, which was inevitable in the light of Patton's past mistakes and the universal furor over this one." She depicted the conversation among the three men as "long and acid," as "one of the stormiest sessions ever staged in our headquarters. It was the first time I ever heard General Eisenhower raise his voice."[18]

On 29 September the telephone rang at Patton's headquarters at Bad Tölz. On the other end was Smith. This time Smith wielded his hatchet. He began by reading a letter prepared by Eisenhower. Patton pointed to an extension phone and told Murphy, who just happened to be there, "Listen to what the lying SOB will say." What Murphy heard was Smith "performing his duty as tactfully as possible. Patton vigorously pantomimed for my benefit his scornful reactions to Smith's placatory remarks."[19] Patton lost his army, and effective 8 October, he would assume command of the Fifteenth Army, literally a paper army dedicated to writing up the lessons of the war. As he confided in his diary, Patton "accepted the job with the Fifteenth Army because I was reluctant, in fact unwilling, to be a party to the destruction of Germany under the pretense of de-Nazification. . . . I believe Germany should not be destroyed, but rather rebuilt as a buffer against the real danger which is Bolshevism from Russia."[20]

Patton's and McNarney's respective appointments called for a reshuffling of senior personnel. Marshall had designated LTG Lucian Truscott as McNarney's eventual replacement in the Mediterranean, but Truscott instead assumed command of the Third Army. Washington wanted to curtail commitments in the Mediterranean and insisted on a British supreme commander; McNarney was currently serving as interim supreme commander. Marshall informed Eisenhower that "Allied Force Headquarters will break up before the end of the year. From the American military viewpoint it is purely a question of rolling up the theater and getting out. We have no qualified senior American officers there to relieve McNarney," and he asked if Smith wanted the job.[21]

The Mediterranean theater staff had just separated from Allied Force Headquarters (AFHQ), so the job of deputy supreme commander amounted to a titular holdover and a real comedown from Smith's present position. Eisenhower quickly replied in the negative. He could not manage without Smith because of his involvement in the "staff reorganization necessitated by the changing administrative situation and the building up of the Control Council staff." As he explained to Marshall, when Eisenhower took over in Washington, he envisioned slotting Smith as assistant chief of staff for operations.[22] So another appointment for Smith went by the wayside, this time to his great relief. The assignment went to LTG J. C. H. Lee, who headed the Communications Zone in northwestern Europe.

One by one, all the senior American officers left the theater. GEN Omar Bradley went to Washington to head the new Veterans Administration, LTG Courtney Hodges redeployed his First Army to the Pacific, LTG William Simpson assumed command of the Second Army in the United States, LTG Alexander Patch headed the review board undertaking a study for the reorganization of the War Department, and LTG Leonard Gerow took the job Patton wanted as head of the Command and Staff College at Fort Leavenworth. The departures climaxed with Eisenhower's in November. After Patton left in December, Smith was the only member of the Old Guard who remained.

In the interregnum before McNarney assumed command, Patton acted as theater commander. "It is very evident that Beadle [*sic*] really runs the show," Patton told his wife, "in so far as it can be said to be run. . . . The chief interest seems to center on doing nothing positive and never going counter to what the papers say. Some one proposes something and Beadle makes a speech against it and ends up by saying that while he is against it in principle he will go along with it just this once." Since Patton loathed Smith, he found the temporary appointment "not very pleasant. . . . It is not a Headquarters, just a chetequa [*sic*]."[23] Frustrated by all the attendant problems of the occupation, Smith would not have disagreed with Patton's assessment, and like Patton, he was worried about his future.

Back in Washington, Eisenhower wrote two letters to Smith. The first assured Smith that he would return to the United States in the near future, "since McNarney has indicated his willingness to fire you almost immediately." In the second, he apologized because he had been "forced to delay [an] exact decision in your case," but he promised Smith, "I will have a critical post for you. We will talk it over after you get here."[24] Smith replied, "in all truthfulness . . . except for my desire to do any job that you particularly want to give me, Washington has no attractions for me." Smith expressed a lack of concern about keeping his temporary rank of lieutenant general, observing, "it might make it easier for some of the others."[25]

McNarney assumed command on 26 November. A week later, Smith gave a luncheon for his new boss. "I have rarely seen assembled," offered Patton in his last diary entry, "a greater bunch of sons-of-bitches." He turned his ire on Clay and McNarney, who "have never commanded anything, including their own self-respect, or if that, certainly not the respect of anyone else." The whole party reminded him of a Rotary Club meeting "where everyone slaps every one else's back while looking for an appropriate place to thrust the knife."[26] Given that Clay and McNarney held the appointments Smith coveted, he had already felt the stab.

Of course, Patton never made it home. On 9 December he suffered fatal injuries in an otherwise innocuous car crash. A number of senior officers rushed to the hospital in Heidelberg where Patton was confined, but they confronted a standing order that the patient would receive no visitors. Smith liked to throw his weight around and got indignant when the attending doctor, a colonel, bluntly informed him that he was not welcome. When the doctor approached Patton about allowing Smith to visit, the general said, "He's never been a particular friend of mine. Colonel, it's up to you to keep him out." Soon Bea Patton arrived from the States. "It may be fatal," Patton told his wife, "if I have to see that old sonuvabitch," in reference to Smith. Mrs. Patton told the medical staff that "under no circumstances" should they allow Smith into Patton's room.[27] Smith had negotiated with some pretty formidable personalities during his tenure as Eisenhower's "foreign minister," but he knew better than to cross swords with the general's wife. The Patton family's bitterness carried beyond the grave. Bea Patton insisted on striking Smith's name from the list of honorary pallbearers, placing the general's faithful African American orderly in his place.

Smith's remaining time in Germany became an ordeal. Eisenhower extracted assurances from his successor that Smith would be released within two weeks of McNarney's taking over. But because Smith labored so hard and generally succeeded in making himself indispensable, McNarney soon realized that he could not run the occupation without Smith pulling the levers. Smith's disposition—foul at the best of times—can be imagined. He worked under McNarney and Clay, carrying out many of the duties incumbent on them in a thankless job that led nowhere. Although he told Eisenhower he did not care about rank, the truth was that he cared very much. Smith was not as selfless as he postured; like every other ambitious and prideful officer who suffered through the deadening interwar years, Smith sought promotion in recognition of his service in the war. He would return to Washington and a new job—not one he anticipated, and definitely not one he desired, but one that would change the entire trajectory of his life.

"Serves Those Bastards Right"

Even after the Potsdam conference, Harry Truman remained committed to pursuing Roosevelt's policy of constructive engagement with the Soviet Union. When W. Averell Harriman signaled his intention to leave Moscow, the administration had to find his successor as ambassador. Truman wanted an experienced and hard-boiled negotiator who would not be bullied by Stalin and his henchmen. In a surprise move, he offered Smith the job.

The chief agent behind Smith's appointment was Secretary of State James Byrnes. Byrnes, then a senator from South Carolina, had met young Major Smith by chance in 1940. Among his many tasks as assistant secretary to Marshall, Smith handled the influential financier Bernard Baruch, whose hobby was advising presidents. Marshall curried Baruch's favor because he lent invaluable assistance to the War Department during the fight with Congress over increased defense appropriations. Baruch and Byrnes were close political associates, and when Smith ferried Baruch down to South Carolina to watch army maneuvers, he met and impressed the senator. During the same trip, Smith made his first acquaintance with another individual who would impact his life and career: Eisenhower. The consummate insider, Byrnes went on to sit on the Supreme Court and then in rapid succession headed Roosevelt's Economic Stabilization Office and the Office of War Mobilization. In July 1945 Truman named him secretary of state. Byrnes served as a justice without attending university, much less law school, and he possessed no experience in foreign relations. He therefore saw no problem with a soldier being named ambassador extraordinary and plenipotentiary to Moscow; indeed, he considered it a positive asset. As Eisenhower's chief of staff, Smith had conducted the negotiations leading to the Italian and German surrenders, and he had routinely dealt with Churchill and the Foreign Office and de Gaulle as head of the Free French and later president of the French provisional government. Pushing for revisions of the unconditional surrender policy and recognition of de Gaulle had placed Smith at odds with Roosevelt and Stimson, but Truman and Byrnes believed Smith's independent thinking could do little harm, given the deteriorating state of Soviet-American relations. "I am hopeful," Truman noted, "that General Bedell Smith will succeed in breaking the deadlock."[28] "Your appointment," Marshall wired Smith from China, "is a splendid choice. I am sorry you are to have such a heavy job with no opportunity for rest but I know of no one who could give a better performance." Marshall's enthusiasm indicates that he had strongly endorsed Smith's nomination. "I would have much preferred a quiet assignment," Smith replied, "but you have set the example of devotion to duty and the rest of us must follow you and do the best we can."[29] Eisenhower told his longtime friend E. E. "Swede" Hazlett, "I know of no one better qualified for the job." More candidly, he also said of Smith's appointment, "serves those bastards [the Soviets] right."[30]

The White House announced Smith's appointment on 14 February 1946, but complications delayed his formal appointment until 22 March. Smith insisted on keeping his military rank, requiring a special act of Congress. On the day of the announcement he made news at a Red Army Day dinner held in Manhattan. Although affirming the enormous debt the Western powers owed to the sacrifices of the Red Army and the Soviet people during the war, and pointing to the mutual desires of the American and Soviet peoples for world peace, he warned the Soviet leadership that they must recognize there were lines beyond which the United States "cannot go."[31]

The only glue holding together the uneasy wartime alliance, with all its mutual suspicions, dissolved with the defeat of Germany. At no time during the war did American leadership employ military force for specific political objectives, and Roosevelt's policy of postponing vital political decisions until after the war left Stalin in the driver's seat. The Soviet premier never comprehended the moralistic legalism in American thinking. Why the United States placed such importance on the political systems of Poland and other eastern European states—where the United States possessed no vital interests—baffled Stalin. By exposing the divisions in the Western camp—made easier because the Americans decoupled diplomatic ends from military means—Stalin won the Soviet Union's greatest successes at the beige-covered conference tables of Tehran, Yalta, and Potsdam.

Truman went to Potsdam with the hope of proving to Stalin that the United States was "on the level" and was interested only in fostering world peace. Stalin could not grasp that the United States entertained no concrete interests and concluded that Truman must be harboring ulterior motives. Told of the Americans' possession of the atomic bomb, Stalin did not blink; in fact, he knew of its existence before Truman did. But in Truman's revelation he could see only a threat. For domestic political reasons, and desiring Soviet participation in the war against Japan, Truman refrained from placing any kind of genuine pressure on

Stalin to achieve a settlement, and threats were the only thing Stalin truly understood.

The paradox of Potsdam rested in the fact that Stalin's belligerence masked the Soviet Union's weakness. After suffering casualties in the tens of millions in the German war—to say nothing of the tens of millions killed in prewar collectivization and purges—and with a third of the European portions of the Soviet Union in ruins, Stalin needed a sustained period of peace. He remained fixed on retaining Soviet conquests and erecting tiers of buffer states on his borders because, despite his bluster, Stalin saw the real possibility of his worst fears being realized: a Western capitalist encirclement with sufficient power, augmented by the atom bomb, to impose its will. He offered no concessions because the Americans demanded none. The American delegation could not disentangle Stalin's Great Russian chauvinism—itself a cover for a traditional and instinctive Russian xenophobia—from his Marxist-Leninist internationalism. The theory of perpetual revolution applied more inside the Soviet Union than outside it, and without the appearance of a capitalist threat, Stalin could not rationalize his tyranny or ask for continued sacrifice from the Soviet people.

Truman still retained notions of cooperating with the Soviets. At Potsdam, Truman, Stalin, and Churchill, avoiding the peripheral issues that had plagued the Versailles conference, consigned the question of Germany and Austria's future, including reparations, to a four-power mechanism, and they delegated determination of the status of Germany's allies and associated states to a future congress. In July 1946 the foreign ministers would convene a peace conference in Paris to hammer out subsidiary treaties. The first attempt in London miscarried. Truman wanted the Paris conference to succeed and rekindle the hope of reversing the downward spiral in American-Soviet relations.

As Smith revealed in Frankfurt on his way to Moscow, the president charged him with finding a modus vivendi for peaceful coexistence with Moscow. He expressed that a "great feeling of doubt" existed among the American public as to "what the Russians want and what the Russian motives are."[32] The world atmosphere grew increasingly tense. On 9 February Stalin made a major speech setting out his vision of the incompatibility of the communist and capitalist systems. He claimed that the recent war had been the creation not of Hitler but of the inherent contradictions in capitalism. "Our Marxists declare that the capitalist system of world economy conceals elements of crisis and war," he said, "that the development of world capitalism does not follow a steady and even course forward, but proceeds through crises and catastrophes."[33]

A month later Churchill made his "Sinews of Peace" speech in Fulton, Missouri. Now head of the loyal opposition, Churchill, with uncanny prescience, adumbrated future American policy. In the interim after Potsdam, the Soviets had consolidated control in their eastern satellites and divided Europe from Stettin to Trieste; the solution rested in containing the Soviet threat through some form of European union and the consolidation of the three Western zones in Germany into a sovereign and rearmed state—all founded on an Anglo-American alliance. "I do not believe that Soviet Russia desires war," Churchill stated. "What they desire is the fruits of war and the indefinite expansion of their power and doctrine."[34] It appeared that the rival systems had received their marching orders.

Churchill's speech did Truman no favors. American and Soviet officials met regularly; American troop levels in Europe markedly declined. Truman instructed Smith to play hardball, but only after exhausting all avenues for reaching some understanding with the Soviets. Smith met Stalin and Foreign Minister V. M. Molotov on 5 April 1946, exactly a month after Churchill's speech. Anticipating that the meeting might prove stormy, Smith went alone. He began by handing Stalin a letter from Truman inviting the Soviet premier to visit Washington. "Neither the American people nor the American Government," Smith assured Stalin, "could take seriously the possibility of aggressive action against the Soviet Union by any nation or group of nations in the world today. We felt certain that no possible combination of powers could threaten the Soviet Union without the active support of the United States, and our entire history precluded the possibility that we would ever lend support to aggressive action." As proof, Smith offered the rapid demobilization of American armed forces. He pointed to Truman's desire to meet the Soviets halfway and stated, "indeed we felt like we had already gone more than half way." Although the United States appreciated Soviet strength, "at the same time we are fully conscious of our own strength." Reinforcing the point, he said, "it would be misinterpreting the character of the United States to assume that because we are basically peaceful and deeply interested in world security, we are . . . divided, weak [or] unwilling to face our responsibilities." Smith cautioned that unless the Soviet Union demonstrated a greater willingness to cooperate within the structure of international law and bodies, chiefly the United Nations, and "if both nations remain apprehensive and suspicious of each other, we may both find ourselves embarked upon an expensive policy of rearmament and the maintenance of large military establishments which we wish to avoid."

Stalin countered Smith's arguments. He pointed to recent American actions in the United Nations designed to forestall any continuation of the Soviet presence in Iran. Stalin said Churchill's speech constituted "an unfriendly act and an unwarranted attack on himself and the USSR." When Smith pushed Stalin and asked why he saw Western actions as threats, Stalin pointed to Churchill as the problem. Rationalizing British intervention in the Russian civil war in 1919, Churchill famously advocated strangling the Bolshevik baby in its cradle and in Stalin's view "was at it again." Smith asked point-blank if Stalin believed the United States and Great Britain "were united in an alliance to thwart Russia." Stalin categorically said he "did so believe." Smith replied that although "the US had many ties with Britain, including common language and many common interests, we were interested primarily in world security and justice; that this interest and responsibility extended to small nations as well as large." Smith also stated that "there was no nation in the world with whom we were more interested in arriving at a basis of understanding than with Russia, as we felt that the future of the world for a long time to come lay in the hands of our two nations." Smith concluded by restating American desires for closer cooperation and mutual understanding with the Soviet Union, "which we considered essential for world peace." "Prosper your efforts," Marshal Stalin replied. "I will help you. I am at your disposal at any time." Referring to Truman's invitation, Stalin said that although he would like very much to accept, "age has taken its toll. My doctors tell me that I must not travel."[35]

Truman's offer of a summit conference went nowhere, and Smith did not meet Stalin again for two years. As a delegate to the Paris Peace Conference, he spent the summer in the French capital. On 10 February 1947 the victorious powers completed treaties with Italy, Romania, Hungary, and Finland. The Paris Peace Treaties represented the last instance of East-West cooperation. By spring 1947 American policy edged from seeking accommodation with the Soviet Union to containing the spread of communism. In March Truman went before Congress and proclaimed, "It must be the policy of the United States to support free peoples who are resisting attempted subjugation by armed minorities or by outside pressures." In April the newly appointed secretary of state, George Marshall, decided Soviet intransigence rendered diplomacy through negotiations a pointless exercise. The Truman administration moved toward solidifying alignments against the Soviet Union. In June the United States launched the Marshall Plan, the economic and political pillars of the containment policy designed to undermine popular support for the communist parties in western Europe by giving direct economic aid to buttress international capitalism and providing covert support for left-of-center parties to revitalize democracy. American policy on Germany moved away from pursuing an all-Germany solution toward forming a Western-oriented state in the American, British, and French zones of occupation. Smith's job centered on convincing the Kremlin, chiefly Molotov and Andrei Vishinsky, that the shift in American policy had evolved as a defensive reflex against the USSR's strategy of playing the Western powers off one another based on the doctrine of the inevitability of conflict among the capitalist states. Smith spent much of his time ameliorating the increasingly severe Soviet policies against internal manifestations of "cosmopolitanism"—mostly attacks on artists, intellectuals, and scientists, many of them Jewish. He also labored to improve and expand the activities of Voice of America and the magazine *Amerika*.

Smith went to Moscow armed with a greater sense of optimism than he encountered in the State Department. Based on his experience dealing with senior Soviet officers during the immediate postwar period, he thought he might achieve some successes. His contacts with Molotov and Vishinsky soon left him disillusioned. When he sat at the table with the Soviet leadership, Smith lamented that during the war he had spoken with "four million men and 15,000 heavy bombers behind [him]."[36] As he told an army official historian in 1947, he deeply regretted that Allied forces had stopped at the Elbe. Eisenhower and the staff of Supreme Headquarters, Allied Expeditionary Force (SHAEF) "frankly wanted water between us and the Russians . . . needed a definitive line of demarcation. We wanted a point where we could you-hoo across at our comrades before embracing them." Churchill bitterly opposed the decision, and Smith "often thought as [he] sat around a conference table how it would have been better to follow him. . . . We leaned over backward to give them a proper deal, and it was a mistake."[37]

Even in the best of times, the posting in Moscow produced a feeling of insulation and remoteness from the outside world. Life in ugly Spasso House, the U.S. embassy a mile from the Kremlin (which some wag aptly named Spasm House), was grim. As tensions between Moscow and Washington worsened, things became more oppressive, with secret police agents following Smith's every movement—even tailing him in a rowboat when he went fishing—and discouraging contact with Soviet citizens.[38] Nonetheless, Smith traveled a good deal, visiting scientific institutes, collective farms, and industrial complexes and generally monitoring the progress of the latest Five-Year Plan. The situation deteriorated further in February 1948 when the Czech Communist Party overthrew the coalition government in Prague. Smith believed "that there never was the slightest intention on the part of Stalin and the Politburo to honor—at any point or in any way—the many agreements . . . to allow the people of Eastern Europe freely to choose their own form of government."[39] Smith made no effort to disguise his frustration and impatience to escape Moscow.

In March 1948 rumors spread in Berlin that Smith appeared to be the "definite choice for high commissioner" in Germany. The State Department planned to assume control in the American zone in Germany, and Marshall pressed for Smith's appointment. The press reported that the decision rested in Smith's hands. Smith told Eisenhower on 1 April that he "accepted General Marshall's suggestion that I go there as High Commissioner," with the "understanding it would be for one year."[40] But for the second time, Smith was passed over as governor of the American occupation of Germany. Given mounting East-West tension in the aftermath of Czechoslovakia, Truman decided to leave Smith in Moscow.

Disheartened over not getting the German appointment—his chief motive being to escape Moscow—Smith took ten days off in the beginning of May for a little soul-searching and fishing in Normandy. Amidst denials by the State Department, a Washington paper reported that Smith had already tendered his resignation.[41] He told the press before heading for France that there was "little doin'" in Moscow. That soon changed; the Soviets began escalating pressure on Berlin in an effort to force a German settlement. Smith hurried back to Moscow and on 24 May made a private call on Molotov at the Kremlin and, as reported in the press, "talked turkey." He warned the Soviet foreign minister that the American economy remained "sound of heart and limb" and the American people "just as determined as ever to oppose Soviet aggression and the spread of Communist ideas." If Moscow thought otherwise, Smith said, it must be "listening too hard to Henry Wallace" in an election year "and swallowing its own propaganda." As Smith told the journalists, he acted on the express instructions of the State Department, which was worried that the Soviets might make "some grievous miscalculations." Smith told *Time* that "Hitler's error in thinking his opponents were 'worms' had plunged him into World War II," and his conversations with Molotov centered on warning the Kremlin not to make the same mistake. Still following instructions, Smith reaffirmed, "As far as the U.S. is concerned, the door is always open for full discussion and the composing of our differences." As a follow-up to Smith's "let's talk it over" exchange with Molotov, Marshall indicated the United States would soften its approach to the Soviets, especially on the deadlocked German question.[42]

Exactly a month after Smith issued his warning, on 24 June 1948, the Soviets made a "grievous miscalculation" by initiating their blockade of Berlin. A war scare gripped the West. Marshall announced to the Kremlin the cessation of all negotiations at the ministerial level while the crisis lasted, and in Berlin, the four-power arrangement collapsed in discord. For the next two months, Smith stood as the focal point of American talks with the Soviets.

Smith flew to Berlin on 25 July for consultations with Clay and his political adviser Murphy, together with the State Department's specialist on Soviet affairs, Charles "Chip" Bohlen.[43] From Berlin he went to Paris and London. On 1 August Smith returned to Moscow, and the next day he, French ambassador Yves Chataigneau, and a representative of the British Foreign Office, Frank Roberts, met separately with Stalin. The routine never varied; senior Soviet officials always met them separately, with Smith always in the lead. Smith opened the discussion by telling Stalin, "the gravity and dangers of [the] present situation in Berlin" demanded "a mutually acceptable solution . . . aware that failure in these talks would render existing dangers even more acute."[44] Stalin offered a compromise: in exchange for the concurrent withdrawal of Western currency and introduction of the ostmark in the Western sectors of Berlin, the Soviets would remove traffic controls in and out of the city. Stalin revealed the real motive behind the engineering of the crisis when he pointed to his "insistent wish" that the formation of a provisional West German government be suspended. Smith described Stalin as "courageous but cautious; suspicious, revengeful and quick to anger, but coldly ruthless and pitilessly realistic; decisive and swift in the execution of his plans when the objective is clear, but patient, deceptive and Fabian in his tactics when the situation is obscure."[45]

On 3 August Marshall conditionally accepted Stalin's currency proposal but ignored his "insistent wish." Smith returned to Berlin and then held further discussions in London. A "pale and tired" Smith returned to Moscow on 9 August. His only remark to the cluster of Western journalists was, "Fine weather you're having here." Smith insisted on seeing Molotov, but the foreign minister was "out of town" on vacation. When he asked to see Vishinsky, he received the same story. One by one, Smith and his colleagues met Molotov's deputy, Valerian Zorin, each handing him an aide-mémoire and asking for meetings with Molotov. At first, it appeared that the Soviets were engaged in another of their delaying actions, but Molotov really was on vacation. He hurried back, and once again the same routine was followed. Smith presented a proposal for convening a four-power conference on Berlin on the condition that the

Soviets lift the blockade. Through Molotov, Stalin showed interest in a conference but refused all prior conditions. Smith's diplomacy produced no immediate results, but Molotov's hurried return "helped to dispel, or at least palliate, a war scare."[46]

Smith, Roberts, and Chataigneau met with Molotov on three other occasions. All four governments signaled their willingness to lift the blockade, accept the ostmark as the sole currency in Berlin, and convene a four-power conference for discussions on all outstanding questions concerning Berlin and even Germany. The only roadblock remained the original obstacle: the conditions under which the ostmark would circulate. As Smith made clear, the Western governments could accept no arrangement resulting in any undermining of their "unquestionable right to be in Berlin or in making it impossible for them to exercise that right, or to discharge fully their obligations as occupying authorities."[47] All four parties labored over the language of a joint communiqué and directives to the commanders of the occupation forces in the hope of narrowing the differences.

All this time, Smith was enforcing a blackout on news releases. With the attention of the world centered on the talks in Moscow, the press hounded him for information. "In five meetings," *Time* reported, "the press got about 120 noncommittal words out of Smith, less than that out of Roberts, nothing but vague smiles out of Chataigneau, not even a smile out of Molotov." In truth, there was little to say and less to smile about. Smith cryptically summed up his last meeting with Molotov by saying, "Molotov, three hours. No Stalin. No comment."[48] Finally, Stalin consented to see the Western diplomats.

The three Western heads of mission carefully rehearsed and coordinated their sales pitches. Journalists noted Smith fidgeting, juggling his attaché case like it was a hot potato, as he made his way into the Kremlin on 23 August. The briefcase contained his new draft. In a carefully prepared opening statement, Smith emphasized that Berlin symbolized to the American government and people the "common allied victory." He continued, "The possibility of peaceful co-existence and collaboration of our respective systems . . . will be largely judged by what happens there. If we are able to get along together in Berlin, we can hope to get along in other spheres too. If we break down over Berlin, then a lot of ordinary folk will give up hope altogether."[49]

Stalin greeted the diplomats genially, but before Smith could open his briefcase, Stalin said, "Gentlemen, I have a new draft." Producing it, he said, "I believe you will find it acceptable to your governments." Smith acknowledged Stalin as an accomplished strategist but stated that the Western envoys also had a new draft, and he suggested that both sides examine the proposed communiqués. To Smith's astonishment, the Soviet scheme was virtually identical to his. The Soviets promised to end all barriers on transportation and communication between the Western zones and Berlin, effective on 25 August, in exchange for the Western powers accepting the ostmark, with arrangements for the mechanisms of exchange, credit, and the settling of occupation costs being left to the four-power representatives in Berlin. Stalin also proposed a conference "in the near future" for negotiations on "any questions which may be outstanding as regards Berlin or affecting Germany as a whole."

Smith thought they had achieved an agreement in "principle." As he told Marshall, "things went so smoothly that I was a little worried, and remembered Stalin's proverb, 'an amiable bear is more dangerous than a hostile one.'" Stalin departed after two hours, leaving Molotov to work out the details. For the next three hours, Molotov acted like the most amiable of bears. "As you will note," Smith informed Marshall, "practically every safeguard on which we have insisted has been included in the final draft," including the reaffirmation "in the strongest possible way [of] our right to be in Berlin." Smith strongly recommended that Washington accept the deal.[50] He gave the press no indication of any "agreement in principle." A grim-faced Smith emerged at nearly two in the morning. "We're always optimistic," he said. "We expect the best and prepare for the worst." Pressed for more details, Smith replied, "Stalin gave us tea and cakes."[51]

Smith's optimism proved misplaced. The next day Marshall rejected the agreement: "As long as the Soviet representatives continue to maintain their thesis that we have no rights in Berlin but are there, in effect, on Soviet sufferance, there is obviously no basis for a satisfactory arrangement with them on the Berlin question." The secretary of state listed his "basic requirements for agreement": insistence on coequal rights in Berlin; no abandonment of the American position with respect to a Western German state; unequivocal lifting of the blockade on communications, transport, goods, and persons; and adequate quadripartite control of the issuance and continued use of the ostmark in Berlin. Ostensibly, the issues in Berlin revolved around control of currency and trade. Stalin challenged the West by provoking a crisis at its most vulnerable point: Berlin. He reckoned that if he pushed hard enough, the fissures in the Western camp might widen; at the very least, he wanted to forestall the formation of a Western German state. This time he seriously overplayed his hand. Marshall remained intent on pursuing no negotiations until, at a minimum, the Soviets unconditionally raised the blockade. In the end, the Berlin crisis lingered; the airlift fostered Western solidarity; and the threat of war spurred the Brussels Treaty, Western rearmament, and, in 1949, the formation of the Federal Republic of Germany and the North Atlantic Treaty Organization (NATO). For Smith, Marshall's rejection of Stalin's proposals brought another impasse.

When the September talks broke down in Moscow, the three Western envoys flew to Paris, where the United Nations General Assembly prepared for sessions. Marshall held a conference with Foreign Secretary Ernest Bevin, French Foreign Minister Robert Schuman, Clay, Smith, Roberts, and Chataigneau. Discussions centered on continuing negotiations with Molotov, if he should appear in Paris, or throwing the Berlin question to the United Nations for debate. The Foreign Office did not want to abandon discussions with the Soviets but argued against bringing the issue before the United Nations. Assured by Clay that the airlift could supply Berlin during the winter, Marshall saw little point in continuing talks with Moscow.[52] From Paris an exhausted Smith flew home.

As soon as Smith arrived in Washington, he traveled to Texas and briefed Truman on his campaign train. Smith told the press he had informed the president that "relations with the Soviet Union had never been more 'critical' than today." He then corrected himself, stating that although the situation remained "serious," he believed "the United States was not 'trembling on the brink of war.'"[53] "It was no secret," the press reported, that "Smith was thinking seriously of getting out." At that juncture in the campaign, it appeared "a new President would make it easy for him to do so in January." After a brief return to Moscow, Smith and Nory flew back to Washington on Christmas. He told the Moscow press corps he had "handed in my resignation according to form. . . . What the New Year will bring I don't know." Newsmen who saw his belongings being stowed on the aircraft "guessed that he was not planning to come back to Russia."[54]

The New Year brought a lengthy stay in Walter Reed Hospital. In part, this serious recurrence of Smith's stomach problems prompted his resignation. The hospital released him on 9 January but readmitted him late in February and again in March. In one of his weekly news conferences, Truman acknowledged that Smith did not want to return to Moscow but would do so "if it becomes necessary." Throughout February and March the question of Smith's status remained a hot topic of speculation. A supposedly reliable source inside the White House revealed, "Ambassador Smith would become Chief of Staff of the Army after finally being relieved of the Moscow post." Although Truman declared Smith "a free agent," he admitted to pressing him to stay on as ambassador. The president denied rumors that Smith was slated as the next chief of staff or commander of American forces in Germany or as head of the Central Intelligence Agency. The press "had him all over the world," Truman remarked, but he refused further comment. On 25 March, after meeting with Smith a second time at Walter Reed, Truman announced that he had accepted Smith's resignation, effective immediately.[55]

Instead of chief of staff or commander of American forces in Germany, Truman offered Smith the post of undersecretary of state for European affairs. The president also may have asked Smith to become the director of central intelligence. Smith declined and stated his preference to return to active duty. On 28 March the Pentagon announced Smith's appointment as First Army commander, headquartered on Governor's Island, New York. Command of the First Army amounted to little more than a sinecure—a post where senior officers sat out their remaining years in the service in the genteel surroundings of New York City. The New York papers talked of Smith arriving for work the first day in a blue business suit; he insisted there be no formal change of command ceremony.[56]

Smith devoted much of his time in New York to writing an account of his time in Moscow. In November both the *New York Times* and the *Saturday Evening Post* began carrying serialized installments of Smith's account. The following year his manuscript appeared in book form under the title *My Three Years in Moscow*.[57] Another American envoy, Joseph Davies, had written a 1941 best seller, *Mission to Moscow*, casting late 1930s Russia in the best possible light and even denying the excesses of the purges. That book influenced American public perceptions of the Soviet Union, and in 1943 Hollywood made a pro-Soviet movie based on the book. Davies went to Potsdam as an adviser to Truman. Davies rejected a balance-of-power approach to Soviet relations and argued instead for accommodating Stalin. Smith's book took the opposite view. Like Davies's book, Smith's provided his impressions of the Soviet Union, his meetings with Stalin and the other members of the *nomenklatura*, his perspective on various points in Russian and Soviet history (before leaving for Moscow, he had embarked on a crash course in Russian history), and a prescription for future Soviet-American relations.

For a short period in 1946, George Kennan served as deputy chief of mission under Smith. They had first met in 1943 when Smith held clandestine talks with the Italians in Lisbon that eventually led to Italy's surrender; at the time, Kennan was serving as counselor in the U.S. embassy. In February 1946, while still in Moscow, Kennan authored the "Long

Telegram," which acted as a catalyst in moving American policy toward containment. Kennan argued for the abandonment of futile attempts at cooperation with the Soviets, favoring instead a realpolitik sphere-of-influence approach. In Kennan's estimate, the admixture of traditional Russian insecurity and the dogmas of Marxist-Leninism produced the Kremlin's neurotic worldview. The United States should strengthen its institutions and act unilaterally based on national interests, but it should also form common cause with the western European states and Japan, with the objective of restraining Russian communist expansion until the internal inconsistencies of the Soviet system forced a mellowing in the regime. Smith's views as expressed in *My Three Years in Moscow* bore too strong a resemblance to Kennan's "Long Telegram" and his famous 1947 "X Article" in *Foreign Affairs* to have been coincidental.[58]

Distilling his ideological underpinning from Kennan, and influenced by his own reading of history—particularly Lord Palmerston's management of the Great Game in containing nineteenth-century Russian expansionism—Smith wrote a book that was, like Davies's, designed for a popular audience.[59] He spoke of a bipolar world divided along diametrically opposed ideological lines and a Cold War "contest of indefinite duration." Though he entertained no doubts of the ultimate triumph of the United States and the demonstrative superiority of democracy and free enterprise, he warned the reading public that victory lay in the distant future. Despite the Soviet regime's oft-repeated assumptions about the inevitability of a final collision with the capitalist West, Smith concluded that Moscow would not risk war unless assured of victory. He expected a Soviet diplomatic war of attrition designed "to exasperate us, to keep probing for weak spots" and warned that the United States "must cultivate firmness and patience to a degree we have never before required." In his view, American strength—moral as well as material—represented the greatest guarantor for preserving the peace. During the Berlin crisis, Smith had detected "some discord" in the ranks of the Politburo. The moderates, led by Georgi Malenkov, believed the West had entered a period of stabilization, requiring the Soviet Union to seek a "closer understanding" with the United States, whereas the hardliners, centered on Molotov and Lavrenti Beria, favored a continuation of the policy of "constant pressure, aggressive action and intransigence."[60] Smith not only predicted the power struggles among the troika following Stalin's death but also adumbrated the succession problems that would confront every post-Stalin regime as it attempted to preserve the strictures of Marxist-Leninist ideology against demands to modify the authoritarian political structure and its command economy. He also emphasized, unlike Kennan, the intertwined nationalities and religious questions that would splinter the Soviet Union forty years later.[61] In June 1950 Smith made another prediction when he appeared on *Meet the Press* and disclosed his suspicions that the Soviets had developed an atomic bomb—setting off a little bomb of his own. His forecast proved correct; the Soviets detonated their first atomic weapon less than two months later.[62]

The best gauge of the accuracy of Smith's analysis rested in the vitriol heaped on it by the Soviet press. *Pravda* called Smith a "slanderer," a "warmonger" with a "petty soul of a diplomat from the infantry." The Kremlin's top propagandist, Ilya Ehrenburg, repudiated Smith's work in a lengthy *Pravda* article on 1 January 1950.[63] Between 1950 and 1953 Smith's book appeared in fourteen languages, cementing his reputation as one of the foremost international experts on Russia.

On 31 March 1950 Smith checked into Walter Reed and remained there for three and a half months. Diagnosed with multiple acute gastric stomach ulcers, a perforated peptic ulcer of the duodenum, and a partial pyloric obstruction, Smith also suffered from chronic gastritis and moderate malnutrition. Once a robust man of 174 pounds, Smith now weighed in at 135. On 3 May surgeons performed a radical gastrectomy, cutting away half his stomach. On the day of the operation, army authorities reported that he was making "very good progress," but his recovery proved slow and difficult.[64] Despite Smith's serious health problems, Truman had another tough job he needed done: the remaking of the fledgling CIA.

Expecting the Worst

Director of Central Intelligence

The Truman administration grew increasingly disenchanted with the struggles of the newly formed Central Intelligence Agency (CIA) to find its niche in the national security structure. In early 1948 the National Security Council (NSC) commissioned three intelligence veterans—Allen Dulles, William Jackson, and Matias Correa—and charged them with undertaking a thorough review and providing a blueprint for reform. The Dulles Report, submitted on 1 January 1949, criticized the CIA for becoming just another bureau "producing intelligence in competition with older established agencies" and called for the CIA's evolution into "a semi-autonomous highly centralized agency with a broad variety of intelligence responsibilities." The report pointed to the "inadequacies of direction" provided by the CIA's current management.[1] Truman knew just the man he wanted to drive the reorganization.

Twice Truman offered Smith the job, but without any luck. Still recuperating in the hospital, Smith realized that taking over the foundering intelligence agency would tax what little reserves he had left. But in light of the CIA's failure to anticipate the North Korean invasion of the south, Smith told Eisenhower he "could not refuse for a third time." To a friend he candidly wrote, "I expect the worst and I am sure I won't be disappointed."[2]

Establishing the U.S. Intelligence Service

When Truman became president, as he noted in his memoirs, one of his strongest convictions "was that the antiquated defense setup of the

United States had to be reorganized quickly."[3] Even before deciding to form a centralized intelligence agency, Truman named a director of central intelligence (DCI). The first appointee was fellow Missourian RADM Sidney Souers, a reserve officer keen on returning to civilian life. Souers, who recognized he was merely occupying a desk, served for only six months but succeeded in establishing the organizational ground-work. The dashing Hoyt Vandenberg, wartime air force commander in Europe and nephew of a powerful Republican senator from Michigan, replaced Souers but served less than a year. Vandenberg set the wheels in motion for legislation that led to the formation of a central intelligence agency. Vandenberg collected remnants of the Office of Strategic Services and other intelligence units and established the Office of Special Operations (OSO), an agency for conducting espionage, counterespionage, and clandestine foreign intelligence operations. During Vandenberg's tenure, his office acquired responsibility for intelligence work in Latin America from the Federal Bureau of Intelligence. Vandenberg left to head the newly independent U.S. Air Force.

On 26 July 1947 Truman signed the National Security Act, establishing—along with the unified Department of Defense, the Joint Chiefs of Staff (JCS), the NSC, and the U.S. Air Force—the CIA. The *New York Times* reported, "one of the final steps before adjournment, largely overlooked in the avalanche of last minute legislation, was the stamp of approval Congress placed on the creation, for the first time in American history, of an effective world-wide American intelligence service of its own."[4] The act charged the CIA with coordinating interagency intelligence activities, primarily with the Departments of Defense and State; collecting, correlating, and evaluating overt and covert intelligence; and producing national estimates for the guidance of the president and policy makers. In addition, the agency would perform other duties and functions related to intelligence, as directed by the NSC. The legislation made the DCI the principal adviser to the president and the NSC on all foreign intelligence matters related to national security, and the DCI was responsible for safeguarding intelligence sources and methods. The DCI also chaired the Intelligence Advisory Committee (IAC), the coordinating body that established priorities among the Departments of Defense and State, the JCS, and the Atomic Energy Commission, whose representative sat on the committee.

Another rear admiral, Roscoe Hillenkoetter, reluctantly succeeded Vandenberg in September 1947. Junior in rank to the brass in the JCS, and lacking self-confidence in his dealings with the State Department, Hillenkoetter proved to be a nonentity. As the Cold War deepened in 1948 (following the coup in Prague and the Berlin crisis), the State Department wanted political and psychological warfare operations initiated against the Soviet Union and its allies. Kennan, as head of policy planning at State, pushed for a covert operations bureau inside the CIA but under State Department control during peacetime. Hillenkoetter restricted CIA activities to information gathering and doubted that the agency possessed the legal right to engage in covert actions. Nevertheless, the White House established a bureau for covert operations in 1948 and placed it in the CIA under Frank Wisner, a well-connected Wall Street lawyer. With little control from above, Wisner rapidly expanded the size and scope of his operations.[5]

Smith Takes the Reins

Two days after his fifty-fifth birthday, on 7 October 1950, Smith inherited an organization in tatters. The agency's multiple failures, climaxing with the North Korean invasion, gave Smith the mandate to reform the intelligence agency.[6] During their entire time together during the war, Eisenhower had stymied all Smith's attempts at restructuring first AFHQ in the Mediterranean and then SHAEF in northwestern Europe. Although Eisenhower had granted Smith what amounted to sovereignty over the operations and staffing of Allied headquarters, until the very end of the war—and then only under duress—he had dithered and ducked and weaved against all efforts to streamline headquarters organization, even those directed by Marshall. For the first time in his career, Smith possessed the authority to build a structure in keeping with his own ideas on how a centralized bureaucracy should operate. His predecessors never overcame the inherent frictions the intelligence agency faced in dealing with the armed services, the FBI, and the State Department; as the CIA rapidly expanded, it became a bureaucratic morass of competing interests.[7] The Washington bureaucratic turf battles—both outside the agency, with national security rivals, and inside, between operations and intelligence sections—deflected the CIA from performing its core tasks. Smith knew he faced formidable political and institutional roadblocks but reckoned that he possessed the prestige, the connections in the Defense and State Departments, and the persuasive powers necessary to effect the required restructuring; he also enjoyed the full support of the White House.

Smith's wartime experience colored his entire approach to the job. As an American chief of staff, he had possessed no grant of executive authority on paper, yet Eisenhower had bestowed on Smith decision-making powers parallel, but always subsidiary, to the supreme commander's. Smith avoided the advice of CIA legal counsel to pursue augmented statutory control as director. Although he preferred clearly defined command channels, Smith knew that pursuing this course would involve time- and energy-wasting wrangles with the Pentagon and on Capitol Hill and would open the CIA to press scrutiny—which he keenly sought to avoid. During the war he had solved problems through personal associations. Rather than worry about the niceties, he visited his friend Omar Bradley, chairman of the JCS, and Dean Acheson, now secretary of state, and hammered out informal arrangements for intelligence sharing.[8] In November Smith met with J. Edgar Hoover with the view of forging better cooperation between the CIA and the FBI. Smith admitted "there had been misunderstandings in the past and thought that a large number of them were the result of personalities rather than any question in policy." He stressed the need for closer collaboration between the FBI legal attachés operating abroad, especially in Latin America, and their CIA counterparts. The next day, 12 November, he issued a directive to overseas operatives instructing them to establish "close and friendly mutual contact" with the FBI. Disputes, he added, would be sorted out in Washington, not by third parties. "FBI and CIA will wash their linen in private at home," he insisted.[9]

The structure he eventually put in place mirrored his wartime thinking. Smith moved to consolidate executive decision making in his own hands. In his first full-dress IAC meeting on 20 October 1950, Smith discreetly but pointedly clarified his intentions by simply reading the relevant portions of the 1947 legislation and NSC 50, which specified the authority incumbent on the DCI.[10] He made it abundantly clear that he would operate independently when appropriate and tolerate no dissent. Smith always referred to the recommendations contained in NSC 50 as his marching orders from the president. In his opinion, Congress and the White House bestowed two principal functions on the CIA: conventional intelligence gathering and analysis, and political and psychological warfare operations. He likened the two to the intelligence (G-2) and operations (G-3) divisions in his wartime headquarters. As Eisenhower's chief of staff, Smith had overseen intelligence and psychological warfare operations and harbored a dim view of covert operations. Smith firmly believed that the CIA's first responsibility was to provide the president and the national security apparatus with the most current and hardest possible intelligence on the strengths, weaknesses, and intentions of potential adversaries. Conducting counterintelligence and aggressive covert operations behind the Iron Curtain and in nations suspected of falling into the Soviet orbit or being susceptible to subversion took a distant second place. He wanted a functionalized headquarters structure with an executive deputy director answering directly to him and supervising two subordinate divisions overseeing intelligence collection and correlation and foreign operations.

Another CIA failure dramatically hastened the process. On 1 November 1950, three weeks after Smith took over, Chinese troops crossed the Yalu in strength, falling on GEN Douglas MacArthur's badly overextended forces. American intelligence—military, diplomatic, and the CIA—suffered its second debacle in six months.[11] Nobody foresaw the size or effectiveness of China's swift intervention. Disaster was narrowly averted, but not without serious losses in American lives and prestige. In January 1951 Smith flew to Tokyo for discussions with MacArthur. One of the factors behind intelligence failures in Korea stemmed from MacArthur's blocking CIA operations in the theater of operations. Smith brought the general around to his view and, on his return to Washington, ordered the formation of a CIA station in the Japanese capital.[12] The intelligence blunder accentuated the pressing urgency of Smith's reforms.

Smith dug in and pushed for his reorganization. He demanded a clear division of functions. Smith recruited William Jackson as his deputy director of central intelligence, created a directory for administration, and placed Allen Dulles in charge of operations as deputy director of plans. Improving the intelligence analysis and dissemination side of his staff proved most pressing, so he tackled it first. Upon joining the CIA, and to his utter amazement, Smith discovered there was no current assessment of the threat in Korea.[13] In October he dissected the Office of Reports and Estimates into three sections: the Board of National Estimates, coordinating intelligence retrieval and the production of national intelligence estimates; a "current intelligence" office, providing the president with daily bulletins; and an office for research. Instead of duplicating the efforts of other intelligence sources, Smith demanded that the CIA integrate and analyze intelligence from across the spectrum. When the armed services balked at surrendering their cryptologic programs, Smith pointed to the failures in signals intelligence in Korea. At his urging, the NSC formed the National Security Agency (NSA), unifying military and naval intelligence inside the Department of Defense. By producing daily bulletins and national intelligence assessments, the CIA evolved into the hub of the Washington intelligence establishment.

Reining in Wisner and his boys proved more difficult. Smith especially resented Wisner's running his own covert operations through the innocuously named Office of Policy Coordination (OPC), which received its direction from the Departments of State and Defense but remained administratively under the CIA. When Wisner asked Smith for a new table of organization and a legal directive, Smith snarled that he required no piece of paper: "Wisner, you work for me." He brought in another hard-bitten general, Lucian Truscott, to conduct a study of Wisner's programs in Europe. "I'm going to go out there," Truscott told Smith, "and find out what those weirdoes are up to." To soldiers like Smith and Truscott, the men who staffed and ran covert operations inhabited a different world—a world out of an F. Scott Fitzgerald novel peopled with privileged scions of wealthy families who attended the same prep schools and Ivy League institutions, joined the same clubs, and entered the same Wall Street legal and financial firms. They saw themselves as gifted amateurs and scorned their less well-born professional colleagues in the OSO, the foreign intelligence analysts. Smith immediately saw the difference between the two sides of his establishment: the operations types drove imported sports cars, while the analysts drove Fords and Chevrolets. The fraternity boy pranks that passed as political and psychological warfare operations astounded Smith, and in Europe these men had virtually unlimited funds, including Marshall Plan money, to underwrite their escapades. In Germany and Italy, operatives set off stink bombs at communist youth festivals. More ominously, they floated the idea of assassinating Stalin should he appear (he did not) in Paris for a four-power summit—a project Smith "rejected out of hand." They thought up inventive uses for rubber products. Balloons dropped 300 million leaflets into eastern Europe. Suggestions surfaced for using balloons to distribute cheap American consumer products behind the Iron Curtain, illustrating the superiority of the capitalist mode of production. Inside the psychological warfare offices at headquarters, CIA officials sat around shooting balloons with BB guns. Famously, another suggestion involved dropping gigantic condoms labeled "medium" into Russia, giving the impression that all American males were supermen. Perhaps it was intended as a joke, but Smith exploded, "If you send me one more project with goddamned balloons, I'll throw you out of here." He organized a "Murder Board" and weeded out the dilettantes, firing fifty of Wisner's people. "I don't care whether they were blabbing secrets or not," he flatly stated. "Just give me the names of the people at Georgetown cocktail parties." Wisner's wife maintained a salon for the Georgetown crowd. When one of the OPC cadre was confined in St. Elizabeth's, a Washington mental hospital, for showing too much affection for barnyard animals, Smith wondered aloud, "Can't I get people who don't hire people who bugger cows?"[14]

Smith's earlier surgery did not solve his health issues. His inability to regain weight—in fact, he continued to shed pounds—nearly led doctors to insist that he step down at the end of 1950. His chronic ill health contributed to his sour disposition, which somebody characterized as always the same—vile. Smith's acerbic tongue and short fuse were already the stuff of legend. He had learned from his mentor Marshall how to put fire to the feet of prospective subordinates to see whether they measured up. Smith wanted there to be no doubt about who the boss was. Even Dulles came in for his share of abuse. "Dulles," Smith routinely roared at his deputy, "Dulles, Goddamnit, get in here." Sherman Kent, who came from Yale to join the Office of National Estimates, remembered Smith's persuasive charms. Uncertain about taking the job, Kent appeared to be on the verge of heading back to New Haven, "whereupon, putting on that annoyed cobra look of his," Smith tore into the young don. Kent stayed, remaining with the CIA until 1967.[15] Douglas MacArthur II reminisced about receiving the Beetle treatment. One time the two men disagreed, and MacArthur stalked out of Smith's office. "Doug, come back here for a minute," Smith said. MacArthur sat down, and they cleared the air. "He liked to stick that shit in the beginning, and make sure you knew he was a force and you were going to play ball. It was a technique."[16]

After contesting against the Abwehr during the war and knowing only too well the ruthless efficiency of the Soviet security apparatus, Smith suffered no illusions about the challenges confronting the CIA. The cold, hard professionals on the other side ran circles around the CIA's not so gifted amateurs. From the beginning, the list of CIA failures lengthened. Foreign operatives in the CIA's pay were betrayed— parachuted to waiting communist agents, interrogated and tortured, marched before people's tribunals, then shot. Moscow radio broadcast the show trials of recruited agents unwittingly delivered up by their CIA handlers. The CIA's track record under Smith showed no great improvement: there were failures in appraising the situation in Iran, anticipating the revolution in Egypt, predicting a series of coups in Latin America, and combating virulent anti-American sentiment in Europe and Latin America.

Korea also demanded an amplification of the CIA's authority over covert operations. In 1948 the NSC authorized the CIA's conduct of "covert action," including the organization of indigenous irregular forces, but in "time of war or national emergency," control reverted to the JCS and the local military command. In the wake of the Chinese intervention and UN retreat, the NSC suspended this provision, at Smith's request, allowing the formation of CIA-organized stay-behind guerrilla bands operating in the enemy's rear. Early in 1951 the NSC discussed options for relieving pressure on UN forces in Korea. The idea emerged of opening a second front by inserting a CIA-sponsored force of Nationalist Chinese into northern Burma, on the theory that Beijing would pull forces out of Korea to deal with the incursion. Smith knew a harebrained scheme when he heard one and angrily stated, "The Chinese Communists have so goddamn many troops, you can't count 'em all; they won't pull anyone out of [Korea]." The secretaries of defense and state overruled Smith, a nonvoting member of the NSC, and pushed the recommendation up to Truman, who approved it. Smith delegated to Wisner the job of initiating the covert paramilitary operation. The Guomindang proved far more adept at trafficking drugs than fighting the Reds; their presence in Burma destabilized the Rangoon government, leading to a temporary breach in U.S.-Burma relations.[17] This fiasco pretty much typified early CIA covert operations.

Reds and Spies

Smith's blunt, no-nonsense communications style served its function in cowing subordinates but proved less efficacious in managing press relations. Unlike Eisenhower, with his highly developed skill of talking but saying nothing of substance, Smith was habitually straightforward. Although no McCarthyite, Smith was a dedicated cold warrior. When Nelson Rockefeller made a lukewarm speech in favor of labor unions, Smith branded him a "Red."[18] In September 1952, with the presidential campaigns at their zenith, Smith set off a furor when he testified at a pretrial hearing in a libel suit brought by McCarthy against Senator William Benton. Smith stated that the State Department had been infiltrated by communists as early as 1945 and that this was widely known in official circles. Under questioning, he acknowledged that communists had no doubt insinuated themselves into his organization; it would be foolish to think otherwise. Here again, he simply told the qualified truth when he said that the CIA "never has detected one spy 'in our ranks.'"[19] Spies outside CIA ranks proved a different matter.

The year before, the CIA had uncovered the activities of the most famous double agent in history, H. A. R. "Kim" Philby. For some time the CIA suspected that a mole had penetrated the highest circles of the agency. In fact, three of the infamous Cambridge Five—Philby, Donald

Maclean, and Guy Burgess—operated out of the British embassy in Washington. In his role as British intelligence liaison, Philby enjoyed access to intelligence on a whole range of CIA operations. Virtually all of the CIA's covert operations behind the Iron Curtain—in Poland, Ukraine, and especially Albania—miscarried. Worse, Philby passed on intelligence about the limited American nuclear stockpiles, which undermined the deterrence threat and contributed to Stalin's pursuit of more provocative policies in Europe—the Prague putsch and the Berlin blockade—and in the rapidly decolonizing Third World. MacArthur's command in Korea also suspected that the other side received operational intelligence. Philby encouraged the CIA's chief mole hunter, James Jesus Angleton, in his belief that the CIA had been penetrated. Angleton turned the agency upside down in his search, disrupting operations, creating a climate of suspicion, and deflecting attention from Philby.

Suspecting one of their own, the CIA allowed Philby, Maclean, and Burgess to continue their activities. When attention finally fixed on Philby, Smith ordered William Harvey to conduct a separate investigation. A gumshoe, not part of the old school-tie set, Harvey never shared the Anglophilia that marked the upper echelons of the CIA. Long before James Bond, British secret service agents enjoyed a global éclat for their subtleness, effectiveness, and aristocratic élan. Before and during the war, the coldly professional British intelligence community made the first American attempts at spying and counterespionage appear clumsy and inept. The U.S. Army in particular suffered under the handicap of an insufficiency of trained intelligence officers; in AFHQ and SHAEF, the British ran the show. Class prejudice blinded the Americans as much as or more than it did the British. Certainly, high-born British gentlemen operatives in His Majesty's secret service—products of the public schools, elite universities, and exclusive clubs that the Grotons, Yales, and Skull and Crossbones modeled themselves after—could never betray their side. Harvey thought otherwise, but Angleton concluded that Philby had been "honestly duped" and advised Smith not to pursue the matter.

Smith and Philby possessed a mutual regard for each other. A curious thing about Smith was that he never developed any deep and lasting friendships with his American colleagues. "Although hundreds of officers call him Beetle," observed a reporter, "only a handful really knows him."[20] He and Eisenhower were friends, but their relationship always remained guarded. Smith worked at being enigmatic because a large part of his effectiveness rested in the unpredictability of his response to problems. He could be subtle, even charming, when the situation demanded; more often, he displayed his explosive irritability. His assignment was to get results, not to make friends. Smith's churlish approach to people and issues won him many enemies and few real friends, and it goes a long way in explaining why he never secured the posts he most desired. With the British it was entirely different; with them, he let his hair down. ACM William Elliott said of Smith, "Bedell was fastidious in his choice of friends but to those he liked he revealed a surprising flame of affection as warm as was, by contrast, the chilling reception which he reserved for those he loved less."[21] His other British friends spoke of his open heart, generosity, and extraordinary loyalty. Except for the last trait, no American saw much evidence of any "flame of affection." The Janus-faced Philby—with his intellect, undeniable charm, disarming upper-class lisp, and brilliant war record—was a master of deception and beguiled a large circle of powerful people. Philby spent a lifetime around intellectually gifted people and respected Smith's "precision-tool brain." "Many times," Philby affirmed, "I saw him read a long memorandum, toss it aside and, without a pause for thought, paragraph by numbered paragraph, rip its guts out—real virtuoso stuff."[22]

With Maclean's cover blown in April 1951, he and Burgess defected. Attention zeroed in on Philby as the "third man" who had tipped off his two comrades. Smith declared Philby persona non grata and dispatched an ultimatum to Stuart Menzies, longtime head of the British Secret Intelligence Service, threatening that if the British did not fire Philby, the CIA would dissolve the Anglo-American intelligence partnership. Menzies sacked Philby but, still not convinced of his guilt, surreptitiously employed him in Beirut until his defection to Moscow in 1963. In the aftermath of the Philby affair, Smith headed a badly shaken organization on the verge of civil war; morale sank as recriminations flowed all around. Smith responded by wrapping a cloak of secrecy around the CIA. He also restructured the flow of intelligence, giving only the uppermost officials a comprehensive picture of the agency's action.

Washington covered up the Philby business, but Smith's admission that communists had infiltrated the CIA—whether true or not—set off a press firestorm and placed the CIA in the middle of a seething campaign issue. The headline in the *New York Times* read, "Gen. Smith Thinks Reds Have Entered All Security Units."[23] Smith flew into damage-control mode, imploring Republican nominee Eisenhower and Democratic candidate Governor Adlai Stevenson to refrain from throwing any accelerant onto the fire of McCarthy's Red Scare. Stevenson immediately responded positively, telling the press that the nonpolitical CIA "must never become a political football." The Eisenhower camp recognized in Smith's remarks a brilliant opportunity to ramp up its attack on the Truman administration as "soft on Communism" and remained noncommittal. Smith informed Truman on 2 September that he had made a second personal appeal to Eisenhower, but the issue did not go away.[24] On 13 October Smith gave more circumspect testimony before the House Committee on Un-American Activities, and later that evening the apolitical Smith told a Philadelphia audience that the country would "have little to worry about" in fighting communist infiltration if the next president cooperated with security agencies "as well as President Truman."[25] As is usually the case, the notoriously short-memoried American public soon focused its attention on other campaign issues. To Smith's relief, the CIA confronted no real press inquiry or congressional investigating groups.

Intelligence Briefings

Truman placed a high priority on receiving current threat assessments and marveled at Smith's facility in providing them. When Truman entered the White House in 1945, the War Department withheld certain strategic and national security information from him. He was president for twelve days before Stimson gave him his first briefing on the Manhattan Project, of which Truman had heard only rumors while vice president. Every Friday, Smith entered the Oval Office and presented a distilled intelligence briefing; he left a boiled-down summary of the *Current Intelligence Weekly Review* in a tidy notebook for the president's perusal. Later Souers, the president's special consultant for national security affairs, joined them for a postmortem over coffee.

In August 1952, after the nominating conventions, Truman and Smith discussed "the propriety of keeping the presidential candidates informed on the situation around the world." Both men decided that Eisenhower and Stevenson should receive their first briefing together; thereafter the CIA would provide updates at regular intervals.[26] Truman invited Eisenhower and Stevenson for lunch with the cabinet and asked Smith to come by and deliver one of his crisp briefings "on the foreign situation." He told Eisenhower, "I've made arrangements with the Central Intelligence Agency to furnish you once a week with the world situation as I also have for Governor Stevenson." Stevenson happily accepted the invitation to lunch; Eisenhower declined, stating, "The problems which you suggest for discussion are those with which I have lived for many years" as Allied supreme commander, chief of staff, and head of NATO.[27]

Eisenhower's curt dismissal greatly angered Truman. Stevenson attended the lunch briefing, and the Eisenhower camp issued what one journalist called "rather a harsh statement" critical of the president for playing partisan politics. Enraged by that charge, Truman held a news conference. When asked about Eisenhower's accusations, Truman replied, "Well, now, let's let that rest for a while, and when the campaign gets to rolling pretty good, I think your question will be answered without much trouble."[28] Truman engaged in some plain speaking in a handwritten letter to Eisenhower. Truman derisively apologized for any embarrassment the invitation had caused Eisenhower and explained his motives for the briefing. In his view, it was vitally important for both candidates to receive current intelligence so that no disruptions occurred in American foreign policy despite the change in administrations. "Partisan politics should stop at the boundaries of the United States," Truman frankly stated. "I am extremely sorry that you have allowed a bunch of screwballs to come between us." He concluded by telling Eisenhower he had "made a bad mistake, and I'm hoping it won't injure this great Republic. There has never been one like it and I want to see it continues regardless of the man who occupies the most important position in the history of the world. May God guide you and give you the light."[29]

Truman's "give 'em hell" letter illustrated the outgoing president's mounting antagonism toward Eisenhower. Aside from the party divide, Truman was from Missouri and Eisenhower from Kansas. There was no love lost between the two border states, and Truman never forgot that his family farm had been despoiled by marauding Kansas Jayhawkers during the Civil War. Beyond that, Truman questioned Eisenhower's character. Truman had made Eisenhower chief of staff and supreme commander and had even offered him, albeit indirectly, support if he led the Democratic ticket. Truman could forgive him the last—Dickinson County, Kansas, had never elected a Democrat to anything—and he could even forgive the blistering attacks on his policies, but he could never condone as "politics as usual" Eisenhower's failure, in an appearance in Wisconsin, to defend Marshall's reputation. Truman considered Eisenhower's Milwaukee speech "the low point in this [Red Scare] hysteria." In Milwaukee, instead of condemning the slander against Marshall, "one of the finest, most honorable, and most patriotic soldiers and public servants we have ever had," Eisenhower endorsed Joe McCarthy for reelection as senator from Wisconsin. Eisenhower may not have been beholden to Truman, but according to the president, he owed "more to General Marshall than he does to any other living man." Worse than engaging in partisan politics and honest disagreement over the direction of foreign policy, Eisenhower stood guilty of the unpardonable sin of disloyalty.[30]

Smith sent Eisenhower a wire congratulating him on the nomination, but he must have had mixed feelings. As DCI, Smith came in for his share of abuse at the hands of the McCarthyites and found himself dragged in front of the Committee on Un-American Activities. He and Truman got on very well; both were self-made straight-shooting midwesterners. Stevenson immediately defended the CIA during the Red infiltration flap and impressed Smith with his command of foreign affairs. Although he never said as much, Smith's reaction to Eisenhower's tacit acquiescence in the personal attacks on Marshall must have mirrored Truman's, and he fumed when the Republicans issued a press release condemning his briefing of Stevenson. Still, with Ike in the White House, Beetle might get that coveted chief of staff's chair.

On 14 August Eisenhower finally acknowledged Smith's note of congratulation but took the opportunity to scold him. "The past two days my whole headquarters has been in a bit of a steaming stew over an incident in which, according to the papers, you were at least briefly involved. It was the meeting that Governor Stevenson had with the President and the Cabinet." It appeared to Eisenhower "like the outgoing Administration was canvassing all its resources in order to support Stevenson's election."[31]

Eisenhower's letter "upset the hell out of Beetle." Two days after Eisenhower received Truman's letter, another one arrived from Smith. Sounding more like a lawyer than a friend, Smith proposed that the CIA provide Eisenhower and Stevenson briefings containing the same information he delivered to the president each Friday morning.[32] Eisenhower was reluctant at first—he told Truman the weekly CIA reports would suffice—but he later changed his mind and accepted Smith's idea. After the last preelection briefing, Eisenhower told the CIA official who conducted the session that he appreciated the agency's efforts but "missed the G-3 information" he had received as a military commander. On parting he said, "When you get back to Bedell Smith, tell him if I get elected I've got a job for him."[33]

Resignation

On 1 November, just days before the election, Smith tendered his resignation. Eisenhower's promise of a job had nothing to do with his decision. Smith had made no secret of his unhappiness with the DCI job and decided to exit with the outgoing administration. As Truman wrote in his last days in the White House, "As Director of Central Intelligence since 1950, following your superior service as Ambassador to Moscow, you have successfully and faithfully accomplished your mission of developing the Central Intelligence Agency into an efficient and permanent arm of the Government's national security structure." Truman felt "sure that future Presidents will benefit substantially from the outstanding work which you have done in developing the Central Intelligence Agency."[34] Smith had taken the faltering agency, applied his typically strong grip, and pounded the disparate intelligence agencies into something resembling an "intelligence community"—a term that had come into usage by the end of his tenure. Although the structure still contained many flaws—the question of which department controlled covert operations in an active theater was never resolved—the CIA organization Smith fashioned survived in many of its parts into the twenty-first century.[35]

In the interval between submitting his resignation and its effective date of 24 January 1953, Smith shouldered a new task: he assumed personal responsibility for the president-elect's national security briefings. In a campaign speech in Detroit on 24 October, Eisenhower pledged he would go to Korea. Now, at the end of November, he prepared to fulfill the promise. On 28 November Smith, accompanied by his assistant Meredith Davidson, took the train to New York, where Eisenhower maintained a residence. Met at Union Station by army security officers, they proceeded on a meandering trip through Manhattan until the car stopped in front of a drugstore. Hustled through the store and out the back door, the little group went up an alley and through another back entrance, arriving in the Commodore Hotel. By this time, Smith was furious with this cloak-and-dagger routine. Then they sat in an outer room while Eisenhower finished lunch. Finally ushered in, Smith gave Eisenhower his frank and pithy personal assessment of the situation in Korea, especially with regard to the stalled peace talks. After the meeting concluded, Smith and Davidson went to the Waldorf Astoria and ran into John Foster Dulles. Dulles knew about Smith's conference with Eisenhower and asked what had transpired. "That's between him and me," Smith snapped, and walked away.

Smith concluded that infrequent briefings would not work and established a CIA facility in New York to provide Eisenhower with information on a daily basis or as desired. Eisenhower's newly appointed chief of staff, Sherman Adams, felt threatened by Smith and limited CIA contact with Eisenhower. Making his point, Adams installed the CIA office in "a broom closet some distance from the President's office."

Truman asked Smith to chair a new NSC appraisal of the global situation as part of a wholesale foreign policy review for the incoming administration. Other than the situation in Europe and Korea, the chief focus of the study was Iran and French Indochina. On 19 December Smith returned to New York and presented the findings of the NSC review. At some point, Eisenhower took Smith aside and revealed what job he had in mind for him. The news floored Smith: Eisenhower wanted him as the number-two man in the State Department under John Foster Dulles. Smith sat silent during the whole train ride back to Washington. He finally said in little more than a whisper, "And I thought that it was going to be great."[36]

Other than his sideways remark to the CIA officer, Eisenhower gave no indication he ever intended to make Smith chief of staff. When Eisenhower was serving as president of Columbia University, he had received a telephone call that interrupted his afternoon game of bridge. The call was from President Truman, informing Eisenhower of his appointment as head of NATO. After he returned to the game, someone asked who he would take as his deputy. Eisenhower replied, "Well, I ought to take Bedell Smith, but I think I'll take [LTG Alfred] Gruenther because he's a better bridge player."[37] Eisenhower's half-joking remark indicated how much he prized the intimacy of his circle of close friends, something he never enjoyed with Smith. Although he often spoke of the great debt he owed Smith, Eisenhower never felt obliged to repay it in kind. The key to Eisenhower's leadership style was his ability to exploit the talents of subordinates; after they had served his purposes, he felt no special compulsion to push too hard for their elevation if it might compromise his own position. Putting aside Smith's other baggage, his precarious health made his appointment as army chief of staff problematic. Whether the bitterness engendered during the 1952 campaign influenced Eisenhower's decision remains unknown. Eisenhower certainly intended to continue to take advantage of Beetle's talents—but in what Smith saw as a blind-alley job.

Whether he would have been a good choice as chief of staff is moot. Smith believed he had earned the appointment and felt betrayed. He had already received his fourth star in summer 1951 while DCI, but the award appeared to be an afterthought. Now with his dreams of holding Marshall's old chair shattered, Smith submitted his paperwork for separation from the U.S. Army. His resignation became effective on 31 January 1954.[38]

★ 3 ★

Dulles's Number Two

Eisenhower made it clear that he intended to give Smith an important role in the new administration. At first he toyed with bringing Smith in as his chief of staff but jettisoned the idea for fear that two generals in the White House might awaken antimilitary sentiment. In the period before the election, John Foster Dulles had engaged in some calculated maneuvers designed to remove any possibility of Smith's remaining at the CIA, intending to replace Smith with his brother Allen. Dulles talked about aggressively "rolling back" communism and envisioned a more proactive role for the CIA; during his tenure, Smith actively blunted many covert operation initiatives. Dulles was also concerned that, given his relationship with Eisenhower, Smith would exercise even more autonomy than he had enjoyed in the Truman administration. Dulles need not have worried. Smith readily resigned as DCI and, according to a Dulles aide, initially turned down the offer to serve as undersecretary of state, reportedly telling Eisenhower, "What I would like to do is get a fifth star and retire."[1] When Eisenhower persisted, Smith gave in, as the president-elect knew he would. Dulles applauded the solution because he could keep a wary eye on Smith; Eisenhower liked it because Smith offered him a separate avenue of communication into the State Department. Nobody much cared what Smith wanted. "For forty years he had taken on assignments," a journalist reported Smith as saying, "and carried them out without thought to whether he enjoyed the work or not."[2] From the outset, Smith gave every indication that he did not expect to enjoy playing number two to Dulles.

Undersecretary of State

Because Smith was a Truman national security team holdover, and given the commotion over his briefing of Stevenson and tacit endorsement of Truman, Smith's nomination presented problems for many Republicans, especially the McCarthy wing. Expecting "a large and strongly opposed minority," the administration placed Smith's confirmation vote before the Senate late on a Friday night. All ten senators present voted in favor.[3] He assumed duties as undersecretary on 10 February 1953.

Smith's appointment occasioned a good deal of speculation over what role he might play aside from his formal duties. Some thought it would parallel the special relationship that had existed between Franklin Roosevelt and Harry Hopkins. In many respects, it did. Smith's office had three phones, one a direct line to the White House. Eisenhower and Smith routinely talked by telephone "maybe several times a day." Whereas relations between Dulles and Eisenhower remained formal—Dulles always addressed Eisenhower as "Mr. President"—Smith could pick up his line and say, "Goddamn it Ike, I think. . . ."[4] Dulles viewed Smith's personal association with the president with suspicion, and he limited Smith's influence inside the State Department. Eisenhower described Smith's wartime role as "general manager of the war," hinting that Smith would play a similar part in the Cold War.[5] As defined by statute, the undersecretary acts as the principal assistant of the secretary of state in formulating and executing foreign policy; in matters not requiring the personal attention of the secretary, he acts for the secretary; and in the absence of the secretary, he becomes the acting secretary of state. Smith went into the job thinking he would act as "the policy chief of staff" and active head of the "thinking side of the State Department as distinct from the actual administrative side."[6] Dulles made sure that never happened. Dulles stayed clear of managerial work, leaving Smith to be the virtual administrative head for the diffuse divisions of the department. The secretary never attended large staff meetings or lengthy, detailed briefing sessions, letting Smith manage the State Department's administrative housekeeping.[7]

As indicated by their chance meeting at the Waldorf Astoria, Smith disliked Dulles, and their relationship was sour from the start. In 1947 Dulles headed a delegation at a conference in Moscow. After hours, the American mission unwound over a few cocktails. The conversation turned to speculation about what jobs their Soviet adversaries would hold if they were capitalists instead of communists. Vishinsky's name came up. Before Vishinsky became a diplomat, he had acted as chief prosecutor and executioner in Stalin's Great Purge. Not missing a beat, Smith said, "Why, there's no doubt about it. He would have been a senior partner at Sullivan and Cromwell."[8] Both Dulles brothers were senior partners at that prestigious international law firm. Smith's animosity stemmed in part from his aversion to Dulles's overbearing Calvinist self-righteousness and patrician self-importance, but mostly, he resented being treated like a patsy. He chafed under the administrative burden, confiding in an acquaintance, "Now that I am out of the intelligence racket, I rather miss it. It did have one advantage—that of being complete czar of all the works with very few people to question one's decisions."[9] Dulles wanted no part of the administrative headaches but showed no hesitation in overruling Smith. Smith fumed and at least once threatened resignation, telling an aide, "I'm not going to take that from Foster Dulles or anyone else."[10]

The differences between Dulles and Smith were strictly personal. From his experiences in Moscow and as DCI, Smith believed the Soviets and Chinese acted as rational players only when faced by overwhelming American strength. "Containment invites a draw," he told the *New York Times*. "I do not think we want a draw." Likewise, he supported the ambitious policy of expanding the American nuclear arsenal. In his estimate, the policy of "passive resistance" must give way to an affirmative foreign policy characterized by "determined opposition."[11]

Eisenhower had other plans for Smith. As president, Eisenhower remained committed to two potentially contradictory aims: to maintain—or even intensify—his administration's pledge to counter the expansion of communist influence while satisfying domestic demands for balancing the budget, cutting the deficit, lowering taxes, and curbing inflation. Eisenhower's foreign policy was bellicose in words but measured in practice. John Foster Dulles's policy fixed on employing the threat of an all-out nuclear attack—later termed "massive retaliation"—coupled with the aggressive use of covert operations to combat the spread of communism. Massive retaliation—and the United States reserved the right to retaliate when faced with any breach of the Truman Doctrine—depended on a policy of pushing the Soviet Union to the threshold of total war. Both Eisenhower and Dulles eschewed costly conventional commitments. By late spring 1953 Eisenhower recognized that the ambitious goals of rolling back communism and liberating eastern Europe were unachievable without the attendant risks of war. On 8 May 1953 he asked Smith to head a select committee and engage in a thorough rethinking of foreign policy, code-named Solarium, after the White House sunroom where Eisenhower held his secret conclaves. Smith, Allen Dulles, and national security adviser Robert Cutler, along with five other senior officials of their choice, weighed the policy options consistent with the fiscal year 1954 budget.

Eisenhower held out three alternatives: (1) "continue the contain-

ment policy . . . [and] generally avoid risking a general war"; (2) determine "areas of the world which the United States will not permit to
become communist" and "draw a line" in Europe, making it clear to
the Kremlin that if a country "on [the American] side of the line" fell
to either overt or covert aggression or subversion, Washington would
consider it a casus belli against the USSR (the same applied in Asia,
with regard to China), "but not necessarily global war"; and (3) genuine
"liberation" based on a vigorous economic response to Soviet political-
military-ideological challenges to Western vital interests, employing
propaganda and psychological and paramilitary operations.[12] The committee recommended a combination of the first two options, confirming
the legitimacy of containment, with reliance placed on nuclear deterrence. Eisenhower apparently agreed with the Solarium findings. From
30 October 1953, national security policy held that "in the event of hostilities, the United States will consider nuclear weapons to be as available
for use as other munitions."[13] Any war involving the United States would
trigger nuclear attacks against the centers of Soviet and Chinese power,
with Washington reserving the right to launch a preemptive first strike.
The American nuclear umbrella, including the integration of tactical
weapons in U.S. ground and naval forces, underwrote the push for a
European Defense Community (EDC), including a rearmed Germany.

In the midst of the policy review, Eisenhower created the Operations
Coordinating Board (OCB) in September. He charged the OCB with
overseeing national security programs and named Smith as its chairman. Although the OCB's role centered on binding the planning and
execution sides of foreign policy strategy—it reported to the NSC—the
board never carved out any real niche because of Dulles's obstruction.
Unhappy with the Solarium conclusions and Smith's principal role in
recasting U.S. foreign policy priorities, Dulles viewed the OCB as a rival
center of influence.

Regime Change—Iran and Guatemala

Although Solarium rejected placing primary reliance on political and
psychological warfare, the United States scored its first successful regime
change operation in summer 1953 and set in motion a second; Smith,
the covert operations naysayer as DCI, played prominent roles in both.
In March 1951 the Iranian prime minister was assassinated and replaced
by the Western-educated intellectual and secular modernist Mohammad
Mossadegh as head of the National Front, the most outspoken opponent
of foreign manipulation of Iran. The new government moved to nation-

alize the Anglo-Iranian Oil Company (AIOC). In summer 1952 friction between the youthful shah, Mohammad Reza Pahlavi (the British had placed his father on the throne in 1941), and Mossadegh over nationalizing AIOC assets prompted Mossadegh's resignation and replacement by Admed Ghavam. Three days of pro-Mossadegh riots broke out. Under pressure, the shah caved in and reappointed Mossadegh. After lengthy and fruitless negotiations with the British, Mossadegh nationalized the AIOC but set aside a quarter of the profits as compensation to British interests. Mossadegh argued that without the oil revenue, Iran could not modernize its economy—build infrastructure, expand education, and fight poverty. The communist Tudeh, the largest such party in Southwest Asia and the Middle East, and the other force for secular modernization in Iran, emerged as a loose political collaborator.

Initially Truman's national security team concluded that Mossadegh represented the best barrier against a communist takeover in Iran and rejected British proposals for overthrowing the democratically elected government in Tehran. As the Iranians moved toward seizing the oil reserves, the Truman administration attempted to mediate a settlement. Under the pressure of British sanctions, the coalition that elected Mossadegh began splintering, and Tudeh became more active. Officials in Washington worried that Iran might fall under Soviet sway. In November, after wide-ranging discussions in the previous months, the Truman administration sanctioned the undertaking of "special political measures" to destabilize Iran—code for covert operations.[14] In his last days as DCI, Smith finalized a detailed plan for covert operations that Truman approved on 8 January 1953, twelve days before Eisenhower's inauguration.

The possibility of ousting Mossadegh gained momentum when a disaffected general approached the assistant U.S. military attaché with the idea of an American-sponsored coup and requested that the attaché pass on the information to the U.S. ambassador. In reply, the ambassador signaled his encouragement but made no commitment of American assistance. When this information arrived in Washington through State Department channels, Smith picked up the ball and ran with it. When Smith met Stalin for the first time in April 1946, the marshal explained how the Soviets had removed Ghavam's anti-Soviet challenger; in Stalin's view, Ghavam was "not unfriendly" to Soviet influence in Iran or to granting the Russians oil concessions. Stalin bitterly complained about American and British pressure and delays in bringing the matter before the UN Security Council—ultimately successful—and he was forced to withdraw his troops from the wartime Soviet sphere of influence in northern

Iran without any oil deal.[15] The Soviet climb-down represented the first instance of Truman's shift toward containment. In Smith's mind, Mossadegh, Ghavam, and any National Front government threatened American interests in Southwest Asia. The Dulles brothers agreed; on 4 April 1953 Allen Dulles approved a budget of $1 million and gave the Tehran station the go-ahead to use the money as the ambassador and CIA station chief saw fit in engineering the fall of Mossadegh.[16]

The CIA dispatched its best operative, Kermit Roosevelt (grandson of Theodore Roosevelt), to Tehran. The coup plan initially called for bribing members of Iran's parliament and leaders of splinter parties, dividing Mossadegh's coalition, and forcing him from office. Money flowed to prominent Iranian clergymen, and the mullahs began denouncing Mossadegh as an atheist and enemy of Islam. Other funds bought off senior military officers. Another $150,000 went as enticements to newspaper owners and editors. If these efforts failed to topple Mossadegh, the last resort was a military coup led by his CIA-picked successor, GEN Fazlollah Zahedi. The British loaned some of their best agents but otherwise deferred to the CIA in staging Operation Ajax.

The CIA completed a comprehensive assessment, "Factors Involved in the Overthrow of Mossadeq," on 16 April, estimating that a combination of the shah and Zahedi, with CIA assistance and financial backing, stood a good chance of ousting Mossadegh. Key would be keeping the army in barracks and mobs on the streets. Operational planning went ahead, disclosed to only a restricted number of individuals in the State Department, chief among them Dulles and Smith. As the political situation in Iran became more confused—in no small measure due to Roosevelt's machinations—the likelihood of supplanting Mossadegh increased. On 1 July the British again approached the United States about launching a coup attempt. This time Washington proved more receptive. On 11 July Eisenhower approved Ajax; he left it to Smith to tidy up the details. Working through the British embassy in Washington, Smith leveraged a promise that the British would remain flexible on the question of control of Iranian oil.[17]

In the meantime, the CIA convinced the shah to dismiss Mossadegh and appoint Zahedi. The shah issued his decree, but the coup failed because, as Smith reported to Eisenhower on 18 August, the shah and the generals vacillated, "during which [time] Mosadeg apparently found out all that was happening. Actually it was a counter-coup. . . . The old boy wouldn't accept [the shah's *firman*] and arrested the messenger and everybody else involved that he could get his hands on." Smith recommended that the NSC "take a whole new look at the Iranian situation and [would] probably have to snuggle up to Mosadeg if we're going to save anything there."[18]

The shah, awaiting the outcome of events in Tehran at a Caspian resort, immediately took flight. Despite receiving orders to leave, Roosevelt nimbly improvised more chaos. On 19 August paid mobs numbering in the thousands took to the streets. By midnight, his house in flames, Mossadegh escaped over the back wall, only to surrender a couple of days later. By then, the shah had returned and duly installed Zahedi as prime minister. A few weeks later, Roosevelt entered Allen Dulles's office, where he was congratulated on the brilliant job of overthrowing the lawfully elected government in Iran. Dulles then asked Roosevelt if he wanted to repeat the performance in Guatemala. Roosevelt declined the offer.[19]

The Iranian coup provided a blueprint for the overthrow of the Arbenz government in Guatemala. Although the outward conditions in the two countries bore little comparison, the dynamics of their internal political situations had remarkable similarities. Jacobo Arbenz Guzman had come to power in March 1951, winning 60 percent of the vote in Guatemala's second universal-suffrage election on a ticket that promised to shed the country's colonial dependence on the United States, end the feudal latifundia landholding structure, and work toward the eradication of poverty. Instead of the AIOC, the United Fruit Company represented not only the symbol but also the reality of foreign economic exploitation of the Guatemalan economy. In 1952 Arbenz legalized the Guatemalan Party of Labor, and communist-affiliated groups quickly infiltrated the peasant co-ops and tiny labor movement. The government embarked on an ambitious program of land redistribution, expropriating 234,000 acres of unused United Fruit Company property and offering the company Guatemalan bonds as compensation. The company vigorously lobbied Washington, including Smith. Although any administration always stood prepared to defend American property rights—and many observers then and after believed that American actions were motivated primarily by economic considerations—the overriding preoccupation in both Iran and Guatemala remained combating the spread of communist influence.

Under Smith's direction, the CIA developed contingency plans (code-named PBFortune) to oust Arbenz. Initially Smith preferred to work with the Central American dictators, funneling aid to opposition groups inside Guatemala to destabilize Arbenz. In April 1952 one of those dictators, Anastasio Somoza of Nicaragua, visited Washington and told Truman he could "clean up Guatemala for you in no time." Somoza floated the idea of arming exiled GEN Carlos Castillo Armas and staging an invasion of Guatemala from Nicaraguan territory with air support furnished by a pirate air force operating out of Nicaragua and Honduras. Truman instructed Smith to pursue the matter, and he in turn delegated Allen Dulles responsibility for organizing the first small shipment of arms and financial backing to Armas. Before signing the order activating PBFortune, Smith sought and received State Department concurrence. On 9 September Smith authorized the CIA action. The plan called for arms to be shipped from New Orleans to Nicaragua in a United Fruit Company freighter in crates marked "agricultural machinery." Smith possessed little faith in Somoza's claims and fretted about security. His concerns proved well founded. In less than a month, the CIA saw its cover plan blown. Neither Truman nor the State Department ever wholly bought into the scheme. Truman and Dean Acheson wanted to preserve whatever remained of Roosevelt's Good Neighbor policy, and the United States had pledged not to interfere in the domestic affairs of other members of the Organization of American States. On 8 October Acheson informed Smith that the operation was off.[20] The arms cache ended up in Panama.

John Foster Dulles evinced little interest in Latin America, and except for showy appearances at conferences, he granted Smith freedom of action in inter-American affairs. In effect, Smith became secretary of state for Western Hemisphere policy. He took on Guatemala as his own pet project. At an NSC meeting on 4 March 1953, Smith said, "the most important question facing the Cabinet [is] to make up its mind that Latin America is important." Pointing to Central America, he emphasized that "timely action [is] extremely desirable to prevent Communism from spreading seriously beyond Guatemala." Eisenhower lamented, "it was a matter of great distress to him that we seem unable to get some of these down-trodden countries to like us instead of hating us."[21] A devout Catholic, Smith employed contacts in the Catholic Church to obtain information on developments inside Guatemala. Given its reactionary defense of its lands and historic hold on the rural population, the Catholic Church hardly provided unbiased intelligence.

Smith kept the Guatemala operation afloat until the Iranian coup convinced the new administration that covert operations offered an effective and cheap means of toppling regimes viewed as unfriendly—and without congressional oversight. On 19 August, the day Mossadegh fell, an NSC paper argued, "A policy of non-action [in Guatemala] would be suicidal, since the communist movement, under Moscow tutelage, will not falter nor abandon its goal."[22] A week later Smith met with Wisner and the chief of the Western Hemisphere division of the CIA, COL J. C. King. Smith gave the go-ahead to restart the mounting phase of the coup. Smith announced the pending appointment of "Smiling Jack" Peurifoy as ambassador; Peurifoy would work in close cooperation with the CIA and begin recruiting disaffected Guatemalan elites and military officers. The new ambassador made his intentions very clear, saying, "I have come to Guatemala to use the big stick. I am definitely convinced that if the President (Arbenz) is not a communist, he will certainly do until one comes along." In Washington, Smith wanted only a select few privy to the program on a "need-to-know" basis. They used "diplomatic preparations" in all communications as code for "other actions in support of CIA actions" and gave "loose harness" to CIA operatives in Central America. "Guatemala," King recorded, "is now number one priority in the Agency."[23]

An 11 September "Memorandum for the Record" claimed that "Guatemala has become the leading base of operations for Moscow influenced communism in Central America . . . [and] now represents a serious threat to hemispheric solidarity and to our security in the Caribbean area."[24] Five days later Smith met again with Wisner. Smith flashed Wisner the "green light" to begin the execution of PBFortune, now code-named PBSuccess, which enjoyed "an extremely high operational priority." Intent that the operation should go ahead, Smith instructed Wisner to engage in no direct discussions with anybody else in the State Department.[25]

At the end of November, fifteen tons of arms sat in New York Harbor. Smith held talks with Allen Dulles and King on 25 November. King wanted the shipment to Nicaragua expedited "to test Somoza's alleged agreement to cooperate." Smith took strong objection to this idea. Remembering the prior security breach, Smith thought "the entire subject of handling arms . . . fraught with peril from a security point of view." Smith trusted Somoza even less than he had the previous year. Smith remained unconvinced when King explained that arms were needed to train cadres. Smith pointed to the logistical problems of getting arms into the jump-off points in Honduras and El Salvador. He considered arms shipments unwise until Washington firmed up military agreements with Nicaragua. "We must first be sure that Somoza has a carrot well within reach," he said, "before we come along with the stick." Eager for the operation's success, Smith worried about leaks. Overthrowing a democratically elected Latin American government undoubtedly would generate significant "blowback," and he insisted the administration retain some measure of "plausible deniability" for its role in the coup if things went south. In the face of Smith's strong objections, King dropped his decision to begin arms shipments.[26]

Senator Alexander Wiley warned of Guatemala becoming a communist beachhead and signaled a need for American intervention. *Time* quoted Peurifoy as saying, "Public Opinion in the United States might force us to take some measures to prevent Guatemala from falling into the lap of international Communism. We cannot permit a Soviet republic to be established between Texas and the Panama Canal." A CIA study admitted that Wiley's threats created a greater storm in Guatemala than in the United States. The Guatemalan ambassador in Washington pleaded for a meeting with Eisenhower. Instead, he met with Smith, and after a ninety-minute conversation, Ambassador Guillermo Toriello left expecting a "clear improvement" in relations between the two countries. The meeting served as diplomatic cover as preparations for the coup continued.[27]

Indochina: Disunited Action

By December, another hot spot supplanted Guatemala as the Eisenhower administration's top foreign policy priority and diverted Smith's attention from Central America: the looming disaster in French Indochina. As DCI, Smith supervised and provided input into the national intelligence estimates evaluating communist threats in Indochina and assessing the French conduct of the war. As principal in the foreign policy reappraisal ordered by Truman for the incoming Eisenhower administration, Smith presented the findings of the NSC review to Eisenhower during that fateful trip to New York. The NSC paper expected that Paris would "continue to try to transfer a growing part of the Indochinese war's costs to the US and the Associated States"—Vietnam, Laos, and Cambodia. In that event, Washington should demand a quid pro quo: in exchange for increased funding, France should grant genuine independence to the associated states, increase troop levels and regain the operational initiative, and develop indigenous forces. "Otherwise the military situation would be stalemated," read the final document, "and the political and economic conditions would deteriorate." Smith also said that any increase in China's active support of the Vietminh might prompt American naval and air assistance, interdicting lines of communication, "including those in China." Smith drew the connection between Indochina and Europe; the war in Southeast Asia blunted French participation in NATO and impacted their decision on joining a western European military pact.[28] Once in office, the Eisenhower administration followed Smith's policy recommendation.

A year later, Eisenhower commissioned another interagency review seeking policy advice on Southeast Asia. Its conclusions varied little from the findings of the last review under Truman. Essentially, the policy recommendations possessed four elements: Southeast Asia was critical to American security; the United States should continue to buttress French military efforts; the United States should not support any negotiations leading to the partitioning of Indochina; and any increase in Chinese participation should trigger American naval and air actions, including interdiction along China's coast and border districts.[29]

On 4 January 1954 Smith met for an "off the record" dinner with a dozen Washington-based reporters. He thought nothing would come of the four-power conference on the German question scheduled for Berlin at the end of the month. The United States saw "no real alternative to EDC," the European military alliance. If France opposed bringing West Germany into NATO, Smith believed the United States might choose Germany over France. He told the journalists, "A successful defense of Europe is probably possible without France but NOT without Germany." When asked about a solution to the Korean problem emerging from an international conference, Smith emphatically replied that he expected "the present armed truce to last indefinitely [and] . . . does NOT expect the truce to be broken by new fighting." As for South Korean leader Syngman Rhee, Smith joked, "Every time he found himself hoping the S.O.B. would drop dead, he looks around and wishes we had three or four more like him." He likened Korea to Germany, "divided for as long as the mind can contemplate." Asked about Indochina, Smith dismissed the Vietminh thrust into Laos as tactically and strategically insignificant but worried about its psychological impact. "It increases the feeling in France that the best solution might be to pull out," and the nightmare "that France might dump the whole problem into our lap" kept him awake at night "in a cold sweat." One of the journalists suggested that France continued to fight in Indochina because without it, "France would fall to the third-rate-power level." Smith answered, "France doesn't care that much about Indochina" but "would fight like hell" in North Africa because Paris thought its Mediterranean colonies made "the difference between [France being] a major and a minor power." On the prospects of a war against China, Smith opined, "The US can never permit itself to get bogged down on the Asiatic mainland as it did in Korea." He did not think the United States could "fight that kind of war—swapping Americans for Chinese, putting up blue chip soldiers against their white chips." He also offered the observation that the United States must guard against the resumption of hostilities with the Chinese because "a

renewal of war would almost certainly lead to a broadening of the war."
He declined to answer when asked whether the United States would
employ nuclear munitions.[30]

On 14 January Eisenhower endorsed Smith's 30 December policy
guidelines as NSC 177, but with additions. NSC 177 rested on a number
of false premises. Allen Dulles argued that the French stood in no danger of military defeat except in the event of Chinese intervention. He
posited that the estimated 24,000 Vietminh troops already in place could
not take the fortified French position at Dien Bien Phu, and their antiaircraft artillery could not interdict supply. NSC 5405, the final revised
draft of NSC 177, assumed British support in the event of American
intervention, but if the United Kingdom and France refused "expanded
military action, the United States should consider taking such action unilaterally," with the understanding that the United States "may become
involved in an all-out war with Communist China, and possibly with the
USSR and the rest of the Soviet bloc, and should therefore proceed to
take large-scale mobilization measures."[31]

If evidence mounted that the military situation in Southeast Asia
was deteriorating, some form of American intervention seemed more
likely. On 18 January Eisenhower, who was not happy with the quality
of the policy recommendations he was receiving, named Smith as head
of an ad hoc NSC Special Committee on Indochina. Smith appeared to
be the ideal choice: his background gave him unparalleled prestige in
the State Department, Defense Department, and intelligence community; the president appreciated Smith's ability to reconcile conflicting
points of view into coherent and succinct assessments; and Eisenhower
trusted him completely. Since the decision would be a military one,
Eisenhower wanted Smith as his point man. The committee consisted of
Smith; Allen Dulles; JCS chairman ADM Arthur Radford; C. D. Jackson, Eisenhower's special assistant; and Roger Kyes, deputy secretary of
defense. The president instructed Smith's special committee to identify "possible alternative lines of action," specifying "who does what and
with what and to whom."[32]

In the meantime, John Foster Dulles traveled to Berlin for the first
foreign ministers' conference since 1947. As Smith predicted, no progress emerged on the German question, but a Soviet initiative for holding
a five-power conference on a political settlement in Korea and the restoration of peace in Indochina carried. The French and British wanted to
test the waters of détente proffered by Stalin's death and the moderate
noises coming out of Moscow; the French wanted British and American
diplomatic support in a desperate bid to end the fighting in Indochina

on the best terms possible; and there could be no agreement on Korea or Indochina without the Chinese. Under pressure, Dulles reluctantly agreed to attend the conference in Geneva, with the understanding that China's presence did not imply American diplomatic recognition. However much he opposed bringing the war in Indochina to the conference table with no victory in sight and with China as a negotiating foe, Dulles felt compelled to approve the Berlin decision, if only to blunt the French threat of scuttling the EDC.

The decision-making process involved in the Indochina problem provides one of the best examples of Eisenhower's passive-negative brand of leadership. It was passive because he always insisted on "multiple advocacy" and high levels of team building before he entertained any departure from established policy lines. This method obscured his hand in the process and shielded him from culpability should things go wrong. The chief of the Australian army attended a five-power military conference on Indochina in summer 1954, and when asked to characterize the president's role, he replied, "Eisenhower was only a figurehead."[33] Quite the opposite was actually the case: behind the screen of the more highly visible Dulles, Smith, and Vice President Richard Nixon, Eisenhower reserved all the important decisions for himself. Eisenhower's style was negative because he proved most decisive when he refused to take policy paths he considered too perilous. Long before he became president, Eisenhower identified the dilemma that confronted him in the first half of 1954. While commanding NATO in Paris in 1951, he discussed the "draining sore" of Indochina with the French commander, GEN Jean de Lattre de Tassigny. Clearly accepting the validity of the Truman administration's "domino theory," Eisenhower recorded in his diary that if the French "quit and Indochina falls to [the] Commies, it is easily possible that the countries of Southeast Asia and Indonesia would go, soon to be followed by India." About the same time, he wrote, "I am convinced that no military victory is possible in that kind of theater."[34] In January 1954 he restated these contrary pressures. At an NSC meeting on 8 January he said that he remained "bitterly opposed" to any unilateral intervention because the Vietnamese would transfer "their hatred of the French to us," and a war in Indochina "would absorb our troops by divisions!" The president added that although no one was more anxious "to keep our men out of these jungles, we could nevertheless not forget our vital interests in Indochina." At another NSC meeting three days later, he exclaimed, "My God, we must not lose Asia—we've got to look the thing right in the face."[35] He never precluded the possibility of direct American involvement in Indochina, but Eisenhower would not commit until he had exhausted all other options and his laundry list of preconditions had been satisfied. In the meantime, as he confided in Swede Hazlett, "There is little I can do except to wait it out and hope for the best."[36]

The question remained, how could he avert a decision? Washington faced a narrowing range of options. The United States could not refuse to engage in negotiations or withhold aid from the French; it could not insist that Paris grant independence to the associated states for fear of undermining Premier Joseph Laniel's government and killing the EDC.[37] Nor could Eisenhower leverage the French into expanding local forces or giving the Americans any role in their training, despite U.S. financial support of $1 billion.[38] All agreed that the Laniel cabinet represented the last French government that would prosecute the war. The United States could not internationalize the war in the United Nations over the veto of the Soviet Union. Smith's special committee examined the conditions under which the United States might intervene in Indochina and identified the means required to effect a positive military and political outcome. As part of that brief, Smith asked the JCS to formulate a "concept of operations" for Indochina. Smith presented the committee's preliminary recommendations to the NSC on 30 January. The conclusions matched those set out in NSC 177. Smith said that the "importance of winning in Indochina was so great that if worst came to worst [he] personally would favor intervention with US air and naval—not ground forces." Radford felt the same way.[39]

Throughout February and March the military situation in Indochina worsened. On 13 March the Vietminh forces began their assaults on Dien Bien Phu, a French fortified position near the triangle of the Sino-Vietnamese-Laotian frontiers. As Smith later remarked, he never expected the French military strategy, the Navarre Plan, to work. "Navarre is stupid and incompetent," he later told journalists. "The United States supported the Navarre Plan for its program of building up the native forces . . . we certainly did NOT support or endorse any tactical system—and certainly NOT the one Navarre employed" at Dien Bien Phu.[40] The French defense minister, René Pleven, told American journalists that he "saw no prospect of satisfactory military solution," and only the Chinese could resolve the Indochina problem. "It seems to me that Pleven has been extremely free with our negotiating position," Smith told Eisenhower. Eisenhower wondered, "Why don't they withdraw request for military aid?"[41] On 19 March, Carrier Division 3 received orders to proceed to the approaches of the Gulf of Tonkin. The next day, at Smith's invitation, GEN Paul Ely, the French chief of staff, arrived in Washington. Only a week into the siege of Dien Bien Phu, the French assessed the situation as beyond retrieval, and Ely requested American intervention. Ely's request set off a flurry of discussions. The Eisenhower administration moved to lay the diplomatic and political groundwork for a possible American entry into the Indochina conflict.

Between 24 March and 6 April, the Eisenhower foreign policy team formulated its response to the crisis. Eisenhower established one overriding ground rule: no unilateral American intervention. Eisenhower, Dulles, and Smith believed the formation of an international coalition consisting of the United States, the United Kingdom, France, Australia, New Zealand, Thailand, the Philippines, and the associated states would bolster the French, deter the Chinese, and constitute a solid front to deflect communist demands at Geneva. The diplomatic initiative, coupled with a strongly worded warning to Beijing implying the threat of a nuclear strike, might render direct American military involvement unnecessary. On 29 March Dulles made a speech before the Overseas Press Club of America, where he sounded menacing. He laid out the domino theory, categorized Chinese involvement in Indochina as "all means short of invasion," and said the imposition of communist control in Southeast Asia "should not be passively accepted but should be met with united action," but he made no commitments.[42]

On 31 March Radford convened a special session of the JCS. For two days Radford tried and failed to drum up any support among the chiefs for launching an air assault to save the French position at Dien Bien Phu (code-named Vulture). All the service chiefs, including the commandant of the Marine Corps, voted not to offer the French any air support at Dien Bien Phu; only Radford voted in favor.[43] The most adamant opposition came from the army chief, GEN Matthew Ridgway. When asked his opinion on whether the United States should conduct a naval blockade and launch strategic air strikes, Ridgway answered with an "emphatic and immediate 'No.'" From a military viewpoint, Ridgway stated, "the United States capability for effective intervention in the Dien Bien Phu operation was altogether disproportionate to the liability it would incur."[44]

Smith still recommended intervention, limited to air and naval support. Eisenhower called Smith and Radford to the White House for talks on 2 April. Resisting aggression was an abstract but guiding principle of American foreign policy, and it melded with the founding premise of the Truman Doctrine, which held that the United States must avert the spread of communism anywhere. Reinforced by the Korean War experience, this magnified areas of peripheral importance, such as Indochina, into regions of vital strategic interest. Containment effectively militarized American foreign policy. In the face of communist armed expansion, the United States had three options: support allies and friendly states in counterinsurgency efforts or in resisting external threats through military and economic assistance; conduct limited conventional operations, mostly entailing aerial and naval interdiction, but including ground troops, if necessary (on the model of Korea); or fight total war, including "massive retaliation." With option one failing, Eisenhower confronted the second alternative: execute Vulture against Vietminh concentrations around Dien Bien Phu. The Eisenhower administration's "New Look" defense policy relied on deterrence—described as "more bang for the buck"—at the expense of ground forces. With ground forces reduced from twenty to seventeen divisions and funding slashed by one-third, the second option appeared unfeasible, even in the unlikely event the administration could secure congressional and public support for fighting another Korea. Radford conceded, "The situation was not one which called for any U.S. participation." Eisenhower made the decision not to authorize Vulture.[45]

For Eisenhower, the British held the key to forging "united action." At the presidential retreat at Camp David, Eisenhower, Dulles, and Douglas MacArthur II, a counselor at the State Department, drafted a letter to Churchill, urging him to press Parliament to support the American diplomatic initiative. They drew a parallel between the present crisis and the situation the prime minister had described "so brilliantly in the second chapter of 'Their Finest Hour,' when history made clear that the French strategy and dispositions before the 1940 breakthrough should have been challenged before the blow fell." Flattering the prime minister further, they alluded to another of his books on World War II, *Gathering Storm*, when "we failed to halt Hirohito, Mussolini and Hitler by not acting in unity and in time." The letter reminded Churchill that "Geneva is less than four weeks away" and expressed concern that the communist bloc remained bent on driving a wedge between the Western democracies. There were no grounds for negotiation; the situation in Indochina could have only one of two results: a "face-saving" French surrender, or a "Communist retirement." "Somehow," the letter stated, "we must contrive to bring about the second alternative." Eisenhower offered to send Smith to London for talks on the question.[46]

Eisenhower and Dulles returned to the White House on 3 April for an unusual Saturday breakfast conference with the congressional leadership; Smith and Radford joined them. The president sought a congressional resolution granting him broad discretionary authorization to employ naval and air forces to forestall the "extension and expansion" of communism in Southeast Asia. The legislators shared the administration's concerns but insisted on conditions. Distrusting French motives in Indochina, they demanded the United States not intervene in defense of colonialism. If the administration secured firm commitments from allied nations, especially from the British, and if France agreed to internationalize the war and grant full independence to the associated states, the congressional leadership promised bipartisan support for the resolution. Eisenhower had no difficulty accepting those terms, since they dovetailed almost exactly with his own thinking. Nevertheless, the conditions virtually precluded any unilateral intervention and tied American actions to British support and French concessions. After the congressmen left, Smith vetted the letter to Churchill and made a number of changes that Eisenhower accepted before dispatching it to London.[47]

On the evening of 4 April Eisenhower held an off-the-record meeting in the upstairs study in the White House attended by Dulles, Smith, MacArthur, Radford, and Kyes. They laid out the ground rules for an eventual American intervention. "Joint action" with the British, including the commitment of Australian and New Zealand troops and, if possible, units from the Philippines and Thailand, headed the list. Second, the French must promise to continue the war, not accept a partition settlement in Geneva, and concede independence to the associated states. If these minimum preconditions were met, Eisenhower would ask Congress for the enabling resolution.[48]

Earlier that day the French foreign minister, Georges Bidault, made the first formal request for American air intervention. Eisenhower rejected the French appeal. As he told Dulles, without congressional support, an air strike "would be completely unconstitutional & indefensible." As Dulles informed the American ambassador in Paris, the "US is doing everything possible . . . to prepare public, Congressional and Constitutional basis for united action in Indochina." The administration remained prepared "to do everything short of belligerency," but until Washington arrived at a full political understanding with Paris and formed a coalition "with active British Commonwealth participation . . . such action is impossible."[49]

While Eisenhower vetoed Vulture again, Smith submitted his committee's final recommendations on Indochina, which called for American opposition to any settlement in Geneva and the pursuit of a complete "military victory" in Indochina, employing its own forces if required. As Smith admitted to the NSC on 6 April, his recommendations "had been overtaken by events." Ridgway argued persuasively against committing American forces. "Such use of United States armed forces," he warned, "apart from any local successes they might achieve, would constitute a dangerous strategic diversion of limited United States military capabilities, and would commit our armed forces in a non-decisive theatre to the attainment of non-decisive local objectives." Still bitter about the diminution of the army's role in national defense, Ridgway ridiculed any suggestion that Indochina would serve as a test case for the new force structure. As he remarked in his memoirs, the "old delusive idea" that the United States could intervene "on the cheap," with only naval and air units, persisted; ultimately, ground forces would be committed, and the overextended army simply lacked the divisions for deployment in Southeast Asia.[50] As Eisenhower told the NSC "with great emphasis" on 6 April, "There was no possibility whatever of U.S. unilateral intervention in Indochina and we had best face that fact. Even if we tried such a course, we would have to take it to Congress and fight for it like dogs, with very little hope of success."[51]

At the same NSC conference, Dulles admitted that intervention was off the table. "We should therefore place all our efforts on trying to organize a regional grouping for the defense of Southeast Asia prior to the opening of the Geneva Conference. If we can do so we will go into that Conference strong and united, with a good hope that we would come out of the Conference with the Communists backing down." He anticipated serious problems securing British support. "The British Government was at present in the doldrums," he said. "The paralysis of the British Government was almost as serious as that of the French." Despite this, Dulles did not exclude the possibility that the British would join in a collaborative effort.[52] The next day the long-awaited cable arrived from London. Eisenhower did not receive the response he needed. The prime minister said the American proposals for joint action in Indochina raised "many problems" for the British, and he knew the president would not expect them "to give a hurried decision." He invited Dulles to London for further discussions. Despite Dulles's warning, Churchill's lukewarm response set off alarm bells in Washington. Without British support, the entire project would collapse. On 10 April Dulles set off for London and Paris to whip the British and French into line in support of American-led "united action."

Dulles made no headway in London. Anthony Eden saw no likelihood that ultimatums and threats of an Anglo-American intervention would force China into a humiliating abandonment of the Vietminh. Faced with a choice between embarrassing retreat and widening its support, Eden believed Beijing would select the second course. Far better, Eden argued, would be to pursue a negotiated settlement in Geneva and reduce the threat of a great power clash.[53] Dulles fared no better in Paris, where Laniel said his cabinet would never survive the appearance of surrendering Indochina, whether by severing ties between France and the associated states, granting the United States a greater political and military say in the conduct of the war, or accepting "united action" troops. France's best option rested in arriving at a settlement in Geneva. Like the British, the French made gestures toward internationalizing the war, but only if Geneva collapsed. Laniel promised never to cede Indochina to the communists, but any manifestation of failure in Geneva would undoubtedly produce a government in Paris that might. Dulles achieved only one concession: a British promise to enter into preliminary talks on a Southeast Asia defense pact in Washington, beginning on 20 April.

Bringing around American opinion makers and public opinion presented another tall hurdle. A Gallup poll indicated overwhelming public suspicion of American involvement in Southeast Asia; just over a fifth of those surveyed favored sending troops, and slightly more than a third supported air and naval actions.[54] On 7 April Eisenhower held a press conference and stated, "The possible consequences of the loss [of Southeast Asia] are just incalculable to the free world." Major news agencies gave the president's news conference uncritical play. Three days later, Smith appeared on television (as acting secretary) on CBS's *The American Week*, where he emphasized the dangers confronting the United States. "Can we allow, dare we permit, expansion of Chinese Communist control further into Asia?" Answering no to his own rhetorical question, Smith underscored that "the human freedom of the masses of people for all that enormous area of the world" stood at risk. By hammering on the human rights issue, Smith sidestepped charges that any American intervention propped up French colonialism. The bellicose rhetoric of administration officials acted as cover for the constraint of Eisenhower's actual foreign policy. Speaking before a gathering of the American Society of Newspaper Editors on 16 April, the day after Dulles's return from Europe, Nixon announced that if the United States could not forge "united action" among the Western powers, it would "take on the problem" alone—he meant at Geneva, but he made it sound as if the United States would enter the conflict in Indochina. He said, "Negotiations with the Communists to divide the territory would result in Communist domination of a vital new area," and the United States stood as "the only nation politically strong enough at home to take a position that will save Asia." When questioned what the United States might do in the event of a French collapse, Nixon replied, "We must take the risk of putting our boys in." Smith hastily offered a statement "clarifying" what the vice president really meant, but it was too late to avoid the damage.[55] Nixon's remarks created a firestorm in Europe and in Congress. Taken as proof of a shift in U.S. policy, Nixon's belligerent remarks handed the British the pretext they needed to avoid getting pinned down to "united action." Two days after Nixon's speech, the British declined to attend the talks in Washington.

Dulles engaged in another round of shuttle diplomacy, heading to Europe on 20 April with a NATO council meeting acting as cover. Despite his frantic efforts, united action was dead. Dulles met with Bidault and Ely, who told him the Dien Bien Phu defense would collapse without massive American air strikes. Bidault now signaled his willingness to internationalize the war. Dismissing the need for British participation, the French foreign minister warned that if Dien Bien Phu fell, "The French would want to pull out entirely from southeast Asia, and assume no continuing commitments and the rest of us would have to get along without France in this area."[56] The final crisis at Dien Bien Phu came and went with no American air strike. On 26 April Dulles went to Geneva for the opening of the Korean phase of the conference.

In a letter to Alfred Gruenther, now NATO commander, Eisenhower expressed his exasperation with the French. France "wants still to be considered a world power, but is entirely unready to make the sacrifices necessary to sustain such a position. She prefers to limit her sacrifices and so, finally, she is bound to be shown up, as in Indo-China, as incapable of doing anything important by herself." He despaired of finding a new and inspirational French leader and stated, "I do not mean one that is 6 feet 5 and who considers himself to be, by some miraculous biological and transmigrative process, the offspring of Clemenceau and Jeanne d'Arc." Eisenhower knew the French "are weary as hell." He told a gathering of Republican congressional leaders on 26 April, "The French go up and down every day," and "they are very voluble. They [think] they are a great power one day and they feel sorry for themselves the next day."[57]

As acting secretary, Smith attended a long and heated NCS conference on 29 April. He painted a dismal picture of prospects for the rapidly approaching Indochina segment of the Geneva talks. He emphasized, "the United States had entered the Geneva Conference with a lesser degree of common understanding . . . with its allies than it had entered any previous international conference." In the lead-up to Geneva, the British remained "very skeptical and pessimistic" about forming a coalition, and "the French position veered as a result of the change in the military situation in Indochina." He then outlined Dulles's present assessment. The British would endorse any agreement satisfactory to Paris, and although they remained open to discussions on forming a joint guarantee of any settlement reached in Geneva, London refused to enter into any regional organization until after the results of the conference became known. "This change of heart on the part of the British had been very disappointing to us," Smith remarked, "since we had been counting on the British to help us buck up the French at Geneva." As he reported, "we could not change the British position, and Mr. Eden had become very irritated when Secretary Dulles attempted to do so." He then read Dulles's latest communication from Geneva, following a private talk with Molotov. Dulles concluded that the fall of Dien Bien Phu would lead to the disintegration of Laniel's cabinet and its replacement with "a government further to the left, which would be committed to liquidate the French position in Indochina." Laniel and Bidault would accept a settlement, provided the French retained Annam and Cochin China—central and southern Vietnam—and an enclave in the Red River delta. He believed that if the United States accepted this scheme, Australia, New Zealand, and Thailand would join France and the associated states in preserving the settlement. "The U.K. attitude," Dulles reported, "is one of increasing weakness—fear of atomic attack has badly frightened them." In view of the Russian and Chinese attitudes at Geneva, Dulles felt that "open U.S. intervention in Indochina would be more likely to be followed by open Chinese intervention, with the strong possibility that general war would result." Although the Western allies remained "very important to us," Dulles believed they would "follow a strong U.S. leadership, not necessarily a warlike one." Smith added his ringing endorsement of the final point.

Eisenhower did not see it that way. He confessed that it lay beyond his comprehension how the United States could consider intervention in Indochina "unless it did so in concert with some other nations and at the request of the Associated States." The best Smith could offer was Thai participation and an expression of his disappointment that Australia and New Zealand had withdrawn their endorsement of the coalition plan. Smith believed the French would hold on at Dien Bien Phu for "three weeks at least," in the hope the United States could solve its "constitutional problems." "The French want, if possible, to avoid a military debacle," he concluded, "and they realize that American intervention would have a highly salutary effect on French morale and French public opinion."

The president again flatly rejected intervention. He expressed his considerable doubt that Congress and the American public would support any such move. To many Americans, and certainly in Asian eyes, if France collapsed, any U.S. intervention would appear to be just another form of Western colonialism. "In short," he asked, "where and how could the United States intervene in Indochina?" Without a pause, he queried, "Where could the United States quickly find military forces to replace the forces which the French would withdraw?" The president then expressed his own conviction that if the United States intervened alone in Indochina, it would mean a general war with China and perhaps with the USSR, which the United States would have to prosecute without allies. He pointed to "our belief that a collective policy with our allies was the only posture which was consistent with U.S. national security policy as a whole." Intervening unilaterally in Indochina or anywhere else "amounted to an attempt to police the entire world." If the United States pursued such a course of action, using armed force "whether we were wanted or not, we would soon lose all our significant support in the free world. We should be everywhere accused of imperialistic ambitions. Without allies and associates the leader is just an adventurer like Genghis Khan." The United States could not be drawn into "brushfire wars in Burma, Afghanistan, and God knows where" and have American power eroded in "piecemeal conflicts, as had been the fate of the British." "The cause of the free world could never win, the United States could never survive," he predicted, "if we frittered away our resources in local engagements. This process would go on indefinitely, with the Communists trying everywhere to involve the United States in indecisive engagements which would ultimately sap its strength." He would not commit "six, eight, ten" divisions in Southeast Asia. To send the six divisions currently under JCS consideration would require the politically unpalatable decision of abandoning the "New Look" and going to general mobilization. An American move into Indochina would trigger renewed fighting in Korea. The president then engaged in a little brinkmanship, not with the communists but with his own NSC. He said before "he could bring himself to make such a decision, he would want to ask himself and all his wisest advisers whether the right decision was not rather to launch a world war"—to hit the head of the snake (the USSR) rather than the tail (China).[58]

Smith interjected that there might be a middle ground between total war and doing nothing. He again raised the question of whether American air strikes might offer a solution short of committing ground forces. Dien Bien Phu need not be decisive. In any case, air strikes could not salvage the situation. The spectacle of American strategic airpower would buoy French morale and enable them to stay in the war. Washington would sanction the use of American air assets only on the condition that the French grant the United States the right to train indigenous forces and have a say in their employment. "After all, there were plenty of ground forces available now," Smith contended, "if they would be properly trained and used . . . we might well avoid having to commit any U.S. ground forces." Smith thought that even without the British, the United States could induce the participation of some of the Asian states in an active coalition. If that happened, "we would meet the basic condition set by the Congress (concerted action) and would be able promptly to give the French what they were asking for—air strikes by U.S. planes." Eisenhower admitted that "this was what he had hoped might come to pass," but Australia's refusal to join the regional grouping dashed the possibility of using diplomatic cover for American air strikes. Nixon supported Smith's assessment, stating that American policy effectively granted the British "a veto on U.S. actions in Southeast Asia," and he characterized "our close tie-up with the British . . . a painful liability." He thought the French would continue the war and endorsed Smith's idea of creating a coalition with Asian nations and perhaps Australia and New Zealand as a means of securing congressional support. The president trimmed; he said when he became convinced the French would stay the course, and if some regional coalition emerged, he would put Smith's proposal up to Congress.[59]

The president made that oblique pledge in the full knowledge that neither would ever come to pass. As White House chief of staff Adams indicated: "Having avoided one total war with Red China the year before in Korea, when he had United Nations support, he was in no mood to provoke another one in Indochina . . . without the British and other Western allies."[60] Eisenhower ended the 29 April NSC meeting with "one word of warning." If the administration wanted to win over congressional and popular support "to an understanding of their stake in Southeast Asia, let us not talk of intervention with U.S. ground forces."

Indicative of Eisenhower's real feelings, in a speech given earlier that day to the U.S. Chamber of Commerce, was his statement that the United States might negotiate a settlement in Geneva aimed at reaching a modus vivendi with the communists.[61]

★ **4** ★

The Geneva Conference

Eisenhower entertained no great expectations for Geneva. He instructed Dulles to "steer a course between the unattainable and the unacceptable." He considered "a general Asian peace in which the free world could have real confidence" unattainable and said, "any division or partition of Indo-China was *not* included in what I considered acceptable."[1] In the end, he got both. The authors of American foreign policy subscribed to a set of firm preconceptions: communists never negotiated in good faith; the Soviet Union and its proxy China pursued foreign policy objectives based solely on strict adherence to the tenets of Marxist-Leninism; and the monocratic communist camp always acted as one. Stalin's death—leading to a power struggle inside the Kremlin and evidence of tension between Moscow and Beijing—did not alter American perceptions. The American foreign policy elite, whose younger members would profoundly influence American diplomacy for decades, fervently believed that the lesson of Munich was that failure to resist aggression early ensured the need to contest it later at far greater cost. The Eisenhower administration worried about the domestic political consequences of American participation in a conference that produced any partition settlement. Given Dulles's vociferous and oft-repeated assertions about "rolling back" communism, any settlement short of complete French success—a virtual impossibility—smacked of another Yalta. Unlike London and Paris, Washington refused diplomatic recognition of Beijing. Dulles, only half jokingly, remarked that the only way he would meet Chinese Foreign Minister Zhou Enlai was if their automobiles somehow collided. Smith would assume the difficult job of representing the United States at the Geneva talks on Indochina. To observers, Smith's attendance indicated that the Eisenhower administration intended to remain on the periphery of the conference—a view not entirely mistaken.

71

Geneva Discords

Before he set off for Geneva, Smith had one other little matter that commanded his attention. He had received a summons to Capitol Hill to appear before McCarthy's Permanent Subcommittee on Investigations. As *Time* reported, Smith "made a terse appearance, crunching out his answers as decisively as he stumped out his cigarettes." Smith testified that Ray Cohn, McCarthy's chief counsel, had approached him seeking a direct commission for David Schine, Cohn's close friend and suspected homosexual paramour—but not with the CIA, because the agency "was too juicy a subject for investigation." When asked if Cohn had attempted any high-pressure tactics on him, the incredulous "hardrock old soldier" snapped, "Not me, Sir!" Cohn had no luck with Smith. "Then Bedell Smith snuffed out a last cigarette," the magazine reported. "McCarthy asked him no questions." Cohn's blatant influence peddling permitted the army to bring charges against McCarthy and Cohn later in 1954. That indignity done, Smith completed his preparations for the conference.[2]

As Smith forecast in his book, Stalin's death generated some new thinking in the Kremlin. The troika dominated by Malenkov moved toward a form of perestroika and domestic reform that required normalization of relations with the West. In early March Molotov told the Chinese ambassador in Moscow, Zheng Wentian, "Although the Americans will try to wreck the Geneva Conference, the representatives of the democratic camp [the communists] will try to make full use of the conference in order to lessen international tensions."[3] Soviet embassies in western Europe and Washington made clear Moscow's intention to pursue political settlements at Geneva. Aware of American resistance to partition in Vietnam or any coalition government, the Soviet embassy in Washington revealed that Beijing would be content with a buffer in the north. None of this made any impression in Washington. Despite Molotov's sometimes provocative pronouncements during the Korea phase of the talks, the USSR wanted no major confrontations at Geneva. Moscow's primary foreign policy objectives centered on improving five-power relations, enhancing Soviet security, and normalizing bilateral relations. Molotov expected that the Chinese would manage the Indochina issue, including moderating Vietminh demands.[4] As the recently opened Soviet and Chinese sources show, Moscow and Beijing wanted an Indochina settlement.

So did the British and especially the French. Churchill and Eden never subscribed to the theory that Indochina was inextricably linked to the security of all Asia or that a settlement at Geneva must end in the surrender of the whole region to the communists. Eden charted a cautious route between the shoals of curbing American aggressiveness and avoiding any unilateral U.S. intervention, with the risk of a broader war, on one side, and the preservation of his independence of action as an honest broker seeking a political rather than a military solution in Indochina, on the other. Paris signaled its intentions: no withdrawal from Indochina, fuller autonomy to the associated states, and an "honorable" settlement at Geneva. As Smith informed Eden, a partition solution "would only be a temporary palliative and would lead to Communist domination of south-east Asia." Although he could not prevent the French from offering concessions, Smith's instructions read that he should dissociate himself from any settlement that included terms unacceptable to the United States: an imposed cease-fire and coalition government in Vietnam, and partition or self-determination through elections the communists would win.[5] All this isolated the American delegation in Geneva; alone among the five big powers, the United States occupied the position of tendering a compromise that might permit a settlement, but these were the very concessions Smith could not make.

The Chinese possessed a clear picture of the divisions inside the Western camp. Reporting to Mao Zedong on his meeting with Eden on 1 May, Zhou noted, "Although the United States fired many blanks [threatening intervention] they could not scare anyone but themselves." Zhou knew of Washington's attempts to form "an alliance of invaders," but the British hesitated, and the Americans refused French appeals for air support. "In sum, it is now impossible for the United States to stop negotiations on the Indochina issue." He interpreted Eisenhower's news conference promise to seek a settlement as evidence of "his retreat [which] embarrassed Dulles." According to Zhou, "Dulles decided to run away and leave the problems to . . . Smith."[6]

On 7 May, the day before the Indochina portion of the Geneva conference opened, French forces in Dien Bien Phu capitulated. Smith saw Dien Bien Phu as more damaging psychologically than militarily, and the shock waves of the fall of the French fortress reverberated in Washington. That evening on a radio and television broadcast, Dulles denounced Ho Chi Minh as a "Communist . . . trained in Moscow." If Vietnam fell "into hostile hands . . . the Communists would move into all of south-east Asia," depriving "Japan of important foreign markets and sources of food and raw materials." Despite that threat, "the present conditions there do not provide a suitable basis for the United States to participate with its armed forces." He dampened any expectations for a settlement in Geneva: "We would be gravely concerned if an armistice or cease-fire were reached at Geneva which would provide a road to a Communist takeover and further aggression."[7] Dulles's address discounted the only ace Smith held—the menace of imminent American intervention.

The conference got off to an unpropitious beginning when, over the strident opposition of Smith and Bidault, the Vietminh representative took his seat. The French opened the conference by proposing that the delegates initially limit discussions to military matters—an internationally supervised cease-fire, regrouping of regular forces into zones, and disarmament of irregular forces—before tackling a political settlement, including future elections. The five powers would guarantee the final agreements. The Vietminh representative, Pham Van Dong, argued the impossibility of decoupling military and political matters or treating Vietnam separately from Laos and Cambodia and made extravagant territorial demands in all three states. Although Smith gave a general endorsement of the French plan, he departed on two important points: he declined comment on whether the United States would guarantee any settlement, and he proposed monitoring of the cease-fire and national elections "under United Nations auspices." In Smith's estimate, the French proposal was tantamount to a permanent partition, and the Vietminh alternative would necessarily lead to a French withdrawal, followed by general elections. The United States preferred the status quo.[8]

The NSC established the guidelines for Smith's actions. "The United States will not associate itself with any proposal from any source directed toward a cease-fire in advance of an acceptable agreement, including international controls." Though empowering Smith to support French efforts toward an armistice, the NSC directive indicated "the United States will continue . . . its efforts to organize and promptly activate a Southeast Asian regional grouping for the purpose of preventing further expansion of Communist power in Southeast Asia." While pushing the British—and, through diplomatic contacts, the Pacific Rim Commonwealth states—toward united action, Smith was charged with buttressing the French with the promise of direct involvement conditioned on Paris's acceptance of a range of "indispensable" concessions and promises. Washington wanted French assurances that they would not yield in the face of communist intransigence, especially in the wake of the fall of Dien Bien Phu. Smith's task was to influence the French not to settle for a quick resolution but, at the same time, not become so embroiled in the bargaining as to link the administration to any final agreement contrary to American interests. Smith received authorization to warn the Chinese that any "intervention would lead to grave consequences which might not be confined to Indochina." Smith held an awkward status: he represented the United States as "an interested nation" but as neither a "belligerent nor a principal in the negotiations."[9] On 12 May Eisenhower approved Dulles's further instructions directing Smith to engage in no direct contacts with the Chinese (or Vietminh) delegation and approve no settlement or cease-fire "which would have the effect of subverting the existing lawful governments of the three [associated] states or of permanently impairing their territorial integrity or of placing in jeopardy the forces of the French Union of Indochina." Rather than sit passively through protracted and purposefully pointless negotiations in a repeat of Panmunjom, Dulles granted Smith permission to withdraw from the conference or restrict his role to observer.[10]

The reference to the Korean negotiations proved accurate. The conference bogged down on a number of peripheral matters—chiefly, determining whether the Pathet Lao and Free Khmer were Vietminh clients or genuine nationalist forces—while the French military situation deteriorated. It was less a conference than an endless set of debates punctuated by Chinese and Vietminh harangues. The real work took place within restricted sessions and circuitous bilateral talks occurring on the sidelines with Eden and Molotov, the copresidents, acting as mediators. Smith's first meeting with Molotov took place on 10 May. Renewing their acquaintance, the two old adversaries talked candidly. Making no secret of his delight that Dulles had returned to Washington, Molotov believed Smith's being a blunt "military man" would hasten the business of the conference. As Smith reported, the Soviets knew the communists need make no concessions.[11]

After the Dien Bien Phu debacle, Washington revived "united action," this time without the British and in combination with France, the ANZUS nations (Australia and New Zealand), and the associated states. The administration reserved the military option in the event the Geneva talks stalemated; once France and hopefully the United Kingdom, Australia, and New Zealand realized the pointlessness of seeking a cease-fire and a political settlement, they would join a coalition. As previously, the promise of direct U.S. involvement came with a price tag, and as the prior negotiations indicated, the longer France deferred, the higher the costs. Washington set out its "indispensable" conditions: France and the associated states must formally request American involvement; Thailand, the Philippines, Australia, and New Zealand must signal their acceptance of united action, together with British assurances that they "would either participate or be acquiescent"; the Asian states must raise "some aspect of the matter" before the United Nations; and the

French must agree to American training of indigenous troops, to a joint command structure, and to not withdraw its Expeditionary Corps, and they must guarantee the independence of the associated states, "including [an] unqualified option to withdraw from the French Union at any time." Laniel must also seek the full endorsement of these conditions by his cabinet and the National Assembly, ensuring a lasting French commitment in the event of a change in government in Paris. Even if the French agreed, American intervention would not immediately follow, because Eisenhower insisted on a congressional resolution. Finally, the United States offered naval and air support, not ground troops.[12]

On 14 May, the day after surviving a vote of no-confidence by two votes, Laniel accepted the conditions in principle but aired his key reservations. First, he expressed dismay at American insistence that the associated states possess the right to withdraw from the French Union. The American refusal to commit ground forces also distressed the premier.[13] As Smith reported after his talks with Bidault, the French provisional acceptance of Washington's conditions did not denote agreement. At the end of the first week of the conference, Smith concluded that the deteriorating French military situation in Laos and the Red River delta, coupled with Laniel's nonacceptance of American conditions for intervention, virtually guaranteed Vietnam's partitioning. Above all, the French sought diplomatic leverage; if the communists, especially the Chinese, sensed any real danger that an anticommunist coalition would be formed to intervene in Indochina, they might prove more pliable in Geneva. This became clear when Bidault suggested that Smith leak the story to the press. "Lightning should not strike," the French foreign minister told him, but "rumbles of distant thunder" could prove most useful.[14] Smith understood that the administration's policy amounted to the same thing; reviving the threat of "distant thunder" strengthened Smith's hand, and should the United States fail to form a coalition for intervention, the administration would have laid the foundation for internationalizing the conflict in the event the talks collapsed. By never totally rejecting intervention but incrementally raising the ante on France, and by promising nothing concrete in return beyond naval and air forces (and then only with international support and congressional sanction), Eisenhower virtually guaranteed that his bluff would never be called. After all, in his younger days, Eisenhower had been such a skillful poker player that he gave it up for bridge, fearing he might lose friends if he took too much money off their hands. In any event, Laniel and Bidault could never agree on fighting a proxy anticommunist war to further an American policy designed to render France dispensable in Indochina.

Someone in the French camp leaked the American conditions, and they appeared in the *New York Times*. An unhappy Eden found out about the new initiative in the press. As Eden noted, Smith was incensed. The story revealed that the United States was moving toward intervention. Worse, the same paper reported a sharp split between Smith and Eden over British refusals to enter discussions on a defense pact.[15] In truth, the Americans never consulted London. Bidault's little plot backfired; the communist delegation hardened its positions, fissures did appear between Smith and Eden, and official negotiations deadlocked for the next two weeks. "Meetings made no progress whatsoever," Smith reported. "Communists appear confident and in no hurry to get down to business."[16] A day later, on 20 May, he wrote, "Communists have not given an inch and I do not believe they will make any concessions. They have a big fish on the hook and they intend to play it out."[17]

Although strained, the Smith-Eden partnership remained firm. Eden later remarked that Smith remained "a splendid friend" throughout the conference.[18] Dulles and the State Department never trusted Eden and concluded that he stood prepared to push the French into a precipitate acceptance of a cease-fire that would lead to a communist seizure of the whole of Indochina.[19] Smith did not see it that way and requested more flexibility in dealing with Eden. He needed to preserve Eden's trust. As happened so often during the war, many in the American camp considered Smith a little too cozy with the British. Walter Robertson, assistant secretary for Far Eastern affairs and Smith's deputy in Geneva, thought Smith preferred Eden's advice to that of his own staff.[20]

Eden's conversations with Zhou convinced him that the Chinese believed the United States would enter the war in any account, and U.S. threats of intervention and talk of creating a regional security coalition rendered political resolution of the Indochina problem doubtful.[21] His assessment proved mostly correct. The Chinese wanted no broadening of the conflict but saw only hostility in American actions. The Central Committee in Beijing believed Smith's intransigence in Geneva was part of a calculated policy to create international tension "for the purpose of further taking over more spheres of influence from Britain and France, of expanding military bases . . . of remaining hostile to our Organization of Defense, and of rearming Japan," all in preparation for war.[22] Chinese diplomacy rested on the twin pillars of breaking the U.S.-Taiwan connection and preventing the formation of a Southeast Asia defense pact. Not so apparent was Beijing's belief that continuation of the Indochina conflict risked a nuclear escalation and favored a settlement, even one unfavorable to the Democratic Republic of Vietnam (DRV; the Vietminh). The Chinese viewed Vietnamese hegemony in Southeast Asia with alarm and favored a "permanent temporary partition," as in Germany and Korea.

Like the French cabinet, Eden saw the Chinese as the fulcrum in the conference. On 20 May he met again with Zhou. Fearing the breakup of the conference, the Chinese foreign minister made an important concession: he agreed to separate military and political matters and admitted that the political settlements might differ for the three Indochinese states. His shift toward the initial French position—undermining Dong's in the process—promised to kick-start the talks. Eden cautioned Zhou that Chinese posturing and violent recriminations against the United States might produce the end China wanted least—U.S. intervention and the formation of an anti-Chinese regional pact. The British foreign minister told his Chinese counterpart that in any confrontation between Beijing and Washington, the British would stand firmly beside their ally.[23]

On 23 May, after another unproductive plenary session, Smith met Molotov over dinner. Smith marveled at the changes in Molotov's negotiating style since Stalin's death. The "old Bolshevik" appeared "completely relaxed, quite friendly, and objective." He made "no charges, by implication or otherwise, no recriminations," Smith reported, "and it was as though he were looking at the whole situation through a magnifying glass." Molotov told Smith he saw no reason why the Americans and Soviets could not solve their many outstanding issues. Turning to the Chinese, Molotov foresaw difficulties—"China is always going to be China, she is never going to be European"—but he made reference to the Korean War, saying that someday the world would discover the restraining influence the Soviet Union had played.[24]

Smith held a news briefing on 27 May. Alluding to the "terrific amount of dust raised about Anglo-American differences," Smith said the only differences involved tactics and timing, not the ultimate objective, which he defined as the "termination of hostilities on [an] honorable basis." He admitted that both the American and British delegations had their "respective positions," and both sides groped "for possible solutions which do not violate our principles," but he categorized the Anglo-American relationship as "extremely good" and noted that he and Eden remained in constant contact. He cautioned the press about expecting a settlement anytime soon. "Dealing with Communists," he pointed out, "takes infinite time. There is unending argument about minutiae." He could never predict if he would encounter complete intransigence or a slight move toward compromise or "find some way out." The next week should be telling, he predicted. "You just cannot ignore [the] fact that

Ho Chi Minh has [a] well-organized, disciplined formidable military force which controls [a] considerable proportion of country. You cannot just wish that out of existence." If the communists stalled and pursued a military solution, he envisaged the talks continuing indefinitely, but not at the ministerial level.[25]

On 25 May Eden proposed handling the three core issues sequentially: first a cease-fire, then a political settlement, and finally the creation of measures for control and supervision. Four days of inconclusive bargaining followed. In the eighth restricted session on 29 May, a breakthrough appeared in the offing. According to the Chinese account, Eden's resolution appeared to be headed for passage when "Smith outrageously stated: 'The government of the United States authorizes me neither to accept nor to object to the principles of the British proposal.'" Smith's statement killed the resolution and revealed the persistent differences between the Americans and the British. "Eden expressed then and there," Zhou told Mao, "that he was not happy with Smith's statement."[26] During the intermission Smith talked with Eden and Lord Reading, the minister of state for foreign affairs and a British delegate, in an effort to explain his position. "Both Eden and Reading gave a startling public exhibition of impatience and pique," Smith reported," including an irate aside by Reading, audible throughout [the] room to [the] effect UK should withdraw its proposal."[27]

Despite what he had told reporters earlier, the gap between the British and American positions had indeed widened. Following instructions, Smith doggedly obstructed progress at Geneva. A gridlocked conference furthered the American objective of forging ahead with united action and, failing that, laying the foundation for some form of Southeast Asian pact. Smith made little headway with Eden because the British foreign secretary believed that any movement toward a collective security agreement heightened Chinese suspicions and weakened rather than strengthened prospects for a salutary outcome in Geneva. Eden knew that Smith acted as Dulles's messenger and was convinced he remained a stalwart ally. Eden told Churchill, "Only Mr. Bedell Smith seemed to have any real comprehension of the reasons which had led us to take our present position."[28] The British did agree to send their chief of staff for a five-power conference in Washington.

Relations with the French remained strained. Smith had known Bidault during the war, when the latter had served as foreign minister in de Gaulle's provisional government. Smith's wartime experience taught him "how extremely touchy and sensitive" the French could be, and it conditioned him to suspect them of "holding out" on him and engaging in "sharp practice." "They have nursed their bruises ever since the war," he told George Kennan, "seeming rather to take pride in the black and blue spots than to make an effort to develop a thicker skin."[29] Smith blamed the lack of firm leadership in Paris for the military situation in Indochina. Any "second rate general," Smith decided, should be able to win, given the proper political guidance from Paris. Following his 23 May meeting with Molotov, Smith fed Bidault information in the strictest confidence that almost immediately found its way into print. An irate Smith accused Bidault of "incredible stupidity" for confiding in his press secretary, and he wired Washington that the episode—following on the earlier leak—"demonstrates [the] practical impossibility of speaking to [the] French with anything like real frankness."[30]

Nevertheless, Smith engaged in some frank talk with the French delegation. He told Bidault's deputy that Washington felt predisposed to support the French position, but the time was rapidly approaching when Paris must make some hard decisions, referring to Laniel's delay in unreservedly accepting American conditions for united action.[31] From his arrival in Geneva on 3 May, Smith recognized the terrible pressure Bidault was laboring under. Smith warned Dulles not to push the French too hard on the issue of guaranteeing the associated states' right to withdraw from the French Union. Pressuring the Laniel government "would not produce sufficiently favorable effects in Vietnam to counterbalance undoubted adverse effects, including diminished support [of the] French Assembly and public opinion."[32] The State Department responded by telling Smith to treat Bidault with kid gloves and avoid doing anything that might intensify French desires to quit Indochina entirely.

On 5 June Smith met with Percy Spender, the Australian ambassador who was en route back to Washington, and with New Zealand's delegate in Geneva, Alistar McIntosh. Washington put high store in wooing Australia and New Zealand away from the British position on Southeast Asia. Smith provided the ANZUS partners with confidential information "about the French-American talks regarding conditions on which American intervention in Indo-China might conceivably take place." Because the French had rebuffed the American conditions, Smith reassured the two diplomats that the United States would take no "hasty action." Smith complained that his "hands are completely tied by Dulles." On the negotiations in Geneva, Smith proved "very pessimistic" about French prospects of achieving "any reasonable settlement," and he detected a noticeable hardening in the Soviet stance following Molotov's return from a short visit to Moscow in late May.[33]

The next day Dulles revealed the state of play to a tired Spender in Washington. He set the odds at fifty-fifty that a settlement would emerge in Geneva, and contrary to the impression Smith had given Spender, Dulles made it clear that the United States now desired a settlement. Dulles confirmed that Smith had performed his difficult role extremely well. Since the United States possessed little negotiating power, Smith's job involved keeping the communists guessing about American intentions, including "the doubt that if they overplayed their hand they might find themselves in armed conflict with United States." Smith came under attack not only in the international press but also in friendly capitals because of the apparent "uncertainties" in American policy. Dulles assured Spender that the United States possessed a clear set of policy objectives and that this appearance of uncertainty "was one of the few factors which would impel the Communists to agree upon some settlement in Indochina." Both Dulles and Smith, in their private conversations with Molotov, urged the Soviets to restrain the Chinese "if possibilities which could lead to war were to be avoided." Paris remained unprepared to request American intervention and sought to use the threat of American intervention to strengthen the French bargaining position in Geneva. The French wanted "the best settlement they could obtain," and "distant thunder" offered "one of the few cards they had to play."[34]

For the "very private information" of the Australian government, Dulles divulged that the situation on the ground in Indochina and in Geneva in no way resembled the state of affairs exant two months before, rendering the prospect of American intervention "less likely day by day." If the United States decided to commit armed forces, that would occur "within the next week or two," but Dulles saw little prospect of that happening. The Eisenhower administration had made it clear under what circumstances the United States would intervene, and it now appeared highly improbable that these conditions would be met. Dulles assured Spender that the United States would not engage in any unilateral actions. The threat of American intervention remained the only viable negotiating lever.

Dulles concluded, as had Smith, that the "French would in the end be unlikely to hold the Tonkin delta." The Americans had little faith in General Ely or in French capabilities of retaining the Hanoi-Haiphong region. "The French had no alternative than to seek the best possible terms they could at Geneva." In accordance, the American stance in Geneva would change to achieve that outcome. Since Dulles remained convinced that the communists would not be satisfied with northern Vietnam, the State Department stepped up the pressure for a regional defense pact to contain Vietminh gains. Dulles reconciled himself to the loss of the Tonkin delta, "the only position of strength left in Vietnam or indeed in Indochina," and he possessed little confidence that a southern regime would endure; the chief concern now centered on holding Laos and Cambodia. Although Dulles acknowledged the importance of influencing Asian official and public opinion with regard to the threat posed by Chinese expansionism, "we should not allow ourselves to be paralysed from acting because we had not the support of any Asian country for everything we did." Solidarity among the Western powers, especially Britain and the antipodean Commonwealth, mattered most. Since it now became clear that Paris must accept a cease-fire, Smith's tasks focused on helping the French "save what they can from the mess." The Australian ambassador left the meeting convinced that Dulles "has about written off Vietnam as lost."[35]

If the administration had undergone any change of heart, it was not apparent in Geneva. On 6 June the Chinese delegate Wang Bingnan complained to Jean Chauvel, the French ambassador to Bern and delegate to Geneva, of Smith's "no objection, but no acceptance" stance, stating, "this continuing negative attitude against the meeting doesn't do any good to the conference."[36] After a three-week hiatus, the plenary sessions resumed on 8 June. Smith reported that after Molotov's return, his position noticeably hardened. Viewing the political ground slipping from beneath Laniel's feet, the Soviets dragged out the conference in the expectation of increasing the pressure on the French government. Molotov attacked Smith, pointing out that the United States had produced all kinds of pretexts for blocking and delaying any agreements, while holding a chiefs of staff conference in Washington to plan an intervention in Indochina. Zhou made a qualified reversal of his previous stance, stating that the interrelated military and political "cannot be completely separated."[37] During the plenary session on 9 June, Smith presented a prepared statement offering chapter and verse on the Soviet record in eastern Europe since the Nonaggression Pact of 1939. "The solicitude I have heard expressed by Mr. Molotov of the people of South-east Asia," Smith bitingly remarked, "apparently does not extend to the Armenians, the Kazakhs, and Mongol." Earlier Smith had threatened the Soviets and Chinese that he would go to the press with the inside story; he did just that on 8 June, stating that the American motive behind attending the conference centered on getting "a clear-cut decision . . . as to whether the Russians and the Red Chinese were going to talk business, and, if not to cut the thing short and go home, and take what measures had to be taken to stop Commie expansion in Southeast Asia." He resented Molotov and Zhou denigrating the conference, turning it into "a propaganda medium." He revealed that the Soviet foreign minister's initial "indication of a willingness to cooperate, and possibly play the part of the slightly left-of-center middleman . . . has vanished."[38]

On 9 June Eden expressed to Smith his extreme pessimism and his belief that the talks would likely recess within a few days. A frustrated Eden told the next day's session that, given their inability to narrow their divergent views, "I think it is our clear-cut duty to say so to the world and to admit that we have failed."[39] That was the verdict in Washington in well. As was his custom during the war, Smith showed Eden selected secret wires from Washington. "Bedell Smith," Eden later divulged, "showed me a telegram from President Eisenhower advising him to do everything in his power to bring the conference to an end as rapidly as possible, on the grounds that the Communists were only spinning things out to suit their own military purposes."[40]

Between 3 and 11 June the chiefs of staff of the United States, United Kingdom, France, Australia, and New Zealand meet in the Pentagon. These five-power talks concluded, "The maintenance of internal security and national independence in South-East Asia is of great significance." The first order of business focused on preventing a "severe reverse" in the Tonkin delta in the face of an expected Vietminh offensive in September. The conference concluded that three "outside" divisions and 300 carrier-based aircraft could hold the delta. In the event of the insertion of "outside" forces, the military objective remained the destruction of Vietminh forces and securing the rest of Indochina, which implied an additional and expanding military commitment. An intervention would not enjoy the sanction of the United Nations or Asian states other than Thailand and the Philippines. Success was contingent on a number of factors, chief among them the Chinese reaction. A Korea-like Chinese entry into the struggle would trigger immediate air attacks on Chinese military targets and a naval blockade. "To achieve a maximum and lasting effect," the Australian summary stated, "nuclear as well as conventional weapons should be used from the onset." Inadequate ground forces, the internal weaknesses of the associated states and Thailand, and the absence of natural barriers—even with the resort to nuclear weapons—would result in the loss of Indochina and Thailand. The chiefs reckoned on a "stop-line" on the narrow Kra peninsula in southernmost Thailand. The conference never concluded whether a Soviet intervention was probable or problematic.[41]

The chief of the Australian army, LTG Sydney Rowell, relayed his observations of the five-power talks. In his view, the Americans acted too cavalier about the potential for broadening the war. "The United States was quite contemptuous of the Russians and did not think that they would come in even if the Chinese got involved." Rowell told the American chiefs that they "were on their own on this point." Rowell also pointed to mixed messages coming from the British. The cabinet was reported as "disturbed . . . that nuclear weapons would be used in the event of war with China," yet their chief of staff, GEN John Harding, "had not expressed the slightest doubts on this point and had in fact agreed that nuclear weapons should be used." Although GEN Nathan Twining, the U.S. Air Force chief, wanted "to have a crack at the Chinese," Rowell believed the American proposals for action in the delta "had been a project of Radford himself." Ridgway "did not conceal his complete opposition to the whole operation."[42]

On 9 June Dulles informed Smith that the United States "could not allow the French to have a continuing option on the situation." At this late stage, the United States must "take into account that with the passage of time and the increasing deterioration of the situation, what was possible at the time of our original proposal could become impossible."[43] Three days later the Laniel government fell to a vote of no confidence, and with it, any realistic hope of forging united action disappeared. On 14 June Smith signaled that he would leave Geneva.

Smith's announcement, Eden's pronouncement, and word that Churchill intended to visit Washington for talks with Eisenhower threatened to collapse the conference and prompted Molotov and Zhou to make concessions in the hope of saving it. In private talks on 16 June, Eden asked Zhou if the Vietminh might withdraw troops from Laos and Cambodia; Zhou replied that it would "not be difficult" if all foreign forces withdrew. China might even recognize the royal governments and agree to allow them to retain ties to the French Union if the United States promised not to establish bases in Indochina. Zhou indicated that the Vietminh were entitled to all of the Tonkin delta, and if they got it, they would soften their demands for territorial concessions in southern Indochina. "What Chou really wanted," Eden told Smith, "was the Geneva Powers to guarantee three little buffer countries to the south of the Tonkin Delta."[44] On his own initiative, Smith announced during the 16 June restricted session that Zhou's six-point comprehensive peace plan (focusing mainly on Laos and the Cambodian situation) "contain[s] a basis for discussion." During the recess, Smith told Molotov he considered Zhou's proposals worthy of careful consideration, and with the addition of proper safeguards, he would not speak against them. He reiterated that the United States had no intention of constructing military bases in Indochina. In his telegram to Washington, Smith indicated he had "listened with interest to [the] Chinese statement which seemed . . . restrained and reasonable." Smith added that "at first glance there appeared to be certain points in [the] Chinese proposal which might be agreed to."[45] Smith also reported that Eden "received a strong impression that he [Zhou] wanted a settlement and I accordingly urged Georges Bidault to have a talk with him and to discuss this new offer."[46] The next day Bidault conferred with Zhou for the first time, as well as with Molotov, and reported that the communists were in a state of great apprehension over the breakup of the conference. Two days later Molotov met with Smith, confirming Soviet support for agreements on Laos and Cambodia. Smith reported that Molotov saw no great obstacle to the Vietminh pulling out its "volunteers."[47]

The thaw came too late. In the next restricted session Smith absented himself, and his deputy, U. Alexis Johnson, denigrated Zhou's offer, under instructions from Washington. Zhou stressed the contradictions in the U.S. position. He pointed out that Johnson's statement differed from Smith's and expressed his understanding that Johnson's duty hinged on instigating controversy. For himself, he would emphasize conciliation in pursuit of an agreement in principle. Wang concluded "that US officials were not a monolithic bloc; Smith, for instance, had his own views."[48] That same day, on 16 May, the National Assembly approved Mèndes-France as premier and foreign minister. He promised a satisfactory end of the war by 20 July. Using the end of the Korean portion of the conference as a pretext, Smith announced that he would leave for Washington on 19 May; many wondered whether he would return.

Feeling the "time had come to sound a note of warning," Smith paid Molotov a visit before he left. The Soviet foreign minister turned the tables on him. Using unvarnished words, Molotov told Smith the United States had isolated itself in the conference. Except for the Americans, "among other delegations present . . . there seemed to be real willingness to reach agreement." Indeed, Zhou's acceptance of Eden's prosposals on a Vietminh withdrawal from Laos and Cambodia and for dealing with the three national questions separately—essentially accepting the original French proposal—represented a significant concession. When Smith said the "US was not one of the principals to [the] Indochinese dispute and did not cast [the] deciding vote," Molotov replied, "Maybe so, but you have [a] veto, that word I hear you use so often." Molotov warned Smith that if the United States continued to take "a one-sided view and insist on one-sided solutions," the conference would collapse. Molotov said the French, not the Vietminh, were making extravagant claims, especially in the Red River delta. He pointed out that the French retained Hanoi and Haiphong only at the sufferance of the Vietminh. In reference to France's territorial claims in both north and south Vietnam, Molotov cited an old Russian proverb: "If you try to chase two rabbits at once you are apt to miss both of them." Smith reported that Molotov appeared to be entirely certain of his position on the delta, Laos, and Cambodia, confirming "Communist intentions to play all the cards they held." Judging from his summary, other than repeating that the United States found "partition repugnant," Smith said little in refutation.[49] Prospects for a resumption of talks at the ministerial level looked bleak.

"Go to Your Corners" and Round Two

Dulles thought Smith should find a nice fishing camp, take a much needed break, and restore his energies before coming back to Washington. Smith thought otherwise. He first flew to Paris and met Mèndes-France at the Quai d'Orsay. The French had been engaged in "underground" negotiations with the Vietminh on arranging a military settlement. Smith emphasized the importance of making no agreements "so that we would not be suddenly faced with a solution from which we would have to publicly disassociate ourselves." Mèndes-France assured Smith that the French delegation in Geneva would keep the Americans apprised of developments.[50] For the third time, Smith turned down an invitation to go to England for talks with Churchill. Eden opposed the two old war buddies getting together; he was not afraid of Smith's influencing the prime minister, but the other way around. Smith's latest refusal stemmed from apprehensions about facing a hostile British press.[51]

Without any respite, Smith met with the congressional leadership at the White House on his first full day back, outlining his grim assessment of the situation. Smith told the president and the thirty gathered congressmen that the conference had run in three cycles: at first, Eden worked for a compromise, Bidault retained "a strong and courageous stand," and the communists remained unbending and unruffled; then, starting on 29 May, the French attempted an end run, conducting underground talks with the Vietminh; finally, after the fall of the Laniel government and Eden's dramatic pronouncement that the conference had failed, the communists employed a new tactic of "apparent conciliation," offering "minor shifts from inflexible positions." He predicted the communists would propose, and the British, French, and associated states would accept, a partition of Vietnam and Laos and an ineffective international supervisory commission, leaving the Vietminh in the position to secure more gains "in the future at such time as the Communists decide." Smith thought Ho Chi Minh would win 80 percent of the vote if free elections were held. When Senator William Knowland, the powerful majority leader, attacked Smith and his conduct of the Geneva conference, declaring it another Munich, Smith angrily replied that no such parallel existed. The Vietminh would gain nothing at Geneva they had not won on the battlefield.[52]

That afternoon, 23 June, Smith held talks with the Australian ambassador, Spender. Smith reported his complete agreement with the findings of the five-power talks. He emphasized the United States would not intervene in Indochina, except possibly to "rescue French forces" in the event of a collapse in the delta. Giving an indication that he planned to return to Geneva, he said his objective now revolved around the difficult task of securing "the best settlement possible." Though admitting that "the Communists were negotiating from strength and knew it," he still entertained hopes of saving a French enclave around Haiphong. Smith then showed Spender a memo he had just completed, "expressing his judgment the United States should directly associate herself with whatever settlement was reached however unpalatable." Spender assumed correctly that "the purpose of the memorandum was to influence Dulles who has been reluctant to commit himself to this proposition." Smith concluded by emphasizing the vital role Australia would play in a regional defensive framework in Southeast Asia.[53]

Smith submitted his memo for Dulles's consideration. Smith appreciated the administration's domestic concerns but concluded that the United States had "no choice other than reluctantly to accept, whether by association or otherwise, the general results of the military defeat," suggesting "it should be our endeavor, at least from a long-term foreign policy point of view, not only to obtain through diplomatic united action as good a settlement as possible, but also to see to it, by participation in the guaranteeing of the settlement, that the other side is not tempted by the weakness and disunity of the opposition to violate the settlement reached." He argued the United States should actively preserve what remained of Indochina's important military and political assets. "I cannot escape the feeling that for us to disassociate ourselves from the harsh reality," Smith concluded, "would accelerate Communist momentum in Southeast Asia, decrease the prestige of the U.S. as a realistic, responsible and reliable ally in the long period of struggle ahead, and thus possibly discredit or weaken our capacity to conduct U.S. foreign policy."[54]

For the next month debate continued over whether Smith would return to Geneva. Smith's line of reasoning made a strong impression, but Eisenhower and Dulles could not easily dismiss the domestic political fallout from being associated with another perceived Munich or Yalta. Every day millions of Americans tuned in to the televised McCarthy hearings. Polls indicated that half the American public viewed McCarthy and his anticommunist crusade favorably. In February the Eisenhower administration, by the narrowest of margins, succeeded in blocking the Bricker amendment. John Bricker, a conservative senator from Ohio and the embodiment of the Republican Old Guard, had sponsored legislation that would have placed serious limits on the president's conduct of foreign policy, specifically restricting the scope of treaty making. Conservatives in both parties rallied around the call for "no more Yaltas." The year before, Smith and Bricker had engaged in a heated public exchange following Smith's speech attacking the pending legislation.[55] Bricker received broad bipartisan support, but his bill failed to win the required two-thirds majority by a single vote. Having just dodged Bricker's bullet, mostly due to Democrats uniting against the amendment, Eisenhower and Dulles shrank from raising the hackles of conservatives in their own party by entering into any agreements with the communists in Indochina.[56]

The intense wrangle over the Bricker amendment also explains Eisenhower's resort to covert operations. Less than a week after Smith's return, the administration had cause for celebration: the CIA succeeded in forcing Arbenz's resignation and flight from Guatemala. As in Iran, the CIA operation had initially appeared destined for failure; the "Army of Liberation" amounted to no more than 400 ragtag volunteers. The pirate air force caused some alarm, but the unanticipated triumph derived mostly from the success of the "Voice of Liberation" and its black propaganda broadcasts, which convinced a rattled Arbenz that the American naval blockade portended the landing of marines. The Guatemalan army withdrew its support, and a tearful Arbenz announced his resignation on 27 June. Smith took great satisfaction from his central role in removing the "Communist beachhead" in Latin America.

Guatemala aside, Eisenhower had other reasons for quiet celebration. On 25 June Churchill and Eden arrived in Washington. The two leaders agreed to form a joint study committee charged with laying the foundation for a future collective security pact for Southeast Asia. Churchill and Eden lobbied hard for American agreement to sign any accord coming out of Geneva, but Eisenhower and Dulles refused; however, they did agree to dispatch a joint declaration to Paris indicating that the United States and Britain might accept a partition, provided the usual preconditions were met. This time, the list included seven principles, most notably that Laos, Cambodia, and southern Vietnam face no impediment in establishing and maintaining stable, noncommunist governments, with effective international machinery to enforce any agreement. The British eventually offered a firm commitment to join the future Southeast Asia Treaty Organization (SEATO), in the words of Eden, as a "sop" to gain American acquiescence on a settlement in Geneva.[57]

Partition predetermined the official American attitude toward the settlement. As Dulles made clear to Eden, the United States almost certainly would not guarantee any Geneva agreement. If the seven-point agreement proved sufficiently strong, and if the French secured a partition arrangement, the United States would not block the proceedings in Geneva. Refusing any association with an agreement that ceded territory to the communists, the communication to Mèndes-France informed him that a low-ranking "observer" would represent the United States in the next round. Smith would not return to Geneva.

The French pleaded with Washington to return a senior diplomat to Geneva; if the United States agreed to do so, Paris assured that "the United States will *not* be asked or expected by France to respect terms which in its opinion differ materially from the attached [seven points], and it may publicly disassociate itself from such differing terms." Dulles argued that Smith should not return to the conference, but Eisenhower, concluding that an American refusal would only add fuel to the domestic political flames, leaned toward sending him back.[58] In a letter to the French premier, Dulles expressed doubts about Smith's return to Geneva. Because the Western powers had failed to forge a united front, "the events at Geneva will expose differences under conditions which will only serve to accentuate them with consequent strain upon the relations between our two countries."[59] Reports from Geneva and on the ground in Indochina left little room for optimism. "The French position is crumbling alarmingly," Eisenhower wrote to Churchill on 12 July. The president considered pulling out of the Geneva talks altogether. Fearing the appearance of a rupture between the United States and its European allies, Eisenhower wanted "to avoid getting into a position at Geneva where we should be forced to disassociate ourselves publicly and on the basis of principle from a settlement which the French feel they had to take."[60] Mèndes-France asked Dulles to come to Geneva for talks; Dulles refused. As reported in *Time*, "To come to Geneva only to 'walk out' again after his conversations, [Dulles] felt, would damage the already weakened French position and provide grist for the Red propagandists." Mèndes-France offered a meeting in Paris. After mulling it over, Eisenhower and Dulles agreed.[61]

The next evening, 13 July, Dulles met Mèndes-France and Eden for dinner at the Hôtel de Matignon, the premier's official residence. Their conversations lasted until after midnight. Mèndes-France outlined what he thought he might achieve in Geneva and how much he stood prepared to sacrifice. He assured Dulles he intended to make no surrender and would accept only a reasonable settlement, but he insisted on Smith's return; without an American ministerial-level representative, Mèndes-France bluntly said, no hope existed for a settlement. If France signed an armistice, Mèndes-France did not expect any pronouncement of American approval. If the conference collapsed, France would continue the war and join the regional defense treaty. Though impressed by what Mèndes-France had to say, Dulles promised only to think the matter over. Returning to the embassy, Dulles, like the good lawyer he was, took out his legal pad and listed the pluses and minuses. The next morning he talked to Eisenhower via telephone. After hearing Dulles's synopsis of what had transpired, Eisenhower decided to send Smith back to Geneva to note, but not guarantee, any agreement. At long last, it appeared that the three Western powers had arrived at a common position.

As events soon proved, so too had the other side. On 9 July Chauvel reported to Johnson, who pinch hit for Smith as head of the U.S. delegation, on his "very cordial" dinner with Zheng Wentian, the Chinese ambassador to Moscow and vice minister for foreign affairs. Zheng told Chauvel that although the Vietminh continued to make "unacceptable proposals wholly out of harmony with . . . Zhou's position," the Chinese foreign minister had had a "very good meeting" with Ho Chi Minh, and the results "would be helpful to French."[62] During the recess, Zhou had extorted Ho's promise that the Vietminh would return to Geneva and make the necessary concessions.

In the days preceding Smith's departure, Zhou met with Molotov and Dong, convincing them of the need to settle the key military issues. On 20 June the Central Committee of the Chinese Communist Party issued an invitation to Ho Chi Minh and GEN Vo Nguyen Giap "to discuss the situation related to the negotiations and the question of the division of zones, so that consensus will be reached and that progress will be made in . . . Geneva."[63] Between 2 and 5 July Zhou held a conference with the Vietminh Central Committee at Liuzhou in southern China. On 5 July the Soviet embassy in Beijing informed Mao that the Central Committee in Moscow "considers it necessary to take advantage of the favourable circumstances developing in France to find a resolution of the Indochina question." The Soviet chargé d'affaires reported that Mao "considers us to be absolutely correct in seeking" a settlement in

Geneva.[64] Although sources on the Liuzhou meeting remain closed, the sudden and dramatic shift in the Vietminh position on the key roadblock issues—the partition line, Laos, and the regroupment areas—indicates that the Vietnamese received an offer they could not refuse. Beijing acted as the chief paymaster of the Vietminh, and the DRV depended on Chinese materiel aid. The specifics of what transpired at Liuzhou remain clouded, but the results soon manifested themselves in Geneva.

When Zhou and Molotov returned to Geneva, they held a series of talks first with Eden and then with Mèndes-France. On 13 July Zhou informed Eden that if the French reconsidered their demand for the eighteenth parallel as the partition line, "the Vietnamese side is willing to make more concessions for a French move." As he told the British foreign secretary, Zhou "exchanged with Chairman Ho Chi Minh our opinions on the issues of Vietnam, Laos, Cambodia, and peace in Southeast Asia, and in the end we achieved a common understanding. I trust that Mr. Eden would be delighted to hear this." He stated his full confidence that the road was now open for harmonizing the positions of China, the USSR, the DRV, France, and Britain. "Everyone hopes for a resolution," Eden replied, "and when I say this I include Washington." Eden confided in Zhou that his American friends thought he had been deceived by Chinese assurances that Beijing possessed no territorial designs in Southeast Asia, "but we are willing to take the risk," he said.[65]

On 17 July Smith returned to Geneva. His return set off a series of meetings. Before getting together with Smith, Eden met again with Zhou. This time, Zhou raised concerns about the Southeast Asia defense pact and its inclusion of Vietnam, Laos, and Cambodia. He wondered whether the Americans had pursued the alliance to sabotage the agreement. The Chinese saw the regional pact as a precursor to new hostilities. Eden told the Chinese that the Americans would not like *any* agreement, but he expressed the hope that they would at least issue a positive statement. "This is what we are trying our best to urge them to do," Eden stated. To the best of Eden's recollection, no mention had been made of including the three Indochinese states in the pact, and he reassured Zhou that the United States had no intention of establishing military bases in any of the states.[66] Zhou then met with Mèndes-France, and they agreed "our opinions are gradually getting closer now," with only two outstanding issues—the demarcation lines and the timing of elections. With Mèndes-France's deadline only three days off, Zhou assured the French premier, "we wanted to push the conference forward for a settlement."[67] Eden and Mèndes-France briefed Smith on their talks with Zhou. Afterward, Smith went to Eden's villa for a private chat.

Smith pushed hard for a firm British commitment on forming SEATO, but the foreign secretary deferred until he could communicate with the Commonwealth states and India. Although Smith expressed deep suspicions about the communists' sudden conversion, he confirmed that the United States would not construct bases in Indochina and would not insist on membership in SEATO for Vietnam, Laos, and Cambodia.[68]

Eden went to work allaying the communists' doubts about American intentions. He met with Molotov and dispatched a member of the British delegation, Harold Caccia, to Moscow for talks with Zheng. Eden and Caccia made the same points: if the Geneva conference could reach an armistice agreement acceptable to all the participants, the establishment of foreign military bases in the three countries of Indochina and the participation of the three countries in a Southeast Asia defense pact would never happen. Both British officials offered strong warnings against engaging in any histrionics at Smith's expense. After Eden's meeting with Molotov, the Soviet foreign minister held talks with Mèndes-France, assuring the French premier that the Soviets fully backed an immediate agreement on the cease-fire.

When journalists asked Smith what communications he had had with Zhou, Smith joked, "The only contact, if you can call it that, was when we were in the men's room and used the same towel." In fact, Smith had decided to engage in some personal diplomacy, skirting the strict prohibition on contact with Chinese officials. During a coffee break in his first session, Smith approached the Chinese translator. The Chinese delegation stood in stunned silence as Smith complimented the linguist on his beautifully spoken English "with just the right American accent." He then effusively praised China's ancient civilization. Just as Smith had intended, the Chinese delegation saw in this "extraordinary gesture" a possibility for a breakthrough. When informed of these events, Zhou remarked, "Since Smith is ready and willing to talk to us, let me reciprocate during tomorrow's break."[69]

All these maneuvers transpired before the restricted session on 18 July. With Molotov in the chair, he opened the session by summarizing the results of the four-cornered private discussions and expressed his belief that if all the parties displayed genuine sincerity, "today's session will help to move forward the solution of problems." The French and Soviet delegations outlined a joint draft on the demarcation line; only minor differences divided the French and Vietminh on military questions. The French had engaged in a series of secret negotiations with the Vietminh, Russians, and Chinese, agreeing on a compromise line at the seventeenth parallel, without consulting the Saigon delegation. Upon hearing of the proposed partition, Tran Van Do, head of the Vietnamese delegation, protested vigorously. Smith then made his statement: "The attitude of the United States toward the Geneva Conference has consistently been that it is willing to assist in arriving at an honorable settlement. Such a settlement will contribute to the maintenance of peace in the area. The United States is not a belligerent in this conflict and is also not willing to impose its will upon others." He continued, "If the agreement concluded here can be accepted by the American government," it would "declare unilaterally that, in accordance with its obligations under the United Nations Charter Articles II and IV, it will refrain from the threat or the use of violence to disturb this agreement."[70]

Smith's statement cleared the way for the rapid conclusion of the conference. Molotov called for an intermission, and the delegates headed for the bar, where, as the Chinese reported, they "energetically carried out diplomatic activities." When Smith went to the bar, Zhou made his move. Smith saw the Chinese foreign minister approaching, hand outstretched. American diplomats were under orders not to shake the hand of any Chinese official. Smith hastily grabbed his drink with his right hand, and in his left he held a cigar—skillfully avoiding any handshaking. "But he was all smiles," a Chinese official remembered, "and he greeted the premier and chatted politely." Smith again talked about Chinese culture and told Zhou about his growing collection of Chinese porcelain. Beyond the idle chatting, Smith said, "I hope that our two countries can move toward a better mutual understanding." Smith indicated the Americans now desired a workable settlement. After Smith sidled away, Eden buttonholed Zhou, hinting that he should not derail the general good feelings by any long-winded speech and reminded his Chinese counterpart that only a few unresolved problems remained—the issues of the partition line, election dates, and Laos. Zhou raised the issue of the composition of the Neutral Nations Supervisory Commission (NNSC) and inquired whether Eden knew about the latest French proposal. Eden said that he did and that he agreed on India as the chair plus Poland and Canada. Zhou readily assented. When the session resumed, Eden and Mèndes-France saw no reason to continue with that day's meeting. Molotov and Zhou concurred, and after settling on the wording of the communiqué, the two chairmen called for an adjournment.[71]

After all the bitterness in Geneva, first in the gridlocked Korean portion and then during the Indochinese phase, the sudden atmosphere of what Smith termed "sweetness and light" produced a race to finalize a settlement that left the delegates a little woozy. Zhou still entertained doubts about the genuineness of Smith's promises. The Cambodians assured him that Smith had refuted any American desire for bases and had even offered economic aid. "Smith can speak like that," Zhou told the Cambodian foreign minister. "However, there are still people like Radford and Vice President Nixon in the American government."[72] Despite lingering mutual mistrust, a final accord emerged on 21 July, only four days after Smith's return. The settlement provided for an immediate cease-fire, a separation of French and Vietminh forces along the seventeenth parallel, and the formation of an NNSC charged with overseeing the armistice and troop withdrawals. Representatives of the DRV and South Vietnam would meet in a year to iron out the details of a general all-Vietnam election set for July 1956. The final settlement mirrored the first French proposal—a military agreement and future negotiations over a final political solution.

Before leaving Geneva, Smith took the initiative and approached Zhou. "As the conference draws to an end, I am very pleased and honoured to be able to make your acquaintance," Smith said. "You have played a major role at this conference. Whether it is Korea or Vietnam, we hope that peace will be restored." He then reached out and, abiding by Dulles's ban on handshaking, shook the Chinese premier's arm, grinned broadly, and walked away.[73]

Despite Smith's pleas for an American guarantee, Eisenhower and Dulles could not bring themselves to associate the United States with the conference declaration, mostly due to apprehension over the domestic political repercussions. In his statement of 21 July, Eisenhower repeated Smith's promise that the United States would not "use force to disturb the settlement" and came close to underwriting the accords by adding that his administration would consider any violation by the other actors a grave matter.[74] Smith had fulfilled his mandate: an "honorable" French retreat, the recognition of Laos and Cambodia as sovereign states, and a provisional partition. Plus, he had helped steer a settlement without associating the administration too closely with its outcome. Finally, as Smith reported on 19 July, the Churchill government agreed to join a Southeast Asia defense pact.[75]

In the end, Eisenhower proved the correctness of his Micawber approach to problem solving. As he remarked in another crisis, experience had taught him that in periods of great stress, "the calamities that we anticipate never really occur," thus confirming what he had always known: sometimes the best decisions are those you never make.[76] The final outcome amounted to a qualified American diplomatic success and represented the last hurrah of the Ike-Beetle team.

★ **5** ★

"Ike's Prat Boy"

Geneva provided the final impetus, spurring Smith's resignation. Never happy serving under Dulles, Smith would have quit long before if not for Geneva. The stress of the first round of the Geneva talks had undermined his health. He joked with journalists he could easily see himself wandering the corridors of the Hôtel du Rhône—where the American delegation (really a miniature State Department) had its headquarters—with a long white beard.[1] Later he assured them that Geneva would not devolve into another Panmunjom. Originally intended to last six weeks, the Korean talks ended up taking twenty-seven months. Smith pointedly said he would not last that long. The deterioration in Smith's health had factored into Eisenhower and Dulles's thinking about sending him back to Geneva. As always, when duty called, Smith completed his task, gave his recommendations—which were rejected—and decided he had finally had enough.

He tendered his resignation on 17 August, effective 1 October, but he asked for "an earlier date if this should be convenient." The president expressed his "greatest reluctance and sincere regret" when he informed Smith that "the best interests of the United States" would not allow him to leave before the first of October. Smith also noted that the terms of his new private-sector job made it possible for him to do "temporary work for the government from time to time" and told the president, "if I can continue to be useful to you in this way it will make me very happy." Eisenhower assured Beetle that he planned to take him up on this offer, observing, "[you give] so completely of yourself to your country that I know you will answer every call promptly and cheerfully and with your never-failing devotion and abilities." The president conveyed his sense of "deep personal and official obligation" for the friendship and advice Smith had provided in peace and in war, which served as

95

"a mainstay to me in trying and difficult times." He extended to Smith and his wife Nory (he misspelled her name) his best wishes on this well-deserved furlough from government service but reminded him, "in the Army a furlough has meant only a respite from active duty."[2]

The president kept Smith's nose to the grindstone for the duration of his tenure. The chief anxiety fixed on Europe. Before Smith left Geneva, he held two meetings with Mèndes-France on the issue of the EDC. The French premier told Smith he would push hard in the National Assembly to win approval for French participation.[3] Initially proposed by France, the EDC offered an alternative to German rearmament by forming a pan-European defense force. The Right and Left both opposed the EDC—for very different reasons—and on 30 August the new French government failed to ratify the 1952 treaty. Eisenhower solicited Smith's advice on policy alternatives on 3 September. Four days later Eisenhower wrote a letter to Churchill, prompted by the apprehension that the death of the EDC might drive "a wedge between ourselves and our principal European allies, especially Britain," and he asked Smith to edit it. "Keeping in mind the principal objectives of the EDC package," Smith replied on 10 September, "we are considering two alternative approaches." The first would bring Germany into NATO after it met "certain voluntary commitments" as a condition for its admission; concurrently, the United States would move toward granting West German sovereignty. The second alternative, if the French blocked the first option, was to forge an agreement among the United States, the United Kingdom (which was not a party to the EDC), Germany, and possibly the Benelux countries and Italy, but excluding France and permitting German rearmament. Smith predicted, "These steps might induce a welcome change in the French position"[4] A week in Walter Reed explains Smith's tardiness in responding.

Before he left the job, Smith had one final opportunity to fire a salvo across the bows of the Dulles brothers. Beijing failed to block the movement toward a Southeast Asia defense pact but now embarked on an effort to fulfill the second plank of its foreign policy agenda, placing pressure on U.S.-Taiwan ties. In August the Nationalists reinforced Quemoy and Matsu islands, and the Chinese reciprocated by shelling the islands. Zhou declared that Taiwan must be liberated.

Reminiscent of the Dien Bien Phu debate, the NSC weighed the options. Dulles argued that the United States must defend the islands, even if they had no military value (assuming they were defensible), and Congress agreed. Smith rejected both the CIA assessment and John Foster Dulles's evaluation, instead supporting the Pentagon's conclusions.

Smith believed the Chinese would make a determined effort to capture the islands, even if they were convinced the United States would commit its armed forces to defending them. And he believed the Chinese could succeed if they were prepared to pay the price in heavy casualties. Though admitting that loss of the islands would represent a blow to American prestige, Smith doubted that Quemoy was "so vitally important" as to require the commitment of U.S. ground forces. He offered another option: the United States should dispatch no ground units but reinforce Taiwanese artillery and antiaircraft defenses while deploying the Seventh Fleet and announcing that the lines of communication would be kept open, but without disclosing American intentions. He thought Beijing would "deduce that more was meant by such a statement than we actually had in mind." In his view, the threat of American intervention would dissuade the Chinese from actually invading. The JCS universally supported Smith's views. The NSC sanctioned the possible use of nuclear weapons three days later, on 12 September, but rejected the commitment of ground forces. The first Taiwan crisis lingered, but Smith's policy guidelines, which were obviously in accord with the president's preferences, were generally followed and proved successful in defusing the emergency.[5]

After the State Department

Smith's retirement prompted a series of farewell fêtes. The doyens of the Washington press corps invited Smith to another off-the-record dinner on 17 September. When Beetle arrived, he asked for tomato juice but was obviously relieved when told there was none, so he ordered a "weak old-fashioned" instead. Smith took the gloves off in these sessions. Preoccupied with the situation in Europe, he lamented, "The trouble is we are betting on old men amongst our strongest allies," referring to Churchill and Konrad Adenauer of West Germany. He expected it would not "be too long before Eden succeeded Churchill, not because of the old man's retirement but because of something more final than that." This prediction missed the mark; the "old man" outlived Smith by four years. Mèndes-France's failure to secure ratification of the EDC launched Smith into a long tirade. "I was had," Smith said. He called Mèndes-France "a lying son of a bitch" whose family was "loaded with Communists or crypto-Communists" and whose advisers consisted of "crack-pots, perverts and assorted nuts." In Geneva the French premier had assured Smith he could pass the EDC "with a decent majority, and without any concessions or changes that would require the other signatories to renegotiate the treaty in their parliaments." Smith saw Mèndes-France as anti-American and deluded in thinking he could "do business with Russia." Shaking his head, Smith again declaimed, "I was had!"[6]

On 22 September Cutler hosted an event aboard the *Sequoia*, the secretary of the navy's official yacht. Vacationing in Denver, Eisenhower sent his regrets, reminding Cutler, "your party this evening does not signify a farewell, but only a change in our particular kind of association." He was sure Smith understood that, "through some means, however devious, we will find ways of profiting from his wisdom, his dedication, and his sense of humor."[7]

The day before he left office, Smith made a plea to the American people to support Eisenhower and Dulles in their foreign policy efforts. He provided the press with an audit of where the United States stood in its confrontation with the Soviets and the Chinese. Smith assured them, "The West has succeeded in maintaining a balance of power with the Soviet bloc." "After forty-four years of service to his country," the *New York Times* reported, "Walter Bedell Smith quietly resigned last week as Under Secretary of State. A spare, gaunt, tired and slightly snappy 59-year-old soldier . . . General Smith went out as he came in—talking straight and making sense."[8]

As *Time* reported, the "able, prickly" Smith left "government work because 1) he is not in good health, and 2) he wants to make some money." Three days after he resigned, Smith joined the board of American Machine & Foundry as executive vice president.[9] Smith knew more than a little about machines and foundries; he had gone to work as a teenager in a car factory and had received training in high school as a machinist. Within a month of resigning, Smith indecorously joined the board of United Fruit, a reward for engineering the Arbenz overthrow. An ardent collector, Smith now stockpiled corporate board memberships. He served as president and chairman of AMF Atomics and Associated Missile Products, as well as board member of Radio Corporation of America and Corning Glass.[10] In 1959 Illinois senator Paul Douglas attacked the procurement abuses in the Department of Defense, showing that 88 of the nation's top 100 defense contractors employed 721 former officers ranked colonel and above.[11] In his last major address before leaving office, Eisenhower famously warned of the formation of a "military-industrial complex." Smith stood as one of the prime exemplars of a former senior officer who exploited his military and government connections for financial gain. Eisenhower took him at his word and appointed Smith to six presidential committees; four of them dealt with procurement and disarmament.[12] An outspoken advocate of nuclear deterrence, Smith's position as chief executive of two firms holding large Pentagon contracts clearly crossed the line between special interests and something worse.

In Smith's estimate, he had grown up underprivileged and saw no reason why he should spend the rest of his life on a pension. During his wartime service, questions arose about Smith's misappropriation of funds; word spread that he had even seriously suggested distributing looted Nazi gold as bonuses for senior officers. An inveterate hoarder since childhood, Smith collected all manner of objects, from primitive weapons and ancient coins to expensive art pieces and various forms of exotica, all as souvenirs of his travels. Visitors always remarked on his good taste. Now he collected money. When he died, Smith left an estate valued at nearly $2.5 million. He never derived much pleasure from his newfound wealth; he and Nory lived modestly. In 1951 the Social Register in Washington added his name, but Smith shunned parties and social functions unless they were "absolute 'musts' from the official point of view." He much preferred to remain at home, either in the company of his wife or, more likely, engaged in private reading, working on his home-crafted fishing rods and flies, gardening, and even needlepointing.[13]

After Smith left the State Department, he consented to serve as cochairman of the American delegation to what became known as the Bilderberg Group. The Bilderberg movement originated in the mind of Joseph Retinger, whom some considered éminence grise in European diplomatic circles. A member of the Polish government in exile during the war, Retinger offered a bewildering mixture of leftist leanings, arch-Catholicism, and anticommunism. He dreamed of a united Europe as part of a wider Atlantic Community and viewed rampant anti-Americanism in Europe as a portent of future catastrophe. Retinger floated an idea to Prince Bernhard, consort to the queen of the Netherlands. He envisioned holding a secret congress with representatives from all the NATO countries aimed at building bridges over the Atlantic and fostering greater American-European understanding. Bernhard made certain entreaties to friends in the Truman administration, who proved receptive, but nothing came of it. One of the people the prince talked to was Smith, whom he knew well from the war. Beetle asked, "Why the hell didn't you come to me in the first place?"[14]

By 1954, anti-American sentiment in Europe reached a zenith. Europeans saw a soldier in the White House and the government in the hands of conservative Republicans for the first time in two decades. Worse, McCarthyism made it appear that the United States might lapse into an

American brand of fascism. Smith considered "the task of persuading friends, allies and the uncommitted that the Soviet Union and NOT the US is the threat to peace, the aggressor" to be "a great, if not the greatest, diplomatic problem facing the United States." Europeans, especially the intelligentsia, viewed the construction of military bases and alliances around the Soviet Union as proof of the United States' hostile intent. "It is hard to convince them," he told writers at one of his off-the-record dinners, that "without such a system of defense, the US and the West would be sitting ducks." He pointed to the successes of Soviet propaganda, beamed to a jittery Europe, "which seem to offer a pledge against atomic warfare while we insist on conditions and controls."[15] For Smith, Bernhard's proposal held a great deal of promise, and as undersecretary he pushed the idea. Smith suggested, and Eisenhower agreed, that the president's adviser C. D. Jackson should take the lead in organizing and attending the first meeting, set for May 1954 in the Bilderberg Hotel just outside the Dutch city of Arnhem, the site of the Allies' only operational setback in the campaign in northwest Europe.[16] Smith confined his activities to chairing the steering committee and eliciting official support. In March 1955 he telephoned Eisenhower and requested that the president encourage American participation. Eisenhower asked Gabriel Hauge, his economic adviser, to attend the 1955 meeting at government expense. Smith remained affiliated with the Bilderberg Group for only two years and never attended any meetings.[17]

The War of Words

Money, honors (four Distinguished Service Medals; membership in fifteen military orders, including two British knighthoods; and fifteen honorary doctorates), and friends in high places could never supplant Smith's bitter disappointment at never having achieved his greatest ambition: to be army chief of staff. As ambassador, DCI, and undersecretary, Smith received a good deal of press—none of it invited—but that only served to turn his wartime service into a footnote. Once out of office, he became yesterday's news, and his reputation sank even lower. Chiefs of staff, unless they sign surrenders, never garner much publicity. Articles about Smith, including a feature in *Life* in 1944, invariably focused as much on Eisenhower as on his chief of staff.[18] Commanders make great copy and, if they possess the common touch, great presidents, but staff officers do not. As Roosevelt told Eisenhower, "Ike, you and I know who was Chief of Staff during the last years of the Civil War . . . but practically no one else knows. I hate to think that fifty years from now practically nobody will know who General Marshall was."[19] That was one reason why Roosevelt had wanted Marshall as supreme commander in northwest Europe. But Marshall stayed in Washington, and Eisenhower went to London and eventually to two terms in the White House. In the second half of the 1950s, Marshall's reputation was blackened by the groundless and scurrilous assaults on him by McCarthy and his ilk. Except for his role as creator of the Marshall Plan, the wartime record of America's greatest soldier has all but disappeared from the popular mind.

Smith chafed that his great contributions to Allied victory in the Mediterranean and Europe went either discounted or unnoted. Within two years of the war's end, the "battle of the books" commenced. The books and memoirs centered on two themes: Eisenhower's conduct of operations in Europe, which, colored by the Cold War, was censured for lengthening the war and missing the opportunity to take Berlin (and Prague); and the contest between Eisenhower and FM Bernard Montgomery over strategy and command. Smith's personality—which produced more friction than warmth—and his role at headquarters engendered little sympathetic treatment if he received any mention at all.

A number of people believed Smith to be the ideal person to set the record straight. Princeton offered him a well-paid fellowship at the Institute of Advanced Study to write his account of the war. He declined. On his way to deliver his famous Iron Curtain speech in Missouri, Churchill visited Smith, then the newly appointed ambassador to Moscow, in Washington. Deeply worried that the race to publish sensationalist books to serve personal or ideological ends would erode the "special relationship" between the United States and Britain in the face of the Soviet threat, the former prime minister used his persuasive powers to convince Smith to write the true story of the wartime alliance. Smith always found it hard to say no, and he agreed. He wrote six articles for the *Saturday Evening Post* that ran serially from 8 June to 13 July 1946.

"Eisenhower's Six Great Decisions" countered the arguments that SHAEF had prolonged the war and the supreme commander had been an ineffectual figurehead. Each segment dealt with one command decision in northwest Europe—D-day, the breakout from Normandy, the Bulge, use of the broad-front approach in closing to and crossing the Rhine and in the Ruhr pocket, and the decision to forgo an advance on Berlin—and all argued the same three premises: the entire campaign in Europe unfolded exactly according to Eisenhower and SHAEF's pre–D-day vision; Eisenhower made all the crucial judgments; and the campaigns in Europe succeeded because of the solidarity of the Allied partnership, for which Eisenhower deserved the lion's share of the credit. Hastily written for a popular audience, Smith's saccharine account avoided all controversy, and other than admitting his own errors—when he disagreed with Eisenhower—he carried self-effacement almost to the extreme.

The serialized version of Patton's "War as I Knew It," which leveled charges that SHAEF had prevented Patton from winning the war in September 1944, prompted Eisenhower to tell Smith, "I am beginning to think that crackpot history is going to guide the future student of the late conflict."[20] Smith apologized for not responding earlier because he had been in London and Paris. He expressed his extreme vexation with those who argued that "SHAEF prevented people from winning the war." While in London, the British press hounded him about Ralph Ingersoll's *Top Secret,* a virulent attack on Eisenhower and SHAEF for winning the war at the cost of losing the peace. Smith declined to comment but informed Eisenhower, who refused to read the book, that the Soviet press exploited Ingersoll's contention that Anglo-American divisions had rent SHAEF.[21]

Eisenhower remained irked by these "so-called histories." He told Smith his *Saturday Evening Post* articles offered a "very definite atmosphere of authenticity" and suggested that Beetle expand them into a memoir that "could not fail to be beneficial to a future historian." Eisenhower recommended that Smith employ SHAEF directives to "cut the ground completely away from some of the arguments made by partisans." The truth, he admitted, was interesting and absorbing enough. A factual, heavily source-laden book might not produce the same kind of sales as "an argumentative, prejudiced account," but "in the long run its value would be definitely recognized."[22]

As had been the case so often during the war, Eisenhower wanted Smith to do the dirty work. In 1947 Smith still hoped to have a future in the army and knew that if he analyzed the divisive issues and antagonistic personalities animating the direction of the war, he would provoke the enmity of scores of highly placed political and military leaders and fan the flames of controversy. Doubtlessly tempted, he balked. Smith wondered why Bradley did not publicly upbraid "Ingersoll's drivel" and then answered his own question by surmising the GI General probably agreed with his former staff officer.[23] Guessing correctly that Eisenhower could not pass up the opportunity to cash in on his celebrity by penning a memoir of his own, Smith recommended that he not "hold back too much and gloss over too much" or "do what you have done so often in the past . . . expose yourself to criticism by assuming responsibility for the controversial matters which come through the personal feelings, weaknesses, and idiosyncrasies of your major subordinates." "I am no Montgomery lover," he wrote, "but I give him his full due and believe that for certain types of operations he is without equal," but he was not "worth a damn for the wide sweeping maneuver where Patton shone so brilliantly." Montgomery's "intransigent attitude and behind the scenes conniving to get his way with regard to military operations, to enhance his own prestige and to obtain a major measure of command are certainly deserving of the most severe censure by any unprejudiced observer." Smith quickly acknowledged that he could never claim to be such an unprejudiced observer. "State frankly and fully," he advised, "your own estimate of the tools with which you were working. By that I mean your commanders like Patton, Montgomery, and Bradley." He exhorted Eisenhower not to "pull a punch," because "I feel so strongly that you owe to yourself, your associates and to history the simple unvarnished truth."[24]

In fact, Eisenhower had already finished his boiler-room first draft of *Crusade in Europe*. Part sedative and part self-promotion, the book perfectly mirrored Eisenhower's self-image as peacemaker and champion of Anglo-American collaboration. Even though he set out to write a sanitized account of his part in the war, designed to calm the waters of personal and nationalistic discord, Eisenhower's retelling of differences over strategy, operations, and command produced plenty of criticism among devotees of Patton, and especially from Montgomery and his following. If Smith expected his reputation to be made, he was sorely disappointed. Eisenhower had often said during the war that if he ever wrote his memoirs, he would devote at least a chapter to the debt he owed Smith. Other than a couple of bromidic mentions, Smith is even more invisible in *Crusade in Europe* than in his own self-abnegatory account.

Eisenhower's reputation took a bashing throughout the 1950s, starting with Chester Wilmot's *The Struggle for Europe* in 1952 and ending with the edited diaries of Lord Alanbrooke, the wartime chief of the Imperial General Staff, in 1957 and 1959, sandwiched around Montgomery's inflammatory memoir published in 1958.[25] In a vain attempt to defend Eisenhower—and perhaps make a little money—Smith did publish a book in 1956, but not the memoir Eisenhower had requested. Smith merely reproduced his original articles, adding an acknowledgment, five superficial "Situation Reports" for each chapter, and a "Prelude to Invasion" and "Epilogue to Victory" as introduction and conclusion.[26] Published in the United States and Britain, Smith's book scarcely reversed the anti-Eisenhower tide.

Stung by the Patton book, nonplussed by Bradley's self-serving

account, and magnanimous toward Alanbrooke, Eisenhower was infuriated by Montgomery's memoir. The book whipped up a furor in Britain.
A number of Eisenhower's wartime British associates—Ismay, Tedder, de
Guingand, and GEN F. A. M. "Boy" Browning, among others—wrote letters in vocal support of Eisenhower's wartime generalship.[27] Avoiding all
personal confrontation remained one of the bedrocks of Eisenhower's
leadership style. He refused to "get down in the gutter" with McCarthy, and he fought the urge to refute Montgomery's claims. Finally, he
revealed his true feelings to Ismay. "I have never before, to my knowledge, put on paper or spoken publicly in a disparaging fashion about any
other public figure—particularly if he was an old comrade-in-arms," but
this time he made an exception. He denigrated Montgomery as a commander. Regardless of how Montgomery had "conducted and expressed
himself during post war years, he would scarcely stand much chance of
going down in history as one of the great British captains." He thought
FM Harold Alexander "much the abler." Eisenhower recalled the "impatience with which we waited for any northern movement of Montgomery's out of the Catania Plain (in Sicily) and the long and unnecessary
wait before he stepped across the Massena Strait." He asked if Ismay
remembered "the great promises that he made during the planning for
Overlord about moving quickly to the southward beyond Caen and Bayeux to get ground fit for airfields, and his post-war assertions that such
a movement was never included in the plan"; or Montgomery's "pre-
posterous proposal to drive on a single pencil-line thrust straight on to
Berlin, and later his failure even to make good his effort for a lodgment
across the Rhine, and this after I had promised and given to him everything he requested until that particular operation was completed."[28]

On 27 October 1958 Smith received an interesting proposition from
his former chief intelligence officer in AFHQ and SHAEF, Kenneth
Strong. In view of the wholesale assault on Eisenhower and SHAEF,
Strong suggested the calling of a colloquy of senior Allied officers.
Strong envisioned such a symposium producing a definitive publication
to refute Montgomery's charges. Smith very much liked Strong's idea
and passed it on to Eisenhower. The president loved the scheme and
even expropriated it as his own. He put together a roster of participants
and proposed the meeting take place at Camp David in October 1959.
Eisenhower and Smith exchanged phone calls and conducted an off-
the-record meeting in the White House on 15 January.[29] The president
delegated to Smith responsibility for pulling the whole thing together.

The seminar never took place in 1959 nor, despite Eisenhower's prodding, in 1960. A number of problems intervened, principally because

many of the British officers had health problems; others, thanks to niggardly British pensions, could not afford the trip. The retrieval of Eisenhower's reputation would have to wait, and whatever hope Smith entertained of having his story revealed dissolved.

The End: No Caissons or Pomp

Instead of attending a reunion at Camp David in October 1959, Smith lay in Walter Reed fighting for his life. As one of Dulles's aides remembered, in "the last ten years of [Smith's] life there never passed a comfortable minute. I mean he was a physical wreck."[30] The army announced that Smith was in "critical condition," but against long odds, he rallied.[31] Characteristically, in the months remaining to him, he soldiered on as best he could. One by one he dropped his memberships in government committees; he remained active in only one, his advisory role in the George C. Marshall Foundation. During this period, Nixon came to visit. Exchanging views over bourbons, they concluded that Eisenhower had exploited them in his rise to the top. Nixon remembered Smith as being "very tired, and he uncharacteristically began showing emotion. Tears began to stream down his cheeks. Summing up his relationship with Eisenhower, Smith stated, 'I was just Ike's prat boy. Ike always had to have a prat boy.'"[32]

When Smith finally died, a *New York Times* writer remarked, "Those who kept in touch with General Walter Bedell Smith during recent years were not surprised to hear that he had died. The wonder was that he stood off death as long as he did."[33] Ever the good army wife, Nory Smith always took a backseat, suffered their long separations in silence, and did everything she could to support her general. As a four-star general, army regulations entitled Smith to a special full-honor funeral, with the army as the sole service represented. The day after Beetle passed, Nory went to the offices at Arlington and insisted that regulations be damned; she wanted Beetle's funeral to be a simple joint service ceremony, identical to the one held for General Marshall in 1959. She then selected a gravesite in section 7, the one in closest proximity to Marshall's. The authorities acceded to her wishes.[34] As Nory well knew, Smith would be happy in the knowledge that he lay buried close to the man he had idolized and to whom he owed so much.

Eisenhower attended the funeral as an honorary pallbearer. He offered no quotes at the time, but earlier he gave what must stand as the best assessment of the Ike-Beetle team: "A very great soldier of France [de Lattre de Tassigny] once assured me that my place in military history was secure since the only requisite for an enduring spot in the history of battles was wisdom in selecting a Chief of Staff. He went on to say that no one in World War II was quite as wise, or at least as fortunate, as I in this regard. And of this circumstance I would of course be forever the beneficiary."[35]

Part Two

★ ★ ★ ★

Officership in the Army of the "Long Generation," 1917–1939

★ 6 ★

Born to Be a Soldier

Americans are a paradoxical people: though wary of foreign entanglements, when drawn into hostilities, they are at once strikingly bellicose
and peculiarly unmilitary. During the years before the Great War—except
for Grand Army of the Republic parades and bursts of patriotism, such
as during the war with Spain—Americans troubled themselves little with
martial thoughts. A citizen could easily live a lifetime without laying eyes
on a soldier of the regular army. Young Ike Eisenhower captured the
national mood. When asked what he wanted to be when he grew up, Ike
answered without hesitation, Honus Wagner. Baseball greats Wagner,
Ty Cobb, and "Christian Gentleman" Christy Mathewson held the thrall
of most young American boys in the first decade of the twentieth century, not military heroes. Unlike other boys, Walter Bedell Smith wanted
nothing else in life than to become a soldier.

Hoosier Boy

Smith described his boyhood as "normal, middle class, substantial," but
that was only a half-truth. The Smiths were a family of moderate means.
Beetle came into the world on 5 October 1895. His father, William Long
Smith, worked as a silk buyer for the Pettis Dry Goods Company; the
family also owned substantial shares in the firm. Beetle's mother, Ida
Frances Bedell, was the daughter of German immigrants. Her parents
emigrated from the Rhine valley, coming to Indianapolis via Cincinnati
and Madison, Indiana. The Smiths lived—together with Ida's parents—
in a two-story wood-and-brick frame house at 1713 Ashland Street on the
verdant north side of Indianapolis.[1]

Christened Walter according to the traditional rites of the Catholic
Church, from infancy everyone called him Bedell (pronounced *BEE-*

dull). He suffered from an onslaught of infant maladies so serious that family members thought he might die. His anxious mother nursed him back to health, and even after he recovered, she carried him about on a pillow bundled in a thick blanket. Under the watchful ministrations of his protective mother—and subjected to a heavy German diet—baby Beetle grew ruddy and fat. Family members began to call him "Boodle."[2]

Family and friends recalled Beetle as a nice, clean-cut boy but with a marked obstinate streak. Other than the chores he performed around the house, Beetle spent his childhood in all manner of outdoor activities. In summer he and his cohorts fished, played sandlot baseball, and roller-skated. Perhaps in anticipation of Indianapolis's famous Brickyard, they constructed a racetrack in a vacant field, where they staged bicycle races all summer. In winter they played skinny, a variant of hockey.[3] Sunday mass featured prominently in the Smith household; Beetle remained a dedicated Catholic his entire life. At Oliver Perry Morton Public School, his third-grade teacher found him a joy to teach. "He was a marvelous reader and a very intelligent child," she remembered; his advanced reading skills were a product of nightly sessions with his mother.[4]

Smith remembered, "I always wanted to be an army officer. I never thought of anything else." His uncle Paul Bedell confirmed this observation: "[Beetle] had been a soldier from the time he was big enough to walk." A member of the Smith clan had fought in every American war since the Revolution. The family traced their ancestry to Samuel Stanhope Smith, a resident of West Jersey. A propertied family, the Smiths numbered MG Thomas Mufflin—aide-de-camp to George Washington, signatory to the Constitution, and governor of Pennsylvania—among their kinsmen. Smith took pride in his military roots. More immediately, his grandfather had seen action in the Franco-Prussian War. A spiked helmet and a needle-gun offered material substance to his grandfather's bloodthirsty accounts of fighting the French.[5]

As further proof of his childhood obsession with militaria, Beetle's favorite playthings were his assortment of wax, wooden, and metal toy soldiers. He spent hours playing with them, arraying them in battle formations. Whenever the Smiths went visiting, Beetle brought along a cigar box filled with his most prized pieces and quietly sat by himself, orchestrating a make-believe battle. Smith would be a loner and an inveterate collector all his life.[6]

His love for the military prompted more than collecting miniatures. A martinet even then, "Boodle" Smith organized and drilled his neighborhood pals. Broomsticks substituted for muskets and hobbyhorses for cavalry. Under the tireless gaze of their captain, the troops marched and countermarched until they achieved Potsdam perfection. A member of the troop, Humphrey Harrington, recalled that Smith occasionally surrendered the commander's baton, but never for very long. Facing a periodic mutiny when the neighborhood boys refused to muster—Beetle preferred drilling to sports—he dragooned his younger brother George into performing the drill. If George escaped, Beetle marched alone. Residents of Ashland Street frequently watched—and probably shook their heads—as the Smith boy goose-stepped down the sidewalk, a broomstick slung over his shoulder. "Military matters were about all that he as a boy ever had on his mind," remembered another friend.[7]

When Beetle commandeered a vacant firehouse as his headquarters and indoor parade ground, he went too far. Fearing trouble with the authorities, his father purchased a ramshackle streetcar from the city and placed it in the backyard. Ida Smith protested—she took great pleasure from the beautiful roses in her carefully tended flower beds—but the eyesore stayed. The Smiths' backyard thereafter acted as the neighborhood gathering spot for the Ashland Avenue Irregulars. "Boodle" no longer sufficed as a nickname, yielding to the more appropriate sobriquet "Brigadier."[8]

One summer it came to Beetle's attention that an officer of the regular army was visiting relatives in the neighborhood. Determined to see this wonder with his own eyes, Smith stationed himself on the stoop. Harrington remembered Beetle spending the entire duration of the young lieutenant's stay sitting on the porch "worshipping his hero." Family members felt this episode inspired Smith to join the army at the first opportunity. His hero turned out to be Hugh Drum, a future lieutenant general and very nearly army chief of staff.[9]

Then his parents decided to transfer Beetle to Catholic school. Leaving his friends at PS 29 proved difficult; unsociable Beetle did not make friends easily. "Brigadier" Smith had already demonstrated the need to control his external environment. In grade school and among his neighborhood circle, Beetle felt compelled to exert his authority. If he did not make the rules, he did not play. If he could not excel in some task, he withdrew. His safe little world abruptly changed when he went to the large parochial school. At Saints Peter and Paul School he found himself, in a popular phrase of the day, a small grape in a big vineyard. He liked nothing about the change.

His friends began to drift away. For a while, the Old Guard continued to meet infrequently in the backyard clubhouse. In a failed attempt to preserve the Irregulars, Beetle inaugurated a new initiation rite: the recruit had to smoke a Sub Rosa cigar down to the nub. The real problem stemmed from the onset of adolescence. The other boys developed different pursuits; they played sports and started showing curiosity in girls—neither of which attracted Beetle. Nor would they bend to his hectoring.[10]

In compensation, Smith started projecting a "tough guy" image. A friend characterized Beetle as "a fighter at heart . . . really a scrapper." His career as a pugilist started early. At age seven he spent a couple of weeks with his uncle Paul Bedell. As the new kid on the block, he soon faced the challenge of a neighborhood mug three years his senior. After taking the first punch, Beetle waded into his assailant with both fists flailing. Soon the other boy retreated into his yard and remained there for the rest of Smith's stay. A pattern emerged. Never looking for a fight, Beetle never backed down. "He would warn him to 'stop or I'll take a poke at you,' and if the bully didn't stop he usually got that poke." Smith must have been good with his hands because he won a boxing tournament at officer training camp in 1917.[11]

With the economy booming, William Smith took a financial risk in 1908; he left the Pettis Company and became a partner in the New York Store. The new venture struggled from the beginning. Under mounting stress, William's health deteriorated. With her husband incapacitated, Ida Frances assumed much of his role as purchaser. Her widowed sister moved in and assumed many of the maternal domestic duties. Now the household numbered seven. The family struggled to maintain its middle-class standing in the face of diminished income. Despite tuition costs, Beetle's parents insisted he remain in private school. By summer 1909 the family found itself in genuine economic straits, struggling to pay the bills. To help with the finances, Beetle, not yet fourteen, went to work part-time as a laborer in the National Motor Car Company. Respectable wives from "normal substantial middle class" families did not work in the first decade of the twentieth century; nor did thirteen-year-old middle-class boys toil in automobile factories.[12]

Beetle spent his first thirteen years in a warm, secure home. His family's suddenly reduced circumstances came as a rude shock. He now shouldered adult responsibilities while still just a boy. This boyhood trauma shattered Beetle's dependence on others but instilled in him the lessons of loyalty and self-reliance. Fidelity to family came first, but Smith paid a price. Relatives remember a sudden and dramatic shift in Beetle's personality. His once lively—if sardonic—sense of humor gave way to a surly moodiness. His aunt remembered that Beetle "never talked unless he had something to say."[13] Estranged from his boyhood friends, exhausted from working and keeping up with school work, and with scant opportunity for recreation, Beetle retreated into himself. He spent what precious little spare time he had alone, sometimes in his room reading military books and popular boys' fiction, but mostly devoted to his new passion for fishing. One friend thought Smith withdrew because "pranks of the Halloween variety" no longer amused him; the real reason was he never had the time or inclination to indulge in normal adolescent pursuits.[14]

Shortly after starting at the car factory, Beetle faced another daunting complication: high school. With his family no longer able to sustain tuition costs, Beetle returned to the public school system. He applied and was admitted to Indianapolis's newest and best high school, the Industrial Manual Training School. Indianapolis numbered among the fastest-growing cities in the United States, fueled by its rapidly expanding transportation sector—railroads and motorcars.[15] The demand for skilled technicians, coupled with civic pride, propelled the creation of a technical secondary school. The jewel of the Indianapolis public school system, the Industrial Manual Training High School opened its doors in 1895. Funded largely by Indianapolis's many German community organizations—the Freethinkers Society and the *Turnverein* in particular—the school's inspiration derived from the model of Germany's technical high schools (*Fachhochshulen*). Other major cities—Chicago and Philadelphia most notably—boasted older technical secondary schools, but Indianapolis, with some justification, claimed that it was "the most thoroughly equipped institution of its kind in this country."[16] The challenging curriculum balanced classic academic subjects—literature, history, English composition, and two and a half years of Latin—with mathematics, the sciences, and vocational industrial courses, both technical and practical.

Beetle performed well in his first year, 1909–1910. He received mostly Bs and, except for gym (with its heavy dose of gymnastics), had a near-spotless attendance record. In 1911 he took on a second job, working as a soda jerk for $6 a week in a drugstore at the corner of College and 16th Street, a busy intersection a couple of blocks from his house.[17] His grades slipped, along with his attendance. Given the demands on his time and energies, Smith now viewed high school as a necessary evil. Although he told nobody, he figured that if he could pull off a little subterfuge, school would enjoy even less priority when he turned sixteen and became eligible to join the Indiana National Guard.[18]

Sergeant Smith

Beetle Smith harbored visions of going to West Point, but harsh reality killed that pipe dream. "My folks didn't have the money or political connections," Smith remembered. At age sixteen his career path appeared set, and he was not the least bit cheered by the prospect. Still he longed for a military career. If the regular army lay beyond his immediate reach, only age stood between him and the second-best thing, the National Guard.

The day he turned sixteen, Smith took the Inter-City downtown to the National Guard armory and signed the enlistment papers. Because of his youth, he needed his parents' approval. Dismayed at the notion of "her hopeful" going off to be a soldier, Ida Frances initially refused. Stretching the truth, Beetle told her the Guard unit amounted to little more than a social organization. Appeased, she stalled but finally consented.[19]

After some typical delays, Beetle swore the oath and entered state service. One can easily imagine his delight when he first donned his uniform. Smith received his posting to Company D, Second Indiana Infantry. Company D also bore the somewhat pretentious designation of the Indianapolis Light Infantry. Beetle did not stretch the truth too far when he told his mother the company was a fashionable gentlemen's volunteer unit. For the officers, the Light Infantry was a social organization. Other than participating in the funerals of dignitaries and other ceremonial occasions, the Indianapolis Light Infantry usually made the papers for the sporting prowess of its members. In 1895 the company completed the first American military cycling relay, riding from Indianapolis to St. Louis. One of its officers won the first citywide golf tournament. The drill and rifle teams toured the country.[20]

Hoosiers justifiably boasted of the contributions of Indiana's volunteer units in American wars. A massive column dedicated to the common soldier and sailor—only fifteen feet shorter than the Statue of Liberty—anchors downtown Indianapolis. Peacetime citizen soldiering never much appealed to Indianans, however. Indiana registered 50,000 on its militia rolls in 1860, less than the Nebraska Territory; in 1910 Indiana stood dead last among the states in per capita enrollment in its National Guard.[21] None of that mattered to Private Smith. Even if few others did, Smith took his Guard drills seriously. Always punctual, never absent, and perfectly turned out, Smith succeeded in impressing his company officers. Beetle quickly made corporal, then shortly thereafter sergeant.

With Beetle holding down two jobs and devoting more and more time to the Guard, something had to give—and that was school. Except for Latin, geometry, and physics, Beetle continued to get Bs and Cs. His grades in the technical courses remained above average, but these accounted for only about a quarter of the course load. Surprisingly, he never obtained higher than a C in history, despite his keen interest in the subject. His performance and attendance indicated a growing indifference to academic work.

He took every opportunity to escape school, factory, pharmacy, and the crowded house on Ashland Avenue. During the week he headed for Riverside Park, where he angled in the White River. On weekends Beetle ventured farther afield, either fishing or hunting birds in the fields and forests in the immediate environs of Indianapolis. Always dexterous—his only As in high school came in free and technical drawing—he spent countless hours in the basement fashioning fishing rods he cut himself and designing and crafting trout and bass flies from simple household items. Any extra money he put aside for the purchase of shotguns.

The year 1913 turned out to be a big one in Smith's life. He graduated from high school, met his future wife, and performed Guard duties that launched his military career. Sometime in 1913 he began dating Mary Eleanor "Nory" Cline. The Clines lived three blocks from the Smiths, but the two families inhabited different social worlds. As Smith later understated, the Clines were "kind of rich." As a standard of wealth in those days, the Clines owned not one but two touring cars, a Wilton and a Stanley Steamer.[22] An extremely attractive and intelligent girl, and a year and a half older than Beetle, Nory attended finishing school and graduated from a private Catholic girls' academy. Beetle, who had previously shown no interest in the opposite sex, fell madly in love.[23] As in all matters, Smith possessed an "all or nothing" attitude. Even though he was punching way above his weight, he decided to woo Nory Cline, whatever the obstacles. And there were many—chiefly Nory's parents, who thought she deserved a suitor with greater expectations. Undeterred, Beetle and Nory continued to see each other.

Mother Nature intervened. The unsettled weather in spring 1913 produced tornadoes and record rainfall throughout the Midwest. The East Fork of the White River breached its levee on 26 March, flooding large sections of Indianapolis and leaving more than 200 dead. The governor called out the National Guard. Beetle drew the assignment of securing the Washington Street Bridge, the largest viaduct in that part of the city, which had collapsed before the river crested. Hearing that the Guard had deployed at the bridge, Beetle's uncle investigated, hoping his nephew might be there. In the gathering darkness, Paul Bedell recognized Beetle, waved, and entered the approach to the bridge. Instead of the greeting he expected, he was met with a stern soldierly warning. If he took another step, he was under arrest. Not the least bit amused, Uncle Paul stomped away. Good soldier Smith had executed his duty.[24]

Whether he liked it or not, schoolboy Smith surrendered to soldier Smith. Beetle missed about a third of his classes during his final semester. His teachers gave him charitable passing grades, but he still fell four credits short of graduating. An enlightened principal, Milo Stuart, recognized that many of his students failed to complete their course work owing to family obligations. Many disadvantaged kids worked to support their families. Beetle would have bristled at the suggestion, but he clearly fell into this category. Although he later claimed to have been "probably one of [the high school's] most stupid students," Smith's senior year academic performance suffered because of his extensive Guard duties. Weighing the circumstances, Stuart awarded Beetle his four credits—in physical education, health, and social studies—for completing National Guard basic training. For whatever reasons, Beetle missed the graduation ceremony and never bothered to collect his diploma.[25]

With Nory's parents in mind, Beetle applied for admission to Butler University, but before the university made a decision, he withdrew his application. William's health had failed completely, and he lapsed into infirmity. Beetle became the primary earner for the family. The aborted attempt to go to college added yet another frustrating failure to a growing list. With no other options, Smith now sought full-time employment.[26]

He joined the Marion Railroad Company as a die maker. A heavy engineering company, Marion built locomotives and earthmoving equipment—including huge tracked steam shovels—for railway construction. The monthly National Guard musters, two-week summer drills at Camp Morton, stolen time with Nory, and his hobbies provided the few escapes from the long, dreary hours at the factory forge. Nor had Beetle made any headway in convincing the Clines of his worthiness for their daughter's hand. Like his plan for attending college, Smith's family responsibilities made marriage virtually impossible.

Not all was bleak. In recognition of Beetle's outstanding performance during the flood, CPT James Hurt promoted him to first sergeant—no small accomplishment for an eighteen-year-old. Later that autumn Indianapolis again garnered national attention when a strike by the streetcar union turned violent. That year and the preceding one witnessed some of the most bitter labor actions in American history—the most famous in Lawrence, Massachusetts—including a number of violent transit strikes. In Indianapolis the municipal railway, facing a halt of services, hired scab labor. Ugly scenes transpired in front of Union Station when the company fired its union employees and imported toughs from Chicago. When the strikers attacked the train carrying the strikebreakers, much of the police rank and file mutinied. The governor immediately mobilized the National Guard, this time statewide. The strike—which polarized opinion in the city—placed the Guard in a difficult position. Company D, the only unit in the city, immediately deployed. Governor Samuel Ralston quickly brokered a preliminary settlement, having employed the Guard less as a coercive force than as a threat. Again, Smith earned commendations for his service.[27]

Perhaps a trifle power mad, First Sergeant Smith, deaf to the angry protests of his apathetic enlisted men, relentlessly drilled the company and strictly enforced discipline, intent on making his unit the best in the state. It was Brigadier Smith and the Ashland Avenue Irregulars all over again—except this time, Smith exercised some real authority. Roundly cursed by his men, Smith doggedly persevered. Beetle made the impression he sought on Hurt, but the constant clashes with his men turned the monthly musters and summer encampments into a torment. He later attributed "some of the less attractive characteristics of [his] personality" to this difficult phase of his career.[28]

Smith always took pride in his label as a "square-wheeled son-of-a-bitch." He was combative, inarticulate when expressing personal feelings, covetous and resentful of those better off, a secretive loner bordering on antisocial; all these characteristics resonated throughout Smith's adult life. Later his supporters blamed chronic ulcers for his famously dyspeptic disposition. Those who favored the other interpretation—that Smith was naturally foul-tempered—came closer to the mark. Adolescence—the crucial period of physical, mental, and psychosocial development—shapes character. Individuals acquire a coherent sense of identity; patterns of behavior and attitudes become routinized and predictable. Smith's family circumstances forged his personality. All of Smith's distinctive and less attractive adult characteristics were molded during this time, undoubtedly the most miserable period of his life. His early adult years merely reinforced predispositions already laid in adolescence.

Smith possessed a first-rate intellect; he was analytical and retentive, yet he never performed well academically. His apathy and crowded calendar provide only partial explanations. Education and a social life would have rounded off the sharp edges of that square-wheeled personality, but Smith never took advantage of the educational and social opportunities offered by a place like Manual High. His father's condition aside, Smith's dream of attending Butler was just that. He possessed neither the grades for a scholarship nor the money for tuition. All these disappointments deepened his resentment aimed at others who lacked his intelligence but enjoyed greater advantages.

Smith's core values remained deeply rooted in family and church. On the surface, Smith exhibited solid Middle American middle-class virtues: he respected authority; worked hard; always appeared clean-scrubbed, mannerly, and plainspoken; and believed in God. The two personality traits that especially stood out—conceded by even his harshest critics later in life—were Smith's unquestioned loyalty and his remarkable capacity for work. These attributes were also formed in his youth. Although bitter about his tribulations, he resigned himself to fulfilling his duty to his family. He held two jobs—three, including the Guard—went to school, and later worked full-time; he performed all these tasks as best he could and never said no, all without a thought for whether he enjoyed his labors. Obviously, he did not, but he never complained. All work and no play made Beetle a dull boy, but it inured in him a powerful work ethic. The period before the Great War was anything but a belle époque for Smith.

War erupted in Europe in summer 1914, but little changed in Indiana, including in the Guard. The episode that succeeded in breathing life into that somnolent body took place along the Mexican border. Interjecting itself into the amorphous political situation in Mexico, the Wilson administration committed a series of blunders that eventually prompted American involvement. With American participation in Europe ever more possible and U.S. intervention in Mexico more probable, Secretary of War Lindley Garrison pushed for the creation of a continental army under federal control. In the face of adamant pro-Guard opposition in the House of Representatives, Wilson killed Garrison's scheme. Pancho Villa's raid into New Mexico in March 1916 forced Washington into action. In June, under the provisions of the National Defense Act of 1916, the Wilson administration called for a fourfold expansion of the now federalized National Guard.

On 27 June 1916 elements of the Indiana National Guard mustered into federal service. For Beetle, the Guard's enlargement and active service in Mexico dangled the likelihood of a commission and perhaps a medal or two. Neither came to Smith. Once again, family circumstances dogged him. Indiana Guard officials perused their rosters and noted that Smith fell into the primary earner category. Orders followed for Smith's attachment to the headquarters staff. This constituted the bitterest pill of all. After all his travails as first sergeant, he would not go south with the Second Indiana. Almost certainly, the enlisted men quietly celebrated the end of drillmaster Smith's reign of terror, made all the sweeter because their gung-ho first sergeant would hold down a despised staff job and never leave Indianapolis.

Confederate soldiers called staff officers "yeller dogs." Staff officers fell far short of the heroic ideal of the American soldier—a stigma that survives in muted form to the present. Chair-bound officers share this deprecatory self-image. Smith was no exception. Worse, administrative chaos attended the National Guard mobilization in Indiana, as elsewhere. Smith ably performed his duties, but his disappointment never slackened.

As events transpired on the Mexican border, Smith need not have fretted. The entire Mexican fiasco demonstrated the United States' woeful unpreparedness for war. The Punitive Expedition spent nine and a half months in a fruitless effort to bring Villa to account. Except for Pershing, no great reputations emerged from this Mexican business. The Indiana troops got no closer to the border than Llanos Grande, Texas—a temporary encampment in the barren rangeland of Nuences County, a few miles southwest of Corpus Christi.

The signposts on an officer's road to the top never appear as they seem. Intangibles—character, luck, personal connections—play more determinant roles than performance. Smith's career proves this law of unintended consequences. Disheartened by missing the deployment to Texas, Smith's frustrating tenure on the Indiana Guard staff eventually served not as a barrier but as a steppingstone in his military career. Nor could he envision that staff duty—not the honors of combat—would carry him to four stars. None of that was remotely predictable in the opening months of 1917.

★ **7** ★

The Summons to War

The year 1917 proved eventful for both the nation and Walter Bedell Smith. Relations between the United States and Germany worsened, and on 2 April President Wilson asked Congress for a declaration of war. This struggle took on the pattern of previous American wars, as large numbers of citizen-soldiers inundated the tiny regular army. The size of the army stood at 127,151 men; the officer corps numbered 5,959. The War Department earmarked prewar officers for leadership and training duties. Platoon and company grade officers were chosen from National Guard cadre and other suitable young men from the general population, many of them "Plattsburg" men, products of the civilian military training camp movement. In the nineteen months the war lasted, the War Department trained 182,000 officers, at a rate of 30,000 in each three-week cycle. By virtue of his "fine work during the flood" of 1913 and his proven leadership qualities as a noncommissioned officer, Hurt recommended Smith for a posting to one of the newly formed officer training schools.[1] Beetle was part of the second series of reserve officer candidates processed through the system. For the twenty-one-year-old Smith, a commission represented the fulfillment of his childhood dream.

Another of Smith's ambitions flowered, perhaps prompted by the romance of war. The Clines relented and gave their consent for Nory to marry. The hurried ceremony took place on 1 July 1917. The honeymoon proved fleeting. Less than eight weeks after his marriage, Smith took the ten-mile trip out to Fort Benjamin Harrison, where he began his officer training course.

You're in the Army Now: Forts Harrison and Greene

The youth of America responded to the call to arms. Fort Harrison came alive with the arrival of each succeeding wave of enthusiastic officer can-

121

didates. The atmosphere of the training camps resembled a college campus the night before a big game. Upperclassmen or recent graduates of the nation's colleges and universities composed the greater proportion of officer candidates. Here many old friends renewed acquaintances in a genuine spirit of collegiate camaraderie. No "college boy," Smith's anxiety eased with the knowledge that he possessed a service background and that his childhood friend Humphrey Harrington occupied the next bunk.[2] The college atmosphere gave way to the rigors of army life. The urgent need to get on with the job animated the training camps. Fort Harrison was a permanent post, completed only in 1910. The Medical Corps occupied the bulk of the permanent buildings. Soldiers not billeted in the hastily constructed wooden barracks lived in sprouting tent cities. As the fair weather gave way to autumn chill, life in the camp became difficult.[3]

With time at a premium, little was wasted. Reveille sounded at 5:15 A.M., and the hectic pace of physical training, bayonet fighting, and field service maneuvers continued until ten at night. Harrison housed two camps, each organized as a provisional training regiment of nine infantry companies. Selected regular officers carried out training, with a captain assigned to each student company. Smith's commanding officer, a hard-boiled regular named B. C. Lockwood, scared the young candidate "to death."[4] Beneath the captain served either a regular first lieutenant or one or more graduates of the preceding course. LT Charles L. Bolté, a "ninety day wonder" from the first batch, remembered that only with extreme difficulty did he keep ahead of his students. "When it came to teaching the .45 automatic pistol," he recalled, "I had to sit up all night long with a manual just learning how you took it apart and put it together again so the next day I could sit down as if I knew all about it and try to teach this company how to do this very complicated task. It was a case of the blind leading the blind."[5] Training was elementary in nature, including close-order drill, weapons handling and marksmanship, and instruction in the conduct of scouting and patrolling. Its purpose was threefold: instill the essentials of military drill, harden the future officers physically, and exorcise the civilian in them. Too rudimentary, this officer training more closely resembled recruit training, lacking sufficient grounding in troop leading and tactical skills.

To enhance competition, the army divided the camps chiefly along state lines: one consisted mostly of candidates from Indiana, the other largely of men from Kentucky. With no love lost between the two states, rivalry was intense. The recurrent scene of cadets drummed out of the corps heightened the sense of competition and inspired the others to even greater efforts. Before "lights out," although fatigued by the day's activities, the cadets studied basic tactical manuals. As the weeks rolled by, pressure mounted. One officer candidate recalled, "Every minute we [are] able to read and are not studying drill regulations or something of the kind, we have that vague fear that someone else [is] getting ahead of us."[6]

As the three months wound down, camp organization changed. New companies formed, based on branch. With his service in the Indiana Guard, Smith drew the infantry. In the last week of the training schedule, his company went into the field for extended training. It was now mid-November, and Smith sloshed through mud, dug trenches, shivered in the cold temperatures, and slept on the ground—all in all, a proper initiation into life in the "poor bloody infantry."[7]

On 27 November Smith received his gold bars. After two weeks' furlough, Lieutenant Smith prepared for his first assignment as an officer in the United States Army. Only two weeks before Christmas, Smith bid good-bye to his wife and family at Union Station. Smith received orders for Camp Greene, North Carolina, one of the newly established training cantonments. Set in the beautiful rolling, pine-covered Piedmont area of North Carolina, Camp Greene at first appeared to be the ideal site for a base. After the horrors of that last week in the field in the teeth of a premature winter, Beetle livened at the promise of pleasant weather in the South. But Fort Harrison was a resort compared to what awaited in North Carolina.

His posting to the Fourth Division, a regular army unit, doubtlessly pleased Smith. First constituted on 19 November, the Fourth Division existed mostly on paper when Smith arrived. By the end of December the division consisted of 13,000 regular troops drawn from three regiments moved from Vancouver Barracks, the Presidio of Monterey, and other West Coast stations. Under a scheme worked out by the War Department, the regular regiments divided into four sections, each providing cadre for new regiments. Smith found himself assigned to Company A, First Battalion, Thirty-ninth Infantry Regiment. The average company numbered thirty-five men, with many having no officers at all. Many regular officers transferred or got siphoned off into other duties. Like Smith, most of his peers were "Sears and Roebuck" officers from the second training cycle. The Ivy Division—derived from the roman numerals IV—would not complete its skeletonized organization until 5 January; the first intake of volunteer and conscripted enlisted personnel did not arrive until the end of February. Until training commenced in earnest after New Year's, little remained for the officers to do except play cards, curse the army, and long for home. Nearby Charlotte opened its doors to the young officers with sporting events and holiday celebrations designed to take the edge off the boredom and homesickness. Smith looked forward to the serious work of putting the division together.[8]

The cool, crisp days of December gave way to what one Charlotte resident remembered as "the worst winter we had ever had, before or since." The War Department had made no provisions for the construction of permanent barracks in the training camps. Making matters worse, tents remained in short supply. Eight men crowded into pyramidal tents designed for five. It frequently snowed during the night, and the blowing wind formed large drifts; then in the afternoon the snow melted, turning the camp "into a vast sea of reddish yellow mud."[9] Incessant rain, intermittent snowstorms, and heavy traffic turned roads into quagmires. With mud knee deep, pack mules brought in food and drinking water. Huddled in their miserable tent cities, the troops cut green pine in mostly futile efforts to heat their overcrowded quarters. Hard to keep lit, the wood yielded little warmth. Given the wintry conditions and the sight of men hauling and cutting timber, the base more resembled a northern lumber camp than a military training installation.

Officers and noncommissioned officers were rotated through special classes directed by British and French officers for most of January. After completing the special schools, they returned to their units as instructors. February brought no relief from the weather. The battle against the mud finally ended in the mud's favor—the entire trench system dissolved. Training virtually ceased for better than two weeks. The impervious clay soil and inadequate drainage, crowded living conditions, poor sanitation, and lack of warm water for personal hygiene combined to produce the perfect environment for the spread of disease. The inevitable happened in late January and February, when Camp Greene suffered through a three-week epidemic of cerebrospinal meningitis. The quarantined camp was cut off from Charlotte, further restricting movement to and from the base. Due to weather and the epidemic, the troops received only sixteen days of training in the first eleven weeks of the division's existence—little beyond the fundamentals of military drill.

Once the epidemic subsided, the War Department commenced the movement of volunteer formations to Camp Greene. The Thirty-ninth, together with its sister regiment the Forty-seventh, had initially been raised at Camp U.S. Troops, a Plattsburg camp outside Syracuse, New York. The other two infantry regiments had been formed at Camp Colt, near Gettysburg, Pennsylvania. The bulk of the troops hailed from northeastern states, principally New York and Pennsylvania. When the newcomers bitterly joked about coming to the sunny South, the veterans of Camp Greene could only smirk. Finally, the weather improved during the second week of March. Along with better weather came relief from the tyranny of the Third Division's MG Joseph T. Dickman, who also commanded Camp Greene. Dickman granted his division priority over training sites and expropriated much of the equipment and arms that filtered into camp. To make matters worse, the remaining regular officers and almost all the regular noncommissioned and enlisted personnel left the Fourth Division to flesh out Dickman's formations. This turnover in personnel made it difficult to build any kind of unit cohesion. The Fourth Division was a "regular organization," Smith dolefully remembered, "in the sense that it was a unit in the regular establishment. A scanty sprinkling of noncommissioned officers represented the training and traditions of the 'old army.'"[10] Only after the four infantry regiments of Dickman's division marched out could the real formation of the Fourth Division begin.

The first three weeks of March brought 10,000 draftees to Greene from National Army training camps in Michigan, Illinois, Washington, Arkansas, and Texas. Many volunteers proved deficient in mental aptitude or physical condition and received discharges or noncombat assignments. Ever so slowly, the companies began to take shape. Ordnance supplies also arrived. The Fourth Division suffered a chronic shortage of rifles. One battalion received a mere 115 rifles, and these were discarded Springfields. March also saw the beginning of serious training in intensive drill and field maneuvers. Three of the four regiments completed the basic rifle course. For most of the troops, this represented their first exposure to firing weapons. The only regiment that did not take part in the course was the Thirty-ninth.[11]

The mobilization plan envisioned the orderly progression from individual to small-unit and finally divisional training. On 30 January 1918 GEN John Pershing agreed to the "Six Division Plan," the movement of American divisions to France in exchange for British promises to provide shipping. The War Department ordered the expedited transfer of divisional infantry and machine gun units to France for preliminary training with the British. The Fourth Division was one of those placed in the pipeline. Several circumstances forced revisions in the training schedule, chief among them the shock of the German spring offensive. On 25 March—four days after the first German offensive opened—Pershing met GEN Philippe Pétain at Compiègne and offered the early deployment of American troops under French command. Although woefully unprepared—without even its small-unit sequence of training complete—the

Fourth Division received orders for deployment to Europe. On 21 April 1918 advance elements began their movement to the New York City area, the port of embarkation. At Camp Mills, Long Island, the men of the division endured a strenuous week of training designed to pound the finishing touches into each company. On 28 April the first units entrained for Camp Merritt, in northern New Jersey, for more hurried training before embarkation. Meanwhile, on 1–3 May the Allied commanders and the Supreme War Council met at Abbeville and decided, in view of the crisis at the front, to rush American infantry and machine gun elements of those six designated divisions to France. Orders went forward for the Fourth Division, minus its artillery, signals, and engineer components, to complete preparations for movement to France.

Before the troops boarded their ships, they received twenty-four hours' leave. Nory and Smith's family made the trip from Indianapolis to see him off. The day he embarked, he had one final chance to visit with his family. At the last possible moment, his grandfather stepped forward on the quay and gave his grandson some sage soldierly advice. "Just remember," the old man warned, "the French Army has never been able to withstand the onslaught of the Prussian cavalry." Amidst the good-natured hoots of his fellow officers, Smith climbed the gangplank.[12]

The Orphaned Ivy Division in France

Advance elements sailed on 21 April, but movement of the division was not completed until the last day of May. The bulk of Smith's Seventh Brigade sailed from East Hoboken, New Jersey, on 7 May. In all, 35,000 men crowded on the sixteen-ship convoy for the Atlantic crossing. Getting the Thirty-ninth Regiment to Europe required a true Allied effort. The bulk of the regiment sailed in an Italian ship manned by an international crew chartered by the British government to carry American troops to France. The convoy divided; the Seventh Brigade was bound for Brest, in Brittany, while the Eighth Brigade made its way to Liverpool. Smith's passage proved uneventful, but the same could not be said for the Liverpool convoy. One ship rammed and sank a U-boat; another, the *Moldavia,* took a torpedo as it entered the western approaches to Liverpool. All but one man of B Company, Fifty-eighth Regiment perished.[13]

After a week in billets in Desvres, Deandeanville, and Bernieville in Picardy—near the Channel coast and close enough to the front to hear the reports of artillery—the Seventh Brigade wedded up with the rest of the division's infantry, less elements of the Fifty-eighth Regiment, at the Samer training area. The original plan called for each infantry division to undergo three-month-long cycles of training under French and British supervision. The first month included preliminary small-unit training; the second phase would see American battalions integrated into quiet Allied defensive sectors "to harden and accustom them to all sorts of fire"; finally, regiments, brigades, and divisions would engage in field maneuvers. At Samer the Fourth Division began its first phase of training under the guidance of the veteran British Sixteenth (Irish) Division. The German offensive obliged the abandonment of the original training scheme. Instead of a full four-week training phase, the Fourth Division remained at Samer for only eight days. First, the American infantrymen dug a trench system. Once that was complete, the British instructors demonstrated the use of weapons and rudimentary trench tactics. The Americans received instruction on Lewis guns and Stokes mortars; the British brought out flamethrowers and trained the men in methods of defense against gas attacks. Eight hours a day, the green American troops suffered through a schedule of rigorous training, climaxing in an unbroken stretch of forty-eight hours in the trenches. In the final day, the battalions practiced tactical exercises under simulated trench warfare conditions. This represented the first realistic training in modern warfare that any of the men, including the regulars, had experienced. Since the infantry regiments and their attached machine gun battalions would immediately brigade with French units, the training never included working with their own artillery and signals.

On 9 June the division marched out of the Samer training area toward predetermined marshaling points along the Hesdin-Montreuil Railway. Two days later the troops detrained at Meaux, on the Marne, in the French Sixth Army sector. On 13 June Smith's regiment attached itself to the French Fourth Division and moved to the Rosoy-en-Meltien training area, north of Meaux on the Oise. For the next two weeks the Americans' training concentrated on the problems of leading troops on the modern battlefield. They learned French methods of stringing barbed wire and passing through barrages with minimal losses, and they had their first exposure to live grenades and the Chauchat and Hotchkiss automatic rifles and machine guns. For the first time the troops of the Thirty-ninth fired their Springfields. With no range available, musketry practice involved shooting at tin cans tied to stakes.[14]

Glaring differences in American and French tactical doctrine and organization soon appeared. American infantry doctrine stressed the rifle and the bayonet as the principal weapons in the assault. The field maneuvers displayed American reliance on tightly packed infantry attacks and the absence of any real appreciation for the power of defensive weaponry, especially the machine gun and field artillery. Though impressed by the ardor of American troops, the dismayed French officers discovered that American doctrine bore striking similarities to the disastrous French infantry tactics of 1914–1915. Having absorbed the bitter lessons of the Frontiers, Champagne, and Verdun, the French army now emphasized mobile infantry tactics combined with coordinated artillery support. After observing the performance of the American infantry, the French command renewed its push to amalgamate American battalions and regiments into French and British divisions.[15]

The Ivy Division earned the dubious distinction of being the only American division in the war that served with both British and French armies. It fought its first engagements apportioned to separate French commands. On 1 July Smith's regiment came under orders of the French II Corps in the northeastern environs of Paris. On 4 July the regiment—the closest American unit to the capital—had the honor of marching in celebration of Independence Day; the next day it occupied a backup position between Autheuil and Varinfroy, guarding the approaches to Paris in the event the Germans made a renewed effort to attack the salient between Montdidier and Soissons. The Thirty-ninth remained in line for only three days, then pulled back to Acy. On 15 July the regiment moved again, and the men believed they were destined for trenches in the rear. That day the Germans unleashed their last offensive impulse, the Second Battle of the Marne. Seventeen divisions of the German Seventh Army attacked the French Sixth Army west of Reims. The assault penetrated nine miles before it ran out of steam.[16]

The Allied generalissimo, GEN Ferdinand Foch, suspected the German offensives had passed their point of culmination, offering the opportunity for a massive Allied counterstroke. Preparations for the counteroffensive continued even as the last German strategic gambit of the war wound down. The German command issued its halt orders on 17 July; early the next morning the French counteroffensive began. American divisions cut their teeth in offensive warfare in this, the Aisne-Marne offensive.

During the night of 16–17 July, the Thirty-ninth Regiment left its position in the rear and attached itself to the French Thirty-third Division. The officers and men expected a quiet tour of the French trenches, but the next night found them trudging along unknown and congested roads in a downpour through the sinister Fôret de Retz toward the western face of the Aisne-Marne salient. As Smith recounted, "Loaded down with packs, rations and ammunition, and blinded by the driving rain, the men were compelled to hold on to one another to avoid losing their way; and the company lines stumbled forward at a snail's pace after their French guides." Just before midnight Smith's battalion, the trailer element, bivouacked and grabbed a furtive bit of sleep. Detached to the battalion scout section, Smith received a quick briefing before moving into a forward observation post, where he checked his maps to ensure that the two companies designated to lead the attack the next morning occupied their correct positions. Ten minutes later a runner from the regimental command post arrived, informing him the attack would commence at first light. No patrol was ordered. Intelligence reported that a battalion of Saxon troops and a machine gun company occupied the objective—the Buisson de Cresnes, a forested spur on the other side of a stream called the Saviéres. "If strongly organized," Beetle concluded, "it would constitute a formidable obstacle.[17]

Originally, the plan called for the Americans to leap off at 5:30, an hour after the initial assault. The French attacks north and south intended to converge at the hamlet of Noroy-sur-Ourcq, east of the wood. The French corps commander sought an envelopment of the German position and ordered the Americans to "occupy" the woods only at "the most favorable moment"—after Noroy fell. American forces would mop up resistance. The French command wanted to minimize American casualties—"in effect," Smith commented, "giving [the American troops] their first taste of war in a comparatively painless dose." The doughboys watched in amazement as the seventy-battery French barrage smashed into the German positions, and they applauded as the Germans were on the receiving end. Their self-congratulations proved short-lived. As soon as the French infantry stepped off, German artillery and trench mortars opened fire on the American lines. With fifteen minutes remaining before the attack, word arrived delaying the move until eight o'clock.

Their objective dominated the terrain between the Ourcq and its tributary, the Saviéres. General Operations Order 200 underscored the "importance of the nest of batteries and Center of Resistance of Noroy."[18] German control of the high ground and forest blocked the advance of the Thirty-third Division and complicated communications along the boundaries of the French armies. Instead of mopping up, the Thirty-ninth received orders to take the vital position.

The first day's fighting illuminated the inadequacies of training, the ambiguities in the tactical doctrine, and the poor quality of American leadership. COL Frank Bolles deployed his three battalions in textbook fashion for an echeloned attack, with the first on the right, leading the way. The two lead companies advanced down a long wheat-covered slope, plunged through a fringe of trees, and descended a bluff to the river.

An eerie silence had engulfed the valley since the end of the German bombardment two hours before. As he watched his comrades' advance, Smith remembered, "The morning was so bright and so still that it became difficult to believe this was anything more than a field maneuver." The night before, the tired regimental staff had hastily examined their maps and, thinking the stream at their front presented no obstacle, ordered no reconnaissance. But the rains had filled the river and swollen the usually sluggish Saviéres over its banks, which were flanked by deep and difficult marshes.

"The two companies promptly became mixed in a hopeless confusion not two-hundred yards from the enemy position," Smith recounted. "Their floundering, splashing, and shouting made noise enough to alarm every German in the Marne salient." A couple of combat patrols managed a crossing and pushed to make contact. They did not have long to wait. Two German machine gun teams emerged from the edge of the forest. One German machine gun opened fire immediately. "The burst of fire expedited the crossing," Smith wryly recollected, "more than any amount of expostulation from the officers."

That same burst of fire inaugurated Smith's combat career, but not the way he fancied. He felt "that some concession to formality was required on the occasion of his first battle" and decided to wear his best uniform. The Germans had strung together logs to facilitate patrolling. Beetle gingerly stepped from log to log, trying not to fall in and soil his uniform. When the first machine gun bullet cracked over his head, Smith found himself submerged in a muddy pool. By the time he crawled out of the muck, the German machine guns had been suppressed. The American forces re-formed and entered the wood. A captured sergeant cleared up the mystery of why the Germans never defended the river line: they assumed that no commander in his right mind would assault across swampy ground and a flooded stream against an enemy commanding the heights in broad daylight. Accordingly, the Germans faced south toward the Ourcq.

Smith's First Battalion encountered scattered but determined resistance as it moved toward a ridge that anchored the defense. Most of the Germans skedaddled—more than 200 of them were collected skulking in the woods—but those that remained manned concealed firing positions that commanded the tracks and firebreaks. Officers lost control as the fighting degenerated into contests between isolated German strong points and extemporized American patrols. Many of the American troops took advantage of the disorder to break away in search of souvenirs. Adding to the confusion, the First Battalion found both its flanks up in the air. Summoned to the command post, Smith received orders to take a patrol, find the Third Battalion, and inform its commander of the situation. Moving into an open flank with Germans lurking about, Smith found no sign of the Third Battalion. He headed back toward the river, finally bumping into elements of the sister unit. What he discovered alarmed him. French division headquarters had delayed the Third Battalion's attack. The First Battalion was on its own. Smith hastened back to inform his commander.

After two more hours of fighting, the Americans secured the ridge; German resistance collapsed. Breaking out of the gloom of the forest, the First Battalion looked down on Noroy, still in German control. Around three o'clock the French division commander, fearing a counterattack from Noroy, requested that the Thirty-ninth storm the village. An hour later, the other two battalions finally arrived. Smith's battalion was ordered to make the assault, but the Third Battalion, responding to the request of a neighboring French unit, launched the attack. Had German defenders been present in force, the unsupported actions of a single battalion might have ended in disaster, but once again, fortune shone on the callow American troops. The town fell after brief hand-to-hand fighting. German machine guns deployed in a gully southeast of the town, and a battery of field guns blocked any further advance. Veterans of a day's combat, the Thirty-ninth dug in, facing the German guns, and spent the night in shallow foxholes under sporadic German shell fire.[19]

Orders called for a general attack at 4:30 the next morning. Smith's unit would spearhead the effort to eliminate the German gunners that had checked the advance the preceding evening. Differences in language, doctrine, organization, and staff methods made it difficult for American formations to operate under French command. The preliminary barrage never materialized, but the Americans advanced regardless. By five o'clock they secured their first objective. Fifteen minutes later, word arrived that the French on the right had never received the attack order, so the advance, preceded by a heavy barrage, was put off until 5:30. Runners were dispatched to inform the French command that the first objective had already been taken, but too late. Nor could the battalions be recalled. Raked by machine gun fire to their front, the American troops held their exposed positions for forty minutes. Rockets and flares were fired, to no effect. Unable to retreat into the creeping curtain of friendly artillery fire, the doughboys had little choice but to grimly assail the German position. The attack dislodged the Germans from the ravine, but at a frightful cost.

Remarkably, the Thirty-ninth re-formed and advanced toward its final objective—the road south of the village of Chouy. A high ridge stood halfway between the jumping-off line and the road. The route of attack crossed one large wheat field rising toward the ridge and down through another toward the village and road. Sheltered by the fog of battle, the two assault companies cleared the ridge and took the village. The Germans manned machine guns in the many thickets that dotted the fields; the open ground remained under artillery observation for guns sited behind Chouy and the same battery that had been dislodged earlier on the flank to the south. The two support companies, slowed by these pockets of "stay-behind" German resistance, fell behind and became separated from the assault units. As battalion scout officer, Smith usually remained close to the battalion command. In this case, the major went forward to link up with Companies C and D on the Chouy road, and Smith attached himself to Company B. As the support companies moved up the rise and over the ridge, they assumed assault formation in accordance with the 1911 Field Service Regulations: Company B in two parallel lines in skirmish order, followed at the proper gap by Company A in section columns.

Every gun of the now alerted Germans trained on the advancing infantry. "None of the officers or men who witnessed the scene which took place during the ensuing five minutes will ever forget it." Smith never would. Company B never saw the "halt—go back" signal flashed by wigwag from the road cutting, and the men marched forward as if on parade: preserving perfect alignment and intervals, never moving faster than a walk, their rifles held at high port. It seemed to Smith that "a shell fell among [us] almost at every step . . . bowling men over like ten-pins." It could just as well have been another memorable wheat field in another war. After advancing halfway to Chouy, the troops broke into a run. The lucky ones made it to the road cutting and safety. Smith was not among them. Second Lieutenant Walter Bedell Smith numbered among the wounded—his combat career lasting less than thirty-six hours.[20]

Baptism into the General Staff

Smith was lucky to survive the maelstrom of shot and shell that descended on his unit during that morning attack beyond Noroy, but no one experiences such horror with impunity. The psychological scars remained. Veterans bore those memories the rest of their days. Smith was carried from the battlefield to an advance aid station, where his wounds were cleaned and dressed. Since his condition was not life threatening, Smith remained at the aid station while the seriously wounded were evacuated. From there, Smith went to a hastily constructed field hospital, a collection of tents concealed in a grove of trees behind the front. As he lay in the hospital tent jammed with the casualties of the first two days of the Aisne-Marne offensive, Smith watched as the medical staff advanced from soldier to soldier, injecting each with a tetanus shot directly into the stomach with a hypodermic needle "the size of a railway spike." After the shell fragments were removed, Smith was transferred to a base hospital housed in a former school. The hospital handled the more serious casualties or, in Smith's case, provided convalescent care. Since his wounds healed quickly and without complications, Beetle's stay proved brief. After a furlough, he awaited orders and fully expected to return to his unit.[21] The army had other ideas.

The crippling shortage of trained staff officers hamstrung the army—in both France and the Zone of the Interior. Under the limitations imposed by the National Defense Act (NDA) of 1916, the General Staff Corps possessed a ceiling strength of forty-one officers for the entire army. In May 1917 the cap rose to ninety-one. Having "first call," Pershing saw to it that virtually all officers with prewar service in the minuscule general staff and graduates of the staff course at Leavenworth came to France. The Leavenworth men staffed the American Expeditionary Force Headquarters (AEFHQ) at Chaumont and served in the headquarters of the major commands, but there were never enough. An extemporized staff school established at Langres trained line and technical officers in staff functions; 537 officers eventually passed through the ninety-day course. Demand far outstripped supply.[22]

In the opinion of George Chamberlain, chairman of the Senate Military Affairs Committee, the War Department "had fallen down" under the burden of mobilization.[23] Three officers occupied the chief of staff's chair after the declaration of war, and all three seemed perfectly content to act as rubber stamps to Pershing. Wilson and his secretary of war, Newton Baker, abdicated executive control over military affairs. Pershing exploited this vacuum in Washington, denying the War Department any measure of coordinate command over the American Expeditionary Force (AEF). The appointment of GEN Peyton March as acting chief of staff in March 1918 challenged Pershing's autonomy.

March ruthlessly restructured the War Department General Staff (WDGS). The Overman Act of 20 May 1918 increased the powers of the executive branch and, with it, the size of the general staff. March moved immediately to reorganize the WDGS and expand its size and functions. Another more sweeping restructuring followed on 26 August.

Described by Baker as "arrogant, harsh, dictatorial, and opinionated," March bypassed the War Council, diminished the influence of the Executive Division, crushed the ancient independence of the bureau chiefs, increased the authority of the War Plans and Operations Divisions, and centralized logistics in the newly created and clumsily named Purchase, Storage, and Traffic Division. Seeing the chief of staff and the general staff as the fulcrum of a modern military structure, March moved to redefine the locus of command in the U.S. military establishment. In late August he issued a general order declaring that the chief of staff "takes rank and precedence over all officers in the Army."[24]

Baker considered these questions of command and staff structure "purely technical" and "unimportant." Wilson remained detached. MG James Harbord, Pershing's first chief of staff, spoke for his boss when he labeled March's claim a "hallucination." Harbord wrote to Pershing, "All you wish from America is such Staff Service there as will insure you a steady flow of troops and supplies. You do not want there a Staff dealing with any phase of your business here." In effect, the U.S. Army was divided—Pershing and the AEF versus March and the WDGS.[25]

Lieutenant Smith stood far removed from this top-brass power struggle, but unbeknownst to him, it influenced his career enormously. On 14 March 1918 the War Department initiated a rotation scheme. March thought it vital to infuse the WDGS with the AEF viewpoint. He asked Pershing to send thirty general staff officers to Washington. Pershing and Harbord interpreted this as a raid on the AEF's monopoly of general staff officers. Pershing had only sixty-four such officers, and March now claimed nearly half of them. Under pressure, Harbord relented. Determined to defend the "Chaumont Circle" from War Department poaching, Harbord dispatched the thirty officers, only three of whom proved suitable for general staff work. That ended the first rotation scheme. The AEF had won this round.[26]

The August reorganization of the WDGS renewed calls for rotation between Washington and France. Pershing instructed his G-1 (Personnel) Division to search the records of junior officers serving in the theater for men with "previous preparation for general staff work." BG LeRoy Eltinge, the deputy chief of staff, directed the tactical commands to detach those officers "who have satisfactorily performed general staff duty for at least two months" for temporary staff assignment. Instead of channeling these officers through the three-month Langres course, they went directly to a headquarters to perform routine duties, releasing experienced officers for more essential tasks. The directive contained an important caveat. In keeping with the desire to maintain the elite status of the general staff, Eltinge instructed that "special care be exercised in the selection of officers not of the regular establishment." Officers so designated served as "attached to" rather than as members of the General Staff Corps. This process, already well advanced, allowed the AEFHQ to fill the quota when the next War Department request came through.[27]

Smith was one of the 296 officers—77 nonregulars—tabbed for temporary general staff duty. Beetle held a reserve commission but had served capably with the regular Fourth Division. What jumped out from his service record was his time spent in the headquarters of the Indiana National Guard during the border crisis. At the time, Beetle had been heartbroken that he could not go to the Mexican border, but that stint on the staff in Indianapolis altered the whole vector of his military career. Instead of returning to his unit for the "big push" in the Argonne, Smith received orders to proceed to Brest and transship to Washington. He also learned of his promotion to first lieutenant.

Smith's circumstances changed dramatically in a dizzyingly short time. Scarcely six weeks before, he had been wounded; on 1 September 1918 he walked down Pennsylvania Avenue in search of the State War and Navy Building, where he would report to the Military Intelligence Division. Less than a week old, the division had emerged out of March's August reorganization. The old saw about military intelligence being an oxymoron pretty much held true for the prewar army. In April 1917 the Military Intelligence Branch, a subsection of the War College Division, consisted of two officers and two civilian clerks. Finding it "unbelievable" that no proper military intelligence apparatus existed, March reorganized the structure in May 1918 and created a separate Military Intelligence Section. Expanded in size and responsibility, the Military Intelligence Section served two masters—the Executive and War Plans (War College) Divisions—making it the only divided section. This change constituted a central part of the chief of staff's incremental reformation of the WDGS. The final reorganization in August saw the creation of an autonomous and enlarged Military Intelligence Division.[28]

BG Marlborough Churchill, one of the thirty officers exchanged by Harbord in March, headed the new division. When Smith reported for duty, the division numbered 173 officers, 23 noncommissioned officers, and 589 civilian employees. In addition to handling conventional military intelligence functions—preparation of strategic estimates and the collection, evaluation, and dissemination of military information—the division dealt with censorship and with sabotage and subversion inside the army and in war plants. In the eleven weeks between the August reorganization and the armistice, 109 officers, 6 noncommissioned officers, and 359 civilian employees—ranging from clerks to university professors—joined the division, swelling it to 1,259 officers and men, a far cry from the 4 men who had staffed military intelligence when the United States entered the war.

Without formal staff training, Smith was thrown into the breach. He was not alone. In November 1918, of the 1,073 officers in the WDGS, only four generals, including the chief of staff, had seen prewar general staff duty. During the hectic days of the summer and autumn of 1918, the staff strained to keep pace with the deluge of administrative details that attended the organization, maintenance, and dispatch of American divisions to Europe. Any staff expedites decision making and routes communications upward toward responsible agencies and individuals within the hierarchy of command. At the lowest level, a staff acts as a clearinghouse for the mass of paperwork and facilitates the flow of documents through the system. Smith resided on the bottom rung.[29]

Beetle's job involved receiving incoming communications, examining the content to determine their proper disposition, and making entries on tally cards outlining subject material, source, date of receipt, and distribution. Routine matters flowed through the division for remarks and concurrence and, when necessary, forwarding to other divisions. Important correspondence went into a special file for the attention of the secretary of the general staff, who determined its disposition. Documents of an urgent nature bypassed this routing system and were relayed by special messengers to the proper agency.[30]

Smith's apprenticeship as a general staff officer proved short-lived. No sooner had he gained an understanding of the systematized framework of staff procedures and familiarized himself with the labyrinthine State War and Navy Building than he received another assignment. Orders came down for him to report to Camp Sherman, Ohio, where he would assume the dual duties of adjutant and intelligence officer to the new 379th Infantry Regiment. In an attempt to rectify the critical shortage of trained staff officers, the War Department established a one-month staff course at the Army War College. Owing to Smith's experience in the WDGS, he proceeded directly to his assignment.

The brief exposure to the WDGS provided Smith with invaluable experience. It served as his initial exposure to official Washington, and service in the general staff improved his chances of gaining the regular army commission he coveted. In addition, Smith's assignment at the War Department expanded his appreciation of the necessity for and functioning of high-level military organizations. Officers who spent time in the general staff came away with an enhanced awareness of the complexities of modern bureaucratized warfare and the essential role of staff organization. March's no-nonsense approach demanded a high degree of decentralization. He expected officers at all levels to exercise their own initiative. Finally, the business methods of the wartime WDGS set the standards for staff procedures for decades to come. Smith's education received during his brief appointment to General March's staff laid a solid foundation for his future development as a staff officer.

During summer and autumn 1918, the War Department prepared for the expected "open warfare" campaign of 1919 and directed the formation of twenty-one new infantry divisions. The Ninety-fifth Division's organization began on 5 September at Camp Sherman. Established in June 1917, Sherman housed an officer training school and served as training center for four divisions. The 190th Infantry Brigade, which included the 379th Regiment, began organizing in September and by the end of October had reached a strength of 6,400 officers and men. Because of the chronic shortage of staff personnel, division headquarters absorbed the regimental and brigade staffs. Smith's section handled the deluge of paperwork involved in the creation of a division. As coordinating authority between the War Department and the division, the adjutant staff dealt with the routine work of issuing assignment, transfer, and discharge papers, as well as overseeing the compilation of headquarters files.

The influenza pandemic hit Camp Sherman in September and October 1918. As at Camp Greene, the living arrangements meant that enlisted men suffered horribly from the sweep of the disease. Healthy men succumbed within days of contracting the flu. The 1,400 cases in September exploded to 5,600 in October. In all, 1,200 men died. A theater in the post town of Chillicothe served as a temporary morgue, where the corpses were stacked like cordwood. Serious training all but stopped. Then in November, the war ended. On 30 November orders arrived initiating demobilization. Three days later, Camp Sherman was designated one of thirty regional demobilization centers.

By November 1918 the War Department had mobilized 3,703,273 officers and men, with 1.5 million in the United States. The first order of business involved rapidly discharging men in units in the Zone of the Interior, clearing the way for the reception and disposition of men and equipment from France. With the public clamoring "to bring the boys home," the War Department expedited the process. Wholesale demobilization proceeded by unit. By 4 January 1919, 732,766 men had been separated from the army; by 1 February, the number rose to 1,026,766;

and by 1 May, nearly 2 million men had been demobilized. Demobilization meant that the adjutant section had to wade through mountains of paperwork, seriously overtaxing the skeleton staff. In December Smith moved to the amalgamated adjutant section of the demobilization center. Camp Sherman discharged 30,527 officers and men; in addition, the adjutant section helped plan for the phased demobilization of the Eighty-fourth Division.[31]

February brought orders for Smith to report to Camp Dodge, Iowa, and the 163rd Depot Brigade. Another training-cum-demobilization center, Camp Dodge prepared to receive and demobilize the Eighty-eighth Division. The depot brigade's responsibilities involved the marshaling and disposal of the vast surplus stocks of weapons, ammunition, equipment, and other materiel. Smith remained in this assignment for less than a month. In March he joined the staff of the Second Infantry Regiment.

Formed in 1808, the Second Infantry boasted a long and storied history; its greatest battlefield honors had come in the storming of Chapultepec in the war against Mexico. American entry into the European war found the regiment garrisoning Fort Shafter in the Hawaiian Islands. It was transferred first to Camp Fremont, California, in July 1918, then to Camp Dodge in September. Along with another regular regiment, the Fourteenth, the Second Infantry provided the foundation for the Nineteenth Division, one of the divisions created by the War Department in summer 1918. On 19 January 1919 Washington ordered the immediate demobilization of all units at Camp Dodge, except the two regular regiments. Smith's transfer to the Second Regiment represented another stroke of good fortune; it guaranteed he would end his wartime service as he had begun it—with a regular army formation.

The rate of demobilization proceeded with such speed that by early summer 1919, Camp Dodge appeared to be virtually deserted. No longer performing the hectic administrative duties connected with demobilization, Beetle had plenty of time to indulge his passion for fishing and hunting. Located a dozen miles north of Des Moines, Camp Dodge was situated in the center of a vast, undulating prairie, presenting plenty of opportunities for the outdoorsman. In spring and autumn ducks abounded, and autumn featured deer and wild turkey seasons. The many streams provided the fisherman with pickerel, pike, catfish, and bass. Smith remained in Camp Dodge until November 1919, when the Second Infantry transferred to Camp Sherman.[32]

At both Dodge and Sherman, Smith found a changed atmosphere. One junior officer spoke for many when he noted, on arriving at his duty station in 1919, "everybody [was] trying to restore the good old days."[33] Prewar officers, especially of field grade, reverted to the rhythms of the "old army"—the comfortable period before the war, France, fighting with allies, and the encumbrances of hordes of National Army officers and unruly citizen-soldiers. With demobilization complete, life in the adjutant section of the Second Infantry settled into a numbing routine. Chillicothe offered few distractions. Smith preoccupied himself with gauging his chances of gaining a regular army commission. He had every reason to be pleased with his war record. He had gone to France, saw combat, visited Paris, and received a Purple Heart, the World War Victory Medal with three campaign clasps, and a Croix de Guerre with Star. He surmised his performance in his many staff jobs improved his prospects; certainly, his stint in the WDGS and his ribbons looked good on his service record, and he consistently scored "excellent" in his efficiency reports.[34] In addition, his current posting in a regular unit might help. Like every officer in the army, Beetle Smith anxiously followed the congressional hearings that would influence the future organization and size of the peacetime army.

Forward into the Past

The army did not come off well in the debates. The nation's wartime enthusiasm soon turned to disillusionment, and traditional sentiments against a standing army resurfaced. In one respect, Wilson had been right: Americans saw themselves as too good to fight in Europe's corrupting wars. Americans wanted to avoid entangling alliances, collective security, and international responsibilities of any sort. They wanted a return to normalcy. Some believed unpreparedness for war a virtue; after all, the war represented a victory over Prussian militarism and the diabolical German general staff. Liberals raised concerns about the place of the army in a democracy, their views colored by the army's strikebreaking during the "Red Summer" of 1919. The National Guard saw conspiracies to disband the organized militia. The influential Military Training Camps Association pushed for an expanded and federally funded national Plattsburg program. Congress balked at the expense of maintaining a large standing army; Republicans assaulted Wilson's internationalism by attacking the army.

The army itself—torn into Pershing and March factions—engaged in its own internecine and highly publicized battles. Behind the scenes, Pershing opposed March's ambitious plan for a half-million-man regular army. One of his AEFHQ men—BG John McAuley Palmer—testified before the Senate Military Affairs Committee. The son of a Civil War general of volunteers, Palmer's one-hour defense of the American citizen-soldier "[tore] Peyton C. March's bill into scraps," according to James Wadsworth, the committee chair.[35] If any doubt remained concerning the future direction of military policy, it ended with Pershing's appearance before a joint session of Congress in October. Even though Baker admitted to Wilson that the NDA of 1920 did not provide for "as effective [a] reorganization as the country ought to have," and despite his belief that "many things the war has taught us . . . we have not learned," the secretary of war advised the president not to veto the final bill.[36]

The Progressive Era (roughly 1890 to 1917) and the expanded strategic responsibilities after 1898 provided an environment for sweeping reform and the first flowering of genuine American military professionalism. The postwar retreat from responsibility into political conservatism and fiscal stringency had the opposite effect. The notion that the United States would not be involved in another great power clash in the next generation—which colored army thinking as much as it did that of the public and Congress—and the rejection of an activist foreign policy provided scant imperatives to maintain high levels of readiness. The army's preoccupations were managerial—principally, maintaining sufficient levels for training an expansible army while preserving some degree of preparedness. Since manpower ceilings averaged 137,300 in the years between 1923 and 1935—less than half that provided for in the 1920 legislation—the army faced a Sisyphean labor. Correspondingly, military appropriations in 1925 stood at one-quarter of 1920 levels. Not surprisingly, the army faced real difficulties retaining junior officers and, as the employer of last resort, experienced problems recruiting adequate numbers to fill its meager manpower authorizations. As standards dropped, so did quality; the army of the 1920s possessed more than its share of social misfits.[37] All this lay in the near future, but the guiding trends had emerged by 1920.

Any army defends the right to regulate itself. Historically, military reforms in the United States followed administrative disasters that fanned sufficient public criticism to prompt hesitant external governmental interventions; the army never reformed itself. Popular isolationism and revulsion of all things military led to the army's segregation from political leaders and civil society; this, in turn, resulted in congressional budgetary strangulation, rendering the army incapable of conducting serious training or acquiring new weapons and equipment. Financial stringency exacerbated age-old interservice and branch rivalries. The lack of money, materiel, manpower, affirmative governmental oversight, and public support offers excuses for why the U.S. Army slouched back into its prewar ways. It does not explain the poverty of American military thinking in 1919–1920, when public and government interest remained high and appropriations were adequate; nor does it explain why the army's leadership rejected the lessons of the war. In the aftermath of the bitter debate over the NDA of 1920, the army enjoyed too much autonomy. Given the absence of external political pressure and any real foreign threat, the senior officers who controlled the army in the interwar period felt no compulsion to confront its defects.

No evidence exists that the U.S. Army would have embraced change if it had enjoyed adequate funding. Resource constraints need not stifle modernization; indeed, scarcity can act as a spur to innovation. The Marine Corps developed the Fleet Marine Force and the doctrine of balanced, combined arms amphibious warfare with fewer assets and coped with stiffer institutional resistance than that which confronted the U.S. Army. The army needed progressive, supple minds in high command instead of old army hangovers. It also needed professional leaders selected on the basis of their ability, not their connections, age, and seniority. The army's bureaucratic politics and corporate culture retarded the internal debate and suffocated any new thinking, virtually guaranteeing the fossilization of the officer corps.

Such obligatory trimming in a democracy demanded a radical reorganization of defense forces. The NDA of 1920 created structural change without any corresponding alteration in the conceptualization of defense requirements. The act established a large and complex organizational structure geared toward the idea of an expansible army: a general staff and the office of the assistant secretary of war to plan; a regular army of 280,000, backed by an organized reserve and National Guard; and force structures designed to raise a mass army of the 1918 type. The legislation apportioned the continental United States into nine corps districts: each contained one regular, two National Guard, and three National Army divisions. The officers of this expansible National Army component would come from a proposed Officer Reserve Corps of 120,000 and a projected Enlisted Reserve Corps—enough to form the first twenty-seven divisions (546,000 men) to be put into the field one year after the outbreak of hostilities. The legislation granted the WDGS statutory expression but never defined command relationships, assigning it the narrowest roles in planning and oversight of mobilization; it also preserved the old bureaus and added new ones for the combat arms. Most of the wartime missions performed by the WDGS were lost under the terms of the 1920 legislation and reverted to the bureau chiefs. Because the "Army of the United States" depended on trained and integrated National Guard and reserve components, the 1920 act tripled the size of the prewar officer corps to 17,717.[38]

Officers concerned themselves with questions such as the role of the National Guard, universal military training, and restructuring of the WDGS, but the core question concerned the size and nature of the postwar officer corps. As part of the demobilization process, National Guard and reserve officers who expressed an interest in remaining in the army took qualifying examinations to determine their fitness for a commission. The competition was intense. Two hundred thousand men held temporary commissions during the war, and 14,565 took the qualifying examination. On 30 June 1920 the new officer lists appeared. Officers of the regular army reverted to their permanent ranks. Colonels became captains overnight. Some received immediate promotions, effective the next day; most did not. Smith's name appeared on the roster, and he was both relieved and surprised. Not only did he receive his commission, but he also retained his rank. Even without a West Point ring or university credentials, Smith now stood on equal ground with every first lieutenant in the U.S. Army.

★ 8 ★

"They Don't Make 'Em Any Better than Smith"

Junior officers like Smith who stayed in the army did so because they wanted to soldier. Some, perhaps the majority, remained in the army because they enjoyed the undemanding lifestyle. The army provided a haven from social change, and the war unleashed plenty of that. For those officers, ambition counted for little; soldiering provided a pleasant occupation rather than a challenging profession. Others sought peer-related status by accepting the norms of military organization and hierarchy, worked at acquiring the practical skills of leadership, and passed through the army's formal and informal educational system. They understood the cultural ambivalence, even hostility, the army faced in a pluralistic and amilitary (even antimilitary) society like the United States. They rationalized their existence as professional soldiers and defended their collegial corporateness as officers by pointing to their selfless devotion to duty, honor, and country and their sense of responsibility to the republic they served. Confronted by glacial advancement under the 1920 promotion structure and scant opportunities for holding line commands, most endured a succession of undemanding postings, knowing the best they could hope for was retirement with a colonel's pension. Despite all the drawbacks—and in the 1920s the allure of private-sector salaries—the "long generation" of officers stayed in the army. Smith was more than happy with his lot. He had always wanted a commission and remained determined to be the best officer he could be; he was equally resolved to make up for lost ground.

Peacetime Soldiering

A year after the passage of the landmark 1920 NDA, Congress pared the size of the regular army. Faced by shrinking manpower and spending ceilings—but required to preserve the mandated nine-corps force structure—the army consolidated many of its tactical units and closed bases. Camp Sherman fell victim to the budget ax. Smith's detachment was merged with its sister components at Fort Sheridan, Illinois.

Unlike Smith's previous postings, Sheridan was a permanent installation, built in the late 1880s. Chicago's commercial and industrial elite had feared a repeat of the 1877 Haymarket violence and petitioned the War Department to build a fort in the environs of the city. Men such as George Pullman and Marshall Fields acquired land twenty-five miles north of downtown, along Lake Michigan; offered it at no charge to the army; and enlisted the support of MG Phillip Sheridan, then posted to Chicago, in winning over the War Department and Congress. The soon-to-be-renowned firm of Holabird and Roche received its first major commission to design the fort. An impressive gate and tower—taller than any extant structure in Chicago—anchored a line of massive stone barracks that dominated the post. The comfortable and stylish officer housing and the fort's proximity to Chicago made Sheridan among the most desirable postings in the army.[1]

For Beetle and Nory, the move to Fort Sheridan allowed them to set up a real household for the first time. Until then, the constant shuffling of assignments had made for long separations. The construction of Camp Sherman had produced an economic and building boom in Chillicothe, whose population shot up from 16,000 to 60,000. Wartime training centers had no accommodations for junior officers who were married, and housing and rental properties in overcrowded Chillicothe stood beyond the price range of lowly lieutenants. The Smiths had to be content with frequent visits; luckily, Chillicothe was not far from Indianapolis. At Sheridan, the couple moved into one of the adjoining brownstone quarters on Lieutenants' Row, across from the parade grounds. The army never placed a priority on maintaining its housing. When the future Mrs. Patton visited her intended at Sheridan in 1910, the shabbiness of the quarters and the fear that she could never become a "good army wife" so frightened Bea that she offered to give George "his freedom." Twelve years later the housing must have been even more dilapidated, but the Smiths did not mind. Nor did Beetle have any reason to complain about Nory's ability to fulfill the duties of a good army wife.

On American posts, where work and residence overlapped, officers' wives played an indispensable social role. For ambitious young officers in the interwar army, having a wife who could "mix and entertain" ranked above high standing on efficiency reports.[2] Books were published (and frequently updated) for prospective army wives to use as manuals of army etiquette. Sheridan featured a lively social scene, both on and off post. Other army installations stood next to rough-around-the-edges post towns; Sheridan lay adjacent to Lake Forest, home to some of the wealthiest families in the country. Officers' families were invited to functions, sometimes lavish affairs, on the grounds of the Lake Forest mansions. It was, after all, the Roaring Twenties. Never comfortable with the soirée set, Beetle could not dodge all social commitments. Fortunately, Nory's social polish compensated for her husband's awkwardness. Described as "always well dressed but not flashy," Nory Smith, a product of finishing school, was perfectly at home with the patrician pretensions of interwar army society. Although Nory performed her mandatory "drop by" visits to senior officers' wives, and the Smiths always returned social obligations, the couple preferred to keep to themselves. For instance, they never attended the Saturday night bash at the officers' club. One officer recalled Nory as reticent, "without a doubt the most meticulous housekeeper," and noted, "She lived for Beetle."[3]

In his spare time, Beetle pursued his passion for the out-of-doors. Beautifully situated on Lake Michigan, the military reserve provided plenty of space for hiking with Nory and bird hunting with the spaniels Smith carefully trained. The trout streams and woods of northern Illinois and Wisconsin also lay within easy driving distance. The four years spent at Sheridan represented some of the happiest times in the Smiths' life together.

Social awkwardness and a brusque personality would not carry Smith far. What he needed was a reputation. In the interwar army—given the small size of the officer corps—reputation meant everything. West Point began—and in some cases nearly completed—the process of reputation formation. When the World War II generation of senior officers thought back over their careers, they always cited West Point as the pivotal juncture when an officer laid the foundation of his future reputation. Cadets could tell even then who would eventually become a general. Character meant more than class standing or the opinion of the West Point tactical officers. Even though West Pointers constituted only 37 percent of the interwar officer corps, the presence or absence of a West Point ring was significant. With no West Point connections, Smith could never gain admission into that "band of brothers" that existed in the army. To make up for the deficiency, Smith settled on outperforming his rivals in whatever billet he held. That tactic had worked with Captain Hurt, and it remained the bedrock of Smith's modus operandi for getting ahead. He believed virtue would be rewarded; if he proved more dedicated, loyal, and efficient than other officers in his grade, he could still win the respect of his seniors and, with it, the preferments necessary for advancement in the officer corps. He resented the West Pointers but employed that bitterness to fuel his resolve. During the next four years, Smith worked tirelessly to build a reputation in the U.S. Army. But hard work would not suffice. A junior officer on the make needed a patron, a senior officer who could spread the good word and pull strings.

George Van Horn Moseley: Mentor and Role Model

As the army withdrew into its old habits, with officers' days ending at noon, Smith wasted no free time. He embarked on a mission to educate himself. He started a new collection—an extensive library. With eclectic interests, Smith devoured everything from pulp detective and spy novels to Joseph Conrad and Ford Maddox Ford. But he reserved the majority of his reading time for military subjects ranging from army training and weapons manuals to the classics of military history and thought.[4] Although he always pursued an autodidactic path, Smith's education also benefited enormously from his relationship with one of those rare interwar senior officers who mentored talented young officers: BG George Van Horn Moseley.

Beetle impressed his regimental commander; COL Frank Watson awarded him a "superior" ranking on his annual report and brought his crackerjack adjutant to the attention of Moseley, the new commander of the parent Twelfth Infantry Brigade. Considering Smith's talents wasted at the regimental level, Moseley made Beetle his aide in mid-October 1922.

Born in nearby Evanston in 1874, Moseley was a member of the West Point class of 1899. A Leavenworth honors graduate, he briefly served as chief of staff in the Seventh Division in France before moving into Pershing's headquarters, first as coordinating chief and then, after the formation of the general staff, as assistant chief of staff for supply (G-4). Among the rising stars, Moseley was considered "the most brilliant mind in the Army" by some, and he was tabbed as future chief of staff material.[5]

Normally, being a general's aide was a thankless job, a glorified "dog robber" in army parlance. But Smith spent a great deal of time alone with the general, and he did not waste the opportunity. A forthright and opinionated officer and never inhibited by superior rank, Moseley openly criticized current policies—particularly the tightfisted and sanctimonious politicians who framed them—and lamented the sorry plight of the army.[6] Moseley used the time to educate Smith. He suggested books for Smith to read, which they later dissected. Smith avidly listened to Moseley's insider stories about Pershing, the other top Allied and American generals, and the leading lights of the "Chaumont Clique." The story Moseley most liked retelling featured his celebrated battle with Harbord.

In the last weeks of the war, Moseley fought a bitter and successful rearguard action, preserving Pershing's "unity of command" in France. March convinced the secretary of war that the near collapse of the American line of communications threatened the very independence of the American armies in France. March wanted a restructuring of the theater command, elevating the Services of Supply (SOS) into a coordinate, not subordinate, command; he had just completed a similar restructuring in the WDGS. Moseley possessed very strong views on the structure and functions of the general staff. In his opinion, the War Department's attempt to elevate the SOS into a coordinate command merely served as cover for forming a bridgehead for March in his assertion of command over the entire army. An independent SOS would evolve into the forward echelon of the WDGS. As G-4 in AEFHQ, Moseley argued that operations should determine logistics—which supplies went forward, and where—not the inverse. Logisticians should never dictate operations; nor should they ever exercise any measure of separate command. March's creation of a unified logistics command in the WDGS that overrode the bureaus and conferred command responsibilities on MG George Goethals raised a red flag. The G-4 in AEFHQ should control supply; the SOS should have been reduced to a mere receiving and forwarding agency for materiel that moved from ports to regulating stations in the advance sections. Moseley would control the flow and distribution of men and supplies to the major field commands. Pershing had placed Harbord, his trusted chief of staff and confederate, in control of SOS in a move calculated to cut off any new appointment from Washington or any attempted restructuring of the theater command. Then on 10 October 1918 Harbord received a fiat from Moseley reorganizing the entire system of supply. AEFHQ would centralize control of all theater logistics. Harbord always stoutly defended Pershing's command prerogatives, but he hit the roof when a mere G-4, a boy brigadier general (Moseley was only forty-four), issued a diktat undercutting his command authority.

Moseley dug in his heels against Harbord and his chief of staff, BG Johnson Hagood. The war ended without any resolution of the heated tug-of-war.

The wrangle with Harbord and Hagood secured Moseley's army-wide reputation; it also reinforced Pershing's high regard for him. Despite Moseley's being a Pershing protégé, March asked him to head the restructured War College. Not seeing "much future in the Army," Moseley rejected March's offer and considered taking one of several good offers in the private sector, but he changed his mind when Pershing succeeded March as chief of staff in 1921.[7]

The army's overriding responsibility, in the estimate of Pershing, centered on ensuring "that our traditional citizen army be organized in time of peace instead of being extemporized, as in the past, after danger had actually come."[8] The NDA of 1920 created an expansible army, with reliance placed on a trained and integrated National Guard and reserve. The War Department saw an opportunity to steal a march on its political adversary, the National Guard and its powerful lobby, by building on its wartime connection with the Military Training Camp Association (MTCA)—the Plattsburg movement (named after one of the 1915 camps held at Plattsburgh Barracks, New York)—and laying the foundations for a ready reserve of trained officers and men.

The training camp movement evolved from two summer camps established by Chief of Staff Leonard Wood in 1911, providing military and citizenship training to college students. By 1914 the number of camps doubled and then expanded to nine in 1915. The encampments attracted not only students but also civic-minded business and professional men. Despite Democratic criticism that the camps represented nests of elitist Republican interventionists, President Wilson told Congress in December 1914: "We must depend in every time of national peril, in the future as in the past, not upon a standing army, nor yet upon a reserve army, but upon a citizenry trained and accustomed to arms. We should encourage such training and make it a means of discipline, which our young men will learn to value."[9]

In 1916 the MTCA emerged. Fueled by war in Europe and trouble on the Mexican border, 10,000 volunteers paid their own way to attend ten camps held across the country. The MTCA vigorously lobbied for a national civilian volunteer reserve component. The Plattsburg movement's leader, Grenville Clark, was a law partner of Elihu Root, the influential former secretary of war who drove the creation of the first American general staff system. The efforts bore fruit. The NDA of 1916 provided the opportunity for college students and Plattsburg enthusiasts to hold junior line and technical commissions in a Reserve Officers' Training Corps (ROTC). Ninety percent of Plattsburg graduates qualified for wartime commissions.

The 1920 NDA gave statutory expression to a system for the continuous commissioning of reserve officers through the campus-based ROTC and the volunteer-based Civilian Military Training Camps (CMTCs). The Harding administration threw its active support behind the civilian volunteer program. "I hope every young man, who can arrange it, will attend one of the Citizens' Military Training Camps conducted by the War Department," Harding announced. "I hope to see established, during my administration, a comprehensive system of voluntary military training for at least 100,000 men each year." In 1921 Secretary of War John W. Weeks appropriated $900,000 for the CMTCs. The first camps opened that year with 11,000 young men attending, one-quarter of the number who applied. The first year's success prompted a doubling of federal money earmarked for the program.[10]

As a CMTC publication trumpeted, the popularity of the voluntary military training programs belied the general drift into isolationism. In the academic year 1922–1923, 100,000 ROTC cadets enrolled in one of the 300 units in some 120 schools across the country. The regular army decided to make a virtue of necessity. The War Department placed top priority on developing the reserve and National Army training components and decided that the Sixth Corps area, centered on Chicago, would serve as the model. Chicago was selected because Fort Sheridan had housed Plattsburg camps since 1915 and ROTC summer camps since 1916, but principally because the city boasted the national headquarters and most active branch of the MTCA. The association's president also served as chief civilian aide to the secretary of war. Pershing selected his best young general, Moseley, to spearhead the scheme. As Moseley described his mission, the army's tasks centered on completing its "own training and hav[ing] direct charge of the training of the organized Reserves, the ROTC, the CMTC and certain field artillery organizations of the National Guard."[11]

Moseley gave up notions of entering the business world because he strongly subscribed to the training camps' mission. The guiding principle behind the Plattsburg movement—aside from rudimentary military drill—involved instilling in young men "the obligation to bear true faith and allegiance to the United States of America . . . [and] all that makes for clean, healthy, vigorous American manhood." Borrowing from Theodore Roosevelt, Moseley thought "the pup tent . . . rank[s] next to the public school among the great agents of democracy."[12] For Moseley,

the Red Scare was real. He equated the upswing in postwar antimilita-
rism to a creeping internationalist conspiracy. As Moseley pointed out
in summer 1923, Trotsky had been an "East Side of New York"—code
for Jewish—pacifist before he transmogrified into a "Bolshevist" leader,
founder of the Red Army, and architect of its military success, who,
according to Moseley, overthrew Lenin. The same could happen in the
United States unless right-minded citizens acted. Moseley declared the
summer camps a future bulwark of American defense against enemies
foreign and internal.[13]

Camp Custer, outside Battle Creek, Michigan, housed the Sixth Corps
training center. A wartime training base, Custer had been deactivated
in 1919. Even though the government designated Custer a "permanent
training center" in 1920, demolition and auctioning of government property continued through 1921. When Moseley arrived, the camp looked
like a ghost town: the barracks had been razed, with only a few permanent quartermaster warehouses left intact, and there was no government
equipment to be issued. The first order of business involved rebuild-
ing the entire encampment. Despite assorted handicaps, the inaugural
year of the training scheme at Custer (1922) saw 15,000 men trained—40
percent of the national total. Indicative of Moseley's influence and the
importance attached to civilian military training, he requested and
received $1 million for construction of a hospital at Custer, in addition
to the already hefty allocation of funds for renovating the camp.[14]

Moseley needed an officer to oversee administration for the summer
training program. Not in the least put off by Smith's junior rank, Moseley
settled on Beetle to wear two hats: one as Twelfth Brigade assistant chief
of staff for administration (G-1), and the other as camp adjutant. As G-1,
Smith not only bore responsibility for the typical adjutant functions—
personnel administration, police and discipline, and recruitment—he
also supervised supply. That meant he commanded the largest staff—in
terms of regular army officers—and shouldered the greatest responsibilities. Smith oversaw a staff of six officers (one of them a captain), eight
enlisted men, and a civilian secretary. The other heads of general staff
divisions were regular army majors and lieutenant colonels.[15]

Custer opened 1 May and closed at the end of August. It processed
reserve officers, third-year ROTC cadets, and CMTC attendees through
three one-month encampments. Regular units, built around the Second
and Sixth Infantry, came from corps area stations in Illinois, Wisconsin,
and Michigan. Custer acted as a staging area for the biennial joint army–
National Guard field maneuvers. One force advanced from Battle Creek
against another retreating toward Lake Michigan. The ROTC cadets—

usually around 120 of them—came principally from the three corps area states, but others were from Minnesota, Indiana, and Kansas. The main focus remained fixed on the August CMTC encampment. In 1923 Custer hosted 3,700 young men aged seventeen through twenty-five.

The encampments more resembled summer sports or church camps than serious military training installations. Military and physical training consumed mornings; sporting events occupied afternoons; and evenings featured lectures on civics by local notables, talks on morals and religious life by army chaplains, and films, all driving home the themes of American patriotism and dread of the Reds. The outstanding baseball player received a bat autographed by Babe Ruth. To qualify for a reserve commission, a CMTC participant completed four yearly courses: the "Basic Red" for infantry, the "Advanced Red" by branch, and the more evolved "White" and "Blue."

The army made no real effort to disguise the encampments' other objective. Although inspired by the Plattsburg movement, the CMTCs were not pitched at the propertied classes. The majority of campers came from the white working classes of Chicago, Detroit, Milwaukee, and lesser industrial cities. In August 1923 Pershing's visit to Custer climaxed his highly publicized tour of CMTC centers. "America's greatest living soldier" told the campers they must combat "Bolshevist and I[ndustrial] W[orkers of the] W[orld] influences," which he categorized as "a menace to the nation." He instructed that campers should take the message back to their neighborhoods, form clubs, and propagate the word. Moseley told them the great general was "preaching the right" and offered a personal homily. Then BG Charles Dawes, held up as the perfect example of the citizen-soldier, denounced labor unions and reminded his listeners to always uphold "loyalty to the government of the United States beyond that of any civil or industrial organization working for the interests of special groups or classes." The last speaker brought in by Moseley, "Soapbox Jack" O'Brien from the League to Uphold the Constitution, continued in the same vein.[16]

"Soapbox Jack" had made a big splash a couple of days earlier at a going-away party for Smith's immediate boss, COL T. J. Powers, Moseley's chief of staff. Moseley staged a little surprise when, to the assembled officers' shock, he introduced a curiously dressed "Bolshevist orator" he had found delivering a pacifist speech on a Battle Creek street corner. The Bolshie launched into an attack on the moneyed interests and their running dog minion. "Officers sat at the tables," reported a Battle Creek paper, "with clenched fists and some were on the point of springing from their seats" when, at Moseley's signal, O'Brien removed his disguise and gave them chapter and verse about the sins of socialists and their fellow travelers. Everyone thought the stunt a brilliant hoax, but the message presumably was not lost on the audience, including Beetle Smith.[17]

Pershing's visit provided the army with an ideal public relations platform. Politicians and dignitaries gathered in Battle Creek. A public live-fire demonstration capped the day's activities. An artillery barrage preceded an infantry battalion assault, complete with Whippet tanks, machine guns, and mortars. High above, nine planes engaged in a mock dogfight. On a hill the campers cheered as the imaginary foe retreated. Pershing's whirlwind appearance and the impressive martial display reaped the desired national press coverage. Always quick to praise worthy subordinates, Moseley heaped commendations on his staff for their exemplary work. Others noticed as well. MG Harry Hale, VI Corps area commander, wrote, "Camp Custer, in administration, in discipline, and in training, is a model."[18]

In early September the Twelfth Brigade headquarters relocated to Sheridan. Only some quartermaster troops and a small guard remained behind at Custer. For Smith, returning to Sheridan meant spending more time with Nory; Custer was an unaccompanied post. Battle Creek lay only 125 miles from Chicago—a short train ride—but Smith's many duties left him very little free time.

Priorities now shifted. Moseley had to sell the program to civic, educational, and church groups, but particularly to the industrial and commercial elites.[19] The MTCA employed a modern publicity campaign to cultivate a positive public perception of volunteer civilian military training. In Chicago, advertisements appeared in department stores and at elevated train stations. In charge of recruitment, Smith coordinated his activities with Charles Pike, the association's president. The MTCA recruited powerful representatives as civilian aides. In Detroit the vice president of General Motors, MAJ Charles Mott, acted as the civilian aide. Major corporations such as GM, General Electric, International Harvester, Marshall Fields, and Montgomery Ward granted employees leave with pay to attend CMTCs and funneled financial support to the MTCA. Smith's job entailed maintaining contact with the civilian aides and keeping them happy.

Civic responsibility was not the only motive for corporate largesse. In the aftermath of the war and demobilization, and in the teeth of a severe postwar recession, the country witnessed a number of bitter wage disputes and strikes and an upswing in racial tensions. As a further foreshadowing of Moseley's later troubles, he harped on the threats posed by immigrants, African Americans, Jewish Bolsheviks, and radicals of any stamp. He wrote to the editor of the conservative *Chicago Tribune*, Tiffany Blake, reminding him why Sheridan had been built in the first place. The army stood "ready for any possible emergency [in] these troubled times." The message did not go unheeded.[20]

Smith profited enormously from his association with Moseley. The junior officer deepened his understanding of army politics, the structure and functions of general staffs and theater commands, and how generals dealt with problems and conducted themselves both formally in the chain of command and informally in public. He learned the importance of balancing command responsibilities with delegation of authority, when to apply the whip and when to soft-soap. Smith saw how a senior officer's deportment influenced his effectiveness. Moseley harbored enmity against his civilian masters but subsumed his own views when selling the army's program to mostly nonreceptive politicians and cynical journalists. Smith accompanied Moseley on his many trips to visit civilian aides, which often involved nights at the club or lavish entertainments. These all smoothed some of the rough edges off the impressionable young lieutenant. Smith's daily contacts with Moseley provided him with the best practical schooling in what it meant to be a general. Smith's war service taught him lessons and provided insights into how staffs operated. His reading added breadth. His time with Moseley laid the real foundation for Smith's developing views. He felt great admiration and affection for Moseley not only for his help as a mentor but also for his many kindnesses to him and Nory.[21] As silent tribute to the debt he owed Moseley, Smith donned the Sam Browne belt, the caste symbol of the Chaumont Clique.

Greatly impressed with Beetle, Moseley confided in Colonel Watson, "They just don't make 'em better than Smith."[22] Beetle performed duties far beyond the ken of a first lieutenant. Service time as assistant chief of staff and adjutant of a brigade counted as "time with troops," improving Smith's chances of getting a good posting in his next rotation. Every year, officers submitted "preference" cards—their wish lists—requesting particular postings. Like most staff officers, Beetle angled for troop duty. Although only a lieutenant, Smith had held a number of captain's billets since 1918 and boasted a personnel file bursting with "superior" and "excellent" ratings.[23] He thought his ace in the hole would be a commendation from Moseley.

As he always did for promising underlings, Moseley wrote Smith a glowing recommendation, but to no avail. Another officer beat him to the punch. "Much against his will," Smith went to "a civilian job" in the

Bureau of the Budget (BOB) in Washington. Powers left Custer to head the army's Office of the Chief Coordinator in Washington and poached Smith.[24] Not for the last time, Smith became the victim of his own hard-earned reputation.

"The Best Regimental Adjutant in the Army"

Attachment to the BOB was not a popular billet. The Budget and Accounting Act of 1921 created a unified federal budget for all executive branch departments under the watchdog BOB. By law, the War and Navy Departments appointed their own budget staffs. The federal government sought a detailed accounting of every appropriation, giving Congress maximum authority over the fiscal process. To emphasize this control function, expenditures approved by Congress remained frozen without additional authorization. Congress could veto any appropriation and earmarked fixed sums for a particular program or piece of equipment; even if conditions changed, the entire sum had to be spent. The unified budget procedures granted the army improved administrative tools for evaluating and coordinating programs to better define institutional objectives; it also tied the already overly bureaucratized army in more reels of red tape. The War Department never embraced the new office. Dawes, now vice president, threatened the recalcitrant bureau chiefs with a letter from Harding promising immediate dismissal if they did not comply with BOB requirements. The army reacted strongly against the bureau, not only out of worry over reduced appropriations and narrowing budgetary limitations but also because it viewed this as another surrender to executive authority.[25]

Smith's job entailed collating all the budget submissions and categorizing them into individual line-item requests for funding. The period between 1 July and the middle of September—between the beginning of the fiscal year and the due date for finalizing budget requests—was an ordeal for Smith and his colleagues. Inputs came from the combat branches and the bureaus, as well as from the joint Army-Navy Munitions Board, the office of the assistant secretary for war, and the Panama Canal Zone, whose costs remained tagged to the War Department. Smith's tiny office prepared long sheets listing the budget requests; beside them, in parallel columns, they tabulated estimated costs (projected expenditures for the year in progress) against the actual amount expended in the last fiscal year. The army presented its requests first to the BOB and then, after revisions, to a subcommittee of the House Appropriations Committee. Inevitably, some estimate sheets bounced back for further revisions and supplemental estimates. Once the process ended, it started all over again.

After Smith learned the ropes, the job did not prove terribly taxing. Between 1925 and 1930 the size of the army remained virtually frozen at 125,000 enlisted men and 14,000 officers. After the drastic budget cuts of 1921–1923, military spending stabilized. As a result, relations between Congress and the army improved. Real power over appropriations devolved to the House committees; the comparable Senate committees acted as courts of appeal. Congressmen knew little about military matters and concerned themselves with local issues—keeping army posts open and preserving contracts awarded to their constituents. Generally accepting the advice of the army, congressional committee members seldom rejected major portions of the army's package. The line-item accounting approach ensured that the army could count costs but could not evaluate the efficiency of its spending. Left with little discretion or flexibility in managing the allocated resources, army administrators made sure they spent every cent—at least on paper—knowing that if they did not, they would face reductions in the next fiscal period. Given the huge stocks of surplus weapons and materiel left over from the war, Congress placed low ceilings on ordnance and quartermaster expenditures. Throughout the 1920s the army made do with obsolescent and rapidly wearing out weapons and equipment. Like the interwar army as a whole, the budgetary process settled into the comfortable trough of routine.[26]

In recognition of Smith's fine work, MG A. E. Smithers made Smith his executive officer and then deputy chief coordinator. He now supervised the compilation of the budget and acted as liaison among the War Department, the BOB, and the congressional committees. Smith's four-year tenure with the BOB provided essential career experience. He saw up close the workings of high-level military administration and major civilian agencies. It also introduced him to the folkways of the capital. In his liaison capacity, he dealt with politicians and senior public administrators. Given the army's political position on Capitol Hill in this period of fiscal retrenchment, Smith developed the skills of subtle diplomacy. The lessons he had learned from Moseley came in handy. Although only dimly perceived at the time, the changing requirements of modern bureaucratic military establishments produced a managerial revolution— a gradual shift in the officer's role from "heroic fighter" to technical or administrative expert. Skill differentials between military and civilian elites narrowed. Beetle's mind tended toward the orderly and concrete, and he always exhibited a passion for organizing. The detailed business of preparing the line-item budgets reinforced these traits. Loyal to the army and committed to rational planning, Smith developed the mentality common to any manager of a civilian organization or business enterprise—the search for more efficient means of managing a changeable external environment. Better preparation for the military manager could scarcely be imagined.[27]

With his service in Washington behind him, and having established his solid standing as a staff officer, Smith again petitioned for troop duty. Instead, the War Department detailed him to the Philippine Islands. Of all the garrisons outside the continental United States—Alaska, the Canal Zone, Puerto Rico, Hawaii, China, and the Philippines—the last two were the most sought after. For one reason, command duty, which was exceedingly difficult to secure in the corps districts, could be more easily obtained in overseas stations. Second, the low cost of living in China and the Philippines meant that even lieutenants could effect gentlemanly lifestyles. Only a quarter of those requesting the Philippines received the assignment. Though pleased with his posting, Smith was less than enthusiastic about his assignment as adjutant of the Forty-fifth Infantry, a Filipino scout regiment stationed at Fort William McKinley.

The Smiths made their way from Washington to New York, where they boarded the army transport ship the *Grant* for the voyage to Manila. Each year the *Grant* made three shuttle trips from New York to the Far East. From New York, the ship traveled through the Panama Canal to San Francisco, where it took on officers and men from western stations; then it made stops in Hawaii, Guam, Tientsin in China, and finally Manila. In all, the trip took fifty-two days at sea. The spartan and cramped quarters aboard the *Grant,* formerly a German passenger ship, proved comfortable enough. For Beetle and Nory, the Pacific crossing and their imagined future time together in the exotic Philippines was an adventure. In common with others, they occupied much of their time reading about their destination.

The coming and going of the *Grant* meant the arrival and departure of officers and enlisted men. Although happy when assigned to the Philippines, officers and men were happier to leave. The Philippines offered all the pitfalls associated with garrison life in Asia—duty far from home amidst an alien culture that cloaked its deep-seated enmity behind a mask of compliant affability. For their part, the Americans—loud, gregarious, overconfident—irritated Asian sensibilities. Misunderstandings and resentments were inevitable. After all, the Americans were the occupiers and the Filipinos the occupied. The admixture of brawling with locals, cheap alcohol and women, and loan sharking and gambling, combined with lax discipline and boredom, ruined many a poor soldier boy and not a few officers. Enlisted men nearing the end of their tours often went over the hill on wild benders. The circuit of officers' "seeing off" parties, though slightly more constrained, meant that most officers suffered from chronic hangovers in the days leading up to the *Grant*'s arrival.

Boat Days—as the locals termed them—occupied pride of place, along with the Fourth of July, on the Manila social calendar. Manila newspapers, especially the social pages, covered the events in detail. A band dressed in gleaming white uniforms played military and patriotic airs as the *Grant* put in at the quay and lowered the gangplank. After the usual formalities, the Smiths loaded into a car for the short trip down Dewey Boulevard to the Army-Navy Club, cited on the esplanade bordering Manila Bay. Called the tropical version of Chicago's Lake Shore Drive, the boulevard more closely resembled Miami's South Beach, with its palms, bougainvilleas, and art deco hotels, clubs, and bars. All along the route, locals lined the street, waving and cheering. Arriving at the posh club (now the U.S. embassy), the Smiths made for the patio and rounds of gin and tonic. After a lavish reception, Beetle and Nory spent the night in the upscale Hotel Manila. Overall, the day served as quite an introduction to life in the "Pearl of the Orient."

The next day the Smiths took the nine-mile drive out to Fort McKinley. At first glimpse—aside from the vegetation—McKinley resembled Sheridan. Built between 1902 and 1904, during the final stages of the Philippines War, McKinley was designed to give the Filipinos the impression the Americans intended to stay. The post contained the usual headquarters building, permanent barracks, officer housing, drill hall, stables, and array of service and institutional buildings. The officers' club came complete with a swimming pool, movie theaters, bowling alley, tennis courts, polo and playing fields, and the ubiquitous golf course. All this looked very good until the Smiths saw their allotted housing. Couples without children lived in the aptly named Beehive, an odd circular structure. The quarters consisted of two rooms with a bath, no kitchen, and a small porch. Beetle must have wondered where he would keep the substantial library he had brought with him.[28]

Not long after arriving in the Philippines, Beetle received some unexpected good news: his promotion to captain, effective on 24 September 1929. In 1920 the regular army granted 5,225 commissions to officers holding wartime temporary commissions. In 1922 troop reductions induced the army to discharge 1,000 "surplus" officers; 140 others were found "unsatisfactory" and dismissed. These reductions did little to alleviate the huge "hump" of junior grade officers. By escaping reduction in rank back in 1920, Smith stood on the forward slope of the postwar lieutenant "hump." He spent less than nine years as a first lieutenant; the average was thirteen. Smith found himself considerably senior to graduates of the West Point class of 1918; it took an act of Congress in 1931 to promote those first lieutenants reduced in rank in 1920. Pleased with his promotion, Beetle now faced an even larger hump. In 1927–1928 captains constituted 40 percent of the entire infantry officer cadre. A 1927 G-1 study concluded that, of the 5,800 officers caught in the hump, 1,259 had no prospect of retiring above the grade of major.[29] The odds were even worse in the infantry; 2,838 officers—almost half the entire hump—held captains' billets. None of this troubled Smith. His promotion did have one immediate effect: it meant he could escape the Beehive by exercising his "ranking out" option and oblige a first lieutenant to vacate his quarters on Officers' Row.[30]

If army life in the interwar years proved undemanding, service in the Philippines might best be described as leisurely. Reveille sounded at 6:00. From 8:00 to 10:00 the troops drilled. One hour of indoor instruction followed; then lunch. The army deemed Americans incapable of exerting themselves in the tropical heat, so from 1:30 to 4:00 in the afternoon, the troops remained confined to "quiet in the barracks." One reason American soldiers might have experienced problems drilling in the heat stemmed from the army's hidebound insistence that troops in tropical stations wear regulation woolen uniforms. Presumably, wool absorbed sweat better than cotton did. The scouts followed the same routine. For officers, duties ended before lunch. After serving as brigade assistant chief of staff at Sheridan and Custer, and given his stint with the BOB, Smith sleepwalked through his daily tasks. In war, the adjutant's office stands on the bottom rung of the staff hierarchy; in peace, it resides at the top. The adjutant serves as conduit for all paperwork, and peacetime armies run on red tape. An officer who served at McKinley remembered Smith as "the best regimental adjutant in the army."[31]

The interwar army placed a high premium on social contact, and that proved doubly true in overseas outposts like McKinley. Officers who served in the Philippines in the interwar years rarely mentioned their soldiering, highlighting their social lives instead. Most officers spent their afternoons pursuing leisure activities—golf, tennis, horseback riding, or training for the next polo match. McKinley fielded two polo teams. Evening entertainments centered on the officers' club. Linen suits, a Panama hat, and a Philippines *rubusto* were de rigueur. Many went to the bar, where a scotch and soda cost 30 cents. If they so desired, they became members of the Army-Navy Club or the Polo Club for $5 a month. Alternatively, they attended a fight or a ball game at José Rizal Stadium, a faux Ebbets Field built by the Corps of Engineers. When Beetle joined in, he played bridge or, if he could find an opponent, chess. This proved increasingly difficult because he soon gained the reputation as one of the best chess players in the army. As was always his practice, he spent most of his free time reading or hunting and fishing; he found the native varieties of bamboo and the plumage of exotic birds perfect for constructing fishing rods and flies.[32]

Officers' wives especially enjoyed their stay in Manila. Hired help looked after all their needs. A servant—an *amah* (combined cook, housemaid, and nanny), houseboy, or gardener—cost $7.50 a month, plus the price of rice and fish. Wives went on shopping sprees, joined cultural and social organizations, volunteered for charitable fund-raising campaigns, and joined their husbands in the constant social whirl of Manila. Other than dealing with servants, merchants, and the odd Westernized Asian gentleperson—and, in Smith's case, his Filipino subordinates—the American community remained insular. Like all interwar posts, McKinley's social life revolved around the horse culture. An infantry partisan, Beetle eschewed everything connected with horses. But Nory loved horses; she rode often and joined in equestrian events.

Far from overworked, and not interested in remaining idle, Beetle exploited every opportunity to visit army installations outside Manila. His duties took him to Fort Santiago, the headquarters of the Philippine Department in the *Intermuros,* the old Spanish citadel and walled city in Manila; to Camps Eldridge and McGrath on Luzon, south of McKinley; to Fort Mills, guarding the entry into Manila Bay on Corregidor Island; and to Fort Stotsenberg, a supply depot and garrison northwest of Manila. He studied the operations of the Spanish-American and Philippines Wars and visited battle sites. Manila's weather has three variations: hot and wet, hot and dry, and hot and saturated during monsoon season. Hot and dry is the worst. To escape Manila's oppressive heat, Beetle took Nory up to Camp John Hay, a hill station in the mountains of northern Luzon, cooled by elevation and by breezes coming off the South China Sea. On at least one occasion he traveled to Mindanao, where he developed an interest in collecting Moro weapons—poison-tipped arrows, blow darts, and the famed bolos.

The chief reason he traveled so much centered on his maneuvering for command time. As at Sheridan and Custer, Smith's service as regimental adjutant counted as "time with troops," but nobody saw it that way. The two scout regiments were maintained at near full troop strength but chronically lacked company grade officers. Conditions in the lone American infantry regiment presented a worse picture. Nicknamed the "American foreign legion"—partly because it was the only unit in the army that had never served in the United States, but mostly owing to its self-image as an orphan outfit—the Thirty-first Infantry remained seriously undermanned. In the late 1920s rifle companies typically mustered two officers and seventy enlisted men. Smith's efforts paid off, and he gained company-level command time.[33]

Smith's duties at McKinley resembled those he had performed at Custer. Every infantryman in Luzon rotated through McKinley once a year for field drills and live-fire training. McKinley also served as the staging area for annual division field exercises. As adjutant, Smith oversaw administrative details and coordinated preparations. Not much urgency attached itself to these maneuvers. The army knew the Philippines were indefensible, but in the 1920s that hardly seemed vital. Japan represented no more than a latent threat. Throughout the 1920s Japan appeared well on the road to building a stable democratic government; it played a conspicuous and constructive role in international organizations. The Washington treaties forbade expansion of the naval base at Cavite or the construction of a new one at Subic Bay. The army and navy developed War Plan Orange in the event of a war in the western Pacific against Japan. It fell to the Philippine Division—in reality, less than a brigade—to defend a nonexistent naval base against a potentially far superior enemy for a fleet the army planners thought unlikely to ever arrive. Under orders from Washington, the division staged annual maneuvers in a mock defense of Luzon. Army planners predicted that the Japanese invasion, if it ever came, would land in Lingayen Gulf, distant from Manila to the north. Lacking adequate money, manpower, and transport, the Luzon command tailored projections of Japanese intentions to circumstances. Instead of meeting a Japanese threat from the north, the exercises defended Manila, the Cavite base, and Nickols airfield from landings in Lamon Bay, thirty-five miles southeast of the city. Although puny and pro forma, the annual maneuvers provided the only true test of the war-fighting capabilities of American and Filipino forces in Luzon. Smith's experience at Camp Custer served him well during his stay at McKinley.

Smith spent less than two years in the Philippines. In March 1931 orders came through, finally clearing Smith to attend the Infantry School. After another lengthy voyage on the *Grant*, Smith looked forward to a long furlough. Beetle and Nory headed back to Indianapolis, and they decided Beetle's widowed mother would join them in Georgia once they secured housing. The Smiths spent most of their time preparing for the move.

En route to Benning, Smith visited Washington and dropped in at the War Department to pay his respects to Moseley, now deputy chief of staff to GEN Douglas MacArthur. Although, as Moseley noted, Smith "made no requests of any kind for himself either directly or indirectly," he surmised his old mentor's current position could only boost his career. Curious about Smith's record, Moseley pulled his personnel file. What he read did not surprise him. Smith had compiled an outstanding record in all his various posts. He had earned "superior" ratings from Moseley; from Smithers and his navy opposite, RADM H. H. Rousseau, during his stint in the BOB; and for both years in the Philippines. Moseley made inquiries about Smith, confirming that he possessed a "fine war record."[34]

The results of a 1935 G-1 study of officer efficiency reports in the infantry for the assessment year 1927–1928—the only one undertaken in the interwar years—put Smith's record into context. Officer efficiency reports had no direct bearing on promotions. The date of appointment—down to the day of the month—determined promotion through the rank of colonel according to a single armywide list. If an officer avoided "syphilis [and] reckless taxi drivers" and refrained from "murder, rape, and peculation," he eventually got promoted.[35] The seniority system and the hump combined to freeze officer promotions throughout the entire interwar period. Still, annual evaluations proved vital to an officer's advancement. Officers who collected consistent "superior" and "excellent" ratings secured competitive placement in command slots, staff appointments, and entry into the army's pyramidal school system. Officers graded "satisfactory" and above remained in the A Pool (promotion eligible); those with successive "unsatisfactory" ratings faced dismissal. Because of the lengthy review and appeals process—all the way to the president—a minuscule number of officers lost their commissions.[36]

Efficiency ratings provided a powerful tool for senior officers. The "West Point Mutual Protection Society," affiliation with the Pershing faction, and branch particularism ensured that the 1920 promotion system protected much deadwood in the higher ranks. The system allowed senior officers to gild the reputations of other field grade officers. In the infantry, overaged colonels and lieutenant colonels represented only 10 percent of officers yet accounted for 61 percent of the "superior" and only 6 percent of the "satisfactory" ratings. Annual reviews granted conservative senior officers the whip hand in enforcing subordination to authority and preserving the status quo by rewarding orthodoxy and punishing nonconformist junior officers. With no fixed criteria for making objective assessments, senior officers employed subjective measurements conditioned by the peculiar agendas of their branches. Zealous in their defense of the horse against the threat of mechanization, the cavalry lavishly handed out "superior" ratings in the expectation that its arm would be overrepresented at Leavenworth, at the War College, in the War Department, and among general officers, thus enhancing its status within the army and defending its autonomy. The opposite held true in the engineers. Senior engineers held subordinates to higher standards of performance; "satisfactory" meant just that. For senior infantry officers, annual performance reviews provided the opportunity to weed out those in the company grade officer hump. The system graded junior officers down, not up. Senior infantry officers used the "superior" and "unsatisfactory" categories only in extreme cases when classifying captains and lieutenants.[37] A couple of "satisfactory" assessments scuttled a career. In 1927–1928, 65 percent of assessed infantry captains and lieutenants scored "satisfactory." Only one of 827 first lieutenants received a "superior" grade—and that officer was Bedell Smith.

Smith thought Moseley had engineered his appointment to Benning. He later confessed to Moseley, "Such success as I have had in the Army I owe to you."[38] In fact, Smith got the appointment to Benning simply because he met the infantry's new requirements: he had eleven years of service, came from a foreign posting, had not been to the basic course, and had no children. The price of housing at Benning ruled out officers with families who lacked private means.[39] Moseley had not pushed for Smith's appointment, but he took the time to include a detailed outline of Smith's service record in a letter to the chief of the WDGS G-1 Division for inclusion in his file. "The only interest I have in this officer," Moseley wrote, "is the Government's interest. I have the very positive and distinct feeling that just as soon as he finishes Benning, he should be sent immediately to Leavenworth. . . . In my opinion," he concluded, "Captain Smith has abilities and talents far in advance of his grade."[40] His practical education now completed, and having stamped out solid credentials as a staff officer, Smith earned advancement into the army's school system, where he would be granted the chance to prove Moseley right.

★ 9 ★

"Expunge the Bunk, Complications and Ponderosities"

External historical determinants dictated that the army and navy traveled on different paths toward modernization and professionalization. The army faced an incubus from which the navy was immune. The U.S. Navy could never threaten the constitutional balance and possessed, at least from the late 1880s, a fleet-in-being. The skeleton army was always held suspect, divorced physically and psychologically from a rapidly changing and mostly unreceptive civil society whose members it would lead in time of war. The navy's trajectory was mostly dialectical; the army's, cyclical.

The story goes something like this: The outbreak of war finds the army woefully unprepared; the hasty mobilization that follows the declaration of war becomes a mismanaged shamble, and the first encounter with the enemy ends in defeat. American wealth and material resources prevail, giving renewed vigor to the "minuteman mythology" that citizen-soldiers always prevail over paid hireling regulars. In the immediate postwar period, popular disgruntlement compels congressional intervention. Budgets are slashed and taxes rise, paying off the war debt. Senior officers grudgingly accept reform but wage a tough bureaucratic rear guard, blunting its worst effects. Popular interest fades, as does that of the politicians. The army recedes into comfortable isolation, reverting to the routines, lifestyles, branch loyalties and antagonisms, and values of the prewar army. In peacetime, the War Department represents little more than a weak confederation of hostile tribes; the senior leadership engages in the traditional bureaucratic wrangling for preference and institutional control and bitterly defends the status quo.[1]

The Root reforms and the 1920 NDA furthered the movement toward creating a corporate military structure, but the officer corps retained its old organic sense of itself as a community. Organizational structures changed, but the undergirding conservative assumptions and attitudes continued intact. As long as the army remained detached from external interference and internally divided, parochial interests precluded the evolution of armywide viewpoints. Such an institution simply could not innovate, much less reinvent itself.

The army schools exactly mirrored this dynamic. Sherman opened the Leavenworth school to educate the rapidly aging post–Civil War hump of officers. It was derisively called the "kindergarten" because commanders, reflecting age-old line versus staff antagonisms and deeply suspicious of "book" soldiers, sent their "idiot lieutenants" off to Kansas. By the 1890s, Leavenworth evolved into a genuine school or, actually, two schools—one for the line and one for the staff. The Spanish-American War renewed the process. The school closed for the duration, and when it reopened, its mission reverted to educating the new hump of officers. The regulars referred to the new intake of officers as "the Crime of '98." In the years before American entry into World War I, the Leavenworth schools threw off their remedial content and again reintroduced the borrowed German applicatory curriculum. Then the war forced the closure of the schools.

March created or reformed the branch schools and ordered Leavenworth reopened, with a restored two-year sequence of courses and a modernized curriculum that sought to incorporate the organizational, tactical, and logistical lessons of the world war. He argued that reduced numbers and funding demanded a progressive system of army schools dedicated to educating—not training—forward-looking and mentally flexible officers so that in the next national emergency the army would not founder, as it had in the past. He wanted a rigorous, meritocratic system that ensured only the best rose through the branch schools, Leavenworth, and the War College to higher commands and the War Department General Staff. The victory of the Old Guard killed March's vision. The structures survived, but the mission changed. The old pattern once again repeated itself.

One important change survived. Whereas the old army had never valued education, the war proved the worth of Leavenworth and the War College, especially the former.[2] "During the World War," Pershing told the War College's graduating class of 1924, "the graduates of

Leavenworth and the War College held the most responsible positions in our armies . . . had it not been for the able and loyal assistance of the officers trained at these schools, the tremendous problems of combat, supply, and transportation could not have been solved."[3] The army's attitude toward education may not have undergone much change, but the message was clear: no officer would rise in the army unless he passed through the army's school system.

Marshall and the Reform of Army Education

Smith's posting to Benning proved to be the most vital in his career. This was true not because it afforded him the opportunity to fashion an armywide reputation as an expert in infantry weapons or because of the grounding he received in the army's war-fighting doctrine—though both were important—but because the Infantry School provided Smith his first brush, albeit an oblique one, with the most influential figure in his life: George Marshall. During his five years as assistant commandant and head of the academic department, Marshall unobtrusively—so as not to arouse external opposition—but steadily effected important changes in the Infantry School—changes he hoped would reverberate throughout the army's school system. That did not take place. Nonetheless, 150 future generals attended Infantry School courses during his tenure, and another 50 taught under his direction. All of them, in varying degrees, left Benning as "Marshall men." Although Marshall forgot about his first encounter with the bright young captain, Smith never did.

Founded only in October 1918 as an amalgamation of the small arms, machine gun, and old Fort Sill infantry schools, Fort Benning emerged from its troubled birth as the largest and most influential of the army's branch and service schools. Benning housed two regiments—two "war-strength" battalions of the Twenty-ninth and the Twenty-fourth, an African American unit that performed maintenance and support roles. Together with artillery, armor, engineers, signals, and other demonstration formations, Benning boasted a garrison of nearly 6,000 men, among the largest in the army.[4]

Throughout the 1920s Benning more resembled a building site than a permanent army post. Faced with educating the officer hump, the infantry funneled large classes through the Benning schools, overburdening instructional facilities and housing. Overcrowded and primitive lecture halls presented "a constant embarrassment to instruction." Housing was a bigger problem. "The present system grows more irksome year by year," Marshall reported, "as living conditions in the army elsewhere stabilize or improve."[5] Some officers quit, refusing to move their families into the allotted housing; noncommissioned officers occupied abandoned sharecropper cabins in the environs of the fort. One reason the infantry balked at lowering the rank of incoming students was because junior officers could not afford the cost of scarce housing in Columbus, nine miles from the post (captains received between $3,000 and $4,000 per year).[6] Columbus was not a very salubrious town, and Phenix City, across the river in Alabama, was worse.

The Smiths, including Beetle's mother, were lucky; they rented a house in Columbus, perched atop a bluff overlooking the Chattahoochee River. Beetle spent a good deal of time with his mother. Helping her in the garden, he developed a fondness for cultivating Red Radiant roses. He even took up needlepoint. Not surprisingly, he spent most of his free time taking advantage of the excellent hunting afforded by the thousands of acres of yellow pine that dominated the Benning reserve. Smith purchased and trained a purebred English setter, and together they ranged across the rolling terrain hunting the quail, pheasants, and raccoons that abounded in southwestern Georgia and neighboring Alabama.[7]

After the death of Marshall's wife, the chief of infantry decided relocation might raise his spirits. Marshall had his choice of three postings. He selected Benning. When Marshall had served with the Fifteenth Infantry Regiment in China, he had participated in a regimental field exercise during which an officer became paralyzed when confronted with a simple tactical problem. "I learnt that he had stood first at Benning," Marshall told a fellow officer, "and I then and there formed an intense desire to get my hands on Benning. The man was no fool, but he had been taught an absurd system."[8]

Marshall was not surprised by what he encountered at Benning. The faculty "had become unconscious creatures of technique." Instructors read canned lectures that had been preapproved by the editorial committee, guaranteeing doctrinal conformity. Barracks discipline was maintained; questions were strongly discouraged, and dissent was not tolerated. Instructors drafted map problems, less to impart a specific tactical lesson than to simplify the meticulous grading regime. Marshall moved quickly to break the mold. As one of his first acts, Marshall ordered that "any student's solution of a problem that ran radically counter to the approved school solution, and yet showed independent creative thinking, would be published to the class."[9] Combating blind reliance on "the book," Marshall insisted that instructors dispense with written lectures, relying instead on note cards. When instructors arrived armed with stacks of note cards, Marshall ordered them to lecture "off the cuff."

As Marshall frequently asserted, the senior officers who developed the army schools' syllabi ignored "the crude, stumbling performances and countless errors of our first year in France"; instead, they based their precepts on the last six months of a four-year war fighting an exhausted foe. "Our officers are almost entirely without practical experience in warfare of movement," he told a class. "Their fighting was confined to the final phases of static warfare. . . . In the hurly burly or rapidly changing situations, their lack of training demanded an appalling toll of life or limb. We have come to view the quality of our participation through roseate glasses, the stumbling, blunderings, failures, appeals for help, and hopeless confusion of the moment have been forgotten in the single thought of final victory."[10] The army schools should produce officers "expert in meeting the confusion and chaotic conditions of the first months of a war when discipline is poor, officers green and information of the enemy invariably lacking." Students never forgot his dictum: "study the first six months of the next war."[11]

Marshall devoted considerable thought to the nature of the next war. Consistent with U.S. Army doctrine, he believed future wars would be fluid, more resembling the first campaigns in 1914 than the siege-like conditions of static trench warfare. As an infantry partisan, Marshall accepted the infantry-centric "open warfare" precepts laid down in the 1923 Field Service Regulations (FSRs). Where he differed was on the question of how best to prepare for a war of movement fought, at least initially, by untrained troops commanded by untested officers. Before the war Marshall held a number of instructor posts attached to the National Guard, volunteer militia, and Plattsburg camps. He recognized the primacy of the citizen-soldier in the post-1920 military structure. The army schools, with their theoretical map and maneuver problems, took for granted the existence of well-trained and equipped full-strength units, the competence of subordinate commands, and the functioning of supply and communications channels—situations officers would "never find during the first years of an American war." Marshall believed the army must develop simplified command, staff, and leadership techniques for "handling [and inspiriting] hastily raised, partially trained" citizen-soldiers.[12]

Marshall constantly hammered on his favorite principle of war—simplicity. He wanted to "get down to the essentials, make clear the real difficulties, and expunge the [Leavenworth-driven] bunk, complications and ponderosities" from the curriculum.[13] He believed a workable decision arrived at quickly was superior to a more correct one that consumed time. "We must be specially trained in when to make decisions rather than concentrating almost entirely on what decision to make," he wrote in 1937. "All these things are far more difficult to learn than the related ponderous technique and formal tactics of Leavenworth."[14] He insisted that orders and intelligence assessments not exceed one page. "A Leavenworth Infantry battalion order would be two or three pages long [and take three hours to prepare], where a similar order at Benning would be less than a page in length. The same applied to G-2 summaries, supply details and so forth. The one was ponderous and cumbersome, while the other at least showed struggle towards simplicity."[15]

As long as Marshall's reforms provoked no outcries from the chief of infantry, the two commandants he worked for supported him. The changes he made produced a great deal of internal bellyaching. Even though much of the teaching staff resorted to passive resistance, over time, the quality of teaching improved. Marshall ended rehearsed tactical demonstrations, replacing them with unscripted field maneuvers. He attempted to wean instructors and students from overreliance on detailed maps. When he still faced defiance, Marshall placed the instructors in command positions during the annual command post exercise and "let them commit errors, some so gross as to be almost amusing, in their blind following of technique." Even "staff officers of brilliant reputation in the Army," he went on, "graduates of Leavenworth and the War College, former instructors at those schools, committed errors so remarkable that it plainly indicated our school system had failed to make clear the real difficulties to be anticipated and surmounted in warfare of movement."[16] Those who never got the message were quietly removed. By the time Smith arrived, Marshall had a handpicked set of officers heading the four sections: LTC Joseph Stilwell in tactics, ably supported by CPT Joseph Collins; LTC M. C. Stayer, backed by MAJ Harold Bull, in the section that handled training, supply, equitation, and signals; MAJ Omar Bradley in weapons; and MAJ Forrest Harding as head of the historical and publications section.

Marshall recognized the basic dilemma growing out of the incongruities of the 1923 FSRs. The foundation rested on training regular officers in peacetime to command citizen-soldiers in an expansible army during war. The army demanded that junior officers demonstrate ascriptive loyalty to the army's hierarchy of authority and its missions and that they practice regularity and uniformity in the application of their duties. Command structures remained vertical and centralized; command was highly personalized. The fixation on "unity of command" left no scope for leadership from below. The army's schools reinforced adherence to prevailing norms in organization and command, staff, and tactical functions; they went to great lengths prescribing "school" solutions to operational and tactical problems. Seeking uniformity, the doctrine taught in the schools underestimated surprise, movement, and improvisation while discounting "fogs" and "frictions" in battle. The doctrine tried to control the uncontrollable. The army's rationale was predicated on the belief that long-service officers uniformly schooled in training, educational, and staff assignments were interchangeable. If one failed, he could easily be replaced. The army's mechanistic doctrine sought to address the problem of how best to train officers for tactical command of a citizen-soldier army. It did not tackle the fundamental leadership and tactical weakness of the AEF—the lack of initiative and flexibility at the tactical level of war. When field grade officers went down, command broke down; the troops took to ground, freezing the advance. When one unit got bogged down, adjacent formations halted, and other forces were thrown into the line to restore movement; confusion blunted the attack. This was what Marshall meant when he wrote, "The technique and practices developed at Benning and Leavenworth would practically halt the development of an open warfare situation."[17]

Marshall was a monument to American empiricism. No original thinker, he never bothered to read the classics of military thought or engaged in academic debates over military theory. Marshall distrusted theorists not because they challenged orthodoxy or undermined authority but because they "muddied the waters." His was an orderly and concrete mind. He wanted officers trained to approach problems like he did—with good old American ingenuity and common sense. Marshall's efforts to make map problems and field exercises more realistic and his pushing instructors and students to think creatively and find spontaneous solutions to tactical problems did not grow out of a desire to make over the army—Marshall was no crusader. Rather, he wanted to address the most pressing shortcomings he had identified from wartime experience. As Pershing's aide and confidant, Marshall helped Pershing prepare his testimony before Congress that initiated the coup that placed the Chaumont Clique in a position of dominance in the interwar army. Marshall understood that Benning's essential mission involved disseminating the mandated tactical doctrine. Although Marshall labored, with limited success, to change pedagogic and troop-leading methods, he made no effort to alter the course content, and nothing he achieved at Benning made any appreciable impact beyond the gates of the Infantry School.

The capstone 1923 FSRs codified the war-fighting principles for the interwar army. Conditioned by their wrangles to stave off Anglo-

French efforts at amalgamating American units and the bitter internecine contest between Pershing and March to centralize command in
the War Department and functionalize staff structures in France, the
Chaumont Clique—of which Marshall was a charter member—assumed
an unequivocally chauvinistic outlook on the lessons learned in the war.
Brigadier General Drum—Smith's beau ideal as a boy and then assistant
commandant at Leavenworth and principal author of postwar doctrine—
extolled the superior "racial characteristics" of Americans, "too distinctive, too enduring, too decisive and too valuable to be sacrificed or to be
subordinated to the teachings and methods of races not so blessed."[18]
The postwar review process—the Superior (AEF) and Lewis (Infantry)
Boards—reflected the experience of the army in France but spurned the
hard-won doctrinal and organizational lessons of 1918. Receiving the
imprimatur of Pershing, the 1923 FSRs vindicated the war-fighting paradigm American senior officers took to France. Except for changes inci-
dental to new weapons—chiefly tanks and aircraft—the FSRs retained
unquestioned faith in the offensive capacity of the traditional combat
arms, especially the inspired American rifleman in "open warfare." "All
other arms," the Superior Board stated, "must be organized and made
subordinate to [the infantry's] needs, function, and methods."[19] Horse
cavalry preserved its operational and tactical roles on the modern battlefield. The army disbanded the Tank and Motor Transport Corps, stifled any prospect of an independent air force by creating the Army Air
Service (designated the Army Air Corps in 1926), and relegated operational logistics back under the narrow control of the traditional bureaus.
The chiefs of arms—created by the NDA of 1920—acted as watchdogs,
exerting jealous control over branch doctrine and officer assignments.
The chiefs were major generals, men in their sixties whose memories
stretched back to fighting Geronimo and the Moros. Each combat arm
developed its own tactical techniques, consistent with the roles assigned
them in the 1923 FSRs. The G-3 (training) section of the WDGS lacked
any mandate for reviewing, coordinating, and disseminating doctrinal
studies emanating from the branch schools. That being the case, the
army possessed no effective system for developing and teaching combined arms doctrine. All this meant that the 1923 doctrine went unre-
vised and unchallenged for sixteen years.[20]

The advanced course was something of a misnomer. In theory, newly
minted officers went to their branch basic courses to learn standardized
small-unit troop-leading and fundamental tactical and training techniques before assuming company-level commands. After a period of time
they rotated back to the branch school as senior captains or junior majors

for the advanced course, which reinforced material covered in the basic course and imparted command and staff procedures for the regiment and brigade. In practice, the hump meant that officers did not proceed to advanced courses until they were majors and lieutenant colonels, men in their mid-forties with better than a decade separating them from the basic course; most, like Smith, held wartime temporary commissions and never attended the basic course. Senior officers believed that education was wasted on lieutenants, but in fact, education proved even less efficacious for officers whose attitudes had already been formed by the war and by long service in monotonous administrative and training assignments.

Marshall did not always get his way. As long as he moved in-house, he enjoyed full rein. When he went higher, his suggested changes were killed by the infantry. Marshall petitioned successive chiefs of infantry to lower the age bar for admission to Benning and permit accelerated entry into the advanced course based on performance rather than seniority. An ardent "selectionist," Marshall believed the promotion structure—particularly the absence of an effective means of eliminating ineffectual officers—produced a decisive "drag on the whole military system." All his efforts achieved nothing.[21]

Smith Goes to School

Smith's class varied widely in terms of educational background and age. At thirty-five, Smith was among the youngest members of his class. Marshall complained that many of the "cast iron" field grade attendees proved "dull mentally," lacked educational qualifications and motivation, and constituted an encumbrance to instruction. Since few students possessed recent command time or much familiarity with their own branches, much less the others, early instruction centered on remedial tactical work at the platoon and company level instead of developing command and staff techniques for the regiment or brigade.[22] About a third of the course consisted of classroom lectures and map problems; the remainder was conducted outdoors, mostly on horseback.

Despite being the bastion of the infantry, Benning had the reputation of being "the horsiest post in the Army."[23] Equitation and horseshoeing were required courses. An avid horseman, Marshall insisted that all his officers ride. Marshall remained, in most respects, very much "old army." The aristocratic pretensions of the officer corps survived World War I and the shock of the Depression. Marshall staged and participated in all sorts of equestrian events. From the beginning of October and lasting into April, formal hunts took place about twice a week. Wives were always included, and Nory took an active part. Polo held center stage on the social calendar. As a measure of its priorities, the army spent $1 million on polo ponies each year, even during the height of the Depression, while it allocated a mere $60,000 for tank development.[24] There was also a practical reason for having horses. The overcrowded and unventilated lecture halls and classrooms required that the majority of course work take place outdoors on the outer ranges and maneuver areas dotting the 97,000-acre reserve. Horses often provided the only means of reaching these isolated sites. "Real" ground-pounding infantry officers eschewed the horsey ethos.

Benning also held a number of shooting competitions. Given his intense interest in firearms, Smith often took part. Bradley organized a trapshooting range for shotgun practice, and Beetle asked if he could shoot.

Bradley possessed even less social acumen than Smith. His unprepossessing appearance—made worse by having to wear ill-fitting dentures after having his teeth removed—and his abstinence reminded people of a small-town preacher or schoolteacher. A 1915 graduate of West Point, he never made it to France. Coming from Leavenworth, Bradley joined the Infantry School faculty in 1929 and headed the weapons section the next year.

Given their reticence, Bradley and Smith did not immediately become friends. Bradley categorized Smith as "a bit of a Prussian, and brutally frank," and compared him to the head of the tactical section, Stilwell, whom another Benning officer thought "pretty close to a misanthrope." Over time, Bradley and Beetle discovered they had things in common: both possessed midwestern roots and unaffected personalities; both treasured the outdoors, shooting, and hunting; both were childless and devoted to their wives; and both loved the infantry. Once Bradley penetrated Smith's tough outer crust, he found the younger officer to be "genuinely modest, shy, humorous and kind." Bradley also judged Smith's performance in the classroom and in the field. He rated Smith the outstanding student in the advanced course. "I was quite taken with this young captain," Bradley later commented. "He had an absolutely brilliant and analytical mind."[25]

Many students wrote papers based on their wartime experience, and Smith followed suit. In the middle of December 1931 Smith made an oral presentation of his essay. In his opening remarks, Smith emphasized that his experiences during the first two days of the Aisne-Marne offensive typified "the partially trained American army of 1918 . . . and the troops which American officers may expect to command in the early stages of any future war." Then, in the twenty minutes allotted, he provided a cogent and gripping narrative of events, interspersed with tactical questions he asked his listeners. Smith concluded with two pointed lessons: "success utterly depended" on small-unit initiative, and the unforeseen and unexpected constitute the rule in war, not the exception.

As luck would have it, Marshall dropped into the classroom that day just as Smith began his presentation. Smith's opening remarks caught Marshall's attention and held it—no easy proposition. Smith's findings perfectly echoed Marshall's views. Marshall returned to his office and told another officer, "There is a man who would make a wonderful instructor and I'll bet no one has asked for him." Bradley scored some points with the boss because his request for Smith's retention and assignment to the weapons section already rested on Marshall's desk.[26] This chance occurrence, and his connection to Bradley, later proved instrumental in Smith's eventual rise in the army.

Smith graduated on 1 June 1932, and after the usual summer furlough, he returned to Benning and took up the post as Bradley's assistant. Before school started, the academic department reviewed the goals for the upcoming year. For the weapons section, the big annual event occurred early in the course—a four-hour demonstration of infantry weapons, including the Browning automatic rifle, mortars, and the 37mm field gun. Smith took charge of the machine gun display.

Fresh from the advanced course, Smith found the teaching load undemanding and exploited the opportunity to carve out a reputation as a weapons expert. He also devoted time to professional development. He continued his habit of reading widely and following his own autodidactic approach to learning. In many posts, roundtables and discussion groups emerged. A number of officers entertained serious misgivings about the legitimacy of established orthodoxies; the debates over movement versus mass and firepower and the roles of mechanization, armor, and airpower in future war percolated through the army schools and separate commands and staffs. Neither Smith nor Bradley ever mentioned sharing books or discussing professional matters. Smith held conventional views. He showed some ambivalence on the armor issue—he accepted the tank's subordinate function in the combined arms team—but adamantly opposed the claims of airpower promoters. Like most junior officers, he did not buck the system and kept his opinions to himself.

That attitude hamstrung professional development, as evidenced by the pedestrian content of the service journals. Given the reigning "never crack a book" anti-intellectualism in the army, many officers, bullied into subscribing to service journals, discarded their copies without removing the mailing jacket. Nor did many officers contribute articles. Many explanations were offered for junior officers' reluctance to write. For one thing, articles were unattributed. Why would anyone take the trouble to write an anonymous article? But "if a lieutenant signed an article," the assistant editor of the Infantry School's *Mailing List* opined, "many an officer of field rank would never read it."[27] More to the point, officers with heretical views—and the least suggestion that the army required change was tantamount to sedition—tended to suppress them. Everyone knew the story of Eisenhower and Patton and their troubles with their respective chiefs of service for having the temerity to write plaintive pieces positing roles for tanks. Even Marshall, with all his rectitude and AEF connections from Pershing on down, pleaded with the commandant at the Command and Staff School to "protect my interests by not quoting" remarks critical of Leavenworth. "A single sentence could be used against me with deadly effect."[28]

While at Benning, Smith's essay on his experiences and observations in the Aisne was published in *The Mailing List,* a semiannual publication "containing the latest thought on Infantry." His presentation and the finished paper had impressed the faculty, and he received top grades for both efforts. Word reached Harding's assistant, LT Buck Latham, who was always in need of copy, and he solicited Smith's permission to publish the essay in its entirety. Under Marshall's direction, the fourth section also produced a manual of small-unit tactical lessons derived from the war, later published as *Infantry in Battle.* A critical success—British military critic Basil Liddell Hart hailed it as "the most valuable instructional military textbook . . . published in many years"—*Infantry in Battle* went through two prewar printings and was translated into German, Spanish, and Russian.[29] An abbreviated version of Smith's monograph on the Aisne-Marne offensive appeared in the section on "surprise."

Smith completed his duties as instructor in May 1933. For the remainder of his Benning tour he served as secretary to Marshall's replacement, COL C. W. Weeks. Beetle requested transfer to the Command and General Staff School. Infantry policy granted priority to officers completing their hitches as Benning instructors.[30] Armed with Weeks's recommendation, Moseley's letter, and another set of "superior" ratings for his work as instructor, Smith received the coveted posting. Since all roads leading to the top went through Leavenworth, Smith anxiously awaited the new challenge that lay before him.

★ 10 ★

The Other Class Stars Fell On

In his inaugural lecture to the class of 1926 at Leavenworth, Commandant MG Edward King summed up the philosophy behind the army's schools. The schools' mission was utilitarian: train the largest possible number of officers for potential command and staff duties in an expansible army, instruct them in accordance with a uniform doctrine, and drive home the primacy of the command function. He used football as an analogy. A team "composed of individuals, indoctrinated in teamwork and led by a real leader, will beat a team of hastily assembled stars." The quarterback is the commander; he gives the signals. All the other specialized players know their roles. "Each player is presumed competent else he would not be in the team." The art of command involves the proper use of staff, but the command function is indivisible. A commander "must, first of all, have character." His staff furnishes advice and frees him from administrative details, but most of all a commander must be decisive; he must lead. "An army is happy under a strong commander," King posited, "but not under a soviet committee."[1]

The Leavenworth approach was quintessentially American, a reflexive hybrid of John Dewey and Frederick Winslow Taylor. Americans are leery of elitism, especially pertaining to the military. Americans think of their society as an egalitarian meritocracy. Consistent with this view, Leavenworth trained the "average middle." The War Department fought off all attempts to raise the intellectual bar by inaugurating entrance examinations. Somehow or other, a Grant or a Pershing always rose to the top without recourse to systematic theoretical education. Americans are also pragmatic. They pride themselves on their ability to improvise solutions and devise new methods derived from a realistic assessment of the elements of a problem. Americans have little faith in programmatic formulas. Their attitude is "just tell me how to do it" and "let me get on with it." Leavenworth emphasized how-to training, the application method. At Leavenworth, officers were not taught; they learned by doing. Schooled according to a uniform methodology, they became interchangeable parts.

King's gridiron comparison was particularly apt. The 1923 FSRs provided a detailed prescription for succeeding in combat based on extant means and conditions. The field regulations provided the playbook. Leavenworth inculcated teamwork; it brought together officers from chiefly the combat arms but also from the technical and support services for a period of one or two years and taught them the playbook and the fundamentals of the game. There was only one way of doing things. Doctrine described the best means of waging a frontal attack to achieve penetration; it detailed the requirements for performing a flanking movement. All the combat arms and supporting services had specified roles. And the army team believed in the controlled ground attack. The quarterback called the plays; he commanded because he demonstrated a superior understanding of the game plan and possessed the right intangibles—the will to win and the character to inspire. If a player lacked the skills, drive, or personal temperament to get the job done, he was replaced. If the offense could not move the ball, the lineup was shuffled or a player came off the bench. Worst case, one changed the quarterback. The Army of the Potomac went through a number of commanders before Lincoln found his general, but once he did, the war ended within a year.

The army's pragmatism can also be seen in Leavenworth's various manifestations during the interwar years. The army confronted a number of hard realities. The 1920 NDA created the framework of the expansible army. In the event of another war, the army needed enough trained officers to staff the corps areas, the War Department, and the mobilization agencies, as well as to train and eventually command a mass army. The officer corps proved far too small and was stretched much too thin to fulfill that mission in addition to its other tasks—maintaining some measure of readiness and defending American overseas possessions, to name but two. But given the meager resources available to the War Department, the officer corps was too large for any orderly passage through the sequential army school system. Finally, the skewed demographics of the officer corps—overaged senior officers and the junior officer hump—bedeviled army planners, and the situation was complicated by the promotion policy. The army wrestled with these problems, tailoring the keystone Leavenworth program to the needs of shifting manpower policies. In 1922 the War Department decided to combine the Line and General Staff Schools into a one-year program. Between 1923 and 1929 Leavenworth funneled 1,686 midgrade officers—the vast majority of them majors—through a pedagogic assembly line. Nearly three-fourths of the officers who commanded corps in World War II attended one of these truncated one-year courses.[2] In 1929 the War Department decided it had enough officers on the general staff–eligible list and ordered that Leavenworth return to a two-year sequence. Seven cohorts went through the two-year cycle. In 1937 the War Department concluded it needed more staff officers and again telescoped the Leavenworth course into a single year. Priorities shifted in tandem. The first one-year course concentrated on command functions; the two-year program redressed the imbalance somewhat, increasing coverage of staff operations but still accentuating command; after 1937 staff work became the focus. Leavenworth never succeeded in reconciling these conflicting missions. Its many critics wondered whether a second year was necessary, but on balance, officers such as Smith who progressed through the two-year program profited from the experience.

"Aides, Adjutants, and Asses"

During the first week of September 1933, Smith and the other members of the 1934–1935 class assembled at Fort Leavenworth, formed into their study consortiums, and began the first-year course. Smith considered himself a "Young Turk"—not because he entertained wild ideas about changing the army but because of his membership in the youngest postwar Leavenworth class. Sixty percent were captains. For the first time, lieutenants were admitted, constituting a respectable 12 percent of the cohort. In another departure, the Air Corps contingent more than doubled over previous years. The younger members dubbed themselves the class of "aides, adjutants, and asses."[3]

No officer arrived in Kansas without some trepidation, and none left without a sense of relief. Everybody knew the Leavenworth legends. The instructors drove the men hard. "School solutions" were canon. Competition for class standing was intense. Many officers succumbed to the pressure; divorces and suicides proliferated. Smith took some comfort in the knowledge that Infantry School graduates enjoyed an advantage. Since the branch schools developed their own doctrine, and because the FSRs defined combined arms as the subordination of all other branches and services to "the mission of the infantry," a large portion of the map problems came straight from Benning.[4] The school's name accurately reflected its mission—to train middle-ranking officers in the fundamentals of combat command, tactical decision making, and the functioning of a headquarters staff. Leavenworth essentially remained a ground combat school.

In the first weeks, most of the time was expended in the field learning how to read maps and aerial photographs, write and interpret intelligence estimates, complete logistical request forms, and compose the five-paragraph order. Lectures and conferences introduced new material, reviewed basic military organizations, and established methodologies for solving tactical problems and conducting historical research. From mid-October until the Christmas break, students formed into committees under the guidance of one or two instructors for the "refresher" course, which dealt principally with the organization, tactics and techniques, and capabilities of the different arms and services, separately and in combination, for the reinforced brigade. Much of this work was remedial because, in the opinion of the deputy commandant in 1938, "the dispersion of the troops of our peacetime army and the large amount of duty with civilian components required result in many of our Regular Officers being ignorant of the tactics and technique of any but their own arm. It is probable that many officers attending the School have never even seen a Field Artillery or a Cavalry unit before their entrance."[5] During the winter months much of the work moved indoors, a portion of it devoted to historical studies.

The second half of the course reiterated and expanded on tactical principles presented in the first half, and schooled attendees in decision making and the details of troop leading at the division level. In addition, students were introduced to the duties and functions of combat command and general staff sections and the principles of movement and supply. Map problems became more frequent and demanding as the year progressed. From the middle of May until the course ended in mid-June, students participated in a series of eighteen general terrain exercises in the field, climaxing in a simulated clash between two divisions operating along the Kansas-Missouri border.[6]

Morning lectures and conferences took place in the academic building, an architectural oddity in the center of the post that had been built in 1859 as a warehouse. By 1935 lectures constituted only about 7 percent of instructional time in the first-year course. In Kansas, autumn lingers and spring comes early. Leavenworth's schedule took advantage of the weather, conducting much of the work outside. Map exercises, maneuvers, and problems and related conferences and discussions absorbed

70 percent of the curriculum; the students investigated subjects such as penetration versus envelopment, attack and defense, and the employment of reinforced brigades and divisions in static and dynamic situations in varying types of terrain. Map exercises were essentially drills, amplifying principles already taught and preparing students for a future map test. Neither critiqued nor graded, students might be called on to give a recitation of the sanctioned solutions. Map maneuvers served primarily as a vehicle for teaching command and staff functions. Students grouped into mock headquarters and moved cardboard markers around their Gettysburg maps against another team, with instructors acting as umpires. Map problems, mostly "written tests solved outdoors," stood as the foundation of the course and the basis for assessment.[7] Students read the "situation and requirement" section and then developed a solution; they had a limited time to complete and submit the exercise for close grading by a faculty committee. Following the map problem, faculty and students gathered in conference rooms to review and reinforce the correct "school solution."[8]

Leavenworth had plenty of critics other than Marshall, including commandants of the two senior army schools. Instead of grooming independent-minded officers, they argued, Leavenworth stifled initiative. The inflexible attachment to doctrine, combined with the rigid system of instruction and evaluation and the competition for class standing, induced students to play to the instructor, "to do what is wanted rather than come to independent conclusions based on study and reason." As a former commandant of both Leavenworth and the War College complained, "conformity to established doctrine [amounted] almost to religion."[9] King, commandant for four of the six years the one-year course ran, aggressively moved to improve teaching quality, instituting more sweeping changes than Marshall had at Benning. He incorporated the latest teaching techniques of civilian universities and divided the students into groups of two instructors and ten students. He combated the poisoned atmosphere bred by the simulated pressures imposed by instructors and the intense competition for grades among students. Numerical grades and class standing remained confidential. Students received SX, S, and U grades, representing exceptional, satisfactory, and unsatisfactory work. Honors and distinguished graduate lists were no longer published. King tried to break down the social distance between faculty and students by inaugurating a mentor tutorial system designed to resist students' tendency to form informal committees that only wasted time and elevated anxiety levels without having any corresponding academic value. He petitioned for higher intellectual standards for both instructors and students.[10] Pedagogic modifications without a wholesale curricular reorientation could not alter a corporate culture inimical to change, and until that occurred, Leavenworth remained fixed in its contented trough.

King's efforts to exorcise the "Leavenworth competition" failed. Even though incoming students knew that everyone who completed the course graduated and that nobody in the army much cared about class standing, they still vied for grades. For starters, officers were schooled always to compete. Drum asserted that officers who fared poorly feared competition. "Competition is the finest and healthiest trait in the American race," he contended, "competition is the life of these schools."[11] Good grades were a means to an end. Students knew the War Department received the class rankings, and they still yearned for placement on honors and distinguished rolls and the general staff–eligible list. Everybody knew Leavenworth "separated the sheep from the goats." Many came to Leavenworth armed with a complete set of annotated notes and solutions provided by friends from previous classes. Nor did antipathy between faculty and students subside. One attendee recorded in his diary, "My class made a joint resolve that if anyone contemplated suicide, he would first kill an instructor."[12]

Leavenworth acted as a proxy for the command and staff experience the officers lacked. Seeking to imitate real conditions, Leavenworth tested students' reactions when exhausted from lack of sleep and irregular eating. Instructors placed artificial pressures on the students, lest the course "degenerate into a series of lectures, lifeless, academic and ineffectual."[13] Students continued to form study groups; they ignored lectures and map exercises, knowing they would not be graded, and burned the midnight oil boning up for map problems. The best students suppressed their independence and acquiesced to the system. The trick involved working backward from the easily deducible school solution and then tailoring the response, not solving the question.[14]

Attendees who were intellectually, emotionally, or physically unprepared for the course suffered under the mounting stress. Married life suffered. Many ate too little or too much, losing or gaining weight. Some took solace in the bottle. Others said, "the hell with it" and spent their time on the golf course. "All the men have a haunted look," Patton told his father.[15] Every student knew who was doing the haunting—the Leavenworth ghosts, specters of students who had committed suicide. In fact, no student took his life—although one instructor did—but everyone believed the stories, revealing a good deal about the warped social psychology of the place.[16]

Army journals often carried primers telling prospective students how to succeed at Leavenworth. Smith subscribed to the *Infantry Jour-*

nal and no doubt read an unattributed essay by "A Young Graduate" advising prospective attendees that they had nothing to worry about. "The ideas and principles [the instructor] enunciates have been carefully scrutinized by the higher authorities of the school to insure that he does not deviate from the accepted teaching." The author counseled incoming students never to question the received wisdom. "Leavenworth places more emphasis on principles than on technique; theory is of less importance than common sense." The student who placed his trust in the "school solutions" and his native common sense need not work deep into the night to succeed in the course and would have a most pleasant time as a result. Those who did not would find their time in Kansas a "mental torture and ceaseless grind." The anonymous author graduated at the top of his class, and his Leavenworth standing remade his otherwise unexceptional reputation in the army: the unnamed author was Dwight Eisenhower.[17] Whether Smith took Eisenhower's guidance or that offered by Patton to CPT Floyd Parks to "never fight the problem or look for 'Niggers in the Wood Pile,' they ain't any," remains a guess.[18] Given Smith's temperament and the fact that he left Leavenworth with an ulcer, it is very likely he opted for the "ceaseless grind" route.

The map problem Smith remembered most from his first year dealt with the Forts Henry and Donelson campaign in the Civil War. Each student had two weeks to prepare a critical analysis of Grant's and BG John McClernand's leadership. Smith read three accounts of the battle written by Lew Wallace, a division commander and later author of *Ben Hur*. The first description was his "after-action report," written a month after the battle; the second version appeared at the end of the war, and the last about fifteen years later. "With each retelling the operations became more perfect," Smith recalled, "so that in the end it became almost perfect—everything went as the general planned it." He took two lessons from this exercise: never trust a single source, as battlefield truths immediately become distorted, and battles never go off as planned.[19]

The first year concluded in mid-June. Most students began working on their Leavenworth papers—the major writing assignment in the second-year course—during the summer furlough. Otherwise, they were free to do as they liked.[20] Late in August, Beetle and Nory returned to their housekeeping apartment on Kearney Street.

Year Two

The second-year course got off to a leisurely start; September was reserved for morning orientation lectures and conferences, with afternoons off. Map problems—usually two each week—started the first week of October and continued through the end of May. The curriculum featured the same core courses as the first year, except that instead of reinforced brigades and divisions, students examined the operational level of war—corps, armies, and, in the last weeks, joint operations in a theater. The structure changed, reflecting a greater weight on staff functions, but the emphasis remained fixed on doctrine and command. The command and operations (G-3) subject areas, devoted exclusively to operational topics, represented 54 percent of the overall course. The intelligence (G-2) module assigned about a quarter of its allotted time to military intelligence topics; the G-2 course served as a catchall for everything from training exercises to military history. Students spent more time in lecture halls in the second year—about a third of the total instructional time, with the G-2 subjects absorbing more than half of it. Historical examples, delivered in lectures, emphasized operational lessons. The supply, logistics, and administrative content accounted for the remaining curriculum. Narrowly focused on troop movement by rail and supply timetabling, the administration and personnel (G-1) and supply (G-4) classes provided combat officers—about 90 percent of the cohort— with their first real exposure to operational logistics.[21]

What Leavenworth taught them exerted a powerful normative influence on the senior officers who rose to high station in World War II. American doctrine, as evidenced by the map problems, consisted of the ratiocinated dedication to the offensive. In problem after problem, the same tenets were driven home: decisive results come only through offensive action; American troops defend or retreat only as a "temporary expedient," preparatory to a general advance; the offensive must continue along a broad and expanding front; frontal attacks must be pressed until the enemy's line is enveloped (preferably) or, failing that, penetrated.[22]

U.S. Army doctrine contained a glaring internal incongruity. While the FSRs spoke of the operational advantages of maneuver, and Leavenworth carried strategic envelopment to the extreme, doctrine insisted that "the ultimate objective is the destruction of the enemy's armed strength in battle."[23] The army never reconciled this divergence between the infantry's avowal of mass, firepower, and decisive battle and the cavalry's advocacy of mobility, speed, and maneuver. Leavenworth taught that both the infantry in a penetrative assault and the cavalry in a flanking movement contributed to a decisive attack. Doctrine called for the "combined employment of all arms," but infantry remained the decisive arm, with artillery, tanks, and air as auxiliaries.

Until 1937, Leavenworth served as the conduit for doctrinal developments originating in the branch schools. A manual on the tactical employment of tanks had been in use at Leavenworth since 1923. In 1931 MacArthur transferred "combat cars"—light tanks—to the cavalry, and two years later Leavenworth published a manual on mechanized cavalry. By 1934 the course included a map problem featuring a mechanized cavalry brigade.[24] All this suggests that Leavenworth stood at the forefront of doctrinal change. In fact, tank doctrine developed along disconnected lines. Infantry tanks provided mobile machine gun platforms in the attack and a counterattacking force in defense. Tanks remained limited by the speed of advancing infantry and the range of artillery. Cavalry doctrine envisioned light tanks playing traditional cavalry roles, including in the pursuit, but subordinate to the horse cavalry.[25] No uniform tank doctrine evolved, and it could not do so as long as the dichotomy persisted between mass and firepower, on the one hand, and mobility and maneuver, on the other—which it did through completion of the 1939 FSRs and beyond. In a lecture at Leavenworth in 1939, the chief of infantry, MG George Lynch, pointed to the "glaring inconsistencies in doctrine" based on "two military philosophies as opposite as night and day."[26]

Leavenworth's treatment of air doctrine proved equally static. As for all the other branches, a first-year text covered the tactics and techniques of the Air Corps. Map problems containing an air component confined themselves to the operational level and assigned the Air Corps three essential roles: win air superiority over the front, perform reconnaissance and gun sighting, and conduct aerial attacks on hostile ground forces, chiefly to isolate the battlefield. None of the map problems assigned aircraft any tactical role in directly supporting the infantry assault, accompanying the cavalry in pursuit, or dealing with enemy tanks. Meanwhile, Air Corps doctrine taught at Maxwell Field, the Air Corps Tactical School, emphasized deep strategic operations; Leavenworth devoted a single lecture to strategic bombing. A 1937 Leavenworth manual and the 1939 FSRs did not materially alter existing doctrine.[27]

American doctrine suffered from no lack of precision on the role of the commander. By tradition and legal precedent, senior officers always exercised jurisdictional authority over the army. Far from altering officers' attitudes, the world war had rendered the officer corps more introverted. Senior officers fled back to the certitudes of the old army; by propagating the ethos and perceptions of the prewar officer corps, they increased their monopolistic control. The fixation on unity of command was a reflexive drive shoring up the hierarchy of authority. As the Superior Board report stated and the 1923 FSRs reiterated, "No greater lesson can be drawn from the World War than that *Unity of Command* is absolutely vital to the success of military operations."[28] The commander was the animating force; sole responsibility rested on him. Ultimately, success in battle depended on the commander's will to win. According to the FSRs, "the morale of the unit is that of its leaders; it is not defeated until he is defeated."[29] A commander exercised untrammeled control over all subordinates, line and staff, within his territorially defined area of authority. Leavenworth graduates dominated the higher staffs in France. The senior line commanders, several years senior to their staff officers, never attended the line and staff courses. The conviction grew that the generals relinquished too much authority to their staffs, sacrificing their command prerogatives. The 1923 FSRs restored the balance. The War Department instructed that Leavenworth and the War College augment the command content in the schools. "The general staff has become necessary in a modern army," Commandant BG Harry Smith told an incoming class at Leavenworth, "but care is necessary that it does not become the controlling force and usurp some or all the duties of the commander."[30]

Leavenworth never particularized command and control functions beyond the assertion of unity of command. A chief of staff supervised the staff and coordinated the actions of subordinate commands in the commander's name. As the personal relationship between the commander and his chief of staff matured from "theoretical to actual intimacy," and as the chief of staff developed greater familiarity with the commander and his approach, more responsibility might devolve to the chief of staff, giving the commander more flexibility to visit subordinate commands and think about pressing problems.[31] Still, a chief of staff possessed no license to exercise any measure of command, even over his own staff.

As a Leavenworth text explained, "our general staff did not get started in the right way. We were confronted with the problem of establishing a General Staff in a country where there were no trained General Staff officers." The text likened the situation to "attempting to establish a college of physicians and surgeons where there were no doctors."[32] The NDA of 1920 expressly forbade the general staff from exercising any superintendence over the functions of the bureaus. Staffs—from brigade up to the War Department—discharged the "function of coordination, direction, and supervision" but possessed "no authority of command." Unity of command held for operational commands, but the doctrine and standards of practice created by the NDA of 1920 and the FSRs created confusion at every staff level between the G divisions on a commander's staff and the attached services and technical staffs. This situation exactly mirrored the uncertain lines of authority in Washington between the WDGS and the bureaus. The "book" never made the staff chain of command explicit. As the same text admitted, the lines of authority remained "obscure." Regulations talked of the ability to advise, administer, coordinate, control, direct, supervise, and outline general policies but not to command or operate. In practice, the actual control over support and logistics echelons remained in the hands of the heads of the administrative, technical, and supply agencies. Since the commander above the staff and the technical and service chiefs below discharged command responsibilities, the precise roles of the chief of staff and his general staff sections remained ambiguous. "The General Staff is supposed to coordinate the Army," so the saying went, "but it can't coordinate itself." One Leavenworth student who studied the question concluded, "Practice varied with the commanding general." This uncertainty rendered actual coordination at every level of command virtually impossible.[33] Nonetheless, officers departed Leavenworth convinced that the American staff system was the envy of the military world.

Military history played a central role in the second-year course, validating doctrinal premises. Although the Civil War and peripheral British operations in World War I received attention, the German offensive in August 1914 loomed largest. The year opened with a series of four conferences dealing with the operations of a German army and two of its corps from Mons through the advance to Le Cateau. In November and December the command course introduced command and staff functions by examining the Schlieffen offensive through the battle of the Marne. A series of lectures and conferences dominated February, climaxing in a major staff exercise.[34] Students received heavy doses of doctrine disguised as military history. In the opinion of Leavenworth, the German concept of "dual command" resulted in the Germans' failure to take Paris. The Schlieffen offensive miscarried because the commanders lacked the will to win, did not preserve the broad front, and relied too much on a general staff possessing too much flexibility and independent authority. German army commanders lacked aggressiveness, failed to achieve the breakthrough, and, with their refusal to employ cavalry at the decisive moment, became prisoners of logistical restraints. Interestingly, students read that the Germans avoided operating in the Ardennes, "a forested highland, with its high hills, deep narrow ravines, [and] relative scarcity of roads . . . [a] difficult area."[35] According to American doctrinal precepts, assertive leadership could overcome any obstacle, material or gestalt. Using the maxims of their own doctrine as the basis for making historical judgments, misinterpretations abounded. In the opinion of one of Smith's classmates, the historical lessons colored the thinking of a generation of officers who went through Leavenworth.[36]

The year ended with a flourish. The penultimate event on the school calendar was the presentation of the Leavenworth papers during the last week of May and first week of June. Smith did not write a paper. As a member of a fifteen-man special group, he helped prepare a dramatized re-creation of the 1914 battle of Tannenberg. The group studied the operations of the German Eighth Army and Russian First and Second Armies from the end of the battle of Gumbinnen through the battle of Tannenberg. The historical narrative was combined with dialogue involving the leading personalities of both the Russian and German staffs. In the four-hour, four-act play, aided by lantern slides and phonographic records, the drive and determination of GEN Paul von Hindenburg, the German commander, were sharply contrasted with the indecisiveness and lethargy of the Russian commanders. Consistent with American doctrine, the overriding lesson centered on the decisive role played by aggressive commanders—Hindenburg at the army level and GEN Hermann von François at the corps level. GEN Erich Ludendorff, Hindenburg's chief of staff, was portrayed as ineffectual and at one point paralyzed "by a case of nerves." Smith played COL Max Hoffman, the interim chief of staff in East Prussia until Hindenburg and Ludendorff arrived on the scene. Although Hoffman masterminded the German strategy of the central position and virtually exercised the command function during the crisis of the campaign, Smith's character remained in a supporting role. He discharged the narrow responsibilities of a chief of staff as prescribed in American practice. By ignoring details not in accordance with American doctrine, such as the central role played by Ludendorff and Hoffman and how the system of dual command actually functioned, the most valuable lessons of Tannenberg were missed.

The group received a "superior" rating, with the recommendation that similar studies become a regular component of the course. In fact, only two years earlier a dramatic production on the same topic had been presented. Members of that class translated Hoffman's *Tannenberg; wie is wirklich war* and wrote a critical examination of François's controversial role in the battle. What Smith's group lacked in originality it more than compensated for in big-name talent. The cast consisted of three future four-star generals—Mark Clark, Matt Ridgway, and Beetle Smith.[37]

The course ended in a weeklong command post exercise. Students manned headquarters, complete with the full array of general and special staff sections; they prepared plans and executed movements, replicating an encounter battle along the Missouri River. The exercise allowed students to show what they had learned in the course and provided the faculty the last opportunity to grade them during a simulated war-fighting situation. After the strain of a week in the field, the students enjoyed a free week before the graduation ceremony on 21 June.

Smith graduated thirty-ninth in a class of 118, a respectable but not impressive performance. Given the rampant grade inflation, the difference between those who earned honors or distinguished rankings—the top 25 percent—and those who narrowly missed out often amounted to decimal points. A student who bucked the school solution and received an "unsatisfactory" or even a couple of "satisfactory" grades placed himself so far back on the curve that he could never recover.[38] Students could "reclaim" their grades, resubmitting their work to the faculty committee, but this rarely changed the outcome. No board selected incoming students based on their fitness for the Leavenworth course, but a board of officers reviewed the results and ruled on an individual's suitability for future admission to the War College and, with it, eligibility for service in the War Department. Although graduating only in the top third of his class, Smith still earned an "excellent" rating on his efficiency report, tapping him for passage to the last level of the army's school system.[39]

Many senior officers lavished praise on Leavenworth in their memoirs and oral histories, claiming that the school saved the army. Although there is a good deal of truth in this assertion, much of this eulogizing was a product of pure nostalgia. Others—including many of the most intelligent but also the most acerbic officers—roundly condemned the course. "The Instructor Staff were a hierarchy, to whom the School doctrine was sacred," remembered Bradford Chynoweth. "They were not teaching War. They were teaching Dogma."[40] John Wood thought so little of the intellectual content that he contemptuously read the newspaper during lectures. As in most things, the truth rests somewhere in the middle. Leavenworth did not exist to cultivate independent thinkers and theorists. It never aspired to replicate the *Kriegsakademie*. After the release of the 1923 FSRs and until the late 1930s—when Leavenworth reverted to the one-year curriculum, long after the bulk of senior World War II officers had graduated—the Command and General Staff School never possessed the authorization to blaze new paths in operational and tactical doctrine. Leavenworth emerged as the doctrinal font; from 1937 onward, it produced simplified tactical manuals of great utility. Leavenworth's mission centered on producing ecumenically trained officers drilled in the same doctrine to follow the mandated procedures with the capacity to discharge a variety of responsibilities in ranks two or three higher than those they presently held. The army required officers who could perform tasks to standard, follow procedures, and harmonize actions. Leavenworth trained officers to assess and solve problems, write orders, and produce results. Preparing a fire plan does not require creative thinking. Tactics involve application, not theory. All these missions the Command and General Staff School performed extremely well. Despite the mediocrity of the teaching staff and the unregenerative course content, Leavenworth inculcated in the "long generation" a common language, a uniform problem-solving methodology, and a heightened sense of their own capabilities.

Leavenworth bestowed intrinsic benefits that were arguably more vital than what it taught. For all the stress, the school served a vital therapeutic function. It took officers away from the tedium of administrative and training jobs with their branches, brought them together, and forced them to think about their profession. Leavenworth built strong fraternal group identities. Careers intertwined like a barbed-wire strand. Men came together, bonded for a short duration, moved to their next posts, but preserved contacts. An officer's reputation—a fusion of character, performance, and coincidence—was his most prized asset. Smith never thought his career had been handicapped because he missed out on West Point, and clearly, he was right. With all promotions based strictly on seniority, Smith stood far in advance of any West Pointer who had graduated after 1917. For men like Smith without a West Point ring—and they constituted the majority of interwar officers—Leavenworth proved crucial. The school provided an officer with the single best opportunity for enlarging or recouping his standing, which was vital in an incestuous body like the interwar officer corps. The shared Leavenworth experience developed an informal system of internalized selection. Senior officers remembered promising juniors and, when the time came, selected them for preferred positions. Junior officers took the measure of one another. These assessments of an officer's abilities and character, together with the strong links of familiarity, exerted enormous influence in deciding who rose in rank in World War II and who did not.

Smith's strong personality either attracted or repelled people. Few responded to him with indifference. Whatever others made of him, Smith widened his circle of connections. Thirty-seven percent of the two-year graduates earned stars in World War II, one in five of them from Smith's class. Of the 113 regular army graduates, 62 became generals, and 4 of them eventually wore four stars (including LT Maxwell Taylor). Just like Eisenhower's famous "Class that Stars Fell On"—the West

Point class of 1915—Smith's "aides, adjutants, and asses" cohort undoubtedly boasted some high fliers. However, the chief reason so many members of the Leavenworth class of 1935 became general officers was simply the luck of the draw. This group was ideally situated and the right age to move up rapidly when the army dramatically expanded. During the war, any headquarters held a number of officers Smith would have known, or at least known of, at Leavenworth.[41]

Although Smith harbored progressive views on armor and mechanization, he left Leavenworth with the same partisan infantry mind-set he had arrived with.[42] In 1934 Smith wrote to Harding, now the editor of the *Infantry Journal,* applauding the efforts of the editorial staff in pushing the debate on the future role of armor. He was enthused enough to give himself a lifetime subscription as a Christmas present.[43] Smith thought Leavenworth produced "loads of good combat leaders," but he was particularly critical of its failure to train high-level intelligence analysts, operational planners, and logisticians. As a result, the army faced an almost debilitating shortage of staff officer talent throughout World War II. "Our service schools simply did not know how to tell us to do real planning," he later recalled.[44] Whatever his feelings about Leavenworth's educative value, the two years Smith spent at the Command and General Staff School provided a thorough grounding in command functions, staff work, and combat doctrine; it gave him the self-assurance to fill a potential command slot or training billet or to man a general staff section. And Leavenworth punched his ticket for admission to the War College.

★ **11** ★

"No One Ever Graduates"

The year Smith graduated from Leavenworth, the U.S. Army's downward spiral finally hit bottom. Strapped for money and men, the army could not properly fulfill any of its missions. As Marshall pointed out, "we have fewer Regular troops in the United States today than twenty years ago, and unfortunately most of our organizations are stationed in the sparsely settled districts along the Rio Grande." After subtracting the 32,000 troops defending American overseas possessions, the 36,000 on detached service or in educational and staff assignments, and the 20,000 policing the Mexican border, the army's paper strength stood at 30,000 scattered in 300 posts and stations throughout the country. If all the combat troops were gathered together, Marshall told an audience in Chicago, they would not even fill all the reserve seats at Wrigley Field.[1]

Fortune ran two articles that captured nicely the plight of the army and its officer corps at its nadir. One was entitled "Who's in the Army Now?" and the other legitimately asked "Why an Army?" The unnamed author accurately portrayed an officer's psychology as "a queer mixture of the clergy, the college professor, and the small boy playing Indian." MacArthur complained that the army schools produced the best "retired" army in the world. The *Fortune* article put a different spin on the issue, describing the officer corps as "a great educational institution from which no one ever graduates."[2] Smith found himself trapped on the army school treadmill. Typical of officers of his age and grade, he would spend eight years in army schools as either a student or an instructor. He feared he might never get off.[3]

Back to Benning

Smith returned to the Infantry School and the weapons section. Little had changed in his absence. The post had taken on more of the feel of a permanent post; the teaching facilities were improved, and the housing crunch had eased. The course remained the same. Most instructors found the first year of teaching challenging; thereafter it lost what little attraction it possessed. Officers used their connections to get into the advanced courses and Leavenworth, and they used them to escape teaching details. As a result, very few officers served out their postings. Many viewed their tenure in teaching assignments as a waste of time. Some officers felt stultified teaching by the book. One officer wanted "to throw the book out the window . . . but you never dared to do it."[4]

Smith had reason for gloom. His chances of getting a command looked bleaker than ever. Officers like Smith applauded MacArthur's drive to improve readiness, press for mechanization, and tackle the "grave embarrassment" of overage senior officers, frozen promotions, and the hump.[5] MacArthur divided the continental United States into four army districts, each with a division attached. In addition, he formed five understrength brigades, giving at least a discernible regular army presence in each of the nine corps districts. To flesh out the reorganization, Congress authorized expansion of the army to 165,000. The War Department thought the restructuring and manpower infusion would open up more officer billets in line units, but the reform had the opposite impact. By consolidating units, entire formations vanished, with a corresponding reduction in command slots. MacArthur's attempt to break the senior officer logjam also miscarried. Newly promoted colonels typically had five or six years of service before they reached the mandatory retirement age of sixty-four; brigadier and major generals averaged sixty-one years of age. The War Department offered inducements for early retirement, and MacArthur lobbied for a reduction in the retirement age. MacArthur pushed for promotion by merit and competitive exams for entry into the army's advanced schools. Predictably, the bureau chiefs dug in their heels and deflected MacArthur's manpower initiatives. Congress passed a package of officer promotion bills, but none of them promised much help for Smith. In 1935 captains constituted 80 percent of the hump. Smith had already benefited from MacArthur's lone minor success in lowering the age of officers entering the advanced schools and Leavenworth.

President Roosevelt extended MacArthur's tenure into 1935. One of the favorite parlor games was guessing who the next chief of staff would be. Given the intensity of branch competition, infantry officers pulled for an infantryman. One thing seemed certain: it would not be Smith's mentor Moseley. During the Bonus March fiasco, Moseley convinced himself and MacArthur that the protesters represented the vanguard of a communist revolution. Evidence suggests that he planned to use the crisis as a pretext for a military putsch. The War Department created color plans to prepare for national emergencies, including Emergency Plan White against a threat to domestic order. MacArthur revised the plan and, in effect, ordered its implementation; ironically, it was the only war plan ever put into operation, even though Hoover never gave his consent. Both MacArthur and Moseley clearly exceeded the president's guidelines. In MacArthur's absence, Moseley ignored an executive order forbidding any pursuit into Hooverville and later lied about it.[6] The sad affair provided neither the spark for revolution nor a military seizure of power, but the army's actions that day blackened its reputation in the eyes of an already antagonistic American public and guaranteed that Moseley would not succeed MacArthur. The army closed ranks; Moseley received no censure or even reprimand, and he held corps and army district commands until his retirement in 1938. Even in uniform he openly opposed Roosevelt and the New Deal and advocated isolationism and extreme rightist policies—forced sterilization, severe limitations on immigration, and federal concentration camps for felons, undesirable aliens, and political (presumably leftist) extremists. To be fair, Moseley's racism, anti-Semitism, and chauvinism, though extreme, mirrored the prevailing attitudes of many officers. Although he retained the friendship of many of his military associates—including Marshall, Eisenhower (who served under him in the War Department), and Smith—he forfeited any real influence in the army.[7]

If career matters were not bad enough, Mrs. Smith's health had deteriorated. Worrying about his mother did not improve Beetle's ulcer. Smith hunkered down at Benning, hoping to spin out one year at the Infantry School before heading off to the War College. He occupied himself with teaching his courses, and he produced another article for *Mailing List*, a rework of his instructional material.[8] He still had his dog, Sport, and the woods and rivers as refuge from his troubles.[9]

All this contributed to Beetle's increasingly foul disposition, as demonstrated in a conference room exchange with a student. During the discussion of a map problem, an attendee questioned the school solution. Not satisfied with Smith's clarification, the student persisted. Smith flew into a blind rage. Following a stream of profanities that left the class dumbfounded, Smith roared, "When I say no, I mean NO!" That was the last question Beetle faced for the rest of the year.[10] As expected, orders arrived clearing him for the War College, bringing an end to the worst year of his career. A year in Washington looked good and promised to shake him out of his doldrums.

The Army War College

Beetle and Nory arrived in the nation's capital in June, where Smith would take his place in what many referred to as the "Gentleman's Course." Away from the Capitol district, Washington still felt like a southern town. The sultry summer heat added to the effect. Since the army did not provide housing, the Smiths had scouted out accommodations—no easy matter on a captain's salary. Adding to the expense, Beetle outfitted himself with a civilian wardrobe. Officers attached to the War Department and the War College wore mufti, a custom growing out of the army's desire not to advertise its conspicuous presence in the capital. Each day Smith, like any minor bureaucrat, trekked to and from Fort Humphreys, situated on a spit of land where the Washington Channel and the Anacostia River flow into the Potomac, about a thirty-minute walk from downtown.

The posting to the War College represented one of the plum assignments in the army. Nothing stood in sharper contrast to the Infantry School. Set aside for military purposes by Pierre L'Enfant in the original plan for the city, the site had housed army installations—an arsenal, then Washington Barracks, and finally the War College—since 1791, making it second only to West Point as the oldest army post in the country. Two long, well-kept quadrangles led up to the ornate beaux arts academic building designed by famed architect Stanford White. The place possessed the look and feel of a real university.

Less than half of Leavenworth graduates went on to the War College. Despite their junior rank, attendees thought they were pretty hot stuff. Among Smith's classmates were two of his collaborators on the Tannenberg project, Clark and Ridgway. The attendees broke into consortiums of six men and at least one assigned instructor. Faculty consisted of officers detailed from the general staff divisions of the War Department and each arm and service, and half a dozen from the U.S. Navy and Marine Corps.

From its inception in 1904 as part of the Root reforms, the War College lacked a clearly defined mission. Before World War I, the War College functioned less as a school than as a planning appendage to the War Department General Staff. Between 1904 and 1917, the War College graduated only 270 officers, and only 57 percent of them wore stars during the war. General March wanted the reconstituted War College devoted to examining national defense policy, international relations, and strategic questions. Beyond constituting the summit of his sequential educational pyramid for producing staff officers capable of moving on to positions in the War Department and higher headquarters, March wanted the War College to study and offer remedies for the worst failings of the War Department in 1917—the debacle of industrial and manpower mobilization. The War College would serve as both an educational institution and a review agency, independent of the WDGS.[11]

Pershing redirected the school's trajectory. Leavenworth, not the War College, emerged as the engine driving the army's school system. Designed as the pinnacle educational institution, the War College filled gaps in the Leavenworth program, recalibrating its curriculum and avoiding duplication with the Command and General Staff School. In both institutions, emphasis shifted to command and staff functions.[12] Leavenworth's adoption of the one-year curriculum set off a chain reaction. Since Leavenworth prepared officers for command, training, and staff duties through the corps, the War College course centered on producing officers suited for future command and staff functions in the corps areas and the War Department.

Although the 1920 NDA removed the War College from WDGS direction, the undermanned general staff took advantage of the school's proximity and assigned it planning tasks until the mid-1930s, chiefly dealing with mobilization. In 1926 the Army Industrial College opened its doors in a building flanking the War College. The new institution was charged with studying the problems of procurement and production as an adjunct to the office of the assistant secretary of war. The War College altered its planning focus to manpower mobilization. From time to time, War College students also war-gamed aspects of the emerging color plans forwarded by the War Plans Division of the WDGS and the Joint Board. The ambiguous association with the WDGS, the Joint Board, and the Army Industrial College, together with alterations in the Leavenworth curriculum, produced uncertainty over the War College's direction. Commandants were never sure whether priority rested with conducting command or staff preparation or in acting as an ancillary planning bureau.

Leavenworth's return to the two-year cycle again forced the redesign of the War College program of study. The War Department directed that the commandant, MG William Connor, tailor the course to provide instruction on the political, economic, and social questions that influenced the conduct of war but retain the prominence of command and staff work, with a secondary emphasis on the problems associated with mobilization. Despite the dizzying array of missions, Connor designed a course far more coherent than anything offered at Leavenworth. Connor reduced war making to two fundamental components: the preparation for war, essentially the staff functions involved in mobilizing, moving, and deploying manpower and materiel into a theater of operations; and the conduct of war, basically a repeat of the Leavenworth command course, but at the operational and strategic levels of war. By the time Smith arrived, the course had been running for nine years.[13]

The Preparation for War sequence consisted of five month-long courses organized parallel to the general staff divisions of the War Department. Student groups examined each phase from mobilization to the movement of forces and materiel from the Zone of the Interior into a theater of operations, through their deployment, and up to the first encounter with the enemy. The G-3 (training) course reviewed the organization, equipment, and training methods for the expansible army. October was devoted to the G-1 (personnel) module, which examined manpower mobilization, followed in November by the G-4 logistics course, again featuring the mechanisms of mobilization but containing a section on supply and movement of materiel into a theater of operations, including the navy's role. In December students prepared intelligence assessments analyzing a potential enemy's political, economic, and social capacity for waging war. After the Christmas break the Preparation for War series ended with a weeklong review of the agencies involved in war planning and an introduction to war gaming.[14]

The Conduct of War portion of the course consisted of a series of four war games conducted on maps. The first map exercise examined the generalship of Lee in the Antietam campaign and Meade's failed pursuit after Gettysburg. These historical case studies were followed by contemporary war games testing the feasibility of elements of the War Plans Division and the Joint Board's color plans. By 1937 the emphasis of War Department planning shifted from Orange—for a war in the western Pacific against Japan—to defense of the strategic triangle of Alaska–Hawaii–Canal Zone. In May the map exercise followed up on the previous scenarios, but this time examined joint army-navy operations. The last set of assignments centered on defending against an amphibious attack in the Chesapeake Bay–Delaware Valley region. The year ended with a command post exercise, conducted on horseback, which played out one of the map exercises in the field. Cutbacks usually meant the staff rides were confined to the environs of Washington—either the Chesapeake Bay or Grant's 1864 Overland Campaign in Virginia. In Smith's year, funding allowed for a return to Antietam and Gettysburg. Almost everyone agreed the staff ride constituted the highlight of the year.

The year in Washington produced none of the angst Leavenworth prided itself on. The War College assumed the mien of a graduate school, except no grades were given and students wrote no thesis. Invited speakers from government, industry, and academe—about three each week—supplemented the lectures and conferences given by the faculty. In the Preparation for War section of the course, groups received problem-solving assignments, many of them current issues of interest to the WDGS. School solutions still applied in the Conduct of War courses, but without the rancor encountered at Leavenworth. The chair rotated among the group participants; individuals conducted their own research. The group then presented its findings to the entire school, and open discussions followed. Attendees produced individual written research projects based on contemporary questions; most of them centered on manpower problems—the War Department's perpetual bugbear. The best ones disappeared unread into the bowels of the War Department. Historical study held an important place in the curriculum; the historical section of the War Plans Division came under War College auspices in 1921. Every student wrote a biography of an important military figure, extracting the correct lessons about leadership.[15]

The War College never occupied a position remotely comparable to that of Leavenworth in the mental universe of World War II generals, Smith among them; their memoirs, oral histories, and letters rarely mention their War College experiences.[16] One reason was the lack of competition for grades and class standing. Officers caught up in the "old Leavenworth competition" felt compelled to work hard. At the War College, individuals profited from the year based solely on what they invested. Bradley thought the War College "wasted his time." In his opinion, many attendees "did not take the work seriously and often the quality of the presentations reflected that attitude." Clearly, he fell into that category.[17] The most ambitious among them curried the favor of their seniors. The faculty board filed recommendations and officer efficiency reports testifying to the graduates' worthiness to fill WDGS slots. Everybody knew that the previous commandant, MG Malin Craig, now occupied the chief of staff's chair.

As at Leavenworth, many of the benefits of the year lay outside the lecture halls and conference rooms. Eisenhower believed he learned more in bull sessions with his colleagues than he ever did in class. Without the pressure of contending for grades, officers enjoyed plenty of leisure for these informal get-togethers or spending time with their families. On an officer's salary, most attendees could not afford to participate in the social bustle of the capital. Other than formal occasions—attendance of the New Year's Day reception at the White House was required—the attendees and their families socialized among themselves. To save cab fare, most lived clumped together in apartments within walking distance of the school. Old friendships were renewed, and new ones formed. In the small interwar officer corps, everyone knew somebody who knew somebody else. Most important, the year in Washington expanded an officer's web of contacts.

Smith was no social lion. He enjoyed bridge and chess, and he always enjoyed downing a couple of old-fashioneds. Beetle and Nory never had children, which excluded them from the many family-oriented activities. Even if they had desired to participate, the Smiths faced other constrictions. They still attended to Beetle's ailing mother, and his stomach condition worsened. Smith never fretted about being left out of the inner circle; he preferred it that way. Beetle knew his way around Washington, having spent four years in the Bureau of the Budget. The capital offered plenty of inexpensive diversions. No doubt he took advantage of the Library of Congress and the holdings of the historical section at the school. If things closed in on him, he did what he always did: he escaped into northern Virginia and western Maryland for some hunting and fishing.

Smith impressed the faculty. BG W. S. Grant evaluated him as "cheerful yet serious" and a "very good team worker" who "appreciates [the] views of others" yet provides "clear cut decisions." He described Smith's work habits as "methodical, thorough, and accurate" and recommended him for "high command and every staff division from division to War Plans Division" of the WDGS.[18]

Graduation on 23 June 1937 marked the end of Smith's formal education, but not his time in army schools. Much to his disappointment, attendance at the War College paid no immediate dividend. Smith received orders for Benning. Summer 1937 also marked Smith's twentieth year in the army. He had completed the infantry advanced course, Leavenworth, and the War College but remained locked in the captain's hump. All he could do was resign himself to another uneventful tour in the weapons section.

Benning Again

Returning to Benning, Smith must have felt as if he had never left. But change was finally in the wind. Smith busied himself with instructional duties. He enjoyed teaching the basic course because most of it took place outdoors. Virtually all his students were West Pointers. Over the course of the year they concentrated on command decision making and tactics, moving up from platoon and company command exercises to the battalion. Students handled every weapon in the infantry's inventory; all qualified on the rifle range. Smith's specialty remained teaching the positioning of machine guns for enfilading fire.[19] The weapons section, in common with the whole infantry, impatiently awaited the introduction of the new standard rifle and the 81mm mortar. Finally, in 1939, the Infantry School received clearance to commence using the M1 Garand rifle. Smith taught the training sections on the Garand. He contributed articles on both his specialties to *Mailing List*. He also picked up some money revising the infantry weapons section for a new ROTC manual.[20]

Something else changed—and not for the better. Smith's foul disposition got worse, in no small measure because of his ulcer. His mother's death hardly improved his attitude. At this stage, Smith's stomach really started plaguing him. Once stocky, he now shed weight. From time to time the Smiths joined other weapons section faculty members at John's Fish Camp on the Chattahoochee to indulge in one of Beetle's favorites, a meal of freshwater fish for 50 cents. They all thought Beetle "a good sport" for coming along, despite his stomach problems. On one occasion the fish disagreed with him, and he barely made it out the door of the restaurant before vomiting violently. Junior officers often felt his wrath. One of them, LT Russell Vittrup, a future lieutenant general, remembered volunteering to go out to a distant range and tune the machine guns for an exercise the next day. Smith had other plans. All during the long drive out to Hook Range, Vittrup feared an eruption of Smith's notorious temper, but it did not come. Nothing happened while they worked with the guns, and Vittrup was feeling relieved as he climbed back into the car for the return trip to the academic building. No sooner had the door closed when Smith launched into a foul-mouthed tirade, berating the lanky Texan the whole way back. Finally, his bile expended, Smith returned to his normal ill-tempered self. Although he frequently lost his temper, Smith rarely held a grudge. The other members of the weapons section respected Smith and abided his stubborn and irritable personality.[21]

A curious element of Smith's persona involved his befriending of younger men. He rarely socialized with his bosses and officers of equivalent rank. It was the Ashland Avenue Irregulars and the streetcar out back all over again. At Benning, Smith often asked junior officers on the faculty to join him for evening possum and raccoon hunts while their wives stayed behind with Nory. When the men returned, their boots caked with red Georgia mud, the young officers hovered at the doorstep. They knew the drill but always hung back, in part out of a reluctance to tread on Nory's spotless floor, but really out of dread of setting off

Smith. Beetle was nothing if not consistent. He marched in, waving the others to follow. Beetle was the master of his own domain.[22]

A past master of sublimating his feelings, Smith never allowed his unhappiness to interfere with the performance of his duties (except for the occasional shredding of a subordinate or student), as indicated by his succession of "superior" ratings at Benning. COL Courtney Hodges noted that Smith "obtains superior results" and possesses the "highest potential value to the service."[23] Smith finally received some good news. On New Year's Day 1939, Smith could finally take off his bars and put on the gold cluster of a major.

Smith enjoyed working under Hodges, the new deputy commandant and director of instruction. Like Smith, Hodges was a mustang, a self-made officer up from the ranks. Hodges had flunked out of West Point, joined the army as a private, earned a commission, served in the Philippines, took part in the Mexican Punitive Expedition, and fought in the Saint-Mihiel and Argonne offensives in France. In Smith's opinion, Hodges was all infantry. The entire infantry branch, and especially Benning, celebrated the news when one of their own, Marshall, succeeded Craig as chief of staff. Many officers (and not only those from the infantry) regarded Craig, a cavalryman, as showing undue favoritism to his own branch.[24] Members of the Infantry School staff anticipated a career boost from Marshall's appointment. Smith remembered his encounter with Marshall but hardly anticipated any windfall, fully expecting to continue his anonymous labors in Georgia.

Marshall once wrote that he regretted not occupying a position of power where he could promote younger officers of "brilliancy and talent damned by lack of rank to obscurity."[25] Now he had his chance. One of those officers so favored was Bradley, now serving directly under Marshall as one of his assistant secretaries.

No section of the WDGS enjoyed closer contact to the chief of staff than the secretariat. Part of Marshall's inner office, the secretaries managed the enormous volume of correspondence that often swamped the War Department Message Center. Bradley, along with the other assistant, LTC Stanley Mickelsen, received incoming communications and judged their significance. They distributed those requiring action to the respective general staff divisions, reviewed staff papers referred to the chief of staff, and briefed the secretary, COL Orlando Ward, in advance of his morning presentation to Marshall. In addition, the office monitored the flow of correspondence by maintaining an official record to keep Marshall informed of the actions of the staff divisions. At the end of each week, the secretariat reviewed the activities of the general staff and submitted statements outlining why certain actions remained incomplete.[26]

Marshall was a stickler for brevity and speed. He insisted that all communications be condensed to a single page, direct, and simply worded. Overburdened by the problems of rearmament, Marshall possessed neither the time nor the patience to deal with correspondence and delegated routine administrative duties to his deputy, BG Lorenzo Gasser, and the secretariat. Bradley and Mickelsen drafted about two-thirds of outgoing messages, but neither proved very adept at it. They had reason to celebrate if one of their letters got by Marshall without revision. The chief of staff bristled when he had to waste time vetting and correcting his secretaries' work, and everyone agreed they needed an officer with some command of the English language. Bradley thought of Smith. When Bradley put forward Smith's name, Marshall replied, "Smith, do I know him?" As tactfully as he could, Bradley reminded Marshall of the episode at Benning.

One of the myths surrounding Marshall is that he kept a little black book that listed all the bright young officers he would promote if given the chance. Nobody ever saw this book, including his biographer and the compiler of his papers.[27] The point is that Marshall could have used such a book, because his mind was a sieve when it came to remembering names. In any case, his encounter with Smith back in 1931 had hardly been memorable.

Bradley felt so strongly about Smith's appointment that he had already checked into Smith's availability. As luck would have it, Smith's stint at the Infantry School was nearing completion. Taking Bradley at his word—that Smith would be the ideal man for the letter-writing job—Marshall forwarded the necessary request to Benning.[28] The memo served as the springboard for Smith's ascent in the army.

Part Three

★ ★ ★ ★

The Towering Figure— George C. Marshall

The Chief's Apprentice

Marshall never acted unless convinced of the rectitude of his decision, and when he did, he exhibited complete self-assurance in his ideas and actions. He thought long and hard about his experiences in France and the interwar years. Upon becoming acting chief of staff, Marshall possessed a clear conception of the changes required to prepare the United States for war: altering the promotion structure, weeding out the deadwood in the senior ranks of the army, and reorganizing the WDGS stood near the top of his agenda. Before he could proceed, he had to clear a number of high hurdles: work out a modus operandi for dealing with Roosevelt and Congress, win public confidence, and surmount the dogged conservatism of powerful senior officers and their influential political friends. Marshall identified his chief mission as bridging the gap in the historic military cycle between peacetime penury and wartime bounty by accelerating the measured rearmament, expansion, and modernization of the ground forces.[1]

His tenure as deputy and acting chief of staff afforded Marshall the opportunity to observe the War Department in action. He did not like what he saw. Marshall valued teamwork, responsiveness, efficiency, and initiative and witnessed little evidence of any. As chief of staff, Marshall wanted a command and staff structure that centralized decision making at the top and decentralized the execution of policy to subordinates. In his estimate, good officers initiated action, found solutions, cooperated across staff lines, and made decisions at or above their level of responsibility; they did not push problems up the staff and command chains. He knew that any restructuring of the WDGS required legislative approval and might well spark a "palace coup" by disaffected senior officers. The congressional process of open testimony would devolve into an extended and rancorous contest, so even if Marshall succeeded in getting his way, it might "do more harm [to the army's prestige and morale] than good."[2]

Content to bide his time, making incremental and digestible changes and selecting and pushing talented younger officers, Marshall exercised his command prerogative and fashioned his own inner headquarters. Marshall's strength rested in character—his determination, integrity, and honesty—not intellect. He wanted subordinates who overcame obstacles through enterprise and common sense and stocked his inner headquarters with some of the best young talent of the "long generation," firm in the resolve to mold them according to his own experience and conceptions.[3]

Marshall never took the time to review Smith's personnel file before agreeing to his appointment to the secretariat. That was not his style. Instead, he relied on the judgment of his subordinates, men he trusted. If Bradley thought Smith was the best choice, that sufficed for Marshall. Had he taken the time, he would have discovered Smith's suitability for the job: his short spell in the WDGS during the war; service as aide, adjutant, and assistant chief of staff under Moseley, an officer Marshall held in the highest regard; his tour in Washington with the Bureau of the Budget; and his string of excellent evaluations and glowing recommendations from superiors. Otherwise, nothing much on paper separated Smith from any number of other officers of his age and grade.[4]

Luck again played a role. Had Drum or some other officer become chief of staff instead of Marshall, the roster of World War II generals would have looked very different. Connections and reputations constituted the vital ingredients. Smith's case illustrates how it worked. Marshall brought Bradley into the secretariat because he knew him from Benning and earmarked him for a future command. Bradley remembered Smith and tabbed him for a specific job in the secretariat. Once an officer received an appointment in Marshall's headquarters, he rose or fell depending on his performance against Marshall's exacting and preconceived standards. Nobody viewed a staff job as an end in itself; every officer selected for a War Department billet saw it as a way station on the road to a field command. Smith proved no different, but fortune had a different path in mind.

Initiation as a Marshall Man

Beetle joined the secretariat in October after completing his tour at Benning. Not long after his arrival, he endured the first of many of Marshall's "tests"—the dreaded summons into the chief's office. No one entered his office without foreboding. One member of the secretariat recalled seeing "many a general officer in [Marshall's] outer office betraying a most unmilitary agitation while awaiting his turn to pass through the door to his office."[5] Everyone feared the initiation rite. It might happen soon after an officer's appearance, or it might take days. No matter how many times other officers told their stories, nothing prepared the new man for the call, once it came. The veterans ushered the unfortunate into the office and gathered within earshot. The acolyte stood in front of the chief's desk and nervously waited as the general finished whatever he was reading. Suddenly Marshall's steely blue eyes, peering over his glasses, fixed on the officer. If not unnerved, the novice outlined the business at hand. Marshall at once appraised whether the new officer could think on his feet under pressure. After listening to the presentation, Marshall asked for a personal assessment and a recommendation on the matter's disposition. The question might involve a routine issue, or it could be of major significance. At the end of the interview, which might last only a couple of minutes, Marshall decided whether the officer deserved greater responsibilities.

Just about everyone on his staff held Marshall in awe. "If George Marshall had a fault," remarked Maxwell Taylor, who later joined the secretariat, "it was that his strong personality had such an unnerving effect on officers around him."[6] The interwar army bred deferential junior officers who were unused to making their own decisions. Some officers tagged for rapid promotion—men such as Leonard Gerow and Robert Crawford—became unglued in the chief's presence. "Those who speak slowly and haltingly and seem to fumble," Smith concluded, "are soon passed by in the rush to get things done."[7] Marshall ruthlessly replaced officers who did not measure up to his rigorous standards. Another of Marshall's faults was a pronounced self-righteous streak that bred a disinclination to change his mind once he came to a conclusion. No shrinking violet, Smith easily passed the test.

The morning briefing of the chief provided the big event of the day. Marshall arrived at his office in the munitions building promptly at 7:30. After studying the logbook and reviewing the précis of communications that had arrived during the night, Marshall buzzed for Gasser and Ward. The deputy and secretary, usually with one of the assistant secretaries in tow, entered Marshall's office and awaited the signal to begin the oral presentation. Marshall listened intently, allowing the presenting officer to state his business. If he detected a problem, Marshall asked why it had not been uncovered before it crossed his desk. After the briefing, Marshall decided what matters required action. If Marshall sanctioned the plan, he expected the necessary orders to be issued and his staff to monitor progress throughout the process. When a problem demanded further attention, such as additional research or refinements, Gasser or Ward delegated the task to one of the assistant secretaries.[8]

The secretariat served as Marshall's private staff. The office discharged a number of functions: collecting statistical data, acting as office of record for the chief of staff and his deputy, and receiving visiting officials in the headquarters.[9] Bradley, Mickelsen, and Smith started their day two hours before Marshall arrived. They held a conference, encapsulated each of the required staff findings for presentation to Marshall in a single typed page, tidied the logbook, and briefed Gasser and Ward. Early in his career Marshall suffered a number of bouts with neurasthenia, or exhaustion from overwork. To safeguard his health, he disciplined himself to exercise and relax. He always returned to his quarters at Fort Myer no later than 5:30 P.M. with instructions that he not be disturbed unless something critical surfaced. This meant that one of the assistants manned the Message Center during the night. The responsible officer read incoming communications, prepared brief summaries of their contents, and entered the particulars into the logbook. Since all officers drew duty during the day, the assistants learned to do without sleep.

Marshall demanded thorough staff work and preparation. Staff officers quickly learned his standards. "When you carry a paper in here," he told Bradley, "I want you to give me every reason you can think of why I should not approve it. If in spite of your objections, my decision is still to go ahead, then I'll know that I'm right." They also learned that he detested erudite staff studies and reports; Marshall insisted on succinct and impartial recommendations. "Every time I turn my back," he lamented, "some staff officer calls on some poor devil for a report or an extra copy of some more damned papers—and I will not have it."[10]

Marshall expected his staff to make prompt decisions beyond their sphere of authority. Staff officers enjoyed wide latitude, and Marshall backed their actions with the full authority of his position. Eisenhower, who joined the War Plans Division in mid-December 1941, later observed that Marshall's "ability to delegate authority not only expedited work but impelled every subordinate to perform beyond his suspected capacity."[11] Marshall complained that his staff contained many able officers adept at analyzing problems, "but [they] feel compelled always to bring them to me for final solution. I must have assistants who will solve their own problems and tell me later what they have done." He repeatedly told his staff, "Gentlemen, don't fight the problem. Solve it." He wanted none of his time wasted weighing problems that those at lower levels could handle. Marshall also wanted staff officers to be confident and enthusiastic about their assignments. He would not give an officer a sensitive job and keep him there unless he evinced genuine enthusiasm for the assignment. He wanted his officers to be positive about a project's successful outcome.[12]

Headquarters acted as a sort of schoolhouse, with Marshall as teacher and role model. Although he countenanced no jockeying for field appointments and often told his subordinates to give up any idea of escaping their desk jobs, both he and they knew that outstanding performance in the War Plans Division and the secretariat would act as springboards to command positions. By insisting that his staff officers be accountable, Marshall groomed them for positions of greater responsibility and leadership.

Smith suffered the disadvantage of lacking any association with Marshall before 1939, but his performance quickly gained the chief's attention. Marshall wanted decisions made on the spot. Not long after joining the secretariat, an automobile salesman approached the army with "a small, low silhouette truck" that had recently been developed by his firm, the Bantam Motor Company. The Quartermaster Corps and the G-4 Division had rejected the model because the army had recently standardized the ton-and-a-half truck for its light transportation needs, but they directed the man to the assistant secretary of war. Instead, he went directly to Secretary of War Harry Woodring, who referred the salesman to Marshall. Smith heard the salesman's pitch and gave the matter careful consideration. Having served as heavy weapons instructor at Benning, Smith thought the vehicle would answer the infantry's need for a weapons and ammunition carrier for frontline units. A flash inquiry confirmed that the infantry and cavalry were interested. Convinced of his position, Smith entered a conference room unannounced, where Marshall was in the middle of a meeting. With only a few weeks in the secretariat under his belt, Smith's actions required real nerve. With a room full of generals impatiently glaring at this upstart major, Smith took three minutes to lay out the case. Asked what he thought of the vehicle, Smith rejoined, "I think it is good." After outlining the costs and recommending that the army purchase forty—Marshall suggested fifteen, but deferred—the chief approved the expenditure and dismissed Smith. A few minutes later Smith reappeared. The vexed Marshall asked what Smith wanted now. "I should have said it before and I say it now," Smith shot back. "That's the first damn time we have been able to get anything for this [salesman] in this whole War Department, and I think it is worthy of special comment." Of all the technical developments occurring during his tenure as chief of staff, Marshall spoke most frequently about how this vehicle, eventually known as the "jeep," gained approval.[13]

This episode demonstrates how the War Department still functioned. The WDGS and the bureaus expended valuable time making decisions; they did not routinely exchange information, no agency enforced cooperation, and all sections routinely pushed unsettled issues upstairs. Ultimately, many problems of no great consequence ended up in the chief of staff's office. The jeep story also illustrates both Smith's self-assurance and Marshall's confidence in his aide's judgment.

A man who accepted responsibilities perfunctorily, Smith dedicated himself to serving Marshall. More than that, he emulated everything about the chief. Smith cultivated the image of being tough, decisive, and tireless. By summer 1940 Smith began demonstrating Marshallesque characteristics. At one point he telephoned an officer whose career very much resembled his own, Charles Bolté. In a testy voice that belied their long acquaintance, Smith told Bolté, "The boss wants to know where you want to go." Taken aback, Bolté replied, "Well, wherever he wants me to go." "No," roared Smith through the telephone, "that's no answer," and hung up. Bolté ended up as operations officer on the staff of a newly organized corps—not exactly the assignment he desired.[14]

Though always "General Marshall" and "Smith," the relationship between the two men had a father and son quality. Marshall kept everyone at arm's length, insisting on old-fashioned, formal relations between superior officers and their subordinates. Marshall knew he placed great demands on those who worked for him, and he often demonstrated his regard through acts of kindness and thoughtfulness, particularly aimed at the wives of his juniors. He was very wary of entering into even the beginnings of familiarity. With Smith it was a little different. Smith spoke to him with an independence Marshall granted few others, particularly in view of his assistant's junior rank. Smith was one of the few men who would joke on occasion with the utterly humorless Marshall.[15]

Marshall enjoyed telling the story of the time Smith brought an important communication to Marshall at Fort Myer, where he found the chief of staff puttering in his garden. A fine drizzle was falling, and as Smith stiffly stood by, his invariably well-starched uniform began wilting. Finally the fastidious Smith muttered, "Do I have to stand here in the rain to make my report?" "No," Marshall replied, "just turn over that pail there and sit on it." This anecdote hardly ranks among the great stories of the war, but it does point to a certain bond between the two men, particularly since it seems so out of character for Marshall.[16]

Smith rose in Marshall's estimate for a number of reasons. Smith understood that knowledge translated into power. In addition to his work at the Message Center and other duties, Smith burned the midnight oil poring over the files, familiarizing himself with their contents. Smith possessed one great advantage—a near-photographic memory. He soon commanded a vast reservoir of information. If he did not know something, he knew where to find it. Being more active, willing to assume duties on his own initiative, and better informed than the other assistants, despite their longer tenure, gave Smith a leg up. The key rested in coming to the chief's attention and staying there. Increasingly Ward brought Smith along to the morning briefings. Soon Marshall turned to Smith when he wanted something. As the jeep episode demonstrated, Smith alone among the secretariat possessed the courage to enter Marshall's office whenever he felt the need. Smith had another intellectual skill Marshall highly prized: Smith could listen to a two-hour presentation and, without notes, boil down the essentials in a one-page exposition. One of his subordinates remembered, "Smith could dictate a two page memorandum without even having to correct so much as a comma."[17] Marshall assigned Smith the added responsibility of keeping the minutes of all his private conferences.[18] Smith's talents came in especially handy when dealing with Roosevelt. The president refused any note taking during private conferences. Once Marshall brought COL John Deane, a later addition to the secretariat, to a meeting with Roosevelt; when the president saw Deane's notebook, he exploded. Smith never made that mistake.[19] Soon Smith graduated from his secretarial tasks and moved on to more important responsibilities.

The Chief's Top Troubleshooter

The officer corps exhibited a paradoxical attitude to the democratic order they swore to defend. American officers considered *politics* a pejorative term; they defined anything not narrowly "military" as political—as outside their purview. They viewed themselves as selfless guardians of the nation, imbued with an ethical sense superior to that of their political masters. Owing to the generally hostile popular opinion of the interwar army, officers paradoxically craved public recognition while holding journalists in disdain. Getting ahead in the army meant avoiding politicians and keeping one's name out of the papers.[20] Though more open-minded than most, Marshall too fell prey to these sentiments, but he understood that the success of his program hinged on his working with the executive and legislative branches and currying favorable press to secure popular support. The burden fell on Marshall, but he needed assistants to run interference. The officer he relied on most was Beetle Smith.

In Roosevelt, Marshall confronted a master politician. In personality and leadership style, the two men stood poles apart. By his own admission "disingenuous, deceptive and devious," Roosevelt employed charm, secrecy, and dissemination; he temporized and trimmed. He told people only what he thought they wanted to hear. Nobody was ever certain where the president stood on any given issue because he constantly shifted position. He told people, "I never let my right hand know what my left hand does." All this hampered efficiency and gave the appearance of disarray, but it effectively contributed to Roosevelt's monopolizing of decision making and disguised his intensely personal style of leadership. Roosevelt accentuated his role as president and downplayed that of commander in chief; he authored a structure that ensured his control over policy without giving the impression that he exercised command. Roosevelt operated in this fashion because he possessed supreme confidence in his mastery over men and institutions that put the levers of power in his hands. Marshall appeared coldhearted; he possessed not an ounce of humor, guile, or skill at prevarication—he told the truth even when it hurt his case. Whereas the president's mind was elastic, and he delayed making vital policy shifts until assured he had the political and popular groundwork in place, Marshall's approach tended toward the doctrinaire, and he placed the highest value on making speedy decisions, then dealing with the consequences. Roosevelt garnered power and, other than Harry Hopkins, trusted few of his own appointees; Marshall's entire system rested on the free delegation of authority and the insistence that those under him make independent decisions and execute them. Roosevelt distanced himself from controversy and jettisoned supporters who outlived their usefulness. He exploited the "pitiless press" to bully his opponents. Marshall loyally defended his subordinates whatever the political or public relations consequences. The two men's leadership techniques shared one vital commonality: both believed that their independence of action depended on insulating themselves from external interference and detaching themselves from detailed administration, ensuring that decision making remained fixed in their hands.

Marshall isolated himself by remaining aloof and apolitical—given his personality and predisposition, not an unlikely tack. He never visited Hyde Park and went to the White House only when invited. He insisted the president call him "General Marshall," not "George." He even refused to laugh at Roosevelt's jokes. Marshall knew his selection as chief of staff over Drum and a number of more senior officers rested on his lack of important political and social connections in the administration. Even though Marshall eventually proved extremely adept at handling Congress, he always scrupulously avoided any appearance of involvement in congressional politics. Marshall might disagree with the president's actions, but he never cultivated outside political support or went to the press. Marshall carefully phrased all his public remarks in the most circumspect military terms.[21]

The army stood low on the rearmament totem pole. Marshall knew he faced an uphill struggle when the president, a former undersecretary of the navy and avid yachtsman, constantly referred to the navy as "we" and the army as "they." In view of the president's reluctance to expand ground forces, favoring instead naval construction and development of the Air Corps, Marshall set his sights on reequipping the existing authorized forces and preparing for further expansion. The highly publicized and ongoing bad blood between Woodring and the assistant secretary of war, Louis Johnson, further complicated his position.

The Woodring-Johnson feud typified Roosevelt's political management style. By 1939 the New Deal had run out of steam, and the outbreak of war in Europe allowed Roosevelt to begin his transformation from "Dr. New Deal" to "Dr. Win-the-War." He reordered his priorities but could not inflame further isolationist sentiments by any precipitate action. The president understood, and in many ways shared, the traditional American dread of centralized authority. The safeguards built into the Constitution guaranteed executive and legislative discord; the backwash of opposition to the New Deal exacerbated the president's problems in selling any rearmament program. Following his New Deal prescription, Roosevelt constructed a crazy-quilt array of agencies for managing economic mobilization and defense production, intentionally confusing spheres of authority. He purposefully appointed men with clashing agendas and personalities to competing positions. Woodring and Johnson fought over the superintendence of industrial mobilization. Woodring was a populist former governor of Kansas and arch-isolationist; Johnson was an outspoken internationalist and advocate of military preparedness. Roosevelt manipulated both men, playing off isolationists against the internationalist lobbies. The Woodring-Johnson imbroglio achieved the president's political ends but drew unfavorable attention to the War Department, hamstrung efforts to secure greater appropriations, and deprived Marshall of a civilian buffer between his office and the White House and Congress.

The Woodring-Johnson standoff obliged the president to deal directly with Marshall more often than either man wished. Marshall had little time for purely military matters, weighed down by the responsibilities of conducting the political battles for increased appropriations and fending off the president's frequent forays into often exceedingly minor War Department matters. Both men needed an indirect communications link. Roosevelt employed his trusted aide Hopkins as his informal connection to Marshall. Hopkins, former executive of the Works Progress Administration (WPA) and later secretary of commerce, literally acted as the president's "legs" and chief troubleshooter. Roosevelt and Hopkins made a strange pair: the wheelchair-bound president and the chronically ailing Hopkins. Their physical conditions belied their relentless drive. Marshall habitually referred to people by their surnames, but in Hopkins's case he made an exception. "Harry," in the general's opinion, stood out as the most courageous man he had ever met. While the president used Hopkins as the conduit to Marshall, the chief of staff employed Hopkins as a buffer and backdoor channel to the White House. Hopkins knew his role and played it extremely well.[22]

In the quiet days of the interwar period, the secretariat acted as liaison between the War Department and the White House and executive branch. Marshall needed a bright young officer as a more formal link with the president and his advisers. The chief also required that officer to obstruct Roosevelt's pipeline into the War Department—the president's longtime military aide and secretary, MG Edwin "Pa" Watson. Marshall selected Smith for the assignment.

Major Smith courted Watson, ever mindful of their difference in rank. Watson was a Falstaffian character, a first-rate raconteur. He acted as a shield for the president, warding off unwelcome callers. People went away from the White House disappointed but not unhappy. In the early part of Marshall's tenure as chief of staff, Watson maneuvered to ensconce himself as the president's chief military representative, but "didn't have the head for it."[23] Head or not, Watson enjoyed the president's confidence and required handling with kid gloves. Watson's favorite "end run" play involved assuring Smith that the president wanted something done but he should not bother Marshall with it. The ploy never worked on Smith. Dealing with Watson called for subtle evasion, but when pressed, he could act tough. When Watson pulled rank, Smith tactfully pointed out that he worked for General Marshall. Although Watson disliked being stymied by an officer of such junior rank, he respected Smith for his integrity, loyalty to Marshall, and intimate knowledge of War Department business. In what might have been a dangerous assignment, Smith succeeded in minimizing political inter-ference in the War Department while providing Marshall with a vital back alley into the White House. After a while, Watson even took Beetle under his wing. As a frequent visitor to the White House, the young offi-cer also came to the attention of the president.[24]

Smith's success in handling Watson prompted Marshall to assign his keen assistant secretary an even more sensitive task as bridge to Bernard Baruch. A man who defied easy categorization, Baruch exerted consid-erable influence in Washington. Born in South Carolina—his Jewish sur-geon father had served on the staff of Robert E. Lee—Baruch had made his fortune in New York by age thirty. His nickname, the "Lone Wolf of Wall Street," highlighted his marked independent stripe. As chair-man of the War Industries Board, Baruch brought order to the chaos of industrial mobilization during World War I. A strong corporatist, he labored in the interwar years, without much success, forging cooperation between the American financial and industrial elites and government. Instrumental in creating the Army Industrial College, Baruch contrib-uted to, and proved highly critical of, a succession of War Department economic mobilization plans. A member of the "Brain Trust" from 1932, Baruch met Roosevelt on a weekly basis. Roosevelt catered to Baruch not only because of his wise counsel but also because of the financier's all-important ability—through lavish handouts—to reconcile hostile south-ern Democrats to New Deal programs. Roosevelt once remarked that Baruch "owned sixty congressmen," among them the powerful senator from South Carolina, James Byrnes.[25]

Baruch's vital role in lobbying for military expansion in spring 1940 provides an example of Marshall working outside the system. Marshall placed the highest priority on gearing up industry for military produc-tion. He remembered the "almost criminal lack of proper preparation" in the last war, when American troops "went into the line . . . [with] everything begged, borrowed, or stolen—certainly not manufactured in America." The memory haunted him as one of his greatest nightmares.[26] Marshall had known Baruch since his days as Pershing's aide in the early 1920s and now employed him as a powerful ally in his struggle with Roosevelt, expediting and bringing greater coherence to the prepared-ness program. As Marshall later remarked, Baruch remained "one of my dear friends and one of the great helpers I had in the war." Baruch frequently visited Marshall and "stood ready to do something for me the minute I wanted it done." Marshall called on Baruch only when he required high-powered leverage. During those junctures, Baruch would meet with Roosevelt and then promptly visit Marshall.[27]

Baruch possessed no official capacity. In a highly publicized attack, Henry Ford accused Baruch of acting as prime agent in the international Jewish conspiracy to control the global economy and subvert the American government. Intent on not handing the isolationist Right any political ammunition, Baruch refused all offers of an appointment. He downplayed his influence, joking that his office was a park bench in Lafayette Park, across from the White House. In other words, he stood proximate to but exercised no power. Underlining the point that he operated in the open, Baruch often held meetings on his bench (in New York, he did the same on his favorite bench in Central Park); in spring and summer 1940, with the rearmament and manpower legislation before Congress, Smith made frequent visits to Baruch's bench.[28]

Effectively, Smith became Baruch's military aide. Day or night, Smith stood ready to fly to New York for consultations or ferry Baruch around Washington. In March, Baruch lobbied against the Senate's efforts to slash the army's appropriations. Baruch argued for a dramatic increase in military spending. Nobody knew the procurement and production side of rearmament better than Baruch, but he had little acquaintance with actual military affairs. Marshall invited him to attend maneuvers in South Carolina and instructed Smith to educate him. Smith's other job involved keeping Baruch's presence out of the newspapers. Marshall voiced his intention not to "circulate the reasons for [Baruch's] presence." As it turned out, weather delayed their departure, and Baruch saw little of the maneuvers. Instead, the party spent a pleasant sojourn at Baruch's estate in the company of Jimmy Byrnes.[29]

In April a Senate committee cut already approved funding for two vital projects. The next month a manpower bill came before Congress. Marshall went up to Capitol Hill and requested, in Baruch's opinion, "a pitiful number of men—280,000" and appropriations to arm and equip them. Once again, Marshall called on his friend Bernie. Baruch asked Smith to prepare a study explaining Marshall's rationale for an immediate increase in the size of the regular army. Smith handed Baruch his memorandum on 10 May. Earlier that day, the Germans opened their offensive against France and the Low Countries. The irony was not lost on either man. Baruch requested that Smith provide data on defense spending over the previous decade.[30]

The same day, Marshall met with the president, Secretary of the Treasury Henry Morgenthau, and several other key officials. The president instructed Marshall and Morgenthau to finalize requirements for the immediate expansion of the army to authorized strength and a budget for fiscal year 1941. They had three days to assemble the package. Marshall assigned the secretariat the job of pulling all the estimates together. By 12 May, after a furious weekend of work, Marshall received the "Summary of Additional Requirements for National Defense." The total, amounting to $640 million, left him giddy. Morgenthau responded, "It makes me dizzy if we don't get it." Smith, who had compiled his estimates for Baruch, played a conspicuous part in preparing the summary.[31] Two days later, Smith handed Baruch the figures on prior appropriations, noting that the total amounted to a third "less than the estimates of minimum requirements made by the Chiefs of Arms and Services." Baruch then worked on convincing his political placemen of the dire need to address the emergency.[32]

The German offensive broke the logjam. Congress voted a large supplemental budget. When France fell in June, Congress tripled defense spending. The money now at the War Department's disposal dwarfed Marshall's paltry requests of only two months before. The aftermath of Dunkirk and the collapse of France bore additional fruit; Roosevelt fired Woodring (and Johnson) and replaced him with Henry Stimson, a Republican war hawk and old friend of the War Department since his days as secretary of war in the Taft administration. In Stimson, Marshall now had an effective civilian intermediary and buffer between him and the president, supplemented by Hopkins. Marshall no longer required Baruch as his backstage manipulator. Smith kept Baruch in the picture, just in case the chief ever needed his special services. Marshall thought Smith had performed his chore "very, very successfully and won Baruch's confidence, and in that way eased my problem because I didn't have to try to settle so many of these things myself."[33]

While Smith's contacts with Baruch lessened, those with Morgenthau increased. Marshall assigned him the delicate task of keeping the powerful treasury secretary happy, informed, and at arm's length. Morgenthau proved exceedingly demanding of Smith's time and required a good deal of stroking. He frequently called on Smith for financial data and other services. Appreciative of the young officer's "considerable loss of time and trouble beyond requirements of duty," Morgenthau wrote a glowing letter of commendation for inclusion in Smith's personnel file.[34]

In May 1940 Congress passed selective service legislation, permitting the expansion of the army to its Protective Mobilization Plan quota of 750,000 men and 250,000 replacements. Under the terms of the Selective Service Act of 1940, African Americans would constitute 10 percent of the draftees—the proportion of blacks in the national population. The War Department geared up for the inevitable political pressure to integrate the army. Marshall assigned Smith the unenviable job of front man in defense of the Jim Crow army.

Needless to say, the interwar army produced few social progressives; MacArthur and Moseley stood at the other extreme and generally represented armywide attitudes. New Deal programs—the Civilian Conservation Corps and WPA—probably contributed more to saving the army in the depressed 1930s than did the army's schools. The army garnered positive press; it expanded in size, providing accelerated promotions for the "hump." Morale improved, and fewer midgrade and junior officers left the army. The army's participation in the WPA, especially the Corps of Engineers, afforded officers the opportunity to gain invaluable experience in planning, managing, and executing mammoth projects involving thousands of men and millions of dollars worth of material and equipment. It was no accident engineers constituted the vast majority of senior logisticians in World War II. But few if any officers saw it that way at the time. The officer corps resented their forced involvement in social and economic programs for which few of them had any sympathy. Similar unenlightened thinking colored attitudes on the race question.

Despite the record of African American soldiers in the Civil War and the role of the famed Buffalo Soldiers in the West, interwar officers almost universally subscribed to the notion that black soldiers would not fight. "Separate but equal" racial segregation was the law of the land, reinforced in the army by tradition and by the conviction that African American combat troops had fought poorly in France. African American soldiers performed menial labor or service jobs—precisely the types of employment open to blacks in the private sector. By June 1940 African Americans composed a scant 1.5 percent of the enlisted strength of the regular army. Another 3,000 served in National Guard units. Smith had more exposure to African American soldiers than most because of his five years at Benning, a base that housed an African American regiment. Nothing suggests that Smith's views on race differed from the norm. The vast majority of white Americans, both inside the army and out, ignored the coiled snake of race relations under the table.

African American activists and their white supporters petitioned the Roosevelt administration to push for integration of the armed services as an important step toward dismantling *Plessy v. Ferguson* and legal segregation. Pressure mounted throughout summer 1940, forcing some kind of War Department announcement. In September Congress passed the Selective Service Act, the first peacetime draft in American history. No longer able to trim, Marshall instructed Smith in late September to draft a memo to Senator Henry Cabot Lodge Jr., spelling out War

Department guidelines regarding the expected roles of African Americans in the army.

The 27 September letter restated that "the policy of the War Department [is] not to intermingle colored and white enlisted personnel in the same regimental organization." Smith acknowledged the "unmistakable evidence of an extensive campaign being conducted at the present time to force a change in this policy." The letter underscored that any movement toward even a measured integration of the combat forces would be "definitely detrimental to the preparations for national defense in this emergency." He reiterated the same point, more forcefully, later: "The present exceedingly difficult period of building up a respectable and dependable military force for the protection of this country is not the time for critical experiments, which would inevitably have a highly destructive effect on morale—meaning military efficiency." He pointed to the no-discrimination language in the draft legislation: African Americans would be drafted up to the required quota, they would be assigned to a variety of military occupations (no mention of the combat arms), and they would enjoy identical housing and services as white troops, but in separate units and facilities. He concluded by making this argument: "Our colored regiments have splendid morale, and their high percentage of reenlistments is evidence of the wisdom of the present system."[35]

Civil rights leaders did not see it that way. The day Marshall signed and forwarded Smith's memo, Roosevelt met with prominent African American activists—including A. Philip Randolph, leader of the March on Washington movement—who challenged the president to use executive authority to end racial segregation in the armed forces. The president proved no more open to integration than the War Department was, and for many of the same reasons. On 9 October the White House issued a press release briefly summarizing the rationale for continuing segregation as presented in Smith's letter to Senator Lodge.

Many of the president's longtime liberal supporters—including his wife—shared in African American leaders' disappointment that Roosevelt failed to tackle the race problem. The president's lurch to the Right constituted a tactical political move. If he wanted the support of the "solid South," he could not hint at playing the desegregation card. Typical of Roosevelt, he offered a couple of palliative appointments in the hope of deflecting swelling criticism. Judge William Hastie, dean of the Howard University Law School, became civilian aide to the secretary of war, and COL Benjamin O. Davis was promoted to brigadier general, the first African American holder of general rank.

The War Department's commitment to no discrimination can best be judged by its manpower and training policies. In December 1941 blacks represented only 6.3 percent of enlisted personnel, most of them classified for unskilled servile duties. Black officers constituted a minuscule 0.4 percent of the officer corps. The army remained separate but far from equal. The policy encapsulated in the Smith-authored letter essentially remained in place throughout the war.[36]

Smith's service as front man for the War Department's race policy did not end there. The old Confederacy housed many of the army's training centers, leading to inevitable clashes with unredeemed southern whites and civil agencies. An incident in May 1941 in Arkansas serves as a typical example. An African American soldier was accused of raping a white woman. Feelings ran so high that the governor, anticipating mob violence, asked for a presidential proclamation and the dispatch of federal troops. Roosevelt signaled his agreement and instructed Watson to contact Marshall. Watson did not linger; he called Marshall, getting him out of bed at midnight. For Marshall, the overriding concern centered on limiting the army's exposure to negative press. He instructed Smith to coordinate contact with Watson, check with the judge advocate on conditions stipulated under the Posse Comitatus Act, and orchestrate communications among the War Department, the Second Army's commander LTG Ben Lear, and the corps and division commanders. In the end, two companies of Missouri National Guard went to Arkansas; the whole episode ended with the defendant's admission of guilt.[37]

By mid-1940 Smith successfully staked out his position as the star of the secretariat. On 18 April he received a promotion to lieutenant colonel. He had spent eighteen years in the ranks of lieutenant and captain and eighteen months as a major.[38] In June, when Gasser retired, his place was taken by BG William Bryden. The new deputy chief quickly fell from grace because of his reticence and refusal to exert control. Marshall rapidly lost faith in anyone who said "show it to the chief." At the end of July Marshall named BG Richard Moore an additional deputy chief of staff for supply, and in mid-November he made MG Henry "Hap" Arnold his deputy for air. Bryden remained as deputy, but he found himself frequently sidelined. As time went by, Marshall increasingly turned to his hard-driven assistant secretary for sensitive assignments, bypassing Bryden.

His duties as recorder of minutes and liaison to the White House and the assistant secretary of war made Smith privy to everything that transpired in Marshall's office. Along with his preoccupation with the trials of manning and equipping the ground forces, Marshall dealt with the associated problem of determining levels of materiel support for France and Britain. In November 1939, under pressure from Roosevelt, Congress placed the Neutrality Act statutes on a cash-and-carry basis, which permitted foreign purchase of American munitions. After Dunkirk, the British pleaded for warships to combat the U-boats and armaments to defend the home islands. The scarcity of weapons—which in 1940 meant World War I surplus—put the War Department in a bind. Many worried that the transfer of weapons to the United Kingdom would seriously impair the U.S. preparedness program. After Dunkirk, the War Department released a million Springfield rifles and some automatic weapons, machine guns, and 75mm guns to help arm the Home Guard. Since the shipments included a mere ten rounds per rifle, the program amounted to little more than a gesture to buoy British morale. By July Roosevelt was satisfied of the British determination to stay in the war, but he waited until after his reelection in November to introduce the "lend-lease" program to Congress. Before he went to Congress, the president made his case to the American public in one of his fireside chats, announcing his intention to convert the American economy into "the great arsenal of democracy." He also used the analogy of not worrying about the price of a hose when your neighbor's house caught fire. Skirting the neutrality laws, lend-lease permitted the sale, transfer, exchange, lease, or loan of war materiel to any nation's defense effort deemed by the president to be vital to American security. Roosevelt sold lend-lease as a means of keeping the United States out of the war; isolationists argued that it made American intervention a certainty. Marshall agreed with senior War Department officials that lend-lease increased the likelihood of American entry into the war and would adversely impact the training of newly organized units, but he concluded that American strategic interests demanded the United States support the British, within limits. He warned that "undue generosity might endanger our security."[39] As recording secretary, Smith played no role in formulating policy, but that did not stop him from adding his two cents' worth. At the conclusion of one heated meeting, he icily remarked that they had better win the gamble, because if they got it wrong and Britain left the war, thus compromising U.S. security, those involved in the decision to arm the British should be prepared to be hung from the nearest lamppost.[40]

Smith continued to perform his valuable liaison services. It came to Marshall's attention that his deputy for air, Arnold, stood in bad stead at the White House. Arnold thought he had lost the president's confidence and found himself cold-shouldered during his infrequent appearances at White House conferences. Marshall walked a tightrope on the air question. He stood ready to grant the Air Corps as much autonomy as it could manage, but he could not announce his intentions because that would create an uproar in Congress, in the press, and within the ranks of the officer corps. Few officers were indifferent on the air issue; the majority of line officers, Smith included, remained hostile to any suggestion of an independent air force. The Air Corps shot itself in the foot by not sending officers to Leavenworth, because when Marshall entered the War Department as deputy chief, air officers had virtually no representation on the general staff. To Marshall, that meant the Air Corps lacked senior staff material. Creating an independent air force on the verge of war would create organizational chaos and render air-ground teamwork all the more elusive. The chief viewed Arnold as indispensable; he was the only senior airman with the requisite presence and administrative ability to push through the air program.[41]

Marshall's concern mounted when Roosevelt refused Arnold's nomination as lieutenant general and intimated that he intended to use a pending retirement bill to oust him. A temporary major general, Arnold was still a colonel on the rolls of the regular army. If Arnold remained in place, he would receive a bump to permanent brigadier general but retire in that grade. That meant Arnold would stand at the top of the Air Corps chain of command but hold a junior rank to the chiefs of the Air Corps and the General Headquarters Air Force.[42]

Marshall set the ball rolling by dispatching Smith to the White House to ferret out what lay behind the president's enmity toward Arnold. Pa Watson proved more than obliging. Back in 1925, during Billy Mitchell's court-martial, Arnold had served as information officer in the office of the chief of the Air Corps. An airpower activist and Mitchell disciple, Arnold had run afoul of the Associated Press correspondent attached to the War Department, Steve Early. Now Roosevelt's press secretary, Early still bore a grudge against Arnold. As even Hopkins later discovered, the president was a faithless friend but a good hater, and as the enemy of his all-important press massager, Arnold found himself persona non grata in the White House.[43]

Smith reported his findings to Marshall and advised him how to fix the problem. Marshall approached Stimson, telling him what Smith had heard from Roosevelt's military aide. He asked the secretary of war to intercede with the president and push Arnold's case. Marshall also requested Stimson "not [to] allow Smith's connection with these matters, particularly in relation to Early, to go further than your personal knowledge." He did not want the powerful Early gunning for his favored assistant. Stimson convinced Roosevelt to promote Arnold to permanent major general and never acknowledged the source of the White House leak.[44]

First Secretary

The post of secretary of the general staff (SGS) customarily went to a senior colonel and normally served as a steppingstone to higher office. Marshall recognized that a modern staff was indispensable and stocked his headquarters with young officers with reputations as thinkers and doers, but he never really shed his veneration for hell and leather heroic leaders. His disappointment at not getting a command in World War I remained fresh in his mind, as did the conviction that his career had been handicapped by too many staff appointments. He also remembered the criticisms leveled against Pershing for rapidly promoting the Leavenworth clique. Marshall determined that promotions would go to field officers, "not the staff officers who clutter up the War Department."[45] Nonetheless, his headquarters—especially in the War Planning Division and the secretariat—afforded Marshall the best opportunity to assess an officer's potential for field command. Marshall insisted on handpicking officers for command positions.

Ward held the assignment as SGS for two years, having been in the post when Marshall took over the War Department. In August 1941 Ward received his reward, command of the First Armored Division. Ward judged Smith "superior" on his officer efficiency report, describing his as "one of the ablest officers I have known." He later recommended Smith for a Legion of Merit medal for his outstanding service as assistant secretary.[46] Considering Smith's standing in the secretariat, and despite his relative youth and junior rank, he loomed as the obvious choice to be Ward's replacement. Mindful that the post promised an immediate promotion and held out the possibility of a future field command, Smith eagerly accepted the proffered appointment. His promotion to colonel came through on 30 August 1941.

Marshall complained that the War Department was the "worst command post in the Army" and stated, "It is a crime the way the higher staffs submerge the staffs and units below them with detailed instructions, endless paper reports, and other indications of unfamiliarities with troop doings." He observed, "I have come almost to feel that my principal duty as a commander is to be out with the troops protecting them against my own staff." Of course, he rarely left Washington, shackled to his desk and a set of "Civil War institutions" he dared not change.[47]

By tradition and doctrine, sixty-one officers had direct access to the chief of staff. With the War Department divided into watertight compartments, each with its own channel to the chief of staff, WDGS division heads and bureau chiefs jealously guarded their prerogatives and oversaw the work of their staffs and commands within narrowly defined jurisdictional boundaries. The heads and chiefs stayed within their respective channels; staff studies moved vertically but not horizontally. "It is astounding to me," Moseley told the secretary of war in 1930, that "the principal members of the General Staff rarely *meet and think;* that, in fact, there is no General Staff conference room."[48] Problems involving two or more divisions or bureaus flowed up the chain to the chief of staff for adjudication. Other problems fell through the cracks without resolution. In the placid interwar years, the fragmented structure lacked cohesion and responsiveness and limped along, but in the hectic buildup stage for a likely American entry into the war, the archaic structure threatened to collapse under its own weight. Other than the office of the chief of staff, no agency coordinated the work of the divisions and bureaus or followed up on decisions to ensure compliance. Marshall wanted his SGS to perform these functions, but colonels like Ward rarely won head-butting contests against major generals.

The SGS acted as the executive agency to the chief of staff. With procedures already well in place, Smith brought to the job an insistence on greater urgency, efficiency, and responsiveness. And he proved far more willing than Bryden and Ward to crack heads to get the required results. Like the other general staff sections, the scope of the secretariat's authority remained poorly defined. Smith entered his new position determined to exploit the unsettled situation to expand his role. He embarked on this path for two reasons: it would raise his status, but primarily, he believed Marshall wanted it that way. His close association with Marshall convinced Smith that he knew the chief's mind better than anyone else in the War Department.

The first order of business centered on isolating Marshall from outside distractions. The chief of staff felt buried beneath the weight of visitors and the flow of paper. In addition to those 61 officers who had direct access to his office, 30 other major and 350 smaller commands fell under his immediate control. Smith became the gatekeeper. The only officers who entered Marshall's office without invitation, aside from Smith, were Stilwell and the WDGS assistant chief of staff for supply (G-4), BG Brehon Somervell. Everybody else went through Smith. Senior officers bristled at being put off by a colonel, but they abided by Smith's dictates.

Smith waged a personal war against administrative red tape. His desk became the nerve center for the entire WDGS. Smith reviewed all correspondence directed to Marshall, except that which he lacked clearance to see. Smith never hesitated to redirect communications to one of the

WDGS divisions or bureaus for action or concurrence without bothering Marshall. He read all letters and memos originating in Marshall's office, made changes, and then returned them to their author for revisions. Once the paper met his specifications, Smith forwarded it to the responsible recipient. Marshall saw only what Smith decided required his attention—and then only after the paper had been thoroughly staffed, studied, and reduced to its barest bones. So complete was Smith's control over the flow of information that Marshall once remarked, "I want this done but don't tell Smith."[49]

Smith applied Marshall's "doctrine of no surprises" to the secretariat. Immediately after assuming duty as the SGS, Smith again restructured and simplified the information retrieval system. Separate folders contained incoming and outgoing communications, divided into Marshall's "eyes only" and general correspondence files. Smith instituted the "two-minute rule." Periodically he took out his watch, insisting that a subordinate produce a set of letters, memos, or staff papers from the files within the fixed time. If the subordinate officer or clerk could not find the required file in the allotted time, he could expect an expletive-laced reprimand in front of the entire section. A second failure usually resulted in the offender's summary transfer from the staff.[50] All this ensured that Smith never got caught short if Marshall made any sort of request for supporting documents or statistics.

Stalin understood that the unwanted, tedious, and decidedly unglamorous job of first secretary conferred real power. The secretary managed the inner center of power, controlled the flow of information, determined its distribution, decided who had access to the boss, defined the agenda for conferences, purged unreliable and ineffectual subordinates, and knew where all the skeletons were buried. Beetle acted as Marshall's first secretary, if not his Stalin. Smith's orchestration of the "morning show" best illustrates his exercise of authority. Smith's day routinely began before 6 A.M. After arranging information that required the chief's attention, Smith met with his assistants and organized the daily meeting with Marshall. The number of officers ushered into Marshall's office increased over time. Usually Bryden, the WDGS deputy chief of operations, and the chief of intelligence attended, frequently joined by other principal officers from the general and special staff sections. Smith started by outlining the various problems that demanded special attention. By adding recommendations, Smith used the morning staff meetings as a showcase of his command of War Department affairs. Most such meetings became a Beetle Smith monologue. Since Smith had hammered out a consensus before they entered Marshall's office, the more senior WDGS officers merely buttressed Smith's points. Through his control of the daily agenda, Smith emphasized completed actions, leaving to Marshall only those questions beyond the competence of the general staff.

Marshall had a fixation about running economical meetings—in terms of both time and words expended—and few could do so as well as Smith. He talked fast but with precision; his words conveyed a sense of conviction. No officer possessed a better understanding of the inner workings of the general staff, and no one came into Marshall's office better prepared; in addition, Smith was nothing if not brutally honest. All this appealed to Marshall, who gauged the success of a conference on how much—or, more to the point, how little—he had to add. The other participants might not have seen it that way, and they no doubt disliked being cast in minor supporting roles, but knowing Marshall's preferences and recognizing Smith's talents, they usually acquiesced.

After the conference, armed with Marshall's directives, Smith initiated actions consistent with his interpretation of the chief's wishes. He delegated responsibility to his assistants to draft letters and memos or oversee research on issues left unresolved during the morning meetings. If things did not run according to the chief's exacting requirements, Smith expedited the process. Constitutionally, the secretariat served as office of record for the WDGS, monitoring the flow of information and instructions throughout the War Department, but it possessed no authority to coordinate staff actions among the various WDGS divisions, sections, and bureaus. Marshall had asked that Bryden and Ward play that role, but little came of their efforts. That changed when Smith took over. The WDGS division and section heads suffered Smith's frequent intrusions into their departmental affairs because they knew he enjoyed Marshall's full confidence.[51] In the process, he made more than a few enemies.

As the WDGS grew, the functions and size of the secretariat expanded. By December 1941 it contained six members, including Beetle's Leavenworth classmates Taylor and Ridgway. Routine administrative duties occupied the bulk of Smith's time. Many of these chores rightfully devolved on subordinates, but Smith only grudgingly surrendered any of his core responsibilities. He defended his hard-won position as the indispensable man, as Marshall's de facto chief of staff. Some saw him as ruthlessly ambitious, an empire builder, and a heartless martinet who demanded too much from his subordinates to aggrandize his own position in Marshall's eyes. All these charges contained more than a grain of truth and would have had more merit if not for the fact that Smith drove himself harder than he did those under his sway. His ulcer condition worsened as a result, and with it his ill temper.

As secretary, Smith injected himself into policy-making discussions involving the senior department, branch, service, and section chiefs of the War Department. As liaison to the executive branch, he set up and sat in on Marshall's meetings with Roosevelt and Stimson. He continued to assist Morgenthau when asked. In addition to meeting regularly with Watson, he increasingly came into contact with Roosevelt's inner circle, Hopkins and Early. Smith was a frequent visitor to the White House, and the president's female staff members all liked him. Beetle could pour on the charm when required. Through these contacts, Smith's stature grew both in the War Department and in the estimate of the men closest to the president.[52]

Smith might have enjoyed a favored position near the centers of American military and political power, but he never gained entry into the top-secret Magic/Purple ring—the small group privy to deciphered Japanese diplomatic communications (too small, as events leading up to Pearl Harbor proved). U.S. Navy cryptanalysts had been reading Japanese intercepts since late September 1940. At one point, precautions to protect the secret became so extreme that even the president was struck from the distribution list when a copy of a Magic message turned up in a White House wastebasket.

On 5 December 1941 Magic traffic disclosed Japanese intentions to rupture diplomatic relations with the United States. The WDGS's head of intelligence, MG Sherman Miles, forwarded the flow of intercepts to BG Leonard Gerow, head of the War Plans Division, with instructions to issue an alert to Pacific stations. Gerow reportedly refused, saying, "I think they have had plenty of notification." COL Otis Sadtler, the Signal Corps officer responsible for the dossier's distribution, later testified that he conveyed the intelligence to Marshall's office. With Marshall out of the office, he handed the sealed pouch to Smith with a similar request. According to Sadtler, Smith replied, "Since War Plans Division had acted, I do not want to discuss the matter further," and he locked the file in the safe.

Smith had a different version of events. As SGS, he often received sealed containers with Magic intelligence. He was acting as the duty officer on the night of 5–6 December. Just before midnight, as he later discovered, he received all but the last of the fourteen-part intercept, which arrived in a locked pouch. Smith had no key, and none was available to him. He never personally saw the decrypted and translated documents and possessed no knowledge of their distribution. Since Smith lacked clearance, as he later stated, Sadtler had no reason to request his involvement.

Smith had followed procedure: during the day, such pouches were immediately taken to Marshall; at night, the secretariat's duty officer locked the dossier in a safe, and Smith would present it to Marshall when he arrived in the morning. At night and on weekends, if G-2 considered the intelligence vital, the pouch went by courier to Marshall, either at Fort Myer or to his retreat near Leesburg, Virginia. In this instance, Smith ignored Miles's recommendation, presumably following Gerow's lead.[53]

Nobody proved culpable for the disasters that befell Pearl Harbor and the Philippines. Nor was it a systems failure, because no system existed. The United States possessed only the most rudimentary structure for correlating and evaluating intelligence, and because of the extreme secrecy surrounding Magic, it proved impossible to integrate decrypted messages with other forms of intelligence. Magic revealed the imminence of war, but it never specified any military targets. Japanese diplomats knew nothing of military and naval planning. Moreover, U.S. Army and Navy commands in the Pacific had received a final war warning as early as 27 November. In any event, Hawaii and Manila received word that Japan would sever relations, even down to the hour, and that Japanese consulates had received instructions to destroy incriminating files and cipher material. Yet RADM Husband Kimmel and LTG Walter Short in Honolulu and MacArthur in Manila still suffered devastating losses from Japanese aerial attacks. If Smith had relayed the decrypts to Marshall, it would not have made a difference.[54]

From mid-1941, Roosevelt maneuvered to build popular support for an eventual and, in his view, inevitable American entry into the war in Europe. After the German victories in the Balkans and the invasion of the USSR, and following the Placentia Bay conference and its Atlantic Charter, the president reckoned that he commanded a majority opinion in favor of American belligerency, but he still fell far short of the consensus demanded for an extended war effort. The Japanese attacks on Pearl Harbor and the Philippines ended the political debate. When the European Axis declared war on 11 December, Roosevelt possessed his overwhelming mandate for forging an alliance with the British. In London, Prime Minister Winston Churchill wasted no time in suggesting an immediate conference in Washington for the purpose of formulating a joint strategy and control mechanisms for the combined war effort. Given his hard-won position in Marshall's headquarters, Smith knew he would play some part in the proceedings. What that would be, he could not divine.

★ 13 ★

Forging the Mold

December 1941 marked one of the turning points in the war. A week into December, Pearl Harbor brought the United States into the war; four days later, the Axis joined Japan against the Western democracies; eleven days later, Churchill and the British Chiefs of Staff opened talks with their American opposite numbers in Washington. The month closed with the basic agreements on Allied grand strategy and the organizational structures in place for the conduct of global war.

The attack on Pearl Harbor produced a firestorm of popular and congressional cries for vengeance against Japan. Marshall worried that Roosevelt might succumb to these pressures and redirect the focus of the approved American strategy from Europe to the Pacific; such a demarche threatened to drive a wedge between the army and the navy. Marshall not only wrestled with a deteriorating situation in the Philippines and MacArthur's pressing requests for aid, but he also faced the impending onslaught of Churchill and his staff—the most threatening British assault on Washington since 1814. Marshall prepared to mount a determined defense. As Stimson recorded, Marshall had his staff hard at work drafting a cohesive strategic proposal.[1]

Although confined on a battleship in the mid-Atlantic, Churchill was far from idle. His initial proposal for the Washington conference centered on forging a cooperative response to Japanese aggression in the Far East and settling ratios of increased American production and the associated shipping requirements. However, Churchill shifted the focus toward deciding on a global strategy and fashioning the mechanisms of command and control for executing it. The day after Germany declared war on the United States, Churchill concluded that American participation "made the end [ultimate victory] certain." The only question revolved around selecting the proper strategic path for accomplishing that end. The British prime minister believed he knew what that was.[2]

Churchill envisioned himself as heir to his illustrious ancestor Marlborough, and he immediately recognized that circumstances proffered an opportunity for fashioning a grand alliance among Britain, the USSR, and the United States, in imitation of the coalition forged by his forebear that had defeated Louis XIV's bid for hegemony in the War of the Spanish Succession. Like Marlborough, Churchill reckoned he possessed the alchemist's admixture of political skill, diplomatic flair, and strategic vision to cement an alliance of mutually suspicious partners with a single aim in common—destruction of the European Axis. He also knew it would require many months before the United States could fully harness its immense war potential. This window of time offered the British leader the prospect of guiding the Western democracies based on his strategic designs.

Throughout the war, the principles of British strategy remained unchanged and predated Churchill's premiership. British strategy in 1939–1940 hung on two assessments. First, a German economy already overstretched by military spending stood vulnerable to economic pressure in the form of a naval blockade and aerial attack. Second, France, supported by British ground and air forces, would blunt any German attack along the frontiers long enough to allow the British, reinforced by the dominions, to construct sufficient ground forces for the invasion of a Germany diminished by the blockade, air bombardment, and internal political discord. All these suppositions proved wrong, and even though the Germans waged the British strategy in reverse—the U-boats and surface raiders preyed on British shipping, and the Luftwaffe subjected British cities to air attack—Churchill never abandoned the underlying principles of the initial strategic design. Germany and Nazi-controlled Europe would remain isolated, while the British conducted opportunistic operations on the periphery, supported the Soviets and subversive groups in occupied countries, and mounted a strategic bombing campaign against the Reich—all designed to grind down German strength. The British fended off the threatened invasion and weathered the blitz, but they strained under the burden of keeping open the sea-lanes on which survival depended. The British, not the Germans, suffered under financial and strategic overstretch. That state of affairs existed before the British faced the nightmare scenario every planner dreaded since 1919: the weight of fighting simultaneously in three widely separated theaters. Japanese aggression in the Far East unmasked the illusion of British global power.

Undeterred, Churchill sailed to the United States fully counting on winning the day. Danger always acted as a catalyst for action in Churchill. Although forced to take the strategic defensive, Churchill came prepared to sell the Americans on conducting offensive operations in the only theater where that remained possible—North Africa. He reasoned the president would warm to the suggestion of going over to the offensive. An unapologetic monarchist and imperialist, Churchill's elemental aim always stayed fixed on preserving the "great" in Great Britain. Eventually, that would require a restoration of the British power that was so obviously waning in Asia, but that would have to wait. Churchill faced no choice but to cede Far Eastern policy to the Americans. To achieve his ultimate objective, Churchill had to win Roosevelt over to the idea of an immediate offensive in North Africa, committing the Americans to the British "grind down" strategy in the Mediterranean in 1942 while holding out the longer-term promise of a return to the Continent in 1943.

Between 16 and 20 December, from aboard the *Duke of York*, Churchill bombarded Washington with a lengthy four-part memorandum detailing his thoughts on the global situation and his robust arguments as to the best course of action to meet the immediate threats and beyond. Churchill got right to the point. In the opening pages of the first dispatch, he reiterated that, despite the crisis in the Far East, Europe remained the decisive theater: "Hitler's failure and losses in Russia are the prime fact in the war at this time," and "an impending victory" by the British in Cyrenaica should result in the total destruction of Italo-German forces in Libya. Such a British success offered glittering strategic advantages in the Mediterranean. The British maintained in readiness a force of 55,000 for dispatch to French Northwest Africa (code-named Gymnast) within twenty-six days of receiving the go-ahead. Should the Gymnast force be committed, Churchill urged that the Americans deploy 25,000 troops to Morocco "at the earliest possible moment," with 150,000 to follow over a six-month period. "The North-west African theater," he concluded, "is [the] one most favorable for Anglo-American operations."[3]

Confronted with Churchill's memorandum, the War Department hastily revised its strategic assessment for review and concurrence by Stimson and the Joint Board. On 21 December, the eve of the conference, Marshall; Arnold; ADM Harold Stark, the chief of naval operations (CNO); and ADM Ernest King, commander in chief of the fleet, conferred with the service secretaries and the president. Stimson thought it "one of the best conferences we have had" and expressed satisfaction at the "great harmony [that existed] on practically all of the problems."[4]

The War Department's paper found plenty of common ground with the British positions. The United States agreed on the "Germany First" grand strategy. Initially the Western powers must maintain the strategic defensive but stand prepared to conduct local offensives in appropriate theaters while building strength for "an all-out offensive against Germany and her European Allies." The Joint Board concurred that essential sea and air communication must remain open and acknowledged the need to adjust Victory Program production priorities and schedules, expand the American armed forces, and increase support to Britain and the Commonwealth, Russia, and China. The American chiefs stood prepared to devise new agencies to superintend the allocation of materiel and shipping and, most important, to create a Supreme War Council complete with Allied committees for planning and supply.[5]

The War Department study, which served as the foundation for the Joint Board's recommendations to the president, evaded the issue of North Africa. A day earlier, Stimson wrote an assessment of the strategic situation after talking it over with Marshall. Marshall stood adamantly opposed to any diversion of ground troops to the Middle East. Stimson remarked that while the Egyptian-Libyan theater remained of "immense importance psychologically to the British Empire," it represented an "unfavorable front for an attack on Hitler in Europe." Stimson listed the Mediterranean as the least vital theater after Europe, the southwest Pacific, West Africa and the approaches to South America, and Syria and Iran. Neither Stimson's memo of 20 December nor the War Department's memorandum mentioned French Northwest Africa.[6]

Although only implied at this juncture, the main fault line between American and British strategic concepts in Europe had already appeared. Marshall liked to keep things simple; for him, "Germany First" meant just that. He envisioned a multistep process. The first priority was to expand production guided by the Victory Program, then to equip and train American forces. In the meantime, the Allies must secure control of the vital sea and air routes that would permit the movement and buildup of overwhelming Allied strength in the United Kingdom. The fastest road to victory was the most direct: a cross-Channel invasion and a decisive defeat of the main German forces in the west. The British, already critically short of resources, could never think in those terms. To them, the path to victory lay in eroding and dispersing German strength before seeking a direct confrontation in western Europe or avoiding it altogether, if executed properly. These differences, soon to erupt into heated exchanges during the talks in Washington, bedeviled Anglo-

American planning for the next two years and created friction in every theater and at every command level until the end of the war.

In the hectic buildup to the conference, Smith labored in the background. As SGS, his desk acted as clearinghouse for vital communications between the War Department and MacArthur's command. He helped prepare the War Department's strategic appreciation, working in harness with Gerow, the head of War Plans, and his new assistant, Brigadier General Eisenhower. Smith's primary function remained rooted in his liaison duties. In addition to briefing Stimson, the assistant secretaries of war, and the White House, Smith acted as Marshall's link with the navy. Marshall attached great significance to bridging the traditional interservice gap between the army and navy. Since he already enjoyed an excellent personal relationship with Stark, Marshall detailed Smith as the go-between with King's headquarters. Smith's opposite number was RADM Richard Turner, newly appointed as King's assistant chief of staff. Even more irascible than Smith, Turner deserved his nickname "Terrible." Since both acted in the names of their willful bosses, and neither possessed any affection for their sister service, the relationship was not a happy one. The Smith-Turner clash, indicative of the depth of animosity between the two services, presaged future difficulties.[7]

Arcadia

In Greek mythology, Arcadia represented utopia and harmony; the conference with that code name did not quite live up to its billing. The British and American staffs held the first of twelve meetings on 22 December. Opposite Marshall, Stark, King, and Arnold sat FM John Dill, until recently chief of the imperial general staff (CIGS); ADM Dudley Pound, the First Sea Lord; and ACM Charles Portal, chief of the air staff. Although the strategic picture looked grim and would soon get grimmer, Churchill enjoyed two advantages. The first was Churchill himself. With his cherubic body and English bulldog face, the cigar clenched in his jaw, and the "V for victory" salute, Churchill was the very emblem of resistance to the scourge of antidemocratic fascism and militarism. His oratory inspired freedom-loving people everywhere. Now he turned the full force of his considerable persuasive powers on the Americans. Behind Churchill stood the well-oiled machinery of the Chiefs of Staff Committee—the principal interservice body that advised the War Cabinet in the formulation of policy and issued directives to the commanders in the field who executed that policy—and its various joint subcommittees, planning and intelligence being most important. The

British Chiefs of Staff (BCOS) offered guidance, constrained their mercurial boss, and generally offered well-reasoned analysis to buttress British policies. First formed in 1923, and with better than two years of war experience, the BCOS organization always gave the appearance of unanimity and efficiency because the chiefs never presented any argument without having already reached a well-calculated consensus.[8]

Right from the opening bell, the Americans found themselves out of their league. Appalled by the lack of organization and procedure demonstrated by the American staffs, the British chiefs found it difficult to do business with a staff structure dating from "the days of George Washington." Dill told his successor, GEN Alan Brooke, that the United States possessed "not the slightest conception of what the war means" and that the American armed forces appeared "more unready than it is possible to imagine." No strangers to interservice rivalry themselves, the British found the enmity between the American services hard to believe. The Americans had no intelligence agency, nothing like the Ministry of War Transport for coordinating shipping requirements, and the toothless Office of Production Management dealt with a jumble of competing bureaus with overlapping responsibilities. In their estimate, the president possessed no adequate links between his will and executive action, and as a result, he made decisions while only haphazardly consulting his service chiefs and the heads of civilian agencies.[9]

Churchill took full advantage of the situation. In an evening meeting at the White House that first night, the prime minister worked on selling Roosevelt on Gymnast. Churchill left the talks convinced that the president was "anxious that American land forces should give their support as quickly as possible . . . and favored the idea of a plan to move into North Africa" with or without Vichy sanction.[10] The American chiefs came to the same conclusion. They worried about the prime minister's influence on Roosevelt, and with good reason. Churchill was staying in the White House and set up his mobile war room down the hall from the president's bedroom. Churchill and Roosevelt were not averse to taking a dram or two before retiring—in Churchill's case, several. These nocturnal chats gave Churchill a gauge on the president's thoughts. Since the prime minister met daily with the BCOS, the British delegation possessed a clearer understanding of the trend of Roosevelt's thinking than did the Americans.

The United States possessed nothing remotely comparable to the British command and staff structure. The Joint Board, created in 1903 as part of the Root reforms, remained the only vehicle for interservice cooperation. The board never achieved "the common understanding and mutual assistance between the two services" called for in the initial legislation. During World War I the Joint Board ceased functioning, only to resurface in 1919. It met intermittently and made recommendations but possessed no legal authority to enforce its pronouncements. Since the Joint Board had no secretariat, the British made the secretarial arrangements for the conference. Captain McCrea, Roosevelt's naval aide; LTC Paul Robinett, intelligence chief of the General Headquarters; and MAJ William Sexton, one of Smith's assistants, served as American representatives in the makeshift secretariat. By monopolizing the secretariat, Brigadier Leslie Hollis drove the agenda and edited the language of the minutes and findings.[11]

Marshall decided Smith was too valuable for the minutes-keeping role. Smith already had too much on his plate: performing his multiple liaison functions and furnishing Marshall with whatever he called for in the way of staff appreciations and supporting evidence in his uphill struggle against the BCOS. Hollis routed all minutes, memos, requests for action, and summaries of decisions to Smith for dissemination and inclusion in the files. Effectively, Smith acted as Marshall's executive officer.[12]

On 24 December the BCOS offered a written strategic overview. Europe remained the decisive theater. "Once Germany is defeated, the collapse of Italy and the defeat of Japan must follow." Like Marshall, the British listed "the realization of the victory program of armaments" and the maintenance of essential sea and air communications as strategic prerequisites. For 1942, as part of "closing and tightening the ring around Germany," the British argued that Russia should receive assistance by all available means, Turkey should be brought into the coalition, and Anglo-American forces should conduct continuous offensive actions against the Axis, including blockade, an "ever-increasing air bombardment," the nurturing of "the spirit of revolt in the occupied countries, and the organization of subversive movements. . . . It does not seem likely," it continued, "that in 1942 any large scale land offensives against Germany, except on the Russian front, will be possible." As for a return to the Continent in 1943, the British paper circuitously avoided any reference to engaging the main strength of the German armed forces in western Europe, offering instead the possibility of offensives into Norway, across the Mediterranean, from Turkey into the Balkans, or even "simultaneous landings in several of the occupied countries of Northwestern Europe." For the Far East, the coalition forces would "safeguard vital interests and deny to Japan access to raw materials vital to her continuous war effort" but otherwise remain on the defensive. In the end, everything hinged on "the scope of the victory programme."[13]

The Joint Board lacked the muscle to dissent very strongly, but behind the scenes they bristled. Their outline strategic forecast appeared very modest, tempered by an awareness of the limitations they faced. In contrast, the British—Churchill in tandem with the BCOS—laid out an expansive vision for the conduct of the war. If the war played out according to the British timetable, the United States would remain on the defensive in the southwest Pacific until 1944. While King agreed in principle to "Germany First," the combative admiral, who had just been designated Stark's replacement as CNO, took a dim view of the Pacific war being sidelined.

Marshall could appreciate the smooth working of the British organization, even if he rejected its committee structure. In contrast to Roosevelt's personal administration, the British system shared authority along formal lines of responsibility. Although Churchill possessed no formal military function as prime minister (he did as defense minister, however), he exercised more effective control through the War Cabinet and the BCOS than did Roosevelt, commander in chief of the American armed forces. To facilitate cooperation among him, the service chiefs, and the respective agencies responsible for production and logistics, Churchill appointed GEN Hastings "Pug" Ismay as his personal chief of staff. After observing the BCOS in action during the Placentia Bay conference in August 1941 and now in Washington, and fearing the prime minister's influence over the president, Marshall recognized the inadequacies of the Joint Board and the pressing need to create an alternative body to influence Roosevelt on grand strategic questions.

During the Christmas Day session, Marshall took the initiative. While discussing the situation in Southeast Asia and the southwestern Pacific, Marshall shocked the conferees by raising the untabled question of a unified coalition command. He never consulted his staff and did not talk to King or Arnold beforehand. "I feel very strongly that the most important consideration," he said, "is the question of unity of command," and he stood prepared "to go the limit to accomplish this." Citing World War I experience, Marshall pointed to the delay in forming a Supreme War Council until 1918, after "much valuable time, blood, and treasures had been needlessly sacrificed." He observed, "We cannot manage by cooperation" and stated, "If we make a plan for unified command now, it will solve nine-tenths of our troubles." Marshall tailored his argument for an Allied joint command in reference to the emergency in the Far East, but his vision involved far more.[14]

Marshall assumed that he would command any U.S. expeditionary force sent to Europe. In 1940 he had reactivated the General Headquarters with a view of its acting as the theater general staff, fleshed out by handpicked officers mostly from his inner staff. If the British won the strategic debate for delaying a return to the Continent until 1943—by which time the United States would provide the lion's share of manpower and materiel—then Marshall would occupy a far stronger position for exercising overall command. Any species of combined or joint command structure must necessarily operate as a committee—generals must run ground operations, airmen the air, and admirals the fleets. Marshall resisted the eventual subordination of any future American headquarters to British higher authority; he desired a single supreme commander over all ground, air, and naval forces as executor of Allied policy. In effect, he sought to centralize policy making in the hands of a Supreme War Council while delegating authority to a supreme Allied theater commander based on the hallowed American doctrine of unity of command.

The next morning he arrived with a draft set of instructions, defining the authority and mission of a theater commander while preserving national control over questions of sovereignty. Marshall proposed that it serve as a model for a Far East command, and as a sweetener, he later recommended a British officer, GEN Archibald Wavell, as supreme commander. The following day produced some heated discussions. Stimson took Marshall and Arnold over to see the president, who approved the scheme for a unified theater command; then the president "spanked" the navy into submission.[15]

The next morning, 27 December, Hopkins engineered a private meeting between Marshall and Churchill. Unbeknownst even to himself, Churchill had suffered a mild heart attack the night before. When Marshall arrived he found the prime minister propped up in bed. Pacing back and forth, an uneasy Marshall stated his rationale for a unified command. The prime minister had been pushing for the formation of a permanent combined supreme command and saw great merit in the idea of a unified command of ground and air forces, but Churchill (who signed his correspondence with Roosevelt "Former Naval Person") had serious reservations about including the navies. He offered an alternative: each service should operate under its own commander, with the designated supreme commander acting as coordinating agent and responsible to the Supreme War Council.[16] As in the case of Anglo-American differences over strategy, the clash between the American doctrine of unity of command and the British principle of command by committee, first raised in Arcadia, remained a stumbling block that dogged Anglo-American theater-level cooperation for the duration of the war.

Marshall expected another stormy session in the morning conference, but to his amazement, the BCOS not only accepted the single command but also argued for a more expansive grant of authority to the commander. The next day Roosevelt won over the prime minister. The ill-fated American-British-Dutch-Australian (ABDA) command, activated on 15 January 1942, became the template for all future Allied combined theaters. Marshall later considered the creation of unified theater commands one of the three great decisions of the war.

Although an attack of angina pectoris normally called for six weeks of bed rest, Churchill continued with his usual hectic schedule. However, he did concede that he needed some rest and decided to take an abbreviated trip to Florida. He convinced the president that Marshall should accompany him. One of Churchill's favorite devices involved isolating an individual he wanted to win over to his point of view. He could then bring the full force of his personality and considerable intellect to bear on an essentially captive audience. A trip with the frenetic prime minister would be anything but relaxing. Marshall knew full well what awaited him and insisted that Smith come along to play his accustomed role as buffer for the chief. They left by plane on 5 January.

Marshall got the full Churchill treatment. Churchill wanted to get the measure of the "quiet unprovocative" man that both he and Roosevelt agreed they could not go forward without. Churchill correctly assessed Marshall as the key to hammering out a lasting collaborative partnership.[17] The prime minister also took the opportunity to press Marshall on Gymnast and the type of organizational structure he envisioned for the Supreme War Council.

Knowing the alliance would prosper only if national suspicions gave way to trust, Churchill determined that no secrets should exist between London and Washington. During the vacation, Churchill took Smith aside and told him he had something to show him. Smith told an official historian in 1947 that Churchill produced several cables containing pre–Pearl Harbor British intelligence assessments. "You won't like this," the prime minister told him, "but I want no secrets." Churchill was right; Smith did not like what he read. According to Smith's cryptic remarks, British intelligence knew more about Japanese intentions than they had shared with Washington. Churchill "went out to get us into the war and he succeeded." Presumably, British intelligence filtered out much of the "noise" and did a better job of connecting the dots from Japanese intercepts and other intelligence sources than did the Americans. At best, the British produced a smoking gun—the Japanese navy's silence in the immediate period before the offensives offered a "case of the dog that did not bark"—but beyond that, as the debacle in Malaya amplified, whatever prior intelligence the British possessed mattered little in the larger scheme of things.[18]

The prime minister took the measure of Smith, correctly deciding that Marshall's de facto chief of staff would play a leading role in forging any new combined apparatus that grew out of Arcadia. He also knew that anything he told Smith would immediately reach Marshall. With the decision on forming a combined headquarters settled, Churchill wanted the joint and combined staffs constructed and run in accordance with British practice. For parallel Anglo-American staff structures to work, the Americans must construct joint organizations over the rubble of the outmoded interservice structures that had produced the pre–Pearl Harbor intelligence fiasco. Smith required no convincing on this point, given his involvement in the intelligence short-circuit. Churchill's confession reinforced the doctrine of "no secrets" but also buttressed the argument for the need to compose truly integrated staffs. Churchill succeeded in one regard. Not easily seduced, Smith was flattered by the prime minister's frankness and the confidence he showed in a junior colonel. Unlike other American officers, who were predisposed to see Churchillian machinations in every British action, Smith, accustomed to the evasiveness of the White House, never doubted the prime minister's integrity or his commitment to victory.

Overshadowed by subsequent conferences—Casablanca, Tehran, Malta, Yalta—that produced more discord, Arcadia deserves greater attention. The first Washington conference produced both the blueprint for Allied grand strategy and the instruments—the Combined Chiefs of Staff (CCS) and the formation of theaters of operation under a unified single command—for orchestrating it. Arcadia continued until 14 January, yielding agreements on a united nations declaration to define Allied war aims based on the democratic principles contained in the Atlantic Charter, the dispatch of U.S. troops to Northern Ireland and Iceland, and, most vital of all, dramatically higher U.S. rates of production as part of a "common pool" of coalition resources. Churchill came away very pleased with the results. The British achieved their essential objectives of securing the basic organizational and strategic frameworks for coalition warfare. Churchill, the amateur stonemason, believed he had succeeded in laying a secure foundation for the alliance. He cemented his personal relationship with Roosevelt, and in his famed address to Congress, he evangelized on his favorite theme of the "natural Anglo-American special relationship," helping to galvanize American opinion in favor of the combined effort.[19] All this rang true, but his euphoria was

misplaced. The British did not secure all they wanted. American acceptance of the "wear-down" strategy amounted to a contingency; over time,
the gap between British strategy and the American insistence on strategic concentration could only widen. The Americans parried Churchill
on Gymnast and never bought "the closing and tightening of the ring"
theory, which left open the timing and location of a return to the Continent; nor did they accept the delay of any genuine offensives in the
Pacific until 1944.

The British offered to leave a permanent Joint Mission in Washington as representative of the War Cabinet and the BCOS, headed by Dill
with ministerial status. The British argued for a parallel combined setup
in London, together with bifurcated Pacific War Councils and Munitions Assignment Boards in the respective capitals. Here too they compromised. Marshall insisted on a single CCS in Washington. During the
13 January meetings, the American chiefs opposed having Dill act for
the War Office with direct access to the president.[20] Discussions over the
munitions boards sparked the most heated debates. At a White House
meeting with Roosevelt and Hopkins on the final afternoon of the conference, Marshall offered his resignation rather than have any agency
beyond the control of the American chiefs dictate the allocation of materiel.[21] He strongly opposed the formation of coequal munitions boards
independent of the CCS structure. With Hopkins in support, Marshall
won the point. The political heads accepted the single Washington-
based CCS command and control framework. Dill would speak for the
BCOS and the Defense Ministry, but not the War Cabinet. The political chiefs agreed to the dual munitions board solution, but under CCS
control. Just as vital, the personal alliance between the two political
chieftains solidified. After seeing the prime minister off, the president
confided in Hopkins that he had grown "genuinely to like Churchill."
Hopkins felt sure the sentiment was reciprocated.[22] Since both parties
left the conference with something, Arcadia built the groundwork for
future Anglo-American collaboration.

Combined Chiefs of Staff

Things did not proceed very well in the initial CCS meeting on 23 January, in large part because of the inexperience of the American section
of the secretariat. Circular letters never completed the circuit, causing
frustration and friction. Hollis considered the combined secretariat "a
sickly plant." "I am afraid," he wired the War Office, "[Brigadier Viv-
ian] Dykes [the secretary of the British Mission] has a number of frac-

tious babies to nurse. Apart from ABDA, GYMNAST, and several joint surveys, our main task has been to try to establish [a] firm US-British machinery."[23] Following a particularly stressful CCS meeting on 27 January, Dykes lamented in his diary, "I wish they [the Americans] would get their secretariat set up."[24]

Marshall knew that the weakness of the American section of the secretariat hampered the labors of both sides during Arcadia, and on 23 January he empowered Smith to organize a Joint Board secretariat and a U.S. Joint Planning Committee (JPC). Embarrassed by the performance of the American secretariat during the first CCS meeting, Marshall decided that parallel secretariats would never work and insisted that Smith move over from the Joint Board and act as first secretary of a combined secretariat. One problem remained: "Dumbie" Dykes was senior to Smith, and as former director of planning in the War Office, he had powerful patrons in Dill and Ismay. Not wishing for another clash, the British consented to Smith's appointment over their man. The job came with a promotion. On 2 February, sporting his first star, Smith took over as chief secretary.

Dykes visited with Gerow and Eisenhower and prodded them into suggesting to Smith (and making it appear to be their idea) that he move all the joint planners and intelligence officers—including the navy and the entire British Joint Mission—into the public health building, where Beetle had set up the combined secretariat. Later Dykes and Smith conferred, and from the beginning, the two men clicked; Smith wholeheartedly agreed to amalgamate the combined staffs.[25]

Smith wore two hats as secretary to both the Joint Board (soon rechristened the Joint Chiefs of Staff) and the CCS. Anxious that there be no hard feelings, Smith treated Dykes as an equal. Both agreed that the combined secretariat must serve as the hub of Anglo-American decision making. To Smith and Dykes fell the vital job for organizing and running the machinery of the CCS committees, but before that could happen, Smith needed to weld together the U.S. JPC and create joint and combined intelligence and transportation committees.

The U.S. Navy provided a formidable obstacle to integration. Stimson pointed to "the peculiar psychology of the Navy Department, which frequently seemed to retire from the realm of logic into a dim religious world in which Neptune was God, Mahan his prophet, and the United States Navy the one true church." Smith needed no reminder that the U.S. Navy was the "problem child."[26] Before Smith's arrival, Turner had bullied the American secretariat, virtually running it. Smith did not wait long to assert his position. He and Turner had a major blow-out during the second meeting after Smith assumed the chairmanship. Smith's calculated eruption sent a clear message to all camps. Marshall wanted unified, centrally directed staffs, and Smith labored to produce that result. Taking his lead from King, Turner then blocked "any kind of joint show." First he insisted on keeping the U.S. joint planners in the Navy Department, where Turner "runs them like a circus of his own." Then he refused to place the navy's planners in the public health building alongside their army brethren and the British delegation. As Dykes recorded, "I fear we are in for a lot of troubles before the show starts to run smoothly," but he applauded Smith's determination in forcing a showdown with Turner. Smith knew if the navy did not come on board, the whole structure would collapse.[27]

The inability to hammer out genuine joint staff thinking necessarily grew out of American service chauvinism. When one service enjoys ascendancy, it invariably behaves badly and then blames the other of obstructionism. This was certainly the case here. Early in March, totally flummoxed by what he saw as the navy's intransigence, Smith advocated bypassing the CCS structure by forming a triumvirate of Marshall, King, and Dill. The weekly CCS meeting would function for formal purposes, merely rubber-stamping decisions arrived at by the inner council and providing window dressing for Commonwealth, Dutch, Chinese, and Soviet consumption. Nothing came from his initiative.

The formation of the American Joint Intelligence Committee (JIC) gave Smith fits. He again jousted with Turner over the navy's refusal to join the JIC. Turner did not play well with others, even those on his own side. As head of the navy's planning division, he fought with the navy's offices of communications and intelligence, contributing to the Pearl Harbor intelligence failure. He made no secret of the fact that a joint intelligence structure would be set up "over his dead body." Marshall replied that "he was sorry to see so young a man must die but that there would be a Joint Intelligence Committee." In mid-March Marshall, at Smith's behest, insisted on Turner's removal. But even after Turner left for a command in the Pacific, interservice cooperation on intelligence sharing did not much improve. King and Marshall interceded, but as Marshall remembered, they "never got the 'peculiar' intelligence people to function peaceably and properly."[28]

The creation of a combined munitions board awaited the final decision of the governments on the placement of the Munitions Assignment Boards. In January Roosevelt finally established the War Production Board (WPB). Its head, Donald Nelson, was no production czar, and he had to navigate his way through a dizzying array of officials and agencies, but the WPB possessed significantly more authority than its predecessor the Office of Production Management. After negotiations in London, the two governments decided to establish munitions boards in London and Washington. In March Smith and Dykes helped set up the Combined Munitions Assignment Board, the agency charged with harmonizing the flow of American materiel to the British.

By April—with Turner out of the picture—the combined organizations began to mesh. On Tuesdays the joint chiefs met over lunch in the public health building. Fridays saw regular meetings of the joint chiefs and the British Mission committees. These conferences covered all manner of strategic and logistical matters and determined the overall "joint" and "combined" requirements.

The first half of 1942 constituted perhaps the most trying period of the war. Japan racked up a series of stunning successes in Asia and the Pacific that secured control of the Philippines, Malaya, Burma, the Netherlands East Indies, and portions of New Guinea and the Solomon and Gilbert Islands. German forces launched renewed offensives against the Soviets and the British in Libya. A Soviet collapse and Japanese thrusts into the subcontinent and the Indian Ocean threatened the loss of India and the oil-rich Middle East and the isolation of Australia and New Zealand. As dual secretary, Smith became intimately involved in discussions at the highest level on the collapse of ABDA, the situation in the Philippines, munitions and aircraft shipments to the British and Russians, and planning for the buildup of American forces in Britain and Northern Ireland. No longer merely a liaison officer, Smith frequently briefed Roosevelt, coming to know the president's views on sensitive military questions. Smith won plaudits from men in high places as an officer of discretion and discernment.

The various joint and combined committees struggled to remain relevant and current. The secretary provided the drive and bore the responsibility for keeping ongoing projects on track. Smith's duties resembled those he had discharged as SGS: as head of the offices of record, he closely monitored the flow of information through the system; he established the agenda for CCS and JCS meetings; and, most vital, he labored to break down the barriers not only between the British and Americans but also across committee lines. He demanded efficiency. He broke out his watch and enforced the two-minute rule. Those who did not produce or proved intractable got the ax. A ruthless expediter, adept at integrating masses of recommendations into effective plans of action, Smith mastered high-level staff procedures and gained familiarity with the personalities of key members of the Joint and Combined Chiefs of

Staff. In the early stages, Smith made numerous adjustments in structure and personnel. By summer 1942, with most of the bugs removed, the joint and combined committees began to operate more smoothly. Much of the credit went to Beetle Smith.

Smith had two other vital chores: promote the American point of view to the British, and defuse divisive quarrels before they rent the combined organizations. The excellent relationship that flowered between Marshall and Dill provided the solid bedrock for Anglo-American cooperation. Smith's friendship with Dykes paralleled and buttressed that of their bosses, providing the other cornerstone relationship during the first pivotal months of the unsettled alliance's existence. Plenty of grounds existed for potential discord. Both powers were suspicious of the other. The Americans charged the British with the unpardonable sin of having their thinking habitually clouded by political calculations connected with preserving the empire. The British suspected the Americans of having designs to supplant the British Empire with one of their own.[29] American impatience for immediate results conflicted with the methodical British way of problem solving. In dealing with the British, Smith displayed a sophistication and affability that few in the War Department thought him capable of. The British saw in Smith a man who exuded an unruffled sense of confidence and decisiveness. Smith proved himself a willing collaborator, skilled at harmonizing his point of view with those of the British representatives. Although Smith often seemed disinclined to work within fixed lines of authority and always remained intensely partisan in his American and army points of view, he knew that cooperating with the British served the highest national interest.

In many respects, Smith encountered fewer problems with the British than he did with his own people. "A large segment of the Regular Army officers," reported the *New York Times,* "has no use for [Smith] and will hear no good about him—except in his professional capacity. Friend and foe alike describe him as a hard man."[30] Few in the British camp saw it that way. Whereas his relations with American officers remained guarded, Smith's contacts with the British were genial and informal, free from the jealousies that strained associations within the War Department and between the services. ADM Andrew Cunningham, briefly a member of the Joint Mission, remembered Smith's "great flair for getting on with people . . . [his] profound sense of humour," and his ready "wise-crack for each and every occasion."[31] Few American officers ever saw this side of Smith. Beetle's acerbic and often self-deprecating humor chafed on some Americans but appealed to the British. Smith marveled at the smooth efficiency of the Joint Mission. In the War Department, Marshall's intimidating personality stifled the atmosphere. In contrast, the collegial atmosphere of the Joint Mission allowed a free exchange of views. Since no officer possessed a more complete picture of War Department and JCS activities, Smith's views carried substantial weight among the British. As 1942 advanced and new British representatives rotated into the Washington organization, Smith, owing to his pivotal role as chief CCS secretary and his unique relationship with Marshall, exercised increased influence in the councils of the British Joint Mission. In the opinion of Dykes's assistant, COL Ian Jacob, Smith, though only a freshly minted brigadier general, emerged as "a power in the land."[32]

From their first encounter, Smith struck the opinionated Dykes as "absolutely sound." Their personalities—blunt-spoken, incisively intelligent, and with similar mordant senses of humor—melded from the beginning. "I am fortunate in having a *first-class* American opposite number," Dykes informed his sister a month into the Smith-Dykes partnership, "who laughs at the same things I do."[33] Famed for his mimicry, Dykes specialized in a bird caricature of his boss, Brooke. Brooke resembled a bird facially, and his lispy, rapid-fire diction and high-pitched voice sounded birdlike; appropriately, his great passions in life were bird watching and bird shooting. Dykes's routine always provoked storms of laughter.

To cement the team, Marshall secured quarters for Dykes next to the Smiths at Fort Myer. Far from home and family, Dykes became less a neighbor than a member of the Smith household. He often ate dinner with the Smiths. Nory usually cooked—fried chicken and strawberry shortcake were frequent features on the bill of fare, along with occasional game dishes such as squirrel—but sometimes Beetle played chef. Whenever a weekend offered a chance to get out of Washington, the Smiths invited Dykes along on their outings. Once they picnicked on the battlefields at Manassas with some of Smith's acquaintances made through Baruch, including toy magnate Louis Marx. Accustomed to British rationing, Dykes came away very impressed. "Drink and food and cigars in profusion," he recorded. "All very thrilled at seeing Smith's 'bird dogs' make a point." Another time they drove into the South Mountains in Maryland for some fishing. The personable Dykes found himself in demand in the Washington social circle. He even encouraged the Smiths to break out of their cocoon and join him. Earlier, Jean Monnet, the French deputy head of the British Purchasing Mission and confidant to both political chiefs, had advised Dykes, "The Yanks won't work to organization—they deal only in personalities."³⁴ No doubt Dykes initially cultivated a relationship with Smith motivated by self-interest, but the friendship blossomed into something genuine and deep.

Without children of her own, Nory mothered Dykes. She officiated in the setting up of his housekeeping and made sure he was well fed and content. She even exhibited some of Beetle's traits. Dykes could not work the furnace and called the Smiths for help. With Beetle away, Nory went over, assessed the situation, and "got on the Utilities officer and roared him up—the fire was lit up inside of a few minutes." The British officer grew much attached to her, attracted by her unaffected personality.³⁵

The Eisenhowers also lived next door. Smith had put the call through to Fort Sam Houston ordering Eisenhower to Washington a couple of days after Pearl Harbor. Although the two officers worked closely together and were neighbors, and although they called each other "Ike" and "Beetle" from the start, their relationship remained reserved. Certainly Nory and Mamie never became friends.³⁶

Smith's partnership with Dykes inevitably led to accusations that he was too "British minded," an intrinsic by-product of any sincere Anglo-American collaboration. Long accustomed to rubbing people the wrong way, Smith ignored the backbiting. He understood that his personal ties with Dykes and other British officers produced results. Through Dykes, Smith emerged as practically another member of Dill's staff. Smith used Dykes as a conduit to London, and in Smith, the British possessed a confidential contact to Marshall. Whether through official channels or private contacts, the first seismic waves of any possible trouble registered in the combined secretariat, and together they defused potentially disruptive clashes. Without entangling their chiefs, Smith and Dykes used their own oblique methods of overcoming obstructions. One means involved "putting the heat" on offenders through their orchestration of the agenda for the weekly CCS meetings. Another lever at their disposal grew out of their minute-taking responsibilities. After each CCS conference they "fixed up" the final version of the minutes and "cooked" the conclusions. BG Thomas Handy remembered observing the two in action. First Dykes wrote his draft and then handed it to Smith, who agreed with the summary except for one point. "Hell, that isn't what he said," Smith exclaimed. Dykes nonchalantly replied, "But it's what he should have said." Manipulating the program of the weekly meetings and massaging the minutes helped avert delays and expedited decisions.³⁷

In his capacity as dual secretary, Smith had three essential duties:

correlate the work of the U.S. joint planners, the War Plans Division, and the intelligence committee; interpret the joint chiefs' views to the British Mission; and maintain constant contact with the British to keep apprised of shifts in their thinking. Each brought its own special problems. Dealing with the capricious political chiefs resulted in the biggest headaches. Roosevelt received frequent private communications from Churchill—as did Hopkins—that never went through channels. Hopkins often conveyed the contents of these cables to Dill but not always to Marshall, and as a result, the British often possessed better information than the JCS did. The Byzantine nature of Roosevelt's leadership created its own set of difficulties. "The White House entourage [proved] extremely cagey," jealously retaining important communications in their own hands. Because the White House short-circuited civilian agencies, the American position could change overnight. Decisions took far longer in Whitehall, and owing to the time delay, the Joint Mission was always a day behind, even in the best of circumstances. To add to Smith's problems, the WDGS's system for circulating memoranda still lacked responsiveness. Often staff sections drafted replies to signals they had never received. Similarly, Dykes complained of having to "play the idiot boy" because the Joint Mission remained in the dark about developments in the War Office.[38]

To remedy the situation, Smith and Dykes devised their own system. Each confided in the other in an effort to remain on top of rapidly shifting circumstances. When Marshall found himself out of the information loop, he asked Smith to work through Dykes. When Marshall wanted to lay the groundwork for a change in American policy, he had Smith leak top-secret in-house memoranda to Dykes. Long accustomed to acting as Marshall's mole in the White House and with Stimson and Morgenthau, Smith knew the rules of the game. He sometimes gilded the lily—usually exaggerating the internal drift toward the Pacific in JCS thinking—nudging the British side into accommodating the American viewpoint. Through Dykes, Smith was virtually placed on the Joint Mission's distribution list. Because they acted with the concurrence of their bosses, Smith and Dykes disseminated confidences on their own. This surreptitious practice had its liabilities. Once Dykes found "poor old Beetle in a hell of a stew" because he had accidentally burned the only copy of a BCOS paper Dykes had loaned him while destroying other secret waste in his office.[39]

The dual secretariats provided Smith with positions of informal power within the official apparatus that far exceeded his rank. As many in the War Department recognized, Smith carved out a special nook for himself in the CCS. Because he enjoyed the respect and confidence of Dill, the other senior British representatives, and the British officers attached to his staff, Smith took certain liberties. With Dykes's assistance, he turned the combined secretariat to his personal advantage. Smith's detractors resented his rapport with Marshall and the British. They accused him of empire building and exceeding his authority. What they never understood was that Smith's actions stemmed entirely from his unreserved loyalty to Marshall. His mission always remained Marshall's mission.

Joint Chiefs of Staff

In January 1942 the Joint Board morphed into the Joint Chiefs of Staff. Although it would not enjoy statutory legitimacy until 1947, the JCS emerged as the chief advisory body to the president, charged with formulating American policy within the CCS framework and having executive responsibility for implementing joint action. The JCS initially consisted of Marshall and Arnold for the army and Stark and King for the navy; then Stark left for England and command of U.S. naval forces in Europe, and King absorbed the CNO's functions. The JCS roster remained unchanged for the rest of the war: Marshall, Arnold, and King.

The creation of the JCS settled two of Marshall's greatest concerns. It gave Marshall a high-level body that could counter the influence of Churchill and the British on Roosevelt and help rein in the maverick president. Arnold's inclusion in the JCS, rationalized as necessary because of Portal and the Royal Air Force's representation at the CCS level, permitted Marshall to grant the Army Air Force an autonomy it already enjoyed without seeking the requisite legislation and its attendant interservice infighting and congressional bickering. Marshall neatly sidestepped the whole question of an independent air force. By mid-January Marshall embarked on the long-delayed restructuring of the War Department—the last piece of the organizational puzzle.

The principal shortcoming of the army's command and staff structure rested in the ambiguity surrounding the role of the chief of staff. The power struggle between Pershing and March colored all army thinking. March's efforts to establish the chief of staff's command authority over the operational commands failed. Pershing reordered the War Department in the image of AEFHQ. The WDGS consisted of five divisions: Personnel (G-1), Intelligence (G-2), Operations and Training (G-3), Supply (G-4), and the War Plans Division (WPD). The chief of staff advised the secretary and assistant secretaries of war, coordinated "planning development and the execution of the military program," and commanded the army in peacetime. The WPD would furnish the general staff personnel for the commander-designate of the field army in the next war. The commander might or might not be the sitting chief of staff, depending on the pleasure of the president. As it evolved, the WPD, charged with planning and coordinating the work of the other general staff divisions, preempted the G divisions. In effect, the WPD became the general staff within the WDGS. Pershing also created a General Headquarters and entrusted it with many of the functions normally preserved for the general staff. The General Headquarters ceased functioning after Pershing stepped down, but by that time, the diminution of the WDGS's authority had become standard practice. The assistant secretary of war oversaw manpower and industrial mobilization planning, which, in effect, rendered G-1 and G-4 subordinate to the assistant secretary. The Military Intelligence Division never developed much of a presence; it remained the redheaded stepson of the general staff. The WPD usurped the planning function, leaving the Operations Division responsible for the oversight of training. The G divisions' weakened status allowed the refractory service and technical bureaus to reassert their old autonomy, supplemented by the powerful new combat arms bureaus. By doctrine and tradition, staff officers exercised no command authority, whereas bureau chiefs exercised armywide command.

Reforming the U.S. Army always proved exceedingly difficult. Despite his immense reputation, commanding general William Sherman gave up in disgust and moved his headquarters to St. Louis. The foremost American military thinker, Emory Upton (who may have suffered from a brain tumor), committed suicide out of frustration following the rejection of his schemes. When he served as chief of staff, GEN Charles Summerall attempted and failed to restructure the WDGS along functional lines; he was motivated not by the wish to increase efficiency and end the compartmentalization of functions but by the desire to short-circuit the influence of the "civilian" assistant secretary of war. His successor MacArthur identified the command disconnect when he remarked, "The War Department has never been linked to fighting elements by that network of command and staff necessary to permit the unified functioning of the American Army," but he made no serious efforts to remedy the problem.[40] In the aftermath of Pearl Harbor and with the formation of the CCS and JCS apparatus, Marshall suddenly found himself in possession of unchallenged hegemony over the U.S. Army, even if his position violated American traditions and practices.

He now moved to refashion the network of interlocking command and staff structures into an agency that would bestow on him unprecedented control over the army and air forces.

Marshall told Smith that "the time was long past when matters could be debated and carried on *ad infinitum*."[41] He needed a hatchet man to stage his palace coup and called in MG Joseph McNarney. Marshall worked out the details of the new setup during a single week in late January 1942. Marshall wanted a simplified and streamlined command and staff structure that freed him to concentrate on the higher direction of the war while liberating him from the day-to-day decisions involving administration, training, and supply. Commanders and heads of staff divisions and sections should make the decentralized decisions, consistent with policy guidelines and appropriate to their level. He demanded more efficiency from the WDGS, removing all the excessive administrative clutter. He gave McNarney a mandate of sixty days for finalizing the reorganization.[42]

While McNarney worked out a new table of organization, Marshall plotted his moves. "The difficulty was how to bring it about," Marshall later remarked, "without so much . . . dissention and opposition within the Army and on the Hill and in the press." He knew he would stir up a hornets' nest. An open internecine turf war would engender "a most unfortunate morale situation at a critical moment and would also be defeating my purpose." Congress granted Roosevelt sweeping authority to restructure governmental agencies under the terms of the First War Powers Act of 18 December 1941. Like March in World War I, the War Powers Act gave Marshall the green light. He planned to use the president's executive power without actually involving the president—at least not until he presented his fait accompli to the War Department. Timing was the key. Marshall knew that the names of the adjutant general and two of the four chiefs of arms were on the retirement list; the other two would move on to more important duties. On 5 February Marshall convened a special meeting of the top War Department brass and presented them with the new organizational chart. Executed brilliantly, Marshall's putsch stunned the entire Washington establishment; even Roosevelt remained in the dark.[43]

The new structure created three new superagencies roughly along functional lines. Marshall had resurrected the General Headquarters in 1940, relieving him of the burden of overseeing the raising and training of ground forces, and had placed MG Leslie McNair in charge. In the new structure, McNair bore responsibility for preparing the combat ground forces—doctrine, organization, equipment, training, and schooling—for deployment overseas as commander of Army Ground Forces (AGF). Arnold, as commander of Army Air Forces (AAF), held even more sweeping responsibility for all air personnel, aircraft development and procurement, training, doctrine, and air-specific construction and logistics. Alone among the new chiefs, Arnold sat on the JCS and CCS, with command authority reaching beyond the Zone of the Interior. He oversaw theater air commands and operations, except for units assigned to other commands. Anything not assigned to AGF or AAF—general administration, construction, and the procurement, movement, storage, and transport of supplies—fell under the control of LTG Brehon Somervell as head of Services of Supply, later renamed Army Service Forces (ASF). The General Headquarters and the offices of the four chiefs of arms were abolished, their staffs absorbed by AGF. Marshall did not eliminate the service and technical bureaus but instead placed them under Somervell.

By statute and convention, the WDGS acted as both a War Department and a general staff. Marshall severed command from the staff functions. The reorganization greatly expanded the size and functions of the War Plans Division—later renamed the Operations Division (OPD)—as Marshall's global command post. OPD's mandate had far-reaching authority. It obtained unprecedented coordinating powers across command and staff lines, orchestrating all phases of the ground, air, and logistical efforts from the formation of units in the Zone of the Interior to their dispatch abroad into the theaters. OPD also absorbed many of the duties of the WDGS and those Smith discharged as SGS: it acted as a clearinghouse for incoming communications from the commands, provided distilled intelligence, and served as a supervising agency to ensure that all orders and directives were distributed, received, and executed. In effect, OPD became *the* general staff. The reorganization retained but neutered the four G divisions of the WDGS. Most of the Operations Division personnel went to OPD; the Personnel, Intelligence, and Supply Divisions, with combined staffs of 661 officers, were reduced to a total of 41 officers, who were tasked with routine administration and acted as watchdogs over the operations of the newly created commands, chiefly those of the ASF.[44]

Next, Marshall went to the president for his sanction. On 28 February, by executive order, Roosevelt approved the work of McNarney's "soviet committee." Nine days later the reorganized command and staff structure began operations. In two months Marshall had dismantled a command structure "age old in custom" and fashioned what he reckoned to be the appropriate "war office of a great power."[45]

A product of haste and compromise, the reorganization achieved a good deal of what Marshall wanted. It provided a more responsive and efficient staff and reduced much of the bureaucratic red tape. In addition, the new structure confirmed air force autonomy while guaranteeing its integration into the command setup. Most vital, the new organization clarified the command authority of the chief of staff. Marshall delegated the detailed responsibility for manpower, training, equipping, and supply to the new commands. Only unresolved issues involving two or more commands went to Marshall; otherwise, McNair, Arnold, and Somervell made the decisions. Liberated from the tyranny of detailed administration, Marshall could focus on questions of policy and grand strategy, operating through his general headquarters, OPD. All this accorded exactly with the ideas he had brought with him to the War Department back in 1938. And therein lay the problem.

Although rightly called the "organizer of victory" and the quintessential military manager, Marshall's organizational concepts never strayed too far from 1918–1920 models. Preoccupied with command and operations, Marshall discounted the vital importance of operational logistics. He retained his Chaumont Clique bias against logisticians. Marshall placed great faith in Somervell; in fact, he admitted, "I would have been rather hesitant to undertake the vast reorganizations . . . had it not been for my confidence in the ability of Somervell to carry the major share of the rearrangement."[46] That did not mean he granted Somervell or his organization any direct input in strategic planning; the logistics section of OPD preempted ASF. The restructuring fell far short of clearly defining the separation of authority along functional lines on questions of manpower and supply. By retaining the truncated G divisions and the old bureaus, the structure contained a set of integral disconnects. OPD's logistical committees, not ASF, planned supply operations. Similarly undercut by OPD, the G-division chiefs exercised what little remained of their authority, interfering with Somervell's operations. They and the disenfranchised bureau chiefs, who had lost their right of direct appeal to the chief of staff, loathed Somervell and fiercely rejected any further restructuring along functional lines. These conflicts—in mindset and in structure—over command and control of manpower and supply remained in place for the rest of the war, complicating planning in Washington and confounding theater commands in organizing the American side of their headquarters.[47]

Smith followed these developments with great interest but confronted his own organizational headaches inside the JCS structure. His obsession with small "Foch" headquarters also revealed Marshall's 1918 thinking.

He disliked the British committee system, in part because it sprouted more and more committees and increasingly tied down scarce officer talent to desk jobs. Smith pulled every book he could find in the War College library on the theory and practice of staff organizations and exhaustively examined the question. Influenced by the restructuring of the War Department and his own observations and experiences, Smith developed ideas not entirely aligned with Marshall's.[48] He concluded that modern military structures required large and diverse staffs. By summer 1942 Smith had organized and staffed five American committees—his secretariat and the office of the deputy JCS, plus agencies for joint planning, intelligence, and psychological warfare—in parallel with those in the CCS structure.[49] He heard a great deal of grumbling, but Smith continually expanded the tables of organization to accommodate the many unforeseen demands placed on the joint committees.

The president pushed hard for the creation of an American centralized intelligence agency. On 9 March COL William Donovan presented his recommendations for the JIC, including the proposed placement of his OSS in the new structure. The War Department viewed Donovan with alarm. An Irish Catholic born in Buffalo, New York, and educated there and at Columbia University, Donovan had gone to law school with the president. A football star at Columbia—where he earned the nickname "Wild Bill"—Donovan won the Medal of Honor in France as a member of the famed "Fighting Sixty-ninth." From there he built a career as a Wall Street lawyer and politician, climaxing in a failed Republican bid for governor of New York. In 1940 and 1941 he undertook thinly veiled secret intelligence missions throughout the Mediterranean and to Britain and Germany, where he met with Churchill, all the top military men and heads of the British intelligence apparatus, and even Hitler. His companion during the Mediterranean tour was none other than Dykes. In June 1941 Roosevelt named Donovan the coordinator of information; in this capacity, Donovan acted as the nominal director of a centralized intelligence program that never functioned because he could not overcome the jurisdictional minefield of coordinating the in-house intelligence activities of the army, navy, State Department, and FBI. In 1942 Donovan reverted to his World War I rank of colonel as head of the OSS. Marshall wanted Smith to handle Donovan.

His rank and war record notwithstanding, the War Department saw Donovan as a "civilian" outsider. Worse, his association with Roosevelt raised red flags in the War Department. The head of the Intelligence Division, MG George Strong, wanted no part of civilian political meddling into military affairs. Although Smith rated the G-2 Division as "a collection of broken down military attachés" and considered Strong pretty weak, he shared the apprehension that Donovan intended to subordinate military intelligence to the OSS. In the lead-up to the 9 March presentation, Smith met with Donovan and prepared recommendations for the president.[50]

The amity between Dykes and Donovan provided Smith with an additional lever. Before joining Donovan for lunch on 14 March, Smith told Dykes he intended to recommend Donovan's appointment as chairman of the JIC. Smith finessed the idea, and much to his surprise, Donovan "swallowed it whole." Dykes thought it "a very satisfactory show." Smith returned to his office and wrote a memo to Marshall and King, expressing concern over the "dangerous possibilities to security" presented by an independent intelligence agency. He suggested that the "simplest way" to solve the problem was to place Donovan under JCS control. Marshall and King agreed. Typical of the slightly duplicitous way transactions were conducted—a natural outgrowth of the president's methods—Smith never bothered to arrange a meeting with Roosevelt. Instead, he composed the necessary order for the White House. On 16 March Smith argued the case before the JCS, reporting that he had removed any obstacles to Donovan's joining the JCS structure. After receiving the joint chiefs' endorsement, Smith forwarded his order, via Hopkins, to the White House, where Roosevelt signed it.[51]

The State Department put up a fuss, delaying the execution of the presidential order. In the meantime, Smith worked out the details of the new structure with Donovan. "Wild Bill" proved tough to break. Smith complained about Donovan's "peculiar position with respect to the President," his freewheeling style, his seemingly inexhaustible funding (Smith estimated it at $100 million), and particularly his refusal to submit to military channels. As a defensive measure, Smith dispatched one of his assistants as OSS secretary, but the ploy failed. "I am afraid Bill is rapidly cooking his own goose by lobbying," Dykes recorded on 4 April. "Smith is getting completely fed up with [Donovan]."[52] Fed up or not, the OSS received its mandate. Charged with civilian (propaganda and political warfare), military (guerrilla warfare), and quasi-military roles, the OSS defied easy categorization. Smith could never clarify Donovan's position or define the OSS's niche within the JCS, nor could anyone else. The OSS succeeded in rebuffing all efforts to bring it under military supervision. His struggles with Donovan deepened Smith's suspicion of irregular and psychological warfare and unconventional operations in general. Somehow the clash never became personal. Donovan liked Smith and thought highly of him as a soldier. Marshall also credited Smith's "missionary work" for the OSS's later successes in the war in combination with the military. "Smith effected a great many adjustments," Marshall remembered, "which were very effective in the long run."[53]

By late spring the hard sledging had mostly ended. Despite dire predictions to the contrary, and despite the many obstructions, the combined and joint committees began to function capably.[54] Problems remained, but they derived less from procedural issues than from the inability of the political heads and the service chiefs to settle on an Allied grand strategy. The lion's share of the credit for the early success of the CCS goes to Marshall and Dill. The American chief of staff and the British field marshal, against long odds, developed a genuine partnership. Monnet was right—personalities proved more important than organizations. Ranking just behind the Marshall-Dill association in importance stood the Smith-Dykes collaboration. Marshall and Dill selected the two best staff officers in their respective services and charged them with designing the staff apparatus and making it work in spite of itself. Strong personalities more often clash than bond. Smith emerged as the quintessential Marshall man, and Dykes enjoyed an analogous relationship with Dill. The choice, though fortuitous, appeared natural enough. No one could have predicted that the charismatic Dykes and the enigmatic Smith would hit it off, but they did. As Alex Danchev, the most authoritative student of the founding of the "special relationship," points out, Smith's and Dykes's great contribution to eventual Allied victory rested in their fashioning the mold for Allied cooperation; their successors never quite replicated their successes, but the mold was never completely broken.[55]

14

"Exceptionally Qualified for Service as Chief of Staff"

Relationships cannot be reconstructed from official records. Documents obscure unofficial lines of influence derived from close personal connections or confidential collaboration. Unrecorded conversations conducted in corridors or over strawberry shortcake often shape events in more decisive ways than can be gleaned from stacks of minutes of meetings or official memoranda.[1] Underlings like Smith and Dykes, working behind the scenes, lacked power but exerted powerful weight. As dual secretary, Smith dealt with the American and British leadership virtually on a daily basis. The secretariat acted as the engine driving the weekly JCS and CCS assemblies. Smith's connections with Marshall enhanced his status and clout within JCS and CCS roundtables; his relationship with Dykes, and through him Dill, opened up alternative avenues of influence. As an intermediary, never a principal, Smith recommended but never decided. Over time—first as Marshall's secretary and confidant, then as secretary to the joint and combined staffs and architect and handler of committees—Smith's stature grew, as did the authority he exerted in the inner circles of coalition decision making. Smith worked long and hard staking out his position as Marshall's indispensable assistant. The more he succeeded, the more he became fixed in the Washington orbit. As events transpired, he almost succeeded too well.

Ike Stakes a Claim for Beetle

At the end of March Marshall ordered that Eisenhower and OPD consolidate American strategic thinking, consistent with what already existed in the American-British-Canadian planning and what had emerged from Arcadia. Eisenhower was another whose star had ascended. He and his staff concluded that only northwestern Europe offered the prerequisites for decisive results; it was the only theater where Anglo-American forces could achieve air superiority and concentrate offensive power against the primary adversary. The OPD plan proposed the Allies assume the defensive in all theaters except the Atlantic, while accelerating the concentration of forces in the United Kingdom for a cross-Channel operation as soon as practicable. The plan envisioned a progression of interrelated operations: Bolero, a year-long concentration of Allied forces in Britain for a forty-eight-division cross-Channel landing in the spring of 1943 (Roundup), or a smaller "emergency" assault of five to ten divisions in autumn 1942 in the unlikely event of German weakening or the more probable collapse of the Soviet Union (Sledgehammer). Japanese successes forced modifications in American strategy and placed greater emphasis on the Pacific war than envisioned at Arcadia. Marshall wanted to stem the Pacific tilt and prevent additional dispersal of American forces. The president readily agreed to the plan and dispatched Marshall and Hopkins to London to sell the British on accepting the strategy "in principle." The JCS sanctioned a policy paper, what the British called the Marshall Memorandum, outlining the plan.[2]

Marshall wanted Smith's assistance in unearthing the latest British thinking. Dykes slipped him a copy of the most recent Joint Mission "Strategic Strategy" paper, on the condition he keep it to himself. Smith read it and not only briefed Marshall on its contents but also forwarded a copy to OPD. When Marshall met Dill on 3 April, the field marshal was shocked to discover the Americans knew the contents of the secret paper and demanded to know the source of the leak. Marshall only said it came from the joint planners' level. The next day Smith returned the favor by showing Dykes the Marshall Memorandum. Dykes wasted no time forewarning the BCOS of the drift in American strategic thinking in anticipation of Marshall's arrival in London four days later.[3]

Marshall and Hopkins's trip to London in early April inaugurated five months of transatlantic military diplomacy in an elusive search for a common grand strategy. The British response to Marshall's program was disingenuous and cynical. Churchill also dreaded a tilt to the Pacific, but he and the BCOS remained unalterably opposed to any cross-Channel operation in 1942. Alerted by Dill, the British prevaricated. As Brooke remembered it, "With the situation prevailing at that time it was not possible to take Marshall's 'castles in the air' too seriously! It must be remembered that we were at that time literally hanging on by our eyelids!" The Japanese raid into the Indian Ocean forced the withdrawal of the Eastern Fleet; the temporary (as it turned out) loss of control of the Indian Ocean menaced the subcontinent, cut the line of communications with Australia, and threatened the British oil supply in the Persian Gulf. Allied shipping losses to the U-boats mounted, and the situation in North Africa looked precarious. Preoccupied with their deteriorating strategic situation, the British merely fobbed off the Americans. On 14 April the BCOS accepted Marshall's proposal "for offensive action in Europe in 1942 perhaps and in 1943 for certain." In reality, the British simply could not envision the coalition being in any position to assume the offensive in 1942. What they really wanted was assistance in the Middle East and Indian Ocean.[4] The British deception campaign worked; Marshall believed that "virtually everyone agrees with us in principle." Perhaps they did in principle, but the devil always lies in the details.

The meetings in London also afforded an opportunity for Marshall's first meeting with Brooke. The American chief of staff, temperamentally incapable of deceit, admitted that the genesis of his proposals lay in countering demands by the U.S. Navy, MacArthur, and the general public to shift the center of American strategy to the Pacific and Australia. He told the British he intended to go "100% all out" for his scheme. That was precisely what worried Brooke. Marshall thought in absolutes—"Germany First" and then the Pacific—and Brooke thought him incapable of prioritizing. The CIGS decided, on the basis of less than a week's acquaintance, that Marshall was "a good general at raising armies and providing the necessary links between the military and political worlds. But his strategic ability does not impress me at all!!" Worse, he thought him "a very dangerous man whilst being a very charming one!" These views remained fixed in Brooke's head for the duration of the war.[5]

The "agreement in principle" acted as only veneer. Coalition strategic thinking diverged because the basic assumptions underlying British and American grand strategy stood in diametric opposition; the British indirect "grind-down" approach remained incongruent with the American insistence on "strategic concentration." Nor was there anything like unanimity in the American camp. Marshall had not exaggerated the pull toward the Pacific. In early May Dykes talked of the "great depression in Joint Planning all round—as we seem to make no further progress at all on combined planning. The US Army and Navy are completely divided, the latter going all out for the south-west Pacific and the former for BOLERO." Smith shared the gloom. He also foresaw an impasse on the allocation of aircraft to the theaters and the British.[6]

On 6 May Marshall wrote a strongly worded message to Roosevelt, bluntly telling the president that he needed a decision on strategic priorities. "If the 'Bolero' project is not to be our primary consideration," he urged its complete abandonment. Further, since the British accepted the "firm understanding" on Bolero, Marshall recommended the formal cancellation of the London agreement. The president replied that day: "I do not want 'Bolero' slowed down."[7]

Everything depended on Bolero, and evidence mounted in Washington that the buildup in the United Kingdom had stalled. In mid-May Marshall ordered that MG James Chaney reorganize the newly formed European Theater of Operations (ETO) headquarters along lines consistent with the reformed WDGS. Toward the end of May Marshall sent a delegation of senior officers to the United Kingdom: Arnold; Somervell; Eisenhower; MG Mark Clark, the AGF chief of staff; and MG John C. H. Lee, commander-designate of SOS in the United Kingdom. The omnipresent Dykes traveled with them. All received the same instructions: gauge the state of Bolero preparations. Eisenhower's job involved discussing command relations for Roundup, assessing the ETO structure, fixing the place of a future SOS organization in the theater, and evaluating British combined operations practices. To his disbelief, Eisenhower discovered that the British did not even know Chaney commanded the theater; the headquarters worked interwar hours and wore mufti. Chaney refused to make the prescribed organizational changes, so clearly, he had to go. In Eisenhower's view, the officer selected as his replacement should be capable of organizing, training, and commanding the combined forces and support services with "absolute unity of command"; he should also be qualified to take up duties as chief of staff to the eventual Roundup supreme commander, widely assumed to be Marshall. "It is necessary to get a punch behind the job," Eisenhower jotted down in his notepad upon returning on 4 June, "or we'll never be ready by spring, 1943, to attack. We must get going!" Marshall agreed and on 8 June told Eisenhower, "It's possible [you] may go to England in command." Three days later he confirmed that Eisenhower "was the guy" to deliver that punch.[8]

Eisenhower knew that, after Marshall's, the ETO command represented the biggest prize in the army. After the wonder abated, he began to think about who he wanted for his staff. He fixed on Clark as commander of ground forces. For chief of staff, he immediately decided on Smith.[9] Working closely with Smith since Arcadia, Eisenhower valued Beetle's abilities as a staff officer. He recognized that Smith possessed a unique set of relationships with the American service chiefs, the British Joint Mission, Stimson and his assistants, the White House, and, most important, Marshall. With Beetle as his chief of staff, Eisenhower reasoned he would have an efficiently run staff and an unequaled intermediary upholding his position with superiors in Washington and with the British in London. Knowing that Eisenhower needed all the help he could muster, Marshall agreed to both appointments. Clark would leave with Eisenhower, but Marshall decided he needed Smith in Washington through the middle of July.[10]

Smith remained of two minds. Out of loyalty to Marshall, he felt a twinge of guilt about leaving Washington. The stronger pull was the desire for a field command. Smith knew his name appeared on the short list for troop duty as an assistant division commander. Although he never admitted it, Smith must have been concerned about his worsening stomach problems. A staff job brought high levels of stress, but so would assuming command of a training division. At least the physical demands would be less in a headquarters than in the field. A move to England also meant a lengthy separation from Nory. Torn in different directions, and even though the appointment to ETO raised some troubling red flags, he accepted the job. "Smith and Eisenhower are curiously nervous about London," Dykes confided in his diary, "just like two boys off to a new school." They had good reason for a case of nerves. They knew ETO was still a mess, and if Bolero did not gain momentum, they would follow Chaney and his staff out the door. For the first time in his career, Smith experienced doubt about his ability to master a job.[11]

Don't Let Go for a Better Grip

Churchill in many ways personified Britain: an aging, once great but declining roué, suffering a long spate of disastrous losses and deeply in debt, looked for salvation from a wealthy, untried relative. Though full of expressions of familial fidelity on the surface, in his heart resided a canker—the knowledge that the unsullied relation must finally eclipse him.[12] Churchill—and the entire British establishment—hoped that if they could not evade that day altogether, they could at least delay it as long as possible. Churchill heard the warnings from Dill, but instead of regarding the Pacific drift as a threat, he saw only opportunity. The gambler knew he had one ace up his sleeve: the knowledge that Roosevelt would remain true to "Germany First." And if the American chiefs split, so much the better. If the American and British chiefs differed, that too worked. In due course the political leaders would decide, and ultimately the choice would fall to Roosevelt. In the end, Churchill remained convinced that he could bring the Americans around to the British view of things. The immediate problem facing Churchill centered on dissuading the Americans from Sledgehammer without provoking a breach over the basic grand strategy.

Churchill dispatched VADM Louis Mountbatten close on the heels of the returning American delegation. The supposed reason for the trip to Washington was to update the Americans on special and combined operations developments. The chief of combined operations since April 1942, "Dickey" Mountbatten embodied the type of officer most admired by Churchill: a young, polished product of a princely family; a dashing, self-confident naval hero; a thruster and not too cerebral. In short, Mountbatten possessed most of the traits Dill and the British service chiefs and senior commanders lacked. Mountbatten's real mission focused on tapping into Roosevelt's thinking and sowing the seeds for a British rejection of Sledgehammer.

The Americans and British were not the only ones engaged in shuttle diplomacy. Amidst the mounting confusion entered Molotov, who traveled to London and Washington in May and June in search of Anglo-American assurances for a second front in 1942. Molotov went away empty-handed, but his circuit through the Western capitals raised the stakes. The second front weighed heavily on everyone's mind. Roosevelt told Mountbatten what Churchill hoped to hear: the coalition could not abide a year of inactivity against the Axis. Mountbatten enjoyed a reputation as a vocal advocate of offensive action and a supposed expert on combined operations, so his views on Sledgehammer carried weight. Mountbatten told the president that the lateness of the season and the critical shortage of landing craft forswore a 1942 cross-Channel operation. With Sledgehammer off, a move against French Northwest Africa offered the only viable alternative to nothing at all.[13]

Churchill struck while the metal was hot, asking for talks in Washington. This time he wasted no time with a sea voyage; he hastened across the Atlantic in a seaplane. Increasingly dissatisfied with Bolero, Churchill appealed to Roosevelt for some concerted effort against the Axis in 1942. At Arcadia, Churchill had boldly talked of destroying Rommel in Libya. Instead, GEN Erwin Rommel preempted the British invasion of Tripolitania with a thrust that forced another humbling British retreat. On 10 June the Germans overran Bir Hakeim and three days later penetrated the Gazala Line. For the British, the question revolved less around destroying Axis forces in North Africa than in salvaging their crumbling position in the Middle East.

What Stimson called "the old War Council"—the civilian secretaries, the joint chiefs, and Roosevelt—met at the White House in preparation for Churchill's visit. Roosevelt felt mounting pressure from public calls for aggressive action against Japan, the plight of the Soviet Union, and the not too distant midterm elections. He and Hopkins wanted American forces engaged against the Axis before the end of September, and if the British blocked any move against the French coasts, Gymnast appeared to be the only option. "It looked as if [Roosevelt] was going to jump the traces over all we have been doing in regard to BOLERO," Stimson recorded in his diary. "He wants to take up the case of GYMNAST again."[14]

Churchill arrived in Washington late on 17 June and flew up to Hyde Park the next morning for talks with Roosevelt. The time for deception regarding Sledgehammer had passed; Churchill adamantly rejected operations in northwest Europe and advocated instead an August Gymnast. Stimson and the American chiefs had every reason for concern. While Marshall, Arnold, and their assistants—chiefly Eisenhower, Clark, and Smith—put together a game plan to head off Churchill's gambit to push his strategic agenda, Stimson made the case for Bolero in a long memorandum to Roosevelt.[15]

The CCS met on 19 June. Only Brooke, making his debut in Washington, and Ismay traveled with the prime minister. Dill and the British Mission joined them. Brooke began by telling the American chiefs that, in the opinion of the BCOS, Gymnast "should not be undertaken under [the] existing situation." His declaration on Gymnast did not resonate in American ears as much as his rejection of a 1942 cross-Channel operation. Despite reassuring the Americans that Bolero should be pushed "with all possible speed and energy," he rejected any 1942 operation— "justified only by reasons that were compelling in nature"—as inevitably "deterring" a Roundup in 1943.[16] From across the table, Dykes saw that "Marshall, Eisenhower and Smith were considerably perturbed." Although Brooke thought he had encouraged the Americans, his words conveyed the impression that "BOLERO had dropped back in the batting [order]."[17]

That afternoon, Smith joined Marshall and Eisenhower in discussions with Dill, Brooke, and Ismay. Nothing illustrates how the two sides remained divided by a common language more than these initial discussions. Part of the confusion stemmed from misunderstandings over what the code words meant. For Marshall and the Americans, Bolero connoted not only the buildup phase but also the cross-Channel designs for 1942 and, more vitally, 1943. The British code names—Sledgehammer and Roundup—were not yet in common use.[18] For example, Roosevelt referred to Sledgehammer as One-Third Bolero. Apparently, no one thought of creating new code names. Again, the British worked on allaying Marshall's apprehensions. They reiterated points made in the CCS meeting. Bolero must remain the overriding operation in preparation for a full-scale invasion of northwestern France in spring 1943. In their opinion, Gymnast would disperse too much naval, air, and logistical strength and not only materially weaken Bolero but also place the entire Anglo-American strategy in doubt.[19] The Americans heard only British waffling on any invasion of the Continent in 1942 or 1943. A rejection of the 1942 crossing translated into a negative response to Bolero. Smith came to Dykes after the meeting "very worried" about a deadlock. Ismay arrived after Smith left, convinced that Brooke "did not in the least intend to write down BOLERO" and that the afternoon talk had cleared the air.

Apparently, Ismay got it right. The next morning the CCS arrived at a consensus; Brooke expressed amazement at the level of concordance. Marshall emphasized that "large scale operations in 1943 would clearly not be possible unless all efforts were concentrated now on their preparation. If we changed our plan now, and opened up another front, we should probably achieve nothing." By September a clearer picture of the Eastern Front would emerge, and by that time, sizable U.S. forces would be deployed in the United Kingdom. Any decision for an offensive should be postponed until then. Whatever transpired on the Russian Front, Bolero ensured British security. Only Bolero offered the coalition any measure of strategic flexibility. "From a military point of view," Marshall concluded, "there seemed no other logical course than to drive through with the Bolero Plan." The British signaled their agreement. All parties agreed on one thing: they strongly opposed Gymnast. Dykes wrote up the minutes while Smith worked on the CCS memorandum for Roosevelt and Churchill at Hyde Park.[20]

Smith's paper stated that the CCS adhered, "without reservation, to our previous decision that continental operations on a large scale at the earliest possible moment should be the principal effort of the United Nations." Since the defeat of Germany required overwhelming superiority, and since "for logistical reasons northwestern Europe is the only front on which this superiority can be achieved" and "logistic factors preclude the mounting of any powerful attack in the theater" before spring 1943, the only solution remained to stay the course on Bolero. The memo strongly opposed Gymnast, producing a long list of arguments—chiefly, the dispersal of "organization, lines of sea communication, and air strength" from the United Kingdom and "the marked effect in slowing up BOLERO." It also made the point that Gymnast's success "depends upon the existence of certain psychological conditions in North Africa which cannot be predicted accurately."[21] Essentially, the CCS's findings mirrored American views. These were best summed up by Stimson, who advised Roosevelt, "When engaged in a tug of war, it is highly risky to spit on one's hands even for the purpose of getting a better grip."[22]

Two clouds hung over these deliberations. After the first meeting, Smith invited Dykes home for dinner. "Sumptuous as usual," Dykes reported, but he could not enjoy the meal. "News from Libya definitely bad," he recorded. "Tobruk is once more besieged and we are where we were last autumn once more." The other worry centered on "plans that the PM and the President had been brewing up together at Hyde Park!" Brooke for one feared the worst, certain that North Africa would reappear even though all the service chiefs were on record as being diametrically opposed to Gymnast in any form.[23]

Brooke knew his man. Feeling cornered, Churchill rose to the occasion. Now back in Washington, the prime minister sent off a sharply worded note to Roosevelt in which he effectively vetoed Sledgehammer. The British government "would not favor an operation that was certain to lead to disaster for this would not help the Russians whatever in their plight, would compromise and expose to Nazi vengeance the French population involved and would gravely delay the main operation in 1943. . . . No responsible British military authority," he continued, "has so far been able to make a plan for September 1942 [landings in France] which had any chance of success unless the Germans become utterly demoralized, of which there is no likelihood." He then followed with a series of rhetorical questions: "Have the American Staffs a plan? What forces would be employed? At what points would they strike? What landing craft and shipping are available? Who is the officer prepared to command the enterprise?" Since no prospect existed for a landing in France on any substantial scale, Churchill asked, "What else are we going to do? Can we afford to stand idle in the Atlantic theater during the whole of 1942?" He suggested a solution: preserve the "general structure" of Bolero while embarking on Gymnast, which would provide "positions of advantage and also directly or indirectly take some of the weight off Russia."[24]

Churchill's arrow hit its intended target. Roosevelt knew that the answer to all the questions was a resounding no. Instead of cabling Marshall and King the full text of Churchill's communication, Roosevelt reduced the prime minister's queries to one: where can American forces be employed against German forces or German-controlled areas before 15 September 1942? The president wanted an answer the next day.[25] The American chiefs had nothing concrete to offer. All they could recommend was Bolero, which at that point was a logistical plan for the American buildup in the United Kingdom, not an operational alternative.

Over lunch on 21 June the two political heads held a powwow at the White House with Hopkins in attendance. Churchill opened with a "terrific attack" on Bolero, while Roosevelt "stood pretty firm." After lunch Marshall, Brooke, and Ismay joined them, and as related by Stimson, the meeting turned into a "rumpus." Marshall launched a spirited defense of Bolero. Then something dramatic occurred. Word arrived that Tobruk had fallen, along with 35,000 troops. The news altered the whole dynamic of the conference. This was a huge blow to British prestige, and Churchill became very emotional. The defeat and Churchill's reaction influenced Roosevelt's stance. From this point, their conversation turned to considerations of how the Americans might best help the British extricate themselves from the disaster in Libya. The situation demanded some sort of decision, but typical of Roosevelt, he sought a compromise that did not commit him to anything. They decided to proceed full blast on Bolero until the first of September, at which time the situation would be reassessed to determine whether Allied forces could make a real attack without danger of disaster. Churchill again pleaded the case for Gymnast, knowing that (again in Stimson's opinion) the North African operation "was the President's baby."[26]

The outcome of the White House meeting disheartened the American side. Until then, they had appeared to be ahead on points. The British had accepted Bolero "as the principal offensive effort," with a target date set for spring 1943. All that went up in smoke. Bolero still enjoyed priority, but the president's mandate for a 1942 offensive against the Axis before mid-September rendered Gymnast the only viable alternative.

That was how the British read the situation too. "Providing that political conditions [in French Northwest Africa] are favorable," Ismay noted, "the best alternative in 1942 is Operation GYMNAST. Accordingly the plans for this operation should be completed in all details as soon as possible." Planning for Bolero would continue in London and for Gymnast in Washington. Ismay's minutes of the meeting differed substantially from what Marshall thought had transpired. The Ismay note contained agreement on Bolero but, in Marshall's estimate, emphasized Gymnast.[27]

Smith tried and failed to reconcile the two views. He met with Brooke and came away only with confirmation that the CCS would discuss the issue the next day. Smith, aided by Handy, chief of the strategy and policy group of OPD, wrote a memo "more in line with [Marshall's] ideas as to the points on which we should agree." Marshall believed that, in the event of a Russian collapse, "immediate and drastic measures will be indicated for the United Nations," involving a 1942 landing in France, whatever the risk. Smith's paper listed the Channel Islands, the Brest and Cherbourg peninsulas, and the Pas de Calais as possible objectives. Gymnast again ranked lowest as proxy for operations in France.[28]

Smith worked with Ismay in an attempt to square exactly what the president and prime minister had decided in their 21 June conclave. Under pressure from Smith, Ismay redrafted his memorandum. Ismay opened by restating, "The United States and Great Britain should be prepared to act offensively in 1942." This time he placed emphasis on Bolero and operations in France or the Low Countries. As for Gymnast, planners in Washington would "carefully and conscientiously" formulate alternatives should operations in northwest Europe prove unavailing. Smith and Ismay forwarded the revised text to Marshall and Brooke, who both concurred on its language. None of the minutes or memos mentions any timetable—neither Churchill's 1 September deadline for a decision between alternative operations nor Roosevelt's mid-September target date for the commitment of American ground forces.[29]

The second Washington conference ended inconclusively. The American chiefs fought off Churchill's Gymnast scheme, but only barely. Just as in April, when the Japanese raid into the Indian Ocean had diverted British attention from the Marshall Memorandum, the Tobruk disaster made it difficult for Churchill and Brooke to view Sledgehammer versus Gymnast as the essential issue. Tobruk and the American reaction convinced the prime minister that Gymnast offered the silver bullet to his problems in the Mediterranean. The American response to the crisis in the Middle East signaled no strategic shift to the Mediterranean, but it increased Roosevelt's tilt toward accepting Churchill's approach.

Beetle Smith resided in limbo as chief of staff–designate to ETO and lame-duck dual secretary of the joint and combined committees. His participation in these discussions signified his entrée into the highest circles of Allied strategy making. His stature had grown a great deal since Arcadia. Smith's central role in the Washington conference confirmed Eisenhower's high estimate of him. Before he flew off to London on 23 June, Eisenhower held a conference with Churchill, who thought there was no better choice for chief of staff than Smith. The prime minister had first taken Smith's measure during Arcadia, and his subsequent dealings with Brooke, Dill, and Ismay spoke to his objectivity. Churchill raised the question of Smith's appointment with Marshall, as did Smith himself, both pointing to the need for an immediate housecleaning of the ETO staff.[30] Marshall remained noncommittal.

"Without Him the Party Would Have Ended in Deadlock"

The British could dissemble no longer. In view of the situation on the Libyan-Egyptian frontier, they wanted strategic consensus and needed Gymnast. On 7 July the War Cabinet confirmed its veto of Sledgehammer. The next day the prime minister cabled Roosevelt at Hyde Park, asserting that "no responsible British General, Admiral or Air Marshal is prepared to recommend SLEDGEHAMMER." In a shameless bit of huckstering, the prime minister tried to convince the president that Gymnast had "all along" been Roosevelt's "commanding idea," calling it "by far the best chance for effective relief to the Russian front in 1942. . . . Here is the true second front." He concluded by pointing to Gymnast as "the safest and most fruitful stroke that can be delivered this autumn."[31]

The JCS meeting two days later opened with Marshall reading a War Office communication rejecting Sledgehammer. Marshall reiterated his rejection of Gymnast as "expensive and ineffectual" while noting that, without British support, Bolero and any cross-Channel operation in 1942 and 1943 were dead issues. As Marshall put it in a memo to the president, the British must decide "at once" if they gave Bolero their full backing. If not, "it is our opinion that we should turn to the Pacific." His objective, he concluded, was "to force the British into acceptance of a concentrated effort against Germany, and if this proves impossible, to turn immediately to the Pacific with strong forces for a decision against Japan."[32] Naturally, King strongly supported the shift.

Churchill and the BCOS ignored repeated warnings from Dill— buttressed by Smith's confidences to Dykes—that the Americans saw Bolero and Gymnast as mutually exclusive. With Dykes out of Washington when the War Office communication arrived, Smith talked to his assistant Jacob, emphasizing the urgent need for London's reaffirmation of its commitment to Bolero. As soon as Dykes returned, Smith cornered him and told him that powerful voices around Marshall, led by McNarney, had concluded that "Britain is going cold on BOLERO, and that these suggestions for side-shows are smoke-screens to conceal this cooling-off." Smith put the worst face on the shift from a "Pacific drift" to a full-fledged "Pacific alternative."[33]

The Pacific alternative represented a ruse on Marshall's part, but it took on a life all its own. King immediately jumped at the opportunity, claiming the British had never been in wholehearted accord with operations on the Continent. In his view, it was "impossible to fulfill naval commitments in other theaters" and do Gymnast. Marshall reinforced these ideas in a memorandum to the president, stating categorically that Churchill's rejection of a cross-Channel operation meant "no BOLERO in 1942 and an inadequate and probably ineffective BOLERO in 1943." He stated, "I believe that we should now put the proposition up to the British on a very definite basis and leave the decision to them."[34] Marshall put the heat on his boss, but the wily Roosevelt never bit.

On 12 July the president called Marshall and King's bluff. "In view of your Pacific Ocean alternative," he telephoned from Hyde Park, "please send me this afternoon by plane, a detailed comprehensive outline of the plans." He also wanted their opinion "as to the effect of such an operation on Russian and Middle East fronts during the balance of this year." Just as in June, Roosevelt knew no such plans existed. And as Marshall admitted, a shift to the Pacific "would require a great deal of detailed planning which will take considerable time." Time was the one thing Roosevelt could not expend. He did follow up on Marshall's other idea. On 14 July he told Marshall, King, and Hopkins to go to London and settle the issue.[35] Marshall told Smith he would be coming along. After a particularly somber JCS meeting, Smith and several members stayed behind, discussing the likely outcome of the London conference. They concluded that whatever the military implications of a diversion from northwest Europe, "apparently our political system would require major operations this year in Africa."[36]

Marshall's deception never fooled Roosevelt, but it frightened the British Mission. On 13 July Dill hurried back from a trip to Ottawa. Smith played on their disquiet. The British knew about Marshall's Pacific alternative scheme and Roosevelt's request for planning details, but not about the president's rebuff. In his conversations with Dykes, Smith proved very economical with the truth. He spoke of his great fear that "this marked the real danger of switching all American effort towards the Pacific." He emphasized that, in American estimates, Gymnast "was quite incompatible with any form of ROUNDUP." Smith's little subterfuge worked. "Apparently the President has seized on the idea of a Pacific offensive," Dykes recorded in his diary, "and it looks very much as if BOLERO is going to be thrown out of the window altogether! London can't say we didn't warn them!"[37]

The next evening Smith invited Dykes over for dinner and some straight talk. Smith discovered that his misinformation blitz had done the trick. Dykes informed him that Dill had written a strongly worded telegram to London, telling Churchill and the BCOS of the "imperative need to convince the Americans of our steadfastness to BOLERO." Hearing this, Smith allayed his friend's apprehensions, but only slightly.

He told Dykes, "Marshall possibly raised the Pacific War as a bogey to frighten [the British], but didn't really mean it. Now however he finds, rather to his surprise, that several people like the bogey!" The following day Smith, fresh from a predeparture conference at the War Department, assured Dykes that "a Pacific offensive is beginning to drop back again in the batting [order]."[38]

In truth, the Pacific option never made it into the lineup. That morning, 15 July, Roosevelt held a stormy meeting with Marshall. The president recognized that Marshall's Pacific alternative amounted to a red herring, and although he understood Marshall's motives, he could not condone what to his eyes appeared to be an abandonment of the British. The next day, as the American delegation left for London, he issued a formal set of instructions to Hopkins and the two service chiefs. "It is of the highest importance that U.S. ground troops be brought into action against the enemy in 1942," Roosevelt directed. "In regard to 1942, you will carefully investigate the possibility of executing SLEDGEHAMMER," but "if SLEDGEHAMMER is finally and definitely out of the picture, I want you to consider the world situation . . . and determine upon another place for U.S. Troops to fight in 1942." Ensuring no further lurch toward the Pacific, he concluded by restating, "This affects the immediate objective of U.S. ground troops fighting against Germans."[39]

Smith, accompanied by Early, flew to Prestwick, Scotland, and arrived in London with the rest of the American delegation on 18 July. Closeted at Claridge's Hotel, Marshall, King, Eisenhower, and Smith were joined by Stark, Clark, and two senior ETO officers—Lee and MG Carl Spaatz, the senior airman. There they prepared the rationale for Bolero and operations in northwest Europe in 1942.

Dill sent Dykes to London with the single purpose of impressing on the BCOS the dangerous situation confronting them. While Smith labored at Claridge's, Dykes briefed the British chiefs. Dykes stressed "the American feelings (a) that some landing could be made on the Continent this year if we really put our backs into it; (b) that GYMNAST and ROUNDUP are mutually exclusive. I gathered that they themselves had by no means made up their minds. Portal is out for GYMNAST; Brooke wants to go ahead with BOLERO but *plan* for GYMNAST; Pound offered no opinion."

Later that day Smith met up with Dykes, Hollis, and Jacob. The three British officers pressed the Gymnast case and the dangers presented by a premature movement into northern France. At that juncture, the strategic situation looked dire. In their view, a Soviet collapse loomed as a real possibility. The Germans had sealed off Rostov, threatening both a drive into the Caucasus and another on the Volga toward Stalingrad. With the Russians defeated or neutralized, any Allied force stranded in a lodgment in northern France would get chewed up by forces moved from the Eastern Front. In fact, the Germans had more than enough ground and air forces in the west to write off any coalition amphibious attempt, which would be limited by the shortage of landing craft to six divisions. In contrast, a successful operation in North Africa provided "the best insurance for the Middle East if things went badly with Russia." They took pains to impress on Smith that an autumn 1942 Gymnast did not rule out a Roundup late in 1943. If the Allies decided on Gymnast, they should strike deep into the Mediterranean, at least as far as Algiers. "Beetle reacted fairly well" to the final point "and said he thought the US COS might accept it, if our people put it over firmly enough. He thought the Pacific idea was definitely *off.*"[40]

The strategic situation also troubled Marshall; Sledgehammer took on even more importance in his eyes. Marshall remained convinced that Gymnast represented a giant diversion of Allied strength into a strategic cul-de-sac. An abandonment of Bolero undermined any realistic hope not only for Sledgehammer but also for a 1943 invasion. He also believed a Soviet collapse would force the United States into abandoning Bolero and Europe in favor of the Pacific. Whatever the cost, the democracies must launch whatever offensive capabilities they possessed, aimed at forestalling a Soviet strategic defeat. He put Eisenhower, Smith, Clark, and Lee to work on drawing up detailed plans for Sledgehammer to present to the British.

Eisenhower had initially been in favor of Sledgehammer; then in his last days in Washington he began to question the feasibility of the operation. Now with the chief in London, he again became its strongest advocate, mirroring Marshall's views. Out of loyalty to Marshall, Smith defended the official American position even while privately entertaining increased reservations about its practicality.[41]

On 20 and 21 July Marshall and King met with the BCOS in closed session. Marshall pressed the suit for Sledgehammer; the British resolutely stonewalled. The British saw little prospect of materially altering the strategic situation on the Russian Front by conducting a forlorn hope amphibious operation in France that at best would gain a small beachhead and at worst might end in utter disaster. Since the greater share of ground and air forces and landing craft would be British, they held the whip hand. Pointing to "the overall scheme" agreed on at Arcadia, the British maintained that Gymnast conformed exactly to the "closing and tightening of the ring" phase of Allied grand strategy.[42] "The US COS have not yet accepted the impracticability of a SLEDGEHAMMER this year," Dykes recorded, "which all our people *have*."[43] Each night Hopkins kibitzed with Churchill. The conference appeared to be headed toward the shoals. If the CCS ship foundered, it might take the coalition with it.

National differences proved difficult to disguise. Any "special relationship" that existed came later—a product of the defeat of Germany and partnership in the Cold War. Americans had grown up reading about Lexington and Concord and the Red Coats burning Washington.[44] Except for northeastern elites, Americans bore no great affinity for things British. Many non–Anglo-Saxon Americans displayed indifference to the British connection; Irish Americans were openly hostile. To members of the American delegation, the British appeared timid, exaggerating the military might of the Germans and their worries about another Somme. For the British, they viewed Cousin Jonathan as naïve. The barely trained units that first arrived in Northern Ireland, the chaos that reigned in ETO headquarters, and the miscarrying Bolero buildup all pointed to American unpreparedness for tackling the Germans. They doubted whether the U.S. Army possessed the officer talent to command large-scale operations and man higher headquarters. Many of them labored to put a lid on their condescending attitudes. The Americans disdained British pretensions of superior military proficiency, given the litany of British disasters in Norway, France, Greece, and Crete; defeats and retreats in North Africa; and utter debacles in Hong Kong, Malaya, Singapore, Burma, and now Tobruk. Britain's "finest hour" simply staved off defeat. Only too aware of their track record, the British labored under the knowledge that one more disaster might finish them, and they saw that disaster looming across the English Channel. Similarly, Marshall feared that a miscarried campaign in a peripheral theater against neutral Vichy France would have catastrophic effects on American civilian and uniformed morale.

On 21 July Dykes took Smith for a tour of the Cabinet War Rooms. Smith confessed that the American chiefs had reached no consensus and, in their frustration, might play the Pacific card again. Smith thought the Americans might dispatch two corps to the Middle East and enough troops to the United Kingdom to guarantee security, with the remainder moved to the Pacific. "Beetle says that political pressures at home may *force* some action by American forces this year," Dykes wrote, "and if it can't be Europe it will have to be in the Pacific." Smith informed him that Marshall remained "extremely concerned at the possibility of irresistible political pressure of this nature." Dykes reasoned this might be a negotiation ploy but decided Smith was dead serious.[45]

At the next CCS meeting on 22 July, Marshall presented the paper prepared by Eisenhower, Clark, and Smith calling for the seizure of a Cherbourg beachhead as a preliminary for a 1943 Roundup. The British raised all the familiar objections. Instead of counterattacking, Marshall pronounced that since the service chiefs could not come to a conclusion, they must refer the question to their political masters.

That afternoon, the combined chiefs met with Churchill at 10 Downing Street. The prime minister declared his opposition to Sledgehammer, repudiated the charge that the Allies had given any firm "second front" promise to the Soviets, and reaffirmed British intentions to launch Roundup when conditions allowed. He announced the matter would go before the War Cabinet later that day. Brooke "had no trouble convincing Cabinet [members] who were unanimously against [the attack on France]."[46] Hopkins dispatched word of the British veto to Roosevelt. He feared that rumors of the disagreement would leak, with disastrous consequences, and pleaded that all appearances of a "united front" be preserved.

Smith returned to Claridge's, where the BCOS would host an ill-timed dinner later that evening. Having worked all that exhausting day without lunch, Smith, Eisenhower, and Clark could not wait and cooked up some dehydrated noodle soup. A few drinks lightened their mood. They discussed the events of the last two days. Smith never shared Eisenhower's dire assessment of the situation. From the onset of the closed American sessions, only Smith consistently argued the merits of a North African offensive as the best of a number of poor options. With Clark, he discounted the charge that Churchill intended to strangle a 1943 return to the Continent. "We should carry out ROUNDUP," Smith opined, "if we have to wait three years." Together they mulled over staff and planning arrangements for Gymnast. Then Dykes dropped in. "Disappointment," he observed, "was intense." "Poor old Ike is terribly fed-up with our refusal." Eisenhower thought it "the blackest day in history."[47]

At the dinner the Americans were still awaiting the president's reply but appeared gracious in defeat. The only untoward moment occurred when Smith rounded on Mountbatten, insisting on the removal of a particularly objectionable British officer, and one of the admiral's favorites, from the Joint Mission staff. Afterward, Dykes "had a long crack with Beetle." Smith expressed relief that Sledgehammer "has been cleared out of the way, never having felt that it was really on." They then discussed planning arrangements for Gymnast.[48]

The following morning Smith attended a downcast meeting among Marshall, King, Eisenhower, and Clark. Later in the morning Smith went to ETO headquarters at Grosvenor Square, where he worked up a staff appreciation of the strategic situation with Eisenhower and Clark. Smith forcefully advanced the case for accepting the North African operation. In the course of their deliberations, they received word that the president had issued a new directive, reiterating his demand that American troops fight the Axis in 1942, with North Africa as the highest priority. That sealed the deal. The "Survey of Strategic Situation," written principally by Smith, advocated a combined Gymnast for autumn 1942.[49]

Marshall called Smith into his office early on 24 July. He wanted Smith's help organizing a formal meeting with the BCOS scheduled for noon. He then handed Smith a rough draft of a new directive proposing the preservation of Sledgehammer and the continuation of planning for Bolero and Roundup. If by 15 September Sledgehammer proved unnecessary or unworkable, a combined Gymnast would go ahead. Smith tidied up the paper.[50]

Beetle called Dykes and arranged the meeting. He seemed antsy, insisting that he talk to Dykes immediately. Dykes hurried over to Claridge's and rode with Smith to the cabinet offices. Smith complained again about Ismay's doctoring of the minutes of private meetings between the American chiefs and Churchill. Marshall wanted amendments made to the record and insisted that Smith and Dykes keep the minutes for the upcoming meeting with Churchill. Smith then handed Dykes a copy of the new American proposals.

Brooke expected more difficulties, but instead he found that the American paper "contained almost everything we had asked them to agree to at the start" of the conference. After some minor amendments, Smith and Dykes produced a draft. The combined chiefs then reassembled to approve a final draft. Ismay, his nose out of joint because of the earlier rebuff, raised the question of whether the paper should bear the stamp of CCS approval without Churchill's signature. Smith rose up in anger. Faced with a stalemate, the Americans had made all the concessions, and the combined chiefs had agreed, yet Ismay raised procedural issues. Smith wondered if the CCS existed as a mere talking shop; the integrity of the whole CCS structure was at stake if the chiefs could not at least make a show of unanimity.[51] In any event, the paper—unsigned in the end—went to Churchill and that evening to the War Cabinet, where it won ready approval. All now hinged on Roosevelt's reaction.

Despite the incendiary clash with Ismay, Smith appeared to be in a good mood when he dined with Dykes and Jacob that evening. Smith regaled them with the story about the internal scum in the American delegation. "Beetle told me that he had a hell of a job selling GYM-

NAST," Dykes noted. "I am quite sure that without him the party would have ended in deadlock."[52]

In the final CCS meeting the next day, arrangements for command and planning for Gymnast—renamed Torch, at Churchill's insistence—came under discussion. No difficulties arose—the supreme commander would be American. To avoid contention between Torch and Roundup, the same officer would command both. In the event Torch went off, the designated supreme commander would lead it, leaving Roundup planning to another officer.

Smith showed Dykes a long cable from Roosevelt, "who had evidently had a sharp attack of strategy the previous evening." Roosevelt proposed "combining GYMNAST with operations against Dakar and God only knows where else." Written before Roosevelt received the CCS agreement, the cable raised eyebrows. Hopkins dispatched a wire, pleading that the president refrain from throwing a monkey wrench into the works. Smith and Dykes cleaned up the minutes of the final meeting over a quick lunch before Smith hurried off to pack in anticipation of the president's approval. When it arrived, the American delegation raced off for a special train to Scotland and flights back to Washington.[53]

Smith emerged from the London conference with his standing much enhanced. In the course of the stress-filled conference, Smith wore his secretary hat when he drafted correspondence to Roosevelt and the JCS, then donned his chief of staff hat when he deliberated with Eisenhower and Clark. His advocacy of Gymnast and his furtive meetings with Dykes convinced many that Smith was "more British than the British." Smith's bushwhacking of Ismay and Mountbatten remained more fixed in the minds of men who counted. Calculated or not, coming as they did at the nadir of American fortunes, and aimed at two of Churchill's favorites, Smith's outbursts salved some of the wounded American pride. Smith's performance in London reaffirmed Eisenhower's desire to secure Smith's services while heightening Marshall's reluctance to part with him. On 25 July Marshall informed Eisenhower that he would probably command Torch as Marshall's deputy supreme commander. Eisenhower restated his position on Smith's appointment. Marshall agreed to Smith's transfer but refused to specify when it would become effective.[54]

Kindling the Torch

Smith thought he should have stayed in London. Soon after returning to Washington, he invited Dykes and Mamie Eisenhower over for dinner. Naturally, the conversation turned to London, a recap of the conference, and news of Eisenhower and his circle. Smith pulled no punches in discussing Eisenhower's staff; he "thought it very poor—it seems to want a lot of strengthening." The next night he expressed anxiety "about planning difficulties in TORCH." According to Smith, "Eisenhower badly needs someone to take a grip on his staff," and he wondered why his orders to join Eisenhower remained on hold.[55]

Torch was very much on his mind. Smith sat down with Cunningham for a long heart-to-heart talk. Smith confessed his enthusiasm for Torch and solicited Cunningham's naval opinion on the strategic benefits presented in North Africa. The U.S. Navy offered little in the way of encouragement. King stated that the occupation of the North African littoral would have little effect on the shipping situation. Few men alive knew the Mediterranean better than Cunningham. The admiral had served in the Mediterranean from 1932 until his recall for service on the CCS in May 1942. The very model of a fighting admiral, Cunningham had preserved British naval supremacy in the Mediterranean throughout his tenure as commander in chief. Cunningham told Smith that the strategic advantages accruing from a successful Torch were incalculable. Control of the south shore would provide air bases and enough air cover to guarantee the free passage of convoys to Suez, saving hundreds of thousands of ship tons. A victorious Torch would open Italy to strategic bombing and eventual invasion. The conversation ranged over a series of other questions, including Cunningham's assessment of likely French reactions in Algeria and Tunisia to Torch. Smith assured the admiral that once Torch had been decided on, it enjoyed the full support of Marshall and Eisenhower. They then discussed command relations. Smith thought there must be an overall naval commander and inquired as to Cunningham's interest in the appointment. An old sea dog like Cunningham—he had joined the Royal Navy three years after Smith's birth—hated being lashed to a desk in Washington; he would like nothing better than to serve under Eisenhower back in his old stomping grounds.[56]

Smith also wanted to escape his Washington desk. Ostensibly, Marshall kept Smith around to coach the new member of the JCS, ADM William Leahy. For five months Marshall worked on Roosevelt, trying to get him to appoint a JCS chairman, but the president always refused. Immediately after Pearl Harbor, his political opponents pressured Roosevelt for MacArthur's appointment as chief of staff. But Roosevelt did not intend to surrender any of his presidential prerogatives as commander in chief, especially to MacArthur. Citing Civil War precedent, Roosevelt flatly refused any appointment of a single uniformed commander in

chief. In the initial JCS meetings, Marshall found himself in the embarrassing position of acting as ex officio chairman. He felt compromised
when troublesome issues arose between the army and the navy. Marshall
decided army policy but felt constrained to push the issue. When Marshall raised the question with the president, Roosevelt answered, "Why?
You are my Chief of Staff." At the end of February Marshall enlisted
Stimson's aid. Marshall considered Leahy a good choice as chairman of
the JCS and chief of staff for the president as opposite number to Ismay
at the CCS level.[57] In his view, after Stark's departure in March, Leahy
would balance the two army representatives. At the CCS level, Arnold
stood as a coequal, but in the War Department, he remained subordinate to Marshall. Marshall knew Leahy's reputation for integrity and for
his ability to get along with the army as CNO on the Joint Board. Leahy
and the president were old friends.

The president stalled, in part because King opposed the appointment.
King feared that Leahy would preempt his position as principal adviser
to the president on naval matters. Finally Roosevelt concluded that he
needed more direct access to the military councils and, with Marshall
in London, appointed Leahy his chief of staff. In the press release, the
president referred to Leahy as his "leg man." The description horrified
Marshall, who cabled back immediately, ordering the preparation of an
office for Leahy. At the first meeting attended by Leahy, Marshall personally sat the admiral at the head of the table, much to King's irritation.

Marshall wanted Smith to "educate" Leahy and figured it would take
two weeks to get the admiral established.[58] Returning to Washington
from his ambassadorial post in Vichy, Leahy, accustomed to interwar
procedures, seemed disoriented by the tumult in the new JCS structure. Smith acted as Leahy's coadjutor, integrating him into the JCS.
Marshall attached much significance to weaning the admiral away from
White House influence, hoping Leahy would emerge as a power broker
between the JCS and Roosevelt. Leahy harbored no such intention. As
the president's man, Leahy received political guidance from Roosevelt
that he did not always share with the service chiefs. Content to play the
role of spokesman for the president in the JCS, Leahy never actually
tried to act like a chairman, primarily because the president wanted it
that way. The JCS organization never devolved into debilitating interservice bickering because of Marshall's personal standing and King's willingness, when pressured, to compromise. The London conference had
one salutary result. As Smith observed, the contest against the British
brought Marshall and King "very close together," which he considered
"a very good thing."[59]

On 5 August Marshall wired Eisenhower with the news that Smith's association with Leahy and King "has made it impossible for me to go through with [the] original plan." He could not release Smith until the end of August, and maybe not then, and he asked if Eisenhower wanted to choose another officer as his chief of staff. "I consider him exceptionally qualified for service as chief of staff for supreme commander," Eisenhower replied, and would make do until Marshall decided "whether or not to spare him."[60]

Smith had another tutoring task—training his replacement as secretary. Since Smith's appointment as ETO chief of staff, John Deane had understudied him. Because Smith had reinvented the secretary's job, no one would ever live up to his expectations, including Deane. He thought Deane lacking in most regards, but they could not find anyone better.[61]

His original orders had Smith proceeding to London on 1 August. Then Marshall delayed his departure to the middle of August, then the end of August, and then maybe not at all.[62] Smith's jobs educating Leahy and Deane, though important, were not the real reason Marshall retained him. During the first week of August, Dill returned to London for an extended period. This coincided with Churchill and Brooke's departure on a three-week trip to the Middle East and Moscow. Churchill assumed the unenviable chore of telling Stalin there would be no second front in 1942, that the Western powers would execute Torch instead. Dill stood in for Brooke during the CIGS's absence. With Dill out of Washington, Marshall needed Smith's pipeline to the Joint Mission and decided to hold on to Smith at least until the chiefs finalized a decision on Torch.

Leahy told the JCS at the end of July that the president had already firmly decided on Torch. There would be no waiting until mid-September for a decision. This left the American chiefs annoyed. Smith felt distressed at the way the London conference had concluded. "If the correct military decision was to go for TORCH they ought to have said so," he lamented to Dykes. He predicted the political heads would now force an accelerated date for the landings on Eisenhower, further undermining the CCS's standing. Churchill and Roosevelt did press for an early date for Torch, and in the absence of a firm decision, the respective chiefs of staff bodies drifted apart. Smith foresaw troubled waters ahead for Torch planning; with no decision on the two vital questions of where and when to land, the planners in London and Washington could not definitely prepare for any operation.[63]

Influenced by a British joint plan, Eisenhower offered his first "tentative and temporary plan" on 1 August. It called for landings sometime after 30 October as far eastward on the Mediterranean coast as possible, designed to "secure the north shore." Marshall rejected Eisenhower's plan; fearful of Spanish intervention and concerned for the safety of Allied communication lines through Gibraltar, Marshall argued for a "short" drive into the Mediterranean at Oran, coupled with simultaneous landings in French Morocco. Dykes concluded that the American chiefs had developed a case of cold feet. "They are beginning to realize their inexperience in the face of difficulties," he surmised. Marshall had fought long and hard for Sledgehammer, an undertaking that even he considered risky or even a "sacrifice" operation, but now he balked at an ambitious British plan aimed at securing Tunisia. The whole thing left Smith depressed. He anticipated another impasse. Suddenly he became apprehensive about Torch. "He is very set on the idea of cleaning up Japan once we have cleared North Africa," Dykes recorded, "as he does not believe we shall defeat Germany in 1944 if we spread ourselves into a new theatre in North Africa!"[64]

Buffeted by strong winds from both London and Washington, Eisenhower tacked again. On 9 August he offered his first formal plan calling for "approximately simultaneous landings" at Oran and Algiers "inside" the Mediterranean and five to ten days later at Casablanca.[65] The British assured him they could complete the mounting operation by 20 September, bringing forward the target date to 7 October—just two months away. American planners, confronting a worsening supply crisis, thought in terms of 7 November. The problem centered on shipping and naval support. If the U.S. Navy pledged ships, simultaneous landings would be possible, but King refused. On 13 August Eisenhower informed Marshall that King's rebuff "clearly calls for deferment of the Casablanca attack."[66]

Smith grew increasingly irritated. "Planning for TORCH is on a rather hit-and-miss basis," Dykes learned through Smith. "Beetle Smith got very shirty," Dykes reported on 14 August. Other than BG Alfred Gruenther, whom Eisenhower had just made deputy chief of staff, Smith thought that Eisenhower "has not yet got a very strong team." That day Marshall solicited Eisenhower's completely frank view on the odds for a successful Torch. Eisenhower responded that, given the imponderables of Spain and Vichy France, the chances Torch would succeed in occupying Tunis stood at "considerably less than 50 per cent." After talking to Smith, Dykes, in something of a British understatement, observed, "This is certainly one of our difficult periods!"[67]

A week later Eisenhower offered a new plan. Obviously influenced by the British, Eisenhower called for two operations—one commanded by Patton, staged out of the United States and aimed at Oran, and another mounted from the United Kingdom against Algiers and Bône, "with a view to the earliest possible occupation of Tunisia." All the landings would be spearheaded by American troops with British follow-on forces. The target date stood at 15 October.[68]

Eisenhower then executed an about-face, principally because Handy arrived posthaste from Washington voicing Marshall's rejection of Eisenhower's latest plan. On 23 August the CCS received a very pessimistic telegram from Eisenhower. The combination of inadequate naval support, incomplete planning for Patton's task force, the state of training for U.S. forces designated for Torch, and mounting uncertainty about shipping schedules for American materiel meant that the target date had to be pushed back. The new plan, consistent with Marshall's directive of 24 August, called for a drastic reduction in the scope of the landings, limited now to Casablanca and Oran on 7 November. Privately, Eisenhower pleaded for more ground forces and logistical and naval support. The British chiefs concurred with the delay, concluding it was better to wait than risk the enterprise if American forces could not execute a mid-October Torch. In truth, the BCOS accepted the postponement in the hope of applying heat to King. "I fear," Dykes confided to Smith, "we are going to have a lot of difficulty over this business."[69]

The next day, 25 August, the British Mission received a memorandum from the BCOS outlining the scaled-down and delayed plan. "A disastrous day," Dykes thought. This time Smith kept Dykes in the dark, even though they had been talking about the twists and turns in the latest installment of what Eisenhower dubbed the "trans-Atlantic essay contest" only moments before the communication arrived from London. Later, a contrite Smith talked to his friend. Dykes argued that the plan for simultaneous landings in Casablanca and Oran, with the former spot 800 miles from Tunisia, was "hopelessly unsound." Smith made no effort to defend the decision and blamed the situation on the U.S. Navy. "King could produce more naval force if he really got down to it." Faced with a mounting Japanese threat in the Solomon Islands, King said he had no ships to spare. Both Smith and Dykes agreed that since Eisenhower, the BCOS, and the American chiefs could not finalize a plan, their political masters must again intervene.[70]

Churchill returned to London on 24 August. Dismayed by the hesitancy and time wasted, Churchill met with Eisenhower and Clark the next night over dinner and again the following evening. Churchill wanted Torch carried out at the earliest date and on the largest scale possible, with ambitious objectives. Churchill discounted American apprehensions: Spain would do nothing, the French would offer negligible resistance, and the Germans would confine their reaction to seizing Tunisia—all of which proved remarkably accurate. Tunisia was the key; an attack on Casablanca amounted to a huge diversion of scarce Allied strength in an operation that was probably undoable because of prevailing surf conditions. Dismayed by the timidity of the service chiefs, the prime minister pressed Eisenhower to assert his command authority. He should attack in mid-October with all available means at whatever sites he determined. Churchill wanted operations as far east as possible "so as to have at least a fighting chance of gaining Tunisia." He signaled his willingness to jettison Bône and Philippeville but would "go it alone" if need be to take Algiers. Despite having just returned from a journey of 15,600 miles, Churchill proposed to jump a plane to Washington to win the necessary backing.[71]

Leahy prevailed on Smith to decipher the intent of Churchill's offer. Other than the obvious—the prime minister circumventing the service chiefs by pressuring Eisenhower directly—Smith recognized the impossible position Eisenhower confronted whether he accepted or refused Churchill's proposition. In either case, rather than enhancing his command authority, Eisenhower would subordinate his military judgment in the eyes of both camps.[72] Smith need not have worried; Eisenhower had no intention of succumbing to Churchill's siren song.

"Beetle tells me that on present form the President is likely to stand fast and not produce more naval forces for TORCH," Dykes remarked on 27 August. "It certainly looks as if the whole thing is going to be a flop."[73] The next day the president met with the service chiefs before the regularly scheduled CCS meeting. As Smith related, they had it out on Torch. The British were right; the American had developed a case of cold feet. They refused to risk landings deep in the Mediterranean for fear "of being cut off inside," with the resultant public backlash. Unless limited to Oran and Casablanca, and unless the attacks were performed simultaneously, the Americans would withdraw from the agreement. Similarly, without at least Algiers, the British saw no compelling reason to proceed. All depended on the U.S. Navy's finding additional ships, and King stated clearly that, without orders, he would move no naval forces from the Pacific in support of Torch. "One strong man with a small brain has sabotaged the whole system," Dykes's diary read. "Beetle and I feel low about it all." That day Churchill also forwarded a letter to Roosevelt containing the same offer he had made to Eisenhower: the British would drop their advocacy for landings at Bône and Philippeville but insisted on Algiers. "Beetle told me King was prepared to produce one battleship but nothing more. We must wait in patience for the President's reply to the PM, but meantime valuable days slip by." As Dykes pithily recorded, "These are grim and anxious days."[74]

On 30 August the president offered his rejoinder. The coalition possessed enough strength for only two landings, and "under any circumstances one of our landings must be on the Atlantic." The initial landings, composed exclusively of American ground forces, should take place no later than 30 October—before the midterm elections.[75] Roosevelt held out hope the French would rally to the Allied cause, which would mean Algeria would fall into their lap without the need to take Algiers and points east.

Eisenhower bemoaned the stress and uncertainty of the past six weeks and longed for a definite decision. As Dykes put it, "I am awfully sorry for Eisenhower—he *has* been buggered about."[76] But a definite decision suddenly appeared to be in the offing. On 1 September Churchill cabled Roosevelt, offering a horse trade—Casablanca for Algiers. This set off a commotion in Washington, and Beetle Smith found himself in the middle of it.

With Dill still in London, the Smith-Dykes partnership took on added significance. Accustomed to brokering deals and working the system, they went to town. Smith showed Dykes copies of the first exchanges between Churchill and Roosevelt received earlier that morning. Then another cable arrived from the BCOS signaling some movement. As Dykes told a British colleague, Smith "went into action hard." The president called a meeting of the service chiefs for five o'clock that evening. Smith hastened to both the War and Navy Departments, briefing the chiefs and their senior staff on the details of the British offer. When Marshall, Arnold, and King arrived at the White House, they had had time to mull over their options. Dykes firmly believed that without Smith's salesmanship, the service chiefs would have come to the president cold and, confronted with Churchill's telegram and its demand for urgent action, probably "would have played [it] safe." At 6:30 Smith rushed in with news that the JCS had agreed to the deal and were currently working on a draft reply for the president's signature, specifying the level of U.S. commitments to the respective landings at Casablanca, Oran, and Algiers. One hurdle remained: the White House had never furnished them with a copy of the prime minister's cables. Marshall told Smith to get his hands on them. While Smith stood at Dykes's desk, a new telegram arrived from London. Smith carried the relevant documents to the JCS and then returned, showing Dykes a copy of the draft reply. Dykes expressed his concern that the allocation of forces—weighted too heavily in Casablanca—tied Eisenhower's hands. Smith assured him that was not the intention. Dykes then sat down and composed an account of all Smith had told him for the BCOS, including his assurance that the force structure ceilings remained negotiable. "Beetle has been an *enormous* help over all this business," Dykes noted. After Dykes dispatched his communication to London, Beetle invited him home for dinner and cooked up some chop suey. "Very good too. They are a grand couple," Dykes decided.[77]

The celebration proved premature. They were not out of the woods just yet. The U.S. Navy had never provided planners in London or Washington with precise details of the naval forces available for Torch, which effectively precluded any realistic planning, and King continued his stonewalling. Even the naval planners in the combined staff in Washington remained "completely in the dark as to what US naval forces are to be provided." Dykes spoke for many: King "is an old shit—he simply won't play at all."[78] Naval estimates offered only one roadblock. As Dykes expected, the BCOS reacted negatively to the margin of safety built into the Casablanca operation at the expense of the landings inside the Mediterranean. Smith guaranteed that this was more apparent than real. The American chiefs, wary of Churchill's influence on Eisenhower, insisted on the imbalance.

A new set of essays crisscrossed the Atlantic, igniting another frenzy in Washington. The British pleaded for adjustments in the force allocations; Eisenhower asked for specific details of U.S. Navy promises. At the BCOS's urging, Eisenhower suggested that either he or Clark, together with Admirals Bertram Ramsay and Mountbatten, come to Washington for conclusive talks to finalize the decision on the apportioning of forces. Cunningham, slated as commander of all naval forces in the Mediterranean, received instructions to remain in Washington. Marshall told Eisenhower that he need not come to Washington, instead offering to dispatch Smith to London. Finally the president weighed in, arbitrating settlements to both questions.[79] On scaling back troop and lift levels for Casablanca in favor of Algiers, Roosevelt reacted positively to the British requests. As for King, he called the admiral to the White House for a conference. As Stimson had observed during a similar episode in June, King "is firm and brave outside of the White House but as soon as he gets in the presence of the President he crumbles up."[80] Once again, the admiral crumbled. By the evening of 4 September, King had drafted a memorandum for the president detailing the substantial U.S. Navy commitment to Torch. The tempest passed, but it left jangled nerves in its wake.

With Torch settled, Marshall decided the time had come to cut Smith loose. As their partnership was about to end, Dykes and Smith performed a postmortem on all that had transpired since January. Both expressed grave concerns for the immediate future. The combined chiefs and theater supreme command structures—the fruits of Arcadia—had been abject failures to date. As evidenced by recent events, all the key decisions devolved to the political heads. "The President is now dictating Eisenhower's plan. The PM," they concluded, "is giving plenty of advice too—poor old Ike!" Dykes wondered about the wisdom of proceeding with the same arrangements. "I think we should be very ill-advised ever to try and repeat this performance but God only knows how we shall ever do a combined ROUNDUP. It would strain good will on both sides to the utmost."[81] Smith could not worry about that. He had spent the last eight months toiling at the combined and joint levels; now he headed toward an uncertain future as chief of staff to a theater supreme commander. His mission would involve whipping Eisenhower's combined and joint staff into shape. If that did not come to pass—and with invaluable time frittered away—Torch would fail and draw down the curtain on Walter Bedell Smith's career.

Part Four

★★★★

The Mediterranean Campaign

15

"Smith Will Save Ike"

At nine o'clock on the morning on 6 September, Nory and Dykes saw "dear old Beetle" off on his flight. Dykes took Nory back to Fort Myer and stayed for a cup of coffee. "She feels his leaving very much," Dykes wrote.[1] Smith doubtlessly felt it too, but a great deal else occupied his mind. With no time for decompressing after the intense pressure of the last few weeks, Smith probably felt like he had jumped from the frying pan into the fire. "This is the first assignment during my service that has frightened me a little," he confided in his old mentor Moseley, "and I hope that General Eisenhower will not be disappointed in his choice."[2] During the long passage he slept only fitfully. In addition to being worked up worrying about what awaited him in London, his stomach issues returned with a vengeance.

It is not known what instructions, if any, Marshall gave Smith before he left Washington. Nobody predicted Eisenhower would command the first combined Allied offensive. He went to London to shake up the headquarters and push Bolero; in the event the coalition staged Sledgehammer, Eisenhower might act as Marshall's deputy. Initially Marshall agreed to Smith's appointment to ETO because he saw it as an investment; Smith probably would have served as his chief of staff. All this changed with the Torch decision. Marshall clung to the hope that "the vicissitudes of war" might revive the cross-Channel operation and prompt his going to London as supreme commander.[3] Although no one admitted it, the scale of the Dieppe disaster proved beyond any doubt the unpreparedness of Allied forces for undertaking any large-scale cross-Channel operation in 1942. Finally on 22 August, Marshall admitted the inadvisability of Sledgehammer. Still Roosevelt balked at announcing Eisenhower's appointment, and he never did until the landings. With Marshall out of the picture, the big command fell to Eisenhower. Now Marshall's priorities shifted toward buttressing Eisenhower. The "trans-Atlantic essay contest" fixed two concerns in Marshall's mind: Eisenhower's hesitancy and his susceptibility to British pressure. Nor had Eisenhower sorted out the command and staff mess—the original reason for his dispatch to London. Evidence accumulated at the end of August that the inadequacies of the American staffs in England might force a postponement of the North African operation. Even if Marshall never specified Beetle's assignment, Smith knew he faced a daunting set of tasks: buck up Eisenhower, resist British influence, and whip the American headquarters structure into shape.

"We're in a Bit of a Tailspin"

One thing Smith need not have fretted about was the reception he would receive from Eisenhower. For two months Eisenhower had grasped the nettle, worried that Marshall might never sacrifice Smith. Indeed, Eisenhower had been "buggered about," and Marshall had done much of the buggering. Marshall's insistence on no slacking in preparations for Roundup "so long as there remains any reasonable possibility of its successful execution before July 1943" meant that, until 22 August, Eisenhower oversaw three separate headquarters—ETO, the combined Torch staff, and a planning staff for Roundup. As he complained to Patton, "I feel like the lady in the circus that has to ride three horses with no very good idea of exactly where any one of the three is going to go."[4] Pulled in different directions, he experienced maddening bouts of indecision. As his letters indicated, Eisenhower increasingly fell prey to a growing sense of insecurity in his relations with Marshall. In part, this stemmed from the fact that Marshall always treated Eisenhower as his executive officer. Eisenhower immersed himself in the details of his command and chafed under the burden of his heavy responsibilities and crushing schedule. Marshall and the JCS's insistence on Casablanca and French Morocco sacrificed the strategic advantages of landings deep in the Mediterranean, threatening yet another impasse with the British and exposing Eisenhower to the countervailing pressures exerted by Churchill. In truth, Eisenhower never entirely bought Torch. In common with other senior American officers, he saw Torch as a "political" operation. From Washington came demoralizing predictions of failure. Handy told him on 23 August that from a strictly military viewpoint, Torch involved an "unjustifiable hazard and should be abandoned entirely or revised and directed toward a less ambitious objective."[5] At the same time, word broke hard about the worsening supply crisis. Uncertain of his position, his relations with his superiors, and Torch itself, Eisenhower's trademark optimism eroded; he experienced problems curbing his furious temper. Irritable and depressed, he grew more irascible and remote.

Eisenhower despaired at Marshall's delay in sending Smith. In the middle of May the British voiced serious disquiet over Eisenhower's haphazard approach to organizing the combined headquarters. The BCOS complained of the "lack of a strong guiding hand," someone to "sort out the tangle and . . . set people on the right road." They could not do it; "it must be done by Eisenhower."[6] But Eisenhower demonstrated no willingness to crack heads. Both Eisenhower and Clark saw the combined staff primarily as a planning agency. Eisenhower expected that Smith would flesh out and organize the full staff, and at the end of July he requested Marshall to direct Smith to select the officers he wanted as heads of the general and special staffs. Nothing came of that while Smith remained in Washington.[7] On 11 August a disheartened Eisenhower fled the office for a drive in the country. "Ike ruminated over the likelihood that Marshall will not permit Beadle [*sic*] to leave Washington," Eisenhower's Boswell, Harry Butcher, recorded, "thus depriving us of a crackerjack chief of staff."[8] Not only did Marshall retain Smith, but he also delayed dispatching American planners from the joint and combined planning committees. On 24 August Dill returned to London for talks with the BCOS. Eisenhower drove out to the airport with one purpose in mind: to plead for Dill's intercession with Marshall on releasing Smith. Dill remained evasive, telling Eisenhower it would constitute "a great sacrifice for [Smith] to be taken away" from the CCS.[9] "We're in a bit of a tailspin," Ike told Mamie on 26 August, "and we're not going to get out of it completely until Bedell gets here."[10]

The next day Eisenhower hit bottom. "Ike ate alone at the flat," Butcher noted, "*perturbed about the uncertainties and changes already made or completed* in his first and his country's biggest prospective action in this war." Whenever Eisenhower experienced one of his "oh, what the hell" days, he withdrew into himself and spent time writing to family members, friends back in Kansas, and old acquaintances in the army. "One of the worst things about high military rank is the loneliness that it imposes on the individual," he wrote to Charlie Harger in Abilene. "Right this minute nothing could give me more pleasure than to drop into Joner Callahan's for a morning Coke with the gang." To Moseley he lamented about his helplessness in unraveling the organizational Gordian knot created by placement of the SOS within his theater and combined headquarters, the "same problems that plagued you a quarter of a century ago," he noted. "It is not the problem itself that always presents the greatest difficulties," he continued, "it is the trouble one has in finding people of sufficient caliber to tackle the job intelligently. I get exceedingly weary of the little people that spend their time worrying about promotion, personal prestige, prerogatives and so on, rather than forgetting everything in the desire to get on with the work." He longed for "the man that can really do a job without eternal supervision." To BG Vernon Prichard, his classmate and a star quarterback, Eisenhower expressed his constant astonishment at "the utter lack of imaginative thinking among so many of our people that have reputations for being really good officers." He pointed to the practice of appointing officers "based upon a number of unimportant factors—among which, personal propinquity, wild guesses, school records, past acquaintanceship, and a number of others, of which few really search down into the depths of character." Eisenhower's command style depended on delegated authority; despite glittering reputations, officers such as Clark and Lee failed to produce the results Eisenhower demanded. He saw in Smith the man who could do the job without interminable direction, and he agonized over Marshall's delays.[11]

As Eisenhower told Marshall on 5 September, "the past six weeks have been the most trying of my life."[12] In the first week of September, the veil of gloom suddenly lifted. For the first time in weeks, Eisenhower could look beyond the strain, uncertainty, and tension that gripped him; a definite decision emerged on Torch, and word finally came that Smith was on his way. At long last he could set his sights on Torch, although the long period of "fence-sitting" made time desperately short.[13] Despite the many tasks demanding his attention, Eisenhower drove out to Hendon airfield and collected Smith and, together with Butcher, ferried him to Telegraph Cottage, Eisenhower's secluded country estate in Surrey, twenty-five miles outside London near Kingston-on-Thames.

"His square jaw and deeply dimpled chin indicate his character," Butcher remarked of Smith; he was "tough in action with the staff but delightfully informal off duty." Butcher never altered his assessment of the "official" Smith, but over time he found Beetle less and less a delight. After dinner, Ike and Beetle sat before a fire and talked. Eisenhower enjoyed getting out of London and into the countryside; Telegraph Cottage served as a retreat in more than one sense. Eisenhower liked kicking back, downing a couple of drinks, and chatting casually. And he and Beetle had a great deal to discuss.[14]

Smith shared with Eisenhower all the inside poop on what had transpired in the War Department, CCS meetings, and the White House over the last six weeks. Now that a decision had finally emerged, both expressed their relief and determination to get down to the nitty-gritty of planning the North African operation and pondered what turn grand strategy might take after Torch. Smith said the coalition leadership must surmount their fumbling over strategy if they sought any real advantage from operations in North Africa. The new CCS directive called for the complete annihilation of Axis forces in North Africa; both agreed that Torch ruled out any 1943 cross-Channel invasion.

The conversation turned to the political aspects of Torch. The two decried that military decisions must conform to the currents of public opinion. Smith conveyed the president's assurances that Vichy officials in Morocco and Algeria would actively support the American invasion. "The President will handle the political angles of TORCH with the French," Butcher recorded Smith as saying, "and he's a master." Smith had recently talked to Robert Murphy, the president's special representative in French Northwest Africa and a man Smith held in high regard, who guaranteed that key civil and military officials in Casablanca and Algeria would come over to the Allies. Smith declared confidently that Torch "will be a pushover."[15]

Eisenhower expressed his irritation with the "one man navy" and King's continual delays in committing to Torch.[16] Smith defended the admiral. King juggled a number of demands—escorts for convoys to Murmansk and for vital bauxite shipments from Brazil, setbacks in night surface actions against the Japanese in the Solomons, and anxieties over naval construction. Eisenhower vaguely spoke of the supply crisis. From Eisenhower's opaque communications from London, Smith had already guessed the depth of the supply problem and sensed it was much worse than Eisenhower indicated. Somervell dispatched his two top assistants to England and charged them with getting to the bottom of the logistics troubles. As Smith soon discovered, supply dictated everything. Eisenhower assured him—taking his lead from Churchill—"come hell or high water" he would attack with whatever he could scrape together and not "whine to the War Department."

Their discussion turned to less pressing matters. They talked about Marshall and the great debt both men owed him. Smith pointed to Marshall's quirks, such as his poor memory, especially for names. Chiefly they marveled at his ability to maintain his equipoise in the storm. Smith mentioned that he expected to receive his second star soon, not knowing that Eisenhower had been pushing for his promotion for weeks.[17]

The fire and the alcohol made Smith dozy, so they took a stroll. They headed toward an adjacent golf course, a feature of any Eisenhower residence. As they walked, Eisenhower got down to brass tacks, explaining what he expected from Smith. Initially Eisenhower planned to place Smith in charge of the ETO staff, but with Torch now set, his thinking changed. Over the preceding month, the center of gravity had shifted from ETO to the combined staff. The scarcity of high-level American staff officers obliged Eisenhower and Clark to move their best officer talent from the ETO to the Torch staff; in many cases, officers held dual appointments on both staffs. Eisenhower wanted Smith to wear two hats—to double in brass, in army jargon—as chief of staff at both headquarters. Eisenhower made a number of points crystal clear. He insisted on a chief of staff "who could direct the organization as a *real* executive," relieving Eisenhower of the headaches of organizing and staffing the headquarters and the mountain of detailed work that went with it. Interestingly, Eisenhower insisted on controlling his headquarters but fled bureaucratic responsibilities. Eisenhower saw no need to issue any directive specifying Smith's authority. Since no "book" existed prescribing the authorities of a chief of staff in a combined headquarters, Eisenhower would grant Smith whatever powers he required. Command relationships and interservice and genuine Allied cooperation had not yet crystallized; Eisenhower would hammer out a solution to the first challenge and expected Smith to handle the second.[18] As commander in chief he insisted on exercising his right to fashion his headquarters as he pleased, and Smith must guard against higher authorities dictating the details of organizational structures. And as theater and supreme commander, Eisenhower would exercise control through the combined headquarters.[19] He asked for Smith's opinion. Even though he had no real knowledge of the internal problems or requirements confronting either headquarters, Smith never voiced any concerns about the dual chief of staff solution and thought it best to shake the slackness out of ETO first; once he got it running smoothly, then he would shift over and assume direction of the Torch staff. Eisenhower agreed.[20] Eisenhower's views—on the relationship between a commander and his chief of staff and on staff organization—remained hard and fast for the duration of the war.

The Supply Fubar

Smith retired early but could not sleep. At 4 A.M. he heard the crowing of a cock pheasant, piquing the interest of the hunter in him. Roaming the pines and rhododendrons that highlighted the ten-acre tract, Smith checked out the hunting prospects. Butcher got up around seven and, while brewing coffee, spied their houseguest emerging from the tree line. After breakfast, Smith accompanied Eisenhower to ETO headquarters.

The chief of staff at work. A typical shot of Smith—at his desk, pen in hand, glasses and spent cigarettes at his side. The bulldog face and razor-sharp creases in his shirt speak to his personality.

The buzz in headquarters centered entirely on the looming supply fubar.[21] With the target date for loading ships for Torch only three weeks away, SOS possessed no firm handle on what supplies and equipment were in hand. The day Smith arrived, Eisenhower forwarded a communication to the War Department, less a whine than a plea: "US stocks on hand in the UK are not balanced," he began. "Time for unloading, sorting, cataloging, and for subsequent boxing, crating, marking and loading simply does not exist. In certain cases therefore, some of our requests will involve items that the SOS in Washington will correctly state have already been shipped here in ample quantity." Somervell handsomely responded, "Give *no* thought to our questioning duplications. Whatever you ask for will be produced if it is within our power to produce it."[22] He made that assurance before seeing the request. On 8 September COL Everett Hughes, the SOS chief of staff, submitted the long-awaited inventory of missing requirements. The catalog left staffs on both sides of the Atlantic astonished. The request took fourteen foolscap pages and 3,000 words enumerating the 244,000 ship tons of missing stocks.[23]

The mounting of Torch exposed the U.S. Army's unpreparedness in meeting the organizational demands of modern war. Bolero suffered from confusion and false starts; matters only got worse after the Torch decision. The scarcity of trained SOS officers, cadre, and men in the port reception centers and depots produced the biggest headache. To greatly complicate matters, ETO and SOS lost their best senior people to the Torch staff.[24] Earlier, Somervell's office had directed that the priority was sending service troops to the United Kingdom and putting in place the necessary infrastructure and basic facilities for receiving, inventorying, and storing the vast quantity of materiel that would eventually flood the theater. Marshall and OPD saw things differently. Since ground combat and air force training required twice as long as that for service troops, the War Department decided to expand AGF and AAF at the expense of ASF. Based on the April 1942 troop basis, ASF's proportion of the manpower allocation stood at a paltry 11.8 percent. With service and support units already in critically short supply in the corps areas, few remained available for overseas deployment. Even though the revised troop basis increased the SOS manpower ratio to 26 percent, the service units assigned to the United Kingdom remained undertrained, and as late as the end of September, the SOS component in ETO represented only 21 percent. Officers and men learned their jobs through trial and error, and there were plenty of both.

ETO/SOS and ASF did not talk the same language. None of the

troop bases or shipping schedules tallied; ASF confessed complete mystification over ETO requirements and requisitions. No agency synchronized the movement of manpower and logistics support. As substance for his advocacy of Sledgehammer, Marshall rushed inadequately trained and equipped ground and air units to the United Kingdom. Troop ships, grouped into fast convoys, arrived far in advance of slow-moving cargo vessels. The hasty movement of ground and air forces precluded the preshipment of weapons. In the first half of 1942, the available lift capacity of the Allied pool of shipping exceeded Bolero requirements. Somervell took advantage of this situation by loading ships "full and down," cramming holds with all available supplies while paying scant attention to balancing requirements. From July, the situation reversed. With time now at a premium, demands for Torch equipment and supplies exceeded lift by 600 percent. ASF accelerated the flow of materiel from the New York port of embarkation by continuing the "full and down" practice on the "first available ships." The army categorized materiel and supplies into classes. ASF set the shipping schedule for Class II (clothing, weapons, and vehicles), Class IV (heavy engineering materials), and Class V (ammunition) supplies based on automatic supply tables, not requisitions from Lee's command. The Transportation Corps—formed only on 1 July, and operating without standard procedures or even manuals—controlled the movement of all materiel and supplies throughout the entire supply chain from New York through the British ports to their assigned SOS depots. Transportation Corps officers drove up tonnages leaving New York, paying little heed to the specifics of what they shipped. New York struggled to meet the monthly targets by class but made only casual efforts, in the case of Class II supplies, to distinguish between types of weapons or vehicles. Shiploads were cut arbitrarily, inventories mixed, and records lost. Ship manifests arrived late if at all, and with rare exception, they bore no resemblance to the cargoes arriving in the United Kingdom. Ships entered British waters in convoys but landed at separate ports. The inadequately trained and undermanned SOS units nearly drowned in the deluge of materiel pouring into the United Kingdom. Owing to critical shipping shortages, ships never lingered in British ports. Unloaded in haste, increasingly by civilian stevedores, the mostly uninventoried supply stockpiles ended up in small warehouses and open storage areas scattered throughout the SOS command. Little time existed for proper record keeping and status reports. Inevitably, huge stocks went missing in the labyrinth of SOS installations.[25]

Critical shortages left units unprepared for active operations. The logisticians reported on 4 September that ETO and SOS could not supply the 55,000 American troops assigned to the Central Task Force in Torch from stocks in the United Kingdom. American forces in North Africa must depend on supplies shipped directly from the United States.[26] Two days later Lee warned that shipping limitations might require reductions in both troop basis and supply levels for the operation.[27]

The story of the First Division best illustrates this. The "Big Red One," the first major ground unit moved to the United Kingdom in early August, arrived without its weapons, vehicles, and most other categories of equipment. On 17 August Marshall wired that "a sizeable portion of 1st Division [men and equipment] left New York" ten days earlier. The War Department's assurance that the ships would arrive in three days' time conflicted with information available in London, which indicated that most of the division's ordnance and heavy equipment remained in New York. Eisenhower replied to Marshall, "1st Division equipment is still on the ocean with some not yet shipped." Under existing circumstances, Eisenhower wrote, First Division would not receive equipment in time to permit its training in amphibious warfare, so "the target date [for the landings] may have to be set back."[28] The month ended with no sign of the missing supplies. As Eisenhower informed Handy on 31 August, as matters stood, there was "no hope of the 1st Division being able to take part in a major expedition from UK."[29] The division began training by borrowing artillery from the British, a source of considerable embarrassment.[30] On 3 September the chief of the Transportation Corps reported that First Division's "stuff" would not arrive for another ten days. The next day a vexed Eisenhower told OPD that the delay in equipping the division would "become a determining factor in fixing date of attack."[31] A few days later, Clark told Hughes that unless he fixed the problem quickly, First Division "will be going in virtually with their bare hands."[32]

Hearing all this must have made the drained Smith wilt even more. Clark placed the blame squarely on Lee and his organization. Officially, Eisenhower backed away from faulting Lee. He told Handy the supply emergency existed "due to conditions beyond the control of the SOS."[33] Privately, Eisenhower could only put the sting on Lee. Preoccupied with settling Torch, Eisenhower, who typically paid scant attention to supply matters, only belatedly realized the seriousness of the escalating crisis. Now Torch hinged not on the French reaction or Spanish intervention or the high surf off the Moroccan coast but on whether the American supply problems would force a postponement, modification, or even cancellation of the operation. Too exhausted to accompany Eisenhower and Clark to 10 Downing Street for one of the prime minister's dinners and debating sessions, Smith retired early in Eisenhower's town flat. Butcher was not around to record how well he slept. No doubt he had visions of Lee dancing in his head.

Smith assumed duties as ETO chief of staff on 8 September. The next day he began settling in, spending most of it in discussions with his predecessor, BG John Dahlquist. Before lunch, he and Clark met with Eisenhower. Smith took the bull by the horns—in this case, the bull being Lee. The night before, Churchill had pressed for an accelerated Torch. Eisenhower had begged off, telling the prime minister the acute logistics shortages required a delay of four days, to 8 November. As Eisenhower, Clark, and Smith well knew, the supply predicament might well push the date back even further. The British expected the new commander of their Eighth Army, LTG Bernard Montgomery, to open a major offensive against Rommel around 22 October. To reap real strategic benefit, Torch could not be delayed long. If the Americans could not answer the bell, the strategic and political consequences of their failure would be incalculable. And failure loomed as a real possibility. Smith argued, backed by Clark, for putting the fire to Lee. Eisenhower could only agree.[34]

John Clifford Hodges Lee was no lightweight. Raised by a widowed mother and two aunts in Junction City, Kansas, the post town of Fort Riley, Lee graduated from West Point in 1909 and entered the Engineers. He boasted an outstanding record in France; he rose to colonel and served on the staff of two divisions, first as the intelligence and operations officer and then as acting chief of staff. In the process he won the Distinguished Service Medal and Silver Star. Another bright young engineer served on Lee's staff with the Eighty-ninth Division: Somervell. In the opinion of Hughes, Johnny Lee was a "queer duck."[35] He was not alone in that assessment. Lee's friends called him Johnny or Cliff, but he carried a number of less flattering nicknames. Known as "Courthouse" because of his frequent volunteering to serve on courts-martial earlier in his career, the imperious Lee impressed fellow officers as a strange admixture of religiosity and pomposity. An intensely devout man, he worshipped daily and twice on Sundays, obliging his subordinates to join him. Behind his back they called him "Jesus Christ Himself," a play on his initials. Obsessed with preserving the outward signs of efficiency and military protocol, Lee rigorously enforced codes of discipline and dress, insisting that everything be "spit and polish." He had already taken to traveling around his domain in a private train. Although Lee capably shouldered an immense workload, his formidable manner and appearance, tactless exercise of authority, and jealous defense of his position made him a target of criticism. He produced results but also animosity.

Eisenhower backed off censuring Lee for a number of reasons. First and foremost, he could ill afford to antagonize Somervell—at this juncture, the last person he wanted to provoke. For two months Eisenhower sang the praises of Lee. Upon assuming command, Eisenhower complained that his faltering headquarters lacked confidence. The one officer who impressed him was Lee, who had "his whole gang going at top speed."[36] Eisenhower told Somervell of his great fortune at having "a man of Lee's ability."[37] In July Eisenhower considered Lee "one of the finest officers in the Army."[38] In mid-August he nominated Lee as his "executive deputy" in ETO "to handle matters in his own name." He told the War Department he "consider[ed] General Lee by far the best qualified" to be his successor as ETO commander.[39] Now Eisenhower faced the prospect of making Lee the fall guy; it all rang rather hollow. Another factor lay behind Lee's difficulties that Eisenhower never acknowledged: his own refusal to weld together the administrative and supply side of ETO.

Eisenhower possessed fixed ideas on how a headquarters should operate. He frequently told people he had served longer stretches on staff duty than anybody else in the U.S. Army and needed no instruction on how a staff should be organized and run. In truth, Eisenhower possessed no special knowledge of headquarters functions, never having spent any appreciable time in a senior staff billet; instead, he had spent most of his career as somebody else's executive officer. Eisenhower and Lee flew to London together at the end of May. Part of Eisenhower's job involved assessing Chaney's failures in restructuring ETO. On 14 May Marshall ordered Chaney to reorganize the London headquarters "along the general pattern of a command post with a minimum of supply and administrative services. All of these services will be grouped under . . . SOS." Theater organization should parallel the restructured War Department, meaning that ETO should feature three strong commands for ground, air, and supply.[40] No doubt Eisenhower and Lee dissected the organizational issue during the long flight.

It became common currency that Somervell had engineered Lee's appointment. In fact, Somervell apologized for "inflicting this job" on Lee, telling him he "wouldn't wish such a job on such a good friend." In 1941 Lee had commanded the Second Infantry Division. Clark, as AGF chief of staff, recommended Lee as the ideal choice for pushing through Bolero. Initially Lee balked, but he backed down when Marshall and Stimson insisted he accept the new assignment in London. Marshall granted Lee a mandate "to take all measures . . . necessary and appropriate to expedite and prosecute the procurement, reception, processing, forwarding, and delivery of personnel, equipment, and supplies" for the buildup in Europe.[41] As commanding general of SOS, Lee held responsibilities equivalent to a corps area commander in the Zone of the Interior. Since Marshall's reorganization left ASF outside the strategic and operational decision loop, Somervell instructed Lee to forge a functionally organized, semiautonomous SOS command inside the theater's highest headquarters. He reasoned that whatever headquarters structure emerged in ETO would influence staff organizations in other theaters. When he arrived in London on 24 May, Lee "carried with him the SOS organizational set-up," complete with a control division and a chief of administrative services.[42]

Chaney's reaction exactly mirrored the sentiment of virtually all senior line officers, including Eisenhower. The artificial elevation of a detached administrative and supply command to a coordinate rather than subordinate status in the headquarters hierarchy appeared "revolutionary" and therefore highly dangerous. A separate SOS command violated prewar concepts of staff organization and command responsibilities; a subordinate officer could not exercise control over any general staff functions.[43] Chaney clung to the "book" linear command system, which assigned a general full authority over all matters in his "territorial" command. Although an airman, he fought a bitter and eventually losing four-month-long rearguard action against the air force's assertion of semiautonomous standing, especially over supply. Chaney denied his classmate Lee the authority necessary to carry out the reorganization. While Marshall's directive instructed that Chaney maintain only a "skeleton [personal] staff," it also provided him with an escape clause: "the organization prescribed . . . need not be slavishly followed."[44] Had Marshall issued a firm directive and vigorously enforced it, the administrative history of the U.S. Army in World War II would have been much different, but he chose not to.

For two weeks an acrimonious contest raged between Chaney and Lee, consuming the attention of much of the staff. In the end, a compromise emerged: Chaney's headquarters retained direction of the administrative branches, while SOS controlled the technical and supply services.[45] Lee decided later in June to move SOS headquarters to Cheltenham, 125 miles northwest of London. Cheltenham provided Lee better access to his bases sections, but SOS's physical separation from ETO created yet another serious obstacle to cooperation. Instead of conserving scarce staff officers, the structure increased the drain; staffs became top-heavy with colonels, many of them serving in liaison capacities between ETO in London and SOS in Cheltenham. Divided authority resulted in overlapping and conflicting jurisdictions between ETO and SOS and within the respective staffs. ETO and SOS submitted separate requisitions to ASF; the technical and service chiefs did likewise, employing their own channels back to the bureaus in Washington. The services and supply chiefs both in Washington and in theater resented reorganization in any form and jealously defended their command statuses, old operating procedures, and control of their staffs. The wedding of manpower (an ETO function) with weapons and equipment (an SOS responsibility) presented difficulties in June; the flood of men and materiel in July and August overwhelmed the bifurcated structure.

None of this surprised Somervell. Before Eisenhower left Washington for ETO, the ASF chief had pulled him aside, warning that "one of the major encumbrances, if not the major encumbrance, upon the progress of the American Expeditionary Forces in France in 1917–1918 lay in bad organizational control of its SOS, and particularly in its being forced to adopt an organization radically different from that existing in the War Department."[46] Lee never tired of using the same analogy. As Eisenhower related to Butcher, "the same issue kept coming up throughout the last war and remains a tough one. There is no perfect solution." Eisenhower's answer involved relying on personalities, not organizational innovations. The discord between ETO and SOS resulted in Chaney's firing, and Eisenhower, though troubled by the inadequacies of the organization, never intervened. Ignoring Marshall's 14 May "instructions" and the dictates of the new field manual, and not knowing what to do, Eisenhower did nothing and simply preserved Chaney's defective divided authority.[47] "In General Lee," Butcher recorded at the time, "Ike felt he had one of the finest officers in the Army and a man who had the best possible qualifications for a job that requires a high degree of human understanding." He now had plenty of reasons to rue that hasty supposition.[48]

Even if Eisenhower proved open to the issue of reorganization—and he was not—little time remained. For Eisenhower, the problem resided in Lee's failure to master the mounting operation. Smith required no prompting taking the lead; he came to London to stir things up and stiffen Eisenhower. On 10 September he drafted a scorching aide-mémoire that Eisenhower signed and forwarded to Lee. It contained the first peremptory order Lee received: "Your basic mission is so to operate the Services of Supply in this theater as to insure adequate support of the American Expeditionary Force now being prepared in the United

Kingdom." Lee should delegate all routine administrative tasks to a subordinate "while you personally devote your attention to the primary mission." Lee would submit daily written reports to Clark, outlining steps taken to deal with the crisis.[49]

Eisenhower activated Allied Force Headquarters (AFHQ) on 12 September, with Smith as chief of staff. Smith immediately directed that chief administrative officer MG Humphrey Gale, the senior British logistician in the headquarters, undertake a survey to answer two questions: the extent to which SOS could support its initial supply requirements, and how much was needed from external agencies to compensate for the deficiencies. Smith made it clear that AFHQ would superintend the mounting operation. That he turned to Gale signaled Smith's mistrust of Lee's entire organization. He wanted an independent source of information; he also put Gale on the spot.[50]

Two days later Hughes detonated an explosion that sent shock waves throughout the American command. Eisenhower considered Hughes the best supply man in the entire U.S. Army and the officer with the best overall picture of theater supply. As one of Eisenhower's closest friends and confidants, Hughes's views carried a punch well beyond his relative low rank. Citing a "multitude of problems," Hughes concluded that Torch as contemplated could not be supported and maintained to a sufficient degree of efficiency within the "limiting dates set." With September 12 "supposed to be the date when supplies were in hand," SOS had not even begun the mounting process. He recommended a six-week delay in staging Torch, until 15 December.[51] Eisenhower called an emergency commanders' meeting for the next day.

At the meeting of the chiefs of staff the next morning, Gale made his recommendations. "Until the SOS reports its condition," he stated, "no final decision can be made." He predicted a gridlock would soon develop and raised doubts that SOS could meet its obligations in initiating the actual mounting operation even if it were pushed back to 5 October—the last possible date to begin the movement of materiel from depots to the assigned shipping. Gale provided Smith with precisely the ammunition he needed; he immediately reported Gale's findings to Eisenhower and Clark.[52]

Before entering Eisenhower's office for the emergency meeting, Clark laid into Lee, accusing SOS of totally failing in its mission. With Smith present, Eisenhower categorized the supply situation as "a major crisis," and with uncharacteristic bluntness he told Clark, Spaatz, and Lee that their careers (he could have added his own) depended on solving the logistics muddle. He accentuated that "failure would mean only that the [faltering] officer's usefulness was ended," and he would be sent home in his permanent rank.[53] Eisenhower talked tough, but he knew that Clark, Spaatz, and Lee—sent by Marshall and protégés of McNair, Arnold, and Somervell—remained virtually untouchable. In any event, Eisenhower meant only to fire a shot across Lee's bow. With good reason, Lee remembered September 1942 as the most trying time of the war. "Not even the driving pressure of the 1944 summer campaign," he remembered, "was as hard on [my] nervous system as the Fall of 1942."[54]

Amidst all the collective angst about supply, another consideration loomed that neither Eisenhower nor Clark had much considered—the response American forces would receive in North Africa. Roosevelt put huge store in giving the invasion every appearance of being American. He remained convinced that Vichy officials were eager to change sides— a confidence that Roosevelt's man in North Africa, Murphy, encouraged. On 16 September Murphy, under a cloak of tight security in the disguise of one Colonel McGowan, arrived from Washington. Because Smith knew him, he met Murphy at the airport and pirated him to Telegraph Cottage.

A career diplomat, Murphy had held minor consular posts in Paris from 1930 until after the fall of France. His responsibilities in the 1930s involved low-level duties requiring little diplomatic skill or deep knowledge of international affairs. A devout Catholic and anticommunist, Murphy associated with the French extreme Right. His otherwise lackluster career received a boost with the formation of the Vichy government, when he became American chargé d'affaires.

Early in 1941 the United States and Vichy France concluded a pact that permitted the posting of twelve vice-consuls in North Africa, ostensibly to facilitate the purchase of American consumer goods with French assets frozen in U.S. banks. Roosevelt selected Murphy as his private representative, supposedly as administrator of the program but in fact to build pro-American support. The interwar State Department resembled the army in some respects. Most senior diplomats came from privileged backgrounds and paid the bulk of their own costs of living in foreign capitals. With pay and promotion prospects so poor for junior diplomats, the service attracted and retained few men of real talent. Amazingly, in the whole State Department, not a single foreign service officer possessed the language skills and background required for this mission. The men selected—mostly the same Ivy League, Wall Street types Smith later encountered in the CIA—had neither diplomatic nor political training. This presented no problem to the president. As with Donovan and the OSS, Roosevelt preferred to go outside normal channels and enlist gifted amateurs for special missions. This proved unfortunate, since the North Africa mission involved gathering military intelligence and generating political support for the United States. Following Murphy's lead, the vice-consuls associated themselves with rightist groups and gained badly distorted impressions of the political situation in French North Africa.[55]

Eisenhower convened a major conference that night at the cottage. Eisenhower, Clark, Smith, AFHQ intelligence chief Brigadier Eric Mockler-Ferryman, the three top men from the AFHQ political and civil affairs sections—W. H. B. Mack, H. Freeman Matthews, and COL Julius Holmes—and Ambassadors John Winant and Averell Harriman attended. Murphy described the various factions, personalities, and possible political complications likely to be encountered in North Africa. Eisenhower, who always played the political "babe in the woods," listened with genuine "horrified intentness."[56] First Murphy had conspired with GEN Maxime Weygand, the last Allied supreme commander in 1940 and implacable foe of the Germans, who had served as Pétain's delegate general in North Africa until the Abwehr insisted on his recall to Vichy. Next Murphy had turned to GEN Charles Mast, chief of staff of the corps stationed near Algiers; Mast possessed clandestine connections with GEN Henri-Honoré Giraud, whose daring escape from German captivity to unoccupied France made him a national hero and a focus of resistance. Murphy believed that Mast, who had masterminded Giraud's escape, could arrange for Giraud to slip out of Vichy France and assume command of French forces in North Africa. If that happened, Murphy assured his listeners, a number of generals, including Louis-Marie Koeltz and Alphonse Juin in Algeria and Charles Noguës and Émile Béthouart in French Morocco, would rally. He believed the French air force would likely follow the lead of the army but doubted that the navy would. Murphy admitted he possessed no connections to the French resident-general in Tunisia, ADM Jean-Pierre Estéva. He said a great deal more, including making promises of active support from committed pro-Allied fifth columnists—in all, painting a rosy picture of what the Anglo-American forces in Torch might expect.[57]

The next morning over breakfast, Eisenhower outlined what Murphy could and could not tell his friends in North Africa. Murphy acknowledged his utter ignorance of military operations and suggested that Eisenhower send a senior officer to North Africa charged with clarifying what steps the French should take in support of the landings. Eisenhower agreed and settled on Smith for the mission. Since the mission required a man with intimate knowledge of the Torch plan, as well as someone who could impress the French and speak with full authority, Smith appeared to be the perfect choice. As Eisenhower knew, nothing Murphy had said the previous night surprised Smith; he had heard it all before. Plus, fresh from Washington, Smith could reinforce what Murphy had been telling the French about Roosevelt's commitment to the liberation of French North Africa and metropolitan France. The venture had the potential to be as exciting as it was important. Traveling under utmost secrecy, first to Gibraltar and then by submarine to the coast of Algeria, the emissary would land in the dead of night on an uncertain beach and be spirited away for a rendezvous with French coconspirators. "Don't think Beetle knows that Ike contemplates putting the finger on him," Butcher surmised, "but he won't mind I'm sure."[58]

With the drama of Colonel McGowan's visit over, attention returned to the sorry state of supply affairs. As Butcher noted, "The whole situation has Ike worried." He was not alone. Following the upbraiding he received in Eisenhower's office, Lee returned to Cheltenham and read the riot act to his staff. Agreeing that it looked "impossible to meet the job," Lee told his supply chiefs they "must support the operations as now set" and challenged each of them to go out there and give it the old college try. "We must play the game as written down in the present book of rules," he told Hughes, "which can't be changed, as I see it and as I accept it."[59] Clark had told Lee he wanted an updated inventory of SOS stocks, and Lee completed a preliminary report on 18 September. "While, as Colonel Hughes indicates, it is difficult for the SOS to meet the dates now set for the operation," he informed the increasingly impatient Clark, "I believe they can be met with *fair* efficiency." He reassured the deputy commander, "The campaign should succeed although the logistical prearrangements be far from perfect."[60]

More bad news followed. Hughes told Clark he could not promise adequate ammunition supplies for Torch. SOS could locate only 21,040 tons of ground forces ammunition. Much of the artillery ammunition proved unserviceable because of mishandling in transit.[61] Then word came that two ships carrying the First Division's 105mm howitzers would not arrive. One had gone aground off the Canadian coast, and the other had put in to Bermuda after its cargo shifted in heavy seas. The SOS also reported that the M-4 tanks would not arrive in time for the assault. Eisenhower advised the War Department that if the ships could not reach the United Kingdom by 21 October, "it means a corresponding delay in D-Day for every day's delay."[62]

The real problem stemmed from Lee's insistence on putting the best possible gloss on his activities and those of his command. His blithe assurances struck the senior logisticians as another example of Lee's Pollyannaism. Hughes noted that Lee supported Sledgehammer in an identical offhand manner. "I am up against Clark who does not want any bad news," he complained, "and Lee who says he can support any operation."[63] BG Thomas Larkin, the officer assigned to command SOS units in Algeria, had the same reaction. He stormed into Clark's office, "obviously highly agitated," and complained that Lee's solution simply involved tossing everything back to ASF. The SOS still had not completed its inventory of stocks in the United Kingdom. "After asking me if I understood what this meant," Clark related in his daily summary to Eisenhower, Larkin stormed out of his office. "The increasingly apparent breakdown of SOS," Butcher observed, "is giving rise to the question of General Lee's ability to run the show." And "in recent days," Butcher continued, "there has been repeated criticism of General Lee's riding around the Island on his special train, handsomely equipped, while the supply situation has been so difficult."[64] Lee's stock hit rock bottom. On 19 September Eisenhower withdrew his recommendation that Lee succeed him as ETO commander.[65]

Lee was not the only one grating on the supreme commander's rattled nerves. "Ike is beginning to have personnel problems at the top," Butcher reported. "The persistent force of ambition is causing difficulties." The rank-hungry Clark, discontented with his role as deputy and chief planner, incessantly lobbied for command of a task force. Smith, who probably wanted Clark out of his hair, endorsed the idea, pointing out that no precedent existed in American tables of organization for a deputy anything. Even though Eisenhower owed Clark, who had been instrumental in engineering the War Plans Division appointment that catapulted his career, his patience began to fray. He also began to question Clark's vaunted reputation as a planner. Eisenhower bought off Clark with a promise to push his promotion. With Smith running the staffs, Clark's sole attention now centered on planning, and despite Eisenhower's concerns, he delegated to Clark full decision-making authority for concluding the Torch operational scheme.[66]

The tightness of shipping space in the convoys induced Clark to make the most crucial decision in the planning phase of Torch. The reshuffling of shipping schedules meant that SOS/ETO supplied American units in the Eastern Task Force, while the Center Task Force drew on support routed from the United States, supplemented by stocks in the United Kingdom and carried to Algeria on British ships. The entirely American Western Task Force, under Patton, would sail from U.S. ports. Limited lift capacity confronted Clark with a hard choice. The logisticians on both sides of the Atlantic argued for a reduction in the troop basis; although smaller, the forces would be fully equipped, supplied, and mobile. Clark ignored their advice. He decided to maintain combat ground strength while sharply reducing vehicles, weapons, supplies, and, correspondingly, service and supply troop levels. Eisenhower met with Clark, Smith, and the senior U.S. Navy commanders on 19–20 September and endorsed Clark's verdict. On 20 September Smith drafted the first consolidated outline plan for Torch.[67] Curiously, Eisenhower never discussed this decision in any of his lengthy correspondence with Marshall. On 23 September Clark and Larkin flew to the United States to finalize planning. Eisenhower correctly guessed that his unhappy deputy would call in his chits in Washington in his campaign to secure a command.[68]

The lone subordinate whose performance matched his reputation was Beetle Smith. Eisenhower wanted freedom from details so he could concentrate on bigger issues; Smith immediately provided it. A week after Smith's arrival, Eisenhower could already detect a huge difference. "The presence of Beetle continues to be a great satisfaction to Ike," Butcher noted on 15 September. "It relieves him from many of the details of staff direction he's been forced to handle ever since his arrival in London."[69] For the first time Eisenhower felt secure enough to leave his office and visit nearby units.

Smith needed no encouragement to assert his control over the staffs. An American command, ETO offered little challenge. The ETO headquarters consisted primarily of a large G-1 staff, now under Dahlquist, and skeleton intelligence and operations divisions with a small G-4 liaison section. The combined headquarters had ruthlessly cannibalized ETO's personnel. AFHQ proved a different matter. When Smith arrived in London, AFHQ had already existed in all but name for more than a month, but it lacked direction because Eisenhower's and Clark's attentions had been focused elsewhere; neither succeeded in putting his stamp on the headquarters. The structure was in place—based on the American system—but it lacked drive. That changed when Smith took over on 12 September. First Smith completed the formation of AFHQ's general staff. He retained Gruenther as his deputy chief of staff for purely American matters and organizations, and he named MG J. F. M. Whiteley as Gruenther's British opposite number. Eisenhower had warned Smith never to concede to the British committee system. Three days after becoming chief of staff, Smith hedged on this injunction and made Gale de facto deputy chief of staff and charged him with coordinating supply and oversight of the entire mounting operation.

Otherwise, Smith left the structure and personnel he had inherited in place. American officers headed three divisions: COL Ben Sawbridge in personnel; BG Lyman Lemnitzer, who had served as interim deputy chief of staff until Smith showed up, continued as chief of the operations division; and COL Archelaus Hamblen directed supply and evacuations. Administration and personnel (G-1) and supply and movement (G-4) contained parallel American and British staffs; intelligence (G-2) and operations (G-3) were combined staffs. A British officer, Mockler-Ferryman, remained at the helm of the intelligence division. Next Smith accelerated the expansion of the staff, manning the American side of AFHQ with officers pinched from other U.S. establishments. On 19 September Eisenhower told a friend, Smith "is a natural-born Chief of Staff and really takes charge of things in a big way. I wish I had a dozen like him. If I did, I would simply buy a fishing-rod and write home every week about my wonderful accomplishments in winning the war."[70]

By the third week of September, the logistics picture suddenly brightened. On 24 September Lee finally produced his "status of supply" report. The situation looked much improved. As Lee informed MG Leroy Lutes, the chief of operations and planning in ASF who was in the United Kingdom to help bring some order to the chaos, "Speaking in baseball vernacular, we lost only vendor supplies—pop, chewing gum—but no bats and balls."[71] In the first half of the month, SOS had unloaded 200,000 long tons, with half as much again due before the end of September. Despite everything, Lee preserved his equanimity, which he attributed to prayer. The solution to the supply mess rested not in divine intervention but in the labors of the War Department, especially ASF. Somervell resorted to extraordinary expedients. Training divisions in the United States returned their newly issued weapons and equipment to ASF—despite the heavy cost in unit morale and delays in training schedules—for transshipment to the Torch forces. By the end of September, it appeared Lee's organization could meet its timetable for mounting Torch. Butcher noted that all the logisticians looked more cheerful.[72] They were not alone.

The Bulldog Almost Sidelined

Eisenhower's liberation from, as he put it, "the backbreaking volume" of detail stood in direct proportion to Smith's absorption in it. Forced to work fourteen-hour days, Smith rushed to complete the thousands of particulars that competed for his attention. In addition to verifying loading schedules, checking air and naval estimates, and overseeing the weaving together of countless other elements of planning, Smith performed the routine duties of chief to two staffs. These responsibilities included screening incoming and outgoing communications with the CCS and Marshall, monitoring the work of the staff sections, handling the assignment of personnel in his rapidly expanding AFHQ, and attending high-level conferences involving the senior American and British officers for Torch, the BCOS, and Churchill.

Smith proved particularly adept at handling the British. In a curious way, the British buttressed Smith's position. When Clark assumed responsibility for organizing and manning the combined headquarters, he began by transferring officers from the ETO planning division. Beyond that, Clark did very little; a table of organization did not appear until 26 August, and the first request for personnel to flesh out the skeleton staffs took another week. Eisenhower held off any real organization of AFHQ, even its activation, until Smith arrived. The AFHQ operations division remained top-heavy in American officers; the War Office agreed to staff the intelligence section and designated some of its top men—Gale, Whiteley, Mockler-Ferryman, and COL A. T. de Rhé Philipe—for service on the combined staff.[73] Things changed immediately after Smith took over. He took charge of the situation, and suddenly AFHQ began to kick into gear. Seeing this, the British rendered Smith all the support they could muster.[74]

Part of that support came in the form of helping the Americans master their logistical problems. Smith appealed directly to Ismay and worked through Gale. AFHQ correlated the revised shipping schedules with ASF, the British supply agencies, and the naval staffs. With it now clear that U.S. forces could not be supplied from American sources, Smith borrowed from British stocks, and Gale coordinated local procurement, including emergency production in British factories. British sources provided the Class I (rations), Class III (petrol, oil, and lubricants [POL]), and most of the Class IV (heavy engineering material) stocks. Many requests involved supplies for the comfort and convenience of U.S. troops; others added to existing reserves. U.S. Army regulations demanded every soldier be equipped with everything called for under prewar tables of supply, even if the articles would have little or no utility in active operations in North Africa. The British, suffering under spartan rationing and shortages, thought American demands excessive but complied nonetheless. The chronic shortage of service manpower meant that AFHQ relied on the assistance of the Ministry of War Transport to clear ports, marshal supplies, and move troops. The British even seconded elements of the Royal Army Ordnance Corps in support. Since these involved Allied as opposed to American matters, AFHQ assumed responsibility for logistical management, merely coordinating these efforts with Lee and his SOS command.[75]

Smith held regular consultative discussions with the British, which required almost daily contact with Ismay and, through him, the BCOS and Churchill. An exponent of close Allied cooperation, Ismay became an invaluable link between the prime minister and AFHQ. Ismay and Smith had butted heads in the past, but those collisions never impaired their relationship. The two men shared one thing in common: both were devoted friends of Dykes. Reinforced by what Dykes told him, Ismay appreciated Smith's strengths and the central role he must play in forging Anglo-American cooperation. In some ways, their relationship mirrored the Smith-Dykes partnership. Together they charted paths of least resistance: Ismay shielded AFHQ from Churchill's interference; Smith gave expression to the British point of view in discussions with Eisenhower and Clark. During this difficult period, they built a close friendship. In his correspondence with Smith, Ismay sometimes signed off "Love, Pug"—a peculiarly unmilitary gesture, but indicative of the bond of trust that developed between them.[76]

Ismay could never contain the prime minister for long. A zealot on the importance of personal contacts, Churchill insisted on weekly dinners at 10 Downing Street with Eisenhower, Clark, and Smith. On 20 September the three American officers went out to Chequers, Churchill's country estate, for meetings with the prime minister and the BCOS. As Brooke commented, the prime minister "never had the slightest doubt that he had inherited all the military genius of his great ancestor, Marlborough."[77] Churchill lectured the senior British and American officers at length on all manner of topics. "It means a long night," reported Butcher, "and these country boys always say how they hate it."[78] "Our relationships with the Prime Minister are on a most informal basis," Smith related to Marshall. "Unfortunately, this happy state of affairs carries with it the obligation for a weekly dinner at No. 10 Downing Street which is usually terminated about 2:00 A.M." Smith took amusement in watching Ismay and Brooke "brace themselves for hours in straight backed dinner room chairs" listening to Churchill's "flights into the stratosphere."[79]

Smith liked things simple. For him, ham hocks and beans represented a culinary delight. After the stresses of the day, he wished only to return to his rooms at the Dorchester Hotel for some downtime alone—an indulgence not easily achieved. Eisenhower insisted on cementing relationships with his closest advisers through intimate social contacts. In the army, an invitation from a superior amounts to an order. This meant that Smith's rare free evenings were consumed with commutes out to Telegraph Cottage or trips to Eisenhower's London flat for dinner, games of bridge, and idle chitchat. Smith was not the idle chitchat type. It also meant he spent his off-hours in the company of men he did not particularly like. Smith and Clark had attended Leavenworth and the War College together but never developed any real familiarity. Smith took an immediate dislike to Butcher, less because of Butcher's ebullient personality than because Smith saw him as a "public relations hound." Smith questioned Eisenhower's wisdom in having a journalist, a civilian adman, keeping his headquarters diary. He worried about leaks to the press and correctly surmised that Butcher intended to profit by publishing the diary after the war.[80] Evenings spent with Eisenhower, Churchill's weekly dinners, and the odd weekend at Chequers provided no relief from the grind, disturbing Smith's routine and robbing him of much-needed rest. The murderous pace of staff duties undermined Smith's already fragile health, and a meal of game pie and the prime minister's homemade onion soup triggered a serious flare-up of his bleeding ulcers.

Smith could no longer hide his ailment. Eisenhower offered to fly in a specialist from the United States. Afraid "the medicos would rule-book him out of the war," Smith finally succumbed to Eisenhower's pressure and took some rest. Despite going on a buttermilk diet, Smith's condition worsened. Fond of the man he called the "American Bulldog," Churchill could not believe how pale Smith looked during a 28 September dinner. Taking Eisenhower into an adjoining room, the prime minister insisted that Smith receive immediate medical attention. Eisenhower replied that he had ordered Smith to bed and arranged for a nurse to attend him at his apartment. With Clark in Washington, Eisenhower knew Smith's absence from headquarters would require his own resumption of staff direction. As much as Eisenhower hated being shackled to his desk, given the option of losing Smith for a week or permanently, his choice was clear.

The next day the theater surgeon general, acting on Eisenhower's directive, issued a verbal order sending Smith to the American General Hospital at Oxford. He refused until he received Eisenhower's promise that he would be allowed to return as soon as his condition improved. Assured that Eisenhower had no intention of sending him home, Smith gave in. The trip up to Oxford did not improve his temper; the ambulance carrying him had two flat tires on the way. Making matters worse, after giving Smith a blood transfusion, the doctors informed him that he required several days of bed rest.

On 1 October Eisenhower took more than four hours from his busy schedule for a trip to Oxford. Recognizing the value of his chief of staff, Eisenhower wanted to put Smith's mind at rest. Finding Smith in a state of agitation, Eisenhower reassured him that he had not let anyone down; although he was badly missed, the most important thing was for Smith to get better so he would be "useful when the big moment comes." Hughes also made the trip up to Oxford. "Tell Mamie that Beadel [*sic*] Smith is sick in bed with two doctors and a nurse," he instructed his wife. "No don't tell her," Hughes concluded, "she believes that Smith will save Ike."[81]

Smith did not remain long in the hospital. Diagnosing himself fully recovered, Smith flew "the coop," as Butcher put it, on 4 October. Alerted of his disappearance, Eisenhower found the fugitive fast asleep in his bed in the Dorchester. Although Smith had violated a direct order, Eisenhower could not bring himself to reprimand his chief of staff and left without waking him. For Smith's birthday the next day, Eisenhower threw a small party. Over a game of craps, Smith loudly announced that his batteries had been charged and he stood "ready to electrify the world." Although Eisenhower thought Smith had rushed his return, he expressed relief at having him back in the saddle.[82]

The prospect of losing Smith worried Eisenhower. He knew word of Smith's serious health problems would surface in Washington, so he propped up Smith's position to Marshall. While in Washington, Clark discovered that Marshall intended to promote Smith. "This would be of tremendous help to me," Eisenhower told Marshall. "Smith seems to have a better understanding of the British and is more successful in producing smooth teamwork among the various elements of the staff than is any other subordinate I have."[83] After Marshall heard of Beetle's bout with ulcers, Eisenhower reassured him of his chief's improvement, reminding him that Smith "will not be exposed to the hardships that front-line soldiers have to bear." And, Eisenhower pointed out, Smith's "organizational and executive abilities are so outstanding that the beneficial effects of his presence are constantly evident."[84] Smith could not be spared.

Marshall shared Eisenhower's anxiety over Smith's condition. In a rare personal letter, Marshall made his displeasure clear. Gratified that Smith was on his feet again, Marshall pointedly informed his former assistant that unless he exercised more discretion, he ran the risk of losing Marshall's favor.[85] Although he made light of his health problems, Smith could not miss the gravity of the warning.

By the time Smith returned to his desk, the supply crisis had eased, and with it anxiety over Torch. While in Washington, Clark fixed planning with the task force commanders and Somervell's people. The plan cut organic materiel by half. The reduced tonnage demands meant SOS could meet its loading schedules, American combat troop levels were preserved, and, according to Lee, "SOS will be able to give a 90% performance on TORCH." As reported to Eisenhower, the American forces would face shortages of equipment, especially vehicles, and SOS troops for at least three months.[86] Preoccupied with getting Torch off the ground, nobody gave much thought to what would happen after the American forces landed. With the supply emergency over and the operational issues settled, the mounting program proceeded with amazing ease. Smith now turned his attention toward organizing the combined headquarters for North Africa.

16

"We Are on the Threshold of a Magnificent Success"

Leadership and command are not synonymous. Leadership is largely the distillate of character. Command is conferred; legally and professionally, subordinates owe loyalty and obedience to the office, not the incumbent. Preindustrial codes of personalized loyalty retain a powerful resonance in the U.S. Army. War produces military leaders who dominate the postbellum army. It was true after the Revolutionary War, the War of 1812, the Civil War, and World War I. World War II was unique because a sitting officer not only embodied the military ideal of leadership but also handpicked the men who exercised command. Marshall exerted an influence over the U.S. Army in wartime unmatched in American history. Unfortunately, his judgments often proved fallible. Witness the long list of Marshall-appointed corps and division commanders who got sacked. As in all wars, the expensive winnowing process removed the ineffectual and unlucky. Arguably, Marshall's most inspired choice for command was Eisenhower, although that was far from apparent in late summer 1942. Before Smith arrived, except for Eisenhower's being better known by the British, little distinguished his faltering leadership from that of his predecessor Chaney. Although other factors intervened, to a large extent, Smith did save Eisenhower; only after he took charge did things start hopping. Eisenhower could not have succeeded as well, or at all, without his hard-driving chief of staff. Had fortune played out differently, both Eisenhower and Smith would have made names for themselves in the war. Both possessed the intelligence, professional background, and personality for an operational command or high bureaucratic office. But fortune—or, rather, George Marshall—fused them together. In combination, Eisenhower and Smith composed a whole much greater than the sum of their parts; each possessed character strengths that compensated almost precisely for the other's weaknesses. Both men were far more than they appeared on the surface.

Ike and Beetle

The key to understanding Eisenhower's leadership style rests in unraveling the layers of his complex personality. The affable Ike that others saw and thought they understood contrasted sharply with the calculative, ambitious operator that lay behind the carefully constructed façade. Eisenhower wore many masks. Raised on the wrong side of the tracks in a small town in central Kansas, one of five brothers with a bitter and distant father and a mother from a nondenominational sect deemed overly zealous even by the standards of the Bible Belt, young Ike learned early how to adapt, competing for attention and acceptance. From adolescence, Eisenhower cultivated the art of manipulating people for his own gain: first influencing the folks in Abilene who mattered, then currying favor to get into West Point and escape Kansas, and finally advancing in the army. An indifferent student at West Point, Eisenhower matriculated at the Military Academy to gain an education at government expense and play football. He never intended to make the military his career, but after World War I he changed his mind, despite his frustrations over never going to France. The watershed in Eisenhower's career was not his spell as understudy of BG Fox Conner in Panama or his year at Leavenworth but an episode that transpired soon after the war, when he ran afoul of the chief of infantry for writing an unremarkable article arguing for a role for tanks. That episode taught him an invaluable lesson: if he planned to move up through the ranks, he needed to conform. Eisenhower decided success entailed uncritical compliance: never rock the boat, and always appear to follow the lead of superiors who could help in his assent. This became his "guiding philosophy," as he told his old file leader from West Point, MAJ Bradford Chynoweth, in 1922. "When I go to a new station I look to see who is the strongest and ablest man on the post. I forget my own ideas and do everything in my power to promote what *he* says is right." The man in that case was Connor, who put Eisenhower through an intensive prep course and pulled strings to get him into Leavenworth. At Leavenworth, Eisenhower graduated first in his class. To Chynoweth, his success came as no surprise. "School Doctrine was sacred. They were not teaching War. They were teaching Dogma," and "Ike had been 100 percent conformist, never deviated, and stood first in his class. School doctrine was his religion."[1] Pershing's Chaumont Clique towered above the interwar army. At one time or another, Eisenhower served under all the leading lights of Pershing's circle: Fox Conner, William D. Connor at the War College, Moseley in the War Department, Pershing in the American Battle Monuments Commission, and finally Marshall. The chameleon routine always worked with varying degrees of success, except for MacArthur. Eisenhower served under the egomaniacal MacArthur for seven years, and the latter's personality template was too variegated to replicate. MacArthur saw through Eisenhower's artifice. He considered Eisenhower "a brilliant executive of someone else's original thought but *not*," as far as he could tell, "in any way an original mind."[2] Eisenhower had his own ideas, but he carefully guarded them.

Eisenhower's best mask was also the easiest to deploy: his winning persona. Eisenhower had a compulsive need to be liked. He possessed an attractive, even magnetic, personality; people were drawn to him and enjoyed being around him. It was easy to like Ike, given the trademark grin and the boyish simplicity and enthusiasm; he even remained physically handsome, despite premature baldness. Eisenhower personified optimism. A skilled poker player, Eisenhower knew how to hide his intentions behind a grinning "poker face." Behind the bonhomie roared a furious temper.

All the Eisenhower boys inherited their father's violent temper. The brothers fought other South Side boys but reserved their real fury for contests among themselves. His mother initiated efforts to curb Ike's pugnacity in what became a lifelong struggle to control his rage. He knew any tantrum aimed at a superior officer might prove fatal. Although his relationship with MacArthur bordered on tempestuous, Eisenhower never crossed the line. In March 1942 Eisenhower exhibited a bout of temper in Marshall's office after being informed that he could forget about a command and a promotion. "I blazed for an hour," he observed, but concluded afterward, "anger cannot win, it cannot think clearly." This episode amounted to another Marshall test of character; he gauged Eisenhower's reaction. Eisenhower passed Marshall's test but failed his own. "For many years I've made it a religion never to indulge myself" in any show of anger.[3]

Eisenhower's ire especially flared whenever he felt imposed on or his prerogatives as a commander came into question. Instead of giving vent to his emotions, Eisenhower sublimated them. He revealed himself only to those closest to him. He became irritable and depressed; he chain smoked, and his health suffered. When Gruenther first saw him in early August, he thought Eisenhower looked ten years older than the last time they had met. When things went wrong, he retreated into his own world. At West Point, it was along the banks of the Hudson; in London, it was Telegraph Cottage.

His ingratiating mien around superiors cast the impression that Eisenhower was a toady, that he owed his success to being a player. His determination never to allow his temper to get the better of him compelled him instinctually to withdraw from personal conflict. Both tendencies—one a "guiding philosophy," the other a religion—bred hesitancy and made it look like Eisenhower lacked moral courage. Eisenhower built a career on parroting senior officers. Now the only officer he answered to was Marshall. Uncertain of himself, Eisenhower approached every problem by asking himself what the chief would do; fearing he deviated too far from that path, he wrote long, self-defensive letters to Marshall in search of reassurance.

Naturally, there existed much substance beneath the veneer. Behind the self-effacing and engaging modesty lay a fierce pride and a keen intelligence. The exterior calm, geniality, and constant buoyancy cloaked an unsentimental operator who manipulated people in pursuit of his own ends. Eisenhower's military ethics consisted of two bedrock tenets: his absolute loyalty to Marshall, and his determination to perform his duty and fulfill his mission. As he told Hughes back in the 1930s, "the word duty is sacred to me."[4] Eisenhower asserted himself by denying himself the role of a decisive actor. He took strong stands against the very notion that he took strong stands. His command style illustrated a high degree of adaptability, but his actions remained obscured by their subterranean nature. He told his old mentor Conner, "I believe in direct methods, possibly because I am too simple-minded to be an intriguer or to attempt to be clever."[5] In fact, he warily disguised his motives. Eisenhower's entire leadership style rested on inspiring trust in his apolitical incorruptibility, good character, righteous intentions, and old-fashioned personal virtues. Eisenhower always made clear his contempt for calculated deceit, yet he engaged in studied machinations when it served his purposes. Eisenhower, who loudly defamed politics, emerged as the greatest political general the United States ever produced—and he came to know it.

But that time still loomed largely in the future. At this juncture, as Cunningham aptly observed, Eisenhower "stood in naïve wonder at attaining the high position in which he [finds] himself."[6] In February 1942 the White House usher's log recorded the visit of "P. D. Eisenhauer" to the Oval Office; six months later, Eisenhower was a household name in command of the coalition's first offensive. He remained very sensitive to charges that he lacked command experience and had never heard a shot fired in anger. He knew politics had motivated his selection as Marshall's caretaker and supreme commander. Owing to Eisenhower's astounding rise, a jealous Patton christened him "Divine Destiny" for his initials. In view of the obstacles he faced in summer and autumn 1942, Eisenhower might have thought he had been consigned to the nether regions.

Mamie was not alone in viewing Smith as a harbinger of success. Eisenhower later told Somervell, "The past months have put everyone under a heavy strain and, without you and your gang to depend upon, I think I'd now be in the nut-house."[7] Smith did more than his share to keep Eisenhower out of the asylum. The two had several things in common. There was the obvious: both were infantrymen who had spent their entire interwar careers tied down in derided nonline jobs on staffs or in education billets. Although only five years separated them in age, Eisenhower stood a decade ahead of Smith on the hump. Because of their humble family backgrounds—which applied far more to Eisenhower than to Smith—both saw themselves as self-made men. Both men hailed from the Midwest, although small-town Abilene—the point where the Midwest becomes the West—bore little resemblance to Indianapolis. Still, they harbored similar sets of values, including self-sufficiency, plain speaking, and firmly rooted beliefs in family, God, and the flag. Both possessed more brain power than their peers. MacArthur described Eisenhower as "ambitious, clever, hardworking" and thought him "the ablest officer he has ever known at absorbing thirty minutes description of an idea (or plan or strategic concept) and getting the whole thing out on paper—orders, arrangements etc. etc.—in ten minutes."[8] People made the same observations about Smith.

The two men possessed diametrically different personalities, which in no small measure explains the success of their collaboration. His many detractors thought Smith possessed all the charm of a rattlesnake. While no misanthrope, Smith remained extremely guarded in his personal relationships. He could never provide Eisenhower what he needed most—a warm shoulder to cry on. Beetle flashed a beguiling gentility when called for—especially around women—but he labored to leave his domineering attitude at the office. Direct to the point of brusqueness, Smith did not suffer fools. Months of experience in Washington taught him how to gauge personal strengths and weakness in an instant; this helped him decide whether he should take an officer—even a superior—seriously or pay him no heed. This ability made Smith an excellent expediter of action and evaluator of individuals, but it never endeared him to anyone.

Smith never revealed how he read Eisenhower, but it is hard to imagine that the many masks of Ike deceived him for long. In many ways, Beetle was born to play his assigned role of "bad cop" to Ike's "good cop." Smith's strong suits—his razor-sharp intellect and maniacal work ethic—predisposed him to judge harshly those who did not measure up to his exacting standards, those less well endowed with smarts or who cringed at twelve-hour workdays. Finally, there was always a palpable smugness about Smith. He saw himself as a mustang up from the ranks who had achieved success by sheer hard work and merit. People tended to see only the mean and hungry look of a younger officer on the make, a grasper for power. Most of all, Smith exuded a sense of empowerment because he viewed himself as the nonpareil "Marshall man." A great many officers shared that label—including Eisenhower and Clark—but none could claim Smith's singular bond to the chief. He might serve under Eisenhower—and never once questioned that role or acted disloyal in any way—but Smith's first allegiance was always to Marshall. Eisenhower knew that, exploited it when he could, but always felt a little threatened by it. The Eisenhower-Smith partnership was born from mutual need, not genuine intimacy. Had not Bellona thrown them together, Eisenhower and Smith would never have become friends.

Untying the Gordian Knot

Smith returned to his office the day after his birthday party. Eisenhower instructed him to take it easy and work half days. The concept of half days proved completely foreign to Smith; he immediately jumped into the fray full bore. He did his best to appear fit, but his stomach continued to tear him up inside. Much to his dismay, and despite his protests, Smith's precarious health ruled him out for the clandestine mission to Algeria. Eisenhower sent Clark instead. His adventures, including fleeing from the police, holing up in a wine cellar, and losing his pants in the surf, made him a celebrity and did nothing to impede his promotion to lieutenant general. Even if Smith's health had not precluded his going, it is unlikely that Eisenhower would have risked Smith's safety. Given the vital tasks still left undone—organizing the AFHQ staff and finalizing plans for Torch—Eisenhower could not manage without Smith.

As soon as Smith returned to his desk, he embarked on untangling the web of AFHQ's organizations. With the supply crisis mostly behind him, Smith placed top priority on accomplishing what Eisenhower had refused to tackle—the complex reorganization of the American logistics apparatus. Smith faced two interlocking questions: how best to coordinate American and British lines of communication and supply in North Africa, and how to structure the American logistics command. In the first instance, Smith intended for Gale to orchestrate combined movement and supply through AFHQ. That proved straightforward enough. The real problem centered on settling the American half of the supply equation.

Smith raised the issue at the morning meeting of the chiefs of staff on 8 October. Prompted by Marshall's May "instructions" to Chaney, and guided by the new Field Service Regulations, Smith issued a circular letter to the American task force and air commanders assigned to Torch, spelling out his intention of organizing a "consolidated SOS [inside AFHQ] for the TORCH theater." The letter gave no indication how this would fit into the American and combined command structure, because that thorny question remained unsettled.[9] Smith agreed with Clark: the logistical problems in ETO derived from a faulty command structure that conferred too much authority on Lee. Although most conceded the need for reorganization, the widely conflicting views expressed by senior members of AFHQ demonstrated the complete lack of consensus on what form the theater logistics structure for North Africa should assume.[10]

Since arriving in the United Kingdom, Eisenhower had waffled on this issue. Butcher noted, "Ike is most worried when he is under strain about an organizational problem. Once the pattern clarifies in his mind his brow unwrinkles."[11] One can only conclude Ike's brow remained tightly knitted throughout the entire period before the North African landings, because he never solved the question of the status of American administration and logistics within an Allied theater of operations. Initially, Eisenhower signaled his intent to restructure his headquarters according to Marshall's instructions, with separate air force and SOS commands. When Somervell refused Eisenhower's request for the release of any of ASF's top four logisticians to head a consolidated SOS command, Eisenhower allowed the question to float.[12] Three critical weeks later, on 16 August, he admitted, "we have not *yet completely crystallized* command lines for TORCH" and tentatively reiterated his aim of forming a consolidated SOS section in his combined general staff, "particularly because of the tremendous importance that will attach to the line of communication—both sea and land."[13] His interim solution involved shuffling men he trusted into responsible positions. Earlier he had made Hughes chief of staff to Lee in ETO/SOS; now Hughes became Gale's deputy, in principle the American chief administrative officer in AFHQ. In the middle of August, Marshall agreed to postpone the formation of a U.S. theater command in North Africa. That ruling allowed Eisenhower to defer making a decision. Because of anticipated communication difficulties in North Africa, Eisenhower estimated that no consolidated SOS command would emerge until two months after the landings.[14] Until then, AFHQ would manage American logistics. That is where matters stood when Smith took over as dual chief of staff.

Marshall's annoyance with Eisenhower's dithering was one reason he had sent Smith to London. On 15 September he insisted that Eisenhower and Smith begin planning for the eventual creation of a North African theater of operations, which again raised the issue of an SOS command. Even though he authored fawning responses to Marshall, Eisenhower refused to compromise any of his prerogatives as commander. As the first Allied supreme commander, no "book" existed as the blueprint for organizing AFHQ. For instance, the new field regulations specified the composition of a U.S. theater command but made no mention of a combined or joint structure. That being the case, Eisenhower ignored it. To Eisenhower, organizational problems always appeared absurdly simple. He bristled at "ritualists" who followed the book and got hung up over fixed chains of command and perfect wire charts specifying exact jurisdictional limits, yet Eisenhower never deviated from well-worn paths. His command style centered not on formal exercise of authority but on managing interpersonal relations. He preferred to deal with problems one-on-one at the highest level. He appointed officers he knew and trusted to key positions and expected them to do their jobs. Eisenhower fervently believed his "people" skills could overcome any major differences in policy or personality. As he told Smith, "while lines of demarcation and chains of command are important, the best results come from mutual understanding and confidence."[15]

Smith never saw it that way; he wanted clear command responsibilities and tight organization. He possessed some definite views on organization but still had not resolved how to meld the American and British staff structures. For starters, he understood the U.S. Army had no experience operating a higher headquarters and possessed few officers with the requisite training in high-level staff work to man them. This he blamed on the inadequacies of a school system that trained officers as operational planners but little else. Like Marshall, he plucked talented young men and trained them in high staff work. For him, the immediate issue revolved around two problems: how to integrate supply functions inside a headquarters when the historical legacy was separation, and how to overcome the resistance of officers schooled and experienced in the old system. These questions bedeviled all his efforts at fundamentally reorganizing his headquarters for the entire war.

Smith's time in the CCS structure convinced him of the advantages of the British committee system—chiefly, its clear division of functions and the simplicity and efficiency of procedures. The British system equalized logistics and operations—in theory, relieving combat commands of administrative and supply matters. British staff officers exercised command over subordinate agencies. Every British headquarters—from the chiefs in London through theater and operational commands down to tactical levels—contained the identical structure. Information ran up the system; commands flowed down. The British army might lack a pool of top-notch operational commanders, but it suffered no scarcity of skilled and experienced staff officers. Already stretched, the British knew the time loomed when they would confront serious manpower and materiel shortages. They could not afford mistakes, which explains their insistence on fighting peripheral campaigns. Manpower and materiel considerations determined British strategy and operational thinking. For these reasons, the British placed many of their best brains in staffs.

Americans—even Americans emerging from the worst depression in their history—believed they came from the land of plenty. Americans took superabundance for granted. There was always "more where that came from." For American officers, the notion that logistics dictated operational decision making was anathema. American doctrine, based on the canons of unity of command, gave commanders at every level complete control over administration and supply. Staffs, which possessed no command function, acted in the commander's name in planning and coordinating the movement of manpower and materiel. Commanders and their operational planners made the decisions, consulting the supply services only after the fact. Clark's decision to cut materiel and support services by half for Torch illustrates this point exactly.

No convert to the British committee system, Smith firmly believed in the doctrine of unity of command. A utilitarian, Smith recognized the inadequacies of the American staff system—the near-run supply disaster made that palpable—and decided to create a hybrid. As AFHQ chief administrative officer, Gale would coordinate American and British administration and supply as Smith's deputy, but without the title. Before Smith's arrival, Gale had petitioned Clark along those lines. But Clark had replied that AFHQ possessed an American-style structure, and the position of deputy chief of staff did not exist in American practice, so Gale must remain content with his position. Since two Americans—Gruenther and Lemnitzer—already held deputy status, Clark's

veto amounted to a transparent rejection of the British committee system. Just what the chief administrative officer did in a combined headquarters remained an open question.[16] Smith's solution answered it. He
had no option—or inclination—but to retain the American G-division
system. Since the American and British structures and procedures differed so widely, the parallel national—as opposed to integrated—sections
would continue in the G-1 and G-4 Divisions; the American components
in each would supervise the work of the U.S. administrative and logistics
services embedded in the task forces. This largely improvised structure
satisfied Eisenhower's prerequisites that he command through AFHQ
and that Smith make no concession to the British committee system.
Eisenhower deferred the question of reorganization until the formation of a North African theater, but Smith hoped the expedient would
become permanent.

Two days after Smith outlined his intentions, a commotion erupted
that guaranteed the tentative restructuring would remain just that.
Eisenhower bristled because he argued for and did not receive clear
operational control over the air forces. A single officer, Cunningham,
commanded Allied naval forces in the Mediterranean. Even though
command lines remained hazy, Eisenhower and Cunningham agreed
"to accept anything that is workable and go to it."[17] The Royal Air Force
proved more difficult. Citing the wide geographic extent of the Mediterranean, the airmen blocked the formation of a unified air command.
Eisenhower would command the American Twelfth Air Force, under
BG James Doolittle, and the RAF's Eastern Air Command.[18] The War
Office then issued a directive to LTG K. A. N. Anderson, the British
First Army commander in Torch, giving him the right to appeal directly
to the British government in the event he felt his forces were exposed to
extreme risk by any decision made by the supreme commander. Eisenhower demonstrated little disquiet over confused lines of authority for
ancillary organizations, but when questions of his control over operational commands arose, he became a lion. He viewed the directive to
Anderson as another British attempt to undermine unity of command
and reacted with vigor. Essentially a repeat of instructions given to FM
Douglas Haig in 1918, the directive generated a great deal of heat until
the British issued a revised document on 20 October. The new instructions retained an escape clause but granted Eisenhower far wider control
than Foch had possessed in World War I. The episode reinforced Eisenhower's determination to blunt the growth of any species of the British
committee system taking root in his headquarters.[19]

Another of Eisenhower's predilections involved his belief in the mythology of the Fochian headquarters. He and Smith had very different views on staff size. Eisenhower wanted a small executive headquarters styled on OPD; Smith understood from his experience in Washington that, as a combined and joint headquarters, AFHQ must inevitably enlarge far beyond anything envisioned in interwar doctrine or called for in American tables of organization. For one thing, organizational and procedural differences between the national components within the headquarters required an expansion in staff size. All headquarters grew because of, and in proportion to, the number and types of functions they performed. Nobody in Washington envisioned the political, economic, and civil affairs liabilities incumbent on AFHQ. Smith added a number of staff sections not included in American tables of organization: public relations and special services on 15 September, a claims section on 3 October, a civil affairs section on 18 October, and a North African Shipping Board two days later. The U.S. Army possessed very few officers experienced in these specialized duties. Faced with these inadequacies, Smith filled these billets with experienced British officers until such time as American officers, seconded from other branches or commissioned from civilian life, became available. As late as the end of September, British officers constituted nearly two-thirds of AFHQ's complement.[20]

As would be the case throughout the war, one of the biggest organizational headaches involved structuring and managing political and civil affairs and psychological warfare. Smith inherited separate civil administration, political affairs, and psychological warfare sections. Mack, from the Foreign Office, headed the political staff; Freeman, seconded from the State Department, led civil affairs. Uneasy about Mack's direct links to the British government, and wanting AFHQ quarantined from political oversight, Eisenhower blocked Freeman's independent avenue of communications with Washington.[21] Mack advised Eisenhower on political and diplomatic matters; Freeman supervised planning for the restoration of law and order, public works and health, and economic life in liberated territories. The third section, psychological warfare, handled propaganda.

Smith recognized that the responsibilities of the three staffs overlapped and decided on an amalgamation. Primarily, he wanted to impose tighter controls on these ill-defined functions and subordinate them to the chain of command. Since the army's schools did practically nothing to prepare officers for these roles, much of the American manpower would come from Donovan's organization. Since his suspicions of Donovan and civilians in and out of uniform had not diminished, Smith placed the restructured civil affairs section directly under his own super-intendence. Even though the British contributed the bulk of the staff, Smith designated Murphy as the section's head. While the headquarters remained in London, Freeman substituted as chief, with Mack reduced to a lesser role as civil liaison officer. Mack continued as Eisenhower and Smith's primary adviser on political matters. The new section began operations on 18 October.

On 20 October Smith chartered the formation of the North African Shipping Board (NASB) as a constituent part of AFHQ. With a coordinated (as distinguished from combined) Anglo-American staff, the board harmonized shipping schedules into North Africa with London and Washington. Two officials from the Ministry of War Transport, Douglas Thomson and J. Gibson Graham, headed the organization. Smith delegated Gale responsibility for overseeing the workings of the NASB.

Smith's final effort at tightening his control over staff activities involved public relations and management of the media. "Before Beetle Smith came . . . there was literally almost no one, except myself," Eisenhower observed, "in the Headquarters that had ever served intimately in the War Department and knew anything at all of the real involvements of press relations, censorship, propaganda and related subjects."[22] The burden of organizing and running press relations fell on Smith. As indicated by his mistrust of Butcher, Smith remained very wary of the press. Late in October he authorized the formation of a separate public relations section, severed from the ETO structure and removed from G-2, and he assumed the added responsibility of acting as final censor for all news releases. The public relations officer answered directly to him.[23]

On 22 October Smith told Marshall he relished the pressure of welding together the Allied headquarters and expressed his general satisfaction with the progress made. Previously, AFHQ had amounted to a "series of associated groups of planners" with no real structure. With time now at a premium, Smith complained that the headquarters still fell far short of being a homogeneous operating staff, and he wished he had the wherewithal to get out of London for a couple of command post exercises to really whip the staff into shape. He complimented the British on their high level of cooperation and expressed his pleasant surprise at how well the two nationalities got along. Smith thought he had made headway in fashioning the beginnings of a combined working team. He confessed that Allied headquarters presented fewer headaches than ETO. The theater staff remained "definitely weak in spots," and genuine integration between the American theater headquarters and

AFHQ remained elusive. Many of the staff sections refused to stay in channel, and complications between ETO and SOS persisted.[24]

Two days later, on 24 October, Smith renewed his campaign for integrating American administration and supply within AFHQ. His operational memo directed: "When AFHQ assumes full operational and administrative responsibility in the theater, task force commanders will be relieved of [British] L of C [line of communications] and SOS functions. L of C and Theater SOS will then operate directly under AFHQ." Smith wanted to head off the formation of a separate Zone of Communication, as called for in American doctrine. Unity of command would function best if Eisenhower exercised authority as supreme commander through AFHQ and as theater commander through the American components of the AFHQ general staff divisions. AFHQ's organization under the American system accomplished precisely those functions. The American G-1 components would handle administration, and G-4 would handle planning and coordinating supply and transportation, with SOS and the chiefs of services operating directly under Smith's control. The memo also outlined a scheme for setting up four separate SOS headquarters during the initial phases of Torch: one for AFHQ-Forward and one for each of the three task forces, all under the direct supervision of Smith and Gale in AFHQ. The proposed organization dealt only with the opening stages of the Torch operation—between the landings and the activation of AFHQ in Algiers—but Smith meant for the structure to become permanent.[25]

Smith's memo set off alarm bells in Washington. Marshall replied the next day, asking for confirmation that Eisenhower intended to create four SOS commands in North Africa. Faced by Marshall's cool response, Smith wired back, emphasizing that as soon as the situation permitted, he planned to withdraw personnel from the base sections to staff an expanded and centralized SOS.[26] Far from pleased with Smith's plan to fragment SOS during the opening phases of the campaign, Marshall accepted the scheme but accentuated the lack of trained officers to man multiple logistics echelons.[27] Somervell also weighed in. As would repeatedly occur during the course of the war, the jurisdictional battles waged between the WDGS and Somervell in Washington over conflicting command and organizational philosophies influenced debates in the theaters. Eisenhower's refusal to create a combined logistics division in Torch alarmed Somervell. Since ETO served as the authorizing agency for all U.S. commands, including those under AFHQ, and acted as a hub for all communications between London and Washington, Somervell solicited AFHQ's opinion on the future functions of ETO when the combined headquarters moved to North Africa. Somervell brought his influence to bear on Eisenhower in the hope he could persuade him to form a single administrative and supply structure in ETO on the model of ASF. The ETO organization would then influence the framework of the future theater structure in North Africa. Chiefly, he desired all American supply organizations to follow a uniform pattern, placing all theater administrative and supply functions on a routine basis.

On 31 October Marshall cabled Eisenhower, decrying the strain that mounting Torch imposed on the manning, training, and equipping schedules of divisions in the United States. Again demonstrating his AEF narrowmindedness and ignoring the lessons of the supply crisis, Marshall wanted to curtail the dispatch of service units to North Africa. Marshall instructed Eisenhower to either form an SOS command or reduce SOS to a "skeleton organization" and "build up SOS forces composed mostly of the natives of that region . . . civilians, ordinary laborers, or what not." This expedient would remove the necessity of deploying supply units to North Africa while winning support of the locals by employing large numbers of them and making them "happy with American pay."[28]

Spurred by pressure from Washington, Smith renewed his bid to push Eisenhower into accepting a sweeping reorganization of American administrative and logistical structures in Torch. He knew the biases of Eisenhower, Clark, and other senior American officers against the ASF's functional organization. In many respects, he shared them. As the current problems with Lee made clear, an independent SOS commander with theater-wide authority and possessing both command and staff functions weakened the authority of the commander and his chief of staff and could only breed conflict at the headquarters level. At a more prosaic level, Smith also knew the U.S. Army did not possess the required number of trained senior staff officers to man parallel headquarters. AFHQ's control of logistics would economize on scarce officers, increase efficiency, and improve responsiveness.[29]

On 2 November Smith issued a new appreciation. It began by stating that "headquarters ETO and the headquarters SOS in Great Britain [had] proven so uneconomical in personnel and so unsatisfactory in co-ordination between the two headquarters that AF[HQ] ought not to repeat the error." Though sound in theory, a functionally organized and relatively independent SOS produced duplication of responsibilities and wasted trained personnel. Either AFHQ should divest all its G-4 and special staff functions and portions of its G-1 responsibilities, or AFHQ should expand its orchestration of administration and supply. AFHQ control required the moderate expansion of the general and special staff sections by withdrawing officers and men from SOS elements embedded in the task forces. The advantages of the second option rested in AFHQ's ability to superintend administrative and supply agencies while tightening Eisenhower's direct control over the manpower and logistics organizations. "There is no need for an SOS headquarters," the study pointedly argued. "Control and co-ordination of administrative functions should properly rest in AFHQ." The proposal ended by recommending that Smith sanction the preparation of plans for a restructured AFHQ "to perform functions otherwise performed by a headquarters SOS."[30]

Confronted by external pressure, Eisenhower dug in his heels and refused all suggestions for altering the command structure. He rebuffed Somervell's lobbying, deciding that ETO would continue to function in its existing capacity until a North African theater command emerged two months after the landings.[31] Not willing to buck Marshall only days before the landings, and still operating under the assumption that American forces would initially play only a static role in Algeria, Eisenhower replied that he would follow Marshall's advice and "at the earliest moment" build up SOS by relying chiefly on local labor.[32] On 2 November, far from centralizing SOS functions into an expanded AFHQ, as Smith had suggested, Eisenhower froze SOS troop ceilings.[33]

For four months Eisenhower deflected all attempts to get him to finalize his supply structure. Not knowing how to proceed, but characteristically blunting all outside challenges, in the end he did nothing. When Clark and the task force commanders stripped the landing forces of their supply and support tails, they reduced the SOS components in the landings to a few signal, transportation, and engineer shore units. Just as in the case of materiel and vehicles consigned to follow-up convoys, it would take months just to balance American troop and equipment levels to the modest projections in the initial Torch plan. The decision also nullified Smith's latest headquarters reorganization scheme and rendered mute any further discussion of centralizing logistics inside AFHQ, since no SOS worthy of the name would exist for an indefinite period after the landings. And as easily predicted, the resort to Arab labor proved an unmitigated disaster. As the logistics debacle in North Africa soon proved, Eisenhower paid a stiff price for his obtuseness.

Left Holding the Fort

According to Eisenhower's original reckoning, Clark and Smith, with a small group of officers, would establish AFHQ-Main in Gibraltar four days before the landings. By mid-October, the calculations changed.

Smith told his senior staff officers that AFHQ would remain in London; he anticipated no move until Christmas Day. A number of factors prompted the delay. As ETO continued to be the authorizing agency for coordinating and requisitioning supplies for North Africa, Eisenhower insisted that Smith stay behind and hold the fort in London. In reality, communications lay behind the decision. Gibraltar's communications would have served the purpose, but the burgeoning size of AFHQ outstripped office space and accommodations. As Eisenhower predicted, it would require two months to build up communications in North Africa just linking Casablanca, Oran, and Algiers. Eisenhower decided he would move to Gibraltar just prior to D-day. Clark would establish a small advance headquarters in Algiers as soon as practicable, primarily to open direct talks with the French and facilitate the movement eastward toward Tunisia. With Smith in London as the link to Washington and the British, Eisenhower figured he had all the bases covered. Smith planned to remain in London for two or three weeks, then move to Algiers.[34]

Eisenhower empowered Smith as his executor in London. On 2 October Eisenhower designated MG Russell Hartle as deputy ETO commander. He originally wanted his pal Gerow for the job, but Marshall remained cool to the idea. Gerow had "not clicked with General Marshall, who Ike says, never changes his mind once it has been made up."[35] Smith remained ETO chief of staff. The British feared ETO affairs would divert Eisenhower's attention. In response, Eisenhower clearly established Smith's broad grant of authority: in Eisenhower's absence, except for narrowly defined theater matters, Smith exercised virtual command in London. As Eisenhower instructed Hartle, Smith "will issue orders in the name of the Theater Commander in matters affecting the TORCH operation."[36]

Smith split his time between his two headquarters. His morning started with a short drive from his apartment at the Dorchester, on Park Lane across from Hyde Park, to Grosvenor Square. After his chiefs of staff conference, he usually met with Eisenhower. Typically, he spent the bulk of the day in his office adjacent to Eisenhower's at ETO headquarters. As the date for Torch approached, he spent more time at AFHQ, installed in a modern office building, Norfolk House, a few blocks away on St. James Square, south of Piccadilly. After his escape from the hospital, Smith had reverted to the old routine: long days in the office, followed by obligatory evenings spent with Eisenhower at Telegraph Cottage and weekly dinners at 10 Downing Street. Now Smith ate a bland diet, fortified with a pocket full of vitamins. The lone upside of being left behind was that Smith inherited Telegraph Cottage for the duration of his stay, which proved much longer than anticipated.

Intelligence from the Mediterranean remained mixed. Montgomery opened his offensive at El Alamein on 23 October, and although it had not gone off as planned, the British expected to score a major victory. On 25 October Clark returned from his secret mission to North Africa flushed with good news. Mast had assured Clark that Oran and Bône would not resist; after initially defending at Casablanca and Algiers *pour l'honneur*, the army would agree to an armistice, provided Giraud appeared in North Africa and issued orders to that effect. The French navy would fight, but if ground and air resistance collapsed, it had no option but acquiescence. Murphy delivered on his promise to line up French collaborators, but his intelligence assessments proved amazingly bad. He blanketed AFHQ with misinformation. The most worrying was that the Germans and Italians expected an Allied movement into French North Africa and had massed troops in Tripolitania for a rapid deployment into Tunisia. Murphy also reported he had entered into negotiations with agents of ADM François Darlan, commander in chief of the Vichy armed forces and Pétain's designated successor, in the hope he could broker a deal with Giraud.[37]

Murphy more than confirmed what he had told Eisenhower at Telegraph Cottage: he possessed not the faintest clue about military matters. As D-day approached, he became panicky. On 1 November, with Eisenhower preparing to leave for Gibraltar the next day, a communication arrived from Murphy that nearly threw everyone into apoplexy. Murphy reported that the Axis had divined Allied intentions; Vichy forces in North Africa stood on alert, and all depended on Giraud, who was delayed in France. Murphy made the unbelievable request for a two-week delay in the landings. As Eisenhower told Marshall, "It is inconceivable that McGowan can recommend such a delay with his intimate knowledge of the operation and the present location of troops and convoys afloat."[38] At this point, Eisenhower could no more cancel the landings than he could calm the swells along the Moroccan coast. It did not end there. On 4 November Murphy relayed the warning that Vichy had issued orders "to defend French Africa at all costs" and recommended, "we should not make the mistake of attacking." The next day Smith received another wire from Murphy via Washington requesting that the Torch landings be "synchronized with British attack on Atlantic and Channel North Sea together with Russian attacks eastern front and Egyptian offensive." Eisenhower dismissed Murphy's "bit of hysteria" as a case of "the big and small jitters."[39]

Others shared Murphy's apprehensions, if not his hysteria. Torch represented the largest amphibious operation ever attempted. One thing Eisenhower did not worry about was the quality of his combined staff. He confided to Marshall on the eve of the landings, "Every member of the staff, British and American, has slaved like a dog" to complete the complex planning for the mounting and staging of Torch. If the landings failed, it would have nothing to do with any failure to achieve an integrated Allied headquarters.[40] Of course, a great deal of the credit should have gone to Smith.

Tension remained high in London. Bad weather delayed Eisenhower's departure for Gibraltar. Refusing to linger any longer, Eisenhower ordered that his six Flying Fortresses make the hazardous trip on 5 November. It fell to Smith to deal with the British. "Prime Minister was hard to hold during your trip," Beetle told Eisenhower. "He called me and everyone else at ten minute intervals during the last hour [of the flight]." When word arrived confirming Eisenhower's safe arrival, Smith and Ismay took the news to Churchill. The prime minister exclaimed, "Don't tell me he has drowned." When Smith affirmed that all was well, Churchill replied, "I never had the slightest idea that it would be otherwise."[41] On 7 November London received the text of a broadcast Roosevelt intended to make. The president emphasized that the Allies had invaded neutral French territory as a reaction to the increasing Axis threat to the region. Roosevelt pointedly said that North Africa would not constitute a "second front." The British vigorously objected, since they hoped to sell the Russians on the idea that Torch *did* represent the long-promised second front. Smith sympathized with the British point of view, but as he informed Mountbatten, "we could do no less than follow [the president's] lead." In any case, Smith calmly proclaimed his confidence that "we are on the threshold of a magnificent success."[42]

The strain took its toll on Smith. As much as he tried to conceal the seriousness of his stomach problems, Smith's increasingly vitriolic mood provided the best barometer of his worsening health. The morning of the landings found Smith in a distinctly foul mood. LTG Frederick Morgan, the officer designated as commander of the Northern Task Force in the event of complications with Spain, witnessed Smith's distress. He recognized that Smith's stomach gave "him very particular hell." While awaiting news relays from Gibraltar, Morgan worked on Smith, trying to raise his spirits and take his mind off his pain. For over an hour the British general engaged "in merry chatter . . . on every subject but that of invasion in general and the invasion of Africa in particular."[43]

Over the course of the day, information began trickling in from

Gibraltar. Dodgy communications created the worst problems, but much of the information proved pretty good. Despite all evidence to the contrary, Torch achieved total surprise. The safety of the convoys stood high on the list of concerns. With the exception of the torpedoing of a troop ship, the convoys arrived in the combat zone without loss. The damaged ship carried a battalion of assault troops from Smith's old unit, the Thirty-ninth Infantry Regiment. Even there the news was not all bad; the vessel was evacuated successfully, and the troops landed at their assigned beaches twenty hours late. On the downside, foul weather and faulty communications turned the airborne operation at Oran into a complete wash. First reports from Algiers were mostly negative; they were spotty from Oran and nonexistent from Morocco, other than indications that the landings had gone in on time. Patton's luck held; reports indicated the calmest surf in decades. The Spanish also remained quiet. Eisenhower had ranked the Moroccan surf, Spanish intentions, and the level of French resistance as his chief apprehensions. The seas cooperated, the Spanish stayed motionless, and only the French remained as a wild card, and an intensely irritating one at that.

The day before the landings, Eisenhower reported that Giraud refused to play ball unless given supreme command. As a weary Eisenhower reported, "He threatens to withdraw his blessing and wash his hands of the affair."[44] Later on 8 November, after two days of frustrating negotiations, Eisenhower finally concluded a gentlemen's agreement with Giraud. The general—aptly code-named Kingpin—agreed to go to Algiers as chief of the French armed forces and civil administration and, in that dual capacity, make a proclamation requesting a cessation of all resistance against Allied forces. The next day Eisenhower told Smith, "In Algiers things are in our hands. . . . At Oran we've had hard fighting. . . . On the West, Patton is having a general battle, all along the line." As a further complication, Darlan, who just happened to be in Algiers, had been taken into protective custody. Even in the face of French resistance and a political mess defying solution, Eisenhower concluded, "The operation—in spite of my resentment that we have to waste *time* and resources fighting people that are *supposed* to become our allies—is proceeding as well as we had any right to expect."[45] It would have been difficult to quibble with that appraisal.

★ 17 ★

"Thank God You Are in London"

Holed up in the fetid catacombs inside the Rock of Gibraltar and grousing about the French (but really fuming at the impotence he felt), an idle Eisenhower advised Smith not to worry about "missing out on the show here."[1] Smith was far too busy to give it much thought. All the political and command channels converged at his desk. When not fielding the enormous flood of correspondence, Smith spent his time running interference for Eisenhower with the British. He stayed in daily, even hourly, contact with Ismay. Meanwhile, Eisenhower keenly felt his isolation in Gibraltar and wiled away his time drawing up lists called "Worries of a Commander" and recording his "inconsequential thoughts . . . during one of the interminable 'waiting periods.'" Letters from Smith offered Eisenhower his "only . . . type of relaxation." "Every time I hear of a pouch arriving from England," Eisenhower told Beetle, "I keep everyone on the jaunt until I find out whether or not it contains a letter for me."[2] He depended on Smith to funnel him news from the gang back in London, including the welfare of his Scottie puppy, for as he told Smith, "I am quite anxious about the black imp!"[3] ETO mistakenly routed one of Beetle's cables about the dog to the War Department, and Eisenhower had to apologize for getting Smith into a jam with Washington because the WDGS had concluded that Telek, the dog's name, represented some unknown code. Apparently, the slip-up caused a great deal of turmoil in high circles. "It is a good thing we get an occasional chuckle out of this thing," Eisenhower offered, "or all of us would probably go a bit goofy." Nobody recorded whether Smith found any humor in this episode. Soon Eisenhower and Smith confronted an issue infinitely more compelling than the progress of Telek's housebreaking. There would be precious

little to laugh about, but a great deal to prompt Eisenhower to think
again about taking up residence in the nuthouse.

The Fixer

Confusion reigned in Algiers, as it did everywhere else in French North
Africa. Darlan's presence compromised the authority of GEN Alphonse
Juin, commander in chief of the French army in North Africa, who
had already signaled his eagerness to cooperate. As Eisenhower later
explained, "The name of Marshal Petain is something to conjure with
here."[4] Darlan supposedly knew the marshal's "secret thoughts," and
only he spoke for Pétain. French officers throughout North Africa
ignored Juin and awaited orders from Darlan. Giraud and Clark arrived
in Algiers at about the same time. Murphy, briefly arrested by pro-Darlan
operatives, immediately entered into negotiations with Giraud backed
by Clark, whose very limited French meant his role consisted mostly
of a lot of table pounding. Giraud made it clear he desired no place
in any provisional government and again insisted on directing all military operations, including a possible invasion of southern France. When
Murphy explained why Darlan should enter the picture, Giraud readily
agreed, offering his services under the admiral. Giraud suggested that
he command the armed forces while Darlan assumed the role of high
commissioner. The French, not Clark or Eisenhower, instigated the deal
with Darlan.[5]

A potential Darlan deal had been on the table since the middle of
October. On 16 October Marshall forwarded the contents of a letter
sent to Roosevelt from Murphy in Algiers. Murphy reported having met
with Darlan's agents, who made it clear the admiral stood prepared to
come to North Africa, cooperate with the Allies, and bring the French
fleet in the bargain. Murphy said a great deal more. Vichy expected an
Allied movement against either Casablanca or Dakar, and the Germans
planned to move into French North Africa through bases in Spain and
Spanish Morocco.

Murphy's letters set off a chain reaction. Roosevelt accepted Mur-
phy's intelligence estimate; it served as the basis for the president's
Torch broadcast claiming that the Allies had moved into North Africa
to preempt the Axis. The claim the Germans intended to operate from
Spanish territory raised the specter of a Spanish intervention, confirm-
ing in American minds the wisdom of committing Patton's forces in
Morocco. In London, Eisenhower jumped at the opportunity to involve
Darlan in the negotiations. He proposed recognizing Giraud as "Gover-

nor of all French North Africa, responsible for all French civil and military affairs," and Darlan as "Commander-in-chief of French military
and/or naval forces," provided some condominium emerged between
the general and the admiral. If Giraud and Darlan brought with them
the French forces in North Africa and the French fleet, Eisenhower
even foresaw the possibility of making one of them deputy supreme
commander.[6] He immediately requested an emergency meeting with
Churchill and the BCOS.

Eisenhower met with Churchill and the British chiefs later that day,
with Foreign Minister Anthony Eden and FM Jan Smuts, the prime minister of South Africa and respected adviser to Churchill, in attendance.
As Eisenhower reported to Marshall, Churchill announced himself in
"full and complete accord" with the essentials of his plan. Eisenhower
informed the British of Clark's mission. The British insisted on certain modifications in Clark's "plan of action," including a separation
of civil and military functions, with Giraud as governor-general; in
addition, they wanted only Darlan to "be considered for . . . [the] position of deputy [supreme commander]."[7] Clark's directive, issued that
same day by the president, insisted that selection of the French command remained "a matter to be handled by the French themselves."[8] On
23 October Eisenhower and Smith went to Paddington Station to greet
Eleanor Roosevelt. The king, who was also there to meet the first lady,
took Eisenhower aside and asked his opinion of the reliability of "D"
and "G." Churchill repeatedly told Eisenhower he would crawl on his
hands and knees to secure the French fleet, which presumably included
kissing Darlan's stern, if required.[9] Clearly, the prospects of Darlan's
playing some role in North Africa had circulated in the highest circles
in London weeks before the landings.

Seeing no danger in offering Darlan a position in the new French
regime, Eisenhower empowered Clark to treat with him. According to
Murphy, none of the American principals ever considered not including Darlan in the bargaining. Eisenhower's preoccupation focused solely
on ending the fighting, rallying the French, securing the Toulon fleet,
and initiating the drive into Tunisia. The problem centered on obliging the French to cooperate with each other. Darlan put Eisenhower
in a tough spot. As Eisenhower told Smith on 9 November, "I've promised Giraud to make him the big shot, while I've got to use every kind
of cajolery, bribe, threat and all else to get Darlan's *active* cooperation."
That same day he informed Marshall of his dealings with the "tempera-
mental Frenchmen" and reported, "Darlan states that he will not talk
to any Frenchmen; Giraud hates and distrusts Darlan. It's a mess! I get

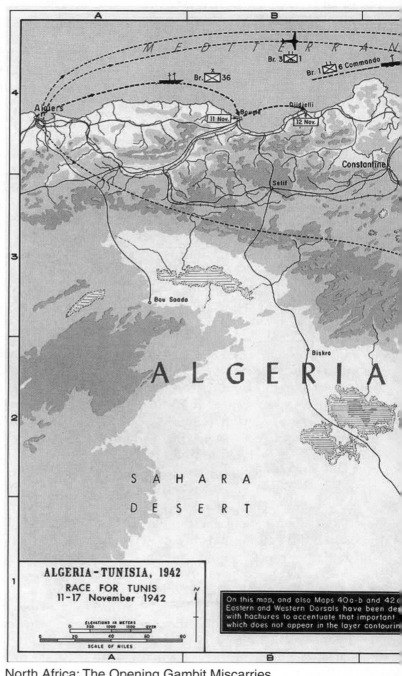

North Africa: The Opening Gambit Miscarries

weary of people that have no other thought but 'ME.'" As he told Smith, Eisenhower grew exhausted by the "petty intrigue and the necessity of dealing with little selfish worms that call themselves men."[10]

It was not quite that simple. None of the senior American leadership remotely understood the psychological baggage borne by their French opposites. The fantasy lingered that the spirit of Lafayette would descend and induce the French to coalesce as one in support of the Allied cause. But for that to happen, the French must forget the humiliation of defeat in 1940, the indignity of Vichy collaboration with the Nazis, and the losses suffered in the face of an unprovoked invasion by the Anglo-Saxon powers on neutral French Northwest Africa. It did not play out that way.

At noon the next day, 10 November, Darlan agreed on an armistice and ordered French forces in Algiers to put down their arms. Oran fell that day—the only objective taken by force of arms. The stumbling block remained Casablanca. Noguès arrested Béthouart and directed the French to resist Patton's forces, which they did, in some places furiously. Nobody outside Morocco on the Allied side knew anything about events there. Patton's force was dubbed the "Lost Western Task Force." "Radio communications has been hopeless," Butcher recorded, "for some reason our sets of codebooks and Patton's do not jibe." Later it was discovered that Patton's staff had brought the wrong codes.[11] At first light on 11 November—coincidentally, Armistice Day and Patton's birthday—the French forces in Morocco accepted a cease-fire.

Events moved rapidly in Algiers. Trying to salvage his tottering regime, Pétain repudiated Darlan's cease-fire and named Noguès his prime representative in North Africa. Clark's plan appeared to be dead, and Darlan dutifully countermanded his cease-fire order. The same day, Hitler ordered his troops into southern France, Italian troops moved into Nice and Corsica, and the Axis rapidly expanded a bridgehead in northern Tunisia. The armistice in Morocco held, and Noguès flew in from Casablanca the next day for talks with Darlan, Giraud, and Murphy. Darlan issued his second cease-fire and ordered French forces in Tunisia to resist the Axis. The powwow among the French officials in Algiers concluded at midnight, but as Butcher remarked, "no peace pipe was smoked."[12] Clark entered the fray, telling Noguès that under no circumstances would the Allied governments recognize him.

"I cannot tell you how much your being in London has added to my peace of mind," Eisenhower confided in Smith. "As you can well see from the messages that flow back and forth between us, I would be completely lost without you there to handle the thousands of tricky problems for me."[13] The trickiest problem involved handling Churchill. Messages traveled between London and Gibraltar, but Eisenhower kept Churchill out of the loop. "PM's extraordinary impatience and desire for personal news" meant he bombarded Smith with incessant requests for information. Repeatedly, Smith requested that Eisenhower send a personal message to Churchill to take the heat off himself.[14] Finally, on 11 November, Eisenhower penned a short note to Churchill, offering congratulations on his "end of the beginning" speech at the Lord Mayor's dinner in London. He obliquely mentioned bringing "prominent French in this region into our camp" and asked for Churchill's assistance in scaring "these French out of their jockeying for position," but he made no reference to Darlan.[15]

Poor communications gumming up the flow of information from North Africa offers only a partial justification for the lack of communication from Eisenhower to the prime minister. The reason Eisenhower gave for avoiding direct communication with Churchill involved his preoccupation with safeguarding "the sanctity" of the chain of command through the CCS and, with it, his claims on unity of command.[16] It is also clear that he purposefully circumvented the combined apparatus. Eisenhower avoided employing radio communications because they required signatures in the body of the text; instead, he used an American channel of communications to which the British had no access. He used this conduit for communicating with Smith and, through Smith, with Marshall.[17] Throughout November Eisenhower wrote long explicatory letters to Marshall but only infrequent and pithy updates using CCS routing.

Smith informed Churchill that Clark had entered into a tentative agreement with Darlan that resulted in the first cease-fire. Following a BCOS meeting on 10 November, Brooke expressed "great hopes of possibly achieving our objectives of ultimately clearing North Africa of Germans." Later Churchill called Brooke in and asked if all necessary steps had been taken to reap full advantage from the situation.[18] The next day Churchill, still unaware of the specifics of developments in Algiers, woke to the sweeping implications of Darlan's assuming the leadership role. In an attempt to head off Darlan, he had Smith wire Eisenhower with the offer to send a Gaullist official to "fix things . . . with KING-PIN." Any pact between Giraud and the Free French—who remained unalterably opposed to any dealings with Vichy—would strengthen the general's position and remove the necessity of depending on Darlan. Eisenhower delayed responding until 14 November—by then, too late.[19]

Eisenhower intended to fly down to Algiers on 12 November and, as he told Clark, "lay down the law with a bit of table pounding" of his

own, but miserable weather grounded him.[20] That morning he received
a cable from Smith that floored him. In view of the successful landings,
Clark's accord with Darlan and Giraud, and the assumption that the
French in Tunisia would ward off the Axis forces, the CCS broached
the idea of expanding operations in the Mediterranean. Smith warned
Eisenhower the chiefs had asked AFHQ to consider employing forces
earmarked for Torch for an alternative invasion of Sardinia.

This line of thinking bore the unmistakable mark of Churchill. There
are those who argue the prime minister suffered from bipolar disorder.
Brooke's diary serves as a veritable case study of the wild modulations
in Churchill's moods, fluctuating between manic highs and bouts of
depression—what Churchill referred to as his "black dog." During hypo-
manic periods, bipolar individuals manifest elevated, expansive, and
petulant moods characterized by the inability to filter emotions, feelings
of euphoria, and inflated senses of self-esteem and self-confidence; they
experience flights of fancy and engage in greater risk-taking behaviors;
they display restless energy, impatience, loquaciousness, and irritability
and are easily distracted; and they require less sleep and tend to abuse
alcohol. Churchill ran the gamut of this symptomatology.[21] Contempo-
raries forgave his many foibles, attributing all these traits to the eccentric-
ity of genius. Whether induced by success or setback, Churchill flew into
his projects with all guns blazing. The only thing he could not abide was
inactivity when great possibilities beckoned, and they always beckoned.
With Torch apparently a success, Churchill wanted forces earmarked
for North Africa employed elsewhere. Since Spain remained passive, an
Allied movement into the Canary Islands and Spanish Morocco (code-
named Backbone) now seemed unlikely, but Churchill saw enormous
potential in rushing forces into Sardinia (code-named Hires). Churchill
wanted Eisenhower to fly back to London for discussions.[22]

Eisenhower emphatically "opposed any suggestion at this time for
reducing contemplated TORCH strength." As he told Smith, they were
already "running some parts of this thing on a shoestring." He stressed,
"The situation is *not* crystallized." The Germans rapidly expanded
their bridgehead in Tunisia, and the French commanders there, caught
between a rock and a hard place, neither resisted the Axis nor followed
Vichy or the conflicting orders out of Algiers and Casablanca. "We
should plan ahead in orderly fashion on strategic matters," he admitted to Smith, "but for God's sake let's get one job done at a time. Rather
than be talking at this time of possible reduction we should be seeking
ways and means of speeding up the buildup with a view of cleaning out
North Africa and then hitting HIRES before defenses are too highly

developed." With the cease-fire hanging by a thread, he demurred to leave the theater for talks in London.[23] Smith wrote back, assuring Eisenhower that he had presented "as forcibly as possible" Eisenhower's views to the BCOS. The next day he went to the BCOS meeting and restated Eisenhower's objections.[24]

Eisenhower finally escaped Gibraltar on Friday the thirteenth. The date did not augur well. Taking Cunningham and Butcher along, Eisenhower flew to Algiers. As he informed Marshall, "Clark needs help."[25] First he met with Clark at his St. George Hotel headquarters. A breathless Murphy arrived with the news that Noguès had agreed to a power-sharing plan that included all the major French players. At 2 P.M. Darlan, Giraud, and Noguès came to the hotel for a meeting with Eisenhower. Through interpreters, Eisenhower acceded, in the name of the two governments, to their arrangement. The French retained administrative control of North Africa, with Darlan as head of a provisional government and naval commander. Giraud would serve as ground and air force commander; Juin would command the eastern sector, and Noguès the western sector as resident general in Morocco. The Allies received military rights in the region. Eisenhower left Clark to work out the details. The supreme commander made one demand: now was the time for the French to "get in and pitch."[26] With that, an immensely relieved Eisenhower boarded his plane and returned to Gibraltar with Murphy in tow. Eisenhower knew the Darlan deal would require some explanation; he had no way of knowing how much.

After arriving in Gibraltar, Eisenhower immediately wired Smith, informing him of the agreement and instructing him to send word to the CCS. But he emphasized, "There is to be *no* publicity until released from here." Smith attended a BCOS meeting that morning, and surprisingly, the topic of Darlan never came up; discussions centered on Churchill's scheme for Sardinia and the shipping problems involved with expanded operations in the Mediterranean.[27] Later that evening Darlan preempted AFHQ and went on the radio to announce the formation of a provisional government, complete with the purported blessings of Pétain. Because in some quarters Giraud's collusion with the Allies opened him to charges of treason, Darlan withheld his name. The omission gave the impression that Darlan had seized power with Eisenhower's compliance.

Eisenhower woke up the next day shocked to discover that Darlan's announcement had set off an explosion in London. In a classic bit of understatement, Smith reported that the British government had received the arrangement "coolly." As Eisenhower explained to the CCS, he could "well understand some bewilderment in London and Washington with the turn that negotiations with the French North Africans have taken." He complained that all the political calculations made before Torch had proved totally wrong. All the senior French officers, including Giraud, agreed that only Darlan spoke for Marshal Pétain. "All concerned profess themselves to be ready to go along with us providing Darlan tell them to do so," he argued, "but they are absolutely *not* willing to follow anyone else." Eisenhower reminded everyone that Darlan had already delivered the goods, and any hope of securing Tunisia, Dakar, and the Toulon fleet depended on French cooperation. "It is extremely important," he pleaded, "that no precipitate action at home upset such equilibrium as we have been able to establish."[28]

Particularly anxious that Smith understand his motives, Eisenhower wrote a long, clarifying letter. Hurt by any suggestion he had naïvely entered into an unholy alliance, Eisenhower could not "believe that the 'bosses' would think us so stupid as to include a known 'slicker' in the proposition unless circumstances forced us to do so." Pointing to the convoy schedules, Eisenhower protested, "It will be a long time before we can get up on our high horse and tell everybody in the world to go to the devil!" He asked Smith to retain that picture in his head "when you feel that the 'hot shots' are getting out of hand on you." He concluded by entreating Smith to take care of his health. "Again, I say thank God you are in London at this particular time."[29]

Smith swiftly tried to repair the damage. He and Ismay spent the whole night together preparing Eisenhower's case. The next day Smith and Gale drove out to Chequers for a scheduled afternoon session with Churchill. The British were in the midst of formulating plans for 1943; future operations in the Mediterranean topped the agenda. Smuts and Eden also attended. Smith presented the justifications for reinforcing Torch. Churchill passed Smith a long letter stating his views on post-Torch strategy, favoring an attack on Sardinia or Sicily, and soliciting Eisenhower's opinion. Conversation inevitably turned to Darlan. Eden voiced his strong opposition to placing Darlan at the head of any provisional government. An emotional Churchill railed, "Is this then what we are fighting for?" After venting his frustration, the prime minister acquiesced, accepting the deal as a fait accompli. "Anything for the battle," he concluded. Smith confessed his surprise at "how deeply disturbed [Churchill] had been by the Darlan agreement." Brooke summed up the situation best when he recorded, "In any case, no alternative for the present." The prime minister promised to send a "fine message" to the president, for which Smith warmly thanked him. Churchill placed much of the blame on Murphy. "For god's sake," he cautioned Smith, "do not let the political people have any more field days. A storm is blowing up over the Darlan affair which further political ventures will intensify." They then turned their attention to what help the French might offer. Churchill thought "the reference to powerful French Armies in Morocco . . . a bit of wishful thinking." Smith readily concurred and argued against building up the French at the expense of American forces—a view Churchill heartily shared.[30] Since Eisenhower could not come to London, Churchill insisted on sending his chief planners to Gibraltar. The next day he asked Roosevelt's opinion on the propriety of holding such a meeting. The president approved, so long as the topics discussed remained strictly military.[31]

The American condemnation of Torch as a political operation appeared well founded. The menacing global situation the Western Allies confronted in summer 1942 elevated Torch's significance. For Roosevelt, any failure to commit American troops in Europe—even if not initially in Europe or against Germans and Italians—raised the likelihood of an enforced reorientation of American grand strategy toward the Pacific; for Churchill, another military setback might bring an end to his premiership. For both, failure meant no second front, with the attendant problems of dealing with Stalin. When the Allies made the Torch decision, the German push into the Caucasus and toward the Volga proffered the gloomy prospect of a Soviet-Nazi accommodation. Even though little discussed, the Eastern Front loomed large in Anglo-American calculations for Torch. In early September, Churchill presaged, "If TORCH fails then I'm done for."[32]

By 1 November the grand strategic landscape had changed significantly. The Red Army's successes now brought the disquieting possibility of a Soviet victory without the assistance of the Western democracies, significantly raising the grand strategic odds should the North African venture miscarry. Taken in concert—Soviet triumphs in the east, Montgomery's victory in Egypt, and successful Allied landings in Morocco and Algeria—the sudden and dramatic improvement in Allied fortunes prompted a greatly relieved Churchill, just two days after the Torch landings, to offer his famed prediction: "Now this is not the end. It is not even the beginning of the end. But it is, perhaps, the end of the beginning." American military tentativeness might have robbed Torch of its ultimate strategic objective—control of Tunisia—but the North African gambit promised immediate political dividends. The German decision to reinforce Tunisia meant American forces would soon confront Axis troops; Torch energized political support for Churchill; and Stalin possessed clear proof of the Western powers' resolve in carrying the war against the Germans and Italians. But just as quickly, the deal with Darlan threatened to offset the gains.

Churchill, euphoric only days before, lapsed into one of his monumental furies. His ability to engineer the tilt to the Mediterranean strategy hung on deflecting the Americans from a genuine second front while funneling their ascending power into a peripheral campaign. He made certain assurances to Stalin about Torch during his visit to Moscow. He expended a great deal of political capital on supporting de Gaulle and the Free French movement. He placed great store in "setting Europe alight" through subversion. Much of his political backing—in Britain and the Commonwealth, in the United States, and among the resistance movements and governments-in-exile on the Continent—grew out of his moral claims as leader of the great crusade against Nazi tyranny. The deal with an arch-corroborationist threatened to unravel Churchill's entire strategic tapestry. The British press had a field day attacking the deal; Churchill might even face another no-confidence vote.

In Washington, Marshall robustly defended Eisenhower's position. Duly warned by Smith, he forwarded Eisenhower's 14 November letter to the CCS to Roosevelt at Hyde Park. Eisenhower's justification moved the president. Hopkins and other close advisers urged that Roosevelt make a public announcement in support of Eisenhower.[33] Marshall immediately called in a select group of congressional leaders and vindicated Eisenhower's position. He read them Eisenhower's letter and elaborated on the problems faced by Eisenhower in North Africa and Smith in London. In Marshall's opinion, his politicking worked; "it gave us defenders on the floor of the Senate . . . and the House."[34] On 16 November Roosevelt held a press conference and announced his endorsement of the "temporary expedient." The same day the CCS cabled Smith, offering their approval.[35]

The tempest subsided but did not die. On 17 November Churchill informed Roosevelt of the "very deep currents of feeling" stirred by the Darlan deal. The more he reflected on it, the more convinced Churchill became that the arrangement with Darlan could "only be a temporary expedient justifiable solely by the stress of battle." He reminded the president not to "overlook the serious political injury which may be done to our cause not only in France but throughout Europe by the feeling that we are ready to make terms with local Quislings." Pointing to Darlan's odious record, Churchill thought any "permanent arrangement with Darlan or the formation of a Darlan government in French North Africa would not be understood by the great masses of ordinary people whose simple loyalties are our strength." The same day Eden added his voice in a similar vein. Cowed by the public and congressional uproar, the State Department recommended Darlan's removal, a proposition ignored by the War Department.[36] Always attentive to fluctuations in the public opinion barometer, Roosevelt could have fired Eisenhower, repudiated the agreement, and scored some cheap political points, but he decided to ride out the storm.

In the meantime, Eisenhower stewed in Gibraltar. Smith sent a series of letters and cables on 15 and 16 November. His personal letters all bore "an ominous ring." Smith reported that the outpouring of opposition in Britain had seriously affected AFHQ morale. De Gaulle added his strident voice to the debate; he opposed the compact and refused to cooperate with any Frenchman in North Africa. Eisenhower decided "things must be in really a bad state," and from the sound of it, only Beetle and Kay Summersby, his Anglo-Irish driver and office assistant, "were sticking." In a transparent ploy to bolster Smith, Eisenhower complained about Marshall's withholding Smith's promised promotion. "I would particularly like to see you come down here with your second star."[37]

With the uproar in his rear, Eisenhower remained frustrated he could not impact developments at the front. British airborne units landed at two spots in Tunisia, and an improvised force advanced eastward from Bône. Anderson informed Eisenhower that he planned to launch attacks toward Bizerte and Tunis on 21 or 22 November. Meanwhile, the Germans clearly enjoyed a wide head start in the race to build up in Tunisia, especially in air assets. Anderson and Eisenhower decided to stage a diversion. Eisenhower wired Smith and asked him to approach the BCOS for permission to employ the airborne forces in Malta for a drop at Sousse (Operation Breastplate) on the Gulf d'Hammamet, astride the north-south coastal corridor in Tunisia.[38] Smith immediately got on the phone to Ismay, who passed the request along to the BCOS. The British chiefs rejected any consideration of Breastplate until a vital convoy reached Malta and safely unloaded. The governor and commander in Malta, Lord Gort, vetoed the plan on operational grounds; any force landing there faced little chance of achieving anything and the real possibility of annihilation.[39]

As Eisenhower told Marshall, communications "tend to tie me rather closely [in Gibraltar]—sometimes to my intense irritation." To Smith he wrote, "You cannot imagine just how much I would like to be down there in actual charge of the tactics of [Anderson's] operation." More anxious than ever to escape Gibraltar, Eisenhower decided to accelerate the establishment of AFHQ in Algiers. He longed for the day "when we get to our own headquarters and can run our own establishment according to our own likes and dislikes, a gang of friends around with whom we can have an hour's conversation a day will be a God-send." Smith thought it was a mistake to rush the move. He argued AFHQ-Main must remain in London for the foreseeable future. He worried about logistical coordination, which could be performed only in London. He also wrestled with what rear echelon functions to transfer to ETO. He thought the best solution lay in building up the ETO planning staffs while maintaining the bulk of AFHQ's planners in London. AFHQ in Algiers should have the final say, but the bulk of the planning and coordination should remain in London until communications facilities improved in North Africa.[40]

Eisenhower rejected Smith's concerns; he saw no reason why the timing of the move to Algiers depended on communications. Nor did he agree on "the necessity of keeping too much of the staff in London after we get ourselves fairly well organized." Acknowledging the need to stay in close contact with the planners and logisticians in London, Eisenhower wanted the mass of the work performed in AFHQ in Algiers. He proposed coordinating programs by creating a liaison group in London. Eisenhower thought once they got to Algiers, they would have to "put on the dog" to impress the French and the locals. He wanted a villa "where I can entertain at will for almost any size of party." "I am going to have a fine layout."[41] Although he still considered it a mistake, Smith expedited preparations for the headquarters move.

The cacophony of criticism increased. Just a few days before, Eisenhower had been a national hero, subject of a feature in *Life* magazine that painted him as the American Everyman. Now the press dubbed him a reactionary and a fascist. He grumbled to Clark about the "barrage that has been hitting me from the rear. For two days here I thought I would simply have to go to a padded cell."[42] Eisenhower avoided responsibility, felt put upon by those who second-guessed and disparaged him, and held grudges against those who made him look bad—even though looking bad is the price leaders must pay for making controversial decisions they believe to be correct.

Eisenhower's irritability began to show. On 18 November Smith wired Gibraltar to inform Eisenhower that he, Gale, and three British planners would fly down in two days' time. While Eisenhower thanked providence for Smith's presence in London, he bitched to Marshall of the "time consuming burden" of keeping him fully informed "on these matters so that he could allay anxieties, at the same time that we are trying to win a battle."[43] "Since this operation started," he complained to Smith in a long epistle written that day, "three quarters of my time, both night and day, has been necessarily occupied in difficult political maneuver in attempting to explain to people, far from the scene of action, the basic elements of the local situation." He wanted to "make perfectly clear [several points] in your mind so that your conversations can be guided accordingly." The list was long:

1. The French must preserve their system of internal control. Historically, no single administration existed for the whole of French Northwest Africa—authority always resided in centralized authority in Paris and then Vichy. The Darlan arrangement now provided for a single agency through which Eisenhower expected to act.
2. Eisenhower assumed he would work through Giraud, but the French general "quickly admitted that he could *not* establish and exercise the necessary control, and agreed that Darlan was the only one that could."
3. Eisenhower made no written or verbal promises about the future administration in the region or any pledge concerning the eventual government of France; he remained guided only by the imperative of controlling the rear and getting on with conducting the campaign for Tunisia.
4. The agreement ended hostilities without upsetting the domestic situation—especially with the tribes in the Rif region—which might have prompted a Spanish reaction.
5. Churchill repeatedly told Eisenhower that securing the Toulon fleet was "worth crawling on hands and knees to get." Darlan offered the only chance of accomplishing that mission.

"I can*not* believe that the bosses want me to throw all this away."

"Another point that you should make clear," he continued, "is that this population is *not* burning with enthusiasm to start a war with the Axis." The *pied noir* benefited economically from the war; they sold their agricultural products at inflated prices to the Axis powers, especially Germany. The Arabs had no stake but reacted negatively to the sudden destabilizing appearance of Anglo-American forces in the region. For urban Algerians, the Allies brought German bombing attacks. "I have tried again and again to assure [Churchill] and others that I know the limitations on the authority of a commander in the field. I am *not* committing ourselves to anything that is *not* essential to immediate operations, and God knows I'm not trying to be a king-maker. I am simply trying to get a complete and firm military grip on North Africa, which

I was sent down here to do." He reminded Smith the Allies still had not won the battle or concentrated the necessary forces or ensured security in Morocco. Finally, Eisenhower requested civilian consumer goods—tea, sugar, cloth—to win over popular support. "Once the population looks to us as their benefactors, I can tell all the turncoats and crooks to go to hell." He fully understood the "crookedness [and] intense unpopularity of Darlan," but the admiral now dangled on his own hook.[44] Later in the day, an obviously agitated Eisenhower wrote again, telling Smith, "My whole interest now is Tunisia. When I can make the Allies a present of that place [Churchill] can kick me in the pants and put in a politician here who is as big a crook as the chief local skunk." Churchill intended to do just that.[45]

Smith and his party arrived in Gibraltar on 20 November.[46] Though glad to have the chance to straighten things out with Smith, Eisenhower felt only irritation at the intrusion. "Unfortunately," he confided in Clark, "one of the things that the Chiefs of Staff want [Smith] to talk to me about is future strategy—the only strategy I am now concerned with is winning Tunisia!"[47] Eisenhower strenuously argued that the coalition must first defeat the Axis in Tunisia and unite the Torch force with Montgomery's Eighth Army. The Anglo-American forces must complete their CCS-mandated mission of clearing the Axis from the North African littoral before allocating forces for secondary objectives. He indicated that he favored the Sardinia project if the CCS decided to continue operations in the Mediterranean. As he had told Marshall earlier, "before that is undertaken, a very broad strategic review by the CCS will probably have been made."[48]

Eisenhower and Smith talked extensively about plans for AFHQ. Eisenhower also solicited Clark's views. Before D-day, AFHQ had 700 officers attached. Clark now thought that number two or three times too many.[49] Eisenhower wanted AFHQ kept as small as possible and confessed he was tired of quarreling with everyone about this question. He was "particularly anxious that we strip down to a working basis and cut down on all of the folderol." Eisenhower admitted that Smith had finally convinced him of the need for a strong logistics setup, and he foresaw the need for a large Operations Division in AFHQ to plan and coordinate supply; otherwise, the American and British army commanders should deal directly with the responsible War Department and War Office agencies. Once again, Eisenhower demonstrated his OPD bias; at the AFHQ level, he insisted that G-3, not G-4, control supply and movement. He reasoned that this arrangement would cut down the size of the combined staffs. Eisenhower recognized that under the iron law of

bureaucracy, every staff division would expand until it had "enough people in the head office to run the whole show." Since this also held true
for subordinate staff echelons, "an enormous number of experienced
officers [were] pinned up in staffs that there is no quality left for the
troop units." Emphasizing the seriousness of the problem, he confessed,
"I have been puzzling my head as to the best way of securing the results
we want." Eisenhower saw no easy solution and again deferred the matter until "we all get together and we can be perfectly ruthless in cutting
out useless portions."[50]

Despite all this tough talk about reducing staff size, and under
pressure from Somervell, Eisenhower authorized the formation of yet
another AFHQ agency—the North African Economic Board, a joint military and civilian committee overseeing civilian supply for North Africa.
He postponed the NAEB's formation until Smith's visit so he could take
the lead. Smith convened the first meeting of the NAEB on 21 November and charged the new agency with coordinating military supply and
shipping through the NASB, in liaison with the Lend-Lease Administration and the various American and British economic warfare boards.
Gale and Murphy, now the active AFHQ chief of civil affairs, would
serve as cochairmen.[51]

"When Beetle returned to London," Butcher recorded, "he carried
numerous problems that needed to be trouble shot." At the top of the list
came more night fighters and aircraft in general. Eisenhower also asked
that Smith intercede with Washington on the theater's behalf to ensure
the dispatch of civilian supplies, especially foodstuffs. In addition, he
wanted Smith to remind the CCS of the present opportunity to hammer
the U-boats now congregating in the Mediterranean approaches. Smith
wired Algiers, advising that he would "catch a plane for the U.S. and get
everything in apple-pie order." Eisenhower agreed, reminding him to
emphasize "with the people in Washington that 'I have no complaints.'"[52]

Smith met with Churchill and Ismay his first day back. He outlined
Eisenhower's views on North Africa versus Sardinia and Sicily. He also
raised the question of the night fighters. They discussed the continued
fallout from the Darlan business. The next day Churchill would face a
hostile Parliament. Smith reported to Marshall, "The situation here is
now good and the Prime Minister and Cabinet are in strong support."
Smith rather overstated the case. The War Cabinet met on 21 November for a full discussion of the Darlan affair. Brooke's views accorded
exactly with Eisenhower's: "As far as I could see there is at present nothing to do but to accept the Darlan situation and get on with pushing the
Germans out of Tunisia." Eden played for more time "before Winston

finally got some form of general agreement." Smith assured Marshall that he remained "in the most intimate touch with the situation here" and had gone over all its implications with Eisenhower.[53]

On 24 November Smith asked Marshall if he should come back to Washington and make a direct report. He saw a breathing spell in the offing; the first echelon of AFHQ had been packed and loaded on transports, and Smith planned to head for Algiers on 5 December.[54] The next day Marshall telephoned, ordering Smith "to come to Washington as quickly as you can arrange your affairs, to discuss the Darlan status but more particularly to assist us in an issue that has been raised by the Prime Minister yesterday with the President . . . all apparently produced by some statement that Hartle made with relation to ROUND-UP." Churchill wanted a full-blown CCS conference in Cairo to decide on Allied strategy for 1943. Marshall shrank from the idea of another conference and wanted Smith's opinion on the state of play in North Africa and prospects for expanding operations in that theater.[55]

The Washington Mission

Churchill once said of John Foster Dulles that he was the only bull he knew who carried around his own china shop; the same applied to the prime minister. The bull got loose again while Smith was in Gibraltar. Hartle asked, in view of commitments to Torch, for guidance on modifications for Bolero. The War Department advised him "not to exceed needs" in the construction program. With the manpower allotment for Bolero trimmed from 1.1 million to 427,000 men, ETO reduced the building program. Churchill interpreted this as indicating a complete shift away from Bolero-Roundup and on 24 November wrote an impulsive (in Smith's estimate) and lengthy remonstrance to Roosevelt. Churchill's protest created another tempest.

Smith contacted Eisenhower, informed him of the new developments, and asked if he should fly to Gibraltar for last-minute consultations before heading to Washington. He promised to "avoid anything like a defensive attitude" and vowed to "present our viewpoint as aggressively as possible consistent with tact" in talks with Roosevelt and Marshall. Eisenhower replied that Smith commanded his full confidence; he requested only that Smith reinforce the benefits accruing from Darlan's aid in gaining French support and push Eisenhower's list of theater promotions.[56]

First Smith had to put out the latest fire. He went over to 10 Downing Street for a late-night conference with Churchill and the BCOS. The prime minister had a long list of matters he wanted to thrash out. Smith began by outlining Eisenhower's thinking on clearing North Africa. He expected a hard fight for Tunisia. Smith predicted Tunis would fall by mid-December. Eisenhower envisioned sending two divisions into Tripolitania to aid Montgomery in Libya. Success in the theater depended chiefly on transportation and shipping. In an expansive mood, Churchill was more optimistic than both Eisenhower and Smith and raised the question of an attack on Sicily. The British provided Smith with a proposed directive for Sardinia (Operation Brimstone) and Sicily (Operation Husky) to present to the American chiefs, as well as their latest intelligence on North Africa. Smith parried any commitments, stating only that AFHQ possessed no appreciation of the forces required for Sicily or Sardinia. He added that Eisenhower favored Sardinia over Sicily but cautioned that either operation must be staged out of the United Kingdom. The discussions then turned to Hartle. The British showed Smith a copy of the minutes of their 20 November meeting, which underscored their perception that the Americans lacked real enthusiasm for either Bolero or Roundup. They concluded no real American buildup in the United Kingdom would occur until Allied grand strategy became firmly fixed. Smith assured Churchill that Hartle simply wanted to calibrate construction with manpower and that this implied no alteration in American strategic thinking about the 1943 cross-Channel operation. On the contrary, the Americans remained committed to staging a 1943 Roundup. Smith thought the matter should have been dealt with by personal contacts and regretted that, in his absence, Hartle's "tactless and ill-considered" actions had prompted a major flare-up involving the political heads over a mere misunderstanding. Reassured by Smith, the prime minister wired Roosevelt, withdrawing his previous complaint but not his request for a full CCS conference.[57]

The topic then moved on to Darlan. Reacting to Roosevelt's press conference and the president's categorization of the agreement with the French as a "temporary expedient," Darlan wrote what Churchill called a "pathetic and dignified" rejoinder. Darlan compared himself to "a lemon which the Americans will drop after it is crushed." He admitted "an agreement with me can be but a temporary one" because once "French sovereignty in its integrity is an accomplished fact," he intended to retire to civilian life. Motivated "neither through pride, nor ambition nor intrigue, but because the place I held in my country made it my duty to act," Darlan argued that the attitude of the American government "spread doubts among Frenchmen" working to reunite in a common cause.

Darlan's stock had already risen in Churchill's eyes. On 27 November the French scuttled the Toulon fleet. At their last meeting before France fell, Darlan assured Churchill the fleet would never fall into German hands. The French admiral in Toulon fulfilled Darlan's promise. Moved by Darlan's appeal, Churchill asked that Smith convey to Eisenhower his opinion that Darlan "has paid and is paying his fare on the bandwagon and is entitled to the ride." In addition, "Squeezed lemon tactics are *not* compatible with the dignity and honor of UK and US," Churchill stated, "and are *unthinkable*." Darlan was "entitled to a pat on the back," and Churchill hoped Eisenhower would do the patting. "All is now serene," Smith reported.[58]

Churchill never remained serene for long. The next day Smith received another summons to 10 Downing Street. Churchill again complained that Eisenhower had blocked vital communications from the theater. On 25 November Anderson advanced in three brigade columns against Axis positions in Tunisia. Three days later, Ultra intercepts indicated that FM Albert Kesselring thought the Axis forces too small to defend both Bizerte and Tunis, and since one was worthless without the other, he questioned the wisdom of committing more troops. "If this is correct," recorded Brooke in his diary, "there should be a chance of pushing him into the sea before long."[59] Yet Churchill received no news from Eisenhower on the First British Army's drive to Tunis. When Eisenhower discovered that Anderson had sent situation reports directly to the War Office, he exploded. Ever protective of the chain of command, Eisenhower insisted that all communications of an operational nature go through AFHQ. Once again Smith arbitrated a settlement. He told the British that even though filing situation reports amounted to standard operating procedure in British practice, henceforth Anderson must forward all communications through AFHQ channels. Smith promised that once he arrived in Algiers, his first priority would center on establishing mechanisms for keeping London better informed of actions in the theater. In fact, Smith again mildly chided Eisenhower while in Gibraltar about Churchill's complaints, but Eisenhower did not back down. Instead, he wrote a lengthy situation report and sent it to Smith with a postscript inviting him to show any or all of it to Churchill.[60] Smith handed the text to the prime minister.

The meager offensive failed, dashing Churchill's hopes for a quick victory in Tunisia. Increasingly rancorous over what he considered the timorousness of his commanders, the prime minister suddenly shifted his fixation to Roundup. At a 30 November meeting of the BCOS, Churchill presented his latest proposals for a reentry onto the Continent in 1943. At the same juncture, the British, already confronting a serious manpower shortage, discussed cannibalizing four divisions. Brooke complained that Churchill "never faces realities, at one moment we are reducing our forces, and the next we are invading the Continent with vast armies for which there is no hope of finding the shipping. He is quite incorrigible and I am exhausted!"[61] No doubt a little exhausted from jousting with the prime minister, Smith avoided this latest spat. On the morning of 29 November he set off on his trip to Washington.

On 1 December Smith arrived in the capital and immediately briefed Marshall, who found his report on Bolero, the Darlan affair, and efforts to pacify the prime minister "illuminating." Marshall also picked Smith's brain on the likely British posture in the event of a new conference, which was now almost certain. Thanks to his Ismay connection, Smith alerted Marshall that the BCOS would likely push hard to expand operations in the Mediterranean, but the prime minister had evinced renewed interest in cross-Channel operations. Marshall arranged for Smith to dine at the White House alone with the president "to make a full presentation of the North African picture as well as . . . British relations in London."[62] It did not quite work out that way. Instead of a private conversation, the president arranged a dinner party including Eleanor Roosevelt, Hopkins and his new wife, and Leahy. The first lady monopolized the conversation over dinner, berating Eisenhower's handling of political affairs in North Africa. After dinner the men happily beat a retreat to the president's study for discussions on a whole range of military and political matters. Churchill and his oscillations and the prospects of a future conference occupied the bulk of the conversation. Reviewing the progress of operations, Smith expected northern Tunisia would be occupied sometime in December, while Tripoli would fall to Montgomery by the end of January. Both predictions proved wildly incorrect.[63]

Smith then made the Washington rounds. The day after Smith left London, Eisenhower had pleaded with Marshall not to detain him for long.[64] The sojourn in Washington took twice as long as expected. Smith talked to Arnold about command relations in North Africa and Eisenhower's continued belief in the necessity of a single Mediterranean air command, probably under ACM Arthur Tedder. Smith held talks with Somervell and his senior subordinates about expediting the shipping of railway equipment and vehicles—especially the deuce-and-a-half trucks Clark had removed from the original shipping schedules—and civilian stocks and about improvements in signals communications. Together with Handy and OPD, they discussed future operations in North Africa, weighing Roundup against a range of Mediterranean options. He held meetings with MG Alexander Surles on establishing censorship policy and the pressing need for officers' training in press and public relations. With Marshall he touched on all these matters; in addition, he pushed for the requested promotions. The promotion he cared most about—his own—happened on 2 December. Marshall presented Smith with his second star the next day. Marshall remained especially troubled by AFHQ's handling of public relations, made all the more urgent by the deluge of negative press still circulating about the Darlan deal. As Smith conveyed to Eisenhower, the "visit here has been most productive and has clarified [the] situation. All matters under discussion have been satisfactorily adjusted." He assured Eisenhower, "You will be pleased."[65]

Before he left, Smith had another conference with the president. Roosevelt and Churchill agreed to hold a major conference in Casablanca, the location selected in part to reap the publicity bonanza presented by the Torch landings. Roosevelt instructed Smith "to check up confidentially on some possible tourist oasis as far from any city . . . as possible." The president raised one other stipulation; as he told Churchill, "One of the dictionaries says 'an oasis is never wholly dry.' Good old dictionary." The president did not have the climate in mind.[66]

The delay gave Beetle more time with Nory. The army had evicted her from Fort Myer as soon as Smith left for London. She now lived in a comfortable place in northwest Washington on Garfield Street. Owing to Eisenhower's plea that Smith return as soon as possible, he boarded a flight for London on 11 December. Smith provided Eisenhower with some other good news; his brother Milton, associate director of the Office of War Information, would accompany him to Algiers. Encountering bad weather over the Atlantic, the plane put down in Bermuda. Smith decided to scrub plans for London and talks with Churchill and the BCOS and instead flew directly to Gibraltar.

★ 18 ★

"We Shall Continue to Flounder"

His time in Washington left Smith disheartened. He found most senior American officers "rather cold" to suggestions about exploiting the possibilities offered in the Mediterranean that so intrigued Churchill and the BCOS. The people he talked to in Washington fixed their attention on Asia and the Pacific region; the "grave danger of a collapse" in China and the heavy naval losses sustained in the vicious fighting around Guadalcanal "colored their entire attitude." American forces in the Pacific required reinforcement and realignment, deflecting interest from Bolero. Smith left Washington more convinced than ever, as he related to Ismay, "of the vital necessity for a determination at the earliest possible moment of a major strategy for the United Nations. Unless our great men set down and reach a definite decision as to whether we exploit the Mediterranean area, push a campaign in the Pacific and Burma, or build up in the United Kingdom for ROUNDUP, we shall continue to flounder and will be absolutely unable to pull together." The situation worried him, but he clung to hopes that the proposed conference would come off and "serve to button up this basic difficulty."[1]

God-Awful Problems in North Africa

The mood was pretty downcast in Algiers too. At the end of November, British units stood within thirteen miles of Tunis, but determined German counterattacks forced the abandonment of the Allied push. Hitler overruled Kesselring and strongly reinforced the bridgehead. Seizing the initiative and backed by a Luftwaffe that operated from hardened airfields in close proximity to the front, German forces inflicted a sharp defeat on Anderson and succeeded in widening their dangerously constricted lodgment. The 17,000 Axis troops in Tunisia—10,000 of them German—easily repelled Anderson's scratch forces.

The Allied attack showed every hallmark of being a first effort. The improvised rush into Tunisia depended on ad hoc command and supply arrangements. The inclusion of French units and the chaotic, piecemeal hustle forward of an American combat command and artillery units, with no attention paid to command or supply lines, led to intermingled combat commands, dislocated logistical operations, and limited resources stretched beyond the breaking point. Inadequate planning, Anderson's "penny packet" tactics, scarce air support, and a tenacious enemy enjoying near total air superiority all contributed to Allied failures. Eisenhower ordered a "breathing space to attempt reinforcement, untangling of supply, and betterment of air support."[2] The pause did not refresh—at least not the Allies.

As Eisenhower confessed to Handy, "our operations to date . . . have violated every recognized principle of war, are in conflict with all operational and logistic methods laid down in text-books, and will be condemned, in their entirety, by all Leavenworth and War College classes for the next twenty-five years."[3] As early as 5 December he reported, "In the rush forward, using every conceivable kind of transportation including air, naval, railway and all types of nondescript vehicles on roads, we have outrun present possibilities of minimum supply, of immediate reinforcement and, what is even more important, of reasonable air support." Anderson could not even evacuate his wounded. Again to Handy he admitted the logistical situation had become "worse from the day we started." Inadequate port facilities, underdeveloped base sections, and the lack of locomotives, rolling stock, and trained operators for the lone single-tracked east-west rail line complicated the supply situation. So did distances: 600 miles of rugged terrain stood between Algiers and Tunis; Oran, the American base, added another 400. To make matters worse, the December rains turned the primitive North African roads into quagmires. The British, Eisenhower reported, "have one God-awful problem," as if he bore no responsibility for the shambles of theater logistics and organization.[4]

Eisenhower ordered Gale down from London on 1 December to straighten out the lines of communication. Under the original plan, AFHQ would not assume control over theater supply until 1 January; until then, reliance would remain fixed on the British lines of communication. The British supported the First Army and attached U.S. units in the field; loaned whatever weapons, vehicles, and materiel they could to the French; and constructed and supplied the accelerated buildup of the RAF in forward airfields. U.S. units, committed in a piecemeal fashion, possessed little or no organic supply capability. Two hundred staff officers from AFHQ—the vast majority of them logisticians—were detached to the operational commands. No forward headquarters had a single American supply officer. Gale immediately went forward and assumed command. As Anderson wrote after the campaign, all this conjured a "nightmare for the administrative staffs, and necessitated a departure from normal maintenance practice."[5] Gale placed a four-day moratorium on all supplies going forward from Algiers, the depot at Bône, and the ancillary ports of Bougie and Philippeville. The receiving units at the ports and railhead unloaded materiel without consideration of priority; all rail traffic went forward to its destinations and off-loaded cargoes. The remedy worked; the kinks in the railroad lessened. But the chief problem remained: materiel accumulated in the ports and at Bône could not be moved forward fast enough.[6] Lack of motor transport constituted the central problem.

Smith could not have been surprised at the situation he found in Algiers, but that did not stop him from getting infuriated. He vented to Ismay. "I know you will respect my confidence," he told him, and excused himself for being so frank. Although he never questioned that the Allies would ultimately succeed in Tunisia, the supply chaos forced an entire reassessment of prospects for the next few weeks. Smith did not point the finger at Eisenhower for not fixing responsibilities; instead, he blamed Clark. Clark and the "tactics-conscious" task force commanders repeatedly cut supply, communications, and transportation units earmarked for the initial landings. Preoccupied with securing the landings and expecting to play only a static role as an occupation force, American operational commanders gave no serious consideration to what might follow. The Western and Central Task Force commanders—MGs Charles Ryder and Lloyd Fredendall—cut all their heavy truck units and reduced other transport allowances by as much as 75 percent. Consigned to follow-on convoys, the first delivery of vehicles and heavy engineering equipment that arrived on D-day + 18 was seriously reduced due to shipping shortages. All this, in Smith's opinion, was "due to the stupidity or cowardice of one of our American commanders." He assured Ismay that Gale had "done much to rectify it."[7]

Eisenhower demanded the dispatch of American reinforcements to Tunisia and ordered AFHQ to manage it. With only a skeleton G-4 staff consisting of inexperienced American officers under Hamblen, Smith superintended the project. Eisenhower had already stripped two divi-

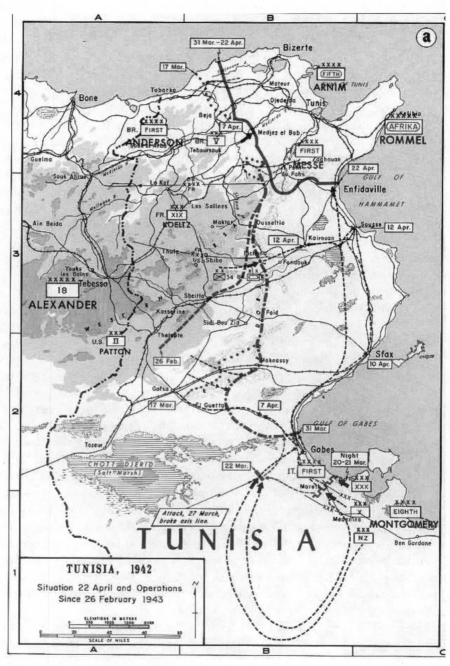

Tunisia: The Tourniquet Closes

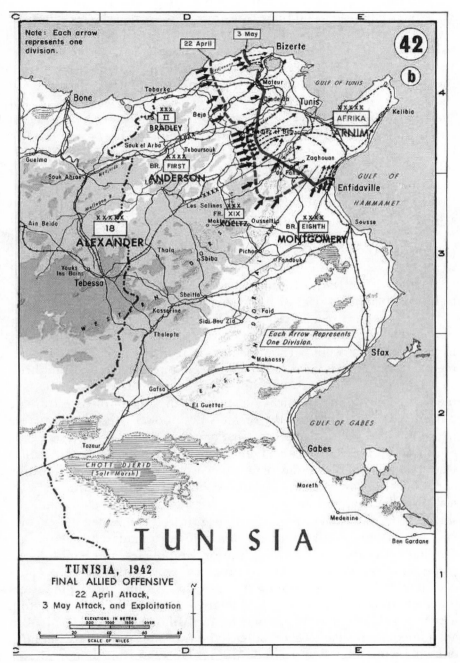

Note: Each arrow represents one division.

42
b

22 April   3 May

Bizerte

GULF OF TUNIS

Bone

Tabarka

Mateur

Djedeida

Tunis

Kelibia

US XXX II
BRADLEY

Beja

XXXX
AFRIKA

ARNIM

Guelma

Souk el Arba

Teboursouk

Zaghouan

Souk Ahras

BR XXXX
FIRST
ANDERSON

El Kef

GULF OF

Enfidaville

Les Salines

HAMMAMET

Ain Beida

XXXXX
18
ALEXANDER

FR XXX
XIX
KOELTZ

Oussellia

Makthar

BR XXXX
EIGHTH
MONTGOMERY

Sousse

Thala

Sbiba

Pichon

Fondouk

Youks les Bains

Tebessa

Sbeitla

Faid

Each Arrow Represents
One Division.

Sfax

Kasserine

Sidi Bou Zid

Thelepte

Maknassy

Gafsa

El Guettar

GULF OF GABES

Tozeur

Gabes

CHOTT DJERID
(Salt Marsh)

Mareth

TUNISIA

Medenine

Ben Gardane

TUNISIA, 1942
FINAL ALLIED OFFENSIVE
22 April Attack,
3 May Attack, and Exploitation

ELEVATIONS IN METERS
300   1000   1600   OVER

0   20   40   60   80
SCALE OF MILES

Tunisgrad: The Final Phase

sions of their organic motor transport to equip provisional units in Tunisia. Now, what little second-line transport—light-scale vehicles at brigade level—that remained was employed to move a second combat command to Tunisia to replace the first, which was so depleted it had to be pulled from the line. AFHQ faced a catch-22: if AFHQ immobilized the two divisions, those units could not provide reinforcements; if it did not, the combat command could not move forward. In other words, it took the transport of two divisions to equip two brigade-sized units at the front. In the end, AFHQ decided on "robbing the Oran force still further."[8] "Our pitifully inadequate L. of C. is *not* an alibi," Eisenhower told Churchill. "I am scraping the bottom of the barrel to build up [the American combat command] to respectable strength."[9]

Eisenhower complained to his West Point roommate that the army schools and prewar doctrine had not remotely prepared him for the rigors of high command. "I am a cross between a one-time soldier, a pseudo-statesman, a jack-legged politician and a crooked diplomat"—all in all, a pretty good definition of his multiple roles as Allied supreme commander. The Darlan business made him feel as if he walked "a soapy tight-rope in a rain storm with a blazing furnace on one side and a pack of ravenous tigers on the other."[10] After the scorching he took, Eisenhower determined never again to leave himself open to condemnation; in the future he would distance himself from overt political involvements, from making any sort of personal commitments, and from direct association with political and diplomatic affairs. He decided the best means of forestalling political and public exposure involved creating a buffer. Now with Smith in the theater, Eisenhower consciously surrendered the lead political and diplomatic roles to his chief of staff. Beetle Smith would act as his primary shock absorber; as chief of staff, Smith would handle the day-to-day operations of his headquarters in addition to the tricky business of press relations and censorship, arbitrating political disturbances, and engaging in direct negotiations of a diplomatic sort, freeing Eisenhower to perform his role as commander.

All this left Smith frustrated and more cantankerous than ever. Dealing with supply, establishing censorship policies, and handling the press, in addition to the myriad other responsibilities he confronted each day, deflected him from his first priority—putting his headquarters together. In fact, he had been foul-tempered since leaving Washington. The trip had not been a happy one; he and Milton Eisenhower had taken an immediate dislike to each other. The two men stayed at Eisenhower's villa when they first arrived. Milton, Ike's favorite sibling, advised his brother to dump Smith and find another chief of staff. Eisenhower demurred, telling Milton, as he told everyone, that Beetle was "strong in character and abrupt by instinct," but one had to overlook his "Prussian" character faults because the man produced results. All this personal angst induced Eisenhower to drop his insistence that Beetle remain part of his social inner circle. As soon as he had secured his own house, Villa Darena, Smith rarely visited Eisenhower's billets. Both men preferred it that way. One reason for the estrangement was the growing antipathy between Beetle and Butcher. Smith's enmity prompted Butcher's conclusion, "He's just a neurotic with an aching ulcer."[11]

A great many others shared Milton and Butcher's opinion. Smith arrived in Algiers on 11 December but could not assemble his full staff for another two weeks. As his first act, prompted by Eisenhower and Clark's concern over the bloated staff, and against his better judgment, Smith announced impending cuts in AFHQ.[12] With the 200 British officers on attached duty, he presided over a rump headquarters. His troublesome ulcer aside, Smith had plenty to be miffed about. First he had to reassemble the disparate portions of his staff. AFHQ in Algiers grew from Clark's tiny staff, augmented by those from Eisenhower's command post in Gibraltar and the phased movement of AFHQ-Main from London. Those beyond his sway in Algiers and Gibraltar adjusted to the more laissez-faire styles of Clark and Gruenther, who accompanied Eisenhower to Gibraltar and acted as his chief of staff. Now Smith busted out the whip and his stopwatch all over again. His bullying tactics initially proved counterproductive, and the already low morale declined even more. He changed methods, but only slightly.

Eisenhower's glib remarks about American and British staff officers coming together initially like dogs meeting cats, only to unify as a team all pulling in the same direction in the days before Torch, can be assigned to the folderol file. American and British officers were more than "divided by a common language," and the setbacks at the front exposed the latent acrimony between the two national groups.

Most of the Americans on his staff who had worked for him in London or knew his reputation resented Smith's bullying tactics. With them he used the Marshall approach, leavened, when necessary, by some vintage Beetle Smith rough treatment. Staff members cringed when they heard him walking down the aisle, for fear he was headed to their desks. They dreaded the summons into his office. Just as Marshall had, Smith made incoming juniors present themselves in his office. They waited, standing stiffly at attention, until Smith finally cast his snake eyes on them. Immediately Smith put the initiate on the spot. If the new officer stood his ground, he passed the test. If he wilted, he already had one strike against him. When an officer of longer acquaintance came into his office, Smith "rattled off questions and orders with the speed of a machine gun." If he was especially disturbed, "the air would be blue with profanity." On one occasion later in the war, his WAC secretary, CPT Ruth Briggs, interrupted a meeting with some matter she thought required his immediate attention. Smith exploded, "Get the hell out of here." Then he commented, "You'll have to excuse her, gentlemen. She's an idiot."[13] Recalcitrant or ineffectual subordinates unceremoniously got the boot, but Smith at least followed the three-strike rule. "If you got the A treatment from Smith," an American staff officer remembered, "you took the afternoon off. If you got the B treatment, you took the rest of the week off. If you got the C treatment, you started cleaning out your desk."[14]

Smith ran a tight ship. He set up his household staff with defined and rigidly enforced procedures. He demanded his headquarters serve as a model of efficiency, discipline, and military courtesy. Eisenhower continually fumed about slack discipline and deportment among the troops; he had no such worries about his staff. Smith expected his subordinates to dress properly, salute, show up on time, and work long hours without complaint. He served as the exemplar with his slicked-down hair, razor-sharp creases in his starched uniform, fastidious punctuality, and attention to detail. American officers thought all this a little overbearing—"chickenshit" in U.S. Army slang—but they complied. The most anyone could hope for was that Smith might stop by one's desk for a casual chat—Smith's way of signaling his satisfaction with an officer's performance.

Smith did have his favorites. He brought in young officers—Carter Burgess and Vittrup, among others—who had worked for him in Washington and placed them in his inner headquarters as aides and members of the secretariat. He appointed COL Dan Gilmer as his secretary. Demanding peak performance, Smith made Gilmer's life hell. "A good staff secretary," Smith remarked, "is a very scarce and precious commodity."[15] Like Marshall, Smith embarked on his own educational program. One of his persistent gripes centered on the failure of the army schools to produce the type and number of officers his staff required. Smith reached out and pulled in promising young officers to man his staff. "We are putting these chaps through an all around course," he told BG Lucian Truscott, "and by the time we are finished with them the Army will have a few thoroughly trained, high level staff officers to get us ready for the next war."[16] Many of the officers plucked from operational commands felt bitter about being yanked out of the "real" war, but Smith paid no attention to their complaints. He felt he owed it to the army to train these men, and it also allowed Smith to put his own stamp on the headquarters.

With British officers, Smith handled things differently. The British, who entertained grave doubts about any American's ability to run a headquarters, were not so easily tossed around. Clark left the headquarters badly divided along national lines, making little effort to cloak his Anglophobia. British officers, from Gale on down, believed Clark played them false. They disliked his arrogance and his habit of issuing contradictory directives. Word filtered back to the BCOS that Clark sowed dissension; his backdoor conniving earned him the reputation as an "evil genius." Many Americans shared this assessment of Clark. Smith enjoyed the best relationships with Ismay and Jacob, now assistant military secretary to the War Cabinet, as well as with Eisenhower's British military aide Stirling—all through Dykes.[17] They trusted him like no other American. Smith exercised more diplomacy with his British underlings, never subjecting them to the full Beetle treatment. He followed Eisenhower's dictum: you can always call them SOBs, provided they deserve it, but never British SOBs.

One episode illustrates how Smith dealt with inter-Allied issues. He called a senior British officer and his American opposite, BG Arthur Nevins, into his office. Unhappy that a G-3 project had not been completed, Smith dressed down both men and then asked that Nevins stay behind. After apologizing for making the American a "whipping post," he explained he had to appear evenhanded in such matters. Unappeased, Nevins indignantly requested a transfer. "No, God-damn it," Smith roared. "You'll stay right where you are."[18] Nevins did, remaining with Smith for the rest of the war.

National stereotypes are dangerous, but they carry some legitimacy; otherwise, they would have no currency. Both the United Kingdom and the United States contain diverse populations. Lowland Scots are different from Highlanders; someone speaking the received accent of the Home Counties is easily distinguishable from a Geordie from Newcastle. The minute a British person speaks, he can be readily identified by region and typecast. The same situation exists in the United States. Still, the "other" often misses these nuances. Americans never understood the workings of the rigid class system that predetermined all social relationships among the British. The British, well-off in comparison to Europeans, but impoverished by U.S. standards, viewed Americans as loud, obnoxious, overly self-confident, superficial in their relations, and overindulgent. Americans saw the British as standoffish, haughty, self-aggrandizing, and prideful out of all proportion to their diminished place in the world. Some Americans bought into the notion of British superiority. Smith's friend Orlando Ward thought many American officers acted like pointer pups around the British. "If someone with a red mustache, a swagger stick, and a British accent speaks to us," he offered, "we lie down on the ground and wiggle."[19]

British condescension toward Americans was not imagined. Harold Macmillan joined AFHQ on 1 January 1943 as British resident and political adviser. He personified a constellation of British stereotypes, and though he never expressed it to an American—he even claimed to be a Hoosier because his mother came from Indiana—he perfectly captured the British attitude toward Americans. As he instructed a British newcomer about to enter AFHQ, "You will regularly enter a room and see an American colonel, his cigar in his mouth and his feet on the table," and in the corner "an English captain, his feet down, his shoulders hunched, writing like mad, with a full in-tray and a full out-tray, and no cigar." Macmillan warned his associate to "never call attention to this discrepancy." Always "permit your American colleague not only to have a superior rank to yourself and much higher pay, but also the feeling that he is running the show." Through that device, "you will run it yourself." Remember, he advised, the British "are Greeks in this American empire." Knowing without asking that his colleague, beneficiary of a public school education, knew his ancient history, Macmillan drew a parallel between Americans and Romans as "great big, vulgar, bustling people," vigorous yet idle, virtuous yet corrupt. "We must run AFHQ as the Greek slaves ran the operations of the Emperor Claudius."[20]

Some British officers proved better at disguising it than others, but from Brooke on down—knowing their empire was in decline and their dependence on American largesse could only grow—this "civilized Greeks conquering the barbarian Romans" attitude colored their routine dealings with Americans. The American officers recognized it and deeply resented it. In a staff like AFHQ, eventually composed in almost equal proportions by selected American and British officers, a clash of nationalities, if unchecked, would wreck any authentic spirit of teamwork. Smith knew this, and he genuinely thought highly of the professional acumen of his British associates; he recognized that he needed their know-how to make the headquarters work. Based on the close bonds he developed with Dykes and Ismay and the trust bestowed on him by the prime minister, Smith earnestly tried to understand the British viewpoint. This prompted some American officers to accuse him of being "more British than the British," but such criticism came with the job. His equanimity in dealing with the British did have limits, however.

In his own right, Smith recognized the differences in makeup and approach between his American and British subordinates. "The American officer is a rapid and aggressive operator, likely to be impatient of detailed planning, willing to let the last details go by default, anxious to get into operation and trusting that he can make up for any planning deficiency by his quickness in improvisation." In some respects, he could have been describing himself. In contrast, the typical British officer, "meticulously training in staff procedure," troubles himself over "the last detail" and tends toward conservatism. "Combined," he believed, "each compensates for the other, and the result is greater strength." But before these strengths and weaknesses could combine, some sense of trust and a common corporate identity must develop. That required time.[21]

Dealing with the British proved a great deal easier than handling the French. With the British, differences could be addressed over a gin and tonic. Not so with the French. Eisenhower usually dealt with Darlan and Giraud when he had no escape, but otherwise, he handed off negotiating with the French to Smith. Smith formed a liaison section under Holmes to formalize connections between AFHQ and the French commands and civil authorities. Eager to strengthen French forces in Tunisia, Giraud planned to move 50,000 African troops from Dakar to North Africa. He also wanted to pass one of his Moroccan divisions through the long, tenuous land lines to the front. Smith diplomatically told the French that without antitank and antiaircraft guns or modern weapons of any sort, these units would overtax the already overburdened transportation and maintenance facilities in the theater. In reality, the American command had other reasons, not connected to logistics, for not deploying African troops.[22]

Rearming the French posed a persistent headache for Smith. During his secret meeting with Mast, Clark had pledged lavish American support for reequipping French forces; these promises were repeated to Giraud in Gibraltar and Darlan in Algiers. In fact, AFHQ discussed the question only once, and then only shortly before D-day. The first convoy brought a token shipment of weapons for the French, but little followed. On 16 December Smith chartered the Joint Rearmament Committee, with French representation, as a vehicle to steer the rearmament program. Initially, the committee had little to discuss. The French leadership began to wonder just who got slickered in the Darlan deal. They stood prepared to rush troops into Tunisia, only to be told there was no transport to get them there and no modern weapons to equip even the forces already fighting there. The French merchant marine went into the Allied shipping pool, but AFHQ insisted that the shortage of ships meant Giraud required patience—another commodity in very short supply.

As discouraging as negotiating with the French military proved to be, it paled in comparison to the political complications. For all his liabilities, Darlan calmed the troubled waters. A skilled opportunist, the admiral's adept political maneuvering meant he cut a pretty good deal with AFHQ, primarily because he knew he held the trump card. AFHQ wanted French forces fighting the Axis in Tunisia but absolutely required that French civil, police, and judicial authorities manage the volatile rear and safeguard the dangerously exposed lines of communication. The vulnerable supply lines presented a serious security worry. A trade-off emerged. The Allies—and that meant the British until mid-January and beyond—would operate the lines of communication with the aid of French civilian agencies, while the French provided security. The system proved eminently successful. The French security forces were past masters in dealing with the Arab population, a role the Americans proved hopelessly ill equipped to handle.

The central problem for AFHQ involved the absence of any agreed-on Allied policy on North Africa. The British talked in terms of a political administration under Allied control; they pointed to their vast experience in managing their empire and called for a colonial administration in French North Africa. Churchill sent Macmillan and expected him, together with Murphy, to gradually exert more political control. A 30 November directive from Marshall had already instructed Eisenhower to surrender political affairs to Murphy, who, in addition to having a direct pipeline to Roosevelt and heading AFHQ's civil affairs section, now enjoyed ministerial rank. British policy veered toward the Free French; Roosevelt and Secretary of State Cordell Hull loathed de Gaulle, viewing him as a would-be Napoleon (or, more likely, a Boulanger), as a "man on horseback" intent on manipulating French divisions, exploiting Allied military victory, and eventually installing a personal regime in France. The British believed a stable postwar Europe depended on a restoration of French power; Roosevelt saw France as a spent force. A principal British war aim centered on regaining lost imperial holdings in Asia; the restoration of French and Dutch dominion in the Far East figured in their calculations. Roosevelt considered formal imperialism obsolete and held up the Atlantic Charter as a universal statement of Allied policy that equally applied to regions outside Europe. It is not hard to see why London and Washington could not reach any accord on policy in North Africa.

The tongue-lashing he received from the first lady convinced Smith something needed to be done to sugarcoat Darlan. Official Washington slowly came around to the notion that the "temporary expedient" might remain for a while. As long as Darlan's regime retained its fascist odor, the White House could never openly embrace it, and opposition in liberal circles would continue. The other problem involved reconciling Churchill and Eden to Darlan. The British press kept up its assaults on Eisenhower.

Just before Smith arrived in Algiers, Eisenhower "wound up the Dakar business." GEN Pierre Boisson, governor-general of French West Africa, opened the Dakar naval and air stations to the Allies. Boisson now tenuously entered the fold but remained deeply mistrustful of the British, in large part owing to their support of de Gaulle. Roosevelt wanted a clear pronouncement from Darlan on plans for dismantling the residual fascist features of the French administration—political prisoners still behind bars, bans on union, and especially prohibitions against the Jewish population. Under pressure from Smith and Murphy, Darlan released a statement to the press on 12 December holding out only the promise of liberal reforms.[23] Darlan's pledge satisfied the White House; Early orchestrated a press campaign emphasizing that the French in North Africa "have definitely allied themselves on the side of liberalism" and against the common foe. With Dakar secured, and given the positive response in the United States to Darlan's gesture, AFHQ sighed collectively in relief. The French problem finally seemed to be under control.

This was not the case—not by a long shot. Churchill still harbored hopes for some modus vivendi between Darlan and de Gaulle and engineered a visit to Algiers by GEN Henri d'Artier de la Vigerie of the French National Committee.[24] Smith had asked Eisenhower back in November if he would consent to the dispatch of a Free French representative to North Africa. Eisenhower had declined on the grounds that the sudden appearance of a Gaullist official would wreck any hope of a settlement among the French factions, and the prime minister had reluctantly concurred. The day after Darlan's announcement, however, AFHQ received a communication from de Gaulle informing it of (not requesting) the dispatch of a representative to Algiers. Churchill renewed his request that AFHQ sanction the visit of the Free French envoy. This time Eisenhower acquiesced. D'Altier arrived in Algiers on 21 December. Smith delegated to Murphy and the newly arrived head of public relations,

BG Robert McClure, the job of orchestrating d'Artier's visit. It turned into a fiasco. First, no one met the general at the airport. Worse, Murphy had neglected to tell Darlan that d'Artier was coming, and when Darlan found out, he ordered the general's arrest. D'Artier's irritation by the slight at the airport turned into outrage; he refused to talk to any Darlan agent, including his brother, who headed police and propaganda in Darlan's administration. Smith then interceded, dispatching Murphy and McClure with instructions to stop Darlan from arresting the general and convince d'Artier to parley with Darlan. D'Artier carried a letter from de Gaulle, introducing him as his *representative en mission* in Africa "to inform himself and to inform me [on conditions in French Africa]. It is necessary for him to have all possible contacts." An unhappy Eisenhower felt obliged to meet the French official and arranged separate discussions with Giraud and Darlan and with Murphy and d'Artier at his villa. When d'Artier insisted on the right to talk to any Gaullist in both North and West Africa, Eisenhower lost his temper. If d'Artier went to Dakar—or to Casablanca, for that matter—an explosion would surely follow. "After much parlez-vooing," d'Artier agreed to hold a brief and inconclusive conference with Darlan; then Murphy hustled him to the airport for a quick return to England.[25]

December 1942 represented the nadir of Allied fortunes; it also marked the low point in Eisenhower's relations with Smith. Eisenhower acted like a caged tiger, impatient with Anderson for pushing back the date to resume the drive on Tunis, intemperate with the French for their bickering and palace intrigues, and irritated at Smith for not whipping the headquarters into shape. All manner of problems plagued Eisenhower. He developed an undiagnosed respiratory ailment in the tunnels of Gibraltar that troubled him for his entire stay in North Africa, which did nothing to improve his temper. On 10 December Churchill held a closed session with the House of Commons and wrote to allay Eisenhower's fears, claiming he had never seen Parliament so unanimous in its support of the Darlan deal. Be that as it may, the British press continued to excoriate the bargain as "revolting" and "disgusting." Brother Milton filled Ike's head with worries about his flagging reputation growing out of his continued cooperation with Darlan and his crew.[26] Eisenhower never developed any rapport with Anderson, a dour Scotsman even by the standards of that taciturn tribe. Referred to as "Sunshine" and codenamed Grouch, Anderson fought with everybody—the RAF, Americans, the French, and his own staff. Eisenhower's corps commander in Tunisia, Fredendall, detested the French and the British in equal measure. Patton stood as the obvious choice to command II Corps, given his experience in setting up and running the desert warfare training center in California, yet Eisenhower gave the command to Fredendall out of deference to Marshall—a decision he would soon regret.[27] The First Army was not an army; it was scarcely more than a corps, and Fredendall's corps consisted of little more than scattered elements amounting to a division. Eisenhower's labors in forming a single command of the Allied air forces produced infighting at virtually every level. He groused at Smith for not relieving him of concerns about rear area discipline, failing to sort out the supply problem, faulty communications, lack of a censorship policy, reluctance in speeding up the accreditation process for journalists in the theater, and any number of other problems, including dealing with the French. Finally, with a new push for Tunis in the offing and with Juin refusing to follow Anderson's orders, Eisenhower decided to flee Algiers for a forward command post in Constantine in the hope of drawing together the twisted lines of command. His presence solved nothing; the advance headquarters stood too far in the rear to monitor operations, further complicating command relations. The offensive miscarried; again the Axis counterattacked and inflicted another sharp defeat on Anderson's forces. On Christmas morning the Germans regained Longstop Hill—a tactically vital position if the Allies entertained any hope of taking Tunis. Eisenhower had already made the "bitter decision" to halt the advance. While in discussions with Juin, he received a call from Algiers. Darlan had been assassinated; Eisenhower needed to return at once.

In Eisenhower's absence, Smith tried to keep a lid on the volatile situation. He imposed a tight blackout on information about the assassination and wired Marshall, requesting that he do the same. Fearing the worst, Smith asked Murphy to sit on the news—not even informing Noguès in Casablanca. He called ahead to Eisenhower and asked him to bring Giraud back to Algiers. None of these initiatives worked; the electric news of the assassination spread so fast that a reluctant Smith authorized an official broadcast.[28]

Eisenhower made it back to Algiers late on Christmas Day. Smith hosted a traditional Christmas dinner at Villa Darena, courtesy of Patton, who "liberated" a couple of turkeys for the occasion. Eisenhower put on his best face. The party allowed him to put the war out of his mind for a while. After a couple of belts, Eisenhower always felt like singing, and this time he favored everyone with "God Rest Ye Merry Gentlemen." With spirits high, Smith thought the moment was right to make an announcement he thought would surely please Eisenhower. Word had arrived that Roosevelt intended to award Ike the Medal of

Honor for Torch. Eisenhower's disposition immediately blackened, however, and he told Smith he did not want the medal, would not wear it if awarded, would not even keep it. He had opposed MacArthur's winning the coveted medal for "sitting in a hole" in Corregidor, and after what he had witnessed at the front, he refused to even countenance that an undeserving rear area desk soldier like him should win an honor reserved for heroism in battle. He might have added that, since nothing had gone right since the landings, he did not merit an award of any sort.[29]

Despite his worsening flu, Eisenhower pulled himself from bed and attended Darlan's elaborate funeral services. Darlan's passing would not be mourned—in most quarters, especially among the British, it was celebrated—but his death reopened the French question. Although he had placed Giraud at the head of the French council, Eisenhower calculated the "big bosses" would have to settle the problem of pulling the French together at their conclave scheduled for mid-January in Casablanca.

Just when Eisenhower thought things could not possibly get worse, they did. On 3 January Smith came into Eisenhower's office with a Roosevelt-issued directive that threatened to scupper the arrangement with the French. The president decreed, "we have a military occupation" in North Africa, and he emphasized that Eisenhower exerted complete control over all military and civil affairs. "Our French friends," he insisted, "must not be permitted to forget this for a moment."[30] If Eisenhower antagonized the prickly Giraud, the entire Allied position in Tunisia might very well unravel, perhaps prompting "passive resistance a la Gandhi or possibly resumption of French fighting Americans and British 'pour l'honneure.'" A downcast supreme commander told his naval aide he had no choice but to follow the president's lead or submit his resignation.[31] The mood in AFHQ got considerably gloomier.

Clean Up the Mess in the Rear

The New Year brought a number of organizational and personnel shifts in AFHQ; some were inaugurated by Eisenhower, but most were forced on him. Clark assumed command of Fifth Army at Oujda; the next day, 6 January, Gruenther left AFHQ as Clark's chief of staff. Fifth Army had two roles: train for future but undecided operations in the Mediterranean, and maintain readiness should Spain become restive. On 5 January the CCS approved Eisenhower's formation of a unified Allied air force command under Spaatz. The RAF wanted a unified air command throughout the entire Mediterranean but deferred to Eisenhower until the CCS met to settle the issue.[32] This tightened Eisenhower's command; Spaatz oversaw the British Eastern Air Command and the U.S. Twelfth Air Force. The direction of coalition grand strategy, French policy, command relations in the Mediterranean, and the nature of the American theater structure were all outstanding questions that awaited solutions in Casablanca.

Eisenhower felt threatened by Macmillan's arrival. He had never requested a British political counselor and wondered why London had sent Macmillan. He admitted that over time, "we will get many of these things centered up into O.W.I, O.S.S., economic boards and so on, and they will be largely separated from the Headquarters" through Murphy, but that time lay in the future.[33] Murphy constituted no problem, but Macmillan—the scion of a wealthy publishing family, a Tory member of Parliament, and an associate of the prime minister with ministerial rank and direct links to the Foreign Office—might compromise Eisenhower's chain of command. While Eisenhower decided on policy, he insisted that Smith handle the management of Murphy and Macmillan. Although the respective domains of these two principal political advisers awaited adjudication in Casablanca, Smith immediately went to work on Macmillan.

Over dinner at Smith's villa, Macmillan assured him that the prime minister accepted Eisenhower's authority over military and civil matters and merely desired a British representative on a par with Murphy. Not undeservedly, the British held a very low opinion of Murphy. To date, his single contribution to Allied success in North Africa had grown out of his bungled covert operations preceding the landings: they had proved so amateurish that the Germans totally discounted any Allied movement into North Africa in 1942.[34] Suspecting Murphy of being a little too friendly with neofascist elements remaining in the French administration, the British also held him responsible for delays in removing the anti-Jewish laws that provoked such negative press. Macmillan pointed out that he and Murphy would relieve AFHQ of much of the burden of local politics. In light of Roosevelt's pronouncement on the "military occupation," the two discussed the wide gulf in official American and British views on the French problem. Smith confessed his sympathy with the British views, including on de Gaulle, but Eisenhower had no option but to uphold the president's policy. Eisenhower and Smith wanted political stability in the rear so they could get on with the business of fighting Germans and Italians. Macmillan assured him that was his principal reason for coming. He also promised Smith that although he needed to safeguard his communications with London, he would apprise AFHQ of British thinking and actions, including covert special operations. Both men promised to treat each other with confidence and not work at cross-purposes. Macmillan left this meeting impressed; he came to consider Smith "a most charming and excellent fellow [and] a friend of Britain."[35]

Smith remained sensitive to charges that AFHQ was still too large. Upon his arrival in Algiers, Smith held daily staff meetings with Gale, Whiteley, the air and naval chiefs of staff, Mockler-Ferryman, and BG Lowell Rooks, who had replaced Lemnitzer as G-3.[36] Not until the day before Christmas did he finally convene his first genuine AFHQ chiefs of staff conference involving all representatives of the general and special staff divisions and sections. When Smith completed fleshing out AFHQ in Algiers by the end of the year, it spilled out of the St. George Hotel into 400 offices in ten adjacent properties. In November, after the three-way split of AFHQ, the headquarters contained 313 American officers, 96 above its authorized strength. After the consolidation of AFHQ in Algiers in mid-January, the staff numbered 3,052, a 48 percent increase over its initial 3 September 1942 authorized strength.[37] As he explained to Hughes, "I have not been here long enough to start using the pruning shears as this must wait until I am settled more firmly in the saddle." Still, he reported, "Things are reasonably satisfactory from a staff standpoint."

One thing Smith avoided was any time-wasting shuttling back and forth between Algiers and London. Eisenhower wanted Hughes as his man in London and asked Smith to arrange for Hughes to "deal with the Prime Minister and the British Chiefs of Staff on the same basis which you dealt with them."[38] Improved communications and Smith's practice of issuing weekly operations and intelligence reports satisfied the British demand that they be informed on developments in the theater. Eisenhower ordered Hughes to Algiers for a "period of indoctrination." His plans for Hughes involved more than acting as AFHQ's liaison in London.

The question loomed whether to sever AFHQ from ETO and form a North African theater command. Disquieted about the continued expansion of AFHQ, Marshall wanted an examination of its structure and solicited suggestions on how to increase efficiency and decrease staff size, as well where an American theater command fit in the structure. Truscott, who had ably served as Patton's deputy commander in Morocco and was now unemployed, received the task. On 30 December Truscott submitted his study to Smith. Truscott thought the allied nature of AFHQ partially explained "the ponderous size" of the headquarters. "Differences in organization, equipment, procedures, and national char-

Allied Force Headquarters. Eisenhower and his commanders, Tedder, Alexander, and Cunningham, pose on the steps of the St. George Hotel in Algiers. Macmillan and Smith are in the background.

acteristics between the British and American forces resulted in much duplication of effort." He also pointed to empire building at all levels, a product of jurisdictional clashes between Smith's level and lower-echelon staffs and a problem he attributed to the "egos . . . of service chiefs." He told Smith, "Every officer with whom I have talked considers the Head-quarters too large and that all sections should be reduced except the one he represents, which usually needs an increase." Although claiming no special expertise, he was "appalled by [AFHQ's] size" and wondered "how it could function effectively." A number of officers expressed similar views. Truscott recommended that Smith undertake a thorough reorganization of AFHQ, ending duplicate organizations, establishing standard operating procedures, and clearly delineating functions and responsibilities of the general staff divisions, sections, and special staffs. Then, once a North African theater command developed, he should remove from AFHQ all administrative and logistical elements not common to both armies.[39]

Truscott told Smith exactly what he wanted to hear. Mindful that Truscott would report his findings to Marshall, Smith sought to exploit Truscott's report and the mounting internal criticisms it provoked as a prod, forcing Eisenhower to make a decision on the form of the proposed theater command and its relationship to AFHQ. Wasting no time, Smith instructed three of his senior staff officers to write memos opposing the creation of a theater-wide SOS headquarters. Gale, Whiteley, and Hamblen all submitted drafts to Smith, who in turn raised the issue with Eisenhower. The complaints reinforced those made by Smith before Torch. Although written separately, the position papers made the same arguments: AFHQ should control American supply through G-4, the creation of an SOS command would not reduce staff size because G-4's many residual responsibilities required a large staff in AFHQ, and a commanding general of SOS outside AFHQ would necessarily complicate coordination. The American administrative and supply structure should parallel the British one, facilitating Gale's ability to coordinate theater logistics without compromising either chain of command.[40]

Smith's timing proved inopportune. Eisenhower confronted far bigger worries than organizing his rear. In fact, he was on the verge of a breakdown. His respiratory ailment worsened, and with his blood pressure skyrocketing, he spent four days confined to quarters. On 11 January Eisenhower dragged himself out of bed and went forward for consultations with Anderson and Juin at Constantine. Upon returning to Algiers, his blood pressure was still dangerously high.[41] As he lay in bed, Eisenhower mulled over all that had occurred since 8 November. Hughes, visiting the theater after a trip to Washington, reassured him that Marshall and the War Department retained full confidence in his command and would defend American interests in the theater at Casablanca. Eisenhower did not expect the outcome of the Casablanca talks to be good. The political fallout from the Darlan deal, the lost race to Tunis, the logistical disarray, and the resultant stalemate in Tunisia convinced him that his days as supreme commander were numbered. In his estimate, the pending amalgamation of Montgomery's victorious Eighth Army with his forces could only result in a British officer being named as his successor.

Many—including close friends—drew the same conclusion. Patton and Hughes spent a night drinking and talking "about the glamour boys." Hughes thought Eisenhower "was on his way out." Patton agreed. Both concluded Ike had been "knifed" by Clark—a view confirmed in Patton's eyes when the new Fifth Army commander spent an hour "cutting Ike's throat" in Patton's presence. Hughes came away from a week in Algiers convinced AFHQ was a failure, a purely theoretical headquarters. "The British are incompetent," he told Patton, "the French mad, and no one commands anything."[42]

During Eisenhower's absences—from 6 to 17 January he spent only parts of two days in the St. George Hotel—Smith ran the headquarters. Initially Smith bore responsibility for finding the site for the Symbol conference—the Anfa Hotel near Casablanca—and overseeing arrangements for security and the care and comfort of the conferees and their attendants. As Eisenhower reported to Marshall, "General Smith has labored earnestly to see that everything possible is done."[43] After having played increasingly important roles in all the conferences from Arcadia onward, Smith sat out Symbol. He stayed behind in Algiers, minding the shop and following the proceedings from daily reports.

All the cards seemed stacked against Eisenhower as he left his sick-bed and flew down to Casablanca on 15 January. First, the plane nearly went down; at one point he put on a parachute and prepared to jump. No wonder he appeared "jittery" to Roosevelt and Hopkins. Eisenhower put on a pretty miserable display during his briefing of the CCS. After providing an overview of operations to date—dismal in their own right—Eisenhower outlined his plans. Instead of assuming the defensive and building up reserves and supplies, Eisenhower proposed inserting a single reinforced American armored division at Sfax on the Gulf of Gabes in central Tunisia between Axis forces in the north and Rommel to the south (Operation Satin). He termed it "Fredendall's plan," but the inspiration was all Eisenhower's. Whatever its origins, Alanbrooke, who later described it as "ridiculous," shot Satin down. Marshall and the other Americans sat in silence.[44] Operational deficiencies aside, logistics alone precluded launching Satin. Eisenhower repeated the performance later that afternoon in front of Roosevelt, Churchill, and Hopkins; all the chiefs; and Generals Harold Alexander, Tedder, and Mountbatten. After holding discussions with Churchill and dining with the president, Eisenhower shared drinks with Patton. As he confided in Patton, he thought "his thread [was] about to be cut."[45]

The thread was not cut, but the outcome of the Casablanca meetings hardly constituted a ringing vote of confidence in Eisenhower's direction of the North African campaign. Eisenhower was not the only American officer left smarting by what transpired in Casablanca. On 18 January the CCS endorsed the British strategy for exploiting success in North Africa with an invasion of Sicily (Husky), leaving open the option of future movements into Italy or against Sardinia and Corsica. That day AFHQ received the first indication from Casablanca of a major reordering of the command structure. Tedder, not Spaatz, would command the Allied air forces in the Mediterranean. The new command accomplished little; Tedder sat over an array of subordinate headquarters but never exercised, not even in theory, control over theater airpower. The British got what they wanted: some measure of policy direction and a vote at the table. Eisenhower did not like it, but he held Tedder in high regard and gracefully accepted the shift.[46] Two days later a bombshell hit Algiers. The CCS agreed to put Alexander in overall command of ground forces in Tunisia and charged him with overseeing the planning and execution of Husky. Cunningham continued as commander in chief of Allied naval forces. The hard fact remained that the British fielded the preponderance of forces in the theater and possessed the right to exercise command over the ground, air, and sea components.[47]

The British "flattered and pleased" the Americans by throwing them a bone—Eisenhower would remain as supreme commander. The British had every reason to question Eisenhower's fitness for supreme command, and his performance in Casablanca did nothing to alter their view. Dismayed by his total lack of combat and limited command experience, Brooke never reconciled himself to Eisenhower's holding the reins as supreme command.[48] The last thing Churchill wanted was a breach with the Americans, and Eisenhower's removal would have created one. The decision to keep Eisenhower in place was entirely political. By elevating Eisenhower "up into the stratosphere and rarefied atmosphere of a Supreme Commander," the British reduced his status to little more than chairman of the Allied board of commanders.[49]

At first relieved he would not be subordinated to a British commander, Eisenhower's calm acceptance of the first directive contrasted sharply with his stormy receipt of the second. He now recognized "that the Chiefs were attempting to issue directives as to how and what his subordinates were to do." Infuriated with this intrusion into his command sphere, Eisenhower dictated a "hot message" to the CCS, resisting the imposition of the committee system on AFHQ and complaining that the new command structure undermined the unity of command by creating four power centers. Eisenhower took exception to the word *coordinate*, which conveyed the impression that the new organization would function as a committee. As was typically the case, Eisenhower strenuously objected to any interference with his most valued prerogatives—the ability to exercise command and determine his own internal organization.[50]

Smith prevailed on Eisenhower not to send the cable. As Smith immediately recognized, if Eisenhower pushed the issue, he would be cutting the thread himself. Not all the news from Casablanca was bad.

The "big bosses" had decided on a grand strategy for 1943 that centered on expanding operations in the Mediterranean, and despite the failures in Tunisia, Eisenhower remained as supreme commander. Despite the amorphous *coordinate*, Eisenhower would still exert command authority. He enjoyed a close collaborative relationship with Cunningham and could expect to forge the same kind of relationships with Tedder and Alexander. Smith knew that Marshall would have strongly objected to any alteration in the command structure if he had deemed it warranted. From all indications, he did not. In any case, Marshall and his entourage would be in Algiers in a couple of days. It would be far better to discuss these matters face-to-face in private than to spark renewed debate in Casablanca on the whole issue of command, which might not augur well for AFHQ. Eisenhower fumed but accepted the inevitable. Instead, Smith wrote a more moderate communication, caustically described by Butcher as "more of an apology" than a protest.[51]

Before Marshall arrived, Smith took the opportunity to make a quick trip to Constantine. On 14 January Truscott assumed control of Eisenhower's command post, and Smith went forward on 20 January by automobile. He soon discovered why the ground forces complained about getting "murdered" by the Luftwaffe. Caught on the road by a strafing German fighter, Smith's driver was killed, and the car veered into a ditch. A badly rattled and banged up Smith continued his trip to Constantine but ventured no farther.[52] When he returned to Algiers he received some shattering news. Dykes—probably Smith's most intimate friend—had died in a plane crash in England on his return from Casablanca. "Next to yourself and the children," Smith wrote to Dykes's widow, "I really think no one feels his loss more deeply than I do."[53]

Marshall arrived in Algiers on 24 January for a brief inspection tour. Dill, Arnold, King, Somervell, and BG Albert Wedemeyer of OPD accompanied him. Brooke congratulated himself on obliging the American chiefs to accept the new command structure, but Marshall was not as quiescent as his British opposite number imagined. He entertained his own growing doubts about Eisenhower's ability to master the situation, and those reservations were not assuaged by Eisenhower's feeble performance at Casablanca.

Since the November landings, Marshall and Handy had continually received long, defensive, self-serving letters from Eisenhower obfuscating his failures and grumbling that logistical problems and his near total immersion in political entanglements and routine administration diverted his attention from exercising command. Although forewarned, Marshall found the situation in the American rear worse than envisioned. The base section in Casablanca and the replacement depot at Oran in particular grabbed his attention. Unkempt troops, lax discipline, officers he described as "drug store cowboys standing around" doing nothing, and no real training in progress greeted Marshall at every turn. Eisenhower was "almost in tears," and Smith, preoccupied with hammering AFHQ into shape, offered little encouragement. Fearing a first-class scandal if the story got home, Marshall read the riot act to Eisenhower, ordering him to get tough, issue unequivocal orders, organize a theater headquarters to relieve himself and Smith of the administrative burden, and, above all, "clean up the mess in his rear."[54] He offered Bradley's services as Eisenhower's "eyes and ears."

Marshall confided in Butcher that Eisenhower's tendency to overwork himself and micromanage problems troubled him. Initially Eisenhower had brought a new approach and energy to OPD, but he started exhibiting the telltale signs of losing his edge in his last days in the War Department. In Marshall's opinion, Eisenhower had to rely on his staff to discharge routine matters and take better care of his health.[55]

Marshall's visit had Smith on pins and needles. He anticipated the chief would not be pleased with what he found. The situation in Algiers and Oran was not good. Idle troops, with too much time on their hands, fell victim to the attractions of the Casbah—cheap North African wine, whoring, brawling, and black marketeering. Eisenhower was obsessed about the lack of discipline and pressured Smith to do something about it. Virtually every day Smith dealt with French civil authorities who were incensed about some outrage committed by American troops against the local population. Smith issued orders, but to little effect; like everything else, the undermanned military justice agencies were overwhelmed by the magnitude of the problem. With Marshall in Algeria, Smith ordered a security lockdown.

After a long day of conferences, Smith decided to walk back to his villa. Along the way he ran into a military police patrol. At gunpoint, the MPs ordered Smith to lay his identification papers on the ground, retreat ten paces, and assume the prone position. Satisfied he was not an assassin, they let him pass. Smith undoubtedly took little satisfaction from the improvement wrought by his security crackdown, and even less when the story made the rounds.[56]

The issue of the American theater command remained unsettled. Before he left for Casablanca, Eisenhower requested a split from ETO and argued, "the assumption of detailed theater functions has now become necessary."[57] The JCS in Casablanca discussed the issue; the consensus favored the formation of a theater headquarters after completion of the campaign in Tunisia. With the president attending the 15 January meetings, Marshall reversed himself and called for the establishment of a separate North African theater. Five days later the joint chiefs forwarded a draft plan to Algiers. There matters stood until Marshall arrived in Algiers.

Somervell came to Algiers determined to convince Eisenhower to rationalize American logistics in North Africa. On 25 January he chaired a meeting attended by Marshall, Arnold, King, Wedemeyer, Eisenhower, and Smith. Somervell had prepared a long catalog of matters for discussion, and the need for a unified SOS topped the list. Given Eisenhower's track record, and knowing that Smith strongly opposed a separate SOS command, Somervell worried that the North African theater would merely replicate the confused ETO structure. Except for the World War I linear structure, based on a single service, no doctrine existed. Only too aware of the organizational disarray and personality clashes in England before Torch, Somervell again made his case for a division of responsibility on functional lines and the consolidation of all theater logistics under a single SOS command. Though far from accepting Somervell's entire package, Eisenhower conceded he had finally come around to seeing the merits of this "SOS business."[58]

Smith made a "call for help" during the session. He detailed the critical shortage of railway equipment and trucks, confessed the errors of Torch planners, praised ASF for saving their bacon, and pleaded that Somervell place priority on these urgent requests. The Americans had landed 117,000 troops in Torch, but a mere 11,800 manned the line in Tunisia. Five divisions stood idle, immobilized by distance and the lack of transport and service personnel.[59] At the end of December, Allied forces in Tunisia numbered 50,000—half the Axis force they opposed. And as Smith could testify, the Germans still enjoyed air superiority. The Allies had clearly lost the race to Tunis, and prospects for any real improvement in the supply situation from resources in the theater looked bleak. Larkin improvised a base section at Oran and had it functioning two days after the landing, but without service units and trucks, he could do little to ease the burden on the British. The situation in Casablanca looked worse. It took BG Art Wilson seven weeks just to activate a base section.

None of this came as news to Somervell. After King promised the escorts, Somervell wired his chief of staff, insisting that "no obstacle will be permitted to interfere with the shipment as directed." Even though the Torch requests had placed ASF behind "the eight ball," it had saved the operation. Now Smith asked ASF to bail out AFHQ again and help solve the logistical logjam in Tunisia. Once again, ASF made good on its promises. Within three weeks, ASF organized a twenty-three-ship convoy of 220,000 ship tons carrying 5,000 motor vehicles. The heavy railroad equipment and engineer stores soon followed, as did an infusion of services and supply personnel. Somervell's chief of staff, BG Wilhelm Styer, cabled AFHQ after the arrival of the convoy and related a "story of unending hours of intensive work to arrange his emergency shipment." The sardonic Styer quipped, "If you should happen to want the Pentagon shipped over there, please try to give us about a week's notice."[60]

Smith resumed his lobbying against the formation of a separate SOS command outside the control of AFHQ. Wilson had talked with Somervell in Casablanca and warned Smith about "something in the wind which may make necessary the breaking up or reorganization of supply staffs." Somervell wanted a rear-echelon commander to "coordinate the whole show and take the whole load off your shoulders," manage "all the odds and ends, and coordinate all supply, training and replacements."[61] Smith argued that until the Americans could bring in the required number of service troops to man the base sections and SOS installations and vastly improve transportation capabilities, AFHQ must retain control of supply through G-4. Any theater headquarters should be limited to administrative matters, relieving AFHQ of all routine details except those required for active and planned operations, rearming the French, and air force requirements.[62]

As Eisenhower informed Somervell on 27 January, a day after the American delegation left Algiers, he had put "the boys to work rapidly on organizing a Command of the SOS and Deputy Theater Authority."[63] Smith advocated a return to a modified version of the extemporized structure that existed before Torch. Guessing that Eisenhower intended to make Hughes the SOS commander, Smith wanted Hughes named as American chief administrative officer (CAO) in AFHQ in harness with Gale. Smith wanted to group administrative and service elements under Hughes, who would act as both a staff officer and commander. As American CAO, Hughes would superintend the American line of communications, operating through the American components in AFHQ. The G-4 Division would function as a watchdog over matters relating to supply and services. In addition, Hughes would handle all theater matters—discipline, replacements, health and welfare, special services—as well as act as the statutory authorizing agency, attending to all routine communications with the War Department and any other responsibilities Eisenhower saw fit to delegate. With Smith serving as chief of staff, Hughes would operate directly under his supervision. Smith's scheme removed the necessity of creating a separate theater staff, with all the attendant duplication in personnel. Smith's scheme possessed the added advantage of replicating and paralleling British supply and administration—which Smith deemed "more simple and direct than our own"—enhancing cooperation.[64]

Eisenhower again rejected Smith's design. "I have had a lot of fun the last two days," he wrote to Handy, "with some grand quarrels with my staff." Hinting at his previous tiffs with Smith, he joked with Handy, "Every once in a while Staff Officers get all confused in a bunch of charts and drawing lines on blank paper. I take a fiendish delight in ripping them to pieces and breaking up their little playhouses." He thought that although the American officer corps preached simplicity, it was "the one thing most frequently violated in our own thinking."[65] After four months of deferring and trimming, Eisenhower was forced to restructure his command, but judging from his letters to Marshall and Handy, he had no clearer idea how to proceed in February 1943 than when he had assumed command of ETO eight months earlier.[66]

Eisenhower, like Pershing before him, possessed an opportunity rarely conferred on an American general: he had the necessary authority to alter the organizational environment of the U.S. Army. Whatever headquarters structure he created would exert powerful normative influences in other theaters. But Eisenhower was a product of the interwar army. The highly fractured military establishment between the wars had proved itself resistant to institutional reform and innovation. Far from altering senior officers' attitudes, the challenges of the new war rendered them even more inimical to change. Eisenhower thought he was different. He ridiculed "ritualistic" officers obsessed with the "book," but he never ventured far from the well-worn paths of U.S. Army convention.[67]

"Simplicity" was a theme very much on his mind at this juncture. He complained to Marshall about "the inevitable trend of the British mind towards 'committee' rather than 'single' command" and their inability "to grasp the utter simplicity of the system we employ." What Eisenhower wanted was a simplification of his own tasks, which explains why he fixed on bringing Hughes to Algiers. Having fallen prey to his own insecurities, Eisenhower made the mistake of drowning himself in the details of his command. He chafed under the burden of his heavy responsibilities and crushing schedule, and his health deteriorated. Eisenhower concluded that, as supreme commander, he could not be bothered with the day-to-day operations of his headquarters or suffer the distractions of the clutter of administrative and logistical liabilities.

To play the only role reserved to him under the post-Casablanca command structure—as a strategic balancing wheel between the British commanders in chief—he must conserve his energies and free himself from theater concerns. When the new command system took effect, each commander would establish his headquarters in widely separated locations. For Eisenhower to exert any kind of direct influence, he would have to absent himself from Algiers, often for long periods. He recognized that nothing could be accomplished without delegating wide authority to competent assistants he trusted. To Smith he delegated executive responsibility for managing AFHQ. The Darlan affair had taught him a critical lesson: a supreme commander could never escape immersion in high-level political frays. To avoid personal commitments, Eisenhower willingly surrendered the lead political and diplomatic role to his chief of staff. In his mind, the lines of authority in the new command structure were clear. As a "strategic headquarters," AFHQ would handle all combined and joint questions—both military and political. Since Eisenhower retained unqualified faith in Hughes's abilities, he decided to make him not commander of a single SOS command but deputy theater commander. The proposed North African Theater of Operations (NATO) would discharge American theater responsibilities—routine administration with the War Department, command of static defense installations, and oversight of manpower. As commanding officer of a separate SOS in charge of supply, he settled on Larkin. In his mind, what could be more straightforward?[68]

Above all, Eisenhower insisted on a command and staff configuration that preserved unity of command. Single command and a linear staff structure conformed to U.S. Army doctrine, but did not fit the requirements of a joint and combined headquarters. By accentuating his role as supreme commander, Eisenhower predetermined that he would exercise command through AFHQ. Had he issued a directive to that effect—that the American component of AFHQ would act as the senior theater staff—there would have been no debate over what role NATO or the SOS would play nor any grounds for difficulties between Smith and Hughes, but no such edict was forthcoming. Here again, Eisenhower's organizational presumptions conflicted with his command technique. The essence of Eisenhower's system of command lay in fashioning a structure that centralized command but delegated authority. He wanted to deal only with key issues, and then only on a personal basis at the highest level. He appointed senior subordinates he trusted, granted them wide authority to act independently, and expected them to identify and solve problems and work out any differences among themselves. Eisenhower remained aloof from the process and intervened only as the last resort. Eisenhower's style focused not on formal exercise of authority through the channels of command but on the managing of interpersonal relations. He trusted that his people skills could overcome any major differences in policy or personality.

Eisenhower expected the creation of NATO and SOS to produce a number of salutary results. He believed a semiautonomous theater headquarters under Hughes and an equally self-regulating SOS under Larkin would relieve him of administrative and logistical responsibilities and limit the proliferation of staffs and staff populations. Smith had finally convinced him that no work could proceed without sizable staffs, but he rued their tendency to "develop diseases that include obesity and elephantiasis." He assured Marshall he would freely wield a sharp knife.[69] As he told Somervell, he need harbor "no fear that ritualistic objections can make any possible difference to me in setting up and organizing this theater for administrative purposes."[70]

At his 29 January chiefs of staff meeting, Smith announced Eisenhower's decision to create NATO and authorize a single SOS command for the theater. Hughes would direct both organizations as the deputy theater commander. Hughes's specific authority and which functions AFHQ would cede to the new headquarters remained undetermined. Smith indicated he would act as the chief of staff in NATO in addition to heading AFHQ. He also pointed out that Hughes's headquarters would be sited in Oran, not Algiers.[71]

His failure to bring Eisenhower around to his way of thinking represented a personal defeat for Smith. Hughes's appointment also concerned him. A 1908 graduate of West Point, Hughes was ten years Smith's senior and had been a colonel in the last war. He had staked out an interwar reputation for rocking the boat as a crusader for reform of the army's advanced schools and changes in officer efficiency reports, and for his advocacy of women in the army. What worried Smith most was Hughes's privileged position as an insider, as an intimate friend of both Eisenhower and Patton. Smith had a hard time reading Hughes. On the one hand, many credited Hughes with being the man in ETO most responsible for bringing together the U.S. supply program for Torch. On the other hand, some viewed him as a long-in-the-tooth colonel who had escaped Marshall's cull because of benefactors in high places. Either way, Smith would have to deal with Hughes. Smith congratulated himself for at least limiting the damage. With Hughes confined in Oran, discharging only housekeeping administrative tasks and a loosely defined supervisory role over Larkin and Wilson—and with Smith ensconced as

NATO chief of staff—Hughes posed no real threat. What Smith under-estimated was Hughes's influence on Eisenhower.

Hughes arrived in Algiers on 3 February. Smith met him and told Hughes the next day he would be named deputy theater command of the yet to be organized NATO. Hughes then reported to Eisenhower. "I've handed [Hughes] a job that has, I think, rather taken away his breath," Eisenhower related to Mamie. "He will get on top of it though, and will relieve me of a tremendous amount of work." He added, "It's a joy to have him around."[72]

Once Hughes caught his breath, he began wondering what he had gotten into. He recognized the anomalous position he would hold. The U.S. Army's table of organization made no provision for a deputy theater commander. His experience in London left Hughes cynical about entering another jurisdictional and personal minefield. He composed a list of complaints and forwarded them to Eisenhower, then followed that up with a personal visit. He told Eisenhower that, as far as he under-stood his responsibilities, the deputy theater commander would exer-cise duties equivalent to the book definition of a commanding general of a communications zone. Hughes wanted his position firmly rooted in traditional terms and requested that Eisenhower designate him as such. Since no new headquarters—distinct from NATO, the base sections, or a future SOS—was required, the communications zone would merely be titular. Second, he rebelled against Smith's acting as chief of staff for both AFHQ and NATO. Hughes had no desire to act as a mere factotum for Smith and insisted on his own chief of staff. He also opposed estab-lishing his headquarters in Oran. As the communications and transpor-tation hub of the northwestern African littoral, Algiers stood out as the logical site for the theater headquarters. Additionally, his separation in Oran would complicate liaison with AFHQ, handicap his ability to con-sult with Eisenhower, and hamstring his communications with the War Department. Finally, to facilitate his superintendence of theater admin-istration, he argued for the transfer in toto of the AFHQ G-1 Division to NATO.[73]

Eisenhower acceded to all of Hughes's requests. Eisenhower's direc-tive to Hughes authorized him, as deputy theater commander, "to estab-lish, operate and command a US Communication Zone for NATOUSA. You will assume all possible US administrative and supply duties now being performed at AFHQ in order to reduce AFHQ to the maximum of supply and administrative matters." As commanding general of a communications zone, Hughes bore additional responsibilities "for the detailed development of supply plans for American forces in future operations to conform to the broad plans of AFHQ." Finally, Eisenhower charged Hughes with establishing close liaison with Gale "in order to insure co-operation between American and British supply operations."[74] Eisenhower directed Hughes to work out the mechanics of AFHQ-NATO cooperation with Smith and Gale.

In theory, Hughes held sweeping responsibilities. Eisenhower empowered NATO as the authorizing agency for all American commands operating under AFHQ and as the conduit for communications with the War Department on administrative and logistical questions. Hughes would directly control the administrative agencies—except the adjutant general's office, which remained in AFHQ—in addition to overseeing Larkin and the SOS, superintending the manpower and replacement systems, commanding rear area units responsible for security (military police, signals communications, and postal and radio censorship), and supervising special services (chiefly mail, army publications, post exchanges, and entertainment).

In practice, the titles of deputy theater commander and head of communications zone conferred little real authority. Both command authorizations contained important caveats. Hughes acted as the theater commander for all purely American administrative and manpower matters, except decisions and policies involving the major U.S. commands— II Corps in Tunisia, Fifth Army, and AAF. These remained the preserve of AFHQ. As the combined headquarters, AFHQ continued to coordinate American and British supply and control of French rearmament and lend-lease, civil affairs, civil defense, and economic policy making; as the joint headquarters, AFHQ regulated all packaged American petroleum allocations and the distribution of materiel and supplies specific to the AAF. After adding together these spheres reserved for AFHQ, little remained of Hughes's zone of authority except control over the SOS, but even there, his influence remained ill defined. Although Hughes controlled the lines of communication, which meant SOS, Eisenhower informed Marshall that Larkin would serve as the "actual head."[75] How that would sort out, like Hughes's relationship to Smith, would presumably evolve over time.

Hughes, Smith, and Eisenhower each tried to draw an organizational chart. They all failed. Over dinner on 10 February, Eisenhower told Hughes, the "organization is too complicated to be placed on paper." "Of course it will make me mad," Eisenhower said, "but what the hell!"[76] In Eisenhower's mind, the formation of NATO fulfilled his promise to Marshall to address the mess in his rear. He had merely handed the problem off to Hughes. He also thought his creation of a consolidated administration and supply command would satisfy Somervell and get him off his back. Having made his decision—which amounted to re-creating the bifurcated structure that plagued ETO—he no longer wanted to be bothered by these questions. Eisenhower knew the organization contained many structural flaws, but he expected any problems that arose to be settled informally among his responsible subordinates— Smith, Gale, Hughes, and Larkin. What preoccupied him were not organizational issues and problems in the rear areas but the stalemate in Tunisia.

Eisenhower did not linger in Algiers to preside over the inauguration of his new theater headquarters; on 12 February, now wearing his fourth star, he set off for a tour of Fredendall's command. Frustration mounted over having to assume the defensive. He remembered his War College days and the commandant's solution to a problem. When the students puzzled over how to conduct a defense, "getting the logistics properly arranged and the necessary forces on the field," Connor corrected them, saying, "Attack with whatever you've got at any point where you get it up, and attack and keep on attacking until this invader realizes that he has got to stop and reorganize, and thus give us a chance to deliver a finishing blow."[77] Smith and his staff projected that if Somervell made good on his pledge to furnish the transportation, and if the promised service troops arrived, then American forces would possess enough strength, backed by sufficient support, to undertake offensive operations in mid-March.[78] That did not satisfy Eisenhower. He went forward looking for ways to attack. Unfortunately, the Germans beat him to the punch again.

★ 19 ★

"Allies Are Very Difficult People to Fight With"

The logic that dictated the decision to embark on operations in North Africa in 1942 still held for the Mediterranean in 1943. Torch offered the only opportunity to employ Anglo-American power that had any likelihood of producing significant strategic and political gains without hazarding a catastrophic defeat. Hitler's decision to prop up Italy was drawing Germany down a strategic dead end; the Allied strategy was opportunistic, to be sure, and it would have been an enormous mistake not to exploit the potential dividends left dangling in the Mediterranean by German strategic blundering. And the Americans—with their own chiefs of staff divided—offered no better alternative. Strategy in the Mediterranean took on an irresistible inertia: Torch magnified El Alamein, Tunisia led to Sicily, and Sicily led to Italy. Although the Mediterranean presented no possibilities for inflicting a decisive defeat on Germany—attrition campaigns are never decisive—the "grind down" theory held out the promise of tying down and eroding German strength, breaking the Axis coalition, and enlivening resistance movements everywhere—all crucial precursors for a successful return to France in 1944. As Eisenhower concluded, he did not "see how the 'big bosses' could have deviated very far from the general course of action they adopted" at Casablanca.[1]

The roadblock remained Tunisia—the bridge to Sicily and Italy. The Desert Fox had learned a very hard lesson at great cost: "the battle," said Rommel, "is fought and decided by the quartermasters before the shooting begins."[2] If that were true, the chaotic state of American logistics guaranteed the Allies' loss of the first rounds in Tunisia. Eisenhower ordered Anderson not to think in terms of a brigade here and a brigade there but rather to concentrate his forces. Anderson failed for two reasons. Throughout January, the German commander in the north, GEN Hans-Jürgen von Arnim, launched a series of limited offensives aimed at blocking Allied access to the passes through the Eastern Dorsals and the coastal plains beyond. Many of these attacks focused on the vulnerable French. Eisenhower ordered the French squeezed out of the line, extending the British First Army south and U.S. II Corps north, stretching the lines dangerously thin. Fredendall's faulty deployments rendered a bad situation worse. The U.S. II Corps remained undermanned owing to the critical shortage of surface transportation. Until ASF made good on its pledge and expedited the shipment of trucks and railway equipment to North Africa, the patchwork deployment of Allied forces in Tunisia and the extemporized supply arrangements continued.[3]

Rommel and von Arnim took advantage of the end of the winter rains and the overextended Allied positions by launching a spoiling offensive in II Corps area. Eisenhower, touring the front, left Sidi Bou Zid only hours before two veteran panzer divisions rolled through. American units, "one packet at a time," were overwhelmed. In the first days it appeared the Germans might roll up the entire Allied line, but stiffening resistance, difficult terrain, and divided German leadership forced the abandonment of the drive. While American losses in manpower, materiel, and confidence were high, the German offensive did not significantly alter the strategic situation. By 24 February, two days after the Germans pulled back, American forces reoccupied Kasserine Pass. Far more menacing, the fallout from Kasserine threatened to open a rift in the coalition.

"Are We Allies or Aren't We?"

Eisenhower and Smith were away from Algiers when the Germans attacked. Smith went to Tripoli for a series of seminars and lectures presented by Montgomery on the lessons of desert fighting. Only three Americans attended the conference—Lee, Patton, and Smith. Montgomery could not help but notice that not a single general officer outside Eighth Army showed up, but Anderson's people had a good reason—they were in combat. Always a keen student of military history, Smith jumped at the chance to meet the "Victor of Alamein" and listen to his "lessons learnt." Just as important, he wanted to cement an association with the general who, in a few days, would command an army under AFHQ, albeit indirectly through Alexander. Naturally, Smith knew all about Montgomery's personality quirks from his British friends, such as how he liked to go his own way and was exceedingly hard to manage.

Montgomery gave the appearance of not caring what others thought of him, but that was pure artifice. He tried very hard to impress people with the forcefulness of his character. The nonregulation cardigan, the baggy corduroy pants, the black beret festooned with badges immediately conveyed the impression Montgomery cultivated: he was not a typical British general. People never knew what to make of Montgomery. Conceited and uncompromising, Montgomery always had to appear to be in charge and have the last word; his hermetic self-absorption prevented him from appreciating anybody else's point of view or feelings. The trouble was, he had a nasty habit of being right. He even managed to transform his virtues—dogged self-assuredness, high-minded professionalism, and undaunted daring—into vices. Montgomery's perplexing persona blinded his contemporary critics (and many historians) to his exceptional gifts as a general. A superb trainer and inspirer of troops, Montgomery, in a remarkably short tenure, transformed a dispirited and defeated collection of imperial units into the victorious army then closing on the Tunisian frontier. Somehow this wispy, homely teetotaler with a foxy face, shrill voice, and repellent personality imprinted himself on an entire army. "He wasn't a nice man," observed one of his staff officers, "but nice men don't win wars!"[4]

Montgomery took the time to have a long talk with Smith. When the conversation turned to expectations for the campaign in Tunisia, Smith asked Montgomery for his estimates. Typically oblivious to Smith's sensitivities over the situation at Kasserine, Montgomery boasted the Eighth Army would "come along and finish it for them [AFHQ]." He predicted he would take Sfax, on the central Tunisian coast, within the next six weeks. This required breaching the formidable Mareth Line and advancing through the defensible Gabes Gap, an assertion Smith regarded as absurd. "Oh, General, come, come," Smith retorted. Confident he would make good on his boast, Montgomery asked what Smith would be willing to wager. Not taking the suggestion seriously, or so he later claimed, Smith replied, "anything you want." Montgomery quickly asked for a Flying Fortress, "complete with an American crew." Smith agreed, and Monty penciled the wager into his betting ledger.[5]

Neither man recorded his first impressions. Doubtlessly, Montgomery lived up to his advance billing. Montgomery typically dismissed other generals; very few quantified as "1st Class chaps," and more often he wrote them off as "completely useless." Certainly none of the British officers on Smith's staff measured up. Whiteley "is no good; he proved a failure here." Mockler-Ferryman "is also not the chap; he is a pure theorist and has no practical experience." After talking to Smith, Montgomery told Brooke, "What Eisenhower ought to have is some 1st Class *practical* chaps," but, he concluded, "the truth is there are not enough 1st Class chaps to go around."[6] A talk with Alexander, then on the verge of assuming command of the Eighteenth Army Group, convinced Montgomery the amateurish Americans "do not know how to fight the battle," and had they "come over here earlier on and asked about how you fight the Germans, these troubles might have been avoided." Smith may not have been "1st Class" in Montgomery's estimation, but at least he made the effort to come to Tripoli to study under the great master of the battlefield; that probably counted for something.[7]

Smith returned to Algiers on 26 February, expecting the worst. Despite having brought his headquarters staff under some degree of control, Kasserine threatened another spate of American and British backbiting. Smith took no comfort in knowing his staff stood as a model of coalition teamwork compared with what existed at the command level. Some heads would roll. But the problem with lobbing off heads is deciding when to start and where to end.

The most obvious head that needed to roll belonged to Fredendall. Smith badgered Eisenhower for weeks about replacing Fredendall. Even in the aftermath of Kasserine, Eisenhower could not bring himself to ax Fredendall and decided he needed bolstering instead. Eisenhower ordered MG Ernie Harmon, the hard-nosed commander of the Second Armored, to AFHQ. Again suffering a bout of indecision, Eisenhower told Harmon he wanted him to go forward and assume command of II Corps or First Armored, whichever he thought necessary. Harmon replied, "Well make up your mind, Ike, I can't do both." Eisenhower admitted he simply did not know. On 22 February Eisenhower and Harmon traveled to Constantine for talks with Alexander and Truscott. Harmon went from there to II Corps as Fredendall's deputy commander, charged with assessing the situation. Eisenhower sidestepped making the decision on Fredendall and Ward, the commander of First Armored. "Fredendall has kept entirely out of the battle," Harmon reported to Smith on 26 February, "and has slept for the last two days. I know this because twice I sent my aide to tell him of the battle progress and he was asleep at 11 AM both times."[8] Four days later he reported to Eisenhower that Fredendall was "no damned good. You ought to get rid of him."[9] Eisenhower offered the job to Harmon, who refused, replying he could not replace the man whose firing he had recommended. In the meantime, Bradley appeared in Algiers to assume the job of helping Smith fix the problems in the rear. But Eisenhower decided he had already solved that problem; the bigger issue lay in II Corps. Eisenhower sent Bradley forward as Harmon's replacement to backstop Fredendall and act as AFHQ's "eyes and ears."

Not pleased with Eisenhower's solution, which solved nothing, Smith decided to accompany Bradley and assess the situation himself. Their automobile passed Harmon's on his way out. During the long trip, Bradley complained that Eisenhower had provided him with no instructions and no authority. What they found exceeded their worst expectations. Fredendall and his staff blamed the British for everything. Bradley reported them "rabidly, if not obscenely, anti-British and especially anti-Anderson." Smith left convinced that Fredendall was either "incompetent or crazy or both."[10] In his mind, Fredendall had to go, if for no other reason than to prevent an open rupture with the British.

Smith gained a reputation as a hard-luck traveler; something always went wrong when he trekked forward. He toured the front and arrived at a forward British battery with "two flat tires and two sore feet from ill-fitting boots."[11] Returning to Algiers, Smith added his voice to a chorus of senior officers—Alexander, Anderson, Harmon, Truscott—demanding Fredendall's immediate relief.

Eisenhower could obfuscate no longer. On 5 March he asked Clark to assume command. Clark declined; three-star generals do not command corps. Clark's decision irritated Eisenhower, widening the estrangement between the two former friends. With no other option, Eisenhower turned to Patton. In many respects, Patton appeared the obvious choice, but his outspoken disparagement of the British made Eisenhower think he might only add fuel to the fire. Smith put in a call to Rabat, telling Patton that he might relieve Fredendall and asking him to come to Algiers. Eisenhower and Smith met Patton on the tarmac at Maison Blanche airfield. Eisenhower told Patton he had been selected because fighting in Tunisia "was primarily a tank show," and he took pains to drive home the point "that criticism of the British must stop." Privately, Patton thought he "would have more trouble with the British than with the Boche," and in his opinion, Eisenhower had "sold his soul to the devil of 'Cooperation,' which I think means we are pulling the chestnuts for our noble allies." He revealed none of this to Eisenhower and Smith.[12]

When Patton arrived at II Corps headquarters, he was surprised to find Bradley there. Bradley did not like forfeiting a corps command in the States; he disliked the task of helping Smith fix the mess in the rear (a job he never actually held) even more, and he was even less enamored of acting as AFHQ's "eyes and ears" and Fredendall's adviser.

Patton was of the same mind. He would not have "one of Ike's god-damn spies" in his command and immediately called Smith. It took little effort to convince Smith; orders went out making Bradley deputy corps commander.[13]

AFHQ did not escape. The first officer to go was Mockler-Ferryman. On 20 February Smith insisted on the removal of his intelligence chief.[14] As he related to Butcher, his "hair stood on end with anger when he was shown one of our intelligence reports after the defeat [at Sidi Bou Zid]."[15] A number of reasons lay behind the intelligence failure. Because of security concerns, the rules for employing and verifying Ultra intelligence presented obstacles. AFHQ G-2 did not possess tasking authority to subordinate echelons, which meant that conventional intelligence sources—contact reports, photo intelligence, and information gleaned from enemy interrogations—did not always make it up the chain. Ultra indicated the Germans intended to attack, but farther north. Smith's rage derived not from Mockler-Ferryman's initial assessments—Smith had endorsed them—but from his insistence that Sidi Bou Zid amounted only to a feint. In fact, American troops had been on alert; faulty intelligence contributed to the defeat, but the real culprits remained the lack of leadership, combat inexperience, and Anderson and Fredendall's flawed deployments. And the Germans could not be relied on to stick to the script. Mockler-Ferryman agreed to stay on until his replacement arrived. "If a man is not wanted," he remarked, "argument won't change the situation." Because of Ultra, the G-2 chief had to be British. Smith requested "an officer who has a broader insight into German mentality and method."[16] Brooke sent him Brigadier Kenneth Strong, an officer Smith came to view as "one of the best intelligence men in the business."[17]

Alexander established Eighteenth Army Group headquarters at Constantine on 20 February. Smith wrote the directive outlining Alexander's mission and defining his relationship with AFHQ. Eisenhower insisted Alexander sort out the confusion at the front, consolidating the forces into national groups. After touring the theater, Alexander found "no policy, no plan, the front all mixed up, no reserves, no training anywhere. No building up for the future. So-called Reinforcement camps in a disgraceful state."[18] He forwarded a sanitized report to Eisenhower. Noting that American troops lacked experience, he diplomatically claimed that over time they would develop into fighting soldiers the equal of any in the world. Left unsaid, Alexander gloomily predicted that this would be a long time coming. In his private correspondence, he exhibited the familiar "Greeks to Romans" mind-set. As he told Montgomery, "I have taken infinite trouble with them—and mind you one has to deal very carefully with them because they are not one of us." For Alexander and Montgomery, "the real trouble is the low fighting value of the troops in Central Tunisia."[19]

Patton commanded II Corps for only forty days—long enough to restore order, discipline, and, most vital, morale. Despite Patton's successes, Alexander's assessment of American troops contained merit. He told Montgomery, "the troops on the ground . . . are mentally & physically rather soft and very green. It is the old story again—lack of proper training allied to no experience in war—and too high a standard of living."[20] Because diversions for Torch and North Africa delayed the division-making assembly line in the United States, the Thirty-sixth Division, which landed in Italy in September, was the first that had completed its entire training sequence. The dispersion of units occasioned by the logistics situation meant that divisions such as the Ninth and Thirty-fourth had long since lost any edge they possessed when they landed. On 19 March Patton, reinforced by elements of the Ninth Division, opened attacks toward Gafsa and Maknassy. Patton's limited objectives involved diverting German strength from Montgomery's offensive against the Mareth Line. Patton petitioned for a bigger mission—an advance to the sea, cutting off the retreat of the First Italian Army—but grudgingly accepted a supporting role. The American forces secured both objectives against light resistance, and at El Guettar the First Division inflicted a sharp bloody nose on the counterattacking Tenth Panzer Division.

With Montgomery positioned for a breakthrough, Alexander requested that Patton renew his drive. The next day Eighth Army pierced the Axis defenses. Now the possibility loomed of pocketing the retreating Axis forces. Two II Corps movements made no headway against tough German resistance: First Armored in front of Maknassy, and First and Ninth Infantry in advance of El Guettar. Smith went forward to Patton's headquarters on 31 March, accompanied by Alexander's chief of staff MG Richard McCreery. Patton made no effort to disguise his lack of enthusiasm about their visit. Smith brought approval for a plan Patton had advanced two days earlier. "It would have worked then," a disgruntled Patton noted in his diary. "Now, as usual with them, it is too late." He also protested about Alexander intruding into his command sphere and issuing "orders that were too detailed."[21] Smith promised to talk to Alexander.

Angered by these infringements on his command, frustrated by his inability to breach the German defenses, and anguished by the death of his favorite aide in an air attack, the mercurial Patton wrote an addendum to a 1 April situation report that set off a powder keg of inter-Allied and interservice acrimony. He attributed his lack of progress to the total lack of air cover, which granted the Luftwaffe free rein over the battle-field. The British head of Allied tactical air forces, AVM Arthur Con-ingham, angrily reacted to Patton's "false cry of wolf" by dispatching a provocative communication to every command in the theater, mockingly suggesting that the report must be someone's idea of an April fool's joke. The real problem, he added, rested not with the air forces, which were winning the battle for air superiority, but with the lack of American battle-worthiness. The exchange created an international and interser-vice brouhaha.

Tedder recognized the potential for "a major crisis in Anglo-American relations" and ordered Coningham to apologize personally. Tedder informed Eisenhower of his actions. Eisenhower had bent over backward to please the British and willingly absorbed all the behind-the-back cavil-ing from even his closest friends about his purported pro-British obses-sion. A deeply deflated Eisenhower drafted a letter to Marshall, stating that since he had failed to control his own subordinate commanders, he could no longer remain as Allied supreme commander. As with Eisen-hower's precipitate reaction to the command shift during Symbol, Smith summoned all his considerable powers of persuasion and finally con-vinced Eisenhower "the damage could be repaired." Eisenhower sat on his resignation.[22]

Tedder and Spaatz staunched the wound. Coningham met with Pat-ton and offered a generous apology, which he duly distributed to all and sundry; Patton replied with a gallant acceptance. Coningham's charges, though patronizing and offensive, stung because they bore legitimacy. On the surface, the waters appeared calmed, but beneath, they remained troubled. The biggest casualty was Eisenhower; although the contretemps had not ended his career as commander in chief, his silence further lowered his standing in the opinion of senior Ameri-can commanders. According to Patton, Eisenhower was putty in British hands. He lamented, "Oh, God, for John J. Pershing." And he spoke for many American officers when he recorded in his diary: "I am fed up with being treated like a moron by the British. . . . Ike must go."[23]

Montgomery's turning of the Mareth Line and his advance through Gabes Gap brought no relief from the internecine squabbling. On 10 April Eighth Army took Sfax. Montgomery immediately dispatched a cable to Algiers: "Have captured SFAX. Send Fortress." His "Little Jack Horner" routine did not play well in AFHQ. Smith first tried to laugh off the matter with a joking reply. He had never told Eisenhower about the bet. In the British army, nothing was more sacred than a mess wager, and Montgomery fully expected payment. Smith now had to go into Eisenhower's office and attempt an explanation. Still reeling from the Patton-Coningham flare-up, Eisenhower flew into a rage. But, "being the past master of cementing inter-allied relations," Eisenhower agreed, even if it meant extracting an aircraft and crew from Arnold and, far worse, informing the humorless Marshall. Two days later, Montgomery had his plane.[24] Two months later, Brooke found Eisenhower still "boiling over internally with anger" at being "bounced in this way by Monty!"[25]

In Brooke's opinion, the episode so intensely annoyed Eisenhower that it "laid the foundation of distrust and dislike [for Montgomery] which remained with Eisenhower during the rest of the war." Eisenhower's aversion to Montgomery predated the Flying Fortress affair, however. Eisenhower had first met Montgomery while touring ETO in May 1942; on a visit to Montgomery's headquarters, and in front of other senior officers, Montgomery rudely upbraided Eisenhower for smoking. Eisenhower stubbed out his Camel but never forgave Montgomery for the slight. The second meeting went no better. Eisenhower flew down to Montgomery's command post on 2 April 1943 and spent the night. With the Eighth Army advancing beyond Gabes, Montgomery was in good form, which meant, in Churchill's characterization, that he was insufferable. Montgomery concluded, as everyone did, that Eisenhower was a "nice chap" and conceded he was "probably quite good in the political line." But Montgomery typically went too far. Eisenhower's "knowledge of how to make war, or how to fight battles, is definitely NIL. He must be kept right away from all that sort of thing—otherwise we shall lose the war." These views remained fixed in Montgomery's mind. Eisenhower's assessment proved both durable and prescient, if more trenchant: "Goddamn it, I can deal with anybody except that son of a bitch."[26]

Eisenhower had no choice but to deal with Montgomery. As he told Marshall, "Montgomery is of different caliber from some of the outstanding British leaders you have met."[27] He eventually decided that Montgomery would produce the desired results as a combat commander so long as he had a strong immediate commander over him. Eisenhower believed Alexander was equal to the task; he was wrong. He also concluded that Montgomery had demonstrated his loyalty "and has shown no disposition whatsoever to overstep the bounds imposed by allied unity of command"—an assessment that proved even further from the mark.[28]

Montgomery thought he and Alexander made a good team. "The requirements of a good team," he wrote, "are that those in the team must, *between them,* have all the qualities and professional knowledge for the job at hand." A duet was essential because only a superman could combine "all the necessary qualities . . . and I do not know any of these." From the day Montgomery arrived in Middle East Command, Alexander surrendered all planning and the conduct of all operations, even control over the Western Desert Air Force, to the Eighth Army commander. "He trusted me completely," Montgomery noted, "and gave me a free hand to do what I liked; the staff at GHQ were ordered to comply with all my demands."[29] The tandem worked because Alexander kept "the party 'sweet' at the top," while Montgomery got "on with the business."[30] In dealing with the Americans and the other services, the affable Alexander compensated for the mischief-making Montgomery. More important, Alexander provided the vital buffer between the prime minister and Montgomery.

Alexander and Montgomery were polar opposites. As GEN Bernard Freyberg observed, "If Montgomery is a cad, it's a great pity that the British Army doesn't have a few more bounders."[31] Once, upon entering a new headquarters, Montgomery famously pronounced, "Gentlemen, out. Players, in." Montgomery frequently used English sporting references, usually to cricket, to make his point. In the nineteenth century, gentlemen's cricket clubs, if they wanted to win, stooped so low as to employ professional ringers. According to the strictures of the British class system, professionals were tradesmen and could never be gentlemen. Montgomery was viewed by the Old Guard as a tradesman. Lord Gort warned Smith, "In dealing with [Montgomery] one must remember that he is not quite a gentleman."[32] For his part, Montgomery thought senior officers like Gort were distinguished only by their "old school tie, the peerage," and he categorized many of them uncharitably as "diseased guardsmen."[33]

Alexander held his position primarily because he personified the image of the squire warrior, especially in the eyes of Churchill, who saw in Alexander some of the traits of a Marlborough. With Hollywood good looks, the tall, suave, superbly well mannered (he considered manners the highest of manly virtues), and always immaculately turned out Alexander certainly looked the part. The son of an earl, Alexander had attended the right school (Churchill's alma mater), played in one of the most famous cricket matches (Harrow versus Eton in 1910), rose to become one of the youngest battalion commanders in World War I in the Irish Guards, and enjoyed an armywide reputation for remarkable courage under fire. In 1937 he became the youngest general in the British army. After commanding a division creditably in France, Alexander assumed command of the British army in Burma in early March 1942 and presided over the last in a string of British disasters in the Far East. The best that can be said of Alexander's conduct of the rout is that he completed the withdrawal—primarily because, unlike MG Christopher Maltby in Hong Kong and LTG Arthur Percival in Singapore, he had someplace, India, where he could retreat. One of his corps commanders and later the general who redeemed the British in Burma, FM William Slim (himself no gentleman, the son of a shopkeeper), thought Alexander never possessed "the faintest clue what was going on."[34] The American liaison officer to the British army in Burma, MAJ Frank Merrill (later of marauder fame), believed Alexander "lacked force and could be talked into anything."[35] The debacle, mythologized into another Dunkirk, did not tarnish Alexander's reputation. He returned to England and promotion to full general. The initial choice as commander of First Army in Torch, Alexander instead went to Middle East Command, where he was later joined by Montgomery.

Alexander emerged as Churchill's favorite general for two basic reasons: he never challenged the prime minister, and he epitomized the Churchillian ideal of what a British general ought to be. Of all the stages in his remarkable life—dashing cavalryman, gentleman adventurer-journalist, politician, man of letters, statesman, and finally warlord—the incurably romantic Churchill remained most fixed on the first. Never having commanded an army in the field, and too old to do so now, Churchill selected pliable commanders he could direct from Whitehall. A large portion of Brooke's job—and the most frustrating—involved blunting the irrepressible prime minister's constant intrusions into operations. What Churchill valued in a general was not intellect but character—the "ours is not to reason why, ours is but to do or die" type. In the diffident *sans peur et sans reproche* Alexander, Churchill found his knight-errant. That Alexander lacked smarts never troubled Churchill; he probably rated it an asset.[36]

Even though Alexander entertained a low opinion of American generals and soldiers—exposure to the opinionated Anglophobe MG "Vinegar Joe" Stilwell in Burma and then Fredendall in Tunisia did nothing to change his mind—he captivated Eisenhower. As Patton put it, "London captured Abilene." Even with the huge social gulf separating them, the two men shared much in common, particularly their insouciance toward the trappings of high command. Both men maintained a certain detachment, preferring to command through persuasion rather than imposing their will on subordinates; this left subordinates unsure of their intentions, allowing the more strong-willed among them to take advantage.

Despite his limitations—which Eisenhower acknowledged as early as May 1943—Eisenhower always considered Alexander superior to Montgomery as a commander.[37]

In some ways, Montgomery's relationship to Alexander paralleled Smith's to Eisenhower. Alexander and Eisenhower sought consensus through personal contacts and proved willing to compromise; both avoided open confrontations. When they needed to fight, they enlisted someone else to do it for them. Consistently, that meant Monty and Beetle. "Whoever embarks on this business of 'fighting for the things that matter' has got to be prepared to be very insistent and to 'thump the table,'" Montgomery observed. "If he does this he will get a lot of 'mud' slung at him, and he will make enemies." Since Alexander never thumped a table, Montgomery did it for him and "took all the 'mud.'" Montgomery recognized that Alexander's greatest asset lay in his charm, "and if he lost that he would go right under as he does not really know much about the business."[38] In Smith, Eisenhower had his own first-class table thumper, who, like Montgomery, got plenty of mud thrown his way.

As Axis forces withdrew behind their Enfidaville defenses, the Tunisian campaign entered its climactic stage. The prospect of almost guaranteed victory brought no end to the infighting. Montgomery's advance left II Corps without an operational mission. Alexander decided First Army would undertake the main effort, leaving II Corps in a holding position. Confronted by Patton's angry response—Eisenhower initially acquiesced—Alexander grudgingly offered II Corps the assignment of taking Bizerte. This required the rapid movement of 100,000 troops across the British lines of communication—a mammoth logistical undertaking. Eisenhower decided on Bradley to head the drive; Patton would return to Husky planning and training.[39]

On 14 April Eisenhower flew to Alexander's headquarters at Haïdra for a major conference on finalizing an accord. While at Haïdra, another storm of inter-Allied discord erupted, this one potentially more damaging than the rest. On 8 April the Thirty-fourth Division, under British command, poorly executed an attack at Fandouk Pass, failing to clear the path for an armored thrust to Kairouan. Except for stragglers, the Axis forces completed their retreat to Enfidaville. Blame fell on American forces for not closing the pocket. The American media broke the story of the failures of the Thirty-fourth Division at Fandouk; columnists contrasted British successes with the "downright embarrassing" performance of Ryder's units.

Eisenhower returned to Algiers, and Smith handed him a letter from Marshall. Resentful of the acclaim afforded the release of the movie

Desert Victory in the States, an embittered Marshall decried the "marked fall in prestige of American troops in minds of pressmen and in reaction of public" and insisted that Eisenhower tighten censorship. Marshall chided Eisenhower for being too passive, for surrendering "too much to logistical reasons with unfortunate results as to national prestige."[40] Badly stung—he called it "practically a body blow"—a defensive Eisenhower informed Marshall of the results of his meetings with Alexander—that is, all four American divisions would form a powerful corps, "even if the logistics of the situation should make the arrangement seem somewhat unwise or risky." In AFHQ's defense, while condemning "the fool censor," Eisenhower argued that Smith had pleaded for qualified censors and public relations officers, without success. He considered firing McClure, the officer directly in charge of press relations and censorship. Eisenhower promised to hold a major press conference to clear the air.[41]

Eisenhower also granted interviews to selected journalists, including Gordon Gaskill, who asked the loaded question: "Are We Allies or Aren't We?" Eisenhower pointed to an irony. "I'm speaking frankly," he started. "You see, we were trying to get Tunisia for nothing. It was a long gamble, but it was worth taking." In the beginning, "we were all like 100s of little Dutch boys, each with his finger in a hole in the dike, trying to hold back the flood." Not surprising, "we lost the first rounds." Now the course had reversed. The current ran strongly in Allied favor. An estimated 150,000 Axis troops were penned up in northern Tunisia; on average, 1,000 enemy troops entered prisoner of war cages each day. Somervell made good on his promises, and the arteries of the American lines of communication pulsated with supplies and materiel. The entire II Corps was being trucked north in preparation for the final drive to Bizerte. Two British armies and a corps each of American and French troops encircled a doomed foe; the Allies had wrestled command of the skies from the Axis and controlled the sea. Together, coalition forces lay poised to inflict a catastrophic defeat on the Axis. Yet journalists insisted on reporting only the negative. In Eisenhower's mind, the answer to Gaskill's question was a resounding yes.[42] The next day a frazzled supreme commander withdrew to the farm, his retreat outside Algiers, for some much-needed rest and to contemplate the next phase of the war in the Mediterranean.

"Husky . . . Has Gotten Planners . . . in a Turmoil"

The campaign in Tunisia took place against the backdrop of turmoil and friction over planning the next chapter in the Mediterranean saga—

the invasion of Sicily. From the outset, Eisenhower was troubled about Alexander's ability to juggle responsibilities as ground commander in Eighteenth Army Group and as superintendent of planning for Husky. On 30 January he informed Marshall the two campaigns had definitely merged and noted, "it is high time that Alexander got on the job and took the tactical reins."[43] His apprehensions proved well founded. Alexander would not arrive in Northwest Africa until 18 February; thereafter he became so involved in the Tunisian fighting he neglected Husky.

Eisenhower railed against the imposition of the committee system on his command, yet he remained curiously disengaged from the one sphere where he could exert influence—over Husky planning. After touring the theater, U.S. senators asked Stimson: "Cunningham commands the naval forces, Tedder commands the air forces, and Alexander commands the ground forces. What in hell does Eisenhower command?"[44] It was a good question. The only area over which Eisenhower exercised direct command was the U.S. rear area, and he had delegated control of that to Hughes. Like Alexander, Eisenhower's attention remained fixed on Tunisia. Every chance he got he went forward, often for days at a time, giving the appearance of being in command without exerting any real authority. Stemming from his absolute faith in unity of command, Eisenhower never treaded on Alexander's "special province."[45] And in common with Alexander, he believed commanders should command and staff officers should plan. So Eisenhower left the supervision of Husky planning to Smith.

Alexander dispatched a senior staff officer, MG Charles Gairdner, the deputy director of plans in Middle East Command, to spearhead planning. The planners, known as Force 141 (from the room number in the St. George Hotel where the initial meeting took place), began working on Husky in late January. Eisenhower instructed Smith to form a parallel Security Council and supervise planning for all operations—including civil affairs for Sicily—except those involving Tunisia. The relationship between Smith and the Security Council and Gairdner and Force 141 remained blurred.

Smith did not like the setup. Even though he was chief of staff to the supreme commander, Smith was obligated to respect Alexander's "special province" over Husky planning. Even though the planners came principally from his G-3 Division, they worked for Gairdner in Force 141. Instead of supervising planning, Smith coordinated it between AFHQ and Force 141 in Algiers and no fewer than five other headquarters—those of the three commanders and the two task force commanders—stretched across the Mediterranean theater from Rabat to Cairo.[46] He also dealt with the War Department and the War Office concerning the deployment of the Forty-fifth and Canadian First Infantry Divisions earmarked for the landings. Eisenhower expected him to orchestrate the entire piece, but not even a military Toscanini could harmonize all these disparate players, especially since Smith possessed no authority beyond acting as surrogate for the supreme commander.

Success depended on Smith's maintenance of personal contacts, primarily with Cunningham and Tedder. He enjoyed the best of relations with Cunningham and his chief assistant, CDR Royer Dick. The opposite prevailed on the air force side. Smith and Tedder did not like each other. Smith thought Tedder pretentious and languid. Tedder accused Smith of being a small-minded soldier hostile to airmen. Under the untidy settlement growing out of Casablanca, command lines over the air forces in the theater remained complicated. Tedder commanded all air forces in the Mediterranean, with Spaatz as his deputy. Tedder answered to AFHQ only for matters concerning the air forces in northwestern Africa. Tedder and Spaatz spent weeks trying to "tidy up the staff and command channels," producing only more confusion and friction. They finally decided to put the wire charts "in the waste paper basket and just go on as we were." Eisenhower would have preferred, as Tedder put it, to have "the divine right to command his own private air force," but he contented himself with working through informal channels.[47]

In mid-August Tedder sent AVM Philip Wigglesworth to AFHQ as his air deputy. Smith and Wigglesworth clashed from the start. Wigglesworth balked at routing RAF communications through Smith. When Tedder paid a visit to Algiers, Wigglesworth went to him and stated, "Oh, this is going to be a bit uncomfortable. I do not like Mr. Bedell Smith very much, and I do not think he likes me very much." Smith jumped Tedder, demanding Wigglesworth's removal for failure to cooperate. Taken aback by the vehemence of Smith's accusations, Tedder refused to replace Wigglesworth or accept Smith's interference with his direct access to Eisenhower. The two held a second meeting to clear the air. Smith strenuously objected to Tedder's claim that he commanded an independent air force organization. Tedder dismissed this row as a by-product of Smith's parochialism and opposition to an independent U.S. air force. "So far as [Smith] was concerned," Tedder believed, "a separate air force in America 'would come over his dead body.'"

Much more than U.S. Army politics lay behind Smith's challenge. Eisenhower had chartered Smith to resist any further encroachment of the committee system. Right after the Torch landings, Smith made a run at integrating the U.S. air command into AFHQ, in effect, making Spaatz chief of an air section inside the combined headquarters. Smith and Spaatz agreed to disagree, and there the matter rested.[48] Beyond that consideration, Smith fashioned the mechanisms of his inner staff around completely integrated joint intelligence and operations staffs; every morning he held a chiefs of staff conference, and the first order of business focused on coordinating air actions, especially strategic assets, with ground and sea operations. As with Spaatz earlier, Smith wanted the air forces to be more responsive to central direction. Wigglesworth's defense of RAF prerogatives undermined what Smith saw as one of his chief duties. Tedder assured Smith he would talk to Wigglesworth. Though not entirely appeased, Smith never took the issue to Eisenhower to adjudicate. Knowing that Eisenhower held Tedder in such high esteem, Smith considered it a fight he might not win. Relations improved between Wigglesworth and Smith, and they eventually became friendly, but genuine integration never occurred. Smith found Spaatz's British chief of staff, AVM James Robb, more pliant. Despite efforts to paper over their differences, the relationship between Smith and Tedder never entirely lost its sharp edge.[49]

The first of no fewer than nine Husky plans emerged in February and bore all the hallmarks of being the work of multilayered committees, an inevitable consequence of Alexander's lack of direction from above. The plan called for three widely dispersed sequential landings: the first, undertaken by the British, aimed at seizing airfields in the southeastern part of the island; then, provided with air support, a second on the southern coast; followed by the final American assault near Palermo on the northwestern coast of Sicily.[50] Cunningham and Tedder insisted on dispersed landings and the seizure of airfields—especially Gela in the south—based on their concerns over neutralizing German airpower. Nevins and BG Thomas Betts, the chief American planners, pointed to logistical constraints. Sufficient supplies could not be brought ashore over the beaches, necessitating the early seizure of ports—Syracuse in the east; Gela, Licata, and Scoglitti in the south; and Palermo in the west. The only other option involved broadening the attacks, but shortages of shipping, naval support, and landing craft ruled out that option. Smith preferred more concentrated assaults, but Eisenhower—influenced by the naval and air commanders' preoccupation with seizing airfields—never intervened.[51]

Predictably, complications arose. In mid-February Churchill, chronically impatient for action, pressed AFHQ for a June Husky. "A delay of three months in the very midst of the campaigning season between the finish in Tunisia and the beginning of HUSKY," he told Eisenhower, "would be a very serious disaster for the Allied cause." Earlier that day Eisenhower had reported to Marshall that because of inadequate shipping, the movement of combat and service troops required for Husky had to be postponed, precluding any June landings. Shipping, the lack of landing craft, the training schedule for amphibious operations, and Montgomery's slowed advance toward the Tunisian border, he informed Churchill on 17 February, combined to make a June Husky impossible.[52]

The shortage of landing craft was only one of the hurdles faced by planners dealing with the vital problem of over-the-beach supply. More vexing, the available landing craft—even the flat-bottomed landing ship/tank (LST), the workhorse heavy loading craft—could not land on the beaches because of the ubiquitous sandbars along Mediterranean shorelines. This situation created enormous headaches for the planners, further limiting operational options and reinforcing the need to seize ports. The sandbar problem created a big stir; various expedients, including using explosives to blast channels through the obstacles, produced no solution.

One of the officers working on this problem was LTC Charles Bonesteel. The son of a major general, Bonesteel served as acting chief engineer planner in Force 141. One day he received a letter from COL Frank Besson, a fellow engineer and West Point friend. Besson served as head of the Corps of Engineers development board. He told Bonesteel about an amphibious truck then in use in the Pacific. ASF had developed this hybrid, the DUKW, to deal with the problem of ship-to-shore supply on small Pacific islands ringed with coral reefs. The aptly named "duck" could transverse the reef, the unfordable lagoon behind, and the sandy beach, delivering 5,000 pounds of supplies, fifty men, or a 105mm howitzer on the beach and beyond.

Typical of the U.S. Army, theater commands did not exchange information, viewing themselves in competition for resources and attention. Nobody in AFHQ knew of the existence of this vehicle, which had been in mass production for a year. Bonesteel knew Smith from Fort Benning; his father had succeeded Bradley as head of the weapons section. Although only a lieutenant colonel, Bonesteel thought nothing of going directly to Smith. The DUKW appeared to be the solution to the problem of supply over the beaches. Recalling his role in the development of the jeep, Smith immediately went to Eisenhower and made the case for the duck. Won over, Eisenhower made a request on 3 March for the speedy dispatch of 400 DUKWs to the theater. The duck so impressed Patton during amphibious exercises near Oran that he called for more. Even though they occupied plenty of cargo space, AFHQ placed a priority on DUKW shipments. By July, more than 1,000 were available for Husky. "This was the secret weapon," remembered Bonesteel, "that completely dumbfounded the Germans when we landed in Sicily."[53]

In early March Eisenhower grumbled about the state of Husky planning, which he termed "most involved and difficult." He thought the solution lay in pulling all the headquarters together. Bizerte was his choice for the eventual site, but he thought Malta would serve in the interim. When Cunningham and Montgomery, the designated Eastern Task Force commander, balked, Eisenhower backed down.[54] Instead, he convened a series of rolling seminars in Algiers. The first major commanders' conference on 15 March accomplished nothing except for an agreement to postpone Husky until July.[55] On 20 March, Smith and Gairdner chaired another conference. "The HUSKY thing," Eisenhower told Somervell, "has gotten planners really in a turmoil."[56] Smith considered the chief stumbling block to be Montgomery's objections to the existing plan. Gairdner confided to his diary, "I can see that Monty is going to be a prima donna who will act as a most unpleasant hair-shirt to me."[57] He was not alone.

Montgomery thought he had deciphered the code of how to beat the Germans, and he could not understand why the other senior Allied officers refused to defer to him. "It very soon became apparent to me," he later commented, "that there was no one on that side who knew the things that are necessary if you are to win battles."[58] He wondered why the British persisted in fighting in "penny packets." Although commanding entire corps rather than brigades, as previously, Anderson's planning for the final offensive in Tunisia again reflected this British penchant for disjointed offensives without sufficient depth. The same "woolly thinking" informed Husky planning. "I am NOT happy about the present plan for HUSKY," Montgomery informed Brooke. "In my opinion it breaks every common sense rule of practical battle fighting, and the present plan would have no hope of success."[59]

Montgomery's objections centered on the lack of concentration; he considered his allotted forces too weak to fulfill their overly ambitious missions of seizing the ports of Augusta and Syracuse while capturing the airfields at Catania, Pachino, and Gela. He wanted one American division placed under his command for the Gela operation, granting him greater depth farther east. In his opinion, the subsidiary landings in the southwest should be canceled, and the move against Palermo delayed until the Allied forces secured the airfields and could provide adequate air cover.

Eisenhower and Smith agreed. Reporting the conclusions of the conference, Smith told the CCS that "without Catania and Gela airfields, the whole plan becomes abortive." Taking Palermo without the airfields was pointless. He saw "*no* recourse" but to accept Montgomery's recommendations. Eisenhower endorsed this view but never issued orders altering the plans accordingly. Cunningham commented, "Here we are with no fixed agreed plan . . . two months off D-Day and the commanders all at sixes and sevens."[60]

The commanders did agree on a couple of things. Smith reported that Alexander, Tedder, and Cunningham unanimously agreed on a July Husky and that without extra landing craft to ferry an additional British division in the eastern zone—in addition to the American division earmarked for Gela—any substantial increase in German ground strength rendered "chances for success . . . practically nil and the project should be abandoned."[61] Smith's communiqué amounted to a thinly disguised plea for more landing craft. It worked; the British eventually responded by freeing up enough shipping to increase Montgomery's assault force by one division. But the letter set off an explosion in London and Washington.

The BCOS "opposed resolutely" the suggestion that the addition of two German divisions in Sicily rendered Husky susceptible to defeat. The British admitted the difficulty of assaulting shorelines bristling with German troops in fixed positions—a dig against the American insistence on Roundup—but Sicily was in no way comparable to France. "We feel it necessary to record our view however that abandonment of HUSKY at any time, wholly because of the number of German troops in HUSKY land had reached a small predetermined fraction of United Nations' strength, could not be considered." The JCS signaled their "complete agreement with the views expressed [by the BCOS]."[62] Churchill thought back to summer 1942 and Eisenhower's robust advocacy of Sledgehammer; less than a year later, he appeared to be spooked by a couple of German divisions. "It is perfectly clear that the operations must either be entrusted to someone who believes in them, or abandoned." He considered the matter "as serious in the last degree" and termed AFHQ's position on Husky "pusillanimous and defeatist." He observed, "What Stalin would think of this when he has 185 divisions on his front, I cannot image." A chastened Eisenhower sent a pusillanimous reply.[63]

Gairdner traveled to London and presented the new plan to the BCOS. He blamed "Montgomery's egotistical outlook" for the lack of coordinated action.[64] Although Montgomery's personality no doubt contributed to the impasse, the real problem, as Montgomery understood it, centered on the lack of "grip," with the result that "HUSKY

planning is in a hopeless mess." Nobody with command authority presided over planning; Eisenhower, Alexander, Cunningham, Tedder,
and Montgomery remained too preoccupied with finishing the Tunisian
campaign to devote the necessary attention to Husky. "Our system seems
to be," Montgomery concluded, "that the staff makes a plan and then try
and force it on the Generals; meanwhile they go on with detailed planning and then tell you that it cannot be changed. I have refused to play
on these lines."[65]

Differing staff methods added to the problem. In the British "top-
down" system employed by Montgomery, the commander makes the
decision, outlines his estimates and intentions, and leaves his staff to
work out the details. A good commander gauges the relative strengths
and weaknesses of subordinates, assigns specific tasks, and allots logistical support. Finally, he analyzes the plan and insists on changes with
a view toward defining how single operations fit into the mosaic of
the entire campaign. American commands followed the Leavenworth
"staff-down" model: staffs create a number of options, leaving the commander to choose. "The British never got used to our staff system,"
Betts observed. "They never quite understood it because, of course, it's
not a very logical thing." Comparing the two systems, Clark remarked in
1970 that when the British made a policy decision, "their whole echelon
of command all the way down [knew] exactly what it [was]. . . . When
[the American staff made] a decision, nobody down the line [knew] anything."[66] As Montgomery quite correctly pointed out, senior staff officers in both camps lacked any real command experience and had never
fought the Germans. Planning took place in a vacuum; theoretical plans
often had unrealistic objectives, overestimating Allied capabilities and
underestimating the combat power of German forces.

On 23 April Montgomery, alarmed by the latest Husky revision, flew
to his headquarters in Cairo, where his staff planned the eastern landings. Horrified at what he discovered, he fired off a telegram to Alexander. Again he criticized the dispersion of effort, declaring that "all
planning to date will land the Allied Nations in a first-class military
disaster." He would participate in Husky, "but must do so in my own
way." He contended that "the first thing to do is to secure a lodgment in a
suitable area and then operate from that firm base," and that demanded
concentrated attacks. He also reminded Alexander that "time is pressing
and if we delay while above is argued in LONDON and WASHINGTON
the operation will never be launched in July."[67]

"My remarks on the plan," Montgomery told Brooke, "have caused
the most frightful tornado at Force 141, and it is clear to me that I am

regarded there as a most unpleasant person." The current plan called for even greater dispersal—no fewer than eleven landings: three in Eighth Army area, four clustered around Gela in the south, and four in the west. The planners "want me to operate in little [battalion groups] all over the place. I refuse." Typically frank, he said, "We cannot go on in this way. Unless we get a good and firm plan *at once,* on which we can all work—*there will be no HUSKY in July.* I hope that is realized [at] your end." He offered his alternative: "The proper answer is to bring two USA divisions in to land at CENT and DIME, on the south coast, and get the aerodromes. And chuck the Palermo landing for the present. If this were agreed to, then we could all go ahead."[68]

Smith called another commanders' conference on 29 April to discuss Montgomery's objections to the existing Husky plan. Since Eisenhower was visiting Anderson, Smith took the opportunity to invite Patton for dinner. "Old Blood and Guts" spoiled for a fight. He had come fresh from a meeting with McNair, recuperating from a wound sustained while observing the fighting in Tunisia. When asked what he made of Allied command, Patton remarked, "Allies must fight in separate theaters or they hate each other more than they do the enemy."

The next day Patton joined the commanders and their deputies and chiefs of staff, VADM Ramsay, MG F. A. M. Browning representing the airborne, and Gairdner and Nevins to hear LTG Oliver Leese, a corps commander in Eighth Army, outline Montgomery's opposition to the Husky plan. Montgomery had intended to attend the meeting himself, but a case of tonsillitis sidelined him; he sent his chief of staff, Brigadier Freddie de Guingand, but his plane crashed en route, so it fell to Leese to voice Montgomery's complaints. The conference predictably ended in stalemate. Patton thought "it was one hell of a performance. War by committee." Patton could not help noting that he and Nevins were the only Americans present.

The conference and the private discussion that followed gave Patton the opportunity to size up the British. He thought Alexander "cut a sorry figure at all times. He is a fence walker." Patton found the British senior officers even more catty about one another than the Americans were of their cousins. "It is bad form for officers to criticize each other," Tedder told him, "so I shall. The other day Alex, who is very selfish, said of General Anderson, 'As a soldier, he is a good plain military cook.' The remark applies absolutely—to Montgomery. He is a little fellow of average ability who has had such a build-up that he thinks of himself as Napoleon—he is not."[69]

Eisenhower returned to Algiers on 1 May. Smith warned him that the standoff among his commanders threatened to escalate, and if it continued, the entire question must be referred to the combined chiefs, with the attendant negative impact on the prestige of AFHQ. Eisenhower ordered Smith to get Montgomery in Algiers and arrive at a decision. Smith concluded, as he indicated to Patton over the phone the next morning, that Montgomery's view would prevail. He asked Patton to come to Algiers as quickly as he could to present his views. The meeting was scheduled for later that day.

Smith met Montgomery at Maison Blanche. Aware of the headaches he caused, Montgomery told him, "I expect I am a bit unpopular up here." "General," Smith retorted, "to serve under you would be a great privilege for anyone, to serve [a]long side you wouldn't be too bad. But say, General, to serve over you is hell."[70]

Weather delayed Alexander's flight, and Tedder and Cunningham shied away from meeting without him. An impatient Montgomery went to Smith's office. Told he had just left for the bathroom, Montgomery proceeded there. Despite the indecorous surroundings, Montgomery forcefully presented his views. Cornered at the urinal, Smith could only listen. Montgomery again argued that the existing plan contravened not only every principle of war but also common sense. Patton and Montgomery should stage massed landings side by side. Only this would ensure successful landings and seizure of the vital airfields. When Smith asked about logistical problems, Montgomery replied that the specialists must find a way to supply the forces over the beaches. Smith shared Montgomery's irritation with the planners, and as he had a month earlier, he accepted the necessity of concentrated landings. They agreed to go to Eisenhower's office.[71]

Eisenhower refused to intervene; he still wanted the concurrence of all three commanders and could not make a decision without Alexander. He did permit Montgomery to meet the planners with Cunningham and Tedder present. Montgomery prefaced his remarks by saying, "I know well that I am regarded by many people as being a troublesome person. I think this is probably true." Nobody disagreed. He then repeated what he had told Smith. As Smith later pointed out, Palermo possessed no real strategic value, "so the changes desired by Monty were readily conceded despite the inherent supply problems."[72] The final decision hinged on Alexander. Before flying back to his headquarters, Montgomery wired Alexander: "Eisenhower will accept this plan if you agree and recommended it. . . . EISENHOWER and BEDELL-SMITH completely in favour."[73] Given how the Alexander-Montgomery team worked, nobody doubted Alexander would sign off on Montgomery's plan.

Patton wanted to align himself with Tedder and Cunningham against Montgomery, but the conference was over by the time he arrived. He reported to Eisenhower and apologized for being tardy, saying he had done his best to get there. Eisenhower replied, "Oh, that's all right. I knew you would do what you were ordered without question and told them so." He told Patton to go over the new plan with Smith.

Patton had no say in the final agreement and expected the worst. He reckoned that Montgomery intended to drop the American landings in Gela, or at least delay them. Instead, he discovered that his forces would land in combination with the British. Even better, to combat the impression American forces had been subordinated to a secondary role, Eisenhower decided to elevate Patton to an army command. Although he had plenty of grounds for applauding the new formula, Patton still entertained serious doubts. He thought it curious nobody had considered what would transpire after the landings and surmised that Montgomery intended the American forces to act as a shield and flank protection for a British drive on Messina. Patton insisted on a clear demarcation of army boundaries; Smith said he would back Patton's demands.

Smith and Patton later discussed "the famous meeting." "So far as I can gather," Patton noted in his diary, "Monty simply refused to play ball; so Alex yielded." Smith stated, "the reason everyone yields to Montgomery is because Monty is the national hero and writes direct to the Prime Minister; and that if Ike crossed him, Ike might get canned. Also that Monty is senior in service to Alexander [not correct] and taught Alex at the staff college [correct], and that Alex is afraid of him."[74]

Montgomery deliberately ignored the issue of command. In the letter to Alexander he argued that the "proper answer would be to put US Corps under me and let my Army H.Q. handle the whole operation of the land battle." He hammered away on the same theme three days later. Under the new plan, he told Alexander, "Only one commander can run the battle." He would command the amphibious and ground operations and "deal direct with Bedell-Smith."[75]

Montgomery's petitioning for command in Husky appeared to be motivated by his monumental ego. Although that entered into the equation, he had other, more legitimate concerns. Alexander had proved his inability and Eisenhower his unwillingness to "grip" Husky. Both remained too fixated on ending the fighting in Tunisia. "Alexander is deeply committed in the tactical battle opposite TUNIS," Montgomery noted in his diary on 6 May, "and I cannot get him to face up to the HUSKY problem." He concluded, "The proper answer is to let Alexander finish off the TUNISIAN war, and to cut him right out of HUSKY."

Montgomery thought that he "should run HUSKY" and "deal directly with Allied Force H.Q." In his opinion, "If this in NOT done, we will be in a grave mess." He decided, "I am going to ALGIERS tomorrow . . . to have the whole matter out with [Smith]." Montgomery considered Smith "a firm ally of mine." His overall conclusion: "There is no doubt that Allies are very difficult people to fight with, especially when political considerations are allowed to over-ride all sound military common sense."[76]

Smith proved less of an ally than Montgomery imagined. He explained that although he agreed with Montgomery, in a strict military sense, on the need for a unified command, Smith vetoed any command shift. Citing civilian morale, Smith pointedly stated, "the American contingent had to be a separate expedition." Left unstated was Smith's surety that any subordination of Patton to the British would spark another bitter round of infighting. Montgomery would just have to accept the complicated and clumsy command arrangements.

With Montgomery in Algiers, Smith wanted the issue of army boundaries settled. He chaired a meeting between Montgomery and Patton, but this time Smith stacked the cards; Patton brought along his deputy, MG Geoffrey Keyes, and two of his staff officers. Unimpressed, Montgomery refused any discussion of boundaries or phase lines. True to his word, Smith pushed the issue, but not hard enough in Patton's estimate. "Smith talked a lot and made nasty remarks," Patton recorded, "but really said nothing. . . . Monty is a forceful, selfish man, but still a man. I think he is a far better leader than Alexander and that he will do just what he pleases."[77] Even though Montgomery got his way again, he came away from the meeting with the conclusion, "Fighting the Germans is quite easy; the tiring thing is the way one has to fight to keep our own show from going off the rails."[78]

"I have probably offended a great many people—outside my own Army," Montgomery supposed. "But I saved Husky from being a disaster for the Allies."[79] Montgomery certainly rubbed people the wrong way, but his intervention ended four months of near paralysis over Husky. He provided the first genuine operational concept for Husky, and he alone brought some sense of realism to the proceedings. The hand missing in all this belonged to the supreme commander. Eisenhower remained passive throughout. There remained only two months for planners to rework their schemes and logisticians to rework their calculations for mounting, staging, and supplying the operations.

Husky would not be a repeat of Torch. As a journalist from the *Chicago Daily News*, Bill Stoneman, put it, "We came into North Africa on a shoestring when we waded ashore at Algiers" and swept into "Tunis on the tail of an avalanche."[80] In the three months following the formation of NATO, the theater received 1.9 million tons of supplies. The arrival on 6–7 March of a twenty-three-ship convoy carrying 6,800 vehicles totally altered the supply situation. ASF also performed brilliantly, supplying North Africa with railroad equipment.[81] The influx of trucks, railroad engines and cars, coal, and railway units coincided with the arrival of SOS manpower. By April, forty-three trains were passing through Constantine each day carrying 10,700 tons. In one seventy-two-hour period, Air Corps engineers built five new airfields; eventually, more than a hundred were constructed. As one American general boasted, "The American Army does not solve its problems, it overwhelms them."[82]

Hughes struggled against the tide of materiel and manpower flowing into the theater to tighten organization. Credit went to Larkin, the best operational logistician produced by the U.S. Army in the war, who made the badly flawed supply system work. In the face of unresolved jurisdictional disputes, Hughes and Larkin's headquarters labored to finalize supply schemes for Husky and stockpile transportation and materiel in support of operations after the landings. All this stood in stark contrast to what had preceded and followed the Torch landings.

On the other side of the hill, von Arnim protested that Tunisia was quickly becoming "a fortress without ammunition and rations." In January and February combined, the Axis forces in Tunisia received 70,000 tons of supplies by sea. Rommel estimated his monthly needs as double that figure.[83] Interdicted by air and sea, the constricted Axis supply lines could never match the flood of American supplies into North Africa. In March the total tonnage of supplies that reached the Axis forces in Tunisia contracted to 29,267. Put differently, by April, Constantine handled as much supply by rail alone (not including that brought in by truck and air) in two and a half days as the Axis had received the entire previous month.[84]

The tourniquet of Allied ground, sea, and air power tightened around the isolated Axis bridgehead. Initially, all the uncoordinated Allied attacks stalled. At Montgomery's behest, an Eighth Army corps reinforced an all-out push (code-named Vulcan) by Anderson's forces in the west. After fierce resistance, German defenses crumbled. Tunis and Bizerte fell on the same day. By 13 May, three Axis armies had ceased to exist. The haul of prisoners exceeded 250,000, 40 percent more than anticipated. Smith was not around to enjoy the kill; Eisenhower had dispatched him to Washington as his representative at the Trident conference.

★ **20** ★

The Many Travails of
an Allied Chief of Staff

Before Smith left on 10 May, he and Eisenhower closeted themselves and reviewed the whole range of issues confronting AFHQ. Eisenhower cautioned Smith against adopting a defensive posture in presenting AFHQ's suit. Ostensibly, Smith went to the conference to report on the state of the French rearmament program and planning for a military government in Sicily. He would also provide details on Husky planning and present AFHQ's thinking on operations after Sicily. As matters stood, the CCS withheld approval of the new Husky plan.

Both men worried that the political heads and the combined chiefs might reject the plan, insisting on expedited landings in Sicily and expansion of the scope of operations to include Sardinia and possibly Corsica. There were plenty of grounds for concern. In the middle of the wrangle between Montgomery and the commanders over Husky, Marshall wired Eisenhower asking for consideration of an extemporized assault on Sicily before the Germans could reinforce the Italians. Marshall again accused Eisenhower of lacking adaptability and listening too much to his conservative planners. He reminded Eisenhower that unorthodox and bold commanders in the past—Nelson, Grant, and Lee—had "won great victories" by ignoring conventional wisdom. The day before Montgomery and Smith brokered the final agreement on Husky, Eisenhower replied, assuring Marshall that AFHQ constantly looked for "ways and means of following up on an exploitation basis" but admitting, "the prospects do *not* look too bright." This was followed the next day by a long rationalization of why he had accepted the Montgomery variant, taking pains to tell Marshall, "these conclusions have *not* been developed by planners."[1] Eisenhower insisted that Smith fight off

413

all attempts to alter Husky, now that an agreement had finally emerged. They also discussed future operations. Even though a follow-up invasion of Italy after a successful Husky ran counter to Marshall's thinking, Eisenhower wanted Smith, in his private conversations, to make the case as forcefully as possible for expanded operations aimed at knocking Italy out of the war.[2]

Additionally, Smith needed to explain to Marshall the reasons for Patton's elevation to army command and convince Marshall to keep Bradley in the theater. Eisenhower wanted Bradley as Patton's deputy in Husky. He also asked that Smith check on promotions, including Butcher's. A great weight rested on Smith's shoulders as he boarded a Liberator at Marrakesh for the flight to Washington.

Trident

Washington offered a pleasant break from Algiers. The cherry blossoms were long gone, but the weather was mild and the skies crystal blue. Smith's flight set a record for the southern crossing; he left Morocco on Sunday morning and landed in Washington at 7 P.M. on Tuesday, in time for the convening of the Third Washington Conference the next day.

Trident began where the Casablanca talks had ended. This conference differed from previous ones because it transpired in an atmosphere animated by Allied success. Except for Burma, the other elements of the coalition's grand strategy staked out in Casablanca had all scored gains: the contest against the U-boats in the North Atlantic; the strategic air offensive in Europe; the expanded, but still limited, offensives against the Japanese perimeter in the southwest Pacific; and, most notably, the victory in Tunisia. The conference's first session coincided with the surrender of Axis forces in Tunisia. Success produced its own problems. For the Americans, the collapse of Axis resistance in Tunisia fueled expectations for an invasion of Italy that would intensify the "suction pump" effect, drawing Allied strength deeper into the Mediterranean and away from northwest Europe; an expanded commitment in Italy would delay rather than hasten the end of the war. It would also increase the dispersion of American strength at the cost of Bolero and the Pacific. For the British, successes in North Africa and the southwest Pacific increased the possibility of being pulled into a revision of coalition strategy that they considered premature and overly ambitious.

From the first meeting of the CCS on 13 May, the two sides drifted further apart. The British came well prepared to push hard for continued operations in the Mediterranean for the duration of 1943. Only by exploiting the advantages offered in the Mediterranean could the essential preconditions for a successful 1944 Roundup be ensured. The victory in North Africa opened Italy to invasion. Given the Allied sea and air power marshaled in the theater, and with some forty divisions available by the end of May, coalition forces could transform the Mediterranean into a first-class strategic liability for the Germans. A decision against Italy and in favor of an accelerated cross-Channel invasion would impose an unacceptable lull in Allied operations against the Axis, just as German forces prepared for a massive offensive against the Russians.[3]

Smith circulated the latest AFHQ staff study on post-Husky operations. Authored by BG Lowell Rooks of G-3, the appreciation outlined two options: an invasion of the boot of Italy, or the seizure of Sardinia and Corsica. AFHQ presented three operations for the movement onto the Italian mainland: one across the Straits of Messina (code-named Buttress), one aimed at the instep of the boot (Goblet), and one aimed at the heel (Musket). A combined Buttress and Goblet or a separate Musket would require four or five divisions in the initial phase, expanding to ten; Naples and the airfields at Foggia would be the immediate objectives. The study pointed to the "considerable forces" required and cautioned, "once we have embarked upon this course we are committed . . . in a major campaign the duration and requirements of which is not possible to foresee." Rooks's report concluded it would be better to accept the alternative, Brimstone (Sardinia) and Firebrand (Corsica), in view of the lesser forces committed and fewer risks taken. In Smith's brief preamble, he stated that Eisenhower and Cunningham endorsed the view that the "course of action which does not definitely commit us to the mainland is preferable." Tedder strongly opposed Rooks's finding. In his view, Sardinia presented as big an operational problem as Sicily, and since Italy would already be within bombing range from Tunisia and Sicily, Sardinia proffered no great strategic prize. Bases in central Italy, in contrast, provided the opportunity to strike Germany and Balkan targets, circumventing the massive German expenditures on air defense against attacks from the United Kingdom. Churchill and Roosevelt weighed the benefits and liabilities of either approach in their discussions on 14 May at Shangri La, the president's camp in Maryland.[4]

On 14 May Smith informed Eisenhower that the conference appeared to be deadlocked and he might not be free to return to AFHQ for a week or ten days. During the day, Smith and Marshall had engaged in a wide-ranging survey of the issues facing the theater, including the unresolved problem of a military government in Husky. After these talks, even in the face of strategic deadlock, Smith told Eisenhower, "the ultimate decision will be to continue operations in our area along [the] general lines" discussed before he had left Algiers. He also warned Eisenhower to expect to become the subject of a "large personal buildup to which you will have to submit." Irked by Montgomery's popularity in the United States, Marshall insisted on publicizing Eisenhower's role in the "the magnificent" victory in Tunisia.[5]

Marshall and Smith drove the sixty miles to spend part of the weekend with Roosevelt, Churchill, Hopkins, Lord Beaverbrook, and assorted guests and Roosevelt family members. Beetle might have preferred to spend the time with Nory, but duty called. Alone with Marshall in the car, Smith took the opportunity to press the theater's case. Although not intended as a working holiday, no doubt the fighting in Tunisia and the plans for Sicily and post-Husky featured in the conversations, all of which made Smith a pretty hot commodity. When he returned to Washington, Smith filled in Eisenhower. While Smith was en route to Washington, AFHQ received a wire from the combined chiefs again raising Marshall's idea—backed by the prime minister—for a sudden demarche on Sicily. They would withhold approval of Husky until Eisenhower responded. Eisenhower replied that all three of his commanders vetoed the option. Perhaps to appease all parties, he informed the CCS he intended to exploit the Axis collapse in Tunisia by seizing the island of Pantelleria, styled the "Italian Malta," midway between the north coast of Tunisia and Sicily. Smith reported that he had strongly backed Eisenhower's position in his discussions with the president, Churchill, and Marshall, and he had succeeded in dissuading Marshall from transferring Bradley out of the theater. Smith also reported that Marshall insisted on having the Army Band tour the theater. The Army Band was one of Marshall's big hobbyhorses. Upset that the Army Band placed a weak fourth behind the bands of the U.S. Navy, Marine Corps, and now the Air Force, he grew obsessed with getting the Army Band some publicity. Although he never said as much, and given the momentous questions confronting everyone at the conference, Marshall's peculiar fixation on the Army Band struck Smith as a little off the wall.[6]

Smith finally made his appearance at a CCS meeting on the morning of 18 May. Discussions centered on French rearmament. Brooke made the point that, though important, arming French units as garrison troops for North Africa, Sicily, and Corsica assumed a low priority in the face of the shipping problem. Marshall underlined that Roosevelt's promises in Casablanca to lavishly reequip the French had been wildly misinterpreted. Smith agreed with Brooke's assessment; shipping limitations retarded the French rearmament program. Giraud fully expected the Americans to live up to their Casablanca promises and demanded 100,000 tons of supply per month, but AFHQ struggled to reach the established monthly quotas of 25,000 tons of military and 35,000 tons of civilian supplies, which Smith categorized as "the maximum which, at present, could be achieved." Smith admitted the French "had fought excellently" in Tunisia with obsolescent weapons supplemented by inadequate allotments of British and American arms and equipment. Giraud had channeled new equipment coming into North Africa not to units in the line but to the construction of new divisions, in the full expectation that French forces would play a prominent role in the liberation of France. The French, he continued, resented being assigned static roles. At present, the French had three combat-ready divisions—one of them mountain troops—earmarked for Operation Firebrand. Smith projected that the French would possess enough troops in three or four months to assume the defense of Morocco, but he cautioned it would be "unwise to count on an adequate return in combat value [from French troops] in the near future," even if supply rates increased marginally. That being the case, he recommended no increase in tonnage to reequip French units. Marshall added that, "in the event of the U.S. divisions being moved to the U.K., their equipment would be turned over to the French." The combined chiefs sanctioned AFHQ's actions and Smith's assessment. They directed that French forces be rearmed and reequipped as rapidly as available shipping allowed, "but as a secondary commitment to the requirements of British and U.S. forces in the various theaters."[7]

The strategic gridlock continued through 18 May. That evening Brooke, despairing over the direction the conference had taken, sought Smith's views. Nothing Smith told him reduced his anxiety. Smith thought the British should take very seriously the threat to reorient American strategy toward the Pacific. If the Americans withheld shipping and landing craft, the Mediterranean strategy would implode. Smith implied the Americans might use shipping and materiel as a lever to reorient coalition grand strategy. These discussions gave Smith scarce comfort; a shift in priorities away from the Mediterranean would shuffle AFHQ from the equivalent of Broadway to Buffalo.[8]

The probability of the British winning the debate alarmed Marshall less than the possibility of an open rupture. Faced with that prospect during the morning session on 19 May, Marshall asked for a closed meeting with only the service chiefs, Leahy, Ismay, and Dill present. Smith and the other two dozen in attendance trundled out the door. The expedient worked; a compromise emerged. The British got their way on Italy. In exchange, the Americans received a formal British commitment for a "second front" in May 1944. Bolero would be accelerated; the bombing offensive extended. Unprepared to specify exactly how to exploit a successful Husky, the combined chiefs passed the decision down to Eisenhower, instructing him to choose "such operations as are best calculated to eliminate Italy from the war and contain maximum German forces." But the CCS added caveats to the directive: no operations could be undertaken without CCS authorization, and they must be wound down by 1 November; on that date, four American and three British divisions would begin their movement to the United Kingdom. Another conference would convene in July or August to assess the prevailing situation in the Mediterranean and determine the strategic and operational roadmap for the second half of 1943.[9]

The other principal questions Smith had hoped to have answered in Washington—an agreed policy on dealing with the French, and definite guidelines on military government and civil affairs in Sicily—went unresolved. Roosevelt's views on de Gaulle had hardened since Casablanca. In the lead-up to Trident, Roosevelt told Churchill, "the conduct of the Bride continued to be more and more aggravated." Characterizing de Gaulle's actions and attitudes as "well nigh intolerable," he suggested, "you and I should thrash out this disagreeable problem and establish a common policy."[10] Throughout Trident, Churchill was under enormous pressure from Roosevelt to dump de Gaulle, who, Roosevelt concluded, suffered from a "messianic complex." In his memoir, Churchill remembered that not a day passed without Roosevelt raising the issue of de Gaulle. Churchill wanted no breach with de Gaulle but dreaded one with Roosevelt even more. Now with a tentative date set for the cross-Channel invasion, which would make France the main theater of operations, some sort of arrangement between the French factions assumed greater urgency. Roosevelt's bulldozing nearly worked. On 21 May the prime minister telegraphed the War Cabinet, asking it to weigh the possibility of withdrawing support from de Gaulle.[11]

Eden convinced the War Cabinet not to take any precipitate action and advised waiting on developments in Algiers. More than a month before, de Gaulle and Giraud had reached an agreement in principle on a power-sharing arrangement.[12] Deeply suspicious of each other's motives, the French leadership in London and Algiers had agreed on the particulars of a settlement but could not concur on the timing and location for a meeting. Finally, on 10 May, Giraud requested that de Gaulle come to Algiers, stating, "the hour of action and of our common responsibilities" had arrived. On 27 May de Gaulle agreed. Eden entertained high expectations for the successful formation of a unified French committee, with Giraud and de Gaulle as co-executives. The Americans took a dim view. Hull concluded, the "British are now primarily interested in an early agreement between Giraud and de Gaulle in order that they may get rid of the entire [Free French] organization and ship it to Algiers where the problem of dealing with them will be placed on our doorstep."[13] Unable to square the circle, the political heads and their foreign affairs chiefs threw the matter back to AFHQ.

The issue of a military government in Sicily remained hung up on the unresolved French question. Some members of Giraud's administration raised the "highly sensitive" issue of Allied plans for military administration in liberated France. Would France be liberated or subjected to military rule—in effect, occupied?[14] Roosevelt's views had not changed since 1 January; he saw all military and civil authority in North Africa as vested in AFHQ, and as he told Churchill, "when we get into France itself we will have to regard it as a military occupation."[15] The British views on liberated France remained moot, but the War Cabinet wanted to work through some legitimate French agency and held up the potential union of de Gaulle and Giraud as the best hope. Deciding on a common policy for Sicily should have been easier, but here too, Washington and London could not agree. Roosevelt wanted benevolent occupation, but with all known fascists arrested. He pushed for the United States to assume leadership but, pressed by Hull and Stimson, accepted a coequal partnership. No sooner had Roosevelt climbed down when Churchill wired the president, making the case for British predominance. The usual round of telegram exchanges followed, but no agreement surfaced.

Since the political chiefs failed to reconcile their divergent views on policy toward the French, the question of a military government in Husky did not exactly command the attention of the combined chiefs. Back in February, AFHQ had requested "at an early date" a clarification of American policy for civil-military administration and guidelines for the relief and rehabilitation of Sicily, the first noncolonial Axis territory slated to come under Allied occupation. As Eisenhower pointed out, Husky "will set the pattern for later operations in Europe."[16] Three months later, AFHQ still awaited an answer, and none emerged at Trident. Smith's directive read: "Without discussion, the COMBINED CHIEFS OF STAFF, agreed that consideration of this matter should be deferred until after TRIDENT conference."[17]

All this while, Smith was not sitting on his hands. He instructed Holmes, as head of the liaison section, to prepare a plan, working in harness with the Security Council. Toward the end of March, Holmes offered a plan for a single joint administration with no "senior partner," but under the direct supervision of AFHQ. The organization—later called the Allied Military Government of Occupied Territory (AMGOT)—would have American and British cochairmen. Not pleased with the arrangement, and still lacking guidance from Washington and London, Smith formed a new civil affairs section in AFHQ and on 6 April put MG Lord Rennell of Rodd in charge of planning for a military government in Sicily. Based on British experience in Italian East Africa and Libya, Rennell argued for indirect rule under the central direction of the senior commander, with the Italian administrative structures retained and headed by nonfascist Italians. Eisenhower and Smith accepted Rennell's proposal and directed him to proceed, based on that starting point. On 1 May Alexander, the designated army group commander in Husky, became the designated governor of Sicily, with Rennell as his chief civil affairs officer and head of AMGOT. Rennell established his headquarters in the mountain town of Blida, thirty-five miles from Algiers. Now Smith had another planning staff to juggle.[18]

On the plus side, Smith held talks with officials from the Foreign Office and headed off the addition of another deputy chief of staff billet for political and civil affairs inside AFHQ. Since the Americans saw staff organization "principally [as] a matter for Eisenhower," the British accepted the clumsy status quo, with Murphy and Macmillan operating in tandem with AFHQ through Smith and the liaison section.[19] In conversations with Marshall, Smith convinced him that commanders in the field must exercise final responsibility and authority over civilian populations during and immediately following the combat phase and that AMGOT should remain under operational headquarters until the situation on the ground stabilized; then AMGOT would revert to AFHQ control. With Marshall's approval, Smith would finalize the organizational structures for a military government; all he lacked was a policy.[20]

While in Washington, Smith beat out another conflagration that grew out of this discordance in Allied political policy on Italy. Roosevelt had proclaimed an unconditional surrender policy at Casablanca. As AFHQ struggled with Husky planning, and with no fixed policy on military government, some senior members of the staff began to view that policy as an obstruction to prosecuting a campaign against Italy aimed at knocking the Axis junior partner out of the war. A G-2 study interpreted the policy as one of "intimidation of the Italians by threat," which could only induce greater Italian resistance. On 17 July McClure's psychological warfare section wrote, and Rooks endorsed, a cable to the CCS strongly recommending "that the statement of policy be amended."

The communication offered instead a three-tiered process: first, the Italian people had to choose between continuing the war and ending the war; second, "a cessation of hostilities on their part will be accepted by the Allies as evidence of good judgment, entitling them eventually to a 'Peace with Honor'"; and third, the Allies would pledge Italy's return to "full nationhood" once the Axis collapsed. If this plan were approved, AFHQ would commence a propaganda campaign presenting Mussolini and the Fascist Party as the only real obstacle to peace.[21]

No doubt if Smith had been on the job, the cable would not have left Algiers. In his absence, Whiteley took the request to Eisenhower, who duly signed it. When the communication reached Washington, it set off an explosion. Eisenhower distanced himself, claiming the cable should never have gone out. This gave the impression that Eisenhower had never read the memorandum closely, which may have been the case. Accustomed to Smith's filtering process, he routinely signed communications involving matters he deemed less vital—and psychological warfare fell into that category—without giving them much consideration. Just as likely, Eisenhower had signed it because he wanted a modification of the policy. As Smith told a postwar interviewer, both he and Eisenhower thought the doctrine "very unfortunate," terming it "a constant hindrance . . . which cost thousands of lives in Italy and Germany."[22]

Whatever the case, Roosevelt and Churchill reacted sharply to Eisenhower's request, and Smith's efforts to mollify the political bosses proved unavailing. On 20 May Smith met with Churchill, who "took strong exception to the 'peace with honor' propaganda to Italy" and voiced his opinion that the Office of War Information constituted the "greatest sore spot in the African Theater."[23] Roosevelt declared: "Most certainly we cannot tell the Italians that if they cease hostility they will have a peace with honor. We cannot get away from unconditional surrender." The CCS forwarded the president's statement, with Churchill's concurrence, to Algiers. Far from relaxing the application of unconditional surrender, Trident concluded with a reaffirmation of the policy as the cornerstone of the Allied war effort.[24]

The Washington trip provided Smith little respite. When not directly involved in the conference, he engaged in talks on the sidelines with many of the chiefs. He met with Portal to arrange more airlift for Husky.[25] He conferred with Brooke. He reopened the backdoor channel with Ismay. He held conversations with MG John Hilldring, the head of civil affairs in the War Department and cochair of the combined civil affairs committee in the CCS. Smith also found time for discussions with Surles about the vexing problems of press relations and censorship.

Whenever he could, he held off-the-record talks with Handy. Although only obliquely mentioned in Husky minutes, developments on the Russian Front loomed large in the minds of people in the know. Ultra indicated, as Smith related to Butcher upon his return, that the "Germans were teed up for an attack on a monstrous scale" in an effort to eliminate the Kursk salient. The giant contest might well prove decisive. Pointing to the Russian defenses, Smith predicted the Germans would lose a million men, and "there was confidence [among the Allied leadership in Washington] the Russians would win the battle." The sheer size of the forces massing on the Central Front in Russia dwarfed Husky. "The big war is still being fought in Russia."[26]

Much of Smith's efforts centered on ferreting out scuttlebutt on what the future held for Eisenhower. The War Department, now housed in the mammoth Pentagon building, was abuzz with rumors. One set focused on the man most responsible for building the Pentagon: Somervell. Described as a stick of dynamite in a Tiffany box, Somervell elicited both admiration and suspicion in equal measure: admiration for his driving intellect and capacity for work, and suspicion growing from his unbounded ambition. Once again Somervell petitioned for a restructuring of the War Department. He advocated the creation of a deputy chief of staff for administration and supply—in effect, an American chief administrative officer who would establish policy and exercise centralized command over manpower, supply, and the services. The reorganization would dismantle the existing general staff structure, abolishing the G-1 and G-4 Divisions and neutering the bureaus once and for all. Although he made a strong case, Somervell ran into a wall of opposition led by McNarney and the resident G-4, BG Raymond Moses. Things came to a head on 21 May when ASF formally circulated a proposal for the reorganization that cited AFHQ as a model.[27] Other than Styer and Lutes inside ASF, everybody else Smith talked to saw Somervell's efforts to rationalize the War Department structure as a thinly disguised cover for his real intent—to engineer his promotion and lay the foundation for his elevation to the chief of staff's chair when Marshall went to England to command the invasion. This speculation gained more traction with the decision to undertake the cross-Channel operation in May 1944. Who would command? Would he be British (Churchill had promised the job to Brooke) or American? If Marshall got the nod, the question arose who would become chief of staff? Would it be Somervell or Eisenhower? Smith thought it was unlikely Marshall would leave Washington. Morgan had headed the cross-Channel planning staff since Casablanca, indicating the eventual commander would be Brooke. Marshall was too big a fish to occupy a subordinate command. As Smith told Butcher, "Ike would be back in England soon after 1 November either as Allied commander-in-chief or as commander of American attack."[28] Smith actively politicked for Eisenhower, defending his record in North Africa. Tunisgrad certainly helped.

Typically, Smith remained mum on his own prospects. He was gratified by all the expressions of appreciation he received for his work in solidifying AFHQ. Eisenhower got credit for welding the Allied team, but those who mattered understood Smith's role. The headquarters' standing was so high, Smith thought, "inevitably it will be kept intact" and in all likelihood would serve as nucleus for one of the headquarters involved in the invasion of France. Smith purposely avoided any speculation about what would happen if Marshall received the command. The Ike-Beetle team now generally served as a model; the assumption was that it too would stay together, whatever command Eisenhower received. But what would happen if Eisenhower replaced Marshall? Surely Smith would not follow him to Washington. And if Marshall became supreme commander—as he fully expected would be the case—who would he name as his chief of staff? Would he accept Morgan? In all probability, the answer was no. Odds remained very good it would be Beetle Smith.[29]

All this meant Smith had little downtime to spend with Nory. On 21 May he stole away to Union Station to meet Mamie and Hughes's wife, returning from San Antonio. Smith always had a way with the ladies. "What a very attractive person his is," Kate Hughes reported to Everett. "No wonder you like him so much."[30] Knowing he had stayed too long, and with the flap over the "peace with honor" episode underscoring the need for his presence in Algiers, Smith boarded a plane on 24 May for the return flight. He brought along CPT John Boeltiger, the president's son-in-law, who would join AMGOT.

Smith had every reason to be pleased with the results of the Washington talks. Eisenhower had wanted him to defend his and AFHQ's record, and Smith had more than accomplished that. With the CCS still far from reaching any consensus on post-Husky operations, a French policy, or military government in occupied territories, all these questions devolved on AFHQ. This signaled a vote of confidence in Eisenhower and Smith; it also greatly increased the burdens placed on their shoulders. Smith's decision to leave the conference early proved prescient. On 25 May Churchill informed Roosevelt of his intention to go to Algiers for talks with Eisenhower and the commanders. Since Trident left the question of what to do after Husky to Eisenhower, Churchill made no bones about his purpose for going—to push Eisenhower into accepting the Italian option. He requested that Marshall accompany him. If a decision emerged in Algiers, Marshall's presence would deflect criticism that Churchill "had exerted an undue influence." Roosevelt dispatched a reluctant Marshall as guardian of American interests.[31]

On 27 May Butcher and Holmes met Smith in Casablanca with instructions for him to proceed directly to Algiers. Over the next week, Algiers would be the site for two simultaneous conferences: one concerning post-Husky operations, and the other involving all the principal French actors, including de Gaulle. Smith arrived in Algiers in time for the first in a series of commanders' meetings. He made a complete presentation on developments at Trident, but the real business focused on preparing for the arrival of Churchill, Brooke, and Marshall. Later that afternoon Smith and Eisenhower mulled over the insider dope Smith had gathered while in Washington, especially Beetle's surmising on their futures.

Meanwhile, Marshall flew down with Churchill, Brooke, and Ismay. Marshall dreaded the trip; it would be like the Florida trip during Arcadia, only much worse. This time there was no escape and no Smith. The interaction between Marshall and Churchill provides insight into how the latter's mind worked. A close acquaintance of Churchill's described how he came to decisions. "In nearly every case," observed C. F. Masterman, "an *idea* enters his head from outside. It then rolls around the hollow of his brain, collecting strength like a snowball. Then after whirling winds of rhetoric, he becomes convinced that he is *right;* and denounces everyone who criticises it."[32] The idea rolling around in his head this time involved the invasion of Italy, followed by subsidiary operations farther east. In principle, Marshall could accept exploiting Husky with operations in Italy, but he remained diametrically opposed to any hint of operations in the eastern Mediterranean. And he refused to discuss anything in concrete terms until he had talked to Eisenhower. After finishing work on the backlog of state papers, Churchill took a seat beside Marshall. "I knew I was in for it," Marshall recalled. To buy time, Marshall engaged in his own peripheral strategy. He knew any conversation with Churchill inevitably turned into a monologue. Marshall needed to deflect Churchill's attention. He had been reading a book about the impeachment of Warren Hastings as a primer on Indian history. Knowing the historian in Churchill could not resist, Marshall solicited his views. Churchill launched into a long dissertation, quoted Macaulay and Edmund Burke verbatim, then vectored into a discussion of bills of rejoinder and sovereign rights. After the torrent subsided, a vastly impressed but now desperate Marshall needed to come up with another topic. He selected Rudolf Hess, his capture in Scotland, and his connections to members of the British establishment. Away Churchill went. When the prime minister ran down, Marshall dovetailed slightly, asking about the repercussions of the succession crisis growing out of the king's marriage to Mrs. Simpson. Again Churchill took the bait. Marshall had inadvertently hit on Churchill's three obsessions: the empire, the British nobility, and the monarchy. No need for any rolling around in the head, the snowball of the prime minister's oratory flowed spontaneously. By this time, dinner appeared, and then the plane landed in Gibraltar. Marshall's stratagem worked brilliantly.[33]

Churchill would not remain sidetracked for long. The prime minister waylaid Eisenhower, who arrived with Cunningham at Maison Blanche to escort Churchill and Marshall to the admiral's villa for dinner. The idea was for Marshall to ride with Eisenhower and the prime minister with Cunningham. Churchill ambushed Eisenhower, however, insisting that Ike ride with him. Churchill immediately pressed his suit for an Italian campaign, dangling before Eisenhower a vision of the strategic bounty that lay before them. After dinner, as Butcher recorded, "The PM recited his story three different times in three different ways." He observed, "He talks persistently until he has worn down the last shred of opposition. Ike is glad to have General Marshall on hand."[34] As it turned out, Marshall offered little succor.

The next day the first of three conferences took place at Eisenhower's villa. Eden, the three commanders, Montgomery, the two chief Husky planners Rooks and BG Cecil Sugden, and Handy also attended. Prepped by Smith, Eisenhower presented his case strongly, favoring expanded Mediterranean operations as the only viable support the Western Allies could offer the Russians in 1943. For Marshall's benefit, he took pains to restate the need to rejuvenate Bolero for a May 1944 cross-Channel invasion. In the discussions that followed, Eisenhower reversed himself on Sardinia, stating that should Sicily prove easier than expected, "we ought to go directly into Italy." He even went so far as to suggest that an invasion of northern France might prove "unnecessary."[35] Whether beguiled by Churchill's "strategic riches" or falling prey to his own ambitions, Eisenhower endorsed the campaign in Italy and left a mostly silent Marshall struggling to preserve his icy calm.

The same day, 29 May, de Gaulle flew into Algiers. That morning Giraud presented Eisenhower with his Grand Commander of the Legion of Honor medal and ribbon, won on the field of battle. Eisenhower announced he would not wear it until they met in Metz, Giraud's hometown. De Gaulle took a dim view of this act of Allied solidarity, indignant that Giraud had made the award without consulting him. Clearly, the road ahead would be rocky. The last time Churchill had been in Algiers after Casablanca, he had asked Smith to arrange a meeting between Giraud and de Gaulle, but that attempt at consummating a "shotgun wedding" had miscarried. This time, Churchill insisted that something positive come from the effort. Involved in the military discussions, Smith was at least exempt from the political negotiations, leaving Murphy and Macmillan in charge, reinforced by Eden. By 3 June, Eden reported the talks had made "great strides."[36]

The second military conference took place on 31 May on the veranda of Villa dar el Ouard. This time, Smith held the floor. He discussed force projections for Buttress and Goblet based on earlier forecasts for Sardinia. Marshall reminded everyone of the Trident decision to withdraw divisions and air assets from the theater on 1 November and requested Smith's opinion on the number of service, signals, and anti-aircraft troops required. He estimated AFHQ would require an additional 63,000 troops from outside the theater. Smith talked about the threat of German airpower and, as it turned out, greatly overestimated antiaircraft artillery requirements. Wanting to put the brakes on post-Husky operations, Marshall raised logistical questions—shipping and landing craft, primarily. Churchill promised to make available the necessary troops from the United Kingdom and to cut further into civilian rations to provide the extra shipping. As he had in Washington in his discussions with Smith, Churchill simply ignored the landing craft issue.[37]

The final session convened on 3 June. The minutes for the last meeting suggest that an agreement emerged reflecting the British position: the Allies should invade the Italian mainland as soon as possible after the conclusion of Husky, with the objective of knocking Italy out of the war. With Italy defeated, its troops would withdraw from the Balkans and the Greek islands, forcing the Germans to draw forces from the Russian Front and accept the strategic liabilities of occupying the Balkans, fighting partisan forces there, and deploying troops into Italy if Hitler decided to mount a campaign to hold all or part of the Italian peninsula. For morale and political reasons, American, British, and French forces could not remain idle during the months between the end of the Sicilian campaign and May 1944. Marshall refused any commitment to an invasion of the mainland until the duration and cost of Husky could be assessed, and he reminded everyone of Eisenhower's Trident directive, which held that the final decision on post-Husky operations required the agreement of the CCS. Churchill glossed over Marshall's objections.

Since "everyone agreed that it would be best to put Italy out of the war as soon as possible," and in view of the accord on the table, Churchill thought it unnecessary to draw up any formal directives for post-Husky operations. Here he exploited the ambiguity in the Trident directive. Convinced that Eisenhower now accepted his views, Churchill wanted the decision left in AFHQ's hands. Eisenhower would decide on the best course of action and so notify the CCS.

The Algiers conferences were more than a mere postscript to Trident. The weeklong talks in Algiers accomplished more in terms of clarifying the trajectory of Allied actions than the CCS conference in Washington. This proved all the more surprising because the whole event sometimes took on the look of a circus. On the one side stood all the glitterati of the military camp—Churchill, Brooke, Marshall, Ismay, and the three commanders and their staffs—and on the other stood Eden, de Gaulle, Giraud, and the other usual French suspects. To add to the atmosphere, King George showed up on 4 June. The disproportionate British representation gave the proceedings an air of being a Churchill tour de force, which was pretty close to the truth. Securing everything he had hoped to accomplish—even a tentative agreement between de Gaulle and Giraud— Churchill reaffirmed his "full confidence in General Eisenhower." Churchill painted a glowing picture of the "confidence and [sense of] comradeship which characterized actions in this theatre." He "had never received so strong an impression of cooperation and control as during his visit [to AFHQ]."[38]

The King and Queen of Hearts

Now that things had "quieted down" after the stress of his "hectic" trip to Washington and the conclusion of the Algiers conference, Smith told Truscott he planned to visit him "and some of the other divisions as well as Georgie Patton's Headquarters."[39] Churchill's views of AFHQ were not far from the mark. AFHQ received the approbation of the combined chiefs in Washington, and the Algiers conference allowed it to strut its stuff. Hiccups still occurred, as witnessed by the "peace with honor" imbroglio, but Smith now felt comfortable spending more time away from headquarters. Time away from Algiers always acted like a balm.

Eisenhower observed, "In this war the team must be developed before any of these large organizations will work."[40] By the time of the Algiers meetings, Smith had succeeded in forging an effective team. Smith maintained "that while we Americans have given lip service to the principle of unity of command the practice was carried out more completely [in the Allied headquarters] than it actually was in some of the Forces composed exclusively of American units."[41] Creating an integrated Allied headquarters proved far easier than reconciling disparate American views on their own staff structures. As Smith later noted, doubtlessly thinking of North Africa, "organization for supply usually presents the greatest difficulties."[42]

The Eisenhower-Smith tandem anchored the AFHQ team. From the very beginning of their relationship, Eisenhower had made it clear to Smith how he wanted his headquarters run. Before Smith's arrival in Algiers, even up to the formation of NATO in February, Eisenhower tried to balance his dual tasks as supreme commander and American theater commander, and he performed neither particularly well. As supreme commander, Eisenhower operated through AFHQ and reserved for himself all questions involving strategic and operational policy making. Everything else that involved combined and joint authority he delegated to Smith, subject to his veto. As the Ike and Beetle partnership matured, and as the number of AFHQ responsibilities multiplied, Eisenhower devolved more and more duties to Smith, who exerted what amounted to total control over the AFHQ staff. To Hughes, Eisenhower passed responsibility for orchestrating administration, manpower, and supply and generally managing theater problems—matters that neither Eisenhower nor Smith saw as terribly vital.

After the war Smith maintained, "the actual organization of the Staff is not particularly important." As demonstrated by his repeated efforts to streamline staff structures, Smith held a very different opinion during the war. He did recognize that "these things are so much [a] matter of personalities."[43] Managing these "intangible factors which do not appear in any of the charts" represented his biggest headaches. Gale remarked that integrating the American and British staff systems was like trying to fit a standard nut into a metric bolt. Smith used a similar analogy. No doubt prompted by his training as a machinist, he compared the workings of AFHQ to an engine. At first the gears did not mesh. If left unchecked, the machine would malfunction. The addition of more wheels and pulleys increased the likelihood of breakdowns; to avoid that, the attendant must exercise vigilance and apply the proper amount of lubrication. The points of friction—he called them "misfits"—"must be eliminated ruthlessly." Over time, the surfaces of the moving parts became "finely burnished," enabling "the machine to run without too much heat." As Husky approached, AFHQ began to take on the aspects of a finely tuned engine.

Smith identified three key ingredients in merging an integrated staff.

The first element was the presence of a supreme commander who set the tone for Allied cooperation. Eisenhower provided that requirement. Second, Smith pointed to the "desirability of keep[ing] the British and American sides fairly well balanced as far as numbers" and claimed, "We do not differentiate one iota between our British and American personnel so far as the assignment of any job is concerned, and we pick officers on merit and ability." He noted that achieving this balance constituted a problem because, as he confided in LTG Henry Pownall, "you will find your British officers will provide the best high level planning and G-2 people." Finally, "there must be the absence of the language barrier." He found, "to our sorrow," the "canned language" taught in the respective command and staff schools "means something quite different to English and American officers." He pointed to one amusing example in North Africa. Eisenhower had received a requisition for 10,000 sleepers. "For Heaven's sake," he asked, "what do they want all these for?" In the United States, a sleeper is a Pullman car; in the United Kingdom, a sleeper is a railroad tie. Over time, American and British staff colleagues began to talk the same language. Generally, the most expressive and shortest term gained general usage.[44]

"Basically," Smith commented, "the chief of staff operates through two deputies: one concerning operations and intelligence . . . the other, the CAO, doing the same for personnel and supply." Each morning began with a staff conference in Smith's office attended by his two deputies, Whiteley and Gale, along with Rooks or Sugden from operations (G-3), Strong (G-2), and the two chiefs of the air and naval staffs attached to AFHQ. When planning for Husky commenced, a representative of Alexander's planning staff also attended. Smith ran the entire show. At these meetings, Smith dealt exclusively with operational matters, the most troublesome being the coordination of air with naval and ground forces. Discussions might involve ongoing operations in Tunisia or planning for Husky. "The real purpose of this conference," he explained, "is to tie in the operation of the strategic Air Force with Ground and Navy operations" and to ensure that Eisenhower's policies "on this, his only real mobile reserve, are carried out." Wigglesworth was not always compliant, so to facilitate integration of the air and naval staffs, Smith formed a Joint Planning Staff—a partial concession to the committee system—under Whiteley.[45] Smith would begin by saying, "Ike wants this," and then he would lay out what Eisenhower wanted done. Not much conferring went on in a Smith-run conference. Eisenhower had already made his decision, most often the product of consultations with Smith. Just as often, "Ike wants this" served as cover for "I want this."

Smith then went around the table asking each individual in turn if he understood precisely the demands placed on him and his section. Invariably the answer was, "Yes, General." If the question at hand demanded inputs from Whiteley or Rooks on operations and planning, Strong on intelligence, or Gale on supply, Smith requested a brief overview. Invariably, all this had been thoroughly analyzed and discussed before the presentation; very little elaboration was required.

"Here we are greatly plagued by political problems," Smith wrote, "and since these are the direct responsibility of the commander-in-chief, the chief of staff handles them himself with the assistance of the Military Government Section and the British and American Resident Ministers." For matters concerning political, economic, and civil affairs or press relations, Smith held discussions away from headquarters, usually on the balcony of his villa over an early breakfast. Normally this involved some combination of Murphy; Macmillan; Jean Monnet, the unofficial French resident; and perhaps other principals with Gale, Holmes, Rennell, or McClure in tow. Here the aim focused on defusing an issue or arriving at a conclusion on a policy matter for presentation to Eisenhower for his consideration. Often these deliberations involved anticipating a looming storm and tailoring a response. Whatever the case, Smith insisted on concurrence before going to Eisenhower. If Eisenhower gave his license, Smith instructed the responsible agencies and initiated planning.

While Smith conducted his staff conference, Eisenhower met with Hughes, usually twice a week. Together they discussed pressing problems, reviewed the manpower and supply situation, and decided the broad contours of theater policy. Since Eisenhower hated to be bothered with detail, Hughes kept most of it from him. If Hughes faced a particularly daunting issue or was putting out some fire, he reserved the right to directly consult Eisenhower. He never abused this privilege.

After Hughes left, Smith would enter Eisenhower's office, usually alone but sometimes accompanied by one or more of his subordinates. Smith set the agenda and did most of the talking, summarizing the main points made at that morning's staff meeting. Smith's vetting procedure meant that Eisenhower gave only cursory attention to staff appreciations that crossed his desk. After concluding the meeting, Smith normally stayed behind to conduct the real business of the day. If some matter demanded immediate attention or an emergency arose, Eisenhower might call Beetle into his office one or two times during the course of the day. Their relationship was collaborative. Together they determined their basic strategic and policy objectives and, after weighing the liabilities, divined the most appropriate means for achieving the desired ends. These daily contacts—direct meetings when Eisenhower remained at headquarters and teletype or telephone communications when he toured the forward areas—reinforced their shared beliefs and perceptions. Since no written record of these meetings exists, the degree to which Smith influenced Eisenhower's day-to-day decision making remains an open question, but it must have been considerable. Smith then returned to his office and drew up a record of action for dissemination to responsible sections of the headquarters. Major policy papers and correspondence with the combined chiefs and War Department bore the initials "D.D.E.," but Smith often wrote them or edited those penned by his subordinates.

On Monday, Wednesday, and Friday, Smith convened a general chiefs of staff meeting for the heads of all general and special staff divisions. Initially, nineteen officers attended. More of a briefing on current developments and a seminar on policy changes than a genuine conference, these general meetings became less frequent over time. As AFHQ expanded and the number of agencies grew, the whole thing became, in Smith's opinion, too ponderous and a waste of valuable time. In addition, three or four times a week, Gale held conferences coordinating the flow of supplies. Smith usually found time to attend. Similarly, Whiteley called meetings twice a week to keep current on the progress of scheduled troop movements and deployments. Smith made a point to reserve time for these as well.

The glue binding all this together was the secretariat. Smith termed his secretariat "the general clearing house . . . this all important cog . . . [and] the one place through which everyone can be reached at any time." Gilmer, who headed the secretariat for the duration of Smith's tenure in the Mediterranean, oversaw the dissemination of staff studies, maintained the vital registry of incoming and outgoing communications, and kept the headquarters diary, among other duties. The diary recorded all decisions emanating from AFHQ, including those made by Smith in Eisenhower's name. When Eisenhower returned after one of his increasingly frequent trips to his commanders' headquarters, he immediately consulted the diary to check on decisions Smith had made in his absence.[46]

The combined headquarters outwardly mimicked Marshall's inner headquarters, but Eisenhower's brand of centralized decision making and delegated authority markedly differed from the chief's. Marshall believed the supreme military virtue lay in a commander making a quick but firm decision and standing behind it; Eisenhower avoided taking such resolute actions. He proved decisive only when he resolved *not* to do something he considered miscalculated or alien to his sense of duty or might expose him to criticism. Like Marshall, he deflected pressure from external agencies. Marshall's stance was always transparent; Eisenhower carefully veiled his intentions and activities. Whereas Marshall always assumed responsibility for any decision made by a subordinate, Eisenhower insisted on multiple advocacies for any policy line he pursued (especially after the fallout from the Darlan deal). The policy remained Eisenhower's, but in its promotion and execution, his role remained shrouded; and if things miscarried, he possessed a ready-made firewall to divert blame.

But none of this was readily apparent to observers. Eisenhower happily relinquished all authority for running the headquarters to Smith. Eisenhower left it to Smith to establish the boundaries of his authority. When Smith moved to expand his authority, opponents accused him of empire building. When Smith exceeded the ill-defined limits—and he never knew precisely where the lines were drawn—Eisenhower reeled him in. Smith did all the heavy lifting. He assumed the lead on all political and diplomatic maneuvering. He settled all but the most important issues; even those requiring the attention of Eisenhower went through Smith. During Eisenhower's extended absences, Smith acted as de facto deputy supreme commander. He authored memoranda in Eisenhower's name to the combined chiefs that often found their way to Churchill and Roosevelt. Smith acted as the all-powerful gatekeeper who not only controlled the flow of information to Eisenhower but also kept out problems and people Eisenhower chose not to deal with. In his hatchet-man role, Smith did the reprimanding and the firing. Smith knew Eisenhower's views so well he made decisions consistent with them. When Smith made decisions or took actions normally reserved for the commander, it looked as though Eisenhower had abdicated authority to his power-hungry chief of staff. Visitors to AFHQ sometimes wondered whether they had been transported to Wonderland: the ineffectual and affable king reigned, but the hair-trigger queen, "blind with rage" and yelling "off with their heads," actually ruled. At one level, this characterization was largely true. Not so evident was that this external appearance camouflaged the true workings of the Ike and Beetle collaboration. Some appreciated that the two men's different personalities and styles—the easygoing Eisenhower and the irascible Smith—complemented each other, contributing to an efficient division of labor, but they remained very much in the minority.

Eisenhower's buffering technique conferred the additional benefit of placing himself above the fray and putting Smith at the center of it. Should any initiative fail, particularly in the political arena, Smith served as lightning rod. Smith confronted a great deal of hostility from senior officers in the theater and, by extension, many in the War Department. Still comparatively young, Smith discharged authority and leverage greatly exceeding that conventionally conferred on a chief of staff, and he exerted influence over many officers who were much senior on the permanent list and better connected in army circles.[47] He earned the enmity of those subjected to his tongue-lashings and sackings. The stories made the rounds, exaggerated with each telling. This might have enhanced his reputation, permitting Smith to extend his preserves, but at a heavy personal cost. Much of the animus directed at Smith was a natural outgrowth of the preeminence of AFHQ—its unprecedented size and authority and the fact that, in American eyes, it appeared to be British dominated. Throughout his career, Smith constantly demonstrated two core traits: a willingness and ability to shoulder responsibilities far beyond his grade, and an unfailing fealty to his superiors. Smith recognized the personal price he paid, but he also knew he needed Eisenhower as much as Eisenhower needed him. Without Smith, Eisenhower's passive-negative leadership style could never have functioned as effectively. Without Eisenhower, Smith might have remained an anonymous staffer caught in the Washington treadmill.

After the war, Smith took pains to depict his relationship with Eisenhower as one based on a near absolute unanimity of viewpoints. This portrait was mostly eyewash. Naturally, differences of opinion emerged, but with one exception, they never left Eisenhower's office. That lone exception involved their ongoing tussle over headquarters and theater organization. The clash generated enough heat in February 1943 that rumors made the rounds that McClure would replace Smith.[48] Matters never got that bad, but Eisenhower chafed at Smith's refusal to take no for an answer. They did not call Smith "Bulldog" for nothing. His defeat in February merely fueled his determination to get his way eventually. The squabble over organization offers the best insights into Eisenhower's command style and how the Ike and Beetle team operated.

Soon after returning from Washington, Smith embarked on a renewed effort to overhaul AFHQ and redefine the position of the American theater command in relation to the combined headquarters. Hughes had won the two preliminary bouts, but Somervell's new efforts to reform the War Department encouraged Smith's belief that he might triumph in the main event. Somervell wanted to close the gulf that separated policy making and planning from policy execution by the "grouping of administrative and service elements under a chief who is both a staff officer and a commander." The ASF memorandum cited the advantages of the British system, which provided in the chief administrative officer a commander who "simply communicates directly with the agency concerned and gives the necessary orders." It condemned the existing American structure, described as "both unnecessary and undesirable" and dangerously unwieldy. American practice meant that "when dealing with matters of . . . supply [a commander in chief] must communicate through three or four different echelons before [his] will . . . has been transmitted through channels to the officer or agency responsible for carrying it into effect." The ASF proposal held up NATO as an example of the failings in the American system. Hughes, a deputy theater commander, held no command responsibility. Conducting "only those functions which the commander himself may see fit to delegate," Hughes "has nothing to do except to get into the hair of the chief of staff, who has enough troubles without this added encumbrance." U.S. Army doctrine "did not take cognizance of the smaller agencies which are the real headaches for a commander and his Chief of Staff." The study cited censorship, press relations, subversive activities, propaganda, and psychological and political warfare as examples. The paper ended by claiming Smith exercised "sufficient control in [Eisenhower's] name to assure continuity of effort."[49]

Smith could not hope for a better endorsement of his proposed reorganization. On 2 June he circulated his restructuring plan. Since the "deputy theater commander's duties [were] analogous to those now carried out at AFHQ by the CAO," Smith again advocated making Hughes the American chief administrative officer inside the combined headquarters. He outlined a number of advantages. Gale and Hughes and their staffs would integrate with AFHQ without abolishing NATO constitutionally. Such an amalgamation would create "one set of general staff sections and one set of special staff sections." Larkin's command would remain unaffected, except for its subordination to AFHQ. Smith argued that the reorganization would not disrupt ongoing staff work; it would preserve independent American and British command, staff, and technical channels and leave the base sections intact. On the American side, Smith's new configuration would create a single staff, ending the duplications and jurisdictional conflicts inherent in the "dual hat" solution, improving the responsiveness of the American line of communications, and significantly reducing the officer overhead. Smith sweetened the bitter pill for Hughes. Under the new scheme, Hughes would exercise genuine command of all American administrative, supply, and services echelons and would supervise the work of a combined G-1 and an enlarged G-4 staff in AFHQ, along with additional duties.[50]

Eisenhower's refusal to establish firm lines of demarcation between Smith and Hughes inevitably produced friction. Instead of being cooperative, their relationship became adversarial, and the lack of familiarity between them degenerated into open antagonism. Since March they had skirmished over control of American supply. Then Hughes got to Eisenhower, convincing him to fire Smith's G-4 Hamblen for failing to cooperate with Hughes's organizations. Both Smith and Hughes wanted no repetition of the problems that had plagued Torch. Hughes complained that NATO and SOS remained estranged from Husky planning. "Finding the situation as it was in the U.K. when TORCH was mounted," Hughes noted in his diary, he "got in Bedell's hair" about it at one of the chiefs of staff conferences. Smith reacted angrily. Later that day he called Hughes, claiming he repeatedly gave way on matters of no concern to Hughes, who continually encroached into AFHQ's preserves. Smith said he "was damn fed up" and "it has got to stop." Smith accused Hughes of being "an empire builder of the first water" and told him, "The staff belongs to me." Hughes believed "things are rapidly coming to a show-down," and it remained to be seen "whether he goes or I do." Later in March, Hughes raised the issue of Murphy's going to Smith on theater matters. "Ike gave me hell because people were interfering with my job," Hughes recorded. "I can't figure it out."[51]

In April Eisenhower withheld Smith's latest reorganization memo until Hughes "had a whack at it." Hughes succeeded in blunting Smith's efforts to limit the size and functions of an expanded NATO.[52] As long as NATO supervised a skeleton SOS, the anomalies and overlapping functions of staff duties implicit in the "two-hat" structure did not create serious problems. In March 63,000 SOS troops arrived in the theater—still far below requirements, but enough to begin the process of fleshing out the base sections and staffing the replacement centers. More poured into the theater during April. Smith understood the need for an expanded NATO to deal with an expanded rear and proved perfectly willing to divest himself of all routine administrative functions, but he refused to transfer G-4 to Hughes's control. Smith considered his G-4, BG Clarence Adcock, the counterpoise to Hughes and built up his staff in anticipation of NATO's expansion.[53] By the end of April the number of officers and enlisted men attached to AFHQ grew to 3,604, a 20 percent increase since January.

Eisenhower assigned MG Ralph Huebner the job of devising a new set of structures for the U.S. side of AFHQ and NATO that would be acceptable to both Smith and Hughes. "If he can get anything but a cockeyed organization," Hughes forecast, "he is good."[54] Smith recruited Huebner for his contest with Hughes, together with his old ally Sawbridge and the AFHQ and NATO adjutant generals, BG Ben Davis and COL Harold Roberts. All authored recommendations for NATO's reorganization consistent with Smith's views.[55] On 24 April Smith launched his attack. That morning, Huebner went to Hughes's office at Smith's request and pushed for "a complete change in the set-up."[56] Then at noon, in front of a collection of senior American and British officers gathered for the chiefs of staff meeting, Smith asked Huebner, "How is your fight with Everett Hughes coming?"[57] Everyone laughed. Later that day Smith drove over to Hughes's headquarters for the climactic shoot-out. Standing before Hughes, Smith told him that Eisenhower "brought you down here to be promoted and a job was made for you. Now that you have been promoted, you can afford to accept this proposed organization."[58]

Hughes was nobody to trifle with. A big man—he stood six foot five—with jet black hair and a saturnine mien, Hughes intimidated people. In addition to being tall in stature, Hughes stood high in the estimate of powerful associates. He had met Eisenhower at Leavenworth, and while associates in the WDGS in the 1930s, they became confidential friends. To Eisenhower's son John he was "Uncle Everett," and Mamie and Kate remained close personal friends. Eisenhower considered Hughes "an officer of outstanding dignity and common sense" and confessed to him in 1941, "there's no one in the Army whose good wishes mean more to me."[59] He was also crony of and drinking buddies with Patton, who deemed Hughes "the most broad-minded and fair thinking man in the U.S. Army."[60] Sworn enemies at West Point—Patton succeeded Hughes as corps adjutant—they became close while serving on Pershing's staff in Mexico. If Smith pushed too hard, he could easily compromise his position.

Hughes saw the trap coming. He wrote a rejoinder to Huebner's study and forwarded it to Eisenhower. As he wrote to his wife, "the opponents thought that they had ample reinforcements. So without consulting me they met and presented an ultimatum. I stood pat but managed to inform Ike of the coming battle." Then after his little face-off with Smith, Hughes went to have a chat with Eisenhower. Though admitting the current setup contained imperfections, Hughes told Eisenhower he found it difficult "to determine just what is wrong with the present system and just how it fails to comply with the repeated clear and concise instructions of the commander-in-chief." Eisenhower replied that Hughes was justified in "organizing slowly in order not to tear apart an on-going organization." Then, when he heard about Smith and Huebner's plot and Beetle's strong-arm tactics, Eisenhower hit the ceiling. "He wanted to send for the recalcitrant members of his staff at once," but Hughes talked him out of it. Eisenhower then informed Hughes not to worry about the outcome of the reorganization.[61]

The next day Eisenhower confronted Smith. "Ike tore into him," Hughes reported. That afternoon Hughes received a call from Smith inviting him to his office. "I went with my chin up prepared to battle to the death. Instead I found two of the meekest MGs it has ever been my good fortune to find." The conference among Smith, Huebner, and Hughes turned into "a love fest and I got without asking . . . everything that I had been standing out for."[62]

Despite his comeuppance, a bitter Smith still resisted "every step of the way." Recognizing that he could not head off Hughes, Smith admitted, "I like to throw my weight around and then quiet down." Hughes remarked, "He doesn't enjoy any more than I would having my job cut into."[63] On 8 May the omnibus General Order #28 expanded NATO's administrative functions and dramatically increased its size. Some staff sections were consolidated in NATO, others were joined to form new sections, and several portions of AFHQ (Inspector General, Judge Advocate, Provost Marshal General, Special Services, Finance, Claims, Chaplain, and Transportation Corps) were transferred to NATO. Hughes's headquarters also established a number of subsections to coordinate with AFHQ and the North African Shipping and Economic Boards.[64]

Smith was far from done. His trip to Washington and the Algiers conference merely provided a respite. Smith seethed, frustrated by his inability to harness the American and British headquarters in preparation for Husky and annoyed by the disruptions in his various staffs produced by the May reorganization. In Smith's view, NATO presented an obstacle to the proper functioning of supply and support services in the theater. On 2 June he took yet another stab at consolidating logistical control inside AFHQ. "The question of organization," Hughes complained, "was raised for the umpteenth time by Bedell Smith."

For the entire month of June, when their time and energies might have been better spent preparing for the Sicilian invasion, Smith and Hughes, their allies, and their competing headquarters engaged in another internecine scum. Complicating matters, a delegation of two major generals from the States toured the theater, stirring up trouble. MG Lloyd Brown represented the WDGS inspector general; MG Gilbert Cook accompanied him. "Apparently Cook and Brown had come to NATOUSA expecting to find a type organization," Hughes reported to his old West Point file mate and Brown's boss, MG Virgil Peterson, "and much to their surprise found an organization depending more or less upon personalities and a great deal on nationalities."[65]

Although stumped, by his own admission, by the organizational riddle, Eisenhower recoiled from surrendering responsibility for restructuring his headquarters to anyone, including Smith. No innovator or initiator, Eisenhower never looked for problems to solve and always reacted with irritated evasion when confronted by a question that defied easy solution. When pushed, he gave the impression of acting under duress, his form of resistance to intrusions into his sphere. When that did not work, he fell back on protective retreats behind regulations and claims of personal integrity. For a month Eisenhower remained quiescent while his headquarters were rent by this renewed power struggle. Constantly called on to referee disputes between Hughes and Smith, Eisenhower doubted the two men could work together. Eisenhower faced two unpleasant options: either alter the command structure or relieve one of his chief subordinates. He knew he could not spare Smith. Hughes made little effort to disguise his hostility to the British, so moving Hughes into AFHQ offered no solution. At the same time, Eisenhower gave Hughes high marks for managing his affairs. His deputy relieved Eisenhower of the burden of daily theater concerns, and he could not have been displeased with Hughes's guarding of American interests in the theater. Eisenhower always sought the path of least resistance. Wishing to avoid the consequences of either course of action—altering the organization with the new campaign looming or changing horses in midstream—Eisenhower made no choice at all. On 24 June Smith struck his colors. Hughes gleefully recorded in his diary, "*Beadle* [sic] *backs down on reorganization.*"[66]

On 25 June Eisenhower called Smith and Hughes into his office to put an end to the bloodletting. Eisenhower told Smith the existing staff structure would remain in place. "There is no necessity for changing the organization," Eisenhower stated, "simply because some person . . . just arrived from the US finds it difficult to understand that the present setup is necessary and finds that the setup is not a type organization and hence it is wrong." Eisenhower emphasized that the difficulties faced by AFHQ were "as difficult as any that has ever faced the American Army." Then he said something that left both Smith and Hughes scratching their heads. "The only point of friction," Eisenhower concluded, "is in parts of the machine where friction should be of no particular moment."

Then their conversation turned to why they faced "so much agitation about our organization." They papered over their differences, concluding that intrusions into AFHQ and NATO reflected power struggles not between Smith and Hughes or over different principles of staff organization but within the War Department. As Hughes noted, "Somervell wants to take over Ray Mosses and eliminate the WD G-4." Eisenhower and Hughes also chafed against Lee's organization in the United Kingdom standing as a model. The new ETO commander, MG Jacob Devers, restructured the theater command along the lines suggested by Smith. "I happen to know," Hughes confided, "Devers set up the present organization in order that he might have Johnny Lee under his thumb." Smith sat in annoyed silence, knowing that Eisenhower's "no decision" blocked his maneuver to place Hughes under his thumb. "Ike's final comment was that he saw the need for an American officer with a strong mind, who was a stubborn son of a bitch," Hughes related, "and since I qualify under one of the specifications, the present situation would continue until there was some real reason for modifying the organization." No real reason surfaced while Eisenhower exercised command in the theater.

Smith remained philosophical about this latest setback. In common with Eisenhower and Hughes, he resented outsiders trying to dictate solutions to problems they did not understand. Closing ranks, Smith reported to the War Department that although "our set-up is cumbersome . . . it is effective."[67]

21

The Road to Messina

The British scored a success in the Algiers talks, winning Eisenhower over to the idea of invading Italy. Before Trident he favored the more cautious route of attacking Sardinia and Corsica; immediately following the Algiers conference, Eisenhower informed Patton, who (curiously) had not been present, "It would be impossible for us to win a great victory unless we should exploit HUSKY by moving ahead, preferably up into Italy." The Straits of Messina represented "the very windpipe of HUSKY," and securing a bridgehead on the mainland "should be considered part of HUSKY." He told Patton to be prepared "to continue moving with *no* stop at all once HUSKY is inaugurated."

At the 29 May meeting, Alexander laid out his plan for the campaign. Beyond seizing the airfields and ports of southeastern Sicily, no concrete plan existed. After a slogging match consuming perhaps three weeks, the Allied forces—read Eighth Army—would "ignore the remainder of the island," drive on Messina, and "secure a foothold on the opposite shore." "All this," Eisenhower repeated to Patton, "will be clarified as the HUSKY operation moved along."[1]

Typically, Eisenhower hedged his bets; he again decided by not deciding. To appease Marshall, he directed Smith to form two new headquarters: one devoted to detailed planning for operations in Italy, and the other for Sardinia and Corsica. Outline plans for all five operations already existed on paper. With no agreed grand strategy in the theater or any overarching operational concept, plans on paper kept staff officers busy but achieved nothing else. Basically, Smith agreed with Alexander; German actions would determine the shape of the campaign in Sicily and beyond. If resistance proved stubborn and the campaign dragged on past 15 August, AFHQ and Alexander's Fifteenth Army Group would face a tough decision. If the Germans held the island beyond the middle of August, the Allies lacked the strength for operations into the toe of Italy. In that event, the whole campaign in the Mediterranean required revision. But if the Axis forces in Sicily collapsed, Eisenhower told the Algiers conferees, "he would immediately undertake operations against the Italian mainland."[2] The obvious problem with allowing the enemy to dictate the flow of operations apparently did not trouble either Eisenhower or Smith.

Tidying Up

In the month between the Algiers meetings and the Sicily landings, Smith wanted to focus his energies on drawing together all the planning threads for the mounting and staging of Husky. Things did not work out that way. Aside from feuding with Hughes, Smith invested much of his effort on the unfinished business of cobbling together some kind of agreement among the French factions. The Allies could not go into Sicily without securing their rear in North Africa.

At Trident, Smith appeared more dismissive of the potential aid rendered by French military forces than he was in private. French units had fought hard and well in Tunisia; their total losses in the North African fighting matched those suffered by U.S. forces. But those forces contained large elements of Arab troops. Moroccan Goums were fine for fighting in Tunisia and perhaps for liberating Corsica, but the forces French generals envisioned marching down the Champs Élysées would not be attired in *djellaba,* the distinctive long woolen cloak worn by the Goumier. The desire to reconstitute the French army and have it play a prominent role in restoring France to great power status constituted the one common denominator between de Gaulle and the French leadership in North Africa. The question of who controlled that army rested at the heart of the political impasse.

Any French union required an accord between two factions representing diametrically opposing legacies of France's defeat in 1940: the *moustachis* (named after the symbolic moustache of the traditional officer), who remained loyal to Pétain, and the *hadjis,* those who demonstrated their faith to eternal France by making the pilgrimage and joining the Free French. The first priority remained forging some kind of modus operandi between Giraud's regime, with its strong associations to Vichy, and de Gaulle, who vowed no cooperation with any elements tainted by the hint of collaboration. If a political agreement emerged, the second step involved amalgamating the *Armée d'Afrique* with the Gaullist Fighting French.

Each faction brought something to the table. Like the pope, de Gaulle did not have any divisions, but his strength rested in his moral and political claims. The Free French represented an unvanquished France; by 1942, de Gaulle had succeeded in forming links with resistance groups inside France, including the communists.[3] He repeatedly proclaimed his attachment to democracy; reiterated his resolve to accept the will of the French people, freely expressed; and promoted a program of social reform for postwar France. All this won him support in France that cut across party and class lines and garnered favorable press in Britain and the United States. Giraud commanded forces numbering 230,000 led by pro-Vichy officers who represented the best pool of professionals; the Free French forces in North Africa represented something on the order of only 15,000 men. For the French to offer any real contribution in Europe, the two factions must combine.

The Algiers conference produced a union of sorts with the formation of the French Committee of National Liberation (FCNL), with Giraud and de Gaulle as joint chairmen. The committee, initially consisting of seven members, agreed on its ultimate political objective. Until the committee transferred authority to a provisional French government, it undertook "to restore all French liberties, the laws of the Republic and the republican regime through the complete destruction of the regime of arbitrary authority and of personal power which is today imposed upon the country."[4] Prodded by Churchill, Roosevelt tacitly recognized the FCNL and accepted de Gaulle's copresidency, but he insisted AFHQ deal exclusively with French military authorities. Churchill informed de Gaulle that henceforth all British transactions "financial and otherwise" would go through the FCNL and not de Gaulle, and he urged AFHQ to work with the committee and not individual French officials.[5]

A week after formation of the FCNL, de Gaulle, "shrouded in sorrow," resigned. He cited two reasons: the continued influence of Vichyites, and the unjustified interference of AFHQ into French affairs. "The real issue at stake," Eisenhower reported, "is apparently a struggle for control of military forces."[6] By his own admission, de Gaulle staged this "calculated outburst" to tilt the committee in his favor. In fact, de Gaulle never really stepped down; he merely asked the committee "to consider" his resignation. As expected, de Gaulle's actions set off a flurry of communications between Algiers and the capitals. Roosevelt applauded de Gaulle's defection and decided to manage matters from Washington. Since, in his view, the Allies still occupied North Africa, he sent directives to AFHQ, bypassing Murphy and the State Department.[7]

AFHQ received three cables from Roosevelt on 11 June. The presi-

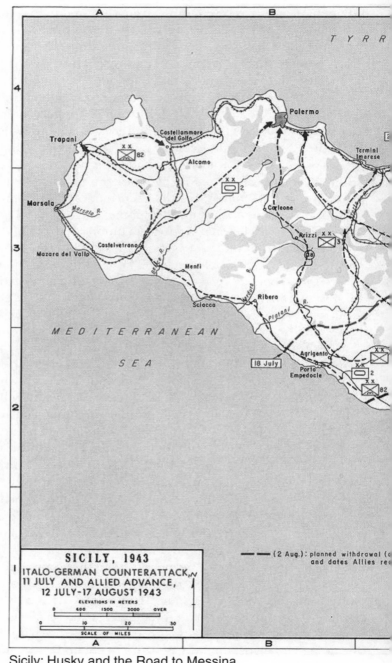

Sicily: Husky and the Road to Messina

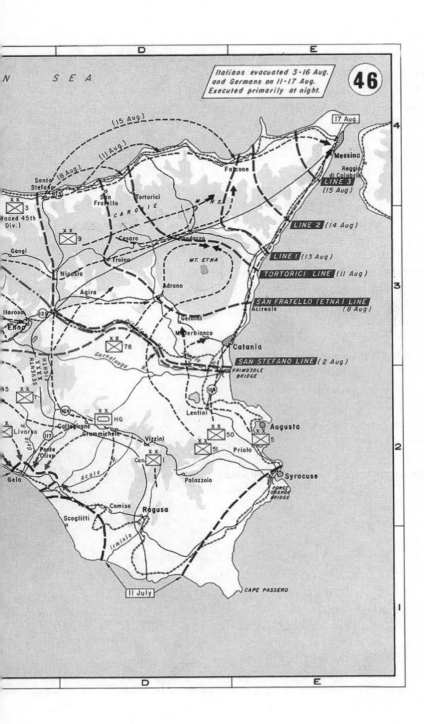

N S E A

Italians evacuated 3-16 Aug.
and Germans on 11-17 Aug.
Executed primarily at night.

46

(15 Aug.)

17 Aug.

(11 Aug.)

Messina

(8 Aug.)

Reggio
di Calabria

Santo
Stefano

Falcone

LINE 3
(15 Aug.)

XX 3

San
Fratello

Tortorici

C A R O N I E

Placed 45th
Div.)

M N S.

LINE 2 (14 Aug.)

XX 9

Cesaro

Randazzo

Gangi

Troina

MT. ETNA

LINE 1 (13 Aug.)

TORTORICI LINE (11 Aug.)

Nicosia

Agira

Adrano

SAN FRATELLO (ETNA) LINE
(8 Aug.)

Acireale

Ilaroso

Enna

Gerbini

Misterbianco

XX 78

Gornalunga R.

Catania

SEVENTH XXXX EIGHTH

SAN STEFANO LINE (2 Aug.)

PRIMOSOLE
BRIDGE

45

IIA

XX

Livorno

Lentini

Caltagirone

XX HG

Vizzini

XX 50

XX 5

Augusta

Grammichele

Priolo

Ponte
Olivo

Can.

XX 51

Gela

Acate

Palazzolo

Syracuse

Comiso

Ragusa

PONTE
GRANDE
BRIDGE

Scoglitti

Irminio

11 July

CAPE PASSERO

dent underscored that de Gaulle's control of French military forces in North and West Africa "seriously jeopardize[d] the safety of British and American operations." Rumor had it that de Gaulle intended to remove Boisson in Dakar. While in Casablanca, both Roosevelt and Churchill had promised Boisson he faced no recriminations for his Vichy past. The president felt Boisson's removal would poison the spirit of cooperation, and he demanded Eisenhower intercede.[8] Eisenhower sent Murphy, who, as Smith reported to the president, "found De Gaulle in a most amiable state of mind." The general talked glowingly of Franco-American ties but admitted he was baffled by Washington's failure to appreciate his vision for the future of France. Still, he could "brook no interference by a foreign power [over] a matter of principle concerning French sovereignty." De Gaulle made "no intimation of this retirement from the Committee" and dispassionately rejected Murphy's appeal that military necessity required unity and not discord. Smith summed up the results of the meeting by saying, "The impasse on the question of French military authority continues."[9]

Negotiations continued, and the climate of crisis worsened. De Gaulle knew how to work the press. Up until the Algiers meeting, Eisenhower repeatedly blocked de Gaulle from coming to North Africa. In April, with the fighting in Tunisia occupying AFHQ's attention, Eisenhower frustrated de Gaulle's attempt to come to Algiers. Newspapers on both sides of the Atlantic, especially Fleet Street, had a field day, attacking Eisenhower for "putting off de Gaulle" again.[10] Journalists argued that Eisenhower preferred to cooperate with Vichyites rather than de Gaulle, whom they portrayed as the true representative of the will of the French people. AFHQ again failed to censor reports coming out of North Africa. "Jesus Christ may have walked on water," a frustrated Smith complained, "but I guess we cannot do the same."[11]

In the midst of the storm, Eisenhower decided to make a long delayed inspection tour of Fifth and Seventh Army areas and Oran. On 16 June Murphy discovered the FCNL had opted to double its membership to fourteen. Giraud signed the decree at Monnet's prompting on 9 June and kept it secret. Just as the U.S. ambassador in London, John Winant, had predicted, de Gaulle's machinations threatened to put Giraud on the shelf. That the politically obtuse Giraud surrendered so easily, and with the connivance of Monnet, threw Murphy into a tailspin. Charging that Monnet had betrayed him, Giraud threatened to resign. At the State Department's behest, Murphy pleaded with Giraud to remain.

Smith hurriedly met with Macmillan and Murphy and set in motion a conference with de Gaulle and Giraud for 19 June. Eisenhower was due back in Algiers late on 17 June. Over the course of 17 June, Smith received two cables from the president. "We will not tolerate," the first insisted, "control of the French Army by any agency not subject to the direction of the Allied Supreme Commander. Nor are we interested in the formation of any committee or government," Roosevelt continued, "that in any way presumes to indicate that it will govern in France until such time as the French people select a government for themselves." He demanded, "it must be perfectly clear that we have a military occupation in North and West Africa and, therefore, no independent civil decision can be made without [Eisenhower's] full approval." Later Algiers received an even more provocative cable, stating, "for your very secret information . . . we may possibly break with De Gaulle in the next few days."[12] Roosevelt fired off an indignant letter to Churchill, forwarded to Algiers, declaring, "It is an intolerable situation. . . . We must divorce ourselves from De Gaulle because . . . he has more recently been interested far more in political machinations that he has in the prosecution of the war and these machinations have been carried on without our knowledge and to the detriment of our military interests."[13]

Trying to calm the waters, Smith wrote to Marshall, cautioning against an overreaction in Washington. "There is no immediate possibility of control of army by De Gaulle," he stressed, "and I think it would be fatal to our plans if matter of military occupation were raised again on very eve of HUSKY." Taken together, these letters not only raised the specter of breaking with de Gaulle but also indicated the president's intention to withdraw recognition of the FCNL, revert to a strict military occupation in French Africa, and suspend the rearmament program. But most explosive of all, they disclosed Roosevelt's aim of subjecting liberated France to direct military rule. If a hint of Roosevelt's scheme for metropolitan France leaked, nobody could foresee the French response.[14]

Eisenhower took a similar tack the next day in a letter to Roosevelt. "The local French difficulties," he assured the president, "have been magnified in certain reports [from Murphy] and in the public press." Ascribing the tempest in Algiers to characteristic Gallic disputatiousness, Eisenhower reassured Roosevelt "that I am fully alive to the potentialities of the situation and that I will not accept any solution proposed by the local French which will jeopardize [Husky]."[15]

Eisenhower and Smith choreographed their meeting with de Gaulle. If they confronted de Gaulle and Giraud with Roosevelt's ultimatum, the consequences could only be imagined. Through Murphy, Macmillan, and Monnet, Smith possessed a good idea of the state of play inside the FCNL. As far as Smith knew, Boisson and Dakar were not even on the French agenda. Smith thought Murphy gave altogether too much credence to rumblings inside French circles concerning de Gaulle's planned putsch of Vichyite officials. Eisenhower concluded de Gaulle had "bigger fish to fry." They decided to ignore political questions entirely, especially those pertaining to Dakar. They shrank from presenting de Gaulle with any grounds for accusing AFHQ of meddling in internal French matters. If the talks remained focused solely on the issue of the command structure of the French forces, and if de Gaulle staged another calculated outburst, Eisenhower reckoned de Gaulle would place himself "in an indefensible position." If de Gaulle remained obstinate, they had other levers—principally, withholding British funding for the FCNL and American materiel for the French armed forces. As Eisenhower reported, "Macmillan has been instructed to cooperate with me 100 percent and we are thus able to present a united front." Eisenhower appealed to Marshall to intercede with Roosevelt and ask the president to refrain from issuing "specific instructions in case French unity strikes a snag."[16]

Smith possessed a pretty formidable duet of political associates in Macmillan and Monnet—one a future prime minister, and the other the prime architect of European union. One of the original FCNL members, Monnet provided Smith with a vital backdoor channel. Unsullied by affiliation with any French faction, especially the Free French, Monnet went to North Africa in February at Roosevelt's request to explain to Giraud why, even though French rearmament held the "greatest importance to all parties," the president's promises at Casablanca could not be fulfilled.[17] Monnet became Giraud's principal political adviser and in April joined Smith's Security Council staff. The Americans regarded Monnet as the fulcrum in their balancing act between the French factions.

Monnet was no American puppet. Murphy regarded him as a firm ally in the struggle against de Gaulle's efforts to gain control over the French armed forces but expressed dismay that Monnet encouraged Giraud's signing of the declaration on FCNL expansion. Only too aware of Giraud's liabilities, Monnet recognized that the old general obstructed the rejuvenation and modernization of French forces. He also thought it was high time to assert greater French autonomy. For all these reasons, Monnet shifted his support toward de Gaulle without actually joining the Gaullist camp. Smith heard a similar story from GEN Georges Catroux, another FCNL member. As Smith discovered, his conduit to Monnet flowed in both directions. Smith always found Monnet a little too well versed on AFHQ thinking. At first he put that down to Monnet's intellectual capacity and his finely tuned political antenna. In fact, Monnet had a mole. AFHQ had assigned a fluent French-speaking American sergeant as an aide to Monnet. Much taken by Monnet, the aide began to leak information to him. Apparently, the sergeant possessed good contacts inside AFHQ. Now suspicious, Smith ordered the spy ring uncovered. After exposing the culprit, as Murphy recounted, Smith "could be heard all through the St. George headquarters shouting: 'Take the **** fool out and shoot him right now.'" The unfortunate noncommissioned officer survived, as did Smith's now more circumspect relationship with Monnet.[18]

It was a good thing Eisenhower and Smith had prepared so well—and that no leaks occurred—because de Gaulle pulled out all the stops. Arriving last and speaking first, the general drew himself up to his full impressive height and announced, "I am here in my capacity as President of the French Government." Nonplussed, Eisenhower stated that, as far as he was concerned, "General Giraud is now—as he has been since last November—the Commander-in-Chief of French forces in North Africa." On that basis, AFHQ would continue to deal only with Giraud. Then Eisenhower threatened to withhold materiel if the FCNL made any more moves depriving Giraud of that authority. De Gaulle reminded Eisenhower that France had provided U.S. forces with the bulk of their materiel and transportation in World War I and had made no attempt to dictate American policy or the choice of commander. As de Gaulle remembered, Smith sat passively as a "silent observer" throughout this exchange.

Although Eisenhower reported no breakthrough, a compromise emerged that became the basis for a settlement. The FCNL promised the formation of a Military Committee, with Giraud and de Gaulle as the rotating presidents and the chiefs of staff of the three French services as members. The Military Committee would merge the *Armée d'Afrique* and the Free French forces, stop Free French poaching of manpower from Giraud's units, and complete a thorough reorganization of the French force structures. Giraud retained control in North Africa; de Gaulle assumed command of everything else. Ultimate authority rested with the FCNL. Boisson and Dakar never came up.[19]

Eisenhower and Smith left the meetings encouraged. As in the case of the establishment of civil and military arrangements under Darlan, the French worked out the details themselves. Because the FCNL sanctioned all that emerged from the 19 June meeting, Eisenhower thought he had won a great coup. He knew—supported by Smith, Murphy, Macmillan, and Monnet—no possibility existed of returning to the status quo ante, depending on "Giraud alone to keep this situation in order." "It should be realized," Eisenhower emphasized, "when the HUSKY forces begin loading within a very few days, there will be practically no troops west of Tunisia that could be employed for insuring tranquility." A breakdown of efforts aimed at achieving French unification might destabilize the situation in North Africa and compromise Husky.[20] Now with Husky just a little more than two weeks away, Eisenhower considered his rear tidied up. Hubris got the better of him. Fundamentally misunderstanding de Gaulle's intentions and underestimating his political shrewdness, Eisenhower reported to Marshall that the irksome general was now neutered.[21] Smith joined in the celebratory mood. "From every point of view," he informed Marshall, "we are certain that the new arrangement is all that we could ask for and I am still surprised that it was put across without a flare-up."[22] Neither Eisenhower nor Smith appreciated that de Gaulle had staged no histrionics because he achieved precisely what he wanted from the deal. Nor did they appreciate the damage they had done to themselves in the eyes of Roosevelt. They had willfully ignored both the letter and the spirit of the president's directives. As their political master in Washington knew, as long as de Gaulle occupied any position of authority, he would never accept any "position of practical impotency." The June compromise left de Gaulle firmly positioned to eventually seize control of the FCNL. It was only a matter of time, as was the next spate of flare-ups.

Husky

Predawn airborne drops on 10 July inaugurated the largest coalition operation to date. Almost 2,600 ships shepherded the landing of elements of eight divisions in an arc from Syracuse on the Ionian Sea to Licata on the Malta Channel. Strong winds and navigational errors badly compromised the airborne operations, and heavy seas in the American sector complicated landings, but by the end of the day, all the Allied forces were ashore and moving toward their objectives. Aided by the success of an elaborate deception plan, the Allies caught the Axis totally by surprise. The Germans deployed only those two divisions that had given Eisenhower such fright back in April. The British XIII Corps took Syracuse, as planned, the first day. American forces in the beachhead repelled a determined German counterattack on 11 July. By that night, the Allies had brought 80,000 men, 3,000 vehicles, 300 tanks, and 900 guns across the beaches. Hard fighting lay ahead, but the final outcome was hardly in doubt.

The "ducks" more than proved their worth. Within four hours of the landings, the DUKWs went into action. On one beach, ducks landed four batteries of howitzers that, within minutes, began firing. One correspondent described "hordes of tiny craft, like water bugs, scooting toward the shore." Ramsay, commander of the Eastern Task Force, spoke for many when he called the duck "a magnificent bird."[23]

Montgomery's push up the coastal road took Augusta on 13 July but thereafter stalled against stiffening German resistance. The next day Montgomery abandoned hopes of "hustling" the Germans toward Messina; instead, he advocated a left hook around the western end of Mount Etna. Once Seventh Army secured its objectives, Alexander ordered Patton's two corps to shield Montgomery's flank and drive north along a separate axis with the objective of cutting the island in half. Montgomery's change in plan required a shift in army boundaries; the British needed the Vizzini road. Bradley protested, but Patton accepted the decision that pushed American forces westward. The Canadian First Division's drive on the vital Leonforte and Enna road networks failed, and loss of the road meant Bradley's II Corps could not take Enna or cut the island, allowing the Fifteenth Panzer Grenadier Division's unmolested retreat into the hardening German defenses.

On 13 July Kesselring arrived on the scene and moved two more German divisions into Sicily. The German field marshal ordered the formation of a bastion anchored on Mount Etna, with the aim of holding as many Allied divisions in place for as long as possible while keeping open the main avenue of escape over the straits. The rugged Sicilian landscape, with its narrow, winding roads, offered ideal defensive terrain, effectively negating Allied advantages in armor.

The muddled command lines hamstrung the campaign from the first days. The basic problem flowed from the lack of any articulated operational concept for the campaign: headquarters—and there were too many of them—simply received tasks, not orders. Alexander never exerted any ground command, and Eisenhower refused to intervene. In frustration, Smith complained that days went by without AFHQ receiving direct communications from any of the operational headquarters.[24] Alexander's decision on the army boundaries removed any pretense of unified command; thereafter, his two headstrong army commanders went their own way. On 17 July Patton flew to Alexander's headquarters in La Marsa in Tunisia, insisting on a greater role for the American forces. Alexander concluded that the impulsive Patton would declare "the hell with this" and do what he pleased anyway, so he sanctioned a move into western Sicily.[25] Ultra had already revealed that the Germans intended to abandon the rest of the island. Patton never divulged that his ultimate objective was not Palermo but Messina. In the back of Patton's mind resonated the advice he had received from de Guingand the day before: "pay no attention to any order from Alexander."[26]

For the next week, all semblance of coordination broke down. Patton regrouped his forces, placing MG Geoffrey Keyes in command of a provisional corps and ordering his movement toward Palermo. Bradley sidestepped Enna and advanced north. Patton's advance—especially that made by Truscott's Third Infantry Division, dubbed the "foot cavalry" after Stonewall Jackson's infantry in the 1862 Valley Campaign—removed whatever tarnish on American arms still lingered from Tunisia, but it achieved no strategic advantage. Meanwhile, Montgomery discarded the strategy of concentration and fought four separate division actions. By 22 July, Patton occupied Palermo, and the Canadians finally took Leonforte. Still no plan emerged for ending the campaign.

Insofar as exerting any direction on the campaign, AFHQ remained silent. From the late afternoon of 6 July, Eisenhower spent the next two weeks away from Algiers. Smith's labors stayed fixed on settling plans for post-Husky operations. Once a week he flew to La Marsa for a commanders in chief meeting. At the 17 July meeting Eisenhower predicted a delay in taking Messina until mid-August. Smith dangled seven possible variations for a move into southern Italy, including a surprise landing in Naples. With Ultra indicating no substantial German reinforcements moving into southern Italy, Eisenhower recommended "carrying the war to the mainland of Italy immediately Sicily has been captured" and requested from the CCS "very early approval in order that no time may be lost in making preparations."[27] But which of the seven options would be chosen was anyone's guess. In the meantime, Marshall threatened to end AFHQ's most favored status and its first call on manpower and materiel, while Churchill called for an operation directed against Rome. "We should attempt only vital blows at this stage of the war," the prime minister advised, "and side shows should be avoided." Eisenhower delegated to Smith responsibility for making the AFHQ's case with Marshall and deflecting the prime minister.[28]

On 22 July Eisenhower returned to Algiers and ordered Smith, who had spent the preceding days at the advance headquarters, to fly to Sicily and appraise the situation. One of the central failings of combined headquarters throughout the war derived from an overreliance on balky signals communications. Thousands of messages flooded the communications center daily, jamming up the works. Smith never formed a corps of liaison officers charged with going forward to component commands to keep AFHQ informed of developments in a rapidly changing situa-

Montgomery (left) explains his plans for taking Messina to Smith and Alexander, with Patton listening on, at Syracuse Airfield, 25 July 1943.

tion. By going forward himself, Smith sent the wrong message to field commanders, affirming their view—in this case, correctly—that AFHQ exerted no influence on events. Given this absence of any direction from above, Montgomery again intervened—someone had to—and asked that Patton come to Syracuse so "we can then discuss the capture of Messina." Just as at the Mareth Line and Enfidaville in Tunisia, Montgomery concluded that his forces could not break out along the coastal road. Facing fierce German resistance in what he termed "a very bloody killing match" south of Catania, Montgomery decided to hold there and "stage a blow about 2 August . . . working round the West and North of ETNA."[29] As early as 19 July, Montgomery conceded he could not take Messina and hoped to "repeat BIZERTA manoeuvre"; in other words, Patton would take Messina.[30]

Patton arrived early for the meeting. Montgomery made every effort to appear complimentary and conciliatory. The two generals immediately got down to business, not waiting for Alexander and Smith's arrival. Montgomery spread a map of Sicily out on the hood of his staff car and laid out his thinking for the drive on Messina. Patton came pre-pared to do battle for priority over the island's meager road network, but much to his amazement, Montgomery not only abandoned any claims on Messina but also proposed that the Seventh Army enjoy complete free-dom in crossing army boundaries—anything to facilitate the pocketing of German forces. A still skeptical Patton readily agreed.

Alexander and Smith finally appeared and discovered the deal already struck. Montgomery's actions stripped away any pretense of Alexander exercising any real authority. "He looked a little mad," Patton recorded, "and, for him, was quite brusque. He told Monty to explain his plan. Monty said he and I had already decided what we were going to do, so Alex got madder and told Monty to show him the plan." Montgomery complied, and a Signal Corps photographer captured the moment. Now with the proprieties observed, Alexander rubber-stamped the bargain.

Patton raised the indelicate question of Huebner's relief as Alexan-der's deputy. In a letter to his wife, Patton had surmised that Huebner got sacked "because he stood up for American interests." Patton made noise about resigning in protest and blamed "Bedell Smith (s.o.b.)" for acceding to Alexander's request.[31] Patton brought along his G-4, COL Walter Maud Muller, who requested landing craft for supplying Pat-ton's movements along the north coast. Smith brewed up, telling him, "AFHQ would make the division [of LSTs] and that he, Muller, was too prone to forget the existence of AFHQ." Patton thought, "So is everyone else, as it never asserts itself."[32]

Alexander and Smith had arrived late because they were monitoring a breaking story in Rome. Following the conference, Smith flew back to La Marsa for a meeting with Eisenhower. When Eisenhower's plane landed, an excited Smith met him with news that something big could be looming: for the first time since 1939, the Fascist Grand Council would convene. The next morning before breakfast, word arrived of Musso-lini's ouster. Totally surprised by this dramatic turn of events, Eisen-hower attached "the utmost importance that full opportunity should be taken immediately." He reckoned a window existed for opening nego-tiations with the king, who had dismissed and arrested Mussolini and formed a government under Marshal Pietro Badoglio, offering "an hon-orable capitulation." Macmillan found Eisenhower "in a great state of excitement and full of plans and ideas for exploiting the Italian situ-ation." As he told his commanders, Eisenhower hoped to foster such a groundswell of public opinion in favor of ending the war that the king would have no recourse but to sue for peace; he even held out the pros-pect that the Italians might drive the German forces from the peninsula.

On Eisenhower's direction, Macmillan composed a five-point message to the Italian people commending the House of Savoy "on ridding themselves" of Mussolini. Eisenhower planned a broadcast announcing the offer of honorable conditions and immediate peace, but first he must secure approval from Washington and London. In the meantime, Smith flew back to Algiers and began compiling a "short list" of "military" terms for a potential Italian capitulation.[33]

Mussolini's exit did not alter concrete Allied operational planning—except for Patton and Montgomery's compact, none existed—but it accelerated the operational timetables. As Eisenhower explained to his military bosses, his "one concern is speed of action and all our efforts are bent on launching the next operation." But which operation: a hop over the Straits of Messina (code-named Baytown), a consolidated drive into the toe of Italy (Buttress), a rush of two divisions into Naples (Barracuda), a major amphibious operation south of Naples (Avalanche), or the opportunistic seizure of Sardinia and Corsica?[34]

Eisenhower flew back to Algiers on the afternoon of 26 July for a dinner with Stimson. The coup in Rome and Eisenhower's cables set off a series of high-level conferences in the capitals and another cross-Atlantic essay contest. In an emergency meeting on 26 July the CCS provided the answer, sanctioning Avalanche at the earliest date possible. As the directive highlighted, AFHQ should exploit the situation and expedite the surrender of Italy.[35] For the next four days the AFHQ message center was bombarded with incoming cables.

The prospect of an Italian collapse or capitulation exposed the gulf between American and British strategic agendas. The British looked toward real strategic advantages in the Mediterranean. The American chiefs could not deny the obvious and immediate gains offered by a limited Allied move into southern Italy—knocking Italy out of the war; posing a threat against the Balkans; and securing air bases to carry the war throughout the Mediterranean, Balkans, and south Germany. For Marshall, the problem rested in limiting British demands for broadening the Mediterranean campaign. But, given the dramatic events in Rome, the speed of the reduction of Sicily, and the imminent conference in Quebec, the American chiefs did not fancy their chances. If Churchill spun his magical web around Roosevelt, as he had during previous meetings, the cross-Channel attack might well be pushed back at least another year.

Not only did the Allies disagree on strategic issues, but the Americans and British also differed on how they might best effect a potential Italian capitulation. Haggling since the last week in June, neither the CCS and the BCOS nor the Foreign Office and the State Department could settle on a program for the Italian surrender or for military administration in "liberated" Axis territories. AFHQ still lacked firm directives for AMGOT in Sicily. The prime minister correctly guessed that the fascist movement would rapidly disintegrate following Mussolini's removal and predicted the king and Badoglio would pursue a separate peace. He urged AFHQ to employ every expedient to knock Italy out of the war. "Now Mussolini is gone," he remarked on 26 July, "I would deal with any non-Fascist Italian government which can deliver the goods . . . even if it is not all we should like."[36] Roosevelt supported the prime minister's views, but with greater circumspection. On 26 July he told Churchill the terms must be "as close as possible to unconditional surrender." The president also stressed that AFHQ should not "fix any general terms without your approval and mine." Two days later in a fireside chat he reassured the American public, "Our terms to Italy are still the same as our terms to Germany and Japan—unconditional surrender. We will have no truck with Fascism in any way, shape, or manner."[37]

While awaiting instructions from Washington and London, AFHQ requested authority to act if approached by the Italian high command. In the absence of direction from above, Eisenhower proposed offering the Italians a "military" armistice without mention of "unconditional surrender." Eisenhower and Smith never bought the unconditional surrender policy. Mirroring their views, Macmillan confided in his diary that no such thing as "unconditional surrender" existed. The political heads demanded "surrender on our conditions." Eisenhower's proposed use of "military" terms amounted to a two-step process: First, Italy would submit without seeing the conditions; then the Allies would present Rome with the formal terms. The British resident did not see how the Italians could accept, but in the absence of any firm directives from the political chiefs, he requested instructions should Italy make gestures.[38]

The ghost of Darlan hovered over all these deliberations, fueling the Foreign Office's resistance to AFHQ striking another "military" bargain and prompting Eden's intransigent insistence on a "long terms" surrender document. The War Cabinet held five meetings in the space of four days (26–29 July). On 28 July the prime minister argued for AFHQ's "two-step" approach and the use of the short terms in Eisenhower's proposed broadcast to the Italian nation. The rest of the War Cabinet voiced their unanimous opposition.[39]

"Poor Eisenhower is getting pretty harassed," recorded Macmillan in his diary on 29 July. Cables inundated Algiers. One would arrive overnight, and Smith would summon Macmillan to the St. George Hotel. No sooner had they assessed the contents of that cable and agreed on the main lines of the reply, after which Macmillan returned to his office, when another arrived. On the morning of 29 July Macmillan went "backwards and forwards between my own office and AFHQ." He recorded, "telegrams (private, personal, and most immediate) pour in on [Eisenhower] from the following sources: (i) CCS . . . his masters. (ii) General Marshall, his immediate superior. (iii) The President. (iv) The Secretary of State. (v) Our Prime Minister (direct). (vi) Our Prime Minister (through me). (vii) The Foreign Secretary (through me)." Each of these cables raised the pressure; all contained instructions, and all were "naturally contradictory and conflicting." Describing these hectic days, Macmillan remembered that he and Smith developed a "parlour game." First they sorted out the communications, and then they replied—Smith to Washington and Macmillan to London—"saying what we think ought to happen." And because "this rarely, if ever, coincides with any of the courses proposed by (i), (ii), (iii), (iv), (v), (vi), or (vii), lots of fun ensues." Exhibiting the British penchant for understatement, he concluded, this business "gets a bit wearing, especially with this heat."[40]

In view of British resistance to a "military" armistice, Eisenhower directed that Smith and Macmillan compose a carefully worded appeal to Marshall and, through the chief of staff, to Roosevelt. The letter emphasized that "a vast but possibly fleeting opportunity" might arise "to accomplish all that we are seeking in the Italian peninsula." Eisenhower requested powers to act decisively. Any wavering—"the absence of an advanced directive or grant of authority to act"—presented the Germans with an opening to preempt Allied actions. Underlining that AFHQ fully appreciated the existence of "corollaries that far transcend military considerations," as well as the limits of the supreme commander's authority, the wire reassured Marshall the armistice would be "limited to military problems." Holding out the prospect that the Allies might end the entire campaign, saving "the maximum number of troops for other commitments," the cable's phrasing appealed to Marshall's insistence on limiting further expenditures in the Mediterranean and the president's thirst for success in the theater. After Eisenhower vetted the document, it went out to the capitals.[41]

The letter did the trick. Only a day after his radio broadcast promising "no truck with Fascists," Roosevelt empowered Eisenhower to treat with the Italian government or high command based on the "short terms." AFHQ's missive arrived in Churchill's hands at 1:30 in the morning. Much exercised by its content, Churchill "considered it sufficiently urgent to turn whole War Cabinet out of bed." Dissuaded against convening the cabinet, Churchill recognized the British could no longer stonewall. Confronted with what amounted to a fait accompli, the British acceded to AFHQ's request. London accepted Eisenhower's "two-step" line on the assumption that plenty of time remained to finalize the long terms before AFHQ had any chance to employ it.[42]

Both political bosses knew they embarked on a dangerous gamble. On 30 July the president wired Churchill, "There are some contentious people here who are getting ready to make a row if we seem to recognize the House of Savoy or Badoglio. They are the same element which made such a fuss over North Africa."[43] Churchill needed no prompting to remember the political price he had paid for supporting the Darlan deal; nor did Eden and the rest of the War Cabinet. But the allure of cheap strategic rewards outweighed potential political hazards. The machinery of coalition warfare by committee ground on mercilessly, to no effect; only the impress of events forced the political heads to resolve the impasse. More rounds of telegraphs between Washington and London followed. Even though the State Department maintained that the illegitimacy of the government in Rome required an unconditional surrender, Roosevelt finally accepted Eisenhower's plea he be empowered to accept a "military" surrender based on the "short terms." As the president explained to Churchill, Eisenhower must be able to "meet situations as they arise" without the encumbrances of terms "oversufficient or insufficient."[44]

A great sigh of relief greeted AFHQ's receipt of permission to proceed with Eisenhower's radio broadcast. The grant empowered Eisenhower to accept only local military surrenders and reminded him that a general armistice involving economic and political questions awaited the decision of the two governments.[45] In effect, without a settled surrender document, Eisenhower's "Message to the Italian People" became the blueprint for the military "short terms."

Having made his radio address and eager to flee Algiers, Eisenhower left on 31 July for the weekly conference with the commanders. First he flew to Tunis, where he talked to Tedder about problems facing the Mediterranean air forces. In anticipation of exploiting the strategic opportunities offered by the change of government in Rome, AFHQ requested the retention of the four heavy bomber groups dispatched to the Ninth Air Force for the raid on Ploesti. The CCS, Arnold, and the BCOS upheld ETO's rejection of the request. Three days after having his appeal denied, Eisenhower received a cable from the prime minister insisting that once the aerial campaign was renewed, AFHQ should "give them [the Italians] all manner of hell if they refused to treat with the Allies."[46] The loss of these units not only weakened the Allied air forces' ability to dish out the required hell but also compromised planning for the various operations into the peninsula then under study. After the meeting, Eisenhower flew to Palermo to visit Patton and then back to Syracuse for talks with Alexander before boarding his B-17 for the final leg of his trip to Malta.

At the conference held the day Mussolini fell, the consensus favored a concentrated drive across the Messina Straits (Buttress) over an amphibious operation south of Naples (Avalanche). In the event of an Italian collapse, planning commenced for a quick dash into Naples (Buccaneer) by two divisions, one of them airborne. Revisiting their discussions of 26 July and the CCS's approval of Avalanche, Eisenhower made a strong case for the Naples operation. Alexander proved less sanguine; he parroted Montgomery's argument that any invasion of the Italian peninsula required a concentration of forces. If the drive into the toe lacked depth, Montgomery believed the Eighth Army could accomplish just as much—tie down Axis forces in the extreme south—by posing as a threat. Why divert strength and landing craft to subsidiary operations? All agreed that a sizable Buttress made Avalanche perilous; the issue remained the availability of landing craft. The CCS's refusal to transfer the B-24s increased the risks faced in launching amphibious operations at the extreme range of Sicily-based fighters. In the end, the commanders agreed that the first priority remained gaining a lodgment across the Straits of Messina. The level of expected Axis resistance would determine whether Alexander ordered Buttress or a scaled-down opportunistic jump across the straits (Baytown). An unopposed Baytown—an unlikely event, given the German buildup there, particularly in artillery—would free up British X Corps, giving Avalanche a green light. Eisenhower also indicated he would renew his request for heavy bombers.[47] The old Husky problems resurfaced: too many headquarters provided too many options, and German reactions still determined Allied responses. Smith should have acted as ringmaster, rationalizing planning inside AFHQ or prevailing on Eisenhower to offer guidance, but neither happened.

During Eisenhower's absence from Algiers, a trough developed in the storm. It did not last long. On 2 August the Italian government, through the Vatican, requested conditions for declaring Rome an open city. Eisenhower delegated Smith the job of dealing with the flood of cables arising from Italy's appeal. Once again AFHQ received precious little direction from Washington and London. Marshall dispatched an ambiguous cable, offering no guidance because the president could not be reached. In the end, after a series of communications, neither the president nor Marshall wanted to "interfere with [Eisenhower's] plans."

That lobbed the ball back into AFHQ's court. Smith replied, stating that Eisenhower reserved the option of bombing Rome but assured Marshall that AFHQ did "*not* intend to overdo operations against Rome." Weather scrubbed the planned 4 August attack; AFHQ decided to suspend bombing missions until 13 August, when attacks resumed against the key Roman marshaling yards.[48]

Smith held a series of meetings with Rooks and Whiteley, finalizing the presentation his chief operations officers would make at the Quebec conference. Smith would have gone himself, but Eisenhower needed him in the theater. On the afternoon of 2 August, Eisenhower met with Smith and his chiefs of operations, firming up their positions. Rooks would update the chiefs on the current situation in Sicily and outline the various plans for operations against the mainland. Mussolini's fall added impetus to these plans but also elevated expectations. More important from AFHQ's perspective, Rooks must drive home to Marshall the point that expectations must be matched by commitments of manpower and materiel—especially landing craft and airpower.

An examination of high-level AFHQ communications after 25 July gives scant indication that a campaign in Sicily was even in progress. By 4 August the advance stalled: the Eighth Army remained stuck south of Catania and west of Mount Etna, Patton's movement along the north coast halted before San Fratello, and Bradley's advance froze at Troina. The lack of communication increased the anxiety felt in Algiers. Attacks were planned all along the line for 5 August.

Operational concerns numbered only one in a long laundry list of pressures on Eisenhower and Smith. On 3 August the CCS again rejected AFHQ's request for the retention of the four bomber groups. The chiefs' blanket refusal complicated ongoing planning for operations in the toe and heel of Italy and in Sardinia and Corsica, and it raised the question of whether and under what circumstance to launch Avalanche. Then there were the twists and turns on whether to bomb Rome and requests for finalized plans on civil affairs and a military government for Sicily. By 4 August, Eisenhower, according to Macmillan, began "to get rather rattled." Finally an ill-considered cable from Churchill unleashed Eisenhower's pent-up fury.

While Eisenhower conferred with his commanders, Smith sanctioned a routine psychological warfare broadcast. A long season of fair weather had permitted the Mediterranean air forces to increase the intensity of the air offensive. By the end of July the strain began to show. Many American aircrews had already exceeded their mission limits. Instead of being rotated—there were not enough trained replacements in the theater—the airmen flew additional missions, with a corresponding fall in efficiency and morale and an increase in losses from fatigue. AFHQ had little choice but to order a reduction in air activity. The temporary bombing halt also allowed for the reorientation of air staff planning from tactical to economic targets. The psychological warfare section, making a virtue of necessity, prepared a broadcast for the Italians, telling them that the bombing hiatus was intended to give them time to consider their options before the air campaign commenced in earnest. The broadcast, authorized by Macmillan and Smith, went out in Eisenhower's name. Churchill peevishly told Hopkins that Eisenhower had no right to delve into political questions. "Politicians should do the talking," the prime minister wrote, "and generals the fighting."[49]

Incensed by the multiple rejections of his pleas for air units, Eisenhower reacted angrily to Churchill's intrusion. Earlier that day Eisenhower sent Alexander an uncharacteristically scorching letter, upbraiding him for sending his situation reports to London and not Algiers, thus giving the BCOS better information on the fighting in Sicily than AFHQ possessed.[50] Algiers had heard nothing from Sicily in two days. After hearing Churchill's complaint, Eisenhower called in Smith and Macmillan and vented on them for two hours. Together they composed letters to Marshall and the prime minister. "I do not see how war can be conducted successfully," the communication with Marshall complained, "if every act of the Allied Command-in-Chief must be referred back to the home government for advance approval." He marveled why, when things went badly, a commander received all manner of material and moral support—here Eisenhower was referring to the Darlan deal and the period following Casablanca—but when things went well, "some individuals who are running the war begin to take an enormous interest in its detailed direction."[51]

The one pillar of Eisenhower's stature as supreme commander rested on his insistence on Anglo-American teamwork. Also that day—with American forces poised to renew the drive on Messina—the BBC reported, "American soldiers [are] eating grapes and meeting no opposition" while the British and Canadians did the heavy fighting. As he heatedly told Churchill, cooperation with the British "has been the guiding precept of my existence." Eisenhower believed the BBC commentary might seriously undermine Allied solidarity at this, a key juncture in the campaign.[52] Hughes for one applauded Eisenhower for finally asserting himself. "I am proud of Ike!" Hughes noted. "He is on his hind legs and growling." His old buddy proclaimed it "Ike's Fourth of July."[53]

The next day Smith flew to Sicily for talks with Alexander. The army group commander now insisted on Buttress as "a necessary follow up for HUSKY." The fortifications and heavy antiaircraft defenses under construction on the Reggio side of the straits impacted, in Alexander's estimate, "our efforts to interfere with his evacuation when the break comes." A full-blooded crossing of the straits (Buttress) would secure navigation and provide a threat and holding action, "materially contributing to a successful AVALANCHE." The problem remained that Buttress precluded the employment of British X Corps from North Africa—earmarked for the Salerno Bay landings—in Avalanche. The British general advised the cancellation of the surprise landings in Naples (Barracuda) but emphasized Naples' vital importance as a port and as flank cover for German forces in the south of Italy. Alexander never considered the possibility that the Germans would not seriously contest in the south. A glance at a map indicated Buttress and Avalanche could never be interdependent operations. A disappointed Smith flew back to Algiers. Eisenhower stored all this away, instructed Smith to wire Washington and London with the results of his conference with Alexander and his staff, but refrained from pushing a more aggressive policy on his subordinate.[54]

The pressures on Eisenhower took a severe toll on his health. Faced with all the aggravations associated with finalizing the surrender terms, determining the parameters for military government in Sicily, and choosing from the long menu of operations for the invasion of Italy, Eisenhower received word his name had been included on the promotion list for colonel in the regular army. British officers could not believe that Eisenhower, a four-star general and supreme commander, remained a permanent lieutenant colonel. One obstacle remained: promotion depended on his passing a physical examination. Smoking sixty Camels a day and not eating or sleeping properly, Eisenhower's blood pressure went through the roof. On 10 August he finally saw a doctor, who, alarmed by Eisenhower's gray visage, ordered bed rest but dared not record his "official" blood pressure. Except for two brief morning appearances at headquarters, Eisenhower spent the next six days in lockdown on the farm. Even on 15 August, when he received a clean bill of health, Eisenhower still suffered from mild hypertension. For obvious reasons, Eisenhower kept his condition secret.[55]

Confined to bed "as much as his nervous temperament" allowed, Butcher reported that Eisenhower "could not harness his brain cells." Plenty occupied his mind. He thought back to Marshall's last visit to Algiers, when the chief had reproached him for listening to conservative planners. Marshall foresaw great advantages in ending Husky as quickly as possible. The rewards, Marshall instructed him, "may justify you accepting calculated risks." Eisenhower remembered the reference to Nelson, Grant, and Lee.[56] Marshall's admonitions preyed on him. Nelson, Grant, and Lee did not refer every decision to their political and military bosses, and they frequently ignored directives from above when these conflicted with their own designs. He lamented the advent of modern communications. "If we were still in the day of sailing ships," he confided in Butcher, AFHQ could act decisively. Instead, Eisenhower must plead with Washington and London for authority to act and "wait for the two capitals to concur and direct."[57]

On 14 August Eisenhower fretted about how history would record his leadership. He vigorously lectured Butcher that in the eyes of history, "his mistakes" numbered two: "landing at Casablanca and our super-cautious approach to Italy." Instead of launching Husky in the south, Eisenhower thought he should have insisted on making "simultaneous landings on both sides of the Messina Straits." Such a Grant-like gambit would have cut off Sicily, obtained wholesale surrenders, saved manpower and equipment (especially all-important landing craft), and "permitted a rapid rush on the mainland."[58]

Eisenhower's confinement coincided with the climax of the Sicilian fighting. The Germans began preparations for withdrawing from Sicily within two days of Mussolini's fall. They fell back into a secondary line and continued resisting fiercely in ideal defensive country. When the First Infantry Division finally took Troina and Eighth Army secured Adrano, compromising the Germans' second line of defense, Kesselring initiated the German evacuation on the night of 11–12 August. As predicted, the Germans dictated the pace of operations in Sicily. Even though Ultra provided plenty of warnings about German intentions, neither the Fifteenth Army Group nor AFHQ intervened, insisting on coordinated action interdicting the German withdrawal. In the north, Patton staged three fruitless amphibious end runs aimed at cutting off the retreating enemy. Eisenhower's insistence on the inviolability of command spheres thwarted his exercise of the full warrant of his authority, and his feelings of impotence produced his edginess. He delegated Torch planning to Clark, and Montgomery drove the decision to launch concentrated landings in southeast Sicily. Now on 14 August, three days into the German evacuation, he ruminated over what he might have done weeks before, instead of asserting his command authority and demanding that the straits be sealed. Three days later he told Hughes how much he regretted deferring to Alexander. "Ike says AFHQ [is] strategic HQ," Hughes noted, "but [he is] not going to raise [his] blood pressure trying to make

[the] idea stick."[59] In the estimate of his most authoritative biographer, Carlo D'Este, "Eisenhower played no role [in closing the Straits of Messina], made no important decisions, and had virtually no impact on Operation HUSKY."[60]

With Eisenhower out of the office, Smith filled the void but possessed no authority to alter the rapidly unfolding events. Most of his attention remained riveted on composing a series of appreciations for the Quebec talks, assessing the state of Allied planning for the invasion of Italy. These offer distilled insights into Smith's thinking. He rued the "terrible inflexibility" of amphibious operations because success or failure depended on the serviceability of available landing craft. In his mind, the greatest uncertainty, other than landing craft, rested in predicting German reactions. Intelligence painted a gloomy picture of the increased flow of German forces into Italy. If the Germans defended southern Italy in strength, Avalanche became problematic, despite the CCS's "very distinct preference for the operation." Baytown and Buttress offered advantages—opening the straits to navigation and forward air bases—but their primary aim centered on holding German forces in place, denying them the ability to move to the Salerno area. Without a major port, Montgomery could sustain only six divisions in Calabria. If the Germans held Calabria, "almost certainly," Smith concluded, "the result would be a stalemate," or at best, a "slow, laborious advance" north.[61]

Smith never doubted that Clark's landings in Salerno Bay—three British divisions followed by U.S. VI Corps—would gain a beachhead; the problem revolved around holding it. "AVALANCHE and succeeding operations" depended on "the build-up race" between Allied and German forces. Once the Germans saw that the Salerno landings lacked real strength, they might "move to the sound of the guns." Everything rode on landing craft and shipping on the Allied side, and the German response and the Italian disposition on the other. Salerno and what followed "depended entirely on the nature of the German reaction." Smith thought if the Allies won the logistics and manpower contest—AFHQ eventually expected to move seven divisions, including one airborne, and tactical air units in or through the Salerno beachhead—they would prevail. But if the Germans received strong reinforcements, the Allied forces would have their hands full "preventing them from ejecting us." Even in the event the Germans abandoned the defense of southern Italy, Montgomery's forces, owing to poor communications and "the physical difficulties of the country and enemy demolitions," could offer little appreciable aid to the Avalanche forces. Even if Naples fell, with its great port, Smith foresaw attritional fighting in the mountains north of the city. The expected losses in landing craft and shipping in Salerno ruled out another amphibious operation on that scale for the rest of the year. Smith grimly predicted the Allies would "fight our way slowly and painfully up Italy."

Ultra intercepts on 13 August rendered Smith into Cassandra—or so it appeared at the time. Intelligence indicated the Germans planned to withdraw to a line at Pisa-Fimini, denying the Allies the Po Valley. The German forces in the extreme south would retire, covered by two divisions in the Naples-Salerno area and another two in Rome.[62] Now prospects brightened. "If German resistance in Calabria weakens," Buttress could be canceled, freeing the British Fifty-sixth Division for Avalanche. In an amazing turnaround, Smith now talked in terms of exploiting Baytown. Montgomery's forces would "move into Calabria and advance north and east with a view of joining up with AVALANCHE forces and occupying the Heel."[63]

Eisenhower's mood scarcely improved with his return to work on 16 August. In the morning he flew to Tunis, where he rubber-stamped the settlement engineered by Smith among the commanders: Baytown would be launched "as early as possible," providing additional lift for Avalanche; Fifth Army would revert to Fifteenth Army Group command; and planning for a rush landing in the Gulf of Taranto (Goblet) was reinstated.[64] Montgomery recognized the obvious flaws produced by what would be termed "mission creep" today, but he stood powerless to change the rush to bounce onto the mainland. Relieved as the "Sicilian phase of the campaign" drew to a conclusion, Eisenhower surveyed the meager fruits of victory. It had taken thirty-eight days for four Allied corps numbering in excess of 480,000 men to defeat four German divisions, never more than 60,000 strong. Despite overwhelming air and naval superiority, AFHQ's forces failed to seal the straits. The veteran German divisions—complete with weapons and transport—completed their evacuation across the straits and added their strength to the growing German order of battle in Italy. A devastated and empty Messina would fall the next day.

Eisenhower rewarded Smith by sending him to Sicily to witness Patton's victorious entry into Messina. Eisenhower flew back to Algiers, where a bombshell greeted him that sent his blood pressure soaring. Word of Patton's assaulting of enlisted men in Sicilian field hospitals had filtered back to Algiers. The fact that it took six days for information about Patton's second offense to reach Algiers underlined how isolated AFHQ remained from the front, in part because Bradley and Alexander sat on the story. The news arrived in Algiers through two

Medical Corps channels. On 16 August Dr. Perrin Long, medical consultant to NATO, returned from an inspection tour in Sicily and notified Hughes about "Patton slapping NPs [neuropsychiatric cases, the U.S. Army's term for battle fatigue]."[65] Confirmation reached Eisenhower that day through BG Frederick Blessé, AFHQ's chief surgeon. Initially, he chalked the story up to "the normal grousing of soldiers" and dismissed it as yet another example of Patton being Patton. But the more Eisenhower thought about it, the more worried he became. Eisenhower might have been reminded of President Harding's remark that it was not his enemies that kept him walking the floors each night; it was his damned friends. The next day he wrote a blistering letter of reprimand and handed it to Blessé with instructions to present the handwritten letter personally to Patton and conduct an investigation.[66]

Smith flew to Fifteenth Army Group headquarters south of Syracuse, where he met Lemnitzer, who had replaced Huebner as Alexander's deputy chief of staff. They drove north along the tortuous coastal road. Because of detours, the drive took longer than the usual two hours, and Smith missed Patton's triumph. That proved the least of his problems.

Patton's convoy of staff cars was greeted by shells fired by German artillery across the straits; the car behind Patton was hit, and a third vehicle carrying Truscott had all its tires blown off from the concussion. Near misses always fortified Patton's sense of destiny, but this episode left him unnerved. The ceremony itself did not amount to much: a nervous Patton accepted the surrender from civil and military authorities and quickly left. Leaving Messina, Patton's car encountered the one carrying Smith and Lemnitzer at the crest of a hill. Patton puzzled over why Smith's car was stopped and guessed, "it would be reasonable to suppose because the road beyond the crest was under fire." Patton's chief of staff, BG Hobart "Hap" Gay, had taken the precaution of sending his aide, LT George Murname, to meet Smith on the road to Messina. As they approached the crest, Smith inquired about the likelihood of coming under fire, and Murname reported it could happen. Just then a battery of Long Toms on the hills above Messina opened up. According to Gay, "Smith thought it was enemy shells arriving and jumped from the car into the ditch in one leap." Lemnitzer and Murname informed Smith it was safe, but he refused to come up. After a few moments, a "pale, gray, and shaky" Smith climbed out of the culvert and got back in the car just as Patton pulled up.[67]

Smith transferred into Patton's vehicle, and they drove to Truscott's headquarters for lunch. Patton pushed Smith on promotions for his staff. As evidenced by Smith's treatment of Maud Muller, AFHQ held a low opinion of Patton's staff. Smith sidestepped the issue, explaining that Eisenhower had formed the Seventh Army as an expedient, and the staff knew there would be no automatic promotions. Patton acknowledged that but stated, "now that we had demonstrated our ability, we demanded recognition, not as a favour but as a right." Patton felt sure Smith would "do his best to prevent it, but I will get them [the promotions] anyhow. Smith is a typical s.o.b." After the meeting, Patton felt "let down. The reaction from intense mental and physical activity to a status of inertia is very difficult."[68] He had no way of knowing how long his inertia would last.

Gay refrained from telling his boss about Smith's case of nerves. The whole island was abuzz with tales of Patton's transgressions, and Gay expected the anvil to drop at any moment. Other than illustrating Patton's mental instability, the episodes in the hospitals were motivated by Patton's perverse warrior faith. As he recorded in his diary and later told Hughes, Patton believed he was doing his "plain duty to a couple of cowards." Patton believed in Valhalla and considered cowardice the worst of all possible sins; he thought he was saving the souls of the two "yellow bastards" he had assaulted.[69] In expectation of the inevitable fallout from his boss's actions in Sicily, Gay wisely decided not to relate the incendiary story of Smith's cowering in the ditch to the voluble Patton. Gay calculated Patton could ill afford to alienate Eisenhower's powerful lieutenant. Whether prompted by memories of his wounding in France or his recent brush with death at the hands of the Luftwaffe, Smith's jitters are understandable. Nonetheless, if the story of "the headquarters hero who had no guts" ever made the rounds, it would have lacerated Smith's reputation, might well have compromised his credibility, and may have undermined his usefulness as chief of staff. It never did.[70]

Smith's eventful day was far from over. A staff officer chased him down to inform him that AFHQ had issued an "all points bulletin" for his immediate return to headquarters. The hurried trip back to Algiers must have been a doleful one; he had ample time to ruminate over the day's events and contemplate what the future held in store. He had no way of knowing he stood poised on the most intriguing episode in his army life.

22

The Italian Job

Badoglio's government promised Italy's "war will go on," but within a week of Mussolini's ouster, it was looking for ways to end it. Three options presented themselves, none of them very attractive. First, Italy could end the alliance with Germany and go over to the Allies. Second, Italy could stay in the Axis but seek an accord with Hitler that allowed it to pursue a separate peace, in the hope the Germans might recognize the strategic benefits of a neutral Italy. Third, Italy could continue the war while pursuing secret surrender negotiations. Considering the Anglo-American policy of unconditional surrender and, more to the point, the likely German response, the Italian leadership rejected the first option. Mussolini's arrest, in German eyes, nullified the "Pact of Steel." Violating Italian sovereignty, the Germans moved quickly, seizing the Brenner Pass and securing vital transportation arteries, airfields, and ports. The German high command initiated the phased movement of eight divisions into northern Italy, doubling the number of German troops "defending" the country. Berlin demonstrated no interest in assuming additional occupation burdens in exchange for any nebulous advantages offered by neutralizing Italy. Instead, the Germans began to intersperse their units with Italian forces in Herzegovina, Montenegro, Albania, Greece (including Crete), and the Dodecanese. The regime in Rome hoped for time to consolidate its power base, but the rapid German reaction meant Italy could not delay. Any hint of an Italian betrayal would trigger an immediate German seizure of power and the installation of a new fascist regime. The Italian government fell prey to a paralysis of dread, prompted not by *what* the Germans might do but *when*. From Rome's point of view, only the last alternative—surrender to the Allies—held any prospect of removing Italy from the war. Wanting to change sides but unprepared to accept surrender, Badoglio decided to initiate contact. On 31 July he dispatched two diplomats—one to Lisbon and the other to Tangier—to sound out the British on Allied intentions.

These peace feelers came to nothing. Deliberately evasive, the Italian envoys stressed the deteriorating situation in Italy, spoke of their fear of a German putsch or a communist rising, and requested diversionary attacks against the south of France or the Balkans, allowing Badoglio time and space to strengthen his position before Italy launched any effort to eject the Germans from the peninsula. No mention was made of peace terms.

Badoglio then decided to employ a military channel. He selected BG Giuseppe Castellano, chief of GEN Vittorio Ambrosio's military office, to travel to Madrid and Lisbon. Moving under cover as a member of a diplomatic party dispatched to the Portuguese capital, Castellano arrived in Madrid on 15 August. He recruited the Italian consul, Franco Mantanari, as his interpreter, and the pair made their way to the British embassy, where Ambassador Samuel Hoare received them. Castellano introduced himself and assured Hoare that he enjoyed the full confidence of Marshal Badoglio. He took the same tack as the diplomats at first, claiming the Italian government could not take action against the Germans until the Allies invaded Italy north of Rome and in force. Then he made a startling proposal: "We are not in a position to make any terms. We will accept unconditional surrender provided we can join the Allies in fighting the Germans." Essentially, he offered a combination of options one and three, and he made this proposal entirely on his own initiative.

As further enticement, Castellano offered intelligence on German intentions and deployments in Italy. Speed was of the essence. Badoglio wanted immediate action. The Germans already had thirteen divisions in Italy, with more troops arriving each week. In essence, Italy was already an occupied country; at the first hint of duplicity, the Germans would seize control. On 6 August the Axis foreign ministers and general staffs met at Trovisto, where the Germans confirmed their intention, in the event of an Allied invasion, to fall back to a line at Genoa-Ravenna. In effect, the Axis and *Supremo Commando* were already dead letters. The Germans operated only in their own interests and were prepared to sacrifice southern and central Italy. Allied amphibious landings north of Rome would find an Italian government and its armed forces fully ready—if supplied and supported—to take up the sword against the Germans. In a nice twist, Castellano painted the Germans—not the Italians—as the betrayers. Without instructions from the Foreign Office, the British ambassador listened to Castellano's pitch and promised only to forward his proposal to London. Hoare penned Castellano a letter of introduction to the British ambassador in Lisbon, wished him good luck, and immediately dispatched a cable to the Foreign Office.

Returning to his hotel, Castellano mulled over what had just transpired. He worried that Hoare might not attach much significance to the offer of military cooperation. Nor had he referred to the Americans. Agitated, Castellano returned to the embassy and requested that Eisenhower send a senior staff officer to Lisbon to join in the talks. Hoare concurred and sent a second wire to London.[1]

Castellano's meeting with Hoare raised the curtain on the melodrama that became the Italian surrender. Full of shady customers, intrigue and deception, "plots, counter-plots and cross-plots," unlikely twists, secret missions, abductions, and exotic locales, and with the destinies of campaigns and ancient dynasties hanging in the balance, the story, according to Smith, possessed "all the elements of an E. Phillips Oppenheim novel," except that fact proved stranger than fiction.[2] And the starring role fell on Beetle Smith—a part that, in some ways, he was born to play.

The Lisbon Show: "Amateur Theatricals"

AFHQ remained in the dark about these diplomatic developments. The Foreign Office and State Department never informed Algiers of the initial Italian peace feelers, and although a representative of the headquarters would now assume the lead in talks with Castellano, it took two days before AFHQ was informed of the events in Madrid and the proposed talks in Lisbon. Then on 17 August AFHQ received a battery of cables that hit Algiers like a bombshell. The Patton affair took the back burner.

Hoare's dispatch reached Algiers via ETO headquarters in London. Hoare gave a full account of the meeting with the Italian general. Unconditional surrender and Italian cooperation were contingent on an Allied invasion north of Rome. Without a move on Rome and a promise of cobelligerent status, Hoare warned, "the Italian Government will not have sufficient courage [or] justification to make a complete volte-face and will drift impotently into chaos."[3]

In a separate cable, Eden raised a red flag. "Although at first sight this offer of cooperation sounds tempting," he advised Churchill in Quebec, "if we accept it it will land us in all sorts of difficulties both military and political with few if any corresponding advantages." He suggested Allied leaders not depart from the "present policy of refusing to make the Italian government any promises or enter into any bargain with them in return for their surrender." The problem was that no such policy existed, and it would not exist until the two political heads fashioned one at the Quadrant talks. In another telegram, Eden reported the Italian emissary's request that a senior staff officer join in the talks in Lisbon. Eisenhower replied that, with Smith in Sicily and time at a premium, he would send Strong. It appeared that Smith's ill-starred trip to Sicily had cost him a chance to play Allied secret agent. However, this time the fates worked in his favor. Not wanting to give the impression of this being a British show, the political heads insisted on the dispatch of two officers—one British and one American. This directive prompted the all-points bulletin for Smith.[4]

Upon returning to headquarters, Smith received a briefing on events and read the correspondence. In the absence of firm instructions from above, Eisenhower acted on the authority granted him in a 6 August directive to employ the "military" terms should the opportunity arise. He instructed Smith and Strong to gather as much intelligence as possible, make no pledge of active Allied cooperation with the Italian army or recognition of the Italian government, and underscore that Badoglio and the armed forces had no recourse but to trust in the decency and sense of justice of the Western democracies.[5]

The next day AFHQ finally received directives for the Lisbon mission—known as the Quebec Memorandum—which varied little from the instructions Eisenhower had already given Smith and Strong. They were to grant the Italians no room for maneuver. Since the final surrender conditions remained undecided, Smith should employ the "short terms." The Italians must understand that their surrender would be unconditional, even though the words never appeared in the document. Badoglio must acknowledge Italy's surrender, announce the armistice in tandem with the main Allied invasion, and send the navy, merchant marine, and aircraft to Allied-controlled territory. Additionally, the Italians must agree to "collaborate with the Allies and resist the Germans." An acceptance of these military conditions obligated the Italian government to consent later to a comprehensive set of conditions. In the event Italy complied with the terms, Eisenhower had the authority to temper the armistice conditions proportionate to the level of Italian assistance.[6]

The Quebec Memorandum clarified certain elements while muddying others. Smith faced a very difficult assignment. AFHQ possessed the authority to accept an Italian surrender but not to negotiate one. Smith could offer few concrete inducements other than holding up Sicily as an example of the benign treatment Italy could expect from Allied forces in the future. Most vital of all, Smith must evade the central question:

could the Allies stage landings near Rome? As Smith knew very well, Avalanche alone stretched Allied resources to the limit.

Smith had little time to prepare before setting off for Gibraltar on the first leg of the trip to Lisbon. Since his passport listed his next of kin as the adjutant general of the U.S. Army, and with no time to secure the necessary American documents, Smith would travel with British papers, disguised as a businessman. This meant a quick trip to a haberdashery, since Beetle had no civilian clothes. He arrived at Strong's quarters outfitted in a new suit. Smith did his best to look the part, dressed in gray flannel pants, jacket and tie, and crowned with a fedora. Much to Strong's astonishment, Smith opened his coat, displayed a holster under each arm, and then produced two other pistols concealed in his hip pockets. "If we were cornered," Strong recalled, "I envisioned a desperate gunfight."[7] The ubiquitous cigarette hanging from Smith's lip topped off the Bogart look.

Apparently, it never occurred to anyone—except perhaps the heavily armed Smith—the huge security risk Eisenhower was taking by sending Smith and Strong to the espionage capital of Europe. Smith was a font of secret information; he had Ultra clearance, attended all the conferences, and ran planning for the next operation.

The two officers then drove to Maison Blanche to board their flight. Macmillan came to see them off, and when he saw Smith, he broke into laughter. For starters, Smith looked odd out of uniform. Macmillan suggested he lose the hat, pointing out that "no British traveler of whatever class would walk about with [that] unusual decoration." No doubt the proper Briton would have been appalled had he known what Beetle concealed under his clothes. On that note, the "amateur theatrical" began.[8]

In Gibraltar, Smith received his traveling papers. The passport read: Mr. Walter Smith, businessman, of No. 10 Grosvenor Square, London—the address of ETO headquarters. After a short stay in Gibraltar, they flew on to Lisbon. The young American chargé, George Kennan, met them at the airport. They drove through the streets of Lisbon in a broken-down Buick to Kennan's flat and awaited instructions. Finally, word came to proceed to British ambassador Ronald Campbell's residence, where they met Castellano and his interpreter. By now it was ten o'clock at night.[9]

In typical Smith fashion, he got right to the point, stating he had come to Lisbon on the presumption the Italian forces intended to capitulate; only then would Eisenhower agree to a cessation of hostilities. Smith made it clear that the terms offered only a military armistice and must be unconditional. He added without emphasis that political, financial, and economic terms would follow.

Clearly caught flat-footed, Castellano replied there must be a mistake. He had come only to confer on how best to orchestrate Italy's joining the Allies in the war against Germany; his government's sole aim was to expel the Germans from Italy in collaboration with the Allies. In any case, Castellano made it clear he lacked the authority to conclude a surrender. In common with the rest of the Italian leadership, Castellano retained the Mussolini myth of Italy's status as a great power. He believed he had something to trade. Smith's intractable posture soon disabused Castellano of that Italian caprice.

Smith informed Castellano that Eisenhower's mandate limited discussions to conditions for terminating hostilities between the Allied and Italian armed forces. Italy's status and any question of Italian participation in the war fell to the political heads. He added that Eisenhower wanted no political interference in military matters. Smith then read the "short terms" paragraph by paragraph, pausing occasionally to amplify points where Eisenhower reserved some elasticity. With the Italian general back on his heels, Smith offered an inducement. He handed Castellano a copy of the Quebec Memorandum and promised AFHQ would lend all possible assistance to Italian forces or citizens who resisted or obstructed German military efforts. Smith also noted that this stipulation would be included in the language of the armistice conditions. Smith took this opportunity to emphasize the humane treatment received by the Sicilian population under Allied occupation. On that note, Smith concluded the first phase of the discussions. The Allied representatives exited the room, leaving Castellano and Mantanari to digest what had just transpired.[10]

Smith conferred with Strong, Campbell, and Kennan. After a calculated interval, the Allied representatives reentered the room and resumed the conference. Castellano rose and informed them he possessed no authority to discuss surrender terms but desired further explanation of the specifics of the conditions. Smith replied that although he might discuss certain points, he could grant no concessions. Castellano took pains to point out that, in view of the presence of German forces on the peninsula, his government might have serious difficulty complying with all the terms, particularly guaranteeing that the Germans would not move Allied prisoners to Germany. Smith assured Castellano that AFHQ understood the difficulties facing the Italian government but expected the Italian armed forces and Badoglio's government to carry out the conditions as best they could.[11]

In common with the majority of Americans of his generation, Smith held Italians in low regard. In the popular imagination, Italians equated, albeit unfairly, with mob bosses and racketeers such as Al Capone. Castellano fit the bill—short, dark, and a little too well dressed. In Smith's opinion, Castellano appeared competent enough and well connected, but since Italian "national traits are different from ours," he never entirely trusted the Italian staff officer. Acting on the Italians' obvious fear of the Germans, Smith and Strong exaggerated Allied strength.[12]

The discussion then turned to the mechanisms for surrendering Italian warships and aircraft. Smith emphasized that the Italian fleet must surrender, and its future disposition would be dependent on the will of the supreme commander. When Castellano warned that fuel shortages would present problems in executing some of the conditions, Smith coldly replied that the Italian authorities must find the necessary petroleum if they wished to preserve their ships and aircraft. Castellano pointed out that the dispersal of German troops in Italy and the Balkans made it unlikely the Italians could guarantee the Allies full usage of airfields and ports or the withdrawal of Italian garrisons outside Italy. The Allied negotiators reassured Castellano they did not expect the impossible.

Castellano broached the issue of Italian sovereignty, but Smith reiterated he had no power to discuss matters relating to the future of the Italian government. Again pointing to the fair and generous military occupation of Sicily, Smith instructed Castellano that the Allies intended to administer "liberated" territories in the same fashion through military government.

Castellano then shifted the conversation to the monarchy and fears for the king's safety. Smith "attached real significance to this point." The Allied representatives took pains to assure Castellano that the king could expect all due consideration if he escaped Rome. All parties assumed the king and government would leave the capital "temporarily." Undoubtedly impressed, Castellano told Smith he would take the surrender document back to his government.[13]

As the discussions continued, Castellano repeatedly tacked back to the question of Italian military collaboration. Smith deflected him, reconfirming that the Italian armed forces must first surrender before the Allied governments would even consider Italian participation in the war. Smith requested that Castellano carefully consider the Quebec Memorandum. Then Smith raised the ante; he told Castellano the Allies never envisioned active Italian assistance in fighting Germany. This pronouncement took the wind out of Castellano's sails. Smith then repeated that he could pledge that the final settlement would contain modifications in Italy's favor, dependent on the level of assistance the Italian government provided against Germany for the duration of the war. Italian forces that fought the Germans, destroyed German property, and hindered German movements would receive all possible support from Allied forces.

Smith recognized the Italians' fear of a German putsch and occupation. At the first hint of an Italian betrayal, the Germans would retaliate with a vengeance; Castellano told the Allied emissaries that his government suspected the Germans would employ poison gas in Italian cities. Smith assured Castellano the Allies would reply in kind. Smith then remarked that in exchange for deliverance from a long war of attrition, the Italians should steel themselves for a few days of German "vindictive action."[14] Doubtless, Castellano took little comfort from Smith's assurances.

Castellano painted a grim picture of the situation in Rome: the streets crawled with German agents; a paratrooper division had moved into the environs; Italian forces had largely withdrawn following the declaration of Rome as an open city; and the population, swollen by residents of other cities who believed the Allies would not bomb the Eternal City, remained critically short of fuel and food. Castellano pointed out that portions of the Italian government would have to leave the capital coincidental with the announcement of an armistice. For that to take place, the Italians must know the time and place of the expected Allied invasion.

Smith informed Castellano that, as a soldier, he must understand the impossibility of divulging the details of Allied planning. If the Badoglio government accepted the surrender terms, AFHQ would grant five or six hours' grace before Eisenhower made the formal announcement, followed by Badoglio's proclamation of the end of hostilities. Aghast, Castellano plaintively indicated that a longer period, something like two weeks, would be required between the Allied invasion and the Italian announcement; otherwise, the Italian government and armed forces could not possibly make the necessary preparations. Very aware of the vulnerability of Avalanche, Smith knew this request was impossible. Smith's negotiating stance had been carefully stage-managed in advance; he now realized he had Castellano on the hook, so the experienced angler decided to give him some line. Smith promised to consult Eisenhower on the question of the timing of the announcement. In reality, Smith knew that Eisenhower placed great significance on Badoglio's making a public announcement only hours before the Allies landed in

Salerno Bay; there was no chance he would budge on the timing of that announcement.

Talks then centered on forging direct contacts between Rome and Algiers. The Italian government must forward acceptance of the deal to AFHQ by 28 August. The British would furnish Montanari with a special radio and cipher. If the Germans compromised the direct link, Badoglio should dispatch a message through the British embassy in the Vatican. If Rome made no reply by 30 August, the Allies would consider negotiations terminated. In the event Badoglio accepted Allied conditions, another meeting between Italian and Allied representatives would take place in Sicily on 31 August. Smith stipulated the exact route information and times.

Campbell and Kennan excused themselves, and discussions turned to strictly military matters. Strong produced a map and questioned Castellano on German troop deployments. At first evasive, Castellano surveyed the map and, observing how accurate it appeared to be, began offering detailed intelligence on the German order of battle. He estimated German troop strength in Italy at 400,000—significantly larger than AFHQ previously thought. Strong did not ask about, and Castellano did not offer, any intelligence on the Italian order of battle. More important, Castellano revealed German intentions. At a recent conference, the German command had revealed they intended to withdraw from southern and central Italy into a line at Genoa-Ravenna. They also planned to retain Sardinia and Corsica. The German leadership worried about the vulnerability of their lines of communication through the Brenner Pass and expected Allied landings near Leghorn. All this came as very good news to Smith and Strong. Suddenly the prospects of a successful Avalanche brightened significantly, as did the possibility of taking Rome much earlier and at a much reduced cost.[15]

Lubricated by a couple whiskey and sodas, Castellano's tongue loosened. He spoke of Italian honor and the widespread disgust among senior officers owing to the Germans' pitiless abandonment of Italian forces in Russia and North Africa. He talked about his role in Mussolini's downfall and portrayed himself as the most vocal advocate in Badoglio's circle of a separate peace with the Western democracies. He told how Dino Grandi had fallen victim to his own ego; how he had been seduced into taking the lead in the Fascist Grand Council, assuming he would be named Mussolini's successor, and had then been double-crossed when the king asked Badoglio to form the new government.

All this talk of double-dealing did little to boost Smith and Strong's confidence in the Italian leadership. They wondered why Castellano possessed no written credentials or formal instructions from Badoglio.

Nonetheless, both came away from the all-night session believing AFHQ had much to gain and little to lose in pursuing the line Smith had taken. With the sun breaking through the window, the talks concluded. They had been at it for nine hours. Smith came forward, shook Castellano's hand, and expressed his hope that their meeting marked the beginning of a new friendship between Italy and the Allies.[16]

The next day Smith and Strong returned to Algiers, confident they had fulfilled their mission. Campbell, a veteran diplomat, thought the negotiations the most brilliant he had ever witnessed. The British ambassador gave 9-to-1 odds that the Italian government would accept the terms offered by Smith "without further parley."[17] Smith and Strong remained less sanguine. The discussions with Castellano revealed the deep rifts existing in Badoglio's government and in the Italian high command. In addition, Smith and Strong appreciated the "intense hatred and intense fear of the Germans" among much of the Italian political and military elite. This knowledge offered a dizzying array of opportunities and possible pitfalls—opportunities for leveraging an Italian capitulation, but also the possibility that all would go up in smoke. Smith thought the Italians would likely make one more attempt to achieve collaboration short of capitulation.[18]

Anxious to hear the complete story, Eisenhower met Smith and Strong that evening at Maison Blanche. Eisenhower wholeheartedly endorsed Smith's conclusions and requested that he forward a report of his findings to the CCS. In the memorandum that appeared over Eisenhower's name, Smith summarized the meeting, concluding that the Italian government evidenced "a complete willingness to cooperate," provided it received "reasonable assurance of protection and support." Badoglio might conclude a peace, but not before making renewed efforts to gain cobelligerent status. Throughout his talks with Castellano, Smith had deliberately avoided using the term *unconditional surrender*. "Our aim was to get Italy out of the war," he later recalled. "But we needed a government in Italy and no government which signed 'unconditional surrender' would have lasted 48-hours."[19]

Since Castellano's return to Rome would take an entire week, there was little to do but wait—or so it seemed. Then on 25 August the story took a bizarre twist. A new player entered the stage in the person of MG Giacomo Zanussi, representative of the chief of the army staff, GEN Mario Roatta. Roatta had come away from the last meeting between the German and Italian general staffs in Bologna on 15 August deeply troubled. Although favoring a continuation of the alliance with Germany, Roatta interpreted the increased enmity he encountered from the chief of the German high command operations staff, GEN Alfred Jodl, and Rommel during the acrimonious talks as convincing evidence that the Germans had no interest in a joint defense of Italy. The next day in a meeting with the king, he finally heard of Castellano's mission. Roatta talked the situation over with his confederate LTG Giacomo Carboni, commander of Italian forces around Rome and soon to be head of Military Intelligence. With Castellano out of communication, nobody knew the results of his meetings in Lisbon. Together, Roatta and Carboni decided to send Zanussi on a separate mission to Lisbon. Zanussi carried no credentials, not even a letter of introduction, but he brought along a noteworthy prisoner of war, British LTG Adrian Carton de Wiart, as a token of good faith. The one-eyed, one-armed de Wiart seemed a singularly odd choice as a companion on a clandestine mission. "We were greatly annoyed at his bringing . . . Carton de Wiart," Smith remarked, "who was known everywhere in Europe." The general was packed off to Gibraltar and kept under wraps.[20]

Campbell initially refused to meet with Zanussi, explaining through an intermediary that since Castellano already had a copy of the surrender terms, no further discussions need take place. He did ask Zanussi to remain in Lisbon in the event the situation changed—and change it did. On 27 August the political heads at Quebec finally agreed on the "long terms." The Foreign Office acted with remarkable speed—first, because diplomatic channels were typically quicker than military routing, and second, because Eden accelerated the dispatch because he had long opposed any "military" armistice. London directed Campbell to present Zanussi with the long terms. Campbell wired London, questioning the wisdom of doing so when the Italian government had probably already received the military terms. In fact, Castellano's return to Rome had been delayed, and he did not present AFHQ's surrender conditions to Badoglio until the next morning. The Foreign Office backtracked: AFHQ could employ the "short terms" if military expediency required it, but the "long terms" now represented the agreed-on policy of the two governments. As party to the Castellano talks, and remembering his prediction, Campbell followed directions, met with Zanussi, and handed him a copy of the "long terms," but he took the liberty of informing the Italian general that the terms now in his possession substantially resembled those Castellano had carried back to Rome.[21]

Zanussi made no comment when he read the opening line containing the words "unconditional surrender." He raised objections that the document made no reference to Italian-Allied military cooperation and informed Campbell that his sole mission was to forge an agreement for Allied-Italian military cooperation to forestall a German seizure of power. Campbell could only read him the Quebec Memorandum, which held out a vague promise of Italy joining the Allies in some form.

AFHQ received the forty-one-paragraph "long terms" document later that day, together with instructions to employ it in all future contacts with the Italians. When Eisenhower and Smith discovered Campbell had given a new Italian negotiator a copy, they felt like they had been cut off at the knees. Smith wrote to Marshall expressing AFHQ's "grave apprehension" that "the secrecy of the whole affair and its ultimately successful result may be seriously compromised." Smith held out the possibility that Castellano might come to Sicily on 31 August "with a signed acceptance of the original short term military instrument," and he asked permission for AFHQ to "close [the deal] on the spot."[22] Roosevelt granted AFHQ leeway in continuing with the two-step program; it could employ the short terms to secure an armistice and then present the comprehensive conditions to the Italian government.[23] The War Cabinet wired its concurrence to Macmillan.

What disturbed Smith most was the fear that Zanussi would use diplomatic channels to inform Rome of the harsh terms contained in the long document, invalidating negotiations with Badoglio and Ambrosio. Smith employed some skullduggery to get Zanussi out of the grips of the diplomats, and he recruited Campbell and the British commander in Gibraltar as accomplices. Campbell called Zanussi from his hotel and asked if he and his aide might enjoy a tour of an Allied military installation. Zanussi readily agreed. Campbell asked him to hand over his copy of the surrender terms, and Zanussi complied. As it turned out, Zanussi never employed Italian diplomatic links. Roatta kept Zanussi's cloak-and-dagger mission secret, and because the Italian foreign ministry remained in the dark, the ambassador to Portugal reacted with unmasked hostility when the Italian officer first arrived in Lisbon. Zanussi could not risk compromising his boss, his mission, or himself by involving Italian diplomats. In the climate of fear gripping Rome, trust was at a premium.[24]

The unsuspecting Italian general boarded a plane early in the afternoon of 28 August and, after a brief stay in Gibraltar, found himself in Algiers later that evening, to his great surprise. Smith guessed the two Italian emissaries worked for opposing factions. Castellano made it clear in Lisbon that Badoglio had intentionally kept Roatta out the picture. AFHQ kept a dossier on the top Italian generals and knew about Roatta's pro-German sympathies. Smith wondered if the Zanussi mission was bona fide and whether Ambrosio and Roatta were simply pursuing the same end. Now he had Zanussi under what amounted to arrest and subjected him to a series of interrogations.

Under close questioning from Smith, Strong, and Murphy, Zanussi, who had attended the Bologna meetings, provided a great deal of valuable intelligence. What he told them did not relieve Smith's anxiety. The rate of German reinforcement seriously altered assessments for Avalanche and emphasized the urgency of cutting a deal with the Italians. Zanussi also presented a number of valuable insights into the Italian leadership; none of them offered much encouragement. Only a small group inside the government and high command favored an armistice. Zanussi described the king, Badoglio—"another Petain"—and those around them as "used men labouring under the handicap of twenty years of Fascism and the embarrassment of past actions . . . helpless in their expectancy that the Allies will deliver them." He warned it would be "too much now to expect spectacular initiative on their part." It was also clear to Smith that the "Italian General Staff have pondered over every possible '*combinazione*' leading out of the morass in which Italy flounders."[25]

Zanussi agreed to write a letter to Ambrosio advising acceptance of the short terms. The letter—vetted by Smith—also referred to the existence of a "full instrument of surrender" whose political and economic clauses possessed only "relative importance." Formulas were not as vital as the general Italian attitude and the extent of their practical assistance against the Germans. He urged Castellano to proceed to Sicily as planned. Either Zanussi or Castellano should remain at AFHQ as a permanent link with the Allies. Zanussi's aide carried the letter to Rome, but not the "long terms."[26]

Cassibile: Act One

Castellano's return set off a series of high-level meetings in Rome that all took the same form: the other participants argued while Badoglio sat silent. Indecision reigned. Finally, on 29 August, Badoglio went to the palace. The king had refused him an audience until the marshal made a decision, but when Badoglio could not make up his mind, the king relented. This time the king remained quiet while Badoglio talked. Still no verdict emerged. With the deadline fast approaching, Badoglio did precisely what Smith had predicted: though not repudiating the Allied offer, he employed it as a mandate for further negotiations.

On 31 August Smith boarded his plane and in the company of Macmillan, Murphy, and Zanussi flew to Cassibile. The party arrived at Fairfield headquarters just as the vehicle containing Strong, Castellano, and his interpreter, Montanari, pulled up the drive. Brigadier Cecil Sugden, acting AFHQ G-3; Cunningham's chief of staff, Dick; and MG Joseph Cannon and Lemnitzer of Fifteenth Army Group met them.[27]

While the Allied officers chatted, Zanussi and Castellano conferred. Zanussi took the opportunity to inform Castellano, in a superficial way, of the contents of the long terms. Then the Italians were motioned by Smith toward a tent, where the conference would take place. Macmillan and Murphy joined Alexander in another part of the sprawling compound.

As in Lisbon, Smith opened the meeting by cutting to the chase; he pointedly inquired whether Castellano had full authority to sign the military conditions. Castellano replied in the negative, but this time he furnished a memorandum of instructions. The document stated that, in view of the increased German deployments in Italy, the Italians were no longer free to accept and announce the armistice. Raising the final point of discussion in Lisbon, Castellano argued that the Italian government required a firm prior commitment that the Allies intended to launch an invasion of at least fifteen divisions as close to Rome as possible, preferably north of the capital. Badoglio could not announce any armistice unless he was assured of the security of Rome, the government, and the king. Italian forces stood no chance of resisting the Germans without direct Allied support.

The Allied officers present must have had difficulty keeping straight faces. They all knew Avalanche would involve only three divisions in the initial landing in Salerno Bay, some 200 miles south of Rome. With a poker face, Smith brusquely rejected Castellano's proposition. The armistice's announcement must coincide with the main Allied invasion. Just when that might happen, Smith could not divulge. Badoglio had two clear options: sign the conditions, including an announcement of the end of hostilities timed to coincide with the Allied landings, or refuse and suffer the consequences. The political heads offered Italy one path to deliverance—the Quebec Memorandum. Eisenhower had it within his power to modify the terms of surrender in proportion to the level of support Italy provided. The Allied invasion would happen with or without Italian support. If Italy had not come to terms by that time, all deals were off. Eisenhower would no longer possess the authority to treat with any Italian official or conclude any peace. Only after great effort had AFHQ received authorization to pursue negotiations limited to military questions. Smith pointedly told the Italians the diplomats would necessarily impose a harsher settlement. This was a calculated ploy on Smith's part. First, it was true. Any future negotiations would proceed based solely on the long terms. Second, Smith knew the Italians' chief concerns were achieving cobelligerent status and, through cooperation with the Allies, saving the regime and the dynasty and ensuring postwar Italy a seat at the peace table. As for the fifteen divisions, Smith mockingly retorted that if the Allies possessed the capability of launching amphibious operations with such forces, they needed no armistice.

Castellano and Zanussi then attempted to draw out an indication of the time and place of the landings. The Italians walked a tightrope, with time being the vital element. Too much time raised the potential for a German putsch; too little meant Rome could not organize any real resistance against the Germans. The timing of the main Allied landing was the key—twined with the threat to withhold the announcement—to the Italians retaining any room for negotiation. Smith gave them the same reply he had made in Lisbon.

At this point, stillness settled over the tent, broken by Castellano's declaration that he had nothing more to say and, in any event, lacked the authority to sign anything. He did raise the question of the Italian fleet: could it proceed to Maddalena off Sardinia, instead of Malta? Smith said no; there could be no modification of the terms. Castellano reminded Smith that the fleet, the only combat-ready arm of the Italian armed forces, would not sit idle as it had during the Sicily campaign. Castellano's bravado made no impression. Smith told him nothing could prevent Italy from becoming a battlefield, and Italian intransigence would only increase the suffering of the Italian population. In retaliation, the Italians refused to update the Allies on German troop movements.

The meeting adjourned at around 2 P.M. The Allied officers put their heads together. Smith noted that Castellano's position had hardened since Lisbon. AFHQ's anxiety over the long terms proved unfounded; the Italians appeared unconcerned about "unconditional surrender" or the harshness of its terms. Smith and Strong concluded that the arrival of additional German forces, now approximately nineteen divisions, placed the Italians in an impossible position. The German troop buildup troubled Smith but horrified the Italians. "A nice balance [prevailed] in their minds," Murphy said of the Italians, "whether we or their German allies will work the most damage and destruction in Italy. They are literally between the hammer and anvil."[28] Smith's chief preoccupation rested in improving the odds for a successful Avalanche. Dick reminded everyone of the great prize offered if the Italian fleet would come over—and he thought the chances were good—especially since planning continued for a rush of the British First Airborne Division into Taranto on Royal Navy ships.

Over lunch, after an embarrassing silence, discussions resumed.

Smith continued the hard sell, but this time more courteously. Smith decided to offer the Italian government something to stiffen its back; otherwise, the whole mess would explode in his face. Armed with Ultra intelligence indicating the Germans continued to plan an evacuation of Rome in the event of an Allied onslaught, Smith reasoned that the key to unlocking the stalemate was to exploit the Italian sensitivity to Rome's security. Italian intelligence knew the extreme range of Allied fighters based in Sicily and had no great difficulty concluding that Allied landings would take place around Salerno. Castellano reiterated that Italian forces could not possibly save Rome. If the Italian army could neutralize the German forces and control the approaches to Rome, Smith suggested that the Allies might consider landing an airborne division in Rome to act in concert with the Italian corps deployed around the city. Together they could stage a coup de main in Rome and trigger the German withdrawal north. Castellano requested that a second division, an armored division, land on either side of the mouth of the Tiber. The chief of staff made no commitments but promised to put the staffs to work studying the feasibility of both operations.

After lunch, Smith conferred with his military colleagues. He thought the Eighty-second Airborne Division—earmarked as Clark's reserve for Avalanche—could make the Rome drop. The idea of an improvised landing of an armored division—even with the availability of landing craft—struck everyone as sheer fantasy. Italian vulnerability to German tanks raised serious doubts. If Castellano proved right and the Italians could not contain the Germans, the lightly armed airborne forces could not long resist determined armor-tipped counterattacks. With an armored division out of the question, Smith wondered whether they could land antitank batteries in conjunction with the airborne drop. Curiously, Smith accepted Castellano's assessment at face value, without much concern for his own intelligence sources.

Smith wrote a memo to Eisenhower in Algiers summarizing the morning talks and plainly outlining his recommendations. First he emphasized that Italy was in fact an occupied country; Badoglio possessed little freedom of action. The Italians were more afraid of the Germans—and with good reason—than of the threat of an Allied invasion or renewed bombing. Why would Italy surrender to the Allies if that meant sacrificing most of the country, Rome, the government, and the king to the vengeful Germans? What good were Allied promises of future humane treatment and amelioration of the terms of unconditional surrender if the reality was a German occupation, and all that entailed, for the majority of the Italian population? Smith recounted how crushed Castellano appeared to be when he divined the Allied landings would take place far south of Rome. As Smith related to Eisenhower, who in turn relayed his views to the CCS, "it appears certain that they will make no attempt whatsoever to agree to an armistice unless assured of some help in the Rome area to stiffen up resistance." Smith recommended the airdrop in Rome as the best way to convince the Italian leadership to leave the war, and Italian compliance was the key to Avalanche's success.

Eisenhower accepted Smith's recommendation on political, not military, grounds; he sanctioned the airborne operation and wired Smith's memo to the CCS, asking for concurrence. Cables also went out to the other headquarters, floating the idea of an emergency landing of antitank artillery. For once, Eisenhower threw caution to the wind. The wheels immediately went into motion: Eisenhower tasked Alexander with planning the airdrop, Tedder with studying the maximum lift of Mediterranean Air Command, and Cunningham with examining the possibility of running antitank ordnance into Rome by sea. The Rome operation—code-named Giant II—took on a life of its own.[29]

While the soldiers conferred, Murphy and Macmillan kept the pressure on their Italian guests. They emphasized the urgency in convincing Rome to sign the surrender; the two diplomats reminded Castellano and Zanussi that this opportunity represented Italy's last chance. If Italy refused, Italian cities, including Rome, would be reduced "to ashes and piles of rubble," and Allied agents would foment "disorder and chaos" throughout Italy. The threats made little impression on the Italians. "The reaction of the Italians remained the same," Murphy recorded, "and in a sense it was like preaching to the converted." Castellano and Zanussi "both said that it is a question of inducing the cautious and frightened men at Rome" to recognize they had more to gain by surrendering to the Allies than they had to fear from the Germans. "As much as they yearned to be rid of the Germans," the Italians agreed, the leadership "lack[ed] the bold initiative to act against them."[30]

Smith's promise of Allied operations to secure Rome broke the deadlock. The afternoon conference quickly moved toward an accord. Now with a real prospect of active Italian cooperation, Smith provided the Italians with a substantive outline of Allied planning. The Allies would land a force of five or six divisions at an undisclosed time and place. The main invasion would take place south of Rome "between one and two weeks" after the initial landings in Calabria. The total forces committed would approximate the fifteen divisions Badoglio considered the necessary minimum. An airborne division would land near the capital, and in lieu of an armored division, naval units would deliver 100 antitank guns on the coast adjacent to Rome. The Italian government had until midnight 2 September to acknowledge acceptance. "In the negative case no communication will be made."[31] "We led Castellano to believe that our invasion would be in greater strength than actually was intended," Smith confided in a 1947 interview. "In war you do not play the game with all your cards down."[32] At 4 P.M. the conference concluded. Despite the appearance of cooperation, Smith knew none of this would come to anything if Badoglio continued to stall. Before Castellano and Zanussi boarded their plane, Smith reminded them if Badoglio made no reply by the deadline, the Allies would unleash the strategic bombers on Rome.

After a day full of tension, Alexander hosted a dinner followed by some libations in his trailer. Smith; MG Alexander Richardson, Fifteenth Army Group chief of staff; Macmillan; and Murphy joined him. Alexander, clearly troubled, gave vent to his apprehensions. The one conclusion drawn from the day's events was the dangerous situation now confronting his army group. Unless the Italians offered active support, Avalanche and the proposed operations in Rome "might fail or at least gain limited success at a very heavy cost in lives." Alexander and Macmillan knew the political stakes. Failure could result in the fall of the Churchill government, "seriously compromising Britain's determination to remain in the war." They talked darkly of fatigue among both British soldiers and the British public after three years of war. Macmillan's recent trip to London confirmed this pessimism. If the Italians remained in the war, Fifteenth Army Group faced thirty-five divisions. Alexander went on, discussing the intricacies of amphibious and airborne operations. Smith needed no reminding; he had recently made the same case to the CCS. All this convinced Alexander that "nothing [can] be neglected to persuade the Italians to cooperate." He went on to say that "he would be quite willing to risk his reputation and, if necessary, to retire from the army should his Government disapprove his insistence on immediate signature by the Italians of the short armistice terms, and Allied acceptance of Italian military cooperation." Smith left the session convinced AFHQ must assume the risk of the airborne assault on Rome.[33]

While this transpired in Cassibile, Castellano and Zanussi flew back to Rome. They had plenty of time to reflect on what had happened that day. Eisenhower relayed Smith's view to the CCS that the two Italian officers were "merely frightened individuals that are trying to get out of a bad mess in the best possible way and their attitude is . . . indicative of that of the whole country."[34] According to Castellano's memoirs, both he and Zanussi agreed that Italy's best hope resided in accepting Smith's conditions. Could they convince the cautious old men in Rome?

The next day Castellano presented himself to Badoglio. After reviewing the conditions offered by Smith, Castellano handed the marshal a copy of his minutes taken at Cassibile. The notes referred to "secondary landings (5 or 6 divisions)" and, after a "short interval (one or two weeks)," a major landing south of Rome. Castellano also reported the initial landings would involve fewer than fifteen divisions.[35]

Smith's assurances, intended to induce Italian confidence in Allied promises, instead produced misgivings. The five or six divisions referred to Baytown and Avalanche combined. The Allies planned to reinforce the Salerno beachhead to five and a half divisions but could not feed another two or three divisions into the beachhead for two or three weeks. Clark's and Montgomery's forces eventually would field fourteen or fifteen divisions, depending on circumstances. Because the Italians still played for time, they interpreted the "one or two weeks" as closer to two than one. The idea became fixed in their heads that the main Allied landings would not occur until 12 September at the earliest, and probably not until the fifteenth. Actually, the Italians were not far wrong; at that juncture, AFHQ planned on a postponement to 11 September, but in the end, circumstances accelerated the timetable by two days. These flawed appreciations informed all Italian calculations in the crucial days ahead.

If Badoglio arrived at any conclusions, he kept them from Raffaele Guariglia, his pro-Axis foreign minister; Ambrosio; and Carboni, all of whom attended Castellano's briefing. Badoglio then met with the king that afternoon. Presented with the facts—or, rather, Badoglio's interpretation of them—Victor Emmanuel accepted the Allied conditions. Ambrosio then forwarded a message to AFHQ stating, "The reply is *affirmative*. In consequence known person will arrive tomorrow two September hour and place established. Please confirm."[36] Owing to delays in transmission and atmospherics, the telegram arrived at AFHQ only a little more than an hour before the deadline.

Relieved, Smith had a long night ahead of him. He sent two wires to Rome. The first acknowledged Castellano's return to Sicily the next day; the second signaled Allied intentions to stage the two Rome operations. Smith requested the Italians provide guidance on which airfields to employ.[37] He then grabbed a couple hours of fitful sleep.

Cassibile: Act Two

Castellano, accompanied by Montanari and a major from the general staff, arrived at Termini airfield outside Palermo on schedule the next morning. A tired Beetle Smith met them. Since the Italians had requested the meeting, Smith assumed Castellano now possessed authority to sign the armistice. The topic never arose during the one-hour flight to Cassibile.

After they landed and exchanged some pleasantries, the officers got down to business. Smith asked if Castellano would sign the instrument of surrender. To Smith's intense shock and dismay, the Italian general demurred. Acting on the understanding reached in Lisbon, the Italians had used the secret channel to signal acceptance. For them, Ambrosio's telegram indicated acceptance of the Allied terms. Castellano informed Smith he had no written authorization; he had returned to work out the details of military cooperation. He revisited the old stumbling block—the timing of the Italian announcement. Badoglio had Ambrosio send the wire and withheld written authorization from Castellano because he still hoped the Allies might offer concessions. As Murphy recounted, "This sounds bad and General Smith indicated great dissatisfaction."[38]

"Despite the Sicilian summer heat," wrote one of the official historians, "there was a sudden drop in temperature."[39] Smith sequestered the Italian delegation in a tent while he figured out what to do next. Both he and Alexander wired Algiers, requesting that Eisenhower come to Cassibile. Originally, AFHQ had intended to fly Castellano to Algiers, but Alexander cautioned, "a move to Algiers might nullify what we have achieved." In the absence of the supreme commander, and in the interest of giving the Italians no pause, Alexander requested that either he or Smith be authorized to sign the surrender.[40] Eisenhower, holed up at the farm, answered through Whiteley. Eisenhower made it clear that only he would sign the formal document—in this he had no option, since the Soviets insisted—but he directed Smith to "go ahead and do everything necessary to make firm all arrangements for collaboration, even signing preliminary documents."[41] Smith knew the Italians operated with a noose around their necks, so he decided to yank the rope. A little more calculated "amateur theatricals" seemed in order. General Alexander now entered the stage.

Startled by a commotion outside the tent, Castellano peeked out to see two files of British troops crisply presenting arms to the shrill commands of a sergeant. A staff car flanked by motorcycle outriders sped forward, a cloud of dust in their wake. Out stepped the tall, impeccably tailored, and finely coiffed commander of the Fifteenth Army Group. The dazzling Irish Guards dress uniform highlighted a chest full of campaign ribbons, medals, and honors. As one observer noted, the "cut breeches, highly polished boots with gold spurs, and the gold peaked cap" all added to Alexander's impressive entrance. "I have come to be introduced to General Castellano," he announced. "I understand he has signed the instrument of surrender." With an expression of anguish on his face, Macmillan said, "I am sorry to say, sir, but General Castellano has *not* signed the instrument, and says that he hasn't the authority from his government to sign such a document."

There was nothing contrived in Alexander's enraged glare at Castellano. "Why there must be some mistake! I have seen the telegram from Marshal Badoglio stating he was to sign the armistice agreement," Alexander chided the dejected Italian officer. Drawing himself up to his full height, Alexander towered over the diminutive Castellano. "In that case," he said, "this man must be a spy. Arrest him!" What would befall Castellano paled in comparison to the horrible fate awaiting his country, Alexander continued. Italian perfidy called for the most ruthless retaliation. By this time tomorrow, Alexander boomed, Rome would lay in ruins. On clue, Macmillan suggested Castellano telegram Rome, confirming his authority to sign the document. Alexander concurred, saying that was "the only way out of this." He ordered the Italian delegation detained until someone signed the document. With that, Alexander spun on his heels and made an equally grand exit.[42]

The ruse worked; it took little prodding from Smith to convince Castellano. The cable went out at 2 P.M. The Italians were left to "stew in their own juice" while the Allied officers nervously awaited a reply from Rome. None arrived. The Italians were not the only ones stewing. Finally a wire arrived, but not from Badoglio. A crestfallen Smith read the communiqué from Ambrosio indicating his acceptance of the airborne operation and including recommendations for three Rome airfields. Correspondence had to be encoded, transmitted, decoded, and, at AFHQ's end, translated. All this took time, but the real reason for the delay rested with Badoglio's indecision. In the early hours of 3 September, Smith lost patience. One hundred miles north, three brigades of Montgomery's XIII Corps boarded landing craft for the first Allied return to the European mainland. Baytown set into motion the timetable for Cunningham's move into Taranto, Avalanche, and the Rome airborne operation. All these depended on the neutralization of the Italian navy and, if not the active cooperation of Italian ground forces, at least their acquiescence and interference with German movements. At 2 A.M. Smith roused Castellano and insisted he repeat his request. That done, Smith went back to his bunk.

In Rome Badoglio convened a conference with the service chiefs and Ambrosio. By the end of the meeting the Italian leadership possessed a clear picture of AFHQ operational intentions, as well as the military

commitments already made to the Allies.[43] Badoglio told them negotiations for an armistice continued, but he neglected to inform them
that his "reply affirmative" wire had already accepted surrender. Italy's
agreeing to the "military" conditions meant little if Badoglio refused
to announce the armistice. Badoglio and Ambrosio kept the surrender
secret for one obvious reason: if too many people knew about the armistice, or if the service chiefs issued written orders expediting troop movements in accord with commitments made by Castellano, the Germans
would pounce and the game would be up. Later that day the new German ambassador, Rudolph Rahn, would present his credentials. A hard-
core Nazi whose record in Bohemia and France spoke volumes, Rahn's
appointment gave ample proof of German intentions. Not so obvious
was Badoglio's ulterior motive. If the Allies guaranteed Rome's and
the government's security, he would announce the armistice. A fifteen-
division invasion near the capital would provide that; a five- or six-
division landing far south of Rome and the drop of a single airborne
division in the city would not. As indicated by the briefings given by the
service chiefs, the Italians accurately deduced Allied operational planning. Moreover, the landing at Reggio that morning set the clock ticking. Badoglio reckoned he had two weeks to complete the movement of
the Fourth Army from southern France, Piedmont, and the Ligurian
coast to the environs of Rome, and a similar interval for negotiating
better terms from the Allies. By issuing no orders to the Italian forces,
Badoglio willfully ignored commitments already tendered at Cassibile,
placing the airborne operation at risk. The Italian marshal decided to
delay military action until events compelled him to make the armistice
proclamation.

At about two that afternoon, AFHQ finally received the long-awaited
cable from Badoglio. The studied obfuscation contained in its ambiguous language called attention to Badoglio's continued efforts to trim and
delay. "Reply affirmative [dispatched two days earlier] contains implicit
acceptance [of] armistice conditions," it read. Implicit acceptance was
not good enough for Smith. He immediately wired Rome, demanding
an unequivocal statement of authorization.[44]

While Smith loitered around the communications tent, Allied planners huddled with Castellano. Lemnitzer for Fifteenth Army Group and
Rooks for AFHQ chaired the meeting that included Strong; Cannon;
Dick; the American operations officer from Mediterranean Air Command, BG Patrick Timberlake; and MG Matt Ridgway, commanding
general of the Eighty-second Airborne Division, the unit designated by
Alexander to execute the airdrop. The mission statement was simple:

cooperate with Italian forces defending Rome. The Germans had two divisions—a parachute division deployed along the coast south of the Tiber, and a panzer grenadier division thirty-five miles north of the city—with a third force south and east of the capital guarding Kesselring's headquarters. Five Italian divisions defended all the approaches to the city. Situated between the German forces and Rome, they held positions well placed for opposing any German drive into the city. Castellano predicted the German reaction to the airborne drop and warned that the Italian forces possessed sufficient numbers for defending forward positions but lacked transportation, fuel, antitank guns, and ammunition. Dick passed on a promise Cunningham had made to Smith that seaborne forces would "land guns up at the first bridge on the Tiber." Rooks, the other planners, and particularly Ridgway were worried about the safety of the airfields and wanted guarantees that Italian antiaircraft batteries would not fire on the low-flying American transports. Castellano gave a number of assurances: the Italians would secure the drop zones, an air route north of the Tiber would minimize German antiaircraft fire, Italian batteries would not fire, a senior Italian general would meet Ridgway and help coordinate actions, various means would be employed to guide aircraft to the correct airfields, and the Italians would safeguard the passage of naval craft up the Tiber.

Ridgway never bought Castellano's glib assurances that the German antiaircraft batteries would remain silent or that enough time existed to spread the word to the Italian gunners not to fire on Allied aircraft. The memories of the Sicily drop and the twenty-four American planes downed by friendly fire remained etched in his mind.[45] Ridgway and his division artillery commander, BG Maxwell Taylor, thought the assigned airfields closest to Rome too exposed and later raised their concerns with Smith. Worse, they remained unconvinced of Italian assurances of cooperation, essential to the success of the airborne mission. Taylor thought Smith had bullied Castellano into making unrealistic promises.[46]

At about five o'clock, a junior officer rushed into the tent and handed Castellano a telegram. The long-awaited authorization had arrived. "General Castellano," it read, "is authorized by the Italian government to sign the acceptance of the conditions of the armistice." The conference broke up as a captain hustled the startled Italian out the door.

Eisenhower had flown down after all. Butcher had interceded the night before, making the case that Eisenhower should sign the document. "Peeved at [Butcher] for butting in," an ill-tempered Eisenhower made the trip not to sign the surrender but because of the problematic communications between Cassibile and Algiers. He could not risk being out of contact. Now present, he ordered the deal consummated immediately.[47]

The improvised stage-managing worked to perfection. Castellano found himself standing in a tent in the middle of an olive glade in front of a camp table covered with napkins. Offered a seat, he received a copy of the short terms and a borrowed pen. Without any fanfare, he and Smith affixed their signatures. Only fifteen minutes had elapsed since the arrival of Badoglio's cable. A bottle of scotch and some dirty glasses appeared. After a toast, a lone Signal Corps photographer captured Eisenhower shaking Castellano's hand. Everyone present stripped souvenir olive branches; Murphy forwarded one to Roosevelt. Eisenhower immediately returned to Algiers.

Castellano forwarded a cable to Rome. Always the gentleman, Alexander congratulated Castellano and invited the Italians to dine with him. Smith waited a decent interval, perhaps allowing Castellano time to digest his meal, before he handed him a copy of the "Instrument of Surrender of Italy." Throughout the torturous negotiations, Smith had avoided the phrase "unconditional surrender." For that matter, so had Castellano and Zanussi. Now when Castellano opened the folio of terms, the first line leaped out at him: "The Italian Land, Sea and Air Forces wherever located, hereby surrender unconditionally." An overwrought Castellano loudly protested: his government had never seen the document and would repudiate the agreement. Smith insisted that Zanussi had received a copy of the conditions in Lisbon, and surely the government in Rome knew of its contents. Castellano retorted they did not. Since neither Castellano nor Zanussi attached any significance to the comprehensive surrender terms—the Allies encouraging them in this belief—Castellano likely told the truth. Smith again countered with the Quebec Memorandum. Castellano parried Smith by saying it contained only the most equivocal promises and that his government had received nothing in the way of a written guarantee. The whole game hung in the balance. Just as Macmillan had predicted, the Italians would renege on step two. Though unprepared for Castellano's démarche, Smith never panicked (but his troubled stomach must have churned) and seized the moment. He calmly sat down, extracted his pen, and wrote on the bottom of the short-terms document: "The additional clauses have only a relative value insofar as Italy collaborates in the war against the Germans."[48]

Later that night Castellano met with an array of Allied officers headed by Alexander and Smith. They discussed how the Italian government might best execute its part of the bargain. An aide-mémoire codified the general actions the Badolgio government must undertake

The Italian deal is sealed. Eisenhower shakes hands with General Castellano, the Italian signatory.

before the announcement of the armistice. Dick handed Castellano a
communication from Cunningham enumerating instructions for the
movement of the Italian navy and merchant marine.[49] With that, the
dramatic day drew to an end.

Ike's Hatchet Man

The photograph of the event conveys a great deal about the Eisenhower-
Smith relationship. A smiling Eisenhower, dressed in a crisp uniform,
extends his hand to a bewildered Castellano, who manages only a forced
half-smile. Behind Castellano stands Smith, clutching the documents,
with a hollow look on his face, his hair disheveled and uniform blouse
plastered to his sweaty chest.

Eisenhower's hand in the Italian surrender was not only hidden; it
was absent. His "4th of July" never marked any genuine move toward
real independence from tutelage from above. He might bristle about
having to clear every detail with his political masters and the CCS, but
in reality, he coveted their approval, particularly on political matters.
Badly burned in the Darlan affair, Eisenhower avoided political entanglements like the plague. His practice of multiple advocacies for any
major initiative reflected his preoccupation with insulating himself from

external criticism. Eisenhower's estrangement from the Italian negotiations alarmed Churchill. The prime minister complained he never knew if the correspondence he read over Eisenhower's name expressed the supreme commander's views or those of his chief of staff.[50]

Eisenhower talked the matter over with Hughes, who advised him "to stay out of politics and appoint a hatchet man."[51] Eisenhower needed no prompting in distancing himself from the Italian negotiations and the preliminary surrender, and he had already designated his hatchet man. Smith also served as a buffer. If the Italian surrender collapsed—and it hung by the thinnest of cords—the fault would not rest on Eisenhower, who stood above a deal he considered "crooked."[52]

A curious thing about Eisenhower was that he could not bring himself to congratulate subordinates face-to-face, especially officers closest to him. This quirk rankled Patton in particular, but others also commented on this facet of Eisenhower's personality. Yet in his correspondence, especially with Marshall, Eisenhower often offered effusive praise of his subordinates. Three days after Smith signed the Cassibile armistice, Eisenhower penned a long memo to Marshall. On 1 September Marshall informed Eisenhower his name appeared on a list of four officers under consideration for promotion to permanent major general. Also included on the list was Patton, and Marshall solicited Eisenhower's opinion. Despite his confinement to the doghouse over the slapping incidents, Patton received a glowing recommendation, and Eisenhower assured Marshall that his "jacking up" of Patton had cured him. On Marshall's list of potential brigadier generals, Smith stood last in a group of nine. The always politic Eisenhower placed two of Marshall's closest associates in the War Department—McNarney and Handy—at numbers one and three, sandwiched around Bradley. Eisenhower ranked Smith fourth.

As chief of staff, Smith contributed "as much—often far more—to win the war than . . . those whose names most often appear in the papers." Eisenhower observed that Smith "comes close to being the ideal chief of staff." Smith served as a vital cog in the Allied machine. "His standing with the British is so high that General Montgomery not long ago remarked that General Bedell Smith was one of the two American generals under whom he . . . would willingly serve . . . at any time." Montgomery never offered the name of the second officer, but it was probably not Eisenhower. He concluded by noting Smith "is in the job for which he is ideally suited and the contributions he has made to Allied success in the past ten months simply cannot be exaggerated."[53]

In the recent past, Eisenhower had pushed for Smith's promotion.

At the end of July Brooke had inquired whether Eisenhower considered promoting Beetle to lieutenant general. Brooke worried that Gale's elevation to that rank might threaten harmony inside AFHQ. Eisenhower explained the War Department's traditional reluctance to promote officers to the highest ranks. Smith was still too junior for three stars, and War Department promotion policy favored combat commanders over staff officers.[54] Smith would have to wait for promotion to lieutenant general, but Eisenhower thought a jump to permanent brigadier general—which American officers valued over temporary rank—suitable compensation for his toil.

The periodic dispatch of promotion lists up Capitol Hill always produced nervousness among senior officer—a product of the sluggish rate of promotions in the interwar army. Because Roosevelt tried an end run around Congress by proposing the promotions during a recess, Marshall warned of a long and bitter confirmation wrangle. Confiding in Hughes, Eisenhower worried that "his promotion would bring on a fight in Congress." Only twelve officers held the rank of major general. Eisenhower's promotion would mean his advancement over 32 brigadier generals and 788 colonels—a higher jump than Pershing's in the last war. Eisenhower's disquiet over his promotion also figured in his decision to dissociate himself from any high-visibility involvement with the Italians. "Of course," Hughes concluded about his friend's apprehension, he was worried about "Darlan [and] Badoglio."[55]

Except for commenting that the Lisbon "party" and the events climaxing in the armistice at Cassibile represented the most interesting episodes in his career, Smith talked little about the Italian surrender. In his report to Roosevelt, Murphy praised the "superb manner in which W. B. Smith has handled these negotiations."[56] Because of the intense secrecy attached to the surrender, Smith's role remained mostly shrouded. His signing of the surrender received a short burst of publicity. MG George Strong told him, "The papers are full of your recent pernicious activities to undermine Hitler's great ally," and queried, "Aren't you ashamed of yourself?"[57] Unlike Clark's exploits in North Africa, Smith's secret mission to Lisbon, the clandestine negotiations with the Italians, and his role in leveraging the surrender stayed hidden. Fears that the delicate threads might unravel resulted in a blanket of secrecy covering the Italian surrender.[58] A story in *Time* appeared later in September; Smith's name was mentioned once in connection to the signing. Castellano got far more ink. A year would pass before an article appeared in the *Saturday Evening Post* that offered a more complete rendering of the Italian capitulation. By then, the story was old news.[59]

Smith had other concerns. Nobody was more aware of the fragility of the Italian deal. All his thoughts and energies now focused on launching Giant II. In many ways, the risky airborne operation—on which so much depended—was his baby. If Avalanche and Giant foundered, Eisenhower and Smith need not worry about promotions or press clippings. Almost certainly, both their heads would roll.

23

"A Feeling of Restrained Optimism"

Except for its nearly disastrous consequences, the sequel to the Lisbon and Cassibile amateur theatricals took on aspects of an *opéra bouffe*. Altogether too much wishful thinking egged on all the chief players. Smith went all out for Giant II because without the promised airborne operation, the Italians would not play ball. As Murphy reported to the president, "all thought the risk was worth taking even if [the Eighty-second Airborne was] lost."[1] All, that is, save the two officers most responsible for Giant II: Ridgway and Taylor. When Ridgway cautioned that the Italians were "deceiving us and have not the capability for doing what they are promising," Smith painted a picture of popular resistance in Rome paralyzing the German defense.[2] Smith never professed much faith in psychological warfare, but he convinced himself that Allied propaganda and the aerial campaign had swayed Italian attitudes. Guilty of mirror imaging, the Allies grossly inflated the potential impact of public opinion on Badoglio's thinking. Allied broadcasts certainly encouraged Italians' belief that the end of the war lay in sight and raised expectations for their deliverance, but they also rendered the Italian population even more inert. Italians wanted an end to hostilities, not a war of liberation. Twenty years of fascism had gutted Italian civil society; there was never any prospect of a national rising en masse. Nor was there an Italian de Gaulle to inspire resistance.

"Situation Innocuous"

Allied airborne operations to date hardly inspired confidence. Ridgway also questioned Allied capabilities in staging Giant II. The Torch landings had amounted to a total wash, and the drops in Sicily brushed with disaster. Still, the airborne forces remained AFHQ's favorite toy. For better than a month, Ridgway's staff prepared for one dubious operation after another, including an amphibious landing in Naples, even though "not one individual in the entire division, officer or enlisted man, had ever had any experience or instruction in amphibious operations."[3] None proved more ill-advised than Giant II. Because of the shortage of lift—a product of the huge losses sustained from friendly fire in Husky— two-thirds of the division would land piecemeal in three stages over two days and nights more than 200 miles from the beaches of Salerno. Professing "full faith" in Italian assurances, Alexander promised Allied forces would make contact with Ridgway's division "in three days—five days at the most." When Ridgway protested the "sacrifice of my division," Alexander sanctioned the dispatch of a mission to Rome for an assessment of Italian preparations.[4]

Smith and Alexander based the plan on two assumptions: the Italian forces could control territory and oppose the Germans, and Giant II and Italian resistance would compel Kesselring's withdrawal into northern Italy. In Rome, that meant Italian forces directly attacking German formations and Kesselring's headquarters, interrupting communications, and providing logistical support. Outside of Rome, the preoccupation remained fixed on securing the Italian navy. The Italians needed to secure the ports of La Spezia, Taranto, and Brindisi. By 7 September, the day the secret mission arrived in Rome, Alexander's faith in Italian promises had faded. After four days of intensive planning with Castellano in Cassibile, and "despite our detailed instructions," Alexander concluded that the Italians "have done nothing."[5] Still, he never intervened and canceled Giant II, presumably because that decision remained a "family affair."

Alexander's anxieties proved accurate. On 3 September Badoglio opened a meeting of his chiefs of staff by announcing, "His Majesty has decided to begin negotiations for an armistice." Only his closest confidants knew he had already authorized the surrender. Badoglio issued no written orders instructing the movement of troops, despite his commitment to defend Rome. The Italian leadership knew Allied plans. As ADM Raffaele de Courten, head of the navy staff, recorded during the meeting: "The British and Americans will mount small-scale landings in Calabria, then a large-scale landing near Naples (six divisions), and finally a paratroop landing of a division near Rome, where Carboni's six divisions and the Italian 4th Army will be concentrated."[6] Reference to the Fourth Army indicates that the Italians presumed a delay in the armistice's announcement until much later. Much of the Fourth Army remained spread out from Liguria through Piedmont and back into France. Neither Badoglio nor Ambrosio forwarded instructions expediting the movement of Italian reinforcements toward Rome, doubtless owing to fear of alerting the Germans. From the outset, Badoglio ignored commitments made to the Allies through Castellano, deferring any action until after the announcement of the armistice.

On 4 September Smith began organizing an Italian military mission to AFHQ and asked Castellano to solicit approval from Rome. He also wanted permission for Taylor's special mission. According to Castellano, Smith took him aside and said, "I understand very well the great anxiety which you have to know these dates, but unfortunately I can tell you nothing; it is a military secret." Then in a whisper, Smith told him, "I can say only that the landing will take place within two weeks." By reaffirming the two-week window, Smith wished to convey the immediacy of the Allied invasion, but Castellano stated in his letter to Ambrosio that although Smith refused to pin down the date, "the landing will . . . take place between the 10th and 15th of September, possibly the 12th."[7] MAJ Luigi Marchesi, who accompanied Castellano to Cassible, returned to Rome on 5 September with the plans for Giant II and the letter for Ambrosio. Castellano promised Italian forces would keep open the Furbana and Cerveteri air bases for the initial landings and secure the port at Ostia and approaches on either side of the Tiber for the landing of antitank ordnance.

Roatta did not receive the operational orders for the airborne landings until 6 September. It suddenly dawned on him that Italian troops would be making the first move against the Germans. Axis intelligence detected the movement of Allied landing craft, signaling the imminence of the amphibious operation in the Salerno-Naples area. Ambrosio dismissed Roatta's concerns based on Castellano's estimate, believing that nothing would happen until 12 September at the earliest. Carboni, commander of the motorized corps and now head of Italian Military Intelligence, rejected any notion of initiating actions against the Germans.[8] The Air Ministry claimed it needed seven days to make the necessary arrangements for securing the two air bases. All this appears even more amazing in light of cables from Algiers warning the Italian regime "of absolute imminence of operation and date already fixed" and advising it to "maintain continuous watch every day for the most important message" and expect a communication "on or after 7 September."[9] Despite all evidence to the contrary, the Italian leadership convinced themselves they still had some latitude. Led by Roatta, they called for a reexami-

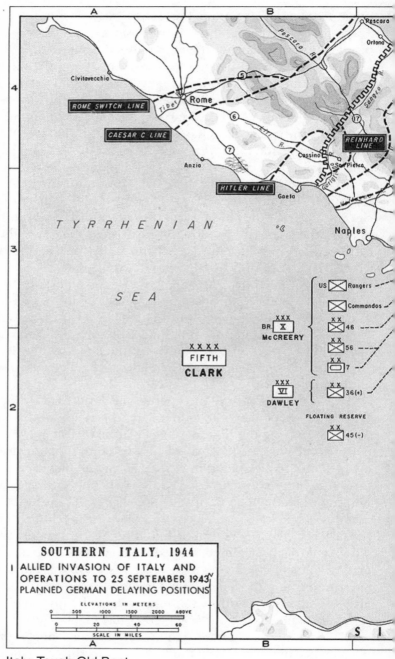

SOUTHERN ITALY, 1944

ALLIED INVASION OF ITALY AND
OPERATIONS TO 25 SEPTEMBER 1943
PLANNED GERMAN DELAYING POSITIONS

ELEVATIONS IN METERS

SCALE IN MILES

Italy: Tough Old Boot

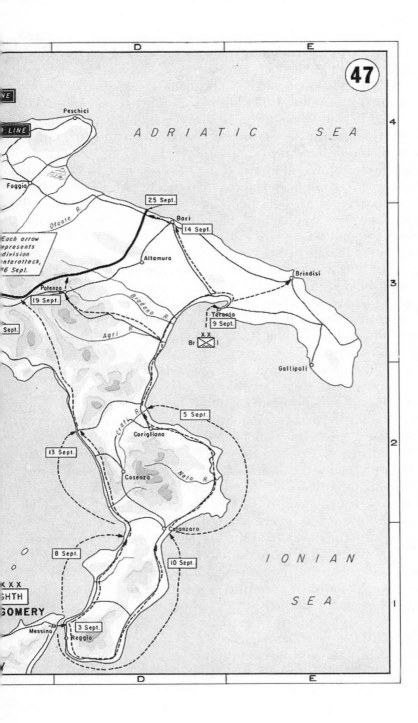

47

ADRIATIC SEA

Peschici

LINE

Foggia

Otanto R.

25 Sept.

Bari
14 Sept.

Each arrow
represents
division
interattack,
16 Sept.

Altamura

Brindisi

Potenza
19 Sept.

Bradano R.

Taranto
9 Sept.

Sept.

Agri R.

Br XX I

Gallipoli

Crati R.

5 Sept.

Corigliano

13 Sept.

Neto R.

Cosenza

Catanzaro

8 Sept.

10 Sept.

IONIAN

SEA

XXX
GHTH
GOMERY

3 Sept.

Messina

Reggio

nation of the airborne drop and the timing of the armistice announcement in light of extant circumstances. Roatta wrote a note to this effect and dispatched it with MAJ Alberto Briatore, one of the officers tabbed to join the military mission in Algiers. The memo reneged on the armistice and accused the Allies of bad faith for landing too soon, too far from Rome, and in insufficient force. "It is necessary," it argued, "not to initiate hostilities [against the Germans]. Therefore the intervention of the airborne division should not take place."[10]

While all this transpired in Rome, Taylor, accompanied by COL William Gardiner, started out from Palermo first in a British PT boat, then an Italian corvette, and finally a Red Cross ambulance. They arrived in Rome at dusk on 7 September. Their mission involved finalizing arrangements for joint action with Italian ground units, but in reality it centered on ascertaining whether Castellano's assurances possessed any substance.[11] The only preparations the Italian leadership made were for a lavish dinner held at the Palazzo Caprara, across from the War Ministry. Ambrosio had conveniently absconded to Turin the previous day, leaving Carboni the unpleasant task of dealing with Taylor. The Italian general finally showed up at 9:30. Taylor requested to inspect the airfields and informed Carboni the operation was set for the following day. Unmoved, the Italian general flippantly opined that the operation should be canceled. He exaggerated the strength of German armor by a factor of ten and diminished the number of Italian troops by half. Carboni lied, telling Taylor the Italian forces possessed virtually no fuel reserves, rendering his so-called motorized corps immobile.[12]

Taylor could scarcely credit what he had heard and demanded an audience with Badoglio. When he arrived at the marshal's sumptuous palace, Taylor learned Badoglio was asleep. When he was finally awoken, Badoglio, in his pajamas, confirmed everything Carboni had told Taylor.[13] To Taylor's astonishment, the old marshal professed surprise "at the rapid course of events" and then repudiated all the agreements Castellano had made in his name. Given the utter unpreparedness of the Italian forces, Badoglio recommended the cancelation of Giant II and the postponement of the armistice announcement. Now incredulous, Taylor pleaded with Badoglio to reconsider his requests. From the marshal's silence, Taylor inferred he already had. Taylor then asked that Badoglio forward a dispatch to Algiers. He complied, stating, "Operation Giant Two is no longer possible because of lack of forces to guarantee the airfields." Taylor wrote a second wire stating, "GIANT Two is impossible." The next morning, Taylor forwarded a third and finally a fourth cable, the last one containing the code words "Situation Innocuous," signaling the cancellation of the operation.[14] On the afternoon of 8 September, AFHQ ordered Taylor and Gardiner's immediate return to La Marsa; they brought along GEN Francesco Rossi, the Italians' deputy chief of staff, to argue for a postponement of Eisenhower's announcement of the armistice.

AFHQ and Fifteenth Army Group never understood the Italians. A master of manipulation, Mussolini had built his regime on an admixture of concoction, co-option, and coercion. He promoted to senior positions only those fascist loyalists who reinforced Il Duce's fanciful worldview—men skilled in veiling their own incompetence and sleaze. With the departure of the puppeteer, it was unrealistic to expect the marionettes to suddenly generate spines. The Allied propaganda blitz had scored successes, chiefly with Badoglio and his ministers, the army commands and staffs, and the king and those closest to him, convincing them of the omnipotence of the Allied armed forces. Fueled by Allied propaganda, the leadership in Rome fixed on the idea that vast Allied armies would land north of Rome, covered by clouds of fighters and bombers and supported by fleets of battleships and cruisers. Now Badoglio believed the Allies could not only cancel the airborne operation but also shift Avalanche, with the convoys already at sea, north to the vicinity of Rome. This was a flight of fancy, but the Italians were accustomed to living in an imagined world.

Eisenhower left Algiers for Amilcar early on the morning of 8 September. Just after his departure, Badoglio's renunciation of the pact and Taylor's initial advisory crossed Smith's desk. For two and a half hours Smith weighed the options; he recognized Eisenhower's sensitivity to depending on direction from above, but he also knew Eisenhower would not carry out the announcement without approval. He decided to dispatch the Rome correspondence to the CCS, together with a request over Eisenhower's signature for advice on whether AFHQ should proceed with the armistice announcement "for the tactical deception value." He added that Giant II would probably be canceled.[15] Smith had never placed much store in Italian fighting capacity. The Italian Seventh Army in Calabria, Campania, and Puglia lay interposed between the German forces in the south. Smith and Eisenhower reckoned an Italian announcement of an armistice would throw the Axis defense into confusion, and even if the Italian troops did not fight, their deployments would at least obstruct German freedom of action. That, in combination with the Salerno landings and the Rome air operation, might just stampede the Germans into a withdrawal.[16] The Allies—placing too much faith in Ultra—were also victims of self-deception. Reality now hit home.

Faced by the Italian double cross—which should not have come as any great surprise—Smith advised proceeding with the announcement.

When Eisenhower read the bundle of dispatches from Algiers, his face flushed as pink as the incoming message form. He picked up two pencils in succession and snapped them in two; then he stamped, "expressing himself with great violence."[17] He was nearly as peeved at Smith for asking for guidance as he was with Badoglio. Eisenhower dictated a scalding reply to Rome, stating his intent to broadcast the announcement as planned; if the Italians refused their cooperation, he threatened "to publish to the world the full record of the affair."[18] He ordered Castellano's return to Tunis, hoping he could influence Badoglio.

Communications in the theater always proved problematic. Alexander issued Ridgway an order canceling Giant II but received no confirmation. Eisenhower ordered that Lemnitzer rush to El Aouina airfield in Sicily. In a commandeered British Beaufighter, Lemnitzer flew to Sicily, but the pilot got lost; he skirted the coast until he sighted circling transport aircraft. Dropping down to treetop level, Lemnitzer fired a flare gun. The controller saw the flare and correctly interpreted its meaning, and the takeoffs ceased. A disaster was averted by the narrowest of margins.[19]

Smith's cable got a lot of very important men out of bed in Washington. Churchill, visiting the White House after the conclusion of the Quebec conference, expressed no shock. "That's what you would expect from those Dagoes."[20] Both political heads approved Eisenhower's announcement. At 6:30 that evening, on schedule, Eisenhower made his announcement on Radio Algiers.

Unreality still reigned in Rome. The Italian leadership understood Eisenhower would make his announcement regardless of their actions. Taylor told them as much. They also knew the Allied invasion was imminent; that morning, 8 September, the Allied air forces launched a massive decapitation raid on Kesselring's Frascati headquarters. Still the Italian leadership dithered. The king believed he still possessed an out: if the Allied invasion triggered a German withdrawal from Rome, the armistice was on; if not, the king believed he could repudiate the surrender, renounce Badoglio, and continue cooperating with the Germans. Only after Eisenhower made his broadcast did the king convene the Crown Council. The king, "a pale, worn-out Badoglio," the foreign minister, the service chiefs, and Carboni considered their options. They called in Marchesi, the officer best informed on Allied thinking. Amazingly, the majority supported continuing with the Axis. Only the lowly major saw the obvious flaw in their hallucination. The Germans would stage their putsch whatever course the Italians took. Deciding to save whatever face he could, the king concluded that Italy could not change sides again and ordered Badoglio to make his announcement.

The Italian command preserved the façade of cooperating with the Germans to the end. The only planning the Italian armed forces engaged in involved meeting the Allied invasion; the only planning in the government centered on escaping Rome. The lone orders that went out facilitated the flight of the king and his convoy of seven vehicles. Otherwise, Italian forces in Rome acted on a single standing order: "in no case . . . take the initiative in hostility against the German troops."[21]

As Smith relayed to Ismay, "the armistice put the Hun into a complete flap for a couple of days."[22] There was plenty of confusion to go around, and in truth, Kesselring did a far better job of cutting through the fog than did AFHQ. The German command structure in Italy suffered from its own internal divisions. Hitler and the high command linked Italy—especially northern Italy—to the defense of the Balkans. A withdrawal to the Alps condemned Croatia and Yugoslavia, with the attendant fear of a domino effect knocking out Germany's satellites—Hungary, Slovakia, Romania, and Bulgaria. Additionally, the agricultural produce and industries of the Po Valley and northern Italy represented valuable economic assets. As early as May, Hitler became convinced that Italy was seeking a separate peace and that fascism in Italy—always the product of a single man—might collapse. Any hint of an Italian betrayal would trigger immediate German action. Units were withdrawn from Russia, and a special staff was created to plan the takeover in Rome and the occupation of Italy.[23] On 25 July the Germans still had only a handful of divisions in Italy; that situation radically changed.

Rommel received command of Army Group North and the task to prepare plans for the defense of Italy. In July he concluded that German forces "cannot hold the entire peninsula without the Italian Army."[24] Rommel planned on a withdrawal north of the Apennines in defense of the Po Valley. Because of Kesselring's warm regard for his allies—many considered his well-known optimism his greatest weakness—and his long-standing rivalry with Rommel, he remained outside the planning loop. Operation Achse (Axis), finalized on 1 August, called for a coup and reinstatement of a fascist regime, the disarming of Italian forces in the north, and a withdrawal from central and southern Italy. Sicily convinced the German high command that the Italian armed forces would contribute nothing in the face of an Allied invasion. In mid-August Kesselring received directives to initiate the retreat in the event Italy moved toward a separate peace.[25] These were the directives intercepted by

Ultra. Those orders still stood when Clark's Fifth Army hit the beaches at Salerno on 9 September.

Unhurt but badly shaken by the attack on his headquarters, Kesselring anticipated Allied landing operations in the vicinity of Rome. On the night of 8–9 September the German embassy burned documents and evacuated most of its staff. LTC Giacomo Dogliani, liaison officer to Kesselring, made a courtesy farewell call to Frascati on the morning of 9 September. Kesselring's chief of staff asked Dogliani for "one more favor. Persuade your headquarters not to oppose the withdrawal of the German troops from Rome." Kesselring then intervened, motioning to say no more.[26] Salerno allayed his anxiety. Kesselring implemented Achse but asked permission to hold in place and defeat the Allied invasion. Berlin wired concurrence.

Smith always regretted the cancellation of Giant II. It was possible the airborne operation might have exploited the confusion and prompted Kesselring's execution of the planned evacuation of Rome. Giant II could have steeled the Italian leadership. The first possibility appears more plausible than the second. Isolated pockets of popular resistance sprang up in Rome, some of it fierce, but in two days the Germans pacified the city. The vast majority of the Italian army either confined themselves to barracks or deserted, proclaiming *tutti a casa*— "let's all go home." Most of the senior officers abandoned their posts and surreptitiously slipped away. "I remain convinced, as do the officers of the planning staff," Smith told Castellano in December, "that this plan could have been carried out and would have been successful had there been in command of the Italian divisions around Rome an officer of courage, firmness and determination who was convinced that success was possible." Clearly, none of the Italian generals possessed any of these qualities. "It might be," he conceded, "that I did not accurately evaluate the situation as it existed on September 3rd."[27]

The Germans quickly roped off the British lodgment and viciously counterattacked against MG Ernest Dawley's VI Corps. Smith authored a situation report to the CCS and BCOS on 9 September. AFHQ had no news from the severely pressed VI Corps. He explained, "demolitions and the Germans' rear guards will prevent [Montgomery] being any real help . . . for some days." On the plus side, Smith told of the rush of the British First Airborne Division into Taranto and the securing of the Italian fleet. "Clark's buildup," he warned, is "now a critical factor."[28] The Wehrmacht, including three of the four divisions allowed to escape Sicily, exploited the seven-mile gap between the Allied forces. By D+3, the situation appeared dire enough for Clark to consider extracting

Dawley's corps and moving it to the British sector—a double amphibious operation fraught with danger. Only Allied firepower staved off disaster. Tedder and Cunningham threw in everything they could get their
hands on. The Northwest African Air Forces, including B-17s, dropped an
impressive 3,020 tons of ordnance on the Germans, but this paled in comparison to the 11,000 tons of accurate naval gunfire directed at the enemy's
armored spearheads and artillery.[29] Fortunately, the Eighty-second had
not been used in Giant II; the paratroopers were airdropped near Paes-
tum on successive nights and played a vital role in shoring up the defenses.
AFHQ informed the CCS on 13 September that the situation remained
"touch and go" and the next week would be "one of anxiety." Three days
later, at the behest of Alexander and Clark, Eisenhower sacked Dawley
for "extreme nervousness under prolonged strain" and replaced him with
Lucas.[30] Dawley paid the price for Clark's inept planning; so too would
Lucas at Anzio. The U.S. Army did not flinch from firing corps commanders; dismissing army commanders proved another story.

With AFHQ, the Allied strategic air forces, and a bulk of the combined fleet preoccupied with saving Avalanche, the Germans began what
turned out to be another brilliantly executed set of evacuations from
Sardinia and Corsica. On Sardinia, despite a huge advantage in manpower, the Italians did nothing. On 9 September the Germans seized the
anchorage at Maddalena and completed their withdrawal to Corsica in
six days. Berlin ordered German forces out of Corsica on 12 September.
Employing air transport and an improvised fleet of ferries, the Germans
evacuated from northern ports as French troops entered from the south.
Despite Allied control of the air and sea and exceptionally good intelligence, by the first week in October another 30,000 German troops, with
arms and vehicles, completed their escape and joined the fight in Italy.

The crisis at Salerno passed, and on 16 September lead elements of
the British Fifth Division contacted a Fifth Army patrol forty miles southeast of Salerno. AFHQ made apologies for Montgomery's tardiness,
but privately the Americans fumed. With typical Teutonic efficiency,
the Germans destroyed the few improved roads and communications,
and Montgomery's forces advanced through very tough terrain. But the
fact remained that, in the two weeks following the landings, the Eighth
Army had faced a single panzer division, losing sixty-two killed in action
and capturing a mere eighty-five Germans. The Canadian First Division
made no contact with the enemy from 8 to 18 September. Illustrative of
the speed of the German drawback and Montgomery's dilatory advance,
the first link actually involved bored journalists in search of copy.[31]

Eisenhower became quite expansive. On 20 September he predicted the Germans were "too nervous to stand for a real battle south of the Rome area."[32] Churchill wired congratulations on "the victorious landing and deployment northward of our armies" and reminded Eisenhower of what Wellington had remarked after Waterloo: "It was a 'damned close-run thing' but your policy of running risks has been vindicated." The next day Marshall "took the starch out of Ike." The chief wondered whether Eisenhower, once he had Naples "under the guns," should bypass the city and make an amphibious dash for Rome. An incredulous Eisenhower struggled to reply, aided by Smith. Eisenhower "grieved to think that General Marshall does not give him credit for cracking the whip. [It] caused him a great deal of mental anguish," Butcher recorded. "We have the paradox of the Prime Minister applauding Ike's willingness to take risks while General Marshall . . . criticize[s] him." During the Salerno crisis, the CCS finally relented and gave Eisenhower those three bomber groups AFHQ had been requesting for weeks. Beetle and Butcher tried to buoy up Eisenhower. Smith half-jokingly thought he should form another staff section with the sole task of keeping the home front constantly frightened. Struggling again to explain to Marshall the impossibility of staging any amphibious operation for at least six weeks—the time required for withdrawing, refitting, restocking, and redeploying landing craft, if they were available (which they were not, because the Germans' destruction of the infrastructure meant they remained tied to supply functions)—Eisenhower and Smith engaged in a little gallows humor. When Butcher suggested the army should alter its training methods and teach GIs to walk on water, Smith retorted that they already could, but not with full packs.[33]

Smith understood the root problem remained AFHQ's inability to direct operations, and as long as that state of affairs persisted, Eisenhower could expect more "mental anguish." On 20 September Smith inaugurated a new scheme asserting the supreme commander's authority. "Beetle states in front of British at his 12 noon conference," Hughes recorded, "that 'The duties and responsibilities of the C in C must be redefined.'" Hughes spoke for many when he wondered, "Why should we worry when apparently even Ike doesn't know what he can tell the other C-in-Cs?"[34] Nothing came from Smith's initiative because Eisenhower never cracked the whip with any real conviction.

While Smith troubled himself over Eisenhower's nebulous hold on supreme command, he congratulated himself on the excellent work of his staff. For him, the inauguration of the Italian campaign marked the coming-of-age of his headquarters. Even at the height of the emergency, Smith told Ismay, "our party here is going very well" and said he retained "restrained optimism" Avalanche would yet succeed. He asked Ismay to come to AFHQ "to see real Allied cooperation and coordination." He boasted, "We still have it and always will as long as Ike is in the saddle."[35] He carried on in a similar vein to Mountbatten after the Germans pulled back. "I tremble to think what our present situation would be if the armistice had not come off but the results so far have been tremendous." He pointed to the long train of successes. "We already have BUTTRESS [the toe], GOBLET [the instep], MUSKET [Taranto], and BRIMSTONE [Sardinia]; that operation FIREBRAND [Corsica] is being done for us and we are about to move into Corsica and that we have AVALANCHE securely, not to mention the fleet, it certainly justifies what the newspapers call 'a feeling of restrained optimism.'" He continued, "I am so desperately proud of this organization that I am quite likely to slop over, but during AVALANCHE and the intricate maneuvering incident to the Italian armistice, I had the supreme pleasure of seeing what started out to be a complicated, unwieldy, creaky machine ticking away like a Swiss watch with every staff division doing exactly the right thing at the right time, constantly thinking ahead and meeting every emergency with a little time to spare." He called it "the high point in my career."[36]

And never had he stood higher in Eisenhower's estimation. "If ever I should write any memoirs," Eisenhower wrote to McNarney, "I should certainly have to devote a full chapter to the debt I owe to Smith. He is a fellow who carries a tremendous load and does it so ably as to excite my admiration every day."[37] His stock was pretty high in Washington too. Stimson's assistant, John J. McCloy, informed Smith, "You are getting a big reputation [in the War Department]." In July Smith received his first Distinguished Service Medal for welding the machinery of the joint and combined staffs as secretary, followed by a second in August for his work organizing and running AFHQ. Amidst all the fanfare, he also received some sage advice from Pa Watson. "Hope you are taking your vitamins," Watson chided, "and keeping your feet on the ground."[38]

Four-Ring Circus

Roosevelt and Churchill told Stalin in August 1943 that an invasion of the Italian mainland would trigger either a German coup and the "setting up a Quisling Government of Fascist elements" or the collapse of the Italian government "and the whole of Italy pass[ing] into disorder." Both occurred.[39] The king's and Badoglio's prevarications and procrastination ensured that the Italian "betrayal" immediately transformed Italy into a battleground. Victor Emmanuel mistrusted the army and dreaded unleashing a popular uprising, for fear it would spark a communist-led revolution and end the monarchy. The prostrated communists offered no threat. The army's orders to avoid any confrontation with the Germans until after the armistice merely delivered unliberated Italy over to the vengeful Germans, who acted with their customary vigor in freeing Mussolini and placing him at the head of the Italian Social Republic (RSI), a puppet regime legitimizing the German occupation and the continuity of the Axis. The partisan uprising did occur in central and northern Italy in the guise of the clandestine Committee for National Liberation (CNL), an umbrella group that emerged to resist the German occupation and the RSI. Although monarchists, Catholics, and former officers took to the hills, the CNL remained dominated by leftist and republican elements. The king and his motley collection of hangers-on made good their escape, but the "flight to Brindisi" virtually ensured a postwar Italian republic.

Except for signing the long-terms surrender document—which he could not avoid—Eisenhower steered clear of any involvement with the Italians. Smith negotiated with the Brindisi government and formed the structures that transitioned Italy from an occupied territory to an Allied military associate. In addition, because of the chronic delay in achieving agreement among Washington, London, and now Moscow, his voice emerged as the most prominent in establishing policy.[40]

Eisenhower and Smith greatly exaggerated the support they expected from the Italian armed forces. The day after the Salerno landings, Smith urged Marshall to prod the president and Churchill into recognizing the Badoglio government, encouraging "the Italians to oppose with the fiercest possible resistance every German in Italy."[41] The next day AFHQ conveyed a message directly to Badoglio, stating, "The whole future and honour of Italy depends upon the part which the armed forces are now prepared to play."[42] The following day the two governments made public a letter to the marshal calling on Badoglio to lead the Italian people against the German invader. All this amounted to little. The Italian ground forces in southern Italy, Sardinia, and Corsica simply disintegrated. The portions of the fleet stationed in Ligurian and Tyrrhenian bases made for Oran, and those in Taranto and Brindisi headed for Malta. About half the Italian fleet made their escape. On 13 September—the day the Germans nearly split the Salerno bridgehead—Smith sent Mason-MacFarlane to Brindisi as head of a military mission. Murphy and Macmillan went along. The day before, Smith had brought his "pet Wop" Castellano to Algiers as head of an Italian military mission at AFHQ. "So you see," he wrote to Ismay, "our two ring circus has developed first into three rings and now four rings, counting the French and Italians."[43]

The Brindisi party consisted of the king, Badoglio, Crown Prince Umberto, Ambrosio, Roatta, and a collection of generals and admirals. All the civilian agencies remained in Rome. The Italians possessed few bargaining chips other than their "unchallenged claim of legality" against the republican regime set up by the Germans. Badoglio also maintained that Italy "is now in a *de facto* state of war with Germany." Acting on Smith's instructions, Mason-MacFarlane dangled the possibility of the Italian government gaining cobelligerent or military associate status and administrative control over the four liberated provinces in southern Italy, in exchange for pledges to broaden the government, restore the constitution, and hold postwar elections. Badolgio must also accept AMGOT's jurisdiction over areas not placed under the control of his government and an armistice commission to oversee Italian compliance with the surrender terms. To make the arrangement more palatable, Mason-MacFarlane opened but never pushed the question of the king's abdication.

After talking to Murphy and Macmillan upon their return to Algiers on 18 September, Smith drafted a long report to the CCS and BCOS. He pointed out that AFHQ intended to use Italian forces in Sardinia and Corsica for coastal defense and portions of the fleet for transport. Smith, in Eisenhower's name, requested that the Badoglio government receive "some form of de facto recognition . . . as a co-belligerent or military associate." Recognizing that such a policy shift was "not at all consistent with the provisions of the long terms armistice" and that it exposed the governments to "considerable opposition and criticism," he recommended that "the burden be placed upon us, on the grounds of military necessity, which I am convinced should be the governing factor." The cable also asked for a decision on the requested modifications before Eisenhower met with Badoglio.[44]

Eisenhower did not like the bit about AFHQ accepting blame for cutting a deal with the Italians. On 19 September—now back at his advance command post in Tunisia after visiting the Salerno beachheads—Eisenhower drafted a new cable. He pointed to two paths the Allies could take in future relations with the Italians: either accept Italy as a military associate and strengthen Badoglio, or assume the heavy liability of establishing an Allied military government. Eisenhower "strongly recommended the first." If Smith concurred, he wanted the cable forwarded to London and Washington.[45] It went out the next day.

Smith's report and Eisenhower's "either/or" request prodded Washington and London to finalize the terms of surrender and define Italy's future status. Though admitting the long terms appeared "somewhat superseded," the British insisted on their use in the final Italian surrender.[46] Roosevelt felt that events in Italy made the long terms "completely superfluous" and wanted the military armistice lightened "in order to enable the Italians, within their limited capacities, to wage war against Germany." Stimson liked nothing about "this Italian business" and influenced the president to grant only temporary approval for AFHQ's withholding of the long terms, pending further instructions. He did offer AFHQ the power to modify the exactions of the surrender if Badoglio agreed to a declaration of war; only then could Italy be considered a cobelligerent.[47]

Acting on Roosevelt's instructions, Smith directed Mason-MacFarlane to arrange an Eisenhower-Badoglio meeting in Malta and warned him against mentioning the long-terms armistice, "as we are instructed to hold it in abeyance." AFHQ instructed that these concessions had no bearing on the requirements for a return to constitutional government in the postwar period.[48] Smith then modified the original title and preamble containing the words "unconditional surrender." After Badoglio signed the "military" surrender, the Italians would be told to expect from time to time additional terms or directives on political, financial, or economic matters under the provisions of the 3 September surrender document. Smith thought Badoglio would accept the two-tier approach.[49]

Macmillan came to the same conclusion. He notified London that Badoglio protested not the harsh terms but the language of the armistice. Advised that Badoglio would sign any document placed in front of him, the British renewed their pressure for the long terms. The Soviets likewise considered "it necessary to expedite the signature of the detailed armistice terms . . . necessary in view of the situation existing in Italy at the present time."[50] Roosevelt gave in and authorized Eisenhower to sign the long terms.

Noting AFHQ's preoccupation with Italian affairs, de Gaulle exploited the situation by manufacturing another crisis. Citing the difficulties involved in dealing with communist resistance elements—and Giraud's political ineptness—de Gaulle insisted that the forces operating in Corsica come under his command. On 25 September he placed before the FCNL proposals to end the system of dual command and form a single executive. Giraud's meek defense convinced the majority to side with de Gaulle. Giraud again played into de Gaulle's hands; he signed a document that effectively deprived him of his nominal authority as com-

mander in chief. Long favoring a greater role for de Gaulle and anticipating a settlement of the French leadership question, Smith raised no
objections to Giraud's ouster as copresident.[51]

As de Gaulle calculated, Smith possessed no time to treat with the
French. The entire deal with the Italians appeared to be in trouble.
On 26 September he received instructions from Washington reversing
American policy on the long-terms document. The same day Mason-
MacFarlane reported that Badoglio had agreed to Smith's agenda and
volunteered to come to Malta. He also indicated the king had suddenly
taken refuge behind the constitution. He could not declare war on Germany, since only a constitutionally established government could do
that. Victor Emmanuel also told Mason-MacFarlane that he expected to
dump Badoglio. He played the communist card, warning, "it would be
most dangerous to leave the choice of postwar government unreservedly in the hands of the Italian people."[52] Accompanied by Murphy and
Macmillan, Smith flew to Brindisi the next morning and explained to
the Italians there would be "no quibbling . . . over details"; they must
sign the long-terms surrender.[53] Smith's first acquaintance with Victor
Emmanuel and Badoglio convinced him "there was something fundamentally lacking in all the top men."[54] He told reporters, "the Italian
government, at the present time, consists of the king, Marshal Badoglio, two or three generals, and a couple of part-time stenographers.
The day that I was there, a couple of cheap help from the Foreign
Office (an under-secretary or two) came down from Rome on foot."
Victor Emmanuel, once described as Italy's "moron little king" in an
AFHQ propaganda broadcast, appeared "absolutely pitiful," in Smith's
opinion. Badoglio "has been a good general but he was an old man—
without decision—and given to crying."[55] Whereas the marshal proved
malleable, the king refused to declare war on Germany or promise free
postwar elections. Smith left with what he came for, however. After
some typical Smith bullying, the king finally authorized Badoglio to
meet with Eisenhower in Malta in two days' time and sign the long
terms. "The King-Badoglio government is a pretty weak affair," confessed Eisenhower, "yet it is the only medium through which Italians can
be inspired to help us."[56]

Badoglio, himself the object of a black propaganda blitz, requested
that the comprehensive terms of the surrender be withheld from the
public. He thought if the Italians knew the full extent of the capitulation, they would reject his government. Smith entertained the same
concerns and worried that release of the surrender text would provoke
resistance and make the work of the Control Commission more difficult.

Smith promised to raise the issue with Eisenhower and intimated the Allies would probably withhold publication.

The surrender itself proved anticlimactic. Aboard the battleship *Nelson* in Valetta Harbor, Eisenhower and Badoglio affixed their signatures to the "Instrument of Surrender of Italy." Cunningham, Alexander, Smith, Murphy, Macmillan, and an array of lesser lights looked on. After the signing Eisenhower handed Badoglio a letter, written by Smith, that stated, "several of the clauses have become obsolescent or have already been put into execution," and others exceeded the current powers of the Italian government. Future conditions remained contingent on "the extent of cooperation by the Italian government."[57] Badoglio appealed, asking that Eisenhower alter the document's title and remove the first clause containing the phrase "unconditional surrender." If the terms became public, his government "would be overwhelmed by a storm of reproach." Eisenhower promised to consult the political heads. As "a matter of the utmost urgency," the next day Smith requested acceptance of his amended title and rewording of Article 1 and suppression of the document "as absolutely vital to our success in Italy."[58] After an exchange of cables, Churchill wrote to Roosevelt on 4 October, "now that Uncle Joe has come in with us about Italian Declaration . . . there should be no nonsense about terms until Rome is taken. It seems to us high time that the Italians began to work their passage."[59] The text of the Italian surrender remained unpublished until November 1945.

"On the Same Track"

For a month Marshall had been requesting Smith's return to Washington for discussions concerning future operations in Italy and manpower and supply requirements, but the unsettled Italian situation and the expected move of AFHQ to Italy kept Smith in the theater.[60] Still smarting from Marshall's criticism of his lack of boldness, Eisenhower wanted clarification on how the Italian campaign could most effectively contribute to the future cross-Channel operation (Overlord). He thought the best solution would be to center all efforts on preserving the initiative in Italy. At the end of September he expected to be "called home for consultation." When the call came and Marshall asked him to come to Washington for talks on "matters pertaining to your theater," Eisenhower begged off. On 1 October the Allies secured Naples, and three days later Eisenhower cabled Marshall, "Alexander and I both believe we will have Rome by [the end of] October. There is nothing particularly bothering us at the moment," he explained, "in spite of the delicate nature of the Italian political problems which Smith handles so well, [so] I think he should come home for a very brief visit in order that our planning for the winter campaign may dovetail perfectly with the larger projects you have in view." He said Smith represented "the only one I have that can come to see you to make sure that we are on the right track." He hoped Smith could conclude his business in two or three days. "I sorely need him back as soon as possible."[61]

Operational matters did not occupy much of Eisenhower's attention. He casually informed Marshall, "We will have Rome by October" and noted, "the greatest possible assistance we can give you is to conduct a vigorous fall and winter campaign to include the capture of the Po valley, from which position we can threaten and actually stage diversionary operations into southern France."[62] Although couching his language in terms of how expanding operations in Italy supported Overlord, Eisenhower's primary interest rested in safeguarding his own theater.

His personal prospects preoccupied him far more. On 1 October the navy secretary, Frank Knox, stopped by El Aouina and informed Eisenhower over lunch that the political heads had decided at Quebec that Marshall would command the cross-Channel operation. Speculation on the appointment prompted a great deal of press. For this reason, according to Knox, the president had ordered a news blackout, and no announcement appeared in the minutes of the Quebec conference. Nonetheless, Knox assured Eisenhower, it was "official." More troubling was the news that, according to Knox, Eisenhower would take over as army chief of staff.[63] Eisenhower immediately called Smith, told him the news, and informed him he was sending Beetle to Washington for talks with Marshall; he then forwarded two letters outlining the points he wanted covered with Marshall.

On 3 October Mountbatten came through on the way to his new theater command. He disclosed a slightly different take on Quebec. Under pressure from Roosevelt, Stimson, and Hopkins, Churchill had bent and agreed that Marshall should command Overlord, and as a sop to Brooke, Hopkins suggested the theater command in the Mediterranean should be British. That left Eisenhower without a command. Mountbatten thought the chances were good that Eisenhower would return to Washington as chief of staff. "Beadle [sic] is being sent home to see what can be done about protecting Ike from becoming US Chief of Staff," Hughes wrote to his wife. "Ike wouldn't like that job—furnish what Marshall wants, do as Marshall says. What Beadle can do is more than I can figure out, but he has gall, nerve, and can talk fast."[64]

To make sure they were on the same page, Eisenhower returned to

Algiers for the first time in a month to brief Smith before he left. In front of Butcher they hashed out all the possibilities. Just about the last thing Eisenhower wanted was a "political" job in Washington, especially becoming the boss's boss. Then there was the equally daunting issue of dealing with another old boss, MacArthur. Eisenhower much preferred commanding an army group under Marshall in Overlord. He told Smith that if the topic came up in his discussions with Marshall, he should convey that message as discreetly as possible. Eisenhower also asked Smith to go to bat for Patton. Despite the Sicilian outrages, Eisenhower had just recommended Patton for an army command in Overlord.[65]

Smith's "official" agenda was lengthy. Eisenhower wanted Smith to convince Washington officials of the paramount importance of propping up Badoglio as "the only leadership in Italy around which anti-Fascist elements can rally." Smith should also make the case for retaining air and airborne units and landing craft in the Mediterranean. Eisenhower envisioned running some amphibious operations to speed the advance up the Italian boot. Questions surrounding the future air command structures in Europe also loomed large. Eisenhower opposed Arnold's idea of creating a single supreme commander for air to conduct the strategic bombing campaign. Spaatz would also go to Washington and settle matters pertaining to the establishment of the Fifteenth Air Force in Italy. Smith's job focused on defending a theater commander's control of air assets. Based on Mediterranean experience, any air commander should coordinate strategic bombing, but Eisenhower considered it more important that he understand the requirements of close air support. Since he considered Tedder the best man for the job, Eisenhower offered to surrender him. As he told Marshall, "our team here has become so well solidified that with Smith and me on the job we can now accept substitutes in some important places."[66] Eisenhower also asked that Smith clarify the theater's opposition to McNair's plan for reducing the combat strength of American divisions by 2,000 men. Also related to the manpower question, Eisenhower insisted the theater's "replacement situation should be thoroughly considered."[67] On 5 October, his forty-eighth birthday, Smith boarded his aircraft for the flight to Washington. Clearly, his mission would take more than two or three days.

Aside from the tasks assigned by Eisenhower, Smith composed his own long list of questions. Many involved dealing with the French and Italians: the impact of Italy's elevation to cobelligerent status on U.S. policy, the vital importance of keeping the Italian surrender terms under wraps, the implications arising from recent developments between de

Gaulle and Giraud, reequipping and training French forces according to the revised Quebec estimates, and finalizing civil affairs policy and organizational plans for military government and the Control Commission in Italy. Others centered on operational issues: amphibious operations, if any, up the Italian boot and their timetable; the invasion of southern France in support of Overlord, an operation Eisenhower thought little of; the effectiveness of airborne units to date and their future use; and AFHQ's opposition to British schemes for operations in the eastern Mediterranean. Smith also needed guidance on a number of issues related to special operations in the theater: how to correlate expanded OSS operations in southern France, northern Italy, and the Balkans with those of the British Special Operations Executive (SOE); the degree of importance attached to special operations, which in turn involved the employment of military, especially air, assets; and whether special operations should be directly under military command.[68]

Before he tackled his official chores, Smith went into undercover mode, tapping into his many sources to try to determine what the future held for Eisenhower. King and Arnold vigorously opposed any suggestion Marshall should leave Washington. Stimson's voice was strongest in making the case for him to go to Europe. Among the senior soldiers he talked to, all believed Marshall would head Overlord, and speculation centered on whether Eisenhower, Somervell, McNarney, or McNair would replace him. Following conversations with Marshall, Smith concluded the chief wanted Eisenhower to stay in the Mediterranean. On 10 October Smith wrote a cryptic letter to Eisenhower, informing him, "you can now concentrate on long range plans."[69]

Hughes detected plenty of indications that Eisenhower planned to leave the theater. "Ike wants me to take Kay [Summersby] with car thrown in. He doesn't want to be Chief of Staff of the US Army."[70] Smith's letter raised his hopes. For one thing, he was relieved that Smith was representing his interests. "Every time you go away," Eisenhower confided in Smith, "I learn again how much I depend upon you."[71] As he explained to the wife of an old army buddy, Beetle was "by all odds the most competent and marvelous Chief of Staff that any Commander was ever lucky enough to have. I don't know how I would carry along without him."[72] Eisenhower began to fret that whichever appointment he received, he might lose Smith.

With that bit of business out of the way, Smith systematically worked through his checklist of assignments. Much of his time was spent handling problems left unsettled by the Italian surrender. On 11 October Smith met with the president and Hopkins. The Malta surrender and the amended surrender conditions had not closed the book on questions pertaining to enforcement of the settlement. Spurred by Churchill, Roosevelt felt no compulsion to cater to the Soviets on the actions of the Allied Control Commission in Italy. Roosevelt stood ready to accept Smith's recommendations. Provisions for control of the Italian fleet remained purposely ambiguous. Churchill wanted a free hand in the disposition of Italian warships; at the very least, he wanted to use the issue as a bargaining chip to induce the Italians to declare war. Now Churchill again raised objections to eliminating the "unconditional surrender" language from Article 1, since it impacted the retention of Italian warships. Roosevelt and Hopkins were prepared to leave matters where they stood. So was Smith.[73] "The matter is becoming too complicated for me to handle at long range," Smith informed Eisenhower. "At McCloy's suggestion, I am filing with the JCS the document as originally signed without any amendments or corrections whatever leaving it to the CCS Secretariat to struggle with matters of protocol."[74]

Smith instructed Whiteley to keep him informed on developments in Italy. On 13 October Badoglio finally made a declaration of war, and Eisenhower ordered Whiteley to expedite Smith's plan for a military government in Italy. Smith orchestrated the selling of the program in Washington. After his trip to Brindisi, Smith had decided the Italian government was incapable of exercising any measure of effective control and that AMGOT and the Control Commission would administer all liberated territories until an Italian government could function in Rome.[75] Smith's plan envisioned three stages. As long as operations continued, ultimate authority remained in Eisenhower's hands; when the Badoglio government proved ready to assume a more active role, supervision would pass to the Control Commission. At that point the Advisory Council, consisting of high commissioners from the United States, United Kingdom, USSR, France, Greece, and Yugoslavia—representatives of all the powers formerly at war with Italy—would operate under the day-to-day management of AFHQ's designated deputy. This third period would begin after the cessation of hostilities. Until then, Italy would be divided into three zones. In the south, the so-called king's Italy took shape in the four Apulian provinces; these areas were under the titular control of Badoglio, with the military mission acting in liaison and supervisory roles. Farther north, in the intermediate zone behind the front, fell those territories under the direct administration of the Allied Control Commission. As the front moved north, so would the zonal boundaries. The final area, the combat zone, remained under AMGOT, directly answerable to Alexander.[76]

The military government program suffered from a host of problems. With the organization settled—the mechanism received the approval of the Allied foreign ministers in Moscow at the end of October—Smith turned to staffing the new structures. Washington only very belatedly placed any priority on military government. Just about the only thing Stimson, McCloy, and Morgenthau agreed on was that they disliked the name AMGOT. They thought it sounded too much like OGPU and Gestapo—secret police.[77] The acronym remained, and given the advanced age of its senior leadership, AMGOT took on the meaning "Aged Military Gentlemen on Tour." The Americans still encountered problems manning AMGOT. Hilldring complained, "I have a lot of willing workers who don't know more about military government than what they read in books."[78] The bigger issue revolved around achieving some semblance of balance between the British and Americans in senior positions. Smith tried to lever McCloy out of Washington as head of civil affairs in AFHQ. As McCloy recounted, he "put it to the Secretary [Stimson] as strongly as I knew how but no luck."[79] Smith asked for Hilldring, who complained of suffering from a dose of "Pentagon pallor" and lobbied hard to escape the War Department, with no luck. After McCloy and Hilldring, Smith had very few options. Eisenhower suggested LTG Kenyon Joyce, whom he had served under at Forts Lewis and Sam Houston. Joyce possessed no experience, but Eisenhower thought highly of him. Smith engineered his appointment as Eisenhower's deputy to the Advisory Council, and another aged military gentleman joined the team on 7 November. Rennell remained chief of civil affairs with an American deputy, BG Frank McSherry. In Smith's view, *military government* was a misnomer. Rennell and Joyce served as his deputies for handling Italian affairs as directed by AFHQ.[80]

The looming manpower crisis triggered the main buzz in the corridors of the Pentagon. Manpower and supply—the two spheres that bestowed the least credit on the army—suffered from almost identical evils, the origins of which lay in the incomplete reorganization of the War Department in 1942. AEFHQ and Pershing's War Department model contained a separate division for training. Under the 1920 NDA structure, G-1 and G-3 shared responsibility for training. Marshall's restructured WDGS not only retained this disconnect, but it also widened it. The War Department's manpower plan called for half the men deployed overseas to enter the theater as members of integrated and trained formations; these units were organized and trained by AGF, AAF, and ASF. The other half would go overseas as individual replacements. Replacements would flow into existing units based on expected rates of attrition.

The system suffered from imbalances from the beginning and never recovered. First, planners greatly exaggerated the percentage of manpower allotted for combat units. Then Torch and North Africa pulled troops from training divisions in the United States as replacements. The critical shortages of service personnel required a number of alterations in the troop basis. The rush of service troops to North Africa and the expedient formation of provisional units in the theater gave the appearance that surplus manpower had been sucked into the rear or lost in the pipeline. Sicily and the movement into Italy placed additional strains on an already faltering system. The army's miscalculations on manpower requirements exacerbated the problem. Responsibility for retraining replacement officers and men placed in redundant or superfluous military occupation slots fell to the theater commands, which suffered under the same organizational constrictions that plagued the War Department. A whole parade of officers toured the theater and always returned to Washington with stories of the unnecessarily bloated rear areas and the extravagant use of officers in headquarters. Marshall saw no need for an independent training command; instead, he placed the organizer of the restructured WDGS, McNarney, in charge of overseeing the army's manpower program. As another by-product of the bureaucratic infighting between the WDGS and Somervell, no agency had control over the replacement structure. Somervell argued for a separate manpower and training command under ASF's superintendence, but McNarney continually blocked any resolution of the standoff. The U.S. Army fought the entire war without resolving the dispute. As a result, the replacement structure became an administrative black hole and a black mark on the record of the U.S. Army.[81]

The War Department's misbegotten manpower program sparked a public outcry, prompting congressional action. Parents complained about their sons languishing for months in retraining depots in active theaters. Others complained that their teenage sons went forward after only a few weeks' training. By summer 1942, the War Department admitted its gross underestimate of manpower requirements and projected serious shortages. As a remedy, the army called for the drafting of eighteen-year-olds and drastic reductions in time in training. In mid-September McNarney went to Capitol Hill to explain the factors behind the projected personnel shortfalls. McNarney sidestepped the issue, affixing blame not on War Department policies or any of his agencies but on the theater commands, especially AFHQ and NATO. Marshall, predisposed to blame rear-area commands, accepted McNarney's whitewashing. On 13 October he placed the fault on NATO and warned Eisenhower that he "must get to the root of the problem immediately." The next day he accused NATO and the SOS of "skimming the cream" of replacement personnel, depriving combat units of the most qualified men.[82] Fortunately for Eisenhower, three days earlier Hughes had submitted a comprehensive study of theater manpower allocations that offered proof to the contrary. Anticipating this turn of events, Smith took pains to meet with Marshall and McNarney, explain the unique problems the theater faced, and defend AFHQ's record. Clearly, his efforts neither pacified Marshall nor deflected McNarney.[83]

By 13 October Smith thought he was "about finished here" and anticipated heading back to Algiers in a day's time. "Just received a report from the commandant of Cadets on Cadet Eisenhower [Ike's son]," he noted. "You will be flattered." The next day he congratulated Ike on his birthday and wished he could be there in person, but owing to complications involving "negotiations over strategic air forces and several other matters," he would be delayed for several more days.[84] He and Spaatz argued that the Fifteenth Air Force must remain under theater command. As Spaatz told Eisenhower, "Smith and I have okayed this plan." Over the next days, their consistent opposition killed Arnold's scheme for forming a unified air command.[85]

The other matters Smith alluded to involved future operations in Italy and the eastern Mediterranean. Smith passed on some bad news to Eisenhower. Production projections for landing craft proved far lower than expected. Eisenhower passed on Alexander's assessment that "the removal of craft as ordered by the Combined Chiefs of Staff will seriously prejudice our operations to gain Rome." Thirty-six landing craft/tanks were currently engaged in supply roles because of the extensive German destruction of infrastructure. Smith initially supported the idea of moving landing craft to Europe based on existing schedules. Eisenhower now wanted him to make the point that without sea lift, the Allied forces in Italy would be forced "into frontal attacks which will undoubtedly be strongly contested and prove costly." Even if the ground attacks succeeded, AFHQ would not possess enough landing craft to sustain the advance. He deflected Smith from raising the question of the transfer of landing craft to the United Kingdom but directed him to argue for increased production.[86]

In between these ongoing discussions about air command and landing craft, Smith received an invitation to Hyde Park for a meeting with the president and Hopkins before he left. In typical Roosevelt style, the conversations covered a wide range of topics—primarily Overlord versus the Mediterranean. From their talks, Smith concluded that Roosevelt had made up his mind on Marshall's going to Europe. The president now appeared "sold" on Eisenhower as army chief of staff.

As was always the case, Smith's hectic schedule allowed little time for Nory. Since the end of August he had been worried about her. Nory's aged mother's health was failing. Torn between tending to her mother and carrying on her various volunteer works with the Gray Ladies at Walter Reed and acting as hostess at USO functions, Nory developed some health problems of her own. As Smith told a Washington friend, "Nory has been used to my carrying the load in cases of this kind and I dread to think of her having to do it alone." As it turned out, Nory managed fine without Beetle. He found her recovered and busy.[87]

Eisenhower described Smith's contributions as "a master of negotiations" as priceless.[88] Aside from Smith's dealing with the British and the associated and enemy powers, Eisenhower relied on his persuasiveness and his connections inside the CCS and the War Department, and especially with Marshall, for defending the theater's prerogatives. Smith scored some successes. As he assured Eisenhower, "most of our recommendations will be approved."[89] Despite mounting pressure from the British to publish the text of the Italian surrender, Washington blocked its release and, in so doing, acknowledged support for Badoglio's tottering government. Although the specifics of command relations never emerged, Smith and Spaatz defended the theater's control over strategic air forces. He talked to the AGF command and expressed Eisenhower's views on the proposed revisions in force structures. He got a hearing with Marshall on Patton and on promotions Eisenhower wanted pushed through. And he finally succeeded in firming up policy and arrangements for a military government in Italy—a vexing problem occupying much of his attention for months.

Not all his efforts achieved results. De Gaulle's latest grab for power confirmed the president's worst suspicions. To Roosevelt, de Gaulle remained a militarist, quasi-fascist, would-be dictator and a very dangerous man. The president had pulled out all his tricks to prop up Giraud, only now to recognize (but not acknowledge) he had backed the wrong horse. The unbendable de Gaulle might offer the only alternative—there was no other contestant—but Roosevelt steadfastly refused to concede anything but a military role to the general. AFHQ's preference for de Gaulle did not go unnoticed by the president. Forewarned by McCloy, who knew only too well Roosevelt's intransigence on the question and the price men paid for obstructing his will, Smith merely made soundings. As Hughes predicted, Smith exerted no discernible influence on anybody's thinking on command billets in Overlord. Nor did he get any solution on the degree to which AFHQ would direct special operations in the theater. Smith would continue to arbitrate among contesting claimants—OSS, SOE, and the commanders in chief—for operations that assumed greater importance and calls on theater, mostly air, assets.[90] And he failed to blunt criticisms of the theater's handling of replacements.

Although it is difficult to gauge what influence he exerted, Smith made the case for continuing offensive ground operations in Italy to the combined and joint planners, OPD, Marshall, and the president. Throughout 1943 the Allies conducted campaigns in the Mediterranean without clearly defined political or grand strategic objectives. In the absence of guidance from above, the campaign in Italy lacked coherence from the start. AFHQ had already fulfilled the objectives assigned it by the CCS: Italy had been knocked out of the war, Naples and the Foggia airfields were secured, and German forces were tied down in Italy and the Balkans. The question now revolved around whether AFHQ should maintain offensive pressure in Italy. Ultra provided evidence in early October that the Germans intended to fight a defensive winter campaign south of Rome; the hardening German defenses already made that obvious. Pressed by the escalating bombing offensive against the Reich, and faced with an irretrievable disadvantage in the air over the Mediterranean, the Germans left only a token Luftwaffe presence in the theater. The Quadrant decision effectively turned the Mediterranean into a strategic backwater. Seven divisions would be withdrawn for Overlord, and a proposed invasion of southern France (Anvil) would subtract two more. Allied air and sea power granted potentially enormous operational flexibility, but the lack of landing craft and the Quebec timetable erected obvious impediments. Why not batten down; maintain enough pressure to compel the Germans to retain forces in Italy, the south of France, and the Balkans; conduct the bomber offensive from Foggia; and begin the process of moving earmarked divisions, air assets, and landing craft to England? To the extent any strategy existed, it seemed directed not at winning the campaign but simply at stretching it out and preventing any redeployment of German forces to France.

The answer rested in the irresistible tug of Rome. Marshall considered Sicily the crossroads of Allied strategy. Once taken, the road inevitably led to Rome. Churchill cautioned Alexander that "no one can measure the consequences" of failing to take the Eternal City. Smith talked up Eisenhower's projection that Allied forces would hold the line at Leghorn-Florence-Rimini by spring 1944. He left Washington with no firm strategic guidelines but, more important, without receiving a shutdown order. AFHQ received the go-ahead to conduct offensive operations, albeit with diminishing assets, for the rest of the year.

★ 24 ★

"We Conduct Our Wars in a Most Curious Way"

Smith returned to Algiers on 21 October. As Hughes reported, he "hastened to report to Ike. Wonder if he knows the answer to Ike's future?"[1] Speculation on "Ike's future" gripped Algiers. All Smith could tell Eisenhower was that nothing had been set in stone. He could forget about a field command in Overlord, however; Marshall thought that would represent too much of a step-down for a theater commander. Smith's best guess was that Eisenhower would return to Washington as chief of staff.[2] That estimate pretty much conformed to what Harriman had told Eisenhower on 15 October. Harriman had spoken of the president's great reluctance in sacrificing Marshall, but if he did, Eisenhower would succeed him as chief of staff.[3] The next night Patton flew in from Sicily. He, Eisenhower, and Hughes ate dinner together. "It was like old times—almost," Patton wrote to his wife. Naturally, they talked about the future. "No one including Devine Destiny knows what is to become of us."[4] Smith may have known more than he revealed. He certainly made no effort to hide the fact that he expected to leave the Mediterranean.

Just before Smith had left for Washington, another major turf battle with Hughes loomed. This time Smith, intent on succeeding, carefully marshaled his reserves, and they were considerable. At the beginning of August the War Department again solicited from Smith an explanation of how NATO fit into the Allied command structure.[5] He made his deputy assistant chief of staff for operations, BG William C. Crane, head of a stacked committee. The War Department demanded a table of organization for both AFHQ and NATO and detailed descriptions of functions and the division of responsibilities. Crane chaired three general meetings interspersed throughout August. To no one's surprise, the committee experienced real difficulty putting on paper a flow chart and an account of how the structure functioned. Finally, at the end of September, the report made its way to Smith.[6] At the same juncture, the senior officers in Algiers were nervous about the impending move of the headquarters to Italy. "Movement of AFHQ growing hotter every day," Hughes noted on 30 September. "Rank, prestige, wishes, desires, hates etc all enter into it. Why can't we concentrate on the war?" Just as Smith was preparing his onslaught, he was called to Washington. Upon his return, everyone expected another bureaucratic bloodletting. It never happened; the urgency disappeared. "Ike tells Beadle he and I are coordinate," Hughes recorded on 27 October, and "any idea that AFHQ is to operate NATOUSA is out." Hughes wondered, "Does Smith like that?" The next day Smith called Hughes on the phone and talked about the organization in Italy. He told a shocked Hughes that he possessed no personal interest in it. The following day a still disbelieving Hughes found "Beadle in cheerful mood. Most agreeable. Must be on his way out." A week later Hughes again predicted, "an explosion due. Beadle has been quiet for three days." But none came. [7]

As far back as the first week of September, Smith was already thinking in terms of his eventually going to England. He exchanged a number of lengthy memos with Moses, now the American G-4 on the cross-Channel planning staff (COSSAC) in London. They discussed supply planning for the cross-Channel operation, Bolero preparations, and the theater command structure. As part of his campaign for restructuring the theater headquarters, Smith presented his rationale for wanting Hughes moved into AFHQ as the American CAO in command of all administrative and supply services; Devers experimented along the same lines in ETO with Lee. The most vocal opponent of functionalized command structures in the War Department was Moses, who raised a number of objections to Smith's proposal. That came as no surprise. What is revealing, although neither officer said as much, was that both proceeded on the assumption that Smith would ultimately exercise an influence in forming the headquarters for Overlord.[8]

Eisenhower assumed he was on his way out too. "Ike wants plan for American operation in event there be a British C in C." Hughes surmised, "I guess Ike is going home." The next evening Eisenhower invited Hughes for dinner. "Sat next to Kay at Ike's invitation," Hughes snidely remarked. "Guess Ike is about to turn over."[9] If he did turn over, he wanted to retain Smith's services. Three days after Smith returned, Eisenhower wrote a letter to Marshall pleading "that you not agree to any assignment for [Smith] that would break up our present intimate association." He continued, "In the long period that he has served as my chief of staff we have developed a team work that I believe is effective and of which the principal ingredient is confidence in each other. It is my hope that, and General Smith informs me that it is also his, that we may continue to function as a team in any task that may be assigned us. I believe that whatever effectiveness I may have in contributing to the war effort, and this applies also to General Smith's effectiveness, are both increased by maintaining our existing relationship." With all due deference, Eisenhower based his request not on personal grounds but on "the best interests of the service." It also served his own best interests.[10]

Lack of Grip

On 24 October Eisenhower called a commanders in chief meeting at La Marsa, specifically for Smith's review of developments in Washington. Based on Smith's appraisal, they voted to maintain the offensive in Italy. Alexander talked about keeping the German "on his heel."[11] With the sanction of Washington and London, AFHQ had inaugurated the longest and bloodiest campaign fought by the Western Allies in Europe. Eisenhower endorsed offensive operations in Italy even though he expected no decisive results. In early October he believed Rome would fall soon and instructed Smith not to initiate any movement of AFHQ-Main to Naples. Now, at the end of the month, German defenses were hardening all along the line; even though he still optimistically told the CCS he expected to be on the Pisa-Rimini line by spring 1944, Eisenhower reversed himself and directed Smith to establish headquarters in Naples.[12] As he had in the winter of 1942–1943 in Tunisia and would again in the autumn and winter of 1944, Eisenhower insisted on maintaining pressure all along the line. The Italian campaign devolved into a World War I–type slugging match. The Allies kept the Germans on their heels, but at a rapidly escalating cost.

After Salerno, the fall of Naples, and the seizure of Foggia, the campaign—void of any clearly defined operational objectives—denigrated into an attritional fight waged at the tactical level. The mountainous terrain, perfect for a delaying campaign, negated the great Allied advantage of airpower and mobility. Sea power might have conferred some operational flexibility, but none of the amphibious end runs Eisenhower alluded to ever happened. As in North Africa and Sicily, Eisenhower deferred to Alexander; Alexander yielded to Clark and Montgomery. "There is no doubt," Montgomery thought, "we conduct our wars in a most curious way." "What we want in ITALY is a proper and firm plan for waging the campaign," he noted in his diary on 27 October. "At present it is haphazard and go-as-you-please." Montgomery complained that he and Clark do "*what* we like, *when* we like; the total military power of the two Armies is not applied on one big plan. In other words, there is no grip or control by 15 Army Group . . . [and] until some very clear directive is issued we shall continue to muddle on."[13] Like Patton in Sicily, Clark followed Montgomery's advice "not to take any notice of what Alexander told him to do because Alexander was a man of straw."[14] If Alexander was the straw man, what did that make Eisenhower?

In December Eisenhower complained about the "eternal pound, pound, pound" and wondered to Mamie whether he could ever live a normal life again.[15] Eisenhower's chronic fatigue and irritability were real enough, but they were the product of nervous tension and his struggle to sublimate his growing angst, not the crushing schedule of the day-to-day management of his headquarters or the many demands of running his vast theater. He developed a near pathological distaste for Algiers. As he told Hughes after the war, "that was one place for which I never expected to experience any homesickness."[16] Instead, he spent as much time as he could at his advance headquarters. He whined about spending half his life in an airplane, but in fact, he remained at Amilcar for weeks at a stretch, returning to Algiers only for meetings with touring dignitaries or infrequent updates on theater matters with Hughes. From the launch of Avalanche to 1 December, he spent less than a third of his time in Algiers. Being away from AFHQ gave him, as Summersby put it, "the illusion of being on the march."[17] He convinced himself the advance headquarters represented the "*true Allied Headquarters.*" There he resided in proximity to his commanders in chief, acting "military." AFHQ became the secondary headquarters, handling "an enormous amount of logistic, civil, political and economic work," all the things he evaded like scrofula.[18] As time went on, Eisenhower became even more disassociated. His instinctive aversion to detail meant his staffs were disinclined to bother him. The less he was bothered, the less he knew. In the last three months of 1943 he reverted to the interwar schedule—finished by noon.[19] The volume of his correspondence slowed to a trickle. He maintained his correspondence with Marshall and Churchill; otherwise, Smith and Whiteley or the operations staff wrote an increasing percentage of the letters and memos that went out in his name.[20]

Smith was the one who spent all his time in airplanes. He estimated he stayed in Algiers half the time; when he was not flying the Atlantic he spent the rest of his air time shuttling between Algiers and La Marsa and Amilcar in Tunisia and Sicily and Naples in Italy. "I now commute

. . . like any suburban tripper," he remarked. "I have developed a perfect drill which consists of boarding the plane, blowing up the air mattress and stretching out with a book."[21] Mostly he read pulp fiction; detective novels remained his favorite. He and BG Theodore Roosevelt Jr. had an exchange going. He found the time to give the newly published *Makers of Modern Strategy*, edited by Edward Meade Earle, careful study.[22]

With AFHQ running up to speed, Smith could afford more downtime. Visitors commented on the lavishness of his Villa Darena, described as "practically a palace," with its vast drawing rooms decorated with mosaics, extensive gardens and terraces, and beautiful views of the mountains. He gave full vent to his predilection for collecting. He filled the house with local art pieces, bric-a-brac mostly, and fine oriental rugs. Many of his guests were amazed at his polished manners and wit. Out of the office, Smith appeared a different person. Summersby described him as "a warm, friendly, and very likeable gentleman." She remembered small parties with expensive champagne and fine food. Others did as well.[23]

One attempt at hospitality backfired. Smith's villa stood near one occupied by Catroux. The general's wife was a harridan. Catroux had six aides—one for himself and five for his wife. The five constantly irritated Smith, always scrounging ham and bacon and sugar for Madame. One day Smith met an attractive young woman visiting with the general and Madame. She liked guns and had lived in the States, and when she expressed a fondness for pancakes and sausage, Smith invited her over for breakfast on the terrace. During the conversation she asked about the FCNL commissioner for foreign affairs, René Massigli. Smith gave one of his unvarnished assessments: Massigli, for all his charm, was as weak as dishwater. No wonder the FCNL's foreign policy wavered in the hands of such a man. After Smith offered his verdict, the conversation lagged. It turned out the woman was Massigli's mistress. Relations between Smith and Massigli never flourished after that breakfast.[24]

Smith spent enough time with a nurse, Ethel Westerman, to set tongues wagging. Eisenhower's relationship with Summersby remained a favorite topic of gossip, and some believed Smith's interest in Westerman was more than platonic. The two first became friendly when she tended him during his confinement in Oxford. He engineered her transfer to Algiers and showed real anxiety when her ship took a torpedo; he assumed charge of superintending the rescue mission. She basically served as his private nurse, monitoring his diet and keeping his ulcer under control. More than that, the Harvard-educated Westerman shared many of Smith's interests. Both were devout Catholics. She provided a companionable source of relief from the incessant grind of his job. An affair would have been out of character—Smith's devotion to Nory ran deep—and Smith possessed little time or opportunity for the pursuit of extracurricular activities of that sort.[25]

With the autumn mornings turning snappy, Smith yearned "to sit in a duck blind." Unable to bring his shotgun from the States, he acquired one from the French Sûreté and ammunition from Ivan Cobbald, a fellow outdoorsman and extremely well-connected friend in London. On 11 November he and Eisenhower took the day off and went partridge hunting in Tunisia. Although he complained Arab beaters could not match his dogs, he always relished getting "out from behind [his] desk for a change and out of doors with a gun in [his] hands." The weather did not cooperate. Just like in Italy, it rained constantly. But they did manage to bag some birds.[26]

Much of Smith's energy remained fixed on presiding over his sprawling headquarters. Between April and October, AFHQ expanded by one-quarter—all of the increase consisting of American personnel. Although he handed off more and more responsibilities to Hughes or civilian agencies, the demands on AFHQ continued to grow. Most of the added staff handled civil, economic, and especially liaison tasks. AFHQ had long been the object of derision. Wags joked in the early days in North Africa, "Never have so few been commanded by so many." When a heavy German air attack left the St. George unscathed, a soldier wondered why they never bombed the headquarters. "Because it is worth fifty divisions to them," came the snide reply. Smith tired of the hackneyed comparison to the mythical Foch headquarters. He carefully studied the question before going to London and concluded that Foch's headquarters amounted to little more than a nineteenth-century suite of officers; it did not possess any genuine general staff functions. The headquarters grew apace with its expanding responsibilities. AFHQ had charge of more than one million soldiers, sailors, airmen, and auxiliaries. Another problem stemmed from American manpower policies; regulations demanded that officers fill staff slots. Large numbers of officers remained in paper-pushing jobs that easily could have been performed by enlisted personnel, especially overskilled and underutilized WACs. Smith still took seriously his job of educating talented young officers. "It is a bit tough on these chaps to condemn them to staff duty," he told Huebner, "but our Army has been so deficient in the past in training high level intelligence and high level planning personnel that I think the need is well justified," even though "it is most likely that after the war these chaps will be put to sorting gun slings or put on ROTC duty, but if so, that is not my fault."[27] In view of the diminished demands placed on AFHQ once the front became stationary, and in anticipation of the move to Naples, Smith trimmed the complement by 710 by the end of November.[28]

The first half of November saw Smith immersed in his role as AFHQ's foreign minister. He retained the belief that "unusual political warfare possibilities to exploit" still existed.[29] On 1 November he redefined policy toward the recalcitrant Italian government, now relocated to Naples. He told Mason-MacFarlane, no more negotiating with the king and Badoglio; if the Italians refused to comply with the dictates of the Control Commission, all recognition and cooperation would cease.[30] Roosevelt had no faith in Italy's "very old top men" and insisted on democratic guarantees, while Churchill wanted the preservation of the House of Savoy. The king rejected any talk of abdication. Initially, he asked for Dino Grandi—an old *squadrista* thug, albeit an intelligent and sophisticated one—as foreign minister. When that went nowhere, he turned to a liberal with impeccable antifascist credentials: Count Sforza. Badoglio tendered his resignation, but the king refused to accept it. In the meantime, Sforza told Victor Emmanuel he would not serve until the king abdicated. The Americans backed Sforza, but Churchill harbored an abiding animosity for him. Churchill thought, "surely we should stick to what we have got till we can get something better and that can only be ascertained when we have Rome in our possession."[31]

Smith traveled to Naples during the first week of November. He and Butcher went there on a scouting mission for a location for AFHQ. He decided on the *grande palais* at Caserta. Smith staked out his claim for an adjacent villa, while Butcher picked the crown prince's hunting lodge for Eisenhower.[32] Smith "noted that there was very little enthusiasm among the people when the King drove through the city." In his view, the best solution lay in abdication by the king and the crown prince, with Badoglio acting as regent and Count Sforza or "some other outstanding anti-Fascist as prime minister." Another reason for Smith's trip to Naples centered on opening the Peninsula Base Section. Exactly one month after seizing Naples, with its port demolished and booby-trapped, the engineers had the harbor cleared, and soon the SOS was processing more tonnage than prewar levels. The Allies simply did not need to placate the king and Badoglio any longer. Smith advised the president that AFHQ should continue operating a military occupation through AMGOT and the Allied Control Commission until a more broadly based government developed after Rome fell.[33]

Almost by default, Smith's policy gained acceptance. A week later, another flap occurred. The Italians rejected AFHQ's control over the Italian fleet and merchant marine. Smith agreed to modify the terms slightly, and if Badoglio refused to accept this quid pro quo, then Smith would invoke the Malta "unconditional surrender" terms. Smith admitted that, other than labor units and police, the only benefit accruing from Italy's cobelligerent status came from the navy and merchant marine. Badoglio signed under protest. As Smith commented to Mason-MacFarlane, "The poor old Marshal came through without much of a struggle. The whole affair is a bit pathetic if it were not so serious."[34]

This Italian maneuvering garnered the attention of very few. Everyone remained focused on what would emerge from the conferences in Cairo and Tehran. Churchill arrived first. Smith met him in Algiers aboard the battleship *Renown*. They had a long talk. The prime minister confessed himself unconvinced of the merits of a spring 1944 Overlord. The British "are persistent in their desire to pursue our advantages in the Mediterranean, especially through the Balkans." He intended to raise the whole question again and settle it in Cairo before moving on to Tehran and the first "Big Three" conference. The conversation turned to command issues. The prime minister explained he had always intended for Brooke to command the cross-Channel invasion and thought the Mediterranean command should remain intact. The stumbling block came when Roosevelt insisted Marshall exercise command in both theaters, while Brooke commanded in England and Eisenhower remained theater commander in the Mediterranean. Churchill bowed to pressure that an American command Overlord, but he totally rejected the idea of Marshall assuming overall command of both theaters. Unable to finalize command arrangements at Quebec, Churchill confided in Smith that if the Americans won on Overlord, the command setup coming out of the Cairo and Tehran meetings would likely have Marshall in London and Eisenhower going to Washington. Smith predicted the upcoming conference would be "the hottest one yet."[35]

The prime minister proceeded to Malta, where Eisenhower met with him on 17 November. The two men covered the same ground. Churchill did not entirely rule out Eisenhower getting the big command and said he would be willing to accept only two Americans in command of Overlord: Marshall or Eisenhower. Always impressed by Beetle, and even more so after their parley, Churchill talked in terms of Smith staying in the Mediterranean as American deputy to the as yet unnamed British theater commander. In addition to providing military advice, Smith's brilliant handling of the French and Italians made him indispensable. Eisenhower dug in, telling Churchill, "this was one point on which I would not yield, except under directions from the President." Eisenhower guessed this was not the last time this issue would be raised.[36]

The president and his party arrived, and on 21 November Roosevelt toured the Tunisian battlefields in the company of Eisenhower. The president told him why Marshall deserved the Overlord command. Roosevelt also informed Eisenhower that he would be coming back to Washington as chief of staff. Later Eisenhower talked with King. The admiral still bet that, when it really came down to a decision, Roosevelt would not allow Marshall to leave Washington. Hopkins thought otherwise; the only way Marshall would not get the command would be if the British succeeded in blocking a 1944 Overlord at the Tehran meetings with the Russians.[37]

Roosevelt flew out late on 21 November; Marshall and King left the next day. With all the tumult of the coming and going of "the Greats," as Montgomery called them, Eisenhower and Smith expected to ride out the eye of the hurricane before they returned. Then another storm suddenly blew in. On 22 November syndicated journalist Drew Pearson reported Patton's slapping of hospitalized enlisted men to a rapt nationwide audience. The broadcast sparked a cry for Patton's scalp that eventually reached the halls of Congress. For Eisenhower, with his future appointment up in the air, the timing could not have been worse. Marshall wired from Cairo and asked for Eisenhower's version of events.

Facing a very angry press corps, Smith tried to mollify them. As he told Patton in a warning letter, Pearson's "very vicious and exaggerated version of the Sicilian hospital incident" produced a "flood of messages from the press associations . . . demanding confirmation or denial." Attempting to avoid a press conference, Smith first issued an official statement that made three points. First, Patton commanded the Seventh Army, had commanded it since its activation, and would continue to exercise that command. Second, he emphasized that "no soldier had ever disobeyed [Patton's] orders." Last, the statement noted that Patton "had never on any occasion been reprimanded officially by the C-in-C." Smith added that Eisenhower had taken "the hide off Patton." But as he told Patton, the statement "was not effective and it was necessary to hold a conference with the press." Smith provided a brief account of the incidents and emphasized that Patton had made full and complete amends for an action "which occurred during the strain and crisis of an important campaign" by apologizing personally to the individuals concerned and collectively to all the Seventh Army divisions. He dwelled at length on Patton's "great accomplishments during the Tunisian and

Sicilian campaigns" and underscored his "irreplaceable value to General Eisenhower and to the Allied armies." "We have *no* knowledge," he finished, "how this leak occurred in Washington."[38] "I got a long wire from Beedle Smith about correspondents raising hell," Patton recorded, "and about his efforts to placate them; also I was told to back up AFHQ and make no statements if I was visited by correspondents." Patton wholly concurred with Smith's actions and the content of his statements, both written and oral.[39]

The press naturally went to one of their own, Butcher, for an explanation. "Beetle was furious" when he discovered Butcher got involved "and wished to withdraw from any consideration of the matter." Butcher went to Eisenhower, advising him to hold an off-the-record press conference. But Eisenhower dodged. He was "trying to cure a bad head cold in anticipation of hard sessions at Cairo," Butcher recorded. "Beetle is an efficient Chief of Staff, but he is also a bit bumbling when dealing with the press, if not bungling, and also I may say, too touchy about his prerogatives as Chief of Staff."[40]

A sheepish Eisenhower replied to Marshall the day after Smith's press conference, defending his own actions more than he did Patton. He recounted that Patton had "momentarily lost his temper and upbraided the individuals in an unseemly and indefensible manner." After receiving verbal and written reports, Eisenhower had dispatched letters to Patton "expressing my extreme displeasure and informing him that any repetition would result in his instant relief." Patton made "proper amends to the individuals involved, and . . . before his whole army." Eisenhower had sent Lucas, his "eyes and ears," to Sicily and ordered Hughes to dispatch the theater inspector general to conduct separate inquiries. After the completion of these "exhaustive investigations . . . I decided that the corrective action . . . was adequate and suitable in the circumstances." In view of Patton's "gallantry, drive and loyalty," Eisenhower still believed "this decision is sound."[41] That evening he flew to Cairo as planned; presumably, he explained to Marshall why he had not confided in him.

Shortly after Messina fell, three senior journalists had come to Algiers insisting that Patton face a court-martial.[42] Explaining Patton's exceptional qualities as a field commander and his value to the war effort, Eisenhower had pleaded with them not to file the story. The journalists— Demaree Bess, Red Mueller, and Quentin Reynolds—agreed, as did the other sixty-odd newsmen in the theater. A month later, Eisenhower received the inspector general's report, confirming Patton's actions and the wide circulation of the story to other members of the press not bound by any pledge of confidentiality. COL Herbert Clarkson, the inspector general, recommended that Eisenhower permit the publication of the story and, to avoid "embarrassment to the War Department," transmit an account of Patton's actions to Marshall and high government authorities. Eisenhower decided not to follow Clarkson's advice. After reading the inspector general's report, Eisenhower sealed and filed it.[43]

Eisenhower was incensed when Smith told the press Patton had never received an "official" reprimand, but he flew off to Cairo on 24 December, leaving Smith to handle the toxic residue of the press conference. Over Eisenhower's name, Smith wrote another warning to Patton. The storm continued, Smith warned, but would soon blow over.[44] "As I told you some time ago," he reassured Patton in a separate letter, "you are slated for UK, and the last message indicates that this will be sometime in February."[45] On 26 November Smith received a cable from McNarney demanding the full story. Smith allowed Hughes, Sawbridge, and Patton's aide, LTC Charles Codman, to read the reply. Together they revised it. "It doesn't tear Geo down so much," Hughes thought.[46]

Alerted by Codman, Patton saw army politics behind his "sad state." He viewed himself as "the means by which McNarney is trying to hurt Ike so as to become Chief of Staff in the event that General Marshall leaves." Despite Eisenhower and Smith's efforts to protect him, Patton concluded, "Ike and Bedell are not at all interested in me but simply in saving their own faces."[47]

The storm built momentum. Patton had committed a court-martial offense and had acted, in Eisenhower's opinion, like a madman, yet Smith ended up in hot water because he exposed Eisenhower's cover-up. Eisenhower need not have worried; because he stood so high in the public consciousness, he escaped censure. Smith, still mostly anonymous, took the hits. Senator Harry Truman weighed in. No fan of the regular army, the old National Guardsman pointed to the "partial denial from Algiers" as evidence of the "highranking officer selfprotective club." He observed, "When soldier strikes officer he's shot. Officer strikes soldier tis denied." Senator Claude Pepper also criticized Eisenhower, although not by name, for failing to formally reprimand Patton. Other members of Congress called for a full investigation; some called for Patton's court-martial.[48] On 30 November LTG Charles Herron wrote from Washington assuring Eisenhower of "a very marked retreat from the virulence and unreason of [the *Washington Post*'s] first attacks on Patton" and noted that Eisenhower's standing had not "suffered in the opinion of the public, except thru the action of the officer who announced that

Patton had not been reprimanded." Herron said, "There is a good deal of interest in what you will do to him."[49]

The press corps in the theater kept the heat on. They deeply resented that Pearson had purloined their scoop, especially after they sat on the story because Eisenhower promised them Patton would receive the toughest punishment, short of court-martial and being sent home. "Beadle got off a very witty saying," Patton told Hughes: "Lately I have been kissing the asses of a lot of correspondents on your account and some of them turned the other cheek."[50] As Smith remarked to Anderson, "I assure you his [Patton's] little escapade has been a serious headache to Ike and myself . . . amazing the furor that an incident like this will cause at home. George gave a transcendent demonstration of poor judgment and lack of self control; but so it goes."[51] The damage cut deeper than Smith expected. Although not compromised in Marshall's estimate or undercut in the public's eye, Eisenhower bore a grudge against Smith for his handling of the affair.

At Cairo on 27 November Eisenhower presented his arguments for retaining landing craft and tactical air assets in the Mediterranean for continued offensive operations in Italy until AFHQ forces reached the Po line. If the CCS decided against these objectives, he believed AFHQ possessed sufficient strength, even with the withdrawal of manpower, lift capability, and air units, to take Rome.[52] After the Cairo talks ended inconclusively, and with Algiers still abuzz, Eisenhower took time out for a little vacation. He toured Luxor, the Valley of the Kings, and the Holy Lands. On 1 December he returned to Algiers. For the next five days he awaited news from Tehran. Finally on 6 December he received a vague communication from Marshall. At Tehran, the British had blocked Marshall's appointment as European supreme commander. Since anything less amounted to a step down—in Roosevelt's opinion, at least—the president had decided on Eisenhower to command Overlord. Assuming that Eisenhower had already been told, Marshall wired AFHQ: "In view of the impending appointment of a British officer as your successor," he asked for Eisenhower's recommendations for American troops "assigned to Allied Force under this new command arrangement." Marshall also informed him that Churchill had pressed hard for Smith's retention in the Mediterranean as deputy to the new commander in chief.

Smith, in an almost trilling voice, relayed the contents of Marshall's communication by phone. Although it clearly indicated that Eisenhower's days in the Mediterranean were numbered, it left open the question of where he would go. Wherever the destination, Eisenhower assured Smith, he would accompany him. Smith volunteered to stay on during the transition period but expressed no interest in remaining in the theater as chief of staff or even as American theater commander.[53] The last thing he desired, even if it came with a promotion, was to be handmaiden to the designated British theater commander.

All doubts evaporated the next day when Marshall forwarded a memo from the final meeting at Tehran. It read: "From the President to Marshal Stalin: The immediate appointment of General Eisenhower to command of OVERLORD has been decided upon." The following day Roosevelt flew back to Tunis. Eisenhower met him, and as they entered a car, Roosevelt said, "Well, Ike, you are going to command OVERLORD."[54]

On 8 December Smith flew to Malta with Roosevelt's entourage. The president presented Lord Gort with an inscribed testimonial from the American people commemorating the brave defense of the island. From there they flew to Sicily, where the president inspected American troops. Eisenhower asked Roosevelt to use the opportunity to award the Distinguished Service Cross to Clark and a Legion of Merit to Smith for his role in the Italian surrender. Because nobody had alerted Smith about the award, he had sneaked away to spend some time with Pa Watson. Finally they found him, and the award ceremony went off without further complications.

The Mediterranean Dénouement

A tired and haggard Churchill arrived in Tunis on 11 December. Physically and emotionally, the prime minister had taken a battering at the Cairo talks and at Tehran; the realization hit home that his days as prime architect of the war had ended. The war's toll was beginning to tell on him. On the drive into Tunis, the enervated prime minister told Eisenhower, "I am afraid I shall have to stay with you longer than I had planned. I am completely at the end of my tether." Churchill's presence in North Africa always alarmed Eisenhower—in part because of the security risks, but mostly because of apprehensions he would meddle and occupy too much time. He had little to fear this time; the prime minister was seriously ill.

With the announcement of Eisenhower's new command, he and Smith began to draw up lists of the commanders and staff officers they wanted. They were like the chief executive and general manager of a sports team with a very large budget surveying a list of free agents, hoping to stock their team with the best available talent. They talked about candidates for the American theater command in the Mediterranean.

Clark appeared to be the likely choice, with Lucas assigned as his successor in Fifth Army. Quadrant sanctioned an amphibious assault on the south of France (Anvil) as a diversion for Overlord. Asked for his comments at the end of October, Eisenhower had endorsed a G-2 reply that raised a number of objections, concluding that using Anvil merely as a threat could achieve as much as an actual operation.[55] Now designated Overlord commander, Eisenhower warmed to Anvil and cooled on bringing Patton to England as an army commander. Instead, he thought "Patton about the only choice to plan and execute the early stages of ANVIL." Bradley emerged as the clear choice as commander of American troops in Overlord and eventually of an army group. The ground commander would be British, with Alexander the preferred pick. Eisenhower made it clear that he would insist on a single command over tactical and strategic air under Tedder. This presented a serious problem, because ACM Trafford Leigh-Mallory had already been tabbed as air commander in Overlord. As for prospective American army commanders, in addition to Patton, the names of LTG Courtney Hodges, Beetle's old boss in the Infantry School, and LTG William Simpson surfaced. What to do with Devers raised a red flag. Smith considered Devers a "good friend," but Eisenhower had developed a strong antipathy to him. Both considered Truscott the best corps commander in the U.S. Army and hoped they could steal him. Smith adamantly made the case for transferring all his senior staff, particularly the British triumvirate of Gale, Whiteley, and Strong. The British readily accepted the reassignment of Whiteley. "Neither General Alexander nor Montgomery like Whiteley," Butcher noted, "whom we have regarded as a most conscientious and effective officer."[56] As anticipated, the British balked at shifting Strong. Smith also raised the old issue of where to place the theater command and the supply and services in relation to the proposed supreme command structure. Eisenhower balked at positioning Lee inside the supreme headquarters, instead signaling his intent to replicate the bifurcated AFHQ-NATO structure, with the SOS commander acting as deputy theater commander, at least during the mounting stage. What would follow once the campaign opened in France, he gave no hint. All of Smith's pressure and maneuvering made not a single dent. Eisenhower's mind was simply closed on this issue.[57]

Who would command the ground forces remained unresolved. No American general possessed the requisite seniority and experience. The process that had turned 1941 majors into major generals obviously produced problems in this regard. Patton possessed the most experience against the Axis, but his command time in active campaigns at corps and army level amounted to something less than three months; for other obvious reasons, he figured in no one's calculations. The only real options remained Alexander and Montgomery. Before a meeting with Churchill that afternoon, Brooke discussed future command relations with Eisenhower and Tedder. Eisenhower expressed his preference for Alexander as ground commander in the cross-Channel operation. As Brooke later noted, Eisenhower knew he could handle Alexander but certainly not Montgomery. The CIGS possessed "little confidence in Alex running that show" but did not push the issue.

While Eisenhower met with Brooke and Tedder, Smith kept Churchill busy touring the site of ancient Carthage. When they arrived, Smith jumped out of his car and motioned for his driver to follow. Lost in thought and intently surveying the ruins, he wheeled and asked the sergeant, "What do you think?" The indifferent noncom took a look and replied, "The Germans sure bombed the Hell out of this place." His astonishment turned to laughter when he discerned the sergeant had been serious. This little episode furnished Smith with his favorite story, one he never tired of telling.[58]

During his talks with Churchill and Brooke, Eisenhower fought off a renewed effort to shanghai Smith. The British remained troubled over the Mediterranean command, which would include the Middle East. Brooke pushed for GEN Henry "Jumbo" Wilson as the supreme commander, arguing Alexander "was not sufficiently high caliber to take on the new centralized Mediterranean Command."[59] Whether Wilson got the nod or not, the prime minister wanted Smith left in the theater. After saying no every way he knew how, Eisenhower "merely grinned and said that is an undebatable subject." Put off, but only momentarily, Churchill expressed his hope that Beetle would stay behind "sufficiently long to indoctrinate the new Allied Commander." Jokingly, Eisenhower made four requests in order of importance: permission for Telek to enter England without quarantine and the retention of Beetle as chief of staff, LTC James Gault as his British military attaché, and Strong as chief of intelligence. The British acceded to all the requests but the last.[60]

Churchill was not himself, and his condition worsened that night. Diagnosed with pneumonia, Churchill suffered another mild heart attack on 15 December. Specialists flew in, as did his wife, Clementine, and son Randolph. Discovering he was in Carthage, a disoriented Churchill said, "What better place could I die than here. Here in the ruins of Carthage." His health recovered, but not his spirit.[61]

After his discussions with Churchill and Brooke, Eisenhower began reevaluating the roster of probable commanders in the Mediterranean and the bounce-on effect in Overlord. He called in Smith for his advice. They talked about future command teams, headquarters structures, and command in Anvil.[62] Eisenhower believed he had solved the problem of Devers. He recommended to Marshall that Devers command American forces in the Mediterranean. His appointment would free up Clark to remain in command of Fifth Army until Rome fell and then assume the planning and execution of Anvil with Seventh Army. Clearly, he remained optimistic that Rome's liberation lay on the horizon. With Clark eventually commanding Seventh Army, Patton "should be brought to England." He reiterated his ideas on the single air command, on Bradley as the eventual army group commander, and on Lee as deputy theater commander. Evidently, Smith's insistence on unifying the theater command and the SOS had made some headway. Eisenhower signaled to Marshall his plan for amalgamating the two in AFHQ; why he made that decision so late in his tenure he never explained. He made no recommendation on army commanders except for Patton. For once, he did not equivocate: "I want Patton as one of my Army Commanders."[63] "With respect to the whole Patton affair," he diverted attention away from Patton and toward Smith. Smith made a "bad mistake," he informed Marshall, but it "was made by my ablest and finest officer and there is nothing for me to do except to keep still and take the brunt of the affair. I hope it has died out by the time you arrive [back in Washington from his tour of the Pacific] as I have no intention of throwing valuable men to the wolves merely because of one mistake."[64]

Anxious to put all this behind him, and rapidly losing interest in Mediterranean problems, Eisenhower embarked on one last tour of Italy and insisted Smith come along. Smith was in a buoyant mood. The day before, Churchill had called him to his sickbed and handed him a document. It was a patent from the king naming Smith a Knight Commander of the Most Honourable Military Order of the Bath. The king would make the official investiture when Smith arrived in London. The cheerfulness did not last, however, and the trip turned into a disaster. They flew to Italy on 18 December, ostensibly to establish the new advance headquarters but really to "get muddy for a week."[65] They met an on-edge Clark in Naples, toured the port, and drove up to Caserta, where they inaugurated AFHQ-Forward, consisting of a small staff, chiefly a war room operations group and signals. A Baroque palace larger than Versailles built as the seat of the Bourbon kings of Naples, the Reggia di Caserta was so cavernous it generated its own internal windstorms. Smith decided the rat- and lice-infested palace was "not so bad, considering it's only thirty-five miles behind the front lines."[66]

The next day they went forward into the Fifth Army area and observed the latest attempt at breaching the German lines. In early November Alexander had issued a directive calling for a three-phase offensive: first the Eighth Army would attack across the Sangro River, take Pecara, and then turn west toward Rome; the turning movement would coincide with a Fifth Army drive up the Liri Valley; and finally, a two-division amphibious force (code-named Shingle) would land south of Rome. Montgomery considered it "a very poor plan," especially the amphibious movement. He doubted it would ever mature. At an 8 November conference, Montgomery convinced Alexander to maintain offensive pressure by the Fifth Army while the Eighth Army launched its breakthrough attempt. As always, Alexander bent to Montgomery's demands. Clark was supposed to attend the meeting, but weather grounded his plane, so the new plan emerged without his input.[67] Montgomery's troops forced crossings of the Sangro, and the Fifth Army cleared the Mount Camino area, but both offensives failed to take their initial objectives. Everywhere along the front the Germans enjoyed the advantage of prepared positions on dominant ground. The near-constant rain and fog and the mountainous terrain negated Allied airpower. It all came down to an infantry slugging match. On 8 December Clark opened a new attack in the hope of penetrating the Mignano Gap. The reconstituted Italian First Motorized Group, marking the first appearance of Italian troops on the Allied side, attacked under the banner *Roma o Morte;* they did not get to Rome, but hundreds died in the attack, the German counterattack, and the rout that followed. In vicious fighting and deteriorating weather, II Corps units ejected the Germans from San Pietro and two key rock masses. Eisenhower, Clark, and Smith arrived in time to see the bloody repulse of the Thirty-sixth Division's assaults on San Vittore.

The party did not linger long. That afternoon, Eisenhower and Smith flew back to Caserta in a Cub. That night, Eisenhower had planned a special dinner, prepared by a famous Neapolitan chef, presumably to celebrate a breakthrough. The group included the president's son Elliott, a colonel in the air force. Eisenhower invited Smith, but after the day's dreary events, he did not feel much like socializing and declined. Eisenhower exploded. Feeling the strain himself, and perhaps giving vent to his festering irritation with Smith, he shouted that no subordinate could refuse his hospitality. Annoyed, Smith shot back that he would quit. Eisenhower replied that was fine with him, adding it could easily be arranged for Smith to remain behind in the Mediterranean. After this childish exchange, both men fell into a sullen silence. Finally Smith

Smith makes a point while Roosevelt, flanked by Eisenhower and Spaatz, listens. The presidential party is dining with the Third Photo Reconnaissance Wing (the president's son Elliott's unit) at La Marsa Airfield, near Tunis.

apologized, and Eisenhower told him to forget about it. As Smith later joked, he had learned a valuable lesson: "never vacation with the boss."[68]

The next morning they set off on a seven-hour journey to Bari for meetings with Alexander, Badoglio, and Joyce. Their business concluded, they drove back that evening. Butcher did not go along, so no record of the trip exists, which might be fortunate. When Smith arrived in Caserta, he received an urgent cable from Algiers. After biding his time, de Gaulle had finally struck; he had arrested the former Vichy officials Boisson, Marcel Peyrouton, and Pierre-Etienne Flandin. Eisenhower and Smith immediately concluded, and so informed the president, "if the Committee presses this affair to its probable conclusion it can only result in the most serious consequences."[69] The next morning, Smith flew back into a maelstrom in Algiers.

For two days a flurry of cables flew between Churchill and Roosevelt.[70] A still weakened Churchill passed on the rumor that the three would be shot. Roosevelt needed no encouragement; he replied that the time had come to remove de Gaulle, complete with his "Jeanne D'Arc complex." The president forwarded a directive to AFHQ: "Please inform the French committee as follows: In view of the assistance given to the Allied armies during the campaign in Africa by Boisson, Peyrouton, and Flandin, you are directed to take no action against these individuals at the present time."[71]

Smith read the president's directive and immediately went out for a chat with Churchill. He explained to the prime minister that the French committee would surely regard Roosevelt's peremptory language as an ultimatum. Undoubtedly, the French would reject the president's demands, triggering an open break and an end to French rearmament. Churchill agreed and sent a wire to Roosevelt suggesting "the actual form of the demarche might be discussed by Eisenhower and Wilson."[72] Following talks with Macmillan and the new American representative to the FCNL, Edwin Wilson, Smith withheld delivery of the president's message. Smith told Eisenhower to stay out of contact; Smith intended to send a communication to Washington and thought it advisable that Eisenhower be in a position to disavow any knowledge of Smith's action, should the thing blow up.[73] Smith then wrote to Marshall, asking for his help in convincing Roosevelt that any French rejection of his demands would appear as "a direct slap at the President which the United States could not accept, [and] its only alternative would be to withdraw recognition of the Committee and to stop French rearmament."[74] Smith considered the situation explosive enough to order up the First Division to safeguard the American lines of communication.

Smith's actions again defused the emergency. Within four hours, Smith received word that Washington would soften the language of the president's letter. On 26 December Roosevelt issued instructions to Eisenhower to notify the FCNL that the United States viewed these events "with alarm" and appealed to the committee to take no judicial action until after a freely elected government formed in France.[75] Although de Gaulle had some objections, he accepted the formula. Just as the campaign in the Mediterranean had begun, so too it ended, with Eisenhower and Smith surmounting yet another French crisis.

Despite evidence of strain between the two, Eisenhower remained adamant about Smith's going to London. Marshall informed Eisenhower of British intentions to create a single Mediterranean command on 4 November, and a month later he indicated Churchill's desire for Smith's retention in the theater as deputy commander in chief and chief of staff.[76] After Eisenhower blunted the prime minister, Marshall complicated matters by suggesting that Smith stay in the Mediterranean at least until the middle of February, "purely because of American interests." Marshall rejected Beetle's dual appointment but stated his belief that Smith should stay in "his present position until a much later date than now seems to be indicated." He noted that Morgan "is a very capable officer and almost seems more American than British."[77] Eisenhower had learned his lesson in Torch: Churchill's and Marshall's insistence that Smith remain in London had delayed the formation of AFHQ by months, with all the attendant problems. As subtly as he could, he explained to Marshall why Smith should not loiter in the Mediterranean. He outlined his plans for Smith. Within the next couple of days, Smith would go to London "to check up on the present organization of COSSAC and to see where it would be profitable for us to make a few trades of experience in the planning and execution of amphibious [operations]." As he told Marshall, after a two- or three-day stay in London, he expected Smith to return to Algiers and remain there while Eisenhower moved to London. Smith would stay behind in Algiers "to clean up details, secure the necessary authority for the transfer proposed, and [then] come on to join me." He anticipated that Smith would serve briefly as Morgan's deputy, but "as quickly as he was in the saddle," Smith would take over, and Morgan would go on to a corps command. At some length, he reassured Marshall that American interests would be safeguarded. "Ever since the QUADRANT meeting at Quebec we have had an inkling that a British commander in chief was to be assigned to the Mediterranean and for this reason have built up Hughes's position as United States deputy theater commander into a rather independent office." He assured Marshall that "any able American commander here, supported by such people as Hughes, Rooks, Lucas and Larkin, to say nothing of our two ambassadors [Murphy and Wilson] and General Holmes, will be fully able to take care of anything that may arise."[78]

What to do with Morgan presented a problem. Morgan visited with Eisenhower and solicited his recommendations for alterations in the COSSAC staff structure, which he dutifully executed. Earlier he had entertained thoughts of serving as Marshall's chief of staff and had gone to Washington with a view of cementing the relationship, but Marshall had kept him at arm's length. Now with Eisenhower named supreme commander, Morgan wrote a warm letter congratulating Eisenhower on his appointment; encouraging him to come to London as soon as possible, since there was no time to waste; and asking whether he wanted him to stay on or would Smith be coming. Eisenhower let Morgan down as easily as he could. "I have become accustomed to working with Beetle Smith and of course, I feel a very great reluctance to terminate the association," he stated. Eisenhower hoped Morgan would initially tutor

Smith and then remain in some capacity in the Overlord operation.[79] The next day Devers wrote to Eisenhower. "COSSAC needs organization and methods of procedure," he warned. "Personalities are good. Morgan fine personality, the best British officer I deal with. [BG Raymond] Barker [Morgan's American deputy] is weak. You will need Bedell Smith."[80]

Shortly before Christmas the British made their announcements regarding command in Overlord. The appointments of Ramsay and Leigh-Mallory were confirmed, and the ground command went to Montgomery. Eisenhower had lobbied as hard as propriety allowed for Alexander, and he thought Churchill agreed, but under pressure from Brooke and the War Cabinet, the prime minister relented and named Montgomery to the post. At Eisenhower's request, Montgomery flew to Algiers on 27 December; together with Smith they dissected the COSSAC plan.

Smith had heard Morgan present a briefing on the COSSAC plan in October in Washington. Smith "nearly fell out of [his] seat" when he discovered that the initial assault consisted of only three divisions. When Smith told Eisenhower about Morgan's estimates, he said: "My God, if I were going to do it I would want [a beachhead large enough to accommodate] ten or twelve divisions."[81] Later in October Eisenhower received an update from a COSSAC planner. Eisenhower told the officer, BG William Chambers, "it was none of my business to pass judgment upon a plan that would presumably be executed by someone else. Nevertheless, I considered that, while the plan apparently made the best possible use of the materiel that could be made available by the proposed target date, the concept involved a plan too weak in numbers and frontage." According to Eisenhower's 1960 account, he called in Smith and they decided, "off the cuff," the initial attack needed a minimum of five divisions.[82]

Controversy swirls around the question of who authored the decision to expand operations in Normandy. The truth is, Eisenhower, Montgomery, and Smith immediately decided the COSSAC outline plan was too small. Husky hit the beaches with seven divisions, and the Atlantic Wall presented a far more formidable obstacle than that encountered in Sicily. Nor was there any mystery that landing craft held the key to success. Airborne forces might compensate for some of the lack of combat sealift, but everyone concurred that if the Allies intended to break through the hard shell of German defenses, they must stage a heavy and rapid buildup, and that required landing craft. Eisenhower instructed Smith to head to London. In addition to checking on staff matters, locations for the new headquarters, and living arrangements, Eisenhower wanted

Smith to talk with Morgan about the state of operational and supply planning for Overlord and with Portal about air command. Eisenhower sent Montgomery to London to press for the necessary changes; Montgomery required little prompting.

Smith had a very busy day on 27 December. Early that morning he attended what everybody hoped would be a breakthrough conference with de Gaulle, Giraud, and GEN Jean J. M. G. de Lattre de Tassigny. De Gaulle proved very agreeable, wanting to cement a rapprochement with Eisenhower before he left the theater. The FCNL agreed to place French forces under Eisenhower's command in Europe. Smith confirmed that French forces would play a prominent role in liberating their homeland, including a "presence" in Overlord. He promised that once the Allies closed on Paris, Eisenhower would prevail on the CCS "to insure the inclusion of a token French force, preferably a division," in the capital's deliverance. Wilson and Macmillan hoped this "military" compact would bear political fruit in encouraging Roosevelt's recognition of the French committee.[83]

Smith engaged in some personal diplomacy. For months, various agents had worked on bridging the personal gulf between de Gaulle and Roosevelt, including suggestions the French general go to Washington for private talks. Smith stated, "I understand you are going to see President Roosevelt." De Gaulle looked askance at Smith and replied, "I had a talk with him at Casablanca." Not put off, Smith acknowledged that the Casablanca meeting had not gone very well, but things would be better in Washington. He suggested de Gaulle and Roosevelt could have a drink together in the Oval Office and talk things over. Smith told de Gaulle that the president could speak understandable French, albeit with an atrocious accent; he knew how persuasive the president was when he wanted to be. Smith thought de Gaulle could pour on the Gallic charm and win the president over. De Gaulle pursed his lips and said, "Who told you to say that to me." Smith replied, "No one," but he thought about telling de Gaulle to go to hell.[84] Nevertheless, a thaw appeared to be in the offing. When Eisenhower met de Gaulle on 30 December, as he told Smith, "it was a love fest and we made mutual promises of great cooperation. I am going to give him a very good send-off with the Bosses."[85]

That evening Smith met with Hughes and Gale, and their conversation focused on Smith's expectations for the future organization of the supreme headquarters in Overlord. As Hughes informed Moses, now Bradley's G-4 in U.S. First Army Group in England, Smith remained determined that the structure would not parallel AFHQ; in his view,

ETO and the SOS amounted to the same thing. He told Moses, "Your duties and function cannot be decided and defined until Smith and Eisenhower make up their minds just what headquarters there will be and what jobs they will have." Hughes never offered a guess, "because Eisenhower and Smith have not yet determined."[86]

Eisenhower again waffled on the organizational question. As Eisenhower informed Marshall, he meant "to disturb the present setup as little as possible." On 27 December Devers explained his organization. Lee controlled all supply and services, and Moses answered directly to him. According to Devers, the "SOS organization is the best I have seen."[87] Eisenhower hoped "that General Lee is big enough for this job . . . that takes a world of ability, not only in technical matters, but in coordinating and operating with Allies." He intended to amalgamate ETO and SOS headquarters to "streamline the organization, save experienced personnel, and cut down the time for red tape." But he stopped short of accepting Smith's model for centralized authority over administration and supply inside supreme headquarters. The expedient of combining the theater headquarters and Lee's command would last only during the buildup and mounting phase.[88]

Smith set off for London on 28 December. Eisenhower sent Smith on a number of missions, but none more vital than this one. To Smith and Montgomery fell the responsibility for establishing the groundwork for a successful Overlord. That meant expanding the operation and, for Smith, laying the foundation for the command structure and staff Eisenhower demanded. On 30 December Marshall insisted that Eisenhower "come on home and see your wife and trust somebody else for twenty minutes in England." A reluctant Eisenhower agreed, and as he explained to Smith, "I would not make this trip except for my complete confidence in you and the way you handle things." He confided in Smith, "There is scarcely anything . . . you cannot handle as well as I."[89] Forgotten were the petty personal clashes; now the Eisenhower and Smith team looked forward to the biggest game of all.

Part Five

★ ★ ★ ★

France 1944

The Supreme Command

Smith updated Eisenhower on developments in London before he left for the States. He expressed his general satisfaction with the COSSAC staff and assured Eisenhower that, with the "substitution of a few individuals," it could be made "to conform to the setup you want." Not wasting any time securing the key players he wanted, Smith met with Brooke's deputy on his first morning in London to request the transfer of Gale, Whiteley, and Strong. He warned, "the organization is very top heavy," especially in British generals. Smith expressed his strong opinion that the headquarters "should get out of London at the earliest possible moment." He found the situation the same as when he had first arrived in London in September 1942, and he talked to Morgan about alternative sites. Aside from the threat of bombing—the Germans had unleashed the "baby blitz"—he felt the staff would never "get shaken down until we get away from Norfolk House."

Laying the Foundation

The air command structure bothered him. On 30 December Smith met with Wigglesworth, whose transfer to England Tedder had engineered. They agreed Tedder's appointment as deputy supreme commander "without portfolio" threatened to throw the air command into disarray. The next day Eisenhower wired Smith: the "integration of Air Forces . . . will be essential to success of OVERLORD."[1] Under the proposed organization, Tedder possessed no "direct Air function." Leigh-Mallory held the position of commander of Allied Expeditionary Air Force and principal air adviser to the supreme commander. The heavy bombers remained tied to Operation Pointblank, the combined strategic bomber offensive. Churchill had assured Smith before he left North Africa, "certainly Tedder was to command," and he continued to think that "Tedder should be the real Air commander and your advisor on air matters," but he warned, "if Tedder assumes command, there is no function for Leigh Mallory." Smith also considered the formation of two tactical air forces "most unsound." They were "now organized on a joint basis. Other than Mallory, who is Air Commander-in-Chief, there is no single commander of the tactical air forces as we had in the Mediterranean." Smith considered these issues to be of the "utmost urgency" and appealed to Eisenhower to wire Marshall immediately and request that no action be taken "on a British proposal to the Combined Chiefs to sanction Air setup." Smith reckoned the CCS would agree to a delay until Eisenhower and Tedder arrived in London and made their recommendations.[2]

Alarmed by Smith, Eisenhower cabled Marshall: "I most earnestly request that you throw your full weight into opposing the tendency to organize in advance the sub-echelons of the OVERLORD operation in such a way as to tie the hands of the command." Eisenhower considered it foolish not to apply the lessons learned in the Mediterranean. "I think it a tragedy to give us such rigid directives as to preclude the application of those lessons."[3] Marshall agreed and shelved the air organization. In the same vein, Eisenhower instructed that Smith blunt higher authorities, particularly the British chiefs, from "dictating details of our organization."[4] Smith acted on that advice.

On New Year's Eve, Smith met with Brooke concerning these issues. Brooke should have been in a good mood. The next day his promotion to field marshal took effect. According to Brooke, Smith and Eisenhower were "most anxious to take all the heads of Staff department out of the Mediterranean!!" As soon as he knew he would be going to London, Smith started petitioning the BCOS on Strong's appointment.[5] In Smith's view, "it was absurd" not to employ Strong, who had served as military attaché in Berlin before the war and was clearly "the best trained man for that job in the armies." Brooke testily replied that responsibility for distributing the staff on all fronts rested with him. "You can rely on me to take their various requirements into account. I will have no string-pulling." At this point, Smith jumped up and made for the door, pausing only long enough to inform the startled CIGS he was "not being helpful." This led to a heated exchange. "You'll get nothing this way," Brooke retorted. There the matter rested. Brooke thought Smith "decidedly bumptious" and wondered if he had "gone off a lot and was suffering from a swollen head." He considered what Smith proposed outright larceny. "I had to put Bedell Smith in his place," Brooke later remembered. "The war is getting on [Beetle's] nerves," Butcher surmised. "Or his stomach. Or both."[6] Never easily put off, the next afternoon Smith went to Ismay to enlist his support.

The next day Smith conferred with Spaatz and LTG Ira Eaker, the commander of Eighth Air Force. Smith thought separate tactical and strategic air forces unworkable and raised the issue. Even though the airmen remained unconvinced of the need for a unified command, Smith reported to Eisenhower that with a little tinkering they could merge the various air commands "into the type organization which was found essential in the Mediterranean," and he requested that Eisenhower bring the matter up with the JCS. In the hope of pushing Eisenhower in the same direction, Smith pointed to Spaatz's formation of a single logistics command. Spaatz had adopted the British system and had two deputy commanders—one for operations and intelligence, and the other for administration and supply.[7]

Smith then laid out his thinking on the new headquarters. He complained that COSSAC amounted to nothing but a theoretical planning staff and would "remain so until they get out of Norfolk House." He compared the situation to the "same as it was at the beginning of TORCH." Knowing Eisenhower's preferences, he selected Bushy Park, the site of Eighth Air Force command, as the best spot for the main headquarters (code-named Widewing). It was located near Kingston, and Eisenhower could again take up residence at Telegraph Cottage. Spaatz would reduce his headquarters, making enough room. "I am sure the setup is just what we want," Smith said. He then set his sights on organizing an advance headquarters (code-named Sharpener) near Portsmouth, adjacent to the headquarters of the naval commander in chief, Ramsay, and Montgomery's eventual command post.[8]

Eisenhower gave up on the idea of Morgan tutoring Smith; he wanted Smith running the headquarters as soon as possible. Still, there was the matter of Smith returning to Algiers to help Wilson in his transition and to bring the newly appointed American theater commander, Devers, into the picture. Eisenhower happily reported that Marshall had "apparently abandoned the argument that you should stay [in Algiers] for any particular length of time."[9] Eisenhower planned to arrive in London in the middle of January and wanted Smith free to join him. Smith went to Morgan for a heart-to-heart. Morgan agreed to stay on as Smith's deputy, which Smith heartily endorsed. He also informed Eisenhower that Morgan "has hurt himself with Brooke by his square dealing with our people." Breaking protocol, Smith made some quiet inquiries about getting Morgan a corps command. Montgomery and Brooke vetoed the proposal, making no effort to disguise their lack of confidence in Morgan.[10] Montgomery intended to bring in proven combat commanders and preferred officers with more command experience and troop time than Morgan.

Smith updated Eisenhower on his efforts to stock the new headquarters with known quantities, but he neglected to mention his dustup with Brooke. In fact, he talked in terms of the CIGS being "most helpful." He felt reasonably sure "we will get Gale" as chief administrative officer and deputy chief of staff and, except for Strong, all the other key British personnel.[11] The addition of Gale made for "a rather overpowering collection of lieutenant generals but it presents no difficulties." He proposed keeping two Americans: Barker would move from deputy chief of staff to head G-1, and MG Harold Bull, who had "his G-3 Section well organized," would stay in his present slot. On the British side, Smith considered MG N. C. D. Brownjohn, the chief logistician, a "fine character and very able." MG Robert Crawford, an old acquaintance of Eisenhower's, served as Brownjohn's American opposite number. Given he could not have Strong, Smith took a jaundiced view of the incumbent head of intelligence. Whitefoord "will not do for us. Can best describe him as another Mockler Ferryman." Other than Strong, the best candidate for the job was Whiteley. Smith had smoothed the way for Whiteley's appointment with Montgomery before going back to Brooke.[12]

Smith, Montgomery, and de Guingand went over a whole range of topics, especially the prospective changes to the cross-Channel operation, in preparation for a full-blown conference with the air, naval, and staff heads the next day. Eisenhower gave Montgomery orders to fix the plan, and he fully intended to use his command authority to do just that. The fact that Montgomery lost sleep—he was fastidious about sticking to an "early to bed, early to rise" routine—indicates the importance he attached to altering the plan. They also discussed command and staff arrangements. Montgomery wanted a separate headquarters as ground commander in chief, distinct from his Twenty-first Army Group staff. Smith beat back Montgomery's suggestion, remaining adamant that no establishment exist between Eisenhower and his commanders. He pointed out that Montgomery's appointment as ground commander coincided only with the assault and lodgment phases, and although it invested him with operational control, it did not confer any specific command authority over Allied forces.[13] As Smith reported, "Montgomery and I [are] equally concerned about faulty air command set-up." They thought the best solution resided in Tedder commanding the air directly under Eisenhower, Leigh-Mallory commanding the tactical air forces, and Spaatz commanding the bombers. "Present arrangement is much more complicated," Smith noted. Finally, he told Eisenhower that he

Supreme headquarters for the Normandy invasion, January 1944. From left to right: Bradley, Ramsay, Tedder, Eisenhower, Montgomery, Leigh-Mallory, and Smith. In an effort to balance the sides, Bradley was included in the photograph despite having no combined role.

and Devers expected to fly to Algiers in two days' time, on 4 January. He finished by pleading with Eisenhower not to loiter in the States. "Here, you are badly needed."[14]

Smith joined Montgomery, Leigh-Mallory, and Ramsay and listened to the chief COSSAC planners—MG Charles West and MG K. G. McLean—present the outline Overlord plan. After an intermission, Montgomery launched into his exposition on all that ailed the COSSAC scheme. He left no doubt who held the ground command. Smith passed on his views to Eisenhower. "There had been much wishful thinking in connection with COSSAC," he began. Recalling the first few days on the Salerno beachheads, Smith thought the "rates of advance after landing . . . [are] entirely too optimistic." Aside from the certitude of heavy German counterattacks, the core problem rested in the rate of buildup. "There is a critical period on D+1 to D+2 during which the enemy can bring stronger forces to oppose us than we can put ashore." He considered "the principal weakness" to be "the proposal to pass an enormous force of men, materiel and equipment in column over narrow and very restricted beaches, already encumbered with the debris of an assault and with limited exits." Montgomery insisted on strengthening the assault to five divisions, with two more as follow-up, and broadening the front-age from twenty-six to forty miles, including landing a division at the southeastern neck of the Cotentin peninsula; otherwise, the invasion forces would lack the strength to secure the key to the operation: Cherbourg. He argued that the additional lift must come from assets allotted to Anvil. Montgomery knew from his discussions with Eisenhower and Smith in Algiers that his views already enjoyed their full support, but he never made that point at the meeting. To the British, including the BCOS, the revisions to the plan appeared to pop virgin from Montgomery's mind. Smith gave his robust endorsement, but curiously, he never mentioned Eisenhower. Later both Eisenhower and Smith deeply resented the new design being tagged "the Montgomery Plan." Whatever its origin, there remains no doubt that Montgomery claimed primary authorship of the evolving Overlord plan.[15]

The problem—as ever—remained the famine of landing craft, which vectored the conversation toward Anvil. Smith concluded, "additional lift [for the critical period D+1 and D+2] can only be obtained at the expense of ANVIL." Montgomery proposed a return to the original concept of Anvil as a threat. Smith went further. He had deep misgivings about Churchill's scheme for an amphibious assault south of Rome to break the stalemate in Italy. In a Christmas Day meeting with Eisenhower, the prime minister revived Alexander and Clark's Operation Shingle plan. All evidence pointed to Churchill's mounting obsession with Italy, Rome, and the Mediterranean in general. The proposed amphibious operation would expend landing craft. If it succeeded, the Germans would retreat and leave destruction in their wake, tying up landing craft as support auxiliaries; if it miscarried and the Germans contained the landings, landing craft would be committed to keeping the marooned forces reinforced and resupplied. In Smith's mind, Shingle should be nipped in the bud. As for Anvil, Smith agreed with Montgomery.[16]

Smith passed all this on to Eisenhower. He assured his chief, "I have refused to [cancel Anvil] during your absence as I think the result of such a recommendation made without your entire knowledge and personal approval would have a very bad effect on our people at home." As events transpired, any such decision would have had a very bad effect on his relationship with Eisenhower. Smith reiterated his complete agreement with Montgomery. "I also believe," he continued, "as do most of the planners who are familiar with the project, that the original ANVIL plan which consisted actually of only a threat, would have just as much effect during the initial stages of OVERLORD as will the present proposed assault with three divisions. I am sure the British COS will support Montgomery's views." Sure in his knowledge that Eisenhower's thinking accorded exactly with Montgomery's, Smith refrained from making any formal recommendations for the changes, but he issued instructions that the COSSAC staff initiate detailed planning on the assumption that additional landing craft would be acquired. Time was of the essence. From long and bitter experience, he reasoned that if they referred the question to the CCS and, by extension, the political heads, weeks would pass before any concrete decision would emerge.[17]

Smith reported that they worked on the plan all night—so late that he had no time to wire the results to Eisenhower before he boarded an early-morning plane for North Africa. He and Devers flew first to Marrakesh, where the prime minister was convalescing, to brief Churchill. As Churchill reported to Roosevelt, "Bedell told me that he and Montgomery are convinced that it is better to put in a much heavier and broader OVERLORD than to expand ANVIL above our pre-Teheran conception and that he is putting this to Eisenhower and your Chiefs of Staff."[18] Smith extracted a promise from Churchill that Tedder would command the Allied air forces in Overlord.[19] Churchill energetically expressed his displeasure that "Anzio [Shingle] would be crippled because of the withdrawal of LSTs for OVERLORD and ANVIL, plus the build-up in Corsica." He asked that Smith organize a major conference with the ground, air, and naval commands for 8 January. "This matter will be thoroughly thrashed out," Smith promised Eisenhower. Returning to the subject of Anvil, Smith urged that Eisenhower talk the matter over with Marshall and Handy. "I do NOT see how we can possibly do both ANVIL and OVERLORD on equal assault scale, and if OVERLORD is to be the main effort, ANVIL will have to be sacrificed."[20]

Smith may have known Eisenhower's mind on Overlord, but he badly overstepped his bounds on Anvil. Initially, Eisenhower thought little of Anvil. An invasion of southern France would subtract manpower, air and sea power, landing craft, and materiel from the Mediterranean command's already dwindling assets. And the plan had changed: first envisioned as mostly a French operation, it had been expanded to two and then three divisions. Now, as he related to Smith, Eisenhower considered Anvil a sine qua non for a successful Overlord. Eisenhower wholeheartedly sanctioned broadening the Normandy landings but rejected the idea that Anvil would be effective as a threat. "Only in the event that OVERLORD cannot possibly be broadened without abandonment of ANVIL," he cautioned, "would I consider making such a recommendation to the Combined Chiefs."[21]

The Anvil debate was put on the back burner; first Smith needed to deflect Churchill from Shingle. The prime minister had felt recovered enough by 27 December to move to one of his favorite spots, Marrakesh. Shaking himself out of the doldrums, Churchill had come up with a "bright idea." His doctor, Lord Moran, noted that Churchill was organizing "an operation all on his own. He has decided that it should be a landing behind the lines at Anzio."[22] On 22 December Clark had already ruled out Shingle. The plan called for a landing of one division—reinforced to 24,000 men—south of Rome. If the amphibious force quickly expanded the beachhead and advanced inland, Kesselring might feel compelled to withdraw forces from the Gustav Line in defense of his vulnerable lines of communication. Fifth and Eighth Armies might then pierce the German defenses and restore movement to the campaign. Eisenhower and Smith saw why Clark had canceled the Anzio landings during their brief tour of the front: there was little prospect of the Fifth Army breaking the German Winter Line defenses.

Eisenhower steered clear of this debate, warning only that Kesselring's actions never conformed to Allied expectations. To Butcher, he complained that Churchill had "practically taken command in the Mediterranean."[23] Churchill, of course, was in his element. Living in a lush olive plantation called La Saadia, he set up his own miniature War Office and bombarded AFHQ via phone, pushing for Shingle. He fumed against conservative planners and wondered why he could not find any commanders willing to fight. He knew time worked against his schemes in the Mediterranean. It would be folly, Churchill proclaimed, to permit the Italian campaign to drag on, and without Rome, the campaign could only be judged a failure. "Winston, sitting in Marrakesh is now full of beans and trying to win the war from there!" Brooke wished "to God that he would come home and get under control."[24] The overbearing prime minister enlisted the support of Clark, who remained ambivalent. Like Churchill, he had a vested interest in preventing the campaign from "peter[ing] out ingloriously," but he also understood the risks.

Churchill lined up his malleable placemen before the 8 January conference. Supreme commander–designate Wilson approved the operation, stating it was "a good idea to go around them rather than be bogged down in the mountains."[25] Alexander lent his support, asserting that the theater could pull off "something big if given the means." Churchill then went about securing those means. Two-thirds of the LSTs were slated for rotation out of the theater by mid-January. Churchill petitioned Roosevelt for a delay, and the president wired his agreement.

"I thank God," Churchill replied, "for this fine decision. Full steam ahead."[26] Clark thought the proposed two-division landing too small, but feeling like "a pistol was being held at [his] head," he endorsed Churchill's scheme.[27] Brooke saw serious trouble brewing and wondered if he should fly down for the conference. "The prospects are not very attractive to say the least," he recorded. He worried Marshall would take umbrage at Churchill's bullying Smith into signing off on Shingle in Eisenhower's absence. Technically, Eisenhower was still commander in the Mediterranean.[28]

Smith flew in and brought Strong with him. Even though he possessed deep-seated views, as a lame duck, Smith decided to play a passive role. He let Strong do the work for him. Strong argued that Fifth Army planners had seriously underestimated German strength around Cassino, and AFHQ planners considered the landing force too small to achieve its dual objectives—secure the beachhead and attack toward the Alban Hills. The Germans enjoyed interior lines; they could pen in the beachhead and still have enough forces to blunt any breakthrough.[29] Smith had received a communication from Badoglio that again indicated a German withdrawal to Spezia-Rimini. But given the old marshal's track record, Smith did not buy it; the Germans would retreat only when they had to. Still, as he told Eisenhower, it offered "some comfort to fight the battle knowing that this is in the back of the enemy's mind."[30] ADM John Cunningham, who had replaced the other Cunningham as naval commander in chief, spoke for everyone present when he pointed out the "serious risks." Churchill would hear none of this. "Of course there is risk," he snapped. "But without risk there is no honour, no glory, no adventure."[31] For Churchill, it was the Malakand Field Force and the charge at Omdurman all over again.

The prime minister withdrew after dinner, leaving the military men to decide. Discussions continued until 1:30 in the morning. Wilson could not handle the pace; he left early to go to bed. "After all," Smith wryly commented, "he is getting old."[32] Finally, they talked themselves into approving Shingle. A delighted Churchill wired Roosevelt, informing him of the "unanimous agreement for action."[33] Anvil also featured in their calculations. Smith reported the emergence of a general agreement "that a reduction of ANVIL should be made to the pre-SEXTANT strength of one assault and one combat loader division in favor of OVERLORD."[34]

Churchill wanted Wilson in command at the earliest possible date and wrote Roosevelt to that effect. Smith had already presided over the official turnover before going to Marrakesh. Returning to Algiers, he set about moving his headquarters files and a year's worth of accumulated booty to London; it weighed two and a half tons—enough to fill two B-17s. With Wilson ensconced as supreme commander, Eisenhower saw no particular reason to return to Algiers and asked Beetle what he thought. Smith urged him to go directly to London, adding that it was "not pleasant to be the guest where you have been the master."[35] Eisenhower took Smith's advice and returned to London on 15 January.

Smith's primary interest was leveraging key personnel away from Wilson and Devers. Wilson proved most accommodating, surrendering Whiteley and Gale. Smith pushed particularly hard for Gale's appointment, telling Wilson that Eisenhower was "unwilling to undertake any large scale operation without Gale's administrative assistance." By way of reinforcement, Smith said, "I should feel greatly handicapped if Gale were NOT working beside me. He has that irreplaceable quality of being able to handle British-American supply problems with tact and judgment and he is also as familiar with the American system as with the British."[36]

Devers proved a far tougher nut to crack. Bad blood existed between Eisenhower and Devers, even though Eisenhower took pains to deny it. He assured Marshall he had "*no* reason in the world to doubt [Devers's] ability and I know that he has enjoyed your confidence for a long time."[37] A certain degree of jealousy had always existed between the two. Marshall had plucked Devers from obscurity and pushed him up the command ladder before Eisenhower. Eisenhower deeply resented Devers's criticism of his management of North African affairs and Devers's appointment to command ETO, which "Ike said flatly . . . was a mistake."[38] As theater commanders, they wrestled over officer appointments, shipping, manpower, materiel priorities, and the allotment of strategic bombers and landing craft. In the aftermath of the Quebec conference, Marshall insisted on picking up the pace of Bolero. Ground and air forces began their redeployment from the Mediterranean to the United Kingdom with growing momentum. Eisenhower bitterly resented having his theater downgraded; Devers took offense at Eisenhower's claims of priority. The two officers and, by extension, their staffs became rivals.

Smith had once considered Devers "an old friend," but that changed.[39] He and Devers engaged in a series of acrimonious free-for-alls over personnel transfers to the United Kingdom. Smith presented Devers with what he considered a "modest list" of officers; Devers considered Smith's "vicious raid on AFHQ's best talent" unjustifiable. According to Butcher, "Devers was approaching his problems in what Beetle considered a narrow point of view" and launched into an "almost wholesale refusal to transfer personnel." Devers wrote, "We have tried to meet your requests for personnel to the utmost possible limit. Sorry we could not do it 100 percent." Eisenhower forwarded the letter to Smith, who returned it with this comment: "This is just swell. I love this 'One idea to assist you' stuff."[40] Devers gladly gave way on Patton, whom he considered finished, but he refused the appointment most desired by Eisenhower—Truscott's reassignment. When Smith caught wind that Devers had assigned an officer to investigate his attempts to purloin AFHQ talent, he exploded. Smith marched into Devers's office and demanded that they go over the list name by name. When defending Eisenhower's prerogatives and his own preserves, rank meant nothing to Smith, as indicated by his scrum with Brooke. There was never any question that BG T. J. Davis, AFHQ adjutant, would go to London; he was a veteran of MacArthur's staff in the Philippines and a close friend of Eisenhower's. Smith wanted Rooks, Holmes, and either Larkin or Adcock, but Devers declined on all of them; Smith managed to pry loose only Nevins and Betts and a number of second-tier officers. An irate Smith described Devers as "a lightweight." Eisenhower required no persuading; he thought Devers "particularly obstinate" and complained to Marshall upon hearing Smith's grumbling that he was "still . . . waiting for the first evidence of real cooperation from the new commander of the African Theater."[41]

On 15 January Hughes invited Smith and Ethel Westerman for dinner. "E. looked lovely in mufti," Hughes thought. They celebrated with Coca-Cola and beer that Hughes had secured from special services. Two days later, AFHQ put on a good-bye luncheon for Smith. Hughes found it very amusing that Smith's replacement, MG J. A. H. Gammel, arrived only to discover no place reserved for him. The next day, amidst pomp and ceremony, Hughes saw his old adversary off at the Algiers airport. Before Beetle boarded the aircraft, he told Hughes not to worry; he would soon follow. Hughes remained doubtful.[42]

"Beetle arrived from North Africa via Gibraltar," Butcher recorded, "after one of his customary exciting air trips." Smith brought along a navigational chart showing where the Flying Fortress, in heavy fog, had "wandered up and down the channel until it practically overran German occupied Guernsey Island." The RAF sent fighters to locate and guide the aircraft to a field in Exeter. All ended well, but not without moments of high suspense.[43]

When Smith returned to London, he learned Eisenhower had already made a major decision on the headquarters structure. On 15 January Eisenhower inaugurated Supreme Headquarters, Allied Expeditionary Force (SHAEF). That day he combined the theater headquarters and

SOS under Lee, simply reproducing the Mediterranean organization. The change fused administration and supply but continued the segregation of logistics from supreme headquarters. Before leaving Washington he had met in the Pentagon with Marshall, Handy, and Somervell, and Eisenhower had explained his plans for organizing his headquarters. During the buildup and mounting of Operation Neptune—the first phase of the invasion—he would place ETO and SOS under Lee; for the campaign in France, he intended to dispense with a deputy theater commander and relegate Lee to command of the Communications Zone (ComZ). For him, the logic appeared inescapable. Until the launching of D-day, the priority rested on readying for the operation—in large part logistical. In effect, except for the U.S. Army Air Force (USAAF) bombing campaign, the United Kingdom constituted a single Communications Zone. Once the invasion started, the priority would shift to operations. What organization would evolve and how ETO and the ComZ commands would relate to SHAEF and the field commands remained unfixed; presumably, Eisenhower intended to follow the North African model. This was precisely what bothered Somervell.

As he had after Casablanca, Somervell faithfully prepared a catalog of priorities and grilled Eisenhower on his plans for the logistics commands for the Continent, particularly after the conjunction of Overlord and Anvil. Somervell strenuously lectured Eisenhower on the need for a functional organization to avoid the problems that had plagued American manpower and supply in North Africa and Italy. Somervell calculated that he occupied a strong position. As they spoke, Lutes was touring the Mediterranean, assessing the leaking supply pipeline, and a four-man delegation from the War Department Manpower Board was evaluating deficiencies in the replacement system. Congress, reacting to adverse public opinion, had been threatening to intervene since September if the War Department did not solve the manpower problem. Many fingers were pointed Eisenhower's way.

Eisenhower listened but did not hear what Somervell said. His mind remained closed on this question, and Somervell's repeated attempts to dictate his administrative organization offended him. What Eisenhower heard was another exercise in Somervell's playing for position. As he told Butcher the day after he arrived in London, Somervell's pressing on the supply organization was "a preliminary to the real thing General Somervell had in mind, namely that officers commanding the supply line, particularly in the big theaters, should have higher rank." Eisenhower "construed this to mean Major General J. C. H. Lee . . . should be a lieutenant general and if this were done, then he should be commanded by a four-star general in Washington." Ascribing Somervell's preoccupation with fixing command relationships as merely a pretext for advancing his own promotion—a view shared by Handy and McNarney—Eisenhower "made no comment."[44]

Given the heat generated by the failures of the logistics commands in the Mediterranean, Marshall took Somervell's concerns to heart. As Eisenhower flew to the United Kingdom, Marshall prepared and issued a directive on 15 January. While a British officer would act as CAO in SHAEF, Marshall instructed, "the number 2 man in administration should be a particularly strong American officer who could later take charge of the section, since it was contemplated that the bulk of supplies would eventually flow direct from the United States to the continent of Europe." Acknowledging that national manpower and supplies would always be a feature of any combined headquarters, but insisting on an improved and balanced coordinating mechanism that had been lacking in AFHQ, Marshall wanted an American CAO in SHAEF from the outset—an officer who would eventually supersede Gale.[45] In Sicily and Italy and during the initial phases of Overlord, British and American forces remained essentially balanced. Once the Allied forces broke out of the lodgment zone and began their advance through France, the preponderance of troops and supplies in northwest Europe would be American. Marshall desired SHAEF both to reflect American manpower and materiel ascendancy and to place the levers of logistical control under a senior American officer inside supreme headquarters.[46]

Confronted by Marshall's directive, Eisenhower uncharacteristically placed the supply organization at the top of his agenda. "I have already instructed General Lee to consolidate all of the Services of Supply activities in this theater and to do it now and not to consider it as merely a plan," Eisenhower informed Butcher. "I have also told him that I will delegate the primary responsibilities of Theater Commander on him."[47] He stopped short of naming Lee the American CAO.

Eisenhower entertained serious doubts about Lee. "Although Ike had made General JCH Lee deputy theater commander," Butcher recorded, "he has some misgivings and does not feel entirely satisfied. His wariness of General Lee flows principally from the fact that Lee has the reputation of traipsing around England and Ireland in a special train consisting of some eleven or twelve coaches."[48] His concerns did not end there. As he repeated to Marshall, "I hope that General Lee is big enough for this job." He did not worry about Lee's technical skills but wondered whether Lee possessed the personal tact for coordinating and cooperating with the Allies.[49] After conferring with Lee, his uncertainty mounted. Sensing that he was finally on the verge of moving Eisenhower toward a far-reaching reorganization, Smith applied his brand of gentle persuasion. On 19 January Eisenhower wired Devers, requesting Larkin's release for a "job I had tentatively in mind . . . for which I consider him personally highly qualified by experience and temperament."[50] Devers first delayed; then he refused Larkin's transfer. Devers's rebuff gave Eisenhower pause, and he decided not to tinker with the overall structure. Contrary to Marshall's wishes, he appointed no American CAO.

The other news Eisenhower had for Smith more than offset his disappointment over the headquarters setup. The day before Smith flew back, Marshall had cabled London asking about Smith's promotion. The topic had never come up in talks in Washington. Eisenhower, after surveying the situation in London, responded that the promotion, though "highly desirable," was not absolutely necessary.[51] Eisenhower may have entertained some misgivings about Smith, and he asked to see Butcher's diary covering November and December 1943, a period of strained relations when Smith had effectively run the theater. Butcher thought it strange. The day Eisenhower got into London, a still angry Brooke confronted him, annoyed by his treatment at the hands of Smith. Eisenhower smoothed the new field marshal's feathers and expressed his shock because Brooke's complaints represented the first criticism ever leveled against Smith by a British officer. According to Smith, Brooke was the only superior officer who ever complained about him. Eisenhower apologized, explaining that Smith "fights for what he wants" and intended no disrespect.[52] In fact, Smith fought for what Eisenhower wanted. Eisenhower expected "a ruckus [over Smith's nomination], certainly in the committee, when his name was presented, but so far have heard of none." There was none. The nomination sailed through the Senate, and Eisenhower pinned on Smith's third star on 28 January.[53]

Eisenhower still could not make up his mind on the roster of American army commanders. Since he saw Patton and Devers as "not compatible," he renewed his request that Patton command Anvil. Hodges would command an army in Overlord. Devers blocked Eisenhower's proposal; he wanted Clark in command of Anvil, with Lucas taking over Fifth Army. With Patton the odd man out, Eisenhower requested that he come to ETO. By the narrowest of margins, Patton assumed command of Third Army.[54] Patton, now in England, dropped by to solicit Smith's support for promotions for fifteen officers he wanted transferred from Seventh Army. "Went to see Bedell Smith," Patton recorded in his diary, "who was in rare form—s.o.b.—had just been made a Lieutenant General and is looking better than I have ever seen him." When Patton needed something, he poured on the charm. "The nurse who takes care of him . . . was present, and I had the opportunity of letting him advertise himself. I let him do all the talking and played him up. Washed mouth out later."[55]

COSSAC into SHAEF

During the preparation phase of Neptune-Overlord, a clear division of labor evolved between the supreme commander and his chief of staff. Eisenhower remained preoccupied with two overriding concerns: finalizing a decision on Anvil, and defending his personalized command structures, chiefly over the air components. These Eisenhower dealt with himself, with Smith playing only a secondary and chiefly advisory role. Smith's primary efforts remained centered on completing the transition from COSSAC to SHAEF, superintending post-Neptune planning, and creating structures for handling civil affairs on the Continent. The pre-Overlord period provides the best examples of Eisenhower's passive-negative leadership style. He initiated nothing, but he absolutely dug in his heels on those matters on which he refused to yield: *not* to cancel Anvil, *not* to accept any diminution in his control of the strategic air forces, *not* to curtail the bombing of French cities, and *not* to alter the supply side of his headquarters. He and Smith did not always agree, but Eisenhower depended on Smith to buttress his positions.

COSSAC bequeathed two legacies to SHAEF: an intact planning staff and an existing plan. Brooke thought he was handing Morgan an impossible task when he assigned him the job of heading COSSAC. Aside from the paltry manpower and lift resource parameters that COSSAC planners labored under, Morgan's biggest problem (as the name of the organization—Chief of Staff, Supreme Allied Command [Designate]—attested) was that the structure lacked any real decision-making capacity. Initially, Morgan worked on the assumption that the supreme commander would be British, probably Brooke. COSSAC's formation followed a modified British staff model. Logisticians enjoyed parity with operational planners not only because the British staff structure demanded it but also, more importantly, because logistical constraints—manpower and supply calculations—dominated planning calculations. To a large extent, Overlord was a logistical plan. Normandy represented only the initial phase and was a springboard for later operations; the ultimate objective in the first three months of the campaign lay in securing the Brittany peninsula and expanding the lodgment area toward the Seine.[56]

Three Allied divisions would land in Normandy: the British on the left would consolidate the lodgment, fend off the inevitable German counterattacks, and expand the beachhead beyond Caen; American forces would do likewise, close the Cotentin peninsula, and secure the port of Cherbourg. Even with the aid of artificial harbors, the Allies would struggle to match the German buildup. Morgan's staff identified the buildup stage as the most critical. The original COSSAC plan assumed a May landing, banking on a lengthy period of good weather prior to opening the ports. Airpower remained vital to all calculations; Allied airpower would lend direct tactical support and impede and inflict damage on enemy divisions and logistical support moving into the sector. A forward advance provided suitable terrain and space for airfields and supply dumps. With the expanded lodgment secure and the buildup gaining momentum, British and Canadian forces would continue to draw German combat power toward them—the bulk of the German forces would move from the reserve and the Paris district and logically work on containing and eliminating the eastern penetrations. It was hoped the elaborate deception plan (Operation Fortitude) and Allied air superiority would delay the movement of German forces from the Pas de Calais long enough for the Allies to complete the first stages of the buildup. Meanwhile, the Americans would assume responsibility for breaking through the German crust of defenses in the west, with the aim of sealing Brittany. Brittany and its ports represented the key to the next and subsequent phases of the campaign. COSSAC planners reckoned the British and Canadian forces would enjoy something like parity with the Americans in Normandy. Thereafter the balance would tilt dramatically to the Americans. Once Brittany fell, the peninsula would serve as a giant gateway for American divisions and materiel flooding into the theater. There was no Liverpool or Antwerp or Rotterdam in France, no single great port. Cherbourg possessed only limited capacity; it served as a holiday port—the equivalent of Southampton—as a debarkation point for transatlantic liners, and it possessed only a single-line rail connection with Paris. Brittany and the Loire contained Brest and Nantes and the secondary ports of L'Orient, St. Nazaire, and St. Malo, as well as the undeveloped anchorage of Quiberon Bay and major railway lines along the Loire and especially toward Paris. As it had in World War I, Brittany would act as a vast reception and training area for incoming divisions, the replacement system, and supply.[57]

Montgomery accepted the general outline for the first phase of Overlord, but before the Allies could contemplate gaining a lodgment, they must first secure and retain the beachheads. Montgomery's revisions did far more than add two assault divisions on two additional beaches and augment the airborne component. The Montgomery Plan also required wholesale alterations in the air, naval, and logistical programs, dramatically increasing Overlord's claims on landing craft, naval fire support, fighters and bombers over the beaches, transport aircraft (tripling the airborne effort), and resources for a much expanded buildup. Since these additional landing craft and air and naval assets could only come at the expense of the Mediterranean, the changes in the Overlord plan called for a realignment of grand strategic priorities, which necessarily must involve the political and uniformed chiefs. This could be expected to reignite the argument over the cross-Channel versus Mediterranean strategies—a crucial month-long delay in staging Overlord and a longer delay or downgrading of Anvil—and engender bitter disputes over naval and air assets, air strategy and command, and materiel.

Given the history of Allied collaboration, it proved little short of amazing that the broadening of Overlord—one of the great decisions of the war in Europe—gained approval almost by acclamation. At the first supreme commander's conference on 21 January, Montgomery reiterated his argument for expanding the beachhead. A three-division assault lacked sufficient staying power; the Germans would easily rope off the narrow beachhead and bring greater forces to bear. He pointed to the benefits of attacking the neck of the Cotentin, taking advantage of the rivers and marshes as additional flank protection for the beaches and the eventual movement on Cherbourg. As the battle for the lodgment developed, the British would hold off German concentrations on the left, allowing the Americans to take Cherbourg and then the Brittany and Loire ports. Montgomery emphasized the crucial importance of the ports; with the ports secure, the Allied forces could then employ their armor and secure the key road centers. He again stated his contention that Anvil should be pursued only as a threat, freeing up the necessary lift and naval support for an expanded Neptune. Eisenhower acknowledged his full agreement on all but Anvil, restating his firm conviction that Overlord and the southern France operation represented a single whole. He did announce his willingness to postpone the cross-Channel attack for a month if sufficient landing craft could be found to mount both operations more or less simultaneously. The next day he offered his recommendations to Marshall, mirroring all of Montgomery's arguments save for Anvil, and endorsed a delay of Overlord until late May or early June. Eisenhower warned Marshall that unless Washington and London resolved the strategic and operational impasse, the Allies confronted "a tremendous crisis with stakes incalculable."[58] SHAEF planners produced the revised outline plan, and on 1 February it received the sanction of the CCS. On 10 February the JCS took the extraordinary step of deferring the question of Anvil to Eisenhower, although no one seriously believed he would render the final verdict.[59]

The details of operational, including logistical, planning for Neptune devolved on Montgomery's Twenty-first Army Group, assisted by Bradley's First Army Group, the headquarters of Leigh-Mallory and Ramsay (Allied Naval Commander in Chief, Expeditionary Force [ANCXF]), and all the subordinate echelons of command. All the commanders made significant alterations in the revised plan—and continued doing so until early May—based on their assessments and reevaluations of changing conditions. On 12 February the CCS issued a mission statement charging SHAEF with overseeing operational and logistical planning for the post-Neptune period. At the next supreme commander's conference, Eisenhower chartered the formation of a Joint Planning Staff under Smith, charged with developing plans for the period following the landings until D+190.[60] The new planning staff received two tasks: select tentative lines of advance into the heart of Germany; and project phase lines on maps, predicting the speed of the advance as a guide in determining future logistical requirements. The danger loomed that the broad contours of SHAEF's strategic forecasts would diverge from operational planning in subordinate headquarters.

Even before leaving the Mediterranean, Smith campaigned for SHAEF's expansion. "I decided to start out with a big staff," he told a postwar interviewer. Smith pointed to a number of factors favoring the centralization of authority in SHAEF. Morgan had reorganized COSSAC according to what he believed the Americans wanted: the so-called Foch headquarters, consisting of a small staff to deal with political matters, with ETO handling the American side and Twenty-first Army Group the British.[61] In British practice, responsibilities gravitated downward to operational and tactical levels of command; the American system acted in precisely the opposite fashion. Divisions, corps, and armies possessed small staffs centered on operations, which pushed administrative and supply tasks up the chain. Bradley stood on unchartered territory as commander of the first American army group organized in the war, but being very much old school, his preference lay in trimming his headquarters to the minimum. Out of necessity, administration and supply and services gravitated toward the center. Nothing could alter the fact that Eisenhower acted as both supreme Allied and American theater commander. Eisenhower made it clear to Smith that he intended to act in his capacity as commanding general of ETO by placing the major theater commands at the disposal of supreme headquarters. Thereafter, he would command without using ETO channels; SHAEF would deal directly with Washington and the operational commands, including ComZ. SHAEF would render final decisions, coordinate actions, and enforce cooperation.[62] Since the dividing line between SHAEF and ETO/SOS remained undefined in Eisenhower's 16 January directive, coordination depended largely on personal agreements between the two agencies and on specific direction from Smith. Smith's dual function as chief of staff of both organizations necessitated the enlargement of the American staff at SHAEF.[63] The overriding concern centered on buttressing Eisenhower's status as supreme commander.

On 19 January Smith forcefully made the case for Eisenhower's assumption of direct command of ground forces, coincidental with the formation of the two army groups in Normandy. "Beetle was realistic in pointing out," Butcher noted, "that Ike again will be the target for those critics who say the British have cleverly accepted an American as Supreme Commander but have infiltrated British commanders for land, sea, and air, even though a majority of the troops are American."[64] Smith and Butcher neglected to consider that the British provided the bulk of the naval support and landing craft and would enjoy rough parity in both ground forces and the buildup until early July. Annoyed with the concept that had evolved in the Mediterranean, with Eisenhower acting as a mere political commander "way up on the pedestal," Smith agitated for him to assert authority from the beginning. If Eisenhower intended to exercise direct command on the Continent, Smith argued against creating intermediate headquarters under SHAEF—and for that, he required a large supreme headquarters. Although he conceded that, politically, Eisenhower could not immediately exercise direct command in Overlord, in hindsight Smith concluded, "We would have saved a lot of trouble if we had started off with Montgomery and Bradley as equals." Smith believed that "with a small staff you couldn't control strategic reserves and through that influence major actions." Finally, Smith explained that he had centralized authority in SHAEF based on a simple premise: "we thought [functions] wouldn't be done as well elsewhere." Smith recollected, "I argued for the full staff, and got Eisenhower to see it my way."[65] On 20 January Eisenhower told Butcher he intended to assume direct ground command once army groups formed in France, "without the cumbersome intermediate command which marked our set-up throughout the 15th Army Group in Italy."[66]

Smith's first priority involved fine-tuning COSSAC and converting it into his staff. From his first briefing of the COSSAC staff, Smith brought two elements to the table. The American deputy chief of intelligence, BG Thomas Betts, remarked that Smith, coming from an active theater, "brought a refreshing air of realism." Even though everyone expected Smith to reshape SHAEF in the image of AFHQ, Beetle reassured the senior COSSAC staff that although he intended to bring some of his people up from Algiers, generally speaking, he would settle for the extant staff. He did announce that Whiteley would take over the Intelligence Division and "was pretty abrupt about this." Otherwise, the basic structure and most of the top COSSAC people would remain in place. Many of the holdovers observed Smith's arrival with trepidation; they all knew his reputation. Many resented that the newcomers were boasting of having "sand in their boots." Brownjohn and Smith possessed very different ideas on staff structures. Smith told him not to trouble himself unduly because he would "not be [around] to carry [the reorganization] out."[67] As C. D. Jackson of the OSS observed, "a considerable reshuffling of top personalities is taking place—people being kicked out of jobs, and all the organizational unrealities that kicking people upstairs always entails."[68] As Betts remembered, the changes Smith made produced "a lot of rancor but it was over very quickly."[69]

Generally, Smith enjoyed excellent associations with his British subordinates. Tedder proved the exception. Just where Tedder fit into the headquarters scheme, especially in relation to the chief of staff, remained unclear. What irked Smith most was that Tedder held a key position inside the decision cycle but possessed no real authority. He exercised influence yet remained above the fray. With Coningham in charge of advance headquarters Allied Expeditionary Air Force (AEAF), Tedder had additional leverage. Tedder also enjoyed the trust and friendship of Eisenhower; the two men frequently spent time together outside the office. By 1944, except for official occasions, Eisenhower and Smith were socially estranged. While Smith "kept the Indian sign on nearly everybody," remembered his SGS, he could "never get General Eisenhower's aides straightened out." Smith never knew what Butcher was up to, and "he and Gault were the only ones who weren't afraid of Beetle."[70] Eisenhower's British aide observed, "Bedell [had] no value outside military business. Not a man who could give Ike that sympathetic aid he needed at some critical moments."[71] Members of Tedder's staff saw Smith as a malevolent agent who was resentful of Tedder's ease around the supreme commander. They also believed Smith viewed Tedder as a threat and kept the deputy commander in the dark as much as possible. Smith never included Tedder in political negotiations, especially those concerning civil affairs. Eisenhower would ask Tedder's advice on something, and he had to confess his ignorance because Smith had never shown him the dossier in question. Tedder never called for a showdown—as members of his staff hoped he would—because the deputy commander felt that as long as he retained Eisenhower's confidence, his contentious relationship with Smith did not matter.[72]

Smith's American subordinates saw things exactly the opposite way. They viewed him as overly solicitous to the British and too quick to accept their counsel—especially that offered by Morgan, Whiteley, Gale, and eventually Strong—over their own. At the same time, men such as Crawford appreciated how Smith complemented Eisenhower. Smith "tried to get everything in his hands, but that was to keep things from Ike." Crawford noted, "Beetle Smith [proved] exceptionally valuable because he knew exactly how Ike would react on most questions and could act for him." Although it was not a universally held view, Crawford concluded that Smith never assumed "power for its own sake."[73] A British officer agreed: "From the standpoint of a person who could take care of the things Ike wanted done, and who would protect Ike's interests, [Smith] was unbeatable."[74]

Smith retained many vestiges of COSSAC's committee system. He named Morgan and Gale as deputy chiefs of staff. He even experimented with a dual secretariat. As in AFHQ, Smith initiated action and worked through his deputy chiefs of staff and the division heads. As CAO, Gale coordinated administration and supply and acted as chairman of a number of joint committees dealing with logistics. Considering the inevitable expansion of the staff, Smith knew the importance of retaining decision making in his hands while granting wide autonomy to his chief subordinates.[75]

Morgan's presence raised a number of questions. For the sake of expediency, American forces entered the United Kingdom through ports in the west; in the COSSAC plan, they would land in Normandy on the western beaches. Morgan pointed to the mounting manpower crisis facing British forces and doubted they possessed sufficient combat power to spearhead the proposed push toward Caen that formed the vital hinge for the later breakout phase. For the same reason, the British and Canadians would occupy the inside track, advancing along the northern axis. Morgan entertained deep reservations about Twenty-first Army Group's ability to sustain its advance in France without significant American support. COSSAC even examined the question of reshuffling British and Canadian divisions with the Americans before D-day. Logistics ruled out what would have been a massive undertaking.[76] None of this sat well with Brooke and many other senior officers and War

Office officials; among themselves, they began saying, "Freddie [Morgan] deserted to the Americans." Although Smith charged Morgan with no specific duties—he would not play the same role Whiteley performed in AFHQ, coordinating intelligence and operations—Morgan received important assignments at the pleasure of Eisenhower and Smith.[77] As time went on, Smith delegated more and more responsibility to Morgan.

Among Morgan's greatest attributes was his talent for balancing Smith. Betts remembered Smith citing Marshall's dictum: "Better to make a decision, even if incorrect, than no decision at all." In Barker's opinion, Smith proved too prone to making "Napoleonic decisions" without weighing all the options. Instead of openly dissenting, Morgan would say, "Yes, Beetle, quite right. I'm sure you're right about that." Then he would tactfully present alternative courses of action. Soon Smith would realize he had "gone off half-cocked" and reverse himself. Barker thought Morgan avoided several potential errors, many of which might have borne serious repercussions. "Nobody knows how much we owe Freddy Morgan," reflected Barker, "for his level headed handling of Bedell Smith."[78] Smith came to the same conclusion. After the war he admitted that Morgan was a man he would not "willingly have dispensed with."[79]

As was his custom, Smith's first act focused on heightening the efficiency of SHAEF's nerve center, the secretariat. He quickly dispensed with the joint secretariat and placed Gilmer in charge. Gilmer's act as the bulldog's bulldog grated on people. Finally Whiteley had enough and threatened to resign unless Gilmer went. Gilmer had served Smith faithfully throughout the Mediterranean campaign, but in the interest of keeping a happy family, Smith transferred the objectionable secretary. LTC Ford Trimble succeeded him in March. Smith regretted the move; the three officers who followed Gilmer all resigned, unable to abide the constant harassment.[80]

As Smith had indicated from the beginning, MG P. Y. Whitefoord got the ax. The two clashed over the organization and handling of intelligence, especially Whitefoord's insistence on preserving close ties with the War Office. Smith thought the division top-heavy with academic types and insisted on Whiteley. After being deputy chief of staff in AFHQ, Whiteley's reduction to intelligence head might have appeared to be a step down. Whiteley thought otherwise; he gladly moved in as G-2, even though he knew Smith had originally wanted that slot filled by Strong.[81]

Smith also brought an Ultra specialist, COL Edward Foord, from AFHQ. Betts had arrived from Algiers back in November, and as the only American officer on the staff with Ultra clearance, he sensed his appointment might create some friction. He approached Smith, asking if he should return to AFHQ. "Quick on the trigger," Smith misinterpreted Betts's intentions, and Betts braced for the expected purple streak of abuse. Instead of reacting in his customary fashion, Smith gently persuaded Betts to stay. This left Betts surmising that Smith had purged Whitefoord as a calculated example for the rest of the headquarters.[82] Only Whiteley, Foord, and Betts knew of the existence of the special Ultra unit. SHAEF received and processed decryptions from the British intelligence complex at Bletchley Park. Charged with preserving supertight security, especially relating to the many elements connected to Fortitude, Smith insisted that he receive prompt updates on all Ultra traffic.[83]

"Pink" Bull presided over the heart of the SHAEF planning staff, the combined Operations Division. Since Montgomery superintended operational planning for Normandy, the G-3 Division developed estimates of the current military situation and drew up assessments and detailed plans for a dizzying number of proposed operations, most of which never went beyond the outline planning stage. SHAEF inherited and worked on a number of plans for the speedy occupations of France, Norway, and Germany in the event of a sudden, 1918-like German collapse (code-named Rankin A, B, and C).[84] The Rankin planning put the Operations Division into direct contact with the associated governments and resistance movements. Borrowing from British procedures, the Intelligence Division prepared estimates and handed them to the operations planning staff. Even though Bull headed the division, Smith brought in Whiteley and assigned him the role of coordinating intelligence and operational planning, as he had in AFHQ. If Bull resented his diminished role, he kept it to himself. Bull and Whiteley developed a close friendship; one officer categorized them "as two peas in a pod."

COSSAC initially possessed a combined Administrative and Supply Division; when Morgan reorganized the staff in November and December 1943, he created separate G-1 and G-4 Divisions in accordance with American practice. Barker took over the Administrative Division, staffed predominantly with Americans, and Crawford headed G-4. As CAO, Gale coordinated administrative and supply planning with the ground and naval commands, but he occupied a position far less influential than that in AFHQ.[85] In Europe, the British and American administrative and supply structures acted independently of one another. From 13 March through the end of April, Gale conducted extensive inspection tours of American and British units, checking on administrative cooperation.

Gale commanded the respect of everyone on the staff. An American member of SHAEF considered Gale "a first-class manager . . . practically a genius."[86] Complications arose with Twenty-first Army Group because Montgomery blamed Gale for the supply mess in Italy. Again, because COSSAC originally possessed a British structure, the planning and operational side of supply passed to subordinate commands. On the American side, Lee's SOS command controlled mounting operations; First Army Group and First Army performed their own logistical planning in conjunction with the nucleus staffs of the advance section (ADSEC) and forward echelon (FECZ) of a future ComZ on the Continent. During the assault phase (D-day to D+14), the ADSEC would be attached to U.S. First Army and operate in the army rear; during the lodgment phase (D+15 to D+41), after the activation of First Army Group, ADSEC would operate immediately behind the combat zone, with FECZ acting as the army group rear; then, during the breakout phase (D+42 to D+90), the ComZ would become operational.[87]

Confusion and friction arose over the precise functions of Lee's command and the SOS's relationship to the various echelons of embedded ADSEC and FECZ planners in First Army and First Army Group. Similarly, Crawford's role in his dual capacity in SHAEF and ETO remained unclear. Smith still hoped Eisenhower would come around to his thinking on restructuring the manpower and supply side of the headquarters, but that possibility virtually died when Devers blocked Larkin's transfer. Confronted by all the other demands on his time and energy, Smith put aside his politicking for reorganization; instead, he merely went about absorbing ETO's planning functions and pirating its staff. SOS already exercised ETO's supply and administrative roles. On 8 February Smith approved a proposal that made Lee ex officio American CAO and sanctioned the plan for the phased formation of a Communications Zone on the Continent.[88] Curiously, Lee never recognized that Smith's reorganization schemes were directed at him. The same day, Lee asked Somervell if ASF would release Clay to command ComZ, on the assumption Lee would remain as deputy theater commander, parallel to the position Hughes held in the Mediterranean.[89] Neither Eisenhower nor Smith countenanced any such development.

Smith conducted all the troubleshooting negotiations with the JCS. Much of his labor focused on leveraging more landing craft out of Washington. On 8 March he phoned Handy, outlining Ramsay's request for American naval units in support of the landings. Washington argued that the Mediterranean could not spare major surface units and suggested the British employ their Home Fleet. Undeterred, the next day

Smith forwarded a formal request to the CCS for American ships and summarized the logistical requirements for Overlord.[90] After a good deal of acrimony, King relented and reinforced ANCXF with three battleships, two cruisers, and thirty-four destroyers. Also on 8 March, Gale completed a study of the number of landing craft obtainable for Overlord and their date of availability. Gale's conclusions sent shock waves through all the planning agencies. On 10 March Eisenhower considered the problem so serious that he told Marshall, "although I badly need him at this juncture," he intended to dispatch Smith on a hurried trip home.[91] In the end, Eisenhower decided not to send him.

The general transition from COSSAC to SHAEF presented Smith with relatively few real headaches. As he told Strong on 7 February, although at times it seemed "like a long uphill pull . . . things are slowly beginning to take shape."[92] The same could not be said of the two nontraditional general staff divisions—civil affairs and publicity and psychological warfare. Morgan remembered civil affairs as "a completely unknown business" that produced the "most vexations" for Smith. "There are plenty of affairs," one of Morgan's assistants quipped, "but the difficulty was to keep them civil."[93]

Immediately upon arriving in London in late December, Smith pushed for clarification on civil relations policy. Any hope of taking advantage of the rapprochement with de Gaulle ended when Hilldring notified Smith in early January that American policy remained unchanged—the president forbade all political dealings with the FCNL. Smith believed the FCNL represented the only viable "vehicle" for cooperating with the French, and with no political understanding, SHAEF could not proceed with civil affairs planning. If the French committee played no role in designing civil affairs policy, de Gaulle would not cooperate militarily.[94] Prompted by Smith, Eisenhower appealed to the combined chiefs, saying it was "essential that immediate crystallization of plans relating to civil affairs in Metropolitan France be accomplished." He assumed his headquarters would operate through accredited representatives of the FCNL. "We will desire to turnover to French control at the earliest possible date those areas that are not essential to military for operations."[95] Pleas from London were ignored. McCloy could not get any movement from Roosevelt. The absence of any sort of political agreement with the French hamstrung all efforts to formulate civil affairs pacts with the Norwegian, Belgian, and Dutch governments in exile until May; military missions to SHAEF and the operational commands were not created until well after the invasion.

Morgan had formed a Civil Affairs Division in COSSAC in October

1943—a small planning staff consisting of six advisory groups and four "country sections" that examined problems related to France, Belgium, the Netherlands, and Norway.[96] In November the War Department had assigned ninety-six officers to the division, but only a handful had appeared by the time Smith took charge. McSherry was already in place as opposite number to MG Roger Lumley. Assessing the COSSAC organization, Smith deemed the "double-headed" leadership team too "ponderous and unwieldy." He wanted a single head and thought he should be a civilian and an American. Uneasy about leaving civil affairs and military government entirely in military hands, Smith again requested McCloy. As a civilian of subcabinet rank, McCloy would administer the organization, provide political advice, and generally act as a lightning rod.[97]

Hilldring told Smith the COSSAC directives were never intended to "prescribe an organization with any idea that it would endure until the end of time," and he indicated the War Department and CCS stood prepared to give Smith carte blanche on organizing the civil affairs setup in London; however, he should forget about McCloy. Smith's request for McCloy caused a "great furor," and Stimson told Hilldring "never to raise the matter again." Stating he would give his "right arm to break out of this jailhouse," Hilldring declined the job, citing Marshall's "forcible" opposition to the idea. He promised the new directives would be "short and non-specific to leave plenty of freedom of action" and assured Smith he could count on Holmes's transfer to London.[98]

After all his tribulations organizing AMGOT, Smith had come to London convinced of the importance of civil affairs; as in the Mediterranean, he wanted military government and civil affairs fused into a single structure under his direct control. In the Mediterranean, Smith had fashioned a tidy organization subordinate to AFHQ but otherwise autonomous. He wanted to centralize and personalize civil affairs and military government as in the Mediterranean, where he had acted as foreign minister, advised and aided by Murphy, Macmillan, and Monnet and working through men such as Rennell and Joyce. Smith had made the decisions and, when required, conducted direct negotiations with the French and Italians. Supreme headquarters would retain policy-making power over civil affairs, surrendering little authority to the restored national governments or the operational commands.

Smith took an instant dislike to Lumley. A former Indian administrator, Lumley acted with too much independence and enjoyed too close a relationship to the War Office for Smith's taste.[99] Eisenhower did not want any fight with the British over the appointment of an American chief and directed Smith to leave Lumley where he was for now. Lumley proposed retaining the COSSAC structure as a separate general staff division charged with policy formulation, coordination of the two subsections for civil affairs in liberated areas, and planning for the occupation of Germany.[100] He also advocated retention of the COSSAC handbook, which delegated discretionary authority to the operational commanders in implementing civil affairs on the ground. Initially, the division would consist of something like forty officers, later expanded to sixty.

On 6 February Smith convened a conference where he reminded everyone he had come from an active theater that had scored some rather notable successes in the field of civil affairs and military government. He laid out his reorganization scheme and announced that it enjoyed Eisenhower's full approval. Smith told Lumley that he opposed the creation of a new staff division, considered Lumley's proposed staff too big, and rejected the idea of delegating responsibility for executing policy to the operational commands. Only a small, high-powered section, "possibly to be designated G-5," would remain under Lumley inside SHAEF, with responsibilities for policies and directives, long-range outline planning, and general coordination. A second and larger staff under McSherry would represent the operating side—training, organization, and detailed planning—at Shrivenham in Oxfordshire, the site of the civil affairs school. Smith also indicated that he intended to remove civil affairs from the tutelage of external agencies, especially the Combined Civil Affairs Committee in London. He though it "apparent we must stand on our own two feet," and as he told Hilldring, "I am afraid I will have to be rather blunt on this subject." He insisted on a clear demarcation between advice and control, and as insurance, he wanted "an American officer of very high quality" as Lumley's deputy. He again asked Devers for Holmes.[101]

Smith was not as self-assured as he appeared. He relayed to Hilldring his apprehensions. "You realize better than anybody else," he admitted, "the complexity of civil affairs problems which will confront us." Although he claimed that "all here agree to this general scheme of organization and I am convinced that it is a sound one," he admitted, "I am NOT quite certain myself and would be guided by your advice." He also appealed for Hilldring's help in his contest with Devers. Smith conceded he could not get along without Holmes.[102]

Not everyone agreed with Smith's new plan. Lumley responded by pointedly rejecting the Mediterranean prototype again. He requested Smith abandon "with finality the concept applied elsewhere which undertakes to execute civil affairs operations through a separate channel either parallel or divergent from the channel of command."[103] After giving the matter some thought, Smith concluded that conditions in northwestern Europe bore few similarities to those in the Mediterranean; civil affairs represented a far more complex proposition in northwestern Europe than in North Africa and Italy. At another conference on 10 February, Smith reversed himself. He sanctioned the formation of a Civil Affairs Division, but not until the headquarters moved out of London. Initially, he was unaware that the political heads had agreed at Quebec that the countries of northwestern Europe would constitute "liberated," not "occupied," territories. The Quebec directives called for the reestablishment of national governments as quickly as possible. The AMGOT model simply did not apply. He wanted to confine liaison with the "country houses" of the governments in exile to another SHAEF agency, the Allied European Contact Section. Organizing the staff around the country branches would create too much duplication of effort and tie up scarce expert personnel. Instead, he decided to functionalize the structure under Lumley; the new Policy Section would deal with supply, public health, labor, economics, and law, without consideration of national frontiers. McSherry's Operations Section still handled training and all planning related to the formation of SHAEF missions to liberated countries and for civil affairs procedures for presurrender and occupied Germany. Smith limited Lumley's inner staff to thirty-five officers and confined it to policy-making and advisory roles. On 11 February Smith issued a memo outlining the need for his tight supervision of the Civil Affairs Section.[104]

Smith requested that the director of civil affairs in the War Office approve the formation of an Allied Control Commission for Germany to take post-hostilities planning off SHAEF's hands. The War Office agreed, and thereafter Smith directed McSherry to coordinate SHAEF planning on Germany with the Control Commission. COSSAC had released a general handbook on civil affairs and military government for Germany in December 1943. Considering it substandard, Smith insisted on a revision and solicited policy guidance from the CCS,[105] which responded by relaying word that the European Advisory Commission (EAC) was preparing a statement and program. The EAC, formed in January 1944 and consisting of representatives from the United States, United Kingdom, and USSR, dealt with problems connected with the termination of the war, including but not limited to drafting surrender terms and establishing zones of occupation. From experience, Smith knew not to expect a CCS directive anytime soon. The Civil Affairs Section continued work initiated by COSSAC, including writing another handbook, but other staff divisions, principally G-1 and G-3, also engaged in similar planning. By the end of March, no fewer than thirty-eight separate studies were under way. Smith attached great importance to this planning and wanted McSherry as his agent synchronizing it.[106]

On 14 March Smith finally authorized formation of the G-5 Division, defined its command and staff channels, and sanctioned its move, along with the rest of SHAEF, to Widewing.[107] Four days later, still intent on dumping Lumley, Smith forwarded a request to the Combined Civil Affairs Committee through the CCS for a highly qualified officer familiar with civil affairs and supply to head G-5.[108] The same day, he dispatched an officer from G-5 to confer with the State Department. For the next six weeks, Smith systematically put Lumley's feet to the fire. Unhappy with Lumley and the entire G-5 structure, Smith bided his time before embarking on another round of reorganization. His jealous obstructionism did nothing to facilitate the division's work.

If Smith experienced problems organizing a separate Civil Affairs Division, he really struggled with how best to handle psychological warfare and press relations. Morgan had formed a section in COSSAC after examining the AFHQ setup. Smith had sanctioned McClure's reassignment in November to organize and head the new section. A related question involved where to place the control mechanism for the OSS. In early February, Donovan came to London to work out the details for employing the OSS on the Continent. McClure argued that OSS activities fell within the purview of psychological warfare and requested the OSS's transfer to the Psychological Warfare Branch. Donovan and Smith talked over the matter and decided McClure's office would serve as the policy-making and control mechanism but stay separate from actual intelligence operations.[109] Because of the importance attached to special operations, Smith used the agreement with Donovan as a vehicle for tentatively accepting the creation of a Publicity and Psychological Warfare Division (G-6) later in February. Agreeing to the creation of the G-6 Division only to "dignify" its functions, Smith still thought it a mistake to pass these duties to subordinates. Like Civil Affairs, McClure's organization would soon face demands for a wholesale reordering of functions.

Smith and Eisenhower had joked in the Mediterranean that the only group they hated more than fascists were journalists. Headquarters faced the dilemma of balancing the need to cultivate good press relations, the home front's hunger for information about their fighting men and women, and the imperative to preserve the tightest security. When deprived of hard information, journalists employed their many contacts and uncovered stories. To SHAEF's alarm, articles appeared that accurately estimated the timing and scope of the invasion. Moreover, in England, Smith could not control press accreditation as tightly as he had in Algiers. Smith made it clear to McClure that he retained final say on certifying journalists and censorship.[110]

American officers avidly followed their own press in the States. Afraid that uneven press coverage might fuel interservice jealousies, as it had in World War I, Marshall often insisted that Smith employ his influence with the press to secure stories for certain officers. Smith resented acting as a press agent and told Marshall he faced more compelling concerns. Not amused, Marshall ordered him to get the job done or he would dispatch a "Marine lieutenant."[111]

Except for logistics planners and a portion of the secretariat, SHAEF completed its move to Bushy Park in the middle of March. A number of motives lay behind Eisenhower and Smith's anxiety about getting the headquarters out of London. In many respects, AFHQ had had it easy in North Africa. In London, Parliament, the Foreign Office, Fleet Street, 10 Downing Street, and the War Office were just around the corner. Escaping to Widewing conferred a sense of getting out from under, but that came with a price. The move out of the capital hamstrung coordination with key British ministries and civil agencies. The government controlled virtually everything—roads, land, airspace, the rail system—which demanded that SHAEF work through these governmental bodies. Civil society and the economy did not disappear just because there was a war on; SHAEF's plans and policies had to accommodate these factors. The move out of London necessarily complicated matters. Intelligence indicated that the Germans stood prepared to unleash their V-weapons on London. A lucky hit on Norfolk House would have disastrous consequences. Because of limited space at Norfolk House and adjacent buildings, SHAEF remained understaffed. After the move, and as planning for the invasion matured, staffs rapidly expanded, prompting a building boom. In early May, Smith authorized the construction of two more wings at Widewing, with the stipulation that this represented the last demand for additional accommodations.[112] Eisenhower thought the intermingling of officers in messes and living quarters would expedite the "welding of all allied command."[113] Smith knew he could never shake the slackness out of his headquarters until they escaped the fleshpots of the capital. In perhaps an unwitting commentary on the different mores of American and British officers, he observed, "Our boys were in the nightclubs every night and the British were always at Claridge's for tea." Smith encountered a good deal of opposition to the move. Officers complained they had nothing to occupy their time at night. Smith typically responded by suggesting, "Why not work? That's what I [do]."

Because Smith was still trying to convince Eisenhower to assume command in France at the earliest possible date, he expanded the Portsmouth command post into an advance headquarters. "We were going to move an echelon across as soon as possible," Smith recounted, "so we needed to train them in living in the field." The officers sent off to Portsmouth to live in tents "thought they would die, of course," but everything stood in place by the time Eisenhower moved to his command post in the days immediately preceding D-day.[114]

A keen observer like Jackson recognized the sharp differences from the first tentative and contentious weeks in Norfolk House. "Now there is a new hustle and bustle," he noted in early April, "and the dawning of a sense that what is put on paper really means something in terms of lives and logistics."[115] As in AFHQ, the forging of a unified headquarters grew from two essential elements: Eisenhower's matchless ability for turning the rhetoric of Anglo-American partnership into something approaching reality, and if that failed, Smith's willingness to bust out his "cat and nine tails and beat [the obstructionists] into line."[116] T. J. Davis remarked that SHAEF "is a honey" and noted, "I think it is even better than the one developed for Allied forces." Although Beetle faced opposition at the outset, Davis reported that the "discontent was put down in 'typical Smith fashion.'"[117] Undoubtedly, creating a unified supreme headquarters constituted one of the most significant accomplishments of the pre-Overlord period, but in the bigger scheme of things, it mattered little if the wider political, operational, command, and landing craft issues went unresolved.

★ 26 ★

"Enough to Drive You Mad"

In the first two and a half months of SHAEF's existence, problems fell into two distinct categories: those under the purview of the CCS, and those that devolved on Eisenhower's commands. At the end of March, Eisenhower believed his headquarters was well on the road toward accomplishing its essential tasks: forming a supreme headquarters and lesser staffs and mastering all the details of organization, the assignment of personnel, and the vast problems of moving troops and supplies. "The matters that have really caused us trouble," he noted in his diary, "are those in which only the Combined Chiefs of Staff can make final decisions." He listed three: the allocation of resources and whether and when to launch Anvil; the organization and command of the air forces; and political matters, especially pertaining to the French.[1] Unless the chiefs could come together, the Overlord ship might never sail.

Hammering Away on Anvil

Aside from the operational value he attached to Anvil as a complement to Overlord, Eisenhower pointed to other considerations. As he explained to Marshall on 17 January, "according to my understanding the British and American staffs at Teheran definitely assured the Russians that ANVIL would take place. Secondly, we have put into the French Army a very considerable investment. Since these troops, plus the Americans and the British, cannot profitably be used in decisive fashion in Italy, we must open a gateway for them into France or all of our French investment will have been wasted. Altogether there would be a great number of American and other forces locked up in the Mediterranean from whom we will be deriving no benefit." There was another factor he omitted:

Marseilles, France's largest prewar port, and Toulon offered alternative points of entry for manpower and materiel coming into the theater.[2]

Whatever the advantages, by 6 February the British restated their opposition to Anvil. On 26 January the BCOS had agreed to the concept of Anvil on the condition it contained two divisions, but by 6 February it became clear the Allies would not possess the requisite landing craft to mount concurrent operations in northern and southern France. As Smith pointed out, the difference of opinion never followed national lines. Cunningham, now first sea lord, sided with Eisenhower, while Smith emerged as the leading doubting Thomas in the American camp. Smith felt Anvil would deflect scarce Allied resources, especially for the vital buildup phase before the lodgments became secure. Intimately involved in assessing the landing craft issue, Smith concluded the strategic debate would necessarily come down to lift, and there was not enough for both operations. Something had to give, and that something had to be the southern France operation: Anvil's demise, its downgrading to a threat, or a delay.

On 6 February Smith received a study from the combined planners in Washington that floored him. Based on their calculations, enough landing craft would become available by 31 May for a seven-division Overlord and a two-division Anvil. This flew in the face of everything his own people had told him and set off another hurried exchange of communications between London and Washington. As Marshall noted, the "battle of numbers" greatly confused the entire puzzle. To Eisenhower, Marshall marveled at the turn of events. "The British and American Chiefs of Staff seem to have completely reversed themselves," he wrote, "and we have become Mediterraneanites and they heavily pro-OVERLORD." Attesting to his continued support, Marshall still wondered if "localitis" had "not warped [Eisenhower's] judgment."[3] A deflated Eisenhower confided in his diary, "looks like ANVIL is doomed. I hate this."[4]

Smith and Handy held marathon telephone exchanges on 8–9 February, trying to narrow the numbers gap. The combined planners in Washington, in Smith's view, badly underestimated the initial force requirements and overestimated the lift capacities of infantry landing craft. SHAEF operated on the basis of division slices, not just combat troops. Divisional assault scales called for 25,000 men, not the 15,000 assumed in Washington. This meant that, according to SHAEF calculations, a seven-division operation called for a lift of 175,000 men, not 105,000. The Washington planners, based on experience in the Pacific, figured on three trips per vessel with 1,400 men in each wave; the London planners' calculated on two trips and 960 men. In addition, calculations for the assault scales did not provide for the immediate buildup phase, which increased the divisional slice to 40,000, or for the vehicles to move materiel, especially ammunition, from the beaches to the dumps and then forward to the troops.

And, as Smith reminded Handy, "Eisenhower was strong for ANVIL." Smith and Handy moved toward a compromise, but the naked fact remained that there would not be enough landing craft for the seven-division cross-Channel attack without a major deployment from the Mediterranean.[5]

The prime minister considered the problem serious enough for a CCS meeting in London; failing that, he wanted Marshall to come over. As Churchill told Roosevelt, "The OVERLORD Commanders-in-Chief must know where they stand and every day counts."[6] Marshall headed off Churchill, and the JCS empowered Eisenhower to negotiate directly with the BCOS. Landing craft constituted only the subtext of the wider issues of Anvil and future Allied strategy in the Mediterranean.

Eisenhower and Smith attended a noon BCOS meeting on 10 February. Nothing much transpired; a full-ranging discussion would await an answer to the landing-craft issue. Marshall and King dispatched MG John Hull of OPD and RADM Charles Cooke Jr., who arrived in London on 12 February. A series of conferences ensued at Norfolk House. On 19 February Eisenhower, Smith, and Cooke, representing the JCS, presented their findings to the British chiefs. As Smith and Strong foresaw, Anzio had accomplished none of its objectives except tying down German divisions. By the middle of February parts of two German corps numbering 100,000 troops launched a vicious counteroffensive against the lodgment. Lucas predicted before the landing that Shingle bore "a strong odor of Gallipoli . . . [with] the same amateur still on the coach's bench." Churchill accepted no responsibility, instead blaming the senior officers. "I had hoped we were hurling a wildcat into the shore," he snidely remarked, "but all we got was a stranded whale."[7] Brooke believed Anzio rendered Anvil impossible and privately concluded that Eisenhower was pushing for the southern France landings merely to please Marshall. Portal thought "the Americans wanted to get all their troops into the European theater and out from under Alexander."[8]

Marshall added to SHAEF's headaches. On 10 February he floated a fantastic airborne scheme that made Giant II look timid in comparison; he proposed "a true vertical envelopment" by establishing an airhead south of Evreux, seventy miles beyond Caen. "We have never done anything like this before," he told Eisenhower, "and frankly, that reaction makes me tired."[9] Not for the first time, Marshall's scheme smacked of the unreal, but Smith put the planners to work.

Montgomery finally added his voice to the debate. Agreeing with Brooke that Anzio made Anvil difficult, he pointed out that "fought out" divisions in Italy could not easily regroup and redeploy for the southern France operation. "No point in saving landing craft in the Mediterranean if ANVIL cannot be staged," he wrote on 19 February. Two days later he argued that the Italian Front had already accomplished its mission by tying down German divisions. "We should now make a definite decision to cancel ANVIL," he stated, and recommended "very strongly that we now throw the whole weight of our opinion onto the scales vs. ANVIL. Let us have two really good major campaigns—one in Italy and one in OVERLORD."[10]

Brooke and Montgomery made an impression. After the meeting with the BCOS, Eisenhower wired Marshall, indicating the situation in Italy probably ruled out Anvil as envisioned. At the meeting he had clearly stated the "utmost urgency" of a CCS decision on "whether the prospects in the Mediterranean can really offer any reasonable chance of executing ANVIL." The BCOS wired Washington recommending "the immediate cancellation of ANVIL."[11]

In the meantime, Smith and Hull talked to Handy on the phone. Echoing Montgomery's assessment that tired divisions and Italian commitments made Anvil doubtful, Smith nevertheless said Eisenhower still believed that "planning for ANVIL and as much of the preparation as possible should go on up [to] the last minute. It may be that ANVIL cannot be launched simultaneously with OVERLORD, but the situation in Italy might clear up and ANVIL might be put on a little later." Pressed, Smith conceded that Eisenhower "is beginning to believe that there cannot be an ANVIL, much as he regrets it." Smith's personal view, he informed Handy, "is that ANVIL as an operation is not going to have any material effect on OVERLORD during the first fifteen to thirty days." Yet Anvil planning must continue because "we may find that we cannot do any OVERLORD." As he explained, "the buffer of German divisions confronting us across the channel is just now approaching the absolute maximum we can handle." If Overlord went by the wayside, the center of gravity must shift back to the Mediterranean in 1944. "I have felt right along," Smith continued, "that we have another month really before we need to make a final decision on ANVIL." Smith and Hull reported good progress in closing the gap on the differing landing craft estimates. Finally, Smith killed Marshall's vertical envelopment plan, explaining that the airborne units must stay fixed on taking Cherbourg "early in the game. Our plans contemplate actually a fast air operation supported by a landing." Hull proved even less diplomatic. He reported the idea had been universally dismissed as unfeasible; "a glance at the map will prove the point."[12]

Smith always proved extremely proprietary when outsiders came to SHAEF lending advice. "The people were all our friends," he remembered, "but we accused them of being desk soldiers." The Hull-Cooke mission fell into that category. Smith resented the War Department using the Pacific as the model. "We had to tell them the facts of life."[13] Smith told them they should forget theoretical capacities of landing craft and look at the beaches. MG Charles Corlett had a similar experience, only worse. Although he was fresh from conducting an amphibious assault at Kwajalein in the central Pacific that, in Marshall's estimate, "approached perfection," Eisenhower passed Corlett over for a corps command in Neptune in favor of Ike's friend Gerow. Eisenhower promised Marshall he would make Corlett available "so that his experience would be available to all."[14] The British proved very keen on exploiting Corlett's expertise, but the Americans made him feel like "a son-of-a-bitch from out of town." He wrote a paper arguing that the estimated rate of fire for artillery was far too low and called for the development of new methods for bringing more ammunition over the beaches in the early phase of the landings. Events proved him right on both counts. Smith had a talk with him, and when Corlett cited Pacific experience, Smith lost his temper. Pounding the table, Smith yelled, "Do I have to defend the plan to you!" Smith exemplified the attitude Corlett found everywhere in ETO. Smith and Bradley both rejected Corlett's advice on flotation tanks. Everybody from Eisenhower and Smith on down, in Corlett's opinion, considered anything that happened in the Pacific as "strictly bush league stuff, meriting no consideration."[15]

On 21 February Roosevelt entered the Anvil fray. At a conference with the JCS, the president issued instructions to Eisenhower "to call attention that we are committed to a third power and I do not feel we have any right to abandon this commitment for ANVIL without taking up the matter with that third power."[16] Despite this communication from the president, Eisenhower admitted to Marshall the next day that the "prospects for ANVIL in the hoped strength . . . have deteriorated in past ten days."[17]

News of Eisenhower's appointment remained classified until 15 February. On 22 February Churchill reviewed the state of the war in a speech before the House of Commons. When he announced Eisenhower's name as supreme commander, the House erupted in cheers. More cheering greeted the prime minister's depiction of the unprecedented unity that existed in the combined headquarters. Then he announced

Tedder's name as deputy supreme commander: more cheers. Finally he revealed the name of the chief of staff, Lieutenant General Walter Bedell Smith: silence. Such is the lot of faceless staff officers.[18]

The next evening Eisenhower and Smith had a rare opportunity to take their minds off their many troubles. The British staged a dinner at Claridge's and presented Eisenhower with a silver salver engraved with all the names of his chief British subordinates from the Mediterranean. Admiral Cunningham made the presentation and, after acknowledging Eisenhower's sterling traits as a man, added, "we must not forget your second self—Bedell—to whom all of us owe a great debt and whose great qualities fill us with admiration."[19] These tributes reminded both men that, despite the immediate stresses, the bonds of the alliance held firm.

After a month of "sweating," Eisenhower intimated to Smith on 26 February that he would reverse his position and call off Anvil in exchange for the release of Mediterranean landing craft for Overlord. Despite his deep reservations about both operations, Smith talked Eisenhower out of sending the cable to Marshall. Another of the pressures on Eisenhower grew out of the relentless British press campaign that elevated Montgomery to the station of Britain's greatest general since Wellington and correspondingly denigrated Eisenhower to affable chairman of the board. Smith had been goading Eisenhower into asserting his command prerogatives. He pushed the idea of Eisenhower's assuming the ground command the day after the landings, and since 11 February he had been quietly expanding the staff of the advance command post at Portsmouth to facilitate the rapid movement of the headquarters across the Channel. He harped on the importance of not repeating what had happened after Alexander's appointment, when Eisenhower and AFHQ had found themselves bypassed and overshadowed by the Eighteenth and Fifteenth Army Groups. "I kept arguing with him on the question and pushing him to take over," remarked Smith. "[I] wanted to handle [Overlord] like a river crossing." Smith also railed against the general impression that the British commander in chief exercised decisive authority over planning and the orchestration of Overlord. Smith feared that if SHAEF gave "the impression of changing our minds too quickly," Eisenhower would sacrifice credibility and ultimately damage himself as supreme commander.[20]

Smith's advice did the trick; Eisenhower agreed that SHAEF should hold on to Anvil for as long as possible. As Smith had argued, until the landing craft dilemma got sorted out, no real decision could emerge. SHAEF suggested a bargain: the Italian Front would enjoy priority for ongoing and future operations in the Mediterranean in exchange for

Wilson's agreement to continue planning and preparations for Anvil. The entire question would undergo reappraisal on 20 March. The political heads readily agreed to the compromise. As Butcher noted, SHAEF decided "to 'saw wood' for a little longer."[21] Just as the Anvil debate subsided, another crisis hit.

At the end of February, Churchill, in another of his "bull in a china shop" moods, suddenly concluded he did not trust Leigh-Mallory. As Brooke noted, "PM had been stepping in and muddling things badly as he has been 'crashing in where angels fear to tread!'" In the middle of February, the first fight over control of the heavy bombers ended in a no decision. Leigh-Mallory advanced his transportation plan—diverting the bombers from attacking German aircraft production facilities and refined petroleum installations (Operation Pointblank) and using them to paralyze the rail networks in northern France, the Low Countries, and western Germany. Spaatz and AM Arthur Harris of Bomber Command opposed the plan and received support from Churchill, Brooke, Portal, and Arnold. Tedder backed Leigh-Mallory. The bomber barons refused to surrender any measure of control over the strategic air forces to Leigh-Mallory, who came from Fighter Command. Churchill wanted Tedder, the "Aviation Lobe of Eisenhower's brain," in command of any air forces assigned to Overlord. Eisenhower blistered at Churchill's intrusion. Eisenhower backed the transportation plan, but he also insisted on his right to employ the strategic air forces in the theater. Even though Spaatz and Harris made it clear they would not willingly follow orders issued by Leigh-Mallory, Tedder also rejected any disruption of the high command.[22] Still with no agreed air plan, Eisenhower ordered Tedder to expedite planning, or "the P.M. will be in this thing with both feet." Eisenhower would control all air units through Tedder, but he emphasized that Leigh-Mallory would actually exercise command of assigned and attached air units for definite periods and specific missions.[23]

How control and command and coordination would function in the absence of an agreed plan and without a fixed chain of command bedeviled the discussions. After a number of meetings, Tedder and Portal cut a deal on 9 March: Tedder would supervise air operations in Overlord, and Portal, as executive agent of the CCS, would superintend the execution of Pointblank as it related to the invasion. Leigh-Mallory remained in command of forces assigned by the CCS to Overlord. The strategic air forces in Europe and the Mediterranean would be at the operational disposal of Eisenhower, subject to the concurrence of Portal. Eisenhower noted to Smith that the deal was "exactly what we want." Smith replied, "I think this is excellent and a most fair solution."[24]

Content the air command agreement went his way, Eisenhower shifted his attention back to Anvil. Eisenhower informed Marshall that planning, down to regimental combat teams, could not proceed without some resolution of the landing-craft issue. "If the matter does not clear up within a couple of days I shall send Smith on a hurried trip home although I badly need him at this juncture."[25]

On 16 March Marshall informed Eisenhower the JCS had proposed reopening discussions with the BCOS on Anvil. "The basis for a final decision appears no better than a month ago," Marshall observed. "The only clear-cut decision would be to cancel the ANVIL operation." Marshall solicited Eisenhower's views, "including your present appraisal of the landing craft situation and the latest dates that you can accept craft for use in OVERLORD." He concluded by saying, "We will support your desire regarding the ANVIL decision, whatever it may be."[26]

The next day Smith got on the transatlantic phone to Handy. Handy thought, "We better hang on to [Anvil] as long as we can. I am afraid you are the people who are going to regret more than anybody else cancelling it in the long run." Smith agreed but complained, "You can't imagine the difficulties here in planning. It is enough to drive you mad with this uncertainty and these changes. When you have to sit down and figure the balance of divisions, the loading tables and everything of that sort and you don't know what kind of craft you are going to load them in or whether you are going to have as many as you think you are going to have, it is enough to drive a man insane." Currently his planners operated on the "very lowest, skimpiest, measliest figure that we can possibly calculate to get by on in the assumption there would be a strong landing in the Mediterranean. Any time anybody will guarantee us there will be a strong landing in the Mediterranean we will stick by that measly figure, but time is getting short."[27]

Eisenhower and Smith reevaluated Anvil on 20 March as promised. "I firmly believe that ANVIL as we originally visualized it," Eisenhower reported to Marshall, "is no longer a possibility either from the standpoint of time in which to make all the necessary preparations or in probability of fresh and effective troops at the appointed date."[28] SHAEF proposed abandoning the concept of a two-division, building to a ten-division, Anvil in exchange for all the landing craft in the Mediterranean except for a one-division lift.[29] A crestfallen Eisenhower complained to Marshall, "More talk seems completely useless." The arguments of the last two months had not changed "the convictions of any single individual." He warned, "Matters must be cleared up soon."[30] They would not be. The BCOS readily accepted Eisenhower's offer, but the JCS balked.

The American chiefs admitted the infeasibility of launching concurrent operations but argued for Anvil's postponement, not cancellation.

That same day, 21 March, the air command deal unraveled. There was never much chance it would survive. Indeed, all throughout the Mediterranean campaign, AFHQ and the tactical and strategic air forces had sought fixed command chains and failed. All the command lines remained tenuous and might have become tendentious except for the fact that Eisenhower's command style worked so well—and then only because of the personalities involved; he enjoyed the trust and admiration of Tedder, Cunningham, and Alexander. Personalized command simply could not function without these feelings of mutual regard. Relations with Montgomery, Leigh-Mallory, Ramsay, Portal, and Harris remained on the whole congenial, but never more. But the British were not the problem. On 14 March Leigh-Mallory forwarded his plan for attacking rail targets in France to Smith, and it mentioned SHAEF's control over the strategic air forces. Smith readily approved Leigh-Mallory's plan and forwarded it to the BCOS.[31] The British exchanged letters with the JCS, and the American chiefs expressed their confusion over the meanings of "supervision" and "command" in relation to the Portal-Tedder agreement.

By 22 March Eisenhower neared the end of his rope. "For two months I have been struggling in every possible way to provide for a real ANVIL but I have come to the conclusion that we are simply striving for the impossible." Despite his and Smith's best efforts, the American and British chiefs remained widely divided. In the first week of March, after weeks of twists and turns, it seemed that he had finally worked out the instrumentality of the air command, but now it flew apart. Without agreements for the distribution of landing craft and naval support, detailed Overlord planning could not proceed. Endless conferences, studies, planning, and revisions of plans—from SHAEF down to regiments—swallowed time and expended energies, while the vital business of preparing troops for combat—discipline, morale, and training—took a backseat. A thoroughly disillusioned supreme commander vowed in his diary on 22 March that if he could not resolve the air command conundrum to his satisfaction, he would "take drastic action and inform the Combined Chiefs of Staff that unless the matter is settled at once I will request relief from this Command."[32]

Things never went that far. The British, who thought the Americans approached the question like lawyers, fastened on the word *direction* rather than command. *Direction* did not constitute *command*, but was much more declarative than *supervision*. Eisenhower exclaimed "Amen!"

when he heard the news. On 25 March he presided over a meeting at the Air Ministry with Portal, Tedder, Spaatz, Harris, and Leigh-Mallory. Tedder made Leigh-Mallory's case for the transportation plan; he argued there was not enough time before D-day for Pointblank to bite enough to disable the Luftwaffe. Portal and Harris gave their tepid and qualified support; MG Lewis Brereton, the acting Ninth Air Force commander, had already approved the plan. On 26 March Eisenhower endorsed the transportation plan, agreeing with Tedder that it provided the best means to "help the Army get and stay ashore."[33] It took another three weeks of wrangling over details, but on 14 April the CCS finally turned the air forces over to Eisenhower's "direction." The next day Tedder issued a directive stating that the primary objective remained the destruction of the Luftwaffe; secondarily, the strategic air forces would be employed against transportation facilities. However, no clear command channels evolved. Eisenhower, Tedder, and Spaatz vowed to stay in personal contact. "In other words," Spaatz commented, "from an organizational point of view it was lousy." Spaatz considered it "the wrong idea in trying to put on paper all complications of lateral staff functions and coordinations between staffs of the organizational setup as now in being." But, he noted, "I have always been able to work satisfactorily with General Eisenhower regardless of conflicts between staff members." As Morgan remarked, "It will, I think, be a considerable time before anybody will be able to set down in the form of an organizational diagram the channels through which General Eisenhower's orders reached his aircraft."[34]

On the morning of 27 March the British chiefs came out to Bushy Park for discussions on the latest JCS proposal for moving landing craft committed to the Pacific to Overlord in exchange for a British pledge to stage a 10 July Anvil. Eisenhower argued that taking Rome bore no significance compared to maximal support for Overlord. Brooke refused any commitment to an unpredictable operation four months in the future. Portal wanted the deal, allowing for a firm decision later when matters clarified.[35] Patton arrived for lunch. The initial reason for the BCOS's visit was ceremonial. In the king's name, Brooke awarded Patton and Smith their knighthoods.[36]

The next day the BCOS signaled their acceptance of the offer of landing craft and agreed that Anvil should be postponed, not abandoned; they conceded that planning should proceed on the basis of a July operation, but no final decision would emerge until a review of the entire problem took place sometime in early June. The BCOS also consented to shift SHAEF's minimum requirements of additional assault craft from the Mediterranean. On Anvil, the British contended no solution could emerge until Fifth Army linked with the Anzio beachhead. After making a real concession toward a settlement, the JCS reacted, in Dill's words, with shock and pain to the testy British response, and on 12 April the JCS withdrew the offer to divert assault shipping from the Pacific. The Americans now insisted the British provide "a firm directive" on Anvil.

Confronted by this bitter altercation, Eisenhower pleaded with Marshall "that no stone should be left unturned in order to achieve an understanding that will allow us to have this additional strength."[37] Brooke noted in his diary, "Marshall is quite hopeless, I have seldom seen a poorer strategist! He cannot see beyond the end of his nose."[38] On 14 April Marshall wired that the American chiefs' acquiescence to the British view amounted to a cancellation of Anvil, and the U.S. Navy refused any diversion of landing craft from the Pacific. Later that day Marshall explained that if the CCS took landing craft from the Pacific, it would slow the momentum of operations against the Japanese; he maintained the cancellation of Anvil at least provided Wilson the flexibility to stage the operation at a later date.[39] Churchill summed up everyone's sense of frustration: "The whole of this difficult question only arises out of the absurd shortages of LSTs. How it is that the plans of two great empires like Britain and the United States should be so much hamstrung by a hundred or two of these particular vessels will be never understood by history."[40]

On 17 April Eisenhower and Smith attended a conference with Churchill, Brooke, and Alexander. They agreed on new wording for a directive to Wilson. The first priority remained tying down as many German divisions in Italy as possible; operations in Italy would center on linking the main battle line with the Anzio forces. Sufficient amphibious lift must stay in the theater in the hope of retaining the initiative in Italy. However, preparations for Anvil must continue, and the operation must be executed "as soon after the beginning of OVERLORD as the situation in the Mediterranean will permit."[41]

To Butcher, Eisenhower seethed at Washington's refusal to provide the added lift. He complained about the "debate reflecting increasing American desire in this election year to prosecute the war in the Pacific." But "if OVERLORD failed," he predicted, "the President couldn't possibly be elected and . . . if he were informed of the seriousness of the situation over here he would quickly . . . make certain that not only OVERLORD but the Mediterranean get the landing craft which are so essential. So far virtually the only additional landing craft we have received for OVERLORD have been at the expense of ANVIL."[42]

After a further exchange of messages between the BCOS and the JCS, King stated he now stood prepared to send the shipping he and Marshall had offered earlier for Anvil. The resultant CCS directive called for an all-out offensive in Italy, with the possibility of future attacks in the peninsula—all designed to neutralize German forces in support of Overlord—and the postponement and possible downgrading of Anvil to a threat. Once again, unable to agree on an overall strategy in the Mediterranean, the CCS sanctioned drift. Events on the ground—and the German response—again dictated the direction and flow of Allied operations. After three months of haggling, the bargain at least guaranteed that operational headquarters could now proceed with detailed planning based on assurances that enough essential assault shipping would be available for the five-division operation.[43]

In the meantime, SHAEF's Joint Planning Staff developed the first draft of the post-Neptune plan. At first Smith had been cold to the idea of forming a Joint Planning Staff, and he never convened a meeting until the middle of March. Betts remembered that the key decision on the outline postlodgment plan took all of fifteen minutes. "We'd break out, we'd cross the Seine, and fan out and advance north." As Betts commented, "the big strategic decisions are usually rather simple."[44] On 11 April the CCS directed that SHAEF undertake planning for the period after completion of the lodgment phase through the capture of the Ruhr, designated as the primary strategic objective. SHAEF replied immediately with its first outline plan forecasting a three-phase campaign: first, secure the Brittany ports and press forward across the Seine to the Somme, merely investing Paris; then advance to the Arras-Laon-Reims line, prompting the climactic armor battle somewhere in Champagne; finally, drive in a northeasterly direction along the Brussels-Venlo-Mülheim axis in the north and through the Aachen Gap toward Bonn in the south. The day before, Eisenhower had requested that operational headquarters and the G divisions of SHAEF prepare estimates for post-Neptune operations, including maps, phase lines, anticipated dates for the capture of ports, the timing and direction of the advance from phase line to phase line, and projected locations for supply echelons. The directive stated that these forecasts would serve as a template for all future planning, particularly pertaining to the computation of supply requirements and logistical organizations. At the same juncture, Eisenhower directed SHAEF to prepare planning for operations in Germany (code-named Eclipse), including the assumption that resistance would continue after the German surrender. The planners anticipated three routes of advance: Hamburg-Kiel in the north, Berlin and Saxony in the center, and Nürnberg-Munich in the south. Initially motivated by requests from AGF and ASF for benchmarks to use in planning the movement of manpower and materiel into the theater, the outline plan, together with the phase lines, evolved into something much more—the first concrete statement of the broad front strategy.[45]

"Damned Well . . . Fed Up"

Smith told COL Frank McCarthy in the War Department, "Things generally are going well—very well—and we are very confident. There is less of the pre-invasion 'jitters' than ever before."[46] With agreements made on the air command and landing craft, the commanders began to finalize planning for the cross-Channel and lodgment phase of operations while SHAEF formulated an overall scheme for post-Neptune strategy. Satisfied that Overlord was now back on track, Eisenhower shifted his focus toward fulfilling his affective role as supreme commander by conducting as many inspection tours as he could manage. He charged Smith with the tedious tasks of harmonizing Overlord planning, coordinating the air program, and, most exasperating of all, dealing with the French and finalizing a policy on civil affairs.

Smith devoted much of his time in April to fashioning a civil affairs program, despite the absence of concrete policy directives from Washington and London. The inability of the political heads to agree on de Gaulle, civil affairs policies for liberated territories, or even basic war aims meant that SHAEF organized and planned in a political vacuum. Without an established French policy and accords with the governments in exile, issues such as cooperating with resistance groups and setting guidelines for the myriad political, social, legal, and economic problems the Allied forces would encounter on the Continent stymied those charged with putting together the civil affairs and psychological warfare programs. The chief of staff carried the burden of these problems on his back.

C. D. Jackson, a perspicuous observer of the French problem and future member of Smith's psychological warfare section, reported, "All circles seem to be agreed that the President's behavior toward the French is pretty outrageous and can only lead to trouble, if not disaster. The French themselves here are so much more realistic and understanding and generally decent than the French in North Africa, that one cannot compensate one's own bitterness over U.S. foreign policy by getting peeved at the Frogs—which was possible to do in North Africa."[47] Roosevelt's unreasoned resistance to recognizing de Gaulle and the FCNL blocked the entire civil affairs program. In the middle of March Roosevelt issued a directive empowering SHAEF to decide "where, when and how [to execute] the Civil Administration in France." Eisenhower could "consult" with FCNL officials and assign civil officials in liberated France, but this conferred no measure of political recognition.[48] The lack of an agreement with the FCNL handicapped efforts aimed at coordinating with French underground groups. On 8 March Smith initiated the execution of the political and psychological warfare plan everywhere in occupied Europe, except in France, where political complications precluded it.[49] SHAEF operated through the special operations section of the SOE, but Eisenhower wanted more formal contacts. He and Smith saw the underground playing a number of vital roles—sabotage in the battle area, disruption of the German lines of communication, and direct cooperation with airborne operations. In the middle of March, Smith approached d'Astier about forging links with the French resistance.[50] Other than promises to make concerted efforts toward the liberation of France, genuine cooperation remained elusive. On 3 April Smith opened discussions on political arrangements that might develop in France in the absence of recognition of the FCNL.[51]

Then in April, Secretary Hull modified the president's injunction: "the President and I [are] disposed to see the French Committee of National Liberation exercise leadership to establish law and order under the supervision of the Allied Commander-in-Chief." This apparent shift in Washington's policy prompted Smith's decision to assume direction of civil affairs, psychological and covert warfare, and public relations. But first the staff divisions devoted to these functions required another overhaul.

At a 4 April chiefs of staff meeting, Smith signaled his dissatisfaction with McClure's organization and his intention to tighten G-3's control over special operations and psychological warfare. Four days later he announced he would redraft the directives to G-5 and G-6. The next day he voiced his displeasure with the War Office for dragging its feet on appointments to G-5. He warned he would fill the slots with Americans—a hollow threat, given the dearth of qualified American officers.[52] On 13 April Smith broke up G-6 into separate public relations and psychological warfare sections. BG T. J. Davis became the new public relations officer, while McClure remained as head of psychological warfare. Taking the lead, Smith ordered that McClure initiate discussions with the FCNL on psychological warfare, especially on propaganda operations.[53] On 19 April he requested authorization from Eisenhower to enter into agreements with the Dutch, Belgian, and Norwegian governments. The next day he created SHAEF liaison missions to each Allied government and charged them with the responsibility for representing headquarters on all operational and civil matters.[54] Finally, Eisenhower succumbed to Smith's pressure and agreed on Lumley's replacement. Smith still wanted an American—he nominated Clay—but again Eisenhower said no. On 22 April LTG A. E. Grassett, a Canadian-born British officer who headed the contact section in SHAEF, took over. Grassett proved even less amenable than Lumley. As he made clear before taking the assignment, Grassett planned to implement civil affairs in strict accordance with the phases of the Overlord plan. Initially, Montgomery's Twenty-first Army Group would control civil affairs; then, with the activation of an American army group, control would devolve to SHAEF. Smith thought political matters could not be subordinated to the chain of command, but for "substantial political reasons," he considered his hands tied.[55] The two men clashed over the timing of SHAEF's handover of civil administration to the reconstituted governments. Churchill and Roosevelt wanted a quick transfer to the national governments; Eisenhower and Smith took the position that military requirements came first.

Smith consolidated understandings with the French through the commander of French forces in the United Kingdom and head of the French Military Mission, MG Pierre Koenig. On 19 April they produced an aide-mémoire.[56] The agreement contained specifics on narrow military arrangements, but since civil affairs and military matters remained inextricably knotted, Smith and Koenig agreed on the inclusion of a civilian FCNL representative in their future deliberations. "It is the Supreme Commander's intention," Smith informed Marshall, "to take the head of the French Military Mission into his full confidence regarding plans for the employment of the French forces in operations in France well in advance of their being committed to these operations." Smith renewed his plea for policy direction; SHAEF needed working agreements on civilian labor, currency matters, custody of enemy property, requisitioning, public safety, public health, displaced persons, and controls on transportation and communications.

At the end of April de Gaulle took offense to a British government ruling, prompted by a SHAEF request, forbidding all governments in exile from sending correspondence in cipher. De Gaulle ordered Koenig to terminate any associations with SHAEF so long as the communications ban applied to the French. The general's reaction threatened to undo Smith's accord with Koenig. Smith got around the problem through a little subterfuge. Koenig submitted copies of transmissions he wanted sent to Algiers; Smith vetted them and transmitted the communications through SHAEF channels. The maneuver satisfied Koenig, who continued his discussions with Smith on a whole range of issues.[57]

Throughout most of April, Hull's undersecretary, Edward Stettinius, conducted a special mission to London, in part expediting agreements on post-hostilities policies in Germany. On 13 April he met with Eisenhower and Smith. The generals had approached Stettinius in the hope the State Department could nudge the president into some modification of the unconditional surrender policy. Without a fixed policy, planning for military government and civil affairs and the whole Allied propaganda program could not move forward. The generals, Stettinius reported, advocated announcing the "principles on which the treatment of a defeated Germany would be based. This seemed to them highly desirable in view of the accumulated evidence that German propaganda is interpreting the words 'Unconditional Surrender' to strengthen the morale of the German Army and people." Eisenhower and Smith believed the terms needed to be defined, emphasizing the protection of law, order, and property rights and creating conditions for the overthrow of the Nazi state. Smith carried the argument. He proposed that, immediately after securing the beachhead, SHAEF should issue a statement of intent, summarizing the terms of surrender and calling on the Germans to lay down their arms. "From all available evidence," Smith stated, "in default of such declarations, it would be impossible to exploit the crisis in the German Army which will undoubtedly arise immediately after a successful Allied landing."[58]

Eisenhower and Smith also approached Stettinius on the question of zonal boundaries for post-surrender Germany. They stated "their conviction that there should be a single Anglo-American zone of occupation in Germany instead of two separate zones. They raised the issue through military channels but received no reply. They ask that the matter be discussed with the President and with the Secretary." Stettinius recommended that, in light of demands that SHAEF initiate planning for the zones of occupation, the State Department should counsel the White House to begin discussions with the British and the Soviets.[59]

Nothing came of these initiatives. As Stettinius explained to Butcher, "the President was far from well and . . . is becoming increasingly difficult to deal with because he changes his mind so often."[60] But recognizing de Gaulle and altering the unconditional surrender formula remained two policies the president refused to reconsider. Roosevelt reacted angrily to appeals for modification in unconditional surrender, instructing Hull that "he did not want the subject to be considered further." On 22 April Hilldring reported that any agreements with the French must remain only tentative.[61] In May Roosevelt reiterated that the "free determination" clause of the Atlantic Charter precluded the recognition of any French group outside of France. There matters rested.

Undeterred, Smith entered into further discussions with Koenig and tightened SHAEF's superintendence over cooperative understandings with the French resistance. Smith convened a meeting to discuss methods for enhancing SHAEF's control over French underground activities.[62] On 26–27 April Smith issued directives to AFHQ, extending control to underground activities in the south of France.[63] On 8 May Smith asked permission to reveal portions of the Overlord plan to Koenig. As Smith explained to the CCS, "the limitations under which we are operating in dealing with the French are becoming very embarrassing and are producing a situation which is potentially dangerous." Despite the liability of having no formal directive, Smith felt he understood the policy "well enough to be able to reach a working way with any French body or organization that can effectively assist us in the fight against Germany." The only body with representation in London was the FCNL. Smith discussed issuing supplemental franc currency and implementing military security and civil policing arrangements. "General Koenig feels very keenly the fact that he is denied even the most general knowledge of forthcoming operations although French naval, air and airborne units are to be employed, and much is expected from French resistance, both active and passive. The sum total of these delays and resentments is, in my opinion, likely to result in acute embarrassment to the Allied forces, and it will be too late, after the event, to correct them."

Smith offered two solutions: either "divulge certain general information to a very few French officers in London only and on the highest level," or allow de Gaulle to come to London. Eisenhower "would then be able to deal with him direct on the most immediate and pressing problem of the initial approach to the French people and their organized resistance groups." Failing that, Smith proposed that he continue working through Koenig, who would then communicate through cipher with de Gaulle in Algiers. He concluded by stating, "from a military point of view coordination with the French is of overriding importance. I request that this matter be treated as of the utmost urgency, and that it be considered, as far as possible, on its military aspects." Eisenhower categorized it as "a pretty sticky mess."[64]

SHAEF's appeal again came to naught. Roosevelt's position remained unchanged: the Allied powers should not assume that de Gaulle represented the French nation, and Allied military leaders should use extreme caution when approaching de Gaulle so as not to appear to support the general's elevation as postwar leader. Roosevelt responded that although de Gaulle might come to London and consult on military matters, Eisenhower could not discuss political topics. "It must always be remembered," wrote Roosevelt, "that the French People are quite naturally shell-shocked from sufferings at the hands of German occupation, just as any other people would be. . . . As the liberators of France we have no right to color their views or to give any group the sole right to impose on them one side of a case." Roosevelt then quoted a message he had sent to Churchill: "I am unable at this time to recognize any Government of France until the French have an opportunity for a free choice, and I do not desire that Eisenhower shall become involved with the Committee on a political level."[65]

Despite the president's reply, Eisenhower called Smith on 13 May, informing him of his decision to invite de Gaulle to London. The general would be compelled to remain in England until well after the landings and possess no channel of communications with Algiers. Smith thought it was a very bad idea; he reckoned de Gaulle would refuse to be muzzled and would angrily rebuff this clear aspersion on his honor, with hard feelings all around. The prime minister agreed. On 18 May Smith attended a meeting of the BCOS as the only American representative. Smith voiced concern about damaging the spirit of cooperation that existed between SHAEF and Free French elements in London, especially Koenig. He pointed to "the great importance of obtaining for the Supreme Commander if possible a clear cut combined directive on relations with the French."[66] The BCOS vetoed Smith's recommendation that de Gaulle be invited to England before the invasion. Since de Gaulle would not be coming to London and had balked at issuing a D-day statement to the French people, Eisenhower charged Smith with writing a proclamation. As Butcher noted, "Beetle said he was 'walking on eggs' to find language which would be effective yet not create a storm of criticism at home as occurred in the Darlan case."[67]

Smith pointed to his reliance on the FCNL to reconcile the French population to the bombing campaign. Portal had first raised the issue of French civilian casualties at a 25 March meeting at the Air Ministry. On 3 April the matter went before the War Cabinet.[68] Eisenhower refused to budge, but he accepted responsibility for monitoring the campaign—a duty he delegated to Smith. On 29 March Smith added a new air staff to SHAEF, headed by another deputy chief of staff, VAM James Robb. On 17 April SHAEF reissued Eisenhower's directive for the strategic bombing forces in preparation for Overlord. Smith established an advisory board composed of officers from Bomber Command, the U.S. Strategic

Air Forces, and Leigh-Mallory's staff to assist Tedder in the direction of these operations. Three days later SHAEF issued the first list of transportation targets.[69]

A week after the bombing campaign opened, Churchill called Eisenhower and announced the cabinet's clear opposition to bombing French marshaling yards. "Eisenhower apparently stuck to his guns & his plan," noted Cunningham, "and apparently said the bombing of the railways was nothing to what was coming." The admiral observed, "if we were not prepared to bomb France we should never have entered on Overlord."[70] As Eisenhower informed Marshall, "the British government has been trying to induce me to change my bombing program against the transportation systems, so as to avoid the killing of any Frenchmen. I have stuck to my guns because there is no other way in which this tremendous air force can help us, during the preparatory period, to get ashore and stay there."[71]

SHAEF responded to pressure. On 30 April SHAEF forwarded a catalog of railway targets, situated in population centers, that were exempted from attack until further notification. A week later Smith ended his supervision of attacks on railroad targets but acknowledged that priority would be given, where options existed, to centers with the smallest populations.[72] As the campaign mounted in intensity, so did French civilian casualties—and with them, anxiety in London and Algiers.

Smith grew increasingly frustrated trying to cope with these interlocking French problems and elicited support from Marshall. Pointing to the military necessity of working through the FCNL, and emphasizing the near impossibility of differentiating between military and civil activities, SHAEF continued to operate under the liability of having no CCS directive. Eisenhower and Smith still worked under the assumption that Hull's April address had altered the framework of American policy. Smith claimed he had "only just learned" that Hull's remarks did not represent the president's views. He stressed the impracticality of acting on a unilateral directive from Roosevelt and complained he could not proceed with basic civil and military agreements with the French. The president left SHAEF no viable alternative to de Gaulle. The only differences between British and American texts, he protested to Marshall in another letter, centered on the British willingness to treat with the FCNL and the American inclination to deal with any non-Vichy group.[73]

Eisenhower added his voice in another letter to Marshall. He mentioned the frustrations Smith confronted in working with the British and French on composing a directive. Churchill now considered deferring de Gaulle's visit to England until after D-day, which provided a

window for reaching an agreement with the FCNL. Eisenhower petitioned Marshall to intercede with the president; he considered it of paramount importance that some joint policy emerge, because command
relations inside SHAEF depended on building a cooperative foundation. He also assured Marshall that the British made no effort to steer
policy decisions.[74]

Marshall offered no comfort; instead, he informed Smith of the
pressures emanating from London and the French Military Mission in
Washington to curtail the transportation plan.[75] Since Marshall threw
the problem back at SHAEF, Smith raised the issue with Koenig. "To my
surprise," Smith informed Marshall, "Koenig takes a much more cold-
blooded view than we do. His remark was, 'This is War, and it must be
expected that people will be killed. We would take twice the anticipated
loss to be rid of the Germans.'"[76] Koenig's sangfroid permitted SHAEF
to soft-pedal the moral issue; the bombing campaign continued.

The constant stress began to eat at Smith. Except for a weekend
trip to Scotland for some salmon fishing in April, Smith had no relief
from the grinding pace of sixteen-hour days. And crises almost always
cropped up when Eisenhower was away on one of his inspections tours.
One example was Patton's latest inability to master his tongue—the so-
called Knutsford incident. On 26 April Smith wired Eisenhower and
Marshall to report that "Patton had broken out again." Smith immediately got on the phone to Patton, who reported he had given a talk to
about sixty people at a private gathering and disavowed speaking for
anybody but himself; he had accepted the invitation on the condition
that no representatives of the press would be present. Smith pointed to
the offensive line: "Since it seems to be the destiny of America, Great
Britain and Russia to rule the world, the better we know each other
the better off we will be." The British press had carried only "innocuous quotes of the blood and guts type," with nothing about "Americans and British ruling the world." In his opinion, it was "not headline
stuff." He also explained to Marshall that SHAEF had released word
of Patton's "unofficial" presence in the United Kingdom as part of the
Fortitude plan to convince the Germans that *Armeegruppepatton* would
spearhead the real invasion of France at the Pas de Calais. Smith had
decided that some unscrupulous journalist would break the scoop
sooner or later and thought it better if SHAEF got out in front of the
story. "Beetle had answered Marshall," Butcher recorded, "taking on
himself the responsibility for releasing Patton's name and reporting
that Ike had steadfastly objected to the release."[77] But as Marshall had
already reported, Patton was very much headline stuff in the United

States, and a *Washington Post* editorial had pretty much killed all the permanent promotions—including Patton's and Smith's—then on the verge of confirmation.[78]

The Smith-Patton relationship was one-sided. Smith admired Patton, defended him during his many scrapes, and, until the end of the war, considered him a close friend. Initially, Patton could not make up his mind about Smith, but by now Smith ranked near the top of his long list of bêtes noires. Privately, Patton declared his dislike for Smith; publicly, he bootlicked. He begrudged Smith's close working relationship with Eisenhower and the fact that Beetle always acted as the bearer of bad news and the supreme commander's instrument for enforcing policy; most of all, he resented having "to bone" Smith in order to "keep things greased." Patton developed a nasty cold sore and attributed it to "all the ass kissing [of Smith] I have to do."[79]

As the rough-and-tough field commander, Patton held all staff officers and rear-echelon types in contempt. He penned a word picture of the typical staff officer as "a man past middle age, spare, wrinkled, intelligent, cold, passive, noncommittal, with eyes like a codfish, polite in contact, but at the same time unresponsive, cool, calm, and as damnably composed as a concrete post . . . a human petrification with a heart of feldspar and without charm or the friendly germ; minus bowels, passions or a sense of humor. Happily they never reproduce and all of them finally go to hell."[80] No doubt Smith served as his archetype.

Patton concluded that he was being framed. "So far as I am concerned, every effort is made to show lack of confidence in my judgment and at the same time, in every case of stress, great confidence in my fighting. None of those at Ike's headquarters ever go to bat for juniors, and in any argument between the British and the Americans, invariably favor the British. Benedict Arnold is a piker compared with them, and that includes . . . Ike and Beedle [*sic*]." Smith called Patton again on 27 April and passed on a verbal order from Eisenhower, which Patton recorded as follows: "I am never to talk in public without first submitting what I am going to say to Ike and himself for censorship, thereby displaying great confidence in an Army commander—if I have not been relieved. Beedle also said that due to my 'unfortunate remarks,' the permanent promotions of himself and me might never come off. How sad. 'God show the right,' and damn all reporters and gutless men."[81]

As he listened to Smith on the phone, Patton glanced at a photograph he had received that day. In the days before D-day, all the senior officers exchanged photographs, and Patton had requested one from Smith for his "rogue's gallery." Smith autographed the photo and included a warm personal acknowledgment. For Patton, the photograph always reminded him of "the Judas trees that grew in Virginia."[82]

Eisenhower would not return to headquarters until 28 April. He attended the disastrous amphibious exercises (code-named Tiger) at Slapton Sands on the Devon coast. German E-boats evaded the naval pickets, sinking two LSTs and disabling a third. The loss of the assault shipping—not to mention the deaths of 749 servicemen—reduced the Overlord reserve to zero and threw a pall of despair over headquarters. The Patton affair added to the gloom.

On 29 April Eisenhower told Marshall, "I am seriously contemplating the most drastic action. I am deferring final action until I hear from you." When Marshall told him the decision on Patton was entirely up to him, Eisenhower stated, "On all of the evidence now available I will relieve him from command and send him home." He would let Patton present his case personally but observed, "after a year and a half of working with him it appears hopeless to expect that he will ever completely overcome his lifelong habit of posing and of self-dramatization."[83] Alerted by Patton, Hughes, since February Eisenhower's special assistant and chief troubleshooter, raced to Bushy Park. "Ike was mad," Hughes recorded. "I read him Geo's explanation in his letter. Don't know what action Ike will take!"[84] To Butcher, Eisenhower estimated that "Patton's chance of retaining his command was only one in a thousand."[85]

"Beedle [*sic*] called up and told me to report to Ike, at Ike's office," Patton noted on 2 May. "It can be anything from a reprimand to a reduction, or a new plan of campaign. These constant pickings are a little hard on the nerves."[86] Patton exhibited bravado but feared the worst. Patton's bipolar symptoms made Churchill's look tame. Patton's posing and self-dramatization were the by-products of a lifetime of playacting. Patton labored so hard to present to the world his own fabricated self-image that he became a caricature of himself. Observers stood aghast at the wild modulations in Patton's mien, from maudlin sentimentality and tears to unchecked exuberance, often in the space of moments. Now he arrived to face Eisenhower, complete with his shiny cavalry boots, creased jodhpurs, gleaming helmet, and ivory-handed pistols. Just like at West Point, when he had curried the favor of the tactical officers by bracing harder and longer than anyone else, Patton stood at rigid attention in front of his old friend.

Eisenhower handed Patton three letters: one called for Patton's relief; the second stated that if Eisenhower could not be trusted to handle the problems of his own officers and troops, he could no longer continue in command; the last, from Marshall, authorized Eisenhower to decide either way. Patton started to sob. This too represented a Patton artifice. On those rare occasions when the golden-tressed Georgie had faced the displeasure of his doting father, he had broken into hysterical crocodile tears. This time, he faced more than going to bed without his supper; Eisenhower could send him home in his permanent grade, with his great destiny derailed. According to the story Eisenhower told one of his staff officers, Patton put his head on Eisenhower's shoulder, and because of the difference in their heights, Patton's helmet fell off and rolled into the corner. "He immediately stopped crying, stooped over, picked up the helmet, replaced it carefully on his head—and started to cry all over again." Eisenhower could no longer stand it. "This was too much for me! I stretched out on the couch in my office and burst into laughter. George couldn't even cry without his helmet! Imagine that!" Patton could not look at Eisenhower without breaking his brace.

Eisenhower had already made up his mind to take another chance on Patton and so informed him. "I expect," he added, "from now on that you will please keep your goddamned mouth shut. When it is time for you to speak, *I will tell you!* I intend to use you to the fullest—you will have every opportunity to get into all the combat you ever dreamed of. That is all for the moment!" Patton dried his eyes, snapped off a salute, and smartly exited the office. Feeling a little sheepish for making "this tough old officer" blubber, Eisenhower "had to tell someone, so I called in Beetle and told him what had happened." Eisenhower remembered it as "the only time in all the years of my long experience with Smith that I saw Beetle really lose himself in laughter!"[87]

An immensely relieved Patton never revealed what transpired in Eisenhower's office, but the customary bluster soon returned. "Everything is OK," he informed Hughes by phone. Patton claimed "he received a note and then a personal telephone call from D. D. who was absolutely charming and reassuring."[88] He never blamed Eisenhower, but Smith would forever remain a thorough "s.o.b."

Relations between Smith and Patton remained strained for another reason. Smith found himself the subject of an inquiry by the inspector general's office for the misappropriation of funds. Eisenhower asked that Hughes investigate the matter. "Beadle [*sic*] looked at his bill," Hughes logged in his diary, "and is now scared." A week later, Patton and Hughes visited a gun shop near Grosvenor Square and found a beautiful shotgun being made for Smith. Smith had befriended the famed gunsmith James Purdey and his family. Upon closer questioning, Purdey revealed that Smith had purchased a toy train for Purdey's son and kept Mrs. Purdey's larder well stocked with U.S. government–issued goods. They also found two U.S. Army carbines Smith had presented to his friend. "Reminds me of Beadle's saying," Hughes recorded: "The photos are expensive. I'll charge them to my entertainment allowance." When Hughes mentioned seeing the guns, Smith flew into a rage and blamed Patton for stirring up trouble. Following up on the story, Hughes uncovered that Smith had been issued two weapons, reported them lost, and paid for them. Hughes decided, "Maybe I's better . . . keep mum on the subject . . . until IG has finished his investigation." The scrutiny continued for weeks. On D-day, when Smith's attention should have been elsewhere, he threatened to fire "IGs who delve too much into his affairs." Patton had nothing to do with Smith's troubles, but he and Hughes reveled in watching Beetle squirm.[89]

All this took its toll. On 11 May Smith unburdened himself to Butcher, of all people. Smith invited Butcher to lunch at his billet and talked of his misgivings about Overlord. Smith thought the Allies would get ashore but calculated their chances of staying as only a fifty-fifty proposition. The key would be the buildup race, and here, SHAEF projections were razor thin. He also worried about the underwater obstacles. Ultra indicated the German high command still had not discovered where the landings would be; Fortitude remained the ace in the hole. "Beetle's professional realism and misgivings," Butcher noted, "rather substantiate the reluctance the British have had about undertaking OVERLORD before we are fully prepared." He groused about all the obstacles to dealing more frankly with the French. All told, Smith confided that "he would never be fit to be Chief of Staff for another campaign; this one had worn him down. Beetle said he was damned well going to get out of the Army after the war. He was fed up."[90]

★ 27 ★

"It's a Go"

During the first week of May the planners finalized outline plans for Normandy, the lodgement area (Neptune) bounded by the Loire and the Seine, and post-Neptune operations. On 7 May Montgomery issued the plan for securing the lodgement area up the Seine (D+90). "Once through the difficult bocage country," Montgomery predicted, "greater possibilities for manoeuvre and for the use of armour." The document clearly defined the respective roles of Dempsey's and Bradley's forces in the first phase and the American and Anglo-Canadian army groups in the second. "Our aim during this [initial] period should be to contain the maximum enemy forces facing the Eastern flank of the bridgehead, and to thrust rapidly [from the vicinity of St. Lô] towards Rennes." Then American forces would drive on Vannes, sealing the Brittany peninsula with a secondary "deceptive" thrust toward Nantes on the Loire. At the same juncture, after acting as the pivot, Montgomery's forces would launch a "strong attack" toward the Seine. The plan reflected Montgomery's preoccupation with opening the Seine and especially the Brittany ports. "The Quiberon Bay project (CHASTITY) offers great scope for surprise," the summary read, and once in American hands, the anchorage would assure "our build-up . . . for some time to come." Earlier, a Second Army appreciation had concluded, "There is no intention of carrying out a major advance until the Brittany ports have been captured." Montgomery placed no great store in phase lines—which began to appear on planning estimates at the end of February—believing them to be only "academic" from an operational point of view but essential for logistical purposes. Typical of Montgomery, the plan lacked nothing in simplicity and clarity.[1]

"Mists of Doubt Dissolved"

A lull descended on SHAEF the next week. After the hectic race to complete the outline plans, everyone could use a break. The day after Butcher's talk with Smith, he recorded, "Ike looks worn and tired. The strain is telling on him. He looks older now than at any time since I have been with him."[2] On 12–13 May Smith dealt with a whole array of accumulated administrative matters, chiefly approving memos and generally tidying up before a major conference set for 15 May. Butcher reported, "SHAEF is as quiet as a farmhouse parlor." All attention focused on the final briefing on the completed Neptune plan.

A glittering array of top brass graced the makeshift briefing room in an auditorium at St. Paul's School—Montgomery's old school and, not coincidentally, his headquarters. When the king arrived and assumed his spot on a bench in the front row of the balcony, Eisenhower took the stage dominated by a huge plaster relief map of Normandy. The St. Paul colloquy acted less as a dress rehearsal for Overlord—all the players knew their roles and how they fit into the bigger picture—than as an exercise in confidence and team building. Gone was the gray visage of a couple days before; in its place stood a smiling and confident supreme commander. Gone too was the tentative Eisenhower of Torch and Husky. He spoke for only ten minutes, and as one observer noted, "the mists of doubt dissolved."

One after another the commanders spoke. Spaatz stiffly read a prepared paper on the results of the transportation plan; Harris talked about efforts to neutralize the V-1 sites and, according to Cunningham, "explained what a nuisance this Overlord operation was & how it interfered with the right way to defeat Germany by bombing"; Leigh-Mallory outlined the air program to cover the landings; Ramsay outlined the hugely complex orchestration of sealift and naval support; Bradley described the tactics he would employ during the landings in the American sectors; and then Montgomery made the focal presentation on what would happen following the landings. Uncharacteristically subdued and guarded, he outlined the rate of buildup and reviewed the expected timetable of the German response. Montgomery assured his listeners the Germans would try to "Dunkirk us," but he confidently stated he had the measure of Rommel. Like a Gulliver he strode over the map and used a pointer to explain the priority objectives of his army group: First Army would capture Cherbourg and then develop the lodgment southward toward St. Lô, in conformity with Dempsey's advance, while Second Army expanded the beachhead south and east of Caen and provided flank protection for Bradley's army while it took and rehabilitated the port of Cherbourg. He spoke of the paramount importance of Cherbourg's port and the tableland beyond Caen toward Falaise as the linchpin connecting the Seventh German Army in Normandy with the Fifteenth in the Pas de Calais. The second image stuck in the heads of Eisenhower and Smith more than any other that day. Montgomery concluded by speaking of the importance of seizing and keeping the initiative, of having faith in the simplicity of the basic plan, and of the robustness of Allied mentality and morale. He talked about sending "the soldiers into this party seeing red . . . [with] absolute faith in the plan; and imbued with infectious optimism and offensive eagerness. Nothing must stop them! If we send them into battle in this way—then we shall succeed."[3]

As was generally the case, Churchill insisted on having the final word. Standing up and clenching his cigar—he defied Montgomery's smoking ban—Churchill announced: "I am hardening to this enterprise. I repeat, I am *now* hardened toward this enterprise." For weeks, Eisenhower and Smith had heard Churchill repeatedly express his great misgivings about Overlord. As Eisenhower recounted to Ismay in 1960, "You will recall his talking of the 'Channel tides running red with Allied blood' and the 'Beaches choked with the bodies of the flower of American and British manhood.' At that time he talked in terms of two years for bringing the war to a successful conclusion, and two or three times he said to Smith and me that if the Allied operations were successful, by Christmas, in capturing his beautiful and beloved Paris, then he would proclaim to the world that this was the most successful and brilliant military operation of all times."[4] Churchill's remarks at the St. Paul conference left Eisenhower feeling ambivalent. "I then realized for the first time," he told an interviewer in 1946, "that Mr. Churchill hadn't believed in it all along and had had no faith that it would succeed. It was quite a shocking discovery."[5] These misapprehensions—Montgomery and Caen and Churchill's lack of faith in the liberation campaign—vindicated later misunderstandings that nearly rent the alliance. But those lay in the future; the St. Paul conclave achieved its objective, and in hindsight, it represented the high-water mark of Allied unity.

After a number of refinements, SHAEF issued "Planning Forecast #1" for post-Neptune operations at the end of May. On 8 May Eisenhower approved the revised "Main Objective and Axis of Advance" study, restating his intention to advance on a broad front. Since the CCS had already assigned the Ruhr as the primary objective, the offensive north of the Ardennes constituted the main effort. He insisted on a secondary offensive in the south, chiefly for the purposes of deception; this would compel the Germans to extend their forces, making them vulnerable to a concerted drive toward the Ruhr. Doubtlessly, the Germans intended to defend the Ruhr as their first priority, which provided the additional benefit of offering the opportunity to inflict a fatal blow on their forces west of the Rhine. As Eisenhower informed the JCS, he predicted the advance to the German frontiers would consume almost a year. Smith reviewed the draft plan at his 19 May chiefs of staff meeting, emphasizing the timeline for breaking out of the lodgment area and noting that determination of the phase lines for continental operations would allow Crawford to formalize supply arrangements.[6]

Smith then moved to revector the center of operational planning for the Continent inside supreme headquarters. He set a list of priorities for future planning based on a number of contingencies: chief emphasis rested on the main advance, followed by the movement to the Siegfried Line in the face of German resistance. Then, in order of importance, came plans in the event of a stalemate in Normandy; for opening the Brittany ports, including the creation of an artificial anchorage at Quiberon Bay (Chastity), and developing the Seine ports; and last, for an immediate German withdrawal from France. He also insisted on establishing methods of circulating planning from inception through the approval process to final distribution. The joint planners forwarded documents to Bull, who passed them on to Smith, who in turn gave them to Eisenhower for approval; Smith then forwarded the distilled directive to the commands for concurrence and direct return to Smith. Bull and Smith could kill a plan before it reached Eisenhower's desk, but once it received the supreme commander's sanction, it became law.[7] The commands remained outside this planning and decision loop. On 26 May Eisenhower sanctioned Smith's memo and approved the outline plan and its publication the following day.

The design, based on the assumption the Germans would conduct a "scorched earth" fighting withdrawal into their frontier fortifications, called for a primary drive through the Aachen Gap, with a secondary movement through the Metz Gap. Planners foresaw the campaign in France unfolding in five phases: the lodgment and Brittany; an advance into the area between the Seine and the Somme, uncovering Paris and the Seine ports, Le Havre and Rouen; then sequential movements forward to the Amiens-Reims, Arras-Mons-Maubeuge-Cambrai, and Antwerp-Aachen-Meuse-Siegfried lines. The main axis of advance wouldbe Amiens-Maubeuge-Liége-Ruhr, with a diversionary secondary drive on the Verdun-Metz line. The plan drew phase lines from D+30 to D+330. By D+120, sixty days after securing and initiating attacks out of the Normandy-Brittany lodgment, the Allies would have twelve divisions across the Seine in the north, another dozen investing Paris in the south, six defending the Loire line, and another four in Brittany. Planners forecast the opening of the main drive on D+270, with twelve divisions north of the Ardennes—no more could be supported logistically—and thirty-three south, with five in static roles guarding the southern flank; they expected the Germans to withdraw from southwestern France and that Antwerp would be opened before that date.[8]

In the three weeks remaining before D-day, Smith expended his energies tying up loose ends. On 17 May he tightened security, sealing off forward areas to all unauthorized officials and the press. The same day he reversed himself on a position taken earlier in a cable to Washington. He now felt that SHAEF should coordinate with Soviet representatives in London on matters of common interest, particularly the pre- and post-surrender periods in Germany. Three days later he provided a list of topics for discussion with the Soviets for CCS review. On 18 May he dealt with special operations and cooperation with the French resistance. He consented to Koenig issuing D-day warnings and action messages to resistance groups without going through Smith, asking only that the French general keep SHAEF informed. The next day he approved a directive to Montgomery and Leigh-Mallory outlining the general principles and procedures governing control of tactical air during Neptune. Essentially, the directive restricted the scope of Leigh-Mallory's independence. Tedder, aided by Coningham, actively politicked for the elimination of Leigh-Mallory's headquarters. On 21 May Smith requested that the BCOS direct Wilson to obtain a statement from de Gaulle for broadcast on D-day.[9]

On 26 May Smith inaugurated daily chiefs of staff meetings. He happily introduced his new chief of intelligence: the British had finally released Strong. Smith moved Whiteley back to operations as Bull's deputy, but he remained in charge of the joint operations planning staff; in effect, Whiteley served as Smith's operations chief and liaison, through his good friend de Guingand, to Montgomery's headquarters. "Bull was a good G-3," Smith said, "but the wheel horse was Whiteley."[10] Smith made other adjustments to his staff. On 18 May he added an Ultra subsection to the SHAEF Operations Division and created the nucleus of a planning and managing staff for deep penetration operations in combination with the SOE, OSS, and resistance groups. The next day he put Grassett back in charge of the European Contact Section and authorized the expansion of G-5 in response to SHAEF's finally consummating civil affairs deals with the governments in exile.[11]

The St. Paul's presentations signified the end of the high-level planning phase for Neptune—all the commanders had their programs in place—and the planning forecast for Overlord offered an outline for operations after the breakout from the lodgment areas. The end of the frantic planning phase did not provide Eisenhower and Smith any breathing space. Appropriately, two familiar issues bedeviled them in the last days before D-day—command and control of American logistics on the Continent, and de Gaulle and the French.

Headaches Redux

The question of supply organization on the Continent had lain dormant for four months. The U.S. Army was a curious institution. Marshall issued directives, and the army changed the service manual, but because of the inviolability of command prerogatives, theater commanders organized their headquarters according to their own preferences. As a result, no two theater commands were the same; among theater commanders, only Devers organized his headquarters consistent with regulations. The essential problem was attitudinal. Officers such as Eisenhower and Bradley saw Marshall's directive calling for the separation of combat and supply functions as contrary to the traditional doctrine of territorial unity of command. Line officers rejected what they termed the ASF theory of organization because it stood contrary to their training and experience in the old structure.[12] Eisenhower had his deep-seated prejudices and advertised them to his subordinates.

In April the hot issue involved creating a single manpower command. Marshall dispatched McNarney and Lutes to the United Kingdom; McNarney would examine the replacement and training structures, while Lutes reviewed logistical preparations for the invasion. The War Department projected a serious shortfall in combat elements, particularly infantry, and wanted no repeat of the problems experienced in the Mediterranean. Lee strenuously rejected ceding his control over manpower. On 13 April Marshall forwarded a "hot" directive calling for the formation of a command "with no other responsibilities than that of handling replacement procedures" in conformity with War Department policies. Marshall wanted to know on what grounds Lee obstructed the creation of such a command; he would accept no "stiff-necked" attitude in opposition to the proposed change. Smith replied that he would arrange a major conference on manpower and assured Marshall that Eisenhower was prepared to establish "a system similar to that you propose."[13] Eisenhower answered he had been considering a move in that direction—he termed Marshall's order a "suggestion"—but as in the case of the American CAO appointment, he claimed he could not settle on the right man for the job. "You may be sure that no objections on the part of subordinate commanders or staffs will deter me from setting up any system that appears to be the most efficient."[14] On 4 May the War Department issued a directive for theaters to establish uniform replacement and training commands; eleven days later it watered down the directive, deleting the term "command" and stating the War Department considered it "desirable" that independent commands be organized.[15] Lee's rearguard effort succeeded; Eisenhower established no new command. Since McNarney blocked the formation of a separate manpower command under ASF in the War Department, Eisenhower saw no imperative for forming one in ETO. By June the Replacement System, ETO—which handled 2.1 million men, half the theater's manpower, before it disbanded—amounted to a corps command, yet a mere colonel headed it.[16]

April's dispute over control and the organization of theater manpower gave way in May to a contest over management of supply on the Continent. "I am so certain that a command problem of major proportions will confront US forces in ETO before many weeks," Hughes memoed to Eisenhower on 3 May, "and I am constrained to outline the problem and prepare a solution for it." He worried the supply structure could not react promptly to German movements and predicted the supply echelons would fail to keep pace in a fluid situation. "The reason is divided responsibilities and uncertainty in the minds of subordinates as to 'whose job it is.'" As Hughes knew only too well from experience in the Mediterranean, "the question of responsibility starts at SHAEF where you are the Commander-in-Chief and also the Theater Commander of ETO. Hence to SHAEF go many problems which in reality are Theater problems." He advised Eisenhower to trust the people in his organizations, delegate authority, and reduce the tendency of "the SHAEF staff to have the last word regardless of the problem."[17]

A week later Moses wrote a memorandum and forwarded it to Smith; he stated his belief "it is a definite mistake to have the Deputy Theater Commander for administration also the Communications Zone Commander." He argued for a reduction in the role of SHAEF, an end to the practice of "doubling in brass," and the restoration and augmentation of the G-1 and G-4 staffs in an independent ETO headquarters. Lee would have his hands full running the Communications Zone. Moses raised a number of issues: whether supply would be a First Army or ComZ responsibility, whether ComZ units would answer to Bradley or ADSEC, when a ComZ would be established in France, who would coordinate supply with the tactical air forces, and who should determine the "economic use" of supply between combat and support units. Moses argued that under the current proposed structure, Lee possessed too much authority; he pointed to the inherent "conflict of interest," fearing the ComZ would defend its interests at the expense of the field commanders. "It appears desirable to have plans for the future general organization laid down at an early date in order that detailed plans may be made and proper personnel acquired to carry them out. In any case, I emphasize my belief that the Communications Zone Commander and the ETO or Deputy ETO Commander should not be the same person."[18] When two weeks went by and nothing happened, Moses forwarded the memo to Hughes and asked him to use his influence with Eisenhower, although he admitted it was "probably too late to be of any possible help . . . the whole matter is pretty much in the mill now."[19]

In the meantime, Lutes completed his survey of American theater logistics. Lutes found things generally satisfactory: the assault forces would receive adequate equipment and supplies, plans existed for forty-one days of supply after the landings, and new plans were under development up to D+90. He also detected grave structural flaws. He reported to Somervell and told Smith that the chief problem rested in gnarled command chains and deep-seated personal antagonisms that "boded ill for the future." Concluding that Eisenhower possessed inadequate time to undertake any serious alterations in organization and personnel, Lutes refrained from "exciting Eisenhower on any deficiencies." He did not shrink from exciting Smith.[20]

Nothing Lutes reported surprised Smith in the least. Smith disliked Eisenhower's expedient replication of the AFHQ/NATO structure, with Lee acting as titular deputy theater commander and commanding general, Communications Zone. In theory, the same system applied as existed before Torch: as chief of staff in ETO, Smith issued instructions to BG Royal Lord, his deputy, who executed them in Lee's name as his chief of staff. In practice, Lee vigorously defended his rights in what amounted to an autonomous command and paid no attention to Smith. Smith would "remind the boys at ComZ he was chief of staff," but Lee ignored him and took his problems directly to Eisenhower. "Smith would get furious" when Lee went over his head, and he complained to Eisenhower. "Ike was always the peacemaker," remembered Smith's SGS Trimble, and would smooth things over, but he resented the distraction and irritation of refereeing these disputes.[21]

According to Smith, he convinced Eisenhower in January to follow

Marshall's directive, fire Lee, and name Larkin as American CAO inside SHAEF, but Devers would not cut Larkin loose. Smith could never secure the services of an officer with sufficient standing and seniority to serve as American CAO. Hughes possessed too much baggage, and the War Department would not release Clay or Lutes; in any case, Clay and Lutes stood too low on the permanent list for consideration. Toward the end of February, Eisenhower read the morning paper and discovered Lee's name on the list of officers slated for promotion to lieutenant general. An incensed Eisenhower penned a testy complaint to Marshall. Seeing Somervell's machinations behind the move, Eisenhower grumbled, "This is the first time one of my chief subordinates has been advanced without consulting me." Eisenhower had told Somervell and Lee he would not recommend Lee for promotion until "completely satisfied [with] the efficiency of his machine." Apparently less than satisfied, Eisenhower made no such recommendation. A sheepish reply came from Marshall, claiming responsibility. He explained that "each advancement or recognition of Smith produced an immediate and emphatic proposal by MacArthur for [MG Richard] Sutherland," his chief of staff. Without checking, and thinking that Eisenhower desired it, Marshall added Lee to his list of promotions. "I hope I have not involved you," Marshall wrote, "in a rank assignment which will be embarrassing." Eisenhower found himself in precisely that position, because Lee's promotion made him virtually untouchable and placed him at the same level as Smith in the command chain.[22]

With Lutes in the theater, Smith came up with a possible solution—name Lutes American CAO and centralize management of logistics in SHAEF. In early May Eisenhower requested Lutes remain in the theater for an additional two or three months as his logistics troubleshooter. Eisenhower wanted Lutes available should he decide to restructure his headquarters along the lines suggested by Marshall and Smith. Eisenhower and Lutes were old friends; Lutes had served as G-4 under Eisenhower in Third Army during the Louisiana maneuvers of 1941, where both of them staked out armywide reputations. In Lutes he had an officer he trusted and one who possessed a wealth of logistics experience and a cooperative spirit—a perfect fit for Eisenhower's personalized command predilection. Somervell rebuffed the scheme, instead suggesting that "Crawford and other suitable officers in your staff should be able to act as your personal representative and troubleshooter with executive authority and as liaison between your headquarters and your SOS."[23] Hughes already filled that role very ably.

More portentous of future problems, the operational commanders—

Bradley and Patton—detested Lee and mistrusted his entire organization. Exhibiting the traditional disdain field commanders harbored for logisticians, Bradley and Patton resented Lee's promotion and theoretically superior position as deputy theater commander; they especially hated being beholden to Lee for replacements and supply. If that situation held true on the Continent, it would represent a world turned upside down, where the logisticians, not the commanders, dictated the pace of operations. In early May they had a long talk with Eisenhower, trying to convince him to remove Lee. They suggested Hughes or the ETO chief quartermaster, MG Robert Littlejohn. Littlejohn, who had served with Hughes and Patton in Mexico and with Eisenhower in the Philippines, dismissed the idea out of hand as sheer fantasy. "John Lee is Somervell's great hero," he told a member of his staff, "and do you think Ike is going to be stupid enough to fire him just [before the invasion]?"[24] Lee's performance raised no red flags. Even Patton admitted, "Gen. Lee certainly is doing a good job in getting us what we need."[25] The problem resided in Lee's peculiarities and his obsession with defending his autonomy.

Lee was obsessively mistrustful. He saw everyone as a potential threat, and that was only partially imagined. Everyone assumed he enjoyed the protection of Somervell, but Lee viewed even the ASF head warily. Lee saw his senior subordinates, officers selected by Somervell, as "friends of the boss" and "headaches" that had to be "watched carefully." As he wrote in his rather bizarre memoir, "As might be expected, there was a certain jealousy or ambition in the hearts of some aspiring officers who would have enjoyed taking over my job with its three stars." "We"—he spoke in the royal plural—"had to expect such conniving and therefore were not surprised or outraged by it. We simply had to do our best and ride such situations through."[26] And if Lee had one talent, it was riding out storms.

Lee did not help his situation by fighting all comers. As combined commanding general of SOS and ETO G-4 under Devers, Lee presided over a structure that enjoyed improved internal organizational integrity but never achieved higher levels of cooperation with COSSAC because Lee never acknowledged Morgan's authority. Instead of concurrence, Morgan got contention. Lee covered it with saccharine, but he handled Smith in a similar fashion, and he clashed constantly with Moses and Crawford.

As Hughes recorded at the end of May, "subject getting hot." On 24 May Eisenhower instructed Crawford and Hughes to fix responsibilities for supply. Two days later Crawford produced a memo calling for SHAEF to act as theater headquarters and for the termination of Lee's role as deputy theater commander. The same day, Eisenhower hurriedly wrote a three-sentence memo to Lee, forwarded to Bradley, outlining how he "desired" First Army Group to cooperate with the supply commands. The memo stated that Bradley held responsibility for making "recommendations" to Lee, the two headquarters would "deal directly with each other," and "in the event of disagreement . . . [or] of conflicting interests the subject will be referred" to Eisenhower for adjudication. In Eisenhower's mind, this settled the matter; he wanted problems resolved on a personal level outside the elaborate command chains. He directed that all concerned—Lee, Moses for Bradley, and Crawford for SHAEF—agree on the specifics and issue a final directive.[27] Eisenhower thought his memo stood as a model of simplicity and grew irritated when his subordinates failed to settle the question. When he returned from an inspection tour on 28 May, Eisenhower called in Smith, Bull, and Crawford and restated his requirements for the command structure. Eisenhower still had no clear idea what he required, but he knew what he did not want. As before Torch, he made up his mind not to radically restructure his headquarters on the eve of the invasion.[28]

Later that day Smith issued a directive in Eisenhower's name establishing the sequence of command shifts in Overlord. Except for specific items, notably gasoline, logistics remained a national responsibility. Planning at every echelon of supply worked toward guaranteeing minimal maintenance levels for combat units by calibrating national tonnage allotments. In the initial stage, FECZ would work in harness with Twenty-first Army Group, and ADSEC would work with Bradley's headquarters. Beyond that, Eisenhower refused to define command chains, other than stating that he would delegate to Bradley "such administrative authority and responsibility as may be practicable and desirable." In the transition stage, SHAEF would activate Patton's Third Army, Bradley would form his army group command, Hodges would assume command of First Army, and FECZ would transition into ComZ headquarters, bringing an end to Lee's tenure as deputy theater commander. Until then, Montgomery's staff coordinated priorities for supply tonnages. Most controversial of all, Lee would initially serve under Bradley, but the memo offered no clue as to how long that expedient would last. The final phase would see ComZ detached from Bradley's command, with its own headquarters; Lee would be placed "under the direct command of the Theater Commander." Even though Lee answered to Eisenhower as theater commander, the memo stated that Eisenhower would control ComZ "through the US element of SHAEF staff." The memorandum directed the dismantling of the existing ETO staff; some of its members would be distributed to U.S. First Army Group, U.S. Strategic Air

Forces (USSTAF), or ComZ, but the bulk of them would go to SHAEF. In effect, ETO would exist only on paper. What precise functions each echelon of command would discharge remained undetermined. The convoluted directive ended by stating, "All communications with the War Department will be through the Theater Commander," but how that would work without an ETO headquarters remained a mystery.[29] Not surprisingly, the confusing memo confounded everybody. All the questions raised by Hughes, Moses, and Crawford went unaddressed. Smith had succeeded in centralizing control of supply in SHAEF, but without any corresponding change in the headquarters structure, and there would be no American CAO.

That night Smith dispatched Crawford to break the news to Lee. There was no love lost between the two rivals. Predictably, Lee reacted negatively and wrote a combative reply to Eisenhower. He began by stating, "This proposal is opposed to your views, as I knew them," and in "the judgment of every Chief of Service, and your staff at Theater Headquarters, the proposal is unsound. It violates the basic logistical principles essential for the support of a military operation." He argued that while "Senior Tactical Commanders must determine operational requirements . . . control *and* responsibility for the logistical support of all combat forces must be established at the highest US level"—the theater command, not SHAEF. Lee pointed to Marshall's directives of 14 May and 24 September 1943 and cited the 15 November 1943 FM 100-10, arguing that faulty organizational structures in Torch and in the Mediterranean proffered "the major lessons learned during this war." He categorically stated that logistical effectiveness would be impaired "by various interpolated headquarters which could only contribute unacceptable delays." Two years of experience pointed to the need to place administration and supply under a single commander "with a complete and experienced staff of sufficient size to insure effective and adequate operations." In SOS, he argued, such a commander and staff already existed. Lee had 21,000 officers and 435,000 troops under his command. "This organization has been preparing for the immediate task for two years," he continued, and "duties have been well defined within the organization." Marshall's repeated directives called for a reduction in the number of headquarters to best utilize scarce trained staff and technical talent; the proposed organization would duplicate staffs, creating confusion and breeding conflict among competing headquarters. Like Smith, Lee thought the cross-Channel invasion "should be considered logistically as a river crossing." He reminded Eisenhower, "This matter is of such importance" that it required a thorough rethinking.

Lee offered his own suggestions: preserve the existing combined ETO and SOS staffs "as organized by you" as the American administrative headquarters "reporting directly to you, as at present." He also recommended a clear delineation of the duties of SHAEF's G-1 and G-4 staffs "to assure that there is a truly integrated conception of the SHAEF organization." To ease the flow of supplies, Bradley's headquarters should determine requirements through the operations and intelligence staffs of ETO, not SHAEF. Finally, he argued ComZ should remain in control of the base sections in the United Kingdom.[30]

Lee's objections set off a number of hurried conferences. The 28 May directive was so fuzzy that even Crawford began to side with Lee. On 31 May an angry Smith ordered that Hughes get together with Crawford and Lee and straighten out the reorganization. Hughes's aide stated the obvious: "It seems rather late in the day to be figuring out how ETO is to be organized."[31] Crawford and Hughes met with Smith on 2 June. Crawford thought that, given the uncertainty of ETO's role, if any, Lee should remain as deputy theater commander, but Bradley should determine the army rear boundary and the timing of the transition of control to ComZ. In any event, he argued, the operational commands must allocate equipment and supplies; the combat zone should pull supplies forward rather than ADSEC pushing from the rear.[32]

Hughes wrote up the conclusions of the meeting. He identified the core problem as "how control is to be exercised by [Eisenhower] over Commanding General, Communication Zone." Would it be through SHAEF or through Bradley's headquarters? The participants recommended abolishing SOS and the title of deputy theater commander. No one knew better than Hughes that a deputy theater commander was a "misnomer in as much as the deputy . . . exercises no portion of the authority of the theater command over combat operations." Lee's ComZ headquarters would control the chiefs of services. To avoid placing an intermediate supply headquarters between Bradley and Lee, the three officers suggested eliminating the FECZ and strengthening the G-2 and G-3 sections of Bradley's staff. Not surprisingly, Smith and Hughes differed over the measure of control exercised by SHAEF. Hughes argued that Lee should control manpower and supply; the G-1 and G-4 sections of SHAEF should confine themselves to supervisory and coordinating roles.[33]

With the invasion only days away, the issue of the theater command remained unresolved. An impatient Eisenhower restated his requirements to Smith. He intended to act in his capacity as commanding general of ETO by placing the major theater commands at the operational disposal of SHAEF. Thereafter, he would command without using ETO channels; SHAEF would deal directly with ComZ. SHAEF would render final decisions, coordinate the operational commands (including ComZ), and enforce cooperation.[34] He ordered Smith to reassemble Lee, Crawford, and Hughes; spell out his requirements; and sequester them until they agreed on the details.[35]

Smith had more weighty matters occupying his mind. One thing even the best-laid plans cannot provide is fair weather. Since 1 June the meteorologists had been painting a somber picture. At 9 P.M. on 2 June, Eisenhower convened a supreme commander's meeting at Ramsay's headquarters at Southwick House. Held in the library, the conference consisted of Montgomery, Leigh-Mallory, Ramsay, Tedder, and Smith. Although Bradley had made a presentation at St. Paul's and appeared in all the official photographs, he held no combined command and played no role in the decision to launch Overlord. Arrayed informally on sofas and easy chairs, they enacted a scene repeated many times over the next couple of days. At 9:30 the SHAEF meteorologist, Group Captain John Stagg, made his presentation in his thick Scottish brogue. He classed the forecast as "untrustworthy" but finely tipped "on the favourable side." The meeting broke up early; the twenty-four-hour window for postponing the landings set for 5 June narrowed.[36]

The next day dawned clear, giving rise to optimism. Eisenhower returned to Bushy Park and Smith to London to deal with the supply command issue. Leaving Lee, Hughes, and Crawford to their labors in Norfolk House, Smith returned to Portsmouth. That night the scene repeated itself at Southwick House, with the same result. Smith raced to the communications building and dispatched the code word to all commands signaling a postponement; he notified the CCS and phoned 10 Downing Street. The weather turned distinctly threatening overnight, and the wind picked up. In midmorning Churchill arrived with Smuts, Ismay, Minister of Labor and National Service Ernest Bevin, and a surprise guest, de Gaulle. The general's sudden appearance took everyone's mind off the weather.

Smith knew he was exposing himself by going so far out on the limb in his bargaining with the French. If the bough broke, he—not Eisenhower—would take the fall. Eisenhower carefully evaded any direct dealing with Koenig and the other senior FCNL officials in London. On 31 May Smith worked out a covenant with Koenig on control of the French Forces of the Interior (FFI). Whiteley and Koenig confirmed the details on 2 June. Koenig would assume command of the FFI once the Allies secured their lodgments and operate under the direction of SHAEF. With de Gaulle in England, the deal looked dead.

Eisenhower noted, de Gaulle "is apparently willing to cooperate only on the basis of our dealing with him exclusively," and concluded, "the whole thing falls into a rather sorry mess." De Gaulle "takes the attitude that military and political matters go hand in hand and will not cooperate militarily unless political recognition of some kind is accorded him. We do not seem to be able, in advance of D-Day, to straighten the matter at all."[37] De Gaulle's sudden arrival revived hope the general would at least address the French people.

Churchill remembered that de Gaulle "was most ceremoniously received. Ike and Bedell Smith vie with one another in their courtesy." Eisenhower and Churchill spent the entire day trying to "secure from [de Gaulle] a statement to galvanize and unify resistance groups in France to help us at this crucial moment." Eisenhower, with the prime minister's concurrence, briefed de Gaulle on the plan. That day Smith attended a meeting with Churchill, de Gaulle, and Koenig. De Gaulle appeared very accommodating; he promised to make a statement and confirmed Koenig's agreement with Smith on the FFI. But the language of the proclamation created problems. Churchill, Eden, Eisenhower, and Smith all tried to reason with de Gaulle. Smith pointed out that de Gaulle would only hurt his own standing in France if he refused to broadcast. De Gaulle wanted the FCNL mentioned in Eisenhower's broadcast; Smith said that was impossible because the speech had already been cleared in London and Washington and recorded, and millions of leaflets had been printed to be airdropped across France. During the course of 4 and 5 June a series of cables told the story: "General de Gaulle will not speak." "General de Gaulle will speak." "General de Gaulle has changed his mind."[38]

To add to these problems, the prime minister was in one of his funks. He wanted to sail with the invasion flotilla and had issued the necessary orders; only a letter from the king dissuaded him. Like a petulant child, he made life miserable for everyone in his circle. And he was drinking too much. Cunningham spoke of the prime minister "in almost a hysterical state," worked up about the invasion and de Gaulle. As was usually the case, the brunt of his bad temper fell on Ismay. Smith took pity on his friend, sheltered him in his caravan, and guarded the door while Ismay stole a little respite from the prime minister.[39]

"A Helluva Gamble"

On the evening of 4 June Eisenhower presided over one of the most important councils of war in military history. Outside, the wind raged and rain fell in torrents; inside, the usual circle sat in comfortable chairs sipping coffee. At 9:30 Stagg made his report. The meteorologists finally agreed; they predicted a thirty-six-hour "break" in the storm throughout 5 June and into the next day. The airmen spoke first; Tedder and Leigh-Mallory, whose grim prediction on airborne losses was well known, hedged. Ramsay pointed out that unless the American task force heard the decision within the next half hour, the ships would return to port for refueling.

Smith always remembered the "loneliness and isolation of a commander at a time when such a momentous decision was to be taken by him, with full knowledge that failure or success rest on his individual decision." The choice hung not on whether to launch the invasion at all but on whether to postpone it. Eisenhower had already made up his mind not to delay; the negatives of doing so outweighed the positives. Postponement meant a deferral until 18 June, and the Germans would use that time to strengthen the Atlantic Wall; more valuable campaigning weather would be sacrificed; and promises had been made to the Soviets. He looked at Montgomery. As ground commander, he owned the greatest responsibility. Any naval or air breakdown would endanger the venture, but failure on the ground spelled disaster. Without a hint of caution, Montgomery declared, "I would say go." He turned to Smith, who agreed and added that the seas might be moderate and the skies open enough. If those conditions held, the weather could actually offer a real break; the Germans had read the same forecasts and might well be surprised. "It's a helluva gamble," Smith stated, "but it's the best possible gamble."

The room fell into a chilling silence. "Finally [Eisenhower] looked up," Smith remembered, "and the tension was gone from his face."[40] Smith knew he had made his choice. Talking almost to himself, Eisenhower asked, "The question is, just how long you can just kind of hang this thing out there on a limb?" After a pause he said, "I'm quite positive that the order must be given." Ramsay rushed from the room to give the order. The room quickly emptied, everyone silent with their own thoughts.

At 4:30 in the morning the conference reconvened. Time still remained to recall the more than 5,000 ships steaming to the assembly point, Piccadilly Circus. When the weatherman walked in to make his presentation, Smith detected "the ghost of a smile on the tired face of Group Captain Stagg."[41] Smith guessed correctly; Stagg gave a more optimistic forecast. Smith, Montgomery, Ramsay, and Tedder all agreed the invasion should go in. Leigh-Mallory saw the enterprise as "chancy" but concurred. After a moment's pause, Eisenhower said, "O.K. Let's go." With that, the decisive campaign in the western European theater commenced.

Within a half minute the room cleared, except for the supreme commander, left alone to ponder his fateful decision. The rest of the assembly hastened off to their command posts. Smith had to hurry back to London to meet with Koenig. The matter of de Gaulle's announcement remained up in the air.

Smith and Koenig met in a final bid to arrive at a compromise. De Gaulle insisted on the deletion of the phrase referring to the "free choice of governmental representatives" following France's liberation. Smith answered that the section could not be altered without the president's approval. Koenig knew that, but he repeated de Gaulle's condition; otherwise, there would be no announcement. Smith tried to Badoglio Koenig, threatening to carry on with the broadcast "minus any statement from General De Gaulle." Koenig recognized the bluff and called Smith on it.[42]

An irate chief of staff talked the situation over with McClure. Smith thought that once word leaked that de Gaulle was in England, people would wonder why he did not speak. "Smith does not propose to have Ike explain why de Gaulle did not make a statement," McClure recorded in his diary. Smith would not "beg de Gaulle." McClure suggested, "We can ruin de Gaulle so he can't get back to France." "As far as I'm concerned," Smith replied, "I would be delighted." McClure wondered if "de Gaulle is fighting the President or the Germans." Smith spat back, "He is fighting anybody not for de Gaulle. I have nothing but contempt for him."[43]

Smith returned to Portsmouth in time to accompany Eisenhower on his visit to Newbury and the 101st Airborne Division. Leigh-Mallory predicted loss rates as high as 80 percent, and Eisenhower felt compelled to witness the division boarding its C-47s. "The light of battle was in their eyes," he told Marshall. Failure was very much on everyone's mind, especially the supreme commander's. Earlier that afternoon he had scribbled a note he intended to release in the event the landings miscarried. "If any blame or fault attaches to the attempt," it read, "it is mine alone." Smith never revealed whether he still thought it a fifty-fifty proposition.

There was no rest for the weary; Smith boarded Eisenhower's train and returned to Norfolk House for an all-night bargaining session with the French. De Gaulle now indicated he would make a broadcast. None of this should have come as a bolt from the blue; Smith had plenty of experience dealing with de Gaulle. Typically, de Gaulle played for time, which he knew was a commodity in very high demand. Just before dawn—ironically, about H hour—and after hurried exchanges with Washington, de Gaulle finally agreed. Once again he got his way; he agreed to speak that morning but emphasized that the French populace should follow only the instructions of the provisional government (the FCNL), without any prominence given to the authority of the Allied command.

For Smith, 6 June held only a sense of letdown. He decided to stay at SHAEF-Main, with its superior communications. Still, he received only spotty reports from the beaches. For the supreme commander and his chief of staff, there was no sea mist in the face, no peering through binoculars at the distant shore, no frenzied command post with telephones ringing and situation maps with division tiles and flags. Eisenhower spent the day downing coffee after coffee and smoking Camel after Camel in his caravan at Portsmouth; Smith spent the day trying to make sense of and write the latest directive on the command and organization of U.S. forces in France.

Amazingly, even though everyone agreed the rate of buildup would ultimately decide the contest, the great invasion began with the Americans still undecided on command relations and organization. Before Torch, Smith had fought to rationalize the headquarters structure and failed; the same thing occurred before Husky. Overlord proved no different. For nearly six months Smith had labored at the epicenter of Allied efforts to launch the cross-Channel attack: broadening the operation, the Anvil debate, coordinating planning, the melee over the transportation plan, civil affairs and the French, the Patton flap, and the many scraps over organizing and staffing SHAEF. All of them piled on stress and frustration. Now, while the greatest gamble of the war played out on the Norman beaches, he added one more aggravation to his long list of complaints: writing a directive that acknowledged his powerlessness in convincing Eisenhower to deal with the logistics mess.

In a typical Eisenhower compromise, both Bradley and Lee got what they wanted most. Bradley preserved his line command in Normandy, including control over logistics, until he decided to relinquish it; Lee retained control of all American theater-wide functions inside a rump ETO submerged within ComZ headquarters. Eisenhower also ceded to Lee any direct control SHAEF might exert over the supply and services commands, except through Smith as dual chief of staff. In the initial phase of operations, the SOS would transform into ComZ, complete with all authority as specified in FM 100-10. During the indeterminate transition phase, ComZ would extend its control to Normandy. "The Theater Commander will delegate all possible authority to the Commanding General, Communication Zone," the directive read, "who reports directly to him. The Communication Zone will be the agency of the Theater Commander for the administration of all US troops and the channel of communications to the War Department excepting on those matters reserved by the Theater Commander himself. For administrative purposes, Com Z headquarters will be considered Theater Headquarters." In the final stage, Lee's command would emerge as an autonomous command equal to those of Bradley and Spaatz. Lee would surrender the title of deputy theater commander, but his duties remained virtually unchanged.[44]

In theory, Montgomery, as ground commander, controlled all supply echelons in Neptune. The directive intended to indicate that the theater retained control over American manpower and supply, but ComZ (SOS would be so designated the next day) would not be activated in France until the formation of the American army group. Until then, Bradley controlled replacements and supply. And the directive made no mention of SHAEF acting as the higher authority after formation of the army group and activation of ComZ. Lee would answer only to Eisenhower. Smith took scant comfort in knowing that this directive—derived from a bargain struck among Lee, Hughes, and Crawford—would not represent the final word because of the conflicting inferences regarding command lines. Smith had faith the Allies could effect the landings, but could they match the German rate of reinforcement and supply with a tangled command web? Would Neptune turn into another Torch, Salerno, or Anzio?[45]

Smith knew that he had succeeding in carving out a prominent niche for himself in the highest circle of decision makers. Back in February, Donovan had told him that Churchill admired Smith's "compulsive quality of service to the common cause" and that the prime minister spoke of Smith "as he did of no other American." Donovan thought it "essential that you should know, and we should know, that you have his trust in your character and his reliance on your ability. It cannot but give you confidence and humility in meeting this greatest test of war."[46] If Smith were in his office at Widewing, he could look up on the wall at the oversized photo of Marshall and read the inscription: "affectionate regards and complete confidence." He could also take comfort in the knowledge that when Eisenhower solicited advice on whether to cancel the invasion, the supreme commander had turned to Smith last and most decidedly.

Yet there remained all the accumulated, maddening strains, not to mention the fact that the inspector general was still hounding him. He joked about the hush in Parliament that had greeted the announcement of his name. Staff officers are supposed to be faceless. Part of Smith's job involved evading the press, not only for security reasons but also because the first rule of being a chief of staff is never to appear to differ with or upstage the boss. True, Marshall, acting as his own marine lieutenant, got a *Life* reporter to interview Smith for a future article. The correspondent thought that, as "a soldier's soldier," Smith cared less for publicity "than probably anybody in the Army."[47] He was wrong. It bothered Smith that he labored in obscurity, that his instrumental role in preparing the invasion was known by only a select few. He had every right to be fed up. But like he told Butcher, he believed he still had one campaign left in him. Like everyone else, he longed to get to the other shore.

★ 28 ★

Normandy Deadlock

In August Beetle Smith pronounced the war in the west "militarily" over. In part motivated by hubris—later diagnosed as "victory disease"—his analysis, though badly timed, proved correct. Two days before launching Neptune, Clark's forces entered Rome. Of far greater significance, the Soviets had completed the destruction of Army Group Center in Belorussia, and the Red Army poured into the Baltic states, Poland, and Romania.[1] Victory in Normandy—combined with Anvil—sealed the fate of German forces in France. From a purely instrumental point of view, Germany was finished militarily. But politically—and American generals rebuffed the commingling of political and military components—totalitarian Germany was far from done.

Unanticipated successes bookended the Normandy campaign. Except for the failure to take Caen and the casualties on Omaha and in the American airdrops, the landings went exceptionally well, and the breakout from the lodgments and the rush to the Seine occurred with amazing suddenness. In between, the picture was not so pretty. The lack of appreciable gains in the fighting before Caen and in the hedgerows prompted much gnashing of teeth and caviling in high places; the final outcome remained problematical. Though never actually stalemated—Allied forces made continual advances— the push inland never matched the fanciful target dates set down in the plan. Smith later admitted, "Without Monty we could never had made the landings," but the idiosyncratic and obstreperous British ground commander and his plan remained at the epicenter of the maelstrom of controversy that swirled around his conduct of the campaign in Normandy.[2]

Monty and "The Plan"

After months of frenetic labors, a strange quiet descended on SHAEF on D-day. Neither Eisenhower nor Smith could do anything; the fate

of Neptune rested in the hands of others, principally the common soldiers, sailors, and airmen fighting to gain, hold, and extend the beachheads. Bracketed by prior airborne drops, five divisions landed on or
near their appointed beaches and, except at Omaha, secured footholds
with surprising ease. Screened by Sixth British Airborne Division east
of the Orne Canal, the British First Corps moved from Sword and Juno
toward its objective—the Norman capital Caen. On the other flank,
two badly scattered American airborne divisions landed in the rear of
Utah in the southeastern shoulder of the Cotentin peninsula. Although
things went unpredictably well at Utah, the American assault units on
Omaha succeeded in carving out only a dangerously thin beachhead by
early evening. With their coastal fortifications breached, the Germans
methodically triggered their defense plans, which chiefly meant shifting reserves from one sector to another. Furious rearguard and local
counterattacks prevented the Allies from advancing toward their inland
objectives or closing the gaps between the beaches; the British never took
Caen, and the Americans made little progress sealing the Cotentin peninsula. By the end of D-day, 133,715 American, British, and Canadian
troops had come through the beaches, and construction of the artificial harbors (Operation Mulberry) and submarine pipeline (Operation
Pluto) were under way—all at the cost of 10,300 casualties, nearly 60 percent American.

"Raining, wind. Supplies being delayed. 1st Div held up," Hughes
chronicled on 9 June. "Not much authentic news," he noted. "SHAEF
(Beetle) doesn't get it until late."[3] Serious holes remained between
the sectors, particularly on either side of Omaha Beach. Alarmed by
the overly optimistic reporting of the invasion, Smith convened an
impromptu press conference and emphasized the great difficulties that
lay ahead. He opened by outlining the serious logistical bottlenecks created by the adverse weather conditions. As predicted, a nasty storm had
entered the Channel. On the plus side, Smith said, the Germans faced
the same problems, and "the bad break of the weather [had] not been
fatal." After explaining the tactical situation in the landing zones, Smith
told the journalists that Caen remained in German hands. Summing up,
he asked the newsmen to exercise restraint in their reporting, so as not
to inflate false hope on the home front of a painless success.[4]

In the days following D-day, Smith could not escape the twin bugbears
that would not go away—the logistics command issue and de Gaulle. Just
as he had guessed, his D-day directive on American command and organization settled nothing. On 8 June Lee went to Eisenhower, asking for
"a little firmer idea of General Eisenhower's personal desires" regard-

ing the delineation of responsibilities in France. As Hughes noted, the "mere redesignation of SOS as a Communications Zone does not accomplish the purpose . . . [of setting] up a Commanding General of the Communications Zone as one of the three officers to aid the Theater Commander in accomplishing his mission. A statement of functions of the Communications Zone appears essential."[5]

Smith called on Hughes for help. He made it crystal clear that SHAEF had no interest in running the theater. Smith "called for a reduction in the activities of SHAEF down to the point of where the only matters to be controlled . . . were matters which the Theater Commander kept under his own personal control." Further, he told Hughes, "the US activities of SHAEF should be a minimum; that [Smith] and other American staff officers at SHAEF had all they could do to carry on their duties of handling Allied problems."[6] Smith never wanted to exert personal control over logistics; he merely desired a clear demarcation of responsibilities for supply. In effect, Smith finally washed his hands of the whole business and threw in the towel. Control of theater, administrative, and supply functions shifted to Lee, who remained deputy theater commander in all but name.

The French bitterly objected to SHAEF's circulation of invasion currency; de Gaulle saw it as a manifestation of an AMGOT-like policy indicating that SHAEF intended to treat France as an occupied nation. The FCNL president viewed the invasion currency as a direct assault on the committee's claim of legitimacy. Smith's attempts to cut off another crisis misfired. On 10 June de Gaulle resorted to one of his most powerful weapons—the Anglo-American press. At a news conference he expressed his offense at what he termed "unilateral action." Whatever Roosevelt and Churchill thought of him, de Gaulle enjoyed widespread popular support as the symbol of an undefeated France. He claimed that the issuance of the "counterfeit" currency, which had begun the previous day, foreshadowed "a sort of taking over of power in France by the Allies' military command." Hurried exchanges of notes between Churchill and Roosevelt raised the temperature but solved nothing. The president supported SHAEF, telling Churchill that de Gaulle could issue his own currency "in any capacity that he desires, even to that of the King of Siam. Prima donnas do not change their spots." What he meant, of course, was any capacity except as premier of France. Roosevelt thought de Gaulle exploited the currency issue "to stampede us into according full recognition to the Comité." Receiving no guidance from the political bosses, Smith worked through Koenig to try to dampen the flame.[7]

Impatient to survey the situation in person, Smith boarded a C-47

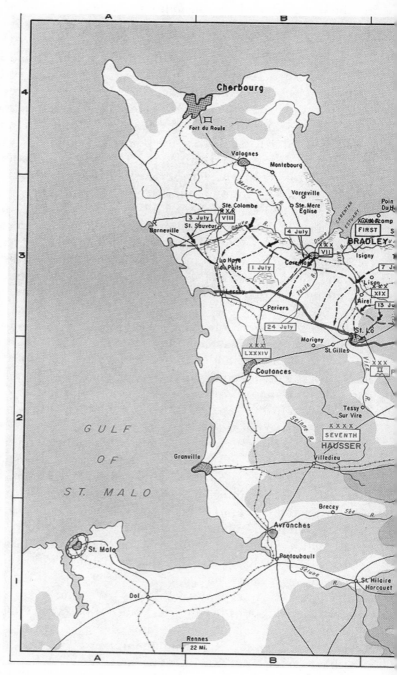

Normandy: D-day to Cobra

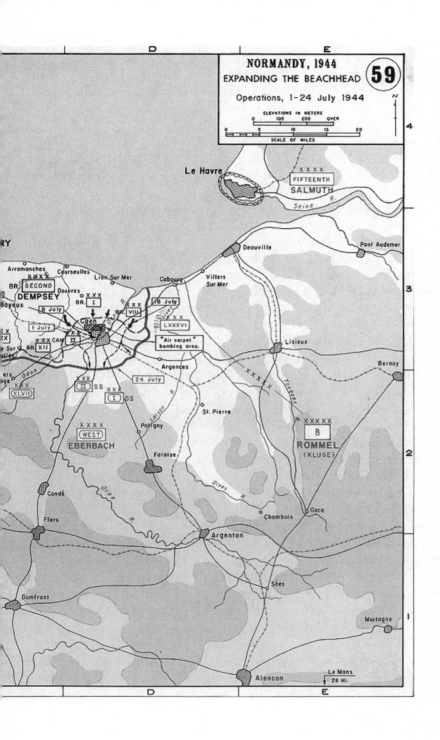

NORMANDY, 1944
EXPANDING THE BEACHHEAD

59

Operations, 1-24 July 1944

N

ELEVATIONS IN METERS
100 200 OVER
0 5 10 15 20
SCALE OF MILES

Le Havre

X X X X
FIFTEENTH
SALMUTH

Seine R.

Deauville

Pont Audemer

RY

Arromanches   Courseulles   Lion Sur Mer

X X X X
BR. SECOND
DEMPSEY

Bayeux   Douvres

Cabourg

Villers
Sur Mer

X X X
BR. I

8 July

X X X
BR. VIII

1 July   Caen

16 July

X X X
LXXXVI

Lisieux

X X X CAN
II
BR. XII

Sur

"Air carpet
bombing area."

Argences

Bernay

w Sur

ge   Odon R.

24 July

X X
II SS

X X
I SS

St. Pierre

X X X X
WEST
EBERBACH

X X X
XLVII

Potigny

Falaise

X X X X
B
ROMMEL
(KLUGE)

Condé

Orne R.

Dives R.

Chambois

Gace

Flers

Argentan

Sées

Domfront

Mortagne

Alencon

Le Mans
28 Mi.

on 10 June for a flight to one of the hastily constructed airfields in Normandy. Soon after taking off at Portsmouth, the plane entered a dense fog bank. After some nervous moments over France, the pilot decided to return to base but neglected to inform his passengers. Much to his amazement, Smith emerged from the aircraft to discover himself back in Portsmouth. "Smart major," remarked Smith.[8]

Marshall, King, and Arnold arrived in London later that day. Smith wanted to give Marshall the clearest possible assessment of the situation. Unable to fly to Normandy for talks with Bradley, Smith instead briefed the Washington mission, based on the still patchy information gleaned from SHAEF's intelligence sources. Both Eisenhower and Smith summarized the situation, which remained mixed. In the simplest terms, Neptune revolved around three questions: Could the Allies complete the landings? Could they hold and consolidate the beachheads against German counterattacks and build up manpower and materiel fast enough? And could they break out of their lodgment, initiate offensive operations, and secure the first strategic objectives—the environs of Caen and Cherbourg—assigned in the Neptune plan?

The answer to the first question was clearly affirmative. The second proved more problematic. Omaha remained thin and exposed; instead of expanding the lodgment outward, Bradley and LTG Miles Dempsey, the British Second Army commander, pushed laterally, eliminating the gaps and pockets of German resistance. The Allies enjoyed uncontested mastery of the skies, but the supply situation looked poor. Bad weather seriously disrupted the discharge of supply over the beaches, and in the American sector, the same set of problems that had plagued previous operations—failures in marking and sorting, ship manifests that never arrived, general confusion, and the lack of established priorities—already placed the discharge timetable at least one day behind. The weather also grounded the Allied air forces. Despite all the difficulties, the tactical situation remained good; the Germans offered stout resistance but only localized counterattacks. The intelligence picture also appeared to be extremely favorable. The single greatest wild card, Fortitude, seemed to be working; Allied intelligence detected no movement of forces from the Pas de Calais into the Neptune area, and only limited movements from Brittany. The efforts of the French resistance were more effective than anyone had hoped. But the fact remained, the expanded beachheads were only one-fifth their projected size, which hampered the buildup and made it vulnerable to the counteroffensive that everyone expected under the cover of bad weather. The answer to the third question was a qualified no.

As of 9 June, the three key towns on the east-west lateral road—Carentan, Bayeux, and, most vital of all, Caen—remained in German hands, although Bayeux fell the following day and Carentan the next. Montgomery had established Caen as a D-day objective and currently planned to employ two divisions and a paratrooper drop north of the city to gain favorable ground for further offensive actions while securing the Orne line. The plan called for both armies to advance in unison. Second Army would rush into Caen if the opportunity presented itself; otherwise, Dempsey would mask the city and lay the groundwork for an eventual envelopment from the west. The situation appeared retrievable: If Dempsey and Bradley pushed in concert in the center and the British took Caen, the Allies would control the key lateral road, which held out the possibility that the Germans might "rope off" the lodgment farther south, obviating much of the fighting to clear the bocage country. (Bocage refers to the system of landholding common in western France, featuring checkerboards of cultivated fields divided by tall, thick hedgerows that restrict movement and observation, affording the Germans a natural system of defensive positions.) With the fusing of MG Joseph Collins's VII Corps and Gerow's V Corps completed, the envisioned attacks to seal the Cotentin and the area toward Falaise might still beat the Germans to the punch.

Despite the failure to take Caen, Montgomery expressed his satisfaction and informed SHAEF, "My general object is to pull the Germans on to Second Army so that First Army can extend and expand." Since the first supreme commander's conference on 21 January, and amplified at St. Paul's, Montgomery had consistently maintained that his primary objective centered on drawing and containing the bulk of the German armor on the eastern flank, permitting Bradley to open the port of Cherbourg, which Montgomery considered more strategically vital than a geographic target like Caen; then, "once through the difficult bocage country," he planned "to thrust rapidly towards Rennes," cutting off the Brittany peninsula.[9]

Dempsey, not Montgomery, made and executed the operational plans. As his 15 May brief clearly indicated, he first needed to secure the Odon–Orne–Caen Canal line and his left before he could launch any general movement south and southeast with Caen as the pivot. Dempsey planned to stage a dual envelopment, advancing in corps-sized bounds conditioned by the weight and range of artillery support, all designed to maintain contact with Bradley, outflank Caen, and gain terrain favorable as the starting lines for a general advance. Second Army's offensive miscarried east of the Orne and at Villers-bocage. Thirty Corps' failure to exploit the Caumont Gap highlighted the British army's "stickiness" in maneuver operations. The attack by a single armored brigade group lacked concentration and infantry support and exposed serious command failures at the division and corps levels. The presence of German armor—soon reinforced by antiaircraft brigades used in the antitank role and separate heavy tank battalions—altered all calculations. Forecasts for the tempo of attacks and distances gained fell victim to deepening German defenses and the tyranny of logistics—troops and supplies landed and shipping—compounded by deteriorating weather and terrain favoring the defense. Villers-bocage ended the post–D-day "scramble for ground," convincing Montgomery and Dempsey that Caen could be taken only by set-piece assaults.[10]

At this juncture (D+8), SHAEF's conception of the campaign began to diverge from Montgomery's. Eisenhower acknowledged Montgomery's 12 June communication and, neither agreeing nor demurring, replied only that he found the message "very helpful." Eisenhower and Smith thought strict adherence to the plan had been nullified by the failure to advance beyond Caen, demanding adjustments. They later maintained they had always believed the plan called for simultaneous offensives on both flanks. Although difficult to credit, Smith told an official historian in 1947 that he and Eisenhower believed Montgomery always intended to make the main effort in the ideal tank country beyond Caen, coupled with Bradley's swing to the right. Caen served as gateway to Paris; it opened into a long, broad plain extending to the scarps northeast of Paris. When Montgomery signaled his intention to go over to the defensive, they interpreted this as being motivated by the general's habitual caution and reluctance to risk heavy casualties.[11]

As their postmortem accounts indicate, Eisenhower and Smith never fully grasped Montgomery's operational thinking. Apart from opposing Nazi aggression, the single British war aim revolved around safeguarding the United Kingdom's standing as a global power. Merely emerging on the winning side beside the two burgeoning superpowers would not suffice; Great Britain must play a prominent part in the defeat of Germany to exert a significant influence on the postwar settlement. Montgomery's army group represented Britain's last great throw of the dice. If disaster befell Allied forces in D-day or Normandy, the Americans would recover—the war would lengthen and they would surely redirect their energies to the Pacific—but Great Britain might not. Another Dunkirk would not end British participation in the war, but it would spell an end to the United Kingdom as a great power.

Montgomery confronted the daunting task of achieving British war aims by preserving a high military profile despite the relative weakness of his armies, both in combat against the Germans and in contributions versus those of the Americans. And he had to accomplish this without incurring heavy casualties. The "shadow of Passchendaele" influenced his thinking, but not as much as the genuine apprehension that the manpower pool would run dry. The RAF hived off nearly 1 million men, principally for the combined bomber offensive; the British also faced commitments in the Atlantic, the Mediterranean and Middle East, and India and Southeast Asia. The manpower demands of war production imposed another constraint. As early as March 1944, the War Office projected that, even with the cannibalization of two divisions and the retraining of men from other branches, Montgomery would face a shortfall of 40,000 riflemen. Five of the nine British and Canadian divisions in Neptune were veterans of the Mediterranean campaigns. The men in these divisions figured they had already done their bit, and they had no enthusiasm for another long and bloody campaign. The rest of the divisions possessed no battlefield experience. As Montgomery understood, jaded veteran and green units could not muster much dash.[12]

Montgomery firmly believed the morale of his soldiers represented the key to battlefield success. Heavy casualties would sap the already fragile morale of British and Canadian combat formations. Montgomery did his best "binging up" his troops, telling them the British Tommy and the Canucks, when properly led, equipped, supplied, and motivated, constituted the best soldiers in the world. Part of the problem was the mediocrity of the British officer corps, especially at senior levels. The officer class was unrivaled in producing the likes of a Lord Hay, a Ponsonby, or a Cardigan, but it lacked the professionalism and common touch for leading and inspiring a mass and imperial army—much of it working class.[13] As the proverbial outsider—with a strong whiff of the Commonwealth man about him—Montgomery excelled at motivating British and Imperial troops under his command. There was nothing of the chateau general about Montgomery; his troops were "not the scum of the earth," and he let them know it. And they appreciated that he would not fritter their lives away; he deeply cared for them, but they also represented a military commodity too dear to waste.

Montgomery's critics pointed to his fetish for preparations and concentration. He reduced his conduct of battle to three elements: "First. I will not have any failures. Second. In order that this is so, I limit the scope of any operation to that which can be done successfully. Third. I do not launch until I am ready. I then hit hard, and quickly" and at a selected place.[14] He believed that with realistic training and rehearsals, well-motivated and competently led troops, backed by copious firepower, could defeat the Germans in spite of Anglo-Canadian weaknesses. If the forces under his command could avoid defeat, morale would be sustained, and the material advantages of the Allies would secure victory.

By inclination and necessity, Montgomery was an attrition general who could not afford to fight attrition battles. He tailored operations both to take advantage of and to compensate for British doctrine, command and force structures, and corporate culture. The British army's forte was the set piece, an operation that allowed Montgomery to concentrate his forces and cautiously and methodically "grip" the battle according to his plan. The top-down command structure permitted him to clearly define his intent while subordinate commands worked toward the plan. By massing more manpower, resources, and firepower he could wear down the enemy forces until he could stage a penetration. This took place in four distinct phases, all of which he clearly identified.

The amphibious operation and staking out of the outer boundaries of the advance inland represented Montgomery's "break-in" phase. First one preserves security, tightens administration, concentrates maximum strength, and hits the enemy a "colossal crack." In Normandy the plan placed the main strength in the center. If the enemy's defenses were broken, all to the good; if not, one could still seize ground vital for developing future offensive operations. The core of Montgomery's thinking on war, a product of his experience on the Western Front in the First World War, remained rooted in his appreciation of the devastating superiority of modern firepower on the defensive. Once the key ground fell, the perimeter must rapidly be hardened and heavily supported by artillery backed by airpower, because the Germans unfailingly counterattacked. German doctrine insisted that decisive results came only through offensive action. Montgomery conceded that German forces, especially armor, possessed superior tactical fighting power, but he understood that the Normandy campaign would be won at the operational level of war. For Montgomery, the key lay in forcing the Germans to fight tactically while he conducted the campaign on the operational plane. Securing ground the Germans recognized as essential obliged them to throw themselves against prepared defenses, sacrificing operational elasticity for local advantage. They might regain lost terrain, but at the heavy cost of surrendering the initiative and committing their armor in static fighting.

The break-in attack seamlessly turned into what Montgomery called the "crumbling" phase. Alamein, the Mareth Line, Gabes Gap, and Enfidaville in Tunisia, as well as Sicily, all reinforced his ideas, but the most instrumental battle of all took place at Medenine, where Eighth Army smashed Rommel's armored-tipped assaults without the loss of a single tank. In each of these battles—except for Medenine, where he fought entirely on the defensive—Montgomery planned to penetrate the Axis position through a set-piece offensive. When the attacks failed—and they failed everywhere except at Gabes Gap—he still succeeded in inflicting heavy casualties on counterattacking German units attempting to eliminate the "break-in" threat. As the Germans committed more men and armor from their reserves to regain the tactical initiative, they unbalanced themselves. Their center of gravity shifted to ground of Montgomery's choosing.

By 14 June Montgomery went over to something resembling the crumbling mode. According to his RAF critics, he optimistically forecast taking Caen and beyond—the Caen-Falaise plain offered ideal ground for forward air bases—to quiet their opposition. Although the failure to seize Caen was a disappointment, in Montgomery's mind, it did not seriously compromise his plan. He guessed correctly that the Germans would mass their armor in the vicinity of Caen and, as Montgomery had predicted at St. Paul's, launch "a full-blooded counter attack" any time after 12 June. In the initial stages, the British possessed more tanks than the Americans, in anticipation of strong counterattacks heavy in armor. As a transportation hub, the city itself was important, but primarily Montgomery wanted good ground as a platform for future operations. While Caen drew German armor, Dempsey and Bradley consolidated and pushed out in the center, all in preparation for a thrust in the west against static infantry opposition sealing the Cotentin peninsula. The port of Cherbourg, not Caen, represented the first great strategic prize.

Like Napoleon, Montgomery comprehended the all-important time and space relationship. Ground can always be regained, but time never. Understanding is one thing; mastering is quite another. Montgomery always gathered his mobile forces in reserve, husbanded his supply, and prepared a plan B—an envelopment—if the penetration failed. Here the Mareth Line served as his leitmotif. While the Germans "crumbled" further—their initiative gone, reserves committed, and flexibility hampered—Montgomery shifted his center of gravity to the new *Schwerpunkt*. Bradley's drive into the Cotentin did not represent plan B; it remained the American half of the "break-in" stage. But once Cherbourg fell and American forces expanded the perimeter beyond the closed bocage country enough to permit the deployment of Patton's Third Army, the breakthrough would come against weakened linear defenses, provided Montgomery kept up the pressure around Caen.

The breakthrough phase—if executed fast enough—held out the

potential of transitioning immediately into a breakout. Speed was the essential element. The Germans must disengage from the eastern sector and move their depleted reserves along exposed external lines to counter the new and more dangerous threat, but they would lack the luxury of time to mass their forces and would have to counterattack piecemeal. Again, the situation forced the Germans into launching tactical attacks, throwing themselves against a buttoned-up enemy that could call down concentrated firepower. If First Army could deliver enough punch and penetrate the German lines, Third Army moved with sufficient tempo, and the bulk of the enemy's armored forces remained pinned and static, the opportunity loomed to stage the planned breakout, sealing the Brittany peninsula. It all would have looked familiar to any German staff officer; it came right out of the playbook of Helmut von Moltke the Elder.

Moltke also famously noted that no campaign plan survives first contact with the enemy. Montgomery was too good a general not to know that, but in part owing to the peculiarities of his mental makeup, he always insisted that all his battles went exactly according to the script.[15] Certainly, Alamein and Mareth had not; all the ingredients presented themselves for a decisive victory, but the British forces lacked the mobility and hitting power to deliver the coup de main. The set-piece battle perpetuated "stickiness" at all levels, the unwillingness to take risks. And Montgomery knew it. But perhaps the less risk- and casualty-averse Americans could stage a maneuver breakout operation. Who better than Bradley, who had distinguished himself fighting in the mountains and stone-walled olive groves of Sicily, for conducting the bocage fight?[16] Who better than a "thruster" like Patton to lead the breakout? What better armies than the highly mobile Americans, backed by overwhelming airpower, for executing an open campaign?

These factors—the limitations of his forces, the unwillingness to incur heavy casualties and the related problem of morale, and the extraordinarily high stakes involved—colored Montgomery's thinking and go a long way in explaining his obsession with following the plan and exerting his "grip over the battle," and they determined his actions as ground commander in Normandy and beyond. Few senior American officers appreciated much if any of this.

American officers were not alone in their mistrust of Montgomery. Senior RAF officers—particularly Tedder and Coningham—reviled Montgomery.[17] Leigh-Mallory and Montgomery got into a squabble over the proposed airdrop near Caen; again Leigh-Mallory demurred and this time won out. Perhaps to mollify Montgomery, Leigh-Mallory promised the future use of bombers to blow a corridor through the German defenses, permitting a renewal of Montgomery's attack against Caen. Tedder, who did not know much about the ground battle, dismissed the scheme as unrealistic and began talking about a crisis in Normandy. He and Coningham also resented the fact that Leigh-Mallory had made this offer to Montgomery at a meeting without the strategic air force commanders present. The Germans briefly retook Carentan, adding to the discomfort at SHAEF. Dismayed by the lack of gains in Normandy, Eisenhower's attention was deflected to other concerns.

The visit of the Joint Chiefs of Staff diverted Eisenhower and Smith from the battle. On 11 June the Combined Chiefs of Staff met in London; the extensive agenda for the four-day conference covered the entire range of Allied grand strategy. The first day Anvil and, more broadly, the relationship between Overlord and the Mediterranean commanded their attention. They agreed on a compromise. Top priority centered on "applying to the enemy, at the earliest possible moment, all our forces in the manner best calculated to assist in the success of OVERLORD." Depending on progress made in Normandy and on the Eastern Front, and on the German reaction to both, the CCS discussed three options for amphibious operations employing forces from the Mediterranean—the south or west coast of France or the Adriatic. In the end, they concluded Marseilles was too heavily defended and the route up the Rhône would be of little direct aid to the campaign in northern France. Instead, the CCS squared the circle and tentatively recommended a landing west of Marseilles, with Bordeaux as the ultimate objective. Based on the advice of Wilson, "we should aim at being ready to launch the operation by the 25th of July," with a three-division lift provided primarily by assault craft already in the Mediterranean. Revealing anxiety over Overlord, Eisenhower confided in Wilson that he preferred a move against the west coast aimed at Bordeaux—an operation nixed by the CCS—but claimed he would accept any operation so long as it could be launched quickly and with a reasonable prospect of success.[18]

The conference adjourned on 12 June; Eisenhower and Smith took the chiefs on a visit to Bradley and a tour of the beaches. Smith made a point of visiting de Guingand, bringing along one of his handmade fly rods as a gift. De Guingand probably wondered when he would get the chance to use it. His critics in British circles said that Monty commanded the armies and de Guingand commanded Twenty-first Army Group. Smith later stated, unfairly and mostly out of spite, that Montgomery punched above his weight as an army group commander. Like Patton, Montgomery's milieu was at the army level. "He liked to go off by himself and fight the corps and army himself," Smith noted. "Montgomery left most of this interaction to de Guingand."[19] In de Guingand, Smith possessed a vital informal back door, and in Whiteley, he enjoyed an additional entrée into Twenty-first Army Group headquarters. De Guingand reminded Smith of Dykes; both men inspired affection and possessed self-deprecating senses of humor, and de Guingand liked his wine. In thanking Beetle for the fishing rod, de Guingand told Smith he was "one who made the hectic days of war so much easier than they might have been."[20] Smith's efforts to cement his friendship with de Guingand paid back in spades later in the campaign.

Montgomery proved a little more generous in his estimate of the Ike-Beetle partnership. He added them to his very exclusive list of "good teams" and wrote in his diary, "Eisenhower is a very 'big' man who takes the large view and keeps clear of all detail. Bedell Smith implements all the big decisions and keeps the whole show on the rails."[21] Montgomery considered Smith a friend, but given the general's ascetic persona, there was no possibility the two men would ever have anything other than a distant, detached professional relationship.

Eisenhower and Tedder flew to Montgomery's headquarters on 15 June "to see whether there really was a crisis."[22] Eisenhower told Smith the best way to get Montgomery moving was to shift emphasis to Bradley's front.[23] Montgomery declared that everything remained under control. The day before, Montgomery had issued his first epistle on the campaign; he "decided to be *defensive in the CAEN sector* . . . to pull the Germans into Second British Army, and fight them there, so that first US Army can carry out its tasks the easier."[24] Montgomery bristled at suggestions he had sacrificed the initiative to Rommel. In tactical fighting like that in Normandy, planning and execution devolved on corps commanders. The master plan assigned specific objectives to both armies. As army group commander, Montgomery oversaw one front and one battle, not separate national armies. He might shift the axis of advance, but only after discussions with Bradley and Dempsey and the corps commanders. In fact, at no point in the campaign did he ever surrender the initiative to the Germans. As matters stood, Dempsey and Bradley simply lacked the forces and supplies for simultaneous offensives on both fronts. Montgomery emphasized that absolute priority must be placed on winning the battle of the buildup. Bradley could not move on Cherbourg and attack south at the same time; he would tackle each task in turn. With Carentan back in American hands, the secure center now allowed Bradley's drive to the west coast of the Cotentin. As soon as British VIII Corps came up, Montgomery fully expected to take Caen. He estimated 18 June as the start date. Tedder left unconvinced, but Eisenhower hoped for the best.

When he returned from Normandy, Eisenhower wrote Smith a memo. Apparently, Montgomery's warning about supply had made little impression. Despite the logistics problems, Eisenhower wanted a cut in supply units in favor of combat troops. He also asked for the timetable for the activation of ADSEC in France. Preoccupied with the supposed operational crisis, Eisenhower attached no particular importance to the looming supply emergency. American units already faced critical shortages of artillery and mortar ammunitions within days of the landings. "Keep me informed from time to time," he told Smith, "of any progress in straightening out all our build-up difficulties."[25] He did dispatch his troubleshooter Hughes to France.

German resistance prompted the accelerated landing of combat personnel far ahead of plan. Initially, Engineer Special Brigades (ESBs) handled the unloading of materiel. Shipping designated for SOS personnel brought in combat troops instead, which meant the ESBs continued in their direct support role. As engineers, they built and improved roads, constructed buildings, and placed lowest priority on their supply functions. The ammunition shortfalls produced frantic efforts to locate and bring ashore ordnance stores, unbalancing stocks of other categories of supply. Receiving units expended little care in cataloging deliveries. Trucks dumped supplies with scant regard for accounting procedures; other trucks appeared and took what they required. Soon First Army depots were awash with ammunition.[26]

The traditional mistrust, even antagonism, between field and supply officers surfaced early and grew over time. Bradley deeply resented that his estimates on the rates of fire, which determined levels of ammunition supply, received short shrift. He considered the War Department's figures—the Mediterranean maximum became the European minimum—about a third of what was prudent. The ammunition shortage in Normandy confirmed his worst fear: Lee's people had decided on levels of support and proved incapable of sustaining even those. Bradley instructed his G-4, COL Henry Wilson, not to keep records of receipts, which meant the supply echelons never knew precisely how much materiel First Army held in hand and in reserve.[27] For Bradley, this practice killed two birds with one stone. Since SOS possessed no firm data on Bradley's stocks, it could not deny his requisitions for more. If he built his own reserve stockpiles of ammunition that appeared on nobody's lists, Bradley would overcome the constraints of the artificially low rates of fire and escape dependence on the ComZ structure he held in such disrepute. Bradley's delay in designating an army rear meant that ADSEC acted not as Lee's advance section but as First Army's rear. To cement that tie, Bradley treated the ADSEC head, COL Eddie Plank, as a member of his staff. These practices continued for the duration of the war.[28]

Bradley's duplicity, bred by his mistrust of Lee, created a domino effect. If the combat commands refused to furnish accurate and up-to-date reports to ComZ, Lee could not provide ASF with the necessary data to inform future planning, regulate production, and adjust the flow of materiel into the theater. ASF controlled production and assigned shipping space, not Lee. As a result, no echelon—not ASF, ComZ, SHAEF, or the commands—talked the same language. The same applied to manpower replacements. About 90 percent of the vast communications between the theater and Washington involved routine administration and supply, and much of that entailed harmonizing misunderstandings over requisitioning, shipping and transportation, storage, stock controls, and the levels and distribution of supplies and manpower. Given the complex relationships and overlapping spheres of authority among SHAEF, ComZ, and the commands, the potential for breakdown became very high indeed.

Hughes's inspection of the rear areas revealed that little was being done; progress was far too slow, officers were not exercising authority, men were acting like it was a WPA project, and organizations still did not know their responsibilities. All the fears he had expressed in early May had apparently been realized. Hughes wondered about the wisdom of Bradley's controlling beach operations; he also entertained doubts about Lee. "General Lee went to the Far Shore with a considerable number of presents for General Bradley," Hughes wrote in his memo to Eisenhower and Smith. "When we arrived at General Bradley's headquarters General Lee opened the conversation by asking if the presents had arrived and made a statement to the effect it was well that the presents had preceded our arrival." Hughes reported, "The general tenor of the conversation was to the effect that General Bradley was accepting General Lee's statement that everything was being taken care of and due to the fact that [Bradley] had just received a nice present did not want to take the offensive, even if he had believed that the offensive was necessary." Hughes told the First Army G-4, "Please tell General Bradley that he must not for the sake of the war convey to General Lee that everything was satisfactory. I told Colonel Wilson that General Lee's whole attitude was of wanting to feel that everything was OK and that everything was being done that could be done. I pointed out that General Bradley had to be very very careful giving such general statements to General Lee." Hughes concluded by stating, "In my opinion it is fatal for the First Army to permit any interference with its control at this time." He emphasized "there is no schedule for the only problem that confronts us . . . whether or not we can build up our forces faster than the Germans can build up theirs."[29] After meeting with Hughes and Lee's chief of staff, Bradley admitted the situation on the beaches was "not entirely satisfactory," but he assured Eisenhower, "we ironed out several things that will help efficiency."[30] Hughes did not agree.

Smith too had other things on his mind. The commotion over currency was only one of Smith's ongoing problems in dealing with the French. De Gaulle was withholding all French liaison personnel from duty with SHAEF and with Montgomery's and Bradley's commands. De Gaulle's intransigence threatened to hamper all of SHAEF's civil affairs programs and handicap operations in Normandy, particularly coordinating actions with the resistance. As de rigueur, Eisenhower evaded responsibility, apologizing to de Gaulle for the impasse on political matters and telling the general he "preferred not to have anything to do with it, that he was a soldier and not a politician; and that none of the present arrangements was his doing."[31] For two weeks Smith carried on running talks with the French. Then on 17 June he concluded a wide-ranging deal with Koenig. The French agreed to provide liaison officers to each headquarters down to division level, along with others to assist SHAEF G-5 and the commands in dealing with French civil administration. Koenig reaffirmed that all FFI units would operate under Eisenhower's command through Koenig, who thereafter enjoyed status as an army commander. Two weeks later Smith and Koenig finally settled the currency problem. Smith reported to the War Department that Koenig had agreed to the supplemental francs.[32] Relations with the French assumed a normalcy that no one would have dared predict in the first week of June, and most of the credit goes to Smith's patient negotiations with Koenig. As a diplomat in uniform, Smith exhibited a tolerance few thought him capable of mustering.

When Hughes returned to London on 17 June, he found that "Hitler has made London more unsafe than France." The Germans had unleashed their V-weapons on England. On 18 June, a Sunday, Churchill made a trip out to Widewing and directly appealed to Eisenhower to divert more strategic bombing assets against Crossbow targets, the launching pads for the buzz bombs. Smith had made plans to attend church services with his friend Ivan Cobbald, but the prime minister's visit obliged him to cancel—and it was very fortunate that he did. A V-1 hit the Guard's Chapel at Wellington Barracks, killing 121, including Cobbald. Quite naturally, Smith developed a real fear of V-weapons; like Eisenhower, he spent many a night racing to air-raid shelters, depriving them both of much-needed rest.

Lack of sleep put Eisenhower on edge, but it was nothing compared to his growing disquiet with Montgomery's handling of the fighting around Caen. Alerted to the unease at SHAEF, Montgomery issued another directive on 18 June, outlining his views on the extant situation and how the battle might progress. He claimed, "We are now ready to pass to other things and to reap the harvest." He pointed out that "the old policy of 'stretch,' which beat [the Germans] in SICILY, begins to emerge." "Once we can capture CAEN and CHERBOURG, and all face in the same direction," he asserted, "the enemy problem becomes enormous." He claimed, "It is then that we have a mighty chance—to make the German army come to our threat, and to defeat it between the Seine and the Loire." "Caen is really the key to CHERBOURG," he announced, and "its capture will release forces which are now locked up in ensuring that our left flank holds secure." Rather than assuming the defensive, Montgomery signaled his intention to launch "a pincer movement from both flanks," seizing Caen as a preliminary for expanded operations in the eastern sector. In the cover letter to Simpson, Montgomery expressed his satisfaction and belief that the Germans confronted "a very awkward situation," and he stated that he intended to "rub in our advantage heavily in the next two weeks."[33]

Montgomery had grounds for satisfaction. His forces confronted unfavorable terrain—a series of ridges, river lines, and thick woods—that canalized armored movements and provided ideal points for German counterattacks against attempts to outflank Caen. Bad weather delayed vital supplies and deprived the attacks of tactical air support, especially vital in pinning down German reserve formations. Nevertheless, Montgomery's limited-objective attacks gained better ground and prevented the Germans from creating a central armor reserve. Under constant pressure, the Germans abandoned schemes for a counteroffensive aimed at isolating the British between the Orne and Bayeux and instead concentrated on containing the expected British breakout toward Paris. The Americans faced immobile opposition in the Cotentin. For months before the invasion, German infantry divisions in northwestern France had lost experienced officers, supply and transport units, and headquarters troops (engineers, bridge-building units, light and heavy artillery).[34] Although weak in the western sector, the German leadership accepted the gamble based on their discounting of American combat power. Bradley initiated his offensive into the peninsula on 10 June. The Germans attacked from Carentan, seeking to develop operations against Collins's flank and rear, but they never even managed to hold the town. A week later, "Lightning Joe" Collins's corps completed its swift drive to the western shore of the Cotentin, isolating Cherbourg. The power and speed of the American push proved irresistible; the German forces found no counter to American air superiority and fully motorized infantry.[35] Hitler ordered an attack up the Cotentin to relieve Cherbourg. The commander in chief, FM Gerd von Rundstedt, thought such a movement impossible in view of the air situation, and Rommel concurred. Thereafter the Germans contented themselves with declaring Cherbourg a fortress and establishing an east-west line at the base of the peninsula.[36]

The rapid advance of Bradley's forces in the west contrasted sharply with Montgomery's apparent failures before Caen—something not lost on American war correspondents and, by extension, public opinion in both countries. It appeared the Americans did the hard fighting and suffered the heavy casualties, while Montgomery's forces sat inactive at Caen. Journalists and the public were not alone in this view; it also colored Eisenhower's and Smith's perspective. The day after Montgomery spoke of taking Caen in a pincer movement he postponed the attacks until 25 June and "scaled down" his objectives. He had good reasons for doing so—the growing depth of the German defenses and difficulties moving his VIII Corps forward—but the delay and scale-down provided fodder for his critics. Worries mounted not only over the lack of gains in the east but also over the health of the coalition. As a rejoinder to Montgomery's "Caen is the key to Cherbourg," Collins suggested to Bradley, "Let's wire him to send us the key!" This remark pretty much summed up the sentiment of most senior American officers.[37]

To make matters worse, a natural calamity struck on 19 June when the worst storm in forty years hit the Channel. For days, nothing moved into Normandy, and not much moved within it. Nearly 800 ships were beached or feared lost; the Americans' artificial harbor was disabled and eventually abandoned. SHAEF worried that the number of lost landing craft would compromise Anvil. The tempest caused another casualty—the further delay of Operation Epsom, Montgomery's planned envelopment of Caen. From a supply standpoint, the "great storm" seriously threatened the buildup. The British found themselves four to five days behind schedule; with the disarray in the American rear areas, no one knew where the American timetable stood.[38] Hughes returned to France on 24 June with a newly minted lieutenant in tow, John Eisenhower. "Uncle Everett," young Eisenhower remembered, "was disturbed." With "his voice choked and eyes moist," Hughes pointed to the wreckage of the artificial harbor and the beached shipping and said, "'See that! That's what's licking your Dad right now.'"[39] The incessant rain topped off by the storm left supply dumps behind Omaha Beach mired in a sea of mud.

Eisenhower's foul mood derived from worry that the campaign had lapsed into a deadlock. He wrote to Montgomery, "Please do not hesitate to make the maximum demands for any air assistance that can possibly be useful to you. Whenever there is any legitimate opportunity we must blast the enemy with everything we have." The same day, 25 June, he requested that Tedder make it his "special province to keep in closest touch with Montgomery" to guarantee he receive "every kind of air support."[40] Despite the logistical problems, Montgomery launched his attacks the next morning. Eisenhower expressed his hope that Bradley "can quickly clean up the Cherbourg mess and turn around to attack southward while you have the enemy by the throat in the east." In the same vein, Smith wrote to Montgomery, informing him that his conduct of the campaign to date constituted a "triumph of leadership."[41] In reply to Eisenhower's letter, Montgomery promised to "continue battle on eastern flank till one of us cracks and it will not be us."[42] Epsom succeeded in carving out a salient west of Caen, but it ended in the face of determined German counterattacks.

An old complication intervened: the Anvil pot began bubbling again. Eisenhower handed off Anvil to Smith. On 22–23 June Smith met with Gammell and made the strong case that Eisenhower "wanted ANVIL and he wanted it quick." Wilson never presented any problem; it was AFHQ that ruled out any operation against the west coast of France, claiming it could not come off in time and with enough power to aid Overlord. Gammell vetoed any operation in the Adriatic until September. "OVERLORD is the decisive campaign of 1944," Smith emphasized to the CCS. "A stalemate in the OVERLORD area would be recognized by the world as a defeat. . . . It is imperative that we concentrate our forces in direct support of the decisive area of northern France." Only Anvil "provides the most direct route to northern France." Smith pointed to a number of advantages derived from an invasion of the south of France: it would contain German divisions, provide ports for incoming American divisions and materiel, and allow the Allies to take advantage of the FFI in a region where it could lend the most direct support.[43]

Wilson supported Anvil and considered it likely to succeed if he received enough sea- and airlift for a three-division landing, follow-on divisions, and an airborne operation. He set a target date no earlier than

15 August. The problem remained sea- and airlift. Eisenhower opposed surrendering the requested fifty landing craft and airlift from Overlord. If Anvil could not be mounted by 15 August, he suggested the American and French units earmarked for the landings be moved into Overlord. At the end of May the joint planners at SHAEF started to work on plans for alternatives in the event the Germans contained Neptune without a port. One contingency outlined in a 7 June appreciation centered on moving Anvil forces into Brittany. Even though Smith and the commanders dismissed any idea of conducting amphibious or airborne operations outside the lodgment area, Eisenhower revived the scheme—a move he later regretted.[44]

Churchill did his best to scuttle Anvil. Both Eisenhower and Smith held private talks with the prime minister, but he remained obdurate on Anvil.[45] That last week in June witnessed a deluge of communications between London and Washington, reminiscent of the great Torch debate. The JCS dug in, supported SHAEF's position, and wired the BCOS that a "decision is necessary at once on Mediterranean Operation." The American chiefs supported Anvil at the earliest possible date, as soon as 1 August. The British joint planners backed Anvil, but Brooke and Portal supported broadening operations in Italy and no Anvil. Cunningham found "the arguments so evenly balanced as to have difficulty in making up my mind. So allowed myself to be guided by the other two." On 26 June the BCOS "took a firm line turning down Anvil," Cunningham recorded. "I fear US COS will have much to say." Instead, the British chiefs took up Eisenhower's idea, favoring the movement of divisions from the Mediterranean and their insertion into Overlord.[46] After assessing the loss of landing craft in the great storm and hoping to break the impasse, Smith found the damage to be less extensive than feared and indicated to the CCS that Eisenhower had decided he could release the shipping Wilson requested. Smith related that Eisenhower now considered Anvil so important that he was "prepared to do [his] utmost to insure its success." He added, "We are convinced of the transcendent importance of ANVIL."[47] Cunningham was right; the American chiefs had plenty to say. The British received a "rather tough" reply on 28 June. "Americans would have none of it," the admiral noted. "It is easy to see that the Americans think we have changed our ground & so we have." He thought the BCOS should have been firmer in discussions with the American chiefs earlier in June.[48]

As with Torch, Churchill went over the heads of the combined chiefs and appealed directly to Roosevelt. He stormed at the "arbitrary" tone of the JCS and petitioned the president to "consent to hear both sides" before deciding. As always, he stood ready to lend Eisenhower all aid, but not at the cost "of all our great affairs in the Mediterranean, and we take it hard that this should be demanded of us." Churchill wanted the Adriatic operation or, failing that, a drive toward Trieste into the Ljubljana Gap. In the event forces withdrew from the Mediterranean, he preferred landing them around Bordeaux rather than the south of France. He categorized Anvil as "bleak and sterile," unable to influence the battle in northern France and guaranteed to throw away great gains in Italy "and all its fronts" and "condemn ourselves to a passive role in that theater." Roosevelt's "very stiff" cable crossed Churchill's and simply stated, "I think we should support the views of the Supreme Allied Commander. He is definitely for ANVIL and wants action in the field by August 30th preferably earlier." When Roosevelt received Churchill's intemperate cable, he appealed to his "dear friend," noting that "history will never forgive us if we lost precious time and lives in indecision and debate." He implored, "I beg you to let us go ahead with our plan."[49] Churchill ordered aircraft readied; "we may be flying off to Washington before we are much older," Brooke noted, "but I doubt it." The BCOS "decided that though militarily we were quite unshaken in our views," Cunningham wrote, "since the Americans appeared so set that we had better agree to carry out Anvil."[50] After much kicking and screaming, Churchill telephoned Eisenhower on 1 July and agreed to Anvil.

The apparent success on Anvil represented the only bright spot in an otherwise gloomy landscape. The Neptune phase effectively terminated on 30 June. Despite horrendous weather and the logistical mess, Montgomery and Bradley landed 850,279 men, 148,803 vehicles, and 570,505 tons of supplies. The lines generally extended twenty miles into the interior; commands and supplies began piling up in the narrow enclave. The airmen complained about their inability to build airfields; those few already constructed remained under German artillery fire. Wheeling north, VII Corps fought through Cherbourg's outer ring of fortifications. On 30 June American forces secured the devastated port and the tip of the peninsula. Progress at Cherbourg fell far behind schedule; German demolition of the harbor proved so extensive it took engineers six weeks just to remove the rubble. Caen remained securely in German hands.

Around his friends, Eisenhower no longer made any effort to disguise his fury. Returning from France on 27 June, Hughes made a beeline to Eisenhower. After he heard what Hughes had to say, Eisenhower put a call through to Lee. Young Lieutenant Eisenhower remembered the call being "blunt and to the point. If Lee wanted to keep his job, Dad said, he had better get over there personally and see to it that things were stepped-up. The call took half a minute." After he read a letter from Bradley that Hughes had brought along, Eisenhower said, "I am tired of talking about that subject and someone had better perform or will be out of a job."[51] He was referring to Lee, but Eisenhower was none too pleased with Bradley either. Cherbourg fell that day, but when Hughes told him that Bradley intended to delay his offensive for twenty-four hours, Eisenhower mused, "Sometimes I wish I had George Patton over there."[52] Butcher remarked that Eisenhower appeared "considerably less exuberant these days. He didn't even seem to get a kick out of the fall of Cherbourg." Hughes told Bradley, "from the frame of mind [Eisenhower] was in . . . things began popping."[53] But things did not pop. Eisenhower adamantly refused any showdown with Montgomery, but he could not escape the conclusion that Neptune was over with Normandy stalled.

July Storms

No month in the war tested Eisenhower and those closest to him more than July 1944. Eisenhower left on 1 July for a five-day tour of Normandy; his mission centered on speeding up operations. He visited Montgomery's headquarters on 2 July, and Montgomery reviewed the existing situation on the ground. Intelligence indicated the Germans had eight panzer divisions deployed in the east. The British general reassured Eisenhower that he planned to immediately resume the drive on Caen in conjunction with Bradley's attempted breakout from the bocage country. Montgomery planned to stage a preparatory attack (Windsor) on 4 July before launching a bigger push four days later (Charnwood). He hoped Caen might fall by 10 July.[54] To Eisenhower, it appeared that Montgomery finally intended to push in unison all along the line. Montgomery complained that the air forces lent inadequate support to his ground operations. Anvil came up, and Montgomery raised a series of objections, which could not have pleased the supreme commander. They also discussed the command structure. As Montgomery reported to Brooke, he convinced Eisenhower to leave the ground campaign in his hands. "I have then explained that if he forms a US Army Group, and SHAEF wants to take direct charge of the battle, he himself must come over here and devote his whole and undivided attention to the battle. Any idea that he could run the land battle from England, or could do it in his spare time, would be playing with fire." Montgomery assured the CIGS, "Eisenhower himself has, I fancy, no delusions on the subject."[55] He fancied wrong.

Both Tedder and Smith pushed Eisenhower to assume ground command. Smith fleshed out the advance command post headquarters in
Portsmouth and readied it for a move to France. Beginning on 1 July
Smith worked out of the forward headquarters, taking his division chiefs
but leaving Morgan and the assistant heads at Widewing. "We have been
moving," Smith reported on 3 July, "and are now swimming in the mud
at the Advance Command Post. Since I am always happy when dirty,
the place fits me to a T."[56] A number of factors explain why Eisenhower
could not exert field command. Initially, he could take only a skeleton
staff with him, and given the communications problems, he would be
out of direct contact with Washington. In fact, Bushy Park never possessed a direct communication link with Washington, which was why
Smith had to leave much of his secretariat in London.[57] Churchill might
have retreated on Anvil, but as Eisenhower guessed correctly, he had not
surrendered. As he explained to Butcher, if he became the ground commander, who would serve as supreme commander? Tedder and Smith's
real motive stemmed from their desire to remove Montgomery's hand
from the operational tiller.

Before Eisenhower returned to Bushy Park on 5 July, he had already
decided that Montgomery would not get Caen; nor did Bradley's attacks
prosper. In a telephone conversation with Churchill, Eisenhower grumbled about Montgomery's refusal to take risks. Eisenhower's complaints
produced a stormy session between an equally impatient prime minister
and Brooke. "I lost my temper," Brooke recorded, "and started one of
the heaviest thunderstorms that we had." An infuriated prime minister
abused Montgomery in front of the War Cabinet. Operations were not
going fast enough to please Churchill. "Apparently Eisenhower had said
that [Montgomery] was over-cautious. I flared up and asked him if he
could not trust his generals for five minutes instead of belittling them."[58]

On 6 July Eisenhower met with Smith and Tedder and discussed
Montgomery's assertion that the air forces lacked vigor in supporting
the ground forces. Nobody understood joint ground-air operations better than Montgomery, who now enjoyed much improved relations with
Leigh-Mallory. His problems were with Stansmore, RAF headquarters.
Eisenhower had first raised the possibility of employing the strategic air
forces in an operational role in his telegram to Montgomery wishing
him luck in Epsom. Montgomery seized on the offer, and Bomber Command reluctantly agreed to employ the bombers in Charnwood. Senior
British airmen openly criticized Montgomery's slow progress. Tedder
"agreed with Coningham that the Army did not seem prepared to fight
its own battles." Returning from France, Portal informed Tedder that

"the problem was Montgomery, who could be neither removed nor moved to action." Smith joined Tedder in requesting Eisenhower to dispatch a letter to Montgomery "which would tell Montgomery tactfully to get moving." The timing appeared particularly ill-advised, with Charnwood set for the next day, and points toward other motives. If Charnwood produced only marginal gains and Eisenhower decided to push for Montgomery's relief, a "get moving" letter would offer written support for doing so. A smoldering Eisenhower directed Smith to take care of it; Smith handed the job to Whiteley.[59]

The letter defended the record of the air forces in gaining air supremacy and in their support of ground operations. "Through Coningham [commanding Second Tactical Air Force] and [VAM Harry] Broadhurst [commanding No. 83 Group RAF] there is available all the air that could be used." The real problem centered on the need for elbow room in the lodgment area. The buildup remained lethargic and would remain so until additional ports became available. It continued by saying that SHAEF understood "your plan for generally holding firmly with your left, attracting thereto all of the enemy armor, while your right pushes down the Peninsula and threatens the rear and flank of the forces facing the Second British Army." SHAEF intelligence had detected the deployment of infantry opposite Montgomery, "allowing the enemy to withdraw certain Panzer elements for re-grouping and establishing of a reserve." Time was vital; the Allies could not allow the Germans any respite that would give them the opportunity to concentrate forces and launch a concerted counteroffensive against a still shallow beachhead. Not so tactfully, the communication pointed out, "We have not yet attempted a major full-dress attack on the left flank supported by everything we could bring to bear." Circumstances had prevented Smith from visiting Montgomery's headquarters on his last quick visit to the lodgment. Knowing how Montgomery felt about visitors to his tactical headquarters in the midst of battle, Whiteley carefully suggested that Smith might come over. "If you get a chance to talk to Beedle [sic], please give him any views you have on these matters, so whatever duties or planning may devolve on [this] headquarters can be expeditiously carried out."[60] At any time Eisenhower could have simply sent Smith to Montgomery's headquarters, but he never did.

Charnwood's objectives called for Anglo-Canadian forces—three infantry divisions and three armored brigades—to clear Caen up to the Orne and, if possible, secure bridgeheads south of the river. The massive firepower of three waves of medium and heavy bombers and naval gunfire, including the 15- and 16-inch guns of the monitor *Roberts* and the battleship *Rodney*, preceded the assault. In the first day of the operation, Montgomery replied to SHAEF's letter, reporting, "I think the battle is going very well." Second Army could not break out in the east, but it could "set alight" the eastern sector. He pointedly issued no invitation to Smith.[61] On 10 July Montgomery launched another thrust (Jupiter) that succeeded in taking Caen north of the river.

At this juncture, Montgomery indicated his intentions to attack in the east not only to mask Bradley's move through the bocage but also as cover for the Americans to stage the main effort in the west.[62] In mid-June Montgomery developed a plan calling for First Army to breach the German defenses between St. Lô and Coutances and initiate two thrusts, one pointed to Vire and Mortain and the other to Villedieu and Avranches. Toward the end of June planners in SHAEF and Twenty-first Army Group worked on a series of studies based on two suppositions: a stalemated Neptune and an accelerated Overlord. The impetus for what became Operation Cobra—the American breakout plan—came from Twenty-first Army Group's prior plan for sealing the Brittany peninsula, which gained renewed impetus with the development of alternative plans in the event Neptune stalled. On 21 June Montgomery and Bradley agreed with SHAEF that all efforts should focus solely on staging a breakthrough from the lodgement area. Montgomery's staff dusted off their breakthrough plan and, in response to SHAEF's call for additional planning to exploit any sudden degradation of German resistance, developed Lucky Strike, calling for a wide envelopment beyond the Seine. Lucky Strike appeared to be wishful thinking at the end of June; opening the Brittany ports—particularly Brest and the Quiberon Bay area—remained the single most vital strategic consideration. Without the early capture and development of Atlantic ports, the entire American buildup would be adversely affected. Planners in SHAEF, Twenty-first Army Group, Bradley's First Army Group, ComZ's FECZ, and Patton's Third Army all played roles in developing plans for Chastity, a scheme to create a giant artificial anchorage in Quiberon Bay, and subsidiary amphibious and airborne operations for opening the Brittany ports. Eisenhower asked that Smith expedite planning "involving every likely objective" in Brittany.[63] Achieving a breakout in the American sector, sealing Brittany, and opening the ports featured largest in Allied thinking.

Eisenhower did his best to steer clear of logistics and manpower details, but the serious supply and replacement problems in Normandy required his attention. Once again he sent Hughes, his primary trouble-shooter and fixer, to First Army. The basic problem revolved around the unsettled question of who commanded the supply echelons in Normandy. On 4 July Hughes composed a list of discussion points to broach with Eisenhower. Heading Hughes's list was "the proposed organization of Theater . . . organization of the Communication Zone as an entity, and the necessity for defining the problems which will be handled by the Theater Commander and hence by SHAEF." Second, he pointed to Barker's proposed organization of a theater manpower command, the need to establish firm replacement guidelines, and the appointment of a senior officer to command the replacement system. After several trips to the American enclave, Hughes complained that neither Bradley nor Lee (nor their staffs) knew the scope of their responsibilities under Smith's 6 June directive. Finally, Hughes recommended that Smith be removed as chief of staff in ETO.[64]

On 5 and 6 July Eisenhower held a series of meetings with Smith, Gale, Lee, Hughes, Barker, and Crawford. He turned to Hughes for an impartial estimate. The central difficulty, according to Hughes, stemmed from Bradley's insistence on defending his territorial command. The plan hung on "the acquisition of territory and phase lines which have not been attained." Bradley's refusal to establish an army rear boundary prevented Lee from exercising direct command. Given the narrow beachhead, supply echelons began stacking up. Anxious to get into the action, Lee moved an advance headquarters to Valognes, just south of Cherbourg. Bradley made no secret of his displeasure; even Lee admitted that his presence "crowded First Army."[65] Hughes recommended the formation of First Army Group and the extension of supply and manpower responsibilities to ComZ. "I am convinced," Hughes told Eisenhower, "that more experienced [supply] men should be gotten into the picture." Patton, no admirer of Lee, agreed. He pointed out to Eisenhower that American combat troops in Normandy exceeded 500,000, and they were "under the command of an army commander and staff who are not trained to handle the big business now existing across the Channel"; he proposed the establishment of an army rear.[66] Eisenhower plaintively told Hughes that he had discussed the problem with Bradley and got nowhere. Bradley never camouflaged his mistrust of Lee. "I would have turned it over long ago," Bradley informed Eisenhower, "if Everett Hughes had been in command of CZ." Eisenhower issued no orders.[67] Eisenhower instructed Hughes to fly back to Bradley's headquarters and hammer out a deal. Armed with instructions from Smith, Hughes enumerated the relative spheres of responsibility between Bradley and Lee's command. Bradley signed the document but made no promise about fixing a rear boundary.[68]

Ramsay and Gale, who thought the buildup would collapse without a deepwater port, stressed the importance of securing the Brittany harbors and increased the pressure on Eisenhower to push Bradley for a breakout in the western sector.[69] The chances for that looked dim. From 3 to 9 July Bradley's attempt to fight through the bocage country made slow progress as casualties mounted, but he succeeded in developing a wide jump-off line for Cobra.

With the fighting at Caen winding down on 10 July, Montgomery met with Bradley and Dempsey and approved Cobra, telling Dempsey to "go on hitting: drawing the German strength, especially the armour, onto yourself—so as to ease the way for Brad." Later that day he issued another directive that stated his first priority, as had virtually all his M-telegrams: "We must get the Brittany Peninsula. From an administrative point of view this is essential; if we do NOT get it we will be greatly handicapped in developing our full potential." He asserted, "I am very anxious to secure the Quiberon Bay area so that we can get a move on with developing it for our administrative needs." He hoped that by the first week in August "Eight US Corps will have turned the corner and be headed for RENNES and ST MALO. This operation is being planned." Montgomery advised, "The great thing now is to get First and Third US Armies up to a good strength, and to get them cracking on the southward thrust on the western flank, and then to turn Patton westward into the Brittany Peninsula."[70] Senior American officers always ridiculed Montgomery for his seeming obsession with "tidying his administration," and many in SHAEF, Eisenhower and Smith included, wrongly saw his conversion to an emphasis on the western drive and the Brittany ports as cover for his failures in the east. This view received a boost when Montgomery redirected Dempsey toward the southwest in direct support of Bradley, away from Caen.

With Cobra now in the works, Bradley experienced no change of heart regarding the turnover of supply and replacements to Lee. Smith went over to First Army headquarters in an effort to inveigle Bradley into relenting on the issue of the rear boundary. Again Bradley refused, and an unhappy Smith returned to Portsmouth. Patton had begun setting up his Third Army headquarters in France, reopening the old question of command spheres. Smith decided to issue a new SHAEF directive and instructed Bull to write it.

On 14 July Eisenhower invited Smith and Hughes for lunch. It opened on a somber note. Earlier that day they heard that assistant division commander Theodore Roosevelt, son of the former president, had died of a heart attack. Roosevelt and Smith had developed a warm relationship in North Africa. Roosevelt had a checkered history and a fondness for the bottle and had lost his position as deputy commander in his beloved First Infantry Division—the unit he had served in during World War I. He buttered up Smith; they exchanged books, mostly detective stories and westerns, and met for drinks. Beetle told him that since Roosevelt seemed so anxious to "get his head blown off," he would see what he could do about getting him a combat post.[71] As deputy division commander of the Fourth Infantry, Roosevelt tried his best to fulfill Smith's prediction; he was the only U.S. general who landed with the first wave on Utah Beach, which won him a posthumous Medal of Honor.

Discussions then turned to the theater and logistics commands. Illustrative of the attention he paid to logistical matters, Eisenhower admitted he had not even read Smith's 6 June directive and had no idea it was in effect. Eisenhower again reiterated that he reserved the right as theater commander to delegate responsibilities as he saw fit, and although he desired no deputy theater commander, he felt secure in farming out all theater responsibilities to Lee's headquarters. Hughes commented, "So lots of fuss and no change." Eisenhower accused Hughes of being egotistical. "Beadle [sic] in joy," noted Hughes. "Says it's all true!"[72]

Later that day Bull completed his task and complained that the existing directives—the ones written and issued by Smith on 6 and 7 June—"to a very large extent . . . abdicated most" of the theater commander's responsibilities to Lee. Since Eisenhower insisted that Lee continue in that role, Smith read Bull's directive over carefully and, still not prepared to surrender, added the phrase "pending the establishment of SHAEF on the Continent." Smith immediately published the new instructions.[73]

Predictably, Smith's latest directive satisfied nobody. Hughes thought it "the worst yet." Eisenhower considered the matter closed and grew intensely irritated when the question refused to die. Given everything else going on—the failures to break through on both fronts and the resultant friction between SHAEF and Montgomery—Eisenhower simply did not want to be bothered. He attributed the trouble to a "personal wrangle between General Lee and Everett Hughes, on the one hand, and Beetle and his staff, on the other."[74] Eisenhower finally took the time and read the 6 June and 14 July directives. As Eisenhower informed Smith that day, "I am not definitely satisfied with [the latest order] and I am personally dictating" a new draft. Amazingly, Eisenhower's design deviated not at all from Smith's order of 6 June, although Eisenhower did clarify the language. When Bradley activated Twelfth Army Group— the designation changed to avoid confusion with First Army—that headquarters stood on an equal footing with Lee as ComZ commander and Spaatz in command of U.S. Army Air Forces in Europe. Lee would control theater duties as Eisenhower's proxy but not his deputy. Eisenhower, in exercising functions reserved to himself—which he never specified—would utilize the American element of SHAEF. "This subject has been under discussion long enough," he emphasized to Smith. He intended to go over to France the next day. In the interim, Smith could talk to Crawford and Bull "and any members of the Staff you want . . . but I will not entertain for a moment the idea of publishing a long-winded series of papers on the subject." When he returned, Eisenhower would give final approval and publish the order. He pointed out that the army issued field manuals covering these issues; they should suffice. The problem was that the field manuals, where they existed (the Transportation Corps conducted operations throughout the entire war in Europe without one), proved wholly inadequate, especially in terms of coordinating actions across agency lines. All Eisenhower wanted was an end to the infighting over chains of responsibility.[75]

That evening, 18 July, Eisenhower invited Lee and Hughes to dinner. They talked Eisenhower out of confirming "his cockeyed order on theater organization." Butcher noted, "Ike said he would re-draft the thing, using nice words but meaning practically the same thing." Eisenhower "seemed miffed . . . Lee and Hughes stayed for dinner, and didn't exactly exuberate happiness." He told Butcher he would call in Smith and they would "draft the thing right once and for all, damned if he wasn't tired of the subject."[76]

Later that night Tedder telephoned Eisenhower and pronounced Montgomery's latest attempt at cracking open the Caen front (Operation Goodwood), begun just that morning, a failure. Tedder categorized Montgomery's attacks as "company exercises," the penny-packet approach Montgomery had railed about in North Africa. "Dempsey's advance," Tedder continued, "had been rigidly restricted." According to Butcher, Tedder claimed that "the BCOS would support any recommendation that Ike might care to make, meaning that if Ike wanted to sack Monty . . . he would have no trouble, officially."[77] The supply command imbroglio vanished.

Smith no longer talked in terms of Montgomery's "triumph of leadership." When Montgomery petitioned for SHAEF's intercession with the RAF, Smith interpreted it as indicative that the ground commander possessed no confidence in senior British air officers. In a similar vein, he reacted sharply when Montgomery complained the navies needed to expedite the clearing of Cherbourg. In a marginal note on Montgomery's M-511, Smith wrote, "I think this is a rather foolish message and I suggest you ask Monty if he's short of any supplies."[78] He became increasingly and openly vocal in his criticisms of Montgomery.

Dempsey found fighting in the bocage as unproductive as Bradley had, and he asked for Montgomery's permission to shift the focus back to Caen. Montgomery approved the request and decided on an expanded version of Charnwood—this time, east of the Orne. Cheered by the news, Eisenhower and Smith went to bat for Montgomery with the air force commands, leveraging the strategic air forces to lend all assistance to Goodwood.[79] The new offensive, timed in conjunction with Cobra, opened before dawn on 18 July. Weather forced a postponement of Bradley's operation, but Montgomery went ahead because intelligence indicated the Germans had started to withdraw armor in anticipation of an American breakout attempt. The rest of Caen fell, and British armor advanced south to Bourguébus Ridge, where it halted against furious German resistance. Tedder thought Montgomery had played SHAEF "for suckers. I do not believe there was the slightest intention to make a clean break-through." According to Butcher, Tedder told Eisenhower that "Monty had, in effect, stopped his armor from going further. Ike was mad."[80]

Sometimes given to embroidery, Butcher vastly understated Eisenhower's reaction. He was livid. Unbeknownst to anyone but Butcher, Eisenhower's short fuse grew out of stress-related health problems. Deprived of sleep, smoking pack after back of Chesterfields (he had changed brands), and not eating properly, Eisenhower's blood pressure went through the roof. "Ike hasn't been feeling so hot these last few days," Butcher wrote in his diary. "I asked if he still had the ringing in his ears and he said yes. It has been bothering him for weeks, but [he] says little about it." The prescribed medicine did not help. Butcher asked for permission to see MG Albert Kenner, head of the SHAEF Medical Division. Kenner suspected Eisenhower was suffering from high blood pressure and prescribed a dose of "slow down medicine" before Eisenhower saw an ear specialist. Kenner worried that "some ear man would not only suspect it but most likely gossip about the fact." Rumormongers abounded, particularly among Lee's people.

Kenner examined Eisenhower and "learned that the pressure really is high again," 176/110. Butcher was not surprised, given Eisenhower's "bad humor . . . being vindictive." The naval aide had no difficulty identifying the cause: the "inward but generally unspoken criticism of Monty for being so cautious [and the] desire to be more active in it himself all these pump up his system," which "ain't good." "What a blow," Butcher concluded, "if he should pull a Teddy Roosevelt."[81]

Using his secret cipher, Montgomery asked Eisenhower to come see him on 19 July and requested that he bring no senior staff and, pointedly, no airmen. In the morning Eisenhower had a brief talk with Smith about the theater and supply command business—which he characterized as a "picayunish problem"—and fielded a phone call from the prime minister, then set off for the flight across the Channel. An overwrought supreme commander impatiently crunched the cinders with his heels awaiting clearance to fly. "Ike has just said he's got to get across, if he has to swim." The flight was canceled. "Ike is like a blind dog in a meat house," Butcher remarked, "he can smell it, but he can't find it."[82]

Whether relieved or disappointed, Eisenhower returned to his lodgings. Presumably, Kenner arrived with his "slow-down" cocktail. Kenner did not shy away from heavy doses of sedatives. He had treated Patton shortly before the war. With his wife sick, his marriage on the rocks, and convinced his career was over, Patton lapsed into the worst depression of his life. Kenner knocked him out with some powerful tranquilizers.[83] Evidently, he did the same with Eisenhower. Eisenhower slept all day. When Butcher got him up for dinner, he "appeared quiet and rested, but blue as indigo over Monty's slow-down." He immediately retreated to bed and slept through to 7 A.M., when an air-raid alarm woke him.

What he discovered that morning did nothing for his blood pressure. Montgomery's advance had indeed halted. Eisenhower carped, "7,000 tons of bombs dropped . . . only seven miles gained—can we afford a thousand tons of bombs per mile?" The RAF's bid to get Montgomery sacked started in earnest with Tedder's call on 18 July and gained momentum. Butcher recorded, "The Air people are disgusted with Monty, Tedder telling Ike . . . 'I told you so.'"[84]

While members of his staff wondered what would transpire, Eisenhower flew off to France. First he saw Bradley, inquired about preparations for Cobra, and pinned oak leaf clusters to the Distinguished Service Medals on Bradley and two of his corps commanders, Gerow and Collins. Then he went on to Montgomery's headquarters for the big meeting. For Eisenhower, this turn of events represented his worst fears realized. For weeks he had burned within and struggled to preserve his impartiality. The mental strain and worry obviously took its toll on his health. At the same time, he dreaded a showdown with Montgomery lest he lose his temper and cause irreparable harm to the alliance and certainly his career. The grim look on his face as he entered Montgomery's map caravan told the story. Neither man ever revealed what transpired, but when he emerged, Eisenhower flashed his trademark smile. Montgomery knew Goodwood put him behind the eight ball; undoubtedly, he remained self-controlled but also self-confident. Nobody ran circles around anybody; Eisenhower was not as facile as some of his British colleagues imagined. Eisenhower's grin reappeared because he left with what he had come for: Montgomery's assurances that the forces under his command would continue offensive action, pinning the German armor on his front. Eisenhower also beamed out of relief; there was no confrontation and no need to take drastic action.[85]

Returning to Bushy Park, Eisenhower faced an irate Tedder. Ultra had detected signs of a putsch following the failed 20 July attempt on Hitler's life, and Tedder bitterly complained that Montgomery's failures around Caen prevented the Allies from reaping the benefits of German confusion. He warned Eisenhower that "his own people would be thinking that he had sold them to the British if he continued to support Montgomery without protest." Earlier that morning Tedder had sat in on Smith's conference, where he raised concerns over the V-1 launching sites in the Pas de Calais and asked when Smith expected them to be neutralized. After Smith's noncommittal response, Tedder replied angrily, "Then we must change out leaders for men who *will* get us there!" On a roll, he questioned the "fighting leadership in the higher direction of the British armies in Normandy," positing that Montgomery needed to weed out the corps and division commanders.[86]

Incited by Tedder, Eisenhower dispatched a caustic letter to Montgomery on 21 July. "A few days ago, when armored divisions of Second Army, assisted by a tremendous air attack, broke through the enemy's forward lines, I was extremely hopeful and optimistic. I thought that at last we had him and were going to roll him up. That did not come about." Eisenhower mentioned his cognizance of the serious manpower problems Montgomery confronted but observed, "Eventually the American ground strength will necessarily be much greater than the British. But while we have equality in size we must go forward shoulder to shoulder with honors and sacrifices equally shared."[87] Still dissatisfied, Tedder told a member of his staff that Eisenhower's note "is not strong enough. Montgomery can evade it. It contains no *order*." Eisenhower's inner staff began to speculate about who would replace "Chief Big Wind." Jimmy Gault noted, "The only man on the horizon who could take Monty's place is Alexander." Butcher chimed in, suggesting that "most well-known British generals, except Monty, Alex and the CIGS, are their has-beens such as Auchinleck and Wavell." It went beyond aides and military assistants. Smith later intimated to de Guingand that his name had come up.[88]

SHAEF's insinuation that the Anglo-Canadian forces never pulled their weight nettled Montgomery, and with good reason. As Montgomery fully understood, taking Caen earlier might have done wonders for his immediate reputation but would have crippled much of Twenty-first Army Group in the process. By mid-July the British had already exhausted their manpower reserves. Montgomery found himself precisely in the position he dreaded. Obliged to conduct offensive operations against the hardening shell of German defenses—he had no room to stage battles of maneuver, even if he wanted to—Montgomery faced mounting morale problems in a number of his divisions. Tough German resistance, their superior armor, and the advantages of fighting on favorable terrain—river and ridge lines and the bocage—inflicted heavy casualties, particularly among junior officers. Epsom and Goodwood produced World War I–like losses. Predictably, morale plummeted, especially in infantry formations, which absorbed more than 70 percent of the casualties. Veteran divisions from the Mediterranean—the Seventh Armored Division, the famed Desert Rats, and the Fiftieth (Northumbrian) and Fifty-first (Highland) Divisions—proved the most brittle, but units newly committed to battle experienced similar difficulties.[89] The 400 British tanks lost testified to the ferociousness of the fighting. The five-division attack advanced as far as 12,000 yards from the start lines, beyond supporting artillery range; ran into another German gun line; and could not filter armor and artillery through the congested funnel to sustain another forward impulse beyond Bourguébus Ridge.[90] Villers-bocage taught the lesson of what happens when the armor advance outpaces artillery support. The Canadians had cleared Colombelles and the Faubourg de Vaucelles—Caen south of the Orne—and on 20 July, while Eisenhower and Montgomery conducted their meeting, assaulted their final objective, the commanding high ground at Verrieres. In the face of resolute German counterattacks and in a driving rain, the Canadian Second Infantry Division, suffering a very nasty baptism of fire, failed in its bid to secure the dominating ground. As the Canadian official historian put it, "the best blood of Canada was freely poured out" in the effort to seize the vital ridge.[91]

Montgomery was his own worst enemy. He always overplayed his self-assurance and, in the eyes of his many critics, practiced a studied dissimulation. According to this view, he "promised" the airfields to the RAF and alluded to "great gains" in Epsom and Goodwood just to get the air support he needed. Even the code names for the offensives—names of famous racecourses in England—gave a false impression. Predisposed to perceive Montgomery as deceitful, senior RAF officers agitated for his removal, and Eisenhower and Smith listened. Similarly, his talk of setting the front alight played to the American doctrine of applying pressure all along the line. The impression grew that he had never sought great gains and declined to put in a big attack. All of Montgomery's declarations that everything was proceeding "according to plan" and his expressions of complete satisfaction with the progress of the campaign sharply contrasted with the limited-objective advances made in the eastern sector. Eisenhower and Smith had not misunderstood Montgomery's "hold the ring while the US expands their elbow-room and attacks in the west" thinking; that would have been virtually impossible, given his numerous M-cables clearly stating his intentions. The constant repeating of the same theme made his assurances sound hollow, seriously eroding his credibility and adding to the charged atmosphere in SHAEF. As his final orders demonstrate, Montgomery never expected a clean breakthrough against a defense arrayed in depth, and on the eve of battle he trimmed his objectives, something he made clear to the War Office and Dempsey but not to SHAEF.[92] Making matters worse, on the first day of the attack, Montgomery held a press conference alluding to a breakout on his front. Montgomery intended that as misinformation for the Germans, but pronouncements of that sort—a foreshadowing of things to come—further alienated officers such as Smith, who reckoned otherwise. Equally damaging for future relations was the fact that Montgomery's operational directives looked like alibis for not breaking through, providing grounds for Eisenhower's and Smith's later claims that the master plan had miscarried and "changes were needed in the original tactical plan," allowing "the full weight of the American strength . . . [to] be used to break out on the right."[93]

Montgomery's conception of Goodwood involved the three essentials that guided his thinking all along: securing key terrain features for forming a line of departure for a future offensive, convincing the Germans the breakout would occur in the east, and tying down and destroying German armor. Goodwood succeeded on all counts. Unprepared to pay the blood price, Montgomery scaled back his objectives in Goodwood without adversely impacting the overall strategy of pinning German strength in the eastern sector. Before his wounding on 17 July, Rommel wrote a stark letter to Hitler, claiming, "the situation on the Normandy front is growing worse every day and is now approaching a grave crisis" and concluding, "the unequal struggle is approaching its end." When FM Günter Hans von Kluge assumed the dual army group and commander in chief west commands, he sat on the letter, but on 21 July, as Goodwood wound down, he decided to forward it with a cover letter agreeing with Rommel. "The moment is fast approaching when this overtaxed front line is bound to break up," he warned. "And when the enemy once reaches the open country a properly coordinated command will be almost impossible, because of the insufficient mobility of our troops."[94] If Goodwood appeared to be a failure at SHAEF, it looked very different from the other side of the hill.

Smith turned his attention back to brokering some agreement on the theater and supply command setup. Smith rewrote the directive and issued it over Eisenhower's name on 19 July. After Eisenhower returned to SHAEF-Main from France on 21 July, Hughes and Lord tried to talk him out of issuing Smith's latest effort. As Hughes noted in the margins of the order, "Ike . . . said he wanted no change from 6 June letter and afterward he laughed and said, 'What is wrong with it?'"[95] Hughes did not know where to begin. Eisenhower agreed to write a letter explaining his last memo.[96]

The letter he wrote to Smith is a model of Eisenhower circumlocution. When Eisenhower wanted to, he could compose prose of crystal clarity; his rise in the interwar army derived in no small part from his skill with the pen. When he did not want to do something, he became a master of garbled text. In the letter, Eisenhower identified all the problems. On the one hand, he pointed to the lack of a "common understanding as to the outline of procedures to be followed in carrying on so-called American administration in this Allied theater of operations. . . . On the other hand it is impossible completely to separate American interests in the theater. Everything that affects the American forces affects the Allied forces." He talked about "imposing" on Lee "all theater duties," yet stated "in the interests of economy in the use of personnel," he would "habitually" turn to the senior American officers in SHAEF as "convenient agents" for advice "on applicable U.S. matters." He stated, "Finally, it is essential that whenever any subject pertaining to American administration comes under consideration by the SHAEF staff, careful coordination with General Lee and his staff be assured. This is particularly true when communication with the War Department is contemplated."[97] Hughes expressed the frustration of all parties when he noted, "The man is crazy. He won't issue orders that stick. He *will* pound on the desk and shout."[98]

What followed was another set of long-winded papers by Smith, Lord, Barker, Betts, Bull, and Crawford trying to decipher precisely what Eisenhower required. "It seems to me," Smith wrote in a circular memo, "that the guiding principle of operations is that General Eisenhower, as American Theater Commander, is using the staff of the Line of Communication to perform the usual functions of a *Theater* staff.

. . . Until routine methods of operation are established, this will require the careful attention of all concerned, particularly in routing telegrams and papers for action." Eisenhower's letter explaining a letter became the final word.[99] Owing to Lee's opposition to the formation of a manpower command or even an oversight board, Eisenhower simply ignored Smith's, Barker's, and Hughes's appeal for one if not the other. Faced with the muddle in SHAEF, Bradley ignored the 14 July directive and continued to exert control over everything in Normandy except the air forces. When he issued an order on 28 July establishing a date (1 August) for the activation of Twelfth Army Group—which simultaneously triggered the formation of an empowered ComZ headquarters—the organizational structure under which the U.S. Army would fight the campaign in France finally took shape—an organization no one quite understood.[100]

Long before this, Smith had given up trying to change Eisenhower's mind on staff theory and practice. Eisenhower misinterpreted Smith's quiescence as a mark of his maturation. He intimated to Hughes, "In North Africa Beadle [*sic*] was young, ambitious, [an] empire builder. Now he is Lt. Gen and willing to do his job."[101] Events in France soon proved that a great deal more than immaturity, ambition, and power seeking motivated Smith's politicking for a rationalized headquarters structure.

Filthy weather pushed back Cobra. Impressed by Montgomery's employment of airpower in Charnwood, Bradley decided to apply the same technique on his front. Behind an intensive air bombardment in a constricted zone (2,500 by 6,000 yards), the infantry would assault in a bid to break the German defensive lines and consolidate the shoulders of the penetration. Mechanized infantry and tanks would then move into the gap. Bradley assigned the task to Collins, who developed the tactical schemes for employing his VII Corps, with three infantry, one motorized, and two armored divisions. The point of attack stood west of St. Lô, with Coutances as the preliminary objective.

The delays in Cobra added to the anxious atmosphere in SHAEF. While awaiting some break in the weather, Smith tried to distract Eisenhower from his many problems by taking him on a little fishing outing. Alone together on a trout stream, the topic of sacking Montgomery inevitably came up. After they returned, Eisenhower retired early; he would fly to France early the next morning to witness the opening of Cobra. That day, 24 July, the weather cleared long enough for the air forces to launch their attacks but then closed over the drop zones, producing dismal results. Expectations mounted that the weather would cooperate the next day. At one o'clock in the morning the phone rang; it was the prime minister. As Butcher left the office tent, he heard Eisenhower ask, "What do your people think about the slowness of the situation over there?" Butcher noted, "the PM [is] also after Monty's scalp."[102]

The next morning Eisenhower revealed that, after a recent trip to see Montgomery, Churchill had come away "impressed with the strength of the military situation. The PM was supremely happy." De Guingand called telling SHAEF that Montgomery had "fattened up" Dempsey's attack in support of Bradley. Before Eisenhower left the headquarters he asked Butcher to call Smith, "get him out of the meeting if he's in it," and caution him against even hinting at "the subject we have been discussing." Smith acknowledged that the situation had changed with the expansion of the British push, "not to mention the PM's satisfaction with the situation."[103] The prime minister invited Eisenhower and Smith to lunch the next day.

Eisenhower returned from France that evening looking glum. The bombers had dropped well short of their targets, inflicting heavy casualties on forward elements of the assault units. One of the dead wore three stars. Bradley called Smith and informed him of McNair's death. As in North Africa, McNair had insisted on going forward as an observer, and this time he ended up dead. His death sent a shock wave through the headquarters. There would be hell to pay from Washington. More important, McNair had acted as cover in Fortitude. With Patton in Normandy—his presence a closely guarded secret—McNair had acted as a beard for the fictional First U.S. Army Group. Smith held an emergency press conference and carefully explained why SHAEF had killed the story of McNair's death. Other reports from First Army remained sporadic and confused; apparently, the bombing runs had had little positive effect. Bradley also told Smith of the modest gains on the ground. "A slow start or a bad beginning," Smith predicted, "might be the harbinger of a good ending."[104]

Tedder had not given up his anti-Monty campaign. On 23 July Tedder wrote an incendiary letter to Eisenhower in which he emphasized that Montgomery clearly had "no intention of making [Goodwood] the decisive one which you so clearly indicated." Tedder pointed out that "an overwhelming air bombardment opened the door, but there was no immediate determined deep penetration whilst the door remained open and we are now little beyond the farthest bomb craters." Declaring his lack of faith in Montgomery's plan, Tedder suggested that Eisenhower either assume command or issue unequivocal orders "for decisive, energetic action." Tedder closed by stating that a letter coming from "your immediate British subordinate may be of some assistance in any action you may consider the situation demands."[105] Three days later Tedder came down to Portsmouth "to pursue his currently favorite subject, the sacking of Monty."[106] Eisenhower told him to forget about relieving Montgomery. "Tedder rather uh-huhed, being not at all satisfied, and implying the PM must have sold Ike a bill of goods." Ever the optimist, Eisenhower replied, "There's nothing so wrong a good victory won't cure."[107]

After meeting Tedder, Eisenhower and Churchill met for lunch. The primary topic reverted to Montgomery's orchestration of the campaign. The prime minister proved as anxious for results as anyone in SHAEF. Eisenhower worried about negative press in the United States, especially in an election year. From the United States, it appeared the Americans did all the fighting and dying while the British and Canadians sat idle around Caen—the inverse of BBC reports about the fighting in Sicily. In addition to pressure from Tedder and Smith inside SHAEF to speed up the timetable and assume direct command in Normandy, Eisenhower confronted similar demands from Marshall and Stimson. Churchill knew a little something about negative press and elections and asked that Eisenhower and Smith come to dinner the next night so they could air their apprehensions to Brooke. The Americans had no choice but to accept, even though it meant a late night and their absence from headquarters while American forces fought desperately to break through around St. Lô.

The prime minister told Brooke the aim of the dinner was to bring him "closer to Ike and to assist in easy running between Ike and Monty." Brooke came away pleased; they cleared the air. But the CIGS left with no better opinion of Eisenhower and Smith. Conceding Eisenhower's great skill in maintaining "the best of relations between British and Americans," Brooke thought, "it is equally clear that Ike knows nothing about strategy and is *quite* unsuited to the post of Supreme Commander as far as running the strategy of war is concerned!" Smith had "brains, no military education in the true sense, and unfortunately suffers from a swollen head." Although "he is certainly one of the best American officers," Brooke admitted, he "falls far short when it comes to strategic outlook." Given the callowness of the two Americans, it was "no wonder that Monty's real high ability is not always realized. Especially so when 'national' spectacles pervert the perspective." Brooke offered to accompany Eisenhower and Smith to see Montgomery, but they declined.[108]

While this scene unfolded in London, in Normandy the thin dike of the German defenses collapsed, and American forces flooded through the breach. Never intended as more than a breakthrough, the American offensive now appeared to be an unfettered breakout. Smith's offhand remark proved prescient: something very big grew from a sketchy start. And although the breakout never quite cured the open sore between SHAEF and Montgomery, just as Eisenhower said, it acted as a pretty good palliative.

★ 29 ★

What Has the Supreme Command Amounted To?

Cobra's success vindicated Montgomery and the plan. Before and during Normandy, Montgomery demonstrated an uncanny ability to see "the other side of the hill." Originally, Rommel never considered holding Caen. He did not want his armor eaten up in a static defensive role, especially on ground unfavorable for panzers. Instead, he advocated pulling back from Caen. After massing the panzers, Rommel felt he could drive along the army boundaries in the center with five panzer divisions and fan out in both directions, isolating the beachheads. Jodl maintained that it would be fatal to voluntarily surrender a connected front in favor of a problematic operation of maneuver for which Rommel lacked the requisite strength. Hitler agreed. Thereafter, Caen served as a magnet for German armor—first in abortive attempts to mass the panzers for a counteroffensive, and then to prevent a British breakout. Despite weakness on the left, the German OKW and the commands in Normandy expected the British to spearhead a breakthrough attempt near Caen. They viewed the British as stronger, more battle wise, and therefore more dangerous. Caen lay nearer to Paris, and the terrain to the south was better. Epsom, Charnwood, and Goodwood reinforced these notions.

At the beginning of July Montgomery faced seven panzer and two infantry divisions on a front of thirty-three miles; Bradley held a fifty-five-mile front and confronted seven infantry divisions. Owing to transportation problems, German divisions were belatedly moved from the Fifteenth Army sector and committed around the Orne and Caen rather than on the weak left flank. Troops moved up from the south of France, even though OKW expected landings there. The four earmarked panzer divisions received orders for Normandy, but because of railroad damage, resistance sabotage, and destruction of the Loire and Seine bridges, this movement took weeks—longer than ever envisioned in planning. "Sometimes we released armored divisions and relieved them with infantry divisions," Jodl told his American interrogators, "and the British would make a heavy attack and we would have to commit the armored divisions as [well as] the infantry." Constant British and Canadian pressure prevented the Germans from extracting armor for any counteroffensive or reinforcing the west beyond elements of two panzer divisions. "So there was a defense-in-depth against the British when we had the armor," Jodl remarked. "Against the Americans we never had any defense-in-depth, and had no divisions in reserve. At most we had local reserves such as a regiment."[1]

Montgomery's "crumbling" also succeeded. The Germans placed new divisions in the line and executed shifts, but the total number of troops never increased. The whole time the average strength of the infantry divisions declined, and armored units suffered severe losses around Caen. The situation in Italy and in the east precluded any infantry reinforcements reaching Normandy; railroad transport remained inadequate, bridges were destroyed, and Allied air interdiction prevented daylight movement.

Failing to either launch a counteroffensive or reduce the Allied lodgment, the Germans concentrated on containing the beachheads. After a month and a half of limiting Allied advances, the German high command thought it had succeeded in stalemating the front. The loss of Cherbourg constituted a heavy blow, but Hitler remained optimistic. "Look at the space they occupy now; what does it mean in comparison with the whole of France?"[2] OKW recognized Allied logistics capabilities and, with the British checked at Caen, fully expected a breakout attempt in the American sector toward Brittany. The Germans anticipated an attack between St. Lô and the Coutances-Cherbourg railroad, but not in such force. They retained little strength against the Americans in the vicinity of the breakout: the bocage fighting left the three infantry divisions as mere remnants, the Twelfth SS Panzers had underperformed, and only one reconnaissance battalion of the Second SS Panzers stood north of Coutances.

As Montgomery predicted, American forces took Avranches on 1 August; three days later they stood twenty miles beyond Rennes while two armored divisions pushed into the Brittany peninsula. "From all reports," Eisenhower informed Montgomery on 31 July, "your plan continues to develop beautifully."[3] Even though Smith failed to see how anyone could portray Montgomery as anything but an SOB, after the war he admitted to Eisenhower, "I give him his full due and believe that for certain types of operations he is without equal. The Battle of Normandy is such an operation."[4]

Before D-day Hitler told Jodl that the Allied invasion would "decide the issue not only of the year but of the whole war. . . . If we don't throw the invaders back we cannot win a static war in the long run" because Germany could never win the *Materialschlact* (the "materiel battle"). "We cannot win a static war in the West for the additional reason that each step backward means a broadening of the front lines across France. With no strategic reserves of any importance it will be impossible to build up sufficient strength along such a line. Therefore, the invasion must be thrown back on his first attempt."[5] Hitler perfectly foresaw the dilemmas faced by the Allies during the campaign in France: Do they follow the plan, seize the Breton and Loire ports, execute Chastity, push the Germans back to the D+90 line along the Seine, and build up along a broad front, with Eisenhower installed as ground commander? Or do they abandon the Overlord scheme, delay opening the logistical lines, and take advantage of the glittering opportunity to pocket and destroy the German forces in northwestern France? The second option involved risks. If they failed to secure the Atlantic line of communications—even if they smashed German forces west of the Seine—could they supply and support the advance of two army groups across France on a broad front? Hitler made the choice an easy one. On 4 August he ordered his forces in Normandy not to retreat but instead to launch a counter-offensive aimed at cutting off the American penetration at its waist at Avranches. Bradley spoke for all the senior Allied field commanders when he said the chance to destroy an entire hostile army group represented "an opportunity that comes to a commander not more than once in a century."[6]

The Normandy Cannae—Almost

On 1 August the move to seal off and occupy Brittany had already commenced. Once Patton pushed two corps—MG Troy Middleton's VIII Corps and MG Wade Haislip's XV Corps—through the Avranches bottleneck, he directed the Sixth Armored Division toward St. Malo and P. Wood's Fourth Armored toward Rennes. The Germans depleted their forces in Brittany down to one understrength corps; Hitler pulled his units back and ordered the ports—St. Malo, Brest, L'Orient, St. Nazaire—defended to the last man. Streaming into the peninsula American forces

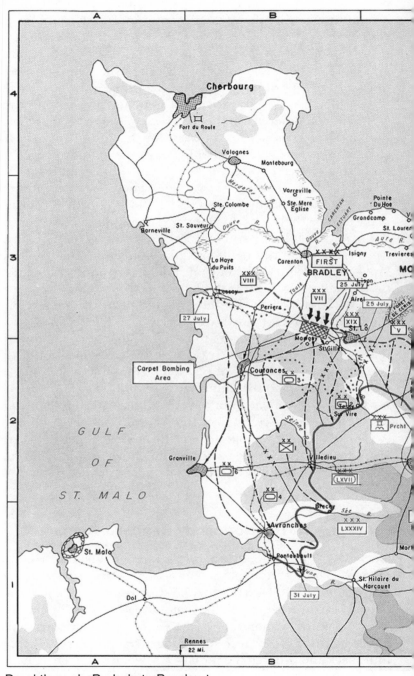

Breakthrough: Prelude to Breakout

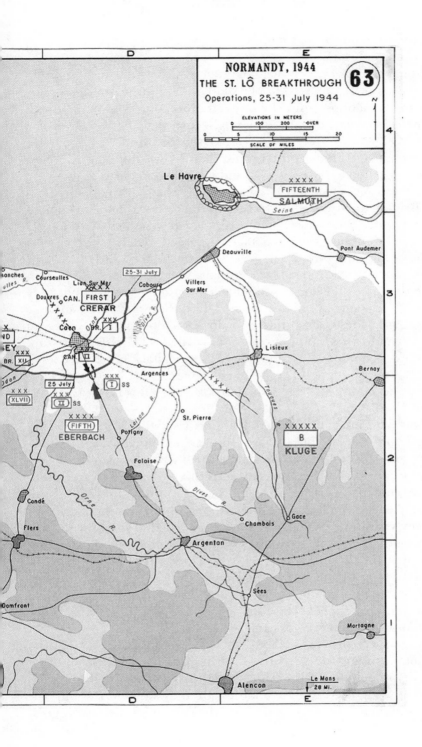

NORMANDY, 1944

THE ST. LÔ BREAKTHROUGH **63**

Operations, 25-31 July 1944

ELEVATIONS IN METERS
0   100   200   ·OVER·

0   5   10   15   20
SCALE OF MILES

Le Havre

XXXX
FIFTEENTH
SALMUTH
Seine

Deauville

Pont Audemer

Courseulles
Lion Sur Mer

Douvres CAN. FIRST
CRERAR

Coen BR. I

Caen

CAN.

BR. XII

XLVII

II SS

FIFTH
EBERBACH

Potigny

Falaise

Condé

Flers

25-31 July

Cabourg

Villers
Sur Mer

Lisieux

Bernay

Argences

St. Pierre

XXXXX
B
KLUGE

Dives R.

Chambois

Gace

Argentan

Sées

Mortagne

Alencon

Le Mans
28 Mi.

faced so little resistance that Patton jokingly asked his officers to keep that fact from reporters.

"Resistance seems to have disintegrated in the Avranches region," a beaming Eisenhower reported to Marshall on 2 August. Any army cook could see the great opportunity looming: if Montgomery's forces pinned the Germans in Normandy, Bradley might turn their flank. "Given the apparent weakness of German forces in the peninsula," Eisenhower assumed that the Brittany ports would "fall like a ripe apple."[7] Now Eisenhower decided to have his cake and eat it too. As he told Marshall, the American forces faced an "open front." He wanted "to operate both into the Brittany peninsula and to roll up the German line." Although Brittany remained the primary objective, "which we must have quickly," he considered "it unnecessary to detach any large forces for the conquest of Brittany and would devote the great bulk of the forces to the task of completing the destruction of the German Army, at least that portion west of Orne, and exploiting beyond that as far as we possibly could." He continued, "If the enemy should succeed in blocking our land advance on the line Avranches-Caen (which I do not for a moment believe he can do) then we would set up a special operation called SWORDHILT to capture Brittany—a combined amphibious-airborne attack north of Brest." He added, "You will note this is a final alternative and I do not believe we will have to mount it."[8] He issued no orders to this effect to Montgomery or Bradley.

The next day Smith returned from a short visit with Bradley infected with a new bug—the "victory disease." From the doldrums of the stalemate emerged the sudden euphoria that, with the breakout, all now seemed possible. Smith issued instructions that he wanted to see Eisenhower "the moment he gets in" from his tour of Bradley's and Montgomery's headquarters. Intelligence sources reported the imminent collapse of Germany's position in Norway. Smith dispatched Morgan to Scottish Command with the view of activating Operation Rankin, a long-standing COSSAC plan for the movement of Allied forces into occupied territories in the event of the weakening or withdrawal of German forces. Rankin never came off; the intelligence proved fanciful. A great deal of wishful thinking fueled Smith's reaction, like that of so many other Allied senior officers in the days and weeks ahead.[9]

Bradley issued orders, cleared by Montgomery, restricting the advance into Brittany to one corps, and he instructed Patton to move east with the remainder of his army. Patton required no prompting; he immediately recognized the possibilities. Bradley worried the impetuous Patton might act too aggressively, but the situation called for aggressive impetuosity, and Patton delivered. Haislip's corps cleared the Mayenne River and pushed toward Le Mans. "All goes well," Montgomery reported to Brooke on 6 August. "In fact everything is working out so much according to plan that one wonders, sometimes, whether it isn't a bit too good."[10] That day he published a new directive. "We will proceed relentlessly, and rapidly, with our own plans for his [the enemy's] destruction," it read. Brittany should absorb no more than the minimum number of troops, "as the main business lies to the east."[11]

Montgomery's M-517 of 6 August envisioned a "wide envelopment," as laid out in Lucky Strike; it would carry Patton's forces, once they cleared Le Mans, to the Seine north of Paris. Patton entertained the same idea but, knowing his probationary status, was reluctant to make the case. The cautious Bradley offered a more conservative approach. On 8 August he phoned Montgomery and proposed that Patton move north from Le Mans through Alençon while the newly activated Canadian army under GEN H. D. G. "Harry" Crerar drove south through Falaise. If Patton took Argentan and Crerar secured Falaise, only fourteen miles would separate the Canadian and American forces. If the Allies closed the gap, an estimated twenty-one German divisions, four of them armored and stalled forty miles to the west (in what became known as the Mortain counteroffensive), would fall into the net. Montgomery disagreed with the decision but never pushed the issue.

Control of the encirclement devolved on Bradley for a number of reasons. For one, Cobra had given him a certain aura of success, whereas Montgomery's image had suffered a serious eclipse after Goodwood. As an army group commander, Bradley stood as Montgomery's equal, and his advisers never tired of reminding him that he was the senior American troop commander. To be fair to Montgomery, while ground commander, he never tried to stage-manage Bradley's orchestration of the campaign in Normandy. As in Sicily and Italy, both generals conducted their own battles, albeit with far greater coordination. As Smith remarked, Montgomery carefully respected Bradley's command sphere; Montgomery "talked to Bradley, solicited his views, and then issued instructions." Bradley and his staff usually dealt with de Guingand. Montgomery remained distant—away at his tactical headquarters—to the point that "sometimes Brad's people thought they were giving instructions to de Guingand," Smith observed, rather than the other way around.[12] These comments underscore the differences in how American and British command and staff cultures operated. Similarly, Eisenhower gave Bradley a free hand. After talking with Smith and Bull on 7 August, Eisenhower wired Marshall, signaling his intention to stage a wide envelopment to and beyond the Seine, with the aim of destroying the German forces "between the Seine and Somme and secure the Seine ports."[13] The next morning he discovered that Bradley had already decided on the "short hook." Despite what he had told Marshall only hours before, Eisenhower "then and there" sanctioned Bradley's plan, commending its tactical soundness.[14] After meeting with Churchill before dinner, Eisenhower went on to Montgomery's tactical forward headquarters to ensure that there were no misunderstandings.

The SHAEF-Montgomery contretemps looked tame in comparison to the disorder in the German high command. On 2 July Rundstedt surrendered his command, in part because Hitler considered him defeatist, but mostly because he had refused, in view of Allied air superiority, to launch a counterattack into the Cotentin to save Cherbourg. When Rommel fell victim to a strafing RAF fighter on 17 July, *der kluge Hans* ("clever Hans") assumed overall command. On 4 August Hitler ordered von Kluge to hold the line and concentrate all the armor he could muster and counterattack toward Avranches. Kluge knew he could not accomplish both, but he also understood, as did the entire German command, that the fate of the German army in France rested on the success of the counterattack.

Hitler did not appreciate the desperate situation Kluge faced, nor did he care. "Again and again the same thing," remarked GEN Walther Warlimont, Jodl's deputy chief who had been dispatched from the *Wehrmachtführungsstab* to Kluge's headquarters. "Hitler grasps an operational idea, without giving any consideration whatsoever to the necessary means, the necessary time and space, troops, and supplies. These are the fundamental elements of strategy which are necessary for success, but Hitler rarely took them in[to] consideration."[15] Hitler set aside the order that the Luftwaffe's primary role was defense of the Reich, promising 1,000 fighters for the counterattack. The orders issued to the Luftwaffe tipped the German hand to Ultra. Hitler believed the counterattack would succeed if Kluge waited for the Luftwaffe and armored reinforcements. As Warlimont informed Kluge, the Führer believed the greater the American penetration, the greater the destructive force of the counterattack. With Patton's forces pushing toward Le Mans, Kluge ignored Hitler's order not to attack until the assembly was complete. Le Mans acted as the primary German supply center, and Patton's drive eastward threatened to unhinge the entire German line. If Kluge waited beyond 7 August, the entire army group faced encirclement.

As Montgomery foresaw, the German counteroffensive, when it came, would be piecemeal and unbalanced. Even though Bradley pierced the

German line at St. Lô, the German command still believed the primary threat resided in the east. When Montgomery sent the Canadian First Army forward, east of the Orne, as a diversion, the Germans heavily counterattacked with armor on 4 August. According to Warlimont, Kluge extracted only one and a half armored divisions from Fifth Panzer Army for the counterattack. Montgomery's and Bradley's crumbling operations at Caen and in the bocage meant that none of the armored divisions used in the counteroffensive possessed anything approaching the strength required; Second Panzer Division fielded no more than fifteen armored vehicles and had no opportunity for reorganization.[16]

Alerted by Ultra, Bradley left a single division guarding the approaches to Avranches but kept two others within supporting range. Meanwhile, manpower and supplies pushed south of the bottleneck. The day the Germans launched the attacks toward Mortain, Montgomery inaugurated the Canadian army's push toward Falaise (Operation Totalize) in conjunction with Dempsey's offensive west of the Orne. On a more negative note, American forces ran into the hard crust of German defenses around the key Brittany and Loire ports.

The Mortain counterattack—too small to be termed a counteroffensive—failed from the outset. Parts of four panzer divisions hit toward Mortain on 7 August with a paltry seventy tanks in the vanguard. They made gains the first day, retook Mortain, and then dug in for the inevitable air retaliation. On Hill 317—surrounded and stormed repeatedly—700 American troops held; from their excellent observation point, they called down withering artillery fire. Adjacent corps filtered in troops. Allied air savaged the Germans. Stopped cold at Mortain, Kluge vainly tried to marshal forces for an attack southeast in an attempt to cut Patton's lines of communication. For four days the Germans maintained pressure in the west; meanwhile, Patton took Le Mans on 8 August and drove north with XV Corps. The Germans attempted to rush a corps north and east of Le Mans to slow Patton, but to no end. They could never match the speed of the Americans. When Patton reached Alençon, Kluge again disregarded Hitler's orders to attack; it now became clear that the whole German Front would collapse.

The race to pocket the Germans again diverted Eisenhower's attention. With Anvil, now called Dragoon, ten days off, the prime minister renewed his efforts to sink the operation. On 4 August Churchill raised the possibility of redirecting Dragoon from the south of France directly into Overlord through Brittany. The prime minister told the BCOS that Eisenhower had sent off a telegram to Washington requesting the same thing. "The upshot was," recorded Cunningham, the BCOS sent a wire "recommending this change and a warning to Wilson that it might come off. All this due to the spectacular advances of the US armoured forces in Brittany." The next day Churchill came down to Portsmouth and pressed his argument, bringing along Cunningham, Ramsay, and RADM William Tennant, the officer charged with operating the artificial harbor.

Butcher remarked that the prime minister was "still a bit pouty over [Anvil]." More than pouty, Churchill had obsessed over Anvil since late June. "The trouble is the P.M. can never give way gracefully," Cunningham observed. "He must always be right & if forced to give way gets vindictive & tries by almost any means to get his own back."[17] Churchill became increasingly preoccupied about the relative decline in British strength and influence. The BCOS, in the midst of defining future strategy in Mountbatten's theater, suddenly confronted this supposed reversal in Eisenhower's thinking. As it became abundantly obvious during the course of the Portsmouth meeting, Eisenhower had made no about-face. "It was very apparent," recorded Cunningham, "that the P.M. knowingly or not had misled the COS and bounced them into sending their telegram to the US COS."[18]

Undeterred, Churchill made his impassioned plea for the Brittany variant. Brittany held out a number of advantages: the amphibious attack would complete the seizure of the peninsula, speed the opening of the ports, and infuse American divisions and materiel directly into the sweep across France. Churchill argued "that history would show that Ike would miss a great opportunity if he didn't have DRAGOON shifted . . . to the ports in Brittany."[19] But Eisenhower had made up his mind and would not budge. "Ike said no, continued saying no all afternoon, and ended saying no in every form of the English language at his command," Butcher reported. Eisenhower pointed to the impossibility of rechanneling the complex operation at this late date. He also sketched out his thinking for a "broad front" advance through France; the Dragoon forces would advance up the Rhône valley and eventually link with Patton. Marseilles and Toulon offered alternative routes for American forces and supply. Cunningham supported the prime minister, while the other two British admirals sided with Eisenhower. "Ike argued so long and patiently that he was practically limp when the PM departed," wrote Butcher, "and observed that although he had said no in every language, the Prime Minister, undoubtedly, would return to the subject in two or three days and simply regard the issue as unsettled." Eisenhower promised Marshall, "I will *not* under any conditions agree at this moment to a cancellation of DRAGOON."[20]

Eisenhower expressed surprise that Smith—off in Normandy that day—agreed with Churchill. The supreme commander's disbelief is curious: Smith had consistently opposed Anvil since January. As Smith later explained, "Churchill was not against ANVIL as an operation but opposed it because of its weakness and believed that the troops should go through Brittany or Bordeaux. We might have been able to bring the troops through Brest more quickly. I was inclined to agree."[21] Smith's inclination grew from apprehension about delays in opening the Brittany ports. The Overlord master plan depended on the ports serving as entryways for American divisions.

For the next four days, communications flew across Smith's desk. On 5 August the JCS weighed in, arguing against any alteration in existing plans. The BCOS cabled Washington, urging the change. Wilson gave Churchill encouragement, indicating that his command could mount a movement into Brittany from the Mediterranean. Complicating matters, Roosevelt was in Honolulu in conference with ADM Chester Nimitz and MacArthur over the future course of Pacific strategy. Churchill wrote an impassioned letter to Hopkins in the hope he could influence Marshall. The CCS solicited Eisenhower's opinion. With Eisenhower in Normandy, Smith wrote the reply. Even though he had never embraced Anvil himself, Smith faithfully outlined Eisenhower's firm conviction that the operation must proceed as planned.[22]

On 9 August Eisenhower met with Churchill at 10 Downing Street. Never easy to handle, capricious and combative at the best of times, Churchill had become more difficult after his bout with pneumonia. Cunningham complained, "What a drag on the wheel of war this man is." The BCOS had completed its review of strategic options in Asia and the Pacific. "The first four paragraphs [were] devoted to the subjects on which we were to approach the US COS & the way it was to be done," Cunningham remarked, "& the 5th arranging to double cross them. I often wonder how we expect the US COS to have any respect for us; we allow our opinions to be overridden & ourselves persuaded against our own common sense at every turn." Brooke was even more emphatic. "I feel that we have now reached the stage that for the good of the nation and for the good of his own reputation it would be a godsend if [Churchill] could disappear out of public life. . . . Personally I have found him almost impossible to work with of late, and I am filled with apprehensions as to where he may lead us next."[23]

In one of his "black dog" moods, Churchill met Eisenhower and launched into an attack on the "bullying" American attitude, portraying the United States as "a big, strong and dominating partner" unwilling to entertain the legitimate ideas of a faithful ally. He wept, cajoled, and, when Eisenhower refused to cave in, announced "he might have to go to the Monarch and 'lay down the mantle of high office.'"[24] Eisenhower had never seen Churchill "so obviously stirred, upset, and even despondent."[25] Less than a week from its launch date—and with German forces now resolutely holding the Breton and Loire ports—Dragoon could not be redirected. A furious Churchill felt ill treated, and Ismay reported to the other British chiefs that the prime minister "was just raving last night & absolutely unbalanced. He cannot get over having not had his own way over Anvil." As Churchill told Ismay, "if we take everything lying down there will be no end to what will be put upon us."[26] In Normandy, the British and Canadian forces enjoyed near equality with the Americans under a British commander; in the campaign in France, no such parity would exist under an American commander. Churchill clearly understood that henceforth the British would be the junior partner, and he recognized the wider implications for his diminished voice in strategic decision making. Making a virtue of necessity, Churchill climbed down, packed his bags, and grudgingly watched the landings.

Smith's attention focused on moving the advance command post to Normandy and getting it operational. Smith commented that during his enforced exile in England during the Normandy fighting, Eisenhower had paced up and down like a football coach on the sidelines exhorting his team. Not content to be the coach, Eisenhower wanted into the game. During that period he made seventeen trips to Normandy. Distracted from his other duties and frustrated by his inability to exert influence on the fighting, Eisenhower wanted a command post in Normandy operational as quickly as possible. Smith selected Tournières, north of St. Lô, as the site for Shellburst, which opened for business on 7 August.

Eisenhower's precipitate move into the advance command post proved to be a serious mistake. Except for a couple of two-day trips to London for conferences with Churchill and an inspection tour in England, Eisenhower spent the month of August in France; when not visiting forward headquarters, he remained at the isolated command post at Tournières. As in North Africa, the move to Tournières did not improve Eisenhower's ability to oversee operations and seriously eroded his superintendence of theater matters. The move provided Eisenhower with more peace of mind but placed additional burdens on Smith to run two headquarters while preserving contacts with Washington; throughout August he shuttled between London, Bushy Park, and Normandy, which pulled him away from more pressing responsibilities. The speed of the American advance left Tournières virtually out of contact with the operational commands, requiring Smith to select another location for SHAEF-Forward. Anxious that Eisenhower assert his full authority—he would take over ground command on 1 September—Smith expedited preparations for a new headquarters near Granville, north of Avranches on the coast.

One reason Eisenhower gave Marshall for delaying his assumption of command was related to the chronic communications problems. "Obviously, communications from the senior fighting commanders to their divisions on the front took precedence over the establishment of communications for SHAEF headquarters," he wrote on 24 August. "Our woeful insufficiency in Signal troops has made it impossible, as yet, to provide for me on the Continent a headquarters which would permit me to discharge all the responsibilities devolving upon me and at the same time take over the broad operational coordination necessary between Army Groups."[27] Smith had located the command post at Tournières on the theory that, as Bradley's first Cotentin headquarters, communication lines already existed there. But those communications connected Eisenhower to Smith in Bushy Park and to British authorities in London; they did not connect him forward. Telephonic communications remained patchy, when they functioned at all. "Once a connection is obtained," Butcher remarked, "one has to shout to be heard." Information from the battle fronts percolated slowly up the chain of command from company to army group "and finally to SHAEF forward—each step being slowed by necessary coding and decoding."[28] To stay informed, Eisenhower traveled in light aircraft to meet with Bradley and Montgomery; he could not expect them to leave their headquarters in the midst of a climactic battle to visit him. He made six such trips in the three weeks following his move to Shellburst. From a communications and transportation point of view, Eisenhower should have remained in England. His presence at the command post served no real purpose.

Montgomery's command style further complicated matters. Smith's contention that Montgomery never really raised his game above that of army command derived in large part from his irritation over the general's command predilections. Montgomery lived in and commanded from caravans at his tactical headquarters, positioned as close to the front as safety allowed. From his forward headquarters, Montgomery might better "grip" the battle and "binge up" his subordinates and troops through frequent visits to the front, but this practice put him out of direct contact not only with SHAEF but also at times with his chief of staff at Twenty-first Army Group Main. In contrast, Bradley rarely ventured far from his headquarters. Aside from the growing personality and national divide, Eisenhower and SHAEF found it physically difficult to communicate with Montgomery. De Guingand acted as intermediary, but he often possessed a less than complete picture of Montgomery's current thinking. Montgomery also utilized a team of military assistants, much as Marlborough had done, whom he dispatched daily on specific missions. He had an American liaison officer for Bradley and Hodges, a Canadian for Crerar, and British assistants he could send to London or forward to serve as his eyes in the combat areas. Montgomery believed that between de Guingand and his liaison officers, he could maintain communications with SHAEF and the other senior commanders without leaving his headquarters. As in the Mediterranean, SHAEF maintained only haphazard liaison with Twenty-first Army Group. Because Montgomery lived and worked forward—and was always busy fighting the battle—he insisted that Eisenhower come forward to see him. This system admirably served Montgomery's purposes—by convention, superior officers always go forward to visit juniors—but it also fortified the impression that Montgomery exercised direct field command at the front, while Eisenhower and Smith remained only rear area staff officers; neither American officer appreciated the insinuation.

Since D-day, Eisenhower had issued no orders; he remained more spectator and cheerleader than supreme commander, giving Montgomery and Bradley free rein. On the cusp of a brilliant success, Bradley wavered. Patton, angered by the halt around Argentan (he mistakenly blamed Montgomery), called Bradley's headquarters and asked permission to bypass the strengthening German south shoulder and begin a wider movement. First Bradley and then his chief of staff refused permission. The Canadians, with their attached Polish Armored Division, made little headway against fanatical German resistance. As Bradley told the story after the war, "Monty had never prohibited and I never proposed that U.S. forces close the gap from Argentan to Falaise." He continued, "Nineteen German divisions were now stampeding to escape the trap," and Patton, whose troops were flushed with victory but short on battle experience, would have to hold a forty-mile front. "The enemy could not only have broken through, but he might have trampled Patton's position in the onrush. I much preferred a solid shoulder at Argentan to the possibility of a broken neck at Falaise."[29] On 14 August he allowed Patton to restart the bulk of Third Army eastward, including part of XV Corps northeast toward the Seine. Patton cursed Bradley's tentativeness and the decision to leave two of his armored divisions in Brittany.

Even the usually pessimistic logisticians fell susceptible to the "victory disease." Somervell happened to be in France when American forces pushed toward the Seine. Not surprisingly, he proved far more interested in operations than in supply. He predicted, "By bold action—no stopping to reorganize or to bring up supplies—we can penetrate Germany by October 1st and finish the war in Europe. . . . The job is swift pursuit. Patton has the right idea—straight ahead, and let the Air Forces take care of the flanks."[30] Somervell came away with this impression: "*Supply is first-rate.* Pipe lines being rapidly built; railroads running, Cherbourg to LeMans; motor trucks in fast motion, with good road discipline and no breakdowns. No shortage of weapons, equipment or rations." In other words, there was no inkling of any impending supply difficulties. Likewise, Lee made sweeping promises that his organizations could handle anything Eisenhower assigned them. Now was not the time to listen to the conservative estimates of planners. In fact, Lee pretty much threw the book out the window. Of course, Lee was not alone in viewing the situation favorably. "Eisenhower very sanguine," Somervell reported, and Patton "has no worry about supply. Certain that he will go fast unless higher command stops him."[31]

The next day the picture became brighter yet: Allied forces landed in southern France. "When I think of all the fighting and mental anguish I went through in order to preserve that operation," Eisenhower confided in Marshall, "I don't know whether to sit down and laugh or to cry."[32] Even though the Germans expected an attack, the fighting in Normandy obliged their withdrawal of one armored and three infantry divisions, half the forces from the defenses already stripped of armor, artillery, and antiaircraft units. Despite that, Dragoon rattled Hitler. He wanted Paris held because it commanded the transportation net for all of France. The Germans started to fortify Paris, but it soon became evident there was too little time to accomplish much; the Paris garrison consisted of administrative and second-line reserve formations that could not hold off the Americans while suppressing an uprising inside the city. The day after the Dragoon forces landed, Hitler ordered German forces first in northwestern and southern France, then in Paris, to concentrate and withdraw. According to Warlimont, Hitler decided he could not hold France; it was the only time he could remember that the Führer did not hesitate to evacuate. Four days earlier Hitler had replaced von Kluge with FM Walther Model. Implicated in the 20 July plot, Kluge chose suicide over facing the so-called People's Court. Known as the "Führer's fireman" for snatching defeat out of the jaws of disaster on the Russian Front, Model was expected to do so again in the west.

The Allies finally closed the gap on 19 August and made poorly executed stabs at cutting off the escaping Germans short of the Seine.

The Fifteenth Army established an *Aufnahmenlinie* along the Seine and exerted great efforts to extract remnants of the Seventh Army and Eberbach Group across the river barrier. Although the Germans suffered a terrible defeat in Normandy, Model still extricated 240,000 troops. Model proposed a line of defense north and east of Paris to control communications radiating out from the capital. OKW had studied the Seine as a possible line of defense but rejected it as too meandering along its lower course. Whatever the case, no senior German officer called for the construction of a line of defense along the Seine. They all knew Hitler's oft-repeated criticism: "Whenever a line of defense is built back of the front line, my generals think nothing but of going back to that line." Hitler instructed Warlimont to tell Kluge not to worry about the details of withdrawing; higher headquarters would take care of building necessary lines into which his army group might retreat. The Somme-Marne-Saone line offered the best defensive option. On 29 August Model ordered a retreat toward the Somme and hastily cobbled together some semblance of a front. He withdrew his armor into the area between Troyes and Chaumont in the hope of counterattacking Patton's exposed flank. Hitler's refusal to construct defensive positions in the rear for fear of undermining morale meant that Model could neither stem the Allied advance nor take advantage of opportunities to hit back. Any chance for improvising a defensive line evaporated. In the south the Dragoon forces under the operational command of LTG Alexander Patch rapidly swept up the Rhône. On 26 August American troops liberated Grenoble; two days later, the ports of Marseilles and Toulon fell under Allied control; and by 3 September Allied spearheads advanced fifty miles beyond Lyon. No German ever heard the term "West Wall" uttered before 31 August. To mention the West Wall before then would have meant "you lost your head." Now the frontier defenses represented the salvation of the Fatherland. Jodl feared the Allies would advance on a "narrow front" on the Paris-Reims-Luxembourg line, crossing the Rhine in a single movement instead of on a broad front with little depth. OKW surmised that—given Hitler's harbor denial stratagem—the Allies would quickly outdistance supply. They were right.[33]

Almost a Disaster: The Great Strategic Debate

As the Allies attempted to close the Argentan-Falaise gap, the top brass began contemplating plans for the advance through France. On 17 August Montgomery developed his ideas for operations following the mop-up of German forces west of the Seine and for the advance beyond the river. As he explained to Brooke, he proposed keeping both army groups together in "a solid mass of some 40 divisions which would be so strong that it need fear nothing." His army group would clear the Channel coast, open the ports and neutralize the V-weapon threat, and secure Antwerp preparatory for a drive on the Ruhr. Bradley's forces would support his drive on a Brussels-Aachen-Cologne line. "Bradley agrees entirely with above conception," he assured the CIGS.[34] Brooke, busy packing for a trip to the Mediterranean, hurriedly approved the plan but began to worry that Montgomery might spark another clash with the Americans. As he confided in Simpson, Montgomery might be the "finest tactical general . . . since Wellington [but] on some of his strategy, and especially on his relations with the Americans, he is almost a disaster."[35] Brooke was not alone in this view. His deputy, GEN Archibald Nye, worried that with Churchill and Brooke away from London, Montgomery might provoke a showdown.

Ismay shared these concerns and made the trip over to spend some time with his friend Smith. He left convinced that Beetle would do his best to forestall any rupture once Eisenhower took over ground command. "I love being with you," Ismay wrote, and remarked on the "absorbing, interesting life" Smith led. "Responsibility and success have ruined more men than whiskey," he offered, but "haven't made the slightest difference in you."[36]

Eisenhower also fretted about a potential rift with Montgomery. In an attempt to salve the wounds between SHAEF and Montgomery, Eisenhower announced to the press corps that the British general remained ground commander. Eisenhower's presence in Normandy received a lot of press. As in North Africa, the press pointed to Montgomery as ground commander, Tedder and Leigh-Mallory as air commanders, and Ramsay as naval commander. Editorialists wondered what precisely Eisenhower commanded. Everyone knew what Bradley accomplished, while Patton's name remained under wraps. Nobody much cared that Smith served as chief of staff. On 18 August Marshall questioned Eisenhower's resolution to delay his assumption of ground command until 1 September. That decision, Marshall pointed out, set off a "severe editorial reaction" in the United States—something Marshall deplored. The chief emphatically stated, "The Secretary and I and all AMERICA are of the opinion that the time has come for you to assume direct command of the American contingent." As Butcher remarked, "The time has come for General Ike to assume and exercise direct command of the ground forces."[37] Goaded by Marshall, Smith, and Tedder, Eisenhower made his first real command decision since that fateful night at Southwick

House: he fixed on initiating the broad-front advance through France, as described in the May Overlord outline plan.

Montgomery kept his plan to himself for the time being, but at a 19 August meeting of army commanders, he discovered that Eisenhower intended to split his forces, sending Twelfth Army Group eastward toward Nancy. Alarmed, Montgomery dispatched de Guingand to SHAEF-Forward for discussions with Eisenhower and Smith. What de Guingand heard would not sit well with his boss. Eisenhower made it clear that he would take over ground command on 1 September and settled on directing Bradley's army group toward Metz and the Saar. The outline plan expected that Patton would advance southeast, securing the Loire. In the absence of any threat in the south, those divisions earmarked for guarding the flank could be employed in the eastern advance. De Guingand requested that Eisenhower consult Montgomery before SHAEF issued any new operational directive. Distressed by what he heard from his chief of staff, Montgomery sat down, wrote "Notes on Future Operations," summoned de Guingand, and instructed him to return to Eisenhower and take along his exposition.[38]

Eisenhower scheduled a major conference for the next morning; he would meet with de Guingand in the evening. The morning discussions brought Bradley, Lee, Koenig, Juin, and Grassett together. Topics ranged from plans for the liberation of Paris to problems related to supplying, policing, and administering the city. They also discussed future operations after clearing the Seine and Paris. Lee assured Eisenhower and Bradley that his organizations could handle all the problems thrown their way.[39]

De Guingand put forward Montgomery's argument, as laid out in his detailed notes. "The [forty-division] force must operate as one whole," they read, "with great cohesion and so strong that it can do the job quickly." The British calculated that, without the Brittany ports, American forces could not advance on a broad front beyond the Seine; with the Seine and Channel ports uncovered, the northern axis of advance offered the only real chance for reaping the benefits of a German collapse. Montgomery not only wanted command of this drive, but he also reopened the question of ground command. Single command had worked in Normandy, Montgomery argued, and any "change in the system of command now, after having won a great victory, would . . . prolong the war."[40] De Guingand soon surmised that his was "a lost cause"; for two hours he made Montgomery's case to Eisenhower but "couldn't get him to budge."[41] Eisenhower said he would fly to Montgomery's headquarters the next day and bring Smith over from London.

Before the SHAEF delegation arrived, Montgomery flew over and saw Bradley at his present headquarters at Laval. The fact that Montgomery left his headquarters reveals the importance he attached to winning Bradley's support for the northern thrust. "I wanted to check up with him again," Montgomery told Nye, "before I saw Eisenhower. I found, to my amazement, that Bradley had changed his views completely; on 17 Aug. he had agreed with me; on 23 August he was a wholehearted advocate of the total American effort going eastward towards the SAAR. He had obviously been 'got-at.'"[42] Another curious aspect of Montgomery's character was his complete lack of discernment of what others thought of him. As Smith remarked, "For a long time Montgomery thought Bradley was very fond of him; didn't know how he couldn't stand him. But Bradley would hold his tongue and [in Normandy] carry out orders."[43] Bradley's days of taking orders from Montgomery had ended. Immediately after Montgomery left, Patton arrived. "Bradley was madder than I have ever seen him," Patton recorded, "and wondered aloud 'what the supreme command amounted to.'" Patton suggested that Bradley and his two army commanders offer their resignations to force Eisenhower's hand.[44] Bradley rejected that suggestion but hopped a plane to Tournières to bolster Eisenhower, fearing that he might buckle under Montgomery's verbal assaults.

Bradley need not have bothered. Eisenhower had made up his mind, and if he could withstand the prime minister's not too gentle forms of persuasion, he feared little from Montgomery. Just before noon, Eisenhower landed at Montgomery's headquarters at Condé-sur-Noireau; Smith and Gale arrived shortly after. Montgomery frequently complained to Brooke he had not seen Smith since before D-day. Smith's nose was out of joint because when he offered to visit Montgomery's headquarters, he had been ignored. When backbiting surfaced in SHAEF, Montgomery imagined that he possessed an ally in Smith and was surprised to discover otherwise. At first reluctant to believe the worst, Montgomery thought, "Bedell Smith is all right. . . . He is intensely 'national,' but I would say he is a good member of the Allied team."[45]

Good team member or not, Montgomery was less than pleased to see Smith. He knew that a formidable array of senior officers at SHAEF, most of them British—Tedder, Morgan, Gale, Whiteley, and Strong— strongly opposed him. He reasoned that the only way he could convince Eisenhower of the military merits of the single front was to get him alone and win him over by the sheer force of his arguments. He bluntly demanded that Smith and Gale be excluded from the discussions.

With all the tact he could muster, Montgomery went over this agenda point by point. Despite his best efforts, he still came off as patronizing—at least Eisenhower thought so. Montgomery wanted nine divisions of Hodge's army placed under his command, while reducing Patton to a holding action. Believing that Eisenhower must remain above the land battle to retain his objectivity, Montgomery thought either he or Bradley should control ground operations. Furthermore, he pointed to the logistical constraints. Montgomery believed that, by trying to be strong everywhere, the Allies as presently deployed were too weak to achieve decisive results anywhere. Montgomery never mentioned Antwerp and the Channel ports, despite an appreciation produced by his planners that argued, "The operation between the ARDENNES and the sea will most profitably take the forms of a powerful drive . . . with right hooks to envelop the enemy and destroy him against the sea." Montgomery and Dempsey rejected the possibility of pocketing the German Fifteenth Army and opening Antwerp; their attention remained fastened on a drive over the Rhine. Montgomery's logistical planners believed that once the Seine and Channel ports came online, Twenty-first Army Group could sustain its eastern advance without Antwerp.[46]

For Montgomery, the debate transcended the question of operational priorities. Montgomery's ego was not the only reason for his petition to retain command of a "full-blooded" northern thrust. If he succeeded, Montgomery would raise British prestige, safeguard British interests, and reduce the probability of incurring shattering British losses that would limit London's political options. Preserving a high operational profile meant higher Anglo-Canadian casualties, and just as Montgomery feared, the fighting west of the Seine rendered Twenty-first Army Group incapable of undertaking any major offensive operations independent of considerable American support.[47] By mid-August nine of his sixteen divisions—the number of Anglo-Canadian divisions deployed in northwestern Europe never rose above sixteen—confronted serious morale problems. The manpower shortage really began to gnaw, especially in Canadian formations. The British resorted to the drastic measure of cannibalizing units to preserve combat strength. And Montgomery had already sacked one corps and two division commanders for being "too sticky." To reap the strategic benefits of the seeming German collapse in France, Montgomery would require operational control over American forces to bend First Army's advance toward the northeast rather than due east on the shortest route to the Rhine.

Eisenhower understood and sympathized with Montgomery's situation. He knew the Overlord plan foresaw that Montgomery's army group would require the attachment of a reinforced American corps if not an entire army.[48] Eisenhower promised Montgomery that he could count on continued American support in the event the British ran into trouble, but he went no further. On the question of command, Eisenhower granted Montgomery the right to exercise "coordination and general operational direction," but he adamantly rejected placing American divisions under British command; American public opinion would not abide it. Not at all pleased, a deflated Montgomery concluded, "Eisenhower in his heart of hearts knows he is wrong; I believe he is being pushed into his present decision by Bedell Smith."[49]

Smith and de Guingand took a walk through an apple orchard and talked matters over. A flummoxed Smith dismissed Montgomery's plan. Whatever Lee might glibly promise, Smith knew that, from a supply point of view, no such drive was remotely possible—a view Gale shared. The Overlord plan called for a twelve-division offensive over the Seine after a month-long hiatus for resupply. All the senior logistics planners in SHAEF and ComZ/ETO flatly stated that any major offensive east of the Seine exceeded transportation and supply capabilities. Given the long lines of communication all the way back to the Normandy beaches, American supply already approached the breaking point. Through extraordinary measures, the best the planners could promise was support for Patton's twelve-division thrust south of Paris if the rest of the army group remained in place along the Seine. In their eyes, Eisenhower's broad-front advance looked equally problematic. Beyond logistics, Eisenhower remained wedded to the Overlord outline plan in which the central group of armies constituted the main effort. And he would never consent to surrendering the ground command, much less continuing Bradley's subordination to Montgomery.[50]

After the conference concluded, Eisenhower and Smith flew back to Tournières to draft a new directive; they brought along de Guingand. That evening Eisenhower chaired a meeting with Smith, de Guingand, Juin, and Bradley. Together they mulled over the various options. Patton offered yet another alternative. Irritated by Bradley's caution and indecision in the bid to close the gap beyond Alençon, and convinced that his plodding infantryman boss had robbed him of the glory he craved in leading a dramatic wide hook, Patton came up with the idea of driving over the Seine to the south and east of Paris and hitting northward in a sickle cut across the Marne and Oise, trapping the retreating Germans. "Mark this August 23rd," he exclaimed to his G-4, "I've just thought up the best strategical idea I've ever had. This may be a momentous day."[51] Patton's notion, though intriguing, was quickly dismissed on logistical grounds. Eisenhower, Montgomery, and all the army commanders save

Patton entertained one thought: push through the Siegfried Line to the Rhine before the Germans could recover. Territory, not the destruction of the enemy, remained their chief preoccupation. But Patton was right on one score. The day was momentous. It marked the arrival of Eisenhower as genuine supreme commander. It also witnessed the widening of the fissure between Montgomery and SHAEF.

But Eisenhower's and Montgomery's thinking was not all that widely separated. As he explained in his directive to Montgomery and in a letter to Marshall, Eisenhower intended to "thrust forward with the bulk of [Bradley's] offensive units along the right boundary of the 21st Army Group so as to assist in the rapid accomplishment of the missions in that area." He informed Marshall, "Because of the fact that we do not have sufficient strength and supply possibilities to do *everything* that we should like to do simultaneously," he thought that "Bradley must rapidly complete the conquest of Brittany so as to provide for necessary maintenance and the accelerated flow of divisions into this theater," while Patton accumulated forces "just east of Paris so as to be ready to advance straight eastward to Metz." He also told Marshall that "Montgomery will necessarily have the right to effect tactical coordination between his own forces and the extreme left wing of Bradley's Army Group." Without mentioning Patton by name, Eisenhower indicated he intended to hold Third Army in a relatively static role east of Paris until adequate reinforcements and supply came forward. Aware of the worsening logistics forecasts, he warned Marshall, "I cannot tell you how anxious I am to get the forces accumulated for starting the thrust eastward from Paris. I have no slightest doubt that we can quickly get to the former French-German boundary but there is no point in getting there until we are in position to do something about it."[52]

Unless the Allies secured deepwater ports—and fast—it would be a long time before they would be in any position to advance into the Reich. Spurred by optimism that the Brittany ports would easily fall into American hands, Eisenhower and Marshall rendered a series of manpower decisions in August that greatly accelerated the flow of U.S. divisions into the theater. First on 2 August they decided on two divisions two weeks ahead of schedule; then nine days later they moved the entire schedule ahead a month; then on 17 August, by two months. Eager to conduct his broad front on an expedited timetable, Eisenhower told Marshall the theater would accept additional divisions, whatever stresses it placed on the lines of communication. Under the revised scheme, sixteen divisions would flood into the theater in the nine weeks between 9 September and 12 November. Given the shipping crisis, the increased flow of combat units translated into severe cuts in cargo shipments, beginning in September. Based on prior experience, there were no guarantees that these divisions would arrive with full complements of support troops and equipment. ComZ's troop allotments already stood far below authorized levels. As in Torch, Bradley cut supply and transportation units "to the limit" in Normandy.[53]

Planners raised alarms. A June study had argued that without the Brittany ports, ETO could support eight fewer divisions by D+150. Now the theater faced the daunting task of supporting an additional sixteen divisions by that date. Without the Brittany ports, Cherbourg and the Normandy beaches would face enormous difficulties trying to accommodate this additional strain. BG George Eyster, deputy ETO G-3; COL William Whipple, the chief SHAEF logistical planner; and COL James Stratton, ETO G-4, all cautioned that the ComZ structure would become overloaded, and they warned of dire consequences if SHAEF decided against a pause for reordering supply. If American forces advanced without their tail, at the very least they faced serious ordnance and ammunition shortages.[54]

The rush to get divisions into the theater explains Eisenhower's persistence in pursuing operations in Brittany. "It is my hope," he told Marshall, "that once we have secured the Brittany peninsula we will find that our total capacity for receiving and maintaining additional divisions has been increased and that we can absorb all that can be brought in to us."[55] Thinking that Brest, St. Malo, and Quiberon Bay were as good as taken already, SHAEF and Twenty-first Army Group canceled all consideration of ancillary operations in Brittany. Later Eisenhower informed Marshall, "Bradley is in position to provide more troops to help clean up the Brittany peninsula," and on 25 August he insisted on "the rapid capture of Brest and the ports on the southern coast of the peninsula."[56] Chastity could not go ahead until American forces held the entire peninsula.

Two insurmountable problems confronted ComZ: the lack of port capacity and the limited capabilities of available transportation. The plan depended on the availability of railway lines leading from Brittany and the Loire ports. After great effort, Lee dissuaded the strategic bomber commands from disabling key marshaling yards, rail lines, and vital viaducts along the east-west corridor; the interdiction campaign cut the north-south routes by blowing the Loire bridges but left the Atlantic trunk lines mostly intact. Planners assumed that bombing, sabotage, and battle damage would leave the French road and rail infrastructure in tatters, but ComZ found more trackage available than expected. The

Germans retreated so quickly that they never systematically disabled the railways, especially east of Paris. The problem was not the amount of rail available but its location. The rail line from Cherbourg could carry only 5,000 tons per day; although that figure eventually doubled, it never matched the discharge rates of the port, to say nothing of the beaches.[57] A second line from Caen to Dreux helped, but only marginally. Motor transport assumed the greatest burden. On 23 August ComZ extemporized a special truck route from Normandy to Chartres and Dreux. Pushing trucks and truckers to the limit, the Red Ball Express delivered 89,939 tons in its first eight days in service, attaining its peak on 29 August. Although Red Bull remained in service for another eleven weeks, its impact steadily declined. Additional problems arose in bridging the obstacles—the damaged marshaling yards and blown Seine viaducts—in the Ile-de-France region. It took five days to move supplies from Chartres and Dreux to assembly points east of Paris. Emergency air supply, capable of bringing forward 1,000 tons each day, could never fill the void. Overlord envisioned the availability of deepwater ports and a steady, orderly movement eastward, affording supply echelons the chance to construct a sound logistical apparatus. Even without the Brittany ports, a reasonable pause on the Seine would have given ComZ the opportunity to put its plans into effect. None of these conditions applied. All the planning came to nothing, and everything depended on Lee's organizations patching together a workable system and pushing enough supplies through a constricting and lengthening line of communications to keep the divisions moving forward.[58]

Even though the tyrant logistics stalked them, Eisenhower and his commanders still had their eyes turned eastward. Eisenhower briefly visited Montgomery again on 26 August. Montgomery made his plea to preserve existing command relations. He argued that command constitutes an admixture of operational planning and the ability and resources to make plans work. If the northern thrust enjoyed priority, Eisenhower should concentrate forces under a single strong ground commander. In addition, given Twenty-first Army Group's dual mission of clearing the coast and advancing eastward—which assigned too much frontage to Canadian First and Second Armies—Montgomery suggested a shift northward of army group boundaries. Eisenhower took this under advisement and then moved on to Bradley's headquarters at Chartres, where he spent the night. Bradley protested vigorously against the idea of surrendering control of any portion of Hodges's army to Montgomery and denied agreeing to any aspect of the British general's narrow-front scheme.[59] Three days later Eisenhower issued a circular directive to all the principals, including Smith (but, interestingly, not Tedder). "The German Army in the West has suffered a signal defeat," it opened. "We, in the West, must seize this opportunity by acting swiftly and relentlessly and by accepting risks."[60]

On 28 August "Bradley and Hodges discussed logistical problems at length" and concluded that shortages had been critical "for the last two weeks . . . with no relief in sight." Bradley's "instructions to General Hodges were to keep going just as far as he could."[61] Far from holding fast, Patton drove east. On the last day of August he had a bridgehead over the Meuse and had pushed a corps south to link with Patch. Despite these gains, Eisenhower still placed precedence on the northern route. By 29 August Eisenhower had given Montgomery virtually all he asked for: the Allied Airborne Army, a bump in supply from American sources, and the right to coordinate directly with Bradley—without having to go through SHAEF—as well as with Ramsay, Leigh-Mallory, Spaatz, and Harris. Although the Allied forces seized vast amounts of French real estate, merely gaining territory no longer interested Eisenhower; his chief preoccupation now shifted to destroying "the bulk of the German forces in the West . . . before they had crossed the Rhine." How that would happen with a broad-front push eastward remained uncertain. Montgomery remained focused on a penetration—break in and break out—rather than an envelopment, although he never made that clear to SHAEF until 10 September.[62]

Montgomery never received what he wanted most, however—a continuation of his command of ground forces or any clear mandate over American forces on his flank. Eisenhower's ideas on command and his commitment to the broad front remained irrevocably intertwined. "Examination will show that there were three areas in which we had to develop our operations against Germany proper and each of these areas demanded a ground commander-in-chief," he argued in 1947. "One of these was the area north of the Ruhr, the other was the secondary line through Frankfurt, and the third was the supporting zone to the south of the Frankfurt area." Each zone required a ground commander with a tactical air force attached. "Above them there was one control only, that over major strategy, and the allocation of the mass of the Air Forces and logistics. That was my function and any thought of inserting a ground commander between those three commanders and myself was not based on logic." With emphasis he wrote, "*It might have been completely logical to replace me* but it was not sensible merely to complicate and encumber the command structure."[63] These were his views after the war, but they also accurately represented his thinking as he assumed the twin roles of supreme and ground command.

He was also averse to monkeying with his headquarters structure. In the days leading up to Eisenhower's assumption of ground command, Smith again proposed a functional reorganization of the American headquarters. He pointed to the problems already encountered in Normandy. Bradley and Lee fought over functions and responsibilities. Close collaboration between First Army headquarters and ComZ never developed because of Bradley's delays and obstructions in Normandy, and it eroded further after the breakout. The rapid advance and the decision to forgo a halt at the Seine left ComZ disordered and without time for a thorough reorganization.[64] Even though Lee no longer held the title of deputy theater commander, his retention of theater-wide control over ETO and the SOS meant he still exercised the deputy's functions. Smith's solution involved renaming Lee deputy theater commander, but only for supply. Theater functions—including manpower—would reside in a separate ETO headquarters directly under SHAEF. The policy-making functions and the task of coordinating supply and adjudicating disputes between the field and air force commands and ComZ over supply priorities, transportation, and facilities would go to Crawford, who would preside over an expanded G-4 staff in SHAEF. The proposed structure would permit SHAEF greater superintendence over manpower and supply and allow Lee to concentrate on the imminent logistics crisis. Smith thought the timing—coinciding with the switch in command—opportune for a restructuring of the American headquarters that would improve efficiency without serious disruption. Preoccupied with, in his view, more vital questions, Eisenhower ignored Smith's argument.[65]

Smith exerted little or no influence on the operational debate. Although he would have much preferred to get his boots dirty in France, Smith spent most of August at Bushy Park dealing with the problems Eisenhower farmed out to him: communicating with the CCS and BCOS, coordinating the flow of manpower coming into the theater with the War Department and air matters with Leigh-Mallory and Spaatz, defining policy with the French, and dealing with civil affairs, public relations, special operations, and psychological warfare.

Throughout August Smith entered into a number of accords with the French through his cordial associate Koenig. On 6 August Smith hammered out agreements covering the employment of FFI units in southwestern France in conjunction with the Dragoon forces, their coordination with air units, and their arming from materiel held in the Mediterranean. SHAEF proved very eager to reduce its civil affairs liabilities, and the French were just as keen to absorb them. The proposed solution centered on creating two spheres—a military zone under SHAEF control, and a Zone of the Interior under FCNL administrative authority, subject only to SHAEF's continued superintendence over military requirements such as the use of ports, naval bases, and Allied lines of communication. The deal remained unconsummated until London and especially Washington agreed.

Relations became less than cordial after Allied forces advanced toward Paris. Against Smith's advice, de Gaulle flew to France on 18 August, intent on forming a provisional government. Five days later SHAEF received a grant of greater freedom in dealing with the French committee on civil affairs matters. But as always, events and personalities got in the way. MG Philippe Leclerc de Hauteclocque, commander of the French Second Armored Division, made it clear that whatever orders he received from Bradley, his division would follow de Gaulle's instructions and advance on Paris. This threatened to rent asunder the Smith-Koenig agreement "in principle" and endangered any kind of political settlement with the FCNL. In the euphoria of Paris's immediate liberation, no little spat over the niceties of command lines interfered. Both Eisenhower and Bradley wanted to avoid sending American troops into the city anyway. Leclerc got his way, but his armored division made little progress—not because of the Germans but owing to the hordes of rapturous French citizens that descended on them. On 25 August Koenig arrived at Tournières and signed the agreement on the zones of control. The next day Smith received a telegram at SHAEF-Main from de Gaulle. The general had already established his headquarters in the city and just as quickly had gotten into a squabble with Gerow. According to de Gaulle, "It was absolutely necessary to leave [Leclerc's division] here for the time being" to preserve order. Anticipating the worst, Smith flew to SHAEF-Forward the next day; by the time he arrived, Eisenhower had met with de Gaulle and straightened out the mess. Leclerc's division stayed until 3 September, with Smith suggesting to Bradley, "The sooner you get it out of Paris the better."[66]

Smith gave a good deal of attention to tightening SHAEF controls over covert operations in France and coordinating psychological warfare efforts aimed at Germany. He opposed breaking up Special Forces Headquarters except in France, where SHAEF would exercise unified control over the resistance groups through Koenig.[67] Never much of a fan of black operations and propaganda drops—he felt they wasted air assets—he suspended Braddock II, a plan calling for the drop of 3 million incendiary packs to foreign workers–cum–saboteurs and resistance groups in Germany, until he was overruled by Eisenhower.[68]

On 21 August Smith approved and filed the finalized tripartite agreements on SHAEF's relationship with the Control Council for the occupation of Germany, but he did not like its findings. The next day he wrote a pointed memo to the CCS, objecting to SHAEF's assigned role once Germany surrendered. "The occupation of Germany will be a continuation of active operations," he argued, "and cannot be based on principles of the pre-surrender directive for the military government of Germany." Smith pointed to the impossibility of SHAEF's controlling or saving the German economic structure. "That structure will inevitably collapse, and we feel that we should not assume the responsibility for its support or control." He requested the CCS apply for guidance and clarification. Smith's vociferous cable was not well received.[69]

One of Smith's preoccupations focused on completing the organization and staffing of his three headquarters. SHAEF-Main completed its transfer from Bushy Park and was activated on schedule at Granville, timed for Eisenhower's assumption of the ground command. Widewing became SHAEF-Rear, while SHAEF-Forward's placement depended on Eisenhower's preferences. Once installed in the new headquarters, Smith knew his primary functions would change. In anticipation of this, he delegated French civil affairs and post-surrender planning to Morgan.[70] Finally, Smith would become a genuine chief of staff to a real commander dealing with operational concerns. Both Eisenhower and Smith were intent on making the supreme command into the very fulcrum of the Allied war effort against the Germans.

End the War in '44

Eisenhower's conception of the tasks of a supreme commander and his headquarters remained circumspect. He confined "the proper and necessary responsibilities" of SHAEF to establishing "broad strategy, the direction of effort, and the allocation of resources, including supplies, troops, and air." Always a stickler for respecting command spheres, Eisenhower left operational arrangements and the decisions carrying out those strategic designs to the army group and army commanders.

To many observers—contemporary and later—Eisenhower appeared limp, vacillating, and indecisive, and some saw him as overly deferential to the British and too prone to agree with the last person out the door. In fact, he was just the opposite. Once he came to a decision, he steadfastly held to his convictions; he proved indecisive only when superiors and subordinates tried to pull him in directions he did not want to go. The problem was not that he changed his mind too often but that he refused to change it often enough. His adherence to the outline plan as indicated to the JCS on 8 May illustrates this point. "I always held to the plan, thoroughly developed long before D-Day, that we would overrun France with the objective of destroying every part of the German force that we could accomplish by vigorous pursuit," he wrote with 20/20 hindsight in 1947. Once the pursuit ran out of steam, "We would then build up our forward bases with our principal ports of entry at Antwerp and Marseilles, in the meantime keeping up an unrelenting series of local offensives to diminish his strength and to gain advantages until we were ready again to stage an offensive which would have practically unlimited objectives."

For him, Normandy provided the paradigm. "I should like to make it perfectly clear that an attack plan of this kind has as its first objective, to which all else must be subordinate, the establishment of a firm and secure beachhead." While "it is true that the initial assault plans hoped for the early conquest of the open ground to the south and southeast of Caen . . . no commander is silly enough to believe that every detail of an assault plan on this scale is going to develop exactly according to his hopes—there must be always sufficient flexibility to go ahead with ultimate objectives no matter what the changing tactical situation may be." The Allies "seized a satisfactory line, went about the business of capturing Cherbourg, bringing in supplies and troops in every possible way, and getting the base that would allow us to make a decisive battle for the destruction of German forces in our front."

Although he succumbed to the "victory disease" and talked about rapid advances over the Rhine, and even to Berlin, Eisenhower maintained that the supply crisis brought him back to reality. "I patiently explained not only to Montgomery but to everybody on my Staff, that support of any campaign, north, south, or in the middle, that could destroy Germany from the West, was impossible from a single inadequate base located as far to the rear as was Cherbourg." According to what Eisenhower wrote in 1947, "the argument was not, in my mind, at the end of August, 1944, a choice as between Bradley or Montgomery in any attempt to end the war by one sudden thrust deep into Germany; I was simply trying to accomplish the greatest possible destruction of German forces pending the time that we could wind up our mainspring and leap forward to the end of the war."[1]

The essential problem rested in the incongruity between his fixed strategic thinking and his conciliatory command style. Eisenhower simply never issued prescriptive and unequivocal orders. Smith knew precisely Eisenhower's thinking; he also recognized that the willful commanders exploited this ambiguity for their own purposes. In their postwar writings, both Eisenhower and Smith declared that no campaign in history unfolded in closer conformity to design than Overlord did—extraordinary assertions, given their marked irritation at Montgomery's claim that all went according to plan in Normandy. Throughout the planning phase for Overlord, both men harked back to their days at Leavenworth. "I know of no single year in my whole service," wrote Eisenhower in February 1944, "that I go back to in my memories more than my student year at Leavenworth."[2] Smith went even further, admitting that the exegesis of the advance through France lay in the Leavenworth command course, especially the study of the Schlieffen Plan. Both men found it ironic that the Allies intended to employ a massive broad-front advance through France as the preliminary to a great "sickle-cut" envelopment of the Ruhr. "This general plan, carefully outlined at staff meetings before

D-Day," Eisenhower maintained, "was never abandoned, even momentarily throughout the campaign."[3]

That Eisenhower maintained fidelity with his strategic concepts appears incontrovertible. That his trouble-brokering command style handicapped him in managing the likes of Montgomery, Bradley, and Patton is equally clear. Eisenhower received virtually no censure for not opening the Brittany ports or not halting on the Seine because everyone succumbed—including Somervell and Lee—to the irresistible allure of the siren song of the Rhine.[4] Eisenhower endeavored to exploit the open warfare situation that existed in September. He recognized the biggest strategic prizes lay in the north; he "did everything that was humanly possible to support Montgomery's attack in those days, but never for one instant at the cost of complete inaction throughout the remainder of the front." Montgomery, Bradley, Patton, Hodges, and Dempsey, like prize racehorses, all chomped at their bits, wanting to run out ahead. Eisenhower's job, the one he assigned to himself, involved harnessing his horses to the Allied wagon and pulling up to the starting line—the Rhine—in tandem. By mid-September Eisenhower's objectives became less ambitious. He wanted the Channel and Mediterranean ports and "a small but safe bridgehead across the Rhine." To him, again writing in 1947, Montgomery's forty-division "single pencil-like penetration to the heart of Germany [to] compel its surrender" sounded not only fantastic but also "so stupid as to have warranted the relief of anyone who would have attempted it."[5] The spare fact remains that the Allies simply lacked the strength on the ground and the transport and supply capabilities—despite extraordinary attempts to furnish them—to achieve more in September than they actually did, especially given the German "Miracle in the West."

Arnhem, Antwerp, or Aachen

Two major announcements were forthcoming on 1 September: Eisenhower took over as de facto supreme commander in charge of ground operations, and Montgomery was elevated to field marshal. Churchill thought "such a move would mark the approval of the British people for the British effort that had led to the defeat of the Germans in France through the medium of Montgomery's leadership."[6] The maneuver did not work entirely; the British press reacted bitterly to Montgomery's apparent demotion. The press campaigns on both sides of the Atlantic augured ill for future relations between Eisenhower and Montgomery.

The day after assuming ground command, Eisenhower met with

Bradley, Hodges, and Patton at Chartres, Twelfth Army Group head-quarters. Eisenhower was in an effusive mood, "very pontifical and [he] quoted Clausewitz at us," Patton recorded. "Ike is all for caution because he has never been at the front and has no feel of actual fighting. Bradley, Hodges and I are all for a prompt advance."[7] Eisenhower wanted Patton held back until the Canadians secured the Channel ports. Hodges should prepare for a drive north and east—a movement Hodges thought unlikely to ever be executed. If the British took Antwerp and Brussels—they had taken Tournai that day without the planned airdrop—First Army would advance eastward toward the German frontier. After Eisenhower left, Bradley issued contrary orders: Patton would "prepare to seize crossings of the Rhine from Mannheim to Coblenz," while Hodges reassembled on Third Army's flank.[8] Hodges complained, "There have been so many changes in the 1st Army direction that indeed there seems at times as if those 'on top' did not have an altogether clear and consistent conception of direction from which they wish to cross the German frontier."[9] Eisenhower possessed a consistent view and repeatedly expressed it, but that never translated into action on the ground. Nor did he go forward to the corps and divisions to follow up on his own orders.

Flying back to Granville, Eisenhower's light observation aircraft developed engine trouble. The small plane landed on the beach, and Eisenhower helped manhandle it out of the sand. Three weeks earlier, Eisenhower had aggravated his bad knee, and now he wrenched his good knee so badly he was fitted with a plaster cast and ordered to stay in bed for at least one day. The injury prevented him from flying to Lailly, near Amiens, for a critical conference with all his senior commanders, and it turned out to be much worse than first thought. As Summersby later commented, for the next several days, "the great Allied army had no trace of its own Supreme Commander."[10]

The first week of September marked another of those turning points in the campaign. Confined to bed, Eisenhower missed the opportunity to assign unambiguous operational objectives. Montgomery complained to Brooke that he had not seen Eisenhower since 26 August "and have no orders from him, so I am making my own plans for advancing against the RUHR and am getting Bradley to lend a hand." Bradley had already reached the same conclusion; he entertained his own ideas, and subordinating himself to Montgomery was not among them. Montgomery came away from the meeting convinced "the Americans are planning to make their main effort via METZ and NANCY directly on FRANKFURT and the First US Army on my flank will be depleted accordingly."[11] Unbeknownst to Montgomery, Bradley had already instructed Hodges to push east, "not drive north to Antwerp or Ghent as was presented as a possibility." All the American commanders ignored the supply issue, blithely thinking they could "lick the gasoline problem."[12]

An alarmed Montgomery dispatched a letter to SHAEF the next day, deploring the separation of the Allies' axes of advance. "I consider we have now reached a stage where one really powerful and full blooded thrust toward BERLIN is likely to get there and thus end the German war," he wrote. Logistical shortages precluded two major drives. That being the case, Eisenhower had to decide on either the northern route or one through Metz and the Saar. "In my opinion," Montgomery continued, "the thrust likely to give the best and quickest results is the northern one." He pointedly concluded by saying, "if we attempt a compromise solution and split our maintenance resources so that neither thrust is full blooded we will prolong the war." Montgomery forwarded another M-cable, announcing the revival of his plan for a "big airborne drop to secure the bridges of the RHINE and MEUSE ahead of my thrust." He requested that Eisenhower come see him: "Do not feel I can leave this battle just at present."A lame Eisenhower could not comply.[13]

Eisenhower rendered his clearest statement favoring the broad front in a 4 September circular directive. "Enemy resistance on the entire front shows signs of collapse. The bulk of the remaining enemy forces estimated as the equivalent of two weak Panzer and nine infantry divisions are northwest of the Ardennes but they are disorganized, in full retreat, and unlikely to offer any appreciable resistance if given no respite." SHAEF reported two panzer grenadier and four badly battered infantry divisions south of the Ardennes. SHAEF intelligence reckoned that the 100,000 German troops pulled from southeastern France possessed the combat equivalence of a single division. The Dragoon forces faced half an armored division and two infantry divisions. In the unlikely event the Germans could hold the Siegfried Line, Eisenhower proposed two axes of advance: one toward the Ruhr, and the other toward the Saar. "The mission of Northern Group of Armies and of that part of Central Group of Armies operating north-west of the Ardennes," he announced, "is to secure Antwerp, breach the sector of the Siegfried Line covering the Ruhr, and then seize the Ruhr." The Central Group of Armies would open Brest, form a solid front with the Dragoon forces, and destroy German forces and penetrate their defenses, with Frankfurt as their objective. Eisenhower placed the First Allied Airborne Army at Montgomery's disposal.[14]

Eisenhower cursed the fates. A day after finally becoming ground commander, his busted-up knee immobilized him in Granville for most of the next eleven days. The hasty move of SHAEF-Main—a decision for which Eisenhower bore as much responsibility as Smith—created huge problems. Even before the move to Granville, Eisenhower admitted he would "not have even minimum communications at my headquarters on the Continent by my target date," but still he insisted on the move.[15] On 1 September Eisenhower repeatedly tried to contact Montgomery by phone to congratulate him on his promotion. As would be the case for the critical three weeks the headquarters stayed in Granville, SHAEF had to rely on RAF communication channels for connections with Twenty-first Army Group. Montgomery told de Guingand, "I do not suppose that IKE or anyone else will be able to telephone me for months."[16] In nineteen days—from 25 August, when Patton crossed the Seine in force, to 12 September, when Hodges's units penetrated the German frontier near Aachen—American forces crossed D+260 phase lines.[17] With each passing day, SHAEF, located north and east of Avranches on the Gulf of St. Malo, became more and more isolated. "We were sort of silent," remembered Betts. Although Smith bristled at the suggestion SHAEF was out of contact, he admitted communications were "atrocious; the worst I have had so far in any of our headquarters."[18] Since D-day Eisenhower had exercised command through fleeting visits and rapid-fire conferences with his senior commanders at their tactical headquarters; now he was trying to conduct operations through lengthy telegraphs via a communications system that had never functioned properly. Illustrative of the problem, Eisenhower's 4 September directive—his first real assertion of ground command—arrived at Montgomery's headquarters late and out of sequence. Montgomery did not respond until 9 September. The same communication did not find its way to the War Department until 19 September. In yet another case, a SHAEF request that the War Department shift the routing of three divisions from Normandy to Marseilles arrived too late in Washington to effect the change. SHAEF presented a pretty feeble visage.

In contrast, Montgomery's "single front" missive arrived promptly at SHAEF. Smith called Morgan, Gale, Strong, and Whiteley into his trailer and read them Montgomery's wire. He asked each man in turn for his comments. Gale stated flatly that the logistical situation alone negated Montgomery's proposal. "We couldn't move the stuff to him in the first place," Gale later remembered. "Besides Monty didn't see that the stuff wasn't his—it was American stuff." Until Le Havre, Rouen, and especially Antwerp became operational, and forward airfields became available, Montgomery would draw the bulk of his supplies from Normandy. In their view, starving Bradley of supply would paralyze too many American divisions.[19] Morgan and Whiteley derided Montgomery's claims; even if the logistical picture had been brighter, Twenty-first Army Group lacked the drive to carry off such a bold maneuver. Strong made the case for Hodges's advance into Belgium in support of a Rhine crossing. The northern advance offered the most advantages—greater ease of supply, shorter distances, and the surety the Germans would defend there. In addition, given the Germans' depleted strength, it offered the best possibility for destroying the bulk of their forces west of the Rhine, and it led to the biggest strategic prize—the Ruhr. Smith passed these recommendations on to Eisenhower.[20]

Eisenhower and Smith went over the same ground. At the end of their talk, Eisenhower asked Smith to fashion a reply to Montgomery. Smith's 5 September letter underscored Eisenhower's general agreement with Montgomery's ideas for a "powerful and full-blooded thrust towards Berlin," but "not to the exclusion of all other maneuver." Just as in the case of Caen, Montgomery had undermined his argument by making exaggerated claims. Even though he knew he lacked the forces and supplies to conduct his present, more modest missions—clearing the Channel ports and opening Antwerp—he raised the stakes by talking about Berlin. SHAEF saw through Montgomery's gambit. Smith pointedly said that until Montgomery opened Le Havre and Antwerp, there could be no consideration of a thrust toward Berlin. Smith referred Montgomery to Eisenhower's directive of the day before (which would not arrive at Twenty-first Army Group headquarters for another two days), stating that the Ruhr and the Saar remained the immediate objectives. Although Eisenhower insisted on closing to and crossing the Rhine on a "wide front," Smith emphasized that the supreme commander recognized the advantages of the northern advance; Montgomery received control of the Allied Airborne Army, and that day SHAEF redirected the flow of supplies via railroad "on the basis of this priority to maintain the momentum of the advance of your forces, and those of Bradley northwest of the Ardennes."[21]

Smith's letter misled Montgomery on a couple of counts. Eisenhower now concluded that Montgomery had received all the support he was going to get. In doctrinal terms, priority translates into primacy, but Eisenhower never granted the northern drive either. Eisenhower noted in his diary that day that he always intended to stick to the script, advancing "rapidly on the Rhine by pushing through the Aachen Gap in the north and through the Metz Gap in the south." He saw "no reason to change this conception," even in the face of maintenance "now stretched to the limit." For him, speed remained the salient factor. "I now deem it important, while supporting the advance on eastward through Belgium, to get Patton moving once again so that we may be fully prepared to carry out the original conception for the final stages of this campaign."[22]

Had Eisenhower attended the 3 September conference or met with Montgomery soon after 5 September, had he issued declarative orders in his 4 September directive instead of relying on problematic communications and couching his language in such general terms, or had he written his own letter to Montgomery and forcefully made the same points he entered into his office diary, the great squabble between SHAEF and the field marshal might well have been avoided. But Eisenhower's knee prevented him from going forward, and Montgomery's insistence he could not leave his headquarters precluded him from flying to Granville. Neither offered a very compelling excuse for not hammering out a firm understanding at this, the most crucial juncture of the campaign in northwestern Europe. Eisenhower, as author of the plan, was responsible for clarifying matters and shaping events. In this he failed, and he received little support from Smith.

The next day Eisenhower and Smith again dissected Montgomery's proposal. From a narrow military point of view, Montgomery's case for granting the northern thrust priority possessed merit. "Long before D-Day," Eisenhower related soon after the war, "I had decided that the 21 Army Group would never be strong enough by itself to do the job I expected it to do and I was quite certain that the American Army, or at least an American reinforced Corps, would normally be necessary to it until we had captured the Ruhr."[23] He had already instructed Bradley to move a portion of Hodges's army northeastward, given Montgomery exclusive use of the Allied Airborne Army, and granted Twenty-first Army Group precedence in supply. In an effort to blur national boundaries, he stopped using numerical designations for the army groups in favor of northern, central, and southern, a further indication he expected to shift American forces north and east.

Both men dismissed Montgomery's talk about Berlin. As Eisenhower related to Marshall, "Montgomery suddenly became obsessed with the idea that his Army Group could rush right on into Berlin provided we gave him all the maintenance that was in the theater—that is, immobilize all other divisions and give their transport and supplies to his Army Group, with some to Hodges." Even if Montgomery's offensive succeeded in forming a deep salient into Germany, the advance would require the compression of the vast bulk of Allied transportation and supply into an ever-contracting funnel that simply exceeded all logistical capabilities. Such a narrow corridor would invite heavy German counterattacks, and with American divisions immobilized, their transport hived off to support Montgomery's thrust, they would stand powerless if the British spearheads became threatened or isolated. Eisenhower categorically rejected the idea of becoming inactive along the rest of the front because it *"would have forced us to establish a defensive flank all the way from St. Nazaire to the Rhine,"*[24] and it would have prevented a speedy link-up with the Dragoon forces and the possibility of reaping the benefits of opening the southern line of communications. "Examination of this scheme exposes it as a fantastic idea," he related to Marshall.[25] In hindsight, Smith more than agreed: "Monty's August proposal for the single thrust was the most fantastic bit of balderdash ever proposed by a competent general." SHAEF executed "the most careful logistical studies which showed us it was impossible."[26] Smith put it down to Montgomery's obdurate backdoor scheming to achieve his real objectives: control the flow of operations, enhance his own as well as British prestige, and obtain command over a considerable portion of Bradley's forces.[27]

Eisenhower always expressed bewilderment that political calculations entered into every major British military deliberation. But Eisenhower could not decide this issue strictly on military considerations. He had just received another letter from Stimson urging him to assert control. He could not immobilize American divisions, move American supplies in support of a British-led drive, and delay the union with Patch and French Army B. As he told Strong, "What can you do in the face of [Stimson's demands]?"[28] As Allied supreme commander, he felt the pull in one direction; as American theater commander, he got yanked in another. In the end, a compromise offered the safest solution. As the days went by, Eisenhower's options narrowed.

For weeks, each time the German troops belatedly received orders for a retreat into a new line of resistance, the Allies had already reached it. In two instances—at Soissons and Laon—German troop trains pulled into their stations only to find the city in Allied hands. The German commanders never expected the British to advance as quickly as they did. "You had barely crossed the Somme," Jodl commented, "and suddenly one or two of your armored divisions were at the gates of Antwerp." The greatest port in Europe, defended by a few recruiting regiments, fell to Dempsey's forces on 4 September. By this time, Patton had crossed the Meuse below Verdun and pushed for Metz, while another corps advanced toward Nancy.

Exhibiting prodigious professionalism, the Wehrmacht rapidly composed a coherent defensive line. In the north, the Fifteenth Army fell

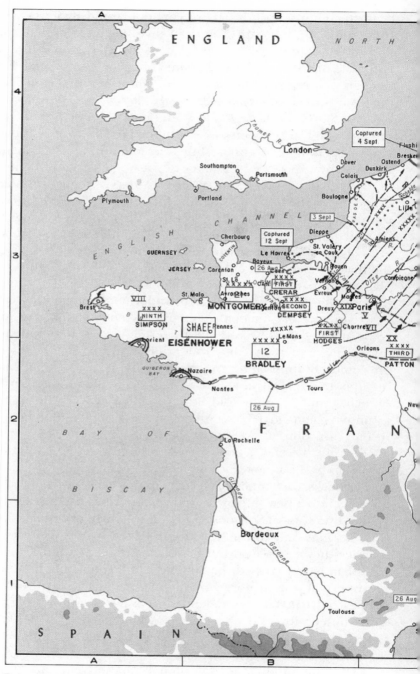

Drive through France: Schlieffen Plan in Reverse

Emden
Bremen
Hamburg
66
Berlin
ZUIDER ZEE
Hanover
Brunswick
Magdeburg
Lek R.
4
Maas
G E R M A N Y
Leipzig
Weser R.
XXXX
FIRST
B
Prcht.
Kassel
Elbe R.
STUDENT
MODEL
Ruhr R.
Dresden
RUHR
Cologne
Erfurt
Rhine R.
C Z E C H O -
OB WEST
Aachen
Bonn
XXXX
Coblenz
Liège
RUNDSTEDT
S L O V A K I A
M
VII
Frankfurt
Schweinfurt
BRANDENBERGER
V
Mainz
Limbourg
Main R.
Trier
Mannheim
Fürth
Regensburg
Thionville
XXXX
Worms
Verdun
Saarbrücken
WITZ
G
XX
Metz
FIRST
Danube R.
Stuttgart
izier
KNOBELSDORFF
Ulm
Augsburg
XII
Strasbourg
Nancy
FIFTH
(Operational 9 Sept.)
Mirecourt
MANTEUFFEL
Munich
ont
XV
Colmar
Epinal
NINETEENTH
A U S T R I A
Vesoul
WIESE
Mulhouse
2 Sept
Belfort
Basel
VI
Besançon
14 Sept.
FR.I
Berne
jon
S W I T Z E R L A N D
2
XXXX
FR.
B
Geneva
Venice
Fr.
2 Mor.
14 Sept.
Milan
Grenoble
I T A L Y
ron
Briancon
Turin
Po R.
VI
elimar
Genoa
Bologna
gnon
XXXX
SEVENTH
PATCH
Ravenna
ence
Nice
Captured
28 Aug.
Cannes
les
Toulon
N O R T H W E S T E R N   E U R O P E, 1940
PURSUIT TO WEST WALL
E R R A N E A N
S E A
Operations, 26 August–
14 September 1944
ELEVATIONS IN METERS
500   1500   ABOVE
50   100   150
SCALE OF MILES

back, charged with guarding the approaches to Antwerp. In the south, Army Group G assembled the Nineteenth Army from the Riviera and LXIV Corps from the Bay of Biscay around the Plateau de Langres, pinning the left wing of the front. Metz offered the best defensive position behind which the Germans rallied retreating units and bought time for the rehabilitation of the West Wall. The fortress city anchored the Nancy-Toul-Epinal-Remirot-Belfort line—combining natural and constructed defenses. Broken units retreated into the West Wall to refit, only to find the installations so overgrown they often could not find their assigned positions.[29]

After a 230-mile advance beyond the Seine, Second Army took Antwerp and halted on the Meuse-Escort Canal. In 1937 the harbor had cleared 57.8 million tons of cargo.[30] Thanks to the rapid advance and the heroism of the Belgian underground, the great harbor complex and the excellent Belgian railway net fell intact into British hands. For the Germans, Antwerp's fall represented a disaster of the first magnitude. Eisenhower and Montgomery talked about their primary mission being the destruction of German forces west of the Rhine, but they and their subordinates remained fixated on advancing to the Rhine— essentially a territorial objective. At this juncture, Montgomery made a serious miscalculation. The day before Antwerp fell he considered the fate of the 150,000-strong German Fifteenth Army sealed. "The bottle is now corked and they will not be able to get out."[31] Proffered a glittering opportunity to pocket the retreating Germans and open the Scheldt estuary, Montgomery remained transfixed on the Rhine. In his view, which was not without merit, crossing the major river obstacle and outflanking the Siegfried Line, invalidating 390 miles of fortifications, presented far greater strategic rewards than opening Antwerp, a port he reckoned Twenty-first Army Group did not require.

LTG Gustav-Adolph von Zangen, the Fifteenth Army commander, occupied a precarious position. Charged with defending the V-weapon sites and the Channel ports, and with little organic transportation and no major east-west road corridor, his army found itself isolated west of the Scheldt. The headquarters diary kept by Commander in Chief West read: "This advance to Antwerp has closed the ring around Fifteenth Army. A thrust to Breda must be expected." A "thrust to Breda" would cut across the Scheldt through Walcheren and the South Beveland isthmus. On 4 September Hitler ordered Zangen to fortify Walcheren, the North Beveland islands, and the South Beveland peninsula. Intelligence summaries proved that Ultra intercepts uncovered German intentions.[32] Montgomery missed the entire point because the Germans never intended to break out. The German high command immediately grasped the decisive importance of denying Antwerp to the Allies: an open Antwerp would provide the necessary supplies and vastly shorter lines of communication for delivering a deathblow against German efforts to hold the northern corridor and the West Wall before the onset of winter. Reminiscent of the Messina Straits, the Sardinia-Corsica evacuations, and the retreat across the Seine, Fifteenth Army improvised a ferrying flotilla and, under the cover of darkness and in the face of overwhelming Allied naval and air superiority, initiated a movement into the forelands and barrier islands.

Montgomery still had time to redirect forces north—the Germans did not complete their movement into the defensive lines south of the Scheldt until 23 September—but his attention was elsewhere. Between 3 and 14 September a preoccupied Montgomery issued individual communications and orders but no new directives to Crerar. On 6 September Montgomery, through de Guingand, told Crerar he "badly" wanted Boulogne "for the rapid development of my plan"—that is, his advance beyond the Rhine. Even without the Channel ports, the British Second Army reported its supply situation as "very favorable."[33] Three days later, Montgomery calculated that with "one good Channel port" and the projected 3,000 tons of supplies coming through Le Havre each day, supplemented by 1,000 tons by airlift, he could reach the Münster-Osnabruck-Rhine triangle, which was his real objective, not Berlin. He reckoned Dempsey could advance into Germany without Antwerp, a port he conceded "may be unusable for some time as Germans are holding islands at mouth of Scheldt." The truth was that without the major Atlantic and Loire ports, the Americans required Antwerp, not the British. On 9 September Montgomery sent a letter to Crerar assigning operational priorities. First on the list was opening Boulogne, then Dunkirk, then mopping up German forces north of Ghent and Antwerp; last was to "examine and carry out the reduction of the islands guarding the entrance to Antwerp."[34] After an army commanders' meeting with Montgomery, Crerar issued a set of six objectives for his corps commanders; the last read: "While constant pressure and close contact with the enemy, now withdrawing North of the River Scheldt, will be maintained, important forces will not be committed to offensive actions." By then, the Germans had begun sealing the bottle on Montgomery.[35]

Although Montgomery deserves the lion's share of the blame for Antwerp, Eisenhower shares culpability. On 9 September he told the CCS, "The hostile occupation in force of Dutch islands at the mouth of the Scheldt is certain to delay the utilization of Antwerp as a port and thus will vitally influence the full development of our strategy." This proved especially true because, as he notified Marshall that same day, the "ports of Lorient, St. Nazaire, Nantes and the area of Quiberon Bay are no longer essential for maintenance of United States forces."[36] "When we got Antwerp so quickly," Smith conceded, "we changed our minds about the necessity of Brittany."[37] Despite the pressing need for Antwerp, Eisenhower stated, an "advance across the Siegfried Line involves a gamble which I am prepared to take in order to take full advantage of the present disorganized state of the German armies in the west." He concluded, "An operation to seize the crossing over the Rhine in the area of Arnhem-Nijmegen" (Comet) offered the best prospects.[38] For the third time in five weeks, Eisenhower made a critical decision that involved subordinating supply considerations to the beguiling prospects eastward. The first had occurred on 3 August, when he sanctioned the move of the bulk of Third Army away from Brittany; the second had taken place two weeks later, with the decision inaugurating the movement beyond the Seine without bringing forward his "tail." Greeted by virtual acclamation, both gambles produced the supply dilemma now confronting the American armies.[39] Smith told an army historian in 1945, Eisenhower "had been the one who decided to employ minimum forces to clear the Brittany peninsula, and he had concentrated on the classic method of pursuit by direct pressure." As Eisenhower admitted to Marshall, "I was always ready to defer capture of ports in favor of bolder and more rapid movement to the front."[40]

The unavailability of the Brittany ports and the Rennes-Vitre-Laval-Segré-Chateaubriand line of supply required ComZ to come up with alternatives for the 24,000 tons a day projected to be discharged from those harbors.[41] Two days after Eisenhower abandoned the Brittany scheme, sixteen American divisions already stood on the D+330 line, most of that ground covered in a span of seven weeks. ComZ—however efficient—could not have been expected to put in place the men, materiel, and transport for 233 days of advance in 49 days. But Lee never insisted that his planners develop a sound long-range program compensating for the loss of the Brittany ports and rail lines. As a result, Rouen and Le Havre (even though in their zone of control, the British handed Le Havre over to the Americans in mid-September) never fully developed as alternatives because ComZ headquarters banked on Antwerp's availability by the middle of October. "The tantalizing hope of gaining Antwerp's huge discharge capacity and short lines to the front," the postwar General Board concluded, "colored Com Z thinking heavily and the color had been rosy."[42] Without Antwerp, Bradley's army group still controlled only one real port—Cherbourg. And by 14 September, the overextended logistics pipeline extended to an Aachen-Luxembourg-Meuse line.

Eisenhower went forward for talks with Montgomery on 10 September. Montgomery steeled himself for this meeting with an intemperate letter to Brooke. He complained that Eisenhower "keeps saying that he has ordered that the northern thrust to the RUHR is to have priority; but he has NOT ordered this." Eisenhower "has taken personal command of the land armies; he sits back at GRANVILLE and has no communications to his commands except wireless/telephone, and this takes over 24 hours to reach him. . . . He is completely out of touch with what is going on; he tries to win the war by issuing long telegraphic directives." Worse, "Eisenhower himself does not really know anything about the business of fighting the Germans; he has not got the right sort of chaps on his staff for the job, and no one there understands the matter." Not without justification, Montgomery complained, "Just when a firm grip was needed, there was no grip. The 'command' factor has broken down. . . . I very much fear that we shall NOT get either the RUHR or the SAAR quickly. In fact if things go drifting along much longer like this, then we shall not get them in time to finish this war off quickly."[43]

The still gimpy Eisenhower loaded himself on his plane and set off for Brussels with Tedder and Gale. Since Eisenhower had such difficulty mounting the aircraft, the meeting took place aboard the plane on the airport tarmac. Montgomery's chief administrative officer, MG Miles Graham, also boarded the plane. An overwrought Montgomery wasted no time; he produced a handful of Eisenhower's "long telegraphic directives" from his pocket and launched into a diatribe. Talking down to Eisenhower as if he were a dull-witted Sandhurst cadet, Montgomery repeated the points he had raised in his letter to Brooke. Montgomery categorized SHAEF's most recent signals as "balls, sheer balls, rubbish!" He portrayed the northern trust as "the last chance to end the war in 1944." Eisenhower curbed his ire, and when Montgomery paused to take a breath, he placed his hand on the field marshal's knee and said in a low voice, "Steady, Monty! You can't speak to me like that. I'm your boss." Realizing he had gone too far, Montgomery muttered, "I'm sorry, Ike."[44]

Earlier that day Montgomery had met with Dempsey, who expressed mounting doubts and queried, "Are we right to direct Second Army to ARNHEM?" Montgomery decided Dempsey was right and raised the stakes; instead of a one-and-a-half-division Comet, he would employ three airborne divisions, two of them American. Eisenhower authorized the increased airdrop but refused to grant Montgomery overall command in the north or absolute priority on supply. "I gave him my opinion of the need to concentrate on one selected thrust," Montgomery relayed to Nye. "He did NOT agree."[45]

"Berlin was not discussed as a serious issue," Tedder remembered, but Antwerp was. Since the question revolved around logistics, Gale and Graham entered the discussion. Gale discovered that Montgomery and his CAO disagreed on the levels of British maintenance. Graham thought Twenty-first Army Group possessed sufficient supply for an advance to the Rhine; Montgomery claimed that, without American assistance, "he could not be supported much farther than he was now." Both made projections for future operations, "which disregarded the importance of clearing the approaches to ANTWERP as a base for our thrust into GERMANY." Gale recorded in his diary that the field marshal obdurately rejected any suggestion Antwerp should assume greater weight. Gale's persistence in stressing the utmost importance of the port to the Americans only provoked a dismissive rebuff from Montgomery, who insisted, "he could not hurry over to it and it would be some weeks before it would fall."[46] Eisenhower held out little possibility of any deep penetration into Germany until the Allies secured deepwater ports and improved the maintenance situation. "We must fight with both hands at present"—Montgomery to open Antwerp and the Channel ports, and Bradley to open Brest—before mounting the left hook. Montgomery made no reply. "I feel the discussion cleared the air," Tedder reported to Portal, "though Montgomery will, of course, be dissatisfied in not getting a blank cheque. It will help ensure that the Ruhr thrust does get the proper priority which all feel it should have."[47]

Tedder relayed the outcome of the meeting to Smith at a commanders' conference the next morning. Smith's attention remained riveted on Antwerp. Brereton, who commanded the airborne army, killed a proposal for airdrops on Walcheren as unfeasible owing to German flak, and Ramsay pushed hard for opening Antwerp. Montgomery's proposal meant the withdrawal of airlift for an expanded Comet, handicapping the movement of gasoline forward by air to support Twelfth Army Group for a bridgehead operation at Arnhem that "did not give them a new port, which was an urgent need." Tedder agreed, stating the opportunity for a quick opening of Antwerp might already have been "thrown away." After much discussion, the conferees agreed: "COMET, if it succeeded in its objective of putting the Army across the Rhine and turning the Siegfried Line, would make the most valuable contribution at the present juncture." Bradley flew in, and he together with Smith, Bull, and Strong held a bedside conference with Eisenhower. "Discussed maintenance of US forces, degree to which 1st Army can be favored over the 3rd so former can go to the Rhine," Summersby noted in the office diary. "Bradley as usual was most cooperative . . . South will be abandoned. Hodges' Army will be maintained to utmost."[48]

After endorsing Eisenhower's decision on Comet, SHAEF received two communications from Montgomery stating that the four-corps "Revised Op COMET can NOT take place before 23 September." After recalibrating the numbers, Graham concluded that Twenty-first Army Group's "very poor administrative condition" ruled out a 17 September operation. "This delay," he warned, "will give the enemy time to organize better defensive arrangements and we must expect heavier resistance and slower progress." The field marshal again protested that Bradley's promised axis of advance contravened the agreed strategy for the main effort in the northeast.[49] Now SHAEF faced the daunting prospect of getting neither the Arnhem bridgehead nor Antwerp. Ratcheting up the pressure on Eisenhower, "Ramsay visited E in the evening, he is much concerned because [Montgomery] seems unimpressed by necessity for taking Antwerp," Summersby noted. "Ramsay plans seeing Monty in a day or so."[50]

As he informed Brooke, Montgomery's letters "produced ELECTRIC results." The next morning Smith brought along Bull, Strong, and Gale for discussions with Eisenhower on operational and logistical matters. Eisenhower insisted that Comet stay on schedule. "After discussing ways and means of supporting flanks, E is sending Bedell to see Monty to find out just what we have to do," Summersby recorded. "Monty's suggestion is simple, give him everything, which is crazy." Smith proved more sanguine, stating his belief that, by combined effort, "we have solved the maintenance problem up to the Rhine."[51]

The next morning Smith set off for talks with Montgomery. Eisenhower now insisted on the expanded airborne operation and authorized Smith to give Montgomery whatever it took to mount Comet on schedule. Montgomery laid out the new two-part plan, called Market Garden: the first part, Market, would lay an airborne carpet on a narrow corridor extending eighty miles from Eindhoven north through Grave on the Maas to Arnhem on the Neder Rijn; Garden involved the simultaneous drive by British XXX Corps up the corridor, crossing the Rhine and pushing on to the Zuider Zee. Montgomery requested 1,000 tons a day supplemental supply flown forward to Brussels.

Smith pointed out that because Market would absorb the vast bulk of air transport, SHAEF could not guarantee air delivery. After talking with Eisenhower the day before, Smith had directed Lee "to make every effort to transport by motor truck" at least 500 tons into the British zone.

To acquire the necessary transport, SHAEF would immobilize three American divisions. Montgomery had already grounded VIII Corps for the same reason. Smith underscored that "such measures are emergency in character and must be temporary," but Eisenhower stood prepared to make these efforts "to enable you to get across the Rhine and to capture the approaches to Antwerp." SHAEF also promised to continue the flow of 500 tons a day supplemental supply after the completion of Market Garden, up to 1 October. Smith assured the field marshal that Hodges would receive adequate supply to continue his advance in support of Montgomery's army group.

Montgomery raised the command issue. Currently he communicated with Hodges through Bradley's headquarters, then sited in Versailles. Given the faulty communications, this proved cumbersome. Montgomery asked permission to deal directly with Hodges, while keeping Bradley informed. Smith could not authorize that, but be pledged to ask Eisenhower to have Bradley establish a forward command post for the duration of the operation. He also assured Montgomery that the weight of Twelfth Army Group would support Twenty-first Army Group's drive toward the Ruhr, just as Eisenhower promised.[52]

Satisfied with Smith's assurances, Montgomery said he could now launch Market Garden on 17 September. Smith brought the conversation around to Antwerp, emphasizing the vital importance of the port. Smith used the pledge of continued priority in supplies beyond 1 October if Montgomery redirected Canadian First Army toward opening Antwerp. Montgomery made no promises.[53] "Thank you for sending Bedell to see me," Montgomery wrote to Eisenhower. "Most grateful to you personally and to Beetle for all you are doing for me." He reiterated, "As a result of the guarantee of 1000 tons a day and of fact Hodges now will get all the maintenance he needs, I have investigated my own [supply] problem again. I have now fixed D Day for Operation Market for Sunday 17 September."[54]

Clearly elated at the results of his talk with Smith, Montgomery told Crerar on 13 September, "We have had a great victory with SHAEF, and the main weight of maintenance is now to be diverted to the northward thrust against the Ruhr." Admitting he felt worn down by his tussles with SHAEF, Montgomery reevaluated the Scheldt question in light of what Smith had said. On 12 September a Brooke-authored CCS memo from Quebec to Eisenhower, but forwarded by Montgomery, pointed to the advantages of the northern thrust but underlined the necessity of opening Antwerp. That day Montgomery cabled Crerar, telling him that although he still wanted Boulogne, "The early opening of the port of Antwerp is daily becoming of increased importance" and solicited his views on taking Walcheren. The next day he asked (a) when Crerar could deliver Boulogne, Dunkirk, and Calais and (b) whether he could simultaneously open operations to clear the Scheldt estuary. "Of the two things (b) is probably the most important." Later that day he instructed Crerar that the "early use of Antwerp [is] so urgent that I am prepared to give up operations against Calais and Dunkirk and be content with Boulogne. If we do this will it enable you to speed up the Antwerp business?" The day after his meeting with Smith, Montgomery's first formal directive to Crerar since 3 September assigned him responsibilities for opening Boulogne and Calais, masking Dunkirk, and then directing "whole energies of the Army . . . towards operations designed to enable full use to be made of the port of Antwerp."[55] Two days later he published a directive to both armies assigning Antwerp "complete priority over all other offensive operations in 21 Army Group, without any qualification whatsoever," and emphasizing that the early opening of the approaches and "early use of Antwerp is absolutely vital. The operations now ordered by me must be begun at the earliest possible moment; they must be pressed with the greatest energy and determination; and we must accept heavy casualties to get quick success."[56]

In the meantime, the reality of the gasoline shortage began to hit home in Twelfth Army Group. Between 1 and 6 September Patton could only edge forward owing to a lack of fuel. "Books will some day be written," he told his wife, "on that 'pause which did not refresh' any one but the Germans." The short-lived surge in supplies—fruits of the Red Ball and emergency airlift—gave reason for optimism. On 6 September Hodges thought, "given ten good days of weather . . . the war might well be over as far as organized resistance was concerned." The rail lines were open as far east as Soissons. The first train brought PX supplies, but the next two carried gasoline and rations. Hodges believed "these acute shortages may soon cease to exist." Both predictions proved wildly optimistic. While Eisenhower and Montgomery met on 10 September, Bradley went forward to First Army headquarters for a staff conference. Hodges's G-4, Wilson, presented an "extremely discouraging" supply picture; there were "no large reserves," and First Army "scraped together enough for issue every 24 hours." Trains arrived in Soissons without manifests, which meant Hodges's staff "can't obtain any accurate information ahead of time as to what they are carrying or when they will arrive." ComZ promised an airlift of gasoline, but "none has as yet been flown in."[57]

Bradley had appeared "most cooperative," agreeing to close down

Patton's advance in favor of Hodges's in his meeting with Eisenhower and Smith, but the next day he turned around and divided the supply allotment at a ratio of 56:44 in favor of First Army—hardly supplying Hodges "to the utmost." Bradley convened a major conference with Hodges and Patton and their G-4s at Twelfth Army Group's new headquarters at Doue. Despite acute shortages, especially in POL, the generals still talked in terms of getting to the Rhine. "It seems likely," recorded the First Army diarist, "that we shall have to halt for a short period once the Rhine is bridged and our troops firmly established on the other side." Patton returned to his headquarters and then went forward to XV Corps, telling Haislip that if he did not cross the Meuse, Third Army would be reduced to a holding action.[58]

After meeting with Bradley and Hodges on 12 September, Patton requested to remain out of contact for at least forty-eight hours. "We got no gas because, to suit Monty, the First Army must get most of it," Patton noted in his diary. "Some way I will get on yet."[59] Aside from sending raiding parties to hijack supplies through "midnight requisitions," Patton employed his "rock soup" ruse—making something from nothing. As Patton related the story, a hungry tramp approaches a farmer's wife and asks for boiling water, which she provides in a dish. He produces two polished stones, places them in the water, and asks for some potatoes and carrots for flavoring, "finally end[ing] up with some meat. In other words, in order to attack we had first to pretend to reconnoiter, then reinforce the reconnaissance, and finally put on an attack—all depending on what gasoline and ammunition we could secure."[60] Patton's rock soup recipe, by his own admission "a very sad method of war making," nonetheless worked, as evidenced by his unsanctioned crossing of the Seine and the Meuse. Now he used it again in his drive across the Moselle toward Nancy.

No subterfuge could disguise the hardening of German resistance twinned with the very real gasoline shortage. On 12 September the First Army diary noted that Corlett "worried over the strength facing him." The next day it reported Collins's corps confronting determined resistance around Aachen. Far from falling back tamely into the West Wall, GEN Johannes Blaskowitz, in command of Army Group G, planned an offensive along the Nancy–St. Dizier line, with the aim of rolling up Patton's flank. Pressure from the newly named Sixth Army Group—the Dragoon forces—in the south forced a delay of the Germans' spoiling offensive. Instead, Blaskowitz strengthened the Metz defenses, fortified the Moselle-Vosges line, and bided his time, looking for an opportunity to strike out at Patton.[61]

On 13 September Eisenhower issued an amplification of his 9 September directive. He rejected Montgomery's variant, calling it "a single knife-like and narrow thrust." Instead, he reiterated his broad-front approach, calling for a "drive forward through the enemy's western frontiers to suitable positions on which we can regroup while preparing the maintenance facilities that will sustain the great bulk of our forces on the drive into Germany." Although he assigned "priority in all forms of logistical support" to efforts directed toward securing bridgeheads in the north and near Cologne and Bonn, Eisenhower consigned Patton responsibility for crossing the Moselle and conducting "continuous reconnaissances." The directive pointed to the primary objective, "one which has been foreseen as essential from the very inception of the OVERLORD plan," of acquiring deepwater harbors, yet he listed as the lowest priority "securing and developing" ports, including Brest. Eisenhower's latest directive contained no direct orders, established no concrete objectives, and allowed Patton's "continuous reconnaissances" in the south while permitting Bradley's diversion of dwindling resources into Brittany, even though SHAEF had already written off the ports.[62]

A 14 September letter to Marshall underscores Eisenhower's overly optimistic conviction that everything remained possible. He expected Montgomery's offensive to carry "up to and across the Rhine." Once Montgomery carved out his bridgehead, "it is absolutely imperative that he quickly capture the approaches to Antwerp so that we may use that port." Eisenhower admitted he had "sacrificed a lot to give Montgomery the strength he needs to reach the Rhine in the north and to threaten the Ruhr." He went on to say that, after Montgomery gained a safe and secure bridgehead across the Rhine, he intended to shift priority into the Central Group of Armies zone, not Antwerp. "The only profitable plan is to hustle all our forces against the Rhine, including Devers' [Sixth Army Group] forces, build up our maintenance facilities and our reserves as rapidly as possible, and then put on one sustained and unremitting advance against the heart of the enemy territory."[63]

One reason for Eisenhower's confidence in the broad front stemmed from a "top secret" letter Bradley had forwarded to him the day before. In it, Bradley reported on his conference with Patton and Hodges and their G-4s. "The picture you paint," Eisenhower replied to Bradley, "is a bit brighter than we thought it was when you were down to see me last." Bradley deeply resented the diversion of logistical support to Market Garden and grossly exaggerated the health of Twelfth Army Group's supply situation. He reported that both Hodges and Patton retained enough fuel and ammunition to get to the Rhine in four or five days.

Hedging the truth, Bradley reported that Hodges would enjoy priority in the allocation of the promised supplies. Patton was then in the process of completing his crossing of the Moselle, and Bradley ordered an attack south of Aachen while Corlett's XIX Corps simultaneously advanced, covering the gap between the Twelfth and Twenty-first Army Groups. He licensed Patton's advance on a separate axis but promised, "if he cannot make real progress to the northeast in the vicinity of Metz, I will have him shift some troops to the north."[64] Patton liked to think he had hoodwinked Bradley, but Bradley clearly knew Patton's intentions and aided and abetted him. Bradley was not alone. As Eisenhower told Patton, he had two days "to become so heavily involved I might reconsider" cutting supply to Third Army.[65] Still livid over what he saw as a bum deal on the divvying up of supply, Patton told Hughes, "Ike through—not a commander. Follows Monty's ideas." Hughes concluded, "Geo jealous."[66]

Smith sought to influence operations through SHAEF's supposed oversight of Lee, but by mid-September, no real reserves existed. Because of Eisenhower's refusal to centralize oversight of logistics in SHAEF, Smith exercised only the broadest sway over the flow of logistics, chiefly through mostly fruitless attempts to establish levels of maintenance and coordinate actions between the American and British supply echelons and between Lee and Bradley. "Patton's ardor for glory led him almost to rashness," Smith commented. "We feared he might stick his neck out too far in the wrong direction and commit us in a direction we didn't want to go. Therefore, we sometimes limited him in supplies."[67] But since Bradley ignored SHAEF in the matter of supply allocations, Smith exerted virtually no influence.

Despite emergency measures undertaken by ComZ to move supplies forward, after a short spike, deliveries of gasoline again declined sharply.[68] On 17 September Bradley again came forward for a "secret conference" with Hodges. The two infantrymen ranted against Lee and his organization. The "only established facts are that supply of POL, ammo, and food continues to become more critical and that we are not even holding our own." Plank and other ComZ representatives attended part of the conference but offered no promises. "Whether we shall see any improvement or not is doubtful," and now Twelfth Army Group faced the doleful prospect that the supply situation would "slow-up, even altogether halt, our drive into Germany and this in the very near future." Now that American ground forces faced serious German opposition all along the line, a new crisis loomed—a serious shortage of artillery ammunition. ComZ pledged 3,000 tons of ammunition via emergence airlifts, but weather grounded all aircraft for three days. First Army—like every other American headquarters—looked for relief in the opening of deep-water ports. "The port of Antwerp *is expected to be in operation soon*," the First Army diary optimistically highlighted, and "Le Havre has opened already to limited shipping."[69] By that date, Boulogne had not fallen, the Scheldt was not open, and badly damaged Le Havre offered no succor.

SHAEF's attention remained welded on Market Garden. On 10 September, the day Eisenhower authorized the Arnhem operation, elements of the Dutch underground reported panzer units refitting in the vicinity of Eindhoven and Nijmegen. As indicated in a SHAEF intelligence summary, Ultra detected a similar pattern of German recovery. The intelligence evaluation pointed to the presence of one and probably two German armored divisions, an assault gun regiment, and units from Model's Army Group B headquarters in the environs of Arnhem, as well as the existence of a main German armor depot in Kleve, just inside the German border a dozen miles from Nijmegen.

These reports so disturbed Smith that he asked Eisenhower's permission to go forward and thrash the matter out with Montgomery. Smith never made the trip, but he forwarded the intelligence assessments and recommended that Montgomery either "drop the equivalent of a second division in the Arnhem area" or move one of the American divisions up to the vicinity of the bridgehead. Montgomery "ridiculed the idea and waved [Smith's] objections airily aside."[70] Dempsey read the same intelligence reports and revived a plan for an alternative airborne operation aimed at securing a crossing of the Rhine at Wesel, which offered the added benefit of drawing U.S. First Army more directly into the fight. Montgomery curtly dismissed Dempsey.

Montgomery's insistence on Market Garden is difficult to fathom. Such an ambitious and outright perilous proposal appeared to be out of character. Montgomery always insisted on building up reserves of manpower and materiel before embarking on an offensive. He always said that logistics represented 75 percent of war; operations the rest. Why then did he leap into the unknown on such a thin line of supply? More to the point, since the early stages in Normandy, Montgomery had considered his British and Canadian forces a "wasting asset." He always harangued, "There must be no mistakes." So why risk debilitating losses on an increasingly problematic operation, especially given the hard intelligence of German strength in the environs of Arnhem?

According to his biographer, a sense of unreality gripped Montgomery. Montgomery bucked all opposition inside Twenty-first Army Group Main. He brooked no opposition and rejected the advice of his chiefs of operations, plans, and intelligence, who all cautioned against the Arnhem operation. One reason for Montgomery's obstinacy was related to the absence of any oversight from above. Churchill and Brooke were away from London—in the Mediterranean or en route to Quebec—when the decision emerged to launch Market Garden. They remained focused on other concerns—Trieste, Greece, Southeast Asia, and another looming set-to with the American chiefs on all of the above. Churchill certainly would not have preached caution, but Brooke might have. Yet Market Garden never got so much as a mention in his diary. Plans for shifting divisions from Europe to India and Southeast Asia demanded his attention. He did send a cable from Quebec alerting Montgomery to the importance of Antwerp, but he never pushed the issue. And one other key individual who might have deflected Montgomery's enthusiasm for Market Garden was also absent. De Guingand, overworked and on the verge of a breakdown, had gone home for a rest. Distressed by the hardening German resistance and the failure to open the Channel ports, which in his opinion rendered the airborne operation ill-advised, de Guingand placed a call to Montgomery from his hospital bed. The field marshal told his chief of staff "he was too far from the scene of action and was out of touch."[71]

Smith came closest to assaying the truth. Montgomery took an uncharacteristic gamble because a successful Market Garden shifted the center of gravity north, away from Eisenhower and Bradley's preferred drives through Aachen and south of the Ardennes. A victory might leverage American manpower and materiel—without which Montgomery and his army group would be consigned to a secondary role—for an eventual forty-division northern thrust under his operational control. Eisenhower came to a similar conclusion. As he relayed to Marshall on 14 September, "I doubt that the [narrow front] idea was proposed in any conviction that it could be carried through to completion." Instead, Montgomery was motivated by "wishful thinking, and in an effort to induce me to give to 21st Army Group and to Bradley's left every ounce of maintenance there is in the theater."[72]

That raises the question of why Eisenhower signed off on Market Garden. In the eyes of many in SHAEF, Montgomery's credibility had been so seriously tarnished in Normandy that they dismissed talk of Berlin and even the Ruhr. Montgomery's airborne-ground operation gained support—from even his most persistent critic, Tedder—for a number of reasons. The sheer audacity of Market Garden surprised the Montgomery naysayers. The biggest strategic rewards lay in the north, and Montgomery's plan held out good prospects of securing a quick bridgehead over the Rhine before German resistance solidified. Eisenhower decided the risk was worth taking. The airborne army burned a hole in SHAEF's pocket. Under immense pressure to use airborne units, especially from Marshall and Arnold, SHAEF approved nineteen airdrops that never came off because the ground troops advanced too quickly. Smith complained it took days to plan and mount an airborne drop, and the allotted airlift was withheld in readiness for a week or ten days.[73] Owing to the many canceled missions, Allied airborne units began to lose their edge; morale and discipline suffered. The conviction grew that the airborne army must be committed, and Montgomery's revived Arnhem scheme held out the best prospects. Although airlift was urgently required for moving POL to Hodges and Patton, SHAEF decided to shift priorities to the north.

There may have been other factors involved. Smith thought Eisenhower lacked the "firmness of will" to handle Montgomery.[74] Eisenhower could ill afford a split at the command level along national lines within weeks of becoming ground commander. No risk taker himself, Eisenhower concluded that Market Garden would accomplish its minimum objectives—a Rhine bridgehead north of the West Wall that posed a threat to the Ruhr. Once Montgomery's offensive wound down, the field marshal would end his hectoring about narrow fronts and Berlin and devote his energies to Antwerp. Unfortunately, Market Garden achieved none of these ends.

Whittling Down a Field Marshal

When Eisenhower approved Market Garden, Montgomery's thrust represented one of three prospective routes into Germany. The sudden manifestation of German strength at Aachen and Metz and east of Nancy narrowed Eisenhower's chances of gaining a Rhine bridgehead down to one. Eisenhower preserved his Pollyannaism. Before the launch of Market Garden, he issued another circular letter to his army group and air and naval commanders, holding out Berlin as the big prize. "There is no doubt whatever, in my mind, that we should concentrate all our energies on a rapid thrust to Berlin."[75] The memo indicated his optimism that the war in the west could be brought to a speedy conclusion, and it gave the impression that he now sanctioned Montgomery's idea of strategic concentration. One day into Market Garden he told Marshall, "This team is working well. Without exception all concerned have now fully accepted my conception of our problem and are carrying it out intelligently and with energy."[76] All this glossed over the fact that none of his senior commanders knew his precise conception of future operations.

Did Eisenhower toy with the idea of conducting a concerted northern drive by Twenty-first Army Group and U.S. First Army? Or was this apparent conversion to concentration just another analgesic to "binge up" the field marshal for his thrust to the Rhine and beyond? The 15 September letter set off another inevitable round of point-counterpoint between Montgomery and Eisenhower. The Eisenhower-Montgomery feud took on a monochrome sameness: the supreme commander insisted, "I cannot believe there is any great difference in our concepts," and the field marshal asserted, "I cannot agree that our concepts are the same." Montgomery again made the case for concentrating in the north. "TIME is so very important," Montgomery stressed, and since logistics ruled out a wide-front advance and the northern advance enjoyed greater ease of supply, it "must have *everything it needed in the maintenance line.*" In reply, Eisenhower swore, "Never at any time have I implied that I was considering an advance into Germany with all armies moving abreast." He maintained, "What I do believe is that we must marshal our strength up along the Western borders of Germany, to the Rhine if possible, insure adequate maintenance by getting Antwerp to working at full blast at the earliest possible moment and [then] carry out the drive you suggest." If Eisenhower remained wedded to closing up everywhere to the Rhine, why the concession on Market Garden? "The net result of the matter," in Montgomery's opinion, "is that if you want to get the RUHR you will have to put every single thing into the left hook and stop everything else. It is my opinion that if this is NOT done then you will not get the RUHR."[77]

Montgomery's frame of mind hardly improved as evidence mounted that Market Garden would fail. The Arnhem operation committed four corps in a bold maneuver strategy designed to resolve Montgomery's many-sided operational predicament. The field marshal claimed he still had "a good sporting chance of getting the bridge at ARNHEM," but the low-risk, casualty-sensitive British ground forces lacked drive. German counterattacks twice broke XXX Corps' narrow corridor while British VII and XIII Corps, attacking to broaden the salient, made little progress.[78] The field marshal ascribed his troubles to Eisenhower's succumbing to Patton's "rock soup" operations at Metz and beyond Nancy, where his forces came under heavy counterattack. Montgomery bitterly complained that Smith's pledge of 1,500 tons of supplies fell short; one-third of the supplemental tonnage arrived on time via road shipments, but rail deliveries fell 12,000 tons behind schedule. The continued demands for airlift in support of the Arnhem fighting—including the emergency drop of the Polish airborne brigade—meant air supply never approached promised levels. An angry Montgomery fired off a cable to Eisenhower stating, "Ground supply situation is *not* healthy and unless it improves then the whole tempo of operations will be affected." He asked if Gale could come forward to "go into the matter" with Graham. The next day Montgomery placed the blame on Gale "for not keeping in touch with the situation." "My own administrative situation is not in blooming health," he chided, "but I can quite well continue the battle and am doing so."[79]

Eisenhower called a major conference at SHAEF's new headquarters in Versailles for 22 September. Montgomery begged off, sending the still shaky de Guingand in his place. MG Frank Simpson, director of military operations in the War Office, flew to Versailles to add weight to Montgomery's case. As Smith reported to Simpson, "we were feeling it very much that the Field-Marshal could not manage to come." Simpson and de Guingand were welcomed, but Eisenhower very much wanted a *tête-à-tête* with Montgomery, and his absence—although completely understandable, given the crisis in Holland—was interpreted as a calculated sign of disrespect.

The night before the conference Smith hosted a dinner in his new quarters. Simpson congratulated him on his wine cellar and liquor stock, "in spite of the extent of my attack on it." After a second drink, Smith got nasty with Simpson, accusing the War Office of an anti-SHAEF bias in its buttressing of Montgomery. The two men did not "see eye-to-eye," and Smith's persistence left Simpson fearing for the survival of their friendship. More to the point, Smith's outburst did not augur well for the next day's meetings. Senior British officers, especially Ismay and Portal, always considered Smith tough and "national" but evenhanded and often an ally. Later Smith apologized, blaming the second old-fashioned cocktail for his bad grace as host, but the episode bore a strong resemblance to his calculated ambush of Ismay during the London conference. Smith agreed with Montgomery's general approach and probably staged this public row with Simpson as a shield against American charges of his being too British.[80]

A worried Simpson sought out Smith the next morning before the conference convened. He laid out Montgomery's assessment. To Simpson's surprise, "Bedell assured me that he quite understood and that Eisenhower understood, and that they fully intended that all resources were to be put behind [Montgomery]. All that Eisenhower was concerned about was that Monty should not go straight off to Berlin on a narrow front." Montgomery never seriously entertained any notion of driving on Berlin—and the sad outcome of Market Garden certainly disabused him of any lingering ideas along that line. Eisenhower was the one suddenly talking about Berlin. Simpson assured Smith, "While an advance to Berlin might come later, Monty's present intention was to capture the Ruhr." Eisenhower had assigned Montgomery that task, and he was merely requesting the required logistical resources for carrying out the mission. "Bedell repeated in a most emphatic way that Monty could rest quite assured that everything possible to support him in capturing the Ruhr would be done." Again, Antwerp never figured in the discussions.[81]

The day before, Montgomery had wired Smith, again raising the command issue. "To achieve success, the tactical battle will require very tight control and very careful handling. I recommend that the supreme commander hands the job over to me, and gives me powers of operational control over First Army."[82] Smith was candid, even for him. He confided in Simpson that Eisenhower faced political constraints that carried up to the highest levels of the Roosevelt administration. Smith told him of Stimson's letter and the president's demand that American forces remain under American command. Despite that, Smith advised Eisenhower to make the move. "Bedell went on to say, 'I think Ike is quite prepared now to disobey this instruction and to put Hodges . . . under Monty.'" Simpson remembered Smith saying, "If it is the best way to get the Ruhr and thus win the war," let "the chips then fall as they will."

Smith grew weary of Eisenhower's refusal to assert command. He acknowledged that "orders given to Bradley and Patton about conserving administrative resources had not been obeyed." As he saw matters, the supreme commander's talent for dissimulation succeeded only in confusing Montgomery and confounding SHAEF's efforts to constrain Bradley, Hodges, and Patton. Smith knew SHAEF lacked credibility. "The trouble with Ike," Smith observed wistfully, is that "instead of giving direct and clear orders, [he] dresses them up in polite language; and that is why our senior American commanders take advantage." Smith expected fireworks that afternoon. He considered inviting Simpson but thought better of it. "So much dirty linen is going to be washed there," he told Simpson, "it would be better if an outsider is not present." Simpson left the meeting with the impression that Eisenhower intended to seize the mantle of leadership and had given Smith full authority to chastise Bradley and Patton for ignoring SHAEF directives.[83]

Bradley flew in for a morning conference with Eisenhower and Lee. Anticipating a renewed effort by the British to push the northern variant, Bradley offered a counterproposal. He agreed the Ruhr constituted the chief strategic objective. On 15 September Devers and Sixth Army Group had come under SHAEF control. Lead elements of Truscott's corps had already completed their link with Patton's forces. Eisenhower now commanded four American armies. The Ninth Army under MG William Simpson would soon enter the line; the question remained where. No question lingered, at least in American minds, of Montgomery becoming ground commander, but if Eisenhower sanctioned a northern pincer against the Ruhr employing British Second and U.S. First Armies, the possibility still loomed that Montgomery would exercise some species of overall command. Bradley adamantly refused to surrender command of Hodges. Bradley's solution involved a two-army envelopment of the Ruhr; Hodges would penetrate through the Aachen Gap and cross the Rhine in the vicinity of Cologne, while Patton cleared the Saar, crossed the Rhine and Main, and executed the main drive north from Frankfurt. Devers would close on the Rhine through Alsace, while Twenty-first Army Group opened Antwerp. Lee, very much in the doghouse for the unauthorized move of his headquarters to Paris, assured everyone that ComZ could support Bradley's scheme.[84]

That afternoon Eisenhower and Bradley joined a glittering array of twenty-two generals, air marshals, and admirals in the Clemenceau ballroom of the Trianon Palace Hotel. De Guingand, armed with Montgomery's prepared script, made the opening remarks. Bradley offered his plan. Smith came down strongly in support of the northern option. Not buying Lee's assurances, Smith said the supply situation ruled out Bradley's ambitious scheme; similarly, he asserted that the objectives of the northern offensives required revision. As de Guingand admitted, Antwerp would not be opened anytime soon. Market Garden had failed to gain a bridgehead but succeeded in carving out a deep salient that offered a pivot for Dempsey's VIII Corps to expand the corridor from Nijmegen to Wesel on the Rhine. From Wesel, Second Army could deliver the left hook, while Hodges moved to consolidate a leaping-off position for the second arm of the pincer farther south on the Aachen-Düren-Cologne line.

Eisenhower found Smith and de Guingand's argument the more convincing. The northern drive held out the promise of a Rhine crossing; Hodges had failed to make any headway against the West Wall at Aachen, and the Metz-Vosges defenses barred Patton from even approaching the Siegfried Line. Except for Ramsay, who argued that opening Antwerp should be the first priority, the rest remained fixated on moving east as quickly as possible before the Germans consolidated their defenses. As Arnhem, Aachen, Metz, and the ongoing German counterattacks east of Nancy proved, the hardening of the German line was already an accomplished fact. Although everyone gave lip service to the vital importance of the Belgian harbor complex, and Eisenhower knew the Allied forces would be "operating on a shoestring . . . until we get Antwerp," the opening of the port was deferred until after Dempsey gained the Wesel bridgehead.[85]

After the conference Eisenhower let his hair down with Hughes and Peterson, the WDGS inspector general. "Ike wants more divisions in line but can't get them trucks," Hughes recorded. "He wants Antwerp but has to depend on Monty. I asked him why he didn't promise Monty a promotion. 'To What?' Then he said that when [the] King was in North Africa he was delighted to discover that Monty wasn't after his job."[86]

De Guingand wired Montgomery, "Excellent conference, IKE supported your plan one hundred per cent."[87] This was not quite true; Eisenhower blocked any command shift but went as far as he dared in giving Montgomery what he recommended. On 23 September he issued written instructions directing that Bradley shift Hodges's "main effort to meet the Field Marshal's developing requirements" for the Ruhr offensive. Eisenhower also granted Montgomery, in an emergency, the right to "communicate his desires directly to Hodges" without the medium of Bradley's headquarters.[88]

In part, Eisenhower's judgment derived from caution and the recognition that American forces were "getting fearfully stretched south of Aachen and may get a nasty little Kasserine if the enemy chooses at any place to concentrate a little strength." Despite that, he engaged in some mirror imaging, assuring Montgomery that the Germans' logistical situation must be worse than that confronting the Allies. "We should be all right," he told Montgomery.[89]

Eisenhower instructed Bradley to place Patton on the defensive and redirect supplies to Hodges. Returning to his headquarters, Bradley again ignored orders and sanctioned Patton's continued attacks. In an amazing display of creative writing—something he was not known for—Bradley explained to Eisenhower how Patton undertook his offensive in the "spirit of your directive to assume the defensive." He stated, "George believes it will be economical in the long-run . . . to eliminate possible areas where the Germans might launch counter attacks . . . as the opportunities present themselves."[90]

As the advance stuttered to a halt, Patton lapsed into one of his depressive moods and blamed SHAEF and ComZ for his problems. To ease the supply burden, SHAEF gave XV Corps to Devers, on the theory that Sixth Army Group suffered less at the end of their overextended lines of communication back to Marseilles than did Twelfth Army Group. At the same time, SHAEF requested Twelfth Army Group to send combat troops to ComZ to police the lines of supply, chiefly against skyrocketing rates of pilferage to feed the burgeoning black market. "Bradley and I are depressed," Patton wrote in his diary. "We would like to go to China and serve under Admiral Nimitz." Patton carped that Lee made "no preparation at all for line of communication troops," and "ComZ [was] using vehicles from arriving divisions because [Lee] has failed in his supply set-up. I cannot understand why Eisenhower does not get rid of him."[91]

Hughes and Peterson visited Bradley's headquarters on 26 September, where they found that Bradley's G-4, Moses, was "not interested in army supply. Always compromising with C[om]Z. Brad on defensive. Supply situation bad. Trucks wearing out."[92] The next day Peterson visited Patton and heard more of the same. "As usual, Lee is a glib liar," Patton recorded in his diary. "Hughes was very much depressed at having to sit at the same table with him." Lee's failure, in Patton's opinion, "will be a scandal some day."[93]

Patton's objections were misplaced. ComZ lacked the manpower to operate and guard the lines of communication, and SHAEF planning had always envisioned as many as five divisions reserved for these functions. SHAEF ordered incoming divisions to surrender their organic transportation. When Smith promised that three divisions would be immobilized to help supply Montgomery during Market Garden, he was really offering nothing, since those units had already been stripped of their quartermaster units. Even with manpower shortages in combat units already beginning to bite, SHAEF simply lacked the transport to move forward those divisions Eisenhower insisted on bringing into the theater ahead of schedule; instead, SHAEF shifted divisions between the armies to balance the supply load. All this pointed not to any plot authored by SHAEF to deprive Third Army of supplies but to Smith's powerlessness in effecting any reorientation of manpower and supply. Eisenhower and Smith had hoped to employ SHAEF's authority over the allocation of reserves to enforce command decisions; instead, Bradley purposefully ignored SHAEF with a wink and a nod from the supreme commander. Bradley disregarded Lee as much as he dared and took his grievances to Eisenhower. Lee insisted on his command prerogatives, paid no attention to Smith, and likewise conveyed his problems directly to Eisenhower.[94] Eisenhower resented being drawn into these scrimmages and expected his chief of staff to handle the details. Smith could only grimace, knowing that the root cause of all these machinations was Eisenhower's refusal to define command chains for manpower and supply inside an authoritative structure under SHAEF, coupled with his habitual compromises, which produced only uncertainty. In trying to keep everybody happy, Eisenhower succeeded only in keeping the pot boiling.

Bradley and Patton's dismay grew mostly from Eisenhower's assigning the northern thrust precedence. Montgomery issued a new directive. Crerar assumed two tasks: open or contain the Channel ports, and attack northward from the Meuse-Escaut Canal, opening Antwerp and reducing Second Army's long frontage on the western face of the Arnhem salient. One Canadian corps would clear the Channel ports and then move to Antwerp, while a second corps opened operations aimed at removing the Breskens Pocket west of the port. Second Army would operate from Nijmegen, clearing the Germans west of the Maas preliminary to a drive north of the Ruhr in conjunction with Hodges's offensive toward Cologne. Consistent with the agreement reached at Versailles, Montgomery returned priority to "the main effort of the present phase of operations," a double envelopment of the Ruhr.[95]

After a "first hasty glance," Eisenhower approved Montgomery's plan. For weeks he had harped on Antwerp but never issued any peremptory orders and always offered one or more caveats. Nor did he present a consistent front. Eisenhower told Smith on 30 September, "I am terribly anxious about Antwerp," yet a week later he insisted, "Both Army Groups must retain as first mission the gaining of the line of the Rhine north of Bonn as quickly as humanly possible."[96]

Tedder believed Montgomery overestimated the Canadian army's ability to perform its missions. In truth, Montgomery knew exactly the limitations faced by Crerar and his army.[97] Canada provided outstanding fighting units. Canadian soldiers were the sons of the famed Canadian Corps, which had won acclaim and the grudging respect of its German adversaries in World War I. Canada received the right to field its own army—a product of British imperial politics—but the country lacked the depth of officer talent, especially in the senior ranks, to command a separate army, and Canada's First Army never commanded the range of resources required to undertake independent operations. The Canadian population—only 11.5 million—offered too small a recruitment base, and conscription inevitably engendered a political crisis between Quebec and the rest of the country. No easy solution to the worsening Canadian manpower shortages presented itself. It took until 1 October for Crerar to disengage from his Channel port missions and initiate the battle for the Scheldt.[98] Hitler appreciated the importance of logistics far more than his opponents did. Middleton finally took *Festung* Brest on 19 September, but not a single American regiment ever came through the port. Boulogne fell on 22 September, followed by Calais eight days later, but Dunkirk, L'Orient, St. Nazaire, the Channel Islands, La Rochelle, and the mouth of the Gironde, which denied the Allies the use of Bordeaux, held out to the end of the war. As von Zangen stated a week into the battle, "The defense of the approaches to Antwerp represents a task which is decisive for the future conduct of the war."[99] The Allied commands never attached the same importance—other than verbal—to the Belgian port complex. Everyone viewed Antwerp as the silver bullet that would solve all the supply woes, but until Montgomery devoted more than an enervated Canadian corps to the task, the port remained blocked.

Following the Versailles conference, Eisenhower and Smith turned their attention to clarifying the muddy air command problem. The British wanted SHAEF to terminate the AEAF command, move Leigh-Mallory to Mountbatten's headquarters, and return the air forces to national control. Eisenhower considered it "a serious mistake" to remove the strategic air forces from SHAEF's jurisdiction.[100] Without AEAF, the air forces possessed no direct command link with SHAEF and no means of coordinating with the army groups. Smith always believed Tedder should serve as air commander in chief. He considered AEAF an unnecessary extra echelon, but once it had been established and was functioning efficiently, he left it alone. "Leigh-Mallory was difficult at first, but we found him after a time to be extremely able, honest and loyal. He stood for what he wanted." And "after he got to working with us," Smith remarked, "we couldn't ask for more."[101] Montgomery much preferred working through Leigh-Mallory (although he once called him a "gutless bastard") than through Portal or Tedder.[102] Now with the CCS insisting on ending what had never truly amounted to a single air command, Smith pushed for Tedder's appointment as head of a unified air command inside SHAEF. Eisenhower agreed, but Tedder refused, viewing the appointment as a demotion. Instead, Smith organized a new air staff under AVM Robb as his deputy chief. Robb assumed the operational duties of the AEAF, while Tedder continued as SHAEF liaison to the strategic bomber commands and took the added responsibility of coordinating the tactical air forces. Tedder's rebuff of Smith added more fuel to the smoldering antagonism between Eisenhower's two senior advisers. "Tedder didn't want to take command," Smith later commented. "He was lazy. He wanted authority without responsibility. Was not a big man."[103]

As was typically the case, the issue lingered until Smith signed the directive dissolving AEAF on 13 October.[104] Nobody particularly liked the new air command arrangement; like the one it replaced, it depended almost entirely on personal contacts among the principals.[105] Under the ungainly new setup, the armies coordinated with their attached tactical air forces; the Troop Transport Command fell under Brereton in Allied Airborne Army; and Spaatz or a senior subordinate personally attended daily meetings at SHAEF "so that all of the operations of Strategic Air forces are likewise coordinated." Arnold could not understand why Eisenhower refused the obvious solution of grouping all American air forces under Spaatz. Eisenhower summed up his philosophy on headquarters reorganization by responding, "It is a bad thing to keep changing organizations just for the sake of change."[106]

Smith's hope that Eisenhower would assert command proved groundless. On 28 and 29 September Eisenhower toured the front, visiting Bradley's, Patton's, and Hodges's headquarters. He and Bradley spent the night at the new SHAEF advance command post at Gueux, near Reims. Soon after his return, Eisenhower, in a classic example of Ike doublespeak, memoed Smith, stating that although he wanted Bradley, Spaatz, Devers, and Lee to solve "their common problems by coordination and cooperation," he expected his chief of staff, "without becoming involved in theater administration," to formulate "decisions and policies" when "inevitable questions arise" that required adjudication among the major American commands. In effect, Eisenhower abdicated command to his senior American commanders and some of his core responsibilities as supreme commander to Smith.[107] How Smith could intercede and arbitrate settlements among the commands "without becoming involved in theater administration" remained a mystery. The 3 October memo signaled Eisenhower's intention, as in the Mediterranean, to spend as little time as possible at SHAEF-Main. A day after the headquarters moved to Versailles, Eisenhower announced, "I am going to be here only very briefly, as I am too far from the battle lines."[108] He may have gone closer to the battle lines, but Eisenhower almost never went forward to the divisions.

On 5 October Eisenhower convened another conference in Versailles, focusing on Allied strategy in the aftermath of Market Garden. Montgomery could not pull his Peck's bad boy routine, because Brooke attended. The seminar began with each of the army group commanders making a statement, followed by Tedder and Leigh-Mallory and concluding with Ramsay. Then Eisenhower took the floor and explained "his future strategy which consisted of the capture of Antwerp, and advance to the Rhine in the north and south, forcing the Rhine north and south of the Ruhr, capture of the Ruhr followed by an advance on Berlin either from Ruhr or from Frankfurt depending on which proved more promising."[109] Once again offering something to everybody, Eisenhower indicated that Montgomery and Hodges would envelop the Ruhr, and in the same breath he talked about Patton driving on Berlin via Frankfurt.

As Brooke noted, "During the whole discussion one fact stood out clearly, that Antwerp must be captured with the least possible delay." Montgomery argued that Antwerp did not represent a sine qua non for seizing the Ruhr. He cited the calculations of his CAO, Graham. With Boulogne, Calais, Dieppe, and Ostend open, the British line of communication could supply Montgomery's proposed offensive. In addition, the British had moved much of their maintenance from the Normandy beaches to an advance base in Belgium.[110] Brooke was not impressed. "I feel that Monty's strategy for once is at fault," he recorded, "instead of carrying out the advance on Arnhem he ought to have made certain of Antwerp in the first place."[111] Actually, Brooke should have done that when Montgomery advanced his plan for Arnhem, but he was asleep at the wheel.

Montgomery's self-assured claims afforded Ramsay "the cue I needed to lambast him . . . and let fly all my guns at the faulty strategy we had allowed." Montgomery's gamble on Arnhem had failed, and "our large forces are now practically grounded for lack of supply." Gazing at the faces of the assembled brass, Ramsay noted, "I got approving looks from Tedder and Bedell-Smith and both of them together with CIGS told me after the meeting that I had spoken their thoughts and it was high time that some one expressed them."[112]

The next day Eisenhower, Bradley, and Smith drove out to Orly airport to greet Marshall and his party, which included Handy and Beetle's old acquaintance Jimmy Byrnes, now director of war mobilization. The chief reason for Marshall's visit revolved around escalating concerns about the American rear. Brooke did not take the opportunity to stay on in Versailles to discuss matters with Marshall; he returned to London to clean up his desk before setting off on a trip to Russia. That evening Eisenhower hosted a dinner for Marshall attended by Smith, Spaatz, Lord, Strong, Bull, and Morgan. Even though Lee had conferred with Eisenhower that day, he judiciously passed on dinner, sending Lord instead.

On 7 October Eisenhower accompanied Marshall on a visit to Twelfth Army Group headquarters. That day Montgomery admitted he lacked the strength to accomplish all his assigned operations simultaneously and postponed the eastern advance, set to kick off five days later. Caught between the pull of the Rhine crossing and the push of Antwerp, none of his drives possessed anything near the strength required to fulfill their missions. The fighting to preserve the Nijmegen salient eventually sucked in Dempsey's army, leaving no reserves for the offensive toward Krefeld on the Rhine. Given its responsibility for the longest frontages and its serious personnel shortages, Twenty-first Army Group could not accomplish either of its core tasks until Montgomery concentrated portions of both armies on a single chore or Eisenhower reduced the Anglo-Canadian liabilities. A third option was to place Hodges under Montgomery. "The operations of Second Army and First U.S. Army are very intimately connected and it is my opinion," Montgomery wrote to Smith, "that the present system of command is most unsatisfactory."[113]

Montgomery met with Bradley on 8 October to discuss altering army group boundaries. Bradley not only accepted a shift north but also instructed Hodges to ready the incoming 104th Infantry Division to help open Antwerp.[114] The same day Eisenhower told Bradley, "under changed conditions commitments of 21 Army Group are too heavy." Although he agreed with a postponement of the twin pincer movement across the Rhine, he maintained that "both Army Groups must retain as first mission the gaining of the line of the Rhine north of Bonn," and he insisted that Hodges's drive toward Düren receive "consistent support," even if Bradley had "to reduce still further the maintenance of Third Army." As an ultimate solution, Eisenhower suggested placing Simpson's army between Dempsey and Hodges. Antwerp never came up; Eisenhower remained absorbed with the goal of pushing to the Rhine.[115]

Later that day Marshall and Tedder arrived at Montgomery's tactical headquarters. The field marshal could not resist the urge to lecture Marshall and cornered him alone in his caravan. "Our operations had, in fact, become ragged and disjointed," Montgomery told Marshall, "and we had got ourselves into a real mess." He returned to his favorite theme: how well the Normandy campaign had transpired with single ground, air, and naval commanders. Tedder informed Montgomery that Leigh-Mallory was departing the theater, and no air commander in chief would be named. Montgomery considered this move another indication of the breakdown of command chains. Marshall sat quietly, but according to Montgomery, clearly "he entirely disagreed."[116] Two more dissimilar personalities than Montgomery and Marshall are difficult to imagine. In the midst of a tour of the entire front, Marshall took immense pride in seeing the payoff for all his labors. Soon four American armies would hold a line from the Netherlands to the southern face of the Vosges, the largest concentration of military power in American history. Behind his placid exterior, Marshall "came pretty near to blowing off out of turn." He fought a "terrific urge to whittle [Montgomery] down," then remembered, "this is Eisenhower's business and not mine."

Marshall simply would not entertain the idea of placing American forces under the command of a man who, in his view, was infected with ego-centrism bordering on megalomania.[117]

Through Royal Navy channels, SHAEF learned that the Canadian army would not have sufficient reserves of ammunition to undertake an offensive until 1 November. Since this estimate contradicted Montgomery's projections, Eisenhower instructed Smith to get to the bottom of this. Writing over Eisenhower's name and with his concurrence, Smith issued what amounted to an order. "You knew best where the emphasis lies within your army group," Smith told Montgomery on 9 October, "but I must repeat that we are now squarely up against the situation which has been anticipated for months and our intake into the Continent will NOT support our battle." He continued, "I must emphasize that, of all our operations on our entire front from Switzerland to the Channel, I consider Antwerp of first importance." The letter asked that Montgomery give the matter his personal attention.[118]

Still not satisfied, Smith went further. He telephoned Montgomery and demanded a date when the field marshal expected the Scheldt to be opened. Heated words followed. Montgomery reminded Smith that the Ruhr, not Antwerp, remained the "main effort." When Montgomery stated that the Americans, not Twenty-first Army Group, needed Antwerp, Smith lost his temper. "Purple with rage," he hurled the receiver to Morgan. "Here," Smith roared, "you tell your countryman what to do." Already sensitive to what the field marshal thought of him, and fully aware he was likely cutting his own throat in terms of postwar British army politics, Morgan calmly told Montgomery that the levels of supplemental supply Twenty-first Army Group received remained tied to the successful opening of the port.[119]

Not without good reason, Montgomery reacted with vehemence. He had assigned Antwerp as Canadian First Army's priority on 14 September, and a major effort against the Breskens Pocket had started three days earlier. Two British divisions—Seventh Armored and part of Fifty-first Highland—reinforced Canadian I Corps. All this indicated to Montgomery that SHAEF remained hopelessly out of touch with what was transpiring at the front. He asked on what authority Ramsay made "wild statements to you concerning my operations about which he can know *nothing*." Montgomery claimed there was "NO shortage of ammunition and present stocks in Canadian Army are a total over 12000 tons." He assured SHAEF that the "operations are receiving my personal attention." Montgomery asserted that Eisenhower had assigned priority to the Rhine crossings on 22 September and reiterated the same in his

8 October letter to Bradley; now, one day later, he seemingly reversed himself and gave Antwerp absolute priority. Montgomery never guessed that Smith, albeit with Eisenhower's full accord, had written the 9 October dictum. In the field marshal's estimate, this represented the first unequivocal order he had received on Antwerp; now clear on the matter, he promised, "You can rely on me to do every single thing possible to get ANTWERP opened for shipping as early as possible."[120]

The next day Montgomery fired off a longish memo to Smith asking for a complete overhaul of the command structure. From prior experience and Simpson's account of their conservation in Versailles, Montgomery believed Smith understood the need for concentration and unambiguous command channels, and despite the charges exchanged the day before, he still hoped the SHAEF chief of staff might influence Eisenhower. Montgomery claimed Arnhem had foundered because SHAEF never enforced cooperation between Twenty-first and Twelfth Army Groups and failed to deliver the promised logistical support. "Eisenhower's idea has always been for the *whole line* to go forward, to capture the Ruhr, *and* the Saar, *and* the Frankfurt area." He stated, "The Americans have outstripped their maintenance and as a result we have lost flexibility on the front as a whole" and "are now unlikely to get the Ruhr *or* the Saar *or* Frankfurt." He opined, "We have 'mucked' the whole show and we have only ourselves to blame." The root of "all our troubles can be traced to the fact that there is no one commander in charge of the land battle. . . . SHAEF is not an operational headquarters and never can be." His accompanying "Notes on Command" covered the same themes, but in more measured terms. It opened by repeating, "The present organization for command within the Allied forces in Western Europe is not satisfactory." He lamented the breakdown of the system that had succeeded so brilliantly in Normandy. With the removal of the air commander in chief, and in the absence of an effective overall ground command, the campaign could only drift. He pointed to the land forces "separated on a national basis and not on a geographic basis." He proposed dividing the front at the Ardennes, with either Montgomery or Bradley in command in the north.[121] Even though SHAEF finally assigned Antwerp as a strategic priority, Montgomery persisted in talking about the pincer drives on the Ruhr.

At SHAEF, Montgomery's reopening of the Ruhr question appeared to be part of a "bait and switch" ploy. Montgomery's campaign for control of U.S. forces had commenced as early as mid-August, when he asked permission to cannibalize Fifty-ninth Infantry, and it had grown apace with evidence that Twenty-first Army lacked the muscle to execute its many missions.[122] Despite waning combat power, Montgomery successfully argued for priority of the northern drive. In early October, Twenty-first Army Group could no longer paper over its limitations. If SHAEF wanted Antwerp, it must make a larger investment than merely shifting army group boundaries and offering Montgomery an American division or two; Eisenhower would have to agree to place Montgomery in charge of much of the theater's ground forces. Smith had long concluded that Montgomery's offer to serve under Bradley amounted to nothing more than a red herring. In his view, Churchill and Brooke, especially the CIGS, would "never have permitted Monty to serve under Bradley and Monty knew it."[123]

Montgomery's latest effort to alter the command structure produced plenty of electricity, but not the type he wanted. Still sizzling over their altercation over the telephone, Smith saw his opportunity to whittle down the field marshal. And with Marshall standing over Eisenhower's shoulder, the supreme commander could no longer prevaricate. They discussed Montgomery's latest proposal, and Smith convinced Eisenhower to await Marshall's return to Versailles before replying. Typically, whenever SHAEF issued any sort of admonishment, Smith or one of his senior British associates wrote it. This time Whiteley got the job.

"I have read your letter to Smith on the subject of command," the dispatch started. Although "the questions you raise are serious ones . . . they do not constitute the real issue now at hand. That issue is Antwerp." It continued, "I do not know the exact state of your supply, but I do know in what a woeful state it is throughout the American and French forces. . . . By comparison, you are rich!" Both Brooke and Marshall informed Eisenhower that "they seriously considered giving [Montgomery] a flat order that until the capture of Antwerp and its approaches was fully assured, this operation would take precedence over all others." Why Eisenhower never issued a "flat order" of his own went without comment. Arriving at the key point, the letter emphasized, "The Antwerp operation does not involve the question of command in any slightest degree." Then came the bombshell: if Montgomery was unhappy with the state of affairs, he could "refer the matter to higher authority for any action they may choose to take, however drastic." On the question of command, the letter observed, "I do not agree that one man can stay so close to the day by day movement of divisions and corps that he can keep a 'battle grip' upon the *overall* situation and direct it intelligently. This is no longer a Normandy beachhead!" Turning to future operations after Antwerp, the letter stated that Montgomery's army group "will be left with such depleted forces facing eastward that it could be expected to do nothing more than to carry out strong flanking operations supporting the main attack upon the Ruhr" by Twelfth Army Group.[124]

Smith reworked parts of the letter and showed it to Eisenhower. Characteristically wary of any confrontation, Eisenhower thought the communication too strongly worded. Smith disagreed, as did Marshall, who reviewed it that night. Eisenhower could do nothing but concur. Smith attached a postscript calling for a face-to-face meeting with Montgomery and Bradley, suggesting 18 October as the date. Knowing the field marshal's predilections, Smith added that if Montgomery found it too inconvenient to come to SHAEF-Forward at Reims, they could meet again in Brussels. According to Bradley, Smith engineered a meeting at Montgomery's headquarters to make "it impossible for him not to attend."[125] To further paint Montgomery into a corner, SHAEF dispatched the letter by hand, ensuring a delay in Montgomery's receipt of it and thus allowing him little wriggle room.[126]

A crestfallen Montgomery received SHAEF's letter on 16 October and immediately responded. To be fair to Montgomery, he had assigned Antwerp to the Canadians a month earlier, and he had added more punch to the operation with British reinforcements. As British theater commander, he possessed the right to defend national interests. In British command and staff practice, a commander expected his subordinates to offer counterarguments, but once the commander decided on a course of action, all discussion ended. In Montgomery's view, he was merely following convention, albeit in SHAEF's view, in an imperious and graceless fashion. Until Smith's 9 October directive, SHAEF had never issued any categorical orders on Antwerp. "You will hear no more on the subject of command from me," Montgomery conceded. He had offered his views, and Eisenhower had given his. "I and all of us here," Montgomery added, "will weigh in 100 per cent to do what you want and we will pull it through without a doubt." He ended the letter, "Your very devoted and loyal subordinate."[127] True to his word, at a conference with his army commanders that day, Montgomery issued a new directive giving Antwerp "complete priority over all operations . . . without any qualifications whatsoever."[128]

Montgomery's climb-down represented a significant personal setback. He not only failed to gain any measure of operational control over American forces, but he also succeeded in getting the northern thrust downgraded to a secondary and supporting role. It would not be the last word Eisenhower heard on the subject of command, but the 13 October letter and the anticlimactic meeting five days later left Montgomery quiescent for the next month.

★ 31 ★

"The Logistical Bottleneck Now Dictates Strategy"

Three factors explain why the Allies failed in their leap toward the Rhine. Two fall into the category of the imponderables of war: the remarkable German recovery and the weather. The third, the apparent logistical breakdown, was the sole element the Allies, in this case the Americans, exerted any control over.

The Allies suddenly faced German forces seemingly conjured out of nowhere. Harking back to German history and the War of Liberation in 1813, when Prussia led a popular national uprising against Napoleon, Hitler called for and received renewed commitment for the defense of the *Vaterland*. The attempt on Hitler's life, the mass bombing campaign, the unconditional surrender policy, and Western and Soviet forces closing to the German frontiers all combined to produce an upsurge in patriotic backing for the regime. For ideological reasons, Germany did not go to a total war footing until 1944; despite intensifying Allied bombing, German industrial output of aircraft, tanks, munitions, and heavy and antiaircraft artillery reached maximal levels that year. Too many senior Allied leaders entertained the delusion that Germany would crack in 1944 like it had in 1918, but the Third Reich bore few parallels to the dying days of the *Kaiserreich*. A totalitarian regime founded on the *Führerprinzip*, terror, propaganda, and a racialist *Volksgemeinshaft* ideology would not collapse from within. Westerners never comprehended Hitler as a social revolutionary, and as leader of a revolutionary state, he could summon up amazing levels of popular support and self-sacrifice. The vast majority of Germans followed Hitler not out of fear but out of adulation and faith in his cause. "In my life," Hitler said in a December 1944 speech, "I have never learned to know the word 'capitulation.'"

735

The regime would survive—and the war would continue—as long as Hitler drew breath.

Bad weather dogged Allied ground, air, and supply operations. The weather paralleled Allied fortunes. The unusually wet June and July of the Normandy deadlock gave way to the glorious weather of August and September and the Allied pursuit, only to end in the wettest autumn since 1861 and finally a bitter and premature winter corresponding to the stalemate along the frontiers. Almost everywhere the German defenses enjoyed the advantages of geography—the polders and the river and canal lines in the Netherlands, and the uplands of the Eifel, Ardennes, and Vosges. Terrain and weather conjoined to degrade Allied advantages in mobility, firepower, and especially airpower. The foul weather spiked nonbattle casualties; soldiers suffered from trench foot, respiratory ailments, and a general malaise that was psychological as much as physical when the realization hit that the war would not end in 1944. Indicative of this gloominess, the number of soldiers with self-inflicted wounds soared into the thousands.

The biggest self-inflicted wound was the supply fiasco, and the main culprit was Eisenhower. During August and September, Eisenhower made four vital decisions that guaranteed American forces would outrun their supply lines: (1) the decision not to open the Brittany line of communications, (2) the decision not to pause on the Seine, (3) the decision to favor Arnhem over Antwerp, and (4) the decision to accelerate the flow of American divisions into the theater far in advance of schedule and without the necessary port and reception facilities. Each was motivated by his resolution to push the advance as far east and on as broad a front as possible—all in accordance with his preconceived attachment to the strictures of the Overlord plan. The first two decisions effectively scuttled the supply plan; the third ensured the lengthening of the supply crisis; the last greatly added to the supply burden without any concomitant operational benefit. All his judgments reflected the traditional American officer's subordination of logistical considerations to operational imperatives. Underlying all this was Eisenhower's obtuse refusal to restructure his American commands. That the logistics plan went out the window need not have been fatal. But his badly organized and internally divided command apparatus ensured that American forces could not reap maximum benefits from the pursuit before the Germans recovered and the frictions of distance, terrain, and weather intervened.

On 18 September Marshall made a speech to the American Legion convention in Chicago in which he painted a glowing portrait of the manpower and supply situation in France. "A conspicuous factor in the sustained successes of the past six weeks," he told his audience, "has been the steady flow of well-trained men to replace combat losses." Divisions remained at full strength, losses were "made good within twenty-four hours and the missing materiel in trucks, tanks and guns is being replaced at the same rate." In comparison, the Germans, with "divisions dwindling in strength and gradually losing the bulk of their heavy equipment, always find themselves beset by full American teams whose strength never seems to vary and whose numbers are constantly increasing. . . . These German deficiencies," he promised, "will bring about their downfall."[1]

The reality on the ground would soon belie Marshall's vision. Despite the debacles in France, the east, and the Balkans, out of a population of 80 million in the Greater Reich, the Wehrmacht still had 10,165,303 officers and men under arms in September 1944. The ground forces fielded 327 divisions and brigades, with 31 divisions and 13 brigades listed as armored. As the Germans fell back, their lines of communication shortened, and their front narrowed; shattered Wehrmacht and SS units reformed around surviving staffs and cadre, formations drawn from other fronts entered the line, and the replacement army raised fifty new Volksgrenadier divisions and static fortress units. These units received the latest and qualitatively superior generation of small arms, antitank weapons, and armor. American units were exhausted after their lightning advance; their equipment was worn out, and their clothes were threadbare. Shorn of much of their organic transport, they were living on K rations and expropriated German foodstuffs; in some cases, they were even firing captured stocks of German and French artillery ammunition. The Americans had long since passed their logistical points of culmination; the combat power of American divisions, not German, waned. Nonetheless, senior American leadership clung to their confidence that the Germans would crack. First Army's attacks had lacked concentration since September, but when Hodges opened his "big attack" toward the Roer in mid-November with only four divisions, Bradley thought it "the last big offensive necessary to bring Germany to her knees." "The Boche are now confronted with a drive along a 400-mile front," recorded the First Army's diarist, "and while he may be able to plug a gap here and there, it is not thought that he can stop for any length of time the combined weight of seven armies."[2] That optimism proved to be misplaced.

Stumped by Supply

From spring 1942, Lee commanded a static SOS establishment in the United Kingdom; the breakout afforded him the long-awaited opportunity to assume operational control. Despite multiple shake-ups in senior staff, virtually none of his senior subordinates possessed any experience in active supply operations. Now they faced the biggest challenge they would confront in the war, and they would have to learn on the job. After the breakout, all ComZ efforts focused on moving supplies forward. Undeterred, Lee seized the moment and made a series of decisions that cast long shadows. The most contentious involved the precipitate move of his headquarters to Paris.

Within days of the capital's liberation, ComZ headquarters initiated its move to Paris. By the middle of September, the transfer neared completion. Illustrative of how much his injured knee debilitated him—or perhaps demonstrative of how little attention he paid to logistical matters—Eisenhower did not know ComZ was operating from its new headquarters in the exclusive Hôtel Majestic, near the Arc de Triomphe, until 16 September. "Eisenhower was furious when he found one morning that they had moved in," Smith remembered. Eisenhower had promised the French there would be no American occupation of Paris; he issued a directive stating, "the main headquarters of L of C is *not* to be in Paris," but it was too late to stop ComZ's move into the city.[3]

Eisenhower instructed Smith to write a sharp letter of reprimand to Lee, insisting that he stop "the entry into Paris of every individual who is not needed at that spot for an essential duty." Eisenhower could not order ComZ out of Paris; that would involve another large expenditure of transport, fuel, and signals equipment, and it would handicap ComZ in its "first priority duties"—funneling supplies forward into the combat zones. "I regard the influx into Paris of American personnel, including your headquarters, as extremely unwise," Smith wrote in Eisenhower's name, "and I want the whole matter readjusted and corrected as rapidly as it can be without interfering with operations of the fighting troops."[4] On 18 September Eisenhower brought Lee to Granville and chewed him out. Lee defended his decision, stating that Paris was the only place he could properly superintend the forward movement of supplies. Because Lee continued to discharge the duties incumbent on a deputy theater commander—maintaining routine communications with the War Department and the New York port of embarkation—he assumed that ComZ headquarters could function properly only in Paris, the epicenter of French transportation and communications. As the head of ComZ—equivalent to an army group command—Lee asserted his right to select the best site for his headquarters, which in any case needed to be in close proximity to SHAEF.[5] Not appeased, Eisenhower fumed for days.

Any hope Eisenhower entertained of keeping Americans out of Paris proved futile. France possessed the most centralized government in the world, and it had been in existence long before the reign of Louis XIV. After living in France while serving with the American Battle Monuments Commission, Eisenhower knew one could not travel by rail anywhere in northern France without transferring at a Parisian *gare*. The same applied for French communications. And there was the allure of the City of Light. Soon Smith confronted an inundation of requests from officials, civilians, press agencies, and representatives of American corporations for permission to establish themselves in the capital and from politicians and various dignitaries wanting to visit the city. Very soon the vast majority of Parisians longed for the day of liberation from the Americans.

In fairness to Lee, Paris was really the only choice for ComZ headquarters. Transferring ComZ from England into a tented headquarters in the Cotentin peninsula would have been like Sears, Roebuck and Company moving its key staff from Chicago, across Lake Michigan, and setting up and controlling its vast distribution system from an improvised head office in the fields around Kalamazoo. Sears, Roebuck offered its customers about 100,000 separate items; ComZ carried and distributed nearly 800,000. Lee simply could not operate from Valognes. In addition, the medical corps had advised Lee that his personnel would experience serious health issues if they remained too long in tents. Certainly the Hôtel Majestic, where Lee staked out three suites for his personal use, had far greater charms than a tent in a Normandy apple orchard. "From rags to riches," is how Hughes described it. "From the heat in Valognes to the [Hotel] King George V—from mud and rain and cold water to rain, beauty rest, and hot water." To be sure, Lee—as was his wont—went overboard. "Too many people for the 655 hotels we took over from the Germans," Hughes remarked.[6] Initially, the communications in Paris proved little better than those in Valognes. As Hughes noted, "Signal communications horrible but that doesn't deter movement of HQ into Paris."[7] At Koenig's insistence, Smith did talk Lee out of requisitioning schools, but ComZ retained its hotels and office buildings. "The personal satisfaction we would have had in throwing them out," Smith concluded, "would not have justified the further disruption of service."[8] Despite all the criticisms, Lee's decision proved sound in the end.

But Lee paid a price. Eisenhower never felt any fondness for Lee. "Ike wants me to continue in the job" as supply troubleshooter, Hughes logged in his diary at the beginning of August, "says he doesn't trust Lee. Queer job."[9] Relations between Lee and Bradley, already strained, deteriorated after word reached Twelfth Army Group of Lee's move into

Paris. "No one can compute the cost of that move in lost truck tonnage on the front," Bradley complained. "Field forces in combat have always begrudged the supply services their rear-echelon comforts," Bradley commented. "But when the infantry learned that Com Z's comforts had been multiplied by the charms of Paris, the injustice rankled all the deeper and festered throughout the war."[10] Lee remained the favorite butt of jokes. Hughes, just back from a visit to the War Department, told Eisenhower an anecdote that was making the rounds in Washington. "Ike enjoyed story about 'having trouble with God who thinks he is Lee.'"[11]

A great many took umbrage at the trucks, manpower, and fuel consumed in Lee's move to Paris, but SHAEF also moved twice in a three-week period in September. Nobody dared take issue with the ill-advised move to Granville, followed by the relocation to Versailles. And no one complained when Ramsay, Leigh-Mallory, and Spaatz moved their headquarters to Paris. No one could deny that Lee's timing left much to be desired, but the hostility against him derived mostly from the typical animosity between real soldiers and rear area denizens. "They always gripe about supply people," Smith remarked. "It is always the contention of the armies," Smith continued, "that the rear echelons keep all the best men and the best supplies. I can't answer whether it was correct or not, but I imagine ComZ ate all right."[12] This view was clearly demonstrated in late September when Eisenhower met with Bradley and Hodges and his corps commanders. "What apparently tickled everybody most," recorded the First Army diarist, "was General Eisenhower's statement he was going to 'chase the SOS out of Paris and make it a well ordered rest center for combat troops.'"[13] That never happened.

Lee remained unfazed by the furor; he had far bigger problems. With his typical "everything is all right" attitude, Lee dismissed the projections of his and SHAEF's planners and assured SHAEF that ComZ could supply the advance. To meet the emergency he embarked on a set of improvisations. In hindsight, none of his organizational expedients solved the basic problem, and many made them perceptibly worse.

The speed of the advance and the lack of ports, coupled with no pause to regroup and amass supplies, induced the abandonment of any attempt to create a system of depots-in-depth and the proper buildup of authorized stock levels in forward installations. According to doctrine, base sections received and stored materiel and moved it forward into the intermediate section, which sorted and classified supplies according to category before distributing them to the issuing agency, the advance section. The intermediate section served as the cornerstone; there, the regulating stations adjusted supply and demand inputs, rationalizing supply from the rear based on predetermined quotas with demands from the combat zone. The plan called for ADSEC to advance with the armies; its place would be taken by FECZ; as the front advanced, FECZ followed, its place assumed by ComZ headquarters. As a result of the standoff in Normandy, Bradley's delay in establishing an army rear, loss of the Brittany line of communications, and ComZ's move to Paris, Lee scrapped plans to establish an intermediate section. Instead, the Seine base section (later combined with the Oise base section) performed intermediate section responsibilities. This expedient might have worked, but Lee never established regulating stations, nor did he form a control division in ComZ headquarters. The improvised structure experienced problems because demands from the front drove the machine—not supply from the rear, as dictated by doctrine. Without an intermediate section and its regulating stations, and with no control division at headquarters, the Transportation Corps effectively regulated the flow of materiel forward.[14] The Transportation Corps, still functioning with no manual and no fixed operating procedures, controlled the ports and the movement of supplies and manpower forward to their ultimate reception centers. According to doctrine, the base sections moved supplies forward with their organic transport and transferred materiel to the intermediate section, where the process was repeated into the advance section. In practice, materiel moved from the Normandy base section to transfer points—Chartres and Dreux—on the borders of the Seine base section, then through Paris to the rear boundary of ADSEC, but with no controls other than those imposed by the Transportation Corps.[15]

By 30 August two main rail lines extended their service into Paris; by 18 September a line connected Paris to Liège. The choke point remained in Paris. Supplies had to be hauled by truck from Chartres and Dreux to points east of the capital—a process that took five days. Not surprisingly, the Transportation Corps' solution to the supply predicament involved moving as much materiel forward as quickly as possible, without regard to category or forward requisitioning. This system succeeded in moving vast quantities of materiel forward, but much of it the combat zones neither requested nor needed. This created huge logjams of unregistered supplies and traffic snarls at the transfer spots, especially east of Paris.[16]

The supply regime had been unbalanced since shortly after D-day. Answering the ammunition shortages in Normandy had misaligned all other categories of supply, and they never regained anything resembling equipoise for the rest of the year. The great lurch forward placed the highest priority on moving gasoline. With supply pipelines filled with

POL, other classifications took a backseat. When the campaign bogged down into tough positional fighting, the armies were awash with gasoline, but the priority shifted to ammunition. Given the systemic problems in the imperfect and already overtaxed supply chain, it took time to realign priorities. The advance proved amazingly hard on soft- and hard-shelled vehicles and on signals, quartermaster, medical, engineer, salvage and maintenance, and ordnance equipment; all this now needed replacement. Clothing wore out at a dizzying rate. The extravagant needs and attendant wastes of American troops multiplied the supply problems. With supply channels clogged with artillery ammunition, not nearly enough of this freight got forward. Pushing more through an already bursting pipeline merely expanded the bottlenecks, geometrically increasing the problem until forward elements were living hand to mouth. Tons of supplies moved forward according to the ledger sheets, but in reality, much of it remained hung up in kinks in the pipeline.[17]

Quartermaster supplies stood at the back of the queue. Littlejohn went to battle against Lee's staff. In Normandy he had fourteen trains loaded with rations sitting on sidings but could not move them without locomotives. Littlejohn inspected Le Havre and found a million blankets or the equivalent in sleeping bags aboard a ship waiting to be unloaded. Five times the vessel was refused a berth because priority went to ammunition. When he got no response from the Transportation Corps, Littlejohn resorted to a little chicanery. He also had a sixty-day supply of cigarettes in ships offshore that he could not land. Littlejohn withheld cigarettes from the ration packs, knowing it would cause a storm when the GIs had no smokes. Littlejohn got his berths for the cigarettes and, more vitally, the winter gear. Next he faced the bigger problem of getting them forward. He "went to the 12th Army Group and the three armies and pled for release of some transportation to advance the center of gravity of the quartermaster supply establishment." He later complained, "Clothing was at the bottom of the priority list until the weather got real bad at the front." When he met with Lee, Bradley, and Moses in late October, Bradley told him, "The men are tough; we must go forward as long as we can. This necessitates ammunition and gasoline be given top priority." When the weather turned foul and nonbattle casualty rates skyrocketed, ComZ rushed winter clothing forward, 60 percent by air.[18]

Throughout October the scarcity of ammunition dictated operations.[19] As indicated by what Bradley told Littlejohn, ComZ expended its energies in forwarding artillery ammunition, especially for the heavies. Lee clearly understood the priority. At the end of September he appealed to the War Department for accelerated shipments of heavy artillery ammunition into the theater. "There is a serious shortage of heavy artillery ammunition for current operations," he stated. "Troops are facing heavily fortified positions and in the opinion of [the] field force commanders concerned only concentrations of heavy artillery fire will reduce these positions without disproportionate loss of life." He made assurances that ComZ could "alleviate the present situation" but pointed out that if the armies continued firing at their desired rates, supply for all sizes of ammunition would be exhausted in fifteen to twenty-five days.[20]

Huge quantities of ammunition went missing during the advance. After the breakout, mountains of ordnance and ammunition stockpiles sat in vast supply dumps in Normandy, where it remained, either lost or inaccessible. As in Tunisia and Sicily, whenever American forces rapidly advanced, they left huge caches of supplies, especially ammunition, in their wake. The sheer size of the forces involved and the length of the supply lines amplified the problem in France. The breakneck speed of Patton's advance meant he created and left behind no fewer than eight army depots before his halt at Nancy. The ADSEC moved supplies forward to army depots; when the armies advanced, ADSEC possessed inadequate transportation to shift forward the materiel left in the army group rear and its own depots. The supply echelons also pressed ahead; staffs and troops familiar with conditions went forward, replaced by the next echelon of undertrained men and untried officers. Complications arose in every echelon because of the lack of fixed and common doctrine—a result of the wholesale indifference to standard operating procedures in the requisitioning, movement, and receipt of supplies, and the absence of uniform stock documentation—and insufficient SOS complements in terms of both numbers and training. The wider the base of the supply pyramid, the more difficult it became to manage. By September, huge quantities of mostly noninventoried supplies simply disappeared off the ledgers. Real ammunition shortages existed in October. ComZ's concerted efforts squeezed the pipeline, moving top-priority artillery ammunition through the system, but creating confusion in the various headquarters and jams in the line of communication. ComZ could not readily fix the problem because according to its records, the system was functioning properly.[21] Since the commands fudged their numbers—in fact, they rarely recorded receipts—nobody knew precisely how much ammunition went forward. If the commands knew, they secreted that fact.

The root of the problem centered on a set of misunderstandings among the War Department, the theater, ComZ, and the commands. At the beginning of the war, the War Department decided the army did not require heavy artillery. Later it changed its mind and started production. After the McCoy Board decided that enough heavy artillery ammunition had been produced and shipped to Europe to meet requirements, many ordnance factories closed down their production lines. The War Department believed the theater possessed ample reserves, the commanders claimed grave shortages, and ComZ maintained it had moved forward adequate stocks. Disentangling this mess was nearly as important as opening Antwerp in cracking the ammunition crisis.

"Shivering, Suffering and Dying up on the Siegfried Line"

"You can be certain this war is not won for the man that is shivering, suffering and dying up on the Siegfried Line," Eisenhower wrote to his wife on 23 September. "My whole time and thought is tied up in winning the bloody mess."[22] A month and a half later, little had changed—except the mess had gotten a whole lot bloodier. Eisenhower suffered a great deal of angst over the lack of movement at the front, but he remained wedded to his broad-front approach and deputized his army group commanders to push through the German defenses. Despite insufficient resources and manpower, Eisenhower rejected any notion of closing down offensive operations until the supply situation improved. Instead, he sanctioned offensives in all three army group areas aimed at inflicting a decisive defeat on the Germans west of the Rhine and gaining bridgeheads for an advance into Germany. Instead of coordinated action, the line advanced in spasmodic jerks and at mounting costs.

Montgomery admitted he lacked the strength to accomplish the three missions assigned Twenty-first Army Group: expand the Nijmegen bridgehead, clear the Germans west of the Meuse, and open Antwerp. Since SHAEF insisted on Antwerp, he conceded his army group could no longer contemplate leading the main effort against the Ruhr. Montgomery's climb-down meant Bradley assumed responsibility for leading the drive across the Rhine.[23] Market Garden succeeded only in delaying the opening of Antwerp. The Scheldt campaign opened on 3 October; gained momentum after 16 October when LTG Guy Simonds, in temporary command, concentrated Canada's entire First Army against the Scheldt forelands; and by 2 November succeeded in clearing the Breskens Pocket and opening Ghent. A set of complicated combined arms operations—using commandos, lavish airpower, naval gunfire, and amphibious landings—finally removed the last stubborn German defenders on Walcheren on 8 November. The campaign took eighty-five days; cost 12,873 casualties, about half of them Canadian; and finally opened Antwerp to shipping. After removing the mines, the first two coasters landed in Antwerp on 26 November; the first convoy entered the port two days later. After completing the clearing of the Scheldt, Twenty-first Army Group, still aided by elements of the Airborne Army, crossed the Waal River and cleared the Venlo Pocket.

Bradley never accepted his role as second fiddle to Montgomery and fought at Aachen and Metz to gain tactical advantage for his movement toward the Ruhr and Saar. Hodges attacked with two divisions north and south of Aachen on 2 October and completed the city's encirclement two weeks later. After bitter street fighting, Aachen fell on 21 October, at a cost of 8,000 casualties. Bradley and Hodges decided the weak German forces holding the Aachen-Düren-Monschau triangle constituted a threat to the flank and rear of the projected breakout attempt toward Cologne. The one thing that guaranteed the strengthening of German forces in the Hürtgen Forest was an American attack. Hodges never saw fit to concentrate his forces. First Army attacked with a single regiment, then two; then it added the rest of the Ninth Division, followed by parts of the Twenty-eighth Division. Finally, two divisions went into the foreboding woodlands laced with mines, tank traps, and concealed pillboxes that brought down interlocking fire. Constant fog, a combination of forest transpiration and the damp, cold weather, ruled out air support. The failures of Ninth and Twenty-eighth Divisions led to another 10,684 casualties and cost Corlett his job; the failed attempts at breaking out pulled in two other divisions, the Fourth Infantry and Fifth Armored.

Finally, on 16 November, Bradley launched his long-awaited breakthrough attempt. Simpson's Ninth Army now occupied the northern end of the American line. Three corps opened the drive: XIX Corps of Ninth Army north of Aachen, Collins's VII Corps south of Aachen, and Gerow's V Corps into the Hürtgen. None of the attacks possessed sufficient depth with real reserves. By 1 December Beetle's old division, the Fourth, emerged from the forest at Gey with 5,200 casualties. Clearing Aachen and the Hürtgen Forest consumed two months of fighting and gutted eight American divisions, to no strategic advantage.[24] By 15 December the push through the Aachen Gap had penetrated the bifurcated West Wall defenses but fell short of the Roer and the vital dams near Schmidt. The First and Ninth Armies sustained 47,039 combat and 71,654 nonbattle losses in the fighting to gain the Roer. Ninety-six days after the first American soldier crossed the frontier, the advance had carried scarcely twenty-two miles inside Germany. In sum, the losses in the frontiers campaign, including the 11,000 incurred under British and Canadian command, amounted to 140,000 men.[25]

Meanwhile, Patton kept slugging away at Metz. Third Army's first attempt in the first week of October at cracking the fortress complex around the city miscarried. From September, when Patton crossed the Moselle, to mid-December, Third Army advanced less than twenty-five miles, at a cost of 50,000 casualties. After Metz fell, Third Army advanced to the Sarre River and prepared for its breakout attempt. Between Gerow and Third Army's northern boundary stood Middleton's corps, holding the hinge of the line in the Ardennes. The razor-thin line in the Ardennes then consisted of two infantry divisions, the recently arrived 106th and the fought-out Twenty-eighth.

The forces under Devers scored the most impressive gains. Attacking on 13–14 November, Seventh Army penetrated through the Vosges and won the distinction of being the first Allied army on the Rhine; it liberated the symbolically important city of Strasbourg in the bargain. Farther south, the French First Army took Belfort and Mulhouse and isolated sizable German elements inside the Colmar Pocket. Despite Sixth Army Group's successes, SHAEF decided to shut down Devers by returning two divisions to Third Army for Patton's offensive into the Saarland.[26]

After a month of incessant fighting in the Eifel, at Metz, and in Lorraine and Alsace, the forces under American command succeeded in inflicting heavy losses on the Germans in attritional fighting but fell far short of achieving any of their strategic objectives; they had not decisively defeated the German armies west of the Rhine, nor had they crossed the river. The problem with attritional warfare is that it cuts both ways, and as the Allies suffered escalating casualties, their already overstretched logistical and replacement structures came under increasing pressure. And with no pause in the fighting for replenishment and reinforcements, the prospects for a breakthrough in renewed offensives in mid-December looked bleak.

All during this period SHAEF remained virtually silent. After the last set-to with Montgomery, SHAEF played no role in detailed planning other than rubber-stamping the designs of the respective operational commands.[27] Eisenhower became the subject of a whispering campaign; many wondered why he spent so little time in Versailles. The judgmental Brooke thought the charms of Mrs. Summersby and the adjacent golf links in Reims proved more alluring than being supreme commander.[28] Tedder's aide Scarman thought Smith encouraged Eisenhower to stay forward—either at his command post or on visits to headquarters—to separate the supreme commander from his staff "until SHAEF was almost solely Bedell's headquarters." Even when Eisenhower remained at SHAEF-Main, he lived apart, and few of the staff ever saw him.[29] According to Montgomery—who got his information from Whiteley—some senior members of SHAEF worried that Eisenhower had lost his grip on command and raised concerns with Smith.[30] Harriman visited SHAEF in late November and saw "no reason in the world" for Eisenhower to remain near Reims with his little entourage, far removed from Versailles but not appreciably closer to the front. Like Scarman, he concluded Smith encouraged this practice because he could accomplish more with Eisenhower out of the headquarters.[31]

In truth, Eisenhower was less of an absentee supreme commander in autumn 1944 than he had been in the Mediterranean. Circumstances—mostly faulty communications—kept him in Versailles far more than he desired. Even then, he spent half his time in Versailles and the rest in Reims, touring the commands, or in London.[32] The situation on the ground resembled autumn 1943 in Italy, with each commander conducting loosely coordinated, limited-objective operations following the general prescription to maintain pressure along as much of the line as possible. Eisenhower saw no reason to intervene because he remained convinced that with the application of unremitting pressure, the Germans would eventually crack. The problem remained that none of the offensives possessed enough oomph to break out, and none had sufficient reserves to exploit the situation even if an opening occurred. As in Italy, the campaign ended in a World War I–type deadlock.

SHAEF failed to harmonize and prioritize operations, and it ignored its own logisticians. Preoccupied with operational questions, Eisenhower expected the supply services to run themselves and never grasped the gravity of the potential crisis until the logistical situation had deteriorated to the point where it hamstrung operations. By then it was too late to do much about it. Even if Smith desired to, except for the contrivance of his appointment as ETO chief of staff, he exerted no real control over Lee's organization. In England, ComZ remained the only American command not subordinated to SHAEF, and Lee continued to operate as if that state of affairs continued in France—and, in the absence of a clear division of responsibilities, it did. In American practice, staff officers do not operate; a chief of staff cannot issue orders to a lieutenant general holding a separate and coordinate command. Smith tried to work through Lord in an attempt to exert some influence in ComZ, but Lord also worked for Lee and spent most of his time "putting out fires" rather than anticipating them.[33] Only once, on 3 November, did Smith authorize the apportioning of supply allocations, granting Twelfth Army Group first priority on the delivery of 16,100 tons per day and 80 percent of the available airlift in anticipation of the renewal of offensives in the Aachen Gap.[34]

Any survey of the SHAEF War Diary for the months September through December indicates that Smith's attention stayed focused on political and civil affairs, almost to the exclusion of operational matters. As always, the biggest preoccupation involved dealing with the French. The formation of a provisional government under de Gaulle and Smith's 25 August agreement with Koenig on zonal responsibilities raised the hope of finally normalizing relations between French officials and SHAEF, but Roosevelt's continued hostility blocked any formal alliance. To Eisenhower and Smith, the president's intransigence made little sense. De Gaulle immediately broadened representation in the provisional administration to resistance groups, including the communists. The general unquestionably enjoyed sweeping popular support, and the French population could not understand why the United States withheld recognition of his government; nonrecognition might well prompt an upswing in anti-American sentiment. Americans in France had difficulty explaining why the United States had maintained diplomatic relations with Vichy but withheld them from de Gaulle.

In the middle of September, Smith met with the American ambassador to France Jefferson Caffery and, arguing from a military standpoint, asserted there was no reason to delay recognizing de Gaulle as the effective head of a French government. His primary worry was the need to preserve security in the rear, particularly in Paris. Caffery appealed through Secretary Hull for a reconsideration of American policy, but Roosevelt refused to budge and pushed Churchill to delay British recognition of de Gaulle, despite pressure from the cabinet, Foreign Office, Parliament, and press. The president insisted on waiting for the liberation of the whole of France; he wanted SHAEF in titular control of civil administration until that time.[35]

Smith treated the provisional government as the de facto authority in France in all but name. He wanted to implement his agreement with Koenig and relinquish all civil control to the French within a Zone of the Interior that now included most of France. Smith held talks with French officials throughout October. Metropolitan France was not North Africa; the French officials in de Gaulle's administration acted in concert, without the endemic infighting that had plagued affairs in Algiers.

Hull, now a convert, asked Roosevelt to reconsider his position. On 14 October the prime minister added his voice. "There is no doubt that the French have been cooperating with Supreme Headquarters," he pointed out, "and that their Provisional Government has the support of the majority of French people. I suggest therefore that we can now safely recognize General de Gaulle's administration as the Provisional Government of France."[36] Roosevelt still stonewalled, refusing to grant recognition until de Gaulle truly increased representation of groups other than the FCNL in the provisional government and formed a Zone of the Interior.

Caffery met with Eisenhower and Smith on 20 October. The generals made a convincing case for the immediate recognition of de Gaulle's government. Smith stated that without such recognition, "there will be increasing opportunity for the forces of disorder to take advantage . . . to break down governmental authority in France thus creating an intolerable behind-the-line situation for our troops at the front." Logistically, the Allied forces lacked the transportation to supply the front as well as cater to civilian demands. Eisenhower and Smith pointed to the onset of "a hard winter"; given the disorder of supply chains, SHAEF could not allot even one-third of the coal supplies for civilian purposes that the Germans provided. "It is obvious that a disaffected population in the rear of the lines might play havoc with our military operations." As matters stood, reserves of coal would not last three weeks in the Paris region. Turning their attention to de Gaulle, Eisenhower and Smith agreed: "Whatever may be said about de Gaulle—and there is plenty to say—there is no opposition leader in sight who would have the slightest chance of overthrowing him at this juncture." Even the communists gave him "lip service." Stated bluntly, the alternative to de Gaulle was chaos. Smith made the obvious point: if Roosevelt insisted on the formation of a Zone of the Interior as a quid pro quo for recognition, why not tie them together? SHAEF and the French could activate the 25 August agreement simultaneously with Washington's announcement of recognition.[37]

Caffery's letter to Hull reporting on his meeting with Eisenhower and Smith broke the logjam. Roosevelt finally accepted the fait accompli but did not like generals meddling in political affairs. In any case, Churchill could not delay any longer; British and Canadian recognition of de Gaulle would leave the United States in an untenable position. On 23 October the Big Three and five other nations recognized the French provisional government, and SHAEF secured its deal on the Zone of the Interior.

SHAEF greeted the recognition of de Gaulle with much relief. The accord lifted from SHAEF's shoulders the huge burden of preserving law and order and providing civilian supply. Smith turned his attention to hammering out agreements on rearming French units. Before the finalization of the zonal agreement, Smith deferred questions of reequipping the French Metropolitan Army to the CCS.[38] On 16 October Smith approved de Gaulle's proposal to replace colonial troops with white French units. As de Gaulle explained to the CCS, he hoped to form a Far Eastern Expeditionary Force to reclaim Indochina for the French empire. The formation of these units required additional supply from American sources, but Smith remained noncommittal.[39] His tune changed on 23 October. With the signed agreement in hand, Smith approved Devers's request for the immediate assignment and shipment of equipment for two French infantry regiments and three armored infantry battalions under a revised and accelerated French rearmament program. At the end of October Smith entered into a number of agreements with the French related to equipping and clothing French regular and FFI units, especially for operations in the Bay of Biscay to open Bordeaux (Operation Independence).[40] With mounting evidence that American forces would face a worsening manpower crunch, Smith suddenly agreed "that training and reconstitution of major French units is of great importance." The problem remained supply, especially meeting the increased demands made by Juin. Between 31 October and 18 November, Smith and Juin conducted sometimes acrimonious discussions, climaxing in an agreement that set priorities for rearming the French.[41] In total, as many as 140,000 former FFI men enlisted as regular soldiers, almost all of them serving as reinforcements in de Lattre's army.

Smith left all routine civil affairs planning, negotiating, and policy making to Morgan and the country missions, reserving for himself the conduct of high-level discussions at the governmental level. Morgan also shouldered responsibilities for clarifying policies on post-surrender Germany. When civil affairs problems hampered military effectiveness, Smith assumed a direct role. Relief of the civilian populations in Belgium and the liberated districts of the Netherlands became one such issue. The daily caloric intake of civilians in the liberated zones stood at less than half that during the German occupation. SHAEF depended on civilian workers for skilled labor in transportation facilities and factories. A strike among transport or port workers would paralyze communication lines; industrial action in the factories would hamstring necessary production. Strikes might easily morph into widespread civil unrest. Though not unmoved by the humanitarian plight of these people, Smith's concerns legitimately centered on the threat these disorders posed to military operations.

As early as mid-September, Smith moved to standardize relief policies for France, Belgium, Luxembourg, and the Netherlands. A month later he had his staff hard at work hammering out the administrative details involved with the speedy reconstitution of governments in the Low Countries. In early November he requested CCS approval to equip Belgian, Dutch, and Luxembourg troops with captured German materiel so they might better maintain internal security. Earlier he had asked Count Pierlot, the Belgian prime minister, to instruct his citizens to turn in their weapons, viewing them as a potential military risk.[42] Although the situation in Belgium caused concern, SHAEF's real worries lay in the Netherlands.

Pieter Gerbrandy, head of the Dutch government in exile, formed a rump government in the southern Netherlands and petitioned SHAEF for urgent action to address the food shortages. Smith informed him that Eisenhower felt sympathy for the plight of the Dutch citizenry and assured him that SHAEF had already studied the relief implications if the Germans opened the dikes, as threatened. As he told the CCS, "assistance provided before liberation [of the rest of the Netherlands] will ease the relief problem subsequent to liberation." He wanted to expedite relief programs through neutral civilian agencies.[43] Through the British, SHAEF discovered that the Swedish government had offered assistance, provided the Germans granted its ships free passage. Smith also considered airdropping relief supplies but rejected the idea for fear of inadvertently supplying German units instead.[44] As much as SHAEF wanted to help, Smith offered the Dutch little in the way of concrete promises.

Bedell Smith's Great Error

Marshall's brief tour of the theater in October proved immensely beneficial. His presence finally galvanized Eisenhower into issuing unequivocal orders to Montgomery, insisting he give Antwerp his overriding attention. The chief of staff also discovered the seriousness of the supply challenges confronting the theater at both ends of the supply chain— the shipping backlog in the Channel, and an acute ammunition shortage at the front. Bradley, Patton, Hodges, and their staffs provided him with chapter and verse on the many failings of Lee and ComZ—that the movement into Paris had deprived combat soldiers of the full benefits of a rest center in the capital; that Lee should not exercise theater-wide control over the allocation of manpower and supply because ComZ possessed a vested interest in satisfying its own establishments' needs in preference to those of the combat zone; that SHAEF could not superintend the flow of replacements and supply because of the submergence of ETO and the chiefs of services inside ComZ headquarters.[45]

Marshall proved all too ready to accept the legitimacy of these complaints. Time and again in his reminiscences he returned to his experiences in France in 1918 as a staff officer in the First Infantry Division and AEFHQ, and his many tussles against a red tape–laden and nonresponsive SOS composed of moss-backed senior officers overly protective of their command privileges. He found the situation little changed from his first tour of North Africa after Casablanca, but this time Marshall placed the blame squarely on Smith. "What made me tired was these things weren't looked into," he later related. "That was Bedell Smith's great error. He was so intent on the forward part of the thing . . . that he didn't have somebody that would do that [clean up the rear] and could break over the restrictions."[46] Since Smith evidently would not perform that task, Marshall decided to send officers who could.

No doubt the topic of firing Lee surfaced. Smith had been working on Eisenhower to do just that—a course of action Eisenhower refused to take. A "dump Lee" movement had already gained traction in the Pentagon, headed by Judge Patterson, Stimson's undersecretary. Patterson had assessed the state of supply in the Mediterranean and European theaters in August with Somervell. They inspected a number of SOS establishments in England with Lee before heading to France, where they looked over the situation in Cherbourg and the beaches. Lee entertained Somervell and Patterson in lavish style at his guest chateau near Cherbourg, then took them forward for meetings with Eisenhower and Patton and a visit to ADSEC headquarters in Le Mans. Lee never went anywhere on impulse; all his trips were choreographed down to the last detail. The units designated for inspection got a heads-up far in advance. As Hughes discovered, the drill was "Dress up—stop all operations—liquor down toilets."[47] Lee made sure his guests observed precisely what he wanted them to see. Somervell bought the Potemkin village Lee sold him, but Patterson did not. As the civilian head of the mobilization effort, Patterson knew a thing or two about logistics structures and functions. Far from being predisposed to swallow Lee's glossy assurances, Patterson saw a supply structure rent by dissension and distrust. In Normandy, it had hobbled from emergency to emergency and then stood on the edge of a far bigger trial. He came away from his brief tour of France convinced that Lee was not equal to the task. Soon after returning to Washington, Patterson petitioned for Lee's removal and nominated three officers he knew well and had confidence in to replace Lee. The three names were Clay, Lutes, and MG Henry Aurand.

Acting on his own assessment of the situation—but colored by what he had heard from the other members of the Infantry School mafia (Bradley and Hodges), plus acting on the advice of Justice Byrnes, the other civilian head of industrial mobilization—Marshall endorsed Patterson's idea. He asked for the permanent attachment of Clay, Lutes, and Aurand to the theater. Somervell agreed to the temporary loan of Clay and Lutes—two officers he considered indispensable to his organization—but he gladly surrendered Aurand. Marshall wanted Lee replaced, but like Montgomery, Lee was Eisenhower's problem.

After Marshall left, Eisenhower toured the commands. At every stop he heard the same complaints about the failures of ComZ: combat divisions had been shorted on ammunition and infantry replacements. The constant chorus of criticism directed against Lee by Twelfth Army Group led Eisenhower and Smith to question Lee's competence. By the end of the month the situation had not improved. On 25 October Marshall stated the obvious: "The logistical bottleneck now dictates strategy."[48] The implication was equally apparent: fix it, and if Lee could not pull it off, replace him.

Personalized command served as one of the bedrock traditions in the U.S. Army. Marshall's respect for the sanctity of command privilege prevented him from issuing direct orders to Eisenhower. An officer received a job, and if the results fell short of expectations, he was replaced. This practice placed immense pressure on commanders, few of whom had ever led more than a company in battle; they suddenly found themselves charged with leading green divisions into war. When the going got tough in Normandy, division commanders got the ax. Between D-day and 13 July, First Army sacked no fewer than five division-level generals.[49] In the fighting along the frontiers, corps commanders also took the fall. The number of commanders relieved of duty corresponded exactly with the mounting impatience for results on the ground. Hodges was the worst offender. Nobody questioned the system that had produced these officers; none blamed faulty organization (with the exception of ComZ). In truth, replacing officers would never solve the basic systematic problems.

Officers bearing three stars presented a different proposition. Pressure intensified on Eisenhower to relieve Lee for the alleged breakdown of the supply structure. As theater commander, Eisenhower confronted two choices: alter the organization, or change personnel. Eisenhower again refused to do either. Though admitting "he had never felt easy about the Communication Zone set-up," Eisenhower said, "in spite of this uneasiness he did not desire to make a change in a Lieutenant General." As his many clashes with Smith demonstrated, he proved just as resistant to all suggestions for modifying command structures. Eisenhower recognized the structural issues. The supply crisis was not the product of mismanagement or misbehavior. Discord naturally arose at points of contact between separate and, in principle, equal headquarters. The American command and staff structures—based on overlapping, shared, and in many cases conflicting responsibilities—inevitably produced friction that hampered planning and the efficient execution of policy. All these problems Eisenhower willingly abided.

As Eisenhower liked to point out, no command and general staff system is perfect, even in theory. In the simplest terms, warfare exists on three planes: strategy defines the end, logistics provides the means, and operations employ the means to achieve the end. A supreme commander's job involves uniting the three, and his headquarters must bridge the gap between combat and supply operations. The evident disconnect between the operational and logistics commands represented the great flaw in all of Eisenhower's organizations. As he later told Lutes, that "was not news to him."[50] Rather than reorganize, Eisenhower choose ad hoc solutions. He never sought to aggregate power; he consciously narrowed his and SHAEF's functions, limiting them to adjusting army group and army boundaries, assigning air missions and ground and airborne reinforcements, and shifting maintenance commensurate with consigned operational tasks. Eisenhower required Smith to integrate wide-ranging opinions and estimates and translate them into policy lines he could accept, reject, or modify. He wanted a system flexible enough to tackle a broad range of decisions, from high-level crisis management to routine administration and supply. SHAEF proved far more effective in dealing with the former than the latter. Rivalry and friction had an adverse effect on efficiency; he and Smith constantly dealt with a multitude of personality conflicts and warring camps within the structure. Eisenhower considered the structure sound but flawed, and he thought the solution lay beyond shifting boxes on organizational flow charts. He feared that a radical solution—restructuring the organization or sacking Lee—would create bigger problems than those it purported to solve. Eisenhower trusted in his subordinates' competence, managerial capabilities, and good faith and relied on informal connections to surmount the bumps in the road.

Eisenhower's system worked admirably when a personal connection existed based on mutual respect, tolerance, and trust. Either he or Smith talked to Bradley via telephone virtually every day, Eisenhower and Patton were old friends, and even the more standoffish Hodges commanded the respect of both Eisenhower and Smith.[51] The technique did not work so well with Montgomery, Devers, and Lee. In the middle of November, Montgomery complained to Brooke that he had met with Eisenhower four times in the preceding four months and had not seen or talked to him on the phone for a month.[52] Much of that derived from Montgomery's repellant personality and the fact that his headquarters was such a soulless place that nobody liked going there. Smith complained he had gone to Montgomery's headquarters only once since D-day and had felt exceedingly unwelcome. He found the situation the direct opposite from that in the Mediterranean, where he had enjoyed the liberty of visiting British units whenever he chose. As he told LTG Brian Horrocks, "I feel the lack of this very much."[53] As for Devers, Eisenhower and Smith viewed him with barely concealed suspicion. Eisenhower resented having Devers foisted on him as an army group commander by Marshall, and there was bad blood from before the time Devers replaced Eisenhower in the Mediterranean. Sixth Army Group always remained at the bottom of SHAEF's totem pole. With the teetotaler Lee, an odd man out in any assembly outside church, the "gin and tonic" solution had no play.

The combination of Marshall's diktat, the ammunition shortage at the front, the hundreds of ships bobbing in the Channel, and the impending arrival of Clay and Aurand made supply the big issue in the last week of October. Meanwhile, Washington was applying a lot of heat on the theater to tackle the Normandy shipping logjam. The lack of a deepwater port and high-volume rail service hamstrung logistical efforts from the beginning. The holdup in capturing Cherbourg, the extensive damage, the maddening delay in restoring the port's facilities, and the fact that it was the only deepwater harbor in northwest Europe solely in American hands created a chronic shipping bottleneck.[54] In September, Cherbourg had cleared just over half the ships piling up in the Channel. By early October, the backlog exceeded 200 ships waiting to be unloaded. The increased flow of divisions into the theater raised arrivals to 265 ships each month for the rest of the year. The problems in Cherbourg—in September as much as 95 percent of known theater stocks remained tied up in the Normandy base section—throttled the pipeline at its point of origin.[55] Red Ball and other emergency measures moved 354,000 tons, but they also threw the logistics structures into greater chaos. In October the daily discharge from American or jointly controlled ports amounted to only 19,735 tons—less than half the projected requirements.[56] In mid-November the two receiving beaches in Normandy would close. Lee came under increasing fire not only in the theater but also in Washington. The backlog of ships standing off

Normandy started to drive a wedge between Lee and Somervell. On 27 October Eisenhower called Lee in and told him in no uncertain terms to remedy the situation.

Clay entered the Trianon Palace Hotel on the morning of 30 October not knowing what to expect. The son of a senator, Clay was an old West Point friend of Eisenhower's. Despite having "no real staff experience" and none in logistics, Clay had held a succession of what he termed "civilian jobs" in ASF since March 1942. In 1944 he served as director of material in charge of procurement agencies. "I couldn't have thought of any job that I'd rather had less," he later remembered. Clay suspected that Marshall and Patterson had sent him to France as Lee's replacement. He also surmised correctly that "the initial moves were made by General Smith."[57] Eisenhower immediately brought Clay into his office and welcomed him effusively. Clay soon discerned that Eisenhower had "made up his mind not to relieve General Lee" because the ComZ commander "was on the whole doing a satisfactory job" and he feared the inevitable fallout. Instead of sacking Lee, Eisenhower decided to go over his head and assigned Clay the job of "speeding up supply" by cleaning up the Normandy base section. The Normandy mission would test Clay's reputation for bringing order to bedlam. Eisenhower sweetened the pot by promising Clay a division if he sorted out the problems in Normandy.[58]

Clay proved more than equal to the task. The War Department had loaned Clay for sixty days; he spent less than half that time in Normandy but effected immediate improvements. Until Clay showed up, the Normandy base section had been commanded by colonels from the engineer establishment that had landed on 6 June. He established a planning group and gave it regulatory authority. Hughes reported, "Clay a bolshevist: 'Too many engineers,' 'Won't take orders from General Staff officers,' 'Will introduce controversial subject at a Lee conference or bust in the attempt.'"[59] After a scuffle with Lee, Clay forced the technical and special services to work for him, not their bosses in Paris. That included the Transportation Corps; Clay assumed direct control of the railroads out of Cherbourg. He assessed the basic problem: "all we were doing was transferring the ship bottleneck into a worse bottleneck on the ground," which in turn created another blockage because the volume of railroad tonnage never approached port discharge rates. During November, beach operations ceased, and the Red Ball service ended. Only the limited train connections out of Cherbourg remained. Clay issued unmistakable priorities: first clear the ports and depots; then increase the flow of sorted material by rail. He was going to host a party at his chateau and told the chief of transportation, "If you make 10,000 tons per day this week, come Saturday night; if not, pack your bag and report to [your boss] in Paris. He came to dinner." The statistics clearly illustrate Clay's impact; the amount of materiel on the Continent in the Normandy base section declined from 73 percent to 46 percent during Clay's short tenure.[60]

Having solved the Clay issue, Eisenhower turned his attention to Aurand. Hughes and Eisenhower had a long talk after Clay exited the office on 30 October. ComZ had again reported, "armies can attack—supplies OK." They both had heard that refrain before. Eisenhower concluded that the chief of ordnance, MG Henry Sayler, "is poor," and he looked forward to "getting Henry Aurand who has done [a] good job running 6th Service Command." Eisenhower then told Hughes about appointing Clay to Normandy. "I'd hate to be Lee and have Ike pick my men," Hughes thought to himself. "Ike says Cliff [Lee] has great faculty of picking poor men and poor organizations. But why shouldn't Ike fire Lee if Lee can't pick proper men. Ike says he didn't want combat failures blamed on CZ. Told Ike he was rare man!"[61]

Smith never placed much store in Aurand's replacing Lee. Eisenhower and Aurand had been classmates, but other than that, the two men remained distant. Smith knew him from Washington, where Aurand had headed the War Department's lend-lease directorate. Aurand had a reputation for efficiency—he had scored high marks while running the Sixth Service Area in Chicago—but also for being opinionated and too full of himself. Unlike Clay, Aurand had no inkling what lay in store when he received a phone call out of the blue from ASF headquarters informing him to prepare for duty in Europe. When briefed in Washington, he "neither asked nor was told why or by whom I had been selected to go to Europe." Aurand did not care. All he knew was that he would be the second ranking general in ComZ after Lee.[62]

Clay got the red-carpet treatment when he arrived in Paris; Aurand got the bum's rush. No delegation greeted him at Orly, and he took a cab to Versailles. After having a hard time entering the SHAEF compound, he cooled his heels at the reception counter. "I guess . . . major generals were a dime a dozen around Versailles," he concluded. After a long wait he was directed to Smith's office.

Aurand found Smith distracted, "busy and not too well." During November Smith's health became an issue again. In addition to the regular ulcer complaints, he began to experience shooting pains. Smith barely gave Aurand the time of day, telling him only that he would be assigned to ComZ and Eisenhower would provide him with instructions.

He handed Aurand a letter of introduction to Lee and showed him the door.

Eisenhower greeted him warmly and immediately laid out his pressing concerns about ammunition supplies. He remembered Aurand had written a manual on ammunition stocks and assigned him the task of getting to the bottom of the ammunition issue. He wanted Aurand to tour the front and ComZ installations, assess the situation, and offer remedies. They exchanged pleasantries; both had sons who had graduated from West Point on D-day.

Aurand made his way back to Paris and the Hotel Majestic. Like everyone else, he wondered about ComZ's setup. The headquarters occupied not only the hotel but also office buildings in both directions off the Rue Kléber on the Champs Élysées. He reported to Lord, who carefully scrutinized his orders and Smith's letter and then shepherded Aurand in to see Lee. A guarded Lee wondered why Aurand had been sent and resented him poking around in his business. After his reception at Orly, SHAEF, and ComZ, Aurand concluded correctly, "I was not asked for by anybody in Europe."

The next day Aurand met Hughes for lunch. Aurand admitted he wished his "mouth hadn't been built so I could put my foot in," and he gave his assessment of the theater after a day in Paris.[63] Aurand told Hughes, "Ike [was] made to carry Beadle [sic]. Lee [is] carried by Somervell, who never made a mistake." He went on to tell Hughes, "POL demands [are] eating into ETO. A lot of b___ s___."[64] Aurand made the mistake of confiding in Hughes, whom he considered a friend. Both were from Ordnance, and Aurand had served under Hughes in an arsenal before the war. Hughes did not share Aurand's high opinion of himself, and wondered how Aurand had ever made major general.[65]

The various Paris headquarters were like a convention of the Daughters of the Confederacy—initiates were intensely loyal to their own organization and cause and deeply suspicious of outsiders, especially those voicing disparagement. Hughes told Eisenhower what Aurand had said. "Ike asked for Beadle," Hughes recorded, and it was not true "that Ike had to take Beadle with [the] job of C in C."[66] Given Hughes's personality and the highly attuned SHAEF rumor mill, word of Aurand's comments almost certainly filtered to Smith.

As soon as he could organize it, Aurand set off on a tour of the commands. He went first to Eagle Rear in Verdun and Twelfth Army Group's supply echelon. Greeted with so many complaints about ComZ, Aurand "couldn't get anything factual." As Aurand discovered at each of his stops, "the dissatisfaction with topside was felt even more strongly the farther down it got." He then proceeded to Luxembourg and Eagle Forward, Bradley's headquarters. The forward areas were crawling with officers investigating the ammunition problem—Crawford and Bull from SHAEF, and Lord and BG James Stratton from ComZ. "Too many observers and 'eyes and ears,'" Hughes thought.[67] Bradley convened a major supply conference on 12 November, and Aurand produced figures furnished by the War Department. Adhering to the McCoy Board recommendations, the War Department had reduced ammunition production based on projections of lower expenditures. Moses trotted out figures he had on U.S. ammunition production. "These schedules won't meet the demands of the 12th Army Group," Moses remonstrated. He had done the math: if you took Twelfth Army Group's projected rates of fire and multiplied that by ninety days, "you haven't got that much in France." Still peeved he had not been consulted since February about ammunition requirements, Bradley "found the information most disturbing" and saw it as another example of ComZ shorting his command.[68] After the meeting Aurand asked Moses how much ammunition Twelfth Army Group held in reserve. Moses admitted, "I don't know. We dropped that from our records as soon as we get it." Aurand replied, "I'll bet you got 90 days up there in front and you are hiding it." Moses quickly denied it.

Aurand got the same story at First and Third Armies. Patton, his chief of staff, and the G-4 were conveniently away on tour when Aurand arrived, so he talked to the chief ordnance officer. At First Army, Aurand met with the entire staff. Hodges and his chief of staff greeted Aurand, but the G-4 was not very welcoming, and Aurand felt he "would just as soon that I hadn't come." As at his previous stops, First Army evaded answering his questions about its artillery ammunition reserves. Since Aurand had written the book on ammunition storage, he wanted to inspect the ordnance depot. No officer received him, and Aurand went into the office and found it vacant. Then the ordnance officer came rushing in and ordered Aurand, with his two stars, out of his office. He had to request permission to enter one of First Army's secreted ammo dumps. "They weren't going to let anybody else count their reserve stocks," Aurand decided. He found the situation entirely different in Ninth Army area. Simpson and Aurand had taught together at the War College, and Aurand remembered that Simpson had given the lecture on supply in a theater of operations. Simpson claimed "supply of ammunition in the 9th Army to be no problem," and he and his staff retained "complete confidence in Lee and his ComZ." On the return trip to Paris, Aurand visited the ammunition depots at Liège in ADSEC and Soissons in the Oise base section. He found them "beautifully laid out . . . just like my book" and brimming with ammunition. He made a quick trip to see Clay in Cherbourg and found mountains of supplies buried in water and mud.[69] On his travels, Aurand discovered huge stockpiles of ammunition along the roads "all across the rear of the First Army," which "was a pretty wide front." He observed, "It looked very much as though First Army was accumulating its own secondary reserves of ammunition instead of relying on ComZ depots for them." Aurand concluded after the war, "I had—and still have—the impression that First Army was determined to discredit ComZ; and its secret weapon for this purpose was its concealed assets of ammunition."[70]

Returning to Paris, Aurand wrote up his preliminary findings and hand-delivered them to Smith on 18 November. He told Smith the report contained incomplete data on Sixth Army Group because he had not visited Devers's headquarters. Aurand informed Smith that Twelfth Army Group and First and Third Armies kept no inventories of ammunition, and the theater's numbers did not tally with those provided by the War Department. He could not reconcile these differences between Bradley's and Lee's headquarters, which held the potential for a serious clash at the highest command levels. Smith avoided that question, instead fixing the blame on ASF. "Very much concerned about the failure of production in the US," Smith "felt that he had to have responsibility for this failure well established." He thought that "someone should present the case of the theater to General Marshall." Crawford, also in attendance, suggested Aurand. Smith insisted that ASF finalize the figures before Lutes came to France.

That afternoon Smith called for an emergency conference on the ammunition crisis. Before he could formulate a theater policy in response to War Department cuts, Smith needed a single theater-wide measure for ammunition. Aurand flatly stated that the War Department and theater numbers did not add up across the board on basic rates of fire, number of weapons, stock levels, and distribution capacity of ComZ. Aurand came under attack; Lord dismissed his calculations and, along with Stratton, strenuously objected to his attempts to hammer out a single rate of supply for artillery with Moses and Plank.[71]

Over lunch, Hughes asked Aurand if he was aware that MG Russell Maxwell, the WDGS G-4, was in Paris. Hughes, Sayler, Maxwell, and Aurand were old acquaintances; all were ordnance officers and major generals. Hughes invited Aurand and the others to dinner in his suite. Over a few aperitifs, Aurand forgot his admonition to watch himself and launched into a graphic description of his tour of the theater. Taken aback, Hughes and Sayler—both old hands—said nothing, but Maxwell, who had never been in the theater, asked Aurand's opinion of the command structure. At first Aurand demurred. He had not been in France very long, and he knew his penchant for shooting off his mouth. But the others assured him that nothing he said would leave the room.

Aurand started by pointing out that Eisenhower wore too many hats. He could not effectively act as both Allied supreme commander and theater commander; Aurand never mentioned ground commander. Aurand thought Eisenhower's use of the American side of SHAEF as his theater headquarters, while ETO remained subsumed inside ComZ, bound to create friction. At the same time, his tour of the commands had proved that Bradley, Hodges, and Patton possessed not a shred of confidence in Lee or ComZ. It appeared to Aurand that the "lack of an independently manned national headquarters on the US side was directly responsible for the lack of cooperation—to put it mildly—between 12th Army Group and ComZ. Good personal relationships were difficult enough to achieve without inhibiting them by poor organization." He opined that Eisenhower should "set up at once a separate ETOUSA headquarters, with an adequate staff and its own commander . . . superior to Bradley and Lee." Generals at the same command levels could not work together, and the existing arrangement offered "a wonderful opportunity . . . for misunderstanding between two coordinate commanders, Lee and Bradley." He thought that, under the circumstances, ComZ had a "well-nigh impossible job" and had done "everything humanly possible to rectify the situation," but all three senior commanders in Twelfth Army Group would hear nothing good about Lee and his organization.[72]

Now on a roll, and "warmed by the fire . . . and some excellent brandy," Aurand became more expansive, offering "words of wisdom . . . so lofty," in Hughes's opinion, "[we] were not supposed to understand—nor did we."[73] He argued that the problem between Bradley and Lee went deeper than a mere clash of personalities. At the core stood the historic "military mind [that] embraced strategy as the highest goal of its learning, and has despised the logistician. This error runs throughout the military of the United States in particular." He saw this reflected in the interwar schools; modules on organization and supply were "badly mauled by a lot of line officers who tried to teach what was known as the 'G-4 Course.'" This bred among "would-be strategists and tacticians [an] evident distaste" for logisticians, which in turn contributed to "the mass ignorance of the regular officers of the US Army concerning this art." As a result, senior American officers possessed "no conception of how to create an overall organization." Aurand thought the interwar dread of large staffs had created a predisposition not to trust them; confronted with the formation of headquarters of undreamed of size and complexity, American officers simply could not run them.[74] In any case, the army lacked trained logistical officers to staff the huge headquarters once they did develop. Aurand deduced that any objective analysis "leads to the inescapable conclusion that those charged with [the conduct of operations] either lacked knowledge of the logistical art, and the basic principles of organization; or they chose to disregard one or both."[75]

Aurand possessed strong views on "the failure to properly organize for operations in Europe." His trip forward convinced him that the schism between Bradley and Lee would never have occurred had command channels and responsibilities been fixed. Fault lines emerged in the American command and staff structures because they were in part line commands and in part functional organizations. This produced a set of built-in disconnects. Aurand thought "it was like running wire across two leads"—short circuits were bound to happen.[76] Working relationships depended on cooperation instead of command, which, in Aurand's opinion, left too much to the vagaries of personalities and not enough on solid organization. Both during his tour and at Smith's conference, Aurand found that a basic mistrust existed between commands and within headquarters. As a result, Moses and Crawford—he could have mentioned Hughes as well—each offered his own set of numbers on production levels garnered by going outside of ComZ channels and back to different agencies in the War Department, none of which matched those Aurand had brought from Washington. It became clear that the theater needed to send a team back to Washington so everyone would be working on the same page.

The command structure Aurand found in Paris perplexed him. Aurand placed the lion's share of responsibility for the faulty organizational structures on Smith. "Smith loved power," Aurand decided, "and dipped in ETOUSA affairs frequently, particularly on those things about which there was no question and he could seem important." Because of Smith's meddling, often through Lord, "any failure of COMZ can hardly be laid at Lee's door." "Lee is a soldier," he continued. "He took it in stride and went on with those things that Smith did not deign to touch. And Bedell himself will deny any part of being a logistician. He hates them."[77]

Unbeknownst to Aurand, from autumn 1942 Smith had constantly pressured Eisenhower for precisely the organizational modifications he advocated. Smith would have agreed with most of Aurand's critique—

except for the barbs aimed at him. Aurand's views mirrored those held by a great many observers: that the power-grasping Smith took advantage of Eisenhower's malleability and, in enhancing his own authority, Smith created the short-circuit among SHAEF, ComZ, and the commands. This provides the perfect illustration of Eisenhower's buffering practice. He made the calls—or, more to the point, refused to make them, such as firing Lee—and left Smith to brandish the stick. When problems cropped up in the rear, even Marshall, who should have known better, pointed his finger at Smith. Eisenhower always got a free pass. Aurand got one thing right: the flawed organization "was ideally suited to the purposes of the skilled 'kniver-in-the-back,'" as he soon discovered.[78]

The next morning Hughes met with Smith, ostensibly to discuss ammunition supply. Smith intended to appeal to the War Department to restart ammunition production. He identified three problems: Eisenhower needed to back Bradley; Smith had to make the combined chiefs aware of the implications of the ammunition shortage, without continuing to alibi; and he had to do that without incurring the wrath of Somervell. The conversation turned to Aurand and his ammunition survey due that day. Hughes produced his notes of Aurand's discourse on the faulty organizational structure of SHAEF and ETO. Plunging the knife in deeper, Hughes told Smith that Aurand had been "advertising [a] list of service chiefs"—Sayler, Littlejohn, and the head of theater signals, MG William Rumbough—"to be fired."[79] He recommended that Auraud be sent home. Just as Hughes had guessed, Smith blew his top and ordered Aurand to get himself over to his office posthaste.

Aurand was working furiously to put the finishing touches on his exhaustive ammunition report when the phone rang. He assumed Smith's summons indicated his eagerness to receive Aurand's recommendations. Entering Smith's office, Aurand received a "cold reception." Smith handed him "a terse memo written in long hand signed by Hughes." Since Aurand "expressed such strong disapproval of the US organization in Europe," Smith informed him, "it would be impossible for [Aurand] to work in it." Aurand should pack his bags; Smith was returning him to Washington, reduced to his permanent rank of colonel. Seeing the shocked look on his face, and calculating that Aurand had powerful associates in the War Department who might stir up trouble (though Somervell was not among them; he intensely disliked Aurand), Smith, who possessed no such authority to send Aurand home, softened. "More mildly," Aurand remembered, Smith "stated that I was a valuable officer and I might be used as a brigadier general on the SHAEF side." Smith asked if Aurand had anything to say. He "had nothing to say about the Hughes memo," but Aurand did want to talk about his ammunition report. Smith shot back that since Aurand "was full of prejudice . . . someone more competent would have to do the job all over again."[80]

Hughes knew he would "not get anything but knife from Aurand" and invited him to his suite to see if he could salvage the situation. Busting out two crates of Lee's champagne, Hughes explained his actions. Deciding he might have to work with Hughes again after the war, Aurand kept things "more or less on [a] friendly basis" and admitted that Hughes had done the right thing. Banished from his suite, Aurand awaited "demotion or deportation or both" for several weeks, until Lee made him Clay's eventual successor in Normandy. Hughes offered him some sage advice on how to get along: "keep my neck in and tongue quiet and say whatever good came my way."[81]

Smith and Hughes ambushed Aurand because he was another redheaded orphan from out of town; they were not going to allow his critical study to make the rounds in the War Department, given the damage it would do to Eisenhower and all the commands in Europe. What Aurand said might have been poorly timed and ill-considered, but he was not wrong. Surveying the situation on 1 December, Hughes repeated Aurand's evaluation, noting, "[MG Frank] Ross [chief of transportation] is dejected over CZ control. John [Lee] is dejected over SHAEF control. Tom Larkin [in command of the southern line of communication] won't let CZ run him. It's all a mess. No discipline by Ike or Lee."[82] Smith never gave Lee the benefit of the doubt. He again agitated for Lee's removal and replacement by Clay.[83] Smith gave up efforts to convince Eisenhower of the need for reorganization; clearly, the timing was all wrong. "Lee was a stuffed shirt," he told a postwar interviewer, "I would have liked someone else. . . . it would have been so much better with a man like Clay." But Eisenhower "couldn't relieve [Lee] over a bunch of little things. So we kept him on. That gave him a semi-independent status. One of the crosses we had to bear. There was no other place for him. After all you have to use the tool you have at the time."[84]

With Aurand's study invalidated, the issue remained how to square the wide variance in ammunition requirements. Smith called in Clay from Cherbourg. At first, Eisenhower attached enough importance to the crisis to contemplate sending Smith to Washington, but then thought better of it. Instead, Clay would go, accompanied by Bull and Lord. Bull would make the case that the ammunition shortage influenced all future plans and operations; Clay and Lord would attempt to rationalize the disparity in the numbers with the War Department, ASF, and Byrnes's agency. Eisenhower reneged on his promise to reward Clay with a division and instead sent him back to a desk job in Washington. "It's very frustrating to have lived through two wars as an Army officer," Clay later lamented, "and to have not been, even for a short period of time, on any active military duty during the war."[85]

SHAEF requested that the army groups submit reports so Smith could correlate them for the three officers to take with them. Bradley complained that the lack of artillery firepower might force him to take the defensive and warned he might not hold his static positions if the Germans attacked. "The crossing of the Rhine with this ammunition is out of the question," he asserted, "unless enemy resistance collapsed."[86] Devers made similar protests, stating that each of his three corps could mass only enough artillery to support a single division in the attack. Sixth Army Group retained control over the southern line of communication (SOLOC) and would not call on SHAEF for materiel until SOLOC amalgamated with ComZ in mid-December. Basically, the War Department believed that enough heavy artillery ammunition had already been produced, huge untapped stocks still existed in the United Kingdom and Normandy, and SHAEF need only squeeze its own supply pipeline. In contrast, the commands in Europe argued, "We hadn't starting fighting yet." Naturally, Smith sided with Bradley and dispatched a carefully worded "cry for help," requesting that the War Department renew and expand ammunition production.[87] Smith's appeal carried the day. On 12 December Somervell reported that the Senate was already moving on increased expenditures.[88] Nothing illustrates the supply disconnect better than this fight over ammunition stocks. As events proved, Somervell got it right. Under congressional pressure, the War Department urgently expanded ammunition production, but many of the factories did not go online until the war in Europe had ended. During the war, American factories produced 408,000 rounds of 240mm ammunition, and American forces expended less than 30 percent of it in combat.[89]

Lee met Lutes at the airport on 5 December and installed him in a suite at the King George V. They talked briefly; Lee appeared "quite subdued and puzzled," unsure of the purpose of Lutes's visit and suspecting the worst. Lutes handed him a letter from Somervell detailing his mission "to perform a general check-up of supply and assessment of organization." That night Lee put on a lavish dinner for Lutes in one of his suites, "of which he seemed to have several."

First thing the next morning, Smith insisted that Lutes come out to Versailles. He wanted Lutes out of Lee's clutches. Lutes quickly detected that Smith was out of sorts, even for him. At the best of times, Smith's nerves tingled, but now they actually did. Smith finally visited a specialist, who diagnosed neuritis, an inflammation of the nerves that produces any number of symptoms, all of them painful. The condition became bad enough for Smith to spend three days in bed. "Smith immediately asked me how long I would be in France," Lutes noted in his diary, "and I told him I was on loan for approximately one month, to which he replied 'That was not enough.'" Lutes assumed that Smith shared Lee's bewilderment at why Washington had dispatched the three officers to ETO. He was wrong. Smith still harbored ideas about putting Lutes in command of ComZ. He told Lutes he very much wanted him attached to SHAEF permanently. Lutes replied he would like nothing more, but Somervell refused to release him "unless the position was of high enough importance." Smith shot back, "How high does it have to be?" Lutes knew where this was headed and gave "a very broad hint," stating, "Unless they were willing to have a new commander in the ComZ I doubted if I would be made available." That was precisely what Smith hoped to wangle.

Then Smith changed gears. He made a voluble defense of the theater's record. "NO one can say that supply here has failed," he declared. "Supply at the front is satisfactory." Turning to the issue of Lee, Smith stated, "Lee was not Ike's choice," and Eisenhower had never recommended his promotion. "BUT at this stage of the war he had no intention of changing him, that the principal difficulties are in clashes of personality." The only grounds for sacking him would be if "a major failure could be laid at Lee's doorstep." Lutes defended ComZ; no major specific failure could be attributed to Lee, and he conceded that combat operations appeared to be "fairly well supported." Smith told Lutes he wanted him to visit the northern group of armies, return to Paris, and then tour the southern group. Smith charged Lutes with determining whether the supply failures—the shipping logjam, the ammunition shortage, and the traffic snarls east of Paris—qualified as a "specific failure." Lutes's role was "to educate myself; to do all I can to advise and keep Lee's staff [from interfering] with operations in any way and to then get out of the way." These mixed messages placed Lutes in a very awkward spot, so to avoid being seen as Smith's hatchet man, Lutes refused the offer of an office at SHAEF.[90]

Lutes's first loyalty remained to Somervell. He never told Smith that his real mission involved discovering if ComZ had fallen short and why, and then ensuring that blame for the failure fell on Lee and not ASF. Certainly Somervell never desired Lee's removal, but he grew increasingly disenchanted with ComZ's failures in managing the shipping problem. Granted, the unpredicted advance of American forces in France threw ComZ into disarray, but the same applied in the Pacific theater, with concomitant demands for shipping. The legitimate claims made by the Pacific placed ASF in an embarrassing predicament: how could Somervell explain the purported shipping shortage when there were hundreds of ships serving as floating warehouses sitting off the coast of France or diverted to British ports? Somervell "was very much interested in what [Lutes] had to say about Smith's report on Lee." He denied playing any role in Lee's promotion. In Somervell's mind, Lee looked increasingly vulnerable.[91]

Lutes looked up Crawford, and "as usual, Bob was in a stew . . . this time it was a traffic jam east of Paris." With Antwerp now open and Le Havre taking in more volume, ComZ sought to shift the supply center of gravity forward. With the rear base sections—especially Clay in Normandy—shifting increased quantities of supply into the Oise base section and ADSEC, a huge backlog of railway wagons bunged the system. ComZ compounded the problem by moving supplies before it redistributed SOS personnel; because it still lacked properly functioning regulating stations, all the old problems of inexact accounting controls resurfaced as well. SHAEF's railroad representative estimated it would take "three weeks or a month to straighten out the matter."

Lee convened a conference of all his base section commanders; Larkin and Art Wilson, head of the advance section of SOLOC, also attended. A "very formal" dinner preceded the meeting. Lee invariably backed his subordinates "to the limit regardless of what happens," but he cut Plank's presentation short. ADSEC faced the biggest obstacles, and Lutes considered Plank "by far the best officer" in ComZ, but Lee viewed him as altogether too friendly with Bradley and Moses. Lutes derived little from the conference, which had obviously been staged for his benefit, and he found the whole exercise too self-congratulatory.[92]

Larkin drew a link between the mismanagement of shipping and the mounting manpower problem. Divisions and replacements earmarked for northern France went instead to Marseilles, but ships with the maintenance for those troops were still held up in the Channel, forcing SOLOC to draw on stocks in the Mediterranean. The shift of divisions from Third to Seventh Army reduced the drain on ComZ but added to his burden—all without any significant increase in supply and support units. The tails of these divisions would not arrive until late January. Delays in reequipping and resupplying divisions and transportation shortfalls suspended the movement toward the front. And there remained the difficulties of equipping the French.[93]

When Lutes toured the forward areas, he discovered the situation just as Aurand had described. At Twelfth Army Group he found Bradley to be "supply and logistical minded and very conservative" but extremely "bitter on the subject" of ComZ. Moses raised the same complaints about the lack of an American general headquarters and reiterated ComZ's faults. Patton was "bitter also on ammunition and dislikes General Lee as much as ever." Patton told Lutes he "trusts no one behind the AdSec and that he doesn't mind saying so to anyone from General Lee on up or down. He is very outspoken." Third Army's surplus of gasoline permitted it to return 1 million gallons to ComZ, but Patton claimed he needed ammunition. He planned to fire all he had and then, when it ran out, dig in, "because the Germans do not have sufficient strength to strike back." Lutes concluded, "Patton does not understand all the problems behind the front." For all of Patton's fire, Lutes found Hodges the most unforgiving. "Of all the commanders on the front," Lutes thought Hodges the most "intolerant of any supply deficiency." He saw Hodges's attitude as "a hangover from the conservatism of the Old Army," and the First Army commander impressed Lutes "as a man who has never studied the supply side of the picture and does not desire to." Like Aurand, he found that Ninth Army area was another world. He reported "problems similar to First and Third Armies" but described Simpson as "a very tolerant understanding type" who harbored "no serious complaints and trusts ComZ to support him."

"The importance of proper logistic organization in the theaters of operations was not understood within the Army," Lute concluded. "The subject received too little attention in peacetime. Lack of doctrine governing logistic activities complicated relationships between theaters and support supply agencies." Like Aurand, Lutes thought that "training in logistic planning and operations before the war had been seriously neglected by the educational system of the Armed Forces," and "nowhere in an officer's training was there a comprehensive treatment of the logistic problems of the War Department or of theaters of operations." Senior officers trained in the "Old Army" way of doing things, especially those who went overseas in 1942, were deeply suspicious of modern managerial methods; they never understood the ASF organization and were perfectly content with the familiar structures. Like the saying goes: "There is the right way, the wrong way, and the army way." Lutes never said it, but Eisenhower clearly fell into this camp.[94]

From 14 to 16 December Lutes traveled from First Army headquarters at Spa to Simpson's headquarters in Maastricht to Aachen, then through the Ardennes to Liège and Namur, and finally Soissons, inspecting the armies' rear areas and ADSEC installations. At Liège he toured vast concentrations of supply, including a huge ammunition dump fed by four railheads. On the way to Soissons he rode "along roads through piles of ammunition."[95]

Lutes guardedly gave ComZ passing grades. He informed Somervell that Smith considered "the supply situation in general is now in good shape at the front and [SHAEF] seem[s] satisfied that the Armies can be supported in the present push." However, given the scale of the logistical effort, "there are bound to be slips." Even though "Generals Bradley and Patton have not changed their minds about the ComZ staff and organization . . . they feel supply is improving." As Lutes informed Eisenhower, "the machine does not move smoothly but it does run." Eisenhower agreed that ComZ had expedited the flow of divisions into the theater and rendered sufficient supply support to the combat zones, but he worried about the general uneasiness in SHAEF and in the field about Lee's organization.[96] Yet Eisenhower felt confident enough to inform the CCS on 3 December that even though Antwerp offered only future relief, the "lines of communications are now adequate to maintain our present offensives and to build up army reserves, as a first priority."[97]

Naturally, Lee stoutly defended ComZ's record against the "aggressive, grasping, fighting natures" of the combat commanders, with their "false suspicions" of commands in the rear. And he promised Lutes that "the pay-off in history will be on the front lines."[98] That payoff was not long in coming.

Après le Déluge

November marked the lowest ebb of Allied fortunes in the campaign in northwestern Europe. Montgomery, whatever his shortcomings, could never be faulted on his professional acumen. As he pointed out, Eisenhower's 28 October outline strategy—it could never claim to be more—amounted to little. Nothing about the autumn fighting along the frontiers reflected well on Allied generalship. The lull in offensive actions in October underscored the supply and manpower constrictions imposed on Allied commanders. Eisenhower's decision to attack every-where—in the Netherlands, north and south of Aachen, in Lorraine, and in Alsace—produced no strategic advantage. Dividing the main American thrusts between Hodges and Patton, separated by the Ardennes, meant that neither supported the other. Despite the German success attacking through the Ardennes in 1940, SHAEF wrote off using this avenue for an advance into Germany. Just as intriguing, the Germans gambled on holding the Ardennes front with minimal forces. By mutual contrivance, the Ardennes became a kind of dead zone.

November also marked the nadir of SHAEF's influence. The September question—what did SHAEF amount to?—was answered by an emphatic not much. Increasingly the object of derision, Eisenhower exerted little discernible influence on events; nor did Smith in SHAEF. Fully convinced of the correctness of his approach, the supreme commander devolved responsibility for the conduct of operations on his field commands. Bradley sanctioned pointless and unproductive offensives based only on the belief that, as in Normandy, the Germans would eventually crack.

Despite ComZ's best efforts, its October deliveries only approached sustainment levels; not until mid-November did circumstances permit the establishment of "on paper" reserves. The opening of Antwerp held out the promise of a daily infusion of 20,000 tons into an American line of communications shortened by two-thirds. Although Antwerp might ease supply worries, there was no easy remedy to the pending manpower crisis. The November offensives lengthened casualty lists. In that month, U.S. forces suffered 62,437 battle casualties—significantly more than those sustained in the ferocious hedgerow fighting in July. Nonbattle losses spiraled up to 56,211—double those of October and more than four and a half times those incurred in Normandy. And just under 90 percent of the casualties fell on the combat arms, 70 percent on the infantry.[1]

As became increasingly evident—and it came as a great shock to SHAEF—the time would soon arrive when the manpower pool ran dry. In September Eisenhower commanded thirty-four American divisions; only twenty-four remained in the United States. In late October Marshall again offered to accelerate the movement of divisions into the theater: three by mid-November, four more by early December, and an additional five by the middle of the month—half of strategic reserves.[2] Eisenhower accepted, even though SHAEF could neither supply the divisions already in line much above subsistence levels nor move forward additional ones already in theater. Divisions went forward with only their three infantry regiments, shorn of their artillery, tanks, and support units. Owing to faltering War Department manpower policies, the unbloodied 1944 divisions lacked the fighting power of their 1943 cousins. Worse, the veteran divisions—especially in First Army—were shells of their former selves. All the veteran divisions faced debilitating shortages in riflemen, an ever-increasing portion of their ranks filled with undertrained replacements. The replacement system itself stood on the verge of collapse.

Amazingly, Marshall reported that the CCS was considering a directive calling for an all-out effort to end the war in Europe "at an early date" before January 1945. In his estimate, the offer of the dozen divisions would put SHAEF over the top. This hubris illustrated just how far removed Washington remained from the realities at the front—a situation never clarified by any of Eisenhower's communications. Brooke scornfully dismissed Marshall's "wonderful telegram" and commented, "He seems to consider that if we really set our heart on it, and bank on its happening, irrespective of what happens in the future should we fail to do so, we ought to be able to finish the war before the end of the year!"[3] By the end of November the Allies held the initiative all along the line, had advanced to the West Wall ahead of the D+360 projections, had eroded German divisions, enjoyed air superiority with an intensifying strategic bombing campaign, and continued their buildup, but the

SHAEF strategy of attrition left the Allied armies confronting a first-class manpower crisis. The uncomfortable question soon dawned: what if the German defenses did not splinter? How long could SHAEF continue "hammering . . . constantly and seriously?" The November offensives and the worsening manpower projections generated the renewal of Anglo-American discord over the conduct of the campaign, which inevitably resurrected the old question of command.

A Plot Fizzles

A predictable monthly cycle emerged in Anglo-American relations. At the Versailles conference it appeared that Montgomery got what he wanted, but when Eisenhower finally published his directive, it fell far short of what the field marshal expected. Montgomery flared up, and a crisis was narrowly averted. On 28 October a new directive appeared that varied little from the previous one. Montgomery's chores consisted of opening Antwerp, clearing the Germans from between the Meuse and the Rhine, and seizing a Rhine bridgehead. The main attack fell to the Central Group of Armies, which was ordered to carve out a bridgehead south of Cologne and then attack northeast in conjunction with Montgomery's forces, while Patton occupied the Saar, Devers occupied Alsace, and both secured their own crossings of the Rhine.[4] Montgomery stewed; things had not gone his way, but since Eisenhower "would hear no more" from him on the issue of command, he remained quiet—at least officially. In his nightly letters to Brooke he berated Eisenhower, but the CIGS admonished him to hold his tongue. By the end of November his disappointment turned to despair as the monthly sequence started anew, with SHAEF preparing another revised but substantively unchanged directive.

Montgomery chafed, but Brooke orchestrated the plot to unseat Eisenhower from ground command. Throughout November the CIGS grew increasingly troubled by the seeming lack of direction in Allied strategy in northwest Europe and identified the command structure as the essential problem. On 2 November Smith flew to London and presented Eisenhower's plan to Churchill and the BCOS over lunch. "Bedell in fine form," reported Cunningham. "There is shortly to be an attack along the whole line." After Smith left, Brooke raised his concerns. "Brooke obviously does not think the main attack has enough weight behind it," recorded Cunningham, "and looks on Patton's attack as too great a diversion of strength." Cunningham proved less certain. "These Americans are often right!!"[5]

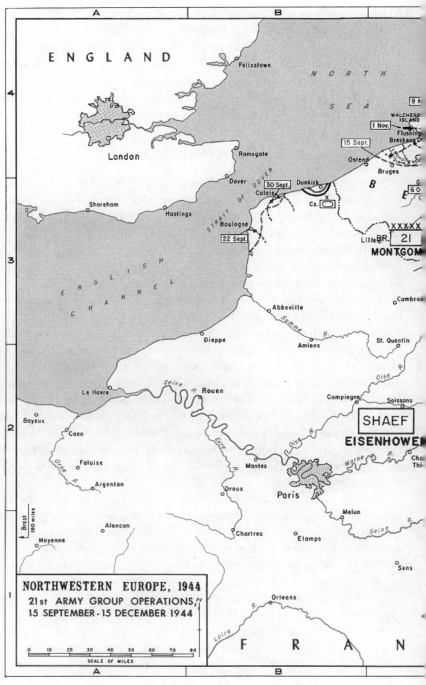

The Frontiers: Antwerp, Arnhem, Aachen, and Alsace

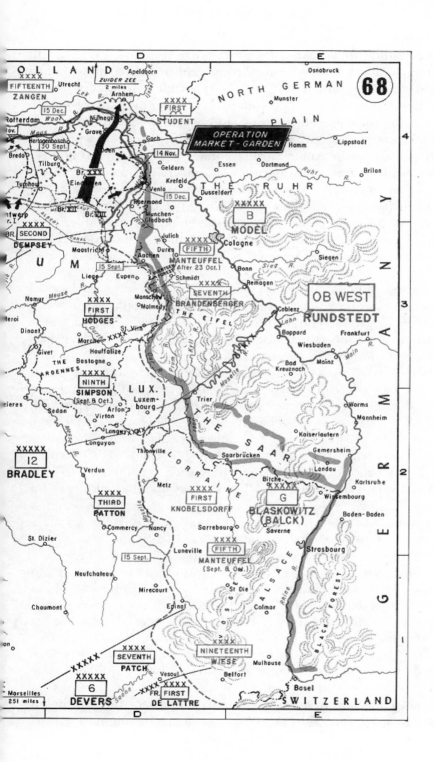

OLLAND

XXXX
FIFTEENTH
ZANGEN

ZUIDER ZEE
2 miles

Utrecht

Apeldoorn

Osnabrück

NORTH GERMAN

Münster

XXXX
FIRST
STUDENT

Lek R.

Arnhem

15 Dec.

Waal

Nijmegen

Rotterdam

Grave

Goch

Nov.

Maas

Hertogenbosch

30 Sept.

Tilburg

Bredo

Turnhout

Br. XXXX

Eindhoven

Venlo

14 Nov.

Geldern

Krefeld

15 Dec.

Roermond

Düsseldorf

PLAIN

Hamm

Lippstadt

Brilon

Essen

Dortmund

Ruhr R.

T H E   R U H R

OPERATION
MARKET - GARDEN

ntwerp

Br. XII

Br. VIII

München-
Gladbach

B

MODEL

Jülich

Cologne

XXXXX

ALBERT
CANAL

BR.

SECOND

DEMPSEY

U   M

Maastricht

15 Sept.

Aachen

Düren

XXXX
FIFTH
MANTEUFFEL
(After 23 Oct.)

Siegen

Ourthe

Liège

Eupen

Schmidt

Bonn

Sieg R.

Remagen

Namur

Meuse R.

Monschau

Malmedy

SEVENTH

BRANDENBERGER

Coblenz

Lahn R.

OB WEST

RUNDSTEDT

eroi

XXXX
FIRST
HODGES

St. Vith

THE EIFEL

Boppard

Frankfurt

Dinant

Marche

Wiesbaden

Main R.

Givet

Houffalize

THE

Bastogne

Bad
Kreuznach

Mainz

ARDENNES

XXXX
NINTH
SIMPSON
(Sept. & Oct.)

LUX.

Luxem-
bourg

Kyll R.

Prüm R.

Moselle R.

Trier

Worms

Mannheim

eres

Sedan

Arlon

Virton

Kaiserslautern

Gemersheim

Meuse R.

Longwy

Longuyon

Thionville

Saar R.

Saarbrücken

Landau

Karlsruhe

XXXXX
12
BRADLEY

Verdun

Metz

T H E   S A A R

Bitche

Wissembourg

Baden-Baden

XXXX
THIRD
PATTON

Moselle R.

Commercy

Nancy

XXXX
FIRST
KNOBELSDORFF

Sarrebourg

Saverne

XXXXX
G
BLASKOWITZ
(BALCK)

St. Dizier

LORRAINE

Lunéville

15 Sept.

XXXX
FIFTH
MANTEUFFEL
(Sept. & Oct.)

Strasbourg

Neufchâteau

Mirecourt

St Die

Colmar

ALSACE

BLACK FOREST

Rhine R.

Chaumont

Epinal

Meurthe R.

on

XXXXX
SEVENTH
PATCH

XXXXX
6
DEVERS

Vesoul

Marseilles
251 miles

Saône R.

XXXX
FR. FIRST
DE LATTRE

XXXX
NINETEENTH
WIESE

Belfort

Mulhouse

Basel

SWITZERLAND

D   E

G   E   R   M   A   N   Y

A week later Brooke had a long talk with Montgomery. "He still goes on harping over the system of command in France and the fact that the war is being prolonged," Brooke reported. "He has got this on the brain as it affects his own personal position, and he cannot put up with not being the sole controller of land operations." Brooke agreed with Montgomery that "the set-up is bad but it is not one which can be easily altered, as the Americans have now the preponderating force in France, and naturally consider they should have a major say in the running of the war." He hoped that once the Americans grasped "the results of dispersing their strength all along the front it may become easier to convince them that some drastic change is desirable, leading to a concentration of force at the vital point." He cautioned that Montgomery must not get involved but should "shove at the back of the scrum."[6]

In Brooke's mind, strategy and command amounted to two faces of the same coin, but he also reckoned the Americans would never accept Montgomery as ground commander. In mid-November Brooke toured the southern front and visited Eisenhower at Reims, and he came away with the conclusion that Eisenhower lacked the capacity "to run the land battle as well as acting as Supreme commander." He also saw plenty of evidence of the futility of the American doctrine of applying constant pressure all along the line. "The French realized these errors only too well," Brooke recorded, "and are fretting at being subjected to their results." At Reims, Brooke found Eisenhower's grasp of the situation at the front "fairly vague as to what was really going on!!" His tour with Churchill left Brooke convinced that the meager results on the front necessitated a thorough review of Allied strategy and the viability of the command structure.[7]

Montgomery naturally added fuel to Brooke's fire. He listed all of Eisenhower's failures as ground commander. "To be quite frank," he wrote, "there is no command at all; the whole affair is disjointed and ragged. The days are slipping by; we are wasting a great deal of precious time." Eisenhower issued directives with "no relation to the practical realities of the battle." Eisenhower should either take "proper control of operations" with a genuine air commander in chief (Tedder), or "he should appoint someone else to do this." Montgomery left little doubt that he thought Eisenhower was in over his head. Eisenhower "has never commanded anything before in his whole career; now, for the first time, he has elected to take direct command of very large-scale operations and he does not know how to do it." A month had passed since Montgomery's pledge not to raise the issue of command again, but alarmed that "we are drifting into dangerous waters," he wondered if he "ought to take the initiative again in the matter."[8]

Brooke knew Montgomery's intervention would add a great deal of high-octane gasoline to the conflagration. For three days Brooke pondered the problem and drafted a number of letters to Montgomery. In one he stated his willingness to launch "a strong attack [on the American chiefs] on our behalf insisting on the necessary changes being carried out without delay."[9] Finally, he wrote a "very secret" letter to Montgomery on 20 November and entrusted Portal to hand-deliver it. Brooke advised Montgomery "not to approach Eisenhower for the present" and "remain silent now, unless Eisenhower opens the subject." He felt "pretty certain that the results of the current offensive will provide us with sufficient justification for requesting the American Chiefs of Staff to reconsider the present Command organization and their present strategy on the Western Front." He thought that within a week or two there would be "ample proof of the insufficiency of present command set-up," validating the BCOS "making the strongest representation to Washington." Given the relative disadvantage of the British position, both politically and militarily, the ground commander must be an American, and Brooke solicited Montgomery's opinion of Bradley. Brooke suffered under no illusions. As he told Montgomery, "I anticipate the greatest difficulties in getting the American Chiefs of Staff to agree to any change in the set-up."[10]

The letter Portal brought back from Montgomery confounded Brooke. Montgomery did not think Eisenhower would accept Bradley as ground commander. Since Eisenhower seemed determined "to show that he is a great general in the field," Montgomery suggested, "let him do so and let us all lend a hand to pull him through." Eisenhower should command the two fronts from a suitable headquarters—not Reims—with Tedder as air commander, Montgomery commanding in the north, and Bradley in the south. Brooke wrote a stinging reply, raising a number of questions. "Ike would allot forces to each front as demanded by his plan," Montgomery suggested. "How is he to do this if he can't make a plan?" Brooke queried. "Can you see Ike judging between requirements of the two fronts, overriding American clamour for their Commander being in charge of the main thrusts, etc., etc.? I can't." He told Montgomery that Eisenhower had affirmed time and time again that the "northern line of advance is the one and only one that has any chance of success," and he asked, "Have you considered whether you are likely to be very acceptable in American eyes for this Command?" Brooke thought the only solution lay in Bradley assuming the mantle of ground commander.[11]

A chastened Montgomery returned to his familiar line. After touring the Roer front, he reported that Ninth Army struggled "to maintain its advance but the troops are wet and tired and the man management is bad and there are not reserves." The same applied in First Army's area. "The whole business is a first class example of the futile doctrine of everybody attacking everywhere with no reserves anywhere."[12]

At a 24 November BCOS conference Brooke cleared out the secretaries and brought up the subject:

> [He] put before the meeting [his] views on the very unsatisfactory state of affairs in France, with no one running the land battle. Eisenhower, though supposed to be doing so, is detached and by himself with his lady chauffeur on the golf links at Rheims— entirely detached from the war and taking practically no part in running of the war! Matters got so bad lately that a deputation of Whiteley, Bedell Smith and a few others went up to tell him that he must get down to it and RUN the war, which he said he would. Personally I think he is incapable of running the war even if he tries.[13]

They discussed the advisability of asking Marshall to fly to London for discussions, "but we are doubtful if he would appreciate the situation." During Marshall's meeting with the BCOS in London in mid-June, a very nasty exchange had transpired over Stilwell's place in the Southeast Asia command structure. It got so nasty, in fact, that Brooke withdrew from the conversation for fear of "irreparably damaging our relationship." Brooke expected far more fireworks if the British attempted any diminution of Eisenhower's status as dual commander. Instead, Brooke decided to go over Marshall's head to Churchill and propose a new command setup. "It is one of the most difficult problems I have had to tackle," he noted. Brooke wanted Bradley named ground force commander, with Tedder as air commander. He also wanted the front divided at the Ardennes, with Montgomery in charge of the northern group of armies and Patton in the south, "whilst Ike returns to the true duties of Supreme Commander."[14]

Two days later Montgomery flew to England. As undiplomatic as ever, Montgomery asserted, "As a commander in charge of the land operations, Eisenhower is quite useless. There must be no misconception on this matter; he is completely and utterly useless." Agreeing with Brooke's proposal for the shift in command responsibilities and the need "to counter the pernicious American strategy of attacking all along the line," Montgomery offered to float the scheme to Eisenhower while Brooke suggested to Churchill that he invite Marshall to London. "Without some such changes we shall just drift on and God knows when the war will end." According to Brooke, Churchill was "evidently beginning to realize that all is not well in France, but incapable of really seeing where the trouble lies!"[15]

On 28 November Eisenhower conferred with Montgomery at his new headquarters at Zonhoven. Montgomery took Eisenhower into his trailer and in unvarnished terms launched into a lecture. For a month the Allied forces had pursued the objectives set down in Eisenhower's last directive, to no strategic end. The Germans not only held the line but also managed to withdraw powerful armored elements into a reserve. Meanwhile, SHAEF possessed no such strategic reserve. He categorized the frontiers campaigns as a strategic defeat and stated that unless SHAEF developed a new plan, Montgomery envisioned no Rhine crossing for months. According to Montgomery's letter that night to Brooke, Eisenhower agreed that his plans had miscarried and "we had, in fact, suffered a strategic reverse." He assented to abandon "the doctrine of attacking all along [the] front" and recognized that we "must concentrate our resources on [a] selected vital thrust." Montgomery then laid out Brooke's proposal for a change in command spheres, with Bradley as ground commander. Eisenhower balked at this. Montgomery claimed that Eisenhower acknowledged, in principle, that the front was divided by the Ardennes, but he saw difficulties in placing the field marshal in command "as [the] main objective lay in [the] Northern zone." According to Montgomery's account, Eisenhower consented to place "a strong Army Group under Bradley north of the Ardennes" under the field marshal's "operational command." Devers would assume a holding action in the south.[16]

Montgomery told Brooke his three-hour conversation with Eisenhower played out "in a most friendly way." Montgomery's military assistant, LTC Christopher "Kit" Dawney, offered a different version of events. For three hours the field marshal harangued Eisenhower and eventually "reduced Eisenhower to a condition of speechlessness," and the supreme commander finally asked to go to bed. Dawney showed Eisenhower to his room and returned to take dictation of Montgomery's nightly letter to Brooke. "Get this message sent to the CIGS," Montgomery instructed. Dawney took down what Montgomery said, including the claim that "Ike had agreed in principle with the single-thrust strategy." Dawney read back the contents of the letter and inquired if Montgomery desired any changes. Montgomery replied in the negative. Taken aback, Dawney asked, "May I say something, sir?" Montgomery said, "Yes, certainly." Dawney pointed out, "Ike does not agree, sir." Montgomery's only reply: "Send that message, Kit."[17]

Brooke met with Churchill that day. "We looked facts in the face," he noted, and concluded "this last offensive could only be classified as the first strategic reverse that we had suffered since landing in France." Brooke identified two essential issues: the faulty American organization, and the misguided strategy of "always attacking all along the front, irrespective of strength available." He considered it "sheer madness." Churchill agreed with much of what Brooke said but doubted the wisdom of a command change. The prime minister agreed that nothing could happen without consulting Marshall and asked for a few more days before anybody attempted anything. Brooke harbored "grave doubts as Ike is incapable of running a land battle and it is all dependent on how well Monty can handle him."[18]

The next morning Eisenhower appeared "worried and ill at ease." As Montgomery told Brooke, "When I suggested last night that Bradley would be suitable as Land Force Commander under him he definitely shied right off it," and in Montgomery's opinion, Eisenhower thought "Bradley has failed him as an architect of land operations. There is no doubt he is now very anxious to go back to the old set-up we had in Normandy and up to 1st September and to put Bradley under my operational command with both our Army Groups north of the Ardennes."[19] Eisenhower and Montgomery agreed that they needed a meeting with Bradley and set the time and place for 7 December at Maastricht.

There are only two explanations of how Montgomery could have come to these conclusions. First, any conversation with Montgomery turned into a monologue. Typically, he presented his opinion, refused to countenance the merit of anyone else's point of view, and heard only what he wanted to hear. When Eisenhower found himself in a situation in which he did not agree, he simply remained silent. He customarily avoided hostile exchanges but never changed his mind under duress. The greater the pressure, the more dogged he became, and silence did not connote consent. The only other explanation is that Montgomery simply stretched the truth. Montgomery always left his one-on-one meetings with Eisenhower sure he had carried the day, and he embroidered his reports of these encounters in his letters, especially to Brooke. But his accounts of the Zonhoven discussions were too emphatic to be mere misrepresentations.

Why Brooke thought Montgomery could handle Eisenhower remains a mystery. On 30 November Montgomery wrote to Eisenhower "to confirm the main points that were agreed on during the conversations": "We have . . . failed," he began, "and we have suffered a strategic reverse. We now require a new plan. And this time *we must not fail.*" SHAEF ought to "get away from the doctrine of attacking in so many places that nowhere are we strong enough to get decisive results. We must concentrate such strength on the main selected thrust that success will be certain." He argued for a division of command on geographic rather than national lines. Clearly, the question of command remained far more unsettled than Montgomery indicated to Brooke; as this letter reveals, Eisenhower made no grant of operational command to the field marshal. Montgomery pointed out what a "good team" he and Bradley made in Normandy but chided, "since you separated us" things did not proceed very well. "I believe to be certain of success you want to bring us together again; and one of us should have the full operational control north of the Ardennes; and if you decide that I should do that work—that is O.K. by me." He ended by insisting, "We want no one else at the meeting [in Maastricht], except Chiefs of Staff: who must not speak."[20]

Churchill and Brooke applauded Montgomery's letter to Eisenhower, "laying down in black and white [the] results of their talk." If everything Montgomery told Brooke materialized—including Montgomery's spurious claim that Eisenhower intended to put Bradley under him—all would be good, but Brooke feared "Ike going back on us when he has discussed with Bedell Smith, Tedder etc!"[21] "Before this offensive was launched," Churchill explained to Smuts, "we placed on record our view that it was a mistake to attack against the whole front and that a far greater mass should have been gathered at the point of desired penetration." All of Montgomery's predictions "have in every way been borne out." Based on Montgomery's 28–29 November letters, Churchill imagined "some readjustments will be made giving back to Montgomery some of the scope taken from him after the victory he gained in Normandy."[22]

The next day Churchill wrote an "off the record" letter to Eisenhower. Though taking pains to point out that Eisenhower retained "the complete confidence of the British armies, of me and of the Chiefs of Staff," Churchill pushed for a division of the front along the lines suggested by Montgomery. "I should hope that the northern front would be given to Montgomery, and the southern front to Devers or whoever is chosen by the American authorities." He emphasized, "I am entirely opposed to the interposition of any command between you and the two commanders of fronts which will be under you." He went on in his flowery prose, describing how Montgomery and Bradley worked "together so well and have mutual liking and confidence" and how "both Bradley and Montgomery have offered to serve under each other, in the true spirit which governs all Anglo-American relations, for the inculcation of which you bear the chief honour."[23] In truth, as Churchill told Brooke, he rejected the idea of placing Bradley between Eisenhower and the army groups. "Ike was a good fellow who was amenable and whom he could influence," Brooke reported Churchill as saying. "Bradley on the other hand was a sour faced blighter and might not listen to what he said."[24]

On 4 December Brooke read Churchill's letter to Eisenhower and another letter for Brooke, with a copy to Montgomery, about the politics involved in any command switch. Stung by British press reports of the Zonhoven meeting—the *Daily Mail* headline read "Eisenhower Holds 'Zero' Talk, Planning Last Battle in Germany, Secret Visit to Montgomery"—and on his not being consulted beforehand, the prime minister now considered the issue "a matter for government decision."[25] Before the BCOS morning conference, Brooke "spent an hour on the phone with the PM about Eisenhower's meeting with Monty & their discussion of the command question." As Cunningham noted, Churchill objected to "being left out of the discussion. He will not realise it is none of his business."[26] Brooke met with Churchill later that day and deflected him from sending the letter to Eisenhower.

Churchill was not alone in reassessing the situation. Eisenhower visited Bradley's headquarters in Luxembourg when Montgomery's 29 November letter arrived. Bradley remembered that "Ike was as angry as I had ever seen him." Incensed that Montgomery persisted in rubbing salt into the wound, Eisenhower responded by writing, "I am not quite sure I know exactly what you mean by strategic reverse." Although Montgomery's letter accurately depicted what the field marshal had said at their meeting, it misrepresented what had been "agreed upon." Although the Ruhr was "an important place," it remained "a geographic objective," whereas the chief aim centered on destroying German forces west of the Rhine. SHAEF intelligence assessments indicated the grind-down strategy was working, and the renewed offensives along the Roer and in the Saar might well accomplish the primary objective. Eisenhower thought they needed a reevaluation of "how much profit there is in the continuation of [Bradley's] current attacks" and should perhaps "recast our future general plan in the light of conditions as they now exist." He made no concession on concentrating north of the Ardennes. In his own mind, he remained unconvinced of the necessity to redefine boundaries or whether, in view of the respective lines of communication, that line should be the Ruhr rather than the Ardennes. On the question of Smith being present but silent, Eisenhower flatly stated, "Bedell is my Chief of Staff because I trust him and respect his judgment. I will not by any means insult him by telling him that he should remain mute at any conference he and I both attend."[27]

As it turned out, Smith's health prevented him from going. Alerted to Smith's latest health issue, Marshall told him he "wished . . . [you] were the type who would turn over to a Deputy for the time being and relax on the Riviera for a couple of weeks," but admitted that "there is no possibility of getting you from your job."[28] As he had during his hospitalization in England, Smith put up a brave front. He informed Marshall the attack of neuritis was "a blessing in disguise" and now that he was rested he had "never felt better."[29] In truth, his condition ruled out any trip to Maastricht; Tedder went in his place.

On 2 December Eisenhower returned to Versailles. Smith dragged himself from bed and handed Eisenhower a copy of Montgomery's testy reply to Eisenhower's chiding letter of the day before. Montgomery denied suggesting that the Allies had failed since breaking out of Normandy; he had only stated that the objectives assigned in Eisenhower's 28 October directive had not been achieved. Since no bridgehead existed, in Montgomery's view, the strategic design had failed.[30] Eisenhower had "a long talk with Bedell re Monty," Summersby wrote. "Monty is most anxious to have Bradley under his command, keeps on saying that there would be a lot of advantages, of course he is completely crazy to even think of such a thing."[31] Crazy or not, Eisenhower and Smith avoided inflaming the situation. Their return letter made "prompt and abject apologies" for misinterpreting what Montgomery had said. Smith produced the most recent G-2 study by Strong, indicating that the Roer fighting "vastly exceeded our expectations" in inflicting casualties on the Germans. The attrition campaign was succeeding, at least from the point of view that more new American than German divisions had entered the order of battle. And as Eisenhower informed the CCS, he had "every intention of continuing these operations as long as conditions permit." The decision to continue the push into the Saar and Alsace effectively negated any talk of concentrating Twelfth Army Group north of the Ardennes. Eisenhower clung to the notion that the northern advance constituted the main show, but he conceded that Montgomery required "at least one very strong American army working with it to conduct that attack."[32]

Eisenhower and Tedder traveled first to Bradley's headquarters in Luxembourg, then on to Maastricht. At some point Bradley told Eisenhower that if he were placed under Montgomery's command he would expect to be relieved.[33] At the Maastricht meeting, Montgomery quickly discerned Bradley's unqualified rejection of the idea of surrendering operational control over any portion of his army group.[34] Hoping to avert an open split, Eisenhower reaffirmed that the Twenty-first Army Group's northern thrust, with Simpson under Montgomery's command, constituted the main effort in the envisioned double envelopment of the Ruhr. First Army would advance on the Cologne-Hamm line. They talked about operations after sealing off the Ruhr and concluded that the northern advance toward Berlin offered the best terrain for the resumption of mobile warfare and access to the most developed transportation corridors, including two autobahns. As in France, if the offensive carried enough momentum, the river lines would not present serious obstacles. In the meantime, Eisenhower stayed the course on fighting winter attritional campaigns in the hope of cracking the West Wall defenses, while the buildup and forward staging of supplies gained momentum with the opening of Antwerp. Simpson and Hodges would push toward the Roer dams, but Eisenhower pinned the biggest expectations on Patton breaking through into the Saarland and the Palatinate toward Frankfurt. Bradley now talked of Third Army thrusting up the Frankfurt-Kassel axis in combination with Hodges's forces crossing south of Bonn.[35]

Montgomery had heard all this before. On 13 September Eisenhower had assigned the northern drive as the main effort, reaffirming this at the Versailles conference on 22 September and again a month later in conference with Bradley.[36] Both those reassurances came in the aftermath of command imbroglios. Eisenhower made pledges but, in Montgomery's eyes, never enforced them. As Bull would later observe, Eisenhower's head told him one thing—the merits of concentration in the north under a single command—and his heart (along with Marshall, Stimson, and American public opinion) told him something else. As Eisenhower explained to Marshall a week later, it remained a "matter of first importance that we get on the Rhine from Bonn northward," but he considered a crossing near Frankfurt "still most vitally important" and reported that "Bradley is confident . . . he will achieve both of these objects."[37] For all these reasons, Montgomery regarded "the whole thing as dreadful." He came away from the meeting convinced, as he told Brooke, "if we want the war to end within any reasonable period of time you will have to get Eisenhower's hand taken off the land battle."[38] Montgomery dispatched similar letters to Secretary of War James Grigg and Frank Simpson, imploring that they bring their influence to bear on the prime minister. Overplaying his hand once again—and considering the depleted state of his divisions, he had few cards to play—Montgomery found himself holding the short end of the stick.

Montgomery received a "top secret" letter by courier from Grigg that day, indicating the anxiety felt in War Office circles. Grigg apologized for not writing sooner and cited his "discouragement of spirit. If you ask what in God's name I have got to be discouraged about I answer: (a) a growing conviction that the Americans and the Russians *intend* that we shall emerge from this war a third rate power. Indeed they no longer take any pains to conceal their intentions, (b) a settled conviction that there is a lack of grip in certain quarters here which makes it quite impossible for us to take a strong line in this or any other direction." The "lack of grip" alluded to Churchill. Grigg steeled himself to the reality of "the German war lasting throughout 1945." In reference to the Maastricht deal, Grigg thought it looked more like an Eisenhower "skid than a wobble. I don't believe he means to deliver the goods."[39]

Brooke decided he must act. The CIGS pinned his fragile hopes on two things: convincing Marshall to journey to London, and persuading him to buck Eisenhower. Fearing Churchill would lurch off on some unpredicted tangent, Brooke waited until after the weekend to send Montgomery's Maastricht letter to the prime minister. Predictably, the prime minister had already waded in. The day before Maastricht, Churchill had written to Roosevelt, pointing to the failure "to achieve the strategic object which we gave to our armies five weeks ago" and "the serious and disappointing war situation which faces us at the close of the year." He wondered if the president might send his joint chiefs to London for a full-ranging discussion on further strategy in Europe.[40]

Brooke had waited too long; Eisenhower had already cut the legs out from under him. The night after Maastricht, Eisenhower requested permission to come to London and make an informal presentation on SHAEF's current thinking. Churchill invited him and Tedder to fly in Tuesday evening, 12 December. On Sunday the president opposed any CCS meeting, emphasizing Marshall's unwillingness to impede Eisenhower's plans. Roosevelt told Churchill he had never shared the prime minister's optimism about a speedy crossing of the Rhine, recalling he had "bicycled over most of the Rhine terrain" as a youth and, given its ruggedness, considered any campaign west of the river a difficult proposition.[41] When Brooke met with Churchill on the morning of Eisenhower's visit, he found the prime minister totally absorbed by the situation in Greece and "quite incapable of concentrating on anything else." The prime minister had not even bothered to read Montgomery's latest discourse. He did not have to, because Roosevelt had already vetoed a CCS conference.

The meeting with Eisenhower went just about as badly for Brooke as it had for Montgomery at Maastricht. "Ike explained his plan which contemplates a double advance into Germany, north of Rhine and by Frankfurt. I disagreed flatly with it, accused Ike of violating principles of concentration of force, which had resulted in his present failures. I criticized his future plans and pointed out impossibility of double invasion with the limited forces he has got. I stressed the importance of concentrating on one thrust." According to Cunningham, "Ike was good," and he "kept an even keel. He was obviously impressed by the CIGS's arguments but refused to commit himself."[42] The petulant CIGS thought Churchill remained in a fog, unable "to even begin to understand the importance of the principles involved." After dinner the conversation resumed, but Brooke made no headway "in getting either Winston or Ike to see that their strategy is fundamentally wrong. Amongst other things discovered that Ike now does not hope to cross the Rhine before May!"[43] Eisenhower had nimbly short-circuited Brooke's little coup. A distraught Brooke considered resigning.

Churchill was not as befuddled as he appeared. He explained to Brooke the next day why he had sided with Eisenhower. With Eisenhower the lone American, Churchill considered it bad manners to gang up on him. He also thought Brooke was too hard on Eisenhower, even though Churchill found what the CIGS said alarming. The day before Eisenhower arrived, the War Cabinet discussed the grim costs of another winter. Bevin, the minister of Labour and National Service, warned of "serious effects on the Coalition Government" and pointed to mounting labor discontent prompted by economic conditions and reactions against Churchill's policy in Greece. The British economy had been in recession since the fourth quarter of 1943.[44] All this played on the prime minister's mind, as did Eisenhower's talk of a May crossing of the Rhine, which "had a profound effect on the Cabinet." The prime minister called a War Cabinet meeting for that night and asked Brooke to present his preliminary assessment before producing a formal paper. But events outpaced Brooke's efforts. The Zonhoven and Maastricht meetings and their aftermath changed nothing, but they deepened British apprehensions for the future and American suspicions of the British. The British opposed the Americans' direct approach against Germany in northwestern Europe for fear it would lengthen the war and threaten their survival as a great power; that anxiety now gave way to worry that lengthening the war would leave Britain too exhausted to extract any tangible fruits of victory, when and if it finally occurred.

"Good Money after Bad": The Manpower Crunch

Unquestionably the blackest mark on the record of the U.S. Army in World War II was the appalling mismanagement of the manpower system. And the officer most responsible for the mess was Marshall. Had the War Department tried to devise a worse system, it probably would have failed. The essential problem derived from Marshall's decision in May 1944 to field only ninety American divisions. As was so often the case, he remained a captive of World War I experience. By the armistice, the United States had brought forty-three divisions to France, but only thirty-one ever went into the line. Marshall wanted to avoid wasting manpower in divisions that might never see active service, not to mention the public outcry that would necessarily follow. He ascribed much of the antimilitary feeling in the interwar years to the public outcry provoked by the army's demobilization efforts in 1919. Marshall wanted a manpower system that paralleled the logistics doctrine of automatic supply, which had already faltered. Once a division entered combat, a continuous stream of replacements would restore losses, maintaining full table of organization (T/O) strength for indefinite periods. According to this logic, divisions would remain in the line longer, without any significant deterioration in combat effectiveness or morale, thereby avoiding the complications involved in forming the 200+ divisions envisioned in the Victory Program.[45] The dearth of Leavenworth-trained officers convinced him that the army could never staff the headquarters of so many divisions. Marshall also worried about the divisions amassing too many troops as overhead—another problem faced in France in 1918.

The War Department's scientific management approach to personnel administration suffered from innumerable defects. Among the worst was its overreliance on sophisticated mathematical models designed to "engineer" manpower. The army grew from 243,000 in 1940 to 8.2 million in 1943, yet the T/O enlisted strength in ground commands on 31 March 1945 hardly exceeded the numbers mobilized in December 1942. The War Department obviously needed some system for managing and organizing first this burgeoning, then static, host. It should have been equally apparent that a priori projections must err. The model determined everything from the military occupation specialty (there were 800 of them) of every soldier in the army to replacement criteria for predicted attrition rates in every arm and service. Even though the manpower system suffered from chronic imbalances from 1942 onward, the War Department contented itself with tinkering with the troop basis, adjusting the duration of training cycles, and altering force structures—

themselves sources of much added confusion. The hypothetical forecasts built into the system in 1942 were already obsolete by mid-1943, when the army exceeded its manpower ceiling, yet they remained essentially in place until the entire system collapsed under its own weight by the end of 1944. Among its many flaws, the system grossly miscalculated infantry casualties.[46]

Not merely a prisoner of his AEF preconceptions, Marshall's thinking also suffered from a set of chauvinistic fallacies. The War Department discarded the infantry-centered force structures demanded by interwar tactical doctrine. This war would be mechanized and mobile. The streamlined "triangle" combined arms division replaced the ponderous "square" infantry division. Artillery, airpower, and armored vehicles would add mobility and decisiveness to the battlefield, reducing casualties and ending reliance on infantry. Marshall presupposed that U.S. divisions would possess exceptional combat power because American troops would enjoy better training, higher motivation, and superior weapons. None of those assumptions proved accurate. Far from producing superior divisions, Marshall's misguided manpower program assembled inferior ones. And as the campaign along the frontiers lengthened, the seriously flawed replacement system—an adjunct to the American gamble of raising only ninety divisions—emerged as the single most important factor in the decline in American combat effectiveness.

If the idea behind the replacement system was to keep combat units at full strength without depleting divisions in the assembly line, the system had already failed by autumn 1942, when divisions in the Zone of the Interior were stripped of manpower and equipment for Torch. The army's solution made a bad situation worse; its remedy seriously eroded the quality of both the divisions sent to Europe and the men assigned to the replacement stream. Owing to public outcry and congressional pressure, the War Department initially withheld eighteen-year-olds from the replacement pool, the thinking being that inductees would be nineteen before they were sent overseas. So the army robbed Peter to pay Paul.[47] The army routinely stripped forty training divisions of privates and most of their noncommissioned officers to flesh out departing units or feed the replacement system; this practice continued up until four months before the divisions sailed. Seventeen infantry divisions lost two-thirds of their infantry privates, replaced by newcomers.[48] The War Department all but dissolved the Army Specialized Training Program (ASTP), transferring 73,000 ASTP trainees to AGF and, at the same time, reassigning 24,000 surplus aviation cadets. Troops in deactivated antiaircraft and tank destroyer units went through an accelerated six-week course in the rudiments of infantry weapons and tactics. Despite those expedients, the War Department still projected a deficit of 120,000 in AGF—more than half that shortfall in infantry. The army then reversed itself, deciding to send eighteen-year-olds overseas. Between 44 and 50 percent of troops in divisions arriving in the European theater in the last five months of 1944 were teenagers.[49]

In theory, the divisions sent to Europe in 1944 should have boasted better-quality personnel than 1943 units, but in reality, the battle-worthiness of divisions entering Europe declined with each passing month. On paper, infantry divisions arriving in Europe after August 1944 had been in training for two years, but they were composed of troops recently arrived in their units, new to the branch, or just entering the army. Seven infantry divisions never took part in maneuvers as a unit; sixteen others participated in maneuvers at 40 to 70 percent strength. In addition to eighteen-year-olds, the army drafted physically and intellectually limited older men and the so-called pre–Pearl Harbor fathers. On average, the 1944 divisions were composed of younger, less intelligent, and less physically fit men compared with their 1943 counterparts.[50] A survey indicated that 40 percent of men assigned to the infantry scored below average in intelligence, which seriously hamstrung the selection of cadre. Instead of filling the leadership void, men drawn from the ASTP, Air Corps, specialist schools, and troops seconded from disbanded combat formations lowered unit morale. These deeply disgruntled soldiers hated surrendering soft billets for the hazards of combat reassignments in the infantry. Yet another survey of 1944 infantry divisions demonstrated that riflemen deprecated their own branch: nearly three-fourths thought "the Infantry gets more than its share of the men who aren't good for anything else," and the majority believed they had the more dangerous job and did most of the fighting for the fewest rewards in terms of promotion and respect from civilians.[51]

The War Department had warned of a severe infantry manpower shortage since 1943 and directed the theaters to commence retraining efforts. Barker attended a major Washington conference on manpower in late December 1943. McNarney drew a stark picture of the breakdown of the replacement structure in the Zone of the Interior: ETO could not be supplied at the expense of other theaters; the army was already significantly overstrength; inductions would come from less propitious manpower pools; and most of the army would soon be deployed overseas, the majority in ETO. Replacements from the United States could not keep divisions at full strength; ETO must squeeze its own personnel pipelines for additional manpower through reconversion training. Eisenhower made no effort to deal with the problem. In April Sawbridge represented ETO at another set of meetings in Washington. Again McNarney pointed to the "present extravagant inefficient personnel conditions which we can no longer afford to maintain."[52] As already noted, Eisenhower sidestepped a directive on forming a theater manpower command, again claiming he could not find the right man to head it. Barker's eleventh-hour efforts to get a manpower command just before D-day failed.

Eisenhower's rejection of a manpower command meant that reconversion training fell between the cracks. The situation demanded a separate command under a senior major general who answered directly to Eisenhower rather than one operating through a virtual ETO under Lee's superintendence. As with supply, it was never clear who commanded the replacement system. Pershing's call for a separate training division in the WDGS went unheeded. In the interwar period, G-1 staff handled routine administration and G-3 handled training. The same division of responsibilities existed in Europe, but the question was which G-1 and G-3—in SHAEF or in ETO/ComZ? In the United States, the War Department never established whether AGF or ASF oversaw the manpower system; AGF trained divisions, and ASF oversaw the armywide replacement structure. In Europe, Lee retained overall command but had neither the time nor the inclination to become involved in the replacement system. COL Walter Layman headed the replacement system in England before D-day, but he could not enforce policy on generals in the base sections who held command jurisdiction over the replacement depots. The stressed and overworked Layman finally received his star but did not have much time to enjoy it; he died of a heart attack in September 1944. Another nondescript junior brigadier general, Henry Matchett, replaced him in November.

Reconversion and retraining did not commence in the theater until July 1944. Another product of the "victory disease," ETO actually reduced its September requisition of replacement troops by 15,000, even though American forces suffered 82,500 battle and 37,964 nonbattle casualties in August and September. Afraid of a raid on his already critically shallow ComZ manpower pool, Lee confined ComZ to conducting a survey to determine whether cuts could be made; he then delegated responsibility down the chain of command for the selection of general service men for conversion training. The Air Corps, the only other untapped reservoir of manpower, proved equally resistant. As with supply, no true theater headquarters existed to enforce War Department policy. Subordinates combed their units and weeded out the goldbricks and hard cases for reassignment. Despite orders to the contrary, field commanders formed provisional units from surplus manpower instead of diverting personnel to the retraining centers. One War Department policy was rigorously enforced—segregation. African American troops represented around 11 percent of all personnel in ETO, but the army entertained no thoughts of dipping into this pool for reconversion training.

Because of the drop in casualties in October—during the comparative lull produced by the ammunition shortage—SHAEF never grasped the seriousness of the situation. When casualties rose dramatically in November, replacement levels fell far below requirements. Eisenhower never issued a declarative order to redirect surplus manpower into the retraining structure until 15 December—far too late.[53] Patton's headquarters had already initiated the "training of 4,000 replacements through [a] 5% cut in overhead of all Corps and Army troops," which still left Third Army "12,000 short [of riflemen]. All divisions were ordered to cannibalize headquarters and anti-tank sections to provide infantry replacements."[54] "The discouraging piece of news was that there is as yet no hope in sight for replacements," Bradley remarked on 10 December. Bradley considered the practice of breaking up new divisions "not very economical. The replacements needed were riflemen and there was a tremendous wastage in breaking up a division, since you had to re-train a large percentage of the men in order to furnish you with the desired number of M-1 carrying replacements." Hodges's chief of staff asked, "Would US Divisions have to fight decimated and in half strength like the German *Kampfgruppens?*" Bradley replied, "Yes, I am afraid that is so."[55]

Sustained combat eroded combat power and undermined morale. Marshall recognized this in Italy, but curiously, he ascribed the problem to British, not American, units. In Anzio "the fighting spirit and aggressive quality of British divisions began . . . to decline, and for the reason of the sheer factor of exhaustion. The British simply could not keep their battalions up to strength and it was very depressing to their men. They had no replacements. The two British divisions at Anzio simply had no punch: it was a very serious situation."[56] American units faced the same problems. By January 1944 Fifth Army, with an establishment strength of 200,000 and 77,000 in the divisions, had sustained 80,000 casualties. Only 24 percent were battlefield casualties; the rest were attributable to sickness, accident, or exhaustion induced by constant contact with the enemy.[57] Soon after assuming theater command, Devers made the same point. Writing to McNair, he recommended, "Divisions should not be left in the line longer than 30 to 40 days in an active theater. If you do this, as has been done in this theater, everybody gets tired, then they get careless, and there are tremendous sick rates and casualty rates. Everybody should know this. The result is that you feed replacements into a machine in the line, and it is like throwing good money after bad. Your replacement system is bound to break down, as it has done in this theater."[58] Devers described the exact state of affairs that existed in November 1944 on the frontiers.

The War Department's dread of "overstrength" units guaranteed that divisions remained understrength. In theory, it required five or six days to move replacements from rear depots into the division areas. Paperwork from divisions to army and group headquarters and eventually to ComZ and finally to the replacement command slowed the entire manpower pipeline to a crawl. With divisions in constant battle, chronic manpower shortages crippled combat efficiency. In the attritional fighting along the frontiers, the rate of casualties overwhelmed the replacement system's ability to fill vacancies in the line. Each day the deficit grew.

Morale at the front plummeted in November. The army reported few cases of "combat fatigue or combat saturation" until November; thereafter, the number shot up dramatically. The dreary weather, continued shortages of winter clothing, length of time in the line, heavy casualties in remorseless positional fighting, and realization the war would continue into 1945 all took their toll. On average, a division suffered 100 percent casualties after three months of continuous combat.[59] As Hughes noted grimly in November, "Men don't like to fight until they are killed."[60] Frontline soldiers, with nothing to look forward to except that elusive "million dollar wound" that would get them sent home, cracked under the stress. The army looked at soldiers as interchangeable parts, which did nothing to inspire any real esprit de corps. Soldiers loved their buddies and fought for them, but they hated the army for placing them in harm's way. They never knew the names of their battalion commanders, much less cared who commanded the division. Any reservoir of pride and devotion to their units quickly dissipated. A September 1944 survey found that "practically all men in rifle battalions who are not otherwise disabled ultimately become psychiatric casualties." A man's resolve wore out, on average, after 200 to 240 days of combat.[61] One soldier with 279 days in combat in North Africa, Italy, and southern France "calmly declared he had done his share" and refused to stay in the line.[62] Not only veterans suffered. A postwar study indicated that troops in recently arrived divisions—men screened out of earlier divisions and teenagers with less training and less orientation to battlefield conditions—were even more likely to become neuropsychiatric cases. The same study found the percentages of combat exhaustion were in direct and reverse proportion to the rates of trench foot (because those with trench foot were removed from the line).[63] Another study concluded that the number of self-inflicted wound cases "ran into the 1000s." The Medical Corps segregated men with self-inflected wounds in special wards, presumably to isolate the contagion.[64]

Morale sank for other reasons. Combat troops bitterly complained about what the army termed "differentials" between officers and enlisted personnel. During summer and autumn 1944, troops in France received no leave; once the front stabilized, units started issuing forty-eight-hour passes. Officers were twice as likely to receive leave. A survey indicated that more than 75 percent of enlisted men believed officers "pulled rank" in gaining greater access to alcohol, PX goods, rest and relaxation opportunities, and the unauthorized use of vehicles. They grumbled that hotels and restaurants—and the higher class of females encountered there—were "off-limits" to GIs. Officers ignored curfews, enjoyed leave and furloughs—privileges denied enlisted men—and generally showed a lack of concern for the welfare of "the average Joe." Hot food rarely made its way forward. GIs complained that German prisoners ate better than they did and received new uniforms, while fighting troops made do with "reclaimed stuff." During rare respites from frontline duty, soldiers still drilled and drew fatigue duty. Negative reports spread by disgruntled soldiers returning Stateside—most of them casualties—began to appear in American newspapers, and the War Department turned up the heat on SHAEF to address the problem.[65]

Without question, individual replacements constituted the most forlorn group of soldiers in the army. The replacement system suffered from the same bottlenecks as supply. Staffs in England before D-day never developed comprehensive manpower replacement plans for operations in France; what plans existed were based on Brittany acting as the staging area. Without plans and without Brittany, the entire system developed as a series of improvisations. The replacement command possessed no fixed tables of organization or supply requirements, no established operating procedures, and no field manual. The War Department and theater never agreed on "authorized strength" versus "troop basis." In November 1944 the discrepancy stood at more than 100,000 troops, but SHAEF admitted it had no idea what the real figure was.[66] The undermanned and poorly officered depots, overburdened by receiving troops, faced the additional encumbrance of retraining. Men arrived in theater without proper papers, essential clothing, and equipment, and those in nonessential specialist billets languished, sometimes for months, in the despised "repple depples," army jargon for the replacement depots. The shortage of transportation also delayed forward deployment. The Third Armored reported some troops hung up in the pipeline for six months.[67]

The repple depples were notoriously bad. Quartered in overcrowded and unsanitary housing—invariably leaky tents—poorly fed, without recreational opportunities, and with their pay in arrears, replacements felt like "lost souls." Friendless and subjected to ceaseless physical conditioning but little real training, individual replacements experienced plunging morale; their discipline and physical conditioning suffered. They frequently went AWOL or succumbed to the temptations of black-market activities; the rates of criminality in the base sections dwarfed those in the combat zones. ComZ supervised the flow of wounded into the hospitals and tabulated how many required evacuation and how many "casuals"— men recovered from their wounds—could be returned to combat units versus those who entered the replacement system for retraining. "Limited service" men received retraining for SOS billets, freeing "general duty"—fit for combat duty—service and supply troops for reconversion training as riflemen. Wounded returnees classed as "general duty" went AWOL if they wanted to return to their original units. Disaffected officer candidates and soldiers culled from ComZ, the Air Corps, disbanded antiaircraft artillery and tank destroyer units, reclassified wounded soldiers and psychiatric cases, and surplus specialists of all types—some of the very troops that should have made the biggest impact—become the worst morale problems.

Without any attachment to other unit members, individual replacements proved more susceptible to combat stress than men who entered battle as part of a unit. They also became casualties in much higher proportions. The experience of going through the replacement system left individuals feeling alienated and hopeless. The morale of individual replacements, already low after a stint in the replacement depots, sank even lower when they entered the line. After interminable delays— or, in the case of riflemen, often immediately—replacements mustered, heard their numbers called, and went forward in "40 and 8" railcars and open trucks to their battalion reception points. Absent orientation, they entered the line without ever seeing the face of the man in the next foxhole. "In their infantry companies, they were buddyless and shunned as almost dangerous strangers" by the long-timers, most of them in their early twenties. "These embittered replacements were a most pitiable group," Paul Fussell, a replacement lieutenant, recalled, "lonely, despised and untrained, deeply shocked by the unexpected brutalities of the front line and often virtually useless."[68]

In the supply crisis, nobody much cared if a few thousand widgets went missing. In February 1945, an amazing 586,369 men in ETO—in transit, in replacement depots or reception centers, undergoing special training, carried as overhead, or simply lost in the pipeline—composed what one general called the "invisible horde of people going here and there but seemingly never arriving." On one side, there was the widely held view that "there is nothing too good for our boys in uniform."[69] On the other side was the replacement system, which dehumanized American soldiers—by autumn 1944, half of them in their teens—and treated them like spare parts. Symbolic of this was the name of the system—men were mere replacements. The name of the structure changed often—indicative of its orphan status—from Field Force Replacement System to Ground Force Replacement System to Replacement System and finally in December 1944 to Ground Forces Reinforcements Command. More revealing were the terms used to describe replacements. They moved between "depots" and were categorized as "stock"; those killed in action went on lists as "dead stock," and Eisenhower referred to rehabilitated psychiatric cases as "salvage."[70]

In a hugely successful 1998 motion picture, Marshall, moved by the deaths of three Iowa brothers in battle, orders a special operation in Normandy to save the one surviving brother. He recalls a similar episode from the Civil War—when Mrs. Bixby gave five sons to the Union cause and received a letter from Lincoln, acknowledging that sacrifice. History always proves infinitely more revealing than fiction. Mrs. Bixby was a charlatan, and the movie portrayal of Marshall was pure hokum. The supreme irony lies in the fact that Marshall, the primary architect of the manpower system, consigned tens of thousands of Private Ryans to anonymous deaths in Europe.[71]

The manpower situation looked equally dire in Twenty-first Army Group. With the withdrawal of the U.S. Eighty-fourth and 104th Divisions and the Airborne Army, Twenty-first Army Group again fielded sixteen active divisions. Montgomery now assumed "an almost purely defensive role" and used the opportunity to refit, retrain, and refresh his troops.[72] That applied especially to the Canadian First Army after the losses suffered in the Scheldt campaign. For three months after the seizure of Walcheren, the Canadian army undertook no major offensive commitments. In fact, Canadian First Army was a misnomer; it consisted of Canadian II Corps, a British corps of variable strength, a Polish armored division, and assorted Belgian units. Hoping to avoid a political split with francophone Canadians over conscription, the Mackenzie King government sent only volunteers overseas. By autumn 1944, Canadian forces faced a critical shortage of 15,000 infantrymen. When King dipped into the 73,000 "home defense" soldiers for replacements, he triggered a political crisis. Nonetheless, Canada dispatched 16,000 conscripts to Europe in late November 1944. The Canadian I Corps transferred into the Low Countries from Italy, a movement not completed until spring 1945. Montgomery disbanded the Fiftieth Infantry Division in late November, sending it back to England as an infantry training formation for replacements. Taking a page from the American replacement system, the riflemen trained in this scheme went directly into divisions at the front. Churchill protested, "finding it very difficult to understand the cutting up of first rate units," and pointed out he was "doing his utmost here to get a bigger intake for the army." As Montgomery explained to Grigg, "The infantry reinforcement situation is bad and with this plan we shall just and only just pull through."[73]

At the beginning of December, Eisenhower took stock of the campaign. He divided it into three phrases: "Normandy and the breakout; the pursuit and the reorganization, attack, and passage through the Maginot line; and the organization and attack of the Seigfried [sic] line." In response to Montgomery's claim that the broad-front approach produced stalemate and a "strategic reverse," Eisenhower wrote a long defense of the decisions made. "I do not agree that things have gone badly since Normandy, merely because we have not gained all we had hoped to gain. In fact, the situation is somewhat analogous to that which existed in Normandy for so long." He stated, "As late as D plus 60 [the situation] was not greatly different than what we hoped to hold in the first week, but I never looked upon the situation then existing as a strategic reverse." By inference, the autumn stalemate might serve as the preliminary to a new breakout campaign that would destroy German forces west of the Rhine and ease the Allies' passage of the river into Germany. He had no intention of abandoning the broad front as "long as [Devers's and Patton's operations] are clearing up our right flank and giving us *capability of concentration*. On the other hand, I do not intend to push those attacks senselessly."[74]

In view of the manpower crisis, Montgomery's fears were not groundless. Eisenhower, of course, was being disingenuous. He was very much worried in late June and July that the Allies faced the sobering prospect of a strategic reverse in Normandy, and in his own mind he conjured up the need to alter operational priorities if not institute a change in command. As during the Normandy stalemate, when casualties mounted and stressed the replacement system, the frontiers campaign produced heavy manpower losses. By early December, evidence mounted that the replacement structure stood on the brink of a breakdown. With the growing manpower crisis came the concomitant decline in the combat power of Allied divisions. Just as surely as logistics determined operational options in October, so too did manpower shortages in December.

The frontiers campaign revealed the asymmetry between American doctrine and force structures. Eisenhower, Smith, Bradley, and Hodges—all infantrymen in good standing—remained true to the "doughboy tactics" of mass and pursuit of the decisive battle called for in American doctrine. As the 1939 FSRs emphasized, "The *ultimate objective* is the destruction of the enemy's armed strength in battle" through the direct application of superior force. "In combat the will and energy of the commander must persist until the objective is attained.[75] The U.S. Army created by Marshall and McNair—its force structures, weapons, and mentality—were geared for mobility and firepower. In 1940 German panzers moved at a 1940 speed against the enemy, fighting at a 1918 pace. By 1944, aside from panzer and panzer grenadier formations, the Wehrmacht still moved with the speed of marching infantry and horse-drawn support. The U.S. Army, by comparison, was fully mechanized and motorized. Virtually every GI was familiar with cars, trucks, or tractors; as long as American forces received fuel and lubricants, they moved with unprecedented tempo. In addition, American armies, with their own attached tactical air forces, could call for immediate tactical air support of a quality, quantity, and flexibility no German commander could even envision. As the push to seal the Cotentin, the breakout from Normandy, and the exploitation drive through France all amply demonstrated, the U.S. Army provided the perfect vehicle for open war fighting, but only when all the tumblers fell into place.

When confronted with positional battles, the force structures and personnel administration policies of the ground forces placed the Americans at a distinct disadvantage, fighting in terrain not conducive to maneuver warfare. American divisions lacked sustained combat power. They had plenty of tail but not many teeth. At full strength, the American infantry division slice stood at 40,000, but its twenty-seven infantry companies fielded only 5,200 riflemen. Impatient for decisive results, all the senior American commanders attacked with inadequate forces; corps and divisions suffered heavy combat casualties in often piecemeal and ultimately costly advances. Subordinates at all levels found themselves facing unrealistic objectives and insistence from above for aggressive action, on the one hand, and the realities of supply, the ground,

weather, fatigue, infantry shortages, and the fighting power of a determined and resourceful foe, on the other.

If the German defenses held—and they showed no sign of breaking—the Allies possessed enough strength to keep up pressure all along
the front, but not enough to break through. In the face of this harsh
reality, American senior generals could conceive of no better solution
than to continue their separate battles of attrition. Eisenhower might
signal his unwillingness to "push those attacks senselessly," but to date,
he had done nothing to stop them. And there appeared little likelihood
that after the attritional fighting ended—and it was by no means certain the Allies would win that fight—Allied forces would still possess the
"capacity of concentration" to stage a breakthrough or to sustain one if
it did come. Even members of Bradley's staff began to dismiss any talk
of breaking the German defenses. "Many people here are resigned to a
static winter," noted Bradley's aide, "which is hard to understand after
the encouraging progress we made during the summer."[76]

The British were not alone in worrying that Eisenhower's attrition
strategy not only threatened to lengthen the war but also raised doubts
about how it might end. Bradley told Lutes, "It is entirely possible for
the Germans to fight bitter delaying actions until 1 January 1946."[77] "But
once you start on attrition," Marshall remarked after the war, "you are
lost, you are ruined." He entertained grave doubts about "the attrition
of a slow, plugging advance" and stated, "I myself dreaded the crossing
of the Roer and the advance to the Rhine more than any other operation
during the war. The terrain there was very difficult. In fact I dreaded
crossing of the Roer more than the cross-Channel attack. I was certain
that we would get across the Channel" but less convinced of getting to the
Rhine without catastrophic losses.[78] If American forces suffered unsus-
tainable losses short of crossing the Rhine, Marshall conjectured, "We
might have had pressure for negotiations [to end the war in Europe].
We still had the Pacific where there seemed to be no surrender of any
kind."[79] The ninety-division gamble looked like a bad bet as Twelfth
Army Group prepared for its renewed breakthrough attempts in mid-
December. And the hard feelings on either side of the Anglo-American
divide boded ill for the future.

Part Six

★ ★ ★ ★

The Victory Campaign

★ 33 ★

One Desperate Blow

Anton Graff's famous portrait of Frederick the Great dominated the Hitler bunker. The Prussian king occupied a prominent position in Hitler's mythical universe, and as the noose of the coalition's armies tightened around the Reich, Hitler drew on Frederick for inspiration. Those who dismissed Hitler as an intellectual poseur were not wrong—except where German history, military thought, and opera were involved. The parallel between Germany's plight in 1944 and Prussia's in the Seven Years' War was obvious enough. Confronted by a constellation of continental great powers—France, Austria and much of the Holy Roman Empire, Russia, and Sweden—and fettered to a perfidious ally, Prussia's position appeared hopeless. But Frederick emerged victorious owing to two products of the imponderables of war: the two "miracles of the House of Brandenburg," and the soldier-king's iron refusal to accept defeat. Frederick's military genius produced the first miracle. Breaking all the rules of eighteenth-century warfare, Frederick exploited interior lines and surprise in conducting an ancien régime version of blitzkrieg in a winter campaign that saw him defeat the western threat, the Franco-Imperial armies, at Rossbach in November; he then moved east and defeated an Austrian army more than twice the size of his at Leuthen in December. Leuthen witnessed the climactic Prussian attack that appeared out of nowhere across fog-shrouded, snow-clad fields. Then two years later, in 1759, *Fortuna* appeared to turn against Frederick; the coalition forces pressed his exhausted army—a shell of its former self—on all fronts, and Frederick suffered a crippling defeat at the hands of the Russians and Austrians at Kunersdorf. His prospects seemed as tattered as his bullet-perforated coat, and Frederick contemplated suicide. But another imponderable intervened—luck. His implacable foe the empress of Russia suddenly and fortuitously died and was replaced by a moron devotee of the king. With Russia's withdrawal, the coalition flew apart, and Prussia emerged from the ensuing tangled diplomacy intact and still a great power.

The lesson for Hitler was clear: military victory, coupled with the will to resist succumbing to one's fears, might yet deliver Germany from defeat. A stunning victory in the west would at least buy time for Germany to mass its forces and smash the Russians in the east; a big enough victory might sever the Anglo-American alliance as the necessary preliminary to successful diplomatic negotiations.

Hitler did not leave off with Frederick; he probably drew guidance from Clausewitz's analysis of the great king's "inner light." The concurrence between the words of the military theorist and Hitler's thinking appear too close to be accidental. "When the disproportion of power is so great," Clausewitz wrote, describing Frederick's 1759 plight, "that no limitation of our own object can ensure us safety from a catastrophe . . . then the tension of forces will, or should, be concentrated in one desperate blow." A leader facing destruction, "expecting little help from things which promise none, will place his whole and last trust in the moral superiority which despair always gives the brave." In such a situation, "the greatest daring" translated into "the greatest wisdom."[1] Backed by the parable of the great Frederick and the wisdom of Clausewitz, and roused by his own sense of intuition that fueled his greatest success in the very locale he meant to attack—the Ardennes—Hitler brooked no opposition from his pedantic generals. Hitler might well have drawn inspiration from his third muse, Wagner. He knew failure would lead not to Clausewitz's "honorable downfall [and] the right to rise again" but to *Götterdämmerung*, the funeral pyre of Germany. The code word *Leuthen* broadcast in the clear, announcing the German offensive in the Ardennes, should have proclaimed Hitler's intentions to his adversaries, but its meaning, as well as other more prosaic forms of intelligence, only confounded his benighted foe.

Turning His Great Gamble into His Worst Defeat

Not everybody in the Allied camp proved somnolent. Eisenhower worried that his lines were getting awfully thin in Alsace, and especially in the Ardennes. Earlier he had warned about "a nasty little Kasserine." But his style of command precluded any intervention. Bradley and his army commanders busied themselves with preparations for the renewal of the offensive against the Roer and into the Saar, gambling that the Germans would not attack in the Ardennes. SHAEF was also optimistic that the November offensives had weakened the German line and that continued pressure all along the front would fracture the West Wall. Commenting to Marshall after leaving his sickbed, Smith said, "There is nothing wrong with any of us that a good breakthrough won't cure."[2]

Smith maintained that SHAEF possessed "every evidence of a counter-operation." Ultra intercepts from U-boats detailing weather conditions in the North Atlantic indicated that at the first four- or five-day span of bad weather, the Germans would launch a "spoiling attack" in either the Ardennes or Alsace. December days in northern Europe are very short. The combination of short days and bad weather would seriously degrade Allied airpower.[3] SHAEF intelligence reported on 3 December that "the outward surface remains comparatively unchanged, but there has been quite considerable stirring within the sepulcher."[4] The next weekly intelligence report noted that the "enemy has continued to withdraw infantry from the quiet sectors . . . some three divisions have given signs of leaving the EIFEL, where replacements in the shape of two fresh Volksgrenadiers have already arrived . . . two further divisions, one infantry and one paratroop, have left HOLLAND for unknown destinations." It also noted the withdrawal of three armor divisions in Fifth Panzer Army area and "the presence of Sixth SS Panzer Army, which remains well up through NOT in [the line]." The assumption remained that the armor divisions had withdrawn for rest and refitting "before they are finally exhausted," but G-2 warned that the Germans might seek "a final showdown before the winter."[5] Privately, Strong grew increasingly anxious about the Germans constructing a strategic reserve, but the intelligence reports continued to relay the message that attrition hurt the enemy more than it did the Allies.

For two weeks, Strong raised concerns about the thin lines in the Ardennes during the morning briefings. Smith expected that the Netherlands between the Waal and Maas, Luxembourg, and the Upper Rhine would remain relatively quiet because no region of strategic significance lay behind them. He assumed the German generals would remain on the defensive, satisfied with stalemating the front. SHAEF still expected the Germans to conduct an active defense, including local counterattacks. Given the weakness of the Ardennes—the Germans knew the divisions deployed there were those chewed up in the Hürtgen or new ones—Smith recognized that the situation offered a textbook opportunity for the Germans to launch an attack to deflect the Allies from restarting thrusts against the Roer and the Saar. Other than a routine rotation of divisions in the Ardennes sector reported by XIII Corps in

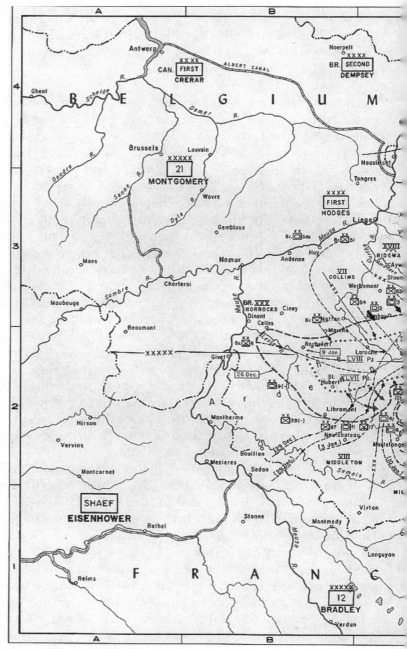

The Ardennes: Squeezing Out the Bulge

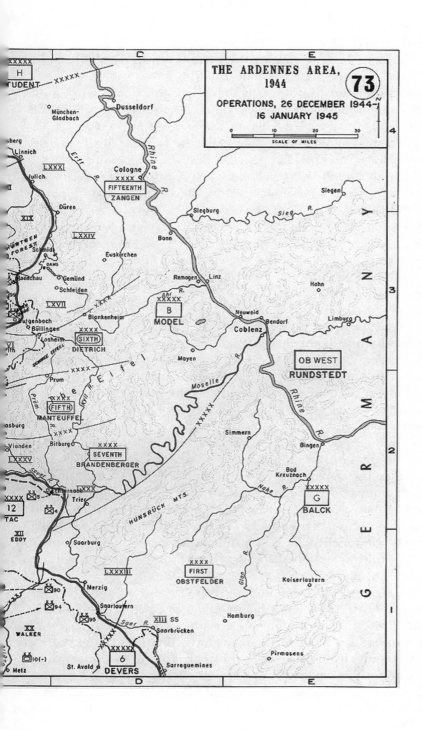

THE ARDENNES AREA,
1944
OPERATIONS, 26 DECEMBER 1944–
16 JANUARY 1945

SCALE OF MILES
0   10   20   30

73

H
STUDENT

München-
Gladbach

Dusseldorf

Linnich

Jülich

LXXXI

Cologne
FIFTEENTH
ZANGEN

Siegen

Düren

LXXIV

Siegburg

Sieg R.

Bonn

XIX

HÜRTGEN
FOREST

Schmidt

DAMS

Euskirchen

Remagen

Linz

Hahn

Monschau

Gemünd

Schleiden

Ahr R.
XXXXX
B
MODEL

Neuwied

Bendorf

Limburg

LXVII

Blankenheim

Coblenz

Wirtgenbach

Büllingen

SIXTH
DIETRICH

Losheim

Mayen

OB WEST
RUNDSTEDT

SCHNEE EIFEL

Prüm

EIFEL

Moselle R.

FIFTH
MANTEUFFEL

Simmern

Bingen

Vianden

Bitburg

SEVENTH
BRANDENBERGER

Bad
Kreuznach

LXXXV

Saar R.

Echternach

Trier

12
TAC

5

4

HUNSRÜCK MTS.

Nahe R.

XXXXX
G
BALCK

XII
EDDY

Saarburg

First
OBSTFELDER

Kaiserlautern

90

LXXXIII

Merzig

Glan R.

94

Saarlautern

95

XIII SS

Saar R.

Homburg

Saarbrücken

XX
WALKER

10(-)

St. Avold

6
DEVERS

Sarreguemines

Pirmasens

Metz

GERMANY

mid-November, SHAEF had detected "no concentration at all." SHAEF knew the Germans had withdrawn their armor and placed it east of the Roer. "This seemed a perfectly normal thing to do in view of our plan for an attack across the Roer, as these divisions would be in position to strike our bridgehead with a good chance of defeating it." The Germans typically rotated three divisions in and out of their Ardennes defenses. For a week during the changeover, the Germans had six divisions in line. "Each time this happened we expected a counter attack," Smith told Handy, "intended to decrease the pressure on the north and south where our own offensive was causing the Germans acute embarrassment." Smith and his staff "never expected the Germans to make an all out offensive, as we thought the strategic risk was far too great considering their limited resources and reserves." Why would the conservative Rundstedt risk crippling losses and perhaps undermine the defense of the West Wall by coming out into the open? Nobody in SHAEF grasped that Hitler called the shots.[6]

The SHAEF G-2 raised three possible uses of the re-forming Panzer Army: (a) for deployment on the Eastern Front, (b) as a counterattack force against an Allied penetration, or (c) to stage a relieving attack through the Ardennes. "Course (c) so impressed General Smith," Strong remembered, "that he asked if General Bradley was aware of this possibility." Strong replied in the affirmative, "but nevertheless General Smith instructed me to go to 12 AG and see General Bradley personally and warn him." Bradley acknowledged that both his and Patton's G-2s had alerted him of the danger, but he assured Strong he had "earmarked certain divisions to move into the Ardennes should the enemy attack."[7] Bradley saw no reason to pull units out of Hodges's and Patton's offensives to reinforce the Ardennes. As he told Smith in November, he hoped the Germans would come out of their holes so the Allies could cut them up.[8] If the Germans attacked in the Ardennes, they would be vulnerable elsewhere. He dismissed Strong by saying, "Let them come." Still worried, Smith telephoned Bradley after Strong's return "but got nowhere. Bradley felt secure."[9]

Hodges also remained sanguine, predicting the war would be over in two months. On 11 December his intelligence chief kept emphasizing "the fact that 6th Panzer Armee is drawing up on the other side of the ROER with at least three of its six armored divisions facing the 1st Army front. Reports from prisoners indicate that moral [sic] is high and that the Boche will soon be ready to stage an all-out counter offensive." Hodges did "not appear unduly concerned over the existence of these Panzer Divisions on his fronts." Simpson arrived for a conference, and

Hodges underscored how vital it was to "keep pushing the offensive. The time is now."[10]

The next day Hodges convinced himself the Germans retained only a "light screen" east of the Roer. The continued shortage of riflemen concerned him. The Fifth and Eightieth Infantry and the Fourth and Tenth Armored reported no replacements. By 13 December, Hodges grew "a little worried tonight that they had over-extended themselves and hoped that the new division [the 106th Infantry in the Ardennes] would know how to button up well." The next day Lutes and Hodges discussed the manpower problem. Lutes complained that the ammunition and manpower shortfalls stemmed from the drain of the Pacific theater and explained that the War Department "was fully cognizant of the critical replacement problem but saw no immediate solution."[11]

Bradley felt confident enough to travel to Versailles on 16 December. Smith pushed for a conference in the hope of infusing a new direction into the campaign. He too thought only in offensive terms; he worried that Bradley had misplaced his emphasis on the Saar at the expense of the Roer attack.[12] The conference's agenda also included a discussion of the worsening manpower predicament. Bradley wanted to fly to Versailles, but weather grounded all aircraft. The drive took most of the day because of the icy road conditions. The Germans got their four- or five-day window of weather; as Bradley drove east, so did three German armies into the vulnerable Ardennes.

Eisenhower attended a morning meeting with Smith, Tedder, Bull, and Strong. Just as they got started, Betts knocked on the door. Strong met with him briefly, then announced the German attack. Neither Eisenhower nor Smith attached a great deal of significance to the German action; both recognized the thinly held Ardennes offered the Germans a tempting target to forestall American plans for offensives. Since the intelligence from the Ardennes remained patchy—communications was still a big problem—nobody exhibited any apprehension.

Initially, Hodges came to the same conclusion. "Today, exactly one month after we launched our attack toward COLOGNE," recorded the First Army diarist, "the Boche began a counter offensive." First Army intelligence expected a pincer movement on Aachen and an attack in Ninth Army sector to follow. "At first it appeared that these counter attacks . . . were only what the General called 'spoiling attacks'" to relieve pressure from V Corps' offensive again the Roer, which had opened simultaneously with the German attack. By 11 A.M. it became clear that "this was a counter-offensive." Although the staff had made nothing of Leuthen, Rundstedt's captured orders removed all doubt. It read in part, "The hour of destiny has struck. Mighty offensive armies face the Allies. Everything is at stake. More than mortal deeds are required as a holy duty to the Fatherland." Hodges appeared neither hopeful nor gloomy, merely saying that the German offensive proffered the "quickest way to bring around the decimation of the *Wehrmacht*." "No one thought the situation critical."[13]

When Bradley arrived, he was told the news and joined Eisenhower and Smith for a tête-à-tête. Tedder's aide Scarman thought Smith appeared "a little panicky," but Eisenhower remained stolid.[14] Even though the picture at the front remained as foggy as the weather, Eisenhower concluded, "That's no spoiling attack."[15] Smith turned to Bradley and said, "Well Brad, you've been wishing for a counterattack. Now it looks as though you've got it." "A counterattack, yes," Bradley replied, "but I'll be damned if I wanted one this big."[16] They pored over the maps. Earlier, Bradley had talked about his earmarked divisions in case the Germans hit in the Ardennes. These divisions—the green Ninth and Tenth Armored—constituted the only reserves First and Third Armies possessed. Despite the German offensive, Bradley still expected his own offensives to proceed. He reasoned that if he pulled his armor divisions from Hodges, Patton, and Simpson, the German would "achieve his primary purpose." Eisenhower warned, "I think you had better send Middleton some help," pointing to the two divisions. Bradley at first balked; Patton would object to losing the Tenth Armored. With more than a little irritation, Eisenhower overruled him.[17]

The Ardennes business did not get in the way of the celebrations planned that Saturday. Eisenhower's orderly and a WAC driver got married that day in the rococo Royal Chapel. Plenty of champagne flowed at a reception held at Eisenhower's quarters. Then the Polish chief of staff, GEN Stanislaw Kopansky, arrived and pinned the Order of *Virtuti Militari* (Military Valor) on Eisenhower and Smith. Hughes came around with a bottle of Piper-Hiedsieck. That day the War Department announced Eisenhower's promotion to five stars. "Told Ike I couldn't bear the idea of having gotten drunk when he received his 4th star and not having a drink with him when he received his 5th," Hughes noted. Even the usually abstemious Bradley joined in. Eisenhower insisted that they play bridge. "Brad says Germans have started a big counter attack toward Hodges," Hughes recorded. "Very calm about it. Seemed routine from his lack of emphasis."[18] During the game Strong arrived to inform them that VIII Corps' front had been broken in five places. The news was bad but not dire enough to end the game. Five rubbers and a bottle of scotch later they retired.

The next morning Bradley conferred with Eisenhower and Smith before returning to Luxembourg. Eisenhower canceled all the American offensives and ordered that the army commanders pull together whatever reserves they possessed. If the Germans could launch a doctrinaire offensive, the American forces could answer with a textbook counteroffensive against both flanks. The first order of business involved canalizing the German penetration and preventing any crossing of the Meuse. Eisenhower wanted a strong shoulder at Monschau in the north and Diekirch in the south. Patton would execute the main counterattacks. Devers would extend his line north, freeing up divisions for Patton's attacks. The two airborne divisions—resting and refitting in camps around Reims after the bitter fighting in the Netherlands—represented SHAEF's only immediate reserve. Eisenhower wanted them committed and left the details to Smith, Whiteley, and Strong.[19]

Smith laid out a large map on the floor of his office. They easily discerned the Germans' intentions—forge the Meuse between Dinant and Liège, where better roads led toward Brussels and Antwerp. Ultimately, the Germans sought to drive a wedge between the Twelfth and Twenty-first Army Groups. SHAEF issued orders for the airborne divisions to ready themselves for immediate deployment; the question remained where. Using a captured German sword as a pointer, Smith motioned toward Bastogne. The town was the obvious choice; like Gettysburg, all roads led through there. The Seventh Armored, transferred from Ninth Army, and elements of the Ninth Armored were already moving toward the other crossroads town, St. Vith; the Tenth Armored would reinforce the southern shoulder south and east of Diekirch, with one combat command redirected toward Bastogne. The only remaining question was whether the airborne movement could get forward fast enough by road. Strong said he thought they could make it.

Smith got on the phone to Lord. Lee had already started for the Meuse crossings, intent on safeguarding ComZ's forward depots. Eisenhower placed him in command of the few available forces to guard the river line. Smith asked how long it would take to get the 101st Airborne to Bastogne. As Smith later related, Lord "gave me a time [and] he beat it by six hours." When the airborne troops arrived, joining elements of Tenth Armored, the razor-thin defensive perimeter was already receiving small-arms fire.[20]

Lee had every right to be worried. Just north of the town of Stavelot, directly in the path of the northernmost German armored thrust, stood a huge gasoline storage area holding 4 million gallons, guarded by only a couple of companies and some Belgian irregulars. If the Germans secured the fuel, they would have more than enough to carry them wherever they wanted to go. As Spaatz remarked only half facetiously, "American supplies of gasoline were so liberal that what was regarded as a Company supply for the U.S. Army could run a German division for several weeks."[21] Illustrative of the chaos at First Army headquarters, Hodges's staff reported "German tanks in STAVELOT" on 17 December. A day after declaring the state of affairs "serious if not yet critical," the First Army diary reported that the "situation is rapidly deteriorating and the position of the enemy is uncertain." The entire headquarters, except for one officer from each section, went forward and took up positions defending the approaches to Spa. A plane stood readied for Hodges to flee. Although reports that the German vanguard advanced to within a mile of Spa proved false—as did the German capture of the gas stores—Hodges gave the order for the hurried evacuation of Spa and the relocation of headquarters to Chaudfoutaine, just south of Liège. Ominously, Hodges's staff wondered "whether 12th Army Group fully appreciates the seriousness of the situation." The German advance cut communications with Bradley in Luxembourg.[22]

A concerned Smith dispatched Whiteley to Twenty-first Army Group and Betts to First Army. Whiteley had visited Montgomery's headquarters the day of the attack; on 18 December he went forward again for talks with de Guingand in Brussels. It came as no surprise when Montgomery reported that Hodges exercised no grip over the battle. As was his custom, the field marshal dispatched his liaison officers to convey his plans and assess the situation. As a result, Montgomery possessed a far clearer picture of the situation than either Bradley or Hodges. Worried about the threat to his southern flank, Montgomery, without direction from SHAEF, initiated the movement of four British divisions south the day after the attack; by 19 December, without alerting Hodges, British patrols crossed army boundaries and took up positions guarding the Meuse crossings.[23] With the front "cut clean in half," Montgomery thought Eisenhower should place the forces north of the German penetration under Twenty-first Army Group's operational control.[24] De Guingand, whom Whiteley trusted, confirmed this view. Betts corroborated what Whiteley had heard about First Army. He found the headquarters in shambles. "They just didn't know what was going on. As far as fighting a war was concerned," Betts informed Smith upon his return, "the First Army was thinking in terms of a battalion here and something else there but they seemed to have no plan at all for meeting the attacks. And I couldn't see any orders going forth."[25]

In the meantime, Lee was finally given the opportunity to exercise command in the field and supervised the removal of stores east of the Meuse, including, by 19 December, the bulk of the dangerously exposed POL stockpiles."Service units have almost completed the move to the rear," First Army noted, "which will prevent any important installation becom[ing] Boche property."[26] Faced with its second great crisis of the campaign in northwest Europe, ComZ performed brilliantly this time. Lee pulled back huge stores behind the Meuse, Lord moved the 101st Airborne to Bastogne in record time, and vital supplies went forward in huge quantities. The Bulge proved Aurand's case conclusively: Twelfth Army Group and the armies had stockpiled vast reserves of ammunition. Third Army moved up 4,500 tons of ammunition per day during the last half of December—43 percent more than it expended. Time and again the lavish use of American artillery broke up German attacks, inflicting heavy casualties; more vital, it seriously delayed the German penetrations.[27]

While the despised ComZ shone, its great detractors Bradley and Hodges foundered. Against all advice, Bradley had insisted on placing his tactical headquarters in Luxembourg. Even under normal conditions, Bradley experienced difficulties communicating with Versailles, and the German advance completely cut his lines to Hodges. For reasons related to prestige, Bradley refused to move his headquarters back. From a morale standpoint, he made the right decision, but it meant he forfeited all command and control over First Army. To make matters worse, the Germans landed parachutists dressed in American uniforms to sow mayhem in the rear areas. Rumors floated that squads of assassins were abroad with the mission to liquidate the senior Allied leadership. Bradley, who never ventured far from his headquarters in any case, became a virtual prisoner in Luxembourg.

He did leave his headquarters to attend an emergency conference with Eisenhower, Patton, and Devers at Verdun on 19 December. The day before, Patton had come to Eagle Forward for discussions with Bradley about launching a relief operation against the penetration's southern flank. To Bradley's surprise, Patton appeared nonchalant about closing down his Saar offensive. "What the hell," he said, "we'll still be killing Krauts." Patton promised he would execute a counterattack, but with only three divisions.[28] The Verdun conference took place, appropriately enough, in a cold, dreary barracks. Eisenhower did his best to raise spirits. "The present situation is to be regarded as one of opportunity for us and not of disaster," he said in his opening statement. "There will be only cheerful faces at this conference table." But even his trademark smile looked forced. Displaying his battle face, Patton riposted, "Hell, let's have the guts to let the sons of bitches go all the way to Paris. Then we'll really cut 'em up and chew 'em up." Everyone laughed nervously except for Eisenhower. "George, that's fine," he said. "But the enemy must never be allowed to cross the Meuse."

Strong and Bull also attended the 19 December meeting; Smith stayed in Versailles. Strong laid out his map and described the latest intelligence picture. A wide wedge appeared on the map; there could be no doubt the Germans had launched a major counteroffensive with three armies and twenty divisions identified, and more in reserve. After Strong completed his presentation, Eisenhower drew a line along the Meuse. There would be no retreat beyond the river. Once the Germans halted, the Allies would counterattack. "George, I want you to command this move," he told Patton. Then as an afterthought he added, "Under Brad's supervision of course." Eisenhower demanded a strong counterattack with at least six divisions. "When can you start?" he asked. "On the morning of 21 December," Patton calmly replied, offering the same three-division attack he had promised Bradley. An impatient Eisenhower retorted, "Don't be fatuous, George." Eisenhower wanted six divisions, not a piecemeal attack with three, and he would be willing to wait until 23 December.

Patton expected this and had carefully rehearsed his sales pitch. In the meantime, his staff prepared three contingency plans. Patton preferred an attack at the shoulder but knew he could not sell that package; instead, he proposed a drive toward Bastogne at the penetration's waist. His only worries centered on the manpower shortage and the ability of ComZ and his own rear to keep him supplied.[29] Eisenhower doubted that Patton could execute the extremely difficult "oblique order" offensive. With Third Army poised to launch its Saar offensive, Patton proposed shifting it north in the teeth of miserable weather on ice-encrusted roads across his lines of communication, attacking within forty-eight hours. Eisenhower instructed Patton to proceed as soon as possible. They set the target date for 22 December. A deflated Bradley "mostly observed . . . saying little, offering nothing."[30]

The day of the Verdun conference marked a significant turning point. In November the status of SHAEF hit rock bottom. Eisenhower and Smith saw themselves eclipsed by the operational commands. The crisis acted like a magic elixir on Eisenhower. His blood was up; Bradley and Hodges had let him down. The broad front was his baby, and he had believed their siren songs of "one more push and we are through." He had accepted Bradley's gamble of leaving the Ardennes exposed. Now the Germans had concentrated their forces, gained total surprise, and appeared to be on their way to the Meuse. The U.S. Army had got kicked in the teeth, and the old scrapper in Eisenhower reemerged. Supposedly at the Versailles meeting on 16 December, when Bradley had been reluctant to take Tenth Armored from Patton, Eisenhower had snapped, "Tell [Patton] that Ike is running this damn war."[31] Apocryphal or not, Eisenhower finally acted like a ground commander—one could even posit a supreme commander—at Versailles and Verdun, casting aside his predilection for consensus building and asserting himself. At Verdun, the only two officers that mattered were Eisenhower and Patton. It was Fort Meade and 1920 all over again, when the two of them had used armor to solve Leavenworth map problems. Patton had predicted, "Ike, you will be the Lee of the next war, and I will be your Jackson." That bit of Patton braggadocio now looked prophetic.[32]

Acknowledging the breakdown of connections between headquarters, Smith informed Montgomery the day of the Verdun meeting that SHAEF would orchestrate communications between the commands.[33] Communications always go vertically, from higher headquarters to lower headquarters, and then horizontally to the commands, but because of the deplorable state of communications in the theater, SHAEF could never exercise its proper command responsibilities. Almost by default, Third Army attached its communications through the rear. But communications were only partially at fault. For months, Smith had chafed at SHAEF's impotence. He knew that "lower headquarters had little use for SHAEF" and agitated for Bradley to resist its directives. Smith never felt welcome at First Army headquarters and detected an unhealthy rivalry between Bradley's and Hodges's staffs; he claimed that "First Army's staff worked against 12th Army Group." Hodges rarely stayed within command channels and was actively aided by his chief of staff, MG Bill Kean.[34] In the crisis, SHAEF started to resemble an operational headquarters.

Apprehension grew at SHAEF that Bradley, in Luxembourg, did not have a full grasp of the gravity of the situation at the front, and evidence mounted that Hodges exerted no control over the fighting. At Versailles, Eisenhower made it clear that the first priority was to prevent any breach of the Meuse line, yet as late as 19 December, Bradley had made no effort to shore up the defenses at the crossings. Eisenhower dispatched a curt reminder to Bradley. Bradley remarked to his chief of staff, MG Leven Allen, "What the devil do they think we're doing, starting back for the beaches?"[35] SHAEF's assertion of authority would amount to little if orders went ignored. Bradley took no action.

All the chief SHAEF players returned to Versailles later that night.

Eisenhower called Smith on the phone and told him the results of the Verdun conference. Betts reported his findings to Strong. "Well, you must go and report this to Beetle Smith," Strong replied. Betts went to Smith and said, "It's my recommendation that you relieve the First Army commander." By now, the crossed rifles of the infantry had lost some of their luster—at least where Smith's old Infantry School chief was concerned. Smith considered Hodges "the weakest commander we had," but relieving a three-star general in the middle of the most desperate battle of the war presented another kettle of fish. "He sort of grunted," Betts recalled, "and that was that."[36]

Not quite. Whiteley thought long and hard about a command shift during his return trip to Versailles. For three and a half months, SHAEF had fought off Montgomery's resolute efforts to command First Army. How could SHAEF turn around now at the peak of the Ardennes crisis and give Montgomery what he had long coveted? And could a British officer make the suggestion? When he arrived he put a call through to Montgomery and asked, "If Ike asked you to take over First Army, when could you do it?" Montgomery needed no time to think; he said he could take command the next morning. Whiteley cautioned the field marshal that no such decision had been made, and Montgomery never pushed the issue.[37] After what he had seen in Verdun, Strong questioned whether Bradley appreciated the seriousness of the situation. After talking with Whiteley, Strong concurred that it was "absolutely essential to inform Bedell Smith about my growing doubts whether the Allies were matching up to the situation. Some German units had penetrated well beyond Bastogne and were getting far too near the Meuse for my liking." Neither British officer was a Montgomery partisan, particularly Whiteley, but both concluded that SHAEF and Bradley would have to swallow the bitter medicine.

The ailing Smith had already retired to a cot installed in the room next to his office. Just after midnight he heard a knock on his door. "Whiteley added some operational details," Strong recounted, "saying that, to his sure knowledge, there had been no contact between General Bradley and the headquarters of his First Army in the north for two days." Whiteley also talked with one of Montgomery's liaison officers, who reported "considerable confusion and disorganization" in First Army's rear. Smith listened to what the two British officers said and then detonated, calling them "limey bastards" and "sons of bitches." "Why is it," he hissed, "whenever there is any real trouble, the British do not appear to trust the Americans to handle it efficiently?" He found their recommendation "completely unacceptable," and since they clearly lacked confidence in SHAEF's ability to manage the battle, they "no longer [were] acceptable as staff officers to Eisenhower and should consider themselves fired."[38]

After he calmed down, Smith assessed the situation. Strong had been suffering from a case of nerves ever since the German breakthrough, but Whiteley's measured opinion carried considerable import. Smith dressed and cabled Montgomery, soliciting his views. Smith expressed his faith that Bradley could master the situation. He reckoned that Bradley could reassert control north of the salient if First Army yielded ground, shortened its lines, and consolidated reserves along its line of communications. The objective focused on "destroying the enemy in Belgium."[39]

By cabling Montgomery, Smith tipped off his thinking. Smith worried most about Whiteley's claim that Bradley remained out of contact with Hodges. If First Army's situation proved as dismal as Whiteley and Betts indicated, Bradley could not possibly exercise command. He also toyed with the notion of Eisenhower taking over direct command. But a glance at a map indicated that could not happen; given the line of communications and the axis of the German penetration, Reims offered no advantages. Nothing like a mobile SHAEF command post existed. Exhausting all the alternatives, Smith confronted the bald fact that Whiteley and Strong were right.[40] Smith also knew that once Montgomery took command of the American armies north of the salient, it would be hell trying to take them away. Giving command to Montgomery would appear like a "call for help." Smith still burned over the British press campaign following the Salerno battle, giving the impression that Montgomery had saved the beachhead. No doubt the same thing would happen again. Yet who better to command a positional defensive battle than Montgomery? Given his views on Hodges's staff, what Betts told him took on added meaning.

In the presence of Strong and Whiteley, Smith put a call through to Bradley. Accounts of what transpired vary. In his 1948 book, ghostwritten by his aide Chet Hansen, Bradley maintained that Smith told him, "Ike thinks it may be a good idea to turn over to Monty your two armies on the north and let him run that side of the Bulge from the 21st Army Group. It may save us a great deal of trouble." Bradley opposed the idea, but Smith persisted, saying the changeover appeared to be the "logical thing to do."[41] In his second memoir, Bradley stated that Smith wheedled, telling him the command shift would be temporary, that Eisenhower was worried Patton might go off "half-cocked" and he wanted Bradley's superintendence of Third Army's offensive; in addition, Montgomery would relieve him of a lot of headaches, and since the British had not committed troops to the fight, they might demonstrate a greater willingness to play a more active role with Montgomery in command.[42] Both sources have Smith asking if the change in command would make more sense if Montgomery were an American. "Beetle," Bradley remembered saying, "it's hard for me to object. Certainly if Monty's were an American command, I would agree with you entirely." Smith's less voluble version is more credible. At this point, Smith was merely testing the waters. Since Eisenhower knew nothing about the proposal, Smith would not have mentioned Ike. But when Bradley admitted he had been out of contact with Hodges for two or three days, Smith concluded, "It was an open and shut case." He decided there and then to make his recommendation to Eisenhower the next morning.[43]

Why Smith waited until morning and wasted valuable time remains a question. Perhaps the case was not so open and shut. A subdued chiefs of staff meeting took place the next morning. Smith remained uncharacteristically low-key. Nobody mentioned anything about a change in command or anybody getting sacked. After the conference concluded and they were walking down the hall to Eisenhower's outer office, Smith reached out and grabbed Strong's arm. A downcast Smith informed him that he intended to make the case for the command shift. The recommendation would be better coming from an American.[44]

In his typically cogent fashion, Smith gave his appraisal of the situation. Eisenhower listened and then asked that a call be put through to Bradley. Naturally, Bradley objected, but finally Eisenhower said, "Well Brad, those are my orders." He then called Montgomery and made the shift official.[45] He neglected to say anything about the command change being temporary. The Germans banked on their offensive throwing the Anglo-American partners into disarray or, at the very least, paralyzing them while SHAEF waited for authority to act from London and Washington.[46] Eisenhower's decision proved them mistaken. Later that day Smith apologized to Strong and Whiteley. "What made me really mad," he admitted to Strong, "was that I knew you were right. But my American feelings got the better of me" because of the storm this would create in the United States.[47]

Montgomery wasted no time; three hours after receiving Eisenhower's phone call, he strode into Hodges's headquarters "like Christ come to cleanse the temple." And the temple needed cleansing. Hodges not only lost grip of the battle, but he also lost grip on himself. One member of his staff remembered Hodges "sitting with his arms folded on his desk, his head in his arms."[48] Even his army diary could not disguise the fact that Hodges had lost the plot, complaining, "the continual traffic moving up and down the main road makes it difficult for the General to obtain the quiet which is necessary in the making of these vast decisions."[49] Observers labored to point to a single major decision made by Hodges since the Germans smashed through his lines. "Neither army commander had seen BRADLEY or any of his staff since this battle began," Montgomery told Brooke that evening. "Ninth Army had three divisions and First Army fifteen divisions and there were no reserves anywhere behind the front. Morale is very low. They seemed delighted to have someone to give them firm orders."[50]

Montgomery wired Smith that, in his opinion, Hodges should be relieved. He could not do it and asked Smith to handle it. Cognizant of what Betts had told him, Smith replied SHAEF would not shy away from making the decision but asked for twenty-four hours. The next day de Guingand called Smith. "Hodges is not the man I would pick," de Guingand frankly reported, "but he is much better [today]." On 22 December Montgomery reported to Smith, "HODGES was a bit shaken early on and needed moral support and was very tired. He is doing better now."[51] Lincoln liked to use the phrase "confused and stunned like a duck hit on the head" to describe his muddleheaded generals. That depiction largely summed up Hodges's performance during the Bulge. For five days in the first week of January he took to his bed with what his diarist called "a slight temperature and a cold" that later got magnified into a case of viral pneumonia.[52] Montgomery wisely avoided getting involved in any intramural American command fight by working through Hodges's staff.

From the beginning of the German onslaught, Smith placed a twenty-four-hour delay on all news releases and a complete blackout on the command switch. His chief of psychological warfare for liberated territories, LTC R. H. C. Drummond-Wolff, went to his boss, COL Ernest Dupuy, and claimed that the delay had a "disastrous effect" on civilian morale. In his opinion, hiding the fact of the Germans' breakthrough and their continuing momentum merely increased rumors of a repeat of 1940. In the absence of reliable news, the French and Belgians listened to German sources, leading to the widespread belief that the Allies had suffered a disaster in the Ardennes.[53] Because he dreaded the press reaction to the command exchange, Smith kept the clamps on. Reports of German assassins and saboteurs in Paris multiplied, adding to the anxious atmosphere. Butcher went out to Versailles for a talk with Eisenhower about the blackout issue. He found Eisenhower "a prisoner of our security police" and "helplessly irritated by the restriction on his moves."[54] Security forces even had a look-alike driven around in Eisenhower's car.[55]

The same applied to Smith. Murphy came over from London and spent the night. A large, wall-enclosed garden surrounded Smith's Versailles quarters. Nine guards, some with submachine guns, patrolled the compound. During the night a startled Murphy awoke to the crackle of gunfire and emerged from his room to find Smith, still in his pajamas, toting a carbine. With Beetle on point, they rushed into the courtyard. Smith joined the fusillade. The next morning the body of an intruder was found—not one of Skorzeny's boys but a stray cat riddled with bullets.[56]

Smith felt confident the Germans would not break out beyond the Meuse. Even as the British moved toward their concentration points around Brussels, Smith had faith Horrocks and British XXX Corps would deflect the German advance short of the river. The chief concern at SHAEF fixed on constricting the German penetration, funneling the German advance, and restricting their lines of communication. The southern flank still concerned him; SHAEF wanted a strong shoulder to cushion Patton's counterattack. Patton's attack with 50,000 troops went in ahead of schedule on 22 December. He argued for a wider envelopment, and Smith agreed, but Bradley overruled them. In Bradley's opinion, the road net—chiefly, reliance on a single artery—made that move too risky. In hindsight, Smith agreed that he was probably right.

Smith later claimed he was never worried about holding Bastogne, although Strong's agonizing played on his nerves. Strong came to Smith three times in one day, expressing his anxieties.[57] When Strong wondered why Smith remained so convinced they would keep Bastogne, Smith replied, "because the commanders there think they can hold today." He thought back to his days as a Young Turk at Leavenworth. The school preached that one division of good troops, properly handled, could hold any position in daylight against any force thrown against it. He conceded that this was unlikely, but he remembered it. In his opinion, SHAEF had its best division in Bastogne, and if the commander on the ground thought he could hold, that was good enough for Smith. He also remembered his study of Tannenberg: "we had been taught the great opportunities offered by a counteroffensive."[58] Tedder spoke for most of the staff when he wrote on 22 December: "The fact that the Hun has stuck his neck out is, from the point of view of shortening the whole business, the best thing that could happen. It may make months of difference. But he might have waited until after Xmas."[59]

"Things look[ed], if anything, worse than before" at First Army headquarters on Christmas Eve. German armor advanced to Celles, less than five miles from Dinant and the Meuse. "The outlook is not good," the First Army diarist opined. If Fifth Panzer Army "pushed northward [the threat] could prove seriously embarrassing." The day's entry ended in a more hopeful vein: "things always look darkest before the dawn."[60] In fact, the dawn had already arrived on 23 December, when the weather broke cold and clear. That morning, aerial resupply dropped artillery ammunition and rations into besieged Bastogne, replenishing the nearly depleted stocks. Tactical air pounded the German ring. Patton's offensive made little progress but nonetheless exerted pressure from the south and blunted the advance of the German Seventh Army. Also that day, British XXX Corps deployed its armor guarding the Meuse crossings from Givet to Namur. Even though confusion still reigned at First Army headquarters, and with plenty of anxious hours yet to come, by 23 December the German penetrations had been contained.

After the war, the German leadership admitted the Ardennes offensive had been doomed from the start. The Allied attrition operations finally paid off; fighting in the Netherlands, along the Roer, at Metz, and in Alsace had whittled German strength to the point they abandoned all hope of attacking on a broader front, as far south as Luxembourg City. According to Jodl, Hitler feared that if the Germans attacked in such a constricted area, the offensive "would form a wedge and might be driven in from the sides in the first Allied counterattack." Because the Germans operated on only two main roads, they echeloned their offensive in depth, not width. Everything hinged on reaching the Meuse by the end of the first day. They never got close. German supply elements began piling up. Göring maintained that "bad weather stalled us more than it helped us," and the SS divisions "had comparatively more maintenance and rear echelon personnel than fighting elements." Jodl and Göring agreed that Hitler's misplaced faith in Josef "Sepp" Dietrich to spearhead the Sixth SS Panzer Army's main thrust was an enormous error. Göring thought Dietrich "had at most the ability to command a division," while Jodl believed only an operational genius could have pulled off the Ardennes offensive, "and Sepp Dietrich was no genius."[61]

How expedient for German leaders to blame Hitler's obsessions and faulty generalship for the breakdown of the Ardennes counteroffensive. The Germans failed because the Americans declined to yield. The Americans' success in delaying the German drives in those first crucial days had little to do with their own generalship—which was mediocre at best—and everything to do with the junior officers and men, often fighting isolated and with open flanks, refusing to give way until eliminated or forced to surrender after being surrounded or expending all their ammunition. Gerow brilliantly refused his flank and stoutly held the northern shoulder. The bitter fight put up by V Corps along the Elsenborn Ridge and by elements of the Twenty-eighth Division at Wiltz and in hundreds of other unrecorded actions fatally threw off the German timetable and channeled their penetrations into the very wedge Hitler dreaded. The Germans had calculated that actions such as the massacre at Malmedy and dropping paratroopers in American uniforms in the rear would undermine American morale; initially, these actions had an effect, but over time, "dirty pool" redounded against the Germans and hardened resistance. The response of the commander of the Bastogne defense to German demands that he surrender—"Nuts!"—perfectly expressed the reaction of the average GI to assertions that he was beaten. Most GIs believed, with Eisenhower, "We cannot be content with his mere repulse. By rushing out from his fixed defenses the enemy may give us the chance to turn his great gamble into his worst defeat."[62]

Field Marshal–itis

Surveying the situation from London on 18 December, Brooke concluded that the Germans offered the Americans "a heaven sent opportunity" to shorten the war. Like SHAEF, he missed the hand of Hitler and identified Rundstedt as the author of the counteroffensive. He concluded that, as a "good officer," Rundstedt executed the risky operation hoping to "offset the Allied plans," but he wondered whether, as a "good German," he accepted the great gamble knowing that its failure would bring "this war to an early conclusion." All depended on the Americans taking advantage of this potential strategic windfall, and Brooke clearly entertained doubts that they could.[63] On the first point, Smith agreed. He considered the strategic miscalculation so obvious that he wondered if the German generals had consented to launch the attack in the hope of hastening the war's end.[64] As to SHAEF's ability to respond to the crisis, he possessed no doubts.

Montgomery disagreed with Smith on both counts. For him, the German counteroffensive represented the third defeat since he had relinquished the ground command, and he had zero faith in SHAEF's ability to manage the campaign. Montgomery never anticipated the German offensive. He had asked permission to go home for Christmas, and on the eve of the German attack, he stopped sending his nightly situation reports to Brooke "until the war becomes more exciting." In his letter to

Eisenhower requesting leave, Montgomery could not pass up the opportunity to make a dig. He reminded Eisenhower of a wager made in October 1943: Eisenhower had bet the war would end before Christmas 1944, and Montgomery expected payment of the £5 bet.[65] Not surprisingly, Montgomery's take on how best to capitalize on the situation differed markedly from SHAEF's. The first order of business centered on containing the German advance east of the Meuse; with German armor committed in the Bulge, "the proper answer . . . is to launch operation VERITABLE as early as possible." For Montgomery, the Bulge was an American affair; he would clean up the mess Bradley made, end the piecemeal splintering of units, consolidate the defense, collect an American operational reserve, and refuse to commit British forces in the counterattack unless absolutely vital for fear that heavy casualties would hamstring Veritable, his planned offensive to remove the Maas salient and advance to the Rhine.[66]

Montgomery left his headquarters and did not return for the next four days, moving between First and Ninth Army areas, visiting Hodges and Simpson daily, and meeting with every corps and many division commanders. He gave ground, took the risk of extending and thinning Simpson's line and reinforcing First Army, overruled Hodges and pulled Seventh Armored out of St. Vith, and by 22 December had assembled four divisions under Collins as the operational reserve. He held back XXX Corps as a strategic reserve but finally moved British elements forward to man the tip of the salient and then sidled them eastward, relieving American forces for a counterattack.

The contention over the timing of the counterthrust revealed the very different thinking of Montgomery versus that of the American commanders and SHAEF. The speed of the American response—the realignment of First Army and Patton's attack—astonished the Germans. Patton's drive north perfectly demonstrated his trademark impetuosity. He appeared everywhere, driving his columns toward Bastogne. Patton abandoned his headquarters and was constantly seen going forward—always forward—in bitter cold by open vehicle; his troops never saw him return to the rear, which he did by air and only after dusk. But had Patton followed Eisenhower's advice, waited, and built up a more powerful counterattack, Third Army would have inflicted greater damage, suffered fewer casualties, and relieved Bastogne just as quickly. On 26 December a relief column battered its way into Bastogne. The fighting there degenerated into a slugging match that involved six American divisions by 31 December. SHAEF, Bradley, and Collins wanted First Army to go over to the counterattack before Christmas, but Montgomery refused. Ultra indicated that Hitler insisted on renewing the offensive toward the north. As he told Brooke, Montgomery wanted to "get the show tidied up and to ensure absolute security before passing over to offensive action." Let the enemy "crumble" himself against prepared American defenses while tactical air smashed his congested logistics and strategic air interdicted his lines of communication. Once Collins's VII Corps completed its assembly, he would "deal a hard blow."[67]

Both Brooke and Montgomery took satisfaction that events and the Germans finally forced Eisenhower to see the light on the command question. But Brooke considered it "most important" that Montgomery "should not even in the slightest degree . . . rub this undoubted fact in [the face of] anyone at SHAEF or elsewhere." Brooke knew Montgomery only too well. Any ill-considered remark would find its way back to Versailles, making "it more difficult to ensure that this new set-up for Command remains even after the present emergency ends."[68] The CIGS's sage advice could not stop Montgomery from being Montgomery.

On Christmas Day Bradley did something he was loath to do: visit Montgomery. He went in an effort to convince Montgomery to counterattack at the earliest possible date. After a circuitous trip, Bradley arrived to find no staff car waiting for him; Montgomery, never a good host, did not even offer him lunch. Bradley's Christmas meal consisted of an apple. At his imperious worst, Montgomery paid no heed to Brooke's injunction. Bradley remembered Montgomery "scolding him like a schoolboy"; he had never seen Montgomery "more arrogant and egotistical." Montgomery rejected out of hand any notion of an early counterattack in the north and returned to his favorite hobbyhorse: the entire campaign since Normandy had been mismanaged; the front was stretched too thin; there were not enough troops; the enemy had seen his opportunity and taken it, inflicting a defeat on the Americans.[69] Bradley remained silent, which, as always, Montgomery took for assent. He could not have been more wrong. Had he demonstrated the same compassion he had shown Hodges, had he appealed to Bradley's sense of soldierly comradeship rather than using Normandy as an illustration of his genius, Montgomery might have produced a different result. Instead, whatever glimmer of feeling Bradley might have retained toward Montgomery flickered out. The next morning an irate Bradley called Smith. Unlike their conversation the night Smith had solicited Bradley's views on a possible command shift, "this time [Bradley] was no shrinking violet." He recalled, "I let him have it with both barrels." Bradley criticized Montgomery, telling Smith that by assuming a defensive posture, the field marshal was "throwing away an opportunity to inflict a devastating defeat" on the Germans. Bradley demanded the return of First and Ninth Armies.[70] Bradley's call ignited another crisis.

Eisenhower decided he needed to go see Montgomery and defuse the situation. Weather prevented his departure on 27 December. Bradley called Smith and said, "Damn it, Beetle, can't you people get Monty going in the north? As near as we can tell the other fellow's reached the high water mark today. He'll soon be starting to pull back—if not tonight, certainly tomorrow." Despite the weather, Bradley made his way to Versailles for a lengthy conference with Eisenhower, Tedder, Smith, Strong, Bull, and Whiteley. How to get Montgomery moving dominated the whole discussion.

That night Eisenhower set off by rail. Eisenhower and Montgomery met on the train at Hasselt Station, and Montgomery insisted they meet alone. Differing personalities, command styles, and army cultures made misunderstandings between the two men inevitable. Montgomery made his professional assessments—always colored by his overbearing conceit—and gave his views ad nauseam in black-and-white terms. Everybody knew precisely where Montgomery stood. Eisenhower's stock in trade was ambiguity and evasiveness. He made opaque statements that always fell just short of concurrence. Two people with different agendas could enter his office and both leave thinking that Eisenhower agreed with them. No meeting between the two men highlights this failure to communicate more than the fateful conference in the railway car at Hasselt.

Eisenhower's sole aim in coming involved pinning down a date for the northern counterattack—no later than New Year's Day. Eisenhower admitted he had been "set back thoroughly on my heels" by Patton's lack of progress.[71] He needed an attack from the north. Montgomery expected one more immediate German push to break through First Army's front. He expected the Germans would replace armor with infantry and marshal their panzers for this effort or for one against Patton; both agreed they could not allow that to happen. In the event the Germans pursued the second option, Montgomery intended to attack immediately. If neither materialized before 1 January, Eisenhower understood that Montgomery would go over to the offensive.[72] But Eisenhower heard what he wanted to hear; Montgomery avoided all commitments, instead deflecting discussions toward Allied strategy after the Bulge. The field marshal's thinking remained focused, as it had from the beginning of the Ardennes, on Veritable followed by a Rhine crossing in the north. Montgomery made the same old pitch: Bradley, Patton, and Devers had steered Eisenhower astray; the northern thrust must be undertaken with "all available offensive power" and with all powers of operational control and coordination vested in one man. If Eisenhower failed to comply with these two basic conditions, he would fail again. As in the last go-round, where Montgomery saw only defeat and assigned blame, Eisenhower glimpsed an opportunity to snatch a signal victory from nothing more than a temporary setback. Whereas Montgomery perceived the Bulge as tacking another six months on to the war, Eisenhower envisioned a glittering opportunity to shorten it.

For Eisenhower, worrying about what might transpire after dealing with the present crisis could wait. He agreed the northern thrust would enjoy priority. Pointing to the inevitable negative reaction in the United States, Eisenhower expressed his doubts about fulfilling the second condition. A tactless Montgomery merely replied that Eisenhower would have even greater difficulty explaining another failed campaign. As always, Montgomery offered his services under Bradley, but after the Christmas meeting, Eisenhower knew there could be no question of either serving under the other. The conference ended with nothing concrete achieved, but both men thinking they had left with something: for Eisenhower, a hazy pledge for a 1 January offensive under the right circumstances; for Montgomery, an indication that the existing command relationships would continue after the Bulge.[73] Before leaving, Eisenhower wired Smith, informing him that with the threat of a Meuse crossing removed, he wanted SHAEF to release the Eleventh Armored and possibly the Eighty-seventh Infantry Division to Bradley as reinforcement for the counterattack in the south. "Make this clear to Bradley," he emphasized. Eisenhower thought he had secured an agreement to initiate a New Year's Day pincer movement north and south against the waist of the salient.[74]

Montgomery was nothing if not predictable. He called de Guingand in Brussels and asked him to finagle an invitation to SHAEF. He figured Eisenhower would once again "run out" on an anticipated agreement and wanted his chief of staff, as reported by Frank Simpson, "to work on Bedell-Smith . . . on the same lines as the Field Marshal had worked on General Eisenhower." When Smith offered de Guingand an invitation, Montgomery penned another of his arson letters. After hearing Eisenhower equivocate at Hasselt, Montgomery went so far as to dictate what Eisenhower should write in his directive on the Ruhr offensive and command.[75]

Eisenhower appreciated being hectored no more than Bradley did. With Montgomery, it was always the same thing. When Eisenhower talked Antwerp, Montgomery talked the Ruhr and command, but this time Eisenhower was determined not to give in. At the morning staff conference on 29 December, Smith applauded Montgomery's success in creating order from disarray in the north but voiced his concern that the field marshal's "inherent overcautiousness was going to cause us to miss the opportunity of inflicting a severe defeat on the enemy in the immediate future." Eisenhower, Whiteley, and Strong all agreed. Montgomery should not wait until 1 January; perhaps they could influence de Guingand to prod the field marshal. In any case, all saw eye to eye that when Collins and Patton linked, Bradley would resume command.[76] After the meeting Eisenhower and Smith discussed how much Montgomery had changed since the Mediterranean, where he had at least made an effort to be a team player. When asked by Kay Summersby how he kept his cool with Montgomery, Eisenhower responded, "If I can keep the team together, anything's worth it."[77] That changed when Montgomery's latest epistle arrived.

The letter brought up the Maastricht meeting again, stating, "Bradley opposed any idea that I should have operational control over his Army Group." Montgomery thought it "necessary for you to be very firm on the subject, and any loosely worded statement will be quite useless." If Eisenhower employed the word *coordination* "it will NOT work." Montgomery insisted on a clear definition of his command authority and suggested that Eisenhower use the sentence "full operational directing control and coordination . . . is vested in the commander-in-chief 21 Army Group." He reiterated his two conditions. "One commanding officer must have powers to direct and control the operations" in the main northern thrust, he restated, and "you cannot possibly do it yourself." It is "absolutely certain that if we do not comply with the two basic conditions," he predicted, "we will fail again." He asked that Eisenhower not divulge his reference to Maastricht. The letter was signed, "Yours, always, and your devoted friend," with the addendum "Do not bother to answer this."[78]

Montgomery's letter set off what Bradley called "a command High Noon." It threw Eisenhower and Smith into a towering rage.[79] They found Montgomery's constant harping on defeat—"the bloody nose" the Americans had sustained—and his aspersions directed against Eisenhower intolerable. Nor did they appreciate his deprecation of SHAEF and its inability to manage operations. The static front and the ammunition and manpower shortages afforded SHAEF little latitude for orchestrating the campaign; the chronic problem of communications did not help. In the Bulge, Eisenhower's self-confidence grew by the day; he asserted his command prerogatives, and SHAEF started acting like an operational headquarters. Montgomery's refusal to attack with American forces—not to mention his rebuff of suggestions that he commit British forces in the offensive—irritated them most. As Eisenhower stressed to Montgomery the day before, "*This is a very important point.* We must break him [the enemy] up while he is out in the open."[80] A "het up" Eisenhower finally lost his temper. After meeting with his inner staff—he always sought consensus—Eisenhower wrote a draft of a "him or me" letter, but at Smith's insistence he sat on it.

Weather canceled de Guingand's flight. For two days he watched the readings on his crisis Richter scale point to an impending seismic eruption. One of Montgomery's liaison officers told him of the depth of the animosity against Montgomery in Bradley's headquarters. Whiteley called de Guingand and informed him, "I am afraid Ike is not going to be able to do quite all your C-in-C wants him to do as regards the set up for Command." Forewarned, de Guingand put a call through to Smith and sounded him out. What de Guingand heard startled him. Risking his life, de Guingand ordered a plane fired up and set off for Versailles.[81]

Smith met de Guingand at Orly airport. The British officer appeared shaken after the hair-raising flight. As they climbed into Beetle's Cadillac, an Eisenhower hand-me-down, Smith told de Guingand that Eisenhower and Bradley viewed Montgomery's delay in launching the counteroffensive insupportable, and operational questions had reached such a point that they must go to a higher authority for resolution. "I think we had better go right over and see Ike," Smith said, "otherwise it will certainly be too late."[82]

They found Eisenhower and Tedder in the supreme commander's office. Eisenhower looked weary and asked de Guingand, "What are you doing here Freddie?" De Guingand replied, "Well, I've come on a very important mission." Smith interrupted, telling Eisenhower that de Guingand wanted to shed some light on the field marshal's position. In a low voice, Eisenhower simply said he had had enough of the whole business and was fed up with Montgomery's dogged campaign aimed at usurping his authority and dictating decision making. At Maastricht he had promised Montgomery eventual control of Ninth Army, but beyond that he would not go. "I think you had better read it," Eisenhower said as he handed de Guingand a piece of paper. "At the moment we've just agreed upon a signal we're sending to General Marshall." De Guingand read the letter recommending Alexander as Montgomery's replacement.

A stunned de Guingand knew what would happen if the letter went out. "I then made my little speech, and I was in deadly earnest," recounted de Guingand. Pointing to Montgomery's isolation in his headquarters, de Guingand was positive the field marshal simply did not know the seriousness of the situation. Completing his plea, de Guingand asked if Eisenhower would withhold the signal for twenty-four hours. He would return to Montgomery and set matters straight.

Tedder emphatically said, "No, we've decided on the signal, it must go." Eisenhower remarked that since the two of them could not work in harness, one would have to go. Everyone knew who that would be. A cable from Washington that day removed any doubt that Eisenhower would win the showdown. Stories demanding a British ground commander dominated the British papers. Guessing the pressure Eisenhower was under, and worried he might crack, Marshall insisted, "Under no circumstance make any concessions of any kind whatsoever." He pointed to the "terrific resentment in this country" if Eisenhower relinquished ground command. Marshall wanted Eisenhower "to be certain of our attitude on this side. . . . You are doing a grand job," the chief assured Eisenhower, "and go on and give them hell."[83] There was no question where that hell was directed at the moment. Beginning to despair, de Guingand looked to Smith. Perhaps mindful of Montgomery's granting a day's grace to Hodges, Smith urged that de Guingand receive his delay. After "quite a time," Smith won out.

As if nothing had happened, they convened a conference, and de Guingand laid out Montgomery's thinking. First Army had taken a pounding, and without extensive preparations it could not immediately go over to the offensive. Any premature attack would go in "half-baked." It would be better to allow the Germans to pound away against prepared defenses and masses of Allied artillery and then come back with a full-blooded riposte with plenty of reserves. Planning for a deliberate counterattack had gone forward since 26 December. Smith said that was all fine and good, but Montgomery had promised an attack on 1 January, and Smith threatened to extract proof from his files. De Guingand saw through that gambit, knowing full well that Montgomery would never commit himself on paper. Smith changed tack, explaining that without an attack in the north, the Germans could employ interior lines and shift armor—intelligence already indicated they were doing just that—against Patton's exposed position around Bastogne. De Guingand conceded that Montgomery could attack sooner, but not until 2 or 3 January.[84]

Relieved and gratified by Smith's actions, de Guingand gladly accepted his colleague's invitation to spend the night. After tidying up some loose ends in his office, Smith took de Guingand back to his comfortable quarters. Simpson had already remarked on the magnificence of Smith's wine cellar and his willingness to share it. A good many people—Caffery, Handy, Arnold, and, of course, Marshall—all testified to

Smith's generosity that Christmas season, given the stockpiles of liberated wine, champagne, and cognac.[85] Smith and de Guingand unwound after the dramatic events of the day, and Smith fortified de Guingand with more than spirits. They both realized that more drama lay in store the next day, especially for de Guingand.[86]

The weather had not improved, but that did not matter. De Guingand was on a mission. On the flight back he experienced "a very bad attack of the nerves." At first incredulous, Montgomery's tough outer crust finally cracked. Now chastened, he asked de Guingand's advice. His chief of staff produced an apologetic letter he had taken the liberty of writing for Montgomery in advance. "What your decision may be," read the key sentence in the single-paragraph cable, "you can rely on me one hundred percent to make it work and I know BRAD will do the same." The wire expressed Montgomery's regret that his letter had caused so much consternation and asked that it be torn up. It was signed, "your very devoted subordinate."[87] Montgomery "looked completely non-plussed," de Guingand remembered. "I don't think I had ever seen him so deflated."[88] What goes around comes around. After the way he had treated Bradley and Eisenhower, it was now Montgomery's turn to eat a big slice of humble pie.

Just before midnight Montgomery sent another message to SHAEF, signaling that the northern counterattack would open "at first light on 3 January."[89] Eisenhower relented, and the cables to Marshall and the CCS never left his desk drawer. Had they been sent, the repercussions of Montgomery's sacking are hard to guess. Certainly the reverberations would have been felt in Whitehall and the White House. Hitler hoped the strain placed on the Anglo-American partnership by his offensive might fissure the alliance. That certainly would not have come to pass, but a first-class crisis at the uppermost reaches of the Allied command structure was the last thing anybody needed as they prepared the counterattacks to pinch out of the Bulge. Fortunately, cooler heads prevailed, and the coolest belonged to the officer most observers considered the biggest hothead in the Allied camp: Beetle Smith.

★ 34 ★

Déjà Vu All over Again

As the end of 1944 approached, prospects brightened. The German attacks in the Ardennes ran out of steam, and Montgomery's pledge to attack from the north on 3 January raised expectations that the Allies would not only regain the initiative in the west but also inflict a telling if not fatal blow on the Germans. Hitler was far from done, and he ensured there was little cause for celebration in Allied circles on New Year's Day. Just before midnight on 31 December, three corps from Army Group G and Army Group Oberrhein attacked the depleted Seventh Army in Alsace (Operation Nordwind). At first light on 1 January the Luftwaffe unleashed a 1,035-plane air blitz (Operation Bodenplatz) against Allied air bases in Belgium and France. Nor was the Kriegsmarine left out. The new snorkel-type submarines launched a U-boat offensive in the coastal waters of the United Kingdom and in the English Channel.

Hitler's attempt to wrestle back the initiative backfired. Bodenplatz achieved surprise, destroying or damaging 495 aircraft—including Montgomery's B-17—and inflicted heavy damage on five airfields, but at a prohibitive cost in planes and irreplaceable aircrew. The Allies quickly made good their losses, and the Luftwaffe never recovered. The U-boats created much alarm in the Admiralty, but the Germans lacked the numbers to sustain the campaign. The Alsace offensive—in common with the Ardennes, Bodenplatz, and the U-boat actions—suffered from the same shortcomings; the Germans marshaled unanticipated strength, caught the Allies napping, inflicted heavy losses, and stressed the Western alliance along its fault lines, yet their audacity proved their undoing. In January SHAEF's attention turned toward defining the best means of exploiting the opportunities presented by Hitler's failed gambles. Before that could happen, Eisenhower and SHAEF had to mend the alliance's fences and put the American household in order.

The Great Allies Are Divided

Before the German Ardennes offensive, SHAEF expected French First Army to eliminate the Colmar Pocket and assume the defensive along the Upper Rhine, freeing Patch to move north in combination with Patton's drive into the Saar. Instead, the Germans reinforced the Colmar Pocket. Eisenhower, Bradley, and Devers held a stormy conference on 24–25 November. Despite Sixth Army Group's successes in gaining the Rhine, Eisenhower remained attached to his idea of closing the length of the river and rejected Devers's scheme for gaining a bridgehead. Instead, he ordered Devers to relinquish two divisions to Patton and drive north in conjunction with Third Army. Eisenhower left the meeting "mad as hell" over Devers's questioning of his strategy, while Devers pondered whether he remained "a member of the team."[1] When Seventh Army complied with the order, and given Patch's steady progress near Wissembourg, Devers believed that, with reinforcements, Sixth Army Group could roll up the West Wall defenses from the south. Eisenhower sent Smith forward to Devers's headquarters at Vittel to tell him he could expect no such reinforcements. When the Germans attacked in the Ardennes, Eisenhower ordered Devers to cease all offensive actions and extend his line, allowing Patton to employ more divisions against the Bulge. Instead of a secure right, Devers's forces were overextended; Seventh Army covered an additional thirty miles, more than doubling its frontage, with one American corps facing north and an additional division employed in containing the Colmar Pocket. Eisenhower knew Devers's position was "inherently weak from a defensive standpoint," but he took the risk.[2]

Sixth Army Group's intelligence alerted SHAEF to the possibility of a German offensive. A worried Devers came to Versailles for talks with Eisenhower and Smith. If the Germans attacked, Eisenhower wanted Devers to shorten his lines, leaving only a weak screen defending Strasbourg. Smith disagreed; Devers should either hold his ground, which he favored, or fall back in detail.[3] Eisenhower remained unconvinced; in the event of a German attack, he ordered a general withdrawal to the Vosges, with Devers pulling back two divisions west of the uplands as a reserve. That meant the abandonment of Strasbourg.[4]

Understandably, de Gaulle experienced an attack of paroxysm when he heard of Eisenhower's intentions, and on 28 December he sent off a strongly worded protest to SHAEF. The day of the German attack, Smith called Devers's headquarters, angrily inquiring why Seventh Army had not followed Eisenhower's order to withdraw and insisting that Devers comply at once.[5] SHAEF recognized that a first-class storm with de Gaulle was brewing, and it did not take long to hit. "The French government," de Gaulle announced on 1 January, "obviously cannot let Strasbourg fall into enemy hands again without first doing everything possible to prevent it"; he sent appeals in the same vein to Churchill and Roosevelt.[6] He intended to insert the French Tenth Division in Strasbourg, whatever orders SHAEF might issue.

On 2 January Smith met with Juin; predictably, things went very badly. The two chiefs of staff had a history of bad blood, stemming back to their butting heads over the pace of French rearmament. Juin told Smith that de Gaulle would withdraw French troops from SHAEF's control if Eisenhower's orders to fall back to the Vosges stood. He decried SHAEF and Eisenhower's generalship in no uncertain terms. "Juin said things to me," Smith related to Eisenhower, "which, if he had been an American, I would have socked him in the jaw."[7]

De Gaulle requested a meeting for 3 January. Eisenhower and the staff discussed Strasbourg during that morning's conference. "E is very definite in his views," Summersby recorded, "that we cannot afford to fight east of the Vosges." Devers's chief of staff reported, "Strasbourg is as good as lost." Churchill and Brooke flew in to smooth the ruffled feathers between SHAEF and Montgomery, but de Gaulle's petition also figured in the prime minister's calculations. Eisenhower met them at the airport—a sad occasion because of Ramsay's death in a crash on the same landing strip only the day before. After lunch, Churchill and Brooke attended the "memorable" conference among de Gaulle, Eisenhower, Smith, and Juin. Churchill remained outside of the discussions. De Gaulle "got heated to say the least of it" and produced an order to de Lattre to hold Strasbourg. "If we were at a Kriegspiel, I should say you were right," de Gaulle admitted. "But I must consider the matter from another point of view. Retreat in Alsace would yield French territory to the enemy. In the realm of strategy this would be only a maneuver. But for France, it would be a national disaster. For Alsace is sacred ground."[8]

After the conference Churchill and de Gaulle separately entered into political discussions. Brooke and Eisenhower conferred about the situation at the front. Eisenhower "seemed worried about the turn of affairs," noted Brooke, and the field marshal "avoided returning to any questions of command-organisation or of strategy, as it is quite useless."[9] In the meantime, Smith, Strong, and Whiteley, who attended the conference, reassessed the situation. Convinced by the weight of French objections, they decided to recommend the holding of Strasbourg. Eisenhower had already come to the same conclusion. As he rationalized to Marshall, execution of the withdrawal order would create far-ranging political repercussions for de Gaulle's government that might threaten its collapse and endanger SHAEF's lines of communication. "It was clearly a military necessity," he deduced, "to prevent this."[10] Smith disclosed to Handy that "at best the French are a constant psychological problem." He judged the French threat of withdrawing from SHAEF's authority another calculated bluff. "But it is difficult doing business on such a basis," he informed Handy, "and it requires a reservoir of tact and diplomacy exceeding my normal level of supply."[11]

From the Verdun conference onward, SHAEF asserted greater direction over operations in Sixth Army Group, including movements down to division level. Sixth Army Group performed well despite being understrength and having a mixed Allied composition; Seventh Army units were on alert when the Germans hit, and German gains remained limited. But neither Eisenhower nor Smith evidenced much faith in Devers's management of the Alsace fighting—a view very much colored by their dislike of the Sixth Army Group commander and amplified by Devers's championing of the holding of Strasbourg. As Robb indicated, "Bedell says don't dare phone Devers because he always interprets a suggestion as an order."[12] To ensure Devers got the message, Smith and Juin would fly to Sixth Army Group headquarters the next day.

That night SHAEF threw a big dinner party for Churchill. As Summersby reported, Churchill was in magnificent form, keeping everybody up until 1:30 in the morning. Doubtlessly fueled by alcoholic intake, he insisted on talking privately with Brooke after the party broke up. The prime minister finally surrendered any notions of pushing through the Ljubljana gap to Vienna. Considering Montgomery's manpower problems, he viewed it wise to transfer divisions out of Italy. After "many patient hours [of] work winning him away from this [Vienna] venture," Brooke thought, "this is very satisfactory." If Italy became a "subsidiary" front, Churchill concluded he could not leave Alexander there. He settled on the idea of moving him into SHAEF, replacing Tedder as deputy supreme commander. Tedder would go to the Air Ministry.[13]

The next afternoon Churchill raised the question of Alexander replacing Tedder. Eisenhower welcomed the change. Tedder had made good sense as deputy supreme commander for the opening phases of the campaign because of the enormous role airpower would play. But the situation had now changed. An experienced ground commander as deputy seemed in order, and he would have to be British. Alexander loomed as the obvious choice. Churchill took "great pleasure" from Eisenhower's ready agreement to the switch.[14]

Questions surrounding what to do with the prime minister's favorite general circulated through the BCOS for a month. As when Brooke had embarked on his design to remove Eisenhower from ground command, the British wrestled with the problem of the supreme command in the Mediterranean. Dill's death set off a domino effect: Wilson would succeed Dill in Washington; Alexander would take over as supreme commander, with Clark replacing him in ground command. To Brooke's utter astonishment, Churchill and Alexander even toyed with the idea of replicating Eisenhower's structure, with Alexander simultaneously holding the supreme and ground commands. Brooke managed to dissuade the prime minister from making this proposal.[15]

Cunningham recognized Churchill's intentions. "Of course the only reason for this," Cunningham concluded, "is to get Wilson out of the way and appoint Alexander Supreme Commander Mediterranean, a post for which he is totally unfitted." The BCOS blocked this move at the Cairo conference, "but it looks as tho' CIGS & PM have agreed on this together." Brooke never intervened, calculating that his opposition to the appointment would appear to be motivated by jealousy. Since all three service chiefs dissented, Brooke asked Cunningham to make the case with Churchill, which he did the next day. Churchill took the admiral's criticisms of Alexander in good grace, then simply told Cunningham that he disagreed. "The tragedy is that [Portal and Brooke] agree with me but decided to take the line of least resistance. The upshot was the PM had his way." Cunningham considered it symptomatic of the way the BCOS operated. "The COS are just told what to do."[16]

Both Cunningham and Brooke agreed that Alexander lacked the requisite qualities of a supreme commander. "I cannot imagine that Alex will ever make a Supreme Commander," Brooke concluded, since "he has just not got the brains for it." Brooke frequently called Alexander a beautiful Chippendale mirror, "with a most attractive and pleasant frame, but when you look into the mirror you always find the reflection of some other person who temporarily dominates him." He wondered if Alexander—soon elevated to field marshal—"has a single idea in his head of his own!" The First Sea Lord was even harsher; he thought Alexander "completely stupid."[17]

Churchill held precisely the opposite view. Recently he had remarked to Brooke, "How wonderful Alex was! What a grasp! What a master mind!" During Brooke's push to remove Eisenhower from ground command, he had reminded Churchill of the situation after Casablanca, "when we brought in Alex as a deputy to Eisenhower to command the land forces for him."[18] The prime minister now latched on to this idea.

On 4 January Churchill and Brooke left Versailles and traveled by train to see Montgomery. Brooke informed Montgomery of the scheme to bring in Alexander. Montgomery replied that "he was all for such a plan which might go some way towards putting matters right."[19]

When Smith returned to Versailles, he encountered Eisenhower in the corridor. Eisenhower produced a draft letter he had written, calling for the command switch. As Smith related in 1947, Eisenhower "actually accepted the notion of a ground commander." A disbelieving Smith strongly resisted this move. He called in Whiteley, whose views Eisenhower valued. Whiteley "vehemently opposed the proposal." Since his two most trusted officers in SHAEF dissented, Eisenhower withheld the cable.[20]

With a change of command in the offing, Smith took the opportunity to raise the air command issue again. "Bedell had a long conversation with E re: the Air Forces," Summersby noted in the headquarters diary on 8 January. "It was agreed that Tedder has just got to take Command of the Air Forces. He has the title, but does not use his authority."[21] Tedder, off on a mission to Moscow, was not a party to these discussions.

The situation looked decidedly better in the Ardennes. On 3 January Montgomery opened the counterattack in the north on schedule. The Germans, having depleted their northern flank by feeding forces into the fighting around Bastogne, yielded ground. While Smith visited Devers's headquarters at Vittel, the Germans crossed the Rhine just north of Strasbourg, raising new concerns about the stability of the Alsace defenses.

On 7 January, at the height of the northern counterattack, Montgomery held an ill-fated press conference. The press agitation in the United Kingdom for a British ground commander reached a crescendo by New Year's, but it had nothing to do with the command shift in the Bulge because Smith kept the censorship clamps tightly closed. SHAEF refused permission on 5 January for an announcement by Twenty-first Army Group. The same day the story was leaked in two New York papers. This prompted a 5 January SHAEF news release that divulged the command arrangements. Since Bradley and Patton held press conferences the same day, SHAEF could hardy prevent Montgomery from conducting one of his own.

British and American newspapers speculated on an impending command switch. Roosevelt told the *New York Times* that Montgomery's command of U.S. forces in the Bulge did not denote that "Marshal Montgomery has become Deputy Commander to Eisenhower." The 6 January story also reported that "any British effort to lessen General Eisenhower's command would meet strong opposition [from Washington]."[22] Eisenhower said later, "No single incident that I have encountered throughout my experience as an Allied Commander has been so difficult to combat as this particular outburst in the papers."[23]

In this highly charged atmosphere, Montgomery strode to the podium wearing a brand-new red paratrooper beret. With characteristic thoughtlessness, he boasted of "straightening out" the command crisis in the northern sector. Summing up the progress of the "very interesting little battle," Montgomery, exhibiting what de Guingand termed his "'what a good boy am I' attitude" to the fullest, explained how he had first "headed off" then "seen off" the German panzer thrusts, and now he busied himself "writing [them] off."[24] The picturesque public school jargon aside, his account of the fighting on the northern flank accurately depicted Montgomery's thinking and his conduct of the battle. He made no claims that the Bulge was a British battle; he intended to give recognition to the American officers and men serving under him, but his remarks produced the opposite impression.

Still smarting from his Christmas Day dressing down by Montgomery, Bradley looked for an incident and found one. Montgomery's press conference received good copy in American papers, which rankled even worse.[25] Montgomery's doctrinal response to the military problem made perfectly good sense, but he totally failed to understand American sentiments. All the Leavenworth-trained officers knew their Civil War history, and many of them likely thought of Grant after the first day at Shiloh: The Confederates had caught Union forces by surprise and pounded them. Sherman found Grant calming smoking a cigar and remarked, "Well, Grant, we've had the devil's own day, haven't we?" Grant replied, "Yes," and, taking another draw, "Yes. Lick 'em tomorrow, though." Americans, from senior officers to the rank and file, assumed they would recover after the initial shock of the German offensive and had no doubt they would come back and "lick 'em." American officers reacted so negatively to Montgomery's rather innocuous statements because, in their view, Montgomery had needlessly delayed launching the northern half of the pincer movement, preventing American forces from reaping the fruits of the counterattack and unnecessarily increasing casualties, especially in Third Army, while refusing to commit more British divisions to the fighting. Montgomery said, "You thus have the picture of British troops fighting on both sides of American forces who have suffered a hard blow. This is a fine Allied picture."[26] The press conference gave the impression that the master of the battlefield and his forces had averted a disaster and pulled Bradley's chestnuts out of the fire. The Ardennes produced 75,482 American casualties; XXX Corps suffered a mere 1,408. Worse, Montgomery implied that American troops fought better under his leadership than under their own generals. The wounds inflicted on the sensibilities of American generals never healed.

Two days before Montgomery went before the press, Churchill inaugurated his campaign to hold a full-blown CCS conference at Malta before the Big Three meetings scheduled for early February in Yalta. A full examination of post-Bulge strategy and command arrangements would obviously feature prominently.[27] On 9 January Brooke unveiled to the other British chiefs "a new scheme of P.M." to substitute Alexander for Tedder. Cunningham told Brooke, "it was quite worthless putting up the suggestion. The Americans would take it as an insult & think that Alex was being sent to hold Ike's hand."[28] Even the prime minister despaired at the long odds. As Churchill gloomily observed, the reaction to Montgomery's statements not only undermined British efforts to install Alexander as ground commander but also "seriously complicate[d Montgomery] being given command of the northern thrust." He placed a moratorium on all BCOS external comments regarding command changes; the matter would be taken up with the American chiefs at Malta if the president agreed to the conference.[29]

Marshall worried about Eisenhower's susceptibility to British influence. The military attachés in London kept Marshall fully apprised of opinion in the War Office and Fleet Street's effort to force the command issue.[30] Marshall guessed that the prime minister's visit to Versailles and "Montgomery's evident pressure to get what he wants in the way of a larger command" had prompted the British insistence on the Malta conference. "I was familiar with his past efforts," he told Eisenhower, "and I was fully expecting him to seize the present temporary assignment as a means to that end."[31]

On 9 January Eisenhower sent two obliquely worded letters to Marshall, dancing around the issue of ground command and the Alexander-for-Tedder trade. In the first cable he admitted that the current structure, though not ideal, was "the most practicable"; a ground commander would not help the situation, but he now concluded it would prove "more convenient if my deputy were an experienced ground officer rather than air." The second communication restated his opposition to any ground command appointment, and as a buttress, Eisenhower proposed bringing Rooks up from the Mediterranean and teaming him with Whiteley as his "eyes and ears" to keep him in closer contact with the commands. Eisenhower also signaled his willingness to assign Spaatz in place of Tedder and make him air commander. Finally, he hinted that Alexander would be "agreeable" if the CCS appointed him deputy supreme commander. He made no mention of his promises to Churchill and Brooke five days earlier.[32] He followed these the next day with a hint that he had already acquiesced to the British on the command shift, laying down conditions under which the new deputy would operate without an "independent charter from my superiors." Acting on Smith's counsel, Eisenhower restated his proposal for forming a new air command with Spaatz as commander.[33]

Based on Eisenhower's waffling, Marshall surmised he had caved in to British pressure. Marshall wired back, stating that Eisenhower's letters indicated "a weakening on your part under the heavy pressure of the press and British officialdom to get some high British military official into your general management of the Ground Forces." Marshall pointedly said he would go to Leahy and the president and block Alexander's appointment. He rejected the command switch for two reasons. First, the British would have "won a major point in getting control of ground operations in which their divisions of necessity will play such a minor part." Marshall dreaded the casualty lists produced by the Bulge and the campaigns to follow. Second, Alexander "being who he is and our experience being what it has been, you would have great difficulty in offsetting the direct influence of the Prime Minister."[34] Faced with Marshall's rejection of Alexander, Eisenhower's position became more awkward.

A chastened Eisenhower replied by assuring the War Department he would "make no shift in our present arrangements," except for bringing in Rooks. Even though his meeting with Churchill and Brooke had occurred only eight days earlier, Eisenhower made it appear that he had only a vague recollection of the British—"I think . . . the Prime Minister"—mentioning Alexander as a replacement for Tedder. If Alexander entered SHAEF, he would do so only at the behest of the CCS, and he would exercise only those duties delegated to him as a "deputy without portfolio." Eisenhower also backed down on the air command.[35]

One reason for Marshall's annoyance was that on 10 January Roosevelt had bent to British pressure and agreed to a full-blown CCS conference in Malta. Marshall informed Eisenhower that the British insisted on a major conference "at the earliest date" and indicated their displeasure that "measures have been insufficient to give full support to the advance on the northern line of approach."[36] Since November, Marshall had fought a number of rearguard moves to block Churchill's requests for such a meeting. Summing up the gravity of the situation, Churchill told Roosevelt, "This may well be a fateful conference, coming at a moment when the Great Allies are so divided and the shadow of the war lengthens out before us. At the present time I think the end of this war may well prove to be more disappointing than was the last."[37]

Piecemeal Reorganization

Reading between the lines of Marshall's correspondence, it seems clear that he began to entertain serious concerns about Eisenhower's steward-ship. Marshall ascribed the mishandling of the ammunition and replace-ments crises and getting caught flat-footed by the Germans in the Bulge to staff failures. He finally lost patience with Eisenhower's refusal to fix the "deficiency in [his] setup." Worried about reports from trusted offi-cers about "what was happening in the rear areas of General Eisenhow-er's command," Marshall grudgingly decided to intervene personally. He dispatched Somervell "to see you in relation to Lee's command."[38]

The heavy losses in the Bulge made the bad manpower situation much worse and gave ETO a bad odor in Washington. For good reason, Marshall no longer trusted the theater's handling of the problem. Curi-ously, Smith, who had fought for months to reorganize the American command structure, proved to be the most dead set against the dictated changes. He was furious that Washington dumped "garbage"—a suc-cession of War Department boards and over-the-hill senior officers—on him.[39] In anticipation of external pressure to reorganize the headquar-ters, Smith attempted some in-house tinkering with assignments. Mar-shall had sent MG Charles Bonesteel to act as Eisenhower's "eyes and ears" in the rear areas. In the hope of appeasing Marshall, Smith made Bonesteel, whom he considered "another excess number," his inspector general and set him to tackling the manpower and morale problems in the army rear areas and ComZ, with the goal of expediting the retrain-ing of replacements.[40] The day before appointing Bonesteel, Smith pleaded with Handy, "in the present emergency, anything you can do to expedite and firm up the flow of replacements to this theater will have a marked effect on our present situation. Please do everything you can." Handy rebuked ETO for its tardy and tepid handling of the replace-ment problem and contrasted the efforts being made in the Zone of the Interior with the poor performance in the European theater. The War Department "no longer [could] bleed itself . . . to meet deficiencies," he warned.[41] Nevertheless, the War Department increased the allotment of infantry replacements to ETO by 18,500, raising the total to 54,500. Meanwhile, Twelfth Army Group suffered 134,400 casualties in Decem-ber, 80 percent of them in rifle units.

As Handy told Eisenhower, Marshall considered the immediate formation of a manpower command imperative. He described Barker and BG Henry Matchett, head of the replacement system, as insufficiently pugnacious in overcoming the resistance of Lee's and Spaatz's commands. Marshall thought MG Lorenzo Gasser "is the tough, experienced individual you need. However, he can only point a finger. The hatchet man must follow close behind. By the time his work is completed we should know what more needs to be done about manpower." Two days later Marshall wrote, "I have thought all the time that you have lacked qualified individuals to offset your tremendous involvements and have tried to assist you." Marshall's solution remained the same: Eisenhower should appoint "eyes and ears and legs" men as his troubleshooters. He offered Bradley and Bull in North Africa and the just-assigned Bonesteel. Each time, Eisenhower consigned them to other roles. Marshall pointed to the "one weak point in our position which I should like you to think over and that refers to the command of the rear areas." He did not think the question rested on whether Lee was the right man; the central problem was incompatible organizational models. "The trouble is [Lee] is involved in both supplying the Front and supplying himself. While the troops on the Front suffer heavily and work with reduced numbers, he has continued apparently to operate with plenty of fat meat," a situation that "awakens an inevitable suspicion in the minds of front line commanders as to the adequacy of the support they are receiving." He said the same situation existed at home. In the previous ten days, Somervell had reopened his campaign to dismantle the WDGS G-4. "Somervell will talk to you about supply matters after he had a brief chance to look over the ground," Marshall stated. The ASF chief would also discuss LTG Ben Lear's appointment as the rear area commander. "The more I think about this the more it impresses me, and Handy is of the same opinion, that Lear who is loyal, stern and drastic, and very soldierly, be made a deputy of yours for command of the rear areas with the head of the supply services subordinate to him."[42]

Marshall assured Eisenhower, "All here are pressing every effort to get you what you need at the earliest possible date." The War Department outlined the arrival schedule of American divisions into the theater: two infantry divisions sailed that week, an infantry and an armored division would enter the theater in late January, and one airborne and two armored divisions would arrive in early February. Two other divisions remained in the United Kingdom. Gasser would aid in combing the theater for manpower. Beyond that, only two training divisions remained in the strategic reserve, and both were earmarked for other theaters. Even an increased flow of replacements would fall far short of casualties. As was always the case with Marshall, the solution involved increasing ground units while cutting support troop levels. He offered an accelerated time-table if SHAEF accepted a reduction in earmarked service units.[43]

This time Eisenhower possessed no room for maneuver. As Summersby noted, "one of E's biggest headaches all the week is the replacement problem. Every commander right down the line had the same story to tell. We are right down to rock bottom." On 20 December Eisenhower sent a delegation of three officers, headed by Barker, to Washington "to insure that we are speaking the same language in matter of replacements."[44] Barker returned from Washington with a dire manpower forecast. He told the War Department, "unless we were supported more strongly we might lose the war."[45] On 9 January Eisenhower replied to Marshall, "send Lear on at once" and signaled his intention to make him deputy theater commander charged with "matters that are currently giving us so much trouble."[46]

The replacement shortage induced SHAEF to increase pressure on ComZ "to produce able bodied men for the front lines." Lee identified a large untapped reservoir of manpower already in the theater: African Americans. Another reason many officers thought Lee unbalanced derived from his long-standing advocacy of greater rights for African Americans in the U.S. Army. At the height of the Bulge, Lee seized on the opportunity and proposed that SHAEF afford black soldiers the opportunity to volunteer for combat duty. After talking it over with Eisenhower, Lee wrote an appeal for volunteers; those answering the call would transfer to a replacement depot as individual replacements "without regard to color or race." It talked about black volunteers "fighting shoulder to shoulder" with "comrades at the front . . . anxious to share the glory of victory," of "relatives and friends everywhere . . . urging that you be granted this privilege," and of "the glorious record of our colored troops in our former wars." Lee's circular went out on 26 December, with instructions that his base and section commanders give it the widest possible distribution.

Two days later, after discussions with Matchett, Lee produced a formal plan. Owing to restrictions imposed by the replacement system—on the numbers of volunteers that could be immediately processed, and because the Ground Force Reinforcement Command was geared to train individuals, not units—the initial quota was capped at 2,000 privates. Those selected were directed to report to the replacement depot at Compiègne no later than 10 January 1945.[47] Aurand, now in command of the Normandy base section, distributed the appeal for volunteers to all black units on 28 December.

Given all his other concerns—the Bulge, the latest Montgomery episode, Alsace, and the confrontation with the French—Smith did not see Lee's directive until 3 January. And when he did, he blew up. Needless to say, he did not share Lee's enthusiasm. He approached Lee first, telling him that having black volunteers serve as individual replacements in white companies contravened War Department policy. Personally, he agreed that African Americans should have the right to fight and to do so in mixed companies, but the theater could not alter policy, especially one with such politically explosive consequences. As Smith told Eisenhower, Lee "can't see this at all." African American leaders pledged themselves to the Double V Program—victory over fascism abroad and racism at home; they knew there could be no real amelioration of racial conditions in the United States unless black soldiers fought in Europe. Lee fully understood that the integration of combat units, with the concomitant press coverage, would push the desegregation debate at home.

Smith never discussed his views on politics—he probably never voted—or race relations. On the surface, evidence suggests he defended the Jim Crow army. He had blocked the deployment of West African troops in Tunisia and insisted that the French division sent to England for Overlord consist of all-white troops.[48] The spectacle of nonwhite combat troops deployed in England could only raise embarrassing questions about the segregationist policies confining African Americans to rear-area support roles and exacerbate already tense relations between the races in the U.S. Army. He also had a proprietary interest in the race policy, since he had played a key role in framing it. Chiefly, he acted in defense of Marshall.

Getting nowhere with Lee, Smith wrote a letter to Eisenhower on 3 January, the hectic day of the de Gaulle conference and Churchill and Brooke's visit. Smith was flying to see Devers early in the morning and would not have a chance to talk to Eisenhower. He began by reminding Eisenhower that he had handled "the negro policy . . . during the time I was with General Marshall." Once the press got a hold of the story, the inevitable "result will be that every negro organization, pressure group and newspaper will take the attitude that, while the War Department segregates colored troops . . . against the desires of the negro race, the Army is perfectly willing to put them in the front lines mixed in units with white soldiers, and have them do battle when an emergency arises." Smith noted, "Two years ago," when he had helped author the race policy, he would have considered Lee's proposal "the most dangerous thing that I had ever seen in regard to negro relations." Smith made no effort to block black recruitment; he merely alerted Eisenhower that this radical departure from policy would place Marshall in "very grave difficulties." He recommended that Eisenhower delay Lee's initiative, giving SHAEF time to notify the War Department that Lee had circulated his appeal and warn officials there "what may happen and [relay] any facts which they may use to counter the pressure which will undoubtedly be placed on them." He also recommended that Lee not issue any further circulars without Smith's concurrence. He made these proposals based on the fact that he knew "more about the War Department's and General Marshall's difficulties with the negro question than any other man in this theater, including General B. O. Davis whom Lee consulted in the matter—and I say this with all due modesty."[49]

Alarmed by Smith's cautionary advice, Eisenhower personally rewrote Lee's directive along with a cover letter instructing all recipients to return or destroy all copies of the original. The revised instructions called for volunteers "without regard to color or race," with preference given to soldiers with "some basic training in Infantry." African American volunteers would fill vacancies in existing black tank, tank destroyer, and artillery units, with the surplus "incorporated in other organizations." "This is replacing the original," he told Smith, and "is something that can not possibly run counter to regs in a time like this."[50]

With more weighty things on his mind, Eisenhower had not given the issue much thought. The phrase "incorporated in other organizations" meant that African American replacements would be assigned to white units. It also illustrated his ignorance of replacement policy. The repple depples were geared up to retrain individuals as infantrymen, with no provisions for reconversion training in other combat specialties.

By the time Eisenhower finally issued his revised directive, 4,562 black troops had volunteered, including many noncommissioned officers who surrendered their stripes. Barker pushed for clarification. On 7 January he met with Eisenhower. Agreeing with Smith that individual black trainees should not be placed in white organizations, Eisenhower wanted to form African American "units which could be substituted for white units in order that white units could be drawn out of line and rested." As he explained to Marshall, although the "more than 100,000 Negroes in the Com Zone" would continue to perform as much of the "back-breaking manual work" as possible, he could not deny African American volunteers "a chance to serve in battle."[51] The SHAEF and ETO G-1s issued a new circular letter through Smith directing that first priority be given to reinforcements for existing black combat units in the theater, with the retraining burden placed on those units, and the leftover manpower formed into infantry units. Initially, the aim centered on creating one battalion. Barker's instructions rescinded all previous ones.[52] The first 2,800 volunteers reported to the Ground Force Reinforcement Command in January and early February. Eisenhower saw black recruitment as a one-off expedient and suspended the program.

Somervell arrived in Versailles on 7 January. He met with Eisenhower the next afternoon, and that evening Somervell and Lee came to dinner. None of the principals left any record of their discussions. Somervell made the trip at the behest of Patterson, presumably to assess the situation himself and recommend Lee's relief if warranted. Perhaps once upon a time Lee had been Somervell's hero, but no longer. The long train of ComZ's alleged failures—the shipping backlog, the ammunition famine, the broken replacement system—reflected badly on Somervell's entire operation. He met with Lutes, who remained in the theater until 13 January. Lutes had come to France to establish whether fault for the ammunition shortfalls resided in War Department production policies or failures in the European theater. In a 31 December letter to Somervell, Lutes surmised that even though his negative report on Lee's operations might cost him "a considerable number [of friends] here in ComZ," he had still "pulled punches [in his meeting with Eisenhower the day before] sufficiently to prevent any serious repercussions."[53] Now in private he gave his boss the lowdown.

Somervell decided that ComZ had failed, but for political and morale reasons, he could not relieve Lee or senior members of his staff. After visiting the operational headquarters and ADSEC and SOLOC, Somervell outlined to Eisenhower the best means of solving the supply problem. Knowing only too well Eisenhower's views on reorganization, he recommended a consolidation of supply under ComZ and the infusion of personnel drawn from Larkin's SOLOC staff into Lee's organization. SOLOC had come under ComZ's jurisdiction in September, and Larkin had held the position as Lee's deputy since late October. But faced by almost universal suspicion, Larkin had made little headway in actually amalgamating SOLOC with ComZ. Somervell's expedient aimed at fixing the structural problems without any undue bloodletting.

Against Eisenhower's advice, Devers had organized his headquarters on the British model. Larkin exercised command over personnel administration and supply, and his staff participated in operational planning at the highest level. The team Larkin and Hughes had put together in 1943 remained essentially intact; most of the top people had been together since Torch. They had long since learned how to function together, and by 1944 they had worked the kinks out of the system. Dragoon would not have come off if not for the efficiency of NATO/

SOS's supply and services commands. Although Larkin's staff structure paralleled that of the British, he ran SOLOC according to the American book. The initial supply echelon went north as an advance section in tandem with Sixth Army Group's movements; the second echelon formed an intermediate section, complete with regulating stations; and the rear echelon acted as the base section. Even though Marseilles' port capacity approximated Cherbourg's at its peak, harbor discharge rates remained consistent with the movement of materiel along the supply lines, producing none of the bottlenecks that so hampered operations in ETO. Larkin's "supply on a shoestring" worked, even though his SOS troop allocations remained far lower than establishment; his command also supplied the French and handled the increased numbers of divisions entering the theater from the south.[54] All this stood in sharp contrast to the state of affairs in ComZ. "Tremendously impressed with the fine job done by SOLOC," Somervell recommended that Eisenhower insert Larkin's people into ComZ headquarters as deputies to the incumbents but in control of actual operations.[55]

Somervell overrode Lee's objections. In a memo to Lee, Somervell underscored the point that the British line of communications and SOLOC outperformed ComZ. He also pointed to the advantages of SOLOC's organization. Lee had no option but to comply with Somervell's solution.[56] The ASF chief brought along his handpicked choice to head a control division, MG Clinton Robinson, and ordered it formed; he also insisted that Lee organize an intermediate section with the normal regulating stations. Somervell convened a meeting of Lee's staff and told them what would happen. Then Somervell explained things to the SOLOC staff: they would exercise control, but without the title. He then pointed to a tree and said, "There's a lot of mistletoe up in that tree. Get a bunch of it and tie it on your coattail, because you're going to need it. They don't like you coming up there."[57]

Lee did not enjoy having his authority undercut, and as expected, the imposition of the deputies on his staff created plenty of friction. On 25 January Somervell, who remained in the theater to ensure his prescribed changes took root, held a mass meeting and laid down the law. "Somervell acting like the Boss that Lee rates him," Hughes noted. He sugarcoated the bitter medicine of the reorganization by acknowledging that supply in ETO "has been one of the most magnificent achievements of the war," but he told the assembled staff they must make the new structure work by applying the book. "Sounded to me," Hughes remarked, "like instructor at Leavenworth talking at chief of staff conference." A contrite Lee admitted that SOLOC had "set the standard since coming into this theater . . . doing more with less, which [is] the highest tribute of efficiency." He said, "These gentlemen," referring to Larkin's former staff, "will leaven the rest of us."[58] Eisenhower signed off on the new structure, which took effect on 29 January. Although it fell short of what Somervell wanted or what Smith tried to engineer, the new configuration consolidated supply and improved ComZ's responsiveness and efficiency.

In the meantime, Gasser arrived on 12 January, followed four days later by Lear. In between, Hughes submitted a stinging indictment of the "piece-meal attack" being made on ETO's personnel problems. "The attack is rapidly resulting in divided responsibility, diversion of effort and loss of time and efficiency." Hughes criticized SHAEF for poorly coordinated staff work, a product of Eisenhower's reliance on Smith, Barker, and Crawford for advice on ETO problems that should have been handled by ComZ. He enumerated specific examples of divided responsibilities and gray areas where no one knew the lines of authority. Hughes concluded by telling Eisenhower: "The result of all this is a great loss of time while everybody scurries around trying to find a solution which they think will be satisfactory to you and to all of those who have access to you. I still believe that your success depends to a large extent upon your reliance on the men *in the organization* who are earnestly and intelligently trying to help you win the war and on men to whom you have delegated as much authority as they can accept. If they cannot accept enough responsibility, get new men."[59]

Eisenhower forwarded copies to Barker and Smith, telling Smith in a handwritten note that Hughes's observations should not "be considered as critical of anyone, including myself!" The memo provided "a lot of food for thought" and alerted Eisenhower to the "confusion that can exist in lower echelons unless we are meticulously careful in fixing responsibility and forcing everybody to do his job." For months, Smith had fruitlessly argued that very case. Eisenhower also indicated that he had already settled on centralizing manpower under Lear but still had not made up his mind on the extent of his authority.[60]

As head of the War Department Manpower Board, Gasser's job was to investigate charges the theater had not made the best use of its personnel and to pressure Eisenhower and Smith to invigorate reconversion training. Smith admired Gasser, his old boss, and set him to work combing out "that goddamned outfit of Lee's." Lear had replaced McNair as head of AGF and had been a favorite for Marshall's job in 1938. Smith thought, since Marshall "had no place for him . . . he sent him to us."[61] On 17 January Eisenhower and Smith had a long talk about what niche

Lear would fill. Given Marshall's insistence on a manpower command, they had no choice but to slot Lear in that billet. Eisenhower went further; as he told Hughes three days later, he wanted Lear as deputy theater commander in charge of ComZ.[62] This meant that Lear would be above Smith in the American chain of command. Unlike when Lee had acted as deputy theater commander, Lear's headquarters would remain inside SHAEF, with much of his personnel drawn from Smith's staff.

Three days after talking with Hughes, Eisenhower backed down. On 23 January he issued a directive giving Lear responsibility for "coordinating, controlling and directing" the functions of the General Inspectorate and Theater Manpower Sections, Gasser's staff, and the Theater Reinforcement System. Ten days later, Lear took over the theater-wide reinforcement section of ETO G-1.[63] Designated deputy theater commander, Lear became the manpower czar, but the directive left open the question of his relationship with Lee's establishment.

The day Eisenhower issued his directive, Lee invited Lear to a splashy dinner. "That settles everything," Hughes concluded. To Lee's surprise, Lear dominated the conversation and explained that his mandate included direct command of ComZ. "Lee [was] hurt," Hughes reported, and he reminded Lear there was more to the job than commanding the services.[64] Undoubtedly, Lee had hit a rough patch. Two days later Somervell clipped his wings.

Lear soon discovered that Eisenhower never really wanted a genuine deputy commander. Somervell's visit left Hughes "groggy," as he informed his classmate Peterson. "Someone has stepped into the picture and is doing all that I have recommended over and over again," reducing SHAEF control and fixing responsibilities. Hughes remained wary and correctly predicted that little would come from Lear's appointment or Somervell's reordering of ComZ. "I am wagering," he told Peterson, "that passive resistance as advocated by Gandhi and practiced by a high ranking friend of ours will win." As a conduit for complaints, Hughes joked, "My office continues to be a wailing wall and I now have a new ashtray where we collect the tears."[65] Smith moved quickly, blocking Lear's raid on SHAEF and ComZ personnel and severely limiting the size of his staff. He met with Lear and made it clear that he "was not here with all [his] War Department rank"; he simply served as a member of a team under SHAEF.[66] Eisenhower loaned Hughes to Lear and assigned him the task of educating the new deputy commander. Hughes considered "Lear's job just a mop up. To clear up after the mistakes are made." Hughes wondered why someone did not "pick a commander who can tell the boys" what to do, "instead of having the boys educate him?" Between Smith and Lee—two well-schooled practitioners of bureaucratic gamesmanship—Lear did not have a chance. "Lear had prostate trouble," Smith later remarked, "so he didn't trouble us much," but he served the valuable function of helping "us outrank Lee." Lear told Hughes that "he always thought commanders made decisions. Ike [was] letting Smith sign letters so that if there was a [blowup], Ike would be in a good position." As a bewildered Lear later noted, he never "saw so much politics as in ETO."[67]

The Bulge and After

Some historians portray the Bulge as marking Eisenhower's coming-of-age as supreme commander and SHAEF's shining moment. The principal actors in January 1945 may not have seen it that way, especially Beetle Smith. The chief of staff's forbearance withered under the combined strain of unsatisfying results at the front, confrontations with American and French generals over SHAEF's assertion of greater operational control, and Washington's intrusions into his cosseted staff spheres. Although he understood why Eisenhower placated, prevaricated, and parleyed, Smith grew increasingly disenchanted with the supreme commander's buffering, his lack of daring, and his refusal to issue authoritative orders.

Marshall never trusted Eisenhower's organizational setup, which explains why he made Clark the deputy commander in Torch and dispatched a series of trusted officers to act as "eyes and ears"—positions that appeared in no U.S. Army table of organization. Indeed, Marshall sacrificed Smith out of the same concern. Yet Eisenhower, as Hughes perceptively observed, passively accepted Marshall's "suggestions" and studiously obfuscated his noncompliance. Eisenhower and Smith possessed very different ideas on organization. Smith was obsessively mission driven; Marshall assigned him the task of realigning Eisenhower's headquarters in conformity with the restructured War Department. Despite dogged efforts, Smith failed, and those failures produced frustration if not rancor. Marshall's and Somervell's eleventh-hour interventions amounted to an unambiguous indictment not of Eisenhower's repeated refusal to follow directives and restructure his command but of Smith's orchestration of his headquarters.

A good chief of staff backstops his boss and understands that he should always remain out of sight; his job centers on making the machine work without giving the impression that he runs things. Problems develop when chiefs think they are partners with their bosses, that they share the same ideas and can act for them. By these standards, Beetle Smith was a very poor chief of staff. But because Eisenhower's greatest skill was his ability to obscure his own use of authority, he required an activist chief who was anything but invisible; he needed a chief of staff who ran the headquarters and made decisions beyond his ken. When things went awry, blame never affixed on Eisenhower. Smith understood this subjected him to criticism that he was a power-grasping minion who did not know his place. Not all the backbiting was unwarranted—too many observers accused him of swellheadedness—but he definitely knew his role and labored to do it justice.

Eisenhower's obscurantist leadership style, his buffering practices, and his avoidance of personal conflict in a hyperpoliticized and -personalized environment placed enormous stress on Smith. Perhaps most maddening of all, Eisenhower's hesitancy—his painstaking pursuit of the middle ground—camouflaged his real aims. To his critics, Eisenhower's path to victory consisted of switchbacks and dead ends; to Eisenhower, it was as straight as a Kansas county-line road. Long before D-day, Eisenhower had conceptualized how the campaign in Germany would play out, and from that general design he never wavered. Now at Malta, the British insisted he provide that road map.

In conjunction with the prime minister's request for a conference in Malta, the BCOS called on the CCS to solicit from Eisenhower a statement of "the progress of operations carried out as the result on your directive of 28th October and the effects of the German counteroffensive," as well as a "detailed appreciation and plan of operations for this winter and next spring, including the general disposition of your forces." The British appeal grew out of the paper Brooke had started to prepare just before the German offensive; Churchill and the BCOS waited until the crisis in the Ardennes had passed before launching their two-pronged effort aimed at jettisoning the broad front for a concentrated northern drive under Montgomery and inserting Alexander as ground commander between Eisenhower and the army groups. As Marshall informed Eisenhower, the BCOS asserted that the Quebec directive, which called for "primary pressure [being] exerted against the Germans in the north towards Berlin[,] had not been effectively carried out." British insistence that Eisenhower account for operations since 28 October, including the Bulge, smacked of Montgomery's "strategic defeat" letter of 28 November. The BCOS document also "discussed the advisability of a single commander for the ground troops and proposed that at least the front be divided into two groups of armies."[68]

Despite all the turmoil in his headquarters, Smith's preoccupation in the middle half of January centered on finalizing plans for post-Bulge operations. In some ways, January resembled the period before D-day. Under pressure to complete the planning, Smith dispensed with the full-blown morning staff conference as too time-consuming and on the whole nonproductive, delegating the chairmanship of these meetings to Morgan or Gale. Smith convened informal brainstorming sessions with Spaatz and his division chiefs. On "a typical day," Robb recorded, "we find Bedell sitting at his desk, Strong and Morgan on the couch, the 'Air,' Spaatz and I, each on an arm of the big easy chair, and Bull, sword in hand, holding the floor, maps with their talc overlays spread before him."[69]

The key element resided in the balance of forces in the west; the biggest variable was the timing and scale of the Soviet offensives. Eisenhower dispatched Tedder to Moscow to glean Soviet intentions. Bad weather in France and Cairo delayed Tedder's departure and eventually rendered his mission pointless, because Churchill extracted from Stalin the information deemed so vital to Allied planning. On 10 January the prime minister sent a messenger to Eisenhower with copies of his correspondence with the Soviet leader. Churchill urged him to "keep the matter entirely to yourself and Bedell, and not let it get in the hands of the Staffs." Soviet forces faced the same adverse weather conditions. "Nevertheless, taking into account the position of our Allies on the Western Front," Stalin replied, the Soviets would open offensives along the entire Central Front no later than the second half of January, regardless of the weather. "You may rest assured that we shall do everything possible to render assistance to the glorious forces of our Allies."[70] The news was exactly what Eisenhower and Smith wanted to hear. Better than Stalin's word, the Soviets unleashed their offensives on 12 January.

By 15 January the first SHAEF plan crystallized. Everything depended on two conjoined conditions: the pull of the Soviet offensive, and the push of Allied forces to the Rhine. SHAEF calculated the Allies could field seventy-one divisions, rising to eighty-five by spring, "with many of the U.S. Divisions seriously understrength in infantry." Given the low combat value of French divisions, SHAEF rated them a "questionable asset." In the event of a "weak and ineffectual Russian offensive," the Germans "could keep on the Western Front about 100 divisions *and maintain them in personnel and materiel*." In the event the Soviet offensives proved strong and sustained, SHAEF planners reckoned the enemy could maintain eighty understrength divisions, and if the Russians "really get to rolling then there *should* be a gradual decline in this enemy strength." Early indicators looked good; Strong reported mounting evidence that the Germans had begun to pull Fifth Panzer Army out of the Ardennes.[71] In that event, and with the return of favorable weather, "it may well be possible to defeat the enemy on our front." But the Allies had to close to the Rhine along its entire length. If they secured the Rhine line, they could place twenty-five divisions in static defensive roles, freeing fifty-four ground and six airborne divisions for the offensive. If the Soviet attacks miscarried, those 100 German divisions in the west might produce a stalemate, with forty-five Allied divisions on the defensive or in reserve, and only thirty-four available for offensive purposes. In Eisenhower's mind, the strategy centered on destroying the maximum number of German divisions west of the Rhine and closing to the river throughout its entire length. If the Soviets succeeded in drawing off those twenty divisions, Eisenhower felt justified in predicting "a quick success only after we have closed the Rhine throughout its length, concentrated heavily in the north and staged a definite supporting secondary attack somewhere to the south of the Ruhr." Worried that he did not possess the strength to break through in the north, since the Germans understood that "north of the Ruhr is the invasion route of first importance," Eisenhower wanted the flexibility to shift the main attack on the Prum-Frankfurt-Kassel line.[72]

Smith did not share Eisenhower's optimism. He remained impressed by the fighting power of German divisions. When he visited Devers's headquarters on 5 January, the Germans staged an amphibious crossing of the Rhine. They pushed across a motorized battalion and reinforced it with a division before the Allies could counter the move. He wondered why Allied leadership and forces lacked that type of dash.[73] Instead, SHAEF's attempts to exert control over operations faced only obstruction on the part of American commanders. On 14 January Eisenhower informed Montgomery that command of First Army would revert to Bradley at midnight, 16–17 January; Ninth Army remained under the field marshal's command. Evidently, Hodges had fully recovered; his first act after Bradley's restoration was to sack one of his division commanders.[74]

On 16 January VII and VIII Corps reestablished contact at Houffalize, pinching out the Bulge. A month after it started, the Bulge ended. The Germans withdrew from the Ardennes, having "suffered a tactical defeat and severe losses in men and materiel," but as Eisenhower admitted, the enemy "will probably manage to withdraw the bulk of his formations." Eisenhower intended to regain the strategic initiative by moving Twelfth Army Group north of the Moselle, but he bent to Bradley's pressure for Hodges and Patton to continue their attacks in the

Shortly after the Germans unleashed their offensives into Alsace, Smith (center) flew forward to Seventh Army's command post, 5 January 1945, where he met with Devers (left) and Patch.

Ardennes and push through the Eifel. He wanted Montgomery to stage Operation Veritable in conjunction with Ninth Army's Operation Grenade as a pincer movement designed to clear the lower Rhine north of the Jülich-Düsseldorf line. Grenade called for four corps and twelve divisions, but on 17 January Simpson's army contained only two corps and five divisions. Eisenhower also grew more anxious about the fighting in Alsace and insisted on eliminating the Colmar Pocket.[75] Veritable, Grenade, and elimination of the Colmar Pocket could not come off as long as American divisions remained committed to Bradley's offensive. "I like to be as bold as anyone else," he told Montgomery, "but I know that we cannot go into a full blooded offensive and worry constantly about security." Smith grew more and more exasperated with Eisenhower's trimming and placating of competing agendas. "We never do anything bold," he vented in his staff meeting on 16 January. "There are at least seventeen people to be dealt with so [we] must compromise, and compromise is never bold."[76]

SHAEF grew increasingly uneasy about Devers's management of the fighting in Alsace. Nordwind and the threat against Strasbourg created "an unholy mess." Like Smith, Eisenhower saw the German offensive in Alsace as proof of the all-important "power of the initiative in war." When Smith hastened to Sixth Army Group headquarters on 5 January, Devers thought he left "impressed with the way we operate."[77] That was far from true; in Smith's view, Devers's staff seemed paralyzed every time a German division moved. As Smith sarcastically told Robb, he did not have "much confidence in our friend Jakey." Eisenhower now spoke openly about replacing Devers with Patch.[78] He again dispatched Smith to Vittel to light a fire under Devers.

Sixth Army Group simply lacked the strength to accomplish its missions. Devers pleaded with Smith for two divisions from what Patton termed "SHAEF's new toy," the strategic reserve. Long before the Ardennes, Smith had advanced schemes for forming a strategic reserve that would permit its employment as reinforcement for either the northern or central thrust under SHAEF's direction. Bull had killed one plan on jurisdictional and logistical grounds, concluding that a reserve would create administrative confusion by overlapping the lines of communications and muddying army and corps boundaries. The U.S. Fifteenth Army had begun organizing under Gerow in Belgium in December, and in early January SHAEF designated it a strategic reserve as part of Twelfth Army Group. Gerow actually commanded only two divisions; the rest of the army would consist of new divisions entering the theater through northern ports and reorganized divisions pulled from First and Third Armies. After the elimination of the Bulge, Smith issued instructions that each army group should keep one division in reserve, subject to orders from SHAEF. Despite talk of a strategic reserve, all Smith could offer Devers were two divisions that had been badly beaten up in the Bulge—the Tenth Armored and the still shaken Twenty-eighth Infantry. On 17 January the Germans, despite mounting pressure in Poland and Hungary, poured reinforcements into Alsace; they continued attacking until 25 January. Devers initially received only the infantry division.[79]

SHAEF issued a new directive over Eisenhower's name on 18 January. It stated that Bradley's offensive "will be pressed with all possible vigor so long as there is a reasonable chance of securing a decisive result," and Veritable and Grenade would "be launched with the minimum delay if and when I decide not to continue with the offensive in the Ardennes." Given Simpson's strength, Montgomery assumed Grenade could not go off until the fighting in Bradley's sector ended. And Veritable sans Grenade made little sense. On 21 January Eisenhower told Montgomery to proceed with Veritable on schedule. He identified the core problem as Devers's inability to straighten out his affairs in Alsace, not Bradley's "continuing to push through the Ardennes."[80]

Bradley never forgave Eisenhower for removing First Army from his command; now with both armies back under him, he persevered in attacking in the Ardennes. Despite the German withdrawals, he made few appreciable gains. On 24 January SHAEF moved to realign American divisions. Whiteley contacted Bradley, informing him that SHAEF would withdraw divisions from his offensive, in part to feed the reserve and in part to reinforce Devers. Patton, who witnessed the scene, saw Bradley lose his temper for the first time in his presence. "If you feel that way about it," he bawled over the phone, "then as far as I am concerned, you can take any goddamned division or corps in the 12th Army Group, do with them as you see fit, and those of us that you leave behind will sit on our ass until hell freezes over. I trust that you do not think I am angry, but I want to impress on you that I am goddamn well incensed." Patton could be heard in the background shouting, "Tell them to go to hell and all three [including Hodges] of us will resign."[81] Bradley's tantrum worked; the divisions remained in place.

On 20 January Eisenhower finally produced his projected plans as demanded by the CCS. The new directive read very much like his 15 January letter to Marshall. What had changed was news from the Russian Front. On 12 January the Soviets launched the single biggest offensive of World War II on four fronts: two across the Vistula and one each into East Prussia and the Baltic littoral. By 3 February Soviet forces stood at the Czech frontier and on the Oder, thirty-five miles from Berlin. SHAEF faced the best-case scenario. Reaffirming that operational priority rested north of the Ruhr, Eisenhower insisted on closing the length of the Rhine before the Allies attempted a crossing. This would force the Germans into defending the entire river line, allowing the Allies to minimize the number of divisions held in static roles while building a powerful reserve. He estimated there would be eighty-five divisions available by 1 May, in addition to eight French divisions later in the summer. According to SHAEF's projections, logistical considerations limited the northern drive to a maximum of thirty-five divisions. A projected twenty would undertake the secondary offensive toward Frankfurt.[82] Eisenhower thought the plan satisfied all British demands. SHAEF knew a Twenty-first Army Group study had concluded that no more than twenty-one divisions could be supported in the northern drive. After conducting careful logistical studies, SHAEF raised that figure to twenty-five, then thirty, and finally thirty-six.[83]

The British remained unconvinced. Eisenhower had made paper pronouncements in the past only to shift operational priorities, and his orchestration of the fighting after pinching out the Bulge confirmed their suspicions. For Churchill and the BCOS, Malta offered an opportunity to wrestle ground command away from Eisenhower. "The best results will be," read the BCOS position paper, "if one Land Force Commander, directly responsible to [Eisenhower] is given power of operations control and co-ordination of all ground forces employed in the main thrust." Failing that, they wanted the CCS to issue ironclad directives so Eisenhower could not deviate from giving the strengthened northern thrust precedence.[84]

"An Acid Conference"

The American service chiefs resented having to participate in what they saw as an unnecessary conference. Since October, the issue of strategy had receded in the minds of the American chiefs, and the question of supporting Eisenhower's command status assumed the fore. The more the British attempted to subvert the command structure, the more adamant became the JCS resistance to any alteration in the command structure. Marshall and King, determined to preserve the status quo, went to Malta resolved to put the British in their place.

Eisenhower knew Malta would produce "an acid conference" and avoided going. "Due to uncertainties of air transportation in winter," he told Marshall, "I do *not* think it advisable for me to go beyond limits of motor and rail transport." He told Butcher he was reluctant to leave headquarters because of uneasiness about Devers getting the situation in Alsace in hand. Smith, backed by Bull, would go in his place. Eisenhower asked Marshall to meet with him in the south of France.[85] They met at Château Valmont near Marseilles on 28 January. Even before they sat down, Marshall raised the question of Alexander's appointment as ground commander. He flatly stated there would be no yielding on the command issue. As Eisenhower recorded in his notes, "General Marshall will not agree to any proposal to set up a Ground Commander-in-Chief in this theater. If this is done he says he will not remain as Chief of Staff." Marshall did acknowledge the necessity of one American army remaining under Montgomery's command. Turning their attention to Eisenhower's conceptualization of the Rhineland campaign, Marshall offered assurances of the full support of the JCS.[86]

In anticipation of Smith's trip to Malta, Handy sent him a chatty letter in the hope of buoying up his friend. He talked about the capriciousness of public opinion; "having completely won the war two or three times," the American public "is now proceeding to lose it just as quickly," he wrote. "If you don't hit a home run every time you come to bat they want your scalp." Handy remarked that the "manpower business is a continual headache which gets no better" and suggested Smith "start swinging the club." He inquired if Smith had gotten over his latest case of field marshal-itis. "Wouldn't it be fine to concentrate on the Germans and not have to spend so much energy in these battles with our own people?" As both Handy and Smith knew, Malta would produce plenty of fireworks.[87]

On 27 December Hopkins came through SHAEF from London on his way to Rome and then Malta. Despite failing health—he ate little and slept a good deal—Hopkins remained his *bonhomme* self, full of schemes and predictions. Smith had spent the last couple of days in bed, dealing with his ulcer and building up reserves for the big conference. De rigueur, whenever sidelined, he made a big show of bouncing back. Butcher remembered him arriving "in something of the manner of the Marines, for he hadn't been there long when he took over the conversation and had the situation well in hand." The president had sent Hopkins ahead to run interference for him. As expected, Churchill remained "volcanic," and Hopkins's chief role centered on promoting in the prime minister "a more amiable mood prior" to meeting Roosevelt. He also met with de Gaulle, who proved neither "very responsive" nor "very conciliatory" to Hopkins's efforts to bring the general and president closer together.[88] Hopkins thought the big issue at Malta would be the Pacific versus the European war. Smith brought up the manpower situation. Hopkins believed the British would agree to close down offensive operations in Italy, releasing two or three divisions for Europe. Assuring Smith he had "thrown [in] his lot with Ike," Hopkins was convinced ETO required more divisions and materiel and promised he would speak to Roosevelt about pulling manpower from the Caribbean, Alaska, Iceland, and the Pacific. He also confided that he believed Stalin would join the fight against Japan "once the Germans were licked," which meant the War Department would look more favorably toward shifting men and materiel to Europe to hasten the end of the war.[89] The insights provided by Hopkins proved invaluable to Smith, greatly aiding his preparation for Malta. Hopkins's visit also reassured Smith that the president, despite heavy pressure from the navy, remained committed to "Europe First."

Smith met with Bradley that day and received affirmation that the attack in the Ardennes "is going well." He called Patton, "who assures

me that if given two more divisions he will go all the way to Berlin."
Although Smith discounted Patton's ebullience, he commended the
general's conduct of the fighting on the southern flank.[90]

Smith flew down to Valmont on 29 December, where he met Marshall. Together they set off on their journey to Malta via Sardinia and
Sicily. The 750-mile trip provided plenty of opportunity for Smith to test
what Hopkins had told him against the chief's assessments of the lay of
the land in Washington and bring Marshall up to date on all that had
transpired since his last visit to the theater in October, especially efforts
at sorting out the manpower issue. Marshall wanted an elaboration on
SHAEF's plans for the Rhineland campaign, and he wanted to hear
Smith's version of British machinations to alter command arrangements
and compare it with Eisenhower's. Given that two of his commanders in
chief had died in plane crashes, Eisenhower's apprehensions about flying were well founded. One of the aircraft carrying the British delegation to Malta did go down off Pantelleria. Marshall and Smith arrived in
Malta without incident.

The conference convened the next day. Smith, Bull, and the American chiefs gathered for a preliminary meeting. Smith opened by stating
that time was increasingly the guiding factor. By maintaining pressure in
the west, the Allies tied down German forces required to stem the tide of
the Soviet advances in the east. Intelligence indicated the Germans were
already withdrawing from both the Ardennes and Alsace. Eisenhower
wanted the Colmar Pocket eliminated but would begin to release American divisions for Grenade. Montgomery would strike southeast and parallel to the Rhine, while Simpson would move from his existing position
north of Aachen in the direction of Düsseldorf. Montgomery would
grasp any possibility that presented itself for seizing bridgeheads on the
lower Rhine during the southerly drive. Operations in Alsace continued;
German attacks petered out on 25 January, and the French, aided by
three American divisions, were in the process of eliminating the Colmar
Pocket. The objective remained fixed on removing the Germans from
the entire west bank; by doing so, the Allies would improve security and
release ten to fifteen divisions for the offensive. Smith then outlined
SHAEF's plan. Operations broke down into three distinct phases: closing to the Rhine and destroying German forces west of the river, establishing bridgeheads, and advancing east of the river into the heart of
Germany for the final defeat of the German armies.

Smith then explained the thinking behind abandoning the Cologne-
Bonn drive in favor of one toward Frankfurt. In SHAEF's estimate,
Montgomery's attack could not succeed without Bradley's offensive.

Eisenhower assumed the Germans would concentrate their best forces in the lower Rhine against Montgomery. The secondary thrust's primary objective centered on forcing the Germans to pull troops from the north to guard against a second penetration. Cologne lay too close to the Ruhr. The Germans could easily shuttle reinforcements against both bridge-heads. In addition, the Cologne area offered fewer good crossing points, and the terrain on the opposite shore was not conducive to mobile oper-ations. The Mainz-Mannheim area offered better crossings sites, the Frankfurt region was vital enough to draw off German forces from the main attack in the north and far enough away to be out of supporting range, and the Frankfurt-Giessen-Kassel axis provided a favorable cor-ridor for the southern arm of the envisioned double envelopment of the Ruhr. If the main drive stalled, Eisenhower considered a secondary operation vital, and Frankfurt clearly held out a number of advantages. The southern thrust could feed in as many as fifty divisions without a rail bridgehead. He also concluded that a threat at Cologne would tie down just as many German divisions as an actual crossing. Smith also pointed out that, despite Eisenhower's marked preference for Frank-furt, a final decision had not been made.

The timetable depended on events. Bull raised the issue of the effect of the spring thaw on water levels in the Rhine; crossings in the north were not feasible until the second half of March. After all the inclem-ent weather, inundated land might delay operations in the Rhineland and make the forward staging of materiel more difficult. Bradley still wanted to push from the Ardennes toward Cologne through the Eifel. Smith explained that Bradley's current operations served as part of the buildup for the main effort in the north. He expected First Army would encounter serious opposition, forcing Bradley to substitute Ninth Army's Grenade for his Prum-Cologne movement. Smith felt sure that if Montgomery initiated Veritable by 8 February, the main thrust across the Rhine could come as early as 15 March. Grenade would go off approximately a week after Veritable if SHAEF decided to mount it. He also warned that if German resistance proved determined west of the Rhine, and Allied forces could not close the length of the river, between ten and fifteen divisions earmarked for the two offensives over the river would remain tied down in static positions. In that case, the crossings might be delayed until June, in conjunction with an expected Soviet summer offensive.

Smith emphasized that regardless of the number of divisions com-mitted, the crossings would still take place on a restricted front of five divisions. The offensives would enjoy greater depth than previously. He expected a SHAEF reserve of ten divisions, and the mobility of American divisions offered flexibility. For the first time, SHAEF could rotate divisions in and out of the line, maintaining the pace of the advance. He petitioned the JCS not to allow the British to tie SHAEF's hands, underscoring the need to preserve operational flexibility. "It would be dangerous to try to define in detail how the battle should be fought," he said. "Too much depends upon the seizing of opportunities as they are presented."

On the question of altering the command structure, Smith assured the JCS that relations with Montgomery were very good. Eisenhower was committed to the main effort in the north, and Montgomery was "quite satisfied with the arrangements." As to Alexander's appointment, Smith doubted the British had come to a firm decision on the question, particularly in view of Montgomery's negative "attitude on this matter."[91]

A full CCS conference assembled at Montgomery House at noon. Bull made the same presentation Smith had given earlier that morning. Smith again emphasized that the only factor that had changed since Eisenhower's 20 January appreciation was time, which assumed greater significance in view of the Russian advance. The threat against Strasbourg had ended, and Devers stood a good chance of clearing up the Colmar Pocket quickly. With German offensive capacity waning, the key remained securing a clearance of the Rhine in the north as quickly as possible. Eisenhower viewed the northern offensive as absolutely essential and the southern operation as "necessary and desirable and to be undertaken if at all possible."

Smith took pains to underline that the northern thrust took precedence and "every other operation must be regarded as subsidiary to the main thrust." He acknowledged the danger of placing "too much into the southern effort and thereby weakening the main northern attack." Pushed hard by Brooke, Smith explained that although SHAEF considered closing the Rhine throughout its length desirable, Eisenhower never intended to do this if German resistance delayed the main attack until June or militated "against an opportunity to seize a bridgehead and effect a crossing in strength on the northern front."

Brooke then took the floor. The British doubted there was enough strength for two major operations. "Of the two," he stated, "the northern appeared the most promising." He rhymed the advantages: Antwerp was closer, the Ruhr was nearer, and the importance of the Ruhr increased with the Russian seizure of Silesia. Southern crossings in the vicinity of Frankfurt might prove easier, but Frankfurt was a long way from the Ruhr. He thought "the plan should be based on the whole effort being made in the North if this was to be certain of succeeding and that every other operation must be regarded as subsidiary to this main thrust." Exploiting what Smith had said about the southern attack, Brooke considered it dangerous "putting too much into the southern effort and thereby weakening the main northern attack." Brooke also voiced his apprehension about Eisenhower's desire to close the entire length of the Rhine. From what Smith had said, the southern front appeared "almost as important as the northern and . . . diverted too much strength from the latter."

Smith responded by saying that although the plan assigned thirty-six divisions for Montgomery's northern crossing, even with the bulk of the airborne army thrown into the mix, the initial northern crossing involved only four or five divisions on a narrow front. It might fail or at least bog down. Nobody suggested that the southern operation competed with Montgomery's in the north, but it must carry sufficient weight to pull German strength into the vital Frankfurt area and "provide an alternate line of attack if the main effort failed." He again drew Brooke's attention to Eisenhower's differentiation between main and secondary thrusts. "Everything that could be put into the main effort would be put there," an increasingly testy Smith said.

Marshall came to the assistance of his beleaguered underling. Trying to bridge the gap between what Smith promised and Brooke deflected, Marshall summed up what Smith and Brooke had said. The northern attack enjoyed logistical advantages, but "it was not safe to rely on one line of advance." Allied forces must clear the Germans from the west bank to gain the necessary security for two crossings because Eisenhower considered it essential to have more than one possible line of advance. SHAEF required the flexibility to feed in reserves, whether "battling through [in the north] or switching the weight of attack elsewhere."

Now on the defensive, Brooke, alive to Marshall's point that the northern attack might suffer heavy casualties, raised the issue of reserves. Smith jumped back in, highlighting that the northern attack would contain thirty-six divisions—and not all could be committed simultaneously—with ten more in strategic reserve. SHAEF could pull tired divisions out of the line; at least twelve other divisions would hold static roles. Additionally, Smith talked about SHAEF's efforts to rearm French divisions. At least three new divisions had already received up-to-date arms and equipment. They would move into the line shortly, and the corps troops would join them later.

The BCOS worried that Eisenhower's insistence on closing along the Rhine would disperse offensive strength. With the Germans defeated in the Ardennes and Alsace, Brooke wanted a concentrated breakthrough in the north backed by adequate reserves, rather than Eisenhower's methodical, sequential operations aimed at getting to the Rhine. Assured that Montgomery's offensive would receive full support and that Eisenhower had abandoned his insistence on clearing the Rhineland before effecting a crossing, Brooke said the whole question took "on a different complexion in the light of General Smith's explanation." What Smith proffered "was very much in line with what we have always asked for," but not what appeared in Eisenhower's 20 January directive. He requested that the CCS be permitted to "examine the record of General Smith's explanation at their meeting the following day." In his diary he confided, "We would probably be prepared to approve Bedell's statement."[92]

Pushing for a settlement, Smith cabled Eisenhower and told him that Brooke wanted "something in writing to clinch the fact that the main effort on the north [is] to be pushed and that you are not to delay other operations until you have eliminated every German west of the Rhine." He suggested that Eisenhower reword his directive, prioritizing his objectives as follows: (1) the northern thrust, (2) the removal of German resistance north of the Mosel, and (3) the elimination of other enemy forces west of the Rhine that threatened the crossings. "If you agree to the above changes," he ended, "we think this will settle the whole matter."[93]

Eisenhower responded by telling Smith he could "assure the Combined Chiefs of Staff that I will seize the Rhine crossing in the north immediately . . . without waiting to close the Rhine throughout its length." Then he quibbled: "I will advance across the Rhine in the North with maximum strength and complete determination as soon as the situation in the South allows me to collect the necessary forces and do this without incurring unnecessary risks."[94]

The next morning's discussions centered on transferring ground and air units from Italy to northwest Europe. Alexander proved very amenable; Brooke promised two Canadian divisions and one British division from Italy and another two from Greece once the situation stabilized in Athens. The British had 80,000 troops in Greece trying to forestall a communist takeover. All this was very good news to SHAEF.

The afternoon session proved less amiable. Unimpressed with Eisenhower's lukewarm response, Brooke clashed with the American chiefs. The CIGS interpreted Eisenhower's cable as yet another example of his subordinating strategy to his concern for balancing competing interests and personalities. Brooke insisted the CCS revise Eisenhower's directive based on Smith's interpretation. If Brooke succeeded, in Smith's opinion, SHAEF would not be able to move American divisions except north of Düsseldorf.[95] Brooke offered the five divisions from the Mediterranean in the hope of inducing the American chiefs to write a binding directive giving the northern variant a clear priority. He also wanted to leverage an agreement on Alexander's future appointment.[96]

That evening the conferees attended a dinner in Nelson's old headquarters. The strained atmosphere of the conference room carried over to the dining table. Smith grew increasingly irritated by Brooke's intransigence. Worn down by his ailments, Smith excused himself, his "stomach going round and round . . . from the ingestion of too much foreign matter." He returned to his quarters and awaited Brooke's return. The longer he waited, the more worked up he became.

Soon after midnight, Brooke had just closed his door when he heard a knock. Without pleasantries, Smith bluntly inquired why the field marshal objected to the SHAEF plan. After all, Eisenhower had given the British virtually everything they asked for: a northern priority with potentially forty-six divisions—including Montgomery's command of Ninth Army—and first call on supply. Brooke said he doubted Eisenhower was "strong enough" to resist pressure from his headstrong American subordinates to reinforce the secondary drive at the expense of the northern thrust. He wanted a CCS directive that left nothing to interpretation. "Goddamn it," Smith flared. "Let's have it out here and now." Asking to speak off the record, he demanded to know exactly what Brooke meant. Brooke replied that Eisenhower was "tolerant to a fault with subordinates including Montgomery." Smith tried to explain how Eisenhower operated, pointing out the Allied team could hold together only through a combination of flexibility and sternness. He told Brooke that any alteration in the command structure amounted to a vote of no confidence in Eisenhower. Since Churchill and the BCOS exhibited so little faith in Eisenhower's leadership, Smith supposed Eisenhower should and would resign. He then informed Brooke he would convey this information to the JCS. Brooke backed down, weakly responding that Eisenhower was a good "chairman of the board" and no one intended to get rid of him.

Ismay's secretary, Jacob, added more to the story. According to him, Smith "announced that, if the British intended to insert a new Ground Force Commander under Eisenhower, then both Eisenhower and Bedell Smith would resign." He noted, "It wasn't everybody who dared stand up like that to Sir Alan Brooke—who was a very formidable character. But that's what Bedell Smith said—and he obviously meant it! Brooke was stunned."[97]

The two then turned their attention to the strategic question. Smith confided in Brooke that SHAEF had erred in France, deflected too often from the objective. He explained that SHAEF calculated on collecting reserves and fully intended to exploit any opportunity for a quick crossing of the Rhine—without waiting to close the river along its entire length. Smith gave Brooke credit "for complete honesty, a tribute I have never paid him before; but he is stubborn as Hell." Relieved, Brooke felt the American general understood the need for concentration in the north and believed Smith would see to it that his boss did not stray from the essential strategy. "I think that the talk did both of us good," Brooke recorded, but it left him feeling "very tired and old."[98]

Smith related the details of his talk with Brooke to the JCS before the 1 February meetings. The session's agenda contained a number of secondary issues. Beneath the surface, tension continued to build. Marshall and King struggled to conceal their antipathy for the uncompromising British chief of staff. The Americans discussed the Brooke-Smith set-to. The vitriolic King strongly voiced his opinion that Montgomery, not Eisenhower, should be relieved of command and insisted he would raise the issue in the CCS meeting. With feelings running high, the Americans looked out on the courtyard and saw the approaching British delegation. Marshall turned to King and said, "Please leave this to me. I will handle it."[99]

Angered by what he saw as Brooke's cynical attitude and the British preoccupation with postwar "political" calculations, Marshall resented most of all the British intrigues aimed at deposing Eisenhower and putting in place a committee command structure. When Brooke aired the issue of Alexander's appointment, the most violent CCS clash of the war ensued. King launched into bitter invectives against Brooke. Failing to end the acrimonious exchanges, Marshall asked everyone except the combined chiefs to leave the room. By constantly asserting the need to reorganize the command structure, Brooke not only questioned Eisenhower's capacity but also, by extension, challenged the professional competence of all senior American officers to direct the war. When Brooke complained about the undue influence exerted by Bradley and Patton on Eisenhower, Marshall lost his temper and "let off rather a tirade about trying to fight the Western front battle by committee." He made it clear the Americans were more worried about Churchill's leverage on Eisenhower: "The President never sees General Eisenhower and never writes to him—that is my advice—because he is an Allied commander. But we are deeply concerned by the pressures of the prime minister," who routinely bypassed the CCS and communicated directly with SHAEF. Marshall then expressed his "dislike and antipathy for Montgomery." Giving vent to accumulated resentments, Marshall called Montgomery an "over-cautious" commander who "wants everything" and "an impudent and disloyal subordinate" who treated all American officers with "open contempt."[100] According to Cunningham, Marshall "said some pretty straight things about Montgomery allowing personal feelings to enter into things." The Americans vigorously defended Eisenhower's independence and were offended by Brooke's demand that the CCS issue a restrictive directive limiting SHAEF's options. For Marshall, the differing concepts of "closing the Rhine" were merely semantic exercises. The real issue remained command.[101]

Before the British delegation left London, Churchill had instructed there should be no "smoothing or smirching to disguise one's true feelings. The closer one's personal relations, the more brutally frank one can be."[102] Relations between the American and British chiefs were not nearly as friendly as the prime minister imagined. Other than Brooke, the rest of the BCOS smirched in the face of Marshall and King's assault. Ismay knew Marshall would never stand for an attack on Eisenhower's conduct of the war, and the BCOS could not sustain their "vote of no confidence."[103] Cunningham thought "Marshall's complaint not unjustified." And "at a time when the defeat of Germany was in view," Cunningham remembered, "we wanted no disagreements as to how victory should be achieved."[104] Every member of the BCOS knew Churchill's methods. They had recently discovered Churchill and Alexander engaged in backdoor correspondence, undermining Wilson's authority just prior to the command switch in the Mediterranean. Unbowed, Brooke rejected Eisenhower's "clarification," simply stating that the British would "take note" of the plan. Cunningham did not think much of Brooke's performance. "Both Portal & myself & King," he noted in his diary, "would have liked, under conditions, to note it with approval."[105] Without a firm agreement, the political heads would decide.

Churchill had developed a serious fever during the flight from England. Confined to bed aboard a British warship, the prime minister pondered the dim prospects of salvaging anything substantive at Malta. And if he left Malta empty handed, he shuddered at his chances in Yalta. On the morning of 2 February, Roosevelt arrived in Valletta harbor aboard USS *Quincy*. Fully recovered, Churchill stood on the deck of HMS *Orion* and waved at the president. Marshall and King came aboard *Quincy* and, together with Leahy and MG Laurence Kuter, who stood in for the ailing Arnold, analyzed the current military situation and discussed the strategic impasse. Marshall and King, who had last seen the president only ten days before, could not believe the deterioration in his health. Shortly after noon Churchill arrived. Churchill and Roosevelt met privately on deck while the chiefs of staff coordinated their respective positions for the briefing that followed.

During the working lunch Churchill monopolized the conversation, reminding the Americans of the wartime problems faced by the British government and expressing his complete devotion to the principles of the Atlantic Charter and the American Declaration of Independence. Roosevelt nodded rather than spoke.[106] After listening to the presentation of the SHAEF plan and Brooke's objections, Roosevelt asked for a map and recounted his bicycle tour of the Rhineland again. He then stated that he understood Eisenhower's views at once and without further elaboration approved the plan. When the new secretary of state, Stettinius, turned the discussion to differences between SHAEF and Montgomery, Roosevelt registered no interest. "The president who is undoubtedly in bad shape & finding difficulty in concentrating," noted Cunningham, "did not rise to the occasion." Not wanting to fatigue the president, Churchill and the chiefs cut the meeting short.[107] During their private talks, Churchill pressed Roosevelt on Alexander's appointment. As Marshall and King stood on deck awaiting a barge to carry them ashore, Roosevelt called Marshall back, and they discussed Alexander's nomination. The president told the not too pleased Marshall that he favored the appointment, but not for another six weeks, "to avoid the appearance of any lack of confidence in Eisenhower."[108]

The final CCS meeting took place aboard the *Quincy* that evening with the political heads in attendance. It proved to be an anticlimactic and rather gloomy affair. Brooke looked on in glum silence as the political heads sanctioned Eisenhower's plan. The British left the meeting still feeling ambivalent, but as Ismay told Churchill after the CCS had endorsed the final directive, "General Eisenhower's intentions are more or less exactly what you and the Chiefs of Staff would have them to be."[109]

The German Is a Whipped Enemy

Not until 28 January 1945 did Allied forces regain the ground lost in the Ardennes. In both the Ardennes and Alsace, Hitler's stubborn refusal to yield ground doubled German casualties, according to one estimate. The manpower and materiel losses debilitated German designs for holding the West Wall, but the greatest casualty of all was that inflicted on German morale. Ideological factors led to Hitler's third fatal decision of the war in northwest Europe. The first, his insistence on the Mortain offensive, undermined any hope of holding in France; the second, his resolve to regain the strategic initiative in the west, grievously wounded his ground and air forces; the last, his determination not to surrender a yard of German territory without a fight, produced the biggest debacle yet, ending any legitimate hope of defending the Rhine and, with it, Germany. With Soviet forces on the Oder and Silesian war production lost, the end was nigh. In rapid succession, the events of the next three months brought the war to an end.

"To Hell with the Planners"

Within a day of the end of the Malta conference, the opening phase of the Rhineland campaign commenced. On 2 February Bradley renewed his drive in the Roer sector. Six days later Montgomery launched Veritable, on schedule, behind the largest artillery barrage of the war in the west. By 9 February U.S. XXI Corps and de Lattre's I Corps completed the elimination of the Colmar Pocket. The next day the Roer dams fell into American hands, but not before the Germans opened the floodgates, delaying Simpson's offensive for two critical weeks. Aside from that lone setback, Allied successes gained momentum.

As a preliminary, Twenty-first Army Group cleared the Roermund triangle (Operation Blackcock) before Crerar's Canadian First Army, with XXX Corps under command, stepped off on the offensive from the Nijmegen salient. Montgomery's forces breached the German defenses the first day and penetrated the West Wall on the second. Anglo-Canadian troops faced a very tough nut. Blaskowitz's Army Group H contained some of the best units in the theater. German morale plummeted after the Bulge, but the paratroopers of First Parachute Army were the exception. On 13 February the Canadians closed the Rhine at Emmerich but encountered some of the heaviest fighting of the war clearing the Reichwald. The bitter fighting drew in many of the Germans' better units; in the end, the Germans committed eleven divisions. Confronting several obstacles—a sudden thaw and heavy rain, coupled with German flooding of much of the area—Crerar made slow and costly progress.

Eisenhower met with Bradley and Montgomery at Zonhoven on 14 February. Montgomery wanted two more divisions in Simpson's attack, which Bradley adamantly rejected. As Summersby noted, "I fear however that there is no love lost between Bradley and Monty. How E. keeps his disposition I really am at a loss to understand."[1] Eisenhower entered the conference with a grim look on his face, prepared to do some table pounding. "There is no doubt that he was worried about something when he arrived," Montgomery told Frank Simpson, now Brooke's number two, "and appeared so during our talk. . . . I have even now no idea at what is at the bottom of his worry." Eisenhower's disquiet grew from his apprehensions about the impending command switch. The meeting produced some minor table pounding over the transfer of forces, but Montgomery got far more than two divisions. Eisenhower restated his determination to stage the main thrust in the north with Simpson's army, with twelve divisions, placed under Montgomery's command for the duration of the war. The quid pro quo was Montgomery's assurance that he would oppose bringing Alexander into SHAEF as deputy supreme commander. As Montgomery reported to the War Office, "It was very obvious that as soon as I had said that I was very well satisfied with the present situation about command, he became a different man; he drove away beaming all over his face."[2]

The field marshal also beamed. As he told Brooke, "All this is very good and I do believe that we are at last all well set with a fair wind to help us into harbour. We have had a few storms, but the sky is now clear." Montgomery correctly guessed that Eisenhower and Smith viewed Alexander as something less than a success in the Mediterranean and resented Churchill's "intrigue," as he termed it in his diary, "to get Field-Marshal Alexander appointed Deputy Supreme Commander."[3]

With Montgomery in his back pocket, the next day Eisenhower talked with Tedder about Alexander. He specified that if the CCS insisted on Alexander, his duties would be limited to the political and economic spheres, not military.[4] He wrote to Brooke on 16 February, claiming that although he recalled promising to make the switch "some time back," he had heard nothing since and assumed the matter "had been dropped." Eisenhower knew perfectly well the president had sanctioned the exchange in Malta, but to Brooke he treated Alexander's transfer as a rumor. Eisenhower outlined his opposition to the move and listed his apprehensions and conditions if the switch took place "some time during the Spring." Given the early successes of the Allied offensive, he "deplored . . . any change in our working team." He foresaw another media blitz in England in the event Alexander came into SHAEF and feared its repercussions on the solidarity of the alliance if the British press misinterpreted "Alexander's appointment here as the establishment of a ground headquarters." Eisenhower reiterated his determination to block any such appointment; if Alexander joined SHAEF, his role would center on "our current problems in liberated manpower, relief, rearmament, and so on." Stretching the truth, he explained that Lear's job entailed the same responsibilities—although the scope of Lear's duties remained in flux, they never involved direct superintendence of civil affairs—and said he expected Alexander to occupy the position as opposite number to the new American deputy theater commander. He asked Brooke to "make certain that both the Prime Minister and Alexander are informed as to my views and intensions."[5]

Eisenhower's letter shocked Churchill, who suggested to Brooke that they make another trip to Versailles. On 22 February Churchill summoned up his best phraseology and penned an impassioned letter to Eisenhower. He prefaced it by mentioning his long talk with Marshall at Malta, with Brooke present; Marshall had confirmed that a change of command would take place in the middle of March. The prime minister reiterated he had always opposed a separate headquarters as "a needless complication" and claimed the right for the British to have a deputy. He wanted Tedder employed elsewhere and underscored that Eisenhower had agreed to name a British general his deputy at Versailles. Now Churchill discovered that Eisenhower intended to create a deputy commander to administer the rear and liberated territories. "Not aware your British Deputy was relegated to such non-military functions," Churchill

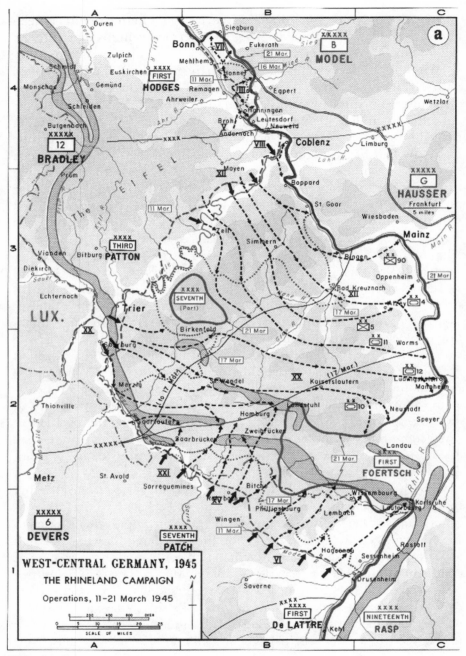

Rhineland

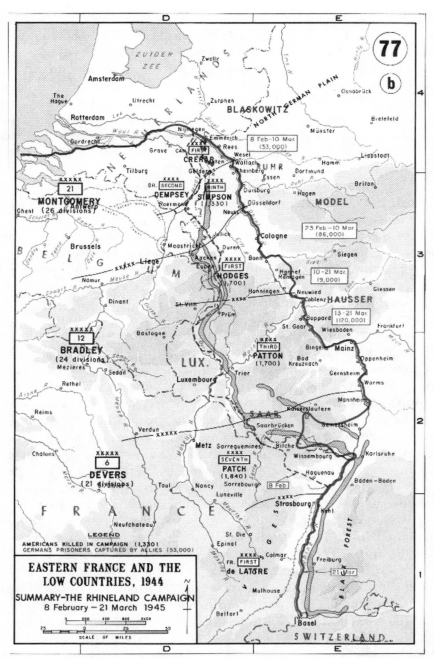

ZUIDER ZEE

Amsterdam

The Hague

Rotterdam

Utrecht

Zwolle

Zutphen

Osnabrück

BLASKOWITZ

NORTH GERMAN PLAIN

Münster

Bielefeld

Dordrecht

Lek R.

Waal R.

Nijmegen

Emmerich

Rees

XXXX
FIRST

8 Feb-10 Mar
(53,000)

Wesel

Lippstadt

Grave

Can.

CRERAR

Xanten

Wallach

RUHR

Hamm

Dortmund

Tilburg

XXXX
BR. SECOND
DEMPSEY

Geldern

Rheinberg

Essen

Duisburg

Hagen

XXXXX
21
MONTGOMERY
(26 divisions)

Antwerp

Ghent

XXXX
NINTH
SIMPSON
(330)

Roermond

Düsseldorf

Neuss

MODEL

Scheldt R.

B

Demer R.

Dyle R.

Brussels

L

E

L

G

I

U

M

Maastricht

Jülich

Düren

Cologne

23 Feb-10 Mar
(86,000)

Liege

Maas R.

XXXXX

Namur

Meuse R.

Aachen

Eupen

XXXX
FIRST
HODGES
(1,700)

Bonn

Honnef
Remagen

Siegen

10-21 Mar.
(9,000)

Sieg R.

Giessen

Dinant

St. Vith

XXXX

Honningen

Neuwied

Coblenz

HAUSSER

Sombre R.

Prüm

13-21 Mar.
(120,000)

Bastogne

St. Goar

Boppard

Wiesbaden

Frankfurt

XXXXX
12
BRADLEY
(24 divisions)

LUX.

Mosel R.

XXXX
THIRD
PATTON
(1,700)

Bingen

Mainz

Main R.

Semois R.

Meziers

Sedan

Luxembourg

Trier

Bad
Kreuznach

Oppenheim

Gernsheim

Worms

Aisne R.

Rethel

Reims

Meuse R.

SAAR

Kaiserslautern

Mannheim

Chalons

Verdun

XXXXX

Saarbrücken

Semersheim

XXXXX
6
DEVERS
(21 divisions)

Metz

Sarreguemines

XXXX
SEVENTH
PATCH
(1,840)

Bitche

Wissembourg

Karlsruhe

Toul

Nancy

Sarrebourg

Haguenau

Baden-Baden

Luneville

8 Feb

Meurthe R.

Strasbourg

Kehl

V

O

S

G

E

S

BLACK FOREST

F   R   A   N   C   E

Neufchateau

St. Die

Colmar

21 Mar

Freiburg

Epinal

XXXX
FR. FIRST
de LATORE

Mulhouse

**EASTERN FRANCE AND THE
LOW COUNTRIES, 1944**

Belfort

Basel

SUMMARY-THE RHINELAND CAMPAIGN
8 February – 21 March 1945

N

SWITZERLAND

25   0   200   400   600   OVER

25   0   25   50

SCALE   OF   MILES

Broad Front along the Rhine

said, and "quite frankly . . . I consider this would be a waste of Field Marshal Alexander's military gifts and experience. I thought he would help you in all your cares and burdens, and that the change would be personally agreeable to you." British and Canadian forces, though smaller than the American contribution, still amounted to 1 million men, and much fighting still lay ahead. "I am sure you would not wish to deny us the kind of representation . . . which is our due." Churchill reminded Eisenhower that "neither you nor I have ever taken a narrow or nationalistic point of view in regards to the High Command," and he now expected Eisenhower to "approach the matter in that spirit of true comradeship of which you are the outstanding exemplar."[6] There matters stood until the prime minister and the CIGS arrived in early March.

With Grenade on hold, and given the slow pace of movement in the Reichwald, Eisenhower remained antsy. "Right now, due to a variety of causes," he wrote to his wife, "we're in a comparative doldrums."[7] SHAEF convened a major conference on 20 February. Intelligence indicated the weakening of German forces south of the Moselle, and Strong posited that an offensive there might reap greater dividends than one in the north. Smith "refused to budge an inch from present plans," reported the visiting LTG Ronald Weeks, Brooke's deputy. Smith said Eisenhower's primary objective remained destroying the German capacity to resist, not avoiding their strengths. The big payoff lay in executing Veritable-Grenade and the preliminary Lumberjack, Twelfth Army Group's attack toward Cologne.[8]

After Smith whipped his staff into line, he and Eisenhower drafted a secret directive outlining the scheme for sequential offensives "so as to secure the maximum possible concentration in ground and air power." Confirming what he told Montgomery, it clearly stated: "The main effort is to be north of the Ruhr; all other operations are to gain secure flanks so as to permit heavy concentration in that area, and eventually to provide secondary threats and thrusts that will assist the main effort." In phase I, Twenty-first Army Group and Ninth and First Armies would "advance to the Rhine in the north." Phase II aimed at clearing the Rhine north of the Moselle (Lumberjack). The last phase would involve the northern crossing, with all other forces holding the Rhine north of Koblenz and Third and Seventh Armies capturing the Saarland and pushing to the Rhine.[9] This time, the bargain with Montgomery held.

The lead-up to Malta and the conference itself triggered another round of ulcer problems for Smith. He soldiered on as best he could, chairing the vital morning chiefs of staff meetings and dealing with the transfer of key staff to the new Reims headquarters in the College Moderne et Technique de Garçons, an institution that must have reminded him of his high school. He cut back on his commitments, even spending a few days in bed. Not the type to be idle, Smith devoted his downtime to completing a history essay. His bouts of field marshal–itis pushed Smith to the limits. Although he stoutly defended Montgomery's northern thrust, whatever personal regard he once held for the field marshal had long expired. Using Eisenhower's correspondence files, Smith wrote an unsolicited, densely worded, nineteen-page account of the Normandy campaign up to the time Eisenhower assumed the ground command. It amounted to a withering attack on Montgomery's claims that he bore chief credit for Allied victory. Exhausted by the field marshal's constant harping on his brilliant orchestration of the battle and management of the Allied team—and how everything went to hell when he lost ground command—Smith argued precisely the opposite. Eisenhower, not Montgomery, made the decision "that the full weight of US strength should be used to break into the open on our right" at a meeting with Bradley on 24 June, six days before Montgomery's directive calling for a breakout in the American sector. Eisenhower, while visiting Bradley's headquarters after the breakout, saw the merits of the proposed "wider envelopment . . . toward the Seine and even to the east of Paris." In the "most prolonged and bitter arguments of the whole campaign," Eisenhower prevailed in preserving Anvil, killing British plans for Brittany, and opening the southern French ports that proved so indispensable in sustaining American forces during the supply draught—a decision Smith saw as eminently correct. Smith's motives are not hard to discern; he wanted to steal a march on the official histories by denigrating Montgomery's generalship and portraying Eisenhower as the decisive supreme commander. The USSTAF historian, Bruce Hopper, recognized the "Boswellian thread of apologia" that must be exorcised "when the material is reworked into definitive history," but Smith's efforts, anticipating the postwar "battle of the books," provided an authoritative first shot in a debate that continues to this day.[10]

Aside from his foray into historical writing, Smith wrestled with the same roster of problems—manpower and civil affairs chief among them. The manpower problem still dogged him. He decided the easiest solution involved expediting the reequipping of French units. "The French are anxious to do their share in the final struggle," he told Handy, reminding him, "the casualties which the French divisions take in the battle will reduce by just so much the number of American casualties." He also thought these new French divisions would be ready "a good deal sooner than it would be possible for us at home to raise and train new

American divisions," which the War Department had no plans to do.[11] This program induced de Gaulle's proposition, with the Colmar Pocket reduced, to withdraw five French divisions and "reconstitute them for future operations." De Gaulle also wanted reinforcements for operations to eliminate the pockets of German troops at Bordeaux. In a marginal note on de Gaulle's letter of 15 February, Eisenhower scrawled, "Does this mean French are ready to assume full responsibility for Alsace with only 5 divisions?" Smith hammered out a deal with Juin. The French would pull out two divisions, but not as far into the French interior as de Gaulle desired—not for use in the Gironde—and they would be held in readiness for employment as reinforcements if the need arose.[12]

Despite all the "field marshal trouble," SHAEF's relations on the whole were better with Twenty-first Army Group than with the American operational commands. Bradley remained hostile, still bitter over SHAEF's having reduced him in the Bulge. As the fighting first to reduce the Bulge and then in the Eifel turned into an inconclusive slugging match, Patton lapsed into one of his deep depressions; he grew increasingly embittered and estranged. Despite all the adulatory press coverage he received for his drive to relieve Bastogne—his standing in the eyes of the American public would never be higher—Patton felt cheated. It was the Falaise Gap and the Seine all over again; his circumspect superiors took the cautious route and—in his skewed view—robbed him of his moment in history. Bradley got his forth star, and he and Hodges got recommendations for decorations for their lackluster roles in the Ardennes; Patton never received so much as a warm word of commendation from his old friend Eisenhower.

The emphasis on operations north of the Moselle reduced Third Army to a supporting role. "You may hear that I am on the defensive," Patton complained to his wife, "but it was not the enemy who put me there. I don't see much future for me in this war. There are too many 'safety first' people running it."[13] Patton decided to resort to his rock soup recipe; he would do what he did best—ignore orders, go over to the offensive, and trust in his destiny. "I am taking one of the longest chances in my chancy career," he wrote on 6 February, "in fact, almost disobeying orders in order to attack, my theory being that if I win, nobody will say anything, and I am sure that I will win."[14] Four days later, Bradley informed him that SHAEF had decided to transfer divisions from Third to Ninth Army for Grenade. A livid Patton again threatened resignation, stating that, in both age and combat experience, he was the senior officer and would be goddamned if he consented to being stripped of his divisions. Once again, under pressure from Bradley, Eisenhower gave in. Simpson would still get his divisions, but he sanctioned Patton "to assume a posture of 'aggressive defense.'" Bradley interpreted "it as an order to 'keep moving' toward the Rhine with a low profile."[15]

Impatient for his "creeping defensive" to kick off, Patton took his first leave since October 1942 and visited his friend Hughes in Paris. Smith took time out from supervising the headquarters move to Reims and invited Patton on a shoot at a former royal hunting preserve. Bradley, Hodges, and Patton all strenuously rejected SHAEF's efforts to withdraw divisions into a strategic reserve. "Reserve for what?" Patton asked himself. "This seemed like locking the barn door after the horse was stolen. Certainly at this period of the war no reserve was needed—simply violent attack everywhere with everything . . . the Germans do not have the resources to stop it."[16] He grudgingly admitted that ComZ had performed admirably in the Ardennes. "The supply situation," he conceded, "was the best it had ever been."[17] Smith raised the issue of SHAEF reserves. "Smith was very eloquent," Patton wrote in his diary, "and said, 'I suppose you don't know the high strategy, but I am convinced that *my* northern effort cannot logistically support more than 35 divisions. As we have 83 divisions, that leaves quite a few I can use anywhere else, and I want you to be prepared to resume the old effort through Saarlautern and Saareguemines. How many divisions would you require?'" Patton replied he could attack with five. Smith said, "I think you should have twelve." A disbelieving Patton joked, "I had never known how great he really is."[18] What Smith neglected to tell him was that his Saar offensive would not receive sanction until the other two operations concluded. Smith intended to keep Patton on a short leash. "Geo gets bellyache while hunting with Beadle [*sic*]," Hughes noted. "It upset him to have Beadle know he was sick."[19]

"I guess Geo is through with this war," observed Hughes, "and has his mind on China and a fourth star. . . . He can't talk about anything except that. He must be getting impotent."[20] This time Hughes read his friend all wrong. Returning to his headquarters, Patton told his staff they should comply with any orders from SHAEF for the transfer of divisions out of Third Army, but he observed, "It would be a foolish and ignoble way for the Americans to end the war by sitting on their asses. And, gentlemen, we aren't going to do anything foolish or ignoble." The staff started work developing plans for an expanded offensive. "Let the gentlemen up north learn what we're doing when they see it on their maps."[21]

Not waiting for the flood-waters to completely recede, Simpson inaugurated Grenade on 23 February. With the Germans concentrating on the fighting in the Reichwald, Ninth Army made immediate and impressive gains. A week later American forces reached the Rhine opposite Düsseldorf; the next day they linked with Crerar's forces. Together, Veritable and Grenade set off a chain reaction. At a cost of 22,500 Allied casualties, two-thirds of them Canadian and British, the combined offensives inflicted losses on the Germans comparable to those suffered in the Ardennes. Only remnants of once proud units escaped across the Rhine into the Ruhr defenses. At long last, Montgomery had in his possession the platform for his northern thrust into Germany.

Hodges opened his offensive timed with Grenade; designed as flank protection for Simpson, the attacks scored some striking gains, and by 5 March elements of VII Corps stood at the outskirts of Cologne. Ultra intercepts the next day indicated Hitler had ordered the evacuation of all German troops east of the river except those opposite the expected Allied crossing points of Wesel, Koblenz, and Mainz. On 7 March a two-battalion task force of Ninth Armored Division probing forward pulled off one of the great coups of World War II; it captured the Ludendorff Bridge intact at Remagen.

Smith had sent Bull to Bradley's headquarters to break the news he would have to give up three divisions and support units for Devers's push into the Saar-Palatinate. True to form, Bradley called the order "larcenous" and openly opposed SHAEF's demands. During the ensuing argument, the phone rang; it was Hodges with news of the seizure of the Ludendorff Bridge. "Hot dog, Courtney," a triumphant Bradley responded, and he ordered him to "shove everything you can across it." Bull dampened the mood by telling an incredulous Bradley, "You're not going anywhere down there at Remagen. It just doesn't fit the plan. Ike's heart is in your sector, but right now his mind is up north." Bradley placed a call to Eisenhower. "Brad, that's wonderful," Eisenhower exclaimed. "Sure, get right across with everything you've got. It's the best break we've had." When Bradley explained Bull's lack of enthusiasm, Eisenhower responded, "To hell with the planners."[22]

To be sure, the terrain east of Remagen—the Westerwald and the Hohe Taunus—offered the worst invasion route, but as Kesselring later remarked, even though "unimportant in itself for the Rhine defenses as a whole . . . never was there more concentrated bad luck at one place than at Remagen." Not only surprised by the bridge's loss, the German commands were also caught in the midst of reorganization. The German corps and division commanders were moving their headquarters when the Americans snatched the bridge. A counterattack with a few tanks might have eliminated the bridgehead, but none came. Eisenhower limited the bridgehead to five divisions, but as Göring stated, Remagen represented "the biggest catastrophe. It made a long Rhine-defense impossible, and it upset our entire defense scheme along the river."[23] It also overturned SHAEF's plan.

Patton's initial attacks fell short of his objective, Trier. He worried SHAEF would pull the plug on his offensive. Bradley, again ignoring SHAEF, gave Third Army back the Tenth Armored Division and told Patton "to keep on going until we receive orders to stop from higher authority." And as Patton noted in his diary, Bradley also said "he would not listen to the telephone."[24] On 1 March Trier fell, and Patton tried to call Eisenhower and Bradley to give them the news. Failing, he called Smith, who congratulated him on his success. "I certainly again proved my military ideas are correct," Patton noted in his diary, "and have put them over in spite of opposition from the Americans."[25] Patton then launched a hook down the Moselle, one armored division advancing to its confluence with the Rhine at Koblenz on 7 March.

Remagen and Patton's drive down the Moselle changed everything. Smith's defense of SHAEF's operational flexibility at Malta paid off. Now Eisenhower could unite his heart and mind and reinforce success. Montgomery continued preparations for his great set piece—a combined amphibious-airborne crossing in the north (Operation Plunder). But attention—and expectations—shifted to the rapidly changing situation farther south. Time became the vital ingredient. If Allied forces moved quickly south of the Moselle, they still might cut off and destroy the mostly immobile German forces before they disengaged from Patch's pinning attacks and effected their retreat across the Rhine. With events unfolding with breathtaking speed, all SHAEF could do was sit back and plot fresh arrows on the situation maps.

By this stage of the campaign, Bradley and Patton seemed almost as intent on upstaging Montgomery as dealing the Germans a death blow. Patton noted to himself, "essential that the 1st and 3rd Armies get themselves so committed down here that they [SHAEF] cannot move us north for the British instilled idea of attacking on the Ruhr Plain." For the next phase of the campaign, Patton reckoned he needed another armored division and approached Smith, remembering the hunting trip promise. He found Smith cool to the suggestion. SHAEF again worried that Patton would get into trouble, and it wanted to exercise greater control over coordinating the actions of Third and Seventh Armies in the Palatinate fighting. Patton did not wait for direction from above. On 11 March he began his drive south, down the *Rheingraben* and across the mostly trackless Hunsrück. Patton again attacked with the thinnest veneer of authority. What the gentlemen up north and at SHAEF saw were Patton's relentless converging attacks—Tedder called them Patton's "Phallic symbols"—simultaneously rolling up the West Wall and enveloping the Saar-Palatinate triangle. "Exact location of our divisions in overrun area impossible to define," Tedder told Eisenhower, "since they have got completely tangled in the rat hunt."[26] Patton drove his exhausted troops at a frantic pace because he knew "a pint of sweat is worth a gallon of blood."[27] He understood the vital time-space relationship in war and fully exploited mobility and firepower to their greatest advantage. The Eifel-Palatinate campaign—not the Bulge—represented Patton's signature claim as a great commander. Gerow wired Patton: "Congratulations on your brilliant surrounding and capturing of three armies, one of them American." Patton recorded, "They did not want me to take Trier nor go to the Rhine nor to cross the Moselle southwest of Coblenz, and now, if we don't cross the Rhine, we may be halted again. . . . [We must] make plans fit circumstance. The other armies make circumstances fit plans."[28] On 22–23 March elements of the Third Army crossed the Rhine in two places—without heavy bombers, airborne drops, ground smoke, or massed artillery.

In six weeks Eisenhower's broad-front strategy paid huge dividends everywhere. In their defense of the Rhineland west of the river, the Germans lost as much as one-third of their remaining combat strength. The loss of a quarter million POWs spoke volumes. Although SS and some Wehrmacht elements fought on tenaciously—as evidenced by the heavy casualties sustained by Allied forces in March and April—the Rhenish campaign and their fruitless efforts to eliminate the Remagen bridgehead effectively broke the back of German ground forces in the west.

The spectacular American successes in March proved as disastrous to British schemes as they did to German designs for defending the Rhine. In anticipation of the arrival of Churchill and Brooke to reopen the push for Alexander's appointment, Eisenhower met with Montgomery at his headquarters in Eindhoven on 1 March. As he had in early December, Eisenhower moved to preempt British attempts to destabilize SHAEF. Montgomery proved as politically inept as Eisenhower was adept. They reaffirmed their Zonhoven bargain. Eisenhower confirmed his intention to concentrate in the north and isolate the Ruhr. Montgomery readily agreed to uphold his part of the deal. He knew Alexander's appointment would spark "another great storm" and revive "the old disagreements." As he recorded in his diary, Montgomery "gave his very definite opinion that Field-Marshal Alexander should be left where he was, and that any further cause of friction should be avoided at all costs."[29]

Churchill, Brooke, and Ismay appeared the next day. Montgomery took the initiative and aired his views; Alexander's appointment would create more problems than it would solve. As recorded in Montgomery's diary, "The Prime Minister was much upset by the Field Marshall's frank opinion." Churchill said "he would not be deterred . . . from fear of hurting the feelings of American generals." Before Churchill got out of bed on 4 March, the day he would travel to Reims, Montgomery forwarded a wire to SHAEF. "The question of Alex was raised by my visitor," it started. Montgomery reiterated the points he had made in discussions with Churchill and finished by telling Eisenhower, "I have no objection to your telling him that you know this is my opinion."[30]

Forewarned by Montgomery, Eisenhower easily deflected the prime minister. With matters progressing so well at the front, Eisenhower saw no benefit in "upsetting the outfit." "It is best to leave Alex where he is," Brooke concluded. "I think that Winston is now of the same opinion." Over dinner that night, Smith made an effort to patch up his relations with Brooke. They confined themselves to a safe conversation about fishing.[31] With Allied forces controlling the west bank of the Rhine from the Dutch frontier to the Moselle, Montgomery wrote to Brooke on 10 March, confirming his complete satisfaction with the existing state of affairs. "We are now on a very good wicket; Ike has learnt his lesson and he consults me before taking any action." The next day, after communicating with Alexander, Churchill finally threw in the towel. Writing to Montgomery, he bluntly said, "Re Alex: I decided not to make the change. . . . The matter is closed."[32]

Although Montgomery never grasped it at the time—he was too busy applauding his victory in extracting assurances that the northern thrust remained the main effort—Remagen and its aftermath ensured that the Allied advance into Germany would follow Eisenhower's broad-front prescription. Despite the massive display of firepower—2,000 guns and hundreds of heavy bombers—and the employment of two airborne divisions in the largest operation since D-day, Plunder was something of an anticlimax. The scenario sketched at Malta was turned upside down. Brooke had insisted on staging the northern main thrust irrespective of whether the Rhine was closed along its length. Now with Remagen and Third Army's crossings—and Patch's crossing near Worms the day after Plunder—Montgomery's offensive no longer topped the bill. Even before Patton got across the Rhine, SHAEF planners began reorienting priority to the Mainz-Frankfurt area. The flexibility Eisenhower and Smith insisted on allowed an opportunistic shift of those ten divisions held in SHAEF reserve to exploit success in the center. Additional crossings, complete with airborne operations, at Boppard and St. Goar north of Frankfurt (Operation Voyage) were planned. The fighting around Remagen pulled in German divisions and frittered away troops in a desperate effort to seal and eliminate the bridgehead. Bad weather, the sorry state of the German rail system, and Allied air interdiction created movement and supply difficulties, compromising German attempts to squeeze out the American bridgehead. The German command withdrew units from Army Group G in the south, but not from Army Group H defending the Ruhr, explaining the ease of Patton's virtually unopposed crossings south of Mainz and his speedy advance to the Main. Without the bridgehead, the Germans could have rested and refit, enabling their divisions to fight at something more than half strength. "The magnetic way in which the Remagen bridgehead drew these divisions," remarked Kesselring, who assumed command from Rundstedt just after the bridge's loss, "prevented their being reinforced for the battle to prevent encirclement of the Ruhr. . . . That was the crime of Remagen," Kesselring told a postwar interrogator. "It broke the front along the Rhine."[33]

No "On to Berlin"

Eisenhower joined Churchill and Brooke in watching Ninth Army's night crossing. He had just come from a five-day retreat at a luxury villa outside Cannes owned by an American tycoon and placed at SHAEF's disposal as a rest and recreation center. Given the great successes scored in the Rhineland campaign, Eisenhower should have been ebullient. Instead, the last week in February and the first week in March proved one of the most nerve-racking periods of the war.[34] A number of pressures ate at him. The delay in launching Grenade loomed large. People close to Eisenhower detected changes in his disposition, a mood Summersby described as "truly vile."[35] He became quarrelsome and argumentative, given to making self-congratulatory speeches. With Smith frequently sidelined by his health complaints, Eisenhower had to stay in Reims and attend to the tasks usually delegated to his chief of staff. Hughes came to his office with a minor problem; Eisenhower first ignored him and then, glaring at him, launched into a bitter tirade. "Ike shouts and rants," Hughes noted. "Says 'I have too many things to do.' . . . He acted like a crazy man." Eisenhower resented Marshall's retreat at Malta on the question of Alexander's appointment, taking it as further indication of the chief's waning confidence in him. He also fretted about Marshall's criticisms of his handling of the manpower problem, especially concerning soldiers' complaints about unfair treatment. Most troubling of all, as he told Marshall, he was "tired of trying to arrange the blankets smoothly over several prima donnas in the same bed."[36] In a letter to Mamie he complained, "Those of us that are bearing real responsibility in this war will find it difficult ever to be restful—serene again."[37] For months his wife had heard rumors about Eisenhower's relationship with Kay Summersby. Demanding reassurances, Mamie gave Ike "hell" instead of comfort. "Ike on defensive," Hughes noted, "guard up, worried, self-isolated." "Beadle [sic] cause of most of trouble," Hughes surmised. "Beadle wouldn't mind being [Army] C of S."[38]

Smith naturally dreamed of someday occupying the chair of his mentor, but he had more immediate problems on his hands. For months he had hidden the extent of his health problems, but the stress of the Ardennes crisis and Malta worsened his bleeding ulcer. Afraid that Marshall would discover the seriousness of his stomach problems, Smith made a point of attending a number of luncheons and dinners at Malta with the chief. "You know the poor view he takes of anybody," he joked with Handy, "who looks as though they even had dandruff or athlete's foot."[39] In February he slowed down the pace, relying more and more on Morgan to run the show. In early March he developed a serious infection that put him in bed under medical supervision for several days.[40] On 16 March Smith felt well enough to go forward with Eisenhower to see Bradley and Patton. Weather diverted the plane to Patton's headquarters. Patton ushered them into the map room, where they discussed the ground situation. At that point, neither of Patton's thrusts had gained much traction; he still needed that armored division. Eisenhower "was quite enthusiastic and complimentary, as was Smith," Patton recorded. Originally, only Smith was supposed to visit Third Army headquarters; because of his health problems, Smith had not been able to come up earlier. To butter up Smith, Patton put on a showy guard of honor, and because the ceremony was intended for Beetle, Eisenhower declined to make the review. "Smith was very much pleased," Patton recorded, "and drove away immediately afterward to visit Bradley." Patton's scheme worked; the Twelfth Armored Division soon joined Third Army.[41]

After touring Third and Seventh Army areas, Eisenhower and Smith returned to Reims on 17 March. The next afternoon Bradley flew in and spent the night. Bradley came to press Eisenhower on sanctioning Voyage and a Rhine crossing near Worms (Operation Undertone). These operations would serve as preliminaries for First and Third Armies' conduct of converging offensives toward Giessen, Bradley's right hook. Bradley found Eisenhower listless. "Ike was beginning to sag badly," Bradley observed. "Beetle and I were very much worried. The General's physical and emotional condition was worse than we had ever known it. . . . Beetle was positive that he was on the verge of a nervous breakdown." Smith insisted Eisenhower take a break. "Look at you. You've got bags under your eyes. Your blood pressure's higher than it's ever been, and you can hardly walk across the room" (his knee was acting up). Eisenhower finally gave in on the condition that Smith, hardly in the bloom of health himself, and Bradley join him.[42]

On 19 March Eisenhower and Smith flew down to the Riviera. The next day Bradley joined the party. For the first two days Eisenhower slept around the clock, emerging only to eat. Afterward, Summersby pronounced him "somewhat human." Despite his languor—likely produced by a liberal dose of slow-down medicine—Eisenhower's mind remained fixated on the war. His monumental rage in the beginning of March stemmed from fears that Veritable would miscarry, refueling British criticism that he had once again failed. Now with the Rhineland campaign all but complete and Montgomery set to uncoil the long-awaited big push, the burning question centered on what to do next. Pondering that question was what bedeviled him. As he remarked, "all I want to do is sit here and not think," but there was no evading the issue. The impromptu conference at Sous le Vents ended with Eisenhower's mind settled: He would fulfill the original CCS directive by undertaking operations into the heart of Germany and destroying the enemy's armed forces. And he would do so as envisioned in the May 1944 SHAEF plan that called for isolating the Ruhr and severing the Reich at the waist. He would sanction no advance on Berlin.

Eisenhower claimed he read Clausewitz three times while attending Fox Connor's "graduate seminar" in Panama. He could trade Clausewitzian bromides with the best of them. He understood that operations served as the instrument and policy guided war, and he fully appreciated that as the war drew to its climax, political considerations would take on heightened importance. Consistent with American war-fighting tradition, Eisenhower never subscribed to the determinant: "No other possibility exists, then, than to subordinate the military point of view to the political." As he told Marshall in late April 1945, Eisenhower never understood why the prime minister was "so determined to intermingle political and military considerations."[43] His two political bosses resided on opposite poles: whereas Churchill viewed war through political glasses and constantly meddled in operational questions, Roosevelt never interceded in operational matters and deferred the hard political questions until after the war.

American war aims rested on two simple threads: a quick victory in

Europe and the redirection of American strength to the Pacific, and the construction of arrangements for postwar cooperation. American policy makers regarded strategy as politically neutral. The conduct of operations served as a purely military mechanism whose sole objective centered on destroying the enemy's armed forces. Roosevelt assigned strategic matters to his joint chiefs, intervening only when the CCS could not resolve differences of opinion; Marshall delegated operational questions to his theater commanders. Other than the unconditional surrender policy, Roosevelt never specified his finite war aims. He wanted to destroy European fascism and Japanese militarism and form a coalition of the "Four Policeman" cooperating together through a world body. True to his Wilsonian internationalist roots, he endeavored to universalize American attitudes and institutions—to spread democracy, free-enterprise capitalism, and the rule of law—and give them concrete form with a global constitution and a bill of rights in a new version of the League of Nations. On occasion he favored collective security; at other times he acquiesced to a more traditional balance-of-power approach. The consummate juggler, he had to educate the American public, wean it away from isolationism and unilateralism, allay suspicions of the Soviet Union, and build a support base for postwar American global leadership. He understood the domestic political obstacles to maintaining American troops abroad after the war. As a result, Roosevelt always employed idealist rhetoric as window dressing to mask his realist agenda. Nobody could quite decide whether his priority rested in domestic or international policy; in his view, they could not be unraveled. He talked about dismantling the world system based on spheres of influence, colonies, and alliances, but he knew he could not dictate a settlement—with Stalin, de Gaulle, Chiang Kai-shek, or Churchill—and must employ American power to ameliorate differences. In the end, all these shifting contours would depend on his personal ability to handle "Uncle Joe," "Joan d'Arc," "Peanut," Winston, and the political Right at home. None of his vision would survive if the global system fractured along ideological lines. American public opinion and cooperation with the Soviet Union constituted the twin pillars of Roosevelt's postwar policy.

Eisenhower possessed two knowables: the CCS directive and the outcomes of the Yalta conference. The CCS directive said nothing about Berlin. Flushed by the "victory disease," Eisenhower talked about Berlin, but that soon passed. His 28 October directive made no reference to the German capital, and in the 20 January statement of purpose demanded by the BCOS, he mentioned an advance on Berlin only once, and then as simply one of three options once the American forces reached Kassel; the other two involved a thrust north to isolate the Ruhr and one eastward toward Leipzig. At Yalta, the political heads agreed in principle on the American-British-Soviet zones of occupation in Germany and Austria and the partitioning of Berlin and Vienna, including French participation. The divided German capital remained deep inside the designated Soviet zone. Issues pertaining to the eastern and western boundaries of Poland did not figure in SHAEF's calculations. Once the primary objective of neutralizing the Ruhr was secured, the secondary aim—completing the destruction of the German armed forces in combination with the Soviets—could best be achieved by advancing on a broad front with Twelfth and Sixth Army Groups, the first on a Thuringia-Saxony line and the second into Bavaria. Before D-day, SHAEF planners had decided the central route offered better terrain and a more essential strategic objective—the industrial region of Saxony—than the northern line of advance, with its numerous and easily defended river lines. Eisenhower agreed with the strategy in May 1944, and the occupation boundaries set out at Yalta, together with the mandate to cooperate fully with the Soviets, confirmed the central thrust as the best possible option.[44]

As always, Eisenhower made up his mind but then insisted on multiple advocacies on any decision that would incite controversy. He knew downgrading Montgomery's advance to a secondary effort and surrendering Berlin to the Soviets would provoke a political conflagration. With the two officers whose judgment he valued most vacationing with him, he elicited concurrence from Bradley and Smith. Relations between the two West Point classmates remained strained, but Eisenhower considered Bradley's "tactical and strategical judgments . . . almost unimpeachable." Both men were conservative by instinct. Bradley remembered the carnage of the street fighting in Aachen and projected far higher casualties in any battle for Berlin. He estimated losses in excess of 100,000, "a pretty stiff price for a prestige objective." Bradley agreed the central push held the greatest advantages.

Eisenhower expected Bradley to say precisely that. Against Bradley's military judgment, Eisenhower had to weigh personal considerations. The stolid "GI General" had emerged from the Bulge with a tarnished reputation and hurt feelings. Beneath the veneer of the hardscrabble, humble Missourian there existed a man thirsting for recognition and revenge. What better path to lasting military fame than leading to victory the largest field armies ever assembled by the United States? Any drive on Berlin would require Montgomery's retention of Ninth Army, the airborne forces, first call on logistics, and some alteration in the command structure, necessitating Bradley's teaming with the field marshal. None of those options sounded very palatable, especially the last. After completing the central offensive and linking with the Soviets, SHAEF could redirect forces to aid Montgomery in fulfilling his missions in the north. Taking Hamburg and Bremen and sealing the Danish peninsula did not offer comparable benefits to securing Saxony. The sooner the central thrust severed Germany in two, the quicker SHAEF could reinforce Montgomery. Eisenhower recognized that, after all the infighting, Bradley and Montgomery could never work together. He decided to return Simpson to Bradley's command once the Ruhr was cut off. Fifteenth Army, tasked with holding the Rhine line opposite the Ruhr and providing security and military governance in the rear of the American advance, also entered Twelfth Army Group's order of battle.

Smith concurred with Bradley's views. The CCS directive called for Allied forces to advance into the heart of Germany. In Smith's estimate, Germany possessed two hearts: Berlin, the political center, and the Ruhr, the economic hub. In his view, the Ruhr constituted "our real target." As he later told the press, "General Eisenhower has always had in mind the classic double envelopment [of the Ruhr] on a large scale." As Smith laid out at Malta, SHAEF insisted on preserving operational elasticity, with the implied option of funneling reserves into the central drive if that alternative held out greater rewards. "We were looking for more" than the "power drive" in the north. Once the northern and southern pincers joined, isolating the Ruhr, the concentration of forces favored the central axis. Logically, with time eclipsing space as the supreme conditioning factor, Allied forces could not involve themselves in any lengthy regrouping of forces and sorting out of supply lines. With the Ruhr, Saar, and Silesia in Allied hands, industrial Saxony took on greater significance. A drive in the center—as foreseen in the SHAEF plan—provided the obvious best option.[45]

Another argument for cutting Germany in two grew out of fear that the Nazi regime planned to hold out and fight an extended guerrilla campaign from the mountain fastness of the Sudetenland, southern Germany, and western Austria. As early as April 1944, Eisenhower expected resistance to continue after the German armed forces collapsed. At the beginning of September 1944 he told Marshall that suspicions developed "in my mind . . . that the fanatics of that country may attempt to carry on a long and bitter guerilla warfare. Such a prospect is a dark one and I think we should do everything possible to prevent its occurrence."[46] In mid-February 1945 SHAEF G-2 stated that, although "no specific details" could be gleaned, "informants are unanimous in their demarcation of the [alpine defense] zone and in their interpretation of its significance." These sources reported the construction of large underground shelters and factories and "the incessant influx of stores and equipment of all kinds," designed "to ensure that the *Gebirgstellungen* will be capable of holding out as the last stronghold of Nazi GERMANY." These sources agreed that the so-called national redoubt represented the regime's last hope; it was where the Nazis intended to hole up in anticipation of the day they could "emerge from their fortress to recapture GERMANY."[47] Negating the national redoubt assumed a greater significance than securing the north German ports, sealing the Baltic corridor, and liberating the Netherlands. Rather than serving as the main avenue for an advance on Berlin, even before he launched Plunder, Montgomery's sector had already slipped from first to last on the American list of strategic priorities.

With the Soviets on the Oder and only the Remagen bridgehead then in Allied hands, any discussion of racing the Russians to Berlin seemed pointless. The Russians bore the brunt of the fighting with the Germans, and without Soviet sacrifices, the war could not have entered its final phase. Even in the extremely unlikely event the Allies beat the Russians into Berlin, they would have to surrender their gains except for the sectors assigned to the Western Allies in the city. In addition, there would be a whirlwind of political repercussions from robbing Stalin and the Red Army of their deserved honor of taking the Nazi capital. Preserving Allied-Soviet cooperation remained a pillar of Roosevelt's postwar policy. The broad-front strategy—crushing the German armed forces, occupying the whole of the Reich, eliminating the national redoubt, all in combination with the Soviets—would strangle in the cradle any future "stab in the back" theory. It was the perfect complement to Roosevelt's stated policies. Not advancing on Berlin appeared to be another "open and shut case."[48]

After his talks with Bradley and Smith, Eisenhower approved Operation Voyage on 21 March, initiating the expansion of the southern pincer. The directive went to Devers, Bradley, and Brereton (but pointedly not to Montgomery) and read as follows: "distribution of this message will be limited to the absolute minimum," to the addressee or his authorized representative.[49] The directive also instructed Patch to execute a crossing (Undertone). Eisenhower's decision changed the whole trajectory of the campaign in Germany.

On 23 March Eisenhower traveled to Rheinburg and, together with Churchill, Brooke, and Bradley, watched Montgomery's set-piece crossings—in Brooke's estimate, "what we clearly saw as the end of the Hitler regime." Eisenhower and Bradley discussed the southern thrust with Brooke and Montgomery. Eisenhower "wanted to know whether I agreed with his present plans of pushing in the south for Frankfurt and Kassel," Brooke recorded. "I told him that with the Germans crumbling as they are the whole situation is changed. . . . Evidently the Boche is cracking and what we want now is to push him relentlessly wherever we can until he crumbles." He admitted that Eisenhower now possessed the strength for the double envelopment but never conceded, as Eisenhower claimed, "Thank God, Ike, you stuck by your plan [for the broad front]. You were completely right."[50] Overjoyed with the success of Plunder, neither Brooke nor Montgomery showed any apprehension that the southern offensive implied a fundamental shift in operational priorities, and Eisenhower and Bradley scrupulously avoided any mention of plans for after the sealing of the Ruhr. In the meantime, Smith went back to Reims to prepare the groundwork for a shift in emphasis to Bradley's front. Logistical timetables and plans for reinforcements and resupply of Bradley's corps were redrawn, including major-ticket items such as reorienting priority on rail lines and extensive preparations for bridging. Much of this work was already in place. As early as 7 February Smith had asked Lee to begin planning and preparations to support an advance up the Frankfurt-Giessen-Kassel axis.[51]

By 25 March Montgomery's bridgehead drove a twenty-five-mile wedge along the Rhine from north of Rees south to Rheinberg, and as much as fifteen miles deep. At the same time, First Army initiated its drive from the Remagen salient between the Sieg and Lahn rivers, and Patton's VIII Corps seized crossings at Boppard and St. Goar south of the Lahn. In the meantime, Patton secured two crossings of the Main east of Frankfurt near Hanau and Aschaffenburg. Both forces staged a race toward Giessen.

The British field marshals still denigrated Eisenhower's strategic competence, but they again witnessed his prowess as a politician. Eisenhower held a press conference in Paris on 27 March. He announced, "I would say the German as a military force on the Western Front . . . is a whipped enemy." Steve Early, who had observed Eisenhower's last press conference in late February, considered him a master dissembler. "Sometimes," Early commented, "he uses a great many words to say nothing at all."[52] Eisenhower's performance at the Scribe on 27 March equaled his best. He avoided any mention of Berlin in his ad-libbed remarks, but when the question arose, he skillfully dampened any idea of a quick advance on the German capital. "I'm not saying that any force, with the maintenance facilities we have now and the obstacles we have to cover, can rush right to Berlin. I don't say that for a minute and I don't want you people by any manner or means to report me as coming here and exalting and over optimistic and ready to start waving flags and ringing bells." When pressed, he conceded that "mileage alone" meant the Russians would take the city. Even though he had told Butcher the day before he thought "there will be long guerrilla warfare after the German armies are beaten," when answering questions on the national redoubt, Eisenhower appeared dismissive. He doubted the Germans could pull their forces from Italy. "Our troops," he assured the press, "will be on their heels so fast they won't know what happened to them. We have a big air force down there too." Eisenhower thought the German armed forces had "no intention of going off like a covey of quail." He said, "If you are of the school who believed they are going to defend the south of Germany"—and he gave the indication he was not—"I would expect them to fight delaying actions in the South."[53]

The next day he put his plan into operation. First, he launched a preemptive strike. Through the American military mission in Moscow—headed by Smith's replacement as SGS, now MG John Deane—Eisenhower dispatched a message to Stalin. As he explained to Deane, "Our operations are now coming to a stage in which it is essential that I should know the Russians' plans in order to achieve the most rapid success." The letter outlined Eisenhower's intentions to encircle and destroy German forces defending the Ruhr and then revealed that the best axis for "joining hands with your forces" would be on an Erfurt-Leipzig-Dresden line. "It is along this axis that I propose to place my main effort." He also alerted Stalin that he planned on a secondary advance in the direction of Regensburg-Linz, "thereby preventing the consolidation of the German resistance in a redoubt in southern Germany." Copies went to the CCS and BCOS. The same day he dropped a bombshell on Montgomery. "As soon as you have joined hands with Bradley in this Kassel-Paderborn area," he explained, Ninth Army "will revert to Bradley's command." Bradley, with Ninth and Fifteenth Armies under his command, "will be responsible for mopping up and occupying the Ruhr and with the minimum delay will deliver his main thrust" on the axis indicated to Stalin. In the cruelest cut of all, Montgomery's mission "will be to protect Bradley's northern flank."[54]

The day before, a buoyant Montgomery had mentioned a hard drive by Ninth and Second Armies to the Elbe; he had informed SHAEF of the intended movement of his tactical headquarters from Wesel to Münster to Hannover, "thence via the Autobahn to BERLIN I hope."[55] Now, there would be no drive across to the Elbe and on to Berlin; instead,

Twenty-first Army Group would move south and east and complete the encirclement of the Ruhr. Then Ninth and First Armies would invest and remove the Ruhr Pocket. Without Ninth Army, Montgomery lacked the strength for an advance toward the Elbe, much less beyond the river. Nor would he possess enough forces to accomplish his ancillary missions, except to contain Blaskowitz's Army Group H north of Montgomery's penetration. As a dejected Montgomery related to Simpson in the War Office, "I received the blow from IKE in which he disagrees with my plan and removes Ninth Army from me; a very good counter-attack!! A very dirty work, I fear."[56] Montgomery faithfully played his role in undermining the Alexander intrigue, and he guessed correctly that Eisenhower and Bradley had already made up their minds when they met with him on 23 March, but they dared not reveal their skullduggery until Churchill and Brooke returned to London. With good reason, the field marshal felt betrayed.

Eisenhower's assessment of the German situation proved accurate. The German high command was "dead sure" the Allies possessed two objectives: isolate the Ruhr and cut Germany in the middle from the Palatinate through Thuringia. In the event the Allies crossed the Rhine north or south of the Ruhr, plans existed for pulling in the flanks and defending along the Dortmund-Ems Canal in the north or in the Main-Frankenwald area in the south. Rundstedt and Kesselring never expected a large-scale envelopment of the Ruhr. Hodges and Patton tore huge gaps of more than sixty miles in the German defenses. Jodl thought the movement from the Frankfurt-Giessen-Marburg penetration northward "strikingly daring" and "faultlessly executed operations taken at a big risk." He admitted, "We were surprised by this rapid breakthrough and had nothing with which to stop it." Jodl said, "From this time we could no longer talk of a general conduct of the war. We had no reserves and could exert no control over the situation." But Kesselring tried. He admitted the American leadership "was bold and made rapid and daring advances. But in other conditions such advances would have been foolhardy. If your enemy had an effective air force and normal anti-tank defenses," he told postwar interviewers, "an energetic counter stroke would have been disastrous to you." But that was precisely the point: the Germans possessed neither. Kesselring attempted to shorten the gaps by continually throwing forces into them while building reserves to hit the flanks of advancing armored units before their infantry could come up. Model, in command of Army Group B defending the Ruhr, improvised a defensive line along the Sieg River. The Americans, seeking space for maneuver, advanced parallel to the Sieg barrier. Kesselring ordered the Ruhr stripped of mobile units for an attack on the Sieg front. His instructions were not executed in time, mostly because of Allied airpower. Because of the speed of the American penetration, the question now revolved around whether Army Group B could break out of the encirclement. Model attacked too soon, too far east, and with only a meager division and a half. The heavy American columns easily stopped it. "Once the opportunity was missed," Kesselring concluded, "there was no way to execute the breakout." In the north, Kesselring called for a counterattack toward Münster to blunt Montgomery's thrust, but when Simpson's forces cut the Dortmund-Ems Canal, it sealed the fate of the Germans in the Ruhr. Blaskowitz pulled his forces north and east to defend the Weser line. Hitler declared the *Rurhgebeit* and Sauerland a "fortress" under Model's command, with instructions that he make no breakout attempt. On 1 April units of Ninth and First Armies joined at Lippstadt, closing the Ruhr pocket. As Smith pointed out, Allied strategic and tactical air forces had accomplished that long before the ground forces achieved their union.[57]

Nory received word of Beetle's confinement to bed. Through the War Department, she said, "Can't stop worrying." But Smith assured her on 2 April, "I am entirely recovered."[58] With his batteries recharged, he anticipated playing an important role in the war's dramatic final act, and he could not have been displeased that Americans now called the shots.

★ **36** ★

Mission Fulfilled

In early January Churchill, in one of his ebullient moods as the emergency in the Ardennes abated, wrote to Roosevelt claiming that 1944 "yielded us results beyond the dreams of military avarice." He spoke of his "complete confidence in General Eisenhower" and of the amity binding the supreme commander with Montgomery "and also Bradley and Patton." He felt animated by "an intense new impulse, both of friendship and exertion, to be drawn from our bosoms and to the last scrap of our resources."[1]

This effusion of sentiment was motivated not by the glowing prospects of victory in 1945 but by the dread that triumph would leave him marginalized. The British expended their last scrap of resources for the coming campaign. Prompted by the Bulge crisis, the British government had called up an additional quarter million men, slashing deeply into Britain's remaining industrial manpower and putting at risk well-laid plans for postwar recovery.[2] Three months later, after failing to reverse Eisenhower's decision to abandon the drive on Berlin, he ended another letter to the president with the Latin phrase *Anantium irea amoris integration est*–"Lovers' quarrels are a part of love"—but love did not fill his bosom. Eisenhower's decision ended one destiny and inaugurated a second. It marked the passing of one global power and the rise of another. The bitter irony could not have been lost on Churchill. His great forebear Marlborough's military genius had catapulted Britain into the ranks of the great powers, and despite the dint of all his efforts, another Churchill presided over a victory that led to the dissolution of the British Empire.

Berlin versus the Redoubt

SHAEF did not have long to wait for Churchill's rejoinder. As expected, Churchill and Montgomery reacted sharply to Eisenhower's decision to deflect the main thrust from the north. Immediately upon learning of SHAEF's 29 March revised orders to Montgomery, the prime minister got on the phone and registered his complaints to Eisenhower. Montgomery wrote a pleading note to Eisenhower: "I pray you not [withdraw Ninth Army from his command] until we reach the Elbe." Promising Whitehall he would not get directly involved, Montgomery again asked de Guingand to work through Smith for a revision. Montgomery suggested that Fifteenth Army complete the investment of the Ruhr, allowing Montgomery and Bradley's army groups, as presently constituted, "to race on while the Germans were in disarray"—Montgomery toward Berlin, and Bradley toward Saxony. According to Montgomery, Smith agreed with Montgomery's alternative plan and promised to present it in a conference scheduled for the morning of 2 April.[3] Smith, Bull, and Strong weighed the military merits of Montgomery's argument, but in the end they rejected his scheme. After the meeting, SHAEF issued orders for the command shift of Ninth Army, effective at midnight on 3 April.[4]

The prime minister made an impassioned appeal, asking that Eisenhower reconsider the command shift of Simpson's army. Without an attached American army, the British would not possess the strength to carry out any offensive action of significance, resulting, in Churchill's words, in "the relegation of His Majesty's Forces to an unexpected restricted sphere." Eisenhower's decision to turn Simpson and Hodges eastward to eliminate the Ruhr meant a delay in driving in force for the Elbe. "If the enemy's resistance should weaken, as you evidently expect," Churchill wondered, "why should we not cross the Elbe and advance as far eastward as possible? This has an important political bearing." If the Soviets took both Berlin and Vienna, "will not their impression that they have been the overwhelming contributor to our common victory be unduly imprinted in their minds, and may this not lead them into a mood which will raise grave and formidable difficulties in the future." The prime minister disagreed that Berlin had lost its military significance. "Whilst Berlin remains under the German flag," he argued, "it cannot in my opinion fail to be the most decisive point."[5]

Eisenhower never conceded that he had altered his basic strategy. As he pointed out to Churchill, the strategy in Europe unfolded precisely as mapped out in May 1944.[6] He made his case to Marshall: "The Prime Minister and his Chiefs of Staff opposed 'ANVIL'; they opposed my idea that the German should be destroyed west of the Rhine." By launching "one main attack calculated to accomplish, in conjunction with the Russians, the destruction of the enemy armed forces," he was "merely following the principle that Field Marshal Brooke has always shouted at me."[7]

Eisenhower easily warded off British objections because the American chiefs stoutly defended his decision to shift the main axis of advance away from Berlin and his right to communicate directly with the Soviets. "The battle of Germany is now at the point," read the CCS memorandum, "where the commander in the field is the best judge of the measures which offer the earliest prospect of destroying the German armies or their power to resist."[8] The president, his health slipping badly, sanctioned what amounted to Eisenhower's carte blanche to stage-manage the completion of the war in Europe.

Eisenhower's letter to Stalin arrived in Moscow just as the American leadership's attitude—if not policies—toward the Soviets showed signs of hardening. In late March the Soviets had signaled their suspicions that the Western democracies sought a separate accommodation with the Germans. Their proof derived from intelligence reports indicating that elements of the German command in Italy had approached AFHQ through Switzerland, seeking a separate surrender. The president assured Stalin there was no effort to conduct negotiations that excluded the Soviets, and any German capitulation would simply constitute a "military" surrender. "It would be completely unreasonable for me to take any other attitude or to permit any delay which must cause additional and avoidable loss of life in the American Forces. You as a military man will understand the necessity for prompt action to avoid losing an opportunity. It is in the same category as would be the sending of a flag of truce to your general at Koenigsberg or Danzig."[9]

Stalin remained unconvinced. He believed these negotiations would provide an opportunity for the Germans to shift forces from Italy to the Eastern Front. He reported three German divisions in the process of doing just that. "This circumstance is irritating the Soviet Command," Stalin posited, "and creates grounds for distrust." He took exception to Roosevelt's use of the examples of Königsberg and Danzig, where Soviet forces had surrounded the Germans. "An entirely different situation is that of the German troops in Northern Italy. They are not surrounded and they do not face annihilation."[10]

Eisenhower's letter appeared out of the blue and threw Stalin into a rage. Stalin met with Marshals Georgi Zhukov and Ivan Konev, two of the three front commanders designated to complete the defeat of Germany. Berlin had lost none of its significance in Stalin's eyes—just the opposite. Stalin read into Eisenhower's letter another Western conspiracy to win the war against their capitalist rival Germany by expending

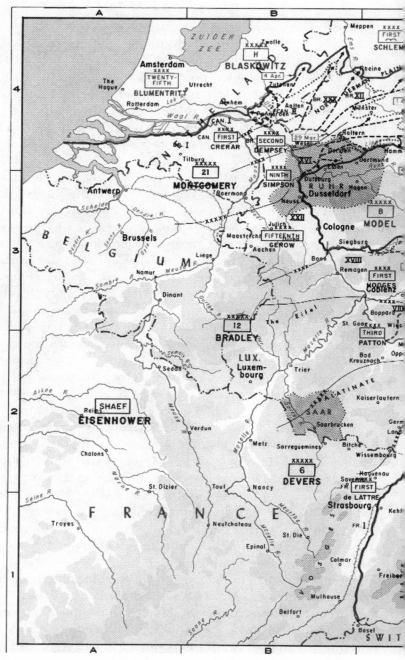

Germany: The Ruhr Pocket and the Push to the Elbe

GERMANY, 1944
ENCIRCLEMENT OF THE RUHR

Operations, 29 March – 4 April 1945

ELEVATIONS IN METERS
200   400   800   OVER

SCALE OF MILES

as much Soviet blood and resources as possible. Why did Eisenhower drive on Dresden—as far east as Berlin and also in the designated Soviet zone of occupation—but not the German capital? On 31 March Stalin ordered a redeployment of the First and Second Belorussian Fronts under Zhukov for a massive frontal drive on Berlin and beyond. Marshal K. K. Rokossovsky and Konev would advance to the Elbe on either flank of Zhukov. Stalin ordered his marshals to unleash their offensives as soon as circumstances allowed. In early February, when Stalin had closed down the drive into Germany along the Oder-Neisse line—a political decision growing out of the Yalta disagreement over the eastern boundary of Poland—SHAEF's forces remained stalled in the Eifel. By 1 April the relative positions of Western and Soviet forces had changed dramatically. American forces had completed their encirclement of the Ruhr, while Soviet forces had halted on the Oder. In many respects, the Germans occupied a stronger position in the east than two months previously. Hitler pulled units from the west and Italy, reinforcing Army Group Vistula on the Oder and Army Group A on the Neisse and Czech border. Stalin unleashed a withering attack in *Pravda* on the Western powers' war aims as a precursor to an explosive letter to Roosevelt claiming that he possessed solid proof the American and British governments had entered into a secret accord with the Germans. In exchange for easier armistice terms, the Germans would cease fighting in the west and harden resistance against Soviet forces.

On 31 March Roosevelt pointed to the existence of "an atmosphere of regrettable apprehension and mistrust." He assured Stalin, "This entire episode [of German peace feelers through Switzerland] has arisen through the initiative of a German officer reputed to be close to Himmler," and there "is a strong possibility that his sole purpose is to create suspicion and distrust between the Allies. There is no reason why we should permit him to succeed in that aim."[11]

The next day Stalin made his reply to Eisenhower. He could not have appeared more accommodating. The Soviet strongman stated that Eisenhower's scheme for a union in the Erfurt-Leipzig-Dresden area "entirely coincides with the plan of the Soviet High Command" and agreed that "Berlin has lost its former strategic importance." Stalin expected his main drive into Saxony would commence sometime in the middle of May. The Red Army planned two secondary offensives: one toward Berlin, and another to link with American forces in the area of Vienna-Linz-Regensburg.[12] Not a word in the message was true, but Stalin's wire removed any lingering doubt in Eisenhower's mind on the correctness of his strategy for ending the war. Stalin was prepared to stake everything on winning the race to Berlin—a contest Eisenhower had already conceded.

Stalin then unleashed another bolt from the blue. Insisting that secret negotiations had taken place in Bern, Stalin claimed that Roosevelt must not be fully informed. "As regards my military colleagues, they, on the basis of data which they have on hand, do not have any doubts, that the negotiations have taken place and that they have ended in an agreement with the Germans, on the basis of which the German commander on the Western Front—Marshal Kesselring—has agreed to open the front and permit the Anglo-American troops to advance to the East, and the Anglo-Americans have promised in return to ease for the Germans the peace terms." For that reason, no Soviet official had been permitted to participate in the negotiations. "As a result of this at the present moment the Germans on the Western Front in fact have ceased the war against England and the United States. At the same time the Germans continue the war with Russia, the Ally of England and the United States." Stalin concluded by saying, "such a situation can in no way serve the cause of preservation of the strengthening of trust between our countries."[13]

Roosevelt replied in kind. "I have received with astonishment your message of April 3," he began. He then restated his "complete confidence in General Eisenhower and know that he certainly would inform me before entering into any agreement with the Germans." Eisenhower's instructions remained the same: "demand unconditional surrender of enemy troops that may be defeated on his front." Roosevelt explained that American success rested mainly on "the terrific impact of our air power resulting in destruction of German communications, and to the fact that Eisenhower was able to cripple the bulk of the German Forces on the Western Front while they were still West of the Rhine." He expressed his amazement that "a belief seems to have reached the Soviet Government that I have entered into an agreement with the enemy without first obtaining your full agreement. Finally I would say this, it would be one of the great tragedies of history if at the very moment of the victory, now within our grasp, such distrust, such lack of faith, should prejudice the entire undertaking after the colossal losses of life, materiel and treasure involved. . . . Frankly," he concluded, "I cannot avoid a feeling of bitter resentment toward your informers, whoever they are, for such vile misrepresentations of my actions or those of my trusted subordinates."[14]

Harriman reported from Moscow: "Russian suspicions, never hard to arouse in the best of circumstances, have now been fanned by reports in our press and radio of lack of German resistance in the west." The Russians concluded the Germans were offering only token resistance to Western advances and suspected they did so either pursuant to some tacit understanding with SHAEF or in the hope of obtaining some assurance of mild treatment from the Allies. Conversely, German resistance in the east would deprive the Red Army "of the glory of being the first to reach the vital centers of Germany, at a time when the forces of the western Allies are winning sensational and—in the Russian view—cheap victories."[15] The State Department asked Harriman's opinion on the state of U.S.-Soviet relations. The U.S. ambassador responded by saying that for many months, Moscow had pursued three foreign policy lines: preserving the appearance of cooperating with the West in the formation of a "World Security Organization," forming buffer states on the Soviet borders, and spreading international communism.[16] None of this augured well for the inaugural United Nations conference, set to open in San Francisco on 23 April.

Churchill wisely remained out of the fray—something that only deepened Stalin's suspicions. On 5 April he weighed in at last. "I am astounded that Stalin should have addressed to you a message so insulting to the honour of the United States and also of Great Britain," he declared. He observed that the Soviet leadership must be "surprised and disconcerted" at the Anglo-American success in inflicting "the almost total defeat of the enemy," especially since they could not "deliver a decisive attack before the middle of May." He continued, "All this makes it the more important that we should join hands with the Russian armies as far to the east as possible and if circumstances allow, enter Berlin." The Red Army had taken Vienna that day. Since the Soviets would likely occupy the whole of Austria, ignoring provisional zones of occupation, Churchill saw no reason why the Western Allies should remain bound by the Yalta accords. The prime minister warned, "the brutality of the Russian messages" foreshadowed "some deep change of policy." He deemed "it of the highest importance that a firm and blunt stand should be made at this juncture by our two countries" as "the best chance of saving the future. If they are ever convinced that we are afraid of them and can be bullied into submission, then indeed I should despair of our future relations with them and much else."[17]

The "Man of Steel" did not back down; instead, he went on the diplomatic offensive. Stalin found it hard "to agree that lack of resistance on the part of the Germans on the Western front can be explained only [by the fact] that they are defeated." The Germans fielded 147 divisions in the east. They "could without harm to their cause take from the Eastern Front 15–20 divisions and shift them to the aid of their troops on the Western Front. However, the Germans did not do it and are not doing it." German forces continued fighting savagely "for some unknown junction . . . in Czechoslovakia which they need as much as a dead man needs poultices, but surrender without any resistance such important towns in Central Germany as Osnabruck, Mannheim, Kassel." Stalin observed "that such a behavior of the Germans is more than strange and incomprehensible." As for the credibility of his intelligence, he pointed to errors made by American sources of information. In February Marshall had informed the Soviet general staff of pending German offensives from Pomerania and Silesia. Instead, the Germans withdrew forces from the west and attacked in Hungary, raising serious doubts about American sincerity and intentions.[18]

In combination with Churchill's letters to Roosevelt, the BCOS stepped up pressure for a revision of SHAEF's strategy. The Soviets were not alone in smelling a rat. Although disappointed the British had received "very much less" in the apportioning of manpower, materiel, and missions than they "first supposed," Churchill considered the issue closed. In sharp contrast to extant American-Soviet relations, he categorized his disagreement with Eisenhower as a "lovers' quarrel." Still, he told Roosevelt, "It was a pity that Eisenhower's telegram was sent to Stalin without anything being said to our Chiefs of Staff or to our deputy, Air Chief Marshal Tedder, or to our Commander-in-Chief, Field Marshal Montgomery." But as indicated in his 4 April letter to Roosevelt, the British were not done. The BCOS asserted the CCS's right to offer guidance on two points: in view of Stalin's mid-May timetable, SHAEF should maintain "momentum in the north, with a view to the capture of Berlin," and it should establish future procedures for "presenting to the Russians matters of high military policy."[19]

The American chiefs again blunted British attempts to redirect operations toward Berlin or muzzle Eisenhower. Just as on 30 March, the JCS voiced their strong opposition to fettering Eisenhower's freedom of action. Some influential voices in the War Department questioned the wisdom of reducing the Ruhr pocket. On 6 April Stimson met with the WDGS operations and intelligence heads and brought up the "problem of the Ruhr." MG Clayton Bissell, assistant G-2, asked, "Should we clean the pocket up now or should we bypass it and let it starve into submission, using the rest of our troops to conquer the rest of Germany?" By then, three American armies had committed four and a half corps to eliminating the Ruhr. Since Hitler had ordered the formation of the Ruhr fortress, Model could not break out, even if he had the means. The 317,000 German troops eventually captured in the pocket constituted no real threat to American forces or their lines of communication. Stimson considered it "a vital big question which lies before Eisenhower today and one in which Marshall apparently felt and I felt it was a case where we should at least discuss it with him." The reduction of the Ruhr held enormous political and economic ramifications for the recovery not only of Germany but also of western Europe. As Stimson noted, "If we bypass it, simply containing it, and finish up with the rest of Germany, it will take time; the Ruhr will ultimately fall in our hands but we may endanger quick success in the rest of Germany by the absence of the troops which we will be obliged to leave around the perimeter of the Ruhr."[20]

Eisenhower had already made up his mind, but Marshall offered him an out. "As yet I have no views whatsoever in this matter," he told Eisenhower, "except that I think the fat is probably now in the fire and whatever the political consequences it is too late, too impracticable to take any action for such reason." Eisenhower robustly defended his decision on the Ruhr. "I repeat . . . I cannot afford to have the German forces remain in that area in their present strength. . . . The attacks will proceed to the point where it is cheaper to contain rather than destroy."[21]

By 7 April the broad-front advance of nine Allied corps had moved forward halfway to the Elbe, to the line of the Weser and Werra rivers, against sporadic resistance. The Ninth, First, and Third Armies narrowed their axes of advance, simplifying logistics, while the British Second Army and Sixth Army Group fanned out, gobbling up territory. Patton's forces entered Erfurt on 10 April; one corps pushed through Thuringia to the Mulde River, while two others advanced into upper Bavaria. Two days later elements of Simpson's army closed to the Elbe between Wittenberge and Magdeburg. On 16 April the strategic air forces declared the air war over; they no longer had any meaningful targets. Two days after that, First Army controlled Leipzig. By that time, elements of all three armies stood deep inside the Soviet zone. In the meantime, Model committed suicide—the third German field marshal who commanded in the west to do so—and resistance collapsed in the Ruhr. All except the seizure of Leipzig transpired before the Soviets unleashed the torrent of their offensive on 16 April. Simpson sent reconnaissance units across the Elbe as early as 12 April and asked permission to drive the fifty miles to Berlin. In his estimate, he possessed all the strength necessary and required only permission from SHAEF. Eisenhower refused to give Simpson the green light.[22]

Starting with Remagen, or really since the launching of Veritable, SHAEF exerted little direct influence on operations. Mostly the G-2 and G-3 staffs spent their time tallying the number of German POWs and updating the giant maps festooning the walls of the War Room at SHAEF. Military operations moved so quickly that divisional commanders often could not locate their own units.[23] This is not to suggest that headquarters went into cruise mode. SHAEF rushed to consolidate civil affairs and political policies for the occupation, a task greatly complicated by the still undecided zonal boundaries. Far more daunting, SHAEF confronted a humanitarian crisis of huge proportions. Given the dire predictions of an impending global food shortage, Western agencies prepared for Europe-wide relief operations, most pressing in the western Netherlands and Germany. With cities in ruins, the infrastructure wrecked, and the German state apparatus in disarray, SHAEF, in combination with the United Nations Relief and Rehabilitation Administration, confronted the herculean task of feeding a German population swollen by 7 million foreign workers, 4 million POWs, 714,000 forced labor and concentration camp inmates, and unknown numbers of German nationals and ethnic Germans who had fled from the Russian advance. On the American side, the War Department pressed ETO to expedite planning for the redeployment of forces to the Pacific. The manpower crisis solved itself, mostly by addition through subtraction. The capture of millions of German POWs translated into a surfeit of American troops in Europe. Smith delegated much of the responsibility for civil affairs to Morgan and for redeployment to Lear, but he still handled coordination with Washington.

Like everyone else, Smith shared the euphoria of the pending victory and used every excuse to escape Reims and go forward. One excuse involved an episode that created quite a flutter. Patton's XII Corps uncovered a horde of Nazi treasure—everything from gold bullion and priceless art to looted silver plate and gold fillings extracted from victims of the "final solution"—secreted in a salt mine at Merkers, near Erfurt. Patton placed a news blackout on the story, but the SHAEF censors missed it. When the story broke, it created a sensation. Questions naturally arose over what to do with it. For one thing, the mine was located in the Soviet sector. Eisenhower decided to move the cache deep into the American zone. After Eisenhower and Bradley viewed the trove, they joked about its disposition. Bradley observed that if they lived in the days of the freebooters, Patton would be among the wealthiest men in the United States. Patton had two suggestions: make medallions "for every son of a bitch in the Third Army," or bury it until the inevitable postwar budget cuts hit, then dig it up and buy new weapons. Smith liked Patton's first idea. He inspected the horde in the company of McSherry, his civil affairs chief. Viewing the 711 bags of U.S. $20 gold pieces, Smith noted they would make perfect souvenirs. "In fact," he added, "we'll give one to McSherry." He even offered to sign a letter of receipt. McSherry thought Smith was pulling his leg but soon discovered otherwise. "You don't trust me, McSherry," he roared, "and I've got to have men around who trust me." Refusing to be pacified, Smith angrily marched off. Still miffed, he told Murphy he "saw no reason why some quiet arrangement could not be worked out to provide bonuses for selected senior officers."[24] Smith's actions left plenty of people scratching their heads.

With journalists clamoring for explanations of why American forces never advanced on Berlin, Butcher asked Eisenhower if he would consent to a press conference. His answer was an emphatic no. When Butcher asked if Smith could do it, Eisenhower readily agreed. As was always the case, in the absence of hard copy, the press invented it, and all too often, their speculations proved too close to the truth for comfort. The American and British publics could not understand why Eisenhower had abandoned the race to Berlin. As a symbol of Prussian militarism and the seat of Nazi power, Berlin occupied a singular place in the popular mind. Elements of Ninth Army had stood on the Elbe, sixty-five miles from the Brandenburg Gate, since 12 April. The Soviet drive on Berlin ran into furious opposition; after three days of making no progress, Rokossovsky and Konev diverted the bulk of their forces in support of Zhukov in a bid to encircle the city. An opportunity still beckoned for Simpson to drive on the German capital, but Eisenhower was no opportunist. He issued a new directive on 15 April. "Present bridgeheads over the Elbe will be secured," it announced, "but offensive operations beyond the Elbe will be undertaken only on later orders." As he explained to Marshall, Eisenhower deemed sealing the Baltic approaches and the "so-called 'Redoubt'" as "vastly more important than the capture of Berlin."[25]

In many ways, the military situation in Germany in mid-April resembled the picture Stalin had drawn at the beginning of the month. To be sure, SHAEF engaged in no secret diplomacy with the Germans. Nonetheless, while the Soviets expended a sea of blood assaulting the "political" objective of Berlin, large portions of Ninth and First Armies spent their time processing the masses of German troops flooding into their lines to surrender. The day of Smith's press conference, 21 April, Red Army troops closed to the outer defenses of Berlin, while Eisenhower informed the Soviets he had ordered a halt along the Elbe-Mulde line.

Smith set himself two objectives in the press conference. First, he wanted to make the case that, under Eisenhower's inspired leadership, the Allies stood on the verge of winning one of the greatest campaigns in history. Second, Smith needed to rationalize SHAEF's thinking behind diverting American strength south to deal with the national redoubt. He stated, "Of all the campaigns I have ever known this one [referring to the one to destroy the Germans west of the Rhine] has followed most exactly the pattern of the commander who planned it." With the lone exception of Cologne—where SHAEF expected a stouter defense—the Rhineland campaign "proceeded exactly as General Eisenhower planned it." Smith even claimed that Eisenhower, not Patton, had authored the drive into the Palatinate and the Rhine crossing at Oppenheim. As for the Ruhr Pocket, Smith said, "We have studied the double envelopment from Cannae down through Tannenberg, but never have [we] seen anything like this before." While advancing to the Elbe against "very little opposition . . . it became increasing apparent to us . . . that Berlin, the second heart of Germany, had ceased to have much military significance." Based on reports from neutral sources—actually, through Ultra—SHAEF had concluded that Berlin was no longer the center of German government.

Then Smith went "off the record" in discussing Eisenhower's thinking behind redirecting Patton's and Devers's forces to the south. "This so-called 'national redoubt' is something we don't know an awful lot about," he admitted. Smith said the only remaining German strength lay in the south. He reminded the journalists of the recently uncovered underground facilities around Schweinfurt, "where we have been just bombing the hell out of the ball bearing plants . . . and finding eighty-five percent [of the tools and machinery] were underground, beautifully underground." He said, "One thing to remember—as long as Hitler or any of his representatives are standing on a rock around Salzburg, proclaiming to all isolated fortress areas holding out that everything is going to come out all right, they are going to hold out." Smith acknowledged the redoubt represented "our target now, if we are going to bring this war to an end in a hell of a hurry. . . . Its capture would bring about the end of the war." He stated flatly, "We don't care who fights their way into Berlin," and the "same thing was true in Vienna." Smith continued, "From a purely military standpoint," the ancient capitals of central Europe held little significance, "not anything comparable to that of the so-called national redoubt."

"I am vulnerable," he joked to the reporters, so "fire away" with questions. The press did. In response to a query whether SHAEF had entered into any deals with the Russians, Smith said the only agreement involved linking with the Red Army in the Leipzig-Dresden area. Again deflecting attention from Berlin, he stated, "At the moment we have other more important things to do. There isn't any place along this front that we are going to try to rush to at the cost of lives and material in order to get there before the Russians do, unless our masters tell us differently."

With Roosevelt dead and the novice former captain of artillery Harry Truman at the helm, there was no likelihood of the masters intervening. "We are handling it as a strictly military campaign." According to Smith, intelligence estimated "possibly 100 to 125" divisions might move into the Alpine districts.[26] One writer inquired into the difficulty of reducing the redoubt. Smith stated the operation should require about "a month's fighting and then guerilla warfare for an indeterminate time. That's not to be quoted. I don't know. That is only a guess." Responding to the next question, he said Hitler was probably at Berchtesgaden, but there was no definite information on the location of the German leader.[27]

Butcher, who knew about such matters, thought Smith "did a bang-up job . . . damned near as good as Ike." The question remains, did Smith actually buy the chimera of the national redoubt? Or was the press conference a rather transparent attempt to dampen expectations about Berlin? The answer to both is probably yes. Just as the skilled fisherman expected, the press took the bait. The *Daily Telegraph* and *Times* warned readers that, in Smith's opinion, the link-up with the Russians would not end hostilities, and it would be a "terrible mistake to announce the end of the war" because "a bitter struggle [lay] ahead in the mountains of the German national 'redoubt.'" Charles Collingwood of CBS quoted Smith as saying, "When we have cut the head from the snake"—killed or captured Hitler and his henchmen—"the tail won't wiggle very long." He also told his listeners, "There is no question but that it is going to take some time to clear them out." The British press simply restated Smith's précis on the conduct of the campaign, but Collingwood made the point that "General Eisenhower is generally thought of as a kind of managing director, a smoother-out of quarrels, but he has not had the credit he deserves as a great strategist." The most inflammatory story came from a journalist named Kingsmith, who reported, "It was estimated some weeks ago that Hitler might be able to mass as many as 200,000 fanatical die-hard troops in the mountain fastness of the Bavarian Tyrol." Judging from the press coverage, Smith masterfully succeeded in sidetracking the whole issue of Berlin.[28]

The saga of the national redoubt had as many plot twists as the spy novels Smith loved to read. And in the end, it amounted to Germany's most successful deception plan, although it accomplished nothing in terms of lengthening the war. It had its origins in the fervent imagination of the amateur spymaster Allen Dulles, the OSS chief in Bern. In September 1944 the OKW established an engineering team in the Tyrol that conducted a ground survey near the border with Switzerland and Liechtenstein. The OSS construed this preliminary work as evidence of German intentions to create a mountain *festung* in the Alps.[29] Thereafter, the story took on a life of its own. The gauleiter for Tyrol-Vorarlberg, Franz Hofer, proposed forming a defensive network, but Hitler dismissed any talk of a withdrawal into the Alps as defeatist. Perhaps not coincidentally, Hofer bore the name of the famous Tyrolean innkeeper-turned-patriot Andreas Hofer, who led a heroic rebellion against France and Bavaria in 1809. The Innsbruck *Sicherheitsdienst* (SD) unit, the intelligence and surveillance organization within the SS, happily fed Dulles plenty of misinformation, including fake blueprints and reports on the construction of underground facilities for supplies and armament production and the transfer of SS units into the redoubt area. Typical of Dulles and the OSS, the story leaked. On 12 November 1944 a feature appeared in the *New York Times Magazine* describing the national redoubt—a term coined by Dulles—as the "Reich's most heavily fortified and closely guarded areas."[30] Josef Goebbels, minister for propaganda, immediately recognized the value of fostering the myth and created a special unit that spun rumors about an *Alpenfestung.* After the Ardennes disaster, Hitler endorsed the idea of a national redoubt—with the fantasy of Andreas Hofer dancing in his head—but he never devoted any resources to the scheme. A detailed article that appeared in *Collier's* in late January 1945 accurately mirrored SHAEF's assessments. Entitled "Hitler's Final V Weapon," the piece pointed to the formation of a Nazi headquarters for sustained guerrilla warfare in the Austrian Alps. "These stories are undoubtedly intended to intimidate the Allies," Erwin Lessner concluded, but "they cannot be lightly dismissed as just another of Goebbels' inventions . . . all signs indicate that the Germans are preparing for intensive guerrilla warfare."[31] The formation of *Die Werwölfe,* a putative Nazi guerrilla organization, in February 1945, led by Ernst Kaltenbrunner, the Austrian head of the dreaded *Reichssicherheitshauptamt,* the Nazi umbrella security structure, lent greater credibility to the theory that the Germans planned to mount organized resistance after the collapse of their armed forces. A spokesperson for the German Foreign Office stated, "Millions of us will wage guerrilla warfare; every German before he dies will try to take five or ten enemies with him to the grave. . . . Millions of Germans will pay back murder with murder."[32] There was just enough substance to the disinformation campaign to give it plausibility. As Bradley later noted, the redoubt "grew into so exaggerated a scheme that I am astonished we could have believed it as innocently as we did. But while it persisted, this legend of the Redoubt was too ominous a threat to be ignored."[33]

Now faced with real evidence of a German collapse, this belief became something of a self-fulfilling prophecy. By March 1945 SHAEF received "a continuous flow of reports that the Nazis intended to stage a final prolonged resistance [in an area known as] the National Redoubt . . . reports of deep dugouts, secret hiding-places, underground factories and bombproof headquarters were confusing and unconvincing. No single piece of information could be confirmed." As Strong pointed out, after the intelligence failures in the Ardennes, SHAEF was taking no chances.[34] SHAEF G-2 reported, "The main trend of German defence policy does seem directed primarily to the safeguarding of the Alpine Zone." The weekly intelligence summary noted that "considerable numbers of SS and specially chosen units are being systematically withdrawn to Austria" and that important ministries and Nazi personalities, including Göring, Himmler, Hitler, "and other notables are said to be in the process of withdrawing to their respective personal mountain strongholds." A large intelligence overlay map titled "Unconfirmed Installations in Reported Redoubt Area" appeared on one wall in SHAEF's War Room.[35] The British Joint Intelligence Committee also bought into the national redoubt, as did Churchill and Eden. The JIC informed a meeting of the BCOS on 27 March, "Hitler will fight to the last and has a sort of fortress area up by Berchesgarten where he will make a last stand." Not everyone bit; a quizzical Cunningham joked that Hitler "would save much trouble" if he collected all his fanatics in one place. "They will be handy to be shipped to Siberia."[36]

Ultra intercepts in April confirmed elements of the German command and government apparatuses leaving Berlin. SHAEF fell victim to reading too much into Ultra decrypts and ground sources, which, by G-2's own admission, ranged "in quality from plausible to wildly fantastic." Strong later conceded that he and his staff started to believe SHAEF's own propaganda that the Nazi regime would flee, leaving the ordinary soldier to die in place. They also accepted an all-out fight to the last as entirely in harmony with Nazi ideology. The interrogations of captured Wehrmacht generals confirmed both these views. Although none of them knew about any concrete plans, "all agree," posited G-2, "that a final withdrawal [into the Alps] is consistent with and most probably part of the National Socialist strategy, and that the *Wehrmacht* will be directed to sacrifice itself."[37] Portions of OKH, OKW, and the SS commands, along with civilian ministries and diplomats, did leave Berlin. Hitler ordered the formation of three echelons—one in Berlin, one in Thuringia, and the third south of the Chiemsee in Bavaria, which included Berchtesgaden. Hitler divided OKW into a northern section—Zossen south of Berlin—and a southern section—Ohrdruf in Thuringia—

to better conduct the defense and relief of Berlin; no plans existed for moving to the national redoubt. As American forces rapidly approached the Ohrdruf-Erfurt area, C Echelon moved south. This was detected by Ultra, and SHAEF misinterpreted these movements as part of a master plan to execute Operation Werewolf.

Eisenhower assigned the task of isolating the redoubt to Sixth Army Group on 31 March; five days later SHAEF G-3 produced the first operational plans. On 14 April Eisenhower reported to the CCS his intention to eliminate the redoubt and issued a new directive. The day before, SHAEF G-4 had produced plans for supporting operations against the redoubt, and on 16 April Bull completed the revised operational planning.[38] Since the substance of what Smith told reporters corresponds almost exactly with SHAEF intelligence assessments and planning activities in mid-April, it follows that fears about the national redoubt confirmed Eisenhower's long-held conviction that the German regime would resort to extreme and unconventional measures to continue the struggle.

The national redoubt as myth soon revealed itself. Ultra discovered on 24 April that Hitler had ordered the remnants of the German government to proceed to Echelon B—lower Bavaria—but also that the Führer insisted on remaining in Berlin. With no Siegfried, there could be no Alpine "twilight of the Gods." American units penetrating into lower Bavaria and western Austria at the end of April met little concerted resistance. The last commander of German forces in the northern alpine front said it best: "The legendary 'Alpine Redoubt' . . . existed merely on paper. It was a slogan and a last act of desperation."[39] But by that time, nobody much cared about Berlin.

Ike's Foreign Minister

April got off to a very bad start personally for Smith. As the war drew to its conclusion, senior officers began jockeying for plum postwar slots. Smith liked his chances of becoming the American proconsul in Germany, but in early April he found out the post had gone to somebody else. Since he enjoyed Marshall's endorsement, he had considered the job—and eventually a fourth star—in the bag.

Washington's indecision on postwar policy in Germany had long plagued Smith's effort to define civil affairs programs. American occupation policy split the Roosevelt administration. Hopkins, Hull, and especially Morgenthau favored the hard line, while Stimson and career State Department officials preferred a firm but brief occupation and speedy rehabilitation of Germany. As always, Roosevelt shifted positions. Throughout late 1944 and into early 1945, Treasury, State, and War Department committees struggled to agree on a directive for SHAEF. McCloy apologized in early October for the lack of guidance on German policy.[40] The wrangle, which still required harmonizing with the British and Soviet governments and correlation with the European Advisory Commission, delayed deliberation on any appointment of the official who would implement occupation policy once it became final. Initially it appeared the job would go to a civilian, but Hopkins was too sick, McCloy had too many big-business connections, and Byrnes did not want it. That left Judge Patterson as the front-runner, but Stimson, based on his experience as secretary of war during the Philippines war, considered it a mistake to name a civilian, even if he put on a uniform. In October 1944 Stimson, Hopkins, and Patterson agreed that Eisenhower should select the officer. McCloy wrote a memorandum to Eisenhower informing him that Washington preferred an army officer undertake the initial stage of the occupation, and he listed four names: Bradley, Lee, Clay, and BG Kenneth Royall. With Allied troops caught up in the frontier battles, the prospect of forming a military government in Germany appeared remote, and Eisenhower asked Smith to make a "non-committal" reply.[41] A week later, on 8 November, Smith expressed shock to Hilldring because he expected McCloy would be offered the job. Eisenhower took the view that administration of the occupation should be a civilian task. Smith suggested if not McCloy, then Patterson with the rank of major general. Smith's specification of the rank of major general indicated that Patterson would operate under SHAEF. Smith pleaded for an early decision.[42] Had Eisenhower shown the least interest and asserted his prerogatives as theater commander, he might have settled the command structure for postwar Germany in early November, but since he viewed military government as political and not military, he failed to take the initiative. The question remained unresolved for another five months.

Roosevelt hinted at his opposition to a military appointment. Stimson remained equally determined to have a soldier in the post and offered another short list consisting of McNarney, now deputy supreme commander in the Mediterranean; Clay; Bonesteel; and Aurand. The president procrastinated and, again remembering his visit to Germany as a youth, suggested he might like the job himself. Word leaked to SHAEF of Clay's appointment. Eisenhower and Smith entertained low opinions of all three alternatives to Clay. Eisenhower wrote to Somervell on 14 March 1945 stating he urgently needed Clay; he entertained the idea of Clay acting as "the Herbert Hoover of this war and would have the job of handling civil affairs in Germany."[43] Eisenhower's letter indicated Clay would be lodged inside SHAEF and under Smith.

Stimson met with his civilian advisers, including Patterson and McCloy, on 14 March to finalize a recommendation for the president's decision, but he never consulted the military side of the War Department. The secretary knew Marshall's view; he wanted Smith made proconsul for Germany. "Smith has indicated that he thinks he could run [German occupation] in addition to his other duties," Stimson noted in his diary the day of the meeting. "That is silly and I won't stand for it." Stimson believed military government must function outside the chain of command, answering only to Eisenhower. They decided Clay should go to Germany, if Byrnes would give him up. That did not present a problem, because Byrnes had already indicated his intention to leave the directory of war mobilization and reconversion, freeing up his deputy. The president accepted Clay's appointment without ever referring the question to either Marshall or Eisenhower. As Stimson noted on 31 March, "Bedell Smith . . . is said to want to have the position himself. . . . Smith has gotten a little bit of a big head and he has also unfortunately let this be appreciated by people as high as the President who has told me several times he has lost confidence in Smith."[44] Smith now reaped the bitter fruit of his not very well camouflaged opposition to Roosevelt's policies on de Gaulle and unconditional surrender.

Against his desires, Clay had emerged as the war's best political general. He came by it honestly; his father held a Senate seat for three terms, and in his youth Clay served as a congressional page. He graduated in 1918 after three years at West Point, benefiting from the decision to shorten the term because of wartime exigencies; it may have saved him the indignity of being asked to leave the military academy and got him into the engineers despite his low class standing. The New Deal made his career. Working under Hopkins, Clay came into contact with the powers behind the Works Progress Administration and the Civilian Conservation Corps and became a familiar presence on Capitol Hill. He paid the price for his politicking because his patrons in the Roosevelt administration and his deserved reputation as an organizer who got results kept him in Washington. He still entertained hopes of seeing action in the Pacific but accepted the German appointment. McCloy preceded Clay to Reims and on 2 April broke the news to Eisenhower.

Eisenhower resented Clay's appointment because nobody had solicited his opinion since late October. Still, he and Clay had bonded during the engineer's one-year stint on MacArthur's staff in Manila, and Eisenhower recognized Clay's excellent work in breaking up the bottleneck in Normandy. Given that the president had already appointed Clay, even if he opposed the move, there appeared to be no going back. Clay "ran into a little rough-neck on the part of Bedell" when he arrived, but beyond that, Smith gave no indication how much not getting the appointment wounded his pride.[45] Had he known the president's view of him, it would have hurt considerably more.

Roosevelt and his chief civilian advisers may have lost confidence in Smith and his political judgment, but the same did not apply to Eisenhower. As the war entered its final act, military diplomacy took the fore. And there remained no doubt Eisenhower would surrender the lead role to his foreign minister, Beetle Smith. In rapid succession—much of it simultaneously—Smith wrestled with the humanitarian crisis in the Netherlands, yet another outburst from de Gaulle, and negotiations with the Germans, first pertaining to relief in Holland and finally the unconditional surrender.

By mid-January 1945 the worsening food crisis in the Netherlands prompted Queen Wilhelmina to approach King George VI, Roosevelt, and Churchill. In identical notes, the queen declared, "Conditions . . . have at present become so desperate, that it is abundantly clear that, if a major catastrophe, the like of which has not been seen in Western Europe since the Middle Ages, is to be avoided in Holland, something drastic has to be done *now,* that is to say *before* and not *after* the liberation of the rest of the country."[46]

Smith had been involved with the thorny question of supplying the Dutch civilian population in occupied Netherlands since October 1944. The month before, Dutch rail workers had gone on strike in support of Market Garden. In retaliation, Reichkommissar Artur Seyss-Inquart imposed an embargo on food and fuel entering Dutch cities. In early October Dutch prime minister Gerbrandy approached the British government with a dire prediction that the Germans intended to systematically strip and destroy the country. On 18 October he arrived unannounced in Smith's office. Smith put him off, called in Grasset for the latest estimates, and promised to meet with Gerbrandy the next day. The Dutch premier was impressed; Smith had done his homework. He assured Gerbrandy that SHAEF had made provisions for rushing food and medicine into the Netherlands immediately upon liberation. When Gerbrandy asked him if the Netherlands would be liberated by 1 December, Smith replied, "Impossible." Already short of food owing to German depredations complicated by the embargo, the Dutch urban population faced the grim prospect of another winter under occupation. The Dutch did not go away empty-handed. Eisenhower signaled his approval of aiding the Dutch, "even if the Germans would benefit," through the agencies of the Swiss and Swedish governments and the International Red Cross, but Smith told Gerbrandy that he must first work out the details at the governmental level. Smith ruled out overland supply and shipment by barge down the Rhine from Basel, since SHAEF saw little prospect the relief would ever get into citizens' hands; he also explained the difficulties presented by airdrops, instead pointing to the advantages of a sealift. The Germans indicated they would not block the shipment into Rotterdam, but plans broke down because the Dutch lacked the means for distributing the aid.[47]

The Dutch kept up the political pressure, especially with the coming of the holiday season. Gerbrandy wrote to Eisenhower, pleading for operations into the Netherlands. "The Dutch government," he wrote, "cannot accept the fact that merely corpses will be liberated." Prince Bernhard, consort of the heir to the throne, and Gerbrandy both made personal appeals to Smith but received only vague promises. "To comply with . . . the Dutch government's [requests]," Smith said, "is impossible. We have no troops for it, and the war may last until autumn 1945."[48] At the end of January two small Swedish ships off-loaded 3,200 tons of supplies, but distribution difficulties delayed these shipments from reaching Amsterdam for two weeks. Another ship, sponsored by the International Red Cross, delivered additional supplies early in March. None of this ameliorated the crisis because the Dutch needed 2,000 tons per day just for minimal requirements.

On 14 March the CCS directed Eisenhower "to liberate Holland as soon as practicable after your Rhine crossing has been secured."[49] Eisenhower, then in the midst of wrestling with the decision of whether to drive on Berlin, rejected the instruction. He refused to divert forces required in Germany into the Netherlands, arguing that the quickest and most painless remedy to the Dutch situation would be the speedy defeat of Germany. Pointing to the risks—collateral civilian casualties in heavy urban fighting and increased hardships produced by the inevitable German breaching of the dikes—SHAEF considered it "militarily inadvisable to undertake operations west of Utrecht."[50] The CCS accepted Eisenhower's conclusions.

On 5 April Canadian First Army sent a corps forward, finally taking Arnhem, and by 18 April it had cleared the Germans from the whole northeastern section of the Netherlands except for the extreme northern coastline and a pocket of inundated polder between Apeldoorn and Zwolle. The Germans still held the core of the country—including Amsterdam, Rotterdam, the Hague, and Utrecht—behind the Greebe

Line and the River Waal. Militarily, "Fortress Holland" held little of consequence, save for the 3.6 million Dutch civilians facing starvation.

The humanitarian crisis in the Netherlands became a political football punted among London, Washington, Moscow, and Reims throughout most of April. "The plight of the civil population of occupied Holland is desperate," Churchill told Roosevelt. "I fear we may soon be in the presence of a tragedy." Churchill believed the Germans would allow relief supplies in through neutral agencies, but if they refused, the prime minister proposed, "We should, at this stage, warn the German Commander in Holland and all the troops under his command that by resisting our attempt to bring relief to the civil population in this area they brand themselves as murderers before the world." The president replied from Warm Springs, Georgia, agreeing in principle but raising the specter of the Soviets. After the Russians' reaction to alleged Allied secret discussions with the Germans in Switzerland, the president insisted on Soviet concurrence.[51] Both the American and British governments offered the Dutch succor; the problem remained working out some kind of modus vivendi with the Germans without raising alarm bells in Moscow. Another two weeks passed; complications arose when the Dutch government proposed a truce.

On 14 April Prince Bernhard wrote to Smith, notifying him that Seyss-Inquart had approached the Dutch underground with a deal. In exchange for the Allies agreeing not to advance beyond the Greebe Line, the Germans would put political prisoners in decent camps, prosecute political opponents in civil courts, execute no more Dutchmen, and open Amsterdam to food and coal shipments. The Germans would not surrender until the Nazi regime ceased to exist and would continue to occupy Holland and Utrecht, but they would stop all fighting and assist in feeding the population in the two occupied provinces. Seyss-Inquart reminded Bernhard that "he had been ordered to hold out under all circumstances, and to carry out the necessary demolitions and inundations for that purpose."[52] If the Canadian I Corps crossed the Greebe Line, the Germans would blow the dikes, flooding everything from Utrecht to the sea.

Marshall wired Eisenhower on 19 April, informing him Churchill had approached Washington and announced his readiness to accept Seyss-Inquart's offer. In San Francisco, Eden raised the issue at the preliminary meeting of the United Nations conference, and to gain greater publicity, he circulated Gerbrandy's latest impassioned petition. The JCS raised no objections in military terms but wondered about the fall-out from trafficking with the enemy and compromising the unconditional surrender formula. Whatever Eisenhower decided, SHAEF must keep the Soviets notified.[53]

SHAEF responded favorably the next day. "Certainly the Seyss-Inquart proposals are the only hope for northwestern Holland," the Bull-written reply stated. From both a military and a humanitarian point of view, SHAEF recommended pursuing negotiations. On 23 April Smith wrote a memo to the CCS and BCOS stating that Canadian I Corps could not initiate operations "for some weeks," and German resistance and sabotage "would inevitably result in even more widespread destruction." Since the question "has assumed increasing urgency and for sheer humanitarian reasons something must be done at once," and since military operations had been ruled out, a truce would kill two birds with one stone: supply the starving Dutch, and free Canadian forces for other missions. "The tragic situation in Holland does not permit further delay," and SHAEF requested "as free a hand as possible" in pursuing truce negotiations.[54]

The CCS immediately granted SHAEF sanction to proceed. The authorization contained a number of conditions: the truce did not preclude the ultimate unconditional surrender of all German forces in the Netherlands; German forces must cease all active operations, freely admit and facilitate the distribution of relief supplies, and refrain from any form of inundation or destruction of capital goods; and German officials must desist in all persecution of opponents. If the Germans complied with all these stipulations, Allied forces would close down all active operations. SHAEF wired Moscow, stating that the Dutch situation was so urgent that if the Soviets required representation, it must be by somebody in the theater, and Harriman received instructions to inform the appropriate Soviet authorities.[55] The Soviets approved, with one minor amendment, and assigned MG Ivan Susloparov, head of the Soviet military mission to France, as delegate to the negotiations. Gerbrandy expressed his full confidence in SHAEF's management of the truce.

The Germans refused airdrops of food but continued underground negotiations. The Canadians received verbal orders to cease firing, beginning on the morning of 28 April. Later that day de Guingand and two senior Canadian officers met with German officials at a schoolhouse in Achterveld. Discussions centered on SHAEF's plans for "free drops" of food supplies beginning that day. The German envoys stated they lacked authority and could not make any definite commitments. A second meeting was set for two days later, this time involving Seyss-Inquart.[56]

Not surprisingly, Eisenhower sent Smith and Strong to arrange a settlement. De Guingand and Brigadier E. T. Williams represented Twenty-first Army Group, Bernhard the Dutch, and Susloparov the Soviets. Both sides drove to Achterveld, but the Germans were forced to walk a short distance to the school. To add insult to injury, Bernhard drove up in Seyss-Inquart's Mercedes. The proceedings started on an unpropitious note. A woman who accompanied Seyss-Inquart irately demanded the return of three parcels left in the vehicle, which the Dutch underground had liberated. With this dispute resolved—to the evident dissatisfaction of the accuser—the real business began.

First Smith read the general proposals for feeding the Dutch and for obtaining, in principle, an accord with the Germans. The Germans—including representatives of the three German services and civilian experts—agreed and even offered suggestions for improvements. Both sides concurred on forming a joint committee to work out the details. The Germans acceded to conveying food supplies by road, air, inland waterways, and sea. The committee would designate ten drop zones, and Allied aircraft could operate from 7 A.M. to 3 P.M. daily; Rotterdam would open for shipping from 4 May; and the Germans would open a single road beginning on 2 May. Relieving Dutch distress provided the pretext for the conference, but Smith's real reason for attending involved the desire to leverage a German surrender.

After concluding the food deal, Smith, Strong, de Guingand, and Susloparov met with Seyss-Inquart and the civilian members of the German delegation. Smith pointed to the hopelessness of the German position and suggested that the time was ripe for an unconditional surrender. He then read a Swiss report stating Bern had received information from senior German officials that a central administration had ceased to function in Berlin. Seyss-Inquart replied that, as a civil administrator, his only authority was related to the food question. Hitler had declared the Netherlands a "fortress," and as long as the German commands remained in contact with Berlin, they would never surrender, whatever advice Seyss-Inquart might offer.[57] The German remained adamant. Nor would he release Allied prisoners of war. "He was, however, fully cognizant of his task to lighten the burden on the Dutch, and to this end he would do everything in his power." Clearly, Seyss-Inquart was no Castellano. Smith changed gears. He talked about his German ancestry and the need to avoid unnecessary bloodshed. "The solemnity [of the occasion]," remembered Williams, "had been spoiled by Bernhard's giggling."[58]

Frustrated and a little embarrassed by his clumsy appeal to German sensibilities, Smith, acting on advice given to him by Seyss-Inquart's doctor, requested that they speak privately. Smith asked if he understood this constituted his last chance. Despite what Williams thought, Smith could see that his arguments citing the futility of further fighting and the human costs had "made a visible and deep impression on Reichkommissar Seyss-Inquart." In barely more than a whisper, the German replied, "Yes, I realize that." "The consequences to you yourself will be serious," Smith continued. "You know what your acts have been here. You know the feeling of the Dutch people toward you. You know you will probably be shot." After a slight pause, Seyss-Inquart grimly rejoined, "That leaves me cold." Not without a certain sense of satisfaction, Smith sardonically replied, "It usually does."[59]

Despite the appeals and threats, Seyss-Inquart refused to yield. He requested permission to visit Berlin to obtain authorization to negotiate the surrender of German forces in the Netherlands and possibly of Germany. Smith refused, stating that if he wanted to surrender in the Netherlands, Seyss-Inquart could do so immediately; if Germany wanted to capitulate, it would have to abide by formal international convention through the supreme commander. With that, the conference concluded. The truce held, and the Germans offered no obstacles to the food deliveries, but there was no surrender.[60]

Eisenhower once remarked that the biggest thorn in his side, even more than the fight over landing craft, was dealing with the French. Fittingly, the war in Europe did not end without another clash with de Gaulle. Seventh Army encircled Stuttgart, and French forces moved quickly into the city. The day before, Devers had realigned the army boundaries and assigned Stuttgart to Patch. Following orders, American units entered Stuttgart on 24 April and found the French apologetic but determined to stay put. De Gaulle ordered de Lattre to "hold and administer the territory conquered by our troops until the French zone of occupation has been fixed." De Gaulle claimed Devers's orders amounted to an "offense to the French Army as well as to the French Government and people" and insisted on the installation of a French military government in Stuttgart. The French president and acting foreign minister told Caffery "he begged, he pleaded" for a definition of the boundaries of the French zone and for French participation in the discussions. France was not represented at Yalta or in the CCS.[61] De Gaulle considered the issue political, not military, and ordered that de Lattre remain in the Württemberg capital. As he explained to Eisenhower, France retained the right to employ French forces in the national interest, "the only interest that they should serve."[62]

Eisenhower distanced himself from the political upheaval. To de Gaulle he expressed his ignorance of ongoing negotiations concerning the French zone of control—a feint, because during a visit to London on 19 April, the prime minister had shown Eisenhower a map indicating French demands for a readjustment of the occupation boundaries. He said he regretted that de Gaulle found it "necessary to inject political considerations into a campaign in which my functions are purely military." Since October, Eisenhower had delegated to his chief of staff responsibility for representing SHAEF in all discussions with the European Advisory Commission pertaining to postwar policy in Germany, including the zones of occupation. On 23 April Smith entered into negotiations with Juin on the issue of French demands for a zone of control as far north as Cologne.[63] Rather than be party to a struggle between the French government and SHAEF, Eisenhower said he would find an alternative solution to Patch's supply problems but would refer the question to the CCS.[64]

On the afternoon of 28 April Smith flew to Paris for discussions with Ambassador Caffery. Smith convinced Caffery that "the French behaved very badly indeed" in what he coined "the Stuttgart Incident." According to Smith, de Lattre repeatedly violated Devers's orders, hampering military operations; Stuttgart was merely the latest example. He also informed Caffery that de Gaulle would be getting more bad news. On 20 April the JCS had decided to end the French rearmament program; now that the war was drawing to a conclusion, the chiefs had no interest in arming the French Metropolitan Army. To avoid any further hard feelings, Eisenhower withdrew American forces from the city.[65]

Smith's negotiations with Seyss-Inquart served as a perfect dry run for what came next. On 25 April First Army troops linked with Soviet units at Torgau on the Elbe, fulfilling the CCS's directive. Forces under SHAEF's command penetrated into the heart of Germany, linked with the Soviets, and crippled the German armed forces in the west beyond their ability to resist. Five days later, with the Red Army overrunning Berlin, Hitler committed suicide. After the official announcement of the Führer's death the next day by his chosen successor, Grand Admiral Karl Dönitz, Smith notified all commands that the end of the war was imminent.[66] On 2 May Alexander reported that German broadcasts were calling for German forces to lay down their weapons in Italy. The same day Twenty-first Army Group secured Wismar and Lübeck, sealing the Baltic. Smith had already started preparations to take the lead in treating with the Germans. Although Eisenhower had not made it official, everyone presupposed the supreme commander would absent himself from any direct dealing with the Germans, leaving that to the experienced duo of Smith and Strong.

At Plön, the temporary seat of the German government, Dönitz convened a conference of his senior military and political advisers to decide whether to continue the struggle and save as much as they could from the Soviets or to surrender. Dönitz decided to do both: resist the Russians while surrendering to the Western Allies, despite the knowledge that the Americans and British would insist on unconditional surrender. The only avenue open to them appeared to be piecemeal surrenders to the Western Allies at army group level, drawing out the process as long as possible to give German soldiers and civilians more time to flee westward. The following day a delegation arrived at Montgomery's headquarters at Lüneburg Heath to discuss the possibility of partial surrenders in the north.

Early on 3 May four German officers appeared in British lines requesting a parley. One of the officers who appeared in front of Montgomery's caravan was Generaladmiral Hans-Georg von Friedeburg, a former Hitler aide and the newly installed commander of the Kriegsmarine. The Germans looked as though they came out of central casting: the cadaverous Friedeburg in his leather greatcoat; General E. Kinsel, chief of staff of Army Group Northwest, the perfect personification of Prussian military arrogance, complete with monocle; Rear Admiral Wagner; and a Major Friedl, who possessed "the cruellest face of any man," according to Montgomery's Canadian personal assistant, LTC Trumbull Warren. True to form, Montgomery met the Germans in his usual dishabille. A past master of humiliating people, Montgomery did not miss his chance to chasten the German officers. Warren remarked that the field marshal was putting on a good show. "Shut up, you S.O.B.," snapped Dawnay, "he has been rehearsing this all his life."[67] Friedeburg offered the surrender of German forces facing the Russians in Mecklenburg. "Nothing to do with me," Monty said. He stated his willingness to accept the surrender of any German soldier entering his lines, but Montgomery wanted the capitulation of German forces in the western Netherlands, Friesland and the Frisian Islands, Helgoland, Schleswig-Holstein, and Denmark. After being harangued by Montgomery on the mercilessness of the Nazi regime and hearing him reject any appeals for safeguarding the lives of German citizens—according to Friedeburg, his reason for coming—the German admiral said he possessed no authority to surrender German forces but requested permission to discuss the field marshal's demands with Dönitz and Keitel, chief of staff of OKW. Friedeburg asked for forty-eight hours, and Montgomery gave him twenty-four.

Dönitz had already decided to surrender unconditionally to the British, but Friedeburg's mission bought another day. Although refusing to surrender on all fronts, in a demonstration of good faith, Dönitz suspended U-boat activities and released King Leopold of Belgium. At the appointed time, Friedeburg returned to Montgomery's headquarters and signed the "Instrument of Surrender." Typical of Montgomery, the document read that the Germans surrendered to the person of the "C-in-C 21 Army Group." Montgomery cabled the news to Reims, including word that he would send Friedeburg on to SHAEF by air. Before the German delegation set off, they privately informed Montgomery that "while the German High Command was prepared to surrender unconditionally, it was most anxious to make this surrender to the Western Allies and not to the Russians of whom all the Germans were profoundly afraid."[68]

Preparations for the surrender negotiations threw SHAEF into a perfect turmoil. Smith remembered the first week in May 1945 as the most hectic of the war. "This period was a single unit of time," he recounted. "Scarcely anyone left headquarters. We ate when we were hungry, slept when we could no longer keep awake. Twelve o'clock on the dial of a watch might mean noon or midnight. A man looked toward the window to find out."[69] Hundreds of loose ends needed tying together: trying to keep current on operations, administer Dutch relief and attend to myriad other civil affairs problems, communicate with the Soviets to ensure there was no confusion, and prepare the instruments of surrender.

The lack of political guidance plagued SHAEF right down to the final act. After eight months of haggling, the European Advisory Commission finally produced a surrender formula approved by Washington, London, and Moscow. At Yalta, the Big Three had agreed on dismembering Germany, but the Russians opposed disclosing that information to the French. On 1 May SHAEF received a surrender document from Ambassador Winant, who represented the United States on the EAC, that included the French amendments but lacked the stamp of approval of the three governments. As a result, SHAEF had two surrender documents: one with and one without the word *dismemberment*. As Smith told Winant in London, he lacked the authority to use either, since SHAEF had received no guidance on the matter from Washington and London or the CCS.[70]

Part of the confusion stemmed from differing command channels. The CCS never issued a directive. Because the EAC stood at the governmental level, its surrender document never went to the CCS for review; nor was there any reason for the CCS to forward the draft for SHAEF's guidance. In January the State Department solicited the JCS's views on the amended terms, including French participation. On 31 January the joint chiefs approved the document and sent it through War Department channels to ETO headquarters. "Nothing further on the matter of including the French," Hull told Smith, "was brought to the attention of the JCS." Smith filed away the EAC document as immaterial until all four governments had approved it.[71]

On 4 May Smith communicated his concerns to Winant. Without an authoritative CCS directive, Smith decided to employ the same gambit used with the Italians and ordered, under Eisenhower's sanction, the preparation of short "military" terms. According to Winant, Smith stated that "Germany was smashed and incapable of continued effective resistance" and that "a quick surrender would save life." Smith thought the Germans would agree more readily to a straightforward military surrender. Matters not adequately covered in the short terms could always be handled in subsequent instructions to the German high command. Smith saw to it that the wording of Article 4 kept open the imposition of unconditional surrender and the declaration of the EAC. Churchill agreed with Smith's approach, and Winant forwarded the short-terms document to Washington and to the Soviet ambassador in London on 6 May. The short terms made no mention of dismemberment.[72] Smith asked Winant to "take immediate steps to invite the attention of Washington to the fact that we had never received a directive from the Combined Chiefs of Staff so that we might receive instructions on it through Combined Chiefs of Staff channels if indeed there was an approved surrender form." Smith proceeded with the drafting of the surrender terms, since "we heard nothing further and in view of the urgent circumstances." SHAEF produced two documents. The first—the short terms— entitled the "Act of Military Surrender," provided for the unconditional surrender of German forces on all fronts. In the second document, the "Undertaking Given by Certain Emissaries to the Allied High Command," the Germans would agree to send representatives to a location and place to be determined by SHAEF, and the Soviets would agree to formally ratify the military surrender. Eisenhower waited on the Soviets' concurrence before giving the documents his approval.[73] As Smith told Murphy, since no recognizable German government existed, SHAEF no longer felt obliged to use the EAC document.[74]

On 5 May Dönitz sent a message to SHAEF asking for permission to send emissaries to arrange surrender terms, but he gave no indication of the scope of the capitulation. Eisenhower responded by telling the Germans he would accept only the simultaneous surrender of all German forces on all fronts.[75] Weather grounded Friedeburg's plane at Brussels; he continued his trip to Reims by automobile. Eisenhower had already told Smith that the only acceptable terms were immediate and uncon-ditional surrender of all German forces, and he made it clear he would not see any Germans until after they had surrendered. To Smith fell the entire responsibility of managing the German capitulation.

With the Germans' arrival delayed, Smith employed one of his clever ruses. The walls of the War Room on the first floor were hung with huge situation maps. In the center, a large swastika dominated the wall, from which rose a graphic thermometer revealing the number of Germans (4,035,051) taken prisoner by Allied forces. Friedeburg would be ushered here to await his interview with Smith. To heighten the German admiral's sense of doom, the staff prepared a new situation map. It accurately showed the current positions of Allied and German forces, but two large red arrows were added—one from the west, cutting off German forces in Bohemia and Yugoslavia, and the other from the east. Although invented, these converging attacks conveyed the sheer desper-ation of the German situation.[76]

When Friedeburg and his associates arrived, the map was ready and laid out on Smith's desk. After a suitable period, the Germans were ushered into Smith's office, where he decided to conduct the prelim-inary discussions. Strong, the only other Allied officer present, acted as interpreter. As Montgomery had warned, Friedeburg tried to limit discussions to surrendering German forces only on the Western Front. Smith merely said there appeared to be nothing to discuss, since the Allies could only accept unconditional surrender. In a scene reminis-cent of the Italian negotiations of 1943, Smith and Strong refused to discuss anything but unconditional surrender while Friedeburg pro-tested he did not have the authority to capitulate. During the course of their discussions, Smith noted Friedeburg's eyes welling up with tears as he scanned the map between them. "Obviously," Smith said, "you do not entirely realize the hopelessness of the German situation." Smith momentarily found himself sympathizing with the pathetic German's plight. It was "a terrible thing for a man to see himself as completely helpless," he remembered thinking.[77]

After his interview with Smith, Friedeburg and his three associ-ates were escorted into a second-floor conference room. The dispirited Germans took their seats opposite Smith, Spaatz, Morgan, Robb, and Strong. A series of detailed discussions ensued. Friedeburg continued to maintain that surrender to the Russians was "unthinkable." Smith replied that if the Germans promptly surrendered on all fronts, they would receive treatment consistent "with the normal dictates of human-ity."[78] If they refused, the Western Allies would close the front to refugees and hold the German command responsible for the needless loss of life and property. Smith told Friedeburg he could either sign the surrender or request that someone be sent with the full authority to do so. Convinced he could stall no longer, Friedeburg asked if he could communicate with his headquarters.[79]

As part of their delaying tactics, the German negotiators had left their ciphers in Lüneburg. The message first went to Montgomery's headquarters, then on to Flensburg, the seat of Dönitz's peripatetic government. The German head of state wanted to buy more time, if only forty-eight hours, to allow more German soldiers and civilians to get into the western zones. He dispatched Jodl, the strongest advocate of continuing the battle in the east, to Reims, hoping the general could convince Eisenhower of the impossibility of surrendering to the Soviets. A confidant of Hitler's, Jodl headed the operations staff of OKW throughout the war, a testament to his political adroitness. The Germans held out the desperate hope that differences would emerge between the Allied powers, providing time for German nationals to make their way westward.[80]

The sixth of May was a day full of mounting tension at SHAEF. Eisenhower spent a sleepless night. "I really expected some definite developments," he wrote to Mamie, "and went to bed early in anticipation of being waked up at 1, 2, 3, or 4 A.M. Nothing happened and as a result I was wide awake . . . with nothing decent to read." His current western novel was "terrible—I could write better ones, left-handed."[81] All afternoon an irritable Eisenhower stayed in his office pacing and chain-smoking, waiting for a Soviet reply to the surrender terms from Deane in Moscow. Summersby described the atmosphere as "electric with his impatience; at the same time I thought it rather lonely and pathetic." Finally, Soviet approval came through for Susloparov to sign the instrument of surrender.[82]

Smith's day was filled with petty irritations. Eisenhower disapproved of the press arrangements for the surrender ceremony. Deciding that the proceedings were "not going to be a Hollywood show," Smith ordered the War Room cleared of cameras and sound equipment. This created a number of headaches for Butcher, who handled press relations. Unhappy with Smith's arbitrary ruling, and concluding that "Beetle's tummy was bothering him," Butcher took the matter up with Eisenhower. Facing bigger issues, Eisenhower simply said the surrender "was Beetle's show," and if he did not want any publicity, "that was the answer." Smith had taken a short afternoon nap, and when he returned to headquarters at 5 P.M., he found Butcher waiting for him.

"The nap had improved his disposition," recorded Butcher, "he was gracious, understanding, and cooperative." They reached a compromise on press arrangements. Heaving a sigh of relief, Butcher told Smith what a "sweat [he] had been in." "Your sweat," Smith retorted sharply. "What do you think the rest of us are doing?"[83] A few minutes later Jodl, accompanied by de Guingand, arrived.

Just as he had made Castellano cool his heels before the final negotiations leading to the Italian surrender, Jodl and Friedeburg waited before being summoned into Smith's office at 6:15. With Strong again serving as interpreter, Smith allowed Jodl to make his presentation. The Germans would surrender to the Western Allies, Jodl told Smith, but they needed twenty-four hours to communicate instructions to isolated units. It was obvious Jodl wanted time. Acting on Eisenhower's instructions, Smith flatly refused the German request, saying the Germans must capitulate on both fronts. He delivered an ultimatum: unless Jodl accepted the terms by midnight, the Anglo-American forces would seal the front. No Germans could cross the line. Smith left the meeting convinced that if granted a day's grace, Jodl would sign. He told Ruth Briggs to send for Susloparov.

Leaving the Germans to contemplate their options, Smith and Strong conferred with Eisenhower. They told him Jodl maintained that Flensburg did not possess adequate lines of communications to the German field commands—a point confirmed by G-2—and it might prove impossible to implement the surrender unless the Germans received a twenty-four-hour cease-fire. Eisenhower agreed to the delay. It was another German ruse—all day Keitel had communicated with units in the east and Bohemia, "authorizing their withdrawal westward within . . . not more than 48 hours."[84]

Though not much discussed, the situation in Bohemia raised a number of unpleasant specters. The Czech crisis and appeasement at Munich had initiated the spiral toward war. The only surviving democracy among the succession states created by the treaties of Paris, Czechoslovakia had endured partition, and Bohemia and Moravia faced annexation into the Greater Reich. Whatever the agreement in Yalta, Churchill saw "remarkable political advantages derived from [the] liberation of Prague and as much as possible of Czechoslovakia." At the end of April Eisenhower rejected the prime minister's appeal, stating he would "*not* attempt any move I deem militarily unwise merely to gain a political prize unless I receive specific orders from the Combined Chiefs of Staff."[85] For weeks, elements of Third Army had sat astride the Czech frontier with Patton pulling on his leash for permission to enter. On 4 May, to put pressure on Dönitz, Eisenhower authorized Patton's movement forward, but only to Pilsen. The American advance—reconnaissance units operated in the vicinity of the Czech capital—prompted bloody street fighting in Prague, but Bradley called Patton on 6 May, repeating Eisenhower's prohibition. "You hear me, George, goddamnit, *halt!*" Despite Patton's appeals that "those patriots need our help," Bradley refused.[86] Uncertainty concerning the state of affairs in Bohemia influenced both parties in Reims.

On their way back to Smith's office, Strong suggested they try a "soldier-to-soldier" approach. Strong had served in Berlin before the war and knew the importance the German officer corps attached to honor. Smith agreed to give it a try. After conceding to the delay, Smith told Jodl the German officers and soldiers had done their best to preserve their military traditions, and the high command "had faced insoluble political pressures." If the German army surrendered, it could salvage a measure of honor and prestige. He reminded the German general that the officer corps could expect all protections afforded by the Geneva Conventions. "It was a good, long speech made with a straight face," Strong recorded, "showing a fine understanding of the German mentality." A fine understanding or not, Jodl maneuvered for an additional twenty-four-hour delay. Strong called Eisenhower, who replied, "You tell them that forty-eight hours from midnight tonight, I will close my lines on the Western Front. . . . Whether they sign or not."[87]

Jodl asked if he and Friedeburg could discuss the matter in private.[88] About an hour later, Jodl emerged from the meeting and requested permission to communicate with Dönitz. According to Montgomery, Jodl already possessed full authority to surrender; his wire to Flensburg—this time he had brought his ciphers—merely played out the string.[89] More important, he wrung the forty-eight-hour concession from SHAEF. After outlining the Allied conditions, Jodl told Dönitz he saw "no alternative other than chaos or signature" and asked for "immediate radio confirmation whether authorization for signing can be put into effect. Hostilities will then cease on 9 May 0001 hours our time." Meanwhile, the German military situation deteriorated as Prague rose up in insurrection, making it impossible to extricate their forces from Bohemia. A little after the midnight deadline, a reply arrived from Flensburg. Dönitz gave Jodl "full power" to conclude the surrender.[90]

While all this transpired, the SHAEF staff raced to complete the surrender documents. "For five days we were typing documents," reminisced Susan Hibbert, a British Auxiliary Territorial Service typist. "We started early in the morning and finished late at night. I typed the English documents; three other secretaries typed the French, Russian and

The final act: the German surrender. Jodl makes his appeal for clemency for the German people to an implacable, ramrod-stiff Smith. Sitting at the table across from Jodl, from left to right: Morgan (obscured), Sevez, Burroughs, Smith, Susloparov, Spaatz, Robb, Bull (on the corner), and LTC Ivan Zenkovitch, an interpreter. Butcher stands behind Burroughs. Strong, acting as interpreter, stands behind Jodl.

German versions." Sergeant Hibbert began typing the final version of the surrender terms on the morning of 6 May. "Staff officers and interpreters were coming and going," she remembered. "We were not allowed to leave the room. There were constant changes and amendments. I often had to start again from the beginning." Finally, after twenty hours of labor, she and her colleagues finished in the early hours of 7 May.[91]

At 2:30 A.M. the Allied delegation, led by Smith, entered the War Room. Morgan found the whole scene slightly unreal. The journalists stationed themselves at the back of the room, manning their cameras and a row of floodlights. "The effect of make-believe was, if anything, heightened by the arrival in the room of the German uniforms." The Germans, escorted by Strong, filed into the crowded room. Jodl bowed stiffly and took his seat opposite Smith. On Jodl's left sat Friedeburg; at his right was his aide, MAJ Friedrich Oxenius. Opposite sat the Allied signatories and witnesses: Susloparov; Spaatz; Robb; Bull; ADM Sir Harold Burroughs, commander in chief of Allied Naval Forces; MG François Sevez, the French representative; and Morgan. Smith formally asked Jodl if he was prepared to sign the surrender; the German general, in a steady voice, replied in the affirmative. Strong, standing behind the Germans, placed the "Act of Military Surrender" before Jodl. After he signed the document, Strong passed it to Smith, who affixed his signature. Susloparov and Sevez followed in turn. Then they signed the second document. Jodl, through Strong, made a brief statement that ended with a plea for the victors to treat the German soldiers and civilians with generosity. There was no reply. The entire ceremony took slightly more than ten minutes.[92] Smith recalled the lack of emotion displayed by the Allied officers around the table and the "stone-like" military bearing of the Germans. Nor were there any outward signs of elation on the faces of the Allied officers. "It was a moment of solemn gratitude."[93]

At the completion of the signing, Smith and Strong took Jodl to see the supreme commander. Entering Eisenhower's office, Smith announced the war was over. Fixing his eyes on Jodl, Eisenhower, flanked by Tedder, asked if the German understood the terms of the surrender. When Jodl replied that he did, Eisenhower told the German he would hold him personally responsible for any breach of the agreement. After the German general said he understood, Eisenhower curtly dismissed him, saying, "That is all." Jodl bowed in compliance and saluted; Eisenhower "stared silently, in dismissal." The interview lasted only a couple of minutes.[94]

Eisenhower gathered his SHAEF team together while photographers captured the historic moment. He held up the two gold-plated pens used in the ceremony in the "V-for-Victory" salute. Afterward, he participated in a short newsreel and a radio recording. As a fitting reward for all their labors, Smith permitted his secretarial staff to witness the historic event. In the back of the room, they shared a bottle of champagne from a single beaten-up army mug. After the journalists left, Eisenhower invited Smith, Tedder, Strong, and Summersby to his quarters for their own champagne toasts. Smith said that, as an appropriate final act, the staff should prepare a message for the CCS. It was natural he would think of Marshall at this moment. Together they struggled to find the correct words. "I tried one myself," Smith recalled, "and like my associates, groped for resounding phrases as fitting accolades to the Great Crusade and indicative of our dedication to the great task just completed."[95] Eisenhower watched in silence. Thanking them for their efforts, he dictated a suitably Grantian message himself. It simply read, "The mission of this Allied force was fulfilled at 0241 local time, May 7, 1945."[96] With that, the war in Europe ended. The next day Smith received a commendation from the secretary of war; the citation read: "It is fitting you should have been the one to sign [the] historic document."[97]

Appendixes

Appendix 1. Marshall's Reorganized War Department General Staff

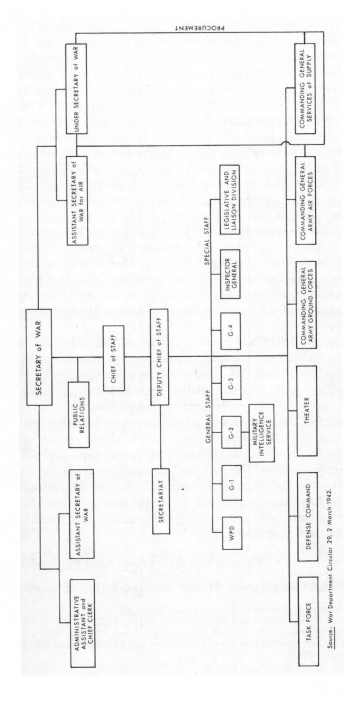

Source: War Department Circular 29, 2 March 1942.

Source: James Hewes, *From Root to McNamara: Army Organization and Administration* (Washington, DC, 1975), 160.

Appendix 2. AFHQ Command and Staff Structure

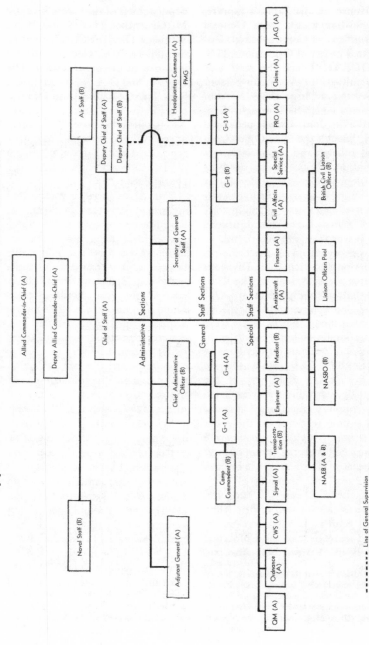

Source: George Howe, *Northwest Africa: Seizing the Initiative in the West*, USAWWII (Washington, DC, 1957), 34.

Appendix 3. SHAEF Command and Staff Structure

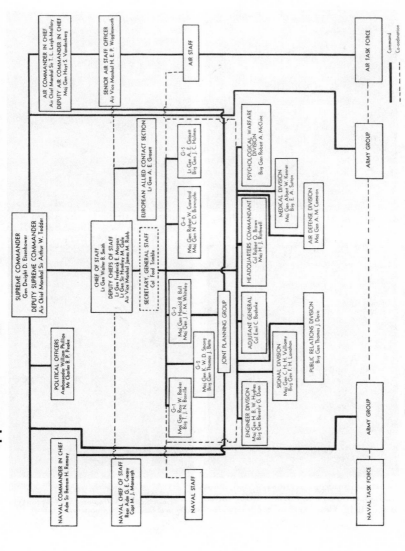

Source: Forrest Pogue, *The Supreme Command*, USAWWII (Washington, DC, 1954), 67.

Notes

Abbreviations

AAFWWII	Army Air Force in World War II series
CAC	Churchill Archives Center, Churchill College, Cambridge University
CARL	Combined Arms Research Library, U.S. Army Command and General Staff College, Fort Leavenworth, Kansas
DDEL	Dwight David Eisenhower Presidential Library, Abilene, Kansas
EP	Alfred D. Chandler Jr., ed., *The Papers of Dwight David Eisenhower: The War Years,* 5 vols (Baltimore, 1970)
FRUS	Department of State, *The Foreign Relations of the United States,* 23 vols. (Washington, DC, 1955–2003)
GBR	General Board Reports, United States Forces, European Theater of Operations
GCMP	Papers of George Catlett Marshall, GCMRL
GCMRL	George C. Marshall Research Library, Lexington, Virginia
GSPP	Papers of George S. Patton Jr., Library of Congress, Washington, DC
ISL	Indiana State Library, Indianapolis
LHCMA	Liddell Hart Centre for Military History Archives, Kings College, London
LOC	Library of Congress, Washington, DC
MHI	Military History Institute, U.S. Army Heritage and Education Center, Carlisle, Pennsylvania
NARA	National Archives and Records Administration (Manuscript Division), Washington, DC
OCS	Office of the Chief of Staff
OPD	Operations Planning Division, War Department General Staff
PPP	Pre-Presidential Papers of Dwight David Eisenhower, DDEL
PRO	Public Record Office
RG	Record Group
SGS	Secretary of the General Staff
USAWWII	United States Army in World War II series
WBSP	Papers of General Walter Bedell Smith, DDEL

1. Soldier Turned Diplomat

1. Smith's death received more attention from British newspapers than it did in the United States. Francis de Guingand, *Guardian and Daily Telegram*, 11 August 1961; Kenneth Strong, *Times* (London), 12 August 1961; *Sunday Telegraph*, 13 August 1961; Hastings Ismay and William Elliott, *Times*, 16 August 1961. Ismay served as Churchill's chief of staff in the prime minister's dual capacity as minister of defense and sat on the British Chiefs of Staff Committee. De Guingand acted as Montgomery's chief of staff, and Strong served under Smith as chief of intelligence in the Mediterranean and northwestern Europe. All were warm personal friends of Smith's.

2. *New York Times*, 10 August 1961.

3. Marshall to Smith, 8 May 1945, GCMP; Churchill to Smith, 25 October 1954, Truman to Smith, 16 January 1953, and Eisenhower, "Supplemental Rating of General Officers" (covering the period June 1940 to date), 12 July 1945, "Officer Career Summary," Smith 201 Personnel File, in Items of Particular Interest to General Smith File, WBSP.

4. Smith to Marshall, 3 December 1945, GCMP.

5. Eisenhower to Marshall, 22 August 1945, *The Papers of Dwight David Eisenhower: Occupation, 1945* (Baltimore, 1978), #282. For ease of referral, cites to the published papers of Eisenhower and Marshall are listed by entry number rather than page number.

6. Eisenhower to Marshall, 8 September 1945, *Occupation*, #311. Eisenhower relayed his doubts about McNarney in a communication with GEN Thomas Handy, Marshall's deputy chief of staff. Marshall informed Eisenhower, "I would not wish seemingly to force his assignment on you." Eisenhower never pushed the issue. Marshall to Eisenhower, 7 September 1945, *The Papers of George Catlett Marshall*, vol. 5, *The Finest Soldier, January 1, 1945-January 7, 1947* (Baltimore, 2003), #226. Eisenhower pushed for Smith's promotion to permanent major general. Eisenhower to Marshall, 11 September 1945, *Occupation*, #320.

7. Eisenhower to Marshall, 5 September 1945, *Occupation*, #307.

8. Smith to Marshall, 9 May 1945, GCMP.

9. Eisenhower to Louis Marx, 8 August 1945, *Occupation*, #242. Marx kept Smith in whiskey during the war. Marx to Smith, 25 January 1944, 1944 Chief of Staff Personal Correspondence, WBSP.

10. Ladislas Farago, *The Last Days of Patton* (New York, 1981), 211.

11. Carlo D'Este, *Patton: A Genius for War* (New York, 1995), 762; Patton Diary, 10 August 1945, in *Patton Papers, 1940-1945*, ed. Martin Blumenson (Boston, 1974), 736.

12. The quote comes from a letter to his wife, but Patton made no effort to disguise his views. Patton to Beatrice Patton, 10 August 1945, *Patton Papers, 1940-1945*, 735.

13. D'Este, *Patton: A Genius for War*, 762. Farago goes into considerable detail on Smith's role. See Farago, *Last Days of Patton*, chaps. 12, 13.

14. *New York Times*, 24 September 1945.

15. Kay Summersby, *Eisenhower Was My Boss* (New York, 1948), 278.

16. "You Don't Know What You Want," *Time*, 8 October 1945.

17. Transcript, Smith press conference, 26 September 1945; copy in GSPP, LOC.

18. The phrase "go to Canossa" alludes to the humiliation of the penitent Holy Roman Emperor Henry IV, who traveled to the Italian village of Canossa

to beg for clemency from Pope Gregory VII in 1077. Summersby, *Eisenhower Was My Boss*, 278.

19. Robert Murphy, *Diplomat among Warriors* (New York, 1964), 294–95.

20. Patton Diary, 29 September 1945, GSPP.

21. Marshall to Eisenhower, 2 October 1945, *Finest Soldier*, #243.

22. Eisenhower to Marshall, *Occupation*, #368.

23. Patton was a notoriously poor speller; he meant Chautauqua. Patton to Beatrice Patton, 15 November 1945, *Patton Papers, 1940-1945*, 807.

24. Eisenhower to Smith, 22 November 1945, *Occupation*, #480, 483.

25. Smith to Eisenhower, 28 November 1945, WBSP.

26. Patton Diary, 3 December 1945, *Patton Papers, 1940-1945*, 812.

27. Dr. R. Glen Spurling, "The Patton Episode," in GSPP. Spurling, the attending physician, kept a diary he later gave to Bea Patton. See also Farago, *Last Days of Patton*, 211, 275, 277–80, 305.

28. "Mr. Truman's Memoirs: Wallace Is Dismissed," Installment 30, "Year of Decisions," *New York Times*, 28 October 1955.

29. Marshall to Smith, 24 February 1946, *Finest Soldier, #373*; Smith to Marshall, 26 1946, Marshall File, WBSP.

30. Eisenhower to Hazlett, 13 March 1946, Edward E. "Swede" Hazlett Papers, DDEL; Stephen Ambrose, *Eisenhower: Soldier, General of the Army, President-Elect, 1890-1952* (New York, 1986), 187–88.

31. "Speakers at Red Army Day Here Last Night," *New York Times*, 22 February 1946.

32. "Smith to Ask What Russia Seeks," *New York Times*, 25 March 1946.

33. Joseph Stalin's Election Address, "New Five-Year Plan for Russia," 9 February 1946, reprinted in *New York Times*, 10 February 1946.

34. Churchill speech, "The Sinews of Peace," 5 March 1946, in Robert Rhodes James, ed., *Winston S. Churchill: His Complete Speeches, 1897-1963* (New York, 1974), 8:7292.

35. Smith to Byrnes, 5 April 1946, *FRUS, 1946, Eastern Europe, the Soviet Union*, 6:732–36.

36. W. H. Lawrence, "Tough Man for a Tough Job," *New York Times Magazine*, 13 March 1946.

37. Forrest Pogue interview of Walter Bedell Smith, 9 May 1947, MHI.

38. "Beedle in Wonderland," *Time*, 21 November 1949.

39. Walter Bedell Smith, *My Three Years in Moscow* (Philadelphia, 1950), 196.

40. Delbert Clark, "Smith Considered for German Post," *New York Times*, 15 March 1948; Smith to Eisenhower, 1 April 1948, Smith File, PPP.

41. "'Little Doing' in Moscow; Smith to Leave on Fishing Trip as News Calm Prevails," *New York Times*, 9 May 1948; "Smith Reported Quitting," *New York Times*, 15 May 1948.

42. "Baited Hook," *Time*, 24 May 1948; James Reston, "Discreet Bids to Russians by Marshall Are Indicated," *New York Times*, 29 May 1948.

43. Drew Middleton, "U.S. Moscow Envoy on Way to Berlin," *New York Times*, 25 July 1948.

44. Smith to Marshall, 24 August 1948, *FRUS, 1948, Germany and Austria*, 1065.

45. Smith, *My Three Years in Moscow*, 51.

46. "Mr. Molotov Comes to Town," *Time*, 9 August 1948.

47. Smith to Marshall, 23 August 1948, *FRUS, 1948, Germany and Austria*, 1061.

48. "Going for the Third Round," *Time,* 16 August 1948; "Moscow Run-Around," *Time,* 23 August 1948.

49. Smith to Marshall, 24 August 1948, *FRUS, 1948, Germany and Austria,* 1065.

50. Ibid., 1065–68; Smith forwarded Stalin's draft to Marshall, ibid., 1069; "Gentlemen, I Have a Plan," *Time,* 6 September 1948.

51. "Visit to the Boss," *Time,* 30 August 1948.

52. "And So to Paris," *Time,* 27 September 1948.

53. "U.S. Moscow Envoy Sees Truman; Takes Grave View but Doubts War," *New York Times,* 28 September 1948.

54. "Gen. Smith Doubtful of Return to Soviet Union," *New York Times,* 24 December 1948; "Smith Quits Moscow, Arrives in Berlin," *Associated Press,* 26 December 1948; "New Face in Moscow?" *Time,* 3 January 1949.

55. "Gen. Bedell Smith Quits Hospital," *New York Times,* 9 January 1949; Transcripts, Truman Press Conferences, 13 January, 17 February, 24 March 1949, Papers of Harry S. Truman, Harry S. Truman Presidential Library, Independence, MO; "Gen. Smith May Return to Moscow Temporarily," *New York Times,* 19 March 1949; "Gen. Smith Resigns as Moscow Envoy" and "A Resignation Accepted," *New York Times,* 26 March 1949.

56. "Smith Takes Over First Army Here," *New York Times,* 30 March 1949.

57. The *New York Times* published twenty-seven installments from 6 November to 2 December 1949; the *Saturday Evening Post* published eight installments from 12 November to 31 December 1950.

58. George Kennan, *Memoirs: 1925-1950* (Boston, 1967), 292–95; X (Kennan), "The Sources of Soviet Conduct," *Foreign Affairs* 25 (1947): 566–82.

59. In 1953 Smith lectured the Foreign Relations Committee on the verity of Palmerston's views on Russia. "Smith Quotes Palmerston on Russian Expansion," *New York Times,* 5 February 1953.

60. Smith, *My Three Years in Moscow,* 64–65, 196, 335. Economist Yevgenii Varga wrote a book arguing that Western capitalism was stabilizing rather than fracturing, undermining Stalin's foreign policy predicated on the assumption of the inevitability of war among the Western states. Far from fighting one another, the Western states, under Moscow's pressure, might unite against the Soviet Union.

Kremlin moderates, employing Varga's work, called for a radical departure from Stalin's policy of confrontation. As Smith told Marshall, the ultimate fate of the Varga group "may therefore well serve as a weathercock of party attitudes toward [the] western world." Smith to Marshall, 6 December 1948, *FRUS, 1948, Eastern Europe; The Soviet Union,* 4:942.

61. "3-Man Soviet Rule Predicted by Smith," *New York Times,* 5 March 1953.

62. "General W. B. Smith Meets the Press," *American Mercury,* June 1949; Richard Severo, "Lawrence E. Spivak, 93, Is Dead; The Originator of 'Meet the Press," *New York Times,* 10 March 1994.

63. "Gen. Smith Scored as Liar by Pravda," *New York Times,* 13 December 1949; "Ehrenburg Attacks Gen. Smith's Memoirs," *New York Times,* 2 January 1950.

64. Smith 201 File, WBSP; "Bedell Smith in Hospital," *New York Times,* 3 May 1950.

2. Expecting the Worst

1. Intelligence Survey Group, "The Central Intelligence Organization and National Organization for Intelligence," 1 January 1949, RG 59, Department

of State, Records of the Executive Secretariat, National Security Council Files, NARA.

2. The press predicted Smith's likely move to the CIA in spring 1950. "High U.S. Post Due for Bedell Smith," *New York Times*, 30 May 1950; Smith to Eisenhower, 7 September 1950, and Smith to John Hickerson, 23 August 1950, 1950 Personal Correspondence, WBSP. Hickerson served as an assistant secretary of state for international organization affairs.

3. Harry S. Truman, *Memoirs*, vol. 2, *Years of Trial and Hope* (Garden City, NY, 1956), 46.

4. Samuel Tower, *New York Times*, 3 August 1947, cited in David Rudgers, *Creating the Secret State: The Origins of the Central Intelligence Agency, 1943-1947* (Lawrence, KS, 2000), 148.

5. Arthur B. Darling, *The Central Intelligence Agency: An Instrument of Government, to 1950* (University Park, PA, 1990).

6. Ludwell Lee Montague, *General Walter Bedell Smith as Director of Central Intelligence, October 1950-February 1953* (University Park, PA, 1992).

7. The wartime Office of Strategic Services never enjoyed complete jurisdiction over foreign intelligence activities. From the early 1930s the FBI held responsibility for intelligence work in Latin America, and the military services jealously protected their areas of responsibility.

8. James Srodes, *Allen Dulles: Master of Spies* (Washington, DC, 1999), 421–22. Although this informal system worked well enough for Smith, the lack of firm command and control channels meant that his successors struggled to fully coordinate national intelligence efforts. Smith did worry about the legalities of covert operations. When he approached Truman with his concerns, the president pulled out a sheet of White House stationery, wrote out a few words, and handed it to Smith without comment. The letter granted Smith a blanket presidential pardon. Peter Grosse, *Gentleman Spy: The Life of Allen Dulles* (Amherst, MA, 1995), 420.

9. Kevin Whitelaw, "National Security Watch: The More Things Change . . . ," *U.S. News and World Report*, 17 November 2005. Whitelaw cited newly declassified CIA records, making the case for the historic disconnect between agencies charged with national security in light of the 9/11 attacks in New York and Washington.

10. NSC, "A Report to the National Security Council by the Secretaries of State and Defense on the Central Intelligence Agency and National Organization of Intelligence," 1 July 1949. Truman accepted this report and issued it as NSC #50.

11. The CIA assessment of the likelihood of Chinese intervention in Korea read: "While full-scale Chinese Communist intervention in Korea must be regarded as a continuing possibility, a consideration of all known factors leads to the conclusion that barring a Soviet decision for global war, such action is not probable in 1950. During this period, intervention will probably be confined to continued covert assistance to the North Koreans." Memorandum by the Central Intelligence Agency, "Threat of Full Chinese Communist Intervention in Korea," 12 October 1950, *FRUS, 1950, Korea*, 7:933–34.

12. Transcript, Truman's Press Conference, 3 May 1951, Truman Papers.

13. Montague, *General Walter Bedell Smith*, 253–54.

14. Ibid., 106–8, 151; Burton Hersch, *The Old Boys: The American Elite and the Origins of the CIA* (New York, 1992), 363–64; Evan Thomas, *The Very Best Men: Four Who Dared: The Early Years of the CIA* (New York, 1995), 64–65.

15. Kent to Harold Ford, May 1980, in Harold Ford, "A Tribute to Sherman Kent," *Studies in Intelligence* (fall 1980).

16. "The Eisenhower Administration and NATO Nuclear Strategy: An Oral History Roundtable," 16 March 1990, National Security Archive, George Washington University, Washington, DC.

17. D. H. Berger interview with Sam Halperin, 13 January 1995, in D. H. Berger, "The Use of Covert Paramilitary Activity as a Policy Tool: An Analysis of Operations Conducted by the United States Central Intelligence Agency, 1949–1951" (U.S. Marine Corps Command and Staff College, Quantico, VA). Halperin, who relayed the story of Smith's reaction in the NSC meeting, served eighteen years in the OSS and CIA.

18. Cited in Townshend Hoopes, *The Devil and John Foster Dulles* (New York, 1973), 379. A member of one of the wealthiest families in the world, Rockefeller chaired the Inter-American Development Commission in the Truman administration and left government service in 1947. He returned as Eisenhower's special assistant for foreign affairs in 1954.

19. Lewis Wood, "Gen. Smith Advises Nominees on Reds," *New York Times,* 1 October 1952; "'Beedle' Smith: Of Spies and Counter Spies . . . An Accidental Glimpse into a Supersecret Agency," *U.S. News and World Report,* 10 October 1952.

20. Harold Hinton, "Soldier, Diplomat, Intelligence Chief," *New York Times Magazine,* 27 August 1950.

21. William Elliott, *Times,* 16 August 1961.

22. Cited in Leonard Mosley, *Dulles: A Biography of Eleanor, Allen and John Foster Dulles and Their Family Network* (New York, 1978), 270, 283.

23. "Gen. Smith Thinks Reds Have Entered All Security Units," *New York Times,* 30 September 1952.

24. William Blair, "Stevenson Warns G.O.P. on Red Fight," *New York Times,* 1 October 1952; "Smith Asks G.O.P. to Stop Spy Talk," *New York Times,* 2 October 1953.

25. "Testimony of General Walter Bedell Smith at a Hearing before the House Committee on Un-American Activities, 13 October 1953," *Congressional Record* (Washington, DC, 1952), 4283–4298; William Wearts, "Gen. Smith Praises Truman for Curb on Red Infiltration," *New York Times,* 14 October 1952.

26. Transcript, Truman's Press Conference, 14 August 1952, Truman Papers.

27. Truman to Eisenhower, 13 August 1952; Eisenhower to Truman, 14 August 1952, Personal File, Truman Papers.

28. Transcript, Truman Press Conference, 14 August 1952, Truman Papers.

29. Truman to Eisenhower, 16 August 1952, Truman Papers.

30. Truman made these remarks on the campaign trail in mid-October. He concluded by saying, "Most of us, I think, believe a man ought to be loyal to his friends when they are unjustly attacked; that he ought to stand up for them, even if it costs him some votes. At any rate, that is a rule of my life. I stand by my friends." Truman, "Address at Symphony Hall," Boston, 17 October 1952, Truman Papers.

31. Eisenhower to Smith, 14 August 1952, 1952 Personal Correspondence, WBSP.

32. Smith to Eisenhower, 18 August 1952, ibid.

33. John Helgerson, "Truman and Eisenhower: Launching the Process," *Studies in Intelligence* 38, no. 5 (1995). Helgerson conducted interviews on 26 March and 25 October 1993 with Meredith Davidson, Smith's CIA assistant. Davidson accompanied Smith both on his weekly visits to the White House and on his trips to brief the president-elect. Helgerson's study and the Davidson interviews, which constitute the

core of the material dealing with Smith, serve a similar function in this treatment for the period August to December 1952.

34. Truman to Smith, 16 January 1953, 1953 Personal Correspondence, WBSP.

35. Smith told a conference of Legionnaires in January 1953, "the United States intelligence service was as good as any in the world—except possibly that of the Soviet Union." Truman proved even more sanguine. He told CIA recruits in November 1952, "We have an intelligence information service now that I think is not inferior to any in the world." "Soviet Espionage Best, Smith Says," *New York Times*, 26 January 1953; Truman, "Remarks at a Meeting of an Orientation Course Conducted by the CIA," 21 November 1952, Truman Papers.

36. The account of the trip to New York comes from Helgerson, "Launching the Process," 7–8.

37. Alan Truscott with Phillip Alder, "Bridge—The Game and Statesmanship," *New York Times*, 18 April 2005.

38. "Central Intelligence Head Is Nominated for 4 Stars," *New York Times*, 16 July 1951; "Gen. Smith to Be Retired," *New York Times*, 22 January 1953.

3. Dulles's Number Two

1. Cited in Hoopes, *The Devil and John Foster Dulles*, 145.

2. "'Beedle' Smith: On Way Up as the Top Aide for Ike," *U.S. News and World Report*, 31 July 1953.

3. Arthur Krock, "When Ten Senators Are the Same as Ninety-six," *New York Times*, 10 February 1953.

4. Hoopes, *The Devil and John Foster Dulles*, 138.

5. W. H. Lawrence, "General Smith Slated to Get Post as Top Aide to Dulles," *New York Times*, 8 January 1953.

6. W. H. Lawrence, "'Beetle' Is Back on the Eisenhower Team," *New York Times Magazine*, 1 March 1953.

7. "Hoover for Smith," *Time*, 30 August 1954.

8. Cited in Mosley, *Dulles*, 194.

9. Smith to Morgan, 18 February 1953, 1953 Personal Correspondence, WBSP.

10. "Memo of Conversation between Smith and Carl McCardle re: Smith's Threatened Resignation," 17 August 1953, Subject File, John Foster Dulles Papers, DDEL.

11. Lawrence, "'Beetle' Is Back."

12. "Memorandum for the Record by the Special Assistant to the President for National Security Affairs (Cutler)," 9 May 1953, *FRUS, 1952-1954, National Security Affairs*, 2(1):323–24.

13. Paragraph 39b of NSC 162/22, "Basic National Security Policy," 30 October 1953, cited in Smith to Eisenhower, 3 December 1953, *FRUS, 1952-1954, National Security Affairs*, 2(1):607.

14. National Security Council, "NSC 136: U.S. and Policy Regarding the Present Situation in Iran," RG 59, Records Relating to State Department Participation in the Operations Coordinating Board and the National Security Council, 1947–1963, 20 November 1952, NARA.

15. Smith to Byrnes, 5 April 1946, *FRUS, 1946, Eastern Europe, the Soviet Union*, 6:733–34.

16. The best source is an in-house CIA history of the coup in Iran written in 1954 that the *New York Times* published online in 2000. Donald Wilber, "Clandes-

tine Service History: Overthrow of Premier Mossadeq of Iran, November 1952–August 1953," CIA Archives, reproduced in *New York Times*, 28 August 2000.

17. British Ambassador Wakins to Smith, "Foreign Office Memorandum," 23 July 1953, in Wilber, "Clandestine Service History," appendix C. Smith engaged in lengthy negotiations with the British on dividing the oil spoils. In February 1954 Smith proposed a 35-30-35 split among Anglo-Iranian, Shell, and U.S. companies. The British accepted Smith's suggestion. Smith to U.S. Embassy in Iran, 19 February 1954, *FRUS, 1952-1954, Iran*, 10:927.

18. Smith to Eisenhower, 18 August 1953, *FRUS, Iran*, 748.

19. Kermit Roosevelt, *Countercoup: The Struggle for the Control of Iran* (New York, 1979).

20. In 2003 the CIA and the State Department both published a limited number of sources on the coup in Guatemala. Based on the mandate, the CIA published very little material from the Truman administration. The best source on PBFortune and its successor PBSuccess is a published CIA study: Nick Cullather, *Secret History: The CIA's Classified Account of Its Operations in Guatemala, 1952-1954* (Stanford, CA, 1999).

21. State Department, "Memorandum of Discussion at the 135th Meeting of the National Security Council," 4 March 1953, *FRUS, Iran*, 699. By early March 1953 the intelligence community had convinced itself that the Arbenz agrarian reforms constituted the first step toward "Communist control over the rural population." State Department, "Intelligence Report Prepared in the Office of Intelligence Research," 5 March 1953, *FRUS, 1952-1954, Guatemala*, 70–72.

22. The same paper warned, "Were it to become evident that the United States has tried a Czechoslovakia in reverse in Guatemala, the effects on our relations in this hemisphere, and probably in the world at large, could be as disastrous as those produced by open intervention." "Draft NSC Policy Paper," *FRUS, 1952-1954, The American Republics*, 4:1083.

23. "Memorandum from King to Wisner," 27 August 1953, *FRUS, Guatemala*, 91–92. Smith's central role in resuscitating the Guatemala operation is covered in Cullather, *Secret History*, 27–33.

24. "Memorandum for the Record," 11 September 1953, *FRUS, Guatemala*, 102.

25. Wisner to Smith, 16 September 1953, ibid., 86 n. 1.

26. "Contact Report," 25 November 1953, ibid., 149–50.

27. "The Americas: The Problem of Guatemala," *Time*, 11 January 1954; CIA, "Guatemala New Notes," 15 January 1954, CIA Historical Review Program (2003). This is another document released under the Freedom of Information Act.

28. "Reexamination of United States Programs for National Security," 19 January 1953, *FRUS, 1952-1954, National Security Affairs*, 2(1):209–11.

29. "United States Objectives and Courses of Action with Respect to Southeast Asia," 30 December 1953, *FRUS, 1952-1954, Indochina*, 13(1):962.

30. Walt Waggoner, "Memo for James Reston: Dinner for General Walter Bedell Smith," 4 January 1954, James Reston Papers, University Library, University of Illinois at Urbana-Champaign. Reston, of the *New York Times*, was the unofficial dean of the Washington press corps.

31. "Memorandum of Discussion at the 180th Meeting of the National Security Council" (NSC 177), 14 January 1954, and "United States Objectives and Courses of Action with Respect to Southeast Asia" (NSC 5405), 16 January 1954, *FRUS, 1952-1954, Indochina*, 13(1):961–62, 971–76.

32. "Memorandum by C. D. Jackson," 18 January 1954, ibid., 981–82.

33. Australian Defense Liaison, "Five Power Planning Report," 23 June 1954, American Relations with South East Asia, 1950–1954, with Special Reference to Indochina File, National Archives of Australia, Canberra.

34. Eisenhower Diary, 17 March 1951, PPP; Robert Ferrell, ed., *The Eisenhower Diaries* (New York, 1981), 190.

35. "Memorandum of Discussion at the 179th Meeting of the National Security Council," 8 January 1954, *FRUS, Indochina*, 13(1):949, 952; Hagerty Diary, 8 January 1954, James C. Hagerty Papers, DDEL.

36. Eisenhower to Hazlett, 18 March 1954, in *The Papers of Dwight David Eisenhower*, vol. 15, *The Presidency: The Middle Way*, #784.

37. Eisenhower to Dulles, 10 February 1954, ibid., #722.

38. LTG James Van Fleet, until February 1953 commander of Eighth Army in Korea, made the case for Asian wars fought by Asians. He dismissed the French plan for Indochina as a complete failure and described the region as a "rathole—bound to be bottomless so long as money goes to pay foreign troops while the natives stand around as bored bystanders, without responsibility for their own freedom." Both Eisenhower and Smith concurred. Eisenhower to Smith, 16 January 1945, *The Middle Way*, #668, n. 2.

39. Smith, "Memorandum of Special Committee," 29 January 1954, *FRUS, Indochina*, 13(1):1003; "Minutes, NSC Meeting," 30 January 1945, in Department of Defense, *United States-Vietnam Relations, 1945-1967*, vol. 9 (Washington, DC, 1972), 235.

40. Walt Waggoner, "Walter Bedell Smith to Thirteen Reporters," 17 September 1954, Reston Papers.

41. Smith to Eisenhower, 12 March 1954, *FRUS, Indochina*, 13:1106–7; Eisenhower to Smith, 15 March 1954, *The Middle Way*, #776.

42. Allen Cameron, ed., *Viet-Nam Crisis: A Documentary History*, vol. 1, *1940-1956* (Ithaca, NY, 1971), 233.

43. Joint Chiefs of Staff to Secretary of Defense, 31 March 1954, *FRUS, Indochina*, 13(1):1198.

44. Ridgway, "Memorandum," 2 April 1954, ibid., 1220-21; Matthew Ridgway, *Soldier: The Memoirs of Matthew B. Ridgway* (New York, 1956), 276.

45. Arthur W. Radford, *From Pearl Harbor to Vietnam: The Memoirs of Admiral Arthur W. Radford*, ed. Stephen Jurika Jr. (Stanford, CA, 1980), 398–406. Eisenhower already knew Radford would not secure support in the JCS for Vulture. *FRUS, Indochina*, 13(1): 1201.

46. Eisenhower to Churchill, 4 April 1954, *The Middle Way*, #816; Dulles, "Memorandum of Conversation," 2 April 1954, *FRUS, Indochina*, 13(1):1210-11.

47. *FRUS, 1952-1954, Indochina*, 13(1):1224-25.

48. Sherman Adams, *Firsthand Report: The Story of the Eisenhower Administration* (New York, 1961), 122.

49. "Memorandum of Presidential Telephone Conversation [with Dulles]" and Dulles to Embassy in France, 5 April 1954, *FRUS, Indochina*, 13(1):1241-42.

50. Ridgway, "Memorandum," 6 April 1954, ibid., 1270; Ridgway, *Soldier*, 276.

51. "Memorandum of Discussion at the 192d Meeting of the National Security Council," 6 April 1954, *FRUS, Indochina*, 13(1):1253-54.

52. "Meeting of NSC," 6 April 1954, ibid., 1254-56.

53. Anthony Eden, *The Memoirs of Sir Anthony Eden: Full Circle* (London, 1960), 105.

54. George H. Gallup, *The Gallup Poll: Public Opinion, 1935-1971*, 3 vols. (New York, 1972), 2:1170–71, 1235–36, 1243.

55. Allan B. Cole, ed., *Conflict in Indo-China and International Repercussions: A Documentary History, 1945-55* (Ithaca, NY, 1956), 174; Hagerty Diary, 16 and 17 April 1954.

56. Dulles to Eisenhower, 22 April 1954, *FRUS, Indochina*, 13(1):1351.

57. Eisenhower to Gruenther, 26 April 1954, *The Middle Way*, #842; Hagerty Diary, 26 April 1954, *FRUS, Indochina*, 13(2):410–11.

58. Three days earlier Eisenhower had told Nixon, "If allies go back on us, then we would have one terrible alternative—we would have to attack with everything we have." If the United States ever went back "to fortress America, then the word 'fortress' will be entirely wrong in this day and age. Dien Bien Phu is a perfect example of a fortress. The Reds are surrounding it and crowding back the French into a position where they have to surrender or die. If we ever came back to the fortress idea for America, we would have, as I said before, one simple, dreadful alternative—we would have to explore an attack with everything we have. What a terrible decision that would be to make." Hagerty Diary, 26 April 26 1954, *FRUS, Indochina*, 13(2):410–11.

59. Unless otherwise noted, the discussion of the 29 April 1954 NSC meeting comes from "Memorandum of Discussion at the 194th Meeting of the National Security Council," *FRUS, Indochina*, 13(2): 1431–45. See also Dwight D. Eisenhower, *Mandate for Change, 1953-1956* (Garden City, NY, 1963), 354–55; Richard Nixon, *RN: The Memoirs of Richard Milhous Nixon* (New York, 1978), 153–54.

60. Cited in Stanley Karnow, *Vietnam: A History* (New York, 1984), 197–98.

61. "Meeting of the National Security Council," 29 April 1954, *FRUS, Indochina*, 13(2): 1445; Hagerty Diary, 29 April 1954, and "Editorial Note," ibid., 1429–30.

4. The Geneva Conference

1. Eisenhower to Dulles, 1 May 1954, *The Middle Way*, #854. He made the same point in his 29 April news conference, "Editorial Note," *FRUS, Indochina*, 13(2): 1430.

2. "The First Day," *Time*, 3 May 1954.

3. Molotov Journal, 6 March 1954, in Paul Wingrove, "Russian Documents on the 1954 Geneva Conference," *Cold War International History Project Bulletin* 16, Woodrow Wilson International Center for Scholars (Washington, DC, 2008), 86.

4. Ilya Gaiduk, *Confronting Vietnam: Soviet Policy toward the Indochina Conflict, 1954-1963* (Stanford, CA, 2003), 50, 61.

5. Eden, *Full Circle*, 102. For Smith's instructions, see "Memorandum of Discussions at the 196th Meeting of the National Security Council," 8 May 1954, *FRUS, Indochina*, 13(2): 1509.

6. Zhou Enlai to Mao Zedong and others, "Regarding a Meeting with British Foreign Secretary Eden," 1 May 1954, and Chen Jian and Shen Zhihua, "The Geneva Conference of 1954: New Evidence from the Archives of the Ministry of Foreign Affairs of the People's Republic of China," *Cold War International History Project Bulletin*, 16–17.

7. Department of State, *American Foreign Policy, 1950-55* (Washington, DC, 1957), 2:2385–86, 2389–90. Illustrative of how the Cold War turned American strategic thinking upside down, Japan went to war against the Western powers in 1941 to secure access to Southeast Asian resources and markets; in the 1950s the United States contemplated intervening in Indochina, and threatening a wider war, at least in part to safeguard a Japanese economy ruined by American arms.

8. Smith referred to the Vietminh as a "nonexistent government." Smith, "First Plenary Session on Indochina," 8 May 1954, *FRUS, 1952-1954, Geneva Conference,* 434–36.

9. Dulles to Smith, 8 May 1954, ibid., 733.

10. Ibid., 731, 733, 778–79.

11. Smith to State, "Memo of Conversation," 10 May 1954, ibid., 755–56.

12. Dulles, approved by Eisenhower, to Embassy of France, 11 May 1954, *FRUS, Indochina,* 13(2): 1534–36.

13. Ambassador C. Douglas Dillon to State, 14 May 1954, ibid., 1566–68.

14. Smith to Dulles, 15 May 1954, and Smith, "Smith-Bidault Meeting," 24 May 1954, *FRUS, Geneva Conference,* 807, 902–3.

15. Eden, *Full Circle,* 119; Thomas Hamilton, "U.S.-British Split on Asia Broadens at Decisive Stage," *New York Times,* 17 May 1954; "Geneva: The Honest Broker," *Time,* 24 May 1954.

16. Smith to Dulles, 19 May 1954, *FRUS, Geneva Conference,* 856.

17. Smith to Dulles, 20 May 1954, ibid., 864–65.

18. Eden, *Full Circle,* 143.

19. NSC, "Memo of 199th Meeting," 27 May 1954, *FRUS, Geneva Conference,* 943.

20. Robertson to Dulles, 1 June 1954, General Correspondence and Memorandum Series, John Foster Dulles Papers, DDEL; Dulles to Smith, 18 July 1954, *FRUS, Geneva Conference,* 1429–30.

21. Eden to Churchill, 15 May 1954, cited in Eden, *Full Circle,* 135.

22. Telegram, CCP Central Committee to Zhou Enlai, "Concerning Policies and Measures in the Struggle against the United States and Jiang Jieshi after the Geneva Conference," 27 July 1954, *Cold War International History Project Bulletin,* 83–84.

23. Smith to Dulles, "Smith-Eden Meeting," 21 May 1954, *FRUS, Geneva Conference,* 874–75.

24. Smith to Dulles, "Smith-Molotov Meeting," 23 May 1954, ibid., 895–99.

25. United States Delegation to the Department of State, "Verbatim Smith Press Briefing," 27 May 1954, ibid., 952–53.

26. Zhou Enlai to Mao Zedong and others, 30 May 1954, *Cold War International History Project Bulletin,* 26.

27. Smith, "Eighth Restricted Session on Indochina," 29 May 1945, *FRUS, Geneva Conference,* 974.

28. Eden, *Full Circle,* 124–25.

29. Smith to Kennan, 11 June 1948, Kennan Papers, cited in H. W. Brands, "Walter Bedell Smith and the Geneva Conference on Indochina," *Cold Warriors: Eisenhower's Generation and American Foreign Policy* (New York, 1988), 85. Brands's chapter on Smith in Geneva helps unravel the many twists and turns Smith faced during the conference.

30. Smith, "Smith-Bidault Meeting," 24 May 1954, and Smith to State, 26 May 1954, *FRUS, Geneva Convention,* 902–3, 936; Smith to Dulles, 24 and 26 May 1954, ibid., 936, 902–3.

31. Smith to Dulles, 4 May 1943, ibid., 689–90.

32. Smith to Dulles, 26 May 1954, ibid., 936. Smith made similar recommendations in Smith to State, 9 and 24 May, 7 June 1954, ibid., 741, 900–901, 1055.

33. Australian embassy cable, 4 June 1954, American Relations with South East Asia, 1950-1954, with Special Reference to Indochina File, National Archives of Australia, Canberra. The Australian sources are particularly helpful for their candid

impartiality and because of the importance of Australian and New Zealand cooperation to the State Department.

34. The material here and in the following paragraphs comes from Australian
sources, chiefly Australian embassy cable, 6 June 1954, ibid.

35. Ibid. Spender gave a lengthy description of his talks with Dulles in the cable.

36. Wang Bingnan, "Meeting with Jean Chauvel," 6 June 1954, *Cold War International History Project Bulletin,* 37.

37. Smith to State, "Sixth Plenary Session," 9 June 1954, *FRUS, Geneva Conference,* 1087.

38. Transcript, *FRUS, Geneva Conference,* 1095, 1098–99; Thomas Hamilton,
"Smith Says Reds Bar Geneva Pact," *New York Times,* 10 June 1954.

39. Smith, "Statement to Sixth Plenary Session," 9 June 1954, *FRUS, Geneva Conference,* 1093; Zhou Enlai to Mao Zedong and others, "Regarding the Seventh Plenary Session," 11 June 1954, *Cold War International History Project Bulletin,* 41.

40. Smith to Dulles, "Smith-Eden Meeting," 9 June 1954, *FRUS, Geneva Conference,* 1083.

41. Australian embassy cables, Washington to Canberra, "Report of the Five
Power Military Conference, Washington, June 1954," and Australian Defense Liai-
son, "Five Power Planning Report," 23 June 1954, American Relations, National
Archives of Australia.

42. Australian Defense Liaison, "Five Power Planning Report." At the same juncture, Dulles told Smith, "If on the basis of collective action, we should get into the
war, we would be in it all the way, and would do whatever seemed necessary to win
the war." Dulles to Smith, 9 June 1954, *FRUS, Geneva Conference,* 1103.

43. Dulles to Smith, 9 June 1954, *FRUS, Geneva Conference,* 1103.

44. Smith, "Smith-Eden-Chauvel Meeting," 14 June 1954, ibid., 1132–34.

45. Smith to Dulles, "Fourteenth Restricted Session on Indochina," 16 June 1954,
ibid., 1157–61.

46. Cutler, "Outline of General Smith's Remarks to the President and Bipartisan
Congressional Group," 23 June 1954, *FRUS, Indochina,* 13(2):1732.

47. Smith to Dulles and U.S. Delegation to State, 17 June 1954, *FRUS, Geneva
Conference,* 1171, 1174.

48. Wang Bingnan, *The Nine-Year Sino-U.S. Talks in Retrospect,* reproduced by Foreign Broadcast Information Service (Springfield, VA, 1985), 11.

49. Smith to Dulles, "Smith-Molotov Meeting," 19 June 1954, *FRUS, Geneva Conference,* 1189–93.

50. *FRUS, Geneva Conference,* 1188 n. 1; Harold Callender, "Mendes-France
Delays Trip after Meetings Smith, Eden," *New York Times,* 21 June 1954.

51. Smith to Dulles, 17 June 1954, *FRUS, Geneva Conference,* 1178 n. 1.

52. Cutler, "Outline of General Smith's Remarks," 1731–32; "Smith Back, Says
Asian Talk Failed," *New York Times,* 22 June 1954.

53. Spender to Prime Minister Sydney Holland, 23 June 1945, American Relations, National Archives of Australia.

54. Smith to Dulles, 23 June 1954, *FRUS, Indochina,* 13(2):1733–34.

55. Charles Egan, "Bricker and Smith Clash on Treaties," *New York Times,* 29
April 1953. Smith complained before the Senate Foreign Relations Committee about
the existing constitutional constraints on the conduct of foreign policy. "I wish we
did not have to tell [our adversaries] that we have no intention of putting ground
troops into Indochina; I wish to God that we could leave that suspicion or that fear

in their minds." Senate Foreign Relations Committee (Historical Series), vol. 6, 83rd Congress, 2nd Session, 1954, 111.

56. Hagerty recorded the president characterizing the amendment as "stupid, a blind violation of the Constitution by stupid, blind isolationists." Referring to McCarthyism and Republican isolationism, Smith told Eden "not to pay much attention to some of the stupid things being said in the USA." Diary of Evelyn Shuckburgh, 1 May 1954, in James Cable, *The Geneva Conference of 1954 on Indochina* (New York, 2000), 70. Shuckburgh was Eden's private secretary, and Cable served on the British delegation.

57. *FRUS, 1952-1954, Western Europe and Canada*, 6(1):1129.

58. Minutes of cabinet meeting, 9 July 1954, Cabinet Series, Staff Secretary Records, Dwight D. Eisenhower: Papers as President of the United States, DDEL; Hagerty Diary, 8–9 July 1954, 86–87.

59. Dulles to Mèndes-France, 10 July 1954, *FRUS, Geneva Conference*, 1330.

60. Eisenhower to Churchill, 12 July 1954, *The Middle Way*, #974.

61. "Reunion in Geneva," *Time*, 26 July 1954; Hagerty Diary, 11 July 1954, *FRUS, Geneva Conference*, 1333–34.

62. Johnson, "Johnson-Chauvel Meeting," 9 July 1954, *FRUS, Geneva Conference*, 1322.

63. CCP Central Committee to Wei Guoqing, Qiao Xiaoguang, and the Vietnamese Workers Party Central Committee, "Regarding the Meeting between the Premier and Comrade Ding [Ho]," 20 June 1954, *Cold War International History Project Bulletin*, 48–49.

64. Journal of V. V. Vaskov (Soviet chargé d'affaires in Beijing), "Top Secret Memorandum of Conversation with Comrade Mao Zedong on 5 July 1954," 27 August 1954, ibid., 88.

65. "Minutes of Conversation between Zhou Enlai and Anthony Eden," 13 July 1954, ibid., 63–65.

66. "Minutes of Conversation between Zhou Enlai and Anthony Eden," 17 July 1954, ibid., 65–68.

67. "Minutes of Zhou Enlai's Meeting with Mendes-France," 17 July 1954, ibid., 68.

68. Smith to Dulles, 17 July 1954, *FRUS, Geneva Conference*, 1026–27.

69. Wang, *Nine-Year Sino-U.S. Talks in Retrospect*, 11–12.

70. Smith, "Twenty-third Restricted Session on Indochina," 18 July 1954, *FRUS, Geneva Conference*, 1431–34.

71. Zhou Enlai to Mao Zedong and others, "Regarding the Situation at the Twenty-third Restricted Session," 18 July 1954, *Cold War International History Project Bulletin*, 72–73; Wang, *Nine-Year Sino-U.S. Talks in Retrospect*, 12; Thomas Hamilton, "Pact Is Tentative; British Concur, but U.S. Waits," *New York Times*, 19 July 1954.

72. "Minutes of Conversation between Zhou Enlai and Cambodian Foreign Minister Tep Phan (Summary)," 20 July 1954, *Cold War International History Project Bulletin*, 82.

73. Wang, *Nine-Year Sino-U.S. Talks in Retrospect*, 12.

74. Text of Eisenhower's announcement, 21 July 1954, *FRUS, Geneva Conference*, 1503.

75. Smith to Dulles, 19 July 1954, ibid., 1448.

76. Robert Ferrell, ed., *Eisenhower Diaries* (New York, 1976), 296.

5. "Ike's Prat Boy"

1. Transcript of press briefing, Smith to State, 2 June 1954, *FRUS, Geneva Conference*, 1007.

2. Smith to Eisenhower, 17 August 1954, and Eisenhower to Smith, 18 August 1954, *The Middle Way*, #1028, nn. 1–4.

3. Michael Hoffman, "Mendes-France Spurs E.D.C. Vote," *New York Times*, 22 July 1954.

4. Eisenhower to Smith, 3 and 7 September 1954, and Smith to Eisenhower, 10 September 1954, *The Middle Way*, #1045, #1050, #1045 n. 3.

5. NSC meeting, 9 September 1954, NSC Series, Ann Whitman File, DDEL. The file was declassified in 2007.

6. Waggoner to Reston, 17 September 1954, Reston Papers.

7. Eisenhower to Cutler, 21 September 1954, *The Middle Way*, #1069.

8. "Gen. Smith Makes Plea," *New York Times*, 2 October 1954; "The Cold War—An Audit by Bedell Smith," *New York Times Magazine*, 10 October 1954. Smith's permanent rank was major general.

9. "Hoover for Smith," *Time*, 30 August 1954; "Expected to Join Board of Machine & Foundry," *New York Times*, 20 August 1954.

10. "Bedell Smith Is Elected to R.C.A. Directorate," *New York Times*, 4 December 1954.

11. "Ringing the Brass," *Time*, 29 June 1959.

12. Smith served as a consultant to the Special Projects Office (Disarmament) in the executive office of the president (1955–1956) and as a member of the President's Citizen Advisory Board on the Mutual Security Program (1956–1957), the Office of Defense Mobilization Special Stockpile Advisory Committee (1957–1958), and the President's Committee on Disarmament (1958). In addition, he contributed to the National Security Training Commission (1955–1957). Between 1958 and 1961 Smith played a part in the advisory council of the President's Committee on Fund Raising. Smith also sat on the board of consultants for the new National War College (1956–1959). However, there is no doubt that serving as adviser to the George C. Marshall Foundation (1960–1961) gave him the most pleasure.

13. "Movers and Shakers," *Time*, 8 October 1951; Lawrence, "'Beetle' Is Back."

14. Eugene Pasymowski and Carl Gilbert, "Bilderberg: The Cold War Internationale," published in U.S. House of Representatives, *Congressional Record*, 15 September 1971, E9616–24. Democratic representative John Rarick of Louisiana inserted the article in the *Record*.

15. Waggoner, "Dinner for Gen. Walter Bedell Smith," 4 January 1954, Reston Papers.

16. Jackson explained how the American political system could cast up a "supercharged, emotional freak from time to time" and predicted, "Whether McCarthy dies by an assassin's bullet, or is eliminated in the normal American way of getting rid of boils on the body politic, I prophesy that by the time we hold our next meeting he will be gone from the American scene." Cited in Alden Hatch, *H.R.H. Bernhard, Prince of the Netherlands* (London, 1962), 218.

17. Smith to Eisenhower and Eisenhower to Hauge, 11 March 1955, *The Middle Way*, #1341, n. 2. Smith has emerged as a favorite among conspiracy theorists. His marginal role in getting the Bilderberg Group off the ground has prompted the notion that Smith, as DCI, undersecretary, and representative of corporate interests, played a prominent part in creating an organization dedicated to forming a single

world government. Smith has also been targeted as the chief agent in covering up the existence of UFOs. As DCI, he thought there existed "one chance in 10,000 that the phenomenon posed a threat to the security of the country, but even that chance could not be taken," so he commissioned a study to assess the risk from UFOs. Primarily, he wanted to determine whether the CIA could exploit UFO sightings as a form of black propaganda to convince the Soviets the United States might be working on a new wonder weapon. Gerald Haines, "CIA's Role in the Study of UFOs, 1947–90: A Die-Hard Issue," CIA study declassified in 1997 and published by the Center for the Study of Intelligence.

18. Charles C. Wertenbaker, "The Invasion Plan: Smith, Eisenhower's Chief of Staff, Worked out the Secret, Closely Guarded Moves," *Life*, 12 June 1944.

19. Dwight D. Eisenhower, *Crusade in Europe* (Garden City, NY, 1948), 197.

20. Eisenhower to Smith, October 1947, *Papers of Dwight David Eisenhower*, vol. 9, *Chief of Staff*, 2014–15. Based loosely on Patton's diary, *War as I Knew It* appeared as a book in 1947.

21. Smith to Eisenhower, 17 November 1947, 1947 Correspondence File, WBSP.

22. Eisenhower to Smith, 28 November 1947, ibid.

23. Ralph Ingersoll, *Top Secret* (New York, 1946).

24. Smith to Eisenhower, 1 April 1948, 1948 Correspondence File, WBSP.

25. Chester Wilmot, *The Struggle for Europe* (London, 1952); Arthur Bryant, *The Turn of the Tide: A History of the War Years Based on the Diaries of Field-Marshal Lord Alanbrooke, Chief of the Imperial General Staff* (London, 1957) and *Triumph in the West* (London, 1959); Bernard Montgomery, *The Memoirs of Field-Marshal the Viscount Montgomery of Alamein* (London, 1958).

26. Walter Bedell Smith, *Eisenhower's Six Great Decisions: Europe, 1944-45* (New York, 1956).

27. Ismay referred to the first volume of the Alanbrooke diaries as "little short of tragedy" and hoped the second volume would "be less a travesty." See Eisenhower to Ismay, 25 January 1958, *The Papers of Dwight David Eisenhower*, vol. 18, *The Presidency: Keeping the Peace*, #550, n. 1. Browning told Eisenhower that although Montgomery's memoirs "stirred up quite a lot of excitement over this side," the field marshal's criticism of Eisenhower did not alter "by one degree the devotion and loyalty we British Generals feel for you as our leader in those great days." The exchange between Eisenhower and Browning is in *The Papers of Dwight David Eisenhower*, vol. 19, *Keeping the Peace*, #979. An entire White House confidential file contains the correspondence dealing with the flap over Montgomery's memoirs.

28. Eisenhower to Ismay, 14 January 1959, *Keeping the Peace*, #1012.

29. Eisenhower to Clay, 1 January 1959, and Eisenhower to Smith, 3 January 1959, ibid., #989, #991, nn. 2, 4.

30. Cited in Richard Immerman, *The CIA in Guatemala: The Foreign Policy of Intervention* (Austin, TX, 1982), 152.

31. "Walter Bedell Smith Is Ill," *New York Times*, 29 October 1959; "Bedell Smith 'Unchanged,'" *New York Times*, 1 November 1959.

32. Nixon, *RN: Memoirs*, 198.

33. Whitney Shepardson, "Bedell Smith Quoted on Russia," *New York Times*, 20 August 1961.

34. B. C. Mossman and M. W. Stark, *The Last Salute: Civil and Military Funerals, 1921-1969* (Washington, DC, 1991).

35. Eisenhower to Cutler, 21 September 1954, *The Middle Way*, #1069.

6. Born to Be a Soldier

1. *Indianapolis Star,* 8 May 1945; "Indiana's Walter Bedell Smith," *Indianapolis Star Magazine,* 18 October 1953. See also *Indianapolis News,* 19 June 1945; "Walter Bedell Smith," *Sons of Indiana; Stories of Indiana's Famous Sons* 25 (1966): 17. During World War II, Indianapolis suddenly discovered one of its native sons had risen to great heights in the army. Throughout the war, particularly after Smith presided over the Italian surrender and later the German capitulation, a number of articles appeared in the Indianapolis newspapers dealing with General Eisenhower's chief of staff. Given that he was an unknown before the war, even in his hometown, and the fact that his meteoric rise in the army shocked even his own family, most of the articles sought to explain the Bedell Smith phenomenon. After the war, Indianapolis newspapers ran a number of pieces on Smith, always containing vignettes of his growing up in the city. These articles, collected in the Clippings File of the Indiana State Library, provide virtually the only biographical material on Smith's life before he entered the military.

2. *Indianapolis Star,* 4 October 1943 and 19 August 1950, Smith File, ISL.

3. *Indianapolis Star,* 8 May 1945, ibid.

4. Mrs. Lucy Wilson Thomas made this observation in *Indianapolis Star,* 8 May 1945, ibid.

5. Wertenbaker, "The Invasion Plan," 94; "Indiana's Walter Bedell Smith," *Indianapolis Times,* 16 September 1943 and 3 April 1949; *Indianapolis News,* 19 June 1945, Smith File, ISL.

6. *Indianapolis Star,* 8 May 1945, Smith File, ISL.

7. *Indianapolis Star,* 4 October 1943, ibid.

8. *Indianapolis Times,* 3 April 1949; *Indianapolis Star,* 8 May 1945, ibid.

9. *Indianapolis Star,* 4 October 1943 and 19 August 1950; *Indianapolis News,* 6 June 1944, ibid.

10. *Indianapolis Star,* 4 October 1943 and 8 May 1945, ibid.

11. *Indianapolis Star,* 4 October 1943, ibid.

12. *Indianapolis Star Magazine,* 18 October 1953, ibid.

13. Mrs. D. S. Callahan, quoted in *Indianapolis Times,* 3 April 1949, ibid.

14. "Indiana's Walter Bedell Smith," *Indianapolis News,* 19 June 1945, Smith File, ISL.

15. The city's population grew from 48,244 in 1870 to 282,677 in 1915. Until Henry Ford built his River Rouge plant in Detroit, Indiana vied with Michigan as the nation's leader in the production of motorcars. As the hub of several railroads, Indianapolis also boasted a wide array of firms serving the needs of the rail system.

16. *Indianapolis in 1915,* Audiovisual Section, ISL.

17. "Smith Left Great Military Record," *Indianapolis News,* 29 January 1965, Smith File, ISL.

18. Smith's high school records, 1909–1913, Emmerich Manual High School. The school's name changed in 1916 in honor of the principal, Charles Emmerich. Richard Grismore to the author, 5 January 2006.

19. "Indiana's Walter Bedell Smith."

20. For mention of the sporting and cultural aspects of the Light Infantry, see *Nation,* 3 December 1885, 3; "Cycling," *Outing,* August 1896, 13; "The National Drill; Infantry and Rifle Competition," *New York Times,* 28 May 1887.

21. John Mahon, *History of the Militia and the National Guard* (New York, 1983),

141. See also William Watt and James Spears, *Indiana's Citizen Soldiers: The Militia and National Guard in Indiana History* (Indianapolis, 1980).

22. "Indiana's Walter Bedell Smith"; transcript, "General Smith," CFAF (Calgary) radio program, 11 April 1946, WBSP.

23. This observation was made by Smith's only real friend in high school, H. F. Weinmann, who remarked that Smith "didn't care much for girls until he was seventeen" (*Indianapolis News*, 19 June 1945). See also an interview with Mary Cline Smith, *Indianapolis Star*, 8 May 1945, Smith File, ISL.

24. *Indianapolis Star*, 26 September 1943 and 8 May 1945, Smith File, ISL. Smith discussed his 1913 service with his old company commander in Smith to James Hurt, 27 January 1944, 1944 Chief of Staff's Personal Correspondence, WBSP.

25. "His Teacher No Longer a Terror to 'Beedle,'" *Indianapolis Star*, 21 June 1945; see also *Indianapolis Star*, 8 May 1945, Smith File, ISL. Emmerich Manual Training High sent him his diploma when he served as DCI.

26. A number of biographical sketches claim that Smith matriculated at Butler. Lawrence, "'Beetle' Is Back." According to the registrar at Butler, Sondrea Ozolins, university records indicate that he never enrolled. Ozolins to the author, 10 January 2007.

27. David Bodenhamer et al., *The Encyclopedia of Indianapolis* (Bloomington, IN, 1994), 106–7, 1122–23; *Indianapolis Star*, 26 September 1943, Smith File, ISL.

28. Smith made this point during a confirmation hearing before the Senate. "Names in the News," *Time*, 16 April 1954.

7. The Summons to War

1. Historical Division, Department of the Army, *Order of Battle of the United States Land Forces in the World War, American Expeditionary Forces*, 3 vols. (in 4 parts) (Washington, DC, 1931–1949), 3:554–55; Hurt, then a colonel in the Indiana Guard, was interviewed in *Indianapolis Star*, 8 May 1945.

2. *Indianapolis Star*, 26 September 1943, Smith File, ISL.

3. The story of Edmund Arpin, an officer candidate at Fort Benjamin Harrison, parallels Smith's to a remarkable degree. His published diary serves as the foundation for much of this chapter. Arpin, "A Wisconsinite in World War I: Reminiscences of Edmund P. Arpin Jr.," ed. Ira Berlin, *Wisconsin Magazine of History* 51 (1967): 3–25.

4. Lockwood rose to the rank of brigadier general and served under Smith in World War II. "Indiana's Walter Bedell Smith."

5. Cited in Edward Coffman, *The War to End All Wars: The American Military Experience in World War I* (New York, 1968), 57.

6. Arpin, "Wisconsinite in World War I," 6.

7. Christian Bach and Henry Noble Hall, *Fourth Division: Its Services and Achievements in the World War* (Garden City, NY, 1920), 18.

8. American Battle Monument Commission, *Fourth Division: Summary of Operations in the World War* (Washington, DC, 1944), 5; Miriam Mitchell, *The Echo of the Bugle Call: Charlotte's Role in World War I* (Charlotte, NC, 1979).

9. Arpin, "Wisconsinite in World War I," 6.

10. Smith wrote a personal experience monograph while at the infantry school. Smith, "Operations of the 1st Battalion, 39th Infantry (Fourth Division) in the Aisne-Marne Offensive, July 18–20, 1918," *Mailing List* (July 1932): 138.

11. Bach and Hall, *Fourth Division*, 23–27.

12. Wertenbaker, "The Invasion Plan," 94.

13. Fourth Infantry "Ivy" Division Association, *4th Infantry "Ivy" Division* (Paducah, KY, 1987), 12–13; Bach and Hall, *Fourth Division*, 39–40.

14. Manton Eddy, who would command a corps in World War II, led a machine gun company in the Thirty-ninth and wrote a personal account of the Aisne-Marne fighting. MAJ Manton Eddy, "Machine Gun Company, 39th Infantry (4th Division) in the Aisne-Marne Offensive (July 18–August 5, 1918)," Advanced Infantry Course, 1929–1930, Donovan Research Library, Infantry School, Fort Benning, GA.

15. Historical Section, Army War College, *Order of Battle of the United States Land Forces in the World War, American Expeditionary Forces–Divisions* (Washington, DC, 1931), 63–64; Fourth Infantry Association, *4th Infantry "Ivy" Division*, 12–14; Harold Fiske, "Report of G-5, AEF," 30 June 1919, cited in Timothy Nenninger, "Tactical Dysfunction in the AEF," *Military Affairs* (October 1987): 180; Bach and Hall, *Fourth Division*, 159.

16. Historical Division, Department of the Army, *Military Operations of the American Expeditionary Forces: Champagne-Marne and Aisne-Marne* (Washington, DC, 1938), 217–18.

17. Most of the account of the First Battalion's actions during the first two days of the Aisne-Marne offensive, as well as the quotations from Smith, are from his personal account, "Operations of the 1st Battalion, 39th Infantry," 137–53. Other than Bach and Hall, Smith cited two other sources unavailable to the author: Robert Cole and B. Eberlin, *The History of the 39th U.S Infantry during the World War* (New York, 1919), and B. A. Poore, *History of the Seventh Brigade during the World War* (Cologne, 1919). An abbreviated version of Smith's infantry school monograph appeared in Smith, "Surprise—Example Two," *Infantry in Battle* (Washington, DC, 1934), 113–16.

18. French II Corps, "*Ordre Général d'Opérations,* No. 200, *Première Partie,* G-3, No. 2563," 17 July 1918, in *Military Operations of the AEF,* 399–401; American Battle Monument Commission, *Fourth Division,* 16, 34; Bach and Hall, *Fourth Division,* 59; Fourth Infantry Association, *4th Infantry "Ivy" Division,* 14.

19. In addition to Smith's thorough account, see Bach and Hall, *Fourth Division,* 66–74; Fourth Infantry Association, *4th Infantry "Ivy" Division,* 14; American Battle Monument Commission, *Fourth Division,* 19–21.

20. Fourth Division casualties in the first two days of the Aisne-Marne offensive were as follows: 2 officers and 93 men killed, 11 officers and 436 men wounded, and 1 officer and 60 men reported missing. American Battle Monument Commission, "Casualties—Aisne-Marne Offensive and Visle Sector," in *Fourth Division,* 34.

21. Arpin's diary discusses the medical attention he received after being wounded.

22. Only twenty post-1900 graduates of Leavenworth served on the prewar general staff. Timothy Nenninger, *Leavenworth and the Old Army: Education, Professionalism, and the Officer Corps of the United States Army, 1881-1918* (Westport, CT, 1978), 135, 159.

23. Chamberlain quoted in *New York Times,* 20 January 1918.

24. War Department General Staff Order #80, 26 August 1918, cited in Historical Division, Army War College, "War Department General Staff," *Order of Battle: Zone of the Interior* (Washington, DC, 1948), 42.

25. Frederick Palmer, *Newton D. Baker,* 2 vols. (New York, 1931), 1:14–15; Donald Smythe, "Your Authority in France Will Be Supreme: The Baker-Pershing Relationship in World War I," *Parameters* (September 1979): 38–45, and "Pershing-March Conflict in World War I," *Parameters* (December 1981): 53–62.

26. March to Pershing, 14 March 1918, and Harbord to Pershing, 16 March 1918, cited in Smythe, "Pershing-March Conflict," 57.

27. LeRoy Eltinge, "General Staff Officers," 18 August 1918, in Historical Division, Department of the Army, *United States Army in the World War, 1917-1919*, 17 vols. (Washington, DC, 1948),12:94.

28. Peyton March, *Nation at War* (New York, 1932), 40, 48-49, 226-27.

29. Historical Division, *Order of Battle: Zone of the Interior*, 43.

30. Edward Coffman, "The Battle against Red Tape: Business Methods of the War Department General Staff, 1917-1918," *Military Affairs* (spring 1962): 1–10.

31. Historical Division, *Order of Battle: Zone of the Interior*, 658–59, 663, 667. Unless otherwise noted, Smith's World War I and interwar service records are derived from his 201 File, WBSP, and "Walter Bedell Smith," *War Department Biographies, American Generals in European Theater*, RG 319, Records of the Army Staff, NARA.

32. C. C. Kenney, "A Prospect of Fort Dodge," *Palimpsest* 13 (1932): 106–30.

33. Several senior World War II officers made these same points. See particularly the oral histories of Henry Aurand, Lucius Clay, and Charles Bonesteel, copies in DDEL.

34. "Officer Career Summary," Smith 201 File, WBSP.

35. Palmer testified before the Senate Committee on 9 October 1919, U.S. Congress, Senate Committee on Military Affairs, Hearings, "Reorganization of the Army," 66th Congress, 1st and 2nd Sessions (Washington, DC, 1920), 1572-651.

36. Baker to Wilson, 3 June 1920, cited in Edward Coffman, *Hilt of the Sword: The Career of Peyton C. March* (Madison, WI, 1966), 209.

37. Appropriations for the War Department sank from $1,008,300,000 in 1920 to a low of $246,092,000 in 1925. *Army Almanac* (Washington, DC, 1950), 696. A private earned 70 cents per day in the 1920s; skilled workers could earn the same in one hour. Robert Griffith Jr., *Men Wanted for the U.S. Army: America's Experience with an All-Volunteer Army between the World Wars* (Westport, CT, 1982), 92–95.

38. "Annual Report of the Chief of Staff, 1920," *Report of Secretary of War to the President* (Washington, DC, 1922), 12–13, 34–35.

8. "They Don't Make 'Em Any Better than Smith"

1. Description of interwar posts taken from Charles Sullivan, *Army Posts and Towns* (Los Angeles, 1942).

2. Lucius Clay oral history, 8 November 1972, DDEL.

3. For the only interview of Nory Smith, see *Indianapolis Star*, 8 May 1945, ISL. Wertenbaker's *Life* article also makes reference to the Smiths' happy stay at Fort Sheridan. An officer who later served with Smith at Fort Benning provided the best insights into Nory Smith's relationship with her husband. Interview with LTG Russell Vittrup, 15 November 1988, Arlington, VA.

4. William Snyder conducted a number of interviews with friends and associates of Smith for a 1984 article. A neighbor in Manila, Irene Ord, the wife of Eisenhower's close friend Jimmy Ord, commented on Smith's reading habits. Smith's WAC secretary, Ruth Briggs, said he continued to read widely during the war. Snyder, "Walter Bedell Smith: Eisenhower's Chief of Staff," *Military Affairs* (January 1984): 6, 13, n. 3.

5. So thought Patrick J. Hurley, secretary of war in the Hoover administration. Don Lohbeck, *Patrick J. Hurly* (Chicago, 1956), 101.

6. Moseley lamented the "damned political partisanship and spirit of evading issues in political platforms and [failure] to give us the leadership with the mind, the conscience, and the heart which American Citizens demand." "Custer Ending Summer Work," *Battle Creek Moon Journal*, 27 August 1927, Fort Custer Vertical Files, Willard Public Library, Battle Creek, MI.

7. Moseley to Jay, 24 May 1919, George Van Horn Moseley Papers, LOC.

8. Pershing, "Our National Defense Policy," *Scientific American* 127 (1922): 83.

9. Cited in MTCA, *The Training Camp Movement* (Chicago, 1924).

10. MTCA, *Preparedness: Sixth Corps Area* (Chicago, 1922–1924), and "The Training Camp Movement," *The Torch: ROTC* (Camp Custer, MI, 1923); William Spiegel, "The CMTC Training Course," n.d., Willard Library.

11. Moseley to the editor, *The Army and Navy Bulletin*, 7 May 1923, Moseley Papers.

12. Spiegel, "CMTC Training Course."

13. "Camp Officers Honor Soldier," 23 August 1923, and "CMTC Real 'Boys Camp,'" 9 August 1923, *Battle Creek Moon Journal*.

14. "Camp Custer News," 25 August 1923, Moseley Papers; *Fort Custer in Story and Picture* (New York, 1941); MTCA, *Preparedness: Sixth Corps Area* (1924).

15. MTCA, *Preparedness: Sixth Corps Area* (1924), 21–22.

16. "Custer Ending Summer Work."

17. "Camp Officers Honor Soldier."

18. "Biggest Day of Year at Custer," *Battle Creek Moon Journal*, 22 August 1923; Hale to Moseley, 30 August 1923, Moseley Papers.

19. MTCA, *Preparedness: Sixth Corps Area*.

20. Moseley to Blake, 4 May 1922, Moseley Papers.

21. Smith to Moseley, 21 February 1942, and Nory Smith to Moseley, 4 March 1946, Moseley Papers.

22. Moseley to COL Frank Watson, 8 May 1925, Moseley Papers.

23. Moseley to G-1, Everett S. Hughes Papers, LOC. While in the Sixth Corps area, Smith received four excellent and two superior ratings, "Officer Career Summary," Smith 201 File, WBSP.

24. Moseley to Watson, 8 May 1925, Moseley Papers.

25. Harold Smith, "The Bureau of the Budget," *Public Administration Review* 1 (1941): 109; Allen Schnick, "The Road to PPB: The Stages of Budget Reform," *Public Administration Review* 26 (1966): 243–58; Philip Present, "Budget and Program Evolution: On the Road to Accountability," in *People and Public Administration,* ed. Philip Present (Pacific Palisades, CA, 1979), 241–50.

26. Elias Huzar, *The Purse and the Sword: Control of the Army by Congress through Military Appropriations* (Ithaca, NY, 1950); Henry Seidemann, "The Preparation of the National Budget," *Annals of the American Academy of Political and Social Studies* 113 (1924): 40–50.

27. Smith discussed his connections with civilian agencies during this juncture in a CBS news program, Dallas Townshend, "Newsmakers," 8 January 1950, transcript in WBSP.

28. Elam Stewart, "Fort William McKinley," *Infantry Journal* 33 (1927): 347–49; U.S. Army, Division of the Philippines, *Annual Report of Major General George W. Davis*, 1930, MHI.

29. Edward Coffman and Peter Herrly, "The American Regular Army Officer Corps between the World Wars: A Collective Biography," *Armed Forces & Society* (November 1977): 69–71.

30. Charles H. Franklin, "History of the Philippine Scouts, 1899–1934," War College Research Paper, May 1935, MHI. For a history of the Forty-fifth Philippine Scouts, see "From Headhunters to Soldiers," *Infantry Journal* 44 (1924):40–43.

31. Unidentified officer quoted in Hinton, "Soldier, Diplomat, Intelligence Chief," 30.

32. Wertenbaker, "The Invasion Plan," 94.

33. Karl Lowe, *America's Foreign Legion: The 31st Infantry Regiment at War and Peace,* http://www.31stinfantry.org/history/htm. See also Richard Meixsel, "American Exceptionalism in Colonial Forces? The Philippine Scout Mutiny of 1924," in *Colonial Armies in Southeast Asia,* ed. Karl Hack and Tobias Rittig (London, 2005), 171–94.

34. Moseley reported that "General Smithers and Admiral Rousseau rated Smith as 'superior throughout'" during his stint in the BOB. MAJ Everett Hughes of the G-1 Division first made the efficiency report study in 1929–1930 and submitted a final version in 1935. Hughes, "Efficiency Reports," 1935, Hughes Papers; Moseley to Assistant Chief of Staff, G-1, 18 August 1931, Moseley Papers. See also "Relative Efficiency of Infantry Officers," *Infantry Journal* (April 1926): 427; "Classification of Officers," *Infantry Journal* (May 1926): 549.

35. "Who's in the Army Now?" *Fortune,* September 1935, 39.

36. In the first seventeen years the system existed, only 350 officers lost their commissions, near 40 percent of them in 1921–1922. In all, 1,428 officers were placed provisionally in Class B: 493 left the service before their cases were finalized, 577 won reinstatement in Class A, 350 were cashiered, and the remaining 8 cases were still pending. Coffman and Herrly, "American Regular Army Officer Corps between the World Wars," 71, n. 7.

37. Officers found "unsatisfactory" on consecutive efficiency reports could be placed on the Class B list. Officers in the latter category lost their commissions, subject to appeal to the president. Because of the lengthy appeals process, few "unsatisfactory" officers were dismissed. Of the 3,519 infantry officers assessed for the year 1927–1928, only 26 received an "unsatisfactory" rating—a minuscule 0.7 percent. "Notes of the Chief of Infantry," *Infantry Journal* 20 (1927): 81.

38. Smith to Moseley, 21 February 1942, Moseley Papers.

39. "Policy for Special Service Schools," *Army Register,* 7 and 28 December 1929, CARL.

40. Moseley to assistant chief of staff, G-1, 18 August 1931, Hughes Papers.

9. "Expunge the Bunk, Complications and Ponderosities"

1. On a number of occasions, GEN George Marshall talked about the pernicious cycle in American military history. He told a Boston audience in 1923, "History is filled—in fact, it almost consists, of remarkable repetitions." In 1939 he addressed the American Historical Association and leveled an attack on historians for their lack of a critical analysis of American wars: "Military history, since it deals with wars, is unpopular, and probably more so today than at any other time." What he said goes to the point of the cyclicality of American military policy:

Historians have been inclined to record the victories and gloss over the mistakes and wasteful sacrifices. Cause and effect have been, to an important extent, ignored. Few Americans learn that we enrolled nearly 400,000 men in the Revolutionary War to defeat an enemy that numbered less than 45,000, or that we employed half a million in 1812 against an opponent whose strength never exceeded 16,000 at any one place, and fewer still have learned why these overwhelming numbers were so ineffective. The War between the States pointed numerous lessons for our future protection, yet seldom has a nation entered a war so completely unprepared, and yet so boastfully, as did the United States in 1898. Veterans of the World War often seem to overlook the fact that almost a year and a half elapsed after the declaration of war before we could bring a field army into being and even then its weapons, ammunition and other materiel were provided by our Allies. And many of them seem unaware of the fact that the partially trained state of our troops proved a costly and tragic business despite the eventual success.

Marshall, "Speech on School History Texts [to the Massachusetts Headmasters Association]," 10 February 1923, *Papers of George Catlett Marshall*, vol. 1, *"The Soldierly Spirit," December 1880-June 1939* (Baltimore, 1981), #196; Marshall, "National Organization for War: A Speech to the American Military Institute, at the American Historical Association convention, Washington, December 28, 1939," *Papers of George Catlett Marshall*, vol. 2, *"We Cannot Delay," July 1, 1939-December 6, 1941* (Baltimore, 1986), #94.

2. Less than 10 percent of regular army officers attended the Leavenworth schools before the war, but "Leavenworth Men" dominated the AEFHQ and the major subordinate commands. Eight of twelve officers who served as chiefs of staff or heads of sections in AEFHQ were graduates of Leavenworth. The chiefs of staff of both armies in France were Leavenworth products; so were nine of the ten corps chiefs of staff. Edward Coffman, "The American Military Generation Gap in World War I: The Leavenworth Clique and the AEF," in *Command and Commanders in Modern Warfare: Proceedings of the Second Military History Symposium, U.S. Air Force Academy, 2-3 May 1968*, ed. William Geffen (Colorado Springs, CO, 1969), 39–48.

3. Cited in Elvid Hunt, *History of Fort Leavenworth, 1827-1927*, updated by Walter Lorence (Ft. Leavenworth, 1981), 155.

4. Paul Malone, "The Need of an Infantry School," *Infantry Journal* (November 1919): 353–59; A. B. Warfield, "Fort Benning: The Home of the Infantry School," *Infantry Journal* (June 1928): 30–31; *History of Fort Benning*, MHI.

5. Marshall, "Memorandum for the Commandant," 19 November 1928, *Soldierly Spirit*, #268.

6. Griffith, *Men Wanted for the U.S. Army*, 75.

7. Wertenbaker, "The Invasion Plan," 94; *Indianapolis Star*, 26 September 1943, ISL.

8. Marshall to Heintzelman, 18 December 1933, *Soldierly Spirit*, #339.

9. Forrest Pogue, *George C. Marshall: Education of a General, 1880-1939* (New York, 1963), 256.

10. Marshall, "Profiting by War Experience," *Infantry Journal* (January 1921): 34–37; Marshall to Heintzelman, 18 December 1933; Marshall, "Infantry School Lecture: Development in Tactics," n.d., *Soldierly Spirit*, #270.

11. Marshall to WDGS G-3 (Training), 13 April 1937, *Soldierly Spirit*, #438.

12. Marshall, *Infantry in Battle*, 5–6; Marshall to Deputy Chief of Staff, "Command and General Staff School," 13 April 1937, *Soldierly Spirit*, #438.

13. Marshall to MG Stuart Heintzelman, 4 December 1933, *Soldierly Spirit*, #338.

14. Marshall to WDGS G-3 (Training), 13 April 1937, *Soldierly Spirit*, #438. He made the same point in a lecture while at Benning. Marshall, "Development in Tactics," *Soldierly Spirit*, #270.

15. Marshall to BG Asa Singleton, 27 February 1939, *Soldierly Spirit*, #563.

16. Marshall to Heintzelman, 4 December 1933.

17. Ibid.

18. Drum, *Annual Report of the Commandant, Army School of the Line and General Staff School*, 30 June 1922, CARL.

19. AEF Superior Board Report, "Organization and Tactics," 1 July 1919, 18, CARL.

20. Interestingly, the disciples proved more orthodox than the high priest. In his "wrapper endorsement" of the Superior Board findings, Pershing thought it "too close to the end of the war" to finalize doctrine, argued against retention of the "too unwieldy" square division, and maintained that "the employment of tanks must be expected to increase many-fold . . . and the necessity for close association (infantry and armor) will increase correspondingly." Pershing to the Secretary of War, 16 June 1920, copy attached to the Superior Board Report, 3, 7. No interwar board reexamined U.S. Army doctrine in the light of technological developments. The British did not create one until 1931. The Reichswehr created fifty-five such committees in the period 1920 to 1922.

21. Marshall, "Selection of Infantry Officers for the Advanced Course," *Soldierly Spirit*, #262; *George C. Marshall Interviews and Reminiscences for Forrest C. Pogue*, ed. Larry Bland (Lexington, VA, 1991), 533. See also CPT John Schwab, "Promotion Study for the Office of the Chief of Infantry," 19 October 1926; COL Lorenzo Gasser, "Memorandum for Chief of Infantry," 1 July 1929; and MAJ Elmer Rice to Gasser, 6 August 1926, 1929, all in RG 177, Records of the Chief of Arms, Chief of Infantry, NARA.

22. Marshall, "Selection of Infantry Officers for the Advanced Course, Infantry School, and for the Command & General Staff School," 9 January 1928, and "Size of Classes at the Infantry School," 19 November 1928, *Soldierly Spirit*, #262 and #268. The problem continued until 1940; Marshall to BG Lesley McNair, 9 April 1940, *We Cannot Delay*, #153.

23. COL Charles Ritchel to Pogue, October 24, 1960, *Soldierly Spirit*, #273, n. 3.

24. Constance Greene et al., *The Ordnance Department: Planning Munitions for War*, USAWWII (Washington, DC, 1955), 189.

25. Omar Bradley and Clay Blair, *A General's Life: An Autobiography by General of the Army Omar N. Bradley* (New York, 1985), 65, 69.

26. Clay Blair interview of Bradley, ibid., 69.

27. Stilwell commented that most officers never cracked a book after leaving West Point. Barbara Tuchman, *Stilwell and the American Experience in China, 1911-1945* (New York, 1970), 90–91; Lanham to Marshall, October 25, 1934, *Soldierly Spirit*, #357, n. 3.

28. Marshall to Heintzelman, 18 December 1933, *Soldierly Spirit*, #339.

29. Smith, "Operations of the 1st Battalion, 39th Infantry." *Infantry in Battle* was first published in 1934. Smith, "Surprise," *Infantry in Battle* (Richmond, VA, 1939), 113–16; Hart's review appeared in *The Army Quarterly*, as cited by Marshall to LT Charles Lanham, 29 October 1934, *Soldierly Spirit*, #357, n. 1; Marshall to Heintzelman, *Soldierly Spirit*, #359.

30. Chief of Infantry, "Policy on Command and General Staff School," *Infantry Journal* (January–July 1927): 63–64.

10. The Other Class Stars Fell On

1. King, "Command," 11 September 1925, published as *Lecture Delivered by Brigadier General Edward L. King, Commandant, the General Service Schools, to the Command and General Staff School* (Ft. Leavenworth, 1925). No doubt the football parallel piqued

the interest of one of King's listeners, a former football standout at West Point by the name of Ike Eisenhower.

2. Twenty-four future corps commanders—four who went on to command armies—attended one of the seven one-year courses. Another eight were products of the seven two-year classes. Only one attended a Leavenworth course after 1937, consisting of only a three-month National Guard course.

3. The reintroduced two-year course opened up Leavenworth to captains. The first two classes averaged less than 30 percent captains; the numbers doubled in 1932–1933 and stabilized at around 60 percent. Between 1929 and 1934, the Air Corps represented 5.4 percent of the class. In Smith's cohort, the Air Corps constituted 12 percent. The heavy infantry bias of Leavenworth doctrine irritated airpower advocates who attended. The Air Corps never sent its quota of officers, which only hurt itself. Without Leavenworth, Air Corps officers could not advance into the WDGS or hold influential posts outside military aviation. If it wanted to enhance its organizational status and win greater branch autonomy, the Air Corps needed to send more people to the CGSS. The doctrinal wall between the Air Corps and the old combat arms began to become more plastic. Maxwell Taylor made reference to his class of "aids, adjutants, and asses" in a 10 December 1984 letter to the author.

4. The FSRs stated: in "the employment of the combined arms . . . the mission of the infantry is the general mission of the entire force. The special missions of other arms are derived from their powers to contribute to the execution of the infantry mission." War Department, *Field Service Regulations, United States Army* (Washington, DC, 1923), 11. Eisenhower, in an unattributed article, stated that the map problems encountered at Leavenworth were identical to those of the Infantry School. "The Leavenworth Course: By a Young Graduate," *Infantry Journal* (June 1927): 589–600.

5. BG Charles Brudel, Annual Report, 22 June 1938, CARL. MG Hanson Ely and his assistant Drum made the same criticism in 1922. Drum wrote, "A great many number of officers here are woefully ignorant of the arms of the service other than their own."Annual Report, 30 June 1922, CARL.

6. *Problems, First Year Course, 1934-1935; Schedule, 1934-1935;* texts for the first-year course, *Tactics and Technique of the Associated Arms, Tactical Principles, Command, Staff and Logistics, Historical Research,* and *General Terrain Exercises,* CARL.

7. The course possessed three core subjects—"Tactics and Techniques of the Associated Arms," "Tactical Principles and Decisions," and "Command, Staff, and Logistics." As a gauge of the relative importance of these subjects, students were graded on fourteen map problems in "Tactics and Techniques," eight in "Command, Staff, and Logistics," and twenty-one in "Tactical Principles and Decisions."

8. MAJ W. G. Simmons, *The Relative Value of Lectures, Conferences, Map Problems, Map Exercises, and Map Maneuvers in a Course of Instruction,* Leavenworth Research Paper, 1932, CARL. See also Orville Eaton, *An Analytical Study of Methods of Instruction at the Command and General Staff School* (Ft. Leavenworth, 1946), 322–33.

9. In 1922 the War Department convened two bodies, the Fiske and McGlachlin Boards, to reexamine the army's school system. BG Edward McGlachlin, "Dissenting Opinion," in War Department, *Boards of Officers Appointed to Study the Army School System: Report of Proceedings* (Washington, DC, 1922); Ely to Adjutant General, 6 November 1925, cited in Harry Ball, *Of Responsible Command: A History of the U.S. Army War College* (Carlisle, PA, 1983), 210.

10. *Annual Reports, 1924–1929,* especially MG Edward King, *Annual Report,* 1 July 1929, CARL.

11. Drum, *Annual Report,* 1922, 12, 28, CARL.

12. Bradford Chynoweth, *Bellamy Park: Memoirs of Bradford Grethen Chynoweth* (Hicksville, NY, 1975), 121.

13. H. H. Pheil, "Why Leavenworth?" *Infantry Journal* (June 1927): 31. One of Smith's first-year texts stated, "The principles and methods taught in our service schools represent the boiled down and studied experience of many people in war. We are well guided if we stay close to those principles and methods." It also maintained, "There must be mental anguish for the solver in a good problem of decision." *First Year Course, Command and G-2 Course, 1934-1935* (Ft. Leavenworth, 1935), 409, 411.

14. Patton wrote to Eisenhower, "I am convinced that as good as Leavenworth is it is still only a means and not an end. . . . I have worked all the problems of the two years since I graduated. . . . I don't try for approved solutions any more but rather to do what I will do in war. . . . But this I know that the present Infantry T[raining] R[egulations] based on super trained heroes is bull." Patton to Eisenhower, 9 July 1926, *The Patton Papers, 1885-1940,* ed. Martin Blumenson (Boston, 1972), 873.

15. Patton to his father, 20 March 1923, George Patton Sr. Papers, Henry E. Huntington Library, San Marino, CA.

16. BG Thomas Betts remarked that Leavenworth prided itself on having at least one suicide a year. MG Bolté reported that five wives attempted suicide when he attended the two-year course in the early 1930s, and two succeeded. Betts and Bolté oral histories, DDEL. In a letter to the Fort Leavenworth Historical Society, 16 February 1967, Eisenhower stated that although nobody in his class committed suicide, "we must have been a very difficult group because one of the instructors did." MAJ Phillip Bagby, an instructor, died on 16 March 1926. Eisenhower's letter is in the Leavenworth County Museum. Bagby's death is reported in *Annual Report,* 1926. Mark Bender found the connection between the Eisenhower letter and the 1926 *Annual Report.* Bender, "Watershed at Leavenworth: Dwight D. Eisenhower and the Command and General Staff School," unpublished, CARL.

17. "The Leavenworth Course." For two other examples, see MAJ Stuart Godfrey, "Command and General Staff School," *Field Artillery Journal* (September–October and November–December 1926), and MAJ E. D. Cooke, "Curves and Fast Balls at Leavenworth," *Infantry Journal* (September–October 1936).

18. Patton to Parks, 28 January 1933, Floyd L. Parks Papers, DDEL. Aside from Harry Collins in the class before his and Lucian Truscott in the class after, the only officer Smith corresponded with about Leavenworth was his classmate Parks. Smith to Parks, 27 June 1944, and Patton to Smith, 6 March 1944, 1944 Chief of Staff's Personal Correspondence, WBSP.

19. Howard Smyth interview with Smith, 13 May 1947, MHI.

20. Albert Wedemeyer, *Wedemeyer Reports* (New York, 1958), 48.

21. Gary Wade, "Conversation with General J. Lawton Collins," Combat Studies #5, CARL.

22. "Combat," *Field Service Regulations,* 1923, 77, 89.

23. *Command Course, 1934-1935* (Ft. Leavenworth, 1935), 203.

24. *The Tactical Employment of Tanks in Battle* (Ft. Leavenworth, 1923); *Problems: Second Year Course, 1934-1935,* MP 222, 14 March 1935. Armor played a defending role, screening for the cavalry and fighting a holding action against an enemy advancing on an exposed flank.

25. A Leavenworth text claimed, "cavalry . . . will contribute most to the success

of the decisive attack." Although tanks increased distance and speed, they did so "without altering the fundamental missions of cavalry." *Command Course, 1934-1935,* 144. The chief of cavalry, MG John Herr, made no concession to armor. He vowed the War Department "would take a single horse soldier over his dead body." Robert Grow, "The Ten Lean Years: From the Mechanized Force (1930) to the Armored Force (1940)," *Armor* 96 (July–August 1987): 38–39. See also Herr, "The Cavalry," lecture, Army War College, 19 September 1939, MHI; "Policies Governing Mechanization and Tactical Employment of Mechanized Forces," *Manual for Commanders of Large Units,* 25 March 1938, WPD 3715, RG 165, OCS, NARA; *Field Service Regulations (Tentative): Operations* (FM 100-5) (Washington, DC, 1939).

26. George Lynch, "The Tactics of the New Infantry Regiment," address to the CGSS, 14 March 1939, CARL.

27. "Tactics and Techniques of the Air Corps (Tentative Text)" (Ft. Leavenworth, 1929); "Tactical Employment of the Air Corps (Tentative)" (Ft. Leavenworth, 1937); *Field Service Regulations, Operations (Tentative)* (Washington, DC, 1939), 132.

28. Superior Board Report, 8.

29. *Field Service Regulations: Operations (Tentative),* 34.

30. H. A. Smith, "Address at Opening Exercises of the Command and General Staff School, Fort Leavenworth, Kansas, 10 September 10, 1923" (Ft. Leavenworth, 1923), 5–7, CARL.

31. For the changed role, and confusion over the functions of, a chief of staff, see General Staff Study, "Staff Organization and Principles," War Department, Document #858 (Washington, DC, 1918); "Division Commander and His General Staff," *Mailing List* 4 (December 1924): 79–155; General Services School, *Field Service Manual* (Ft. Leavenworth, 1925); CGSS, Instructional Circular #1, 1932–1933; CGSS, "Command and Staff Principles" (Ft. Leavenworth, 1937); War Department, "Staff Officers' Field Manual" (Washington, DC, 1940); and E. C. Harwood, *Staff Principles and Procedures* (Washington, DC, 1945), all in CARL.

32. *Command, Staff and Logistics* (Ft. Leavenworth, 1926).

33. Aurand oral history, DDEL.

34. "Army in Attack," conferences, Command Course, I-201, 203, 11 and 13 September 1934; "Corps in Attack," conferences, Command Course, I-202, 204, 12 and 14 September 1934; "The Role of Corps and Army Cavalry and a Cavalry Corps," lecture, Command Course, I-228, 14 November 1934; "Plan of Campaign," conference, Command Course, I-230, 16 November 1934; "Plan of Campaign—Logistic Factors," conference, Administrations and Logistics Course, IV-229, 19 November 1934; "Plan of Concentration," conference, Command Course, I-232, 19 November 1934; "Corps Concentration," conference, Command Course, I-233, 21 November 1934; "Tactical and Strategical Operations of an Interior Army," conferences, Command Course, I-253–56, 8, 11, and 13 February 1935; "Tactical and Strategical Operations of a Flank Army," conferences, Command Course, I-257–58, 260, 15, 18, and 20 February 1935; Map Problem 200, 25 February 1935; "Highlights of Tactics and Strategy Series" and associated map exercises, Command Course, I-261, G-2 Course, II-247, G-3 Course, III-247, Administrations and Logistics Course, IV-251, 25–27 February 1935, all in CARL.

35. "Operations of an Interior Army," Problem and Solution, Command Course, I-253, 8 February 1935, CARL.

36. Maxwell Taylor made this point in *Swords and Plowshares* (New York, 1972), 30, which he expanded on in his December 1984 letter to the author.

37. "Battle of Tannenberg," filed under Walter Weible, 1935; C. A. Willoughby, "Reviews in Research Papers," 31 May 1935; Troup Miller, "Individual Research Studies, Class of 1935." For the 1933 class, see Feodor Schmidt, *Critical Analysis of the Battle of Tannenberg Based Primarily on the Translation Tannenberg; wie is wirklich war by General Max Hoffman;* Herman Kramer, *Was General von Francois Justified in His Actions during the Battle of Tannenberg?* and Marcus Ming, *Critical Analysis of the Battle of Tannenberg,* all in CARL.

38. Commandant King reported on the harmful effects of the grading system. Officers failed to earn honors and distinguished standing "due to an infinitesimal difference in grade with no appreciable difference in ability." King, *Annual Report,* 1928–1929, 1 July 1929. Eisenhower was at the top of his 1925–1926 class, with a final average of 93 percent; his study partner Leonard Gerow came eleventh in the cohort, although his average was only 1.7 percentage points lower than Eisenhower's. Typically, two-thirds received "excellent" grades, with the remaining third evenly divided between "superior" and "satisfactory." "Unsatisfactory" grades were rarely given. *A Brief Outline History of the General Service Schools,* CARL.

39. Faculty Board Proceedings, 16 June 1935, CARL.

40. Chynoweth, *Bellamy Park,* 121.

41. CPT Roger Cirillo executed a study of the two-year courses and concluded that age at the time the war broke out and a Leavenworth diploma were the primary determinants of elevation to general rank, and that "branch and combat experience were almost irrelevant." Cirillo to Deputy Commandant, 4 October 1983, CARL.

42. In an exchange of letters, Harry Collins, a strong proponent of armor, made reference to Smith's forward-thinking ideas. Smith replied that many of Collins's "opinions have been triumphantly vindicated. In a few others, and particularly in the matter of the importance of Infantry on which we never entirely agreed, I believe that events have proven that I was right." Collins to Smith, 23 January 1944, and Smith to Collins, 29 February 1944, 1944 Chief of Staff's Personal Correspondence, 1941–1944, WBSP.

43. Smith to Harding, 27 December 1934, Harding Memorial Museum, Franklin, OH.

44. Smith to MG Lucian Truscott, 15 December 1943, Chief of Staff Personal Papers, 1941–1944, WBSP. Smith made the same points in Smith to MG Ralph Huebner, 21 September 1943, Smith 201 File, and in a 25 September 1945 interview with BG Ray Moses, General Board Report, "Organization of the European Theater of Operations," 32, 86. Smith vetted Moses' report; many of the points raised in the conclusion are Smith's, emphasizing the inadequacies of the interwar training of qualified staff officers. The shortage of high-level staff talent is a recurring theme in most of the General Board Reports.

11. "No One Ever Graduates"

1. Marshall, "Speech on the Illinois National Guard," *Soldierly Spirit,* #343.

2. "Who's in the Army Now?" 39, 136.

3. The average division commander in World War II—the group that parallels Smith's career most closely—spent three and a half years as a student and slightly more than five and a half years as an instructor. Three-quarters of corps commanders spent more than ten years in the army school system. Where Smith's career path diverges from that of the average division commander is "time with troops," which

averaged over eight years. Gary Wade, "World War II Division Commanders" (Combat Studies Institute, 1983), and Robert Berlin, "U.S. Army World War II Corps Commanders" (CGSS, 2002), CARL.

4. Clay oral history, 8 November 1972, 17, 21.

5. MacArthur's reactionary predecessor, GEN Charles Summerall, used the phrase "grave embarrassment" to describe the situation. Summerall, War Department Annual Report, 1930, 141–42, CARL.

6. For Moseley's views, including his advocacy of a military putsch, see Moseley to Patrick Hurley, assistant secretary of war, 9 October 1930; Moseley to Grenville Clark, Law Firm of Root, Clark & Buckner, New York, 3, 6, and 7 June and 15 July 1932; Clark to Moseley, 6 June and 15 July 1932. Clark served as president of the CMTC movement when Moseley headed Camp Custer. Moseley whitewashed his part in the affair, claiming he sympathized with the Bonus marchers and delivered the message to MacArthur. See Moseley, "The Bonus March," Military Reports, Statements, and Notes, 1899–1938, and his four-volume unpublished biography, *One Soldier's Journey*, 2:138–45, all in Moseley Papers.

7. Moseley firmly believed in the international Jewish conspiracy. An active promoter of American-style fascism, Moseley served as spokesman for the American First movement and had ties to groups such as the *Amerikadeuscher Volksbund*, the Ku Klux Klan's Silver League, the Christian Mobilizers, and the Paul Revere Sentinels. His actions earned him a summons to appear before the House Committee on Un-American Activities—then called the Dies Committee—in 1939 and two FBI files (HQ-1510001063 and HQ-0620049867).

8. "The Caliber 0.22 Machine Gun," *Mailing List* 12 (summer 1936): 113–40.

9. Wertenbaker, "The Invasion Plan," 95.

10. Otto Nelson to Smith, 4 March 1944, WBSP.

11. Unlike Leavenworth, the interwar War College generated little controversy or academic attention. For example, in his superb 705-page biography of Eisenhower, Carlo D'Este devotes a single page to Eisenhower's year at the War College. The War College has produced two in-house histories: George S. Pappas, *Prudens Futuri: The U.S. Army War College, 1901-1967* (Carlisle Barracks, PA, 1967), and Harry P. Ball, *Of Responsible Command: A History of the U.S. Army War College*, rev. ed. (Carlisle Barracks, PA, 1994).

12. MG E. F. McGlachlin, "Address at Graduation Exercises for the Class of 1923," 28 June 1923, MHI.

13. "Course at the Army War College, 1928–1929," MHI.

14. *Course at War College, Course of Instruction, 1936-1937;* Troup Miller, "Correspondence with the Commandant, War College," June 1936, MHI.

15. Lytle Brown, "The United States Army War College," *Military Engineer* 19 (July–August 1927): 294–97; Oswald Saunders, "The Army War College," *Military Engineer* 26 (March–April): 101–4.

16. The lone exception is Collins, who spent two years as an instructor after completing the course in 1938. J. Lawton Collins, *Lightning Joe* (Baton Rouge, LA, 1979), 90–94.

17. Bradley and Blair, *A General's Life*, 74.

18. "Officer Career Summary," Smith 201 File, WBSP.

19. Hayden Twiggs to Smith, 25 January 1946, WBSP.

20. The army adopted the M1 in 1936, but owing to manufacturing glitches, real production did not start until 1939. Smith, "Machine-Gun Indirect Laying Using an

Aerial Photograph," *Mailing List* 16 (July 1938): 239–50; "The M1 Rifle" and "Individual Training with the M1 Rifle," *Mailing List* 18 (July 1939): 159–204.

21. Eight of the ten officers in the weapons section rose to general rank.

22. Much of the material on the Infantry School and accounts of Smith during this period derive from two lengthy interviews with General Vittrup, 15 and 23 November 1988, Arlington, VA.

23. "Officer Career Summary," Smith 201 File, WBSP.

24. Noting the preponderance of cavalry officers on the faculty of the War College, an instructor, MAJ Henry Aurand, commented that he hoped another cavalry officer would not succeed Craig as commandant. His cavalry colleagues charged him with defaming the chief of staff. Aurand termed the cavalry "a pernicious influence." Aurand oral history, DDEL; John Reese, "Supply Man: The Army Life of Lieutenant General Henry S. Aurand, 1915–1952" (PhD diss., Kansas State University, 1984), 21–23.

25. Marshall to LTC Edwin Harding, 31 October 1934, *Soldierly Spirit, #358.*

26. Aside from Bradley, Collins and Taylor served at various times in the secretariat. They all left personal accounts discussing how the section functioned under Marshall. Bradley and Blair, *A General's Life,* 83–85; Collins, *Lightning Joe,* 95–97; Taylor, *Swords and Plowshares,* 38–41; Robert Gallagher, "Memories of Peace and War: Interview with General Maxwell Taylor," *American Heritage* (April–May 1981): 4–17.

27. In the interviews of Marshall by Forrest Pogue, Marshall admitted he "always had difficulty remembering names" but made no mention of any little book. Pogue told Larry Bland, the coeditor of Marshall's published papers, that the "little black book" was a myth. Bland and the author discussed the matter in 1988. No "little black book" turned up in Marshall's papers. *Marshall Interviews,* 473–74.

28. Marshall to Commanding General, Ft. Benning, 14 August 1939, GCMP.

12. The Chief's Apprentice

1. This chapter and the next one draw heavily on the works of Pogue, particularly *George C. Marshall: Ordeal and Hope, 1939-1942* (New York, 1966). A number of the official histories in the *United States Army in World War II* collection; the "War Department" series, especially Mark Watson, *Chief of Staff: Pre-War Plans and Preparations* (Washington, DC, 1950; reprint ed., 1974); and Ray Cline, *Washington Command Post: The Operations Division* (Washington, DC, 1951; reprint ed., 1970) complement Pogue.

2. Marshall to LTG Daniel Van Voorhis, 22 August 1940, *We Cannot Delay,* 293–94; Marshall to BG John McA Palmer, 12 March 1942, *The Papers of George Catlett Marshall,* vol. 3, *"The Right Man for the Job," December 7, 1941-May 31, 1943* (Baltimore, 1991), 129–31; Otto Nelson, *National Security and the General Staff* (Washington, DC, 1946), 328–34.

3. In a number of public addresses, Marshall made no secret of his intentions. Marshall, "Address at the Opening of the Air Corps Tactical School, Maxwell Field, Alabama," 1 October 1938; "Address at the Annual Banquet of the National Guard Association of Pennsylvania," 13 October 1939; "Testimony before the House Appropriations Committee," 1 May 1940, Broadcasts, Statements, and Speeches File, GCMP. See also Marshall to Ralph Immell, 14 September 1939, *We Cannot Delay, #50.*

4. In most respects, Smith's career up to 1940 mirrored the profile of officers

who went on to command divisions in World War II—the most comparable sample group. He was a forty-five-year-old (average age, forty-seven) native-born Anglo-American, an infantryman (the largest group, 44 percent, came from the infantry), who had spent eight years in the 1930s as a student or instructor at the army's schools (average, a little less than nine). That Smith never attended university did not make him a rarity; nearly one-quarter of World War II division commanders had no college education. Slightly more than half graduated from West Point. Smith differed from the norm in three respects: his urban background, his Catholicism, and his service in France in World War I (20 percent of division commanders went to France; 68 percent of corps commanders served in the AEF, 47 percent saw combat). Coffman and Herrly, "American Regular Army Officer Corps between the World Wars," 55–73; Wade, "World War II Division Commanders."

5. Taylor, *Swords and Plowshares*, 40.

6. Ibid.

7. Ambrose interview with Eisenhower, 14 December 1964, cited in Stephen Ambrose, *The Supreme Commander: The War Years of General Dwight D. Eisenhower* (Garden City, NY, 1970), 8; Harry C. Butcher, *My Three Years with Eisenhower* (New York, 1946), 277. Smith is also quoted making the same point in Edgar F. Puryear, *Nineteen Stars: A Study in Military Character and Leadership* (Orange, VA, 1971), 82.

8. The best description is in Forrest Pogue, *Organizer of Victory* (New York, 1973), 60, 65–66. Pogue also gave two lectures, "The United States General Staff" and "Marshall and the War Department," at the War College, describing how Marshall's inner headquarters functioned; theses lectures were derived from Pogue's work, including a series of interviews with the principals, on the Marshall biography. The lectures are available in the Audio-Visual holdings, MHI. Pogue provided more insights in two letters to the author, 30 November 1984 and 15 January 1985.

9. War Department, *Staff Officers' Field Manual* (Washington, DC, 1932).

10. Omar N. Bradley, *A Soldier's Story* (New York, 1951), 20.

11. Eisenhower, *Crusade in Europe*, 56.

12. Ambrose interview with Eisenhower, 11 October 1967, cited in Ambrose, *The Supreme Commander*, 6; Eisenhower, *Crusade in Europe*, 51.

13. Smith to Marshall, 29 July 1943, 210 File, WBSP; Pogue, *Marshall Interviews*, 267.

14. Bolté oral history, DDEL.

15. Wedemeyer, *Wedemeyer Reports*, 121–22; Pogue, "United States General Staff."

16. Dean Acheson, *Sketches from Life of Men I Have Known* (New York, 1961), 159.

17. Vittrup interviews.

18. These minutes are contained in Smith, "Notes of Conference in Chief of Staff's Office" RG 165, OCS, NARA.

19. Pogue, *Marshall Interviews*, 623.

20. "Thirty-two years in the peacetime army had taught me to do my job, hold my tongue, and keep my name out of the papers." Bradley, *Soldier's Story*, 147.

21. Pogue, *Marshall Interviews*, 282, 417, 620.

22. The assessment of Roosevelt's leadership style, especially as it related to Marshall, the War Department, and the wartime alliance, derives mostly from the works of Warren Kimball and Mark Stoler: Kimball, *The Juggler: Franklin Roosevelt as Wartime Statesman* (Princeton, NJ, 1991) and *Forged in War: Roosevelt, Churchill, and the Second World War* (New York, 1997); Stoler, *The Politics of the Second Front* (Westport, CT, 1977), *Allies and Adversaries: The Joint Chiefs of Staff, the Grand Alliance and U.S.*

Strategy in World War II (Chapel Hill, NC, 2000), and *Allies in War: Britain and America against the Axis Powers, 1940-1945* (New York, 2006).

23. Pogue, *Marshall Interviews*, 620.

24. Pa Watson confessed himself "warmly attached" to Smith. MG Allen Gullion to Smith, 9 May 1944, Chief of Staff's Personal Papers, 1942–1944, WBSP.

25. *The Secret Diary of Harold L. Ickes*, 3 vols. (New York, 1945), 2:164.

26. Marshall, "Speech to the Committee of the Community Chest, Washington, DC," 16 November 1939, *We Cannot Delay*, #76; Marshall, "Remarks at the Opening of the Army Industrial College," 9 September 1939, "Address at the Army Ordnance Association Meeting, Washington, DC," 11 October 1939, and "Address at Brunswick, Maryland," 9 November 1939, *Selected Speeches and Statements of General of the Army George C. Marshall*, ed. H. A. DeWeerd (Washington, DC, 1945), 9, 18–26.

27. Pogue, *Marshall Interviews*, 484–85, 609–10.

28. Baruch's efforts to keep his role under wraps evidently failed. In a December 1943 poll, respondents voted on the effectiveness of American wartime leadership. Baruch ended up at number six. Roosevelt received the most first-place votes, but because of the lack of any weighting in the tabulation, Marshall was ranked at number one. "We Tested Our Leaders: These Are the Ten Rated Topmost by a Panel of Authorities," *Newsweek*, 6 December 1943.

29. Marshall to BG Asa Singleton, 11 April 1940, *We Cannot Delay*, #155.

30. Smith to Baruch, RG 165, OCS, Emergency File, NARA; and Baruch to Smith, 11 May 1940, Bernard M. Baruch Papers, Seeley G. Mudd Manuscript Library, Princeton University.

31. "Summary of Additional Requirements for National Defense," 12 May 1940, RG 165, OCS, Emergency File, NARA. John Morton Blum, *From the Morgenthau Diaries*, vol. 1, *Years of Urgency, 1938-1941* (Boston, 1965), 1:275–81, 291–92.

32. Smith to Baruch, 14 May 1940, RG 165, OCS, Emergency File, NARA.

33. Pogue, *Marshall Interviews*, 485.

34. A copy of the letter is in Smith's 201 File, WBSP.

35. Smith [for Marshall] to Lodge, September 27, 1940, Pentagon Office—Selected File, GCMP.

36. Ulysses Lee, *The Employment of Negro Troops*, USAWWII (Washington, DC, 1966), 75–79; Morris J. MacGregor Jr., *Integration of the Armed Forces, 1940-1965*, Defense Studies Series (Washington, DC, 1981), 5–15. In June 1941 Randolph's threat to stage a mass march on Washington extorted the creation of the Fair Employment Practices Committee within the Office of Production Management to enforce more equal access to employment for African American workers. Roosevelt's executive order—the first affirmative presidential order since Reconstruction—improved the economic prospects of black workers in defense factories. No such executive order followed for the integration of African Americans in the armed services.

37. Marshall, "Memorandum for the Staff," 2 May 1941, *We Cannot Delay*, #438.

38. Smith received a regular army promotion to lieutenant colonel three weeks later on 4 May 1941.

39. Pogue, *Marshall Interviews*, 317–19.

40. Smith to Marshall, 11 June 1940, in Watson, *Chief of Staff*, 312.

41. Marshall to Van Voorhis, 22 August 1940, *We Cannot Delay*, #245; Marshall interview, 11 February 1949, conducted by Colonels Guyer and Donnelly, GCMRL.

42. Pogue, *Marshall Interviews*, 276, 310–13, 340.

43. Henry Arnold, *Global Mission* (New York, 1949), 186.

44. Marshall to Stimson, "Memo for the Secretary of War," 16 May 1941, *We Cannot Delay,* #456.

45. Eisenhower was on the receiving end of this admonition, cited in Ambrose, *Supreme Commander,* 21.

46. "Officer Career Summary," Smith 201 File, WBSP; J. Ulio to Ward, 29 September 1943, Chief of Staff's Personal Papers, 1942–44, WBSP.

47. Marshall to Paul Peabody, 6 April 1937, *Soldierly Spirit,* #437; Marshall to Hjalman Erickson, 18 March 1942, cited in Pogue, *Ordeal and Hope,* 289.

48. Moseley, "Memo for Secretary of War," 16 July 1930, Moseley Papers.

49. Pogue, "United States General Staff."

50. Sometimes called the three-minute drill, the length of the exercise was not as important as its effect on staff efficiency. Pogue, *Ordeal and Hope,* 408.

51. Pogue interview with Smith, 25 July 1958, GCMRL.

52. Watson to Smith, 19 August 1943, Chief of Staff's Personal Papers, 1942–44, WBSP.

53. Smith, "Affidavit of Lieutenant General Walter B. Smith," 15 June 1945, in *Pearl Harbor Hearings, United States Congress, Joint Committee on the Investigation of the Pearl Harbor Attack,* Chief of Staff's Personal Papers, 1942–44, WBSP. Sadtler's testimony is contained in Smith's affidavit. Smith wrote a memo for Marshall, explaining the purveyance and routing of messages from the War Department to the Pacific commands. Smith, "Memorandum for the Chief of Staff," 20 January 1942, RG 165, OCS, Chronological, Miscellaneous File, NARA.

54. Six wartime investigations and the postwar congressional inquiry that Smith testified before all failed to pin the blame on Roosevelt or anybody else in Washington. Nevertheless, some continue to believe the conspiracy thesis that holds the president responsible for bringing the United States into war "through the backdoor."

13. Forging the Mold

1. Since Roosevelt adamantly refused to permit minutes to be taken during private meetings, even with the Joint Board, reliance must be placed on diary extracts. The most valuable is the diary of Henry L. Stimson, Stimson Papers, Sterling Memorial Library, Yale University, New Haven, CT. Whenever possible, published sources are employed. Stimson Diary, 18 December 1941, in *FRUS, The Conferences at Washington, 1941-1942, and Casablanca, 1943,* 37–38.

2. Roosevelt to Churchill, 8 December 1941, and Churchill to Roosevelt, 9 December 1941, in *FRUS, Washington and Casablanca,* 4–5.

3. Churchill, "Part I—The Atlantic Front," 16 December 1941, Roosevelt Papers, ibid., 21–24.

4. Stimson Diary, 21 December 1941, ibid., 56.

5. Joint Board, "Tentative U.S. Views on British Memorandum," 21 December 1941, ibid.

6. Stimson to Roosevelt, "A Suggested Analysis of the Basic Topics and Their Attendant Problems," 20 December 1941, ibid., 44–47.

7. Lewis Morton, "Germany First: The Basic Concept of Allied Strategy in World War II," in *Command Decisions,* ed. Kent Roberts (Washington, DC, 1960; reprint ed., 1971), 33–47; Watson, *Chief of Staff,* 117–18; Maurice Matloff and Edwin M. Snell, *Strategic Planning for Coalition Warfare, 1941-42,* USAWWII (Washington, DC, 1953; reprint ed., 1970), 43–46.

8. The minutes of the twelve Arcadia meetings are in "Proceedings of the American-British Joint Chiefs of Staff Conferences," Washington, DC, 24 December 1941 to 14 January 1942, in Combined Chiefs of Staff: Conference Proceedings, 1941–45, DDEL.

9. Dill to Brooke, 3 January 1942, Alanbrooke Papers, LHCMA, cited in *War Diaries, 1939-1945: Field Marshall Lord Alanbrooke,* ed. Alex Danchev and Daniel Todman (Berkeley, CA, 2001) (subsequently cited as Brooke Diary). See also Danchev, *Very Special Relationship: Field Marshall Sir John Dill and the Anglo-American Alliance, 1941-44* (London, 1986), 56–76. Dill's views are also highlighted in Pogue, *Ordeal and Hope,* 262. Both ADM Andrew Cunningham, who attended Arcadia, and ACM John Slessor, who went to the Casablanca conference, commented on the intensity of American interservice antagonisms. Cunningham, *A Sailor's Odyssey* (New York, 1951), 466–67; Slessor, *The Central Blue* (London, 1956), 494.

10. "Meeting of President Roosevelt and Prime Minister Churchill," 22 December 1941, in *FRUS, Washington and Casablanca,* 64.

11. An example of Hollis setting the agenda nearly led to a serious breach. At a Christmas Eve dinner at the White House, Roosevelt and Churchill discussed the possibility of diverting American reinforcements to Singapore if Japanese naval power precluded their going to the Philippines. Hollis sent out a memo adding the question to the agenda. Stimson very nearly resigned over the issue. Stimson Diary, 25 December 1941, in Pogue, *Ordeal and Hope,* 265–66.

12. For organizational matters related to the secretariat, see "Minutes, British War Cabinet," 17 January 1942, cited in Richard Steele, *The First Offensive 1942: Roosevelt, Marshall, and the Making of American Strategy* (Bloomington, IN, 1973), 91. For communications directed to Smith, see *FRUS, Washington and Casablanca,* 9, 267, 301, 304.

13. BCOS, "Memorandum by the British Chiefs of Staff," 24 December 1941, *FRUS, Washington and Casablanca,* 210–16.

14. "Meeting of the United States and British Chiefs of Staff," 25 December 1941, ibid., 92–93. Eisenhower also kept minutes: "Notes Taken at Joint Conference of Chiefs of Staff on Afternoon December 25," 28 December 1942, *EP, #*23. Marshall provided insights into his thinking and dealing with the British in Marshall interview, 25 July 1949, conducted by Sidney T. Matthews, Howard Smyth, et al., GCMRL.

15. Eisenhower sketched the first draft: "Supreme Commander, Southwestern Pacific Theater," *EP, #*24; "Meeting of the United States and British Chiefs of Staff," 26 December 1941, *FRUS, Washington and Casablanca,* 92–93.

16. Pogue, *Marshall Interviews,* 595. On Hopkins's role, see Robert Sherwood, *Roosevelt and Hopkins: An Intimate History* (New York, 1948), 457.

17. John Moran, *Churchill: Taken from the Diaries of Lord Moran* (Boston, 1966), 22.

18. For Smith's version, see Pogue interview, 9 May 1947, MHI. Precisely what Churchill showed Smith remains a matter of conjecture. The British intelligence apparatus was far more advanced than its American counterparts. Churchill read the joint intelligence assessments daily. Some have speculated he withheld information from the Americans. James Rusbridger employed Australian sources, chiefly the diary of CPT Eric Nave, to construct this case. Rusbridger and Nave, *Betrayal at Pearl Harbor: How Churchill Lured Roosevelt into WWII* (Orangeville, ON, 1991); Ian Pfennigwerth, *A Man of Intelligence: The Life of Captain Eric Nave, Codebreaker Extraordinary* (Lancaster, UK, 2006). Neither book is convincing. A huge gap existed

between signal intelligence officers in the field, such as Nave, and the Joint Intelligence Committee in London. Smith's tantalizing comments to Pogue suggest there might be something to the story, but like all other conspiracy theories arising from Pearl Harbor, no hard supporting evidence exists.

19. Churchill penned a euphoric report to the Cabinet on 17 January.

20. "Meeting of the United States and British Chiefs of Staff," 13 January 1942, *FRUS, Washington and Casablanca,* 198.

21. Sherwood, *Roosevelt and Hopkins,* 471–72.

22. Hopkins, "Memorandum by the President's Special Assistant," 15 January 1942, *FRUS, Washington and Casablanca,* 209.

23. Hollis to William Stirling, 14 January 1942, cited in Alex Danchev, *Establishing the Alliance: The Second World War Diaries of Brigadier Vivian Dykes* (London, 1990), 90–91 (subsequently cited as Dykes Diary). Two of Dykes's notebooks turned up in the offices of the British Defence Staff in Washington in the early 1980s. Danchev received others from family members. The published diaries provide unparalleled entrée into Smith's thinking and actions from January to September 1942.

24. Dykes Diary, 27 January 1942.

25. Ibid., 3, 5, and 7 February 1942.

26. Henry Stimson and McGeorge Bundy, *On Active Service in Peace and War* (New York, 1947), 281; Smith to LTG Henry Pownall, 23 November 1943, 1943 Correspondence File, WBSP.

27. Dykes Diary, 22 January and 3, 5, 7, and 14 February 1942.

28. For Marshall's insisting on Turner's removal, see Eric Larrabee, *Commander in Chief: Franklin Delano Roosevelt, His Lieutenants, and Their War* (New York, 1987), 190. Marshall interview with L. M. Guyer and C. H. Donnelly, Historical Section, Joint Chiefs of Staff, 11 February 1949, Modern Military, Reference Collection, NARA; copy also in GCMRL.

29. Smith fueled British suspicions. At the end of April 1942, he foresaw "a very militaristic spirit developing in America as a result of the war," according to Dykes. "He quite seriously thinks that America will have to absorb Canada and all the British West Indies even by force if necessary." Dykes remained skeptical. "I doubt America's capacity for going tough and *staying* tough," he stated, but wondered if Smith might be right. Dykes Diary, 28 March 1942.

30. Hinton, "Soldier, Diplomat, and Intelligence Chief," 30.

31. Cunningham, *A Sailor's Odyssey,* 466.

32. Danchev interview with Jacob, 12 August 1981, in Danchev, *Establishing the Alliance,* 9.

33. Dykes Diary, 7 February 1942; Dykes to Mary Ravenshear, 8 March 1942, cited in Danchev, *Establishing the Alliance,* 8.

34. Dykes Diary, 11 January 1942.

35. Dykes Diary, 27 February, 22 and 23 March, 11 April, 27 June, and 24 September 1942.

36. Townshend, "Newsmakers."

37. Dykes Diary, 10 and 17 February, 7 April, and 25 July 1942; Thomas Handy oral history, MHI; "Minutes of Meetings of the Combined Chiefs of Staff," POST-ARCADIA, vol. 1, 23 January to 19 May 1942, in Combined Chiefs of Staff: Conference Proceedings, 1941–45, DDEL.

38. Dykes to Hollis, 21 November 1942, in Danchev, *Establishing the Alliance,* 107.

39. Dykes Diary, 2 July 1942.

40. MacArthur to Commanding Generals of the Four Armies, 22 October 1932, cited in Cline, *Washington Command Post,* 28.

41. Marshall to Secretariat of the WDGS, cited in Pogue, *Ordeal and Hope,* 289.

42. Marshall outlined his ideas to McNarney on 25 January. McNarney put together a committee and completed the draft for Marshall's approval on 5 February. For the reorganization, see Nelson, *National Security and the General Staff,* 347–48, 378–96; Cline, *Washington Command Post,* 92–95; and John Millett, *The Organization and Role of the Army Service Forces,* USAWWII (Washington, DC, 1954), 23–33, 37.

43. Marshall to BG John McA Palmer, 12 March 1942, *The Right Man for the Job,* #123.

44. Cline, *Washington Command Post,* 107–11.

45. Marshall first made this point back in 1939 and again two days after Pearl Harbor. "We must fight the fact that the War Department is a poor command post," he told his staff on 9 December 1941. Marshall to Gasser, 4 August 1939, *We Cannot Delay,* #24; Frank McCarthy, "Notes on Conference in General Marshall's Office," 9 December 1941, RG 165, OCS, Chief of Staff Conference File, NARA.

46. Marshall to Edward Stettinius Jr., 27 March 1942, *The Right Man for the Job,* #126, n. 3.

47. Somervell, then in the midst of reorganizing G-4, reacted negatively to McNarney's original organizational structure. According to Somervell, McNarney did not understand logistics functions. He took his complaints directly to Marshall. Though conceding that Somervell should control services and supply, and seeking greater collaboration between the logistics services and operational planning, Marshall never insisted on genuine integration. The reorganization did not go far enough to satisfy Somervell, who petitioned endlessly but unsuccessfully for a further restructuring of the War Department.

48. Smith to Deane and Deane to WBS, 9 and 17 September 1943, Chief of Staff's Personal Papers, 1942–44, WBSP.

49. The JPC met first on 13 February 1942. In addition to representing the Joint Chiefs of Staff within the JPC, the American portion of the committee furnished the War and Navy Departments with strategic guidance.

50. For his views on military intelligence officers, see Smith to Lucian Truscott, 15 December 1943, Chief of Staff's Personal Papers, 1942–44, WBSP; "Minutes, JCS 5th Meeting," 9 March 1942, and Smith to Marshall and King, 12 March 1942, RG 218, Records of the US Joint Chiefs of Staff, JCS/CCS 385, NARA; Dykes Diary, 14 March 1942.

51. "Minutes, JCS 6th and 7th Meetings," 16 and 22 March 1942, and Smith to Marshall and King, 14 and 23 March 1942, RG 218, Records of the US Joint Chiefs of Staff.

52. Dykes Diary, 4 April 1942.

53. Pogue, *Marshall Interviews,* 468. How OSS functioned remains something of a mystery because many of the sources remain unopened—not because of security issues but because of the bureaucratic clutter of the documents.

54. Brooke's negative attitude presented perhaps the single biggest obstacle to functional cooperation inside the CCS. When the British returned from Arcadia, he brusquely told Portal and Pound that they "sold our birthright for a plate of porridge." He rejected combined theater commands and the fact that the war would be run from Washington, and he took a dim view of Dill's work inside the CCS. Brooke Diary, 9 February 1942.

55. Danchev, *Very Special Relationship,* 25–26.

14. "Exceptionally Qualified for Service as Chief of Staff"

1. The Dykes diary reveals this process. The archives—including Smith's papers—permit a mute reconstruction of what Smith did in his official capacities but offer no real insight into the kind of influence he actually wielded, as attested to in the memoir literature and postwar interviews. Dykes's chronicle is in many ways also Smith's diary.

2. Operations Division, "Draft Memorandum for the Chief of Staff," n.d., RG 165, OCS, OPD File. COL Albert Wedemeyer was part of a joint team that drafted the memorandum, which included inputs from Eisenhower and COL Thomas Handy from WPD. Eisenhower's initials appear on some of the preparatory documents. Wedemeyer, *Wedemeyer Reports*, 97–130.

3. Dykes Diary, 3 March 1942.

4. Brooke Diary, 9–16 April 1942; Marshall to McNarney, 12 and 13 April 1942, *The Right Man for the Job*, #155–56; War Cabinet/Chiefs of Staff Committee, "Comments on General Marshall's Memorandum," 13 April 1942, GCMP.

5. Brooke Diary, 15 April 1942.

6. Dykes Diary, 4 May 1942.

7. Marshall to Roosevelt, "The Pacific Theatre versus Bolero," 6 May 1942, and Roosevelt's reply, *The Right Man for the Job*, #179, nn. 1–3.

8. Eisenhower, "BOLERO Trip," 30 May 1942, and "Notes," 4, 8, and 11 June 1942, *EP*, #318, 320, 328, 333.

9. Butcher, *Three Years with Eisenhower*, 61.

10. Dykes Diary, 11 June 1942.

11. Ibid., 20 June 1942; Townshend, "Newsmakers."

12. The phrase "canker of the heart" comes from William Clark, *Less than Kin* (London, 1957), 146.

13. Mountbatten, also elevated to a seat on the BCOS, expressed opposition to Sledgehammer in early May. Brooke Diary, 8 May 1943.

14. Stimson Diary, 17 June 1941, *FRUS, Washington and Casablanca*, 417.

15. Stimson Diary and Stimson to Roosevelt, 19 June 1942, ibid., 457–60.

16. CCS Secretariat, "Meeting of the CCS," 19 June 1942, ibid., 417, 422. Marshall to Roosevelt and Stimson, Stimson Diary, 19 June 1942.

17. Dykes Diary, 19 June 1942.

18. Churchill wrote to Roosevelt in July, complaining that "our code-words need clarification." Despite its Wild West connotation, Roundup was a British plan developed in 1941. The president replied with specific definitions for Bolero, Sledgehammer, and Roundup; thereafter the code words became fixed. Churchill to Roosevelt, 6 July 1942, and Roosevelt to Churchill, 8 July 1942, in Warren Kimball, *Churchill and Roosevelt: The Complete Correspondence*, 3 vols. (Princeton, NJ, 1984), 1:519, 523.

19. Eisenhower, "Combined Chiefs of Staff Memorandum for Information," 19 June 1942, *FRUS, Washington and Casablanca*, 427–28; Dykes Diary, 19 June 1942.

20. "Minutes of the Combined Chiefs of Staff Meeting," 20 June 1942, RG 165, OCS, CCS 334, NARA; Dykes Diary, 20 June 1942.

21. Smith, "Combined Chiefs of Staff Memorandum for Information," 19 June 1942, *FRUS, Washington and Casablanca*, 427–28. See also Minutes, Eisenhower draft, edited by Smith, 19 June 1942, *EP*, #344.

22. "Offensive Operations in 1942 and 1943," 21 June 1943, RG 218, JCS Files, NARA; Stimson to Roosevelt, 19 June 1942, *FRUS, Washington and Casablanca*, 465–

67, 459–60. Although Marshall always vetted important memoranda, Dykes reported that "Offensive Operations in 1942 and 1943" was produced mainly by Smith. Dykes, "Note on the Development of American Thought in Favour of Offensive Action in the Pacific Theater," 15 August 1942, in Danchev, *Establishing the Alliance*, 189.

23. Dykes Diary, 19 June 1942; Brooke Diary, 20 June 1942.

24. Churchill to Roosevelt, 20 June 1942, *FRUS, Washington and Casablanca*, 461–62. The letter is also reproduced in Kimball, *Churchill and Roosevelt*, 1:515.

25. Roosevelt's Naval Aide (McCrea) to Marshall and King, 20 June 1943, *FRUS, Washington and Casablanca*, 462.

26. At the meeting, the Americans offered the British an armored division to be sent to Egypt. The War Department called MG George Patton from California to plan the movement. In the end, the Americans stripped units of armor and anti-tank weapons for the Middle East. No official minutes were taken. Marshall did make some notes after the afternoon meeting and informed Stimson, who pointedly was not invited, about the outcome. Hopkins also talked to Stimson. Churchill and Ismay discuss the meeting in their memoirs. Stimson Diary, 21 June 1942, *FRUS, Washington and Casablanca*, 443; Churchill, *The Second World War*, vol. 4, *The Hinge of Fate* (Boston, 1950), 382–83; Ismay, *The Memoirs of General Lord Ismay* (New York, 1960), 254–55. Perhaps too shocked by the fall of Tobruk, Brooke never mentions Gymnast. Brooke Diary, 21 June 1942.

27. Ismay, "Memorandum," 21 June 1942, in *FRUS, Washington and Casablanca*, 443–44. See also Ismay, *Memoirs*, 254–55.

28. Marshall outlined his views in a letter to Roosevelt on 23 June 1942. Smith and Handy drafted the original, which went through a number of revisions before being sent to the president. Marshall to Roosevelt, 23 June 1942, *The Right Man for the Job*, #229–30. Smith's memo to Marshall, outlining the policy line the American delegation should follow in the 22 June CCS meeting, is in Smith, "Memorandum for the Chief of Staff," 21 June 1942," *FRUS, Washington and Casablanca*, 468–69.

29. Smith's revised "Offensive Operations in 1942 and 1943" on 24 June outlined the final inconclusive findings of the Washington conference, with Ismay's amended minutes attached. JCS Files reproduced in *FRUS, Washington and Casablanca*, 477–79.

30. Eisenhower to Marshall, 26 June 1942, *EP*, #353. The early Eisenhower-Smith connection is "Newsmakers."

31. War Cabinet Offices to Joint Staff Mission, 8 July 1942, RG 165, OCS, OPD File; Churchill to Roosevelt, 8 July 1942, in Kimball, *Churchill and Roosevelt*, 1:520–21.

32. "Minutes, JCS Meeting," 10 July 1942, RG 165, OCS, CCS 334; Marshall, "Memorandum for the President," 10 July 1942, *The Right Man for the Job*, #251.

33. Dykes to Sterling, 10 July 1942, in Danchev, *Establishing the Alliance*, 166–67; Dykes Diary, 10 July 1942.

34. "Minutes of the JCS Meeting," 10 July 1942; Marshall, "Memorandum for the President," 10 July 1942, RG 165, OCS, CCS 334.

35. John Deane, "Memorandum for Admiral King," 12 July 1942, and Marshall, King, and Arnold, "Memorandum for the President," 12 July 1942, RG 165, OCS, OPD File.

36. Roosevelt to Marshall, 14 July 1942, RG 165, OCS, BOLERO File; Wedemeyer to Handy, 14 July 1942, RG 165, OCS, OPD File.

37. Dykes, "Note on Development of American Thought," 189; Dykes Diary, 13 July 1942.

38. Dykes Diary, 14 and 15 July 1942.

39. Marshall, "Memorandum for Admiral King," 15 July 1942, *The Right Man for the Job*, #255; Roosevelt, "Memorandum for Hopkins, Marshall, and King," 16 July 1942, F. D. Roosevelt Papers, Franklin D. Roosevelt Library, reproduced in Sherwood, *Roosevelt and Hopkins*, 603–5. See also Marshall interview, 11 February 1949, GCMRL.

40. Dykes Diary, 18 July 1942.

41. Eisenhower to Butcher, 20 July 1942, *EP,* #384; Eisenhower, "Memo," 22 July 1942, Diary of Harry C. Butcher, PPP. The diary contains portions of Eisenhower's memos and notes, along with many entries by Butcher withheld from publication. Dykes Diary, 20 July 1942.

42. Leo Meyer, "The Decision to Invade North Africa," in *Command Decisions*.

43. Dykes Diary, 15, 18, and 20 July 1942.

44. Eisenhower observed, "The seeds for discord between ourselves and our British allies were sown, on our side, as far back as when we read our little red school history books." Eisenhower to Marshall, 5 April 1943, *EP,* #927.

45. Marshall told Dill on 16 July that the president had rejected the Pacific scheme. Dykes Diary, 21 July 1942; Dykes, "Note on Development of American Thought."

46. Brooke Diary, 22 July 1942.

47. Butcher, *Three Years with Eisenhower*, 29–30; Dykes Diary, 22 July 1942.

48. Dykes Diary, 22 July 1942.

49. Dykes attests that the CCS "Survey of Strategic Situation" was authored mostly by Smith. "Survey of Strategic Situation," 23 July 1943, *EP,* #389; Dykes Diary, 24 July 1942; Dykes, "Note on Development of American Thought," 15 August 1942.

50. Marshall to British Chiefs of Staff, 24 July 1942, *The Right Man for the Job*, #257. Dykes recorded that the paper was written "mainly by Smith, who had a great deal of difficulty putting over the idea of TORCH at all." At Churchill's suggestion, the code name was changed from Gymnast to Torch. Dykes Diary, 24 July 1942.

51. "Minutes, CCS 32nd Meeting," July 24, RG 165, OCS, CCS Minutes; Marshall and King to Roosevelt, 24 July 1942, RG 319, Records of the Army Staff, Chief of Staff File; Dykes Diary, 24 July 1942; Brooke Diary, 24 July 1942. Minutes are also contained in "Minutes of Meetings of the Combined Chiefs of Staff," POST-ARCADIA, vol. 1, 23 January to 19 May 1942, in Combined Chiefs of Staff, Conference Proceedings, 1941–45, DDEL.

52. Dykes Diary, 24 July 1942; Dykes, "Note on Development of American Thought."

53. Dykes Diary, 25 July 1942.

54. Eisenhower to Butcher, 26 and 27 July 1942, *EP,* #393, #396. For Butcher's summary, see *Three Years with Eisenhower*, 32.

55. Dykes Diary, 29 and 30 July 1942.

56. Cunningham, *A Sailor's Odyssey*, 466–67.

57. Stimson Diary, 25 February 1942, Stimson Papers.

58. Marshall to Eisenhower, 30 July 1942, *The Right Man for the Job*, #284; William Leahy, *I Was There* (New York, 1950), 97.

59. Dykes Diary, 30 July 1942.

60. Marshall to Eisenhower, 5 August 1942, *The Right Man for the Job*, #267; Eisenhower to Marshall, 7 August 1942, *EP,* #15.

61. So Nory told Dykes. Dykes Diary, 24 September 1942.

62. Smith received orders on 7 July to proceed to London on or about 1 August. Adjutant General to Smith, 7 July 1942, Smith 201 File, WBSP.

63. Dykes Diary, 30 July 1942.

64. Ibid., 3 August 1942.

65. Eisenhower ruled out landings at Bône and Philippeville but proposed a ranger battalion drop on the former. Eisenhower to Marshall, 9 August 1942, *EP,* #418.

66. Eisenhower to Marshall, 13 August 1942, *EP,* #424.

67. Dykes Diary, 13 and 14 August 1942.

68. Eisenhower to Ismay, 22 August 1942, and Eisenhower to Combined Chiefs, 23 August 1942, *EP,* #444–45; plan summarized in Matloff and Snell, *Strategic Planning,* 288–89.

69. Eisenhower to Combined Chiefs, 23 August 1942, and Eisenhower to Marshall and OPD, 24 August 1942, *EP,* #445, #447; Dykes Diary, 24 August 1942.

70. Dykes Diary, 25 August 1942.

71. Eisenhower to Marshall, 26 August 1942, Eisenhower to John Deane, 27 August 1942, Eisenhower to Marshall, 29 August 1942, *EP,* #453, #455, #463.

72. Smith to Leahy, 27 August 1942, RG 218, Records of the U.S. Joint Chiefs of Staff, CCS 381.

73. Dykes Diary, 27 August 1942.

74. Ibid., 28 August 1942.

75. Roosevelt to Churchill, 30 August 1942, in Churchill, *The Hinge of Fate,* 531–33.

76. Dykes Diary, 1 September 1942.

77. For copies of Churchill's letters to Roosevelt, see Churchill, *The Hinge of Fate,* 534–35. Dykes Diary, 1 and 2 September 1942; Dykes to Stirling, 2 September 1942, in Danchev, *Establishing the Alliance,* 197.

78. Dykes Diary, 3 September 1942.

79. Eisenhower sent three cables to Marshall on 3 September 1942, *EP,* # 475–77; Handy to Eisenhower, 4 September 1942, *EP,* #478. Copies of all these communications are in Eisenhower Miscellaneous, Cable File, DDEL. The exchange between Churchill and Roosevelt is reproduced in Churchill, *The Hinge of Fate,* 541–42.

80. Stimson Diary, 17 June 1942, *FRUS, Washington and Casablanca,* 417.

81. Dykes Diary, 4 September 1942.

15. "Smith Will Save Ike"

1. Dykes Diary, 6 September 1942.

2. Smith to Moseley, 4 July 1942, Moseley Papers.

3. Eisenhower to Marshall, 15 August 1942, *EP,* #429; Marshall to OPD, 19 August 1942, *The Right Man for the Job,* #282.

4. CCS Directive, 24 July 1942, Butcher Diary; Eisenhower to George Patton, 31 August 1942, *EP,* #468.

5. Handy to Eisenhower, 23 August 1942, Butcher Diary. Patton was another who saw Torch as political and therefore ill-fated. Patton traveled to London for talks on Torch. His friend Hughes visited him on 8 August and found Patton behind a desk with his head buried in his hands. "Without taking his head out of one hand," Hughes later remembered, "he tossed me a document and said, 'Read that.' I did. It was the order to P[atton] to return to the US and organize the Western Task Force for the N[orth] A[frican] campaign." For his entire career, Patton had longed for the opportunity to lead a major force in battle, and now he commanded an operation he saw as a forlorn "political" operation. Death—he never feared defeat—would

defuse the great destiny he believed lay before him. Patton's views, though typically more extreme, mirrored the sentiments of most senior American officers. Hughes, "Notes of Patton," n.d., Hughes Papers; Hughes Diary, 8 August 1942.

6. MG Joseph Haydon, Mountbatten's vice chief, made these complaints on 8 August. Mountbatten passed Haydon's memo on to Eisenhower. On 11 August the JCS approved Clark's appointment as deputy supreme commander; Eisenhower instructed Clark to focus on Torch. Eisenhower to Mountbatten, 11 August 1942, *EP,* #421; Marshall to Eisenhower, 11 August 1942, *The Right Man for the Job,* #3204; Eisenhower Manuscripts, Cable File, DDEL.

7. Mark Clark, *Calculated Risk* (New York, 1950), 48.

8. Butcher Diary, 11 August 1942.

9. Reginald MacDonald-Buchanan, "Notes on General Marshall," MacDonald-Buchanan Papers, GCMRL.

10. Eisenhower to Mamie, 26 August 1942, in *Letters to Mamie,* ed. John D. Eisenhower (Garden City, NY, 1978).

11. Butcher Diary, 27 August 1942; Eisenhower to Charlie Harger, Moseley, and Vernon Prichard, 27 August 1942, *EP,* #456–57, 459.

12. Eisenhower to Marshall, 5 September 1942, *EP,* #484.

13. Butcher Diary, 3 September 1942, *EP,* #473.

14. The chief sources for the rest of this chapter are the published and unpublished Butcher diaries.

15. Butcher, *Three Years with Eisenhower,* 91,104.

16. Eisenhower used the "one man navy" expression repeatedly. Butcher Diary, 10 August 1942.

17. Eisenhower recommended Smith's promotion at the end of July and again early in October. Eisenhower to Marshall, 27 July and 3 October 1942, *EP,* #395, 534.

18. Butcher Diary, 11 August 1942; Eisenhower to Operations Division, 16 August 1942, *EP,* #433.

19. Eisenhower's insistence that he alone determined the structure of his headquarters emerged as a leitmotif throughout his tenure as supreme commander. Butcher, *Three Years with Eisenhower,* 45; Eisenhower to Smith, 31 December 1943, *EP,* #1469.

20. Butcher's account of Smith's first day is in *Three Years with Eisenhower,* 90–93.

21. FUBAR is army slang for "fucked up beyond all repair."

22. Eisenhower to Handy, 7 September 1942, *EP,* #488; Somervell to Eisenhower, 8 September 1942, *EP,* #490, n. 1.

23. Lee, BG Thomas Larkin, and Hughes put together the list. Hughes [for Eisenhower] to War Department, 8 September 1942, Hughes Papers; Butcher Diary, 9 September 1942.

24. J. C. H. Lee, *Service Reminiscences,* unpublished manuscript, Hoover Institution, Stanford University, Stanford, CA (a copy is in MHI); Somervell to Marshall, 24 September 1942, *The Right Man for the Job,* #334, n. 4.

25. Leroy Lutes, who headed operations and planning in ASF, provides some of the best insights into the logistical and organizational problems experienced by the U.S. Army in World War II. Lutes to Lee, 12 September 1942, Hughes Papers; Lutes, "Army Supply Problems," 23 September 1946, Industrial College of the Armed Forces lecture; "The Effects of Logistics upon Strategy," 29 January 1951, Army War College lecture; "Supply in World War II: The Flight to Europe in 1942," *Antiaircraft Journal* 95 (May–June 1952): 8–10, Leroy Lutes Papers, DDEL. Hughes's unpublished manuscripts also offer firsthand insights. See Hughes, "Organization," "Impetus of

Supply from the Rear," and "Supply from the Rear," Hughes Papers. See also Carter Magruder, *Recurring Logistical Problems as I Have Observed Them* (Washington, DC, 1991), 27, and Magruder oral history, MHI. The confused state of American logistics is discussed in Millett, *Organization and Role of Army Service Forces*, 60–61; Roland Ruppenthal, *Logistical Support of the Armies*, 2 vols., USAWWII (Washington, DC, 1953), 1:96–99; and Richard Leighton and Robert Coakley, *Global Logistics and Strategy, 1940-1943*, USAWWII (Washington, DC, 1955), 368–73.

26. Butcher Diary, 4 September 1942.

27. Ibid., 6 September 1942; Ruppenthal, *Logistical Support of the Armies*, 1:96.

28. Eisenhower to Marshall, 17 and 19 August 1942, *EP,* #434, #437; Butcher Diary, 17 August 1942.

29. Eisenhower to Handy, 31 August 1942, *EP,* #468.

30. Butcher Diary, 2 September 1942.

31. Eisenhower to OPD, 4 September 1942, *EP,* #479.

32. Hughes Diary, 12 September 1942; Lida Mayo, *The Ordnance Department: On Beachhead and Battlefront*, USAWWII (Washington, DC, 1968), 104.

33. Eisenhower to Handy, 7 September 1942, *EP,* #488.

34. Smith [for Eisenhower] to Marshall, 10 September 1942, *EP,* #491.

35. Hughes to Kate Hughes, 10 September 1942, Hughes Papers.

36. Eisenhower to Somervell, 26 June 1942, *EP,* #355.

37. Eisenhower to Somervell, 27 July 1942, *EP,* #398.

38. Butcher, *Three Years with Eisenhower*, 7.

39. Eisenhower to OPD, 16 August 1942, *EP,* #433; Butcher Diary, 16 August 1942.

40. Marshall to Chaney, "Organization Services of Supply," 14 May 1942, cited in GBR, "Organization and Function of the Communications Zones," annex. See also Ruppenthal, *Logistical Support of the Armies*, 1:36.

41. Lee, *Service Reminiscences*, 81.

42. GBR, "Organization and Function of the Communications Zones," 1; Hughes, "Organization," Hughes Papers.

43. GBR, "Organization of the European Theater of War," 84.

44. Marshall to Chaney, "Organization Services of Supply."

45. The administrative services were Adjutant General, Senior Chaplain, Inspector General, Judge Advocate, Provost Marshal, and Special Services Office. The supply services were Army Exchange, Chemical Warfare, Depot Services, Engineers, Finance, Ordnance, Quartermaster, Medical, Signal, and Transportation.

46. Historical Division, U.S. Forces, European Theater, "Organization and Command in the European Theater of Operations," in *The Administrative and Logistical History of the European Theater of Operations*, 2 vols. (Paris, 1946), 1:64.

47. The field manual issued less than a week after Eisenhower assumed command directed as follows: "The theater is organized for tactical control and administrative control to the extent dictated by War Department instructions." "Theater of Operations," 29 June 1942, *FM 100-15, Field Service Regulations, Larger Units*, para. 11. For three weeks, Eisenhower issued no directive on theater organization. Finally, on 20 July, he issued General Order 19, preserving Chaney's structure. Ruppenthal, *Logistical Support of the Armies*, 1:44.

48. Butcher, *Three Years with Eisenhower*, 7.

49. Smith [for Eisenhower] to Lee, 10 September 1942, *EP,* #494.

50. Gale to Smith, 15 September 1942, Hughes Papers.

51. Hughes to Clark, 14 September 1942, Hughes Papers.

52. Gale to Smith, "Ability of SOS to Meet Initial Supply Demands," 15 September 1942, Hughes Papers.

53. Eisenhower Diary, 15 September 1942, *EP,* #502.

54. Lee, *Service Reminiscences,* 81.

55. Murphy tells his own story in *Diplomat among Warriors.* Leon Blair, "Amateurs in Diplomacy: The American Vice-Consuls in North Africa, 1941–43," *Historian* (August 1973): 607–20.

56. Murphy, *Diplomat among Warriors,* 104–5.

57. For an account of Murphy's diplomatic maneuvering, see Murphy, *Diplomat among Warriors,* 124–61; Eisenhower, *Crusade in Europe,* 86–88; George Howe, *Northwest Africa: Seizing the Initiative in the West,* USAWWII (Washington, DC, 1957), 77–83.

58. The account of the meeting comes from Butcher, *Three Years with Eisenhower,* 103–4, 106–10, and Murphy, *Diplomat among Warriors,* 155.

59. "Minutes of Conference, SOS Headquarters," and Lee to Hughes, 18 September 1942, Hughes Papers.

60. Lee to Clark, 18 September 1942, Hughes Papers.

61. Hughes to Clark, "Estimate of Supply and Administrative Aspects of Proposed Operation," 14 September 1942, Hughes Papers.

62. Eisenhower to War Department, 19 September 1942, Hughes Papers.

63. Hughes's marginal note, Lee to Clark, 18 September 1942, Hughes Papers.

64. Butcher Diary, 19 and 21 September 1942.

65. Eisenhower to Marshall, 19 September 1942, *EP,* #509.

66. Butcher Diary, 18 September 1942; Butcher, *Three Years with Eisenhower,* 113.

67. Smith, "Outline Plan, Operation TORCH," 20 September 1942, in "Operation TORCH," Combined Chiefs of Staff File, WBSP.

68. Butcher Diary, 18 September 1942; Eisenhower to Marshall, 3 October 1943, *EP,* #534.

69. Butcher, *Three Years with Eisenhower,* 104.

70. Eisenhower to Charles Gailey, 19 September 1942, *EP,* #510.

71. Lee to Lutes, 21 September 1942, Hughes Papers.

72. Butcher Diary, 24 September 1942.

73. Eisenhower, "Staff Requirements, Future Operations," [27] July 1942, *EP,* #397; Eisenhower to Marshall, 17 August 1942, EP, #435; Smith to Marshall, 22 October 1942, Chief of Staff's Official Correspondence File, 1942–1944,WBSP. An entire file is devoted to the Smith-Marshall correspondence from the time of Smith's arrival in the theater until after he moved to London.

74. COL Ben Sawbridge, "Organizational and Functional Chart, AFHQ," 26 August 1942, AG AFHQ: 323 35-1, in Allied Force Headquarters, Historical Section and U.S. Army, North African/Mediterranean Theater of Operations, Historical Section, *History of Allied Force Headquarters,* ed. E. Dwight Salmon, Paul Birdsall, et al. (1945).

75. Ruppenthal, *Logistical Support of the Armies,* 2:90–91.

76. Ismay, *Memoirs,* 262–63.

77. Brooke Diary and "Notes for My Memoirs," 26 June 1942. Between 1951 and 1956, Brooke wrote commentaries on his diary ("Notes"), presumably for an eventual biographer. Danchev inserted these notes in *War Diaries;* they do not appear in Bryant's books based on the Alanbrooke diaries.

78. Butcher, *Three Years with Eisenhower,* 117.

79. Smith to Marshall, 22 October 1942, Personal Correspondence File, WBSP.

80. Carter Burgess interview by author, 19 November 1988, Roanoke, VA. Burgess, Smith's aide who came to London with him, later served as secretary of the general staff.

81. Hughes to Kate, 30 September 1942, Hughes Papers.

82. For an account of Smith's hospitalization, the escape, and the birthday party, see Butcher, *Three Years with Eisenhower,* 124–27, 132, 143.

83. Eisenhower to Marshall, 3 October 1942, *EP,* # 534.

84. Eisenhower to Marshall, 12 October 1942, *EP,* #544.

85. Marshall to Smith, 19 October 1942, and Smith to Marshall, 22 October 1942, Chief of Staff Correspondence, WBSP.

86. Butcher Diary, 27–28 September and 3–4, 6 October 1942.

16. "We Are on the Threshold of a Magnificent Success"

1. Chynoweth to George Pappas, 24 October 1987, and Chynoweth to Patton, 16 July 1926, both in Chynoweth Papers, MHI. See also Chynoweth, *Bellamy Park,* 100, 121–25.

2. MacArthur made these observations to BG Gerald Wilkinson, the British liaison officer to MacArthur's command in Australia in 1942. N. Gerald Hugh Wilkinson, "War Journal," CAC.

3. Eisenhower Diary, 21 March 1942, Eisenhower Diary, January 1–July 6, 1942 File, Eisenhower Diaries, DDEL.

4. Eisenhower to Hughes, 9 September 1934, Hughes Papers.

5. Eisenhower to Conner, 21 August 1942, *EP,* #442.

6. Oliver Warner, *Cunningham of Hyndhope, Admiral of the Fleet: A Memoir* (London, 1967), 185.

7. Eisenhower to Somervell, 31 October 1942, *EP,* #574.

8. Wilkinson, "War Journal."

9. AG AFHQ to Commanding Generals of American Task Forces and Air Forces, 3 October 1942, in Salmon et al., *History of Allied Force Headquarters,* and European Theater of Operations, U.S. Army Historical Division, *The Administrative and Logistical History of the European Theater of Operations* (Washington, DC, 1946).

10. Butcher Diary, 8 October 1942.

11. Ibid., 9 August 1942.

12. Eisenhower to Marshall, 29 July 1942, *EP,* #399.

13. Eisenhower to OPD, 16 August 1942, *EP,* #433.

14. Eisenhower to AG WDGS, 3 September 1942, *EP,* #474.

15. Butcher Diary, 24 September 1942.

16. Eisenhower to OPD, 16 August 1942, *EP,* #433; Eisenhower to Marshall, 17 August 1942, *EP,* #435; Butcher Diary, 27 August 1942.

17. Eisenhower to Marshall, 3 October 1942, *EP,* #534.

18. Eisenhower believed the failure to create a unified air command was one of the errors of the North African campaign. Eisenhower, "Commander-in-Chief's Dispatch, North African Campaign, 1942–43," copy in WBSP. Frank Craven and James Cate, eds., *Europe: TORCH to POINTBLANK, August 1942-December 1943,* AAFWWII (Chicago, 1949), 56–60.

19. Eisenhower to Ismay, 10 October 1942, *EP,* #541; Eisenhower to Marshall, 20 October 1942, *EP,* #559; Eisenhower to Handy, 23 October 1942, *EP,* #563.

20. Salmon et al., *History of Allied Force Headquarters.*

21. Eisenhower to AG WDGS, 21 August 1942, *EP,* #443; Butcher, *Three Years with Eisenhower,* 68.

22. Eisenhower to Charles Gailey, 1 January 1943, *EP,* #751.

23. An American major, Joseph Phillips, held the position.

24. Smith to Marshall, 22 October 1942, Marshall Correspondence File, WBSP.

25. AFHQ Operational Memo #30, 24 October 1942, AFHQ, 1942–1944 File, WBSP.

26. AFHQ to War Department, 26 October 1942, Cable R 4129, AFHQ, 1942–1944 File, WBSP.

27. Marshall to AFHQ, 25 October 1942, Cable R-2409, and Marshall to Eisenhower, 30 October 1942, Cable R 2593, AFHQ In-Coming Cable Log, WBSP.

28. Marshall to Eisenhower, 30 October 1942, *EP,* #572, n. 1.

29. Smith's views are thoroughly laid out in GBR, "Organization of the European Theater of Operations," 63–64, 78–84.

30. Sawbridge, "Staff Study," 2 November 1942, AG AFHQ: 323.35-66, AFHQ File, WBSP.

31. Leighton and Coakley, *Global Logistics and Strategy,* 466–67.

32. Eisenhower to Marshall, 31 October 1942, *EP,* #572.

33. Sawbridge, "AFHQ Memo #37," 2 November 1942, AFHQ 0100/21/144, stated: "Effective at once, no additional requests for personnel or troop units for service in TORCH area will be made upon the War Department without the personal approval of G-1 and the Chief of Staff."

34. Eisenhower to Marshall, 19 September 1942, *EP,* #509; "Minutes of Chief of Staff Meeting," 13 October 1942, Hughes Papers; Eisenhower to Anderson, 7 November 1942, *EP,* #584; Butcher, *Three Years with Eisenhower,* 159.

35. Butcher Diary, 2 and 5 October 1942.

36. Eisenhower to Hartle, 27 October 1942, *EP,* #568; Smith to Handy, 29 October 1942, AFHQ, Out-Going Cables, WBSP.

37. Eisenhower to Marshall, 29 October 1942, *EP,* #569; Butcher, *Three Years with Eisenhower,* 152–56. The Axis had no troops in Tunisia and only a few understrength and immobile Italian divisions in western Libya.

38. Eisenhower to Marshall, 1 November 1942, *EP,* #576.

39. Marshall to Eisenhower, 5 November 1942, RG 492, Mediterranean Theater of Operations, United States Army, NARA; Smith to Eisenhower, 7 November 1942, Eyes Only Cable File, WBSP; Eisenhower to Marshall, 7 November 1942, *EP,* #585; Butcher Diary, 7 November 1942. See also ETOUSA Historical Section, Pre- & Invasion Planning File, WBSP.

40. Eisenhower to Marshall, 7 November 1942, *EP,* #585.

41. Smith to Eisenhower, 7 November 1942, *EP,* #579, n. 1.

42. Smith to Mountbatten, 7 November 1942, Smith 201 File, WBSP. As was the practice among senior officers, Smith removed a number of sensitive letters and placed them in his 210 File.

43. Frederick Morgan, *Overture to Overlord* (Garden City, NY, 1950), 9.

44. Eisenhower to Marshall [through Smith], 7 November 1942, *EP,* #585.

45. Eisenhower to Smith, 9 November 1942, *EP,* #592.

17. "Thank God You Are in London"

1. Eisenhower to Smith, 11 November 1942, *EP,* #609.

2. Eisenhower to Smith, 16 November 1942, *EP,* #631.

3. Eisenhower to Smith, 6 November 1942, *EP,* #583.

4. Eisenhower to CCS, 14 November 1942, *EP,* #622.

5. Murphy, *Diplomat among Warriors,* 136–38.

6. Murphy forwarded three letters; the other two involved meetings with Mast concerning command arrangements between Eisenhower and Giraud. Mast told Murphy the general did not trust Darlan and dismissed any cooperation between the two men. Eisenhower to Marshall, 17 October 1942, *EP,* #557.

7. Eisenhower to Marshall, 17 October 1942, *EP,* #558; Brooke Diary, 17 October 1942.

8. Cited in Howe, *Northwest Africa,* 81.

9. Butcher, *Three Years with Eisenhower,* 251; Eisenhower, *Crusade in Europe,* 116.

10. Eisenhower to Smith and Eisenhower to Marshall, 9 November 1942, *EP,* #592, #594.

11. Butcher, *Three Years with Eisenhower,* 188.

12. Ibid., 190. Macmillan told Smith that Noguës possessed "a wonderful skill in grazing the edge of treason." Macmillan to Smith, 15 April 1943, Smith 201 File, WBSP.

13. Eisenhower to Smith, 11 November 1942, *EP,* #609.

14. Eisenhower to Marshall, 11 November 1942, *EP,* #607.

15. Eisenhower to Churchill, 11 November 1942, *EP,* #604.

16. Eisenhower to Marshall, 11 November 1942, *EP,* #606; Eisenhower to Smith, 11 November 1942, *EP,* #609.

17. Eisenhower made these intentions clear to Smith before Torch commenced. Eisenhower to Smith, 6 November 1942, *EP,* #583.

18. Brooke Diary, 10 November 1942.

19. Smith to Eisenhower, 11 November 1942, Chief of Staff, TORCH, November 8–December 9, 1942 File, WBSP. Smith had his staff collect all the correspondence in a single file.

20. Eisenhower to Clark, 12 November 1942, *EP,* #613.

21. Bipolar disorder is so common among the general population that there is no great stigma attached to those who suffer from it. Noted British psychiatrist and author Anthony Storr makes the valid point that, had Churchill been "stable and equable," he "could never have inspired the nation. In 1940, when all the odds were against Britain, a leader of sober judgment might well have concluded that we were finished." Churchill revisionists make the same argument, without the psychological categories. Anthony Storr, *Churchill's Black Dog and Other Phenomena of the Human Mind* (New York, 1997).

22. Smith to Eisenhower, 12 November 1942, TORCH, WBSP.

23. Eisenhower to Smith, 12 November 1942, *EP,* #615, #616.

24. Smith to Eisenhower, 12 December 1942, TORCH, WBSP; Brooke Diary, 13 November 1942.

25. Eisenhower to Marshall, 13 November 1942, *EP,* #619.

26. Butcher, *Three Years with Eisenhower,* 190–93.

27. Brooke Diary, 13 November 1942.

28. Eisenhower to CCS, 14 November 1942, *EP,* #622.

29. Eisenhower to Smith, 14 November 1942, *EP,* #625.

30. Smith gave a complete account of the Chequers meeting to Eisenhower. Smith to Eisenhower, 16 November 1942, TORCH, WBSP. See also Brooke Diary, 15 November 1942.

31. Smith to Eisenhower, 16 November 1942, TORCH, WBSP; Eisenhower to Smith, 17 November 1942, *EP,* #638.

32. Cited in Roy Jenkins, *Churchill: A Biography* (New York, 2001), 702–3.

33. Sherwood, *Roosevelt and Hopkins,* 651.

34. Pogue, *Marshall Interviews,* 488–89.

35. Smith to Eisenhower, 16 November 1942, TORCH, WBSP.

36. Churchill to Roosevelt and British Foreign Office to British Embassy in Washington, 17 November 1942, *FRUS, Foreign Relations, 1942, Europe,* 2:445–47; Eisenhower to Clark, 19 November 1942, *EP,* #645.

37. Eisenhower to Smith, 16 November 1942, *EP,* #631.

38. Ibid., #634.

39. Brooke Diary, 19 November 1942.

40. Eisenhower to Marshall, 17 November 1942, *EP,* #640; Eisenhower to Smith, 17 November 1942, *EP,* #638; Eisenhower to Smith, 11 November 1942, *EP,* #609; Smith to Eisenhower, 16 November 1942, TORCH, WBSP.

41. Eisenhower to Smith, 16 November 1942, *EP,* #631; Eisenhower to Smith, 17 November 1942, *EP,* #638.

42. Eisenhower to Clark, 19 November 1942, *EP,* #645.

43. Eisenhower to Marshall, 18 November 1942, Marshall Correspondence File, DDEL.

44. Eisenhower to Smith, 18 November 1942, *EP,* #641.

45. Ibid., #642.

46. Aside from Gale, Smith brought MG F. H. N. Davidson, director of British Military Intelligence; Brigadier Cecil Sugden, the British G-3 in AFHQ; and Dykes's old friend Colonel Stirling, now assigned as Eisenhower's military assistant. Smuts flew down separately and also attended the conference.

47. Eisenhower to Clark, 19 November 1942, *EP,* #645.

48. Eisenhower to Marshall, 17 November 1942, *EP,* #640.

49. In fact, AFHQ had only 403 officers attached (313 American and 90 British), with another 200 British logisticians detached from headquarters for service with the First Army and the British line of communications command. Salmon et al., *History of Allied Force Headquarters.*

50. Eisenhower to Clark, 20 November 1942, *EP,* #649.

51. Somervell to Eisenhower, 11 November 1942, TORCH, WBSP; Sawbridge [for Eisenhower] to Somervell, 21 November 1942, *EP,* #655; Salmon et al., *History of Allied Force Headquarters.*

52. Butcher, *Three Years with Eisenhower,* 201.

53. Brooke Diary, 21 November 1942.

54. Smith to Marshall, 24 November 1942, TORCH, WBSP.

55. Marshall to Smith, telephone transcript, 25 November 1942, TORCH, WBSP.

56. Smith to Eisenhower, 25 November 1942, TORCH, WBSP; Eisenhower to Smith, 25 November 1942, *EP,* #665.

57. "Minutes, BCOS Meeting" and Smith to Eisenhower, 25 November 1942, TORCH, WBSP. See also Brooke Diary, 25 November 1942.

58. Smith to Eisenhower, 26 November 1942, TORCH, WBSP. The full text of Darlan's letter is reproduced in Butcher, *Three Years with Eisenhower,* 206–7. Butcher also reported that Marshall instructed Eisenhower to write a note to Darlan expressing his own appreciation but not that of the American government.

59. Brooke Diary, 26 November 1942.

60. Smith to Eisenhower, 27 November 1942, TORCH, WBSP; Eisenhower to Smith, 27 December 1942, *EP,* #672.

61. Brooke Diary, 30 November 1942. Three days later he presented a new paper. Churchill repeatedly said that "North Africa must act as a 'springboard' and not a sofa to future action! After urging attacks on Sardinia and Sicily he is now swinging away from these for a possible invasion of France in 1943!" Reflecting back on this period, Brooke remembered Churchill saying, "You must not think that you can get off with your 'sardines' [referring to Sardinia and Sicily] in 1943, no—we must establish a western front, and what is more we promised Stalin we should do so when in Moscow." Brooke Diary and "Notes," 3 December 1942.

62. Marshall to Eisenhower, 1 December 1943, *The Right Man for the Job,* #430. On 7 January Ismay confirmed the BCOS had arrived at a "definite decision" to exploit the situation in the Mediterranean. Ismay to Smith, 7 January 1943, Chief of Staff Official Correspondence, 1942–1944, WBSP.

63. Leahy, *I Was There,* 137.

64. Eisenhower to Marshall, 2 December 1942, *EP,* #681.

65. Smith to Eisenhower, 3 December 1942, TORCH, WBSP.

66. Roosevelt to Churchill, 11 December 1942, *FRUS, Washington and Casablanca,* 499.

18. "We Shall Continue to Flounder"

1. Smith to Ismay, 15 December 1942, Chief of Staff Official Correspondence, 1942–1944, WBSP.

2. Eisenhower to Churchill, 5 December 1942, *EP,* #692.

3. Eisenhower to Handy, 7 December 1942, *EP,* #698.

4. Eisenhower to Robert Littlejohn, 12 December 1942, *EP,* #712.

5. K. A. N. Anderson, "Home Forces, Subject: Administrative Lessons of the Campaign in North Africa," 27 July 1943, in Allied Interoperability File, MHI.

6. Gale sporadically kept a diary in which he chronicled his efforts to disentangle the supply lines. War Diary of Chief Administrative Officer, Allied Force Headquarters, Papers of LTG Sir Humphrey Myddleton Gale, LHCMA.

7. Smith to Ismay, 15 December 1942, WBSP. For a discussion of this question, see U.S. Army, Mediterranean Theatre of Operations, Supply (G-4) Division, *Logistical History of NATOUSA/MTOUSA* (Naples, 1945), chap. 1, and Leo Meyer, "Strategy and Logistical History: Mediterranean Theater of Operations," MHI.

8. Eisenhower to CCS, 12 December 1942, *EP,* #711. The high attrition rates for vehicles in Tunisia—many of them bogged down in a sea of mud—were not anticipated.

9. Eisenhower to Churchill, 16 December 1942, *EP,* #724.

10. Eisenhower to Paul Hodgson, 4 December 1942, *EP,* #687.

11. Butcher Diary, 12 and 20 December 1942. For Eisenhower's estimate of Smith, see *Crusade in Europe,* 54–55.

12. "Minutes, Chiefs of Staff meeting," 10 December 1942, AFHQ, WBSP.

13. Ruth Briggs interview with William Snyder, cited in "Walter Bedell Smith," *Military Affairs* (January 1984): 9–10.

14. Carter Burgess and Dan Gilmer oral histories, DDEL; Vittrup and Burgess interviews. Gilmer served as Smith's secretary of the general staff in AFHQ. A graduate of the Virginia Military Institute, Burgess served as Smith's aide in Washington and traveled with him to London and Algiers; he later acted as Smith's secretary of

the general staff. Vittrup also served in the secretariat in Washington and later in AFHQ.

15. Smith, "Problems of an Integrated Headquarters," *Journal of the Royal United Services Institute* (November 1945): 455–62; original transcript in WBSP.

16. Smith to Truscott, 15 December 1942, Personal Correspondence, WBSP. Truscott tried unsuccessfully to retain one of his prized staff officers and keep him out of the big headquarters. He argued that a staff appointment would curtail a promising career. It did not; the officer in question, Theodore Conway, rose to four-star rank. Conway, Senior Officer Debriefing Program, MHI.

17. Jacob Diary, "Operation Symbol," 30 December 1942, unpublished personal diary of LTG Ian Jacob, cited in Carlo D'Este, *Eisenhower: A Soldier's Life* (New York, 2002), 379.

18. Nevins oral history, DDEL.

19. Russell Gugeler, unpublished biography of Orlando Ward, and Ward Diary, Orlando Ward Papers, MHI. See also Rick Atkinson, *An Army at Dawn: The War in North Africa, 1942-1943* (New York, 2002), 279.

20. This quote appears in several sources but not in Macmillan's account, *The Blast of War* (London, 1967). See Nigel Fischer, *Harold Macmillan* (New York, 1967), 100–101. The recipient of this advice was Richard Crossman, who headed AFHQ's psychological warfare section and became a prominent voice of the Labour Left in the postwar period.

21. Smith, "Problems of an Integrated Headquarters."

22. Eisenhower to Marshall and Eisenhower to Churchill, 16 December 1942, *EP,* #711, #724.

23. Eisenhower to Marshall, 8 and 9 December 1943, *EP,* #700–701; Smith to Marshall, 13 December 1943, Eyes Only, WBSP.

24. A meeting was held on 12 December between a member of Darlan's staff and GEN Georges Catroux, the most noteworthy Vichy officer to join the Free French. This meeting planted the seed of hope for a rapprochement between the French factions in Churchill's mind. Eisenhower to Harold Stark, 13 December 1942, *EP,* #713.

25. Butcher, *Three Years with Eisenhower,* 226; Eisenhower to de Gaulle, 21 December 1942, *EP,* #733.

26. Butcher, *Three Years with Eisenhower,* 225–26; Murphy, *Diplomat among Warriors,* 149–51.

27. Eisenhower to Marshall, 31 December 1942, *EP,* #748.

28. Smith to Marshall, 24 December 1942, Eyes Only, WBSP.

29. Eisenhower later related to his friend Robert Eichelberger, "I knew a man who had received one for sitting in a hole in the ground and [I] refused to accept it." Unpublished Eichelberger manuscript, Eichelberger Papers, MHI. See also D'Este, *Eisenhower: A Soldier's Life,* 372–73.

30. Roosevelt to Churchill, 1 January 1943, *FRUS, Europe, 1943,* 2:23–24.

31. Butcher Diary, 4 January 1942.

32. Eisenhower to Portal, 4 January 1943, *EP,* #757.

33. Eisenhower to Gailey, 1 January 1943, *EP,* #750.

34. Interrogation of GEN Walter Warlimont, in Historical Section, USFET, "Interview statements General Warlimont, Deputy Chief of Staff (German General Staff), and Generals Jodl, Keitel, Field Marshal Goering, and other German General Staff Officers," copy in WBSP (hereafter cited as Interviews of Senior German Officers).

35. Macmillan, *Blast of War,* 346.

36. Hamblen stood in for Gale during his extended absences from headquarters.

37. AFHQ Staff Size

Date	Total	Officers	Enlisted Men
September 1942	2,068	549 (205 U.S., 344 British)	1,519 (793 U.S., 726 British)
November 1942	1,646	507 (217 U.S., 290 British)	1,139 (362 U.S., 777 British)
Actual strength	1,270	403 (313 U.S., 90 British)*	867 (90 U.S., 777 British)
January 1943	3,052	1,060	1,992
April 1943	3,604	1,480	2,124
October 1943	4,782**	2,066	2,716
November 1943	4,072	Relative parity: U.S. 2,012; BR 2,060	

* In addition, 200 British officers, chiefly logisticians, served on detached duty to First British Army and the British line of communication.
** The entire increase—586 officers and 592 enlisted personnel—consisted of Americans.

Figures compiled from Salmon et al., *History of Allied Force Headquarters.*

38. Smith to Hughes, 24 December 1942, Smith 201 File, WBSP.

39. Truscott to Smith, 30 December 1943, in Salmon et al., *History of Allied Force Headquarters.* See also Truscott, *Command Missions: A Personal Story* (New York, 1954), 129.

40. Gale to Smith and Hamblen to Smith, 3 January 1943; Whiteley to Smith, 4 January 1943, in Salmon et al., *History of Allied Force Headquarters.*

41. Butcher Diary, 12 January 1943.

42. Hughes Diary, 8–10 January 1943; Patton Diary, 9 January 1943, GSPP.

43. Smith [for Eisenhower] to Marshall, 29 December 1932, *EP,* #744; Eisenhower to Marshall, 10 January 1943, *EP,* #765. Smith delegated most of these responsibilities to his aide, Major Burgess, who had performed many of the same responsibilities during the Washington conferences. Patton, always looking for ways to impress his superiors, took charge of the preparations for and management of the conference, even though Clark, as Fifth Army commander, was the official host. Burgess interview.

44. Brooke Diary, 31 December 1942, 15 and 16 January 1943. All the minutes of the Symbol conference are in CCS, ANFA File, WBSP.

45. Patton Diary, 15 January 1943.

46. CCS 163, "System of Air Command in the Mediterranean," 18 January 1943, ANFA, WBSP. Eisenhower to Arnold and Eisenhower to Marshall, 19 January 1943, *EP,* #778, #779.

47. CCS 171, "Operation HUSKY, Directive to Commander-in-Chief, Allied Expeditionary Force in North Africa," 21 January 1943, ANFA, WBSP.

48. During the Casablanca conference, Brooke noted in his diary his apprehension that Eisenhower lacked the "basic qualities required from such a Commander." He expressed these views earlier and held them throughout the war.

49. Brooke Diary and "Notes," 20 January 1943.

50. Eisenhower Memorandum, 23 January 1943, Butcher Diary.

51. Butcher Diary, 23 January 1943. Eisenhower's stock fell pretty low in the estimate of both the president and Marshall. When Marshall asked the president if Eisenhower should be promoted to four stars, Roosevelt replied that "he would not promote Eisenhower until there was some damn good reason for doing so." Sherwood, *Roosevelt and Hopkins,* 688.

52. Marshall interview by Matthews, Smyth, et al., 25 July 1949, Interview III: Part 2, GCMRL.

53. Smith to Mrs. Dykes, 30 January 1943, Danchev, *Very Special Relationship*, 25.

54. Marshall interview by Matthews, Smyth, et al., 25 July 1949, Interview III: Part 1, GCMRL.

55. Ibid.; Butcher Diary, 26 January 1943; Butcher, *Three Years with Eisenhower*, 247–48.

56. Butcher Diary, 27 January 1943.

57. Smith [for Eisenhower] to Marshall, 14 January 1943, *EP*, #768.

58. Somervell's long undated memo, "Matters to Be Discussed with General Eisenhower," ANFA, WBSP; Eisenhower to Somervell, 27 January 1943, *EP*, #795.

59. The U.S. First Division in Oran, the Thirty-fourth in Algiers, and the Second Armored and Third and Ninth Divisions in Morocco.

60. Leroy Lutes to Hughes, 16 March 1943, Hughes Papers; Lutes, "The Effects of Logistics upon Strategy," Lutes Papers; Eisenhower, *Crusade in Europe*, 149.

61. Wilson to Smith, 18–19 January 1943, Eyes Only, WBSP.

62. Wilson was busily campaigning for the job of deputy theater commander. Wilson to Smith, 1 February 1943, Chief of Staff Official Correspondence, 1942–1944, and Smith to Wilson, 3 February 1943, Smith 201 File, WBSP.

63. Eisenhower to Somervell, 27 January 1943, *EP*, #795.

64. Smith discussed his views on organization in a long letter to Marshall. Smith to Marshall, 8 July 1943, Smith 201 File, WBSP.

65. Eisenhower to Handy, 28 January 1943, *EP*, #796.

66. Soon after returning to Washington, Marshall authorized the formation of the North African Theater of Operations (NATO). Marshall to Eisenhower, 3 February 1943, WBSP.

67. Eisenhower frequently used the term *ritualistic* to denigrate other officers. It had a number of applications. For example, a ritualistic officer depended on fixed chains of command, enforced martinet discipline, unthinkingly relied on conventional methods, and refused to delegate authority to the men he selected as his subordinates. Commanders too attentive to logistical constraints—to tidying administration—he also categorized as ritualistic. He considered "the slow, methodical, ritualistic person . . . absolutely valueless in a key position." Eisenhower saw none of those traits in himself. Eisenhower to Marshall, 30 November 1942, *EP*, #673; Eisenhower Manuscript [in Butcher Diary], 10 December 1942, *EP*, #705; Eisenhower to Handy, 19 January 1943, *EP*, #782; Eisenhower to Somervell, 19 March 1943, *EP*, #896.

68. Eisenhower to Marshall, 8 February 1943, *EP*, #811.

69. Ibid.

70. Eisenhower to Somervell, 28 January 1943, *EP*, #795.

71. "Minutes of Chief of Staff Meeting #19," 29 January 1943, AFHQ Secretariat, Chief of Staff Conference File, WBSP.

72. Eisenhower to Mamie, 2 and 3 February 1943, in *Letters to Mamie*.

73. Hughes to Eisenhower, 6 February 1943, Chief of Staff NATOUSA: Organization File, Hughes Papers.

74. Eisenhower to Hughes, 9 February 1943, Hughes Papers.

75. Eisenhower to Marshall, 8 February 1943, *EP*, #811.

76. Hughes Diary, 10 February 1943.

77. Eisenhower to Connor, 22 March 1943, *EP*, #902.

78. As late as the end of February, U.S. service troops in North Africa num-

bered a mere 2,500; the complement of ground and air forces in the theater stood at 180,000.

19. "Allies Are Very Difficult People to Fight With"

1. Eisenhower to Handy, 28 January 1943, *EP,* #796.
2. Basil Liddell Hart, ed., *Rommel Papers* (New York, 1995), 328. Along the same lines, another German general called the campaigns fought in North Africa "a tactician's dream and a quartermaster's nightmare."
3. Eisenhower manuscript, Butcher Diary, 25 February 1943, *EP,* #843.
4. Brigadier Edgar Williams, Montgomery's chief of intelligence in northwest Europe, cited in Nigel Hamilton, *Monty: The Man behind the Legend* (London, 1987), 114. Hamilton steers clear of any speculation about Montgomery's psychological makeup in his three-volume biography. But in a book published in 2001, Hamilton portrays Montgomery as an emotional cripple, tormented by barely repressed "homosocial" desires and deep-seated feelings of inadequacy produced by a physically and psychologically abusive mother (who dressed him up as a girl and briefly sent him to a girls' school) and by the brutalizing boarding school environment marked by "the English vices" of bullying and buggering. To what extent Montgomery was affected, if at all, by these influences remains pure speculation and of no great import, but there is no question of Montgomery's bullying traits. Nigel Hamilton, *The Full Monty: Montgomery of Alamein, 1887-1942* (London, 2001).
5. Montgomery to Brooke, 12 April 1943, in *Montgomery and the Eighth Army: A Selection from the Diaries, Correspondence and Other Papers of Field Marshal the Viscount Montgomery of Alamein, August 1942 to December 1943,* ed. Stephen Brooks (London, 1991), 207.
6. Montgomery to Brooke, 15 February 1943, ibid., 135-36.
7. Montgomery to Brooke, 16 and 23 February 1943, ibid., 150, 153-54.
8. Harmon to Smith, 26 February and 5 March 1943, Chief of Staff Official Correspondence, 1942-1944, WBSP. Harmon also took the opportunity to defend Ward. He complained it would be a "cruel injustice to relieve Ward" of the First Armored Division. Patton later relieved Ward after the fighting at El Guettar and Maknassy. Others also got the sack in what was fast becoming "a professional graveyard." COL Alexander Stark, a regimental commander in the First Infantry, and BG Raymond McQullan, who commanded a combat command in First Armored, were relieved.
9. Harmon's account of his meetings with Eisenhower and his assessment of Fredendall are in Ernest Harmon, *Combat Commander* (Englewood Cliffs, NJ, 1970), 111-21.
10. Bradley and Blair, *A General's Life,* 135.
11. LTC L. Gayer to Smith, 11 May 1944, Chief of Staff's Personal Papers, 1942-44, WBSP.
12. Patton Diary, 5 and 7 March 1943; Butcher Diary, 7 March 1943. As an indication of Marshall's obtuseness, he asked Eisenhower on 4 March if Fredendall merited consideration for promotion to lieutenant general. Fredendall went home in grade and received his promotion and command of a training army. Amazingly, in 1944, Marshall even proposed Fredendall to command the First Army in France. Eisenhower tactfully declined the offer. Eisenhower to Marshall, 3 and 4 March 1943, *EP,* #680-81.
13. Eisenhower to Patton, 6 March 1943, *EP,* #865.

14. Smith [for Eisenhower] to Brooke, 20 September 1943, *EP,* #831.

15. Butcher, *Three Years with Eisenhower,* 266.

16. Smith requested the change be made "without prejudice." Mockler-Ferryman went back to London and a post in SOE there. Mockler-Ferryman did have experience dealing with the Germans; he had served as head of the German intelligence section of the War Office in 1939–1940. Mockler-Ferryman's version is contained in a typescript account of his service in AFHQ, Eric Mockler-Ferryman Papers, LHCMA.

17. Smith to Pownall, 23 November 1943, Correspondence File, WBSP.

18. Alexander to Montgomery, 5 March 1943, *Montgomery and the Eighth Army,* 164.

19. Alexander to Montgomery, 29 March 1943, ibid., 188.

20. Montgomery to MG A. F. Harding, 25 February 1943, ibid., 156.

21. Patton Diary, 31 March 1943; *Patton Papers, 1940-1945,* 203.

22. Arthur Tedder, *With Prejudice: The War Memoirs of Marshal of the Royal Air Force Lord Tedder* (London, 1966), 411.

23. Patton Diary, 11 and 12 April 1943; *Patton Papers, 1940-1945,* 207–8, 211. Privately, Eisenhower scolded Patton, telling him "the great purpose of complete Allied teamwork" would not "be furthered by demanding the last pound of flesh for every error." Eisenhower to Patton, 5 April 1943, *EP,* #928.

24. Montgomery to Brooke, 12 April 1943, *Montgomery and the Eighth Army,* 207.

25. Eisenhower and Smith told Brooke the entire story when the CIGS visited Algiers in early June. Brooke Diary and "Notes," 3 June 1943.

26. Montgomery to BG F. E. W. Simpson, 5 April 1943, *Montgomery and the Eighth Army,* 195–96; Hanson Baldwin oral history, "Reminiscences of Hanson Weighman Baldwin," U.S. Naval Institute, Oral History Department, Annapolis, MD. In March and April, Baldwin toured North Africa as the military correspondent for the *New York Times* and succeeded in worming his way into the major headquarters. He "accosted" Montgomery on 28 March, telling the British general that American soldiers lacked "heart in the war, & were not fighting properly." Montgomery concluded Baldwin was "a dangerous chap" and got rid of him. Alexander replied, "Perhaps Mr. Baldwin is right." Montgomery to Alexander and Alexander to Montgomery, 29 March 1942, cited in *Montgomery and the Eighth Army,* 186, 367–68 n. 68.

27. Eisenhower to Marshall, 5 April 1943, *EP,* #927.

28. Eisenhower Diary, 11 June 1943, Butcher Diary.

29. Montgomery, "The Basic Need if Operations Are to Be Successfully Carried Out," August 1943, *Montgomery and the Eighth Army,* 264–65.

30. Montgomery to Simpson, 8 September 1943, *Montgomery and the Eighth Army,* 279–80.

31. Cited in Colin Baxter, *Field Marshal Bernard Law Montgomery, 1887-1976: A Selected Bibliography* (Westport, CT, 1999), 5.

32. Blumenson, *Patton Papers, 1940-1945,* 239.

33. Montgomery to Percy Grigg, 14 October 1943, *Montgomery and the Eighth Army,* 303.

34. Nigel Hamilton interview with Ian Jacob, cited in Hamilton, *Full Monty,* 490.

35. Merrill, "Notes on Burma Campaign," in Marc Bernstein, "A 'Black and Dismal' Record," *Quarterly Journal of Military History* (winter 2004): 81.

36. Brooke's diary is littered with references to doubts about Alexander's intelligence. Even more pointed are the views of some of Alexander's subordinates. LTG

Jacob served under Alexander for a year immediately after the war, when Alexander succeeded Brooke as CIGS. Jacob could not remember Alexander ever "once producing a single idea, or suggestion during the entire time I served as his chief staff officer." Hamilton interview with Jacob, in Hamilton, *Full Monty*, 490. A Canadian division commander who fought under Alexander in Italy thought the field marshal "was bone from the neck up."

37. He told Hughes, "Alex isn't as good as he thinks he is." Hughes Diary, 1 May 1943. As Eisenhower recalled to Ismay in 1960, "Shortly before I left the African Theatre—but after I had been informed that I was to be commander of OVERLORD—I learned that Montgomery was to be my British ground commander, even though I had told the Prime Minister, who earlier had said I could have my choice between Alexander and Montgomery, that I should prefer to have Alexander." Eisenhower to Ismay, 3 December 1960, *Keeping the Peace*, #1722. See also Eisenhower, *Crusade in Europe*, 211.

38. Montgomery, "The Basic Need," 207.

39. Butcher, *Three Years with Eisenhower*, 285.

40. Marshall to Eisenhower, 14 April 1943, *The Right Man for the Job*, #603.

41. Eisenhower to Marshall, 15 and 16 April 1943, *EP*, #945–46. McClure not only managed public relations and military and political censorship, but he also oversaw psychological warfare and propaganda. He brought six censors, both British and American, to Algiers with him in December. He and his overburdened office could never keep up with the demands of the press.

42. A copy of Gaskill's draft article is contained in the Butcher Diary.

43. Eisenhower to Alexander, 29 January 1943, *EP*, #799; Eisenhower to Marshall, 30 January 1943, *EP*, #800.

44. Ambrose, *Supreme Commander*, 214.

45. Eisenhower to Alexander, 23 March 1943, *EP*, #906.

46. In British practice, a commander had two or more chiefs of staff in addition to a chief administrative officer. Montgomery received command of the Eastern Task Force on 16 February. He sent BG Freddie de Guingand—soon promoted to major general—to Cairo to plan the Eighth Army's part in Husky. Meanwhile, he retained BG Charles Richardson as chief of staff in Eighth Army headquarters.

47. In the question-and-answer segment of Smith's lecture to the Royal United Services Institute, Tedder talked about his relations with Spaatz and Smith. Smith, "Problems of an Integrated Headquarters," 16.

48. "Minutes of Conference, Smith, Spaatz, BG L. S. Kuter," 12 November 1942, TORCH, WBSP; Arthur Ferguson, "Origins of the Combined Bomber Offensive," in Craven and Cate, *Europe: TORCH to POINTBLANK*, 65.

49. Tedder's comments in Smith, "Problems of an Integrated Headquarters"; Tedder, *With Prejudice*, 404–5; Eisenhower to MG Frank Andrews, 19 February 1943, *EP*, #828.

50. The basic problem remained the shortage of lift, both at sea for the landings and in the air for airborne operations. Eisenhower to Marshall, 15 March 1943, *EP*, #888.

51. Tedder, *With Prejudice*, 433–34.

52. Eisenhower to Marshall and Eisenhower to Churchill, 17 February 1943, *EP*, #821, #824.

53. Bonesteel oral history, MHI; Eisenhower, *Crusade in Europe*, 168; Mayo, *Ordnance Department*, 156–57, 162. Bonesteel and Besson both went on to earn four stars.

Smith was not always so open to suggestions. Before Torch, Bonesteel approached Smith and pointed out that American troops had no training in the use of camouflage. Smith dismissed him, claiming a chief of staff had bigger concerns. Then, when the Germans held air superiority in North Africa and inflicted serious losses on exposed American troops, a hue and cry went up for camouflage nets and training.

54. Eisenhower, "Notes," 7 March 1943, *EP,* #867.

55. Eisenhower to Marshall, 15 March 1943, *EP,* #888.

56. Eisenhower to Somervell, 19 March 1943, *EP,* #896.

57. Gairdner Diary, 1 April 1943, in *Montgomery and the Eighth Army,* 369.

58. Montgomery, "The Basic Need," 207.

59. Montgomery to Alexander, 3 April 1943, *Montgomery and the Eighth Army,* 191; Montgomery to Brooke, 17 March 1943, ibid., 176.

60. Cunningham, *A Sailor's Odyssey,* 536–37.

61. Smith [for Eisenhower] to CCS and BCOS, 20 March 1943, *EP,* #898.

62. JCS to ETOUSA AG, 10 April 1943, *EP,* #942, n. 1.

63. Tedder, *With Prejudice,* 429–30.

64. Brooke Diary, 9 April 1943.

65. Montgomery to Simpson, 5 April 1943, *Montgomery and the Eighth Army,* 196.

66. Betts oral history; David Irving interview with Clark, 4 January 1970, in David Irving, *Papers Relating to the Allied High Command, 1943-1945,* copy in author's possession.

67. Montgomery discussed his trip to Cairo in Montgomery to Mountbatten, 12 August 1943, *Montgomery and the Eighth Army,* 263; Montgomery to Alexander, 24 April 1943, ibid., 217–18.

68. Montgomery to Brooke, 30 April 1943, ibid., 221–23.

69. Blumenson, *Patton Papers, 1940-1945,* 234–37.

70. Cited by MG Brian Horrocks, one of Montgomery's corps commanders, in Horrocks, *A Full Life* (London, 1971), 159.

71. Montgomery gave his own account of his trip to Algiers and the famous "lavatory conference" in Montgomery, *Memoirs,* 153–65.

72. Sidney Matthews interview with Smith, n.d., MHI.

73. Montgomery to Alexander, 2 May 1943, *Montgomery and the Eighth Army,* 223.

74. Blumenson, *Patton Papers, 1940-1945,* 236–40.

75. Montgomery to Alexander, 5 May 1943, *Montgomery and the Eighth Army,* 224–26.

76. Montgomery, "Diary Notes, 3-6 May 1943," ibid., 226–27.

77. Blumenson, *Patton Papers, 1940-45,* 244.

78. Montgomery, "Diary Notes, 7-17 May 1943," *Montgomery and the Eighth Army,* 229.

79. Montgomery, "Basic Points: For a Talk with CIGS in June 1943," ibid., 230–31.

80. Butcher, *Three Years with Eisenhower,* 299.

81. By the end of the campaign, 250 locomotives and 4,500 railcars were added to the Transportation Corps' inventories.

82. Cited in John Ellis, *Brute Force: Allied Strategy and Tactics in the Second World War* (New York, 1990), 525.

83. Liddell Hart, *Rommel Papers,* 417.

84. Howe, *Northwest Africa,* 498–99; Leighton and Coakley, *Global Logistics and Strategy,* 474–75; Joseph Bykofsky and Harold Larson, *The Transportation Corps: Operations Overseas,* USAWWII (Washington, DC, 1957), 148.

20. The Many Travails of an Allied Chief of Staff

1. Marshall to Eisenhower, 30 April 1943, and Eisenhower to Marshall, 4 May 1943, *EP,* #968; Eisenhower to Marshall, 5 May 1943, *EP,* #970. In mid-April Marshall floated the idea of attacking Sicily in June—according to the original timetable—to the BCOS, even if the Allies were stalemated in Tunisia. Brooke thought the proposal "quite mad and quite impossible," but the prime minister was delighted, calling the idea "a high strategic conception." Brooke Diary, 17 April 1943.

2. Butcher, *Three Years with Eisenhower,* 301. On 27 April Marshall emphasized to Eisenhower that expanded operations in the Mediterranean "are not in keeping with my ideas of what our strategy should be" and warned him of the possibility of moving "a large part of your forces to the United Kingdom." Marshall to Eisenhower, 27 April 1943, Marshall File, DDEL.

3. Ismay offers a full account in Ismay, *Memoirs,* 293–300.

4. Allied Force Headquarters, "Memorandum by Chief of Staff," 14 May 1943, with attachments; BG Lowell Rooks to Smith, 7 May 1943; and Tedder to Eisenhower, 8 May 1943, in *FRUS, Conferences at Washington and Quebec, 1943,* 253–55.

5. Smith to Eisenhower, 14 May 1943, Correspondence File, WBSP.

6. Eisenhower to CCS and BCOS, 11 May 1943, *EP,* #982; Smith to Eisenhower, 15 May 1943, WBSP.

7. Smith pointed out that enough materiel reached the theater each month to equip a division to 50 percent of requirements, sufficient for training. The French had eleven divisions in formation. "Minutes of CCS Meeting," 18 May 1943, TRIDENT, WBSP. See also *FRUS, Washington and Quebec,* 103–4.

8. Brooke Diary, 18 May 1943.

9. *FRUS, Washington and Quebec,* 281–82, 367.

10. Roosevelt to Churchill, 8 May 1943, *FRUS, Europe, 1943,* 2:111.

11. Churchill, *The Hinge of Fate,* 801.

12. Giraud and de Gaulle would serve as copresidents. De Gaulle insisted on the separation of civil and military affairs. If Giraud chose to serve as "first president," he forfeited control of the military. The American ambassador in London, John Winant, recognized this as a device "to shelve" Giraud. The executive committee would have five to seven members, including the first and second presidents. Winant to Hull, 15 April 1943, *FRUS, Europe, 1943,* 2:94–95.

13. Hull to Wiley [for Murphy], 17 May 1943, ibid., 118.

14. Wiley [for Murphy] to Hull, 20 April 1943, ibid., 97–98.

15. Roosevelt to Churchill, 8 May 1943, ibid., 111.

16. Eisenhower to Marshall, 8 February 1943, *EP,* #812.

17. "Directive on Organization and Operation of Military Government for HUSKY," 21 May 1943, *FRUS, Washington and Quebec,* 187.

18. The twists and turns of organizing the civil affairs section are covered in Harry Coles and Albert Weinberg, *Civil Affairs: Soldiers Become Governors,* USAWWII (Washington, DC, 1964), 160–68.

19. William Hayter, "Memorandum by the First Secretary of the British Embassy," 21 May 1943, *FRUS, Washington and Quebec,* 284.

20. Marshall to Eisenhower, 14 May 1943, and Eisenhower to Marshall, 18 May 1943, *EP,* #1012.

21. Eisenhower to CCS, 17 May 1943, Eyes Only File, WBSP. The initial plan, authored by Strong, emerged in mid-April. "Psychological Warfare Plan for

HUSKY," 16 April 1943, WBSP. Eisenhower expressed himself "exceedingly irritated" by the "peace with honor" incident. Sidestepping any responsibility, he informed Smith it fell to him to vet all such future communications. Eisenhower to Smith, 30 May 1943, *EP,* #1030.

22. Smyth interview with Smith, 13 May 1947.

23. Smith to Eisenhower, 20 May 1943, Chief of Staff's visit to Washington, May 1943 File, WBSP.

24. CCS to Eisenhower, 24 May 1943, TRIDENT, WBSP.

25. "Minutes of CCS," 19 May 1943, *FRUS, Washington and Quebec,* 118.

26. Butcher, *Three Years with Eisenhower,* 314.

27. Wilhelm Styer, "Proposed Organization of Service Activities," 21 May 1943, Smith 201 File, WBSP.

28. Smith filled in Butcher on all he had learned in Washington during a flight from Casablanca to Algiers. Butcher, *Three Years with Eisenhower,* 313–14.

29. Ibid., 314–15.

30. Kate Hughes to Everett Hughes, 21 May 1943, Hughes Papers.

31. Churchill, *The Hinge of Fate,* 810–11.

32. Cited in John Pearson, *Citadel of the Heart: Winston and the Churchill Dynasty* (London, 1991), 141.

33. Pogue, *Marshall Interviews,* 552–54.

34. Butcher, *Three Years with Eisenhower,* 316.

35. Proceedings in "Minutes of a Meeting Held (May 31–June 3, 1943) at General Eisenhower's Villa (dar el Ouard)," AFHQ Subseries, WBSP. Churchill's account of the three meetings was based on these minutes (*The Hinge of Fate,* 817–30).

36. Brooke Diary, 3 June 1943.

37. "Minutes of a Meeting Held at General Eisenhower's Villa," 31 May 1943, AFHQ, WBSP; Butcher, *Three Years with Eisenhower,* 314.

38. "Minutes of a Meeting Held at General Eisenhower's Villa," 3 June 1943, AFHQ, WBSP.

39. Smith to Truscott, 6 June 1943, Chief of Staff Personal Papers, 1941–1944, WBSP.

40. Eisenhower to Marshall, 3 March 1943, *EP,* #860.

41. Smith, "Problems of an Integrated Headquarters," 5.

42. Ibid., 5, 8.

43. Smith's views on staff organization and functions derive chiefly from three sources: a long letter he wrote to Marshall expressing his views on the proposed reorganization of the War Department, the explanatory letter he wrote to Pownall, and his lecture to the Royal United Services Institute. Smith to Marshall, 21 June 1943; Smith to Pownall, 23 November 1943, Smith 201 File, WBSP; Smith, "Problems of an Integrated Headquarters."

44. Smith, "Problems of an Integrated Headquarters," 3–4.

45. Smith to Pownall, 23 November 1943, WBSP.

46. In addition to the oral histories and insights gleaned from Forrest Pogue's interviews conducted for *The Supreme Command,* USAWWII (Washington, DC, 1954), housed in the MHI, much of the preceding material comes from a detailed summary of AFHQ's staff mechanisms and Smith's role in fashioning and running them written by Smith for LTG Henry Pownall, chief of staff in the Southeast Asia Theater of Operations. Mountbatten solicited a similar description of the roles of a supreme commander from Eisenhower. Smith to Pownall, 23 November 1943, WBSP.

47. In terms of seniority, on the major generals list, Smith stood 226th in the U.S. Army and 12th in North Africa. The roster appears in Hughes Papers.

48. Hughes Diary, 10 February 1943.

49. Styer, "Proposed Organization of Service Activities."

50. Smith, "Reorganization Plan," 2 June 1943, Hughes Papers.

51. Hughes Diary, 9, 12, 28, and 29 March 1943.

52. Smith to Hughes, 6 April 1943, Smith 201 File, WBSP.

53. Smith to Marshall, 8 July 1943, ibid.

54. Hughes Diary, 23 April 1943.

55. Sawbridge to Hughes, 25 April 1943, AG NATOUSA: T/O Hq NATOUSA; Davis to Smith, 29 April 1943, AG AFHQ:323.35–1; Roberts to Hughes, 24 April 1943, AG NATOUSA:321–87, in Salmon et al., *History of Allied Force Headquarters.*

56. Hughes to Huebner, 25 April 1943, Hughes Papers.

57. Hughes, "Memo to Myself," 26 April 1943, Hughes Papers.

58. Hughes, "Notes for My Diary," April 1943, Hughes Papers; Hughes Diary, 26 April 1943.

59. Eisenhower to Marshall, 5 December 1942, *EP,* #691; Eisenhower to Hughes, 14 October 1941, Hughes File, PPP.

60. Patton to COL Kent Lambert, 12 May 1943, GSPP.

61. Hughes, "Notes for My Diary."

62. Hughes, "Draft of Memo," April 1943, and Hughes to Kate Hughes, 26 April 1943, Hughes Papers.

63. Hughes Diary, 5 May 1943.

64. These subsections were G-1 NATO with Civil Affairs and Psychological Warfare; G-3 NATO with Civil Defense; and liaison sections to AFHQ G-4 to coordinate planning and cooperation with the Petroleum and North African Shipping Board and the North African Economic Board. Salmon et al., *History of Allied Force Headquarters.*

65. Hughes provides the only account of the lead-up to the 25 June meeting and the meeting itself in Hughes to MG Virgil Peterson, 25 June 1943, Hughes Papers. Material in the following paragraphs is taken from there, supplemented by Hughes Diary, 24 and 25 June 1943.

66. Hughes Diary, 24 June 1944. The next day he noted, "Ike puts stop on Beadle."

67. Smith, "Proposed Organization of Service Activities in a Theater of Operations," June 1943, Smith 201 File, WBSP. Smith wrote this in response to Marshall's soliciting his advice on Somervell's proposed reorganization. Marshall to Smith, 21 June 1943, ibid. Smith's undated memorandum, attached to Styer's 21 May proposal, was obviously written after Eisenhower made the decision not to alter the headquarters structure. On 8 July Smith replied more specifically to Marshall, and his ideas on staff organization remained the same. "I have always believed that the Commanding General Army Service forces should be a commander just as the Commanding General AGF is a commander"; he agreed "in principle to the general idea of grouping administrative and service functions under a staff officer who also has administrative authority" but opposed abolishing general staff supervision. Smith to Marshall, 8 July 1943, ibid.

21. The Road to Messina

1. Eisenhower to Patton, 4 June 1943, *EP,* #1038.

2. "Minutes of Meeting," 3 June 1943, AFHQ File, WBSP.

3. The fact that he enjoyed Communist Party support did nothing to elevate de Gaulle in the eyes of Roosevelt and Hull. Hull to Roosevelt, 10 May 1943, *FRUS, Europe, 1943*, 2:113.

4. *FRUS, Europe, 1943*, 2:134–35.

5. Winston Churchill, *Closing the Ring* (Boston, 1951), 173–76.

6. Eisenhower to CCS and BCOS, 10 June 1943, *EP,* #1050.

7. For de Gaulle's motives, see Charles de Gaulle, *The War Memoirs of Charles de Gaulle*, 3 vols. (New York, 1955–1960), 2:126–27.

8. All three communications are in Roosevelt to AFHQ, 11 June 1943, Eisenhower Manuscripts, DDEL.

9. Smith [for Eisenhower] to Roosevelt, 12 June 1943, *EP,* #1054.

10. Winant to Hull, 6 April 1943, *FRUS, Europe, 1943*, 90–91.

11. Macmillan, *Blast of War*, 364.

12. Roosevelt to AFHQ, 17 June 1943, cables 493 and 511, Roosevelt Correspondence, Eisenhower Manuscripts, DDEL. See also Murphy to Roosevelt and Hull, 16 June 1943, *FRUS, Europe, 1943*, 2:152–55.

13. Roosevelt to Churchill, 17 June 1943, with the first letter to AFHQ attached, *FRUS, Europe, 1943*, 2:155–57.

14. Smith to Marshall, 17 June 1943, Eyes Only, WBSP.

15. Eisenhower to Roosevelt, 18 June 1943, *EP,* #1057. Murphy's stock fell again. As Eisenhower told Marshall, "My two strongest and able assistants in this matter are General Smith and Mr. Macmillan. They are both sound, respected by everybody, and are not hysterical." Eisenhower to Marshall, 26 June 1943, *EP,* #1075.

16. Eisenhower to Marshall, 18 June 1943, *EP,* #1058.

17. Hopkins to Monnet, January 1943, Smith 201 File, WBSP. Monnet was in London, representing France on an economic mission, when Paris fell. He went to Washington and served on the Combined Munitions Board under Hopkins. Roosevelt dispatched him to Algiers to help steer the rearmament program.

18. Murphy, *Diplomat among Warriors*, 224.

19. Eisenhower to Marshall, 19 June 1943, *EP,* #1064; de Gaulle, *Memoirs*, 2:131–33.

20. Eisenhower to Marshall, 22 June 1943, *EP,* #1069. Boisson resigned "out of the clear blue sky" on 24 June.

21. Eisenhower to Roosevelt and Eisenhower to Marshall, 22 June 1943, *EP,* #1068–69; Smith [for Eisenhower] to Marshall, 22 June 1943, *EP,* #1070.

22. Smith to Marshall, 23 June 1943, Eyes Only, WBSP.

23. Jack Belden, *Still Time to Die* (New York, 1943), 269; Mayo, *Ordnance Department*, 163.

24. Smith [for Eisenhower] to CCS and BCOS, 4 August 1943, *EP,* #1163.

25. Matthews interview with Alexander, MHI.

26. Patton Diary, 24 July 1943, based on his 16 July conversation with de Guingand.

27. Eisenhower to CCS and BCOS, 18 July 1943, *EP,* #1119.

28. Marshall to Eisenhower, 5 July 1943, in *The Papers of George Catlett Marshall*, vol. 4, *Aggressive and Determined Leadership, June 1, 1943–December 31, 1944* (Baltimore, 1996), #37; Tedder, *With Prejudice*, 186–87; Smith [for Eisenhower] to Marshall, 9 July 1943, *EP,* #1005.

29. Montgomery to Brooke, 27 July 1943, *Montgomery and the Eighth Army*, 254–55.

30. Montgomery to Alexander, 19 July 1943, ibid., 249.

31. Patton to Beatrice Patton, 24 July 1943, *Patton Papers, 1940–1945*, 300–301.

32. For Patton's account of the meeting, see Patton Diary, 25 July 1943, *Patton Papers, 1940-1945*, 301–302.

33. DDE to CCS and BCOS, 26 July 1943, *EP,* #1138; Butcher Diary, 27 July 1943; Macmillan, *Blast of War,* 307; Harold Macmillan, *War Diaries: Politics and War in the Mediterranean, January 1943-May 1945* (London, 1984), 164.

34. DDE to CCS and BCOS, 27 July 1943, *EP,* #1141.

35. Albert Garland and Howard Smyth, *Sicily and the Italian Surrender,* USAWWII (Washington, DC, 1965), 269.

36. Churchill to Roosevelt, 26 July 1943, in Kimball, *Churchill and Roosevelt,* 2:348–49. Devers forwarded the cable from London, which is in AFHQ, *Capitulation of Italy,* 9, WBSP. *Capitulation of Italy* is a set of bound folios, a compilation of telegrams and other documents relating to the Italian surrender assembled for Smith by Gilmer. See also Churchill, *Closing the Ring,* 55–56.

37. Cited in Herbert Feis, *Churchill–Roosevelt–Stalin: The War They Waged and the Peace They Sought* (Princeton, NJ, 1957), 157.

38. Macmillan, *War Diaries,* 164.

39. Churchill to DDE, 29 July 1943, Eisenhower Manuscripts, DDEL; Brooke Diary, 26, 28, and 29 July 1943.

40. Macmillan, *War Diaries,* 29 July 1943.

41. Eisenhower to Marshall, 29 July 1943, *EP,* #1147.

42. Brooke Diary, 30 July 1943.

43. Roosevelt to Churchill, 30 July 1943, in Kimball, *Churchill and Roosevelt,* 2:366; Churchill, *Closing the Ring,* 64.

44. Roosevelt to Churchill, 2 August 1942, in Kimball, *Churchill and Roosevelt,* 2:372.

45. Marshall to Eisenhower, 29 July 1943, Eisenhower Manuscripts, DDEL.

46. Churchill to Eisenhower, 29 July 1943, ibid.

47. Eisenhower to CCS and BCOS, 27 July 1943, *EP,* #1141; Tedder, *With Prejudice,* 456–63.

48. Smith [for Eisenhower] to Marshall, 3 August 1943, *EP,* #1159–61.

49. Marshall relayed Churchill's complaints to AFHQ. Eisenhower to Marshall, 4 August 1943, *EP,* #1164 n. 1.

50. Eisenhower to Alexander, 4 August 1943, *EP,* #1167.

51. Eisenhower to Marshall, 4 August 1943, *EP,* #1164–65; Macmillan to Churchill, 3 August 1943, Eyes Only Cable File, WBSP.

52. Eisenhower to Churchill, 4 August 1943, *EP,* #1166.

53. Hughes Diary, 6 August 1943.

54. Smith [for Eisenhower] to CCS and BCOS, 5 August 1943, *EP,* #1168. On 7 August a reply went forward from AFHQ, written by Smith, suggesting a simultaneous Baytown and Buttress, complete with British X Corps. At the next commanders' conference on 9 August, despite the decision on Buttress, they agreed on Avalanche, with a target date of 7 September. Barracuda was canceled.

55. Eisenhower's blood pressure registered 142/90. Thomas Mattingly and Live Marsh, "A Compilation of the General Health Status of Dwight D. Eisenhower," Mattingly Collection, DDEL. Hughes recorded that although Eisenhower was "satisfied with doctor; he didn't follow Dr's orders. What would Mamie say? Ike says high blood pressure, too many cigarettes. He had a lot of alibis but concluded that he had to take care of himself and do what the Dr. said. But all has to be so secret." Hughes Diary, 12 August 1943.

56. Cited in Garland and Smyth, *Sicily and the Italian Surrender,* 67.

57. Butcher, *Three Years with Eisenhower,* 372.

58. Ibid., 386–87.

59. Hughes Diary, 17 August 1943.

60. D'Este, *Eisenhower: A Soldier's Life,* 438. As Montgomery scathingly remarked, "The truth of the matter is that there is *no* plan." Fixated on the invasion of the peninsula, Eisenhower and the senior commanders never discussed means to obstruct the German escape. Montgomery cited in Ralph Bennett, *Ultra and the Mediterranean Strategy* (New York, 1989), 234–35.

61. "Summary of Recent Correspondents with AFHQ," 19 August 1943, *FRUS, Washington and Quebec,* 1065.

62. F. H. Hinsley et al., *British Intelligence in the Second World War,* 2 vols. (New York, 1981), 1:106–8.

63. "Summary of Recent Correspondence with AFHQ," 10 August 1943, and Smith to Whiteley, 10 and 14 August 1943, *FRUS, Washington and Quebec,* 1065–67; Smith [for Eisenhower] to Marshall, 12 August 1943, *EP,* #1181; Smith to Whiteley, 22 August 1943, in Martin Blumenson, *From Salerno to Cassino,* USAWWII (Washington, DC, 1967), 41. Whiteley made these same points in his presentation in Quebec. See Minutes, "AFHQ Briefing to QUADRANT," 24 August 1943, *FRUS, Washington and Quebec,* 956–57.

64. Smith to Whiteley, received 17 August 1943, *FRUS, Washington and Quebec,* 1068; Eisenhower to CCS and BCOS, 16 August 1943, *EP,* #1185.

65. Hughes Diary, 16 August 1943. For a number of complex sociological reasons, American troops were far more likely to be psychological casualties than their British counterparts. In North Africa, American casualties of this sort were six times higher than British losses: 66 per 1,000 in II Corps, compared with 11 per 1,000 in Eighth Army.

66. "Report of Lt. Col. Perrin H. Long, M.C. to the Surgeon, NATO," 18 September 1943, Patton File, PPP. Blessé had already received a report from COL Richard Arnest, II Corps' chief surgeon. Bradley placed a separate report in a sealed envelope in his safe. Upon receipt of similar reports, Alexander steered clear of the affair and told Patton: "George, this is a family affair." D'Este, *Patton: A Genius for War,* 533–36. For Eisenhower's receipt of the news and his initial reaction, see Butcher, *Three Years with Eisenhower,* 390, 395–96. On 21 August Butcher recorded, "Ike is deeply concerned and has scarcely slept for several nights, trying to figure out the wisest method of handling this dilemma."

67. Gay is not an unimpeachable source. Although his handwritten diary entry reads 17 August 1943, he refers to Lemnitzer as "now a 4 star general." Lemnitzer did not achieve four-star rank until 1955. Gay obviously edited his diary and engaged in some after-the-fact character assassination aimed at Smith. Gay's intense antipathy derived from Smith's supposed role in Patton's removal from Third Army command after the war. Gay Diary, 17 August 1943, Hobart R. Gay Papers, MHI.

68. Patton Diary, 17 August 1943, *Patton Papers, 1940-1945,* 323–24.

69. Patton Diary, 10 and 20 August, 21 September 1943; Patton to Hughes, 21 September 1943, Hughes Papers. In November Patton wrote a letter of explanation to Stimson in which he affirmed his belief that he had saved the souls of the two soldiers he attacked. Hughes talked him out of sending it. Hughes to Kate Hughes, 30 November 1943, Hughes Papers.

70. Gay finally told Patton the story in May 1944. Patton Diary, 22 May 1944; *Pat-*

ton Papers, 1940-1945, 324. Patton never used the story against Smith; he never even told Hughes, who would have loved getting some dirt on his bête noire.

22. The Italian Job

1. Hoare to Foreign Office, #1404, #1406, 15 August 1943, as repeated in Devers to Eisenhower, 17 August 1943, in AFHQ, *Capitulation of Italy,* 76–77, 79–80, WBSP. See Samuel John Gurney Hoare, Viscount Templewood, *Ambassador on Special Mission* (London, 1946), 212–16.

2. Smith to Mountbatten, 21 September 1943, Smith 201 File, WBSP. Little read today, Oppenheim, a self-styled "prince of storytellers," wrote 150 novels and invented the "rogue male" school of spy thrillers.

3. Smyth interview with Smith, 13 May 1947, MHI.

4. The exchanges among Madrid, London, and Quebec and AFHQ's four replies are contained in *Capitulation of Italy,* 76–82.

5. Eisenhower to CCS, 17 August 1943, *EP,* #1187.

6. CCS to Eisenhower, 18 August 1943, *Capitulation of Italy,* 82–83; the Quebec Memorandum is printed in full in Garland and Smyth, *Sicily and the Italian Surrender,* 556–57.

7. Kenneth Strong, *Intelligence at the Top: The Recollections of a British Intelligence Officer* (Garden City, NY, 1968), 145.

8. Macmillan, *Blast of War,* 313.

9. This account of the secret meeting in Lisbon is based principally on the minutes recorded by George Kennan. Smith [for Eisenhower] to CCS, 21 August 1943, *FRUS, Washington and Quebec,* 1070–74. A condensed summary of the first phase of the meeting is in "Minutes of a Conference Held at the Residence of the British Ambassador at Lisbon on August 18, 1943 at 10 P.M." Kennan wrote the summary but got the date wrong; the meeting took place on 19–20 August. For the military portion of the conference, see Smith [for Eisenhower] to CCS and BCOS, 20 August 1943, *EP,* #1200; Smith [for Eisenhower] to Marshall, NAF 335, 21 August 1943, all in *Capitulation of Italy,* 85–88, 112–17, 126–27. See also Eisenhower, "Allied Commander-in-Chief's Report, Italian Campaign, 1942-1943," 116–18, copy in WBSP; Smyth interview with George F. Kennan, 2 January 1947, MHI; Smyth interview with Smith. Neither Smith nor Strong kept minutes, but both jotted down salient points in their respective notebooks. Strong wrote a complete account of the Lisbon meetings and subsequent AFHQ negotiations with the Italians in *Intelligence at the Top,* 137–59.

10. Strong, *Intelligence at the Top,* 148.

11. Smyth interview with Strong, 29 October 1947, MHI.

12. Smyth interview with Smith.

13. Ibid.

14. Smith told Whiteley and Rooks in Quebec, "The Italians expect bitter reprisals from the Germans, whom they both hate and fear." Smith to Whiteley and Rooks, 22 August 1943, RG 319, Records of the Army Staff, NARA.

15. The military discussions were outlined in Smith [for Eisenhower] to Marshall, 21 Aug 43, *Capitulation of Italy,* 126–27; Smyth interview with Smith.

16. Smith to CCS, 22 August 1943, *Capitulation of Italy,* 126–27; Smyth interview with Strong.

17. Smyth interview with Kennan; Strong, *Intelligence at the Top,* 147.

18. Smith [for Eisenhower] to CCS and BCOS, 20 August 1943, *EP,* #1200.

19. Smyth interview with Smith.

20. Ibid.; Adrian Carton de Wiart, *Happy Odyssey: The Memoirs of Lieutenant-General Sir Adrian Carton de Wiart* (London, 1950), 230.

21. In Zanussi's testimony before a 1944 Italian commission, he stated that Campbell "informed me that Castellano had performed his mission and had left with a draft armistice of which I had a copy." Cited in Elena Agarossi, *A Nation Collapses: The Italian Surrender of September 1943* (Cambridge, 2000), 160 n. 77. Given the prevarications offered by the leading Italian players in the memoir literature and before various Italian commissions, it is exceedingly difficult to determine who knew what and when. In addition, highly charged and ideologically slanted histories dealing with the events leading up to Italy's surrender skew interpretations. Agarossi collected documents pertaining to the Italian surrender for the Italian State Archives and published them as *L'inganno reciproco. L'armistizio tra l'Italia e gli anglo-americani del settembre 1943*. From these documents, as well as British and American sources and a careful sifting through the memoirs, she constructed a convincing and balanced analysis of the period between the fall of Mussolini and the collapse of the Italian state in September, known in Italian historiography as "the forty-five days." Since her research in Italian sources postdates and surpasses similar work performed by Garland and Smyth, Agarossi's book is employed to supplement the official history and color Italian participation in the events covered in this chapter.

22. Smith [for Eisenhower] to CCS and BCOS, 28 August 1943, *EP,* #1213.

23. CCS to Eisenhower, 27 August 1943, CCS Cable File, PPP, with text of the long terms; Smith [for Eisenhower] to CCS and BCOS, 28 August 1943, *EP,* #1213; War Department to Eisenhower, 29 August 1943, all in *Capitulation of Italy,* 137, 160–64.

24. Smith [for Eisenhower] to Mason-MacFarlane, 28 August 1943; AFHQ to Gibraltar, 28 August 1943; Gibraltar to Lisbon, copy to AFHQ, 28 August 1943, all in *Capitulation of Italy,* 156–57, 160–64; Smyth interview with Smith.

25. Smyth interview with Smith; Garland and Smyth, *Sicily and the Italian Surrender,* 463–65.

26. AFHQ forwarded three cables to Washington relating the information provided by Zanussi. Eisenhower to Marshall and Hull, 30 August 1943, *EP,* #1217–19. Smith told a postwar interviewer, the "long terms were a source of annoyance to us at AFHQ and we tried as much as possible to avoid using them." Smyth interview with Smith.

27. Murphy kept a record of the meetings he attended and gave the president a lively account of the Cassibile negotiations. Murphy to Roosevelt, 8 September 1943, *FRUS, Washington and Quebec,* 1275–83. The most complete narrative is provided in Howard Smyth, "The Armistice of Cassibile," *Military Affairs* (spring 1948): 12–35. Smyth's account draws heavily on Castellano's version of the story and the reprint of his notes taken at Cassibile, *Come firmai l'armistizo di Cassibile* (Milan, 1945), 135–37, 219–23. Castellano came under a great deal of fire in Italy for his actions leading to the armistice. He wrote a sixteen-page discussion, really a justification, of his actions. Smith read "Report on the Activities Explicated by General Castellano during the Negotiations which Brought about the Conclusion of the Armistice" and confirmed the veracity of Castellano's account. Smith to Castellano, 5 December 1943, Official Correspondence, 1942–1944 File, WBSP.

28. Murphy cited in *FRUS, Washington and Quebec,* 1276.

29. Smith to Eisenhower, 1 September 1943, *Capitulation of Italy,* 202–3; Eisen-

hower to CCS, 1 September 1943, *EP,* #1221; Eisenhower to Alexander, 2 September 1943, *EP,* #1227.

30. Murphy to Roosevelt, 8 September 1943, *FRUS, Washington and Quebec,* 1277.

31. A summary of the conference and its conclusions are in NAF 346, 1 September 1943, *Capitulation of Italy,* 198–202. Castellano reprinted his minutes in *Come firmai l'armistizio,* 219–23.

32. Smyth interview with Smith.

33. Murphy to Roosevelt, 8 September 1943, *FRUS, Washington and Quebec,* 1277–78.

34. Smith, aided by Strong, Murphy, and Macmillan, described the outcome of the 31 August conference with Castellano and Zanussi. Smith to Eisenhower, 1 September 1943, *Capitulation of Italy,* 202; Smith [for Eisenhower] to CCS and BCOS, 1 September 1943, *EP,* #1221.

35. Castellano, *Come firmai l'armistizio,* 223–24, cited in Agarossi, *A Nation Collapses,* 78–79.

36. AFHQ to War Department, 1 September 1943, *Capitulation of Italy,* 205.

37. Smyth, "The Armistice of Cassibile," 17.

38. Murphy's account of the 2–3 September meetings is a good narrative of events. Murphy to Roosevelt, 8 September 1943, *FRUS, Washington and Quebec,* 1279–83.

39. Smyth, "The Armistice of Cassibile," 18.

40. Alexander to Eisenhower, 2 September 1943, Earl Alexander of Tunis Papers, War Office 214/36 File, National Archives, Public Record Office, Kew. The War Office 214 File contains Alexander's papers for April through December 1943.

41. Whiteley [for Eisenhower] to Smith, 2 September 1943, *EP,* #1228; Butcher, *Three Years with Eisenhower,* 405.

42. Macmillan, *War Diaries,* 187; Macmillan, *Blast of War,* 322; Sidney Matthews interview with Alexander, 10 and 15 January 1949, MHI; Strong, *Intelligence at the Top,* 157; Murphy, *Diplomat among Warriors,* 240–41; Murphy to Roosevelt, 8 September, *FRUS, Washington and Quebec,* 1279.

43. ADM Raffaele de Courten kept notes that clearly dispel, in Agarossi's words, "the network of lies constructed by Badoglio and the senior military leaders," who claimed the heads of the armed services knew nothing of Allied intentions before 8 September. Agarossi, *A Nation Collapses,* 82–83.

44. AFHQ Advanced to AFHQ, 3 September 1943, *Capitulation of Italy,* 252.

45. Smyth interview with Lemnitzer, 3 March 1947, MHI.

46. "Report of General M. B. Ridgway to C in C.A.F.," 25 October 1943, in Smyth, "The Armistice of Cassibile," 23. Taylor told an interviewer that Castellano "was under great pressure from Beedle Smith—who said, 'Of course you can do it: You know you can!' I suspect that while there was no physical arm-twisting there was a lot of psychological arm-twisting. Castellano may well have been agreeing to things which in his heart he knew couldn't happen." Nigel Hamilton interview with Taylor, 17 October 1981, in Hamilton, *Monty: Master of the Battlefield, 1942-1944* (London, 1983), 390.

47. Eisenhower got even with Butcher; he refused to bring him along to witness the historic event. Butcher, *Three Years with Eisenhower,* 405.

48. Smyth interview with Smith.

49. Copy in *Capitulation of Italy,* 221–23.

50. Marshall to Eisenhower, 1 September 1943, Eyes Only, WBSP; Eisenhower to Marshall, 2 September 1943, *EP,* #1225.

51. Hughes Diary, 10 September 1943.

52. Murphy, *Diplomat among Warriors,* 237; Butcher, *Three Years with Eisenhower,* 405.

53. Eisenhower to Marshall, 6 September 1943, *EP,* #1233.

54. Eisenhower to Brooke, 29 July 1943, *EP,* #1149, n. 1.

55. Eisenhower to Dan Gilmer, 6 September 1943, *EP,* #1236; Hughes Diary, 4 September 1943.

56. Smith to Ismay, 12 September 1943, Chief of Staff's Personal Papers, 1942–44, WBSP; Murphy to Roosevelt, 8 September 1943, *FRUS, Washington and Quebec,* 1282.

57. Strong to Smith, 22 September 1943, Smith 201 File, WBSP.

58. Eisenhower to Whiteley for CCS, 3 September 1943, *EP,* #1229.

59. David Brown, "The Inside Story of Italy's Surrender," *Saturday Evening Post,* 9 and 16 September 1944.

23. "A Feeling of Restrained Optimism"

1. Murphy to Roosevelt, 8 September 1943, *FRUS, Washington and Quebec,* 1280.

2. Ridgway to Smith, 5 December 1955, and Ridgway to Castellano, 20 December 1955, Clay Blair Collection, MHI; Smyth interview of Smith, 13 May 1947; Clay Blair, *Ridgway's Paratroopers* (Garden City, NY, 1985), 126. In his memoirs Ridgway wrote, "I knew in my heart [the Italians] could not, or would not, meet the commitments they were making." Ridgway, *Soldier,* 80.

3. James Gavin, "Airborne Plans and Operation Giant," *Infantry Journal* (August 1946): 22.

4. Ridgway, "Development of Operation Giant," 9 September 1943, Blair Collection; Ridgway, *Soldier,* 81.

5. Alexander, "Tasks in Order of Priority," 7 September 1943, Alexander Papers, cited in Agarossi, *A Nation Collapses,* 82.

6. De Courten's memorandum, housed in the Italian Navy Archive, is cited in Agarossi, *A Nation Collapses,* 83. The Italians had four infantry and two armored divisions, organized in three corps, in the environs of Rome, plus two coastal divisions and numerous auxiliary units. Two other divisions of the Fourth Army were not expected to deploy until 12 September.

7. Castellano, *Come firmai l'armistizio,* 170–71, cited in Smyth, "The Armistice of Cassible," 25. Smith confirmed Castellano's version in his interview with Smyth.

8. Roatta, *Memoria sulla difesa di Roma,* cited in Agarossi, *A Nation Collapses,* 84–85.

9. *Capitulation of Italy,* 281–82, 311–17.

10. Cited in Smyth, "The Armistice of Cassible," 30–31.

11. The outline plan provided for two days of rations and enough gasoline for a single day. Aside from Italian units actively fighting the Germans, the entire operation depended on the Italians providing the necessary logistical support. The Italians made no provisions to supply the Eighty-second Airborne with anything.

12. The Italians controlled a large POL reserve, but not for long. Within one hour of the armistice's announcement, the Germans seized it from a corporals' guard of defenders.

13. History repeated itself. At Caporetto, the 1917 defeat that nearly knocked Italy out of World War I, Badoglio had retired to his bed without redeploying the Italian artillery, contributing to the Italian rout.

14. The story of the secret mission received a great deal of press. On the first

anniversary, the first installment of two articles appeared in the *Saturday Evening Post*. The next month *Harper's Magazine* carried the story. Earlier, in England, it appeared in book form. David Brown, "The Inside Story of Italy's Surrender," *Saturday Evening Post*, 9 September 1944; Richard Thruelsen and Elliott Arnold, "Secret Mission to Rome," *Harper's Magazine* (October 1944): 462–69; Alfred Waggs and David Brown, *No Spaghetti for Breakfast* (London, 1943). See also Garland and Smyth, *Sicily and the Italian Surrender*, 480–84.

15. Smith [for Eisenhower] to CCS and BCOS, 8 September 1943, CCS Cable File, DDEL.

16. "Our greatest asset now," Eisenhower reported on the day of the landings, "is confusion and uncertainty which we must take advantage of in every possible way." Eisenhower to CCS and BCOS, 9 September 1943, *EP*, #1246.

17. David Hunt, *A Don at War* (London, 1990), 224.

18. Eisenhower to Badoglio and Eisenhower to CCS, 8 September 1943, *EP*, #1244, #1248.

19. Smyth interview with Lemnitzer, 4 March 1947, MHI; L. James Binder, *Lemnitzer: A Soldier for His Time* (Washington, DC, 1997), 113–14.

20. John Hull, unpublished autobiography, MHI.

21. Agarossi based her account on the memoir literature of participants on the Crown Council. De Courten's version, written immediately after the flight from Rome, is reproduced in the notes. Agarossi, *A Nation Collapses*, 95–96, 166.

22. Smith to Ismay, 12 September 1943, Personal Correspondence, WBSP.

23. Denis Mack Smith, *Mussolini: A Biography* (New York, 1983), 289–90, 293.

24. Ralph Mavrogordato, "Hitler's Decision on the Defense of Italy," in *Command Decisions*, 56.

25. Albert Kesselring, *Kesselring: A Soldier's Record* (Westport, CT, 1970), 212. Amazingly, at the Bologna conference on 15 August, the Germans surrendered the defense of central Italy and Rome to the Italians, only to be refused. Even though Roatta and Ambrosio recognized the Germans intended to stage a coup, and Ambrosio knew Castellano had been dispatched to Madrid to open talks with the AFHQ, they requested *more* German troops. As Roatta weakly explained, he did not desire "our game be known." Roatta, *Storia di un armistizio*, cited in Agarossi, *A Nation Collapses*, 62.

26. Giacomo Dogliani, *Relazione sugli avvenimenti dell'8 settembre 1943 dal tenente colonnello Giacomo Dogliani*, cited in Agarossi, *A Nation Collapses*, 99.

27. Smith to Castellano, 5 December 1943, Chief of Staff Official Correspondence, 1942–1944, WBSP. As Smith told a postwar interviewer, an officer with real authority should have been sent to Rome—someone who would have threatened to line the Italian leadership up against the wall and shoot them if they did not live up to their bargain. His intelligence chief, Strong, believed Smith was the ideal man for that job. Smith thought otherwise but agreed that sending Taylor had been an error. "It is a good example . . . that it is a mistake to send a specialist when what is needed is someone who can make a decision and enforce it." Taylor thought Giant II was the perfect example of why staff officers should not exercise control over operations. Eisenhower told Smyth in 1949, "I wanted very much to make the air drop in Rome, and we were all ready to execute that plan. . . . Certainly we were prepared—all ready to make the drop in Rome. I was anxious to get in there." Smyth interview with Smith; Smyth interview with Strong, 29 October 1947; Smyth interview with Eisenhower, 16 February 1949, MHI; Hamilton interview with Taylor.

28. Smith [for Eisenhower] to CCS and BCOS, 9 September 1943, *EP,* #1246.

29. Samuel Elliot Morison, *Sicily-Salerno-Anzio,* History of the United States Naval Operations in World War II (Boston, 1964), 280.

30. Eisenhower to Marshall, 16 September 1943, *EP,* #1261.

31. AFHQ G-3, "Operations against Italy," 15 September 1943, Arthur Nevins Papers, MHI; C. J. C. Molony, *The Mediterranean and Middle East,* vol. 5, *The Campaign in Sicily, 1943 and the Campaign in Italy, 3rd September 1943 to 31st March 1944,* History of the Second World War (London, 1973), 252.

32. Eisenhower to Marshall, 20 September 1943, *EP,* #1271.

33. Butcher, *Three Years with Eisenhower,* 424–25; Marshall to Eisenhower, 22 September 1943, *Aggressive and Determined Leadership,* #115; Eisenhower to Marshall, 24 September 1943, *EP,* #1284.

34. Hughes Diary, 20 September 1943.

35. Smith to Ismay, 12 September 1943, Chief of Staff Personal Papers, 1942–1944, WBSP.

36. Smith to Mountbatten, 21 September 1943, Smith 201 File, WBSP.

37. Eisenhower to McNarney, 16 September 1943, *EP,* #1262.

38. McCloy to WBS, 17 September 1943, Smith 201 File, WBSP; Watson to Smith, 19 September 1943, Personal Correspondence, WBSP.

39. Roosevelt and Churchill to Stalin, 19 August 1943, Hopkins Papers, *FRUS, Washington and Quebec,* 1062.

40. AFHQ first suggested its own set of policy guidelines for Italy on 19 July; the CCS did not sanction them until 6 September. AFHQ had already implemented its own AMGOT plan in Sicily; the CCS merely endorsed the program after the fact.

41. Smith [for Eisenhower] to Marshall, 10 September 1943, Cable File, PPP.

42. Rooks [for Eisenhower] to Smith, 10 September 1943, *EP,* #1247. Smith forwarded the letter to Badoglio.

43. Smith to Ismay, 12 September 1943, WBSP.

44. Smith [for Eisenhower] to CCS and BCOS, 18 September 1943, *EP,* #1264.

45. Eisenhower to Smith, 19 September 1943, *EP,* #1266; Butcher Diary, 21 September 1943.

46. Churchill to Roosevelt, 21 September 1943, in Kimball, *Churchill and Roosevelt,* 2:458–59.

47. Roosevelt to Churchill, 21 September 1943, ibid., 470. McCloy passed on the story of Stimson's role in deflecting the president. McCloy to Smith, 17 September 1943, WBSP.

48. Smith to Mason-MacFarlane, 24 September 1943, Capitulation of Italy File, WBSP.

49. Smith [for Eisenhower] to Marshall, 25 September 1943, *EP,* #1287.

50. Chargé in the Soviet Union to Hull, 26 September 1943, *FRUS, Europe, 1943,* 2:377–78.

51. De Gaulle, *Memoirs,* 2:158–66; Milton Viorst, *Hostile Allies: FDR and Charles de Gaulle* (New York, 1965), 180–81.

52. Mason-MacFarlane to Smith, 26 September 1943, Capitulation of Italy File, WBSP.

53. Eisenhower to Marshall, 26 September 1943, *EP,* #1288.

54. Smith gave his account in his interview with Smyth.

55. Press conference transcript, 30 September 1943, WBSP.

56. Eisenhower to Dill, 30 September 1943, *EP,* #1301.

57. Smith [for Eisenhower] to Badoglio, 29 September 1943, *EP,* #1298.

58. Smith [for Eisenhower] to CCS and BCOS, 30 September 1943, *EP,* #1299.

59. Churchill to Roosevelt, 4 October 1943, *FRUS, Europe, 1943,* 2:383–84.

60. Eisenhower to Marshall, 4 and 7 September, Eyes Only, WBSP.

61. Eisenhower to Marshall, 4 October 1943, *EP,* #1316; Eisenhower to Marshall, 13 October 1943, *EP,* #1335.

62. Eisenhower to Marshall, 2 October 1943, *EP,* #1311; Eisenhower to Marshall, 13 October 1943, Eyes Only, WBSP.

63. Eisenhower Diary, 6 December 1943, *EP,* #1408.

64. Hughes to Kate Hughes, 5 October 1943, Hughes Papers.

65. Butcher Diary, 5 October 1943; Butcher, *Three Years with Eisenhower,* 428.

66. Eisenhower to Marshall, 2 October 1943, *EP,* #1311.

67. Eisenhower to Smith, 2 and 3 October 1943, *EP,* #1310, #1312.

68. Smith, "Questions for Discussion," 12 October 1943, Chief of Staff Conference Notes, Washington Trip, October 1943 File, WBSP.

69. Smith to Eisenhower, 10 October 1943, Conference Notes, WBSP. On 7 September the United Press carried a story entitled, "Report Marshall to Head Big Push," Patton File, PPP.

70. Hughes Diary, 8 October 1943.

71. Eisenhower to Smith, 13 October 1943, *EP,* #1333.

72. Eisenhower to Ethel Wyman, 16 October 1943, *EP,* #1341.

73. Smith to AFHQ, 11 October 1943, Conference Notes, WBSP.

74. Smith to Eisenhower, 13 October 1943, Conference Notes, WBSP.

75. Whiteley [for Eisenhower] to CCS, Smith, and BCOS, 18 October 1943, *EP,* #1343; Coles and Weinberg, *Civil Affairs,* 246.

76. Coles and Weinberg, *Civil Affairs,* 253–55.

77. Hilldring asked Smith to "soft pedal the use of AMGOT. . . . It will be useful in taking the heat off me." Hilldring to Smith, 7 August 1943, Chief of Staff Official Correspondence, 1942–1944, WBSP.

78. Hilldring to Smith, 20 September 1943, Official Correspondence, WBSP.

79. McCloy to Smith, 17 September 1943, WBSP.

80. Smith to Taylor, 7 November 1943, Official Correspondence, 1942–1944, WBSP.

81. Marshall warned Eisenhower that at the end of October, Congress would open investigations into the replacement system. Marshall to Eisenhower, 21 October 1943, Eyes Only, WBSP. On 13 December 1942 the WDGS G-1 categorized the replacement channel as suffering from "confusion, complication, inefficiency, serious lack of coordination." So it would remain until the end of the war. The War Department never established which agency—WDGS or ASF—was responsible for the overseas replacement system until 29 June 1945; ASF got the job. U.S. Army Center of Military History, *The Personnel Replacement System in the US Army* (Washington, DC, 1954), 263–65. See also Kent Greenfield, Robert Palmer, and Bell Wiley, *Organization of Ground Combat Troops,* USAWWII (Washington, DC, 1947), 300–318.

82. Marshall to Eisenhower, 13 and 14 October 1943, Eyes Only, WBSP; Eisenhower to Marshall, 14 October 1943, *EP,* #1339.

83. Smith to Eisenhower, 13 October 1943, Conference Notes, WBSP. As deputy theater commander, Hughes absorbed most of the beating for the theater's problems with replacements, promotions, and the formation of service and support provisional units and for the failure of the rotation policy for officers. Sawbridge [for

Eisenhower] to Marshall, 22 May 1943, *EP,* #1017; Hughes [for Eisenhower] to Marshall, 3 July 1943, *EP,* #1099; Eisenhower to Hughes, 31 August 1943, *EP,* #1220; Sawbridge to AFHQ, "Review of Replacement Situation in NATO," 11 October 1943, in U.S. Army Center of Military History, *Personnel Replacement System,* 275.

84. Smith to Eisenhower 14 October 1943, Conference Notes, WBSP.

85. Spaatz to Eisenhower, 14 October 1943, Conference Notes, WBSP.

86. Eisenhower to Smith, 13 October 1943, *EP,* #1337; Smith to AFHQ, 13 October 1943, Conference Notes, WBSP.

87. Smith to Russell Reynolds, 22 August 1943, and Paul Stone to Smith, 25 October 1943, Personal Papers, 1942–1944, WBSP.

88. Eisenhower, "Associates," unpublished memo, 5 July 1967, Dwight D. Eisenhower: Post-Presidential Papers, DDEL.

89. Smith to Eisenhower, 13 October 1943, Eyes Only, WBSP.

90. One such example occurred in July and August. Donovan complained about the lack of support for OSS operations in the theater. The Mediterranean Air Command refused to free up aircraft for airdrops to resistance groups in the south of France. Smith replied, "We work here as one force without a dividing line between British and American units or functions." Smith intervened to get the OSS the necessary aircraft. He categorized the responsible air officer as an ass. Donovan to Smith, 21 July 1943; Smith to Donovan, 29 July 1943; Donovan to Smith, 5 August 1943, Official Correspondence, 1942–1944, WBSP.

24. "We Conduct Our Wars in a Most Curious Way"

1. Hughes to Kate Hughes, 24 October 1943, Hughes Papers.

2. Smith, "Chief of Staff Notes, Washington Trip," Conference Notes, WBSP; Butcher Diary, 28 October 1943. On his way back to Washington from China, Somervell could offer no insider hint as to Marshall's thinking. Butcher Diary, 30 October 1943.

3. Eisenhower Diary, 6 December 1943, *EP,* #1408.

4. Patton to Beatrice Patton, 22 October 1943, GSPP.

5. AG WDGS to Smith, "AFHQ Organization and Its Relationship to NATOUSA and the British L of C," AFHQ File, WBSP.

6. Crane to Smith, 28 September 1943, AFHQ File, WBSP.

7. Hughes Diary, 27–29 October and 3 November 1943.

8. Moses to Smith, 8 and 19 September 1943, Raymond G. Moses Papers, MHI. Smith's two letters could not be located, but their contents were thoroughly discussed in Moses' memoranda.

9. Hughes Diary, 9 and 10 November 1944.

10. Eisenhower to Marshall, 24 October 1943, *EP,* #1359. Four days later, anxious about Smith's future appointment, Eisenhower asked Marshall if he had received the message. Marshall replied, "Yes," but offered nothing further. Butcher Diary, 28 October 1943.

11. Smith [for Eisenhower] to COS and BCOS, 25 October 1943, *EP,* #1360.

12. Eisenhower to Marshall, 4 October 1943, *EP,* #1316; Eisenhower to CCS, 29 October 1943, *EP,* #1369.

13. Montgomery Diary, 27 October 1943, *Montgomery and the Eighth Army,* 313–14.

14. Dominck Graham and Shelford Bidwell, *Tug of War: The Battle for Italy, 1943–45* (New York, 1986), 99.

15. Eisenhower to Mamie, 2 December 1943, in D'Este, *Eisenhower: A Soldier's Life*, 457.

16. Eisenhower to Hughes, 10 May 1950, in *The Papers of Dwight D. Eisenhower: Columbia University* (Baltimore, 1984), 797.

17. Summersby, *Eisenhower Was My Boss*, 108.

18. Eisenhower to Mountbatten, 14 September 1943, *EP*, #1256.

19. Eisenhower's daily appointment log, in "Chronology," *EP*, 5:104–40.

20. Based on letters published in *The Papers of Dwight D. Eisenhower*, between 22 October (Smith's first day back from Washington) and 6 December, Eisenhower wrote eight official and nineteen personal letters; Smith, Whiteley, G-3, and the military government section wrote sixteen official letters, signed by Eisenhower. Also noteworthy is the diminished volume of correspondence. Thirty-six pieces of correspondence went out in Eisenhower's name in the slightly more than two weeks Smith spent in Washington; the same number was produced in the six weeks after his return.

21. Smith to Ismay, 12 September 1943, Chief of Staff's Official Correspondence File, 1942–1944, WBSP.

22. Smith to Theodore Roosevelt, 30 December 1943, and Smith to Earle, 3 October 1943, Personal Correspondence, WBSP.

23. Summersby, *Eisenhower Was My Boss*, 50; Kay Summersby, *Past Forgiving: My Love Affair with Dwight D. Eisenhower* (London, 1986), 88–89.

24. Pogue interview, 8 May 1947.

25. Interview with Burgess.

26. Smith to Paul Stone, 21 November 1943, and Smith to Ed Merkle, 14 February 1944, Chief of Staff's Personal Papers, 1942–44, WBSP; Butcher, *Three Years with Eisenhower*, 441.

27. Smith to Huebner, 21 September 1943, Smith 201 File, WBSP.

28. Salmon et al., *History of Allied Force Headquarters*.

29. Smith to Eden, 2 November 1943, Smith 201 File, WBSP.

30. Smith [for Eisenhower] to Mason-MacFarlane, 1 November 1943, *EP*, #1371.

31. Churchill to Roosevelt, 8 November 1943, *FRUS, Europe, 1943*, 2:420.

32. Butcher, *Three Years with Eisenhower*, 440.

33. Smith [for Eisenhower] to Roosevelt, 10 November 1943, *EP*, #1382.

34. Smith [for Eisenhower] to CCS and BCOS, 15 November 1943, *EP*, #1389; Smith to Mason-MacFarlane, 15 November 1943, Chief of Staff's Personal Papers, 1942–44, WBSP.

35. Butcher Diary, 17 November 1943; Butcher, *Three Years with Eisenhower*, 442.

36. All the various permutations are in Eisenhower Diary, 6 December 1943, *EP*, #1408.

37. Sherwood, *Roosevelt and Hopkins*, 770–71; Butcher, *Three Years with Eisenhower*, 445–49.

38. Smith to Patton and press transcript, Seymour Korman, 23 November 1943, Patton File, PPP.

39. Patton Diary, 23 November 1943, *Patton Papers, 1940-1945*, 377.

40. Butcher Diary, 23 November 1943.

41. Eisenhower to Marshall, 24 November 1943, *EP*, #1396.

42. Demaree Bess of the *Saturday Evening Post* wrote a thoroughly investigated report and handed it to Eisenhower on 19 August 1943. Bess, "Report of an Investigation," submitted 19 August 1943, Patton File, PPP.

43. Clarkson to Hughes, "Report of Colonel Herbert Slayden Clarkson," 18 September 1943, Patton File, PPP. Hughes's handwritten marginal note on Clarkson's report read: "Read by Gen. Eisenhower at La Marsa on 22 Set. 43. He directed these papers be placed in AG's secret file." Hughes Diary, 18 and 21 September 1943.

44. Smith [for Eisenhower] to Patton, 24 November 1943, *EP,* #1397.

45. Smith to Patton, 25 November 1943, Smith 201 File, WBSP.

46. Hughes Diary, 26 November 1943.

47. Patton Diary, 28 November 1943.

48. The Office of War Information sent excerpts of press coverage of the fallout in Congress. WAR OWI—43/2, n.d., Patton File, DDEL. Truman chaired the powerful Senate Special Committee to Investigate the National Defense Program. Interestingly, Pepper gave Truman only lukewarm support in 1948, instead petitioning Eisenhower to run on the Democratic ticket.

49. Herron to Eisenhower, 30 November 1943, Patton File, DDEL.

50. Patton to Hughes, 9 December 1943, Hughes Papers.

51. Smith to K. A. N. Anderson, 15 December 1943, Chief of Staff's Personal Papers, 1942–44, WBSP.

52. *FRUS, The Conferences at Cairo and Teheran, 1943,* 359–62.

53. Butcher, *Three Years with Eisenhower,* 454. On Churchill's request for Smith's retention in the Mediterranean as dual deputy supreme commander and chief of staff, see Marshall to Eisenhower, 23 December 1943, *Aggressive and Determined Leadership,* #172.

54. Eisenhower, *Crusade in Europe,* 206–7; Butcher, *Three Years with Eisenhower,* 454–55.

55. G-2 [for Eisenhower] to CCS, 29 October 1943, *EP,* #1369.

56. Butcher Diary, 5 December 1943.

57. Eisenhower reviewed his initial choices in consultation with Smith in Eisenhower to Marshall, 17 December 1943, *EP,* #1423.

58. Burgess interview.

59. Brooke Diary, 4 December 1943.

60. Butcher, *Three Years with Eisenhower,* 458.

61. Carlo D'Este, *Warlord: A Life of Winston Churchill at War, 1874-1945* (New York, 2008), 635–37.

62. Smith to Bull, 19 December 1943, COSSAC File, WBSP.

63. Eisenhower to Marshall, 16 and 17 December, *EP,* #1422–23; Smith to Hull, 19 December 1943, COSSAC File, WBSP.

64. Eisenhower to Marshall, 17 December 1943, *EP,* #1423.

65. Smith to Truscott, 15 December 1943, Chief of Staff's Personal Papers, 1942–44, WBSP.

66. Butcher, *Three Years with Eisenhower,* 460.

67. Montgomery Diary, 6–8 November 1943, *Montgomery and the Eighth Army,* 317–18.

68. Burgess interview.

69. Smith [for Eisenhower] to Roosevelt, 22 December 1943, *EP,* #1425.

70. Churchill to Roosevelt, 21 December 1943, Hull to Council General in Algiers, 22 December 1943, *FRUS, Europe, 1943,* 2:193–95.

71. Roosevelt to Churchill, 21 December 1943, text of exchange in Matthews, "Memo," 22 December 1943, *FRUS, Europe, 1943,* 2:195.

72. Churchill to Roosevelt, 23 December 1943, *FRUS, Europe, 1943,* 2:196.

73. Pogue interview with Smith, 8 May 1947.

74. Smith to Marshall, 24 December 1943, Eyes Only, WBSP.

75. Roosevelt to Eisenhower, 26 December 1943, *FRUS, Europe, 1943,* 2:197.

76. Marshall to Eisenhower, 4 November 1943, *Aggressive and Determined Leadership,* #155; Marshall to Eisenhower, 6 December 1943, Eyes Only, WBSP.

77. Marshall to Eisenhower, 23 December 1943, *Aggressive and Determined Leadership,* #172.

78. Eisenhower to Marshall, 25 December 1943, *EP,* #1428.

79. Morgan to Eisenhower, 20 December 1943, and Eisenhower to Morgan, 26 and 27 December 1943, Morgan File, PPP.

80. Devers to Eisenhower, 27 December 1943, COSSAC File, WBSP.

81. Pogue interview with Smith, 9 May 1949.

82. Eisenhower to Ismay, 3 December 1960, *Keeping the Peace,* #1722.

83. Réne Massagli to Wilson, quoted in Eisenhower to CCS, 4 January 1944, *EP,* #1489, n. 1. Hughes also attended the conference. Hughes to Larkin, 27 December 1943, Hughes Papers.

84. Pogue interview with Smith, 8 May 1947; Hughes Diary, 27 December 1944.

85. Eisenhower to Smith, 30 December 1943, COSSAC File, WBSP.

86. Hughes to Moses, 28 December 1943, Hughes Papers.

87. Devers to Eisenhower, 27 December 1943, COSSAC File, WBSP.

88. Eisenhower to Marshall, 28 December 1943, *EP,* #1445.

89. Marshall to Eisenhower, 29 December 1943, *Aggressive and Determined Leadership,* #187; Eisenhower to Smith, 30 December 1943, COSSAC File, WBSP.

25. The Supreme Command

1. Eisenhower to Smith, 31 December 1943, Eyes Only, WBSP.

2. Smith felt so strongly about the faulty air command issue that he sent two cables to Eisenhower that day. Smith to Eisenhower, 30 December 1943, COSSAC File, WBSP. See also Pogue interview with Smith, 9 May 1947.

3. Eisenhower to Marshall, 31 December 1943, *EP,* #1470.

4. Eisenhower to Smith, 31 December 1943, *EP,* #1469.

5. F. H. N. Davidson to Smith, 22 December 1943, Chief of Staff Official Correspondence, 1942–1944, WBSP. Major General Davidson served as deputy head of military intelligence.

6. Smith's account is found in his interview with Pogue, 8 May 1947. Brooke Diary and "Notes," 31 December 1943. Butcher provides a blow-by-blow description of the meeting. Eisenhower thought Smith "certainly would not intentionally be rough with the CIGS." Butcher Diary, 20 January 1944; Butcher, *Three Years with Eisenhower,* 472.

7. Smith to Eisenhower, 1 January 1944, COSSAC File, WBSP.

8. Smith to Eisenhower, 30 December 1943, ibid.

9. Eisenhower to Smith, 31 December 1943, *EP,* #1469.

10. Pogue interview with Smith, 8 May 1947.

11. Smith to Eisenhower, 31 December 1943, COSSAC File, WBSP.

12. Smith to Eisenhower, 2 January 1944, ibid.

13. Pogue interview, 9 May 1947.

14. Smith to Eisenhower, 2 January 1944, COSSAC File, WBSP.

15. Pogue interviews with MG Raymond Barker, 16 October 1946; MG K. G. McLean, 13 February 1947; and MG C. A. West, 19 February 1947, MHI.

16. Smith had all the cables, memos, minutes of meetings, telephone summaries, and documents related to the Anvil debate for the period December 1943 to April 1944 in one file, Overlord-Anvil Papers, WBSP.

17. Smith provided a full version in Smith to Eisenhower, 5 January 1944, COS-SAC File, WBSP. Ramsay gives his account in "Report by the Allied Naval C-in-C, Expeditionary Force on Operation Neptune," November 1944, copy in WBSP; Pogue interview with West.

18. Churchill to Roosevelt, 7 January 1943, *FRUS, Cairo and Teheran*, 865.

19. Pogue interview, 9 May 1947.

20. Smith to Eisenhower, 5 January 1944, COSSAC File, WBSP.

21. Eisenhower to Smith, 5–6 January 1944, *EP,* #1473.

22. Moran, *Diaries of Lord Moran*, 170.

23. Butcher, *Three Years with Eisenhower*, 465.

24. Brooke Diary, 7 January 1943.

25. H. M. Wilson, "Report of the Supreme Allied Commander Mediterranean," 7, copy in WBSP.

26. Roosevelt to Churchill, 28 December 1943, in Kimball, *Churchill and Roosevelt*, 2:638.

27. Clark oral history, Senior Officers Oral History Program, MHI.

28. Brooke Diary and "Notes," 5 January 1944.

29. Strong, *Intelligence at the Top*, 177; Matthews's interview with Strong, 30 October 1947, MHI.

30. Smith to Eisenhower, 9 January 1944, COSSAC File, WBSP.

31. Michael Carver, *Harding of Peterton, Field Marshal* (London, 1978), 123.

32. Butcher Diary, 20 January 1944.

33. Churchill to Roosevelt, 8 January 1944, in Kimball, *Churchill and Roosevelt*, 2:657.

34. Smith to Eisenhower, 9 January 1944, COSSAC File, WBSP.

35. Smith to Eisenhower, 5 January 1944, McCarthy [for Eisenhower] to Smith, 10 January 1944, and Smith to Eisenhower, 11 January 1944, COSSAC File, WBSP.

36. Smith to FREEDOM, 9 January 1944, COSSAC File, WBSP.

37. Eisenhower to Marshall, 25 December 1944, *EP,* #1427.

38. Butcher Diary, 9–10 May 1943.

39. Smith to Ivan Cobbald, 15 July 1943, Chief of Staff's Personal Papers, 1942–44, WBSP.

40. Butcher Diary, 8 February 1944.

41. Butcher Diary, 20 January and 8 February 1944. Smith considered Truscott the best American division commander. Smith to F. B. Shaw, 29 February 1944, Chief of Staff's Personal Papers, 1942–44, WBSP.

42. Hughes Diary, 15, 17–18 January 1944.

43. Butcher Diary, 20 January 1944. Burgess accompanied Smith on the flight. Burgess interview with author.

44. Butcher Diary, 16 January 1944.

45. Marshall Directive, "Designation of SHAEF," 15 January 1944, in GBR, "Organization of the European Theater of Operations," 20.

46. Eisenhower related all this to Butcher the day after he arrived in London. Butcher Diary, 16 January 1944.

47. Ibid.

48. Ibid., 27 January 1944.

49. Eisenhower to Marshall, 28 December 1943, *EP,* #1445.

50. Eisenhower to Marshall and Eisenhower to Devers, 19 January 1944, *EP,* #1487–88. Eisenhower told Marshall that he found Devers's attitude "a great disappointment."

51. Eisenhower to Marshall, 18 January 1944, *EP,* #1484.

52. Pogue interview, 9 May 1947; Butcher, *Three Years with Eisenhower,* 472–74.

53. Butcher Diary, 20 and 28 January 1944. The promotion dated from 13 January.

54. Eisenhower to Marshall, 18–20 January 1944, *EP,* #1486–87, #1492; Marshall to Eisenhower, 18 January 1944, Eyes Only, WBSP.

55. Patton Diary, 27 January 1944; *Patton Papers, 1940-1945,* 410.

56. LTC Frank Osmanski, "The Logistical Planning for OVERLORD," *Military Review* (November 1949): 31–40.

57. SHAEF, SGS, History Sub-Section, "History of COSSAC," copy in WBSP.

58. "Minutes, Supreme Commander's Conference," 23 January 1944, Supreme Commanders File, WBSP; Eisenhower to Marshall, 22 January 1944, *EP,* #1496; Smith [for Eisenhower] to CCS and BCOS, 23 January 1944, *EP,* #1497.

59. "Neptune Initial Joint Plan," 1 February 1944, SGS Files; Smith to Secretary, BCOS, 10 February 1944, SHAEF War Diary, both in WBSP. The Smith Collection has the whole run of Neptune plans.

60. CCS to SHAEF, 12 February 1944, "Minutes, Supreme Commander's Conference," 18 January 1944, in GBR, "Organization of the European Theater of Operations," 20.

61. Smith told Montgomery in December in Algiers about his plans to create a large headquarters. Montgomery to Brooke, 23 December 1943, in Hamilton, *Monty: Master of the Battlefield,* 465. Pogue interview with Brownjohn, 28 March 1947, MHI.

62. Eisenhower and Smith discussed their thinking behind SHAEF's organization in Eisenhower conference with Moses, 27 September 1945, and Smith conference with Moses, 25 September 1945, GBR, "Organization of the European Theater of Operations," 36.

63. GBR, "Organization and Function of the Communication Zone," 78.

64. Butcher, *Three Years with Eisenhower,* 474.

65. For Smith's views, see Pogue interviews, 8, 9, and 13 May 1947.

66. Butcher Diary, 20 January 1944.

67. Pogue interview with Brownjohn, 28 March 1947. Pogue conducted interviews with all the major actors in COSSAC and SHAEF in preparation for his official history, *The Supreme Command;* that excellent volume and many of those interviews are relied on here.

68. Jackson, a former executive for *Time,* later joined the SHAEF Psychological Warfare Division. Jackson to Henry Luce, 3 April 1944, J. D. Jackson Papers, DDEL.

69. Betts provides the best insights into the creation of SHAEF and the planning phase. Pogue interview with Betts, 19 May 1950, MHI. There are also three oral history interviews with Betts, 18 October 1973, 20 November 1974, and 25 June 1975, all in DDEL. The oral history of Arthur Nevins, also in DDEL, is valuable as well. Betts remained as deputy G-2; Nevins headed a subsection of the Operations Division.

70. Pogue interview with Ford Trimble, 17 December 1946, MHI.

71. Pogue interview with COL James Gault, 13 February 1947, MHI.

72. Pogue interview with Group Captain Leslie Scarman, 25 February 1947, MHI.

73. Pogue interview with Crawford, 5 May 1948, MHI.

74. Pogue interview with Group Captain T. P. Gleave, 9 January 1947, MHI. Gleave served as chief of the air mission to France.

75. T. J. Davis to H. V. Roberts, 12 February 1943, Thomas J. Davis Papers, DDEL.

76. COSSAC, "Operation OVERLORD—Command and Control," 11 September 1943, "History of COSSAC." In May Morgan suggested that the British home forces be combed to contribute troops for a strategic reserve for Overlord. Morgan to BCOS, 21 May 1944, SHAEF War Diary.

77. Ruppenthal interview with Smith, 14 September 1945, MHI. After the war the British treated Morgan very shabbily. In 1963 C. D. Jackson reported to Eisenhower that Morgan "was living in a state of abject poverty . . . without heat, without money to buy more than a few pieces of coal . . . a half frozen old man." Jackson to Eisenhower, 28 February 1963, C. D. Jackson Papers, DDEL.

78. Betts oral history; Barker oral history, 15 July 1972, DDEL.

79. Pogue interview with Smith, 13 May 1947.

80. One such officer was his longtime aide, Colonel Burgess. Burgess interview; Pogue interview with Smith, 9 May 1947.

81. Pogue interview with Smith, 9 May 1947.

82. Betts oral history.

83. Ibid.

84. SHAEF transferred Rankin planning to headquarters, Scottish Command, on 4 March.

85. Gale [for Smith] to Ramsay, 6 March 1944, SHAEF War Diary.

86. Betts oral history.

87. SHAEF to FUSAG, "Operation OVERLORD," 10 March 1944, and Lee to Deputy Commanding General, Communications Zone, 14 March 1944, GBR, "Organization of the European Theater of Operations," 53.

88. Smith to Chiefs of All Divisions, "Organization of US Forces (Administration)," 8 February 1944, SHAEF War Diary; Smith to Bradley, 18 February 1944; SHAEF Directive, 10 March 1944, in GBR, "Mechanics of Supply," 8, 73.

89. JCH Lee to Somervell, 8 February 1944, COSSAC File, WBSP.

90. Smith to CCS, 9 March 1944, SHAEF War Diary.

91. Eisenhower to Marshall, 10 March 1944, *EP,* #1585.

92. Smith to Strong, 7 February 1944, Chief of Staff's Personal Papers, 1942–44, WBSP.

93. Morgan, *Overture to Overlord* (New York, 1950), 227–28; Pogue interview with Morgan, 3 February 1947, MHI.

94. Smith to Hilldring, 7 January 1944, Official Correspondence, WBSP.

95. Signed by Eisenhower to CCS and Combined Civil Affairs Committee, 19 January 1944, *EP,* #1489. Smith sent a copy to Ismay.

96. Morgan, *Overture to Overlord,* 227–29.

97. Coles and Weinberg, *Civil Affairs,* 674–75. For an examination of the formation of the Civil Affairs Division, see Earl Ziemke, *The U.S. Army in Occupation of Germany,* USAWWII (Washington, DC, 1975), chap. 4.

98. Hilldring to Smith, 27 January 1944, and Holmes to Smith, 29 January 1944, Chief of Staff's Personal Papers, 1942–44, WBSP. Smith instructed the secretariat to collect all pertinent files in a folio, "Civil Affairs Northwest Europe." The two volumes are in WBSP. Other documents appear in COSSAC, Civil Affairs Diary, in SHAEF G-5, SHAEF Selected Records, RG 331, Records of the Allied Operational and Occupation Headquarters, World War II, NARA.

99. For Smith's views, see Smith to Hilldring, 7, 12, and 22 January 1944, Eyes Only, WBSP.

100. In the COSSAC structure, the Civil Affairs Division consisted of six advisory groups composed in part by staffs designated by the governments in exile—France, Norway, the Netherlands, and Belgium-Luxembourg. These groups offered guidance on legal, fiscal, supply, intelligence, governmental, and economic affairs. Because the FCNL enjoyed no official recognition, relations with the French proved more difficult. The German section not only prepared plans for post-hostilities Germany but also served as a nucleus for a military government staff.

101. Lumley to Smith, 5 February 1944, and Smith to Lumley, 7 February 1944, Civil Affairs Northwest Europe, WBSP.

102. Smith to Hilldring, 6 February 1944, Eyes Only, WBSP.

103. Lumley to Smith and Smith to Lumley, 8 February 1944, SHAEF War Diary.

104. Smith memo, 11 February 1944, SHAEF War Diary; Pogue, *Supreme Command,* 347.

105. Smith to Director, Civil Affairs, War Office, 25 February 1944, and SHAEF Directive, 3 March 1944, SHAEF War Diary.

106. Pogue, *Supreme Command,* 347.

107. Smith, "Organization of Civil Affairs Section," 14 March 1944, SHAEF War Diary.

108. Smith to Combined Civil Affairs Committee, 18 March 1944, SHAEF War Diary.

109. Donovan to Smith, 8 February 1944, 1944 Chief of Staff's Personal Correspondence, WBSP.

110. Smith to McClure, 29 March 1944, SHAEF War Diary.

111. Pogue, "U.S. General Staff," MHI.

112. "Minutes of Meeting," 4 May 1944, SHAEF War Diary.

113. Butcher Diary, 20 January 1944.

114. Pogue interview with Smith, 9 May 1947.

115. Jackson to Henry Luce, 3 April 1944, Jackson Papers, DDEL.

116. Pogue interview with Trimble.

117. Davis to Roberts, 12 February 1944, Davis Papers, DDEL.

26. "Enough to Drive You Mad"

1. Eisenhower Diary, 22 March 1944, *EP,* #1601.

2. Eisenhower to Marshall, 17 January 1944, *EP,* #1483.

3. Marshall to Eisenhower, 6 February 1944, *Aggressive and Determined Leadership,* #232.

4. Eisenhower Diary, 7 February 1944, *EP,* #1536.

5. Summaries of the conversations between Smith and Handy are in Marshall, "Memo for FM Dill" and "Memo for Admirals Leahy and King," 9 February 1944, *Aggressive and Determined Leadership,* #233–34.

6. Churchill to Roosevelt, 6 February 1944, in Kimball, *Churchill and Roosevelt,* 2:705.

7. Lucas's diary entry cited in Lloyd Clark, *Anzio: The Friction of War: Italy and the Battle for Rome, 1944* (London, 2006), 76; Churchill's remark cited in John Colville, *The Fringes of Power—Downing Street Diaries, 1939-1955* (London, 2004), 456.

8. Brooke Diary, 19 February 1944; Pogue interview with Portal, 7 February 1947, MHI.

9. Marshall to Eisenhower, 10 February 1944, *EP,* #1558, n. 1.

10. Montgomery to Eisenhower, 19 and 21 February 1944, Montgomery File, PPP.

11. Eisenhower to Marshall, 19 February 1944, *EP,* #1556.

12. Transcript, "Conference between General Handy and General Smith," 20 February 1944, OVERLORD-ANVIL File, and Smith to Handy, 21 February 1944, COSSAC File, WBSP.

13. Pogue interview, 9 May 1947.

14. Eisenhower to Marshall, 19 February 1944, *EP,* #1557.

15. Charles Corlett, *Cowboy Pete: The Autobiography of Major General Charles H. Corlett,* unpublished manuscript, 245–46, 248, 250, Corlett Papers, MHI.

16. Roosevelt [through Leahy] to Eisenhower, 21 February 1944, Roosevelt File, PPP.

17. Eisenhower to Marshall, 22 February 1944, *EP,* #1562.

18. Butcher, *Three Years with Eisenhower,* 494–95.

19. Eisenhower to Cunningham, 23 February 1944, *EP,* #1564, n. 1.

20. "Minutes, Supreme Commander's Conference," 26 February 1944, OVERLORD-ANVIL, WBSP; Pogue interviews with Smith, 8–9 May 1947; Butcher, *Three Years with Eisenhower,* 474.

21. Butcher, *Three Years with Eisenhower,* 497; Butcher Diary, 29 February 1944.

22. Tedder, *With Prejudice,* 508–12.

23. Eisenhower to Tedder, 29 February 1944, *EP,* #1575.

24. Both these comments were marginal notes made on the letter Portal wrote outlining the agreement. *EP,* #1577, n. 1.

25. Eisenhower to Marshall, 10 March 1944, *EP,* #1585.

26. Marshall to Eisenhower, 16 March 1944, *Aggressive and Determined Leadership,* #296.

27. Transcript, Smith to Handy, 17 March 1944, OVERLORD-ANVIL, WBSP; Eisenhower to Marshall, 18 March 1944, *EP,* #1591.

28. Eisenhower to Marshall, 20 March 1944, *EP,* #1593; Eisenhower Manuscript [in Butcher Diary], 22 March 1944, *EP,* #1601.

29. Smith [for Eisenhower] to Marshall, 21 March 1944, *EP,* #1595.

30. Eisenhower to Marshall, 21 March 1944, *EP,* #1596.

31. Smith to BCOS, 14 March 1944, SHAEF War Diary.

32. Eisenhower Manuscript, 22 March 1944, *EP,* #1601; Smith to Handy, telephone transcript, 17 March 1944, OVERLORD-ANVIL, WBSP.

33. Tedder, *With Prejudice,* 519–20.

34. Spaatz Diary, 23 April 1944, Papers of Carl Spaatz, LOC.

35. Eisenhower to Marshall, 27 March 1944, *EP,* #1608.

36. Patton Diary, 27 March 1944.

37. Eisenhower to Marshall, 12 April 1944, *EP,* #1641.

38. Brooke Diary, 1 April 1944.

39. Marshall to Eisenhower, 14 April 1944, Eyes Only, WBSP.

40. Handy reported that Wilson promised to give Anvil priority after completion of the link with the Anzio beachhead. Handy to Eisenhower, 5 April 1944, Eyes Only, WBSP; Churchill cited in Matloff and Snell, *Strategic Planning,* 424–26.

41. Eisenhower to Marshall, 17 April 1944, *EP,* #1645.

42. Butcher Diary, 17 and 18 April 1944.

43. Eisenhower had an unlikely ally in Wilson. Devers reported, "Wilson never has indicated that he desired to put troops into Balkans, but rather that he expected to make that an air war." Devers to Eisenhower, 9 May 1944, Devers File, PPP.

44. Betts oral histories, 18 October 1973 and 20 November 1974, DDEL.

45. SHAEF Planning Staff, "First Draft," 11 April 1944; War Department from Joint Staff Planners to U.S. Planners, SHAEF, 13 and 17 April 1944; SHAEF G-3, "Post-NEPTUNE Planning Forecast," 15 April 1944; SHAEF Forward G-3, "ECLIPSE Plan," 16 April 1944; SHAEF G-3, Plans Sub-Section, "Progress Report," 19 April 1944, in Historical Division, U.S. Army Force, European Theater, *The Administrative and Logistical History of the European Theater of Operations*, pt. 5, vol. 2, *Survey of Allied Planning for Continental Operations*, 71–80. The planners produced multiple revisions of "Post-NEPTUNE, Courses of Action after Capture of Lodgment Area." The first section, "Main Objective and Axis of Advance," went through three revisions on 17 and 25 April and 3 May; the second section, "Method of Conducting the Campaign," was also revised three times, on 27 April and 12 and 20 May. GBR, "Strategy of the Campaign in Western Europe, 1944–1945," 42–48.

46. Smith to McCarthy, 15 April 1944, Frank McCarthy Collection, GCMRL.

47. Jackson to Henry Luce, 3 April 1944, Jackson Papers.

48. Coles and Weinberg, *Civil Affairs*, 667–68.

49. Smith to Leigh-Mallory and McClure, 8 March 1944, SHAEF War Diary.

50. Smith [for Eisenhower] to d'Astier, 17 March 1944, *EP*, #1590.

51. Minutes of Meeting, 3 April 1944, SHAEF War Diary.

52. Minutes of Chiefs of Staff Meeting, 5, 8, and 9 April 1944, SHAEF War Diary.

53. Smith, SHAEF Directive, 13 April 1944, and Smith to McClure, 15 April 1944, SHAEF War Diary.

54. Smith [for Eisenhower] to CCS, 19 April 1944, and Smith, SHAEF Directive, 20 April 1944, SHAEF War Diary.

55. Cited in Pogue, *Supreme Command*, 82 n. 26.

56. Smith [for Eisenhower] to Marshall, 26 April 1944, *EP*, #1653.

57. Forrest Pogue, "High Command in War: Two Problems from the Second World War," *Military Affairs* (December 1951): 332.

58. The Under Secretary of State (Stettinius) to the Secretary of State, 13 April 1943, *FRUS, 1944, General*, 507–9; Butcher Diary, 14 April 1944. The first draft of the "unconditional surrender" terms emerged in late January, authored by the European Advisory Council. Smith commented, "This is counting chickens before they are hatched." Butcher, *Three Years with Eisenhower*, 481.

59. Stettinius, "Report on Conversations in London, April 7 to April 29, 1944," *FRUS, 1944, British Commonwealth and Europe*, 6–7.

60. Butcher, *Three Years with Eisenhower*, 518.

61. Hilldring to Smith, 22 April 1944, 1944 Chief of Staff Personal Correspondence, WBSP.

62. Minutes of Meeting, 23 April 1944, SHAEF War Diary.

63. SHAEF to AFHQ, 26 and 27 April 1944, SHAEF War Diary.

64. Smith [for Eisenhower] to CCS, 8 and 11 May 1944, *EP*, #1675, #1681; Eisenhower to McNarney, 11 May 1944, *EP*, #1682.

65. Roosevelt to Eisenhower, 12 May 1944, GCMP.

66. Butcher Diary, 18 May 1944.

67. Butcher, *Three Years with Eisenhower*, 538.

68. Eisenhower to Churchill, 5 April 1944, *EP*, #1630.

69. Robb to Spaatz and Harris, "Direction of Operations of Allied Air Forces against Transportation Targets," 17 April 1944, and Robb to Spaatz and Harris, 20 April 1944, SHAEF War Diary.

70. Cunningham Diary, 2 May 1944, A. B. Cunningham Papers, British Library, London; copy in the author's possession.

71. Eisenhower to Marshall, 29 April 1944, *EP,* #1658.

72. Robb to Spaatz and Harris, 30 April and 6 May 1944, SHAEF War Diary.

73. Smith to Marshall, 14 and 16 May 1944, Eyes Only, WBSP; Butcher Diary, 16 May 1944.

74. Eisenhower to Marshall, 16 May 1944, *EP,* #1691.

75. Marshall to Smith, 16 May 1944, *Aggressive and Determined Leadership,* #386.

76. Smith to Marshall, 17 May 1944, Eyes Only, WBSP.

77. Butcher, *Three Years with Eisenhower,* 531.

78. Smith to Marshall, 27 April 1944, Eyes Only, WBSP. Eisenhower related his conversation with Smith in Eisenhower to Marshall, 29 April 1944, *EP,* #1657. Marshall to Eisenhower, 26 April 1944, *Aggressive and Determined Leadership,* #372.

79. Patton Diary, 18 February and 2 March 1944; *Patton Papers, 1940-1945,* 417, 420.

80. Paul Munch, "Patton's Staff and the Battle of the Bulge," *Military Review* (May 1990): 46–54.

81. Patton Diary, 27 April 1944; *Patton Papers, 1940-1945,* 444.

82. Patton to Smith, 6 March 1944, Chief of Staff's Personal Papers, 1942–44, WBSP; Patton Diary, 24 May 1944.

83. Eisenhower to Marshall, 29 April 1944, *EP,* #1657–58.

84. Hughes Diary, 29 April 1944.

85. Butcher Diary, 9 May 1944.

86. Patton Diary, 30 April 1944; *Patton Papers, 1940-1945,* 447–48.

87. "Some Personal Memoirs of Justus 'Jock' Lawrence, Chief Public Relations Officer, European Theater of Operations," 4, 145–47, Miscellaneous Box, Patton Papers, GSPP.

88. Hughes Diary, 2 May 1944.

89. Ibid., 6, 14, 16, 17 May and 6, 28 June 1944. Gunmakers to the Royal Family, James Purdey and Sons proudly displays photographs of its more noteworthy patrons. Amidst the photographs of kings and royalty hangs one of Smith. Drew Middleton, "A Home of Guns Fit for a King, *New York Times,* 9 June 1985. On 18 June Eisenhower told Smith, "There is nothing to indicate a need for disciplinary measures against any officer, although I hope that a number [presumably including Smith] have received good lessons in good judgment. Eisenhower to Smith, 18 June 44, *EP,* #1762.

90. Butcher, *Three Years with Eisenhower,* 538.

27. "It's a Go"

1. Twenty-first Army Group, "Appreciation on Possible Development of Operations to Secure a Lodgement Area," 7 May 1944; Second Army, "Outline Plan, Fourth Draft," 21 February 1944; Twenty-first Army Group, Map, "Planning Forecast of Development of Operations," 26 February 1944, in C. P. Stacey, *Victory Campaign: The Operations in North-West Europe, 1944-1945,* Official History of the Canadian Army in the Second World War (Ottawa, 1960), 83–84.

2. Butcher, *Three Years with Eisenhower*, 539.

3. Cunningham Diary, 15 May 1944; Montgomery, "Address Given by General Montgomery to the General Officers of the Four Field Armies on 15 May 1944," in Hamilton, *Monty: Master of the Battlefield*, 570–78. Twenty-first Army Group's operational priorities were spelled out in "Appreciation on Possible Developments of Operations to Secure a Lodgment Area," 7 May 1944, RG 331, Records of the Allied Operational & Occupational Headquarters, NARA.

4. Eisenhower to Ismay, 3 December 1960, *Keeping the Peace*, #1722.

5. S. L. A. Marshall interview with Eisenhower, 3 June 1946, in D'Este, *Eisenhower: A Soldier's Life*, 502.

6. Nevins [for Eisenhower] to War Department for U.S. Planning Staff, 8 and 26 May 1944; Bull to Vulliamy, 9 May 1944, both in *Survey of Allied Planning*, 2:84–91; Chiefs of Staff Meeting, Minutes, 19 May 1944, SGS File, WBSP. Eisenhower's approved plan is in AGWAR for U.S. Joint Planning Staff, 8 May 1944, in Steven Ross, ed., *U.S. War Plans, 1938-1945* (Boulder, CO, 2004), 237–38.

7. Smith, "Memo on Future Planning," SHAEF/18001/Plans, 25 May 1944, in *Survey of Allied Planning*, 2:90–91.

8. SHAEF, "Planning Forecast No. 1," in *Survey of Allied Planning*, 2:78–81, 84–89. After several revisions, the forecast was finalized on 27 May.

9. Smith to War Office, ETOUSA, Canadian Military Headquarters, and Smith to CCS, 17 May 1944; Smith to Koenig, 18 May 1944; Smith to Montgomery and Leigh-Mallory, 19 May 1944; Smith to BCOS and Smith to CCS, 21 May 1944, all in SHAEF War Diary. Smith approved the latest revision of "Method of Conducting the Campaign" on 20 May; see GBR, "Strategy in Western Europe," 47–48.

10. Pogue interviews with Robb, 3 February 1947; Whiteley, 18 December 1947; and Smith, 9 May 1947, MHI.

11. Smith to War Office, 19 May 1944, SHAEF War Diary.

12. GBR, "Organization of the European Theater of Operations," 64.

13. Marshall to Eisenhower, 13 April 1944, *Aggressive and Determined Leadership*, #348; Smith to Marshall, 15 April 1944, and Eisenhower to Marshall, 25 April 1944, Eyes Only, WBSP. See also Ruppenthal, *Logistical Support of the Armies*, 2:336.

14. Eisenhower to Marshall, 17 April 1944, *EP*, #1646; Butcher Diary, 15 April 1944.

15. U.S. Army Center of Military History, *Personnel Replacement System*, 291, 294.

16. The Replacement System, ETO contained 100,000 men in training, with a cadre of 6,000 and a reinforcement unit cadre of more than 20,000 in thirteen centers in England.

17. Hughes, "Memo for Eisenhower," 3 May 1944, Hughes Papers.

18. Moses, "Organization," 10 May 1944, Hughes Papers.

19. Moses to Hughes, 26 May 1944, Hughes Papers.

20. Lutes to Somervell, "Report on ETO," 29 April 1944; Lutes to Somervell, 4 May 1944; Lutes to Somervell, "Personal Report," 8-9 May 1944; and Lutes to Somervell, 11 May 1944, Lutes Papers, DDEL.

21. Pogue interviews with Smith, 13 May 1947, and Trimble, 17 December 1946, MHI.

22. Eisenhower to Marshall, 3 March 1944, and Marshall to Eisenhower, 9 March 1944, *Aggressive and Determined Leadership*, #280, n. 1; Pogue interview with Smith, 13 May 1947.

23. Somervell to Eisenhower, 11 May 1944, Lutes Papers, DDEL.

24. David Irving interview with Buel Weare, 28 October 1979, in Irving, *Papers Relating to the Allied High Command.*

25. Patton to Beatrice Patton, 20 February 1944, *Patton Papers, 1940–1945,* 418.

26. Lee, *Service Reminiscences.*

27. Eisenhower to Lee, 26 May 1944, *EP,* #1714.

28. Hughes Diary, 22, 24, 26 May 1944.

29. Smith [for Eisenhower] to Bradley, Spaatz, and Lee, "Organization and Command of US Forces on the Continent," 28 May 1944, Hughes Papers.

30. Lee to Eisenhower, 29 May 1944, Hughes Papers.

31. Hughes Diary, 31 May and 1 June 1944.

32. Crawford to Smith, 2 June 1944, Hughes Papers.

33. Hughes, "Organization of ETO," 2 June 1944, Hughes Papers.

34. Eisenhower conference with Moses, 27 September 1945, and Smith conference with Moses, 25 September 1945, GBR, "Organization of the European Theater of Operations," 36.

35. Hughes Diary, 3 June 1944.

36. Most of the participants and observers of these fateful meetings—Eisenhower, Tedder, Ramsay, Strong, de Guingand, Stagg, and Smith—offered their own published accounts. See Smith, *Eisenhower's Six Great Decisions.* Robb took notes and immediately wrote an account; a copy is contained in Pogue's interview collection, MHI.

37. Eisenhower, "Memorandum," 3 June 1944, *EP,* #1732.

38. Eisenhower to CCS, 4 June 1944, *EP,* #1733. The best account is François Kersaudy, *Churchill and de Gaulle* (London, 1981), 34–36.

39. Cunningham Diary, 5 June 1944; Ismay, *Sunday Telegraph,* 13 August 1961.

40. Smith, *Eisenhower's Six Great Decisions,* 55.

41. Ibid., 53.

42. Smith to Eisenhower, 5 May 1944, Chief of Staff's Official Correspondence File, 1942–1944, WBSP; Butcher, *Three Years with Eisenhower,* 562–63.

43. McClure, "Journal, 1943–45," 5 June 1944, MHI.

44. Smith [for Eisenhower] to Bradley, Spaatz, and Lee, "Organization and Command of United States Forces on the Continent," 6 June 1944, Hughes Papers.

45. Given the rivalries that emerged in Europe between operational headquarters and the Communications Zone, the General Board Reports—one with Bradley's G-4 as the lead author, the other authored by Lee's chief of staff—differ sharply but agree on the confusion emerging from Eisenhower's unwillingness to define spheres of command and control. GBR, "Organization of the European Theater of Operations," 56–57, 73–74; "Mechanics of Supply," 1, 7–8; "Organization and Function of the Communication Zone in the European Theater," 5–8.

46. Donovan to Smith, 8 February 1944, 1944 Chief of Staff Personal Correspondence, WBSP.

47. Wertenbaker, "The Invasion Plan."

28. Normandy Deadlock

1. GEN Alfred Jodl commented, "after the destruction of Army Group Center, there could no longer be any question of reinforcements from the East." The view from the "other side of the hill" is derived from the interrogations of German generals, principally Jodl. Combined interview with Keitel and Jodl and Warlimont, in Interviews of Senior German Officers, WBSP.

2. Drew Middleton, review of Richard Lamb's *Montgomery in Europe, 1943-1945*, *New York Times*, 4 March 1985.

3. Hughes Diary, 7 and 9 June 1944.

4. Butcher, *Three Years with Eisenhower*, 574–75.

5. Lord to Crawford, 9 June 1944, and Hughes, "Memo for Lee," 8 June 1944, both in Hughes Papers.

6. Hughes, "Memo for Lee," 9 June 1944, Hughes Papers.

7. Ambassador John Winant to Hull, 8 June 1944, and Roosevelt to Churchill, 12 June 1944, *FRUS, 1944, The British Commonwealth and Europe*, 701, 707; Smith [for Eisenhower] to CCS, 9 June 1944, *EP*, #1745.

8. Burgess interview.

9. Excerpts from Montgomery's text at the St. Paul's conference are from Hamilton, *Monty: Master of the Battlefield*, 577.

10. Roger Cirillo provided invaluable help in clarifying command and operational questions in this chapter. In addition to offering advice and documentation, he gave me a copy of his "Numbers and Operational Decision Making in Normandy," an unpublished paper he presented in Calgary.

11. Pogue interview, 8 and 9 May 1947. In Smith's opinion, Normandy went according to type but not to plan. Montgomery always planned for penetration battles; he favored direct attacks because they were manageable. "But he wins his battles by wide envelopments he never planned." Montgomery, M-501, 14 June 1944, Orlando Ward File, PPP. Ward served as chief of military history immediately after the war, and this file contains most of Montgomery's M cables.

12. Later, in August, de Guingand's American aide, CPT William Culver, was asked, "What really stopped Montgomery's attack?" He replied that the British commanders "feel the blood of the British Empire, and hence its future, is too precious to waste in battle." Butcher Diary, 10 August 1944.

13. Lord Hay invited "the Gentlemen of the French Guards, [to] fire first" at the battle of Fontenot; the British lost. Lord Ponsonby died in command of the Union Brigade at Waterloo; he lost a race against a Polish Lancer because he left his best mounts back in his stables in Ireland. Cardigan commanded the Charge of the Light Brigade.

14. Montgomery to Brooke, "Some Notes on Morale," August 1943, *Montgomery and the Eighth Army*, 268.

15. As Smith told Drew Middleton, "As the British say, 'Monty wasn't everybody's cup of tea' but everybody including the Germans, they knew his quality and, of course, they didn't have to suffer that supreme ego. We did." Cited in Middleton's review of Nigel Hamilton's *Monty: Master of the Battlefield, New York Times*, 16 April 1984.

16. Some historians claim the bocage caught the Allied commanders off guard—another example of not looking beyond the beaches. Smith discounts this. He told Pogue that Brooke was always dismissive of plans for offensive operations in the American sector. He had retreated through the bocage country in 1940. Pogue interview, 9 May 1947.

17. As Smith remarked in 1947, "You can't depend absolutely on the airmen in regard to Monty. They hated him and were inclined to overlook his abilities." Pogue interview, 8 May 1947.

18. Eisenhower to Wilson, 16 June 1944, *EP*, #1755; Cunningham Diary, 13 June 1944.

19. Pogue interview, 8 May 1947.

20. De Guingand to Smith, 13 June 1944, 1944 Chief of Staff's Personal Correspondence, WBSP.

21. Montgomery Diary, 17–22 August 1943, in Hamilton, *Monty: Master of the Battlefield*, 371.

22. That day, Coningham told a commander's meeting, "The Army plan had failed." Tedder, *With Prejudice*, 553.

23. Pogue interview with Morgan, 3 February 1947, MHI.

24. Montgomery, M-501, 14 June 1944, in Hamilton, *Monty: Master of the Battlefield*, 645. Montgomery informed the War Office's director of military operations on 14 June, "All quite O.K. and I am very happy about the situation." Montgomery to MG Frank Simpson, 14 June 1944, in Hamilton, *Monty: Master of the Battlefield*, 653.

25. Eisenhower to Smith, 16 June 1944, *EP*, #1754.

26. GBR, "Mechanics of Supply," 14–15.

27. Ibid., 39–40.

28. The army groups did not command ComZ elements but were charged with maintaining close liaison with the advance sections of Lee's organization. SHAEF, "Organization of US Forces on the Continent," 14 July 1944, in GBR, "Mechanics of Supply," 7–8.

29. Hughes memos, 14 and 16 June 1944, "Far Shore—SOS," 19 June 1944, Hughes Papers.

30. Bradley to Eisenhower, 15 June 1944, Bradley File, PPP.

31. De Gaulle sent his account of his conversation with Eisenhower through SHAEF channels to Algiers, as reported by the acting U.S. representative to the FCNL. Chapin to Hull, 10 June 1944, *FRUS, The British Commonwealth and Europe*, 704–5.

32. Winant to Hull, 19 June 1944, *FRUS, The British Commonwealth and Europe*, 715; Pogue, *Supreme Command*, 231–36.

33. Montgomery, M-502, 18 June 1944, in Hamilton, *Monty: Master of the Battlefield*, 663–65; Stacey, *Victory Campaign*, 147; Montgomery to Simpson, 18 June 1944, in Hamilton, *Monty: Master of the Battlefield*, 663.

34. Keitel and Jodl interviews, Interviews of Senior German Officers, WBSP.

35. Interview with MG von Gersdorff, Seventh Army chief of staff, ibid.

36. Keitel and Jodl and Warlimont interviews, ibid.

37. Montgomery, M-504, 19 June 1944, in Stacey, *Victory Campaign*, 145; J. Lawton Collins, *Lightning Joe* (Baton Rouge, LA, 1979), 220.

38. *The Administrative History of the Operations of 21 Army Group on the Continent of Europe, 6 Jun 1944–8 May 1945* (Germany, 1945), 10.

39. John S. D. Eisenhower, *Strictly Personal* (New York: 1974), 56, 66.

40. Eisenhower to Montgomery and Eisenhower to Tedder, 25 June 1944, *EP*, #1774, #1778.

41. Smith to Montgomery, 22 June 1944, Montgomery Diary, in Hamilton, *Monty: Master of the Battlefield*, 584.

42. Montgomery, M-30, 25 June 1944, Ward File, PPP.

43. Smith [for Eisenhower] to CCS, 23 June 1944, *EP*, #1770.

44. SHAEF, "Stabilization of NEPTUNE Area," 7 June 1944, in *Survey of Allied Planning*, 2:101–2.

45. Eisenhower to Marshall, 29 June 1944, *EP*, #1785.

46. Cunningham Diary, 26 June 1944; cables in John Ehrman, *Grand Strategy*,

August 1943-September 1944, History of the Second World War (London, 1956), 351–52.

47. Smith [for Eisenhower] to CCS, 26 June 1944, *EP*, #1780.

48. Brooke categorized the American note as "rude." Brooke Diary and Cunningham Diary, 28 June 1944.

49. The exchange is in Winston Churchill, *Triumph and Tragedy* (Boston, 1953), 352–58, 723. Marshall to Eisenhower, 28 June 1944, Chief of Staff's Official Correspondence File, 1942–1944, WBSP.

50. Brooke Diary and Cunningham Diary, 30 June 1944.

51. Eisenhower to Bradley, 27 June 1944, *EP*, #1782.

52. Hughes Diary, 27 June 1944.

53. Butcher Diary, 27 June 1944; Hughes to Bradley, 28 June 1944, Hughes Papers.

54. Montgomery, M-505, 30 June 1944, in Stacey, *Victory Campaign*, 653.

55. Montgomery to Brooke, "System of Command in France," 7 July 1944, in Hamilton, *Monty: Master of the Battlefield*, 693.

56. Smith to BG T. J. Davis, 3 July 1944, 1944 Chief of Staff's Personal Correspondence, WBSP; Butcher, *Three Years with Eisenhower*, 604.

57. Gilmer to Burgess, 14 January 1944, SGS File, WBSP.

58. Brooke Diary, 6 July 1944.

59. Tedder, *With Prejudice*, 557, 559; Butcher, *Three Years with Eisenhower*, 605.

60. SHAEF [for Eisenhower] to Montgomery, 7 July 1944, *EP*, #1807. Smith and Bull discuss SHAEF's concerns in "Answers by Smith and Bull to Questions Posed by Members of the Historical Section, ETO," 14 and 15 September 1945, Office of the Chief of Military History, in Martin Blumenson, *Breakout and Pursuit*, USAWWII (Washington, DC, 1961), 5.

61. Montgomery to Eisenhower, 8 July 1944, in Hamilton, *Monty: Master of the Battlefield*, 706–7.

62. Interview with Dempsey, Papers of Reginald William Winchester ("Chester") Wilmot, LHCMA, provided by Roger Cirillo.

63. Smith to Montgomery and Bradley, "NEPTUNE: Capture of Area Required to Implement the Project of CHASTITY," 23 April 1944, and Twenty-first Army Group Plans to Bradley, "Responsibility for Planning Operation CHASTITY," 19 May 1944, in *Survey of Allied Planning*, 2:93–95; SHAEF War Diary, 22 June 1944; Twenty-first Army Group, "Operation No. 1 APDC," 27 June 1944, GBR, "Strategy on the Campaign in Western Europe," 30; Eisenhower to Smith, "Future Operations," 6 July 1944, SGS File, WBSP.

64. Hughes, "Points of Discussion with General Eisenhower," 4 July 1944, Hughes Papers.

65. Lee, *Service Reminiscences*, 94.

66. Patton to Eisenhower, 7 July 1944, Patton Papers.

67. Hughes Diary and "Memo for Eisenhower," 7 July 1944, Hughes Papers.

68. Hughes Diary and "Relationship between the Communications Zone Commander and the Senior US Field Force Commander on the Continent," 9 July 1944, Hughes Papers.

69. Butcher Diary, 11 July 1944; Tedder, *With Prejudice*, 559.

70. Montgomery, M-510, 10 July 1944, in Hamilton, *Monty: Master of the Battlefield*, 709–10.

71. Theodore Roosevelt to Smith, 23 October and 30 December 1943, 1944 Chief of Staff's Personal Correspondence, WBSP.

72. Hughes Diary, 14 July 1944.

73. Eisenhower to Bradley, 14 July 1944, *EP*, #1828; SHAEF to First Army, Communication Zone, USSTAF, "Organization of US Forces on the Continent," 14 July 1944, SHAEF File, WBSP.

74. Hughes and Butcher Diaries, 17 July 1944.

75. Eisenhower to Smith, 18 July 1944, *EP*, #1842.

76. Hughes Diary, 17 and 18 July 1944; Butcher Diary, 19 July 1944.

77. Tedder, *With Prejudice*, 562; Butcher Diary, 20 and 25 July 1944.

78. Ibid., 13 and 14 July 1944.

79. Ibid., 13 July 1944; Butcher, *Three Years with Eisenhower*, 612.

80. Butcher, *Three Years with Eisenhower*, 614. Tedder used the same language in a 25 July letter to Lord Trenchard; see *With Prejudice*, 571.

81. Butcher tells the whole story of Eisenhower's high blood pressure scare in his diary, 17, 19, and 20 July 1944. It never made it into the book, other than Butcher's comment that Eisenhower slept almost the entire day of 19 July. Butcher, *Three Years with Eisenhower*, 617–18.

82. Butcher, *Three Years with Eisenhower*, 618–19.

83. For Kenner's treatment of Patton, see Ruth Ellen Patton Totten, *The Button Box: A Daughter's Loving Memoir of Mrs. George S. Patton* (Columbia, MO, 2005), 306; and D'Este, *Patton: A Genius for War*, 368.

84. Butcher Diary, 19 July 1944.

85. Simpson of the War Office thought Eisenhower refused to confront Montgomery because he "knew jolly well that if he went to Monty, Monty would run circles round him with a clear exposition of his strategy and tactics." Hamilton interview with Simpson, cited in *Monty: Master of the Battlefield*, 752.

86. Tedder, *With Prejudice*, 566–67.

87. Eisenhower to Montgomery, 21 July 1944, in Pogue, *Supreme Command*, 190.

88. Butcher Diary, 20 July 1944. On de Guingand, see Hamilton interview with de Guingand, 7 May 1978, in *Monty: Master of the Battlefield*, 724–25. De Guingand was shocked by the suggestion: "I couldn't have done it: there is all the difference in the world between being a chief of staff and a commander." Cited in Charles Richardson, *Send for Freddie: The Story of Monty's Chief of Staff* (London, 1987), 158–59. Brigadier Richardson served as chief of plans in Twenty-first Army Group.

89. Montgomery made this point to a postwar interviewer. Nigel Hamilton, *Monty: The Field Marshal, 1944-1976* (London, 1986), 33.

90. Brigadier A. L. Pemberton, *The Development of Artillery Tactics and Equipment. The Second World War, 1939-1945* (War Office, 1950), 225–26. On 24 July the commander of British First Corps told Crerar that the Highland Division was "not fit for battle." Crerar, "Memo of Conversation," 24 July 1944, cited in Stephen Hart, "Montgomery, Morale, Casualty Conservation and 'Colossal Cracks': 21st Army Group's Operational Technique in North-West Europe, 1944-45," in *Military Power: Land Warfare in Theory and Practice*, ed. Brian Holder Reid (London, 1997), 137–38.

91. Stacey, *Victory Campaign*, 174–76.

92. Dempsey told Pogue, "Monty realized that the attack was open to exaggeration and for this reason gave me one of the first written orders I ever received, in which the limited nature of the attack was made clear." Dempsey interview with Pogue, 4 February 1947, MHI.

93. Smith, *Eisenhower's Six Great Decisions*, 73. Smith made the same argument ten years earlier in the *Saturday Evening Post*, 15 June 1946. Eisenhower provided a

similar account in his *Report by the Supreme Commander to the Combined Chiefs of Staff* (Washington, DC, 1946), 41. In truth, virtually all planning that contained a component for the sealing off of Brittany foresaw a breakout in the vicinity of St. Lô, including one presented by the Free French as early as October 1941.

94. Rommel's letter and Kluge's cover letter are in Liddell Hart, *Rommel Papers*, 486–87.

95. Smith [for Eisenhower] to First Army, Communication Zone, USSTAF, "Organization of U.S. Forces," 19 July 1944, Hughes Papers.

96. Hughes Diary, 21 July 1944.

97. Eisenhower to Smith, "Memo to Chief of Staff, SHAEF," 21 July 1944, Hughes Papers.

98. Hughes Diary, 21 July 1944.

99. WBS to Barker, Betts, Bull, and Crawford, "Administration of American Theater," 22 July 1944, and Lord to Chiefs of General and Special Staff Sections, 23 July 1944, Hughes Papers.

100. Lee had already activated his headquarters on 17 July. "In spite of directives and agreements" a GBR stated, "there was still considerable question as to just what the US administration set-up actually would be on the continent after the early days of the invasion, and when FUSAG became operational on the continent." The board concluded, "in retrospect . . . each of these decisions led to uncertainties with respect to functions and responsibilities." GBR, "Organization and Function of the Communication Zone," 73, 78.

101. Hughes Diary, 26 July 1944.

102. Butcher Diary, 25 July 1944.

103. Butcher, *Three Years with Eisenhower*, 623.

104. Ibid., 625.

105. Tedder to Eisenhower, 23 July 1944, in Tedder, *With Prejudice*, 568–70.

106. Butcher Diary, 25 July 1944.

107. Butcher, *Three Years with Eisenhower*, 624.

108. Brooke Diary, 26 and 27 July 1944. Percy Grigg, the British secretary of state for war, warned Montgomery about the ongoing RAF attack against him. "Bedell—who seems to have become very conceited and very sour—listens too readily to the poison." Grigg to Montgomery, 27 July 1944, Papers of Sir Percy Grigg, Correspondence with Montgomery, CAC.

29. What Has the Supreme Command Amounted To?

1. Jodl, Interviews of Senior German Officers, WBSP.

2. Warlimont, Interviews of Senior German Officers, WBSP.

3. Eisenhower to Montgomery, 31 July 1944, *EP,* #1873.

4. Pogue interview, 8 May 1947; Smith to Eisenhower, 1 April 1948, Smith File, PPP.

5. Warlimont interview.

6. Bradley, *Soldier's Story,* 375–76.

7. Butcher, *Three Years with Eisenhower*, 632.

8. Eisenhower to Marshall and CCS, 2 August 1944, *EP,* #1876.

9. Butcher, *Three Years with Eisenhower*, 632.

10. Montgomery to Brooke, 6 August 1944, in Hamilton, *Monty: Master of the Battlefield,* 760.

11. Montgomery, M-517, 6 August 1944, ibid., 761.

12. Pogue interview, 8 May 1947.

13. Eisenhower to Marshall, 7 August 1944, *EP,* #1886.

14. Eisenhower memo, 8 August 1944, *EP,* #1884. The editors of Eisenhower's published papers date the memo 6–7 August, despite references to 8 August, including "on a visit to Bradley today." Eisenhower spent 6 and 7 August in Portsmouth; his meeting with Bradley took place on 8 August. Tedder, *With Prejudice,* 575; Bradley, *Soldier's Story,* 369–72.

15. Warlimont interview.

16. Interview with GEN Johannes Blaskowitz, Interviews of Senior German Officers, WBSP. Blaskowitz commanded Army Group G.

17. Butcher Diary, 11 August 1944; Cunningham Diary, 5 July 1944.

18. Cunningham Diary, 4–5 August 1944.

19. Butcher, *Three Years with Eisenhower,* 634–35.

20. Ibid., 614–15; Eisenhower to Marshall, 5 August 1944, *EP,* #1883.

21. Pogue interview, 9 May 1947.

22. BCOS to JCS, 5 August 1944; Wilson to SHAEF and CCS to Eisenhower, 7 August 1944; and Smith [for Eisenhower] to CCS, 8 August 1944, Incoming Cable Log, WBSP.

23. Cunningham Diary, 8–9 August 1944; Brooke Diary, 15 August 1944.

24. Butcher, *Three Years with Eisenhower,* 639.

25. Eisenhower to Marshall, 11 August 1944, *EP,* #1892.

26. Cunningham Diary, 11 August 1944. See also Ehrman, *Grand Strategy, August 1943–September 1944,* 362–67.

27. Eisenhower to Marshall, 17 August 1944, *EP,* #1898; Eisenhower to Marshall, 24 August 1944, and Eisenhower to Smith, "Command Organization," 22 August 1944, SGS File, in Blumenson, *Breakout and Pursuit,* 685.

28. Butcher Diary, 19 August 1944.

29. Bradley, *Soldier's Story,* 375–78. Bradley doubtlessly exaggerated the number of German divisions because SHAEF and the commands possessed no clear picture of the German order of battle. For starters, nineteen divisions would not fit into the space. Smith and Bull defended Bradley's decision to army historians. Exercising the license of hindsight, they maintained that a more ambitious plan would have disrupted efforts to get "U.S. and British forces lined up and started together going east." Smith and Bull are cited in Blumenson, *Breakout and Pursuit,* 506 n. 2.

30. Somervell Diary, 22 August 1944, RG 160, Records of Headquarters/ASF, NARA.

31. Somervell Diary, "Trip to Europe 8–27 August 1944."

32. Eisenhower to Marshall, 24 August 1944, *EP,* #1910.

33. Interviews with senior German generals, chiefly Jodl, Warlimont, and Blaskowitz.

34. Montgomery, M-99, 17–18 August 1944, in Hamilton, *Monty: Master of the Battlefield,* 784.

35. Recollections of GEN Frank Simpson, in Hamilton, *Monty: Master of the Battlefield,* 785.

36. Ismay to Smith, 17 August 1944, Chief of Staff's Personal Papers, 1942–44, WBSP.

37. Marshall to Eisenhower, 17 August 1944, *Aggressive and Determined Leadership,* #480; Butcher, *Three Years with Eisenhower,* 647.

38. Francis de Guingand, *Operation Victory* (London, 1947), 411–12.

39. Eisenhower told Montgomery, "All the supply people have assured us they can support the move, beginning this minute." Eisenhower to Montgomery, 24 August 1944, *EP,* #1909.

40. A summary of "Notes on Future Operations" is in Hamilton, *Monty: Master of the Battlefield,* 793–94.

41. Montgomery, *Memoirs,* 266–69; de Guingand's account of the day's proceedings is in his *Operation Victory,* 411–12.

42. Montgomery to Nye, M-521, 26 August 1944, in Hamilton, *Monty: Master of the Battlefield,* 797. In 1979 Belchem insisted that Bradley had agreed with Montgomery's 17 August directive. Brigadier David Belchem served as chief planner in Twenty-first Army Group. Belchem to David Irving, 29 December 1979, in Irving, *Papers Relating to the Allied High Command, 1943-1945.*

43. Pogue interview, 8 May 1947.

44. Blumenson, *Patton Papers, 1940-1945,* 526–27.

45. Montgomery to Brooke, 9 August 1944, in Hamilton, *Monty: Master of the Battlefield,* 781.

46. Twenty-first Army Group War Diary, "Appreciation," 22 August 1944, War Office, WO 205/8, PRO, in Hamilton, *Monty: Field Marshal,* 13.

47. In a review of *Crusade in Europe,* de Guingand remarked that after Normandy, Twenty-first Army Group could not undertake any major offensive using its own resources. De Guingand, "Eisenhower's Own War Story," *Sunday Graphic,* 2 January 1949.

48. Days before D-day, a SHAEF directive foresaw the necessity of attaching at least one American reinforced corps to Twenty-first Army Group. Smith [for Eisenhower] to Montgomery, Bradley, Ramsay, and Leigh-Mallory, "Command and Organization after D-day of OVERLORD," 1 June 1944, *Survey of Allied Planning,* 2:98–99.

49. Montgomery to Nye, M-521, 26 August 1944, in Hamilton, *Monty: Master of the Battlefield,* 799–802. See also Eisenhower to Montgomery, 24 August 1944, *EP,* #1909.

50. Smith told Pogue that SHAEF executed "the most careful logistical studies which showed us it was impossible." Perhaps guilty of too much hindsight, he said the best Montgomery could hope for was a bridgehead over the Rhine at the expense of the failure to open Antwerp. In Smith's estimate, Montgomery could not possibly have stayed across the Rhine without Antwerp, and it is doubtful that he could have reached the Rhine. Pogue interview, 9 May 1947.

51. Patton Diary, 23 August 1944.

52. Eisenhower to Montgomery, and Eisenhower to Marshall, 24 August 1944, *EP,* #1909–10.

53. Eisenhower to Marshall, 2 and 9 August 1944, *EP,* #1876, #1889; Marshall to Eisenhower, 11 August 1944, in Ruppenthal, *Logistical Support of the Armies,* 2:277.

54. SHAEF G-4, "Aide-Mémoire on Quiberon Bay Project," 15 June 1944, in Ruppenthal, *Logistical Support of the Armies,* 1:470; SHAEF G-3 [Bull] to Com Z, "Analysis of Build-up from D to D Plus 90," 9 August 1944, Harold R. Bull Papers, DDEL; Brigadier G. C. Ravenhill, "Logistics in Northwest Europe, 1944-1945," *Journal of the Royal United Service Institute* (November 1946), reprinted in *Military Review* (November 1947): 73–78; Frank Osmanski, "The Logistical Planning for OVERLORD," *Military Review* (November 1949): 31–40 and (January 1950): 50–62; Seymour Potter, "Quiberon Bay," *Military Review* (September 1951): 45–53; Harold Mack, "The Critical Error of World War II," *National Security Affairs,* Issue Paper 81-1, February 1981; Roland Ruppenthal, "Logistical Limitations in Tactical Decisions," *Military Review*

(August 1957): 3–9. Ravenhill, Osmanski, Potter, and Mack all served on logistics planning staffs.

55. Eisenhower to Marshall, 2 August 1944, *EP,* #1876.

56. SHAEF abandoned Operations Beneficiary and Handsup in mid-July. SHAEF, "BRITTANY," 14 July 1944, and Twenty-first Army Group, "Summary of Conclusions," 9 August 1944, in *Survey of Allied Planning,* 2:110–11; Eisenhower to Marshall, 17 and 22 August 1944, *EP,* #1898, #1907.

57. ComZ established a discharge rate of 21,800 tons per day on 24 July; on 16 August, a month after the first ships arrived in Cherbourg, the Normandy base section cleared 10,000 tons. Henry Aurand, "History of Normandy Base Section," unpublished manuscript, Henry S. Aurand Papers, DDEL.

58. GBR, "Mechanics of Supply," 11. Another report concluded that "all the [Overlord] planning came to nothing." GBR, "Supply and Maintenance in the European Theater," 23–24.

59. Bradley, *Soldier's Story,* 312–13.

60. Eisenhower to Ramsay, Montgomery, Bradley, Leigh-Mallory, Brereton, Spaatz, Harris, and Smith, 29 August 1944, *EP,* #1920.

61. Major Sylvan, First Army Diary, 28 August 1944, MHI.

62. Eisenhower to Ramsay, Montgomery, Bradley, Leigh-Mallory, Brereton, Spaatz, Harris, and Smith, 29 August 1944, *EP,* #1920.

63. Eisenhower to Pogue, 10 March 1947, Pogue File, PPP.

64. By 28 August, ComZ had formed four base sections: Normandy (7 August), Brittany in Rennes (16 August), Seine (27 August), and Loire (28 August). ComZ's FECZ was never activated. According to the plan, the FECZ would develop into the intermediate section, complete with regulating stations, but this did not take place until late March 1945. The ADSEC moved forward, providing direct support for Twelfth Army Group. Lee's headquarters remained at Valognes, just south of Cherbourg.

65. Smith conference with Moses, 25 September 1945; GBR, "Organization of the European Theater of Operations," 36, 64–65, 75–78, 81; GBR, "Organization and Function of the Communication Zone," 5.

66. Pogue, *Supreme Command,* 240–43, 319–20; Smith to Bradley, 3 September 1944, Outgoing Cable Log, WBSP.

67. Smith to Donovan, 8 August 1944, Morgan to Donovan, 24 August 1944, in SHAEF War Diary.

68. Smith to Lord Shelbourne, 9 August 1944; Smith to BCOS and Shelbourne, 14 August 1944, SHAEF War Diary. Smith later joked about finding a good use for propaganda drops. The Psychological Warfare Division dropped four tons of propaganda in Marseilles and managed to sink a ship. Smith to Handy, 23 September 1944, Personal Papers, 1943–44, WBSP.

69. "Relationship between SHAEF and the United States and British Elements of the Control Commission/Council for Germany," 21 August 1944, and Smith to CCS, 22 August 1944, SHAEF War Diary.

70. Smith to Hilldring, 4 July 1944, Chief of Staff Personal Papers, 1942–1944, WBSP.

30. End the War in '44

1. Eisenhower's clearest exposition of his thinking, stripped of the saccharine language that appears in *Crusade in Europe,* appears in a five-page memo he wrote for

Pogue. After Pogue completed his interviews with senior British officers in February 1947, he passed them on to Eisenhower for comment. Badly stung by the opinions expressed, particularly by Brooke, Belchem, and LTG Guy Simonds, on his conduct of the campaign in France, Eisenhower answered their charges with uncharacteristic candor. Belchem served as director of plans and later as chief of operations in Twenty-first Army Group; Simonds commanded a Canadian corps and, for a period, Canadian First Army. Eisenhower to Pogue, 10 March 1947, Pogue File, PPP, copy in WBSP.

2. Eisenhower to MG Herbert Brees, 28 February 1944, *EP*, #1573.

3. Smith, *Eisenhower's Six Great Decisions*, 211; Eisenhower, *Crusade in Europe*, 229.

4. The lone major exception is the muted criticism offered by Ruppenthal in his official history and an article in *Military Review*.

5. Eisenhower to Pogue, 10 March 1947.

6. Brooke Diary, 30 August 1944.

7. Blumenson, *Patton Papers, 1940-1945*, 537.

8. Diary of Chester B. Hansen, 2 September 1944, MHI.

9. First Army Diary, 2 September 1944.

10. Summersby, *Eisenhower Was My Boss*, 180.

11. Montgomery to Brooke, M-156, 3 September 1944, in Hamilton, *Monty: Field Marshal*, 21.

12. First Army Diary, 3 September 1944.

13. Montgomery, M-160, 4 September 1944, *EP*, #1935 n. 1; M-161, 4 September 1944, in Hamilton, *Monty: Field Marshal*, 24.

14. Eisenhower to Ramsay, Montgomery, Bradley, Leigh-Mallory, Brereton, Spaatz, and Harris, 4 September 1944, *EP*, #1933.

15. Eisenhower to Marshall, 24 August 1944, *EP*, #1910.

16. Twenty-first Army Group War Diaries, War Office 205/5B, PRO, cited in Hamilton, *Monty: Field Marshal*, 12.

17. Ruppenthal, "Logistics and the Broad-Front," in *Command Decisions*, 419–28.

18. Betts oral history; Smith to Hilldring, 6 November 1944, Chief of Staff Personal Papers, WBSP; Pogue interview with C. H. H. Vulliamy, 22 January 1947, MHI. MG Vulliamy served as chief signals officer in SHAEF.

19. Pogue interview with Gale, 27 January 1947, MHI.

20. Pogue interview, 9 May 1947; Strong, *Intelligence at the Top*, 199–200.

21. Smith [for Eisenhower] to Montgomery, 5 September 1944, *EP*, #1935. Whiteley and Bull also had a part in composing the letter.

22. Eisenhower, Office Memo, 5 September 1944, *EP*, #1936.

23. Eisenhower to Pogue, 10 March 1947.

24. Eisenhower to Pogue, 10 March 1947; Eisenhower's emphasis. A Smith-authored 1 June directive to the commanders foresaw the necessity of attaching at least one reinforced corps to Twenty-first Army Group. Smith [for Eisenhower] to Montgomery, Bradley, Ramsay, and Leigh-Mallory, 1 June 1944, in *Survey of Allied Planning*, 2:98–99. The same communication designated Montgomery's and Bradley's forces as the northern and central groups of armies, respectively.

25. Eisenhower to Marshall, 14 September 1944, *EP*, #1953.

26. Pogue interview, 9 May 1947.

27. Smith to Eisenhower, 1 April 1948, WBSP.

28. Strong related his story to Brooke's military assistant, MAJ Peter Earle. Earle Diary, 7 September 1944, in Hamilton, *Monty: Field Marshal*, 25–26.

29. Interviews with Jodl, Warlimont, and Blaskowitz.

30. By way of contrast, Marseilles, the largest French port, cleared less than 4.4 million tons annually.

31. Montgomery to Brooke, 3 September 1944, in Hamilton, *Monty: Field Marshal*, 23.

32. War Diary, Army Group D and Second Army Intelligence Summaries Nos. 94 and 96, 7 and 9 September 1944, in Stacey, *Victory Campaign*, 302; Ralph Bennett, *Ultra in the West* (London, 1979), 143.

33. Second Army to SHAEF G-4, 30 August 1944, Records of 21 Army Group, WO 219/259, PRO, as cited in Twenty-first Army Group, *Administrative History* (London, n.d.), 47.

34. Montgomery to Crerar, 9 September 1944, in Hamilton, *Monty: Field Marshal*, 56–57.

35. Crerar's directive is reproduced in Stacey, *Victory Campaign*, 330. Stacey refers to the escape of the Fifteenth Army as "a considerable misfortune." He covers this period in a section entitled "The Germans Lose Antwerp but Save an Army," 301–3, 306–10.

36. Eisenhower to CCS, 9 September 1944, *EP*, #1939.

37. Pogue interview, 9 May 1947. Bradley told Patton: "I would not say this to anyone but you, and have given different excuses to my staff and higher echelons, but we must take Brest in order to maintain the illusion of the fact that the U.S. Army cannot be beaten." Patton fully concurred with this view. Blumenson, *Patton Papers, 1940-1945*, 532.

38. Eisenhower to CCS, 9 September 1944, *EP*, #1939.

39. Ruppenthal, "Logistical Limitations in Tactical Decisions," 3–9.

40. Interview statement of Smith, in *Survey of Allied Planning*, 2:143; Eisenhower to Marshall, 14 September 1944, *EP*, #1953.

41. According to a 30 July estimate, the Brittany ports of Brest, L'Orient, and St. Malo and the adjacent beaches at Cancale would off-load 13,800 tons of supply each day by D+120 (4 October). The Chastity plan for the facility in Quiberon Bay potentially added another 10,000 tons. Even with the Brittany ports, planners maintained that port capacity would not equal requirements until after D+180. Instead, all the Brittany ports unloaded something less than 3,000 by that date. Aide-mémoire, "Quiberon Bay Project," 15 June 1944, in Ruppenthal, *Logistical Support of the Armies*, 1:470.

42. GBR, "Supply and Maintenance in the European Theater," 23–24.

43. Montgomery to Brooke, M-524, 9–10 September 1944, in Hamilton, *Monty: Field Marshal*, 43–45.

44. Graham gave an account of the meeting to war correspondent Chester Wilmot on 19 January 1949. Wilmot, *Struggle for Europe*, 544.

45. Montgomery to Nye, M-186, 10 September 1944, in Hamilton, *Monty: Field Marshal*, 53. Tedder's account is in *With Prejudice*, 590–91.

46. In discussing this meeting, Montgomery engaged in some calculated deception in his *Memoirs*. He stated that the topic of Antwerp "was not, in fact, ever mentioned at our conference." He also claimed that only he, Eisenhower, and Tedder joined the discussions, purposely excluding Gale. Clearly, based on Gale's diary entry, he not only attended but also featured prominently in the deliberations. Montgomery, *Memoirs*, 289; Gale Diary, "Brussels," 10 September 1944, Gale Papers.

47. Tedder to Portal, 10 September 1944, in Tedder, *With Prejudice*, 591.

48. SHAEF War Diary, 11 September 1944.

49. Montgomery, M-192 and M-194, 11 September 1944, SGS File, in Hamilton, *Monty: Field Marshal,* 57.

50. Summersby Diary, 11 September 1944. Summersby kept an office diary from June through the end of 1944, copy in Summersby File, PPP.

51. Summersby Diary, 12 September 1944.

52. Smith reinforced these points with a new SHAEF study: Smith to Montgomery, "Supply Problems of Allied Advance," 15 September 1944, SGS Files, cited in Hugh Cole, *The Lorraine Campaign,* USAWWII (Washington, DC, 1950), 212.

53. SHAEF to Montgomery, 13 September 1944, *EP,* #1945.

54. Montgomery to Eisenhower, 12 September 1944, Montgomery File, PPP; Montgomery to Eisenhower, M-205, 14 September 1944, in Charles MacDonald, *The Siegfried Line Campaign,* USAWWII (Washington, DC, 1955), 129.

55. Crerar Diary, September 1944; Montgomery to Crerar, 12 and 13 September, and the 14 September directive are in Crerar File GOC-in-C, in Stacey, *Victory Campaign,* 330–31, 336.

56. Montgomery, M-532, 16 September 1944, complete text in Stacey, *Victory Campaign,* 655–56.

57. First Army Diary, 10 September 1944.

58. Hughes Diary, 12 September 1944.

59. Patton Diary, 30 August 1944.

60. George Patton, *War as I Knew It* (Boston, 1947), 125.

61. Blaskowitz interview, WBSP.

62. Eisenhower to Bradley, Leigh-Mallory, Brereton, Spaatz, Harris, Ramsay, and Montgomery, 13 September 1944, *EP,* #1946.

63. Eisenhower to Marshall, 14 September 1944, *EP,* #1953. He made the same points, with greater accentuation, in his 10 March 1947 memo to Pogue. The next day Devers assumed command of Sixth Army Group.

64. Bradley to Eisenhower, 14 September 1944, Bradley File, PPP.

65. Cited in David Eisenhower, *Eisenhower at War, 1943-1945* (New York, 1986), 466.

66. Hughes Diary, 13 September 1944.

67. Pogue interviews, 8 and 13 May 1947. "Patton screamed 'Give me the gas and I'll go to the Rhine,'" Smith told Pogue. Smith thought Patton might have done it, "but we wanted to go to the Rhine where we could cross into the area where we wanted to fight." Patton's axis of advance led to a strategic dead end.

68. Third Army required 450,000 gallons of gasoline a day; between 4 and 7 September it received 1.6 million gallons. After 4 September, with Haislip across the Meuse, supplies of POL fell back to about half of requirements.

69. First Army Diary, 6, 10–13, 17, 19–20 September 1944.

70. Hinsley, *British Intelligence in the Second World War,* 2:282–87; SHAEF, "Weekly Intelligence Summary," 16 September 1944, WBSP. None of this is as clear and dry as it appears. Wilmot, who enjoyed inside connections in Twenty-first Army Group headquarters, made the claim about the Dutch report, but no one has ever found any concrete documentation. Similarly, the official history suggests that Smith went forward and issued a warning to Montgomery, based on postwar interviews. Smith made no such trip. Wilmot, *Struggle for Europe,* 488; interview by ETO historians with Smith and Bull, 14 September 1945; S. L. A. Marshall interview with Smith, 18 April 1949, MHI, cited in MacDonald, *Siegfried Line Campaign,* 119–20.

71. Richardson, *Send for Freddie*, 165.

72. Eisenhower to Marshall, 14 September 194, *EP*, #1953.

73. Pogue interview, 9 May 1947.

74. Ibid.

75. Eisenhower to Montgomery, Bradley, Devers, Ramsay, Leigh-Mallory, and Tedder, 15 September 1944, *EP*, #1957.

76. Eisenhower to Marshall, 18 September 1944, *EP*, #1968.

77. Montgomery to Eisenhower, 18 September 1944; Eisenhower to Montgomery, 20 September 1944, and Montgomery to Eisenhower, M-223, 21 September 1944, Montgomery File, PPP.

78. Montgomery to Brooke, M-219, 20 September 1944, in Hamilton, *Monty: Field Marshal*, 76. Two British corps commanders suffered under the liability of prior service in the Mediterranean: LTG Brian Horrocks of XXX Corps (replacing the previous commander sacked in mid-August) was seriously wounded, and LTG Richard O'Connor of XIII Corps was captured and imprisoned. O'Connor attributed the lack of initiative in British units to the "victory disease." Nobody wanted to be the last casualty in a war already won. The British forces were not "prepared to take the same risks as they had earlier." Cited in Hart, "Montgomery, Morale, Casualty Conservation and 'Colossal Cracks,'" 138.

79. Montgomery to SHAEF-Forward, 20 September 1944, Butcher Diary; Montgomery to Eisenhower, 21 September 1944, Montgomery File, PPP.

80. On 3 October Smith apologized "for speaking out of turn" and admitted it was "most ungrateful to criticize the War Office which has helped us in every possible way." He maintained there existed "a lack of close contact which should exist" and wanted to correct the situation by extending an invitation to War Office officials to visit SHAEF. "You chaps are rather sensitive," he said, "and require a special invitation in each case." For the exchanges between Smith and Simpson, see Simpson to Smith, 24 September 1944, and Smith to Simpson, 3 October 1944, 1944 Chief of Staff's Personal Correspondence, WBSP; Eugene Wason interview with Simpson, in Hamilton, *Monty: Field Marshal*, 79–81.

81. Wason interview with Simpson.

82. Montgomery to Smith, 21 September 1944, Butcher Diary, reproduced in *EP*, #1979, n. 2. Montgomery omitted any mention of this letter in his *Memoirs*.

83. Wason interview with Simpson.

84. Bradley, *Soldier's Story*, 422–23.

85. Eisenhower to Montgomery, 25 September 1944, *EP*, #1994.

86. Hughes Diary, 22 September 1944.

87. De Guingand to Montgomery, 22 September 1944, copy forwarded to SHAEF, SGS File, WBSP.

88. Eisenhower to Bradley, 23 September 1944, *EP*, #1989.

89. Eisenhower to Montgomery, 24 September 1944, *EP*, #1993.

90. Bradley to Eisenhower, 25 September 1944, Bradley File, PPP.

91. Patton Diary, 23 and 27 September 1944, *Patton Papers, 1940-1945*, 557.

92. Hughes Diary, 26 September 1944.

93. Patton Diary, 27 September 1944, *Patton Papers, 1940-1945*, 557.

94. Pogue interview with Ford Trimble, 17 December 1946, MHI.

95. De Guingand to Smith, 26 September 1944; Montgomery, M-527 and Twenty-first Army Group, "General Operational Situation," 27 September 1944, all in SGS File, WBSP.

96. Eisenhower to Montgomery, 27 September 1944, SGS File, WBSP; Eisenhower to Smith, 30 September 1944, and Eisenhower to Bradley, 8 October 1944, *EP,* #2012, #2028.

97. At this juncture, Crerar was convalescing in England. Simonds held command of Canadian First Army.

98. De Guingand to Smith, 26 September 1944, SHAEF SGS File, WBSP.

99. Cited in Stacey, *Victory Campaign,* 424.

100. Eisenhower to Marshall, 2 September 1944, *EP,* #1930; Eisenhower to Arnold, 3, 14, and 27 September 1944, *EP,* #1931, #1954, #2004.

101. Pogue interview, 8 May 1947.

102. Pogue interview with Robb, 3 February 1947, MHI.

103. Pogue interview, 9 May 1947.

104. Smith, directive, 13 October 1944, SHAEF War Diary.

105. Frank Craven and James Cate, eds., *Argument to V-E Day,* AAFWWII (Washington, DC, 1983), 622.

106. Arnold to Eisenhower, 18 October 1944, and Eisenhower to Arnold, 26 October 1944, *EP,* #2070 n. 2.

107. Eisenhower to Smith, "Utilization of U.S. Elements of Supreme Command for Co-ordination of Activities in Which More Than One Major U.S. Command Is Involved," 3 October 1944, *EP,* #2020.

108. Eisenhower to Stark, 21 September 1944, Stark File, PPP.

109. Brooke Diary, 5 October 1944.

110. "I personally have no doubt from a purely administrative point of view," Graham wrote in 1947, that "it would have been possible to carry out successfully the operation which Field-Marshal Montgomery desired." Graham, *The Times,* 24 February 1947.

111. Brooke Diary, 5 October 1944.

112. Ramsay Diary, 5 October 1944, Papers of Admiral Sir Bertram Home Ramsay, CAC.

113. Montgomery to Smith, 7 October 1944, Eyes Only File, WBSP. Marshall and Tedder visited Montgomery's headquarters on 8 October. Montgomery reviewed the operational situation and furnished Tedder with his "Notes."

114. Bradley blocked the SHAEF-inspired transfer of the underperforming Seventh Armored. Bradley to Eisenhower, 7 October 1944, Bradley File, DDEL.

115. Eisenhower to Bradley, 8 October 1944, *EP,* #2028.

116. Montgomery, *Memoirs,* 254.

117. Pogue, *Marshall Interviews,* 345.

118. Smith [for Eisenhower] to Montgomery, 9 October 1944, *EP,* #2031.

119. De Guingand, *Generals at War* (London, 1964), 202; Stephen Ambrose interview of Morgan, 17 July 1965, cited in Ambrose, *Supreme Commander,* 525. In early November Montgomery told Grigg, "The Americans regard the acquisition of Antwerp as the solution to all our difficulties. I am afraid they will be greatly disappointed." Montgomery to Grigg, 3 November 1944, Grigg Papers.

120. Montgomery to Eisenhower, M-268, 9 October 1944, Eyes Only, WBSP. In the official history, MacDonald maintained Montgomery did not give Antwerp "unequivocal priority" until 16 October; Montgomery made the case in his memoirs that he received no such direction from Eisenhower until 9 October. MacDonald, *Siegfried Line Campaign,* 220; Montgomery, *Memoirs,* 256.

121. Montgomery to Smith, 10 October 1944, Eyes Only, WBSP; "Notes on Com-

mand in Western Europe," 10 October 1944, in Hamilton, *Monty: Field Marshall*, 110–11.

122. This point was made by Carlo D'Este, *Decision in Normandy* (New York, 1983), 262–63.

123. Pogue interview, 8 May 1947.

124. Whiteley and Smith [for Eisenhower] to Montgomery, 13 October 1944, *EP*, #2038.

125. Bradley, *Soldier's Story*, 433.

126. Smith drew Eisenhower's attention to the postscript in a margin note.

127. Montgomery to Eisenhower, M-281, 16 October 1944, Eyes Only, WBSP.

128. Stacey, *Victory Campaign*, 389.

31. "The Logistical Bottleneck Now Dictates Strategy"

1. Marshall, "Speech to the American Legion," 18 September 1944, *Aggressive and Determined Leadership*, #514.

2. First Army Diary, 16 November 1944.

3. Pogue interview, 13 May 1947.

4. Smith [for Eisenhower] to Lee, 16 September 1944, *EP*, #1963.

5. Lee defended his move to Paris in an unpublished manuscript. "Since [Eisenhower] held me responsible for communications with the War Department in Washington as well as with our ports through New York City, we tried and succeeded in maintaining promptly and effectively the best communications. Such could not have been done except in Paris." Lee, *Service Reminiscences*, 94.

6. Hughes Diary, 5 September 1944. Hughes exaggerated; ComZ headquarters and the Seine base section requisitioned 296 hotels.

7. Ibid.

8. Pogue interview, 13 May 1947.

9. Hughes Diary, 4 August 1944.

10. Bradley, *Soldier's Story*, 405–6.

11. Hughes Diary, 4 September 1944.

12. Pogue interview, 13 May 1947.

13. First Army Diary, 29 September 1944.

14. Lutes to DDE through Lee, "Official Report: Mission to European Theater of Operations, 4 December 1944–13 January 1945," 25 December 1944, RG-160, Records of Headquarters, ASF, NARA.

15. Lee thought the "need for integration [was] apparently forgotten between the wars" and used the Transportation Corps, formed only in 1942, as an example. The Transportation Corps, in Lee's view, acted as "almost the regulating factor in supply of both materiel and personnel replacements." Lee to Commanding General, General Board, 17 December 1945, GBR, "Organization of the European Theater of Operations," addendum.

16. GBR, "Mechanics of Supply," 32–33. As Brigadier A. E. Walford, Crerar's senior administrative officer, remarked on 7 September, a ten-ton truck was now worth more than a Sherman tank. Stacey, *Victory Campaign*, 300.

17. Lutes, "Army Supply Problems," 5 February and 23 September 1946, and "An Appraisal of the Logistical Lessons of World War II," 31 October 1946, Industrial College of the Armed Forces lectures, Lutes Papers.

18. Littlejohn to Lee, 20 August 1947, Littlejohn File, PPP.

19. Ruppenthal, *Logistical Support of the Armies,* 2:246–75, especially 255.

20. Lee to War Department, 23 September 1944, GCMP.

21. Lutes, "Army Supply Problems" and "An Appraisal of the Logistical Lessons of World War II."

22. Eisenhower to Mamie, 23 September 1944, in *Letters to Mamie.*

23. Montgomery to Eisenhower, 14 October 1944, Ward File, PPP.

24. An official historian who fought there found the Hürtgen "a misconceived and basically fruitless battle that could have, and should have, been avoided." Charles MacDonald, *The Battle of the Huertgen Forest* (New York, 1984), 205.

25. The rate of November casualties marginally exceeded those suffered in July in Normandy: 1,598 per day compared with 1,529. GBR, "Reinforcement System and Reinforcement Procedures in the European Theater of Operations," 20–21.

26. On 23 November Smith claimed that SHAEF lacked the resources to justify transferring any units from Bradley's command. Smith to Devers, 23 November 1944, SHAEF War Diary.

27. Pogue interview with Belchem, 2 February 1947, MHI.

28. Brooke Diary, 24 November 1944.

29. Pogue interview with Scarman, 25 February 1947, MHI.

30. Montgomery to Brooke, 17 and 21 November 1944, in Hamilton, *Monty: Field Marshal,* 139, 143–44. Brooke told a closed-door meeting of the BCOS on 24 November that Smith had been a party to telling Eisenhower "he must get down and RUN the war," but Montgomery mentioned only Whiteley in his correspondence to the CIGS.

31. W. Averell Harriman and Elie Abel, *Special Envoy to Churchill and Stalin* (New York, 1975), 773–74.

32. In the two months following the opening of his command post, Eisenhower spent thirty-two days in Versailles, seventeen visiting the front, nine at Gueux, and two in London.

33. Lutes to Somervell, 20 December 1944, Lutes Papers.

34. Smith, "Approval of Tonnage Allocations," 3 November 1944, SHAEF War Diary.

35. Caffery to Hull, 15 September 1944, and Hull to Roosevelt, 17 September 1944, *FRUS, 1944, The British Commonwealth and Europe,* 733–36.

36. Churchill to Roosevelt, 14 October 1944, and Roosevelt to Churchill, 19 October 1944, ibid., 740–41.

37. Caffery to Hull, 20 October 1944, ibid., 742–43; Smith to JCS, 20 October 1944, Eyes Only, WBSP.

38. Smith to GEN Roger-Alexandre-Louis Leyer, 2 October 1944, Morgan to Leyer, 7 October 1944, and Smith to GEN Alphonse-Pierre Juin, 12 October 1944, SHAEF War Diary. On 13 November 15,000 Senegalese troops were withdrawn from French First Army.

39. Smith memo, 16 October 1944, SHAEF War Diary.

40. Smith to French War Ministry, Juin, and de Gaulle, 29 October 1944; Smith to Juin, 31 October 1944, SHAEF War Diary.

41. Smith to SHAEF Mission to France, 6 November 1944, SHAEF War Diary; Marcel Vigneras, *Rearming the French,* USAWWII (Washington, DC, 1957), 229–34.

42. Smith to CCS, 14 September 1944; 19–23 October 1944; Smith to Pierlot, 27 October 1944; Smith to CCS, 4 November 1944, all in SHAEF War Diary.

43. Smith to CCS, 29 October 1944, *EP,* #2079.

44. Smith, memo, 29 October 1944, SHAEF War Diary.
45. According to Lutes, the suggestion that Marshall dispatch Clay, Lutes, and Aurand to Europe came from the combat commanders, most forcefully from Bradley. "Marshall had toured the theater and while visiting the field commanders received complaints about ComZ's failure." The senior commanders "knew all three of us and apparently wanted to see our services used in the ComZ of the European Theater." Lutes Notebook, 6 December 1944, "Mission to European Theater—Log of Trip to France," Lutes Papers.
46. Pogue, *Marshall Interviews,* 539.
47. Hughes Diary, 3 October 1944.
48. Marshall to Eisenhower, 25 October 1944, Marshall File, DDEL.
49. MG MacMahon, and BGs McKelvie, Martin, Barber, and Bohn.
50. Lutes to Somervell, 31 December 1944, Lutes Papers. Lutes reported on his long talk with Eisenhower on 30 December.
51. Smith told Horrocks that he "admired [Hodges] very much." Smith to Horrocks, 3 October 1944, Chief of Staff's Personal Papers, 1942–44, WBSP.
52. Montgomery to Brooke, 17 November 1944, in Hamilton, *Monty: Field Marshal,* 142.
53. Smith to Horrocks, 3 October 1944, WBSP.
54. Dragoon opened Marseilles and Toulon, but the SOLOC equipped Sixth Army Group and did not come under direct SHAEF control until the end of October.
55. The best brief discussion of the shipping bottleneck is in Randolph Leigh, *48 Million Tons to Eisenhower: The Role of SOS in the Defeat of Germany* (Washington, DC, 1945).
56. GBR, "Mechanics of Supply," 11, and "Supply and Maintenance in the European Theater," 23–24, summary.
57. Clay oral history, 14 December 1972, DDEL.
58. In addition to Clay, Eisenhower met with Hughes, Lord, and Gale on 30 October. Summersby Diary, 27 and 30 October 1944.
59. Hughes Diary, 15 November 1944.
60. Clay oral history; Aurand, "History of Normandy Base Section"; Frank Elder to Aurand, 14 September 1960, both in the Aurand Papers, DDEL. Colonel Elder served as chief of staff to both Clay and Aurand. The statistics are from Leigh, *48 Million Tons.*
61. Hughes Diary, 30 October 1944.
62. Unless otherwise noted, the account of Aurand's arrival in Paris, his inspection tour, and his clash with Smith are based on his oral history.
63. Aurand to his wife, 21 November 1944, Aurand Papers.
64. Hughes Diary, 31 October 1944.
65. Aurand listed himself, along with Clay and Lutes, as the best logisticians in the U.S. Army. Aurand oral history. Objecting to the inflation of major generals, Hughes pointed to "Henry Aurand for example." Hughes to Kate Hughes, 5 November 1942, Hughes Papers.
66. Hughes Diary, 4 November 1944.
67. Ibid., 9 November 1944.
68. Aurand to Henry Sayler, 12 November 1944, Aurand Papers. MG Sayler was the theater chief of ordnance and technically Aurand's superior.
69. Aurand to Sayler, 18 November 1944, Aurand Papers.
70. Aurand wrote an unpublished manuscript detailing his service in France; for

his account of the trip and his observations, see book manuscript, 15–19, Aurand Papers.

71. Aurand to Sayler, 18 November 1944, Aurand Papers.

72. Aurand to Sayler, 2 December 1944, Aurand Papers.

73. Hughes Diary, 18 November 1944.

74. Before the American entry into the war, Aurand produced a manning table for the WDGS G-4 Division calling for 700 officers. Senior War Department officials dismissed his estimate as wildly excessive. By summer 1944, the G-4 section had a complement of 2,400 officers. Aurand oral history.

75. Aurand, "SHAEF-ETOUSA-COMZ: A Lesson in Organization for National Defense," 1. Aurand submitted the article to *Logistics*, a publication of the Army Ordnance Association. The editor considered the piece too controversial for publication, especially Aurand's comments directed at Smith. John O'Connor, cover letter, 17 July 1946. Aurand's unfinished manuscript on his experiences in the European theater, also tentatively titled *SHAEF-ETOUSA-COMZ*, raised the same criticisms, especially the chapter "The Regular Army Officers vs. Logistics." All these sources are in the Aurand Papers.

76. Aurand oral history.

77. Aurand, "SHAEF-ETOUSA-COMZ: A Lesson in Organization for National Defense," 21.

78. Aurand, "The Regular Army Officers vs. Logistics."

79. Hughes Diary, 19 November 1944.

80. Aurand, book manuscript, 20–26.

81. Hughes Diary, 19 and 20 November 1944; Aurand, book manuscript, 26; Aurand to his wife, 21 and 30 November 1944, Aurand Papers.

82. Hughes Diary, 1 December 1944.

83. Ibid., 21 November 1944.

84. Pogue interview, 13 May 1947.

85. Clay oral history, 14 December 1972, DDEL.

86. Bradley to SHAEF, 21 November 1944, *EP,* #2130, n. 1.

87. Clay oral history; Lutes, "The Effects of Logistics upon Strategy," and "Army Supply Problems," Lutes Papers.

88. Somervell to Lutes, 12 December 1944, "Records Relating to Various Overseas Missions," Lutes Papers.

89. Hughes, "Army Ordnance Wartime Production Problems," lecture at Industrial College of the Armed Forces, 12 February 1948, Hughes Papers.

90. Lutes Diary, 6 December 1944, and Lutes to Somervell, 6 December 1944. Lutes wrote a memo to himself, "Comments in Private," 6–7 December 1944, recounting his meeting with Smith, in "Mission to European Theater—Log of Trip to France," Lutes Papers.

91. Somervell to Lutes, 12 December 1944, "Records Relating to Various Overseas Missions."

92. Lutes Diary, 7 and 8 December 1944, "Mission to European Theater."

93. Eisenhower memo, 23 December 1944, Butcher Diary, *EP,* #2198.

94. Lutes, "Army Supply Problems," 5 February 1946, 11–12; "An Appraisal of the Logistical Lessons of World War II"; and "Army Supply Problems," 6–7, 9.

95. Lutes Diary, 14–16 December 1944.

96. Lutes to Somervell, 6, 7, 17, 20, and 31 December 1944, Lutes Papers.

97. Eisenhower to CCS, 3 December 1944, *EP,* #2148.

98. Lee to Commanding General, General Board, 17 December 1945, GBR, "Organization of the European Theater of Operations," addendum; Lutes to Somervell, 20 December 1944.

32. Après le Déluge

1. Ruppenthal, *Logistical Support of the Armies*, 2:316; GBR, "Reinforcement System and Reinforcement Procedures," 20–21. Infantry's proportion was 70.3; armor's, 5.6; field artillery's, 7.2; and engineers, 5.5, for a total of 88.4. The number of armor losses increased over time, and artillery losses decreased after Normandy.

2. Eisenhower to Marshall, 21 and 23 October 1944, *EP,* #2054, #2063; Marshall to Eisenhower, 22 October 1944, *Aggressive and Determined Leadership,* #552.

3. Brooke Diary, 26 October 1944.

4. Eisenhower to Ramsay, Montgomery, Bradley, Devers, Coningham, Vandenberg, and Brereton, 28 October 1944, *EP,* #2074.

5. Cunningham Diary, 2 November 1944.

6. Brooke Diary, 9 November 1944.

7. Ibid., 13 and 14 November 1944.

8. Montgomery to Brooke, 17 November 1944, reproduced in Bryant, *Triumph in the West,* 264–65.

9. Draft, Brooke to Montgomery, 17 November 1944, Papers of Field Marshal Viscount Alanbrooke, LHCMA.

10. Brooke to Montgomery, 20 November 1944, in Bryant, *Triumph in the West,* 265.

11. Brooke to Montgomery, 22 November 1944, ibid., 266–67.

12. Montgomery to Brooke, M-344, 23 November 1944, in Hamilton, *Monty: Field Marshal,* 154.

13. Brooke Diary, 24 November 1944.

14. Ibid.; Brooke Diary, "Notes," 15 June 1944.

15. Brooke Diary, 26 and 27 November 1944.

16. Montgomery to Brooke, M-351, 28 November 1944, in Bryant, *Triumph in the West,* 270.

17. C. P. Dawney, "Inside Monty's Headquarters," in *Monty at Close Quarters: Recollections of the War,* ed. T. E. B. Howarth (Bath, UK, 1987), 21.

18. Brooke Diary, 28 November 1944.

19. Montgomery to Brooke, M-352, 29 November 1944, in Bryant, *Triumph in the West,* 270–71.

20. Montgomery to Eisenhower, 30 November 1944, Montgomery File, PPP, partially quoted in *EP,* #2145, nn. 2, 4.

21. Brooke Diary, 1 December 1944.

22. Churchill to Smuts, 1 December 1944, cited in Martin Gilbert, *Winston Churchill: Road to Victory, 1941-1945* (Boston, 1986), 1080.

23. Churchill to Eisenhower, 2 December 1944, cited in G. E. Patrick Murray, "Eisenhower and Montgomery: Broad Front versus Single Thrust. The Historiography of the Debate over Strategy and Command, August 1944–April 1945" (PhD diss., Temple University, 1991), 205-7.

24. Brooke Diary, 4 December 1944.

25. Churchill to Brooke, 2 December 1944, as noted in Brooke Diary, 4 December 1944.

26. Cunningham Diary, 4 December 1944.

27. Bradley and Blair, *A General's Life*, 346; Eisenhower to Montgomery, 1 December 1944, *EP*, #2145.

28. Marshall to Smith, 29 November 1944, GCMP.

29. Smith to Marshall, 3 December 1944, GCMP.

30. Montgomery to Eisenhower, 2 December 1944, in Hamilton, *Monty: Field Marshal*, 157.

31. Summersby Diary, 3 December 1944.

32. Eisenhower to CCS, 3 December 1944, *EP*, #2148.

33. "I told General Eisenhower that, of course, if he put the Twelfth Army Group under Marshal Montgomery, he would of necessity have to relieve me of command, because it would be an indication that I had failed as a separate Army Group Commander." Bradley, "Memorandum for Record," 13 December 1944, cited in Hamilton, *Monty: Field Marshal*, 163.

34. Montgomery to Eisenhower, 29 December 1944, Montgomery File, DDEL.

35. SHAEF, "Notes on Meeting at Maastricht on 7 December between SAC, Field Marshal Montgomery, and D/SAC," 8 December 1944, SHAEF File, WBSP.

36. SHAEF to Montgomery and Bradley, "Decisions Reached at Supreme Commander's Conference, 18 October 1944," SHAEF File, WBSP.

37. Eisenhower to Marshall, 13 December 1944, *EP*, #2163.

38. Montgomery to Brooke, M-537, 7 December 1944, in Hamilton, *Monty: Field Marshal*, 162–63.

39. Grigg to Montgomery, 7 December 1944, Grigg Papers.

40. Churchill to Roosevelt, 6 December 1944, cited in Pogue, *Supreme Command*, 314–15. Brooke's diary makes no mention of Churchill writing to Roosevelt.

41. Churchill discusses the exchange with Roosevelt in *Triumph and Tragedy*, 231–33.

42. Cunningham Diary, 12 December 1944.

43. Brooke Diary, 12 December 1944.

44. Cunningham Diary, 11 December 1944; John Ehrman, *Grand Strategy, October 1944-August 1945* (London, 1956), 20.

45. Marshall outlined the War Department's "new policy" at a CCS meeting in June 1944, "by which divisions at the front were being kept at full strength throughout operations with resultant increase in morale and in the length of the periods possible for units to operate without relief." "Minutes of the Combined Chiefs of Staff Meeting," 10 June 1944, RG 165, OCS, CCS 334, Combined Chiefs of Staff Minutes, NARA.

46. The problems arising from overreliance on the inflexible replacement criteria are discussed in Replacement Board, *Replacement System World Wide, World War II* (Washington, DC, 1946), book 2, pt. 45. See also Millett, *Organization and Role of Army Service Forces*, 252–53.

47. By February 1944, AGF units lost a net total of 52,625 enlisted men, 35,249 of them taken from combat units as overseas replacements.

48. William Keast, *Provision of Enlisted Replacements*, Army Ground Forces Historical Section, Study No. 7, 1 September 1945 (Washington, DC, 1946), 20–21.

49. Millett, *Organization and Role of Army Service Forces*, 245–53.

50. The physical quality of men received by AGF was so poor that 14 percent of trainees already in replacement training centers in December 1944 were reprofiled downward after six weeks of training. The case of Eddie Slovik was exceptional in

one regard—he was the first American soldier shot for cowardice since 1864—but in other respects, he was not atypical of the bottom-of-the-barrel draftees entering the army in 1944. A school dropout and repeat offender, Slovik left prison in April 1942, and his Detroit draft board classed him 4-F. By November 1943 the army had lowered its standards; reclassified 1-A, Slovik went through training as a replacement and joined the Twenty-eighth Infantry in France on 20 August 1944. Immediately after experiencing his first taste of artillery fire, he went AWOL, turned himself in on 9 October, and refused to go back into the line. His trial took place on 11 November, at the height of the Twenty-eighth Division's ordeal in the Hürtgen Forest, and the review took place in the midst of the Ardennes fighting. He faced a firing squad on 31 December, eight days after Eisenhower signed the warrant.

51. War Department, "What New Inductees Think About the Infantry," in *What the Soldiers Think*, 20 April 1945, Study No. 13, 11.

52. U.S. Army Center of Military History, *Personnel Replacement System*, 289, 294-97, 299-300.

53. Ruppenthal, *Logistical Support of the Armies*, 2:310, 313, 320.

54. Headquarters, Third Army, "Notes on Bastogne Operation," 12 December 1944 entry, published 16 January 1945, GSPP.

55. First Army Diary, 10 December 1944.

56. Matthews and Smyth interview with Marshall, 25 July 1949.

57. McNair to Marshall, "Infantry Strength in the Infantry Division," 1 February 1944, in Keast, *Provision of Enlisted Replacements*, 16.

58. Devers to McNair, 4 February 1944, in Keast, *Provision of Enlisted Replacements*, 16-17.

59. Russell Weigley, *History of the United States Army* (Bloomington, IN, 1984), 438.

60. Hughes Diary, 7 November 1944.

61. Office of the Surgeon General to LTG Ben Lear, "Prevention of Manpower Loss from Psychiatric Disorders," 16 September 1944, in Keast, *Provision of Enlisted Replacements*, 32.

62. GBR, "Military Offenders in the European Theater of Operations," 3.

63. GBR, "Combat Exhaustion," 3-4.

64. GBR, "The Military Justice Administration in the Theater of European Operations," 14.

65. War Department, "Some Morale Problems Overseas," in *What the Soldiers Think*, 25 February 1945, Study No. 12, 3-4; Eisenhower to Bradley, Devers, Lee, Spaatz, and Smith, "Correction of Troop Conditions in the Rear," 6 November 1944, *EP*, #2106. Eisenhower apparently identified the problem with rear areas because they housed the recreation, rest, and comfort facilities.

66. SHAEF G-3 to Handy, 17 November 1944, *EP*, #2125.

67. War Department Observer Board, "AGF Report," 1 January 1945, in GBR, "Reinforcement System and Reinforcement Procedures," 33.

68. Paul Fussell, *The Boys' Crusade: The American Infantry in Northwest Europe, 1944-45* (New York, 2003), 98.

69. U.S. Army Center of Military History, *Personnel Replacement System*, 285-87.

70. Eisenhower to Handy, 17 November 1944, *EP*, #2125; Eisenhower to Marshall, 29 January 1944, *EP*, #1521.

71. In a postwar interview Marshall remarked, "We did make rather intelligent use of manpower." Matthews and Smyth interview with Marshall, 25 July 1949.

72. Eisenhower to CCS, 3 December 1944, *EP*, #2148.

73. The exchange of correspondence is in Hamilton, *Monty: Field Marshall*, 158–59.

74. Eisenhower to Marshall, 27 November 1944, *EP*, #2144; Montgomery to Eisenhower, 30 November 1944, and Eisenhower to Montgomery, 1 December 1944, *EP*, #2145, n. 2.

75. "Conduct of Battle," in *Field Service Regulations (Tentative): Operations* (FM 100–5) (Washington, DC, 1939), para. 91.

76. Hansen Diary, 22 November 1944.

77. Lutes Diary, 13 December 1944, "Mission to European Theater."

78. Matthews and Smyth interview with Marshall, 25 July 1949.

79. Pogue, *Marshall Interviews*, 625.

33. One Desperate Blow

1. Karl von Clausewitz, *On War* (New York, 1943), 236.

2. Smith to Marshall, 3 December 1944, GCMP.

3. Smith to Handy, 28 December 1944, Thomas Handy Papers, GCMRL; Pogue interview, 8 May 1947.

4. SHAEF G-2, "Weekly Intelligence Summary," 3 December 1944, WBSP.

5. Ibid., 10 December 1944.

6. Interview statement of Smith, in *Survey of Allied Planning*, 2:146; SHAEF G-2 Intel Summary 35, week ending 19 November 44; Twelfth Army Group Intelligence Summary 15, 18 November 44, WBSP. In his letter to Handy, Smith went into some detail explaining why the German offensive had caught SHAEF napping. "I must say that while he may have made a real strategical blunder, Rundstedt's counter offensive was handled with the greatest possible technical skill." Smith to Handy, 28 January 1944; Pogue interview, 8 May 1947.

7. Pogue interviews, 8 May 1947 and 1 November 1951; Strong to Pogue, 31 August 1951, cited in *Supreme Command*, 365 n. 20; Bradley, *Soldier's Story*, 461–64.

8. Bradley, *Soldier's Story*, 441–42.

9. Strong, *Intelligence at the Top*, 210–12; Pogue interview, 8 May 1947.

10. First Army Diary, 27 November and 11 December 1944.

11. First Army Diary, 12–14 December 1944.

12. Strong, *Intelligence at the Top*, 213.

13. First Army Diary, 16 December 1944.

14. Pogue interview with Scarman, 25 February 1947, MHI.

15. Eisenhower, "Memo," 23 December 1944, Butcher Diary, *EP*, #2198; John Eisenhower, *The Bitter Woods* (New York, 1969), 215.

16. Bradley, *Soldier's Story*, 449–50.

17. Hansen Diary, 17 December 1944.

18. Hughes Diary, 16 December 1944.

19. Eisenhower retold the story to Patterson in Eisenhower to Patterson, 18 December 1947, Patterson File, PPP. He outlined his plans for dealing with the German offensive in Eisenhower to Bradley and Devers, 18 December 1944, *EP*, #2178.

20. Smith wanted to move both airborne divisions to Bastogne, but Bradley refused. Smith, *Eisenhower's Six Great Decisions*, 91–92; Pogue interview, 8 May 1947.

21. "Minutes, Chiefs of Staff Conference," 20 December 1944, SHAEF War Diary.

22. First Army Diary, 17–18 December 1944.

23. Montgomery to Brooke, M-380, 17 December 1944, in Hamilton, *Monty: Field Marshall*, 186–88.

24. De Guingand, *Generals at War*, 106.

25. Betts oral history.

26. First Army Diary, 19 December 1944.

27. In total, ComZ removed 3 million gallons of gasoline. Perhaps 100,000 gallons fell into German hands. For a discussion of supply in the Ardennes, see Hugh Cole, *The Ardennes: The Battle of the Bulge*, USAWWII (Washington, DC, 1965), 661–68, 670.

28. Bradley, *Soldier's Story*, 469.

29. Pogue interview with Strong, 12 December 1947.

30. Strong, *Intelligence at the Top*, 219–22. The irony here is that Frederick won Leuthen in his most famous "oblique order" attack.

31. Eisenhower, *Bitter Woods*, 215.

32. The two old friends could even joke with each other. "Funny thing," Eisenhower remarked (recalling Kasserine), "every time I get a new star I get attacked." "And every time you get attacked," Patton retorted, "I pull you out." For the Verdun conference, see D'Este, *Eisenhower: A Soldier's Life*, 643–46.

33. Smith to Montgomery, 19 December 1944, Eyes Only File, WBSP.

34. Pogue interview, 8 May 1947. Whereas Patton told Smith he had a staff of mediocrities that worked as a team, Smith always thought Third Army boasted an excellent staff; in the next few days they proved Smith right.

35. Eisenhower to Bradley and Lee, 19 December 1944, *EP*, #2183; Bradley, *Soldier's Story*, 476.

36. Betts oral history.

37. Pogue interview with Whiteley, 18 December 1946, MHI.

38. Strong, *Intelligence at the Top*, 164–66; Pogue interview, 8 May 1947.

39. Smith to Montgomery, 20 December 1944, *EP*, #2184.

40. Pogue interview, 8 May 1947.

41. Bradley, *Soldier's Story*, 476.

42. In *A General's Life*, a different story emerged. The book claimed that Smith's call had "an Alice in Wonderland air" about it, as if "SHAEF was losing its head." Bradley claimed, "I had things under control, and [was] reassuring [Smith] that Hodges was performing magnificently under the circumstances." The assertion that Hodges acted magnificently raises the question of who resided in Wonderland. Bradley and Blair, *A General's Life*, 362–65.

43. Pogue interview, 8 May 1947.

44. Strong, *Intelligence at the Top*, 226.

45. Eisenhower to CCS, 20 December 1944, *EP*, #2182; Eisenhower, "Memo," 23 December 1944, *EP*, #2198.

46. Jodl interview.

47. Strong, *Intelligence at the Top*, 226. Both Strong and Whiteley told almost identical stories to Pogue; Pogue interviews with Strong, 12 December 1946, and Whiteley, 18 December 1946, MHI.

48. David Hogan Jr., *A Command Post at War: First Army Headquarters in Europe, 1944-1945* (Washington, DC, 2000), 212.

49. First Army Diary, 20 December 1944.

50. Montgomery to Brooke, M-383, 20 December 1944, in Hamilton, *Monty: Field Marshal*, 213.

51. Pogue interview, 8 May 1947; Montgomery to SHAEF-Main, 22 December 1944, Eyes Only, WBSP.

52. First Army Diary, 4 and 8 January 1945.

53. LTC R. H. C. Drummond-Wolff to COL Dupuy, 21 December 1944, C. D. Jackson Papers.

54. Butcher, *Three Years with Eisenhower*, 727–28.

55. "All papers this morning featuring General Smith's statement that [Eisenhower's] car and a double were used last winter in an attempt to capture would-be German assassins." Associated Press, 1 June 1945, SHAEF, WBSP.

56. Murphy, *Diplomat among Warriors*, 239.

57. Brigadier Edgar Williams, Montgomery's intelligence chief, told Pogue, "Bedell told a direct lie when he said there was no flap at SHAEF over the Ardennes. They kept calling us until we thought we would go crazy. Strong . . . got hysterical over the Ardennes." Pogue interview with Brigadier Williams, 30–31 May 1947, MHI.

58. Pogue interview, 8 May 1947.

59. Tedder, *With Prejudice*, 629.

60. First Army Diary, 24 December 1944.

61. Interviews of Senior German Officers, WBSP.

62. Eisenhower, "To Troops of AEF," 22 December 1944, *EP*, #2195.

63. Brooke Diary, 18 December 1944.

64. Pogue interview, 8 May 1947.

65. Montgomery to Brooke, M-379, 15 December 1944, in Hamilton, *Monty: Field Marshal*, 181; Montgomery to Eisenhower, 15 December 1944, *EP*, #2173, nn. 1–2.

66. Montgomery to Brooke, M-380 and M-383, 17 and 20 December 1944, in Hamilton, *Monty: Field Marshal*, 187, 217.

67. Montgomery to Brooke, 21 December 1944, ibid., 222.

68. Brooke to Montgomery, 21 December 1944, ibid., 219.

69. Montgomery related his version of the meeting in Montgomery to Frank Simpson, 25 December 1944, ibid., 240–41.

70. Bradley, *Soldier's Story*, 480–81.

71. "Notes of Command Meeting," 26 December 1944, Robb Diary, J. M. Robb Papers, DDEL.

72. Eisenhower to Montgomery, 29 December 1944, *EP*, #2206.

73. That night Montgomery reported to Brooke that Eisenhower gave way on the second condition. Montgomery to Brooke, M-410, 28 December 1944, in Hamilton, *Monty: Field Marshal*, 262–63. In London Brooke did not "like the account [of the meeting]. It looks to me as if Monty, with his usual lack of tact, has been rubbing into Ike the results of not having listened to Monty's advice! Too much of 'I told you so' to assist in creating the required friendly relations between them." Brooke Diary, 23–30 December 1944.

74. Eisenhower to Smith, 28 December 1944, Eyes Only, WBSP.

75. Frank Simpson arrived after the Hasselt meeting and remained through 31 December; he made a full report to Brooke. See Simpson to Brooke, 31 December 1944, excerpts in Hamilton, *Monty: Field Marshal*, 266.

76. Robb Diary, 29 December 1944.

77. Summersby, *Eisenhower Was My Boss*, 188–89.

78. Montgomery to Eisenhower, 29 December 1944, Montgomery File, PPP.

79. Bradley and Blair, *A General's Life*, 376.

80. Eisenhower to Montgomery, 29 December 1944, *EP*, #2206.

81. Simpson to Brooke, 31 December 1944, in Hamilton, *Monty: Field Marshal,* 266.

82. The story of de Guingand's trip to Versailles is in de Guingand, *Generals at War,* 106–11.

83. Marshall to Eisenhower, 30 December 1944, *Aggressive and Determined Leadership,* #632; excerpt in Pogue, *Supreme Command,* 386.

84. Robb Diary, 30 December 1944.

85. Smith to Caffery, 24 November 1944, WBSP; Frank McCarthy to Marshall, 24 November 1944, Frank McCarthy Papers, GCMRL.

86. Soon after the war de Guingand wrote an effusive letter to Smith, thanking him for going out of his way to help and for always rendering unwavering support. Everyone in the British headquarters had "always known that any of our problems & difficulties would receive from you the fairest of attention and the wisest of counsel." He concluded by saying, "I, probably before all others, know what our headquarters and our Armies owe to you." De Guingand to Smith, 25 May 1945, in Richardson, *Send for Freddie,* 175.

87. Montgomery to Eisenhower, M-406, 31 December 1944, in Hamilton, *Monty: Field Marshal,* 279.

88. De Guingand, *Operation Victory,* 435; de Guingand, *Generals at War,* 112–14; Montgomery, *Memoirs,* 286–89.

89. Montgomery to SHAEF, M-408, 31 December 1944, in Hamilton, *Monty: Field Marshal,* 279.

34. Déjà Vu All over Again

1. When Smith visited Devers's headquarters on 4 December, he heard about the contentious disagreement from Sixth Army Group's chief of staff, BG David Barr. BG Daniel Noce, "Notes," 4 December 1944, cited in Jeffery Clark and Robert Ross Smith, *Riviera to the Rhine,* USAWWII (Washington, DC, 1993), 440.

2. Eisenhower to Marshall, 6 January 1945, *EP,* #2224. After the Verdun conference, Devers thought it a "tragedy" that Eisenhower "has not seen fit to reinforce success on this flank." Devers Diary, 19 December 1944, cited in Clark and Smith, *Riviera to the Rhine,* 491.

3. Robb Diary, 1 and 3 January 1945.

4. Eisenhower to CCS, 31 December 1944, *EP,* #2209.

5. Devers Diary, 1 January 1945, in Clark and Smith, *Riviera to the Rhine,* 497.

6. De Gaulle, *Memoirs,* 3:166.

7. Robb Diary, 3 January 1945.

8. Summersby Diary, 3 January 1945; de Gaulle, *Memoirs,* 3:169.

9. Brooke Diary, 3 January 1945.

10. Eisenhower to Marshall, 6 January 1945, *EP,* #2224.

11. Smith to Handy, 12 January 1945, 1944 Chief of Staff's Personal Correspondence, WBSP.

12. Pogue interview with Robb, 3 February 1947, MHI. Asked by Marshall to rank the senior officers under his command, Eisenhower placed Devers twenty-fourth. He explained, "The proper position of this officer is not yet fully determined. . . . But he has not, so far, produced . . . that feeling of trust and confidence that is so necessary to continued success." He ranked Patch tenth. Eisenhower, "Memo," 1 February 1945, Butcher Diary, *EP,* #2271.

13. Brooke Diary, 3 January 1945.

14. Churchill to Eisenhower, 22 February 1945, Eyes Only, WBSP.

15. Brooke Diary, 7 November 1944.

16. Cunningham Diary, 4 and 6–7 November 1944.

17. Brooke Diary, 17 November 1944, 12 January 1945, and "Notes," 18 January 1945; Cunningham Diary, 4 November 1944.

18. Brooke Diary, 28 November 1944.

19. Ibid., 28 November and 12 December 1944, 4 January 1945.

20. Pogue interview, 8 May 1947.

21. Summersby Diary, 8 January 1945.

22. Sidney Shalett, "Roosevelt Explains Shift," *New York Times,* 6 January 1945.

23. Eisenhower to Brooke, 16 February 1945, *EP,* #2284.

24. De Guingand, *Operation Victory,* 434.

25. More than a month later, Eisenhower was still engaged in damage control. Montgomery's press conference "is still rankling in Bradley's mind and I must say I cannot blame him," Eisenhower told Marshall. Eisenhower to Marshall, 9 February 1945, *EP,* #2276.

26. Tac HQ 21 Army Group, "Press Conference," 7 January 1945, in Hamilton, *Monty: Field Marshal,* 312.

27. Churchill to Roosevelt, 5 and 8 January 1945, in *FRUS, The Conferences at Malta and Yalta,* 29, 31.

28. Cunningham Diary, 9 January 1945.

29. Churchill to Ismay for COS Committee, 10 January 1945, PREM 3, 431/2, 185–86, National Archives, Kew.

30. Military Attaché Report, "Criticism Command Organization SHAEF," 27, 30 December 1944 and 26 January 1945; Military Intelligence Division, WDGS, RG-165, War Department General and Special Staff, Operations Division 1942–1945, NARA.

31. Marshall to Eisenhower, 8 January 1945, *Finest Soldier,* #15.

32. Neither appears in Eisenhower's published papers. Eisenhower to Marshall, 9 January 1945, Marshall File, PPP.

33. Eisenhower to Marshall, 10 January 1945, *EP,* #2233.

34. Marshall to Eisenhower, 11 January 1945, *Finest Soldier,* #18.

35. Eisenhower to Marshall, 12 January 1945, *EP,* #2235.

36. Marshall to Eisenhower, 10 June 1945, Marshall File, DDEL.

37. Churchill to Roosevelt, 8 January 1945, in Francis Loewenhem, Harold Langley, and Manfred Jonas, eds., *Roosevelt and Churchill: Their Secret Wartime Correspondence* (New York, 1975), 647.

38. Marshall to Eisenhower, 6 January 1945, *Finest Soldier,* #12; Pogue, *Marshall Interviews,* 532.

39. Pogue, *Marshall Interviews,* 532.

40. Hughes Diary, 30 December 1944.

41. Smith to Handy and Handy to Smith, 21 December 1944, SGS File, WBSP.

42. Marshall to Eisenhower, 6, 8, and 11 January 1945, *Finest Soldier,* #12, #14–15, #18.

43. Marshall to Eisenhower, 8 January 1945, *Finest Soldier,* #14.

44. Eisenhower to Handy, 19 December 1944, *EP,* #2182.

45. Summersby Diary, 7 January 1945.

46. Eisenhower to Marshall, 9 January 1945, Marshall File, DDEL.

47. Lee to Commanding Generals, SOLOC, U.K. Base, and Section Commanders, ComZ, 26 and 28 December 1944, in Lee, *Employment of Negro Troops,* 689.

48. Morgan to G-3, 14 January 1944, Bull to G-3, 15 January 1944, and Smith to Chiefs of Staff Committee, War Office, "French Participation in OVERLORD," 28 January 1944, COSSAC File, WBSP.

49. Smith to Eisenhower, 3 January 1945, SHAEF OCS File, WBSP.

50. Eisenhower to Lee, "Draft," 4 January 1944, *EP,* #2218; Eisenhower to Smith, 4 January 1945, in Lee, *Employment of Negro Troops,* 690. The new directive was issued in Lee's name.

51. Eisenhower to Marshall, 7 January 1945, *EP,* #2227.

52. Barker to ETOAG, 8 January 1945; ETO G-1 to Commanding Generals through Smith, 9 January 1945; Headquarters ETO to Lee, 9 January 1945, in Lee, *Employment of Negro Troops,* 692.

53. Lutes to Somervell, 31 December 1944, Lutes Papers.

54. GBR, "Supply and Maintenance in the European Theater," 48–54, 66–67. By 1 January 1945 SOLOC outstripped ComZ in daily deliveries, even though Marseilles and Toulon combined boasted a fraction of Antwerp's harbor capacity. In December the southern French ports discharged 501,568 tons, compared with 427,592 for Antwerp.

55. Somervell to Eisenhower, 12 December 1944, Somervell File, PPP.

56. Somervell to Lee, 24 January 1945, Hughes Papers.

57. GBR, "Organization of the European Theater of Operations," 61. Hughes recorded plenty of instances of friction caused by Somervell's action. The best insights are in MG George Craig Stewart oral history, U.S. Army Transportation Museum and Research Library, Fort Eustis, VA.

58. "Minutes of Command and Staff Conference, Communications Zone Headquarters," 25 January 1945, Hughes Papers; Headquarters ComZ, "G-4 Action on Somervell Memo of 24 January 1945," in GBR, "Mechanics of Supply," 37; Hughes Diary, 25 January 1945.

59. Hughes, "Memo for DDE," 14 January 1945, Hughes Papers.

60. Eisenhower to Smith, 16 January 1945, *EP,* #2246.

61. Pogue interview, 13 May 1947.

62. Hughes Diary, 20 January 1945.

63. Ruppenthal, *Logistical Support of the Armies,* 2:326–27, 334–47.

64. Hughes Diary, 23 December 1945.

65. Hughes to Peterson, 3 February 1945, Hughes Papers.

66. Pogue interview, 13 May 1947.

67. Hughes Diary, 24 December and 3 April 1945; Pogue interview, 13 May 1947.

68. Marshall to Eisenhower, 8 January 1945, *Finest Soldier,* #14.

69. Robb, "Higher Direction of War," unpublished article, Robb Papers, DDEL.

70. For the correspondence, see Churchill, *Triumph and Tragedy,* 278–79.

71. Robb Diary, 15 January 1945.

72. Eisenhower to Marshall, 15 January 1945, *EP,* #2242.

73. Robb Diary, 15 January 1945.

74. First Army Diary, 17 January 1945.

75. Eisenhower to Montgomery, 14 and 17 January 1945, *EP,* #2240, #2247.

76. Robb Diary, 16 January 1945.

77. Devers Diary, 5 January 1945, cited in D'Este, *Eisenhower: A Soldier's Life,* 670.

78. Robb Diary, 10 and 15 January 1945.

79. SHAEF-Forward G-3, Memo, 4–6 October 1944, with Bull's marginal note, "Kill this," and interview statements of Smith and Bull, in *Survey of Allied Planning,*

2:159–60. Eisenhower paid a visit to Devers on 27 January. He called the Colmar Pocket the only "sore" along the entire front and reinforced Sixth Army Group with five divisions and 12,000 service troops. Clark and Smith, *Riviera to the Rhine*, 556.

80. Whiteley [for Eisenhower] to Montgomery, Bradley, Devers, and Brereton, 18 January 1945, *EP*, #2248; Montgomery to Eisenhower, M-547, 19 January 1945, in Hamilton, *Monty: Field Marshall*, 334–35; Eisenhower to Montgomery, 21 January 1945, *EP*, #2257.

81. Gay Diary, 24 January 1945, in D'Este, *Eisenhower: A Soldier's Life*, 671.

82. Eisenhower to CCS, 20 January 1945, *EP*, #2254.

83. Eisenhower used the figure thirty-five in his cable. Crawford warned Smith that projections for a thirty-six-division drive in the north seemed extreme rather than optimistic. Crawford to Bull, "Logistical Implications of Operations in the Northern Bridgehead," 7 January 1945, in *Survey of Allied Planning*, 2:153; Bradley Commentaries, MHI.

84. Reprinted in Ehrman, *Grand Strategy, October 1944-August 1945*, 78.

85. Eisenhower to Marshall, 21 January 1945, *EP*, #2256; Butcher, *Three Years with Eisenhower*, 749.

86. Eisenhower, "Notes on Conference with Marshall," 28 January 1945, *EP*, #2264; Pogue, *Organizer of Victory*, 516–18.

87. Handy to Smith, 26 January 1945, 1945 Chief of Staff's Personal Correspondence, WBSP.

88. Sherwood, *Roosevelt and Hopkins*, 846–48.

89. Butcher, *Three Years with Eisenhower*, 349–51.

90. Smith to Handy, 28 December 1944, Handy Papers.

91. JCS, "Minutes of Meeting," 30 January 1945, in *FRUS, Malta and Yalta, 1945*, 464–66.

92. "Minutes of CCS Meeting," 30 January 1945, in *FRUS, Malta and Yalta*, 469–74; Brooke Diary, 30 January 1945.

93. Smith to Eisenhower, 30 January 1945, Eyes Only, WBSP.

94. Eisenhower to Smith, 30 January 1945, *EP*, #2268.

95. Smith to Handy, 9 February 1945, Handy Papers.

96. "Minutes of CCS Meeting," 30 January 1945, *FRUS, Malta and Yalta*, 485–88.

97. Nigel Hamilton interview with LTG Ian Jacob, 28 June 1984, in Hamilton, *Monty: Field Marshal*, 450–51.

98. For Smith's account of the late-night meeting, see Smith to Handy, 9 February 1945; Summersby Diary, 31 January 1945; Summersby, *Eisenhower Was My Boss*, 218–19; Pogue interview, 8 May 1947. For Brooke's version, see Brooke Diary and "Notes," 31 January and 1 February 1945.

99. Smith to Samuel E. Morison, 1 April 1957, GCMP.

100. Pogue, *Organizer of Victory*, 516–17.

101. "Minutes of CCS Meeting," 1 February 1945, *FRUS, Malta and Yalta*, 522. Ismay noted, "One can read the official minutes of these meetings without suspecting that a single harsh word had been exchanged." Ismay, *Memoirs*, 385; Cunningham Diary, 1 February 1945; Pogue, *Marshall Interviews*, 540–41.

102. Ismay, *Memoirs*, 385.

103. Pogue interview with Ismay, 20 December 1947, MHI.

104. Cunningham, *A Sailor's Odyssey*, 626.

105. Cunningham Diary, 1 February 1945.

106. Leahy, *I Was There*, 346; Ernest King and Walter Muir Whitehill, *Fleet Admiral King: A Naval Record* (New York, 1976), 586.

107. Cunningham also said, "The President does not appear to know what he is talking about and hangs on to one idea." Cunningham Diary, 2 February 1945. "Report to the President and the Prime Minister of the Agreed Summary of Conclusions Reached by the Combined Chiefs of Staff at the ARGONAUT Conference," 2 February 1945, RG-319, Records of the Army Staff, NARA.

108. King and Whitehill, *Fleet Admiral King*, 586.

109. Cited in Ehrman, *Grand Strategy*, 6:93.

35. The German Is a Whipped Enemy

1. Summersby Diary, 14 February 1945.

2. Montgomery to Simpson, M-556, 14 February 1945, in Hamilton, *Monty: Field Marshal*, 379.

3. Montgomery to Brooke, 14 February 1945, in Bryant, *Triumph in the West*, 328; Montgomery Diary, "Notes on the Campaign in North-Western Europe," in Hamilton, *Monty: Field Marshal*, 380–81.

4. Tedder, *With Prejudice*, 663.

5. Eisenhower to Brooke, 16 February 1945, *EP*, #2284.

6. Churchill to Eisenhower, 22 February 1945, Churchill Files, PPP.

7. Eisenhower to Mamie, 19 February 1945, in *Letters to Mamie*.

8. Summersby Diary, 20 February 1945; LTG Ronald Weeks to Simpson, 24 February 1945, in Hamilton, *Monty: Field Marshal*, 388. Weeks had recently become deputy CIGS while Simpson moved up to assistant CIGS.

9. Eisenhower to Bradley, copies to Montgomery and Devers, 20 February 1945, *EP*, #2291.

10. Smith to Chief, Historical Section, "LT GEN W. B. Smith Memorandum of 22 February 1945," Carl F. Spaatz Papers, LOC. Dr. Hopper sent a copy, with his comments, to Spaatz on 5 April 1945. COL W. A. Ganoe, the theater historian, proved less critical. In his cover letter he called this "personal contribution by a very busy general the 'Milk of Paradise to a historian.'"

11. Smith to Handy, 28 December 1945, Handy Papers.

12. De Gaulle to Eisenhower, 15 February 1945; Smith [for Eisenhower] to de Gaulle, 19 February 1945, *EP*, #2289, n. 1.

13. Patton to Beatrice Patton, 4 February 1945, *Patton Papers, 1940-1945*, 634.

14. Patton to Frederick Ayer, 6 February 1945, ibid., 636.

15. Bradley and Blair, *A General's Life*, 392.

16. Patton Diary, 2 and 22 February 1945.

17. Patton Diary, 29 January 1945; Patton, *War as I Knew It*, 219.

18. Patton Diary, 14 February 1945, *Patton Papers, 1940-1945*, 639.

19. Hughes Diary, 17 February 1945.

20. Ibid., 15 and 16 February 1945.

21. Patton Diary, 26 February 1945.

22. Hansen Diary, 7 March 1945; Butcher Diary, 11 March 1945; Bradley, *Soldier's Story*, 511–13.

23. Kesselring and Göring interviews, Interviews of Senior German Officers, WBSP.

24. Patton Diary, 27 February 1945.

25. Ibid., 1 March 1945, *Patton Papers 1940-1945*, 649.

26. Patton Diary, 9 March 1945; Tedder to Eisenhower, 22 March 1945, Tedder File, PPP.

27. This was one of Patton's favorite aphorisms, dating back to his first "Blood and Guts" speeches at Forts Benning and Knox.

28. Patton Diary, 19 March 1945, *Patton Papers, 1940-1945*, 658.

29. Montgomery Diary, 1 March 1945, "Notes on the Campaign in North-West Europe," in Hamilton, *Monty: Field Marshal*, 398–99.

30. Montgomery Diary, 2 March 1945; Montgomery to Eisenhower, M-1012, 4 March 1945, ibid., 399.

31. Brooke Diary, 5 March 1945.

32. Montgomery to Brooke, 10 March 1945, and Churchill to Montgomery, 11 March 1945, in Hamilton, *Monty: Field Marshal*, 401.

33. Kesselring interview, WBSP.

34. "I'll confess to you now," he told a press conference on 28 March, "that those were the two most anxious weeks I have spent in this campaign." Transcript in Butcher, *Three Years with Eisenhower*, 780.

35. Summersby, *Past Forgiving*, 248.

36. Eisenhower to Marshall, 12 March 1945, *EP*, #2330.

37. Eisenhower to Mamie, 28 April 1945, in D'Este, *Eisenhower: A Soldier's Life*, 679.

38. Hughes Diary, 4–5 March 1945.

39. Smith to Handy, 9 February 1945, Eyes Only, WBSP.

40. Summersby Diary, 27 March 1945.

41. Patton Diary, 16 March 1945, *Patton Papers, 1940-1945*, 656.

42. Bradley and Blair, *A General's Life*, 410–11; Summersby, *Past Forgiving*, 217.

43. Eisenhower to Marshall, 23 April 1945, *EP*, #2440. After two terms as president, he still held the same view, as expressed in Eisenhower to Ismay, 3 December 1960, *Keeping the Peace*, #1722.

44. The publication of Ismay's book prompted a "rather lengthy dissertation" from Eisenhower (see *Keeping the Peace*, #1722) defending his prosecution of the broad-front strategy; in it he provides some unadorned insights into his thinking about the final campaign.

45. Smith discussed the reasoning behind the Ruhr double envelopment and the decision not to go to Berlin in an April press conference. He used the personal pronoun "we," denoting Eisenhower, Bradley, and himself. Butcher reproduces the transcript in *Three Years with Eisenhower*, 806–15. He repeated the reference to the Ruhr and the "heart of Germany" used in Eisenhower's first statement on his broad-front approach in 8 May 1944.

46. Eisenhower to Marshall, 31 August and 4 September 1944, *EP*, #1925, #1934.

47. SHAEF G-2, "Weekly Intelligence Summaries," 11 February 1945, WBSP.

48. Bradley's account is in *Soldier's Story*, 535–36, and *A General's Life*, 410–11. Eisenhower does not mention the discussions at Sous le Vent in his memoir, saying only, "As soon as American forces had begun to establish themselves firmly in the Remagen bridgehead Bradley and I had started to develop our plans for deriving the greatest usefulness from this development." In reference to the northern versus southern thrust, he wrote, "Equally important [as the northern objectives] was the desirability of penetrating and destroying the so-called 'National Redoubt.'" Eisenhower, *Crusade in Europe*, 392, 397. Eisenhower did discuss his rationale for not advancing on Berlin in postwar letters to Wedemeyer and Pogue. To Wedemeyer,

he said he made the decision before Patton crossed the Rhine. In his view, it would have been the "height of folly for us to concentrate everything upon a race toward a destroyed city such as Berlin, particularly when we appeared doomed from the beginning to lose the race." Eisenhower also told him that SHAEF was "terribly anxious" about closing to the Baltic and preventing the Germans from manning the redoubt. In the letter to Pogue he listed distance, the obstacle of the Elbe, the cost in American lives, and the established zonal boundaries as the key determinants. "In the absence of directives from higher authority, I limited our efforts to the attainment of strictly military objectives and to the best possible positioning of Western troops in those areas of which political agreements had made no mention." His objective remained to "crush the enemy on the broadest possible front—to seal off the Danish peninsula by reaching Lubeck, at the same time, penetrate the Bavarian 'Redoubt,' and make the greatest possible advance into Austria." Eisenhower to Wedemeyer, 2 May 1947, Wedemeyer File, and Eisenhower to Pogue, 20 February 1952, Pogue File, PPP.

49. Eisenhower to Devers, Bradley, and Brereton, 21 March 1945, *EP,* #2348.

50. Brooke Diary, 25 March 1945.

51. Smith, *Eisenhower's Six Great Decisions,* 147; Smith to Lee, "Administrative Preparations for Spring Offensives," 5 February 1945, in GBR, "Strategy of the Campaign in North-West Europe," 83.

52. Butcher Diary, 26 February 1945.

53. Butcher, *Three Years with Eisenhower,* 778. Butcher reproduced the transcript of the press conference, 779–90.

54. Eisenhower to Montgomery, 28 March 1945, *EP,* #2364.

55. Montgomery to Eisenhower, M-562, 27 March 1945, in Hamilton, *Monty: Field Marshal,* 440.

56. Montgomery to Simpson, 8 April 1945, ibid., 443.

57. Jodl and Kesselring interviews, WBSP.

58. War Department [from Nory Smith] to Smith, 31 March 1945, and Smith to Nory, 2 April 1945, 1945 Chief of Staff's Personal Correspondence, WBSP.

36. Mission Fulfilled

1. Churchill to Roosevelt, 5 April 1945, in Pogue, *Supreme Command,* 443–44.

2. Smith told his staff he should "go on record to our Masters in Washington that if they want us to win the war over here they must find us another ten Divisions." Robb, "Notes," Robb Papers.

3. Montgomery to Frank Simpson, 2 April 1945, in Hamilton, *Monty: Field Marshal,* 456.

4. Bull [for Eisenhower] to Montgomery, Bradley, and Devers, 2 April 1945, *EP,* #2385.

5. Churchill to Eisenhower, 31 March 1945, *EP,* #2374, n. 2.

6. Eisenhower to Churchill, 3 April 1945, *EP,* #2387.

7. Eisenhower to Marshall, 30 March 1945, *EP,* #2373.

8. CCS, "Memorandum by the United States Chief of Staff: Plans of Campaign in Western Europe," 30 March 1945, *Finest Soldier,* #77.

9. Roosevelt to Stalin, 24 March 1945, *FRUS, 1945, European Advisory Commission, Austria, Germany,* 738.

10. Stalin to Roosevelt, 29 March 1945, ibid., 739–40.

11. Roosevelt to Stalin, 31 March 1945, ibid., 740–41.

12. Bull [revised by Smith for Eisenhower] to CCS, 5 April 1945, *EP,* #2394, n. 1.

13. Stalin to Roosevelt, 3 April 1945, *FRUS, European Advisory Commission, Austria, Germany,* 742.

14. Roosevelt to Stalin, 4 April 1945, ibid., 745–46.

15. Harriman to Stettinius, 2 April 1945, *FRUS, 1945, Europe,* 5:816.

16. Harriman to Stettinius, 6 April 1945, ibid., 821.

17. Churchill to Roosevelt, 5 April 1945, *FRUS, European Advisory Commission, Austria, Germany,* 746; Churchill, *Triumph and Tragedy,* 449–51.

18. Stalin to Roosevelt, 7 April 1945, *FRUS, European Advisory Commission, Austria, Germany,* 749–51.

19. Reproduced in *EP,* #2400, n. 1.

20. Stimson Diary, 6 April 1945.

21. Marshall to Eisenhower, 6 April 1945, *Finest Soldier,* #91; Eisenhower to Marshall, 7 April 1945, *EP,* #2399, n. 2.

22. Simpson oral history, DDEL.

23. A General Board study concluded that, after 8 February 1944, operations developed so rapidly and unexpectedly "so as to make impracticable the preparation of detailed plans for operations east of the Rhine." GBR, "Strategy in North-West Europe," 91.

24. Drew Pearson told the story, timed to coincide with congressional confirmation hearings, to raise questions about Smith's suitability as ambassador to Moscow. Pearson, "Washington Merry-Go Round," *Atlanta Journal,* 21 February 1946, in Moseley Papers, LOC. See also Murphy, *Diplomat among Warriors,* 293, and Jean Edwards Smith interview with Murphy, 23 February 1971, in Smith, "Selection of a Proconsul for Germany: The Appointment of Gen. Lucius Clay, 1945," *Military Affairs* (October 1976): 128.

25. Eisenhower to Montgomery, Bradley, Devers, Brereton, Burroughs, Coningham, Vandenberg, and Webster, and Eisenhower to Marshall, 15 April 1945, *EP,* #2415, #2418.

26. As late as 22 April, SHAEF G-2 foresaw potential German ground forces in the southern region amounting to almost 100 nominal divisions, including the greater part of the remaining armored and SS formations and perhaps thirty mechanized divisions. SHAEF, "Weekly Intelligence Summary," 22 April 1945, WBSP. Eisenhower made the same claim in United States Army, *Report by the Supreme Commander to the Combined Chiefs of Staff on the Operations in Europe of the Allied Expeditionary Force: 6 June 1944 to 8 May 1945* (Washington, DC, 1945; reprint, U.S. Army Center of Military History, 1994), 112.

27. Transcript in Butcher, *Three Years with Eisenhower,* 806–15. Smith's statements reflected the most recent intelligence summary and SHAEF Joint Intelligence Committee, "The National Redoubt," 10 April 1945, provided by Roger Cirillo. The JIC reported "at least twenty underground areas" for the production of war materiel and numerous supply depots. The committee also considered it likely the Germans would use Allied POWs as hostages.

28. Butcher, *Three Years with Eisenhower,* 806; "General Eisenhower Changed Allied Plans," *Daily Telegraph,* 23 April 1945; "How the Ruhr Was Enveloped," *Times,* 23 April 1945; Charles Collingwood, CBS broadcast, 21 April 1945; Kingsmith, *Deferred Press Internews* (New York, n.d.), copies in WBSP.

29. Hans Wolfgang Schoch, "National Redoubt," U.S. Army European Com-

mand, Historical Division, Military Study B-212 (1946), 7. In mid-April air reconnaissance confirmed isolated stretches of fieldworks east of the Swiss frontier and antitank obstacles, ditches, and canals near the Liechtenstein border. Nobody offered an explanation why the Germans chose to construct defenses against Switzerland and Liechtenstein; the answer rested in the fact that those areas were the only ones that received preliminary work. SHAEF, "Weekly Intelligence Summaries," 15 April 1945.

30. Harry Vosser, "Hitler's Hideaway," *New York Times Magazine*, 12 November 1944.

31. Erwin Lessner, "Hitler's Final V Weapon," *Collier's*, 27 January 1945, 14.

32. Monitored in London, the 13 February 1945 speech by Dr. Paul Schmidt was published the next day in the *New York Times*. "Nazis See Project for 'Mass Murder,'" *New York Times*, 14 February 1945.

33. Bradley, *A Soldier's Story*, 536.

34. Strong, *Intelligence at the Top*, 187, 255–56.

35. SHAEF Planning Staff, "Operations against the German National Redoubt," 5 April 1945, in *Survey of Allied Planning*, 2:206; SHAEF, "Weekly Intelligence Summary," 11 March 1945, WBSP.

36. Cunningham Diary, 27 March 1945.

37. SHAEF, "Weekly Intelligence Summary," 22 April 1945, WBSP.

38. Eisenhower to CCS, 31 March 1945; SHAEF G-4, "Study of Movement Requirements and Potentialities for Support of Projected Operations," 15 April 1945; SHAEF, "Message for General Eisenhower to CCS," 14 April 1945; Bull, "Supreme Commander's Decisions and Details with Reference to Directives for Gen Eisenhower," 15 April 1945; SHAEF G-3, "Operations against the German National Redoubt," 16 April 1945; GBR, "Strategy in North-West Europe," 97–98, 101–2.

39. Interrogation of LTG Georg Ritter von Hengl, "National Redoubt," U.S. Army European Command, Historical Division, Military Study B-461 (1946), 13.

40. McCloy to Smith, 2 October 1944, Eyes Only, WBSP.

41. McCloy to Eisenhower, 24 October 1944, and Smith [for Eisenhower] to McCloy, 1 November 1944, *EP*, #2087, n. 1.

42. Smith to Hilldring, 8 November 1944, Eyes Only, WBSP.

43. Smith [for Eisenhower] to Somervell, 14 March 1945, *EP*, #2339.

44. Stimson Diary, 14, 16, and 31 March 1945.

45. Clay oral history, 16 January 1971.

46. CCS to SHAEF, 15 January 1945, in Historical Section, G-5 Division, SHAEF, "Relief for the Netherlands," June 1945, 43, copy in WBSP.

47. SHAEF War Diary, 6, 14, and 20 December 1944. Dutch attempts to gain SHAEF's support for food relief is covered in Henri van der Zee, *The Hunger Winter: Occupied Holland, 1944-1945* (Lincoln, NE, 1998).

48. Cited in Walter Maass, *The Netherlands at War, 1940-45* (London, 1970), 206.

49. CCS to SHAEF, 14 March 1945, in "Relief for the Netherlands," 66.

50. Smith [for Eisenhower] to CCS, 27 March 1945, ibid., 68.

51. Churchill to Roosevelt, 9 April 1945, and Roosevelt to Churchill, 10 April 1945, *FRUS, 1945, Europe*, 5:19–20.

52. Bernhard to Smith, 14 April 1945, Eyes Only, WBSP.

53. Marshall to Eisenhower, 19 April 1945, and Churchill to Eisenhower, 20 April 1945, Eyes Only, WBSP; Churchill to Eden, copy to the JCS, 18 April 1945, RG 218, Records of the U.S. Joint Chiefs of Staff, Leahy Papers.

54. Bull [for Eisenhower] to Marshall, 20 April 1945, *EP,* #2431; Smith [for Eisenhower] to CCS and BCOS, 23 April 1945, *EP,* #2439. Bernhard requested the Germans cease all inundations until after the completion of the negotiations. De Guingand to Smith, 25 April 1945, Eyes Only, WBSP.

55. Smith [for Eisenhower] to Moscow Military Mission, 24 April 1945, and CCS to Eisenhower, 24 April 1945, Eyes Only, WBSP; Acting Secretary of State to Harriman, 24 April 1945, *FRUS, 1945, Europe,* 5:21–22; Gerbrandy to Eisenhower, 24 April 1945, Eyes Only, WBSP. For Susloparov's accreditation, see Military Mission in Moscow to Eisenhower, 25 April 1945, Eyes Only, WBSP.

56. Twenty-first Army Group to SHAEF, McClure to Smith, SHAEF to Twenty-first Army Group, 25 April 1945, and SHAEF to Seyss-Inquart, 25 April 1945, all in Eyes Only, WBSP.

57. Caffery [from Murphy] to Stettinius, 2 May 1945, *FRUS, 1945, Europe,* 5:23–24.

58. Pogue interview with Williams, 30–31 May 1947, MHI.

59. Smith, *Eisenhower's Six Great Decisions,* 197–99.

60. Smith gave a full account of the meeting with Seyss-Inquart in Smith to Eisenhower, "Meeting with German Representatives in Holland," 1 May 1945, Smith File, PPP. See also de Guingand, *Operation Victory,* 450–51.

61. Caffery to Stettinius, 28 and 29 April 1945, *FRUS, 1945, Europe,* 4:680.

62. For de Gaulle's version of events, see de Gaulle, *Memoirs,* 2:192–95.

63. Winant to Hull, 18 October 1944, *FRUS, 1944, General,* 1:354.

64. Smith [for Eisenhower] to Marshall, 19 April 1945, *EP,* #2425; Eisenhower to Marshall, 23 April 1945, *EP,* #2440; Eisenhower to de Gaulle, 28 April and 2 May 1945, *EP,* #2457, #2473.

65. Caffery to Stettinius, 29 April 1945, *FRUS, 1945, Europe,* 4:681. In the end, the French zone of occupation in Württemberg did not include the northern part, including Stuttgart.

66. Smith to Commanders, 2 May 1945, Cable and Messages Dealing with Negotiations for the Surrender of Germany Files, WBSP.

67. Trumbull Warren, "The Surrender of the German Armed Forces," in Hamilton, *Monty: Field Marshall,* 501–2.

68. Montgomery Diary, "Notes on the Campaign in North-West Europe," ibid., 525.

69. Smith, *Eisenhower's Six Great Decisions,* 200.

70. Smith had viewed the original EAC surrender document in late March 1944, but he considered it not only premature but also invalid, since France had entered the alliance. Winant to Stettinius, 10 May 1945, *FRUS, 1945, European Advisory Commission, Austria, Germany,* 283–84. Murphy claimed Smith "suffered a rare lapse of memory" and forgot about the "big blue folder" containing the EAC document. The exchange between Smith and the State Department officials indicates otherwise. Murphy, *Diplomat among Warriors,* 296–97.

71. Hull to Smith, 11 May 1945, *FRUS, European Advisory Commission, Austria, Germany,* 283–84. Pogue interview, 9 May 1947. See also Strong, *Intelligence at the Top,* 269–71; Murphy, *Diplomat among Warriors,* 240–41.

72. Winant to Stettinius, 10 May 1945.

73. SHAEF to Military Mission in Moscow, 4 and 5 May 1945, Surrender of Germany Files, WBSP; Eisenhower to CCS, 4 May 1945, *EP,* #2485.

74. Smith received a lot of flak for not employing the EAC document. McCloy thought it "simply incredible" that Smith ignored the approved text. Smith insisted

that SHAEF, mostly Whiteley and Bull, draft the surrender terms. Smith "made up his mind to restrict these conversations to the military," Murphy reported, "and to exclude Foreign Office and State Department participation." As Smith admitted, "if we had brought [Murphy] into the picture we would not have missed this bet." Memo of phone conversation, McCloy and Matthews, 12 May 1945, Murphy to Matthews, 14 May 1945, and Smith to Hull, 10 May 1945, *FRUS, European Advisory Commission, Austria, Germany*, 289–90, 294–97. The consequences for Susloparov proved much worse. He received a "reprimand" for signing the SHAEF surrender and, according to Smith, all subsequent inquires about Susloparov were met with embarrassed silence. Cited in Eisenhower, *Eisenhower at War*, 803.

75. Eisenhower to CCS and BCOS, 5 May 1945, *EP*, #2492.

76. Smith, Strong, and Butcher all provide full accounts of the negotiations. Smith, *Eisenhower's Six Great Decisions*, 206–29; Strong, *Intelligence at the Top*, 268–82; Butcher, *Three Years with Eisenhower*, 821–34.

77. Pogue interview, 9 May 1947.

78. Butcher, *Three Years with Eisenhower*, 826.

79. Friedeburg to Dönitz, 5 May 1945, SHAEF to War Department, 5 May 1945, Surrender of Germany Files, WBSP; Eisenhower to CCS, 5 May 1945, *EP*, #2494.

80. Butcher, *Three Years with Eisenhower*, 826.

81. Eisenhower to Mamie, 5 May 1945, in *Letters to Mamie*.

82. Summersby, *Eisenhower Was My Boss*, 242. Deane to SHAEF, 5 May 1945, Surrender of Germany Files, WBSP; Eisenhower to Military Mission in Moscow, 6 May 1945, *EP*, #2495; Strong, *Intelligence at the Top*, 276.

83. Butcher, *Three Years with Eisenhower*, 828–30.

84. Wilhelm Keitel, *The Memoirs of Field-Marshal Keitel* (London, 1968), 440.

85. Bull [for Eisenhower] to Marshall, 29 April 1945, *EP*, #2462, n. 1.

86. D'Este, *Patton*, 727–28.

87. Butcher, *Three Years with Eisenhower*, 831.

88. Strong, *Intelligence at the Top*, 277–78; Smith, *Eisenhower's Six Great Decisions*, 206.

89. Jodl appeared in Montgomery's headquarters before going on to Reims. According to the field marshal's account, Jodl indicated he "was armed with full authority from Doenitz to surrender." Montgomery reported this to the War Office, and Simpson passed along the information to Brooke. Simpson to Brooke, 6 May 1945, in Hamilton, *Monty: Field Marshal*, 525.

90. Eisenhower to CCS, 6 May 1945, *EP*, #2498.

91. Kathryn Westcott, "I Remember the German Surrender," *BBC News*, 4 May 2005. Hibbert was one of two surviving witnesses of the German surrender.

92. Strong, *Intelligence at the Top*, 280–82.

93. Smith, *Eisenhower's Six Great Decisions*, 210.

94. Strong, *Intelligence at the Top*, 282; Butcher Diary, 7 May 1945; Summersby, *Eisenhower Was My Boss*, 242–44.

95. Smith, *Eisenhower's Six Great Decisions*, 229.

96. Eisenhower to CCS, 7 May 1945, *EP*, #2499.

97. Secretary of War Commendation, 8 May 1945, Smith 201 File, WBSP.

Sources and Further Reading

Unpublished Sources

The principal sources of information for this book are contained in the massive collections housed in the Dwight D. Eisenhower Presidential Library in Abilene, Kansas, primarily the Walter Bedell Smith Papers and Eisenhower's Pre-Presidential Papers. There are essentially two sets of Smith's papers in the Eisenhower Library that correspond with Smith's two careers—chief of staff to Eisenhower, and diplomat and intelligence chief. The Walter Bedell Smith, Military Associate, Diplomat, Director of the C.I.A., and Under Secretary of State Papers hold materials pertaining to his post-1945 career, with two very important exceptions. Boxes 7 to 10 contain Smith's personal papers and correspondence for 1942 to the end of 1945, and Boxes 27 and 28 include Smith's "210" Personnel File and a file entitled "Items of Particular Interest to General Smith." Consistent with the practice of other World War II generals, Smith filed many of his most revealing letters in his 201 dossier. The second compilation of papers, the Walter Bedell Smith: Collection of World War II Documents, 1941–1945, houses the official documents during his tenure as chief of staff in AFHQ and SHAEF. The most important are the Cable Log and Eyes Only Cable Files for the headquarters and the correspondence files for Smith. Duplicates exist in the Modern Military Records Division of the National Archives and in British archives for AFHQ cables but not for SHAEF. The Eyes Only cables involve communications between AFHQ and SHAEF and superior bodies in Washington and London. The "official" correspondence files supplement those found in Smith's personal papers.

The single greatest handicap in writing a biography is the absence of family correspondence—in Smith's case, letters to his wife Nory. Presumably he withheld them when his collections of documents made their way first to the War Department Library, then to the War College, and finally to the National Archives. In his will he deeded his papers to the Eisenhower Library, apparently minus the letters to his wife. For more than a quarter of a century I have sought in vain to unearth these letters and must now conclude that Smith destroyed them.

The Eisenhower Pre-Presidential Papers are used primarily as a supplement to material contained in the first four volumes of *The Papers of Dwight David Eisenhower*. In addition to the Combined Chiefs of Staff, Eisenhower/Marshall, and Supreme Commander, Allied Forces cable files, the Supreme Commander, Allied Forces and D-day conference files are of particular importance in distilling Smith's contributions, especially from his first chiefs of staff meeting on 21 January 1944 through the end of July 1944. The Eisenhower correspondence files also constitute a valuable source, principally those of Lord Alanbrooke, Harold Alexander, Henry H. Arnold, Omar Bradley, Harry C. Butcher, Winston S. Churchill, Mark W. Clark, Andrew B. Cunningham, Jacob Devers, James Gault, Leonard Gerow, Alfred Gruenther, Charles Hager, W. Averell Harriman, Arthur Harris, Everett Hughes, Hastings Ismay, William Leahy, Ben Lear, Trafford Leigh-Mallory, Robert Littlejohn, George C. Marshall, Lesley McNair, J. C. McNarney, Bernard Montgomery, Frederick Morgan, Louis Mountbatten, Robert Patterson, George S. Patton, Forrest C. Pogue, Charles Portal, Matthew Ridgway, Franklin D. Roosevelt, Walter Bedell Smith, Brehon Somervell, Carl F. Spaatz, Harold Stark, Henry Stimson, Kenneth Strong, Kay Summersby, Maxwell Taylor, Arthur Tedder, Harry S. Truman, Lucian Truscott, Orlando Ward, A. C. Wedemeyer, Henry Maitland Wilson, and John G. Winant.

Additional collections employed include the papers of Henry Aurand, Ray Barker, Harold R. Bull, Harry C. Butcher, Thomas Davis, John Foster Dulles, James Hagerty, Courtney Hodges (including First Army Diary by MAJ William Sylvan and CPT Francis Smith), Julius Holmes, C. D. Jackson, Leroy Lutes, Floyd Parks, James Robb, and Kay Summersby-Morgan; and the oral histories of Aurand, Barker, Thomas Betts, Charles Bolté, Charles Bonesteel III, Carter Burgess, Mark Clark, Lucius Clay, Jacob Devers, Dan Gilmer, Lutes, Arthur Nevins, and William Simpson. Of special interest are two diaries: the Desk Diary kept by Summersby, particularly for the period 1 June 1944 to 10 March 1945, and the original manuscript of Butcher's *My Three Years with Eisenhower,* taken from his headquarters journal. Until Butcher's assignment to the public relations section—undertaken by Eisenhower in part to curb Butcher's access—the diary offers the best insider's view of Eisenhower's thinking on the issues he confronted and the personalities of the men closest to the supreme commander. The contents of the Butcher diary—really Eisenhower's household and headquarters journal—differ substantially from the published version. Angered by some of the too candid entries, Eisenhower vetted the diary and insisted that the objectionable items be removed. After Eisenhower went to London, he sporadically wrote or dictated entries for inclusion in his diary. These, as well as important documents Eisenhower wanted set aside and a collection of media clippings, are also contained in the Butcher Papers. Since Smith mistrusted Butcher and Butcher disliked Smith, both the published diary and the censored excerpts provide unvarnished insights into Smith's thinking and actions as chief of staff.

In many respects, the Combined Arms Research Library at the U.S. Army Command and General Staff College, Fort Leavenworth, Kansas, parallels the Military History Institute, U.S. Army Heritage and Education Center, Carlisle, Pennsylvania. Both contain a complete collection of U.S. Army publications, including periodicals, manuals, large collections of unpublished items, and materials on the interwar army, including commandant annual reviews, rosters, curriculum schedules and texts, and other relevant sources for the Command and General Staff School. Of particular value are the interviews conducted by the authors of volumes in the United States Army in World War II series, housed at the Military History Institute: Forrest Pogue interviews with Alanbrooke, David Belchem, N. C. D. Brownjohn, Arthur Coningham, Robert Crawford, A. B. Cunningham, Humphrey Gale, James Gault, T. P. Gleave, Ismay, Alphonse-Pierre Juin, Alan Moorehead, Frederick Morgan, Charles Portal, James Robb, Leslie Scarman, Arthur Tedder, Ford Trimble, C. H. H. Vulliamy, Charles West, J. F. M. Whiteley, and E. T. Williams; Howard Smyth interviews with Alexander, Eisenhower, Lyman Lemnitzer, Smith, and Kenneth Strong; Roland Ruppenthal interview with Smith; Sidney Matthews interviews with Smith and Strong; and Pogue and G. A. Harrison interview with C. H. Bonesteel III. Additional sources include the Raymond Moses collection and memoranda; the Robert Colglazier Papers and oral history; the papers of Bradford Chynoweth, Charles Corlett, Robert Eichelberger, Hobart Gay, Chester Hanson, Robert McClure, Arthur Nevins, and Orlando Ward; the Clay Blair and John Hull collections; and the oral histories of Mark Clark, Theodore Conway, Thomas Handy, and Carter Magruder.

A reviewer once labeled Everett Hughes the "deep throat" of the Allied commands in Europe, and he did not mean it as praise. He did Hughes a disservice. A man of considerable gravitas, Hughes enjoyed unparalleled access to Eisenhower and Patton, and his diary and papers, housed in the Manuscripts Division of the Library of Congress in Washington, DC, provide the best insights into the structural problems besetting American headquarters and commands, as well as the foibles of the men who headed and staffed them. I also possess an edited and annotated copy of the Hughes diary. George S. Patton's unexpurgated diary contains material exorcised from the published *Patton Papers*. Aside from the papers and diaries of Hughes and Patton, the Library of Congress also houses the papers of Carl F. Spaatz and George Van Horn Moseley. The papers of Smith's mentor, Moseley, are an especially important source.

The George C. Marshall Papers con   a good deal more than appears in the published papers. The holdings of the   ge C. Marshall Research Center and Library at the Virginia Military Academy   Lexington, Virginia, also include the papers of Thomas T. Handy, Reginald MacDonald, and Frank MacCarthy. In addition to the Pogue interviews with Marshall, the library contains an interview conducted by L. M. Guyer and C. H. Connelly and two by Sidney Matthews, Howard Smyth, Roy Lemson, and David Hamilton.

Papers relating to Smith at the National Archives in Washington contain relatively little concerning his tenure in Washington. The Records of the Office of the Chief of Staff (RG 165.2) provide the best information on Smith's time in Marshall's secretariat and as secretary to the Combined and Joint Chiefs of Staff committees. A second records group (RG 218, The Records of the Joint Chiefs of Staff) provides minutes of the CCS and JCS meetings, as well as material on the Italian surrender and planning for Anvil and Overlord and the deception plan. RG 218 also contains the Leahy Papers. Other collections of importance are RG 59, Records of the State Department; RG 160, Records of the Headquarters, Army Service Forces; RG 319, Records of the Army Staff; RG 332, Records of U.S. Theaters of War, World War II; and RG 338 Records of U.S. Army Commands. The core collection is contained in RG 331, Records of the Allied Operational & Occupational Headquarters, World War II, including the General Records of AFHQ and SHAEF; the records of the General Staff Divisions, Committees (especially the Joint Intelligence Committee), and Special Staffs; correspondence and plans emanating from the air, naval, army group, and airborne army headquarters and AMGOT; and, most vital, the SHAEF Secretary of the General Staff Files. A large percentage of the pertinent files in RGs 319 and 331 (for 1944 and 1945), including material contained in the SGS files, are duplicated in the Pre-Presidential Papers and Smith Collection at the Eisenhower Library.

I made every effort to cite from published sources whenever possible. However, in true British empiricist fashion, Nigel Hamilton carefully employed the full range of Montgomery's papers in his massive and authoritative three-volume biography of the field marshal, so I found no case where I needed to cite directly from Montgomery's papers. Likewise, the Alanbrooke papers have been reproduced twice—once by Arthur Bryant in the late 1950s, and more comprehensively by Alex Danchev and Daniel Todman in 2001—so I had little reason to cite archival sources.

Other unpublished sources include the following: the papers of Viscount Montgomery of Alamein CBE, Imperial War Museum, London; the diary of Admiral of the Fleet Viscount Cunningham of Hyndhope, British Library, London; the papers of Sir Percy James Grigg, Admiral Sir Bertram Home Ramsay, and N. Gerald Hugh Wilkinson, Churchill Archives Centre, Churchill College, Cambridge University; the papers of Forrest Harding, Harding Museum, Franklin, Ohio; the papers of FM Alan Francis Brooke, 1st Viscount Alanbrooke of Brookeborough, LG Sir Humfrey Myddleton Gale, and Brigadier Eric Mockler-Ferryman, Liddell Hart Centre for Military Archives, King's College, London; the George S. Patton Sr. Papers, Henry E. Huntington Library, San Marino, California; the James Reston Papers, University Library, University of Illinois at Urbana-Champaign; American Relations, Indochina Files, National Archives of Australia, Canberra; Classified Naval Archives, containing transcripts of telephone communications between Smith and Handy, Naval Historical Center, Washington Navy Yard, Washington, DC; Bernard M. Baruch Papers, Princeton University, Princeton, New Jersey; the papers of Harry S. Truman, especially the Public Papers of Harry S. Truman, 1945–1953 and President's Personal Files, Harry S. Truman Presidential Library, Independence, Missouri; Henry L. Stimson Papers, Sterling Memorial Library, Yale University, New Haven, Connecticut; and Fort Custer Vertical Files and newspaper collection, Willard Library, Battle Creek, Michigan.

Published Sources

Whatever people think about David Irving, nobody can fault him for a lack of industry in conducting broad-ranging documentary searches. He reproduced a vast collection of primary sources gathered for his book *The War between the Generals*. I purchased that collection sometime in the early 1980s. Chiefly, I used these papers to cite a number of British sources: the papers of Sir James Grigg, Churchill Archives Centre, Churchill College, Cambridge University; the diary and papers of Lord Alanbrooke and the Hastings L. Ismay Papers, Liddell Hart Centre for Military Archives, King's College, London; and War Office 205, Records of 21 Army Group and WO 214, and copies of documents from the Montgomery and de Guingand files from the National Archives (Public Record Office), Kew, London.

SHAEF's five general staff divisions, the combat arms and services branches, and the publicity and psychological warfare sections wrote a total of 133 General Board Reports. Seldom utilized by historians, these reports, written immediately after the war, provide a wealth of information and, in some cases, collections of documents in their annexes. Many of the reports reflect the contentiousness that existed during the war, particularly over command and staff structures. Several of the principals—including Eisenhower, Smith, and Lee—carefully vetted some of the reports. I employed the following General Board Reports, listed with the issuing agency: General World War II European Theater of Operations, G-3, "Strategy of the Campaign in Western Europe, 1944–1945," and G-4, "Study of the Organization of the European Theater of Operations"; G-1, "Reinforcement System and Reinforcement Procedures in European Theater of Operations"; G-4, "Study of the Administrative Functions of the Army Group Headquarters," "Mechanics of Supply in Fast-Moving

Situations," and "Service Troop Basis"; G-5, "Civil Affairs and Military Government Organizations and Operations"; Judge Advocate, "The Military Justice Administration in the Theater of European Operations" and "Military Offender in Theater of Operations"; Medical Corps, "Combat Exhaustion"; Ordnance, "Ammunition Supply and Operations, European Campaign"; Provost Marshal, "Stragglers and Absentees without Leave"; and Theater Service Forces, "Organization and Functions of the Communications Zone," "Mounting the Operation OVERLORD," and "Supply and Maintenance on the European Continent D-Day to VE-Day." Copies are in my possession.

The point of departure for any research on the military history of American participation in World War II is the Army's "Green Series." *The United States Army in World War II* series currently numbers more than 100 volumes. The following, listed in chronological order by year of release, were employed in this study: Kent Greenfield, Robert Palmer, and Bell Wiley, *Organization of Ground Combat Troops* (1947); Hugh Cole, *The Lorraine Campaign* (1950); Ray Cline, *Washington Command Post: The Operations Division* (1951); Maurice Matloff and Edwin M. Snell, *Strategic Planning for Coalition Warfare, 1941-42* (1953); Roland Ruppenthal, *Logistical Support of the Armies*, 2 vols. (1953, 1959); John Millett, *The Organization and Role of the Army Service Forces* (1954); Robert Coakley and Richard Leighton, *Global Logistics and Strategy, 1940-1943* (1955); Charles MacDonald, *The Siegfried Line Campaign* (1955); Constance Greene et al., *The Ordnance Department: Planning Munitions for War* (1955); George Howe, *Northwest Africa: Seizing the Initiative in the West* (1957); Marcel Vigneras, *Rearming the French* (1957); Joseph Bykofsky and Harold Larson, *The Transportation Corps: Operations Overseas* (1957); Martin Blumenson, *Breakout and Pursuit* (1961); Harry Coles and Albert Weinberg, *Civil Affairs: Soldiers Become Governors* (1964); Albert Garland and Howard Smyth, *Sicily and the Italian Surrender* (1965); Hugh Cole, *The Ardennes: The Battle of the Bulge* (1965); Ulysses Lee, *The Employment of Negro Troops* (1966); Lida Mayo, *The Ordnance Department: On Beachhead and Battlefront* (1968); Earl Ziemke, *The U.S. Army in Occupation of Germany* (1975); and Jeffery Clark and Robert Ross Smith, *Riviera to the Rhine* (1993).

The following select bibliography contains other published sources consulted during the writing of this book or works that may be of interest to readers:

Agarossi, Elena. *A Nation Collapses: The Italian Surrender of September 1943*. Cambridge: Cambridge University Press, 2000.

Ambrose, Stephen. *The Supreme Command*. New York: Doubleday, 1970.

Atkinson, Rick. *An Army at Dawn: The War in North Africa*. New York: Henry Holt, 2002.

———. *The Day of Battle: The War in Sicily and Italy*. New York: Henry Holt, 2007.

Bland, Larry, ed. *George C. Marshall: Interviews and Reminiscences for Forrest C. Pogue*. Lexington, VA: George C. Marshall Foundation, 1991.

Bland, Larry, and Sharon Ritenour Steven, eds. *The Papers of George Catlett Marshall*. 5 vols. Baltimore: Johns Hopkins University Press, 1981-2003. *The Soldierly Spirit, December 1880-June 1939* (1981); *We Cannot Delay, July 1, 1939-December 6, 1941* (1986); *The Right Man for the Job, December 7, 1941-May 31, 1943* (1991); *Aggressive and Determined Leadership, June 1, 1943-December 31, 1944* (1996); *The Finest Soldier, January 1, 1945-January 7, 1947* (2003).

Blumenson, Martin, ed. *Patton Papers*. 2 vols. Boston: Houghton Mifflin, 1972-1974.

Bradley, Omar N. *A Soldier's Story*. New York: Holt, 1951.

Bradley, Omar N., and Clay Blair. *A General's Life*. New York: Simon and Schuster, 1983.

Bryant, Arthur. *Triumph in the West.* London: Collins, 1959.

——. *The Turn of the Tide: A History of the War Years Based on the Diaries of Field-Marshal Lord Alanbrooke, Chief of the Imperial General Staff.* London: Collins, 1957.

Butcher, Harry. *My Three Years with Eisenhower: The Personal Diary of Captain Harry C. Butcher, USNR, Naval Aide to General Eisenhower, 1942 to 1945.* New York: Simon and Schuster, 1946.

Cameron, Allen, ed. *Viet-Nam Crisis: A Documentary History,* Vol. 1, *1940-1956.* Ithaca, NY: Cornell University Press, 1971.

Chandler, Alfred D., Jr., ed. *The Papers of Dwight David Eisenhower: The War Years.* 5 vols. Baltimore: Johns Hopkins University Press, 1970.

Chandler, Alfred D., Jr., and Louis Galambos, eds. *The Papers of Dwight David Eisenhower: Occupation and Chief of Staff.* 3 vols. Baltimore: Johns Hopkins University Press, 1978.

Chen Jian and Shen Zhihua, eds. "The Geneva Conference of 1954: New Evidence from the Archives of the Ministry of Foreign Affairs of the People's Republic of China." *Cold War International History Project Bulletin,* Issue 16. Washington, DC: Woodrow Wilson International Center for Scholars, 2008.

Churchill, Winston. *The Second World War.* 6 vols. London: Cassell, 1948–1954.

Chynoweth, Bradford. *Bellamy Park: Memoirs of Bradford Grethen Chynoweth.* Hicksville, NY: Exposition Press, 1975.

Clark, Mark. *Calculated Risk.* New York: Harper, 1950.

Collins, J. Lawton. *Lightning Joe: An Autobiography.* Baton Rouge: Louisiana State University Press, 1979.

Cunningham, Andrew B. *A Sailor's Odyssey.* London: Hutchinson, 1951.

Danchev, Alex, and Daniel Todman, eds. *War Diaries, 1941-1945: Field Marshal Lord Alanbrooke.* Berkeley: University of California Press, 2001.

De Gaulle, Charles. *The War Memoirs of Charles de Gaulle.* 3 vols. New York: Simon and Schuster, 1955–1960.

De Guingand, Francis. *Generals at War.* London: Hodder and Stoughton, 1964.

——. *Operation Victory.* London: Hodder and Stoughton, 1947.

Department of State. *The Foreign Relations of the United States: Diplomatic Papers.* 23 vols. Washington, DC: Government Printing Office, 1955–2003. In order of publication: *The Conferences at Malta and Yalta* (1955); *The Conferences at Cairo and Teheran, 1943* (1961); *1942, Europe* (1962); *1943, Europe* (1964); *1944, British Commonwealth and Europe* (1965); *1944, Europe* (1966); *1944, General* (1966); *1945, European Advisory Commission, Austria and Germany* (1968); *1945, Europe* (1968); *The Conferences at Washington, 1941-1942, and Casablanca, 1943* (1968); *1946, Eastern Europe, the Soviet Union* (1969); *Conferences at Washington and Quebec, 1943* (1970); *Council of Foreign Ministers; Germany and Austria* (1972); *1948, Eastern Europe, the Soviet Union* (1974); *1950, Korea* (1976); *1952-1954, Geneva Conference* (1981); *1952-1954, Indochina,* parts 1 and 2 (1982); *1952-1954, Western Europe and Canada,* part 1 (1983); *1952-1954, The American Republics* (1983); *1952-1954, National Security Affairs,* part 1 (1984); *1952-1954, Iran (1989); 1952-1954,* Guatemala, (2003).

DeWeerd, H. A. *Selected Speeches and Statements of General of the Army George C. Marshall.* Washington, DC: Infantry Journal, 1945.

De Wiart, Adrian Carton. *Happy Odyssey: The Memoirs of Lieutenant-General Sir Adrian Carton de Wiart.* London: Jonathan Cape, 1950.

Eden, Anthony. *The Memoirs of Sir Anthony Eden: Full Circle*. London: Cassell, 1960.

Eisenhower, Dwight. *Crusade in Europe*. Garden City, NY: Doubleday, 1948.

——. *Letters to Mamie*. Edited by John D. Eisenhower. Garden City, NY: Doubleday, 1978.

Farago, Ladislas. *The Last Days of Patton*. New York: McGraw-Hill, 1981.

Ferrell, Robert, ed. *The Eisenhower Diaries*. New York: Norton, 1981.

Galambos, Louis, ed. *The Papers of Dwight David Eisenhower: The Chief of Staff*. 4 vols. Baltimore: Johns Hopkins University Press, 1978.

——. *The Papers of Dwight David Eisenhower: Columbia University*. 2 vols. Baltimore: Johns Hopkins University Press, 1984.

Galambos, Louis, and Daun van Ee, eds. *The Papers of Dwight David Eisenhower: Keeping the Peace*. 4 vols. Baltimore: Johns Hopkins University Press, 2001.

——. *The Papers of Dwight David Eisenhower: The Middle Way*. 3 vols. Baltimore: Johns Hopkins University Press, 1996.

Griffith, Robert. *Ike's Letters to a Friend, 1941-1958*. Lawrence: University Press of Kansas, 1984.

Hamilton, Nigel. *The Full Monty: Montgomery of Alamein, 1887-1942*. London: Penguin, 2001.

——. *Monty: Master of the Battlefield, 1942-1944*. London: Hamish Hamilton, 1983.

——. *Monty: The Field Marshal, 1944-1976*. London: Hamish Hamilton, 1986.

Hinsley, F. H. *British Intelligence in the Second World War*. Vol. 3, pts. 2–3. London: Her Majesty's Stationery Office, 1984, 1986.

Hoare, Samuel John Gurney. *Ambassador on Special Mission*. London: Collins, 1946.

Hobbs, Joseph. *Dear General: Eisenhower's Wartime Letters to Marshall*. Baltimore: John Hopkins University Press, 1999.

Irving, David. *The War between the Generals*. New York: Congdon and Lattès, 1981.

Ismay, Hastings. *The Memoirs of General Lord Ismay*. London: William Heinemann, 1960.

Kaplan, Diana, ed. *Microfilm Edition of the Diaries of Henry Lewis Stimson in the Yale University Library*. College Park: University Libraries, University of Maryland, 2006.

Kennan, George. *Memoirs: 1925-1950*. Boston: Little, Brown, 1967.

Kennedy, John. *The Business of War*. London: Hutchinson, 1957.

Kimball, Warren. *Churchill & Roosevelt: The Complete Correspondence*. 3 vols. Princeton, NJ: Princeton University Press, 1984.

——. *Forged in War: Roosevelt, Churchill, and the Second World War*. New York: Morrow, 1997.

Kimball, Warren, and Mark Stoler. *The Juggler: Franklin Roosevelt as Wartime Statesman*. Princeton, NJ: Princeton University Press, 1991.

King, Ernest, and Walter Muir Whitehill. *Fleet Admiral King: A Naval Record*. New York: Norton, 1952.

Leahy, William D. *I Was There: The Personal Story of the Chief of Staff to Presidents Roosevelt and Truman*. New York: Whittlesey House, 1950.

Liddell Hart, Basil, ed. *Rommel Papers*. New York: De Capo, 1953.

Macmillan, Harold. *The Blast of War, 1939-1945*. London: Macmillan, 1967.

——. *War Diaries: Politics and War in the Mediterranean, January 1943-May 1945*. London: Macmillan, 1984.

Montgomery, Bernard. *The Memoirs of Field-Marshal the Viscount Montgomery of Alamein*. London: Collins, 1958.

Montgomery and the Eighth Army: A Selection from the Diaries, Correspondence and Other Papers of Field Marshal the Viscount Montgomery of Alamein, August 1942 to December 1943. Edited by Stephen Brooks. London: Army Records Society, 1991.

Morgan, Frederick. *Overturn to Overlord.* New York: Doubleday, 1950.

Murphy, Robert. *Diplomat among Warriors.* Garden City, NY: Doubleday, 1964.

Murray, G. E. Patrick. *Eisenhower versus Montgomery: The Continuing Debate.* Westport, CT: Greenwood Press, 1996.

Pogue, Forrest. *George C. Marshall.* 3 vols. New York: Viking Press, 1963–1973.

———. *The Supreme Command.* Washington, DC: Office of the Chief of Military History, 1954.

Radford, Arthur W. *From Pearl Harbor to Vietnam: The Memoirs of Admiral Arthur W. Radford.* Edited by Stephen Jurika Jr. Stanford, CA: Hoover Institution Press, 1980.

Richardson, Charles. *Send for Freddie.* London: William Kimber, 1987.

Ridgway, Matthew. *Soldier: The Memoirs of Matthew B. Ridgway.* New York: Harpers, 1956.

Sherwood, Robert, ed. *The White House Papers of Harry L. Hopkins.* 2 vols. London: Eyre and Spottiswoode, 1948–1949.

Slessor, John. *The Central Blue: Memories and Reflections.* London: Cassell, 1956.

Smith, Walter Bedell. *Eisenhower's Six Great Decisions: Europe, 1944-1945.* New York: Longmans Green, 1956.

———. *My Three Years in Moscow.* Philadelphia: J. B. Lippincott, 1950.

Stacey, C. P. *Victory Campaign: The Operations in North-West Europe, 1944-1945.* Official History of the Canadian Army in the Second World War. Ottawa: The Queen's Printer, 1960.

Stimson, Henry, and McGeorge Bundy. *On Active Service in Peace and War.* New York: Harper, 1948.

Stoler, Mark. *Allies and Adversaries: The Joint Chiefs of Staff, The Grand Alliance and U.S. Strategy in World War II.* Chapel Hill: University of North Carolina Press, 2000.

———. *Allies in War: Britain and America against the Axis Powers, 1940-1945.* London: Hodder Arnold, 2005.

———. *The Politics of the Second Front.* Westport, CT: Greenwood Press, 1977.

Strong, Kenneth. *Intelligence at the Top.* London: Cassell, 1968.

Summersby, Kay. *Eisenhower Was My Boss.* New York: Prentice Hall, 1949.

Summersby-Morgan, Kay. *Past Forgiving: My Love Affair with Dwight D. Eisenhower.* New York: Simon and Schuster, 1975.

Taylor, Maxwell. *Swords and Plowshares.* New York: Norton, 1972.

Tedder, Arthur. *With Prejudice: The War Memoirs of Marshal of the Royal Air Force Lord Tedder.* London: Cassell, 1966.

Truman, Harry S. *Memoirs.* Vol. 2, *Years of Trial and Hope.* Garden City, NY: Doubleday, 1956.

Truscott, Lucian K., Jr. *Command Missions: A Personal Story.* New York: Dutton, 1954.

Wedemeyer, Albert C. *Wedemeyer Reports!* New York: Henry Holt, 1958.

Wilmot, Chester. *The Struggle for Europe.* New York: Harper and Row, 1952.

Wilson, Charles, Baron Moran. *Churchill: Taken from the Diaries of Lord Moran.* Boston: Houghton Mifflin, 1966.

Wingrove, Paul, ed. "Russian Documents on the 1954 Geneva Conference." *Cold War International History Project Bulletin,* Issue 16. Washington, DC: Woodrow Wilson International Center for Scholars, 2008.

Index